THE PARTITION OM

The present collection brings together four classic accounts of the Partition which reflect in different ways how religious, cultural, and territorial boundaries were redefined, leaving a lasting impact on South Asian politics.

The first book in this collection, *Prelude to Partition* by David Page examines the forces responsible for the Pakistan movement, with the eye on Indian Muslim politics in the 1920s. He discusses how Muslim rule in Punjab and Bengal became a real possibility with the Communal Award, which in turn was an outcome of the constitutional reforms of 1920. *The Origins of the Partition of India 1936–1947* by Anita Inder Singh investigates the process of decolonization by the British and its far-reaching consequences for their international status. The core of *Divide and Quit* is Moon's account of the creeping communal unrest in Bahawalpur ... the way in which a princely state which had been prosperous and at peace was caught up in powerful forces of vengeance and avarice, and the efforts made to prevent the breakdown of the civil government. Based on the reports of a government fact-finding organization, *Stern Reckoning* documents in great detail the riots, massacres, casualties, and political occurrences that led to the partition An insightful introduction by Mushirul Hasan puts the issue of the Partition in historical perspective.

David Page is Co-Director, Media South Asia Project, Institute of Development Studies, Sussex University, England.

Anita Inder Singh is Fellow at the Center for Socio-Legal Stidoes at Wolfson College, University of Oxford.

Penderel Moon was an officer in the Indian Civil Service until his resignation in 1943.

G. D. Khosla graduated from the University of Cambridge, and served in the branch of the Indian Civil Service, until his retirement as Chief Justice of the Punjab High Court in 1961.

Mushirul Hasan is Professor of Modern Indian History at, and recently appointed Vice Chancellor of the Jamia Millia Islamia, New Delhi.

The Partition Omnibus

Prelude to Partition
The Indian Muslims and
the Imperial System of Control 1920–1932
David Page

The Origins of the Partition of India 1936–1947
Anita Inder Singh

Divide and Quit
Penderel Moon
With contributions from Mark Tully and
Tapan Raychaudhuri

Stern Reckoning
A Survey of the Events Leading Up To and
Following the Partition of India
G. D. Khosla

with an Introduction by Mushirul Hasan

OXFORD
UNIVERSITY PRESS

OXFORD
UNIVERSITY PRESS

YMCA Library Building, Jai Singh Road, New Delhi 110 001

Oxford University Press is a department of the University of Oxford. It furthers the
University's objective of excellence in research, scholarship, and education
by publishing worldwide in

Oxford New York

Auckland   Bangkok   Buenos Aires   Cape Town   Chennai
Dar es Salaam   Delhi   Hong Kong   Istanbul   Karachi   Kolkata
Kuala Lumpur   Madrid   Melbourne   Mexico City   Mumbai   Nairobi
São Paulo   Shanghai   Taipei   Tokyo   Toronto

Oxford is a registered trade mark of Oxford University Press
in the UK and in certain other countries

Published in India
By Oxford University Press, New Delhi
© Oxford University Press, 2002

Prelude to Partition
© Oxford University Press 1982
The Origins of the Partition of India
© Oxford University Press 1987
Divide and Quit
© The Estate of Sir Penderel Moon, 1961
© Introduction, Mark Tully, 1998
© Re-reading *Divide and Quite*, Tapan Raychaudhuri, 1998
Stern Reckoning
© Oxford University Press 1989

ISBN 0 19 567176 7

Printed at Saurabh Printers Pvt. Ltd., NOIDA, UP
Published by Manzar Khan, Oxford University Press
YMCA Library Building, Jai Singh Road, New Delhi 110 001

Contents

Partition Narratives—*Mushirul Hasan*

❁

Prelude to Partition
The Indian Muslims and the Imperial System of Control 1920–1932

Introduction to the Paperback Edition

Acknowledgements to the Paperback Edition

Preface

Introduction

1. The Montagu-Chelmsford Reforms and the Changing Structure of Politics

2. The Growth of Communalism and the Polarization of Politics

3. The Emergence of Punjabi Dominance

4. The Muslim Conference and the Reforms

Conclusion

Glossary

Bibliography

Index

Maps
India 1920 • The United Provinces • The Punjab

❦

The Origins of the Partition of India 1936–1947

Preface

Abbreviations

Acknowledgements

1. Elections and the Congress in Office:
   April 1936 to September 1939

2. India and the War: September 1939 to December 1941

3. Provincial and All India Politics: Currents and
   Cross-Currents—December 1941 to April 1945

4. The Success of the Muslim League—June 1945 to March 1946

5. The Cabinet Mission: March to July 1946

6. Negotiations for The Interim Government and Direct Action

7. Prelude to Partition: November 1946 to February 1947

8. Divide and Quit

Conclusions

List of Important Persons

Bibliography

Index

❦

Divide and Quit

List of Illustrations

Introduction to Divide and Quit—*Mark Tully*

Brief Biographies of Key Figures

Introduction

1. The Genesis of Pakistan
2. The Punjab and Pakistan
3. The Cabinet Mission
4. The Mountbatten Plan
5. The Punjab and Partition
6. Bhawalpur State
7. Journey across the Punjab
8. Outbreak of Disturbances in Bhawalpur State
9. Restoring Order—I
10. Restoring Order—II
11. Disturbances in Bhawalpur City
12. Events in Rahim Yar Khan
13. Resettlement
14. Summing Up
    Note on Casualties
15. Re-reading Divide and Quit—Tapan Raychaudhuri

Bibliography

Index

Maps
The Punjab • Bhawalpur State

꠸

Stern Reckoning
A Survey of the Events Leading Up To and Following the Partition of India

Foreword

1. The Parting of the Ways
2. Direct Action Day and After

3. The Punjab
   Lahore District • Sheikhpura • Sialkot • Gujranwala • Gujrat •
   Montgomery • Lyallpur • Shahpur • Jhang • Multan •
   Muzaffargarh • Rawalpindi • Jhelum • Attock • Mianwali • Dera
   Ghazi Khan • Bhawalpur State

4. Exodus

5. Sind

6. North-West Frontier Province

7. Retaliation

8. Conclusion

Appendix I—Notes to Chapters

Appendix II—Tables and Statements

Bibliography

Partition Narratives*

Mushirul Hasan

Partition was the defining event of modern, independent India
and Pakistan, and it is hardly an exaggeration to say that
partition continues to be the defining event of modern India
and Pakistan ... Partition [moreover] was and is a profoundly
religious event for both sides ... and most of the agony over
religion throughout the South Asian region is to a large extent
traceable to it. Partition is at the heart not only of the great
regional conflicts ... [but] it is also an important component
or factor in a whole series of religious-cum-political conflicts
reaching down to the present time ... To be sure, partition as a
defining *religious* event is not by any means the only event or
condition for an appropriate analysis and explanation of [these]
great religious controversies currently tearing the fabric of
India's cultural life, but ... it is, indeed, one of the necessary
and central events or conditions for understanding India's
current agony over religion. In many ways it is the core plot in
the unfolding narrative of modern, independent India.

> Gerald James Larson, *India's Agony Over Religion*
> (New Delhi, 1997), pp. 182–3.

At the beginning of this millennium, the great ideological debates
between the proponents of 'secular' and 'Muslim' nationalisms are
waning. A sense is abroad that the Partition story, hitherto dominated

---

*It may be useful to read this introduction as a sequel to my recent writings on the
Partition. I have therefore avoided any reference to the arguments in *Legacy of a
Divided Nation: India's Muslims Since Independence* (New Delhi, 2001 reprint with a new
preface), and the three anthologies, namely, *India's Partition: Process, Strategy and Mobi-
lisation* (New Delhi, 2001 reprint); *India Partitioned: The Other Face of Freedom*, in 2 vols.
(New Delhi, 1997, rev. & enlarged edn.); *Inventing Boundaries: Gender, Politics and the
Partition of India* (New Delhi, 2000).

by grand narratives, needs to be told differently.[1] Attention is drawn
to comparisons across space and time, to theoretical issues of import
well beyond the confines of South Asia,[2] and to partitions restructuring
the sources of conflicts around borders, refugees and diasporas.[3]
There is even talk of the need for a new language to deal with the
historical traumas of the past,[4] of rethinking 'Partition', necessitated
by the shift away from the high political histories.[5] The legacy of
Partition for India, Pakistan and Bangladesh is, suggests Ritu Menon,
the 'fragility of nations; the porosity of borders; the reality of migration.
The migrant/refugee/*muhajir*—the person displaced—has become
the new metaphor of the subcontinent.'[6] According to the French
scholar Jean-Luc Nancy, the gravest and most painful testimony of
the modern world, the one that possibly involves all other testimonies
to which this epoch must answer, is the testimony of the dissolution,
the dislocation, or the conflagration of community.[7]

Whatever the approach and howsoever diverse the interpretations,
the fact is that Hindu-Muslim partnerships exploded in the 1940s,
and the weakness of the secular ideology—an emblem of the desire
to create a world beyond religious divisions—became all too clear
to that generation. Their association with majoritarianism and

---

[1]For example, Tai Yong Tan and Gyanesh Kudaisya, *The Aftermath of Partition in
South Asia* (London, 2000); Sucheta Mahajan, *Independence and Partition: The Erosion of
Colonial Power in India* (New Delhi, 2000); D.A. Low & H. Brasted (eds.), *Freedom, Trauma,
Continuities: Northern India and Independence* (New Delhi, 1998); Alok Bhalla (ed.), *Sto-
ries About the Partition of India*, 3 vols. (New Delhi, 1994); D.A. Low (ed.), *The Political
Inheritance of Pakistan* (London, 1991); Niaz Zaman, *A Divided Legacy: The Partition in
Selected Novels of India, Pakistan, and Bangladesh* (New Delhi, 2000).

[2]Mushirul Hasan (ed.), *Islam, Communities and the Nation: Muslim Identities in South
Asia and Beyond* (New Delhi, 1999).

[3]Radha Kumar, 'Settling Partition Hostilities: Lessons Learnt, the Options Ahead',
in *Transeuropeennes* (Paris), nos. 19/20, winter 2000–2002, p. 24.

[4]Rustom Bharucha, 'Between Truth and Reconciliation: Experiments in Theatre
and Public Culture', *Economic and Political Weekly* (Bombay), 29 September 2001, pp.
3763–72, and Ranabir Samaddar, 'The Last Hurrah that continues', *Transeuropeennes*,
pp. 31–48.

[5]Suvir Kaul (ed.), *The Partitions of Memory: The Afterlife of the Division of India* (New
Delhi, 2001), p. 25.

[6]Ritu Menon, 'The Dynamics of Division', *Transeuropeennes*, p. 171.

[7]Jean-Luc Nancy, *The Inoperative Community* (Minneapolis: Minnesota, 1991), p. 1.
See, for example, the brilliant stories of Abdullah Hussein, *Stories of Exile and Alienation*. Translated by Muhammad Umar Memon (Karachi, 1998).

minorityism discredited it, they were badly led and, at the moment of great peril, Hindu, Muslim and Sikh organisations proved more than a match for the tepid enthusiasm of Congress' secular wing. The Communist Party of India not only acknowledged the importance of the national question for politics, but also unequivocally embraced the principle of national self-determination. The idea was drummed into the heads of people with little recognition of the consequences it could have for the party itself, and for the accentuation of the communal process at the level of the masses. Finally, the colonial government's conciliatory policy towards the Muslim League bore fruit during the Second World War, and stiffened Mohammad Ali Jinnah's resolve to achieve his Muslim homeland. 'It was the outbreak of war in September 1939,' writes Anita Inder Singh, 'which saved the League. Even as Linlithgow put federation into cold storage for the duration of the war, Jinnah set out to exploit the British need for the support of the Indian parties for the war effort.'[8]

When the war ended, the engine of communal politics could no longer be put in reverse.[9] This is what happened, in the words of the Urdu writer, Ismat Chughtai (1915–1991):

The flood of communal violence came and went with all its evils, but it left a pile of living, dead, and gasping corpses in its wake. It wasn't only that the country was split in two—bodies and minds were also divided. Moral beliefs were tossed aside and humanity was in shreds. Government officers and clerks along with their chairs, pens and inkpots, were distributed like the spoils of war. ... Those whose bodies were whole had hearts that were splintered. Families were torn apart. One brother was allotted to Hindustan, the other to Pakistan; the mother was in Hindustan, her offspring were in Pakistan; the husband was in Hindustan, his wife was in Pakistan. The bonds of relationship were in tatters, and in the end many souls remained behind in Hindustan while their bodies started off for Pakistan.[10]

Pluralism, the bedrock of secular nationalism, could no longer contain hatred, religious intolerance, and other forms of bigotry.

[8]Anita Inder Singh, *The Origins of the Partition of India 1936–1947* (New Delhi, 1987), p. 238.

[9]Eric Hobsbawm, *Age of Extremes: The Short Twentieth Century 1914–1991* (London, 1994), p. 220.

[10]Ismat Chughtai, *My Friend, My Enemy: Essays, Reminiscences, Portraits*. Translated and introduced by Tahira Naqvi (New Delhi, 2001), p. 3.

xii *Introduction*

Some of the anxieties Indians faced while formulating strategies for political survival reappeared with a force that could not have been anticipated at the turn of the century. They came into sharp focus only a decade or so before the actual transfer of power. The League, the Akali Dal and the Hindu Mahasabha rejected the once seemingly unassailable pluralist paradigm, while religious fundamentalists, who were at any rate wary of the corrosive effects of secular ideologies, turned to the creation of a Hindu state or an Islamic theocracy. The outcome was a cataclysmic event—India's bloody vivisection. As the historian of Islam pointed out, 'a few years after the extermination camps and incendiary and atomic bombs of the Second World War seemed to have confirmed the worst condemnations Indians had levelled against [the] materialistic modern West, Modern India, Hindu and Muslim, confronted horrors of its own making.'[11]

Mohandas Karamchand Gandhi was the person most sensitive to this reality, though his reactions scarcely figure in post-modernist narratives on Partition. One almost gets a sense, in the writings of many historians, of Gandhi's premature demise well before his assassination on 30 January 1948. That being the case, it is important to recover Gandhi's voice, and attach some importance to his responses in the discussions over Partition violence.

Although the literature covering his last years is rich, it is hard to comprehend how and why a man, having dominated the political scene for three decades, could do so little to influence the Congress to take firm and effective steps to contain violence. Even if this illustrates Gandhi's diminishing political influence, we can still ask why he became, as he told Louis Fischer, 'a spent bullet', and what turned him into 'a back number'. What led him to conclude that he could not influence, much less lead, India on the eve of Independence? Why tell the Mahatma to shut up at a time when the nation's unity was at stake and the eruption of large-scale violence widely anticipated? Was it because, as Acharya Kripalani pointed out, that Gandhi had found no way of tackling the communal problem, and that 'he himself [was] groping in the dark?'[12] This is an extraordinary comment from

[11]Marshall G.S. Hodgson, *The Venture of Islam: Conscience and History in a World Civilisation* (Chicago, 1974), vol. 3, p. 355.
[12]D.G. Tendulkar, *Mahatma: Life of Mohandas Karamchand Gandhi* (New Delhi: Publications Division, Government of India), vol. 8, p. 19.

a man who had himself displayed little political clarity during his long years in public life.

What is missing in such explanations is the sense of the great ideological fissure dividing the upper echelons of the Congress party between popular support in its rank and file for Partition, and acquiescence in violence as an unavoidable consequence of the communal rupture. It was, after all, G.D. Birla who had told A.V. Alexander, member of the Cabinet Mission, that 'in such a big country specially when power is to be transferred, such clashes (he referred to 10,000 deaths), however deplorable, cannot be made impossible.' Implicit in the same letter was the ominous warning: 'These riots, however, have impressed one thing clearly on the minds of all reasonable people that this mutual killing cannot help one side. This is a game which both sides can play with disastrous results. So I am not taking a pessimistic view.'[13]

Is it then the case that the otherwise well-tested Gandhian methods were now so out of place in the new political culture nurtured by the Congress that it led the Mahatma to distance himself from the Congress' decision to accept Partition;[14] or, do we see the balance of power tilting against him from the time he suggested the dissolution of the Congress and 'before the rot set(s) in further'? He had stated at the Congress Working Committee meeting, which finally approved the partition plan, that he 'would have declared rebellion single-handed against the CWC if he had felt stronger or an alternative was available.' That he did not feel strong enough to carry out his threat is a powerful indictment of the Congress party and its tall poppies.

Writers poignantly detail Gandhi's heroics in riot-torn Noakhali in East Bengal and dwell on his fasts unto death in Calcutta that began in September 1947 and on 13 January 1948, respectively. But most pay scant attention, especially during this period, to his moral dilemma resulting from the Congress party's desire to achieve freedom at all cost. It is fair to argue that the colonial context, the complex legacy of history, and the potentially explosive legacy of social and economic

---

[13]16 December 1946, Nicholas Mansergh (ed.), *The Transfer of Power 1942–47* [*TF*] (His Majesty's Stationery Office, London), vol. 9, p. 406.

[14]'Let posterity know,' he said, 'what agony this old man went through thinking of it [Partition]. Let not the coming generations curse Gandhi for being a party to India's vivisection.'

inequalities between the two communities handicapped him.[15] Nonetheless, we also need to understand the dialectics of the Partition *movement*, and not so much the consequences, that enfeebled the Mahatma's initiatives to resolve the Congress-Muslim impasse, and in the end, hastened his political death.

Doubtless, Gandhi did not have a ready-made answer to allay Jinnah's anxieties or curb the stridency of Hindu militants. He could not have produced a magic formula to extinguish the flames of hatred. Yet, he still commanded the allegiance of millions across the subcontinent, including the Muslim communities, to reconcile competing political aspirations. Doubtless, he lacked the political resources to prevent Partition in 1945–46, but the transfer of power may not have taken such an ugly and violent turn had his Congress colleagues allowed him to wield his moral stick. With non-violence being so very central to his life-long mission, he had every reason to reaffirm its efficacy in the twilight of his career. Worn out by the rigours of an active public life, an ageing Gandhi had every reason to expect that his colleagues would provide him the space to pursue his moral crusade against violence. Darkness prevailed, but he still hoped that the country would 'survive this death and dance', and 'occupy the moral height that should belong to her after the training, however imperfect, in non-violence for an unbroken period of 32 years since 1915.'[16] Violence had engulfed the country, and yet he hoped, as he stated in Calcutta, that 'the goodness of the people at the bottom will assert itself against the mischievous influence.' His goal was 'to find peace in the midst of turmoil, light in the midst of darkness, hope in despair'.[17] Pyarelal describes this quality of hope:

By an almost superhuman effort of the will he was able in the midst of all this to preserve his balance and even his good humour ... He seemed to have access to some hidden reservoir of strength, optimism, joy and peace, which was independent of other circumstances.[18]

Finding peace amidst turmoil became an integral part of Gandhi's inner quest, his inner journey that had a goal but no destination.

[15]Bhikhu Parekh, *Gandhi's Political Philosophy* (London, 1989), p. 184.

[16] Louis Fischer, *The Life of Mahatma Gandhi* (New York, 1983 edn.), p. 486.

[17]Pyarelal, *Mahatma Gandhi, Life of Mohandas Karamchand Gandhi* (New Delhi: Publications Division, Government of India), vol. 8, p. 587.

[18]Pyarelal, *Mahatma Gandhi*, p. 685.

Pacifying enraged mobs was relatively simple, for the Gandhian charisma still worked, as in Bihar, where his presence did much to reassure local Muslims.[19] But Jinnah, as he had discovered during the course of their many previous encounters, was a hard nut to crack. Allaying his apprehensions proved to be a nightmare for his political adversaries. Meeting his demands was doubly difficult. With their conflicting visions and perspectives surfacing during their talks in the autumn of 1944 (the talks began on 9 September) and later, the main stumbling block remained Jinnah's insistence on having his 'Pakistan', and Gandhi's moral indignation at the very idea of India's 'vivisection'. 'What made his [Jinnah's] demands even more incongruous,' wrote Madeline Slade (Mira Behn),

was that he maintained that the Moslems as a separate nationality had the sole right to decide, in the areas he chose to describe as Moslem-majority Provinces, whether to separate from India or not, regardless of the rest of the population which, except for the North-West Frontier regions, formed only a little less than half of the total population.[20]

Gandhi did not expect to convert Jinnah *Sahib* to his creed, but he counted on his party comrades to pay heed to his warnings. What, if they had done so? The fact is that they did not. Though Jawaharlal Nehru and Vallabhbhai Patel pressed his services to restore peace and harmony in the riot-stricken areas, they wilfully disregarded his views on crucial issues. Though the historian Sucheta Mahajan laboriously attempts to prove otherwise, Gandhi was deeply hurt,[21] complaining to friends about his estrangement from those very Congress leaders whose careers he had nursed assiduously.[22] When Pyarelal joined Gandhi in December 1947, barely six months before his death, he found him isolated from the surroundings and from almost every one of his colleagues.[23] Sometimes he would ask himself, 'had India free no longer any need of him as it had when it was in bondage'.[24] A month before his assassination, he stated:

[19]H. Dow to Mountbatten, 25 March 1947, *TF*, vol. 10, p. 19.
[20]Madeline Slade, *The Spirit's Pilgrimage* (London, 1960), p. 262; Stanley Wolpert, *Jinnah of Pakistan* (New York, 1984), pp. 231–36.
[21]Mahajan, *Independence and Partition*, pp. 374–79.
[22]Gandhi to G.D. Birla, n.d. (Probably at the end of 1946), *CWMG*, vol. 86, p. 295.
[23]Pyarelal, *Mahatma Gandhi*, p. 681.
[24]Bose, *My Days with Gandhi*, p. 250.

I know that today I irritate everyone. How can I believe that I alone am right and all others are wrong? What irks me is that people deceive me. They should tell me frankly that I have become too old, that I am no longer of any use and that I should not be in their way. If they thus openly repudiate me I shall not be pained in the least.[25]

The sun had set in Noakhali village and the rioters had retreated to their den to prepare themselves for an early morning assault. While the *lathis* were readied and the knives sharpened, a weary Mahatma, leaning upon a *lathi* that had stood him in good stead during his political journeys, had to prove to the world that personal courage, moral fervour, and commitment, more than formalistic ideologies, could soothe violent tempers. He had demonstrated the force of his methods in the past, but there was now a greater and more compelling obligation to drive home this message across the country. He had written to G.D. Birla from Srirampur:

It is my intention to stay on here just as long as the Hindus and Muslims do not become sincerely well-disposed towards each other. God alone can keep man's resolve unshaken. Good-bye to Delhi, to Sevagram, to Uruli, to Panchgani—my only desire is to do or die. This will also put my non-violence to the test, and I have come here to emerge successful from this ordeal.[26]

In Noakhali, he would have said to his restless audience basking in the morning sunshine that violence breeds more violence. Hatred, he would have reiterated in his low and soft voice, betrayed weakness rather than strength, generated fear, heightened anxieties, and created insecurities. Gandhi told his companion, Nirmal Kumar Bose, 'I find that I have not the patience of the technique needed in these tragic circumstances. Suffering and evil often overwhelms me and I stew in my own juice.'[27] And yet the world outside the Congress arena listened to only one man, eagerly awaiting the outcome of this belated but extremely important mission. Never before had a political leader taken so bold an initiative to provide the healing touch not just to the people in Noakhali but to the warring groups across the

---

[25] *Harijan*, 18 December 1947, *CWMG*, vol. 90, p. 253.

[26] Gandhi to Birla, 26 November 1946, G.D. Birla, *In the Shadow of the Mahatma: A Personal Memoir* (Bombay, 1968), p. 288.

[27] Nirmal Kumar Bose, *My Days with Gandhi* (Calcutta, 1974), p. 84; Manubehn Gandhi, *Last Glimpses of Bapu* (Agra, 1962), p. 284.

vast subcontinent. And yet, never before did so earnest an effort achieve so little. In Noakhali, Gandhi wrote on 20 November 1946:

I find myself in the midst of exaggeration and falsity, I am unable to discover the truth. There is terrible mutual distrust. ... Truth and Ahimsa, by which I swear and which have, to my knowledge, sustained me for sixty years, seems to show the attributes I have ascribed to them.[28]

After Naokhali, Gandhi was caught up in the whirlpool of hatred, anger and violence. Jinnah, on the other hand, steered his ship through rough currents seeking a secure anchorage. Riding on the crest of a popular wave, he, the Quaid (leader), seemed oblivious to the human sufferings caused by his cry for a Muslim homeland (though he signed a statement with Gandhi condemning violence on 15 April 1947). The one-time disciple of Dadabhai Naoroji, a staunch Home Rule Leaguer, architect of the Congress-League Pact (December 1916) and Sarojini Naidu's ambassador of Hindu-Muslim unity, firmly rejected Gandhi's vision of a united India. 'By all canons of international law,' the Lincoln's Inn-educated barrister told Gandhi during his talks in early September 1944, 'we are a nation.' 'We are a nation,' he reiterated, 'with our own distinctive culture and civilization, language and literature, art and architecture, names and nomenclature, sense of value and proportion, legal laws and moral codes, customs and calendar, history and traditions, aptitudes and ambitions.' [29]

Though spoken from the commanding heights of power, this was small talk based on ill-founded theories and assumptions that Jinnah had himself repudiated a decade ago. Gandhi did not agree. He asked Jinnah whether or not they could agree to differ on the question of two nations, and find a way out of the deadlock. Predictably, Jinnah said 'no'. Whether this was a titanic clash of ideologies is debatable, but what is worth discussing is whether, in the political climate of the 1940s, they could have acted differently. Was there even the slightest possibility of mediating their differences within or, for that matter, outside the party structures? Were they politically equipped to push through a negotiated settlement against the wishes of their following?

---

[28] *The Collected Works of Mahatma Gandhi* (New Delhi: Publications Division, Government of India), vol. 86, p. 138.

[29] Quoted in Wolpert, *Jinnah of Pakistan*, p. 233.

Even at the risk of entering the realm of speculation, it is hard to conceive the meeting of the two minds taking place at *that* juncture. Even if that had happened, it is hard to visualize their capacity to deliver. The pressures from below, as indeed the exertions of their senior leaders, were too strong for reversing attitudes and strategies. A groundswell of rural Punjabi support for the League was in evidence.[30] In Bengal, the League captured, in the 1946 elections, 104 out of 111 seats in the rural areas. The Great Calcutta Killing of August 1947, followed by the violence that rocked Noakhali seven weeks later, completed the convergence between elite and popular communalism.[31] With the League ideology of securing adherents in the countryside and the urban-based professional classes mounting their campaigns masquerading as defenders of the faith, Jinnah could ill-afford to backtrack. For him, achieving 'Pakistan' became a matter of life and death.

Similarly, Gandhi could not single-handedly negotiate a Hindu-Muslim agreement without incurring the hostility of his own Congress colleagues. The Hindu Mahasabha and the RSS, too, had burst on the political scene with their Hindutva ideology. Having maintained their distance from the liberation struggles for years, they emerged out of their dark corridors to ensure that Gandhi and the Congress did not yield to Jinnah's demands. G.B. Pant expressed their sentiments, and perhaps also his own, to Mountbatten in May 1947:

The repercussions of events in the Punjab and Bihar and Bengal were beginning to make themselves felt in the U.P., and that [sic] he could not regard the situation as entirely satisfactory. They had gone out of their way in the U.P. to give the minorities more than a fair deal, but the Hindus were gradually becoming opposed to such generous treatment towards a community which was proving itself to be so brutal and vital in other Provinces.[32]

As the new men—some having access to top Congress leaders— arrived equipped with their heavy but coarse ideological baggage,

[30]David Gilmartin, *Empire and Islam: Punjab and the Making of Pakistan* (London, 1998), p. 73.

[31]Suranjan Das, *Communal Riots in Bengal, 1905–1947* (New Delhi, 1991), ch. 6.

[32]Interview between Mountbatten and Pant, 3 May 1947, *TF*, vol. 10, p. 590; and the criticism of B.S. Moonje, the Hindu Mahasabha leader, Judith M. Brown, *Gandhi: Prisoner of Hope* (New Delhi, 1990), pp. 380–1..

the Indian ship began its slow but inexorable drift into muddy waters without a boatmàn. The captain, having safely steered many a ship through the rough currents in the past, saw nothing but fire and smoke around him. Though Nehru told Gandhi, 'we do often feel that if you had been easier of access our difficulties would have been less',[33] the Mahatma's own belief, which he shared at his prayer meeting on 1 April 1947, was that 'no one listens to me any more ... True, there was a time when mine was a big voice. Then everybody obeyed what I said, now neither the Congress nor the Hindus nor the Muslims listen to me. Where is the Congress today? It is disintegrating. I am crying in the wilderness.'[34] Again, on 9 June, he conceded that the general opinion, especially among the non-Muslims, was not with him. That is why he decided to step aside.[35]

Gandhi was not the only one to sense the drift, the volatile political climate, and the unhindered movement towards chaos and disorder. As the war clouds dispersed and the British government began taking stock of the situation, the rapid turn of events, rather than the inexorable logic of history the League invoked to legitimise the two-nation theory, caught activists napping. Liberal and secular ideologies received a beating: the untidy communal forces, on the other hand, had a field day. The RSS, the Mahasabha and the League seized the opportunity, denied to them during the Quit India movement by the rise of anti-colonial sentiments, to regroup themselves into cohesive entities. With the Congress rank and file divided and dispirited, they gained the space to intervene. The activities of the Muslim National Guards, the stormtroopers of the Muslim League, the swayamsevaks, and the sword-wielding Sikh jathas amply illustrate this. Eventually they, the inheritors of divided homelands, fouled the path leading to the newly created capitals of free India and Pakistan—Delhi and Karachi.

At the cross-roads of communal polarisation, India became a fertile ground for the idea of a *divided* India to nurture. Most found, willy-nilly, and that included powerful Congress leaders who had until now paid lip service to the conception of a united India, the partition as a way out of the impasse. Patel had said: 'Frankly speaking, we all

[33]*SWJN*, vol. 1, New Series, p. 111.
[34]*CWMG*, vol. 87, p. 187.
[35]Ibid., vol. 88, p. 118.

hate it, but at the same time see no way out of it.' The options, if any, were foreclosed.[36] The Congress agreed to the Partition because, as Nehru stated at the All India Congress Committee meeting on 9 August 1947, 'there is no other alternative'.[37] This was not an admission of failure but a recognition of the ground realities that had moved inexorably towards the polarisation of the Hindu, Muslim and Sikh communities.

For Jinnah, the real and ultimate challenge was to translate his otherwise nebulous idea of a Muslim state into a territorial acquisition that he could sell to his partners in Punjab—termed by Jinnah the 'cornerstone' of Pakistan—Bengal and UP. When the Lahore Resolution was adopted in March 1940, Jinnah's Pakistan was undefined. He hesitated placing his cards out in the open not because he feared a Congress backlash, but because he could not predict the reactions of his own allies in Punjab (the Muslim League showing in the 1937 elections was pitiful), the United Provinces (UP), and Bengal. But once the edifice of resistance and opposition crumbled, especially in Punjab after the deaths of Sikander Hayat Khan and the Jat leader Chhotu Ram (both had kept the Punjab Unionist Party intact), and popular support for the Pakistan idea gathered momentum, Jinnah had no qualms in defining his future Pakistan. His greatest strength lay, a point underlined by David Gilmartin, in transcending the tensions in the provinces and localities and directing Muslim politics towards symbolic goals, even as he compromised to build political support. His 'genius' lay in forging what in fact approximated to a marriage of convenience between the professional classes of the Hindu dominated areas and the landlords of the future Pakistan regions.[38]

At every critical moment after the resignation of the ministries in September 1939, Jinnah's great asset was the government's readiness to negotiate with him as an ally rather than as an adversary. This had not been the case earlier, though Nehru had pointed out that the third party could always bid higher, and what is more, give substance to its words. The Quit India movement (August 1942) turned out to be yet another milestone. From that time onwards the League bandwagon

[36]Mahajan, *Independence and Partition*, pp. 358–9.

[37]*Selected Works of Jawaharlal Nehru* (Jawaharlal Nehru Memorial Fund: New Delhi), Second Series, vol. 3, p. 134.

[38]Ian Talbot, *Pakistan: A Modern History* (London and New Delhi, 1999), p. 5.

rolled on, and Jinnah developed the habit of reminding senior British officials—many turning to him to take sweet revenge on the Congress—of their obligations towards the Muslims. Whenever he found them dithering or tilting slightly towards the Congress, he, conjuring up the self-image of a wounded soul, raised the spectre of a civil war.

Words were translated into deeds on Direct Action Day on 16 August 1946. This ill-advised call did not exactly heal communal wounds, but proved to be, as was the undeclared intention, Jinnah's trump card. The Quaid, says Ayesha Jalal, was forced by the Muslim League Council to go for Direct Action; otherwise he would have 'swept himself aside.[39] What remains unexplained is how this decision, besides leading to the Great Calcutta Killing, sounded the death-knell of a united India. If the resignation of the Congress ministries allowed Jinnah to jump the queue and gain proximity to the colonial government, direct action confirmed his capacity to call the shots and create, with the aid of his allies in Bengal particularly, the conditions for civil strife on a continental scale. H.S. Suhrawardy, the Bengal Premier, ensured that this reckless call paid off.[40] Ironically, the same Suhrawardy, who toyed with the impractical idea of a united Bengal[41] in the company of a handful of tired bhadralok leaders, accompanied Gandhi to extinguish the flames of violence in Bengal.

Meanwhile, the colonial government—the 'third party'—nursed its wounds. Bruised and battered by the impact of World War II, it had little or no interest in curbing violence. As the sun finally set on the empire, the imperial dream was over. It was time to dismantle the imperial structures and move to the safety of the British Isles. 'Your day is done', Gandhi had written. The British, having read the writing on the wall, had no desire or motivation to affect a *peaceful* transfer of power. Having bandied around the view that Hindu-Muslim violence resulted from a civilizational conflict between Islam and Hinduism, they now put forward the thesis that it could not be contained once Pakistan became inevitable. Penderel Moon, the civil servant, argues

[39]On July 1946, the Muslim League Council withdrew its acceptance of the Cabinet Mission Plan. Direct Action Day was celebrated on 16 August.

[40]Viceroy Wavell recorded on 5 November 1946: 'Suhrawardy, looking as much of a gangster as ever, described to me the measures he proposed for stricter enforcement of law and order.' *TF*, vol. 9, p. 16.

[41]Record of Interview between K.S. Roy and F. Burrows, *TF*, vol. 10, p. 6.

that the holocaust in Punjab was unavoidable without a Sikh-Muslim settlement, and that 'by the time Lord Mountbatten arrived in India it was far too late to save the situation'.[42] H.V. Hodson makes similar assertions.[43] There is little reason to subscribe to their thesis: Sudhir Ghosh, the young executive from the Tata firm, rightly told Stafford Cripps: 'if the Governor-General and the Governor say that this kind of killing and barbarity [following the Direct Action Day] is inevitable in the present circumstances of our country, I look upon that argument as an excuse put forward by men who have failed to do their duty.'[44]

Wavell had stated in early November 1946 that 'the long-term remedy and the only one which will really improve matters is of course an improvement of relations between the two communities.'[45] Such a view offered to the government an escape route. According to Moon's own testimony, 'you couldn't prevent [the Hindu-Muslim conflict], but you might if you were sufficiently prompt and on the spot at the time, prevent it from assuming a very serious form.'[46] The fact is that the administrators were unprepared to risk British lives being lost at a time when their departure from India was all but certain. Quickening their retreat from civil society, they sought the safety of their bungalows and cantonments. While large parts of the country were aflame, they played cricket, listened to music, and read Kipling. For the most part, the small boundary force in Punjab stayed in their barracks, while trainloads of refugees were being butchered.

It is debatable whether this was 'a creation-narrative, an epic founding myth, of sheer agony over religion'.[47] There is no denying, however, that in the histories of imperial rule, the retreat of the British administration, once the source of Curzonian pride, was an act of abject surrender to the forces of violence. 'We have lost,' wrote Wavell,

[42]Penderel Moon, *Divide and Quit* (New Delhi, 1998), pp. 276–7. Introduction, Mark Tully; 'Re-reading *Divide and Quit*', Tapan Raychaudhuri.

[43]H.V. Hodson, *The Great Divide: Britain-India-Pakistan* (Karachi, 1997 edn.), pp. 402–7.

[44]31 October 1946, *TF*, vol. 9, p. 26.

[45]*TF*, vol. 9, p. 19.

[46]Quoted in Charles Allen (ed.), *Plain Tales from the Raj* (London, 1975), p. 246.

[47]Larson, *India's Agony Over Religion*, p 191.

'nearly all power to control events; we are simply running on the momentum of our previous prestige.'[48] When the dead count was taken, the people of the subcontinent paid the price—and that too a heavy one—for the breakdown of the law and order machinery. Eventually, a beleaguered Congress government faced with a civil war like situation, cleared up the debris of death and destruction.

The colonial thesis was, as indeed its more recent endorsement in certain quarters, based on false assumptions, for neither then nor now does the 'clash of civilizations' theory carry conviction. If anything, the cause of extensive violence had its roots in the structured imperial categories designed to differentiate one community from another. The categories thus created were translated into formal political arrangements. So that the issue at hand is not to question the motives or the intentions behind the constitutional blueprint—for these are by now well established in secondary literature—but to assess the consequences of carving out special religious categories and extending favours to them on that basis. As David Page puts it:

In the consolidation of political interests around communal issues, the Imperial power played an important role. By treating the Muslims as a separate group, it divided them from other Indians. By granting them separate electorates, it institutionalised that division. This was one of the most crucial factors in the development of communal politics. Muslim politicians did not have to appeal to Muslims. This made it very difficult for a genuine nationalism to emerge. [49]

Again, concludes Page succinctly,

With each stage of devolution, Indian was set against Indian, caste against caste, community against community. But as each area of government and administration was ceded to Indian control, it was followed by demands for more concessions. Ultimately, even the Raj's closest allies were only allies for a purpose. In 1947, the Raj withdrew, ceding its dominant position to those who had triumphed in the electoral arena. But the final act of devolution was also a final act of division ...[50]

[48]Penderel Moon (ed.), *Wavell: The Viceroy's Journal*, p. 402.
[49]Page, *Prelude to Partition*, p. 260.
[50]Ibid., p. 264.

II

Murder stalks the streets and the most amazing cruelties are indulged in by both the individual and the mob. It is extraordinary how our peaceful population has become militant and bloodthirsty. Riot is not the word for it—it is just sadistic desire to kill.

Jawaharlal Nehru to Krishna Menon, 11 November 1946.

The four books included in this omnibus cover not only the prelude to and the consequences of Partition, but also illustrate, equally, the evolution and changing trends in partition historiography. This single volume may well carry the *imprimatur* of an authoritative historical series.

Nobody knows how many were killed during Partition violence. Nobody knows how many were displaced and dispossessed. What we know is that, between 1946 and 1951, nearly nine million Hindus and Sikhs came to India, and about six million Muslims went to Pakistan. Of the said nine million, five million came from what became West Pakistan, and four million from East Pakistan. In only three months, between August and October 1947, Punjab, the land of the five great rivers, was engulfed in a civil war. Estimates of deaths vary between 200,000 and three million.

G.D. Khosla, an enlightened civil servant, describes the colossal human tragedy involving, according to his estimate, the death of 400,000 to 250,000 people. Appearing in the shadow of Independence and Partition, his book offers an overview of the sequence, nature, and scale of the killings. For this reason, it is of invaluable documentary importance, and useful for many events that took place on the eve of the transfer of power. A work of this kind can hardly be scintillating, though it captures the trauma of a generation that witnessed unprecedented brutalities, all in the name of religion.

For one, *Stern Reckoning* belies the claim aired in certain circles that Partition violence has remained outside the domain of critical scrutiny. The issue is not the sophisticated approach or interpretation (the subaltern studies siege of the existing citadels of knowledge had yet to begin), but the overriding concern with violence. Public men, social scientists, especially historians, writers, poets, and journalists shared this concern, in equal measure, and, contrary to

Gyanendra Pandey's contention,[51] represented violence, pain and struggle in such a way as to reflect the present-day language of historical discourse. This was true of historians at Aligarh, Allahabad, Patna and Calcutta, and exemplified by, among others, Krishan Chandar (1913–1977), Rajinder Singh Bedi (1910–1984), Saadat Hasan Manto (1912–1955), the *enfant terrible* of Urdu literature, and other creative writers both within and outside the Progressive Writers' Movement. In fact it was their preoccupation with mob fury and its brutal expression that led first-generation social scientists to pin responsibility, identify the 'guilty men' of the 1940s, place them in the dock, and ask them to account for their public conduct. Hence we see the makings of public trials with the aim of discovering not so much the genesis of Pakistan but the factors leading to the violent conflagration. Implicit in this concern is a sense of moral outrage, an unmistakable revulsion towards violence, the fear of its recurrence, and, at the same time, the hope of its being prevented in free India and Pakistan. 'Perhaps', concludes Khosla,

there are some who will take warning from this sad chapter in our history and endeavour to guard against a repetition of these events. So long as sectarianism and narrow provincialism are allowed to poison the minds of the people, so long as there are ambitious men with corruption inside them, seeking power and position, so long will the people continue to be deluded and misled, as the Muslim masses were deluded and misled by the League leaders and so long will discord and disruption continue to threaten our peace and integrity.

Another noteworthy point, as evident from Khosla's portrayal, is that violence is not celebrated (as was done by the Serbs and Croats in Bosnia-Herzegovina) but decried in the narratives I have accessed. Doubtless, there is a great deal of fuming and fretting over Jinnah's call to observe 'deliverance day' after the Congress ministries resigned in September 1939, and anger and indignation, as in Pakistan, over the Boundary Commission Award. Doubtless, such episodes are recounted to reinforce arguments in favour of, or in opposition to, the demand for a Muslim nation. And yet Hindu-Muslim-Sikh violence and its perpetrators are not valourized except in polemical literature.

[51]'The Prose of Otherness', David Arnold and David Hardiman (eds.), *Subaltern Studies VIII: Essays in Honour of Ranajit Guha* (New Delhi, 1994), p. 221.

Violence is, in fact, not only condemned but is so often attributed—often as a means to disguise the collective guilt of a community—to anti-social elements, unscrupulous politicians, and religious fanatics.

It is worth reiterating that the 'heroes' in the Partition story are not the rapists, the abductors, the arsonists, the murderers and the perpetrators of violence, but the men and women—living and dead—who provide the healing touch. The silver lining is that it is they who emerge, in the twilight of Delhi, Lahore, Calcutta and Dhaka, as the beacon of hope in riot-torn cities; and it is their exemplary courage, counterpoised to the inhumanity of the killers, that is celebrated. Khushdeva Singh, a medical doctor who saved many Muslim lives, kept repeating to himself as he returned from Karachi after his visit to Pakistan in 1949:

Love is stronger than hatred, love is far stronger than hatred, love is far stronger than hatred, love is far stronger than hatred, and love is far stronger than hatred at any time and anywhere. It was a thousand times better to love and die, than to live and hate.[52]

In the secularized discourses too, there is a tendency to invoke those who, regardless of their standing in the political spectrum, fostered inter-community peace.[53] It will not do to ignore the fact that Nehru, Azad and Rajaji, occupying the secular site, capture the imagination far more than their detractors. Whatever one might say, this bears some relevance to the support for a secular polity and the marginalization of, at least a decade after Independence, the communal forces.

Even at the risk of oversimplification, I conclude by arguing that the general tenor of the literary and political narratives, both in India and Pakistan, is to emphasise that Partition violence sounded the death-knell of those high moral values that were essential components of Hinduism, Islam and the Sikh faith. Naturally, the definition of such values, rooted in diverse traditions, varied. But the consensus, though unstated and unstructured, is to invoke diverse religious,

[52]Hasan (ed.), *India Partitioned*, vol. 2, p. 112.
[53]The trend continues, for example, Rajmohan Gandhi, *Revenge Reconciliation: Understanding South Asian History* (New Delhi, 1999); the essays/stories in Ahmad Salim, *Lahore 1947* (New Delhi, 2001); and Syed Sikander Mehdi, 'Refugee Memory in India and Pakistan', in *Transeuropeennes*, pp. 123–5, 127.

intellectual, and humanist traditions to serve the crying need of the hour—restoration of peace and inter-community goodwill. Thus Nanak Singh, the Punjabi writer, invokes Guru Gobind Singh to lend weight to his moralistic plea for communal amity (he had ordained, 'every one of the [sic] humankind is same to me');[54] Amrita Pritam, the Punjabi poet, vividly recalls the dark nights on the train and the images of death and destruction which Haji Waris Shah had seen in Punjab at the end of the eighteenth century, with the butchery and rape that accompanied Partition; Kamaladevi Chattopadhyaya (d. 1990) and Aruna Asaf Ali (1909–1996) invoke the composite tradition to lament how the birth of freedom on that elevated day— 15 August 1947—did not bring India 'any such ennobling benediction';[55] the Delhi-based writer and social activist, Begum Anis Kidwai (1902–80) pleads in her book *In the Shadow of Freedom*:

We have lived through the times. An epoch has come to a close and my generation has either retired to their corners or is preparing to leave this world. Throughout this piece of writing, I can only say this to the younger generation:

Look at me if your eyes can take a warning
Listen to me if your ears can bear the truth.

Builders of tomorrow, keep away from that chalice of poisons which we drank and [sic] committed suicide. And if you build anew on the foundations of morality, strength, dignity, and steadfastness, you will be esteemed.[56]

For scores of writers, social activists and publicists, secularism, in the sense of anti-communalism, was a deeply held faith, an integral face of nationalism, a value to be upheld even during the difficult days of August 1947 and thereafter.[57] One of them, the writer Attia Hosain who preferred living in London rather than going to Pakistan, recalled years later:

---

[54]S.S. Hans, 'The Partition Novels of Nanak Singh', Amit Kumar Gupta (ed.), *Myth and Reality: The Struggle for Freedom in India, 1945–47* (New Delhi, 1987), p. 367.

[55]Kamaladevi Chattopadhyaya, *From Outer Spaces: Memoirs* (New Delhi, 1986), ch. 10; Aruna Asaf Ali, *From Fragments from the Past: Selected Writings and Speeches* (Delhi, 1989), ch. 25–26.

[56]*India Partitioned*, vol. 2, pp. 158–9.

[57]Mahajan, *Independence and Partition*, p. 23.

Events during and after Partition are to this day very painful to me. And now, in my old age, the strength of my roots is strong; it also causes pain, because it makes one a 'stranger' everywhere in the deeper area of one's mind and spirit *except where one was born and brought up.*[58]

III

Living as I was in a mixed Hindu-Moslem region, where the two communities had dwelt together for centuries and where the Moslem peasants were, if anything, better off than the Hindu peasants, all that talk had, for me, a most unhealthy ring.

Mira Behn, *The Spirit's Pilgrimage*, p. 262.

Penderel Moon (1905–1987) joined the I.C.S. in 1929. Prior to his resignation in 1944 to join the Bahawalpur State, he had served in Punjab for fifteen years, rising from Assistant to District Magistrate in Multan, Gujrat and Amritsar. He played an active role in Punjab affairs. In 1945, he submitted a note to Stafford Cripps contending that the general support of the Muslims for Pakistan meant that 'the emphasis on the unity of India which has hitherto characterised official utterances and official thought [was] no longer opportune.' The disadvantages of division and the advantages of unity were doubtless great but 'it is no use crying for the moon'. It should be Britain's 'working hypothesis' that 'to come down on the side of Pakistan is likely to be the right decision.' Jinnah was now strong enough to block all constitutional progress except on his own terms. However, if the Pakistan principle were conceded, he might welcome arrangements for collaboration with Hindustan. 'The concession of Pakistan in name would be the means for approximating most nearly to a united India in fact.' Again, among the Congress leaders were realists who would recognise that: 'An India united otherwise than by consent is an India divided *ab initio.*'[59]

Around the same time, his other concern found tangible expression in his efforts to persuade the Sikhs 'to throw in their lot with their brethren in Punjab and take their place in the new Dominion or

[58]Anita Desai, Introduction to Attia Hosain, *Phoenix Fled* (New Delhi, 1993 edn.), p. xiii.

[59]I have reproduced a summary of the note—'The Pakistan Nettle'—from R.J. Moore, *Escape from Empire: The Attlee Government and the Indian Problem* (Oxford, 1983), p. 59.

State of Pakistan.' In return for this, the Muslims, so he believed, would offer considerable concessions to the Sikhs to make them feel secure in Pakistan.[60] He discussed his proposals with Ismay, Chief of Staff to Mountbatten (March–November 1947), who arranged a meeting of the two Sikh leaders, Giani Kartar Singh and Sardar Baldev Singh, with Mountbatten. But their encounter turned out to be a damp squib. Moon was bluntly told that 'all the emphasis at the interview [was] on concessions to be obtained from the Union of India and not from Pakistan.'[61] At the end of June 1947, Moon proposed the realignment of boundaries that would establish the province of East Punjab with the strongest possible Sikh complexion. Ismay and Mountbatten were sympathetic to his views, but as Ismay commented, 'things have now gone much too far for HMG to be able to take a hand.'[62]

The earlier part of Moon's book, first published in 1961, traces political events in India and Punjab from 1937 until their tragic de-nouement ten years later. The second half, starting roughly from chapter five, is confined to the disturbances occurring from the end of August 1947 onwards in the Bahawalpur State, a territory imme-diately adjacent to Punjab. These chapters are quite instructive. 'When the clash came,' writes Moon in *Divide and Quit*,

my position in Bahawalpur was like that of a battalion commander in an obscure outlying sector of the field of battle. But during part of the preceding ten years I had held a staff appointment which gave me an insight into the movement and massing of forces leading to the conflict in which I was subsequently involved. Thus, to change the metaphor, I ended by playing a small part in a tragedy the preparation for which I had long watched moving to their appointed but unpurposed end.

The scale of the work necessitated extreme condensation, and the treatment of certain themes is very slender and the material elementary, though most readers may find new points made on Bahawalpur. The text is explicit and concise, and the plan simple and clear. The intrinsic value of *Divide and Quit* lies in a senior British

[60]Moon to Master Sujan Singh, 8 June 1947, Kirpal Singh (ed.), *Select Documents on Partition of Punjab 1947* (Delhi, 1991), pp. 103–4.

[61]Ismay to Moon, 3 July 1947, ibid., p. 138.

[62]Ismay to Moon, 3 July 1947, ibid., pp. 330–1.

civil servant telling the story as it unfolded itself to him at the time. It can be read either as an observant record of the more complex periods in modern Indian political history, or as an account of a senior civil servant on the threshold of old age.

All this said, and with the respect due to a learned man who also edited Wavell's journal, the author has not much to add to earlier conclusions about the genesis of Pakistan, the Cabinet Mission, or the Mountbatten Plan. Besides, he is by no means a neutral observer. Many of his categories, Tapan Raychaudhuri points out, reflect the colonial stereotype. And yet one hopes that, used with necessary caution, this book will be of help to scholars and teachers alike.

IV

The year Penderel Moon died, Anita Inder Singh, an Oxford graduate, published her absorbing account of the years 1936 to 1947. There is much in her study that is refreshingly new and interesting. At a time when some of the old debates relating to Partition are being revived, it is worth revisiting *The Origins of the Partition of India* for a corrective to certain misplaced suppositions, and for gaining fresh insights. For example, it is worth considering her thesis that the demand for a Muslim nation was proclaimed from above, and 'so it held no great significance or effect on the divisions among Muslim politicians in the majority provinces before 1945–46.'[63] There is, furthermore, merit in her argument that the elections of 1945–6 provided the League's opponents with an opportunity to defeat it, but they failed to rise to the occasion. True, the result of the election (Muslim League won 70 per cent of the Muslim votes) gave a boost to the partition movement—the political unification and solidification of the Muslim community. Yet the extent of this unification, adds Inder Singh, 'need not be exaggerated into a communal mandate for a sovereign Pakistan.'[64] This requires elaboration.

Nehru's perception of the election campaign runs contrary to the weight of evidence marshalled by several historians of Partition. The key factor he highlighted in his exchanges—one that was suppressed by the eventual triumph of the League—is the favourable response

---

[63]Singh, *Origins of the Partition*, p. 241.
[64]Ibid., p. 243.

of the Muslims to the Congress campaign. In November 1945, he told Vallabhbhai Patel: 'I want to repeat that the recent election work has been a revelation to Congress workers so far as the Muslim areas are concerned. It is astonishing how good the response has been. Have we neglected these areas! We must contest every seat.'[65] He shared this assessment with Azad, referring in particular to the 'extraordinarily favourable response from the Muslim masses' in the Meerut division.[66]

Did Nehru exaggerate the pro-Congress sentiment among Muslims at that juncture? I believe he did. Was his enthusiasm misplaced? If not, what went wrong? Is it the case that the Congress deliberately and systematically avoided reaching out to the Muslim masses with the aim of weaning them away from the League? If so, why? Is it because they felt that it was a no-win situation with Jinnah, or is it that they were pressured by Hindu communalist groups to let the Muslims stew in their own juice? Or, possibly, the Congress strategy was dictated by the single-minded purpose of facilitating the speedy transfer of power to two sovereign nations. The point is not to attribute blame but to recognise the dilemmas and predicaments of a party that was, besides being horizontally and vertically divided, caught up in its own quagmire.

Nehru explained the League's success in the 1946 elections to officials actively helping the League candidates, and to the Congress, which was continually under ban and in prison during those five years, giving the League a field day to pursue its propaganda.[67] The historian Sarvepalli Gopal has pointed out that the Congress was ill prepared for the elections. Though popular among the masses, its party machinery was out of gear, many of its supporters among the narrow electorate—about 30 per cent of the adult population—had not been registered, and 'its leaders at every level were tired, unenthusiastic and pulling in contrary directions.'[68] I have argued elsewhere that the Congress could have made some additional gains if it had put up Muslim candidates in the general and urban

[65] 26 November 1945, *SWJN*, vol. 14, p. 123.
[66] 27 November, 1945, ibid., p. 124.
[67] To Stafford Cripps, 27 January 1946, ibid., pp. 140–1.
[68] Sarvepalli Gopal, *Jawaharlal Nehru: A Biography* (New Delhi, 1975), vol. 1, p. 305; and Nehru to Azad, 31 October 1945, *SWJN*, vol. 14, p. 115, complaining of lack of Congress organization and 'small cliques controlling Congress committees'.

constituencies, and if its nominees in the Muslim urban constituencies were chosen with greater care.[69]

Accepting office after the elections was the last straw—'the greatest tactical mistake' made by the Congress.[70] It was clear from Jinnah's statements that the League ministers entered the Government not to work it out but because they feared that they would be weakened if they kept out. Hence Jinnah's statement on 14 November that his ministers were 'sentinels', who would watch Muslim interests.

In his seminal essay, Asim Roy places the writings of Stanley Wolpert, R. J. Moore, and Inder Singh in the category of 'orthodox historiography'. He regards Ayesha Jalal, on the other hand, as the principal advocate of the revisionist position on Pakistan and Partition in relation to Jinnah and the League (*The Sole Spokesman: Jinnah, the Muslim League and the Demand for Pakistan*, Cambridge, 1985). What then is the dividing line between the conventional and the revisionist positions? Asim Roy's answer is: 'On both chronological and thematic grounds the Lahore Resolution of 1940 clearly emerges as the divide between the two distinct interpretative approaches.'[71]

Students of high politics may well discover that Inder Singh and Jalal complement each other, though this view may not go down well with the authors themselves. The former provides us with the big picture, focusing on the national arena. Jalal explores the happenings in the provinces, linking them judiciously with all-India politics. Unlike Inder Singh's uncomplicated narrative, there is, in *The Sole Spokesman*, a much fascinating and complex discussion on the extraordinary configuration of forces in Punjab and Bengal, and readers have therefore found stimulation, as well as opinions to question, in this highly interpretative account. In sum, both these books have earned their place on the college and university bookshelves, and in the homes of the historical-minded reader.

Inder Singh's interpretations are based on wide-ranging sources; in fact, the factual and interpretative contents of certain portions of her book are impressive. Jalal's source base is less broad-based, and yet this does not inhibit her magisterial analysis. At the same time,

[69]Introduction, Hasan (ed.), *India's Partition*, pp. 40–1.

[70]Singh, *Origins of the Partition*, p. 251.

[71]Asim Roy, 'The High Politics of India's Partition: The Revisionist Perspective', in *India's Partition*, p.106.

it constrains her ability to negotiate with the Congress story, and to tie up loose ends in describing the political domain outside Jinnah, in particular, and the League circles generally. This is a major omission, for the story of the Congress does not merely rest on a few hotheaded individuals out to wreck Jinnah's plans, and ultimately, preside over the liquidation of the Muslim communities in the subcontinent. It is also the story of Gandhi, Nehru, and Azad and Khan Abdul Ghaffar Khan, the symbols of plural nationhood, and of a powerful movement—with its high and low points—embracing many sections of the society, including Muslims. Between the two distinct phases—from the benign politics of petition until the swadeshi movement in Bengal to sustained agitation—lie a rich variety of ideas and movements. Even if the Congress career ended ingloriously during the dark days of Partition, it is still a compelling historical necessity to decipher the Congress script afresh, account for the flaws in its mobilization strategies, and point to the inconsistencies in its conception of secularism and plural nationhood.

Together with the works of Jalal and Inder Singh, the book *Prelude to Partition: The Indian Muslims and the Imperial System of Control* forms a natural unity. David Page, an Oxford graduate like Inder Singh, examines the period from 1920 to 1932 when political interests were consolidated around communal issues and Muslim attitudes were framed towards the eventual withdrawal of Imperial control. Before the Montagu-Chelmsford Reforms (Act of 1919) came into operation in 1920, cross-communal alliances took place, notably in Punjab and Bengal, but Dyarchy foregrounded communal antagonism and deepened inter-community rivalries. Page proceeds to explain how and why disparate communities came to regard Pakistan as a common goal in the 1940s. Even with his broad canvas, he probes deep into the political alignments in Punjab, a Muslim majority province. He argues how Punjabi Muslims took the lead in working against a responsible government at the Centre, and extracted, under the terms of the Communal Award (1932), a major concession—control of their own province under the new constitution. He profiles Mian Fazl-i-Husain to illustrate how he and other Punjabi Muslim leaders came to lead 'Muslim India' in the complex constitutional arrangements that resulted in the Act of 1935, and how their perspective mattered during the fateful negotiations of the 1940s.

When published in 1982, *Prelude to Partition* was a major break-through. Its author travelled through the dark alleys to make sense of the nitty-gritty of power politics in the provinces of British India. Unlike some of his predecessors, he was not swept by the rhetoric of Islam skilfully used by the *pirs* of Punjab and Sind to legitimise the predominance of one group over the other. Doubtless, religious boundaries existed and communal consciousness came into play in the public arena, but its impact was felt only when political and economic interests conflicted but not otherwise; and they did not conflict markedly before the introduction of reforms in the 1920s. In this way, Page introduces a nuanced discourse around imperial policies, and their profound impact on elite groups and their changing political alignments. The very nature of those alignments and their shifting character lies at the heart of his explanation for the rise of Hindu-Muslim antagonism. Concurring with the view that well-established traditions of Muslim political thought (he does not discuss the role of the Arya Samaj) and socio-economic disparities shaped communal consciousness in the localities, Page argues that,

if these streams of thought and consciousness fed into the river of all-India politics, the Imperial system was like a series of dams, diverting the waters to left and right to suit its own purpose. Structures may not tell the whole story but they tell an important part of it.

A great deal more has appeared since the publication of *Prelude to Partition*. David Gilmartin, Ian Talbot and Iftikhar Malik have traversed the muddy terrain of Punjab to unfold vital aspects of its polity and society on the eve of the transfer of power; Sarah F.D. Ansari uncovers the world of the *pirs* of Sind to reveal how their influence proved decisive in swinging the support of the province's Muslims in favour of the League's demand for Pakistan; Joya Chatterjee,[72] Suranjan Das, Taj ul-Islam Hashmi, Tazeen Murshid, Harun-or-Rashid, and Yunus Samad reflect on aspects of Bengal politics and society and, in the process, raise new questions that remained unanswered by historiography in the 1970s and 80s. Their interventions offer insights, open up new vistas of research, and enhance the value of studying the region and the locality.

[72] *Bengal Divided: Hindu Communalism and Partition, 1932–1947* (Cambridge, 1994).

With regional and local studies drawing greater attention, the all-India picture is increasingly out of focus. The role of major political actors is, likewise, eclipsed by the foregrounding of regional and local brokers in the world of politics. The answer lies not in the reversal of existing historical trends or in the tendency to ignore or rubbish other people's work,[73] but in a judicious mixing of the multiple levels at which partition studies can best be studied, analysed and integrated. This exercise may prove rewarding in the long run, especially because some post-modernist scholars in the West are beginning to seek new avenues for self-expression.

V

A major lacuna in existing accounts—and this is true of the books included in this omnibus—is the absence of major studies on the United Provinces (UP), a region that nurtured the ideology of Muslim nationalism.[74] Unlike Punjab, Sind, and Bengal, UP did not have the advantage of numbers. It did not have leaders of Fazl-i Husain or Fazlul Haq's stature who could, on the strength of their respective constituencies, bargain with the colonial government for political concession. Unlike Punjab, with its powerful landed gentry concentrated in western districts, UP did not have so large and unified a landlord community that could make or break a coalition. And unlike the vast peasant communities in Bengal that were mobilized around Islamic symbols from the days of the Faraizi movement to the khilafat-non-cooperation campaigns,[75] the Muslim

---

[73]The falling out of old friends and allies often leads to acrimonious exchanges. Notice, for example, the polemical debates between Gyanendra Pandey and Ayesha Jalal, and the bitter encounters between Pandey and Sumit Sarkar. Often, the divide is so thin that one tends to conclude cynically that such debates are conducted to attract attention in the West.

[74]The importance of UP is often overstated, but it is worth recording the opinion—romantic and exaggerated—of Jinnah's biographer. 'This was the area,' observes Saad R. Khairi, 'where all Muslim movements, whether of revolt or regeneration, had regenerated and flourished ... The area was also the cradle of Urdu, which had now become, after Islam, the strongest bond between the Muslims of India. Any scheme that would make this land totally "foreign" could not easily be contemplated.' Saad R. Khairi, *Jinnah Reinterpreted: The Journey from Indian Nationalism to Muslim Statehood* (Karachi, 1995), p. 352.

[75]Partha Chatterjee, 'Bengal Politics and the Muslim Masses, 1920–47', Hasan (ed.), *India's Partition*, pp. 60–62.

peasantry in UP was scarcely mobilized, even during the khilafat movement, on purely religious lines. Some element of religious rhetoric came into play, but that too coalesced, though sometimes uneasily, with peasant grievances resulting in a partnership between local khilafat committees and the kisan sabhas. Even at the height of the Pakistan campaign, with its religious symbolism, the towns rather than villages remain the foci of mobilization. 'There is no doubt,' wrote Nehru on the eve of the 1946 elections, 'that as a rule city Muslims are for the League.' He added, however, that in UP and Bihar the Momins (chiefly the weaving class) and the Muslim peasantry were far more for the Congress because they considered the League an upper class organization of feudal landlords.[76]

What is equally noteworthy—a point that may be of some help in locating the areas and directions of future research—is the role of religious leadership in minimizing the impact of the Muslim League campaign. Unlike Punjab, Sind, and Bengal, the major segment of the Muslim divines, headed by the *ulama* of Deoband, the Jamiyat al-ulama, and the Shia Political Conference, hitched their fortunes with the Congress. The *ulama* at Lucknow's Firangi Mahal were divided; their influence in Muslim politics had at any rate steadily dwindled after the khilafat campaign petered out. The Barelwi *ulama*, too, were scarcely united: for example, Shah Aulad-e Rasul Mohammad Miyan Marahrawi and the Barkatiya *pirs* firmly opposed the Muslim League, though not on secular grounds. It is not without significance that regardless of their positions, none of the *ulama* whose lives Usha Sanyal has studied, left for Pakistan.[77] One has to look beyond the 'personal exigencies', i.e. insecurity, uncertainty, and sheer danger to life at the time, and turn to the many ambivalences that characterized the decision, both before and after Partition, to remain in Hindustan or to leave for the so-called Muslim haven.

During the 1946 elections, the Hapur-born (in Meerut district) Syed Manzar Hasan (b. 1934) canvassed for the Muslim League without knowing that soon he would leave India. He, whose father's maternal grandfather had taken part in the 1857 revolt, did indeed leave for Pakistan. He recalled his arrival:

[76]Nehru to Krishna Menon, n.d., *SWJN*, vol. 14, p. 97; for the responses of the All-India Momin Conference, see Papiya Ghosh, 'Partition's Biharis', Hasan (ed.), *Islam, Communities and the Nation*, pp. 229–64.

[77]Usha Sanyal, *Devotional Islam and Politics in British India: Ahmad Riza Khan Barelwi and His Movement, 1870–1920* (New Delhi, 1996), pp. 302–27.

There, under the shade of peepal trees in the school yard, we chanted *Hindi hain ham vatan hai sara jahan hamara* [We are Indians; the entire world is ours]. Later, after I'd migrated to Pakistan, I asked my school mates, 'What did you chant on 14 August?' I'd guessed right: they had chanted *Muslim hain ham vatan hai sara jahan hamara* [We are Muslims; the entire world is ours]. What a fine poet he [Mohammad Iqbal] was. God bless him! He served two warring powers equally well. Anyway, we'd become Pakistanis overnight, but somehow it was hard to get rid of the feeling of being strangers in this new country of ours.[78]

So what explains UP's decisive role in the making of Pakistan? The Paul Brass-Francis Robinson debate has run its full course,[79] and it is time to pay special attention to the dialectics of ideology and material interests in UP, the ideological stormcentre of the Pakistan movement. It is no good harping on the 'distinct differences between Hindus and Muslims', the inherited traditions of Muslim thought and Islamic culture that were supposedly incompatible with democracy and secular nationalism, or the ideology of the Mughal ruling-class culture rooted to the idea of Mughal inheritance and the common assumptions of a divinely revealed faith.[80] What we need is a comprehensive social and economic profile of Muslim groups and how their changing profile in the 1930s, rather than the essentialized image of Indian Islam and its followers, influenced the Muslim elites to make their choice.

In this context, three points are salient. First, the Congress agrarian programme and the responses of the Awadh taluqdars; second, the middle-class perception of the Congress Ministry in UP, and the insecurities generated by some of its policies; and finally, the concern over future social alignments in a federal polity with adult franchise. The fear of being overwhelmed by the masses had prompted Jinnah and the Muslim League to reject the Nehru Committee Report in 1928.[81] The same anxiety gripped the Muslim elite once the process

[78]Introduction by Muhammad Umar Memon, Hasan Manzar, *A Requiem for the Earth: Selected Stories* (Karachi, 1998), p. xxxii.

[79]*Journal of Commonwealth and Comparative Politics*, November 1977, pp. 215. See also Paul Brass, *Language, Religion and Politics in North India* (Cambridge, 1974); Francis Robinson, *Separatism Among Indian Muslims* (Cambridge, 1974); Robinson's new Introduction to the paperback version (Delhi, 1993).

[80]Farzana Shaikh, *Community and Consensus in Islam: Muslim Representation in Colonial India, 1860–1947* (Cambridge, 1989).

[81]Mushirul Hasan, *Nationalism and Communal Politics in India, 1885–1930* (New Delhi, 1991), ch. 9.

of devolving power to India was consummated in the Act of 1935. The symbols of Islam, howsoever evocative, had a limited role to play in translating their anxieties into forging a coalition with the Muslim League. At best, they were a catalyst to, rather than the cause of, the UP Muslims' drive to secure their homeland.

Some answers may still lie in what, Lance Brennan described, as the 'Illusion of Security';[82] some in the manipulation of symbols of Muslim unity and Hindu-Muslim separateness by an elite concerned with preserving its political privileges;[83] and some in the fears engendered by the rising tide of aggressive Hindu nationalism. In *Legacy of a Divided Nation*, I analysed the Pakistan movement in terms of group interests, delineated the political context in which the Muslims were encouraged to develop separately by the colonial authorities, and pointed out nationalist narratives that rested on mistaken suppositions. I argue that prior to 1947 it was possible for fervent advocates of Indian nationhood to thwart majoritarianism and minorityism through a well-orchestrated campaign that Nehru always talked of but hardly ever translated into practice. My prescription for the Congress—to evolve an independent/autonomous discourse free from colonial narratives; to discard communal categories, the mainstay of religious mobilisation; to ignore the Muslim elite's self-image and perceptions, and act unitedly with the socialist and communist groups to erode the ideological foundation of the Hindutva and Islamist forces.

This did not happen. The Congress, with its eye fixed on the transfer of power, muddled through to occupy the commanding heights of state power on 15 August 1947. The pace of change outwitted the left forces, which could have otherwise put up a people's front. Lack of ideological coherence, combined with their mistaken assumptions about the Muslim League movement, reduced them to political impotence. To discern a democratic core in the demand for Pakistan was a huge miscalculation. 'Who killed India?' asked the left-wing writer Khwaja Ahmad Abbas. Among others, 'India was killed by the Communist Party of India which provided the Muslim separatists with the ideological basis for the irrational and anti-national demand

---

[82]Lance Brennan, 'The Illusion of Security: The Background to Muslim Separatism in the United Provinces', in Hasan (ed.), *India's Partition*, pp. 322–60.

[83]Brass, *Language, Religion and Politics in North India*, p. 120.

for Pakistan. Phrases like "homeland," "nationalities," "self-determination" etc. were all ammunition supplied by the Communists to the
legions of Pakistan.'[84]

VI

Setting out an agenda for the future historian of Partition is not an
easy proposition. The literature that has appeared during the last
decade or so points to the possibilities of charting new territories, and
breaking free from the boundaries defined by partition historiography. Using fiction to portray the other face of freedom, and
introducing poignant and powerful gender narratives has, likewise,
triggered lively discussions that go far beyond the limited terrain
explored during the last few decades.[85] When artfully undertaken,
invoking popular memories, too, shifts the burden of the argument
outside the familiar realm of elite manoeuvres and high politics to
local specificities and personal and family traumas.[86] It is this—the
interplay of emotions with the societal forces beyond the control of
an individual or family—that lends both a human and realistic touch
to partition studies.

Realistically speaking, however, gender narratives and personal
and collective memories can at best enrich partition debates and not
constitute an alternative discourse to the existing ones. Oral interviews
can only go that far; they cannot be a substitute for archival research,
especially because they are conducted over space and time by writers
who have an agenda of their own. Historians, too, have their agenda,
but their script can be read and interpreted differently. The same
cannot be said of gender narratives and other accounts, often
contrived, of pain and suffering. In 1995, I put together a cultural
archive of first-hand information, experiences and impressions in a
two-volume anthology to underline the other face of freedom. The
effort has been intellectually rewarding. At the same time, I realise,

---

[84]K.A. Abbas, *I am not an Island: An Experiment in Autobiography* (New Delhi, 1977),
p. 281.

[85]For gender narratives, Ritu Menon & K. Bhasin, *Borders and Boundaries: Women
in India's Partition* (New Delhi, 1998); Urvashi Butalia, *The Other Side of Silence: Voices
from the Partition of India* (New Delhi, 1998).

[86]Nonica Datta, 'Partition Memories: A Daughter's Testimony', Mushirul Hasan
& Nariaki Nakazato (eds.), *The Unfinished Agenda: Nation-Building in South Asia* (New
Delhi, 2001).

more so after the proliferation of recent partition literature, that our preoccupation with the pain and sorrow that resulted from Partition has doubtlessly limited our understanding of many other crucial areas, including the political and civic fault-lines revealed then—fault-lines of religion, gender, caste and class that still run through our lives.[87]

All said and done if one is located in South Asia—the issue of location is so central to the post-modernist discourse as illustrated by the polemical and personalized Aijaz Ahmad-*Public Culture* encounter—it may not be easy displacing the dominant intellectual discourses.[88] Whether this can or should be done is not the issue at hand. The reality, one that I have no special claims of knowing, is that South Asian readers everywhere—from colleges and universities to the platform of the Indian History Congress—still earnestly desire to understand a lot more about the triangular narrative, with the British, Congress and the League occupying centre stage. Its segments, on the other hand, arouse limited interest. One may want to change such concerns and reading habits (you can't be doing that from the vantage point of Columbia, Chicago or Baltimore), though at present most readers in South Asia do not pay heed to the historian's plea to eschew preoccupation with national leaders and national parties. Most studiously follow who said what at the national level, and at what juncture. We can fault them for that, but they nonetheless want to fathom how a slight slant in a statement or a twist in an event— for example, the abortive talks over the Congress-Muslim League coalition in UP—changed, in their perception, the course of the subcontinent's history.

Though sensitized to alternative discourses, most people in the subcontinent discuss not so much the high price for freedom or the enormity of the tragedy in 1947, but the factors that led to the country's division. They want to know about the intractable stubbornness of one or the other leader, and make sense of the ill-fated talks in Delhi and Simla. In short, they wish to unfold the great drama being enacted, with the spotlight on their 'heroes' and the 'villains'. They want to learn how the principal actors—Gandhi, Nehru, Patel and Azad on the one side, and Jinnah, Linlithgow, Wavell and Mountbatten on the other—fared during the negotiations. Uppermost in their mind are

[87]Kaul (ed.), *The Partitions of Memory*, p. 5.

[88]Aijaz Ahmad, *In Theory: Classes, Nations, Literatures* (London, 1992); *Public Culture*, 6, 1, Fall 1993.

the questions: Where did they falter and where did they go wrong? What, if they had said this and not that? What, if they had taken recourse to this or that particular action? Consequently, they follow the moves and countermoves of the 'major' actors performing on the grand Indian stage to satisfy both plain and simple curiosity, or to reinforce ideas inherited from family and friends, and school and college textbooks. This may or may not be bad news, but that is how it is.

While searching for answers and explanations, some give up midway. Others are more persistent. But most, perhaps, end up echoing the views of George Abbell, private secretary to the last two Viceroys, who told the historian David Page: 'I was in India for twenty years and I didn't manage to get to the bottom of it and you certainly won't in three.'[89] Yet the dialogue between the historian and his reader must go on. In the words of Ali Sardar Jafri (d. 2000), who himself wrote creatively on Partition:

Guftagu bund na ho
Baat se baat chale
Subh tak shaam-e-mulaqaat chale
Hum pe hansti hui yeh taron bhari raat chale

Keep the conversation going.
One word leading to another,
The evening rendezvous lasting till dawn,
The starry night laughing down with us.

Hon jo alfaaz ke hathon mein hain sung-e-dushnaam
Tanz chhalkaein to chhalkaya karen zahr ke jaam
Teekhi nazrein ho tursh abru-e-khamdaar rahein
Bun pade jaise bhi dil seenon mein bedaar rahen
Bebasi harf ko zanjeer ba-pa kar na sake
Koi qaatil ho magar qatl-e-nava kar na sake

Though we hurl our stones of abuse,
Pass around poisoned cups brimming with taunts,
Gaze steely-eyed at each other; none of this matters.
Though we are helpless, just keep our hearts warm and beating.
Don't let words be stifled with helplessness.
Don't let voice be murdered.

Subh tak dhal ke koi harf-e-wafa aayega
Ishq aayega basad lagzish-e-pa aayega

---

[89]Introduction to the paperback edition, p. 1.

Nazrein jhuk jaayengi, dil dhadkenge, lub kaanpenge
Khamushi bosa-e-lub bun ke mahak jaayegi

By dawn some word of love is bound to emerge,
Love will be victorious, it surely will.
Our hearts will stir, mouths tremble, and eyes well with tears
Silence will perfume like a kiss,
And will resound with the sound of opening buds.

Sirf ghunchoan ke chatakne ki sada aayegi
Aur phir hurf-o-nava ki na zaroorat hogi
Chashm-o-abroo ke ishaaroan mein mahabbat hogi
Nafrat uth jjayegi mehmaan muravvat hogi

No need then for talk,
When eyes glow with love.
Hate will leave forever,
Giving way to affection.

Haath mein haath liye, saara jahaan saath liye
Tohfa-e-dard liye pyaar ki saughaat liye
Regzaaron se adavat ke guzar jaayenge
Khoon ke daryaon se hum paar utar jaayenge

Holding hands; with the world in our hands,
Bearing the gift of love and pain,
We shall cross the deserts of hate,
And ford the rivers of blood.[90]

VII

At the beginning of this millennium, the gulf separating India and
Pakistan, widened by four wars and by the after-effects of the 11
September attack on the World Trade Centre in New York and the
Pentagon in Washington, seems unbridgeable. As Pakistan struggles
to define its national identity, sections in India, though enjoying
the fruits of secular, parliamentary democracy, continue to harp on
Partition's 'unfinished agenda'. The pot is kept boiling. During the
Babri masjid-Ramjanumbhumi dispute, the popular slogan, *Babar
ki santan, jao Pakistan* (children of Babur, go to Pakistan), reflected
the deep-seated distrust of Muslim loyalty to the Indian State and its
imaginary affinity with Pakistan.[91] Today, the unending turmoil over

---

[90]'*Guftagu*' (Conversation), Anil Sehgal (ed.), *Ali Sardar Jafri: The Youthful Boatman
of Joy* (New Delhi, 2001), p. 234–5.
[91]Sudhir Kakar, *The Colours of Violence* (Penguin Books: New Delhi, 1996), pp. 162–3.

Kashmir, the worsening Indo-Pakistan relations, and the resurgence of Islamist ideas and trends are conveniently attributed to Partition's unfinished agenda.

Even Gandhi's assassination has acquired sinister overtones as the tiger growls in Maharashtra and the Mahatma is vilified and Nathuram Godse hailed as the saviour in Gandhi's own Gujarat. 'The politics of the assassination was this contest on the terrain of nationhood—the contestations have not abated over the years, they are fiercer.'[92] The more David Page became associated with South Asia, the more he realised that the battle over its history is far from finished; it was almost as contested in 1998, as it was in 1947. For the historian's located in South Asia there is no escape route: they have to whet the appetite of their readers. Though it may take a long time for the scars to heal, it is important to sensitize them to the Partition as the defining moment in South Asian history, and in the words of Intizar Husain, 'the great human event which changed the history of India'.[93] The Lahore-based Urdu writer goes a step further. The agony of India's partition, he suggests, could be lessened—perhaps— by exploiting the event's potential creativity: 'to salvage whatever of that [pre-partition] culture, if only by enacting it in literature. To preserve a memory, however fugitive, of that culture before time and history have placed it beyond reach.'[94]

Purists in the world of academia may choose to stay out of these disputations, but this will not do. Partition's impact on the individual and the collective psyche of the two nations is too deep-seated to be wished away. Both as an event and memory, it has to be interpreted and explained afresh in order to remove widely held misconceptions. This is both a challenge and a necessity, and it is indeed a theme where the historian's craft must be used deftly. As I write these lines, I know that this is easier said than done. The only hope lies in what Mirza Asadullah Khan Ghalib wrote long ago:

My creed is oneness, my belief abandonment of rituals;
Let all communities dissolve and constitute a single faith.[95]

[92]Mahajan, *Independence and Partition*, p. 16.
[93]Intizar Husain, *The Seventh Door and Other Stories*. Edited and with an Introduction by Muhammad Umar Memon (Boulder Co., 1998), p. 13.
[94]Ibid., p. 16.
[95]Ralph Russell, *The Pursuit of Urdu Literature* (London, 1992), p. 71.

PRELUDE TO PARTITION

The Indian Muslims and the
Imperial System of Control 1920-1932

DAVID PAGE

To my parents

Contents

Introduction to the Paperback Edition   v

Acknowledgements to the Paperback Edition   xlix

Preface   1

Introduction   1

1. The Montagu-Chelmsford Reforms and the Changing Structure of Politics   30

2. The Growth of Communalism and the Polarization of Politics   73

3. The Emergence of Punjabi Dominance   141

4. The Muslim Conference and the Reforms   195

Conclusion   259

Glossary   265

Bibliography   269

Index   279

MAPS

India 1920   Facing page 1

The United Provinces   "   "   16

The Punjab   46

Introduction to the Paperback Edition

Fifty years of independence have done little to diminish the scale of interest in the events which led to the end of the British Raj and the division of India into two sovereign independent states. The fiftieth anniversary itself produced a welter of commemorative events and publications, both in Britain and in the Subcontinent, much of it celebratory in character, but a good deal of it devoted to the rights and wrongs of Partition, to responsibility for the bloodshed which accompanied it and the unresolved legacy of bitterness between the two successor states. Partition continues to have an impact: in the memories of millions of individuals and families affected by communal slaughter and ethnic cleansing, in the continuing dispute over Kashmir, and in the costly military and nuclear standoff between the two countries which diverts scarce resources away from human development.

Preamble to Prelude

It is now almost twenty five years since *Prelude to Partition* was written—an attempt by a young British scholar to answer the deceptively simple question: why did relations between Hindus and Muslims deteriorate to the point where partition became a necessity? It was undoubtedly a presumptuous and foolhardy quest, as I was told quite firmly by Sir George Abell, private secretary to the last two Viceroys whom I met in his later incarnation as Chief Commissioner of the British Civil Service. He said: 'I was in India for twenty years and I didn't manage to get to the bottom of it and you certainly won't in three!'. His words were still ringing in my ears five years later and do so even today.

The question had become important to me during a year spent at Edwardes College Peshawar in the mid 1960s teaching English and History for the British charity, Voluntary Service Overseas. It was just after the 1965 war between India and Pakistan and the college garden bore witness to hurried and very amateur efforts to create some kind of air raid shelter. Most of the staff and students were still talking about the days the Indian jets came over—to bomb the Pakistan Air force headquarters. The 1965 war lasted only twenty-three days and came to an end as a result of Soviet mediation, but most Pakistanis were proud that they had held their own against their much larger adversary. It was commonly boasted by my students—and by Pakistanis in general—that one Pakistani soldier was worth nine Indians; that Muslims were better fighters than Hindus—the kind of bravado that the experience of Bangladesh was later to silence. For me it was an intriguing introduction to the Subcontinent, its conflicts and its stereotypes, but it raised more questions than it answered.

It was these experiences which prompted me a year later to begin the research which led to the book. As I sat in Peshawar reading about the history of the area, about Mughal rule in India and about the long mutual association of different communities, I became determined to understand how the subcontinent had come to be divided and how the young college students I was teaching had developed such definite views about Indians and Hindus, of whom, almost without exception, they had no personal experience. It was an attempt to explain the contemporary in terms of the historical which took me down a number of blind alleys before I developed a thesis which I thought began to stand up. But in the process I discovered I had hit on a subject of endless interest—not just to me but to Indians and Pakistanis themselves. The more I became associated with South Asia—and when I finished the thesis I began working for the BBC making programmes for South Asian audiences—the more I realized that the battle over its history is far from finished; it is almost as contested today as it was in 1947.

In the relatively prosperous 1960s, the main political contest in Pakistan was between an apparently progressive military dictatorship and the demand for democracy and regional autonomy. It was not about Islam. The country's ruler, Field Marshal Ayub Khan, looked benignly at us every morning from the front page of the Pakistan Times, sporting a suit and tie and encouraging everyone to work hard for the economic development of the country. The fact that Pakistan was a Muslim country was taken for granted. Friday was a half day so that students could go to the mosque, but most of them did not.

Coming from neighbouring Hazara, Ayub Khan was reasonably popular in Peshawar. But the merging of the provinces of West Pakistan into one unit was not. The North West Frontier had its own strong regional identity; Khan Abdul Ghaffar Khan, then in exile in Kabul, and his son Wali Khan exerted a powerful influence over many of the students. Most Pashtoons took the view that in the name of national unity, legitimate regional self-government and expression were being suppressed. Their language and culture, their traditions of hospitality, their links with their Afghan brothers across the border were all of great importance to them. They may have been pleased that Pakistan had held its own against India, but they wanted to hold their own in Pakistan.

A visit to East Pakistan strengthened these reservations. After Peshawar and the deserts and mountains beyond, landing in Dhaka after a flight of a thousand miles took one into a completely different world. They were all Pakistanis, but geographically, ethnically, culturally, linguistically, they were very far apart. And they felt it. Two or three years before the political crisis came to a head, there was a sense of a country run from elsewhere, of a lack of equality, of a highly politicized Bengali culture out of tune with the management of the state.

This was in 1967—twenty years after the foundation of Pakistan— during which time the democratic foundations of the country had more or less collapsed and been replaced by military and bureaucratic government. The two nation theory survived; indeed in many ways it had been reinforced. But what had first been voiced by a democratically elected Muslim League leadership had been appropriated by the new rulers of the state, powerful military and civil service interests.

As I began my research, the most striking contrast for me was between my own experience of Pakistan and much of the writing on Pakistan history. My experience had highlighted the conflicts within Pakistan between nationalism and regionalism, dictatorship and democracy, secularism and Islam, whereas most Pakistani historians seemed to concentrate on the emergence of Muslim nationalism, the central role of Mahommed Ali Jinnah and the importance of the ideology of Pakistan in the construction of the new state. For them, as Ishtiaq Hussain Qureshi has written 'the attitude of the Muslim community towards the idea of Pakistan was the logical consequence of its history'.[1] They argued that the Muslims had always been a distinct community, always wanted to maintain their separate identity, and that Pakistan was the natural if not inevitable crystallization of that desire.

This teleological approach to Pakistani history, though helpful in bolstering the new state's identity, seemed to ignore political complexities. In the first place, it treated the British Raj and the Hindu and Muslim communities as monoliths which they patently were not. It took nationality for granted without showing how it emerged. It took very little account of the differences within the Muslim community in the run up to Partition. It downplayed completely cooperation between Muslim communities and the Raj. In short, it did not deal with the realities of power in early twentieth-century India. It concentrated on periods when the storyline was strong—particularly the period after 1937—and glossed over much of the rest.

If this sense of official history was strongest in Pakistan, writing in India and Britain on the subject of nationalism and partition was similarly affected by the immediacy of events and the self-justification of many of the leading players. In India the official narrative of nationalism laid the blame on the British for creating division and saw Jinnah not as the father of Pakistan but as a collaborator of the Raj. The British, on the other hand, prided themselves on fostering the unity of India and blamed primordial divisions among the Indians for the re-emergence of division and bloodshed in the last days of empire. Such views, as expressed in the memoirs of politicians or civil servants, though valuable as insights into personal or political experience, were not easy sources for an historian trying to work out what actually happened. Indeed, in those days even a reliable chronology was lacking.

By a happy coincidence, as I began my research, the introduction of a new thirty year rule for British government archives meant that the documents of the inter-war period were opened for the first time and it was possible to find out in detail how the process of decolonization had been managed. Ten years later, almost all the British documentation on the run up to the transfer of power in 1947 had been made available. Over the same period, remarkable archival work was also done in India, particularly by the Nehru Memorial Library, to preserve the papers of nationalist leaders, while the Indian National Archives and the different state archives enabled scholars to explore the work of government in the localities over the same period. Pakistan has been slower to open up its archives and many of the key provincial records on political developments before 1947 are still not available. But the papers of Jinnah and the Muslim League have added greatly to knowledge of the Pakistan movement, even if they have not been as extensively consulted.

As a result, a huge amount of new and interesting work has emerged on the last phase of imperial power. Much of this work has concentrated—like my own—on the structure of empire and separatist and nationalist responses to it, with policy makers and leaders the main focus of attention. But other historians—and more recently, anthropologists and feminists as well—have investigated how political movements were understood and interpreted at different levels of society and have greatly extended our understanding of the range of social, cultural and political reactions to British rule, the complexity of nationalism and the human impact of Partition. What follows is a review of some of this recent work which touches on themes investigated in *Prelude to Partition*. It begins by looking at responses to the book and some new interpretations of Muslim separatism and of Jinnah's role in the demand for Pakistan. It then examines the influence of Imperial strategies and structures on successor states. It deals first with recent writing on the development of Pakistani nationalism and its problems accommodating regional forces, notably in Bengal. It then looks at the dominant Nehruvian nationalist narrative in India and the criticism it has faced from the Subaltern school. The review concludes with a discussion of new feminist and anthropological perspectives on Partition and the continuing value of Partition studies for an understanding of contemporary South Asia.

Responses to Prelude

The explanation of Muslim separatism that I put forward in *Prelude to Partition* owed a good deal to newly available British documentation on the inter-war years. Though I sought to balance the British viewpoint by interviewing surviving Indian and Pakistani politicians and their families, the main focus of the book was on the way in which the British Raj attempted to manage the challenge of nationalism in that period. It looked particularly at the development of representative institutions, which during those years provided first partial and later substantial provincial autonomy, and it argued that these very significant constitutional developments should not be seen simply as concessions to Indian nationalism but rather as a means of offsetting the nationalist challenge and perpetuating Imperial control. According to this theory, the way in which political power was devolved—the balancing of rural against urban, of Muslim against non-Muslim, and the encouragement of the provincial at the expense of the national—played a role in shaping the character of politics, whether among the Muslim separatists or the Congress nationalists. Further, it was argued that the matching of power and population—the beginnings of responsible government, however limited the franchise—introduced a new dynamic into politics which sowed the seeds of important political and economic change. In particular, it changed the balance of power within Muslim India, giving new importance to the Muslim majority areas and displacing the old leadership which had come from the traditional Muslim centres of power in North India.

The aspect of the book which attracted most attention was its location of the roots of Punjabi dominance in Pakistan after 1947 in the close political alliance between the Punjabi Muslims and the Raj during the interwar period. The transformation of the military alliance between the Raj and the great landowners and tribal leaders of Punjab into the politically dominant Unionist party and the key role played by its leaders in shaping the destiny of Muslim India under the auspices of the British were seen to foreshadow the emergence of the Punjabi Muslim interest politically and militarily in Pakistan itself.[2] Though most official Pakistani historiography has tended to concentrate on the role of the minority provinces in the demand for Pakistan, *Prelude* shows how the Punjabi Muslims, under the guidance of Mian Fazli Husain, came to lead Muslim India in the complex constitutional negotiations which resulted in the Government of India Act of 1935. It also shows how the demands of the All India Muslim Conference, which was the most influential Muslim organization during the period, were conceded by the Raj as a means of stabilizing its rule in the face of growing Congress opposition. This was in many ways a key period in the emergence of a consolidated Muslim North West, with Sind separated from Bombay, the Frontier transformed into a Governor's province and the Punjab Muslim majority safeguarded by the continuance of separate electorates under the terms of the communal award. By the end of the 1920s it was clear that the Punjabi Muslims were at one with the Raj in not relishing the prospect of a democratic central government dominated by the Congress party. Rather, they were thinking in terms of maximum provincial autonomy, with residuary powers at that level, and only the loosest control from the centre. Here in embryo was the very same battle over the future shape of India which was to dominate the negotiations of the mid 1940s which ultimately led to Partition.

What some critics found more difficult to accept was that this foreshadowed Partition. For them, it was not the Punjabi Muslims who collaborated with the Raj in the inter-war period who were responsible for Partition but the Muslims of the minority provinces, and particularly the United Provinces, who provided the shock troops of the Muslim League in its demand for a separate state. They argued that it was a weakness of the book that it did not deal more thoroughly with the cultural and religious dimension of Muslim separatism, those important underground tributaries of Muslim political thought which burst into the open in the 1940s. As David Lelyveld put it: 'There is a gap between 1932 and the creation of Pakistan in 1947 and no one will understand it without a healthy respect for the power of symbols'.[3]

Others welcomed what the book had to say about the structure of power, seeing it as a more sophisticated version of the old theory of Divide and Rule, but thought that it went too far in trying to explain communalism in these terms. For historians of the Subaltern school, for example, it was a moot point whether politicians instigated the trend towards communalism after 1920 or were simply beneficiaries of it. For them, the popular roots of communalism were to be found not in the constitutional manipulations of the Raj but in the socio-economic changes brought about in Indian society by the impact of colonialism over a much longer period.[4]

In defence of the position put forward in *Prelude*, it was never argued that a structural approach to Muslim politics in the inter-war period offered a total explanation of separatism; it was always intended to complement existing ideological explanations which tended to concentrate either on developments in North India running up to the formation of the Muslim League or the period after 1937. There are some glimpses in the book of the way in which separatist thinking developed within the realities of power opened up by the Reforms—in Iqbal's strong support for a guaranteed Muslim majority in the Punjab or in the alignment of the Ali brothers with the Punjab Unionists on the platform of the Muslim Conference—but the interconnectedness of the intellectual and the political could certainly have been explored more thoroughly.

At the time, I was conscious that my knowledge of Urdu was too limited to do justice to the complexities of Muslim writing on issues of religion and history and law. As a result of reading and of meeting politicians and clerics, I was aware that there was a body of religious and political thought which stressed the separate identity of Muslims, the superiority of their religion and laws and the need to safeguard their culture in a changing world; it was clear that 'Islam in danger' was a potent rallying cry. It was also evident, however, that the Indian Muslim community was much more differentiated socially, economically, culturally, even religiously, than the concentration on Sir Syed Ahmed Khan and the products of Aligarh might lead one to believe. I found it difficult to accept that separatism was inherent in the Muslim condition or that Pakistan was in some sense inevitable; as I saw it, there needed to be a more structured explanation of why disparate Muslim communities came to regard it as a common goal in the 1940s.

In retrospect, in the attempt to illuminate the working of 'previously neglected factors', *Prelude* may have overemphasized the importance of structures. Obviously political structures do not create community or communalism; separate electorates were a means of mediating power which acknowledged existing religious divisions. But I would argue that in the process they also changed perceptions of community, encouraged the consolidation of a Muslim political identity and intensified political competition around communal issues. Moreover, because the Raj was in the process of devolving responsibility to Indians—first at the provincial and subsequently at the national level—the way it handled Muslim politics played an important role in the emergence of an all-India Muslim community and the kind of choices its leaders made. It was in relation to the Imperial structure of power that they had to define themselves. This is not to deny the importance of well-established traditions of Muslim political thought or of the socio-economic forces which shaped communal consciousness in the localities. But if these streams of thought and consciousness fed into the river of all-India politics, the Imperial system was like a series of dams, diverting the waters to left and right to suit its own purposes. Structures may not tell the whole story but they tell an important part of it.

Other interpretations of Muslim separatism.

Paul Brass and Francis Robinson, both specialists in U.P. Muslim politics, debated some of these issues in the 1970s. Brass asserted that despite a strong sense of their own religion there was no automatic reason for Indian Muslims to adopt what he called an ethnic identity, while Robinson argued that Brass underestimated the 'distinct differences between Hindus and Muslims'. Significantly, the two men disagreed most profoundly about the role of the Muslim political elite. Brass took the view that it was important to look at the political elite as an independent variable because skill and quality of leadership varies and this affects political choices. Robinson argued that Brass exaggerated the role of the Muslim political elite in winning support for separatism and underestimated the part played by religious institutions, by widely held religious values and by government interventions. Robinson, whose early work attributed a considerable role to British policy in the development of separatism, has since modified his views to give more importance to inherited traditions of Muslim thought and Islamic culture.[5]

A more recent attempt to delineate the influence of Muslim political thought on the emergence of separatism is Farzana Shaikh's *Community and Consensus in Islam.* In her investigation of reactions by the North Indian Muslim elite to the introduction of notions of representative government in India, Shaikh shows them to have been influenced by a Mughal ruling class culture, anxious to maintain their special status and social distinction, wary of democracy, particularly its emphasis on individual rights, and supporters of separate electorates because they were in keeping with their sense of Muslim community. Her thesis is that attitudes evolved at that time continued to dominate Muslim thinking right up to independence. These included the notion of political power as trust, the dichotomy between Muslim and non-Muslim, the belief that only Muslims should rule over Muslims, all of which she represents as part of a dominant Indo-Muslim tradition which drew on the Mughal inheritance and the common assumptions of a divinely revealed faith. Though she does not underestimate British influences—indeed she goes as far as to say that 'without an official policy which encouraged Muslims to organise politically as Muslims, there might well have been no Muslim representation to speak of'—she argues that the elements which sustained the politics of Muslim representation were also grounded deep in this tradition.[6] In her working out of this thesis, however, she comes very close to adopting the same kind of teleological approach to Muslim separatism which has influenced 'official' Pakistani history. One may sympathize with her rejection of the view that the demand for a separate homeland was 'no more than a bold attempt to play a dangerous hand of cards' without accepting the contention that Jinnah's every move drew upon 'a view of the political community as an extension of religious fellowship' or that the Muslim League somehow embodied that view even in the 1920s when it was more or less moribund.[7] Her analysis provides useful insights into the kind of traditions drawn on by the UP Muslims in resisting Congress dominance and in demanding Pakistan. But the failure to explore the socio-economic context in which those choices were made in the 1940s or to assess them in the light of Partition itself leaves important questions of context and leadership unanswered. As she herself makes clear, the 'dominant Indo-Muslim tradition' was not as fully accepted in the Muslim majority areas, where the arithmetic of democracy was less hostile, and were the urban traditions of UP and even of East Punjab were balanced by the 'ruralism' of folk Islam. In Shaikh's political analysis of the 1920s and 30s, Fazli Husain's 'spectacular gains'—and indeed the victories of 'ruralism' and 'provincialism' in the 1937 elections—are achieved at the expense of the Indo-Muslim tradition,[8] while the achievement of Pakistan is seen as its successful reassertion. She is right to the extent that the ideology of Pakistan has drawn strongly on that tradition, though the realities of power in the new state have been shaped more by the victories of ruralism and provincialism. It was only when those provincial forces were converted to Pakistan that it became a territorial reality, even if the demand was more vociferous elsewhere.

Recent research on the course of the Pakistan movement in the Punjab has tended to reinforce the view advanced in *Prelude* that the creation of Pakistan was as much about the preservation of established political interests as about the implementation of a new vision of society. David Gilmartin's book *Empire and Islam*, which looks at the emergence of the Pakistan movement in the Punjab from the late 1930s, succeeds extraordinarily well in exploring the interplay between *Din* and *Dunya*, religious consciousness and the political world. Gilmartin shows that the emergence of provincial autonomy on a substantially widened franchise after 1937 found even the apparently impregnable Unionists casting around for a new popular justification for their rule. It was this which first pushed Sikunder Hayat into a closer association with Jinnah and the Muslim League, though in the end they fell out because of the contradiction between Sikunder's commitment to the colonial system and the Muslim League bid to replace it.[9] Gilmartin argues that Jinnah's greatest strength lay in his ability to transcend such tensions, 'to direct Muslim politics towards symbolic goals, even as he compromised to build political support'. He shows how Jinnah could at the same time be compromising with the Punjab Unionists, in order to improve his representative status, and encouraging groups like the Punjab Muslim Students federation who had adopted the demand for a separate Muslim state as early as 1937. These students, who were in the forefront of the Muslim League campaign, came mostly from the urban centres of central and eastern Punjab and were inspired by Iqbal, whose idea of a Muslim political community defined by 'the active ... intensely personal... almost mystical commitment of each individual to Islam' transcended not only formal political structures but also the ulema's preoccupation with the *shariat*. According to Gilmartin, it was this idea, conveyed by Iqbal in his last days, which Jinnah incorporated into his vision of Pakistan in the 1940s. However, though Gilmartin sees the success of the Muslim League in the 1946 elections as 'a new public expression of Muslim community... that justified a cultural redefinition of the state', he also acknowledges that, despite the rhetoric, the elections did not transform the structure of local politics. *Din* and *dunya*—exemplary personal ideals and the world of rural politics—had been publicly joined, with pirs and rural magnates playing critical roles. But, as he himself admits, 'for all its outward political trappings and public ideological identification with Pakistani nationalism, the power of the Muslim League rested largely on the same bases as had the Unionist party.'[10] It was a contradiction that was to affect not just the Pakistan movement but the future of the state itself.

Ian Talbot, who has also worked extensively on Punjab Muslim politics, comes to very similar conclusions. In his early work, he explains the collapse of the Unionist citadel largely in terms of power politics. Providing ample evidence of the late conversion of the Unionists to the Muslim League, he shows how in fielding candidates for the 1946 elections the League frequently preferred recent converts from Unionism with substantial vote banks to League activists of longer standing but less influence. Talbot's analysis of the role of *pirs* and *sufis* in support of the Muslim League reinforces the same point. He finds that most of the *pirs* of the older established shrines deserted the Unionist party because of the Muslim League's rise in status in all India politics. Like the landlords, they wanted to protect their local influence by being on the winning side.[11]

More recently, Talbot has sought 'to restore the popular dimension to our perceptions of the Pakistan movement'.[12] In his book *Freedom's Cry*, he reviews some of the literature on Partition and examines different aspects of the mass movement in Punjab, including the role of the crowd and popular perceptions of Mr Jinnah as the embodiment of political sovereignty. In the light of this, he argues that the failure of the Muslim League to bring about a permanent transformation of local politics after 1947 should not be allowed to obscure the existence of mass participation in the movement. However, though there is no doubt that there was a 'groundswell of rural Punjabi support for the Pakistan demand',[13] and that despite Mr Jinnah's predilections, many *pirs* and *sufis* in west Punjab put the message across in millenarian terms, what the masses made of it has yet to be explored. In some ways the shallowness of the Muslim League movement in West Punjab makes that area a less fertile area of enquiry for this kind of research than East Punjab or the traditional heartlands of Muslim influence in North India, where the Pakistan movement found firmest root among the middle class and where pursuit of the Pakistan ideal led to dramatic changes in the pattern of life.

Reinterpreting Mr Jinnah

Though *Prelude* focused largely on the development of Muslim separatism, it also tried to explain the development of all-India politics—whether nationalist or separatist—in terms of the trend towards provincialization introduced by the Reforms. It showed, for example, how national politicians pressing for concessions at the all-India level after 1920 had to deal with a completely different set of political pressures from their predecessors in the pre-war period. The Lucknow Pack of 1916 was not repeatable in 1928 because by then the divisions between provincial politicians and their political opponents were too deep to be papered over at the national level. What the Muslim Conference was demanding of the British to safeguard Muslim majorities and minorities could never be delivered by the Congress without alienating its own supporters and potential supporters among other communities. As Nehru himself put it. 'Whatever offer we make, however high our bid might be, there is alway a third party which can bid higher, and what is more, give substance to its words.'[14]

This was also the dilemma of Mahommed Ali Jinnah, whose attempt to built an alliance for reform at the national level foundered during the same period. Throughout the 1920s, Jinnah's political ambition remained at the all-India level, where for some years he and his liberal allies cooperated with the Congress Swaraj Party in demanding the introduction of political responsibility. However his efforts to forge another Hindu–Muslim pact to pressurize the Raj fell foul of the escalating demands of Muslim political interests in the provinces and their increasingly vociferous Hindu nationalist opponents. By the end of the decade, with the Indian National Congress abandoning efforts to reach new deals because the terms were too high, Jinnah had to admit that no new pact was possible. He had reached the 'parting of the ways' and retired to London to lick his wounds.

Some reviewers found this treatment of Jinnah as a political broker between Muslim provincial interests and the Congress a useful new way of looking at his career, freeing him from the interpretative constraints imposed by his eventual emergence as the father of Pakistan and showing him dealing with the politics of the central assembly or the all-party conferences in his search for power at the all-India level.[15] The distinctive contribution of Ayesha Jalal's work on Jinnah—*The Sole Spokesman*—is that it pursues this idea right up to Partition itself, arguing that until 1947 Pakistan was only a bargaining counter and that what Jinnah really wanted was power at the centre in a union of Pakistan and Hindustan.[16] The novelty of the book—and the controversy it has provoked—stems from the fact that it portrays Jinnah in this last period as a man with an inward mission of his own, one which he could not communicate even to his own followers. As in the inter-war period examined in *Prelude*, Jinnah is shown as an all-India figure working to reconcile and represent disparate Muslim provincial interests and for much of the time facing tough opposition from the powerful chief ministers of Punjab and Bengal. Jalal shows how these interests were constantly raising the stakes in their demands to the British for special treatment, but she argues that Jinnah continued to look for some accommodation at the centre. She portrays the Lahore resolution of 1940 as a serious setback for Jinnah, envisaging as it did the creation of two Muslim federations, abolishing the centre, and leaving the minority province Muslims high and dry. She says Jinnah had to go along with it, but he knew that it was unacceptable to both Congress and the British, and he also knew that the Muslims were not the sole arbiters of their destiny.[17]

Jinnah's acceptance of the Cabinet Mission plan is seen as part of the same strategy. It offered him what Jalal argues he had wanted from the beginning, a chance to find a solution within the unity of India by giving maximum autonomy to the regional units and allowing for a federal government at the centre with limited powers. The plan explicitly rejected Pakistan but the Muslim League Council, under Jinnah's leadership, accepted it. The problem, as everyone knows, was that Congress did not want a weak centre, and Congress, unlike the Muslim League, had the power to resist it. Jalal says the Cabinet mission had forced Jinnah to reveal his hand but in doing so he had shown his own weakness and aroused suspicions among his own supporters. In the end, she argues, it was not a change of heart on his part but pressure from the rest of the Muslim League Council which forced him to go for Direct Action; otherwise he would have been swept aside himself.[18]

Ayesha Jalal's work has brought home the tentative nature of Pakistan as an objective during the 1940s, but she seems to go too far in arguing that Jinnah had a secret agenda of his own which he could not communicate to his followers. Given the diversity of his following, Jinnah had good reason not to define Pakistan too precisely. He needed to maintain a united front in negotiations at the all-India level and precision would have been divisive. But there is no evidence to suggest that he was not working sincerely to obtain the best terms possible for Muslim India. He may well have continued to hope for an all-India agreement, but by 1946 the only kind of central government he was prepared to accept was not one in which he would have enjoyed any substantial power. Moreover, by the time of the Cabinet Mission plan, trust between the League and the Congress had more or less completely broken down.

Anita Inder Singh has shown in her work on Partition that Jinnah entered into negotiations willing to consider the preservation of some sort of centre but most reluctant to see the establishment of either a central legislature or a constituent assembly for India as a whole. In accepting the Cabinet Mission plan, he wished the three zones to be given primacy and the centre to be delegated only those powers which the zonal constituent assemblies were prepared to relinquish. His demand, moreover, for parity with the Congress in the interim government implied a recognition of the sovereignty of the zonal units; it made no sense at all in a united India, where the Muslims were only thirty percent of the population. For these reasons, Singh seems closer to the mark in arguing that by 1946 'Jinnah and the League intended the claim to a sovereign Pakistan to be more than a bargaining counter...' It was, she argues, a tactic which Jinnah played at Simla 'so that both the other parties had to concede Pakistan, before or when power was transferred to Indians.'[19]

Though the argument about what was meant by Pakistan and whether it was a bargaining counter or not will continue, the revelations of the official records on the transfer of power have made it clear that its emergence as a separate Muslim state was a much more hesitant development than the country's official historians would have us believe. For Jinnah, the long drawn out negotiations were a lawyer's attempt to obtain the best deal for his clients in the last days of empire, with a confederal solution on the right terms among his possible options. But there was an obvious conflict between his openness to such a solution and the sanctions developed to pursue that end. It seems extraordinary in retrospect that Jinnah should have argued that Hindus and Muslims constituted two nations and still expected Pakistan to include undivided Punjab and Bengal with their substantial Hindu and Sikh minorities. Yet there is no doubt that he was deeply disappointed with what he called the 'truncated' and 'motheaten' Pakistan he eventually had to accept.

The same paradox seems to lie at the heart of the continuing controversy in Pakistan over Jinnah's famous speech to the constituent assembly on 11 August. Having achieved Pakistan, he seems to be saying clearly in that speech that it is to be a secular state in which religion will be regarded as a private matter. As he put it: 'You are free to go to your mosques and your temples... that has nothing to do with the business of the state.' And in the same spirit he looked forward to a time when 'Hindus would cease to be Hindus and Muslims would cease to be Muslims, not in the religious sense, because that is the personal faith of each individual, but in the political sense as citizens of the state.' Because this flies in the face of subsequent efforts to make Pakistan an Islamic state, it has proved an uncomfortable inheritance. In the early 1980s, Sharif ul Mujahid, the Director of the Quaid i Azam Academy and biographer of Jinnah, even went as far as to say that it represented ' a serious lapse on his part',[20] while Stanley Wolpert in his biography of Jinnah portrays the whole speech to the constituent assembly as a surreal experience: 'What was he talking about? Had he simply forgotten where he was? Had the cyclone of events so disoriented him that he was arguing the opposition's brief? Was he pleading for a united India on the eve of Pakistan?'[21]. Yet all liberal and secular Pakistanis give this speech an absolute centrality in their interpretation of Jinnah—the founder's guarantee, as he put it himself, of 'equality of rights, privileges and obligations irrepective of colour caste or creed'.

It seems clear that until 1947 itself, Jinnah visualized Pakistan in terms of greater autonomy or independence for existing provinces of British India rather than a strict redrawing of boundaries according to religion. As the Pakistani author Saad Khairi has argued in his *Jinnah Reinterpreted*, 'the presence of non-Muslims was an essential part of Jinnah's Pakistan. Their presence was in fact a guarantee of safety for the Muslims left behind in India.'[22] Moreover, even after 1947, though Jinnah had negotiated the separation of Pakistan from India he did not initially abandon the legal and constitutional framework in which he had lived his earlier political life. As late as mid 1947, Jinnah was still investing in shares and property in India[23] and according to Muhammad Ali Chaiwallah, the man who acted as his solicitor in Bombay, he even had a plan to retire to Bombay after being Governor General of Pakistan.[24] He left his house and furniture there, and in 1947 saw nothing illogical in the thought. It was the killings and riots and the exchange of population of Partition itself which set the seal on the new divided subcontinent and left Jinnah with a great sense of bitterness and betrayal.

The Raj and its nationalist successors

Pakistani sensitivity to the suggestion that Jinnah was prepared to consider a confederal solution to the communal problem is not difficult to understand. However in the 1940s when the post-colonial shape of the Subcontinent was being negotiated, the choice was not just between one state and two; there was a great patchwork of princely states and autonomous provinces and a range of different ideas about how India might be governed once the British departed. It was not a foregone conclusion that the British Raj would be succeeded by a unitary Indian government. Indeed, as *Prelude* demonstrates, the whole trend of constitutional development from 1920 onwards had been encouraging a more federal solution. It was as much the Congress vision of itself as the successor of the Raj as the intransigence of Mr Jinnah which stood in the way of that particular resolution of the Muslim problem.

Prelude does not deal with Congress politics in detail, but it does attempt to show how the Congress strategy of the late 1920s was reaction to the systemic pressures introduced by the Montagu-Chelmsford Reforms. The Congress decision at the time of the Nehru report to abandon its earlier commitment to cross-communal alliances, to withdraw the concessions which it had made in the Lucknow Pact and to stake a new claim to be the premier nationalist organization and the natural successor of the Raj, are all seen as responses to the growing communalization of politics under the reformed constitution. Moreover, though the book deals more with the politics of Motilal Nehru than of Jawaharlal, it does suggest that the final shape of the Nehru report reflected the growing ascendancy of Jawaharlal and his political philosophy, his impatience with religion, his contempt for communal politics and his emphasis on the economic rather than the political character of nationalism. It was a vision of India which met the Congress need to transcend the competing demands of different communities and it marked the beginning of a new confrontation between the Congress and the Raj, in which the centrifugalism induced by the constitution had to be matched by a centripetalism on the part of the Congress if it was to hold nationalist forces together and successfully challenge the British in New Delhi.

It was also a watershed for Congress relations with the Muslims. If it was a serious mistake for the British to make the overriding principle of their programme of constitutional reform outmanoeuvring the Congress, it was arguably an equally serious error on the part of the Congress to take the view that the Muslim question was a colonial creation which would disappear with independence. To refuse to think in terms of coalitions, to attempt to undermine the leadership of the community, however conservative it may have been, by means of the mass contact movement, to insist to the end that Congress represented the whole of India may have been necessary for the rhetoric of nationalism and bargaining with the British, but it had serious consequences for India's plural tradition.

It was argued in *Prelude* that the manner in which power was devolved to the provinces without any corresponding devolution at the all-India level encouraged centrifugalism. The trend was discernible after 1920; it became crystal clear after 1937. Muslim separatism was reinforced by the emergence of autonomous Muslim majority provinces and the Congress had to develop new strategies and new mechanisms to keep the nationalist movement united. Robin Moore's very thorough exploration of the British role in the making of the 1935 Act and the eventual transfer of power reinforces the importance of these themes. In his view, the introduction of provincial autonomy without central responsibility set the Congress a new challenge in its bid to succeed the Raj. In order to maintain the coherence of the national movement, it had to set up a unitary party structure to control the Congress provincial governments. As Moore expresses it: 'Instead of the Congress provincial ministries operating as autonomous governments within a federal structure, they accepted the Congress working committee as the legitimate directorate of a unitary government. The monolithic Congress stood in the place that the unitary Raj had vacated.'[25] Moore sees this as the beginning of a new 'unitarianism' in the Congress which seriously affects its relations with the Muslims and the princes.[26] The Muslim mass contract movement in the United Provinces alienated the Muslim leadership in the Congress provinces, while the Congress call in 1938 for the same democratic rights for states' peoples as for the rest of India, changed attitudes towards the viability of the proposed federal centre. As the Aga Khan put it in 1940, just one month before the Lahore resolution was passed: 'The sugar had come off the pill the moment the states' representatives were to be elected by the states' peoples rather than nominated by the rulers, for under such an arrangement the Muslims would not get from the states in the central legislature the support they required to balance the Congress votes.'[27]

As far as the development of Muslim separatism is concerned, Moore shares the view that the emergence of powerful provincial interests in the Muslim majority provinces was a stepping stone to Pakistan. He believes that 'the very creation of autonomous Muslim provinces under the 1935 Act encouraged and validated the demand for separate nationhood. The Muslim League's achievement was to convert the process of provincialization into the process of separation.' Moore certainly does not see Pakistan as inevitable, but he documents the steady trend towards separation from the late thirties onwards, pinning much of the blame for this on the Congress party. In his view, the Congress converted what he calls 'latent propensity for separate nationhood into strident insistence by its recourse to crude approaches to national integration...'.[28]

Moore's insights into the reactive character of both Indian and Pakistan nationalism reinforce the thesis put forward in *Prelude* that British constitutional strategies helped to shape both the forces of Muslim separatism and of Indian nationalism. It was the British retention of power at the centre under the 1935 Act and the absence of any elected responsibility at that level which evinced an authoritarian response from the Congress and it was this Congress authoritarianism which in turn shaped the response of the Muslim League. As Moore graphically puts it: 'In Jinnah's hands the two nation theory became a psychological weapon to be wielded for political advantage. It was a tyrannical idea formulated to prevail over the Congress totalitarian claim to be the Indian nation in microcosm.'[29]

Given what is known of attitudes in the British parliament, it is questionable whether it would have been possible to establish even a partially responsible central government for British India in 1935, but the debate in the Viceroy's council over this issue shows a wide awareness of what was at stake. By retaining absolute control of the government of India, by pinning their faith on a federal system involving the princes which never took effect, the British created the conditions for a political vacuum at the centre when they eventually ceded power. Ultimately, succession to the Raj meant succession to a system of government which was totalitarian in key areas of imperial control—despite its overt support for democratization elsewhere—and which had no established democratic tradition in dealing with centre-state relations. In 1947, the vacuum was filled by successor governments trying to cope with communal bloodshed and mass migration on an unprecedented scale. It was not surprising in those conditions that they continued to wield many of those powers, despite their own more democratic credentials. However, the problems of over-centralization of power have proved of longer duration than those crises and very difficult to remedy. The successor states inherited the political structures, some of the perceptions and many of the problems of the Raj and they have both found centre-state relations among the most difficult to solve.

Pakistani nationalism and the challenge of regionalism

The view that the attitude of the Congress party was as much responsible for the partition of India as the intransigence of Mr Jinnah has been supported by recent researches on Bengal. Joya Chatterji's *Bengal Divided* may go too far in blaming the *bhadralok* for the communalization of politics, but she shows clearly that the prospect of permanent subordination to a Muslim majority converted many of them to the idea that Bengal must be partitioned and that Nehru and Patel in opting for a truncated Pakistan had the strong support of the provincial Congress.[30] It is also beyond dispute that immediately before partition Jinnah gave his blessings to efforts by Shaheed Suhrawardy and Sarat Bose to float an independent united Bengal. That venture was vetoed by the Congress High Command as well as by the Congress in Bengal, and according to Chatterji was 'never more than a pipe dream' but Jinnah's acceptance of it was a sure sign that even in the last stages of the transfer of power he was not opposed to a future for the Bengalis built around their ethnic rather than their religious identity.[31]

Once the decision to partition India and to create Pakistan had been taken, however, Jinnah and those who worked with him embarked on a policy of centralization of power which was in effect the mirror image of the very trends he had objected to in the political behaviour of the Congress. From the late 1920s onwards, as *Prelude* demonstrates, Mr Jinnah had been arguing for maximum provincial autonomy and a weak central government. But in Pakistan—no doubt partly because of the circumstances of partition itself and the need to build up the new state in the face of hostility from India— he argued for strong central government and he and his successors used the extraordinary powers of the Governor General's office to impose the centre's will on the provinces. Within a matter of months of East Bengal becoming part of Pakistan, the centralizing imperative had taken effect and Jinnah was in Dhaka promoting Urdu as the national language and setting off a long process of disillusionment which was eventually to lead to the emergence of Bangladesh.

Concepts of statehood in the two new dominions had more in common than either side might like to admit not in terms of ruling ideologies but in terms of the structures of power. Just as Nehru and Patel wanted a strong central government to put their stamp on newly independent India, so the official ideology of Pakistan has drawn more on the imperatives of the centralizing Governor General than on those of the liberal politician and the advocate of minority rights. It has emphasized the need for unity and discipline, the binding power of Islam and the primacy of the armed forces in defending the state, and it has been used at various stages of the country's history to justify action by the managers of the state against their critics, particularly those demanding more regional autonomy.

Not surprisingly, therefore, Pakistan governments since 1947 have faced a very similar kind of opposition from their own constituent units as Muslim provinces waged against a strong centre in India before Partition. In Pakistan, however, the issue has not been the rights of Muslims in a Hindu-dominated India but the rights of the country's ethnic minorities in a state dominated by the Punjabis. Over the past fifty years, all the other ethnic groups in Pakistan have revolted against the centre at one time or another over their right to a proper share of power and resources: most notably the Bengalis, who broke away to form their own state in 1971, then later the Baluch and Pashtoons, the Sindhis, and more recently even the Muhajirs

who were in the forefront of the demand for Pakistan in the 1940s
and left their homes in north India to make it happen.

If *Prelude* showed how all-India Muslim politics during the 1920s
and early 30s was the sum of the politics of Muslim provincialism,
with the Punjabis playing the dominant role, other works have shown
how the forging of Muslim unity, whether under the leadership of
Jinnah during the 1940s, or in Pakistan after 1947, continued to
involve a problematic suppression of regional and ethnic identities.
Yunas Samad in his book *Nation in Turmoil* traces this conflict between
Muslim unity and regional identity back to the colonial period and
argues that 'there is an element of continuity in the tension between
centrifugal and centripetal forces between pre-independence and
post-partition Muslim politics.'[32] Samad takes the unusual step of
studying the period from 1935 to 1958, a perspective that enables
him to pursue the provincial divisions which existed before 1947
into the new state. His chapter on the period from the 1946 elections
to the creation of Pakistan is entitled 'A brief moment of political
unity', underlining the argument that the unity created around the
demand for Pakistan defined the new country in terms of what Indian
Muslims did not want, rather than what they did.

Samad points up the contrast between the support for a weak
centre by dominant Muslim interests in Punjab and Bengal before
1947 and the League leadership's conviction afterwards that a strong
centre was essential for its survival. He also shows how due to
authoritarianism in Pakistan, centrifugal forces soon re-emerged,
with the rights of Bengal the key issue in the early years. In looking
at pre-partition politics, Samad shows that Abul Hashim, the Bengal
provincial League secretary who built up a mass movement on an
anti-zemindari platform after 1943, was opposed to the two nation
theory and favoured a multi-nationality concept for India. Like
Suhrawardy, he was a strong supporter of the idea of an independent
Bengal in 1947 and warned that the formation of a united Pakistan
from the Muslim majority areas would result in the imposition of an
alien bureaucracy on the Bengal Muslims. The course of politics in
East Bengal after 1947 confirmed many of these presentiments.[33]

Not surprisingly, scholars from Bangladesh have seen the origins
of the eventual rupture with Pakistan in these different approaches
to Muslim separatism before Partition. In *The Foreshadowing of
Bangladesh*, Harun-or-Rashid argues that 'the Pakistan ideal of the

larger section of the Bengal Provincial Muslim League was completely different from that of Jinnah, for they developed the ideals of either an independent East Pakistan or some kind of greater Bengal well before 1947'.[34] He says that for Abul Hashim and Suhrawardy, the two nation theory was not an article of faith but 'a strategic framework for the united struggle of Indian Muslims against the common principal enemy' and he contends that what really motivated them was 'the goal of a separate state for North East India'. However, though it can be shown that the two men had developed such a vision by 1944, they appear to have kept it largely to themselves. Harun-or-Rashid describes it as 'incredible' that they did not publicize their ideal, even during the 1946 elections, but he points up the complexity of the choices facing the Bengali Muslims when he says that this was a matter of strategy. As he puts it, they carefully avoided direct confrontation with the League leadership on the form of Pakistan because that would have torpedoed the whole idea. Harun-or-Rashid argues that Suhrawardy's proposal for an independent united Bengal was not just a counter move to prevent Partition but he also has to admit that until early 1947 Suhrawardy gave primacy to the demand for a separate Muslim state and that in any event because of economic differences between the two communities 'a clear and powerful sense of common Bengali nationalism...was not there'.35

Taj ul Islam Hashmi's *Peasant Utopia* concentrates less on high politics and more on the role of the Muslim peasantry, whose politicization was central to the growth of the Pakistan movement in Bengal. Hashmi follows others in highlighting the radical economic agenda of the Bengal Muslim League which went into the 1946 elections promising the abolition of zemindari and major improvements in the lot of the peasantry and he explains the disillusionment with Pakistan after 1947 in terms of the failure of this utopia to materialize. Much of the value of his work lies, however, in the critique it offers of Marxist and Subaltern interpretations of peasant politics.[36] Hashmi argues that before 1947 the Muslim peasantry proved to be less autonomous and less differentiated in its political reactions than many such analysts have suggested; the poorer peasants accepted the leadership of the more prosperous and the peasantry as a whole trusted the ulema, the urban professionals and the Muslim aristocracy to represent their interests at the provincial level. Hashmi does not accept that communalism was instilled in the rural areas from the top downwards; in his view, the re-emergence of the ulema during the Khilafat movement was a major factor. But he argues that from the 1920s the British played an important role in communalizing the peasantry by increasing Muslim representation in local bodies and by taking measures to regulate usury and to increase security of tenure.[37] He follows *Prelude to Partition* in holding that the political power accruing to the Bengali Muslims under the Reforms encouraged the communalization of politics—what he calls' the communalization of the class struggle'—but he argues that the creation of this separate Muslim identity transcending economic divisions turned out to be short-lived. If the 1940s saw the emergence of an alliance between the urban *ashraf* and the richer peasants in support of Pakistan, the coming of the new state brought a new alliance between the *ashraf* and the West Pakistan elite which left the richer peasantry and the Bengali middle class out in the cold. It was their disillusionment which ultimately led to the creation of Bangladesh, though according to Hashmi the 'first victims' on both occasions were the poor Bengali peasants.

While Hashmi concentrates on the economics of communalism, Tazeen Murshid's *The Sacred and the Secular* highlights the complex interplay of religion, culture and language from the late nineteenth century onward. Her work is a useful reminder of the cultural schizophrenia which affected Bengali Muslims, split between the appeal of North Indian role models—the upper class Urdu speaking leaders of the community—and the pull of Bengali culture, which inevitably grew stronger as education and politics spread to the middle class and the rural areas. She acknowledges the role of British constitution-making in consolidating the sense of Muslim community, but she also stresses the impact of Hindu revivalism and chauvinism as seen in the rejection of plans for a united Bengal. Murshid detects a continuing ambivalence about their identity among the Muslim intelligentsia even on the eve of Partition, something which she says persisted after 1947 and deprived them of the initiative in Pakistan. In terms of social and economic change, the emergence of Pakistan temporarily strengthened conservative forces, though it was not long before the Bengali language became a rallying point for the new middle class in their resistance to political and economic domination by the Western wing. The emergence of

Bangladesh in one sense marked the triumph of ethnicity over religion, but Murshid's study makes it clear that old contradictions persist. Religion remains a key marker of identity and has been politically exploited in Bangladesh just as it has in Pakistan.[38]

Indian nationalism: the Nehruvian narrative

While much of the debate in Pakistan since 1947 has been about the extent to which the state defines itself in religious terms and the extent to which other allegiances—of ethnicity, language and class can be accommodated, in India Nehru's commanding influence in the first two decades of independence ensured that his vision held sway. Unlike Jinnah, who committed few of his innermost thoughts to paper, Nehru left an extraordinary corpus of writing, personal and political, which has successfully communicated the thinking of the nationalist and statesman to a very wide readership over several generations. Such works as *An Autobiography* and *The Discovery of India* show how he viewed Indian history and how he re-interpreted it to create a modern secular nationalist discourse for the emerging independent state. It was a process heavily influenced by his own education at Harrow and Cambridge, by his agnosticism and his socialism, by critiques of colonialism coming out of Europe and by what was being done under the Communists to build a modern state in Russia. The result was a new vision of India which downplayed religious and cultural difference and put the emphasis on the elimination of vested interests and economic progress for all under the auspices of a modernizing state. For Nehru, 'the real struggle in India' was 'not between Hindu culture and Muslim culture but between these two and the conquering scientific culture of modern civilisation'. Communal leaders were merely 'a small upper class reactionary group' which exploited religion for their own ends and made every effort 'to suppress and avoid the consideration of economic issues'. As to claims by the Muslim League that the Indian Muslims formed a nation, Nehru wrote: 'Politically, the idea is absurd, economically it is fantastic; it is hardly worth considering...To talk of a Muslim nation... means that no nation in the modern sense must be allowed to grow... that modern civilisation should be discarded and we should go back to the medieval ways...'.[39]

Of course, running alongside the Nehruvian modern, secular nationalist narrative—albeit in a minor key for most of the time—

was a Hindu nationalist narrative which portrayed India as the land of the Hindus and the British as only the last in a long line of conquerors, among whom the Muslims featured most prominently. Sarvarkar's influential work *Hindutva*, scrawled on the walls of a prison in the Andaman islands during the first world war, was an early rallying cry to Hindus to reclaim their birthright after many centuries of foreign domination; it also foreshadowed prophetically the growth of militant Hindu organizations like the RSS and the kind of strategies of organization and proselytization, particularly the demonization of the Muslim, which has been their hallmark since that time. The cohabitation of these two narratives—and others—within the Congress party, which was a feature of the early phase of the nationalist movement, proved more uncomfortable from the 1930s onwards, when Nehru at least was openly intolerant of communalism in all its forms. But even at this stage public posture often disguised tacit tolerance. As all-India politics became communalized, Congress support could not go unaffected, and once the Muslim League was openly demanding a homeland for the Muslims, this trend became more marked. Arguably it was only the assassination of Mahatma Gandhi at the hands of a Hindu extremist that brought India to its senses and gave Nehru the upper hand in suppressing the Hindu right and establishing the ascendancy of his own secular vision of the future.

Much Indian history since 1947 has taken its cue from Nehru's own writings. To read Bipan Chandra's work on communalism, for example, is to be struck by the extraordinary identity of view between the country's first prime minister and one of its most noted Marxist historians. According to Chandra, 'not only did Hindus or Muslims or Sikhs or Christians not form a nation or a nationality, they did not even form a distinct and homogeneous community, except for religious purposes... Hindus and Muslims as such were divided among themselves by economic interest, class, caste, social status, language, culture and social practices and even in religion. In fact an upper class Muslim had far more in common culturally with an upper class Hindu than with a lower class Muslim.'[40] Chandra argues that nationalism emerged in the nineteenth century to express 'the common interests of the Indian people for modern social, economic, political and cultural development ... for liberation from the colonial state and for the formation of an independent state.' He describes this as 'valid or legitimate consciousness' whereas he characterizes communalism, which emerged at the same time, or indeed casteism, as 'false consciousness'.[41] For Chandra, as for Nehru, it is only class consciousness that is valid and communalism is seen as an attempt by vested interests to forestall its growth. Consequently, he agrees with Nehru that a compromise with communal forces was neither feasible nor desirable because 'the terms on which it was available would have destroyed the secular integrity and identity of the nationalist forces themselves, leading to the creation of a Hindu communal, possibly fascist India.'[42] At the same time, he is critical of the Congress for not pursuing the logic of its own analysis. Nehru himself had accepted that 'many a Congressman was a communalist under his national cloak',[43] but Chandra takes the view that it was an 'ideological weakness of the national movement' that 'socially reactionary and obscurantist ideas... were never frontally opposed or rooted out by the Congress leaders.' He supports Nehru's view that national unity should be 'a unity between the masses and not an artifically arranged marriage of convenience between the leaders', but he points out that Nehru's Muslim mass contact campaign in the late 1930s, which was intended to bypass the Muslim middle class and upper class communal leaders, was not only 'ill planned and ill organised' but also opposed by the Congress right wing. As he says, 'it was not possible to heighten the class understanding and social consciousness of the Muslim masses without doing so also in case of the Hindu masses.'[44] For Bipan Chandra's nationalist ideal to have been realized, the Congress party would have had to be less dependent on the middle class, with a stronger social and ideological base among the mass of peasants and workers, and more committed to a policy of socialist transformation. But as he admits himself, this did not happen either before independence or afterwards. He does not find it surprising that the process of modernization should have given rise to all sorts of false consciousness, but he regrets that communalism, regionalism and casteism have remained so powerful.

Historians of the so-called nationalist Muslim school have tended to share these perceptions, though for them Partition has presented more acute dilemmas of identity. As Muhammad Mujeeb wrote in his magnum opus *The Indian Muslims*, Partition did not solve their problems. On the contrary, 'they became a much smaller minority in India, physically not less but more vulnerable by the creation of the separate state of Pakistan, with their loyalties obviously open to suspicion and doubt, and their future nothing but the darkness of uncertainty.'[45] Mushirul Hasan, the leading contemporary historian of the nationalist Muslims, holds virtually identical views. 'For the Muslim communities that remained in India', he writes, 'Partition was a nightmare... the so-called Islamic community in India, which had no place in Jinnah's Pakistan, was "fragmented", "weakened" and left vulnerable to right wing Hindu onslaughts.'[46]

Mushirul Hasan rejects the idea that the Indian Muslims prior to 1947 were 'a monolithic community with common interests and aspirations'. Rather he sees them as 'a disparate, differentiated and stratified segment of society'. So how could so many disparate groups strive for and eventually accomplish their goal of partition? He gives a number of answers, some drawn from an analysis of the Pakistan movement itself and its appeal to the masses in terms of Muslim values and history, some from a political context in which the Muslims were encouraged to develop separately by the British colonial authorities. In his view 'the colonial government created a community in its own image and allowed its war-time ally, the League, to transform a segmented population into a "nation" or "juridical entity".'[47] But he argues that the ground had already been made fertile by Muslim thinkers and clerics themselves. He accepts the point made by Aijaz Ahmad that many so-called Orientalist constructions of the Muslim community had their origins within the community itself and, after an account of the development of separatist Muslim thinking after 1857, he even goes so far as to say that 'by the close of the nineteenth century, the "community", separate and distinct from the "Others", had arrived with its accompanying baggage of concepts *bearing no relation to realities on the ground*' (my italics).[48] Mushirul Hassan's commitment to secularism—as exemplified by Nehru's own thinking and practice— shines through his writings. But his examination of the two most significant episodes in the history of the contemporary Indian Muslim community—Partition itself and the demolition of the Babri Musjid in 1992—reveals a vision under serious threat if not overwhelmed by strong communal currents. He passionately believes that prior to 1947 there was a possibility 'for fervent advocates of Indian nationhood to thwart Hindu majoritarianism and Muslim nationalism'. But his prescription for achieving this—'to evolve an independent/autonomous discourse, discard communal categories, the mainstay of religious mobilisation, and ignore the Muslim elite's self-image and perceptions of its role and destiny and history'[49]— makes clear the enormity of the task.

The Subaltern challenge

The Nehruvian consensus in Indian politics, though still shared by many Indian commentators, particularly those on the left, has suffered, not just from the re-emergence of communalism, but also from a loss of faith in the ability of the state, both in India and more widely in communist or socialist countries, to effect the kind of social transformation on which Marxists previously pinned their hopes. Consequently, with the emergence of all sorts of political challenges to Congress dominance—based on ethnicity, religion and caste— attention has inevitably focussed on the shortcomings and misuses of state power and the viability of the secular, scientific model of nationalism. Various kinds of 'false consciousness' are now the order of the day and while defenders of Nehru's vision attribute this situation to failures of the system, others argue that the vision itself was too limited to do justice to the diversity of India.

In terms of Indian historiography, the steady decline in Congress power has been matched by a questioning of the traditional nationalist discourse—in which the role of the great Congress leaders and the importance of national integration always had pride of place—and a search for alternative explanations which focus less on the unity which was imperative in confronting the Raj and more on the diversity which often underlay it. In this quest, historians of the Subaltern school have been particularly important. Drawing their inspiration from the work of the Italian Marxist Gramsci, they have sought to provide a counterbalance to traditional elite histories of nationalism by looking at the role of subordinate groups, whether as participants in the nationalist movement or rebels against it or indeed as rebels in their own right.

Subaltern history emerged in the late 1970s, criticizing traditional nationalist historiography for concentrating on leaders and institutions and for ignoring a wide range of other responses to colonialism, and finding fault with much European and American scholarship for portraying nationalism too narrowly. What is left out of such history, they argued, is 'the politics of the people... the subaltern classes and groups constituting the mass of the labouring population...' which, at least initially, was their main subject for study. It is important to realize, however, that the Subalterns offered a critique not just of historiography but of Indian nationalism itself. In their view, the leadership of the nationalist movement had failed to speak for the nation; in other words the movement was a social and political revolution that did not happen.[50] As Sumit Sarkar put it in *Modern India* : 'the social and economic contradictions that had provided the deeper roots of popular anti-imperialism had not been resolved, for the privileged groups in town and country had been able to successfully detach attainment of political independence from radical social change.'[51] For the 'subalterns', this failure constituted 'the central problematic of the historiography of colonial India.'

The first phase of Subaltern studies was devoted largely to writing history 'from below' but the second phase has paid more attention to political theory and to the re-examination of key concepts such as nationalism and communalism. In this phase, the influence of Edward Said's *Orientalism,* of Michel Foucault and of post-modern theory has been more marked and the resulting scholarship more contested. However the intellectual critique of Indian nationalism offered by scholars like Partha Chatterjee and Gyanendra Pandey has stimulated a very wide debate about the Nehruvian legacy and about the role of the state in independent India.

In his *Nationalist Thought and the Colonial World,* Partha Chatterjee offers a theoretical perspective on Indian nationalism which focuses on three important personalities—Bankim Chandra Chatterjee, Gandhi and Nehru—who are taken to characterize moments of departure, manoeuvre and arrival in the development of nationalist thought. Chatterjee acknowledges Gandhi's remarkable contribution to the development of mass politics and the originality of his critique of western industrial civilization, but he argues that Gandhi's politics of non-violence was not what he claimed it to be— a means to power for the masses—but a struggle conceived and directed by others which opened up 'the historic possibility by which the ...peasantry could be appropriated within the evolving political forms of the new Indian state'.[52] The role of Nehru, representing the Indian bourgeoisie, was to complete that process, becoming the author of what Chatterjee calls a 'supremely statist' utopia, in which the 'omnipotent and supremely enlightened state' is responsible for planning the progress of the country. In Chatterjee's words, this means that '... the world of differences, of conflict, of the struggle between classes, of history and politics, now finds its unity in the life of the state'. As he puts it 'Nationalism has arrived; it has now constituted itself into a state ideology; it has appropriated the life of the nation into the life of the state.'[53]

Chatterjee argues that nationalism is itself a child of the same post-enlightenment influences as colonialism. In his view, Reason—in which is subsumed science and technology and the power of the European nations to colonize the rest of the world—has always been 'parasitic upon... the universalist urge of capital.' Nationalism may have succeeded to some extent in checking capitalism. But nationalism was 'a derivative discourse'; its arguments were derived from the discourses of the enlightenment; it did not possess the ideological means to challenge the nexus of reason and capital; it merely resolved the contradiction by absorbing the political life of the nation into the body of the state, which then made its peace with global capital.

In Chatterjee's analysis the nation state, as an instrument of capital, is incapable of suppressing the unresolved tensions which are the product of an incomplete revolution. These may take the form of peasant populism or ethnic separatism but whatever the form Chatterjee says they 'bear the marks of the people-nation struggling in an inchoate, undirected and unequal battle against forces which have sought to dominate it.'[54]

This is a theme to which he returns in *The Nation and its Fragments*, where he argues that: 'The modern state, embedded as it is within the universal narrative of capital, cannot recognize within its jurisdiction any form of community except the single, determinate, demographically enumerable form of the nation. It must therefore subjugate, if necessary by the use of state violence, all such aspirations of community identity. These other aspirations, in turn, can give to themselves a historically valid justification only by claiming an alternative nationhood with rights to an alternative state.' For Chatterjee, more explicitly and more controversially in this second work, in the unresolved struggle between capital and community, it is community 'persistent in its invocation of the rhetoric of love and

kinship against the homogenising sway of the normalised individual'
which has right on its side.[55]

Chatterjee and other 'Subalterns' have been accused by those
who support Nehru's secular vision of India of encouraging other,
more partial and more dangerous allegiances. Chatterjee's
condemnation of the nation-state and his preference for the
narrative of community have even been read as an encouragement
of the forces of Hindu nationalism. Such criticisms are undoubtedly
oversimplified, given the intellectual influences on the Subaltern
group, but they do point up the negative character of much
Subaltern theorizing, which has for the most part been more
proficient in providing critiques of nationalist discourses than in
suggesting viable new ones.

Though there is wide agreement on the state of Indian politics
which Chatterjee is interpreting—notably the failure of the Congress
party to introduce far-reaching economic reforms after
independence and its compromises with the capitalist sector—it is
by no means clear that the problem of authoritarianism in the 1970s
and 80s and the emergence of serious and often violent regional,
ethnic and communal challenges to the state at that time arose from
the same causes. Nehru certainly embodied the traditions of western
'rationality' in his vision of the post-colonial state, but he also handled
the challenges of 'community' during his period of office more
democratically than many of his successors. The challenges faced
by his successors were arguably more to do with their
authoritarianism and the collapse of internal democracy in the
Congress party than with the imposition of an ideology which
rejected alternative allegiances. There is a danger here of mistaking
the discourse for the reality.

There may also be a problem in putting upon Nehru's shoulders
the burden of representing nationalism at the point of 'arrival'. My
own reading of the pre-independence period is that Nehru emerged
as a key nationalist voice in the late 1920s because his theory of
economic nationalism and his resistance to appeals in the name of
religion and community fitted the needs of Congress political
strategy at the time. His scientific socialism and his secularism were
not fully shared by his Congress colleagues; indeed, many
Congressmen remained very communal in their thinking, as became
clear at Partition. By the same token, though Nehru's vision certainly

held sway in independent India in the planning of development, the pressures of community and caste continued to bear on the implementation of policy at other levels.

If Nehru carries too heavy a burden in Chatterjee's interpretation of Indian nationalism, the same may also be said of the narrative of 'Capital' and 'Reason' in the post-colonial period. Though European influences have continued to have a major impact on India, not least in the preservation after 1947 of the instruments of colonial government—the civil service, the judiciary and the army—there are obvious dangers, as Sumit Sarkar has pointed out, in ascribing too much influence to ruling forms of power-knowledge; it may mean that power relationships are oversimplified, and subordinate groups are robbed of agency.[56] Chatterjee may be right in pointing up the dichotomy between Nation and Community, but he is unhelpful in locating the problem in the realm of imported ideas rather than in the use made of those ideas by Indians themselves.

If Chatterjee's main thrust has been the deconstruction of Indian nationalism, Gyanendra Pandey in his book *The Construction of Communalism in Colonial North India* looks from similar philosophical perspectives at the growing rift between the two main communities from the late nineteenth century onwards. In a series of essays, he focuses particularly on the role of the British colonial authorities in perpetrating the idea that communalism was inherent in the Indian condition. He argues that this essentialist view—that India was a country of primordial if not primitive allegiances—served imperial purposes and justified colonial rule as the harbinger of enlightenment. However, as Pandey points out, it was not just the Imperialists who rewrote history. Nationalist politicians and historians also rewrote it to serve their purposes, stressing Akbar rather than Aurangzeb, Ashoka and the Buddha rather than Shivaji, the unifying and the syncretistic rather than the plural and the divisive, while on the Hindu right a similar vision of the fundamental unity of India was also emerging, very different in its inspiration but sharing the same perceptions of India's political geography.[57]

Though approaching the subject from a more theoretical perspective, Pandey supports the thesis put forward in *Prelude* that the 1920s are a watershed in terms of changing attitudes to nationalism and communalism. In the late nineteenth century concepts of nation and community had overlapped. India had been

seen as an aggregate of its different communities—Hindu, Muslim,
Sikh, Christian and Parsi. How else could Gandhi have said w:.:.
such evident admiration for the Ali brothers: 'The brave brothers
are staunch lovers of their country, but they are Mussulmans first
and everything else afterwards. It must be so with every religiously
minded man.'[58] But the 1920s bring a change—with the growing
politicization of both communities and more communal violence
and rioting. It is in this period that Hindu and Muslim communal
organizations grow in importance and that Congress leaders begin
to characterize communalism as the antithesis of nationalism—the
result of colonial manipulation which will only disappear with the
coming of independence. Pandey explains the growth of communal
consciousness in terms of the mass mobilization of Muslims in
support of the Khilafat, subsequent evangelical movements in both
communities and the growth of rioting in the mid 1920s, whereas
Prelude places more emphasis on the way in which constitutional
change—the introduction of political responsibility in the provinces
and the growth of communal politics—underpinned this process.
It is common ground that the new Congress approach to nationalism,
which was pioneered by Nehru, was a response to this growth of
communalism, but Pandey opens up a new field as a result of his
analysis of the reconstruction of history which accompanied this
process. Pandey argues that much of this rewriting, with its emphasis
on unity and synthesis and the role of great leaders, with its discovery
of the early roots of secularism in the reign of Akbar, was intrinsically
oversimplified. There was no sense of the common people as
historical agents, no room for the accommodation of local loyalties,
no place for continued attachment to religion or for class or regional
perspectives on the Indian national movement. On the contrary,
'...nationalism was forced into the kind of statist perspective that
colonialism had favoured and prompted for its own reasons. In
nationalist historiography, as in the colonial construction of the
Indian past, the history of India was reduced in substance to the
history of the state.'[59]

Recent explorations of the intellectual origins of nationalism have
confirmed that in the late nineteenth and early twentieth century
there was an overlap between nation and community. At that stage,
many Hindu writers produced work in both Urdu and Hindi—
Persianized and Sanscritized—and were champions of the religious

and the national. Sudhir Chandra in his work *The Oppressive Present* has shown how Hindu writers on the one hand characterized the Muslim as alien and on the other argued for political cooperation among all the communities in the wider interests of nationalism. He makes it clear, however, that for most Hindus—whatever Nehru's formulation may have been—there was a strong cultural dimension to their perceptions of nationalism which made it an ambiguous inheritance.[60] Moreover, the more politicians attempted to reach out to the masses, as they did from the 1920s, the more important this cultural dimension became.

Attempting to portray nineteenth century Hindu approaches to nationalism during a period of 'ominously rapid Hinduisation of the Indian polity' makes Chandra particularly sensitive to these nuances. We must not forget, he warns us, that in India, as in other nation-states, 'a kind of teleology is at work. Taking its cue from the present, it works backward to confirm the belief that the nation-state, as it is, marks not only an inevitable, but also an inviolable stage in the nation's historical evolution.' Chandra deplores the 'centralising viewpoint' which 'underlies not only the communal Hindu but also certain secular conceptions of Indian nationalism', the tendency to cast the nation-state in a monolithic mould, to project narrow group identities as the only possible Indian identity, to assume that there is an essential opposition between nationalism and all other identities. He laments the disappearance of the earlier harmony between Indian nationalism and regional nationalisms and the fact that 'despite the plurality of Indian society... and the federal spirit of the Indian constitution, the idea of a multi-national Indian state finds no place in these conceptions.' For Chandra, nationalism as an historical phenomenon was a rich mix of the economic, the political, the religious and the cultural, and attempts to reinterpret it more narrowly have been the cause of many of India's subsequent political problems.[61]

New feminist perspectives

In much of this analysis of nationalism and community, Partition, with all its violence, bloodshed and dislocation, has been for many years a spectre at the feast. The lost lives of the partition victims and the traumas of the survivors have reinforced the ideologies of nationalism, justified the centralization of power and the suppression of challenges to it, and helped to perpetuate divisions between the two states and their peoples. But until recently they have not been the subject of extensive historical analysis. Now however, a new generation of scholars has begun to look at Partition from this perspective.

This new work owes its origins partly to the interest of the next generation in answering questions previously too painful to be asked, though perhaps more influential has been the experience of a new wave of communalism in Indian politics, on a scale not seen since Partition, affecting Sikhs and Muslims in particular. It is no accident that a number of those who have begun to re-examine Partition from the perspective of sufferers and survivors were involved in dealing at first hand with the victims of indiscriminate violence against Sikhs in Delhi after the assassination of Indira Gandhi.

It is also significant that this new research has been pioneered mostly by women authors, who have seen Partition as a male narrative, in which women were sacrificed or abducted or recovered in a conflict which gave primacy to community and hierarchy at the expense of individual rights. Their work first attracted attention in 1993 with the publication of two articles in the *Economic and Political Weekly* looking at the role of the Indian state in the recovery of women abducted during Partition.[62] These articles point up the extraordinary sufferings that women went through at that time, in some cases killed by their own families to prevent them from falling into the hands of the other community, in other cases raped and abducted, then recovered and rejected by their original families, in yet others settling for a new life with their abductors only to have their choices overturned by tribunals set up by agreement between the two new states.

Ritu Menon and Kamla Bhasin in their article argue that 'it was a particular construction of the identity of the abducted women that determined the entire recovery operation, one that raises serious questions regarding the Indian state's definition of itself as secular and democratic.' If the tribunals appointed by the two states so decided, the individual woman had no right of appeal; she was in effect deprived of her fundamental rights. Action by the state 'entailed representing the women as ill-treated and humiliated, without volition or choice and most importantly without any rights that might allow her to intervene in this reconstruction of her identity and her life... Only thus could social and moral order be restored and national honour vindicated.'

Urvashi Butalia in her article looks in more detail at the harrowing stories of some of the women caught up in these crises, but her conclusions are very similar. As she puts it: 'This vocabulary of recovery, rehabilitation, homeland was actually a euphemism for returning Hindu and Sikh women to the Hindu and Sikh fold and Muslim women to the Muslim fold. On this point... both countries were agreed. Thus even for a self-defined secular nation (India), the natural place/homeland for women was defined in religious, indeed communal terms, thereby pointing to a disjunction between its professedly secular rhetoric... and its actively communal actions in regard to women. Women who had been taken away by the "other" community, had to be brought back to their "own" homeland: both concepts that were defined for women by the men of the respective countries. They did not have a choice.' Butalia also points up the way in which the crisis caused by Partition, the collapse of civil society and the killing and brutality which ensued, in some sense emasculated the men who would normally protect the women in their own families and forced the leaders of communities to look to the state to intervene on their behalf. In her view, this explains why the issue of gender became so important and why the state 'now provided coercive backing for restoring and reinforcing patriarchy within the family.'[63]

This concentration on the role of women—as sufferers and victims—during the Partition violence has raised important new questions about how community, religion and nationality have been defined, whether at that crucial moment or subsequently, and about the balance between the rights of the state, of communities and of individuals. In her recent book, *Critical Events*, the Indian anthropologist, Veena Das, has examined these questions—and the role of anthropology in addressing them—in relation to this work on Partition and to certain other key episodes in recent Indian history which pitted communities against the state. These include: the Shah Bano Affair, which raised questions about the place of Muslim personal law in a secular state, the revival of *sati* in Rajasthan, which highlighted the tension between the state and the Rajput community in the interpretation of cultural rights, and the growth of militancy among Sikhs in the Punjab in the 1980s, with its discourse of sacrifice and martyrdom and its definition of Sikh identity at odds with both Hinduism and the Indian state. The value of Veena Das's approach—as that of Menon, Bhasin and Butalia—is that by her focus on the victims she puts competing discourses of state and community into a more humane perspective. In fact she puts the case for what she calls a new 'anthropology of pain', 'an anthropology which can be seen as forming one body with the victim',[64] to replace traditional anthropology, which she sees as heavily Eurocentric in its approach and inclined to accentuate the 'otherness' of Indian society.

Das accepts many of the criticisms of the state which have emerged in India over recent years. She delineates very clearly how the state has arrogated or attempted to arrogate to itself rights which have thrown it into conflict with communities and individuals. However she does not see this as a reason to champion the community—as many academics as well as politicians have tended to do—because in her view champions of community rights very often fall into the same trap as the state itself, making absolutist claims which are equally restrictive of individual rights and freedoms. She says the community has traditionally been seen as an area of face to face relationships and therefore a humane counter to the growing power and impersonality of the modern state, but she finds that in India 'community is emerging as a political actor which seeks to reshape not so much the face to face intimate relations of the private sphere but control over law and history in the predominantly public sphere of life.' For this reason she believes that 'unless a very different theory of community emerges, the language of cultural rights cannot help us to remoralise those areas of life which have become denuded of meaning by the dominance of technologies of governance within modern states'.[65] As to the resolution of the conflict between the state and the community, her view is that it will only be possible 'if the state ceases to demand full ideological allegiance from the various collectivities which constitute it; and if communities, instead of demanding complete surrender from individual members on the pretext of preserving their culture recognize the paradoxical links of confirmation and antagonism from their members. An individual's capacity to make sense of the world...presupposes the existence of collective traditions; but indviduals must be able to experiment with these collective traditions by being allowed to live at their limits. The simultaneous development of the **rights** of groups and individuals will depend on the extent to which these paradoxes can be given voice, both in the realm of the state and the public culture of civil society.'[66]

Intellectually, Veena Das's call for the rejection of 'the seduction of consensus' in the name of either modernity or tradition,[67] and her sceptical treatment of claims to allegiance by both state and community constitute a powerful appeal for more attention to individual rights and more space for individual development. But as she herself makes clear, her main quest has been for a more humane and useful role for the anthropologist, not to provide a blueprint for legal or constitutional reform. By her emphasis on the victim she succeeds remarkably in injecting a new moral urgency into an area where polemics and violence have all too often had the field to themselves. It is a longer term project, however, to reshape state and community to such a prescription and one which will require significant changes in public opinion and much practical thinking in the legislative and judicial field.

Postscript

One of the reasons why Partition remains so absorbing a subject is that it continues to cast its shadow over relations between India and Pakistan. As the recent nuclear escalation in South Asia has proved so dramatically, fifty years of independence have done little to alleviate the rivalry and suspicion between the two countries. Nationalism remains a very powerful force.

But it has not gone unchallenged. In terms of the writing of history, Indians have enjoyed more freedom to call official ideologies into question, but there are obvious comparisons to be made between the kind of reflections emerging from historical research into the independence movement in India and the regular questioning of centralized state power which has taken place in Pakistan, even if in Pakistan the questioning has been done more by politicians than by historians. Nationalism remains powerful, but in both countries it has had to find new clothes, new weapons and new enemies in order to perpetuate itself in the face of serious ethnic, regional and other challenges.

New historical writing has carried research well beyond the areas explored in *Prelude to Partition*. But there are some common

assumptions and preoccupations. There is a broad recognition that
the 1920s were a crucial period in the shaping of the subcontinent,
in preparing the ground for the emergence of Pakistan and in casting
the character of Indian nationalism. There is also widespread interest
in deconstructing the narrative of nationalism, in arguing the case
for a more genuine pluralism and in pointing up the inhumanity of
too narrow a definition of citizenship.

What *Prelude* has to say about those years is only part of a complex
story. A study of colonial strategy and structures cannot explain how
people were mobilized to achieve Pakistan or the continued
centrality of those ideas in the future history of the state. But I believe
it does help to explain how the building blocks of Pakistan were put
in place, how it became possible for Muslim communities from
different parts of India to see it as a common goal, and the kind of
contradictions involved, not only during the Pakistan movement
but in Pakistan itself.

I would also argue, as others have done from different
perspectives, that the character given to Indian nationalism—in
response to the communalization of politics and the challenges
thrown down by imperialism—produced a mirror-image Muslim
nationalism. Both these nationalisms have interpreted India and
Pakistan in ways which have often proved too narrow to incorporate
the diversities which fall under their sway. This is also to some extent
an inheritance of the Raj and the way it handled the process of
decolonization.

Partition is an event of such momentous significance for states,
for families and for individuals, that it needs to be examined in
many different ways and re-intepreted by every new generation.
Structures do not tell the whole story. But they tell an important
part of it. The impact of British imperialism in south Asia continues
to be felt long after 1947. *Prelude to Partition* is an attempt to
understand that impact at a critical stage in the region's history.

London
June 1998.

Notes

1. Ishtiaq Hussain Qureshi, *The Muslim Community of the Indo-Pakistan Subcontinent (610–1947)* (New Delhi 1985), p. 349.

2. See for example the review by I.A. Rehman in the *Herald*, Karachi, June 1987

3. David Lelyveld's review in the *American Historical Review*, vol. 89, number 2, April 1984.

4. See David Hardiman's review in the *Economic and Political Weekly*, 11 September 1982, and Gyanendra Pandey's review of writings on communalism in *Economic and Political Weekly*, 15 October 1983.

5. See *Journal of Commonwealth and Comparative Politics*, November 1977, pp. 215–34 in which Robinson comments on Brass's views on Muslim separatism and Brass replies.

See also Paul Brass, *Language, Religion and Politics in North India* (Cambridge 1974); Francis Robinson, *Separatism among the Indian Muslims* (Cambridge 1974); and Robinson's new introduction to the paperback version (Delhi 1993).

6. Farzana Shaikh, *Community and Consensus in Islam, Muslim Representation in Colonial India, 1860–1947* (Cambridge 1989), p 233

7. Ibid., pp. 175, 199–200, 207

8. Ibid., pp. 189–93

9. David Gilmartin, *Empire and Islam* (London 1988), chapter 5.

10. Ibid., chapter 6 and conclusion, particularly pp. 205–7 and 221–7.

11. Ian Talbot, *Punjab and the Raj 1849–1947* (New Delhi 1988), chapters 9 and 10.

12. Ian Talbot, *Freedom's Cry: The Popular Dimension in the Pakistan Movement and Partition Experience in North West India* (Karachi 1996), p. 1.

13. Ibid., p. 97.

14. Jawaharlal Nehru, *An Autobiography* (New Delhi 1988), p. 137.

15. See for example Dr Gopal's review of work on the transfer of power, *Hindustan Times*, 11 August 1985.

16. Ayesha Jalal, *The Sole Spokesman: Jinnah, the Muslim League and the Demand for Pakistan* (Cambridge 1985), p. 122.

17. Ibid., p 57

18. Ibid., chapter 5, particularly pp. 191–207 and chapter 6, pp. 211–13.

19. Anita Inder Singh, *The Origins of the Partition of India 1936–1947* (New Delhi 1987), chapter 5, particularly p. 143.

20. Sharif ul Mujahid, *Quaid i Azam Jinnah, Studies in Interpretation* (Karachi 1981), p. 268.

21. Stanley Wolpert, *Jinnah of Pakistan* (New York 1984), p. 340.

22. Saad R. Khairi, *Jinnah reinterpreted, the journey from Indian Nationalism to Muslim statehood* (Karachi 1996), p. 460.

23. I am indebted to Dr. Z.H. Zaidi for this information.

24. Interview with Mahommed Ali Chaiwallah, Bombay, September 1970.

25. R.J. Moore, *The Crisis of Indian Unity* (Oxford 1974), p. 307.

26. Moore shows that prime minister Clement Atlee also subscribed to this diagnosis. As a member of the Simon commission, Atlee had been concerned from its inception that the 1935 Act was 'deliberately framed so as to exclude as far as possible the Congress party from effective powers', though later, as prime minister, trying to maintain the unity of India in the face of the growing rift between the Congress and the Muslim League, he found fault with the Congress for its unwillingness to meet the legitimate fears of the Muslims. At that stage, he took the view that the failure to establish responsible government at the centre had facilitated 'totalitarian dictatorship by the working committee of the Congress party'. See *Escape from Empire: The Atlee Government and the Indian Problem* (Oxford 1983), p. 5.

27. Linlithgow to Zetland, 27 February 1940. This and the following quotation from *The Crisis of Indian Unity*, p. 312.

28. *Escape from Empire*, p. viii.

29. Ibid., p. 53.

30. Joya Chatterji, *Bengal Divided: Hindu Communalism and Partition 1932–1947* (Cambridge 1994), p. 222.

31. Ibid., pp. 259–60. Mountbatten asked Jinnah on 26 April 1947 for his views on Bengal remaining united and outside Pakistan. He is reported to have said without hesitation: 'I should be delighted. What is the use of Bengal without Calcutta; they had much better remain united and independent; I am sure they would be on friendly terms with us.' See Mansergh, *Transfer of Power*, vol. x, pp. 452–3.

32. Yunas Samad, *A Nation in Turmoil: Nationalism and Ethnicity in Pakistan, 1937–1958* (New Delhi 1995), pp. 10–11.

33. Ibid., pp 71—2, 106–7.

34. Harun-or-Rashid, *The Foreshadowing of Bangladesh: The Bengal Muslim League and Muslim Politics 1936–47* (Dhaka 1987), p. vii.

35. Ibid., pp. 344–6.

36. Taj ul-Islam Hashmi, *Peasant Utopia, The Communalisation of Class Politics in East Bengal, 1920–47* (Dhaka 1994), pp. 1–21, 263–70.

37. Ibid., See Chapter 4, pp. 83–123.

38. Tazeen Murshid, *The Sacred and the Secular, Bengal Muslim Discourses 1871–1977* (Calcutta 1995), particularly pp. 204–10, 286–7, 437–41.

39. Jawaharlal Nehru, *An Autobiography* (New Delhi 1988), pp. 467–70.

40. Bipan Chandra, *Communalism in Modern India* (New Delhi 1984), pp. 13–15.

41. Ibid., p. 21.

42. Ibid., p. 290.

43. Jawaharlal Nehru, *An Autobiography*, p. 136.

44. Bipan Chandra, op.cit., pp. 299–304.

45. Muhammad Mujeeb, *The Indian Muslims* (London 1967), p. 440.

46. Mushirul Hasan, *Legacy of a Divided Nation: India's Muslims since Independence* (New Delhi 1997), p. 6.

47. Ibid., p. 98.

48. Ibid., p. 236.

49. Ibid., p. 52.

50. See Ranjit Guha's article 'On some aspects of the Historiography of Colonial India' in *Subaltern Studies I* (New Delhi 1982) pp. 1–8.

51. Sumit Sarkar, *Modern India* (New Delhi 1990), p. 453.

52. Partha Chatterjee, *Nationalist thought and the Colonial World, a Derivative Discourse* (New Delhi 1986), p. 124.

53. Ibid., pp. 160–1.

54. Ibid., pp. 168–70.

55. Partha Chatterjee, *The Nation and its Fragments: Colonial and Post-colonial Histories* (New Delhi 1997), pp. 238–9.

56. See his 'Orientalism revisited: Saidian Frameworks in the writing of Modern Indian history' in the *Oxford Literary Review*, vol. 16, nos 1–2, 1994, pp. 205–24.

57. Gyanendra Pandey, *The Construction of Communalism in Colonial North India* (New Delhi, 1990), chapter 2, pp, 23–65, and chapter 7, pp 247–54.

58. Ibid., pp. 210, 233, 238.

59. Ibid., chapter 7, particularly pp. 235, 253.

60. Sudhir Chandra, *The Oppressive Present* (New Delhi 1992), chapter 3, pp. 116–154.

61. Ibid., pp, 155–9.

62. *Economic and Political Weekly*, 24 April 1993: Ritu Menon and Kamla Bhasin, *Recovery, Rupture and Resistance, the Indian State and the Abduction of Women during Partition;* Urvashi Butalia, *Community, State and Gender, on Women's Agency during Partition.*

63. These authors have since published books elaborating these themes: Ritu Menon and Kamla Bhasin, *Borders and Boundaries: Women in India's Partition* (New Delhi 1998) and Urvashi Butalia, *The Other Side of Silence: Voices from India's Partition* (New Delhi 1998). Gyanendra Pandey is also writing a book on Partition based on interviews with survivors which examines some of the same issues.

64. Veena Das, *Critical Events, An Anthropological Perspective on Contemporary India* (New Delhi 1995), chapter 7.

65. Ibid., p. 17.

66. Ibid., p. 116.

67. Ibid., p. 54.

Acknowledgements to the Paperback Edition

This book was begun more than thirty years ago during a year spent teaching at Edwardes College, Peshawar. It was during that first experience of the subcontinent that I became interested in the origins of Partition and I owe a huge debt to the Principal, the late Dr Phil Edmunds, and to the staff and students with whom I worked.

In writing the original thesis, I received assistance, both financial and academic, from a very large number of people and institutions. The Department of Education and Science supported my first year of studies. The trustees of the Hildebrand Harmsworth Scholarship Fund of Merton College, Oxford, awarded me a three year senior scholarship from 1968–71. The Beit Fund and the Bartle-Frere Fund of Oxford University made possible my research visits to India and Pakistan in 1969 and 70. I was also greatly helped by the staff of the Indian Institute Library, Oxford, the India Office Library in London, the National Archives of India, the Nehru Memorial Museum and Library and the Jamia Millia Islamia, New Delhi, the U.P. Secretariat Archive, Lucknow, the Research Society of Pakistan, Lahore, and Karachi University Library.

In those days, my tutor at Merton college, Dr Roger Highfield, and Dame Lucy Sutherland, historian of the East India Company, with whom I worked on Warren Hastings for my first degree, were important influences. The late Professor Jack Gallagher, the father of the so-called Cambridge school of Indian history, acted as my supervisor during his stay in Oxford and on his return to Cambridge. In his habitually irreverent and thought-provoking way, he encouraged me to keep digging for answers to what sometimes seemed impossibly large questions. I am also indebted to Professor Peter Reeves and Professor Ronald Robinson for helping me to put some of my ideas into a better perspective; to Chris Bayly and Francis Robinson for the opportunity of talking to them about their work; and to Bruce Cleghorn, Peter Kelly, Margaret Macmillan and Gynendra Pandey, for their friendship and for many helpful discussions. Dr Sarvepalli Gopal has been a source of encouragement and advice over many years. I also owe a great deal to my friends Anthony and Ursula King, under whose roof in West Dulwich the thesis was finally completed.

In the preparation of the introduction to the paperback edition, Anthony King and Gynendra Pandey have made valuable comments on several drafts. Urvashi Butalia, Barun De and Sudipta Kaviraj have given me helpful advice on parts of the text. Ruth Kirk-Wilson has demanded greater intelligibility on behalf of the general reader. The section on the historiography of Pakistan was discussed in London at a seminar at the School of Oriental and African studies in December 1995 and at a meeting of the Pakistan society in May 1997.

Finally, my thanks to the Oxford University Press in New Delhi, for seeing the paperback into print.

London
September 1998

Preface

Until the creation of Bangladesh in 1971, most Pakistanis saw the emergence of their country primarily as a religious or ideological phenomenon. This view was shaken by the secession of East Pakistan, which raised important questions about Pakistan's identity as a homeland for the Muslims of the subcontinent. However, it was not rejected. Indeed over the past fifteen years, the rulers of Pakistan have continued to stress the country's Islamic identity, whether in the development of closer ties with the Muslim world, or in an effort to establish an Islamic state in Pakistan itself. Furthermore, the mass media within Pakistan, as well as the educational system and the ulema, have continued to reinforce this perspective.

This book does not seek to question the part played by religion in the formation of the state. For the belief that Islam was in danger was clearly crucial to the growth in support for the Muslim League on the eve of Independence. However, though it is possible to explain in such terms how men were mobilized to achieve Pakistan, such a theory is plainly insufficient to explain how disparate Muslim communities throughout India came to see Pakistan as a common goal.

Many Muslim historians have been aware of this themselves, at least subconsciously, for they have concentrated their attention on two main historical periods: firstly, the period dominated by Sir Syed, from 1857 to the foundation of the Muslim League, and secondly, the period after 1937, when the movement which led to Pakistan began to gather momentum. This book contends, however, that the intervening period was crucial, and it seeks to provide a structural explanation of Muslim politics in that period to complement existing ideological explanations.

It does this by concentrating attention on the formal structure of politics—the Imperial system of control and the manner in which it was modified. In particular, it examines the constraints on political development imposed by the introduction of electoral institutions. This process, which was the chief means by which the government modified its system of control in the last stages of Empire, is seen as crucial both to the quickening pace of politicization and to the steady increase in communal awareness among the Muslims of the different provinces.

The value of this approach is that it illuminates the working of factors previously neglected. In the process, however, important elements in the development of Muslim politics have necessarily been treated less thoroughly. Little is said, in particular, about the cultural context of politics, or about the social and psychological tensions produced by the process of 'modernization'. This is a subject in itself, and one which requires a more detailed study of Muslim society.

Those who open this book in the hope of discovering a detailed examination of Muslim politics in every part of the subcontinent also deserve an apology. The main focus of the work is on political developments in the United Provinces and Punjab, the two provinces with the lion's share of all-India leadership during the period under study. Considerations of time, space and coherence have made necessary this degree of specialization.

The theoretical basis for the analysis is explored in detail in the Introduction. The Introduction also contains an examination of political developments under the Morley – Minto Reforms as an illustration of the working of the theory during that period. It shows how the linkages provided by the Reforms between provincial and district levels of politics drew local issues into the orbit of provincial politics, and how the introduction of a substantial elected element in provincial councils acted as a spur to political confrontation with the Raj. Both the participation of the Muslim League in the politics of confrontation and the rise of communalism in the localities is explained in these terms. The rise of Panislamic politics is treated briefly as a separate theme.

The book itself concentrates on the constitutional Reforms introduced in 1920. These Reforms are considered the most important stage in the process of electoral innovation. For the first time, an element of political responsibility is introduced at the provincial level, and by the time these Reforms give way to the Government of India Act of 1935, provincial autonomy has become a reality and the Congress has emerged as the obvious political successor to the Raj. In the period before 1920, the Muslim League works with the Congress to further the cause of constitutional reform, but by 1937, the dominant Muslim interests in most

Indian provinces have been alienated from the Congress and the scene is set for the emergence of the Pakistan movement.

Chapter 1 examines the effect of the Montagu – Chelmsford constitution on the structure of all-India politics. It suggests that the weight given to the rural interest and the efforts made to balance the representation of different communities within individual councils were deliberate attempts to offset the challenge of the 'nationalist' politicians. It also suggests that these devices were to have an important effect on the nature of respondent political activity, both encouraging the development of communal blocs within councils, and ultimately dictating the logic of the Congress appeal to the countryside. Where all-India Muslim politics are concerned, chapter 1 argues that the Reforms were instrumental in bringing the majority-province Muslims into prominence. By distributing power, at least in some measure, according to population, the Reforms made numerical superiority a political asset. But because the Bengali Muslims were economically and politically weaker than the Punjabis, they were less well-represented within their own council and less capable for that reason of utilizing the Reforms for their own advantage. Chapter 1 concludes with an analysis of the Muslim political interest which emerged in the Punjab under the new dispensation—its leadership, and its tactics for consolidation.

Chapter 2 examines the growth of communal tension which followed the introduction of the Reforms, and assesses its implications for political co-operation between the two communities at the all-India level. Because this tension was most marked in the Punjab and the United Provinces, attention focuses on these two provinces. An attempt is made to explain the worsening communal situation in political terms. In the Punjab, it is suggested that the use of political power by the majority community penalized the urban Hindus and provoked a communal reaction. In the United Provinces, Hindu interests with an eye on office at the local and provincial levels appear to have used communal appeals to undermine the political dominance of an inter-communal alliance. The effect on all-India politics of the resulting polarization of communal relations is then discussed. Where the Khilafat movement is concerned, the growth of communalism in the provinces is shown to have undermined the hold of the Ali brothers on the all-India organization. Where constitutional politics are concerned, Jinnah's career illustrates the same trend. Anxious for a measure of responsibility at the Centre, Jinnah endeavours to produce a new Lucknow Pact to strengthen his hand. But the rise of communalism in the provinces obliges him to demand a higher price than the Congress is prepared to pay. Finally, the same phenomenon is shown to have affected the Congress. The Congress has to compromise with communal parties in order to maintain its coherence and in the process loses much of its Muslim support.

In Chapter 3, a study is made of the process of polarization at the all-India level induced by the appointment of the Statutory Commission. The government's strategy is to encourage provincial ambitions, and particularly Muslim provincial ambitions, to offset challenges to its authority at the Centre. It is at this time that the Punjabi Muslims appear on the all-India stage as the leaders of provincial Muslim opinion.

The exclusion of Indians from the Statutory Commission provokes a re-alliance of all-India interests and gives new momentum to the politics of confrontation. However, support from provincial interests enables the government to stand by its decision, and communal dissension re-emerges. In March 1928, the Muslim League withdraws from the all-parties conference and the Nehru report is drawn up without its assistance.

The formulation of the Nehru report is examined in detail. By this stage, the terms on which the Congress is prepared to frame a constitution are shown to be unacceptable even to important nationalist Muslims. The report's demand for a strong unitary government at the Centre intensifies Muslim demands for safeguards within a Federal framework. It also forces minority-province Muslims to come to terms with the eventual withdrawal of the Imperial power. At the all-parties convention at Calcutta in December 1928, with Jinnah's failure to secure amendments to the Nehru report, the possibility of a genuine all-India agreement between the two communities disappears. The scene is set for the Congress one-year ultimatum to government and the emergence of the All India Muslim Conference, an alliance of provincial Muslim interests, under Punjabi leadership.

The final chapter examines the role of the Muslim Conference during the period of constitutional revision. Attention is drawn to the importance of the Punjabi Muslim leader, Fazli Husain, as the organizer of the Conference and to the value of his membership of the Viceroy's Council. An examination of Fazli Husain's role in shaping the Government of India's proposals for Reform shows he was chiefly concerned to secure Muslim control of the majority provinces and to forestall the introduction of responsible government at the Centre. At the first round-table conference and immediately afterwards, the Muslim Conference faces serious all-India challenges. Liberal efforts to secure Muslim support for a Federal Centre and government overtures to the Congress prompt negotiations on the communal question which threaten the Conference position. But continuing communal tension and astute Conference leadership prevent agreement from being reached on Liberal or Congress terms. The acceptance of the Federal idea also favours the Conference. The princes acquire a virtual veto on constitutional advance, and the establishment of a responsible Centre is made less likely. By the beginning of 1932, with the failure of the second round-table conference and Congress resumption of civil disobedience, Muslim support has become vital to continued Imperial control at the Centre. An increase in Muslim belligerence at this time forces the government to settle the main communal questions according to Conference demands. The Communal Award makes Muslim Raj in Punjab and Bengal a real possibility. It also strengthens those provinces against the emergence of a national government at New Delhi.

The Conclusion examines the implications of the Award for the future of Muslim politics. It suggests that Pakistan only became a reality when the most important provincial interests created by the Reforms had been converted to it. It also points to the continuing importance of the Punjab interest once Pakistan had been achieved. The study ends with an assessment of the role of Imperial policy in the creation of communal consciousness.

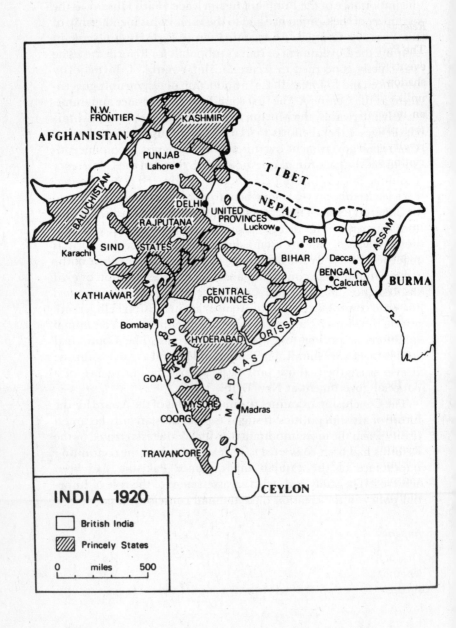

INDIA 1920

☐ British India

▨ Princely States

0   miles   500

Introduction

Relevance of a study of pre-Partition politics

The Partition of India can lay claim to be one of the most significant events of modern history. Indeed in many respects it has over-shadowed the release of the subcontinent from colonial rule, for unlike that event, which is now taken for granted, it continues to be an important factor in the political complexion of South Asia. It took place in 1947 because it seemed the only way of alleviating the rivalry of Hindu and Muslim. But it was accompanied by bloody rioting and the transfer of populations and far from laying discord to rest, it merely institutionalized that discord at an international level. Where party opposed party, state has since opposed state, and on three occassions war has broken out. For this reason, an investigation of the reasons for Partition has a relevance beyond the event itself. It is also important to an understanding of subse-quent relations between the two countries.

But the relevance of Partition does not stop there. India was the first major colonial dependency outside the white Dominions to gain its independence, and the communal problems which it faced as it evolved towards that state have since occurred in similar, if not identical forms, in many other countries. In Northern Ireland, communal tension has long been a political problem. In Malaysia, there has been friction between Malays and Chinese. In Nigeria, the Ibos tried to secede from the Federation. In Cyprus, there have been serious divisions between the Turkish and Greek Cypriots. And more recently in Sri Lanka, political differences between Tamils and Sinhalese have erupted into violent confrontation. Consequently, the problem of Hindu-Muslim antagonism in India in the last phase of Empire has a relevance beyond the confines of that particular time and place, and an examination of how it arose may throw light on similar situations elsewhere.

Imperialism and political integration

One of the most important questions for the student of nationalism, whether of Indian or Pakistani nationalism, is: how did politicians succeed in building bridges between district and district and

between province and province? In other words, is there a funct-
ional explanation for the growth of national consciousness? If one
merely looks at the map of India and meditates on the variety of
races, castes and customs, the disparities of social and economic
development, not to mention the huge physical distances which
separated one Indian from another, the question seems impossible
to answer. What had the Parsee businessman in common with the
Jat farmer? The Allahabad Brahmin with the untouchable of
Nagpur? The Moplah with the Pathan? Apparently nothing. But
there is an answer. What they all had in common was that they
came under the political authority of the Imperial power. Long
before the foundation of the Indian National Congress or the All
India Muslim League, there existed in India a 'national' organization whose ramifications extended into the remotest village—the
Imperial power itself. Rather than asking, therefore, what it was
that bound together men of different races, languages and customs,
and created Indian or Pakistani nationalism, the historian might
more profitably ask in what ways the Imperial power itself contributed to the bridge-building process.

In the years immediately after 1857, the Indian Empire might be
described as a three-tiered autocracy. From the 'national' level,
where Imperial authority was wielded by the Viceroy in Council,
orders travelled down to the next tier in the hierarchy, the provincial level, whence they were relayed by the Governor in Council to
the district officers and their assistants, who gave them executive
effect. Some decisions were made at the national level, some at the
provincial level and some at the district level, and laws regarding
what could be decided where were laid down in great detail. But
the strength of the system, as of any autocracy, was that the relations
between the Raj and its subjects were conducted almost entirely at
the district level. India was run by the district officers and each
district officer was the 'mother and father' of his district.

From the point of view of the preservation of Imperial rule, the
value of this system was that it confined points of irritation within a
small compass. Because each district officer was both the embodiment of Imperial power within his own district, and the channel by
which men were obliged to approach the provincial and national
governments, there was little chance of undermining his authority.
And because each district officer ran his district along individual

lines, choosing his own allies, dispensing his own justice and utilizing his own methods to keep the peace, the management of provinces was made easy. The greater the number of individual units the provincial government had to deal with, the easier it was to maintain Imperial authority, for with each district run along individual lines, the chances of province-wide agitation were small. Only at times of great economic distress or religious disturbances was this not the case, and in both these instances the causes of province-wide concern were essentially temporary in character.

So what disturbed the placid waters of autocracy? This book suggests that an important part of the answer to this question may be provided by a study of the introduction of electoral institutions. It suggests that this process, which was the main means by which the Imperial power modified its system of control between 1857 and 1947, contributed, in its various stages, to the focusing of district grievances at the provincial level, and to the focusing of provincial grievances at the national level. Moreover, it suggests that the introduction of electoral institutions, by providing permanent political links between the different levels of government, encouraged the settlement of grievances at higher levels than had previously been the case, and so contributed to the building of parties first at the provincial level and subsequently at the national level. Finally, it suggests that the devolution of power to Indian hands, which took place within this electoral framework, by encouraging competition for power, also encouraged an extension of political activity, with the result that new classes, castes, communities and interests were drawn into the political process.

Electoral innovation and political catalysis

Electoral institutions with a substantial elected element were first introduced in local self-government, at the district and municipal level, in the 1880s. But from the point of view of the preservation of Imperial control, this stage of devolution, even when it came to involve real responsibilities, did little to throw the Raj off balance. The same institutions were introduced in most towns and districts but the system did nothing to focus grievances at a higher level of government. Each district board and each municipality continued to be treated as an individual unit. The district officer remained the main vehicle for Imperial control and patronage, and even though many boards were empowered to elect non-official chairmen, they generally made sure that the district officer occupied this important position. In their relations with the provincial government, he was the man most capable of getting things done.

In 1909, with the introduction of the Morley-Minto Reforms, this system began to change. Except in the Punjab, where reasons of military security dictated otherwise, the Reforms introduced a substantial elected element at the provincial level and made election to the provincial councils the prerogative of district and municipal boards. The powers of the new provincial councils were not extensive. Except in Bengal, the elected members were everywhere in a minority. They only had the right to ask questions, to speak in the Budget debate and to introduce private members' bills subject to government approval. Yet their inauguration made a substantial difference to the Imperial system of control. For the first time, the grievances of the districts and municipalities were brought to a permanent provincial focus, with the result that the Raj could no longer deal with such grievances on an individual basis. It became obliged to discuss local grievances in provincial terms and, as a result of the pressure which it faced in the council, to make decisions at the provincial level which it would previously have left to the jurisdiction of its local officers.

Another important feature of the Morley - Minto Reforms was that they gave those with purely provincial grievances their first opportunity to achieve representative status and to confront provincial governments with those grievances. For such politicians, however, there was a price to pay for participation. Because local self-government bodies formed the electorate for the provincial councils, politicians with provincial grievances were obliged to involve themselves in municipal and district board politics. Consequently, competition for power at that level increased; conflicts emerged between provincial and local interests; and, as a by-product of this process, politicization was enormously speeded up.

In the decade after the introduction of the Morley-Minto Reforms, the confrontation with government assumed a new intensity, and at the end of that decade, signs of national consciousness were beginning to appear. But the Reforms did not give anything away at the provincial level. The power to remedy provincial grievances continued to lie in the hands of the Raj, and if the Raj had stood firm at the provincial level, the political spotlight might have shifted back to the district officer. But the Raj did not stand firm. In 1920, the system changed again. In that year, by the terms of the Montagu-Chelmsford Reforms, each provincial council was given a majority of elected members, the franchise was greatly extended, and most important of all, the patronage of such important departments as Education, Agriculture and Local Self-Government was handed over to ministers responsible to the legislatures.

From the point of view of the relations between the districts and the province, this first stage of political devolution at the provincial level was of crucial importance. In those areas of control which had been handed over to Indian ministers, the ground under the district officer's feet began to give away. Patronage ceased to be the prerogative of the district officer. The district officer became the servant of the minister; and the patronage which he had distributed became the reward for political organization. Consequently, in certain important areas of government, those who were not receiving satisfaction at the district level could no longer look to the district officer for redress. Just as their opponents were enjoying the fruits of government patronage because they had allies in the provincial government, so they were obliged themselves, either to find similar allies or, failing that, to join a provincial opposition party. In certain important areas of government, there had ceased to be a local solution to local grievances.

But if the position of the local politician had changed, so had the position of the provincial politician. Under the Morley-Minto Reforms, because no power had been devolved at the provincial level, it had been possible, indeed it had been expedient, for provincial politicians to resolve local conflicts for the sake of provincial advantage. After 1920, however, the council chamber became a battleground between those who had access to the transferred departments and those who did not. This gave local grievances a new importance. Just as those who worked the Reforms were able to consolidate their power province-wide by the distribution of patronage, so those who wished to unseat the ministers were obliged to develop a similar organization themselves. Consequently the exploitation of local divisions, the recruitment of local opponents of ministers and the politicization of new sections of the electorate proceeded apace. The localities were drawn increasingly into the ambit of provincial politics, and the fortune of local and provincial politicians became correspondingly interdependent.

But what of the growth of nationalism? This book suggests that the politicization of the provinces was an essential prerequisite for its emergence. An arena for the expression of 'nationalist' grievances existed at the all-India level at a very early stage, and particularly after 1909, when an Imperial council was instituted along the same lines as those in the provinces, there was never any shortage of eminent men to fill the seats which had been created. Yet though the Morley-Minto Reforms had the same catalysing effect at the national level as they did in the provinces, the demands of 'nationalist' politicians for a share of power at that level fell on deaf ears. In 1920, under the Montagu-Chelmsford Reforms, the Central Legislature was expanded and an elected majority created, but no devolution of power took place. All the departments of the government of India remained firmly in the hands of the Raj and its agents until the very eve of Independence. This had important implications for the nature of nationalist politics. Whereas the devolution of power at the provincial level, both in 1920 and in 1937, had the effect of sharpening conflict at that level between 'in' groups and 'out' groups, causing a polarization of political interests around provincial issues, the failure to devolve power at the all-India level prevented the same yeast from working in nationalist politics. After 1920, confrontation with the Raj continued to be the *leitmotif* of Central Assembly politics, but in the face of Imperial recalcitrance on this issue, the mainspring of nationalist politics remained competition of interest at the provincial level. The assault on the Centre, the last stage in the emergence of nationalism, came not from the nation itself but from the provinces. The Congress party only won its right to succeed the Raj when it had captured a majority of provinces in 1937.

The Imperial system of control: beneficiaries and opponents

The introduction of electoral institutions and the devolution of power to Indian hands *per se* provide a framework for explaining the pace of politicization and the building of bridges between different levels of government. But they do not explain the nature of the bridges which were built and the kind of politicization which was done. They do not explain why certain groups, castes, classes and communities found themselves among the 'nationalists' at any given stage of the process of devolution, nor why certain others did not. More particularly, they do not explain what this book attempts to explain, namely why Muslim separatism became so important a political force. In order to explain these things, one has got to look at the introduction of electoral institutions and the devolution of power not as an autonomous process but in relation to the existing system of Imperial control.

In the system of control which Britain inherited from its predecessors, a man's importance in the eyes of the Imperial power lay in his social and political influence at the local level. No Imperial power could run a country of India's size without the help of local agents, and in the British case, the absence of intensive European settlement and the relative paucity of European personnel made it very necessary for the Imperial power to recruit to its service those who already possessed an established position in society, whether on account of their personal wisdom, their economic influence or their authority as social or religious leaders. In practice, the main criterion for an individual's usefulness was the ownership of land. It was from land that men derived the political and economic leverage necessary to ensure compliance with their wishes, and it was also from land that the government derived the bulk of its income. These were both excellent reasons for the government to develop a firm alliance with the landed class. It confirmed it in its possession of the land, by legal and, if necessary, by military means, and in return the landed class collected the land revenue and delivered a portion of it to the Imperial power. But the ramifications of this system of control did not stop there, for the Imperial power cemented the alliance even more firmly by recruiting the scions of landed houses into the Imperial bureaucracy. It endeavoured, in fact, to create an administrative machine which reflected the established social structure of the country, a machine which operated not only in the collection of land revenue, but in the day-to-day administration of every district, *tehsil* and *pargannah*.

The position of the Muslims within this system of control depended on their social and economic importance in the different provinces. Where they were influential landowners, they formed an important element in the Imperial system. Where they were small farmers and traders, the part they played was less significant. In North India, in the area around Delhi, which had been the centre of Muslim power since the twelfth century, and in the Gangetic plain to the East, where Muslim settlement had been most intense under the Moghul Empire, the Muslim share of land was great and their role within the Imperial system proportionately great. In this area (the United Provinces), and to a lesser extent in Bihar, the decline of the Moghul Empire did not radically disturb the Muslim share of landownership, and even where landed families were coming under pressure as a result of the working of new economic forces, they continued to play a similar role under the British Empire to the one they had played under the Moghuls. In 1913, as Table I shows, though only fourteen per cent of the population, the U.P. Muslims had thirty-five per cent of the most important jobs.

TABLE 1

Hindus and Muslims, by province and population:
their share of executive and judicial services, 1913
(Shown in percentages)

Province	Hindus				Muslims			
	Pop.	Exec.	Jud.	Total	Pop.	Exec.	Jud.	Total
Madras	88.90	73.5	91.3	82.9	6.67	11.8	1.3	6.3
Bombay	76.02	81.3	89.1	84.4	20.32	4.9	1.7	3.7
Bengal	44.80	72.9	97.5	84.7	52.74	18.1	2.5	10.6
Bihar and Orissa	82.40	54.3	76.1	60.2	10.63	22.6	22.7	22.7
United Provinces	85.32	50.7	73.9	60.1	14.11	41.3	24.8	34.7
Punjab*	33.46	38.2	37.5	38.0	54.85	38.2	39.6	38.6
Central Provinces	82.62	53.0	88.2	64.9	4.06	28.0	3.9	19.9
Assam	35.55	62.7	91.7	67.6	50.25	18.6	8.3	16.9

*In the Punjab the Sikhs formed 10.48% of the population and possessed 10.3% of the executive posts and 6.2% of the judicial posts.

Source: Report of the Public Service Commission 1912, vol, i (Calcutta 1917), p. 191.

In Western India, on the other hand, Muslim landowners had suffered at the hands of the Mahrattas, and in the South, where they had been largely confined to the princely state of Hyderabad, they remained so confined at the turn of the twentieth century. Both in Bombay (except in Sind) and in Madras, the most influential Muslims were merchants, and the community did not qualify for special consideration.

In Bengal, though for different reasons, Muslim influence was also negligible. Until the coming of the British, Bengal had possessed a substantial Muslim aristocracy. But as a result of the resumption proceedings of the East India Company, this aristocracy was virtually eliminated. At the turn of the century, despite the emergence of a parvenu aristocracy in the Dacca division, the community consisted primarily of peasant farmers and it was not favoured for government service. In 1913, though over fifty per cent of the population, the Bengali Muslims had only ten per cent of the prestigious jobs.

Outside the United Provinces, the Punjabis were the only community of great importance to the system of control. In the Punjab, Muslim fortunes improved under the British, for after the 'Mutiny', because the Muslims of West Punjab played so notable a part in putting it down, the Punjabi Muslims became a vital element in Imperial military strategy. For this reason, the Raj bolstered Muslim interests in the Punjab, and when irrigation schemes led to the reclamation of large areas of West Punjab in the later nineteenth century, the Muslims of that area were among the chief beneficiaries. This development marked the most important accession of landed wealth to the community during the British period. It gave the Punjabis a landed position to rival that of their co-religionists in the United Provinces, and in the years after 1920, because of their numerical strength, it was to make them politically more powerful.

Opposition to this system of control (and to the Muslim position within it) came from a multitude of sources. It came from the trader facing restrictions; from the landlord refused a revenue remission; from the oppressed tenant who found the administration siding with his oppressor; from the government servant facing a block in promotion; from the unsuccessful job applicant; from the religious zealot with theocratic beliefs; and from all those who felt they suffered discrimination. But particular grievances were not a substantial source of irritation to government. They only became so when they could be generalized—when the same grievance united a large number of opponents, or when a number of different grievances could be brought together under the same umbrella.

In the early stages of the nationalist movement, before the working of electoral institutions began to assist this process, one of the most important sources of generalized opposition to the Raj was the growth of an educated and professional élite, united by a common education, a common language, in many cases by the practice of a common profession, and increasingly, as the volume of graduates grew, by a common search for personal fulfilment in a system loaded against it. For those who were recruited as agents of the Raj were not educationally competitive. They were recruited not on the basis of qualifications obtained in the colleges, but on account of their family background and tried loyalty to Government. In the United Provinces, for example, in 1886, out of 161 Deputy Collectors, only fifteen had passed their intermediate examination and only nine had degrees. Of 225 *tehsildars*, only four had passed the intermediate examination and only one had a degree.[1] Moreover, even after 1886, despite the recommendations of the Public Service Commission that entry into the provincial services should be by competitive recruitment 'wherever the Government of India thinks it not inexpedient', the same system continued. Prior to 1917, the only 'competitive' examination for entry to any provincial service took place in the Punjab, where two jobs were awarded as a result of a competition among nominated candidates.[2] Thus, even though colleges in the Presidency towns were producing hundreds of graduates, the majority of prestigious jobs remained outside their reach unless they fulfilled the broader requirements of Imperial recruitment policy. This inevitably created resentment; and as the number of graduates grew, so did the demand for a change in the system. The foundation of the Indian National Congress was in part the result of these resentments—a recognition that the system would only be changed if a more concerted political approach was adopted, and if pressure was brought to bear not only on the Indian Civil Service but also on the British Parliament and people.

The Muslim part in challenging the system was not initially very

---

[1] *Report of the Public Services Commission 1886-7* (Calcutta 1888), pp. 34-5.

[2] *Report of the Public Services Commission 1912*, vol. i (Calcutta 1917), p. 29.

large. College education first made headway in the oldest centres of British rule, Calcutta, Bombay and Madras, and the Muslims of those areas were in no position to benefit from it. In Bengal, the community was impoverished and concentrated far from Calcutta in the province's Eastern divisions. In Bombay, and to a lesser extent in Madras, though adequate funds were available, they were invested chiefly in trade, an occupation for which English education was unnecessary. When the Indian National Congress was founded to express the grievances of this class, therefore, the Muslims took virtually no part of it. Those of the Presidencies were not educated enough, and those of North India, though keenly aware of the importance of education, were too far behind to compete with the Presidency elites. By the turn of the century, however, North India had become part of the educational mainstream. In 1911, as Table 2 shows, there were more pupils in colleges in the United Provinces than in either Madras or Bombay; and the Punjab was not far behind. Moreover, because the North Indian Muslims had the funds to invest in education, they also benefited from this process. In the same year, there were more Muslims in colleges in the U.P. than in any other province and the ratio of their share of college places to their share of the population was also considerably higher. By the turn of the century, therefore, insofar as the United Provinces had joined the educational mainstream, the U.P. Muslims had also joined it, and insofar as the educated elite was in the vanguard of the nationalist movement, the U.P. Muslims were also qualified to take part.

The Morley-Minto Reforms: political manipulation and electoral response

It is sometimes assumed in discussions of the introduction of electoral institutions in Britain's dependent territories that Britain's only role was to bestow on her subjects as a free gift a system of government which had been tried and tested by the 'Mother of Parliaments'. Such an assumption belongs more to the realm of myth than of reality. In Britain, parliamentary reform and the extension of the franchise was a positive if reluctant response by the ruling class to a demand for a change in the political system. In 1832, for example, Parliament took note of the social and economic changes wrought by the industrial revolution and gave the vote to

TABLE 2

*English education in colleges and secondary schools, showing total
numbers of pupils (A), total numbers of Muslim pupils (B), and the
percentage of Muslim pupils (C), by province in 1911/12*

Province	A		B		C	
	Colleges	Schools	Colleges	Schools	Colleges	Schools
Madras	5,801	110,336	103	5,519	1.8	5.0
Bombay	4,958	74,601	183	5,543	3.7	7.4
Bengal	11,620	205,931	792	20,364	6.6	9.8
East Bengal	3,156	186,641	381	59,439	12.0	31.8
Punjab	3,549	99,418	872	24,774	24.5	24.9
U.P.	5,844	97,056	1,357	10,561	23.2	10.8
C.P.	716	55,295	33	2,054	4.6	3.7
NWFP	38	9,332	23	3,362	60.5	36.0

Source: Progress of Education in India, Sixth Quinquennial Report,
Cmd. 7485 (1914), Table 16, p. 203, and Tables 217-18, p. 286.

those whom it had brought into prominence. By the terms of the
Reform Bill of that year, the country's ruling class admitted the
new industrial and commercial bourgeoisie to a share of the rewards
of the political system and so avoided the development of extra-
parliamentary confrontations. In India, on the other hand, those
who were loudest in demanding reforms were rarely those who
benefited from them. In India, as this book will attempt to show,
the introduction of parliamentary institutions was not a concession
intended to absorb those 'on the outside trying to get in' but an
attempt to extend and improve the existing system of control by a
new method.

The Morley-Minto Reforms are the first significant electoral
monument to this strategy.[3] They endeavoured to put power not into

---

[3] In the 1880s, when electoral institutions with a substantial elected element were
first introduced in local self-government, it was chiefly for financial reasons. It was
decided that the localities should bear more of the cost of local administration and it
was considered necessary to increase popular participation to make this change more
palatable. Lord Ripon, the Liberal Viceroy, did hope that these measures would
provide India's emerging élite with a training ground for greater responsibilities.
But the élite was still small and the matters in which it was most interested could not
be settled at the local level.

the hands of those who demanded reform but into the hands of those on whose co-operation the Raj had long relied. They did this chiefly by making local self-government bodies the electorates for council seats. In the United Provinces, for example, twelve seats were created along these lines. Each of the eight divisions elected one member, the weight of the responsibility lying with the more conservative district boards, and the eight most important municipalities were given the right to elect a member at alternate elections. The aim of this arrangement was to secure the return of the government's allies in the localities. The eight divisional seats were expected to elect 'sound' members of the landed interest, and from the major cities were expected nominees of the substantial indigenous commercial interests whose political influence had hitherto been dominant.[4] The Raj had succeeded for nearly three decades in managing the municipalities and districts with their help, and it hoped to manage the provincial councils in the same style. For those outside the system of control, therefore, and particularly for India's growing educated and professional élite, the Reforms were as much a challenge as a response. If they wished to be returned to the provincial council, either they had to make themselves amenable to dominant local interests or they had to take up arms and oppose them.

Additional constraints were imposed on Muslim political activity by the introduction of separate electorates. Separated by religious conviction and social customs from the bulk of the Hindu community, the Muslims had always received special consideration from government, and particularly in North India, where they formed a vital part of the system of control. But separate electorates had never been generally demanded before, and they had only been introduced in one or two municipalities in the Punjab. Why then were they introduced at this time? Hitherto the debate on this question has been about whether the Muslims really wanted them. Most Pakistani historians have said they did. Many Indian historians have accused the government of pulling strings behind the scenes to arrange for them to be demanded. This scenario is too simple. It does not make sense to suppose that the Simla deputation demanded concessions its members did not want. Nor that the government

[4] To date, the most thorough study of urban politics at this time is C.A. Bayly's *The Local Roots of Indian Nationalism* (Oxford, 1975).

introduced a new system of election without being sure that it would be worked positively by those it was designed to assist. On both sides of the debate, the weakness is the assumption that 'the Muslim community' can be treated as a coherent unit at this time.

From the turn of the century, divisions had begun to emerge between the traditional leaders of the community—those who had a place within the system of control—and the growing body of educated Moslems. This was nowhere more so than at the Aligarh Mahommedan Anglo-Oriental College, the institution founded by Sir Syed Ahmed to bring Muslim India into line with the new educational demands of the Imperial system. There, the increasing interest of Muslim youths in the Congress threatened the credibility of the community's traditional leaders, and if Harcourt Butler, at that time Joint Secretary to the U.P. Government, is to be believed, it was in order to harness these enthusiasms to their own cause that these leaders founded the Muslim League in 1906.

There never was any splendid loyalty. Moshin ul Mulk and others came to see me at Lucknow to take my advice. They were quite frank. They could not hold their young men and feared their joining the Hindus, which meant ultimate absorption of the Mahommedans. It was purely in their own interests that they formed the Muslim League. I said at that time: What if you can't control the young men in the League? They recognized the possibility of this but regarded the danger as remote.[5]

Seen against this background, the granting of separate electorates appears to have been an attempt by the Raj to shore up a crucial part of its system of control. As in the case of the general electorates, it was an attempt to extend and broaden the base of its rule by extending and broadening the support of its traditional allies. For those Muslims outside the system of control, however, and particularly for the Muslim professional and educated élite, this innovation had serious implications. For it meant that they could only work the Reforms successfully if they came to terms with the grievances of the Muslim localities. In the years after 1912, when the Muslim League began to develop an alliance with the Congress, this was to be a potential source of conflict between the two organizations.

[5] Harcourt Butler papers (IOL MSS F 116) 71: Butler to Allen, 6 April, 1913.

In 1911, the Muslim League moved its headquarters from Aligarh to Lucknow, and shortly afterwards it came to be dominated by a group of politicians, chiefly of the Shia sect, who lived and worked in that city. The group's patron was the Raja of Mahmudabad, one of the largest *taluqdars* of Oudh, and one of the few members of his class with an interest in nationalist politics. In 1914, he became the League's permanent President. Apart from the Raja, most members of the group were lawyers and professional men. Most prominent among them was Wazir Hassan, a man of exceptional intellectual and organizational abilities, who became the League Secretary in 1912. To him belongs the credit for changing the League's creed in 1913, and according to the Raja he was also one of the chief authors of the scheme of Reforms which the Congress and League submitted to the government.[6] Another important member was Samiullah Beg, an advocate of the Lucknow Bar and the group's link-man with the U.P. Congress. The older statesman of the group was Syed Nabiullah, the Chairman of the Lucknow Municipal Board, who had been called to the Bar in England in the 1880s. Within the U.P., the group's political ambitions were focused on the provincial council, and from 1912 to 1914, it was engaged in building up its influence within the province. But after the outbreak of the World War, in co-operation with a number of other politicians, it came to assume all-India importance. Prominent among the politicians with whom the Lucknow group co-operated at that time were Mahommed Ali Jinnah, an ambitious Bombay lawyer with his sights set at the all-India level; Hassan Imam, once a judge of the Calcutta High Court; Ali Imam, his brother, from 1910 Law Member of the Government of India; and Mazhar ul Haq, their protégé, a man of more radical views. The Raja, Jinnah, Ali Imam and Mazhar ul Haq all sat on the Viceroy's Council in the years before the War, and their association with other Indian political leaders in that body provided a basis for subsequent Congress-League co-operation.

But Congress-League co-operation was not achieved easily. Indeed in many parts of the U.P., the policies adopted by the Lucknow group only met with qualified approval. This was because of the different levels of development of the Muslim community in different parts of the province. The province of Oudh, of which

---

[6] Ali Imam papers (Karachi University Library): Wazir Hassan to Raja of Mahmudabad, 20 July 1917; Raja of Mahmudabad to Ali Imam, 25 July 1917.

Lucknow was the capital, was in two ways an exception: firstly, in that the landed leadership of the community was in a fairly thriving condition; and secondly, in that Lucknow, both as a traditional Muslim centre and as a service centre for the colonial regime, was naturally a focus for the more educated and intelligent Muslims. In the province of Agra, on the other hand, both in the more populous western divisions of Meerut and Rohilkhund, and in the divisions further east, the landed position of the community was under severe attack, and educational advancement, particularly in the highly urbanized Rohilkhund division, was very limited.[7] It is, of course, difficult to claim overwhelming reliability for such generalizations. The evidence for degrees of educational advancement is by no means exhaustive. Nor is it true to say that all Muslims were losing land in the province of Agra. The Sheikhs appear to have been gaining in many districts,[8] demonstrating in all probability that those Muslims who were increasing their holdings were also changing their titles to register their claims to higher social status. But if one examines the sort of questions asked in the U.P. Legislative Council by Muslim members from the different constituencies, it is noticeable that those representing the more economically and educationally backward divisions tend to demand more special treatment for their community. Syed Raza Ali, the member for the backward Rohilkhund division, is the most communal politician in the Council.[9] Samiullah Beg and Wazir Hassan, on the other hand, advocate a better deal for those with higher educational qualifications almost

---

[7] The evidence for these generalizations has been taken from the U.P. District Gazetteers and the Censuses. See *DG Bahraich* (1903), p. 80; *DG Kheri* (1905), p. 97; *DG Barabanki* (1904), p. 102; *DG Fyzabad* (1905), p. 97; *DG Lucknow* (1904), p. 90; *DG Bareilly* (1911), pp. 98, 100-1; *DG Bijnor* (1909), pp. 107-8; *DG Badaun* (1907), pp. 82 and 84; *DG Moradabad* (1911), pp. 84, 87, 93, 97; *DG Shahjehanpur* (1910), pp.87-8; *DG Bulandshahr* (1903), p. 92; *DG Aligarh* (1909), pp. 91-2; *DG Muzaffarnagar* (1903) p. 120; *DG Meerut* (1904), pp. 83-5; *DG Saharanpur* (1909), pp. 116-17; *DG Allahabad* (1911), pp. 103-4; *DG Fatehpur* (1906), p. 101; *DG Jaunpur* (1908), p. 94; *DG Ghazipur* (1909), p. 95; *DG Azamgarh* (1911), p. 107, *NWP and Oudh Census 1901*, part ii, table viii, pp. 116-120; *U.P. Census 1911*, part ii, table viii, pp. 148-51; *U.P. Census 1921*, part ii, table viii, pp. 130-3.

[8] See *DG Aligarh* (1909), pp. 91-2; *DG Saharanpur* (1909), pp. 116-17; *DG Meerut* (1904), pp. 83-5.

[9] See for example, *UPLC Progs. 1913*, p. 215; *UPLC Progs. 1914*, pp. 515-17; *UPLC Progs. 1915*, p. 449; *UPLC Progs. 1916*, p. 738.

The Punjab (1920), showing districts and divisions

without reservation.[10] Nor is it simply a coincidence that loyalist leadership throughout the British period—from Sir Syed to the Nawab of Chaththari—comes from the province of Agra. It reflects the inherently less competitive character of the community in that province.

But if loss of land to the moneylender and educational backwardness were important sources of communalism, they were not activated significantly at the provincial level at this time. The main reason for this was that in these fields no points of distribution were reached. The emphasis of the politicians was on securing concessions, not on distributing them, and on this basis it was possible for very different interests to combine. In the demand for an Executive Council for the United Provinces, for the replacement of Europeans by Indians, for greater financial devolution to the provincial level, for the expansion of educational opportunities, and for an improvement in the status of the legal profession, Raza Ali was as spirited an advocate as the Lucknow leaders.[11] On these issues, moreover, he stood shoulder to shoulder with the very Hindus who opposed his demands for special treatment for the Muslims of his locality. This was a paradox of the Morley-Minto constitution which was to be removed when Indians were given control of government patronage at the provincial level.

The same kind of paradox is also noticeable in the relations of the professional elite and the landed class. Though accusations of subservience were common enough, the landed class was still far from being the main target of the politicians and it did not consider it necessary to organize itself. Despite the introduction of a new system of representation at the provincial level, the government still had a monopoly of decision-making, and those who already formed part of the system of control had no need to compete for its attention. This is a twilight period between two systems of government and a study of overt political activity only provides one half of the political equation. This paradox was also to be removed in the years after 1920.

During the Morley-Minto Reforms, the most significant challenge

[10] See *UPLC Progs. 1916*, p. 681; *UPLC Progs. 1917*, pp. 146 and 908-18.

[11] The annual Council debates on the Budget give an indication of political feelings on these questions. For Raza Ali's views, see, for example, *UPLC Progs. 1913*, p. 59; *UPLC Progs. 1915*, pp. 203 and 387; *UPLC Progs. 1916* pp. 472-3 and 738.

to the ambitions of the provincial politicians developed as a result of the working of the constitution itself. For by making membership of municipal and district boards a stepping stone to representation at the provincial level, the Reforms awakened a new interest in municipal politics. The result was many more hotly contested elections, much more rivalry for seats on municipal and district boards, and a distinct increase in communalism in the localities. In the U.P. municipalities before 1909, despite the existence of general electorates, there does not appear to have been any persistent communal friction. The municipalities of the Rohilkhund division may have been an exception to this, particularly after the turn of the century, but except in that one division, Muslims did not suffer any severe losses as a result of the working of the general electorate. Indeed in several of the larger towns, just before the 1909 Act was introduced, they made a number of gains.[12] After 1909, however, Muslim losses increased, particularly in the eight most important towns with the right to elect a member to the Council.[13] Quite why this happened is uncertain. Whether it was, as a report from Mirzapur suggests, that the more established members of municipal boards were enrolling members of their own religion to offset the challenge of the *vakils*,[14] or whether it was the *vakils* themselves who were indulging in communal appeals to cut across the electoral alliances of the traditional urban élites, is a question which can pro-

[12] To date, the most detailed examination of Muslim politics in the U.P. municipalities is to be found in F.C.R. Robinson, 'Municipal Government and Muslim Separatism', in Gallagher, Johnson and Seal (eds.), *Locality, Province and Nation* (Cambridge 1973), pp. 69-121. But I have differed from him in his assessment of the effect of the working of general electorates on the Muslim community before 1909. Dr Robinson contends that the Muslims were losing seats in the Meerut, Agra, Rohilkhund and Allahabad divisions from 1883 onwards. But in computing his statistics he does not take the Municipal Reform Act of 1900 into account. This Act reduced the membership of municipal boards in order to provoke keener competition for election. Prior to that time, many municipalities had a record of poor electoral response and infrequent meetings. See annual *Reports on Municipal Taxation and Expenditure in the North Western Provinces and Oudh*, 1891/2-1898/9; *Reports on Municipal Administration and Finances*, 1900/1901-1908/9.

[13] Between 1909 and 1916, the Muslims lost three seats at Meerut, two at Bareilly, four at Benares, three at Lucknow and two at Fyzabad. At Allahabad by 1913, there were no Muslim members on the Board at all. See *Report on Municipal Administration and Finances, 1908/9*, appendix A, pp. ii-v; *U.P. Gazette*, part viii, 2 Sept. 1916.

[14] See *Report on Municipal Administration and Finances 1909/10*, p. 2.

bably be answered in a different way in each locality.[15] What is certain, however, is that except in the very limited number of municipalities where they formed a majority of the electorate, the Muslims, as a minority community, could not help but suffer, and this undoubtedly explains why the demand for an extension of separate electorates increases in volume after 1909.[16]

While the Muslim League leaders pursued their policy of political co-operation with Congress, this rise of communalism in the localities forms a sombre backcloth to their activities. At the All India Muslim League at Agra in 1913, when Jinnah and Mazhar ul Haq attempted to persuade the League not to pass its regular resolution in favour of separate electorates in local self-government as an earnest of its intentions to work with the Congress, they were voted down by the politicians of the U.P. municipalities.[17] At Bombay in 1915, the first year that both Congress and League held their sessions in the same city, local opposition almost wrecked the possibility of a joint approach to the question of Reform, and Jinnah and his colleagues only carried the day against Cassim Mitha and his 'goondas' by locking themselves up in the Taj Mahal hotel and holding their session in private.[18] Finally, in 1915 and 1916, these local conflicts emerged on to the provincial and national stage most threateningly of all as a result of a Government decision to introduce a substantial measure of reform in the U.P. municipalities. The U.P. Municipal Bill, which proposed a large-scale devolution of power to the municipalities, sharpened communal demands in the localities at the very time that provincial and national leaders

[15] C.A. Bayly, in his work on Allahabad, sees 1909 as a definite landmark in the involvement of the professional classes in politics. Before that date, they acted as brokers and publicists, pursuing their ambitions under the umbrellas of dominant *rais* factions. Afterwards the professionals came into their own and electioneering based directly on caste and creed became more frequent. Dr Bayly sees electoral reform as one of the main causes for the change, but he believes it was assisted by modifications in the structure of local taxation. (op.cit., pp. 226-244.)

[16] Syed Raza Ali was the main leader of the communal faction. The campaign to secure separate electorates began in earnest after the provincial council elections of 1912. See *UPLC Progs. 1913*, pp. 20, 60, 214 and 393; *UPLC Progs. 1914*, pp. 410-11, 492 and 517-18.

[17] See S.S Pirzada (ed.), *Foundations of Pakistan, All India Muslim League Documents 1906-47*, vol. i (Karachi 1969), pp. 315-17.

[18] Ibid., vol. i, pp. 324-61.

were anxious to keep them out of sight. It brought the 'separate electorate issue to a head, it embittered relations between the communities throughout the province, and it came very close to sabotaging the Lucknow Pact itself.[19]

But the scope of the argument goes somewhat beyond the assertion that the working of the Reforms imposed important constraints on the activities of the politicians. It would also suggest that the nature of the Reforms influenced the capacity of such politicians to overcome these constraints, to compose communal divisions, and to produce a united front against the government. Where the controversy surrounding the U.P. Municipal Bill was concerned, it was the fact that there had been no real devolution of power at the provincial level which enabled provincial leaders of both communities to surrender local advantage in the hope of provincial gain. As Tej Bahadur Sapru put it when the final compromise was being debated:

Were it not that I believed in and hoped for higher things to come, were it not that I hoped that we are not going to rest contented with merely local self-government, I should not be so willing to accept an amendment which I know is not approved of by my friend, the Hon. Babu Brijnandan Prasad[20].

Moreover, when the same controversy re-emerged during the negotiations prior to the Lucknow Pact, it was because of the operation of similar factors at the all-India level—because the Presidency politicians were in no mood to be baulked in their own ambitions—that the recalcitrance of the U.P. communal Hindu party was not allowed to stand in the way of a national agreement[21].

However, even after the Lucknow Pact had been agreed, even after the Congress and the League had met Mr Montagu in joint

[19] For an account of the Municipal Bill controversy, see Robinson, 'Municipal Government and Muslim Separatism', op.cit., pp. 106-15.

[20] *UPLC Progs. 1916,* pp. 217-18. Brijnandan Prasad was the member for Rohilkhund and Kumaon. The Rohilkhund Hindus lost twenty-six seats as a result of the compromise.

[21] For details of the efforts of Mrs Besant, Tilak, Surendra Nath Bannerjee and Bhupendra Nath Basu to produce the Lucknow Pact, and of Jinnah's strategy for ensuring continuing compliance with it, see GUPGAD140/1917. CID report on the Lucknow sessions of the League and Congress.

deputation, the power to modify the constitution still lay with the Raj. How would the Raj respond to their demands? What modifications would it make to the system of control? These were the questions which preoccupied the politicians as first Montagu and then the various constitutional committees toured the provinces. They only met with a definitive response with the passing of the Government of India Act of 1919. But long before that time, as the Raj mobilized its allies to present their case,[22] it had become clear that the politicians did not face a rosy future. For the opponents of the system of control, the Montagu-Chelmsford Reforms, like their predecessors, were to be as much a challenge as a response.

Panislamism: an agitational alternative

Those involved in constitutional politics were hopeful that modifications to the existing system of control would give them a new importance in their own society. But there were other political and quasi-political elements in Muslim society which shared neither their hopes nor their interests. Some considered it inherently unlikely that constitutional methods would secure Reform. Some felt that Reform was not likely to benefit them, whatever methods were employed. Others—notably the religious elements in Muslim society—were not fundamentally interested in the system, except insofar as it imposed limitations on their own areas of activity. In the period before and after the First World War some of these political and religious forces contributed to the rise of Panislamism in India. This development, which owed its impetus to the problems faced by Turkey as a result of European expansionism, reached maximum intensity after the War, when the fate of Turkey was being settled by the victorious allies. At that time in India, the Khilafat movement obtained massive support and presented a serious threat to the stability of government.

The dependence of the Khilafat movement on circumstances outside India necessarily limited its long-term importance. But it was not without significance for political developments inside India. Firstly, it did have a bearing on the constitutional situation. Both before the First World War, in co-operation with the constitutiona-

---

[22] For details of the U.P. government's efforts in this field, see GUPGAD 553/1917, *passim.*

lists, and afterwards, in co-operation with Gandhi, the Panislamists play an important role as the shock troops of Reformist politics. Secondly, the religio-political alliances formed at this time in some respects foreshadow the Pakistan movement itself. The Khilafat movement was the most significant mass movement among the Muslims before the 1940s, and many of the politicians involved in it were later to figure on the Muslim League platform.

The most convenient place to begin a study of Panislamist politics is the Aligarh Mahommedan Anglo-Oriental College, which was the initial political focus for the two most prominent Panislamists, Mahommed and Shaukat Ali. The structure of power within the college was remarkably similar to the structure of power in Muslim society at large. The management was dominated by the Rajas and Nawabs who figured largely in the Imperial system of control, whilst the students themselves, and particularly the scholarship boys, were in many cases attracted to more radical politics. The Ali brothers, both former scholarship pupils, had their strongest links with the students and the old boys, and their chief aim in college politics was to democratize the court of Trustees in such a way as to gain a position of greater prominence for themselves and their followers. In 1907, Mahommed Ali drew up a scheme of Reforms with this in view; and in 1910, when the Aga Khan launched a campaign to make the college into a university, the two brothers were among his most ardent supporters. They appear to have hoped that the university would be controlled more democratically than the college and that they would benefit from the reorganization.[23]

The coincidence of the Secretary of State's veto on the community's plans for the university and the outbreak of the Balkan wars makes it difficult to assess the precise reasons for Mahommed Ali's involvement in Panislamist politics at this time. Like many Indian Muslims, he took pride in the independence of Turkey as a compensation for the Muslim fall from power in India, and he had great hopes of the Committee of Union and Progress as a vehicle for the revitalization of the decaying Ottoman Empire. As an English-educated Muslim, moreover, he saw in the expansion of European power in the Balkans an exaggerated form of the subjugation which Indians suffered in their own country. It is significant, however,

[23] See G. Minault and D. Lelyveld, 'The Campaign for a Muslim University 1898-1920', *Modern Asian Studies*, 8, 2 (1974), pp. 145-189.

that the Italian invasion of Tripoli in 1911 provoked far less reaction in India than the Balkans wars. It was only after the veto on the university that Mahommed Ali began to campaign politically on Turkey's behalf; only then that the Ali brothers began to develop an alliance with the ulema, and to argue in favour of confrontation with the Raj and co-operation with the Congress. Prior to the veto, Mahommed Ali had argued that the fate of Tripoli and Persia made no difference to the realities of Indian politics.[24] Afterwards, he was to say that the treatment meted out to Tripoli, Persia and Turkey justified the Muslim League's acceptance of self-government as an ideal.[25]

The political alliance which the Ali brothers developed at this time had two poles—Aligarh and Delhi, the first the seat of the college, and the second, the capital of India, where Mahommed Ali edited and published the *Comrade*. At Delhi, Mahommed Ali's chief allies were Ajmal Khan, a hakim with a lucrative practice among the princes, and Dr Ansari, a younger man who had studied and practised medicine in England. These two men shared Mahommed Ali's concern for the position of Turkey, and they co-operated with him in a number of ventures both before and after the War. What gave the Delhi-Aligarh axis a new dimension, however, was the adherence of a number of Punjab and U.P. ulema, chief among whom was Maulana Abdul Bari of Firengi Mahal, Lucknow. An *alim* of a traditional mould, Abdul Bari was apprehensive that secular education would undermine religious allegiances, and he saw the Balkan wars as fertile ground for the extension of ulema influence. In the first decade of the century, he had founded a number of evangelical organizations to recall Muslims to the correct observance of Islamic law, and together with Mushir Hussain Kidwai, a taluqdar of Barabanki, he had made efforts to improve the religious instruction of the English-educated. Abdul Bari was also quicker than most ulema to grasp the political implications of the Balkan wars, for he had visited Mecca and Constantinople only two years before. His association with the Ali brothers, which was to last for over a decade, began in the winter of 1912/13.

Before the First World War, the Delhi-Aligarh axis was involved

---

[24] See Afzal Iqbal (ed.), *Select Writings and Speeches of Maulana Mahommed Ali*, first edition, (Lahore 1944), p. 70.

[25] *Comrade*, 24 May 1913.

in two main enterprises, the organization of a Medical Mission to Turkey, and the developments of the *Anjuman-i-Khuddam-i-Kaaba*, a society designed to protect the heartland of Islam, and to strengthen the faith by preaching and teaching. Both enterprises enjoyed a measure of success. The Medical Mission, which was led by Dr Ansari, was appreciated by the Turks, and proved a formative experience for a number of Aligarh students who were later to figure prominently in nationalist politics.[26] The *Anjuman* opened an office at Bombay to provide a service for *hajis* en route for Mecca, and under the leadership of Shaukat Ali and Abdul Bari, established branches in Punjab, the United Provinces, Sind and Kashmir. According to one source, it had a membership of 17,000 by 1915.[27]

These activities were brought to an end when Turkey entered the War on the German side. Most Muslims understood that Britain was a reluctant opponent of Turkey, and were reassured by the Allied guarantee that the Holy Places would be immune from attack. Far from campaigning on Turkey's behalf, they concentrated on averting a confrontation, taking it as a foregone conclusion that Turkey would be the loser if one took place. But this was not the attitude of the Ali brothers. At a time when the government was empowered to deal more effectively with challenges to its authority, the Ali brothers campaigned unreservedly on Turkey's behalf and quickly got into trouble. The *Comrade* was obliged to cease publication, and in April 1915, the brothers were interned for the duration of the War.

However, as the War progressed and Turkey came under pressure from the Allies—as the Sharif of Mecca repudiated Turkish rule and Baghdad fell—Muslim anxiety increased and the Ali brothers came to assume a new importance. Their internment in these years becomes symbolic of the plight of Turkey, and the demand for their release a vicarious plea for the restoration of Turkey to her former strength. In September 1917, as preparations were being made for the Congress-League deputation to Montagu, Panislamist pressure on this question was very embarassing to the League leaders, and at Allahabad in October they embarassed the

[26] See Chaudhuri Khaliquzzaman, *Pathway to Pakistan* (Lahore 1961), pp. 20-7.

[27] GI Home Poll., June 1915, B 549-52; Weekly Report of the Director of Criminal Intelligence, 1 June 1915.

Congress by insisting that the issue be given priority.[28] By December, however, with communal organizations marshalling their forces for the revision of the constitution, and feelings embittered by a bout of rioting in Bihar, the situation had changed noticeably. By that stage, the League leaders were under pressure to break with the Congress, and the Ali brothers began to take their place as the symbols of Hindu-Muslim unity. At Calcutta in December, as the League leaders attempted unsuccessfully to renegotiate the Lucknow Pact, the Ali brothers' mother was given royal treatment on the Congress platform.[29] In this lay the embryo of post-War developments.

The prime mover in the development of an agitational alliance between the two communities was Mahatma Gandhi. By February 1918, he had made contact with Abdul Bari; by March he was petitioning the Viceroy for the brothers' release; and by November, he was quite explicit in his strategy. 'My interest in your release', he wrote to Mahommed Ali 'is quite selfish. We have a common goal and I want to utilize your services to the uttermost in order to reach that goal. In the proper solution of the Mahommedan question lies the realization of Swaraj.'[30] But early efforts at co-operation were not successful. Gandhi's hopes that Abdul Bari would be able to mobilize the Muslims to participate in the Rowlatt Satyagraha proved ill-founded. At that time, the plight of Turkey was not serious enough for the Muslims to be allured by offers of a joint front against Government, and it was only after the Delhi riot of 30 March 1919, in which members of both communities were shot dead in police firing, that a joint front developed.[31] The Khilafat movement itself only began to attract serious attention in September 1919, when a decision at the Peace Conference was believed to be imminent. At that stage, meetings of protest were held both in Bombay and in North India, and Gandhi was accepted as a mentor by the Khilafatists of both areas. Under his guidance, a *hartal* was organized on 17 October, and he was also responsible for suggesting a boycott of the

[28] GI Home Poll., Nov. 1917, B 471-74; Weekly Report of the Director of Criminal Intelligence, 3 Nov. 1917.

[29] GI Home Poll., Jan. 1918, B 487-90; Weekly Report of the Director of Criminal Intelligence, 12 Jan. 1918.

[30] *Collected Works of Gandhi,* vol. xv (Ahmedabad 1965), pp. 63-4: Gandhi to Mahommed Ali, 18 Nov. 1918.

[31] See GUPGAD 262/1919.

peace celebrations.[32] By December, when the Ali brothers were released from internment, the Khilafat-Swaraj alliance was already well established.

The Khilafat movement itself was the result of a genuine religious concern for the position of Turkey. To most Muslims, it seemed that the Kaaba really was in danger, and in those circumstances, the call to prayer became a call to action. All over India, there was a spontaneous and widespread groundswell of agitation, and religious leaders mushroomed to give it voice. The problem for the political leaders of the movement was how to harness these religious feelings to a movement directed against the government. For on a question of such moment, the nature of Quranic instruction was one of blunt alternatives. If the government did not interfere with the practice of the Muslim religion, India was to be considered *Dar ul Islam* (Land of peace), but if it did, and no redress was obtained by appeal, India became *Dar ul Harb* (Land of war), and the immediate response of the Muslim people had to be one of *jihad* (war) or *hijrat* (migration). In the nature of things, however, the Raj was too strong to be successfully opposed by *jihad*. Very few people imagined that the Khilafat movement could succeed in an outright war with the administration. And *hijrat* was really a counsel of despair. For the political leaders of the movement, this presented a very real dilemma.

The leadership's answer to this dilemma was the alliance with Gandhi and the adoption of his programme of non-co-operation. This alliance had the obvious strategic advantage that it held out hopes of Hindu support, and it had the practical advantage of providing a stage-by-stage programme for putting pressure on the Government of India. The success of this policy, however, depended on efficient organization and shrewd leadership by the Khilafatists themselves, and the history of the movement suggests that these qualities were lacking. Khilafat committees sprang up all over India. Vast amounts of money were sent to the Central Khilafat Committee at Bombay. The Ali brothers toured India making speeches. Mahommed Ali went to Europe and played the Grand Moghul. The popularity of the brothers was enormous. But the control of the Central Khilafat Committee over the rank and file

<hr>

[32] See IOR/L/P and J/6/6594/1919: Viceroy to Secretary of State, 16 Oct. 1919; GI Home Poll., Jan. 1920, D 5: Bombay FR I Nov. 1919.

was very circumscribed. Such control as the leadership did exercise was dependent on their ability to convince the ulema and the workers that peaceful pressure according to Gandhi's programme was being successful, and once it became clear that this was not the case, as it did by April 1920, the ulema and workers began to champion a resort to religious solutions. At this point, the deficiencies of the political leadership became most apparent. Because they had failed to organize the movement, they found it difficult restraining the ulema, and because they lacked the necessary political initiative, they failed to take the one step—immediate commencement of all stages of non-co-operation—which might have kept control of the movement in their hands. Instead, they themselves gave voice to the same views which the ulema were propagating, and by doing so encouraged a movement which they hoped to contain. By May 1920, the leadership was in fact following the masses. The Khilafat movement had assumed a momentum of its own. This loss of control by the leadership is shown most graphically in the *hijrat* movement to Afghanistan.[33]

The political dominance of Gandhi in the counsels of the Central Khilafat Committee is the other side of the same coin. This dominance, which was as much personal as political, was not always to the leadership's disadvantage because Gandhi had a shrewder awareness than they of how to organize a political movement. But Gandhi's advice was not principally related to the need to save the Khilafat. His own ambitions were more related to the Indian situation. His reluctance, for example, to give way to Khilafatist demands for full-scale non-co-operation in April and May 1920, when the Khilafat movement began to escalate, was principally motivated by his desire to bring Congress under the same umbrella over the issue of the Hunter report.[34] Delay in the publication of the report thwarted him in this ambition. But even then he only eventually began non-co-operation when it had become clear that the Congress would not come in over the Hunter report, and that the only way of cowing

[33] For the dilemma facing the political leadership and their reactions to it, see Weekly Reports of the Director of Criminal Intelligence, March, April and May, 1920: GI Home Poll., March 1920, D 89; April 1920, D 103; June 1920, D 78. The government's reactions to the *hijrat* movement can be found in IOR/L/P and J/6/5703/1920.

[34] Gandhi's tactics emerge most clearly at the Allahabad meetings of Khilafatists and Congressmen early in June. See Reports of the Commissioner of Police, Bombay, GI Home Poll., July 1920, B 109.

his opponents into submission was by starting the movement unilaterally with Khilafat support. In this plan he was successful. At
Calcutta in September, with the Khilafatists strongly behind him,
he captured the Congress organization, and he consolidated this
victory at Nagpur in December.[35] Yet once he was established in
firm control of the Congress organization, Gandhi's political priorities changed. Having obliged the Congress to reject the new
constitution, he began reshaping the organization to cope with the
new political situation. Party-building became the most important
aspect of his political work and it brought him increasingly into
conflict with the Khilafatists. In March and April 1921, when the
Ali brothers began to throw off Gandhi's leadership and incite their
audiences to violence, Gandhi began to dissociate himself from
them. In July, when the Khilafat Committee pronounced it *haram*
to serve in the Army, Gandhi took no part in the proceedings, and
by September, when the Ali brothers were arrested, the most significant phase of Hindu-Muslim co-operation had come to an end.

As a result of his alliance with the Khilafatists, Gandhi increased
his political prestige, captured the Congress organization, and reformed and revitalized it so as to give nationalist politics a new
sanction. As a result of their alliance with Gandhi, however, the
Khilafatists had little effect on British government attitudes towards
Turkey. When the government made concessions, it was chiefly
due to the resurgence of Turkish military power and not to Panislamist support for her position. Within the context of Indian politics, moreover, the Khilafatists made fewer gains. The movement
had derived its impetus from events outside India, and it had acquired support for primarily religious reasons. Once the Turks settled
the Khilafat question themselves, religious feeling abated and the
movement died away For many politicians, however, participation
in the Khilafat movement was a formative experience which continued to affect their political outlook long after the Khilafat had
been abolished. The belief that Hindu-Muslim unity was the only
basis for Swaraj was fostered and strengthened, and the alliance
between Gandhi and the Ali brothers, between Congressmen and
Khilafatists, which was cemented in these years, continued, though
with varying degrees of intensity, well into the 1920s. After the

[35] See J.M. Brown, *Gandhi's Rise to Power: Indian Politics 1915-1922* (Cambridge 1972),
pp. 250-304.

Khilafat movement subsided, however, the context of the Khilafat-Swaraj alliance became more exclusively political and pressures on the Khilafat leaders sprang more from the working of purely Indian forces. By the time the Ali brothers were released from gaol in 1923, the new constitution was already beginning to make an impact, and many Congressmen had recognized that they could no longer afford to continue with a policy of boycott. Gandhi himself was never converted to this view, though he did not always oppose those who were; and the Ali brothers, who had built up their careers as Panislamist politicians, continued to work in the same field after their release. In the long run, however, the working of the new constitution prompted political developments which neither Gandhi nor the Ali brothers could afford to ignore, and it was ultimately in relation to those developments that their political future had to be worked out.

CHAPTER 1

The Montagu-Chelmsford Reforms and the Changing Structure of Politics

The changing structure of all-India politics

During the Morley-Minto Reforms, though the introduction of a substantial elected element in most provincial councils did prove a spur to political organization, the councils offered no real power to those elected to them. Except in Bengal, the elected members were nowhere in a majority and even the possession of a majority was not sufficient to move the government to action. The government was not responsible to the Council and it was under no obligation to implement a majority decision. After 1920, however, by the terms of the Montagu-Chelmsford Reforms, provincial councils were enlarged, provision was made for a substantial elected majority, and under a system known as Dyarchy, certain departments of government, notably Local Self-Government, Education, Agriculture, Health, Commerce and Industry, were transferred to the control of ministers responsible to the legislatures. After 1920, therefore, the government no longer possessed a monopoly of power at the provincial level. Very real power had been transferred to Indian hands and the government became dependent on the goodwill and co-operation of others for the administration of important departments.

In many respects, however, the devolution of power which took place in 1920 was less important than the terms under which it took place. Those who had been most active in calling for constitutional reform had been the English-educated professionals of the cities; and what they had demanded was that the urban areas should be given more substantial representation. The power of the government, however, lay in its alliance with the rural élites—the landed families whose offspring filled the ranks of deputy-collectors, *tehsildars* and *naib-tehsildars*. In its formulation of the Morley-Minto Reforms, the government had deliberately used these élites as a counterbalance to the 'advanced' urban politicians, and in framing the Montagu-Chelmsford constitution it continued with the same policy. There were two main techniques. Firstly it kept the number of urban seats at a minimum. Secondly, it extended the franchise beyond the canvassing power of the politicians. An examination of the situation in the United Provinces will illustrate the point.

When the U.P. Congress Committee met Mr Montagu, its main complaint was that under the Morley-Minto Reforms the towns were insufficiently represented:

It is there that the largest measure of public spirit and capacity can be found and the desire for progress and the comprehension of political questions are keenest. Yet the present system all but ignores them. It allows of the nomination of persons ignorant of English, and ruling chiefs who have no concern with the affairs of British India, but rigorously limits the number of men who can be worthy representatives of their country.[1]

But when the U.P. government's Reform proposals were formulated, this complaint was ignored. In a house of 100 members, the government proposed that there should be seventy elected seats, of which ten were to be for urban interests. The only towns which were to receive such representation were the very largest ones — Lucknow, Benares, Allahabad, Agra, Kanpur, Meerut and Bareilly. All the others—and these included such substantial towns as Moradabad, Shahjehanpur, Aligarh and Jhansi—were to be represented within rural constituencies.[2] As a result of pressure from the politicians, these proposals were subsequently modified. Provision was made for two more urban seats, and the claims of Moradabad, Shahjehanpur and Aligarh were recognized. But this modification did little to alter the substance of the government's proposals. The government kept the urban politician at a disadvantage by ensuring that the balance between urban and rural seats remained the same.

The government's proposals for the franchise also put the urban politician at a disadvantage. The Congress and League scheme had demanded that members of Council be elected 'directly by the people on as broad a franchise as possible'.[3] But at that stage the

---

[1] Montagu papers (IOL MSS Eur. D 523) 35: Address presented by the U.P. Congress Committee, 26 Nov. 1917.

[2] IOF/L/Parl./409B: The Reforms Committee (Franchise), Proposals of the U.P. Government, pp. 71-3.

[3] S.S. Pirzada, (ed.), *Foundations of Pakistan, All India Moslem League Documents 1906-47*, vol. i (Karachi 1969), p. 492.

politicians were primarily concerned to secure the uniform introduction of direct election[4] and when they spoke of 'as broad a franchise as possible' they appear to have envisaged at the very most giving
the vote to zemindars and tenants paying fifty rupees land revenue
or rent.[5] The government decided, however, to give the vote to
zemindars paying twenty-five rupees land revenue, and not only to
secured tenants paying fifty rupees rent but also to non-occupancy
tenants paying the same amount.[6] Neither the Congress nor the
League protested strongly at these additions, and for very obvious
reasons, but the concern both parties showed at the prospect of so
large an electorate suggests that the government's proposals went
considerably beyond their expectations. The addition of those paying between twenty-five and fifty rupees land revenue added 125,000
to the electorate,[7] and the number of non-occupancy tenants paying
over fifty rupees rent was 430,937.[8] The government's proposals
thus enfranchised over 500,000 more electors than the politicians
had anticipated; and this number constituted almost fifty per cent
of the new rural electorate. Why had the government gone beyond
what the nationalists demanded? There is no explicit evidence on
motivation. But if an argument can be made from the effect of the
proposals, the government was attempting to extend the electorate
beyond the canvassing capacity of the politicians and to secure the
return of its old allies in the districts. The existence of a more
limited franchise would have made it possible for urban politicians
to manage the rural electorate and get elected themselves. By extending the franchise beyond what was demanded, this possibility was
considerably reduced.

Another important manipulative device was the distribution of
seats between different interests in each council. The Lucknow Pact
had stipulated that each council should consist of eighty per cent
elected members and twenty per cent nominated members. But the

---

[4] Under the Morley-Minto Reforms, only the Muslim seats were filled by direct
election. Non-Muslim members were elected indirectly by municipal and district
boards.

[5] Montagu papers, 35: Address presented by the U.P. Congress Committee, 26
Nov. 1917.

[6] IOR/L/Parl./409B: The Reforms Committee (Franchise), Proposals of the U.P.
Government, p. 71.

[7] Ibid., table vii, pp. 90-1: Statement of persons paying land revenue.

[8] Ibid., table vi, pp. 86-7 and table vii, pp. 88-9: Statements of all tenants and of
secured tenants.

government laid down that at least thirty per cent of the seats in each council should be allocated to nominated and special interests. The Lucknow Pact had kept the nominated element low for good reason. In granting the Muslim community substantial weightage in Muslim minority provinces, the Hindu community had no intention of depriving itself of its majority position. The government, however, was not concerned to give either Hindu or Muslim majority communities a dominant share in their respective councils. Its main concern was to preserve its own position. Table 3 shows that only in the Central Provinces, where the non-Muslims formed 95.4 per cent of the population, were the elected members of a majority community in a position to command a majority in a legislature. In Bombay, the elected non-Muslims were given 40.4 per cent of the total number of seats; in the United Provinces 48.8 per cent; in Bihar and Orissa 46.6 per cent; and in Madras 49.2 per cent. In the Muslim majority provinces of the Punjab and Bengal, the elected members of the Muslim community were given 34 per cent and 27.9 per cent respectively.[9] Furthermore, even as a proportion of the total number of elected seats, the number of elected seats allocated to majority communities was considerably lower than the percentage laid down at Lucknow—34.2 per cent and 45.1 per cent for the Muslims of Bengal and the Punjab, and 66.3 per cent, 53.5 per cent, 60 per cent and 63.2 per cent for the non-Muslims of Madras, Bombay, the United Provinces and Bihar and Orissa. Only by the addition of nominated Muslims and non-Muslims to the totals for elected Muslims and non-Muslims was it possible to approach the Lucknow proportions.

The significance of this constitutional arrangement is obvious. It meant that in default of a combination of Muslim and non-Muslim elected members the government held the balance of power in all the most important provincial councils. Except in the Central Provinces, the elected members of a majority community could not work the Reforms without government support, whereas the government, provided it could win the support of the minority community and the special interests, was capable of running the

---

[9] In Bengal, this low figure in some measure reflected the agreement reached at Lucknow whereby the Muslims, though a majority, were awarded only 40 per cent of the elected seats. But the Bengali Hindus, though awarded 60 per cent of the elected seats, did not fare much better. They received only 32.9 per cent of the total number of seats in the council.

TABLE 3A
Provincial representation under the Montagu-Chelmsford Constitution

Province	Elected M	Non-M	Others	Special	Total	Nominated	Total
Madras	13	65	7	13	98	34	132
Bombay	27	46	2	11	86	28	114
Bengal	39	46	7	22	114	26	140
U.P.	29	60	1	10	100	23	123
Punjab	32	20	12	7	71	23	94
B and O	18	48	1	9	76	27	103
CP	7	41	0	7	55	18	73
Assam	12	21	0	6	39	14	53

TABLE 3B
Elected members of provincial councils and their influence

Province	Muslims A	B	C	D	E	Non-Muslims A	B	C	D	E
Madras	6.7	15	13.2	9.8	10.6	90.0	85	66.3	49.2	73.3
Bombay	19.8	33	31.3	23.7	25.4	78.9	67	53.5	40.4	53.5
Bengal	54.6	40	34.2	27.9	30.8	45.1	60	40.4	32.9	47.9
U.P.	14.3	30	29.0	23.6	26.0	85.4	70	60.0	48.4	58.6
Punjab	55.2	50	45.1	34.0	40.4	32.0	50	28.2	21.3	25.5*
B and O	10.9	30	23.7	17.6	18.5	88.2	70	63.2	46.6	61.2
CP	4.4	15	12.7	9.6	9.6	95.4	85	79.2	56.2	78.0
Assam	32.3	—	30.8	22.6	30.2	65.9	—	53.9	39.6	47.1

The Sikhs, who formed 11.1% of the population in the Punjab, were awarded 16.9% of the elected seats. This gave them a 12.8% share of the entire council, exclusive of special and nominated members.

A Percentage of population.
B Lucknow Pact proposals.
C Elected members as percentage of elected total.
D Elected members as percentage of total.
E Elected and Nominated members as percentage of total.

Source: *Indian Statutory Commission*, vol i (*Cmd. 3568*, 1929-30), part ii, ch. 4, appendices iii and iv, pp. 144-7.

administration in the face of a hostile majority community. The distribution of seats ensured, therefore, that the government was in a position to extract the maximum advantage from its enormous powers of patronage. Implicit in the whole structure of the new constitution was the maxim that co-operation with government was a precondition for constitutional success.

But despite the existence of these constraints, the main effect of the introduction of ministerial responsibility was to increase competition for power at the provincial level. Before 1920, though there had been distinct differences of attitude amongst the members of the educated elite, competition for power had been restricted to the municipal and district level where actual power had been devolved to Indian hands. At the provincial level, politicians had stressed the need for unity as a prerequisite for political reform, and they had been prepared, in order to achieve that unity, to adjust their differences and even to sacrifice local advantage to hopes of eventual provincial profit. Once devolution had taken place, however, the objective was no longer to convince the British public that India was ready for reform, but to gain a majority in any given legislature. The desire to obtain office or to prevent others from obtaining office became the mainspring of political activity, and men who had worked together for political reform became competitors in a struggle for power.

This growth of competition at the provincial level provincialized all-India politics. Between 1909 and 1920, all-India politics had been dominated by the educated elites of the most advanced provinces and because they were not competing for power at the provincial level, either amongst themselves or with other interests, they presented a united front at the all-India level. After 1920, however, except during a brief period of successful non-co-operation within the legislatures, the Reforms were worked in all provinces, and political interest groups supported by the Raj established a lien on the resources of government. The Raj needed them to work the Reforms and in most cases they needed the Raj to remain in office. In all provinces, therefore, parties with a vested interest in the continuation of the existing political dispensation came into being. Where a consolidated party worked the Reforms, this vested interest was well-entrenched. Where they were worked by a shifting alliance it was less well-entrenched. Throughout India, however, the exercise of power in the provinces transformed the nature of the all-India confrontation with the Raj. That confrontation nc longer derived its strength from those who had no chance of power in the provinces. It drew its support instead from those temporarily excluded from the power which others enjoyed. Consequently it was subject to a greater degree of instability. The magnetic attraction of provincial office drew political energies away from the all-India level, and the all-India confrontation with government lived uneasily under the axe of constitutional collaboration in the provinces.

The changing structure of all-India Muslim politics

The Montagu-Chelmsford Reforms also changed the nature of all-India Muslim politics. Before 1920, Muslim political organization at the all-India level had been in the hands of the Muslims of the United Provinces, Bihar and Bombay. In these provinces, a Muslim educated élite had shared the political aspirations of the Hindu educated élite and had masterminded a political alliance with the Congress in pursuit of constitutional reform. Almost as soon as the government's Reform proposals were formulated, however, the League leaders saw the writing on the wall. There was no need for special representation for the landlords, Raza Ali told the U.P. government, because even without such representation, they would be 'in the ascendant in the first two, maybe three, councils'. 'At present their interests are not imperilled', he said. 'Rather there is a remote danger of their imperilling the interests of others.[10] Raza Ali obviously realized how difficult it would be to canvas such huge constituencies. 'It is important to consider', he wrote, 'whether a huge extension of the vote without a corresponding increase in the size of the councils will not lead to a breakdown of the system.'[11] Wazir Hassan made many of the same points. In his view, the franchise proposed by the government was too low and ought to be raised :

The danger of a constituency becoming too large to be workable can be very much reduced by enhancing the property qualification to double figures. I think it would be pertinent to observe that in as much as we are not considering the question of franchise in relation

[10] IOR/L/Parl./409B: The Reforms Committee (Franchise), Syed Raza Ali's proposals, p. 143.
[11] Ibid., p. 141.

to complete self-government but only in relation to a step towards it, the broadening of the franchise should be commensurate with the step.[12]

On second thoughts, however, he concentrated his efforts on increasing the number of urban seats. The government had allocated thirty seats for the Muslims, of which three were to be for the towns. In an additional note submitted to the Franchise Committee, Wazir Hassan demanded twelve, including three for Lucknow.[13]

But these protests went unheeded. In the U.P. Council, under the new constitution, twenty-five out of twenty-nine Muslim members were returned by rural electorates, and a majority of these were leading zemindars of their districts.[14] Kunwar Jamshed Ali Khan, the Nawab of Baghpat, was returned from the Meerut constituency for all four councils.[15] The Nawab of Chhatari, a leading Lalkhani Rajput and one of the richest Muslim landowners in the Western divisions, was returned from Bulandshahr;[16] and from the Aligarh, Muttra and Agra constituencies the member for three out of four councils was Mahommed Ubedar Rahman Khan, a close relation of the Nawab of Bhikampur, a man renowned for his loyalty to the Raj.[17] From Muzaffarnagar, the member for the first two councils was Kunwar Inayat Ali Khan, a *Khan Bahadur* with an encumbered estate;[18] and from Bijnor, Chaudhuri Amir Hassan Khan, a leading zemindar paying 18,000 rupees land revenue.[19] From Bareilly, the member for the second and third councils was K.B. Hakim Mahboob Ali Khan, 'a big zemindar of good status';[20] and from Shahjehanpur, the

---

[12] By 'double figures', Wazir Hassan appears to have meant that the voting qualification should be double what the government was proposing. This would be in line with the suggestions put forward by Sheikh Habibullah, and by Raza Ali. Ibid., pp. 100 and 143.

[13] Ibid., pp. 140-1: additional memorandum submitted by Wazir Hassan.

[14] For the election returns for the United Provinces during the Montagu-Chelmsford Reforms, see *Cmd. 1261* (1921); *Cmd.2154* (1924); *Cmd.2923* (1927); *Cmd.3922* (1931).

[15] GI Home Public 953/1924: Summary of information received about new members of the U.P. Legislative Council, p. 254.

[16] *DG Bulandshahr* (1903), pp. 103-4; *DG Aligarh* (1909), p. 108. Chhatari paid 67,620 rupees land revenue in Bulandshahr and 12,318 rupees in Aligarh.

[17] GI Home Public 953/1924, p. 255; *DG Aligarh* (1909), pp. 110-12. The Pathans of Bhikampur were the wealthiest Muslim landlords in Aligarh.

[18] GI Home Public 953/1924, p. 254.

[19] Ibid., p. 254.

[20] Ibid,. p. 256.

member for all four councils was Fazlur Rahman Khan, 'one of the biggest Mahommedan zemindars in the district'.[21] In the Eastern divisions and in Oudh, a similar pattern was reproduced. Nawab Mahommed Yusuf, the son of Nawab Abdul Majid was regularly returned for Allahabad, Jaunpur and Mirzapur;[22] and Shah Badre Alam for Benares, Ghazipur, Ballia and Azamgarh.[23] From Hardoi, Lucknow and Unao, two taluqdars, Lt. Sheikh Shahid Hussain, a former member of the Morley-Minto council, and the Raja of Salempur were returned for two sessions each. The Fyzabad and Barabanki seat was filled by the Rajas of Pirpur and Jehangirabad and their relations,[24] and the Kheri and Sitapur seat, presumably with the approval of the Raja of Mahmudabad, initially by a Swarajist lawyer,[25] and subsequently by Sheikh Habibullah, the manager of his estate. For the most part, these men were zemindars, not lawyers, but even those who did have legal pracices generally took a conservative stand in politics. Furthermore, because of the nature of the electorate, even in the constituencies where landowners were not returned, the members were conservative intellectuals and educationalists—men like Dr Ziauddin,[26] Sheikh Abdullah,[27] and Professor Shafaat Ahmed Khan[28]—or men like Hafiz Hidyat Hussain of Kanpur, whose earlier dalliance with Panislamism gradually gave

[21] Ibid., p. 256. Fazlur Rahman Khan was also a *vakil* and chairman of the Shahjehanpur Municipal Board. See also *DG Shahjehanpur* (1910), p. 94.

[22] Nawab Mahommed Yusuf was 'the biggest and most influential landholder in the Eastern districts of the United Provinces'. See Nurul Hasan Siddiqui, *Landlords of Agra and Avadh* (Lucknow 1950), p. 273. Siddiqui's work is an invaluable source of information on U.P. landlord politics.

[23] Shah Badre Alam was a member of 'the chief Musulman landowning family of Ghazipur' and one of the leading supporters of the Muslim Defence Association. *DG Ghazipur* (1909), p. 98; GUPGAD 553/1917.

[24] The Raja of Pirpur filled the seat in the first council; the Raja of Jehangirabad's brother-in-law in the second; and the Raja of Jehangirabad himself in the fourth.

[25] Mahommed Habib Ashraf, the famous Aligarh Muslim historian [and brother of Mahommed Mujib], was elected to the seat as a Swarajist in 1923. Gl Home Public 953/1924, p. 257.

[26] Ziauddin was returned for Mainpuri, Etah and Farrukhabad in the second council.

[27] Sheikh Abdullah was returned for the same constituency in the third council.

[28] Professor Shafaat Ahmed Khan of Allahabad University, member for Moradabad South in the second and third councils, married into Sir Mahommed Safi's family. He was the leading U.P. Muslim political strategist at the time of the round table conferences.

way to more stolid conservative sentiments.[29]

The League leaders' reactions to this situation varied from person to person. Few were prepared to dance to the rhythms of landlord politics; and even fewer to embrace the logical alternative—agitational politics. The only one to follow this course was Mazhar ul Haq, who participated in the Khilafat movement and subsequently disappeared from national politics altogether.[30] So they were faced with a very limited choice—either to take what jobs they could get from the government, whether political, administrative or judicial, or to opt out of British Indian politics and seek a new future in the States. The Raja of Mahmudabad and Wazir Hassan chose the first course of action; Sir Ali Imam and Samiullah Beg chose the second. The Raja was persuaded by Harcourt Butler to serve for a short while as Home Member in the U.P. government. Wazir Hassan accepted a job as Assistant Judicial Commissioner of Oudh. Ali Imam and Samiullah Beg, on the other hand, deserted British India for Hyderabad, the first to become the Nizam's Prime Minister and the second his Chief Justice. The only League leaders to remain actively involved in the politics of confrontation after 1920 were those whose ambitions were focused at the all-India level. Jinnah was the most notable of such men. He had been working for central responsibility since 1909 and his objective remained the same. It is a measure of the effect of the Reforms in the provinces, however, that many politicians whose interests had previously been strictly provincial should have attempted after 1920 to build themselves a new future at the all-India level. Syed Raza Ali, for example, moved into the Council of State; Mahommed Yakub into the Legislative Assembly. Even at the all-India level, however, politics were not the same, for the non-co-operation movement had taken the initiative, at least temporarily, out of the hands of the constitutionalists, and it was only when non-co-operation was suspended that the constitutional battle could be resumed.

So where did the leadership of the Muslim community lie after

---

[29] Hafiz Hidayat Hussain joined the U.P. Muslim Defence Association in 1917. In the years after 1920, he was one of the most vociferous protagonists of Muslim rights in the Western U.P. See for example, GUPGAD 429/1925, 246/1926, and /03/1927.

[30] In 1926, after spending the mid-1920s in district politics, Mazhur ul Haq failed to secure election to the Bihar and Orissa Provincial Council. Shortly afterwards, he retired from politics altogether, and spent the rest of his life living in an *ashram* as a virtual recluse.

1920? Certainly not with the landlord politicians of the United Provinces. Of course, these men did share in the responsibility of government. Men like the Nawab of Chhatari and Nawab Mahommed Yusuf, because of the support they commanded among the Muslim landlords in the U.P. Council, were given charge of the transferred departments and even appointed to the highest offices of state.[31] They held these honours, however, not as leaders of the Muslim party *per se*, but as leaders of the Muslim arm of the U.P. landed interest. It was only in combination with the Hindu landed interest that they secured their ministerships, and whilst their participation in the responsibilities of office undoubtedly preserved the position of their community within the collaborative system, it was not possible for them to make radical changes in the distribution of political patronage without the consent of the Raj.

This is not to imply that the Muslim landlord in the Muslim minority province was not concerned with communal advantage. Even if he was not involved in communal politics himself, he was certainly subject to pressures from below and at times when communal tensions exercised a polarizing infuence on politics, he followed his religion like everyone else. But while a Hindu landlord in a Muslim minority province could choose to join a communally oriented party in the hope of securing majority support for a solely Hindu ministry, a Muslim landlord, even taking into account the distribution of seats within the legislature, had only the slenderest hope of achieving office as the leader of communally oriented block. In the Muslim minority province, the exercise of power by the Muslim landlord was dependent on the solution of communal difficulties in a spirit of compromise under the auspices of the Raj.

The real power of the Muslim community after 1920 lay with the Muslim majority provinces of Punjab and Bengal; and the main reason for this was that under the Montagu-Chelmsford Reforms, for the first time, power began to be distributed, at least in some measure, according to population. The criterion for distributing power was no longer solely the social standing of the community's leaders in the districts, though the government did its best to ensure that they continued to thrive. Numbers began to matter. Consequently, the Punjabis and Bengalis, simply because they possessed

[31] Chhatari was appointed a Minister in 1923; he became Home Member in 1926; he acted as Governor in 1928. Nawab Yusuf served as a Minister from 1926 to 1937.

a greater share of the seats in their respective councils, were put in a better position to work the Reforms for their own advantage than their co-religionists in the minority provinces. After 1920, therefore, the political spotlight moves away from the United Provinces and Bihar, and focuses instead on the North-West and the North-East.

The Reforms in Bengal

Of the two Muslim majority communities, the Bengali Muslims were in the weaker position. They had been given a minority share of the elected seats under the terms of the Lucknow Pact and despite both the protests of their leaders and the recommendations of the government of India their position did not improve when the constitution was finally framed. They received only 34.2 per cent of the elected seats and even if they could secure the support of the government bloc this low figure put them in a less commanding position than their Punjabi co-religionists.

The main stumbling block to their enjoyment of power, however, was not the poor deal they had received at Lucknow but the existence of internal divisions within the community itself. These were threefold. Firstly, in the Dacca, Mymensingh and Murshidabad districts there was a small but influential aristocracy which collaborated closely with the Raj and provided the community with its loyalist leadership. Secondly, in the other rural areas of Northern and Eastern Bengal, in default of an aristocratic leadership, political power was in the hands of small proprietors who were closely in touch with the mass of Muslim and Namasudra tenant farmers. Thirdly, in Calcutta itself, and in Barrackpore, Howrah and the municipalities of the twenty-four *pargannahs,* there was a Muslim educated class akin to that of North India. Between these groups there were three main lines of division. Firstly, there was a division of economic interest between the aristocracy of the Dacca division and the mass of Muslims elsewhere. The aristocrat was favoured by the Raj; the *raiyat* was not. The aristocrat collaborated closely with the Raj; the *raiyat* was more likely to join the forces of opposition. Secondly, there was a cultural difference between both the urban educated Muslim and the aristocrat on the one hand and the *raiyat* on the other. The first spoke Urdu and looked nostalgically towards North India; the second spoke Bengali and shared a common culture with his Hindu counterpart. Lastly, between the urban élite of West Bengal and the rural society, whether landlord or peasant, of the North and East, there was a gulf created by hunger for employment and the innumerable waterways of Southern Bengal. The urban élite had co-operated with the Congress in the years before 1920 and given the right terms it might do so again.

These divisions within the community were not politically significant during the first council because the elections of 1920 had been boycotted both by the Congress and by the Khilafat committee, and the floor had been left to co-operating interests. By 1923, however, the All India Congress Swaraj party had been formed, and in Bengal, under the leadership of C.R. Das, it was advocating a policy of non-co-operation within the council. Because of the manner in which the seats in the council were distributed, however, the success of this policy depended on a combination of Muslim and non-Muslim members, and Das was therefore obliged to make a bid for the support of those Muslim interest groups which were least closely allied with the government. These fell into two categories—firstly the Muslim *raiyats*, and secondly the urban educated Muslims—and of the two the first were the more important. Long before the elections, Das directed his attention to the Muslim majority areas of the province and utilizing the connections which he had built up during the Khilafat movement, he succeeded in securing the return of an appreciable number of Swarajist Muslims. It was significant, however, that where the aristocracy was strong, Das was not successful. Of the fifteen Swarajists returned from the rural areas, five were returned from the Rajshahi division, four from the Chittagong division and four from the Presidency division. From the Dacca division only one was returned, and the Dacca, Mymensingh and Murshidabad districts returned seven loyalists and a Minister.[32] After the election had been fought, Das also secured the support of a number of urban Muslims. These men had supported the campaign for Reforms but once the Reforms had been granted they found themselves with an unattractive range of choices. For those like Sir Abdur Rahim who were taken into government, personal advancement was not impeded, but for others like Dr Abdullah Suhrawardy and Hussain Shahid Suhrawardy,

---

[32] See R.A. Gordon, 'Aspects in the history of the Indian National Congress with special references to the Swarajya party 1919-1927', unpublished D.Phil. thesis (Oxford 1970), pp. 152 and 336-9.

hopes for political success were small in a council so largely dominated by the rural interest. When Das produced the right terms, therefore, they were not slow to join him.

Though the Pact by which Das secured the support of these Muslim interests was only ratified by the Bengal Provincial Congress Committee on 16 December 1923, its terms were known to Das's Muslim supporters during the campaign, and they were so enormously to the Muslim advantage that they almost certainly exercised an important influence on the polling. The Pact laid down that the Muslims should be represented in the Council according to population and by separate electorates; it divided the spoils of local self-government on a sixty: forty basis according to which community was in the majority in each district; it gave the Muslims fifty-five per cent of the services, and an eighty-per-cent share of recruitment until this quota was complete; and it ordained that music should not be played before mosques, and that the Muslim right to slaughter cattle should be respected.[33]

The Muslim support which Das won as a result of this Pact enabled him to make Dyarchy unworkable. In March 1924, supported by twenty-one Muslims, he defeated the government over many important heads of the Budget. The demands for ministerial salaries and for the salaries of civil servants in the Medical and Education department were rejected and the government was obliged to have recourse to extraordinary powers to keep the administration running.[34] Yet though Muslim support for Das made the difference between success and failure, the alliance which he had created was a very unstable one. The educated Hindu middle class adhered to the Pact with reluctance because it struck at their preponderant share of the services. The Hindus from the Muslim majority areas did not relish the prospect of permanent minority status; and the Hindu landlord dwelt uneasily in a camp overflowing with Muslim *raiyats*. Das's alliance, therefore, was essentially an alliance for opposition. Promises could produce a temporary unity, but any attempt to implement those promises was bound to create divisions.

As far as opposition was concerned, Das proved his point. He

---

[33] For an account of the making of the Pact from the Muslim point of view, see Maulvi Abdul Karim, *Letters on Hindu-Muslim Pact* (Calcutta 1924).

[34] J.H. Broomfield, *Elite Conflict in a Plural Society* (Berkeley and Los Angles 1968), p. 249.

made Dyarchy unworkable and despite the instability of the alliance he managed to maintain his majority and to prevent any ministry from functioning for more than a matter of weeks. He did not succeed, however, in bending the government to his will. Indeed, far from offering to negotiate with Das, the government sought to undermine his hold over the Council by driving a wedge between the Hindu and Muslim Swarajists. No better example exists, in fact, of the power of patronage enjoyed by the government under the Reforms than that provided by the creation in Bengal between 1924 and 1927 of a homogeneous community working closely with the government out of the disparate material of pre-1920 Muslim politics.

In March 1924, when the demand for ministerial salaries was rejected, the government made much of the fact that the two ministers were both Muslims, and it retained them in office and encouraged them to make communal profit out of this issue.[35] A Muslim supporter of government was given the task of moving a resolution calling for the implementation of that clause of the Bengal Pact which referred to the Muslim position in the services; and though Das prevented a split over this issue by moving for an adjournment, the communal atmosphere became fouler as a result.[36] By April 1924, a communal party which included the two Suhrawardys had come into existence, and Das's majority began to look shaky. The government's efforts to secure majority support for a ministry, however, did not meet with success. Both in August 1924 and in March 1925 Das succeeded in defeating the government over this issue by exploiting factional differences within the Muslim community. In August 1924 he won back the support of the urban Muslims,[37] and in March 1925, when the inscrutable Fazlul Haq and his eight followers put their votes up for auction, Das appears to have been the highest bidder.[38] Even so, these successes brought no tangible rewards. The net result was merely the suspension of the constitution and an increased determination on the government's part to win the support of the Muslims by unilateral concessions.

The man most responsible for separating Das from his Muslim

[35] Ibid., pp. 252-3.

[36] Ibid., pp. 254-5.

[37] Ibid, p. 256.

[38] IOR/L/P and J/6/1193/1925: Chief Secretary, Government of Bengal, to Home Secretary, Government of India, 28 March 1925.

followers was Sir Abdur Rahim, a former judge of the Madras High Court and an executive councillor in the Bengal government. He saw where Das was strongest and persuaded government to offer the Muslims of those areas more tangible concessions. Firstly, in order to win back the support of the urban educated, he persuaded government in July 1925 to review the Muslim position in the services. In October, it was agreed that the Muslims should receive more favourable treatment, and in December, the terms of this new deal were made public. Secondly, he encouraged government to make concessions to the agriculturalists; to extend primary school education to the rural areas, and to amend tenancy legislation in favour of the *raiyats.* Both these measures were opposed tooth and nail by Das's Hindu supporters and served to alienate his Muslim supporters from Northern and Eastern Bengal. Thirdly, he supported government's efforts to organise communal organizations in the districts; and in late 1925, following his resignation from the Executive Council, took up the task of political organization himself, making communal appeals through the press and building up a communal party to contest the 1926 elections. In all these activities Rahim had remarkable success. But the event which did most to polarize the two communities was the Calcutta riot of April 1926, which raged for a fortnight virtually unchecked, and which saw whole bazaars razed to the ground and the death of over fifty citizens, both in open combat and in isolated revenge killings. The part played by Hussain Shahid Suhrawardy both in the April riots and in the July riots[39] casts grave suspicions on Rahim's own role, because Suhrawardy was Rahim's son-in-law and the two men worked closely together. Nor can the government itself be entirely cleared of responsibility because the ineffectiveness of the administration, both in preventing the riot and in bringing it under control, suggests at best a culpable degree of negligence and at worst an element of political vindictiveness.[40] Whilst the responsibility for the riot must remain a matter for conjecture, however, its effect need not. By the time of the 1926 elections, the Muslims had been thoroughly alienated from the Congress party, and the Congress itself was so aware of its poor standing with the

[39] For a discussion of Suhrawardy's activities at the time of the July riot, see GI Home Poll. 209/1926.

[40] See GI Home Poll. 11/vii/1926: Note by Haig, 11 July 1926; also Hailey papers (IOL MSS Eur. E 220) 9A: Craik to Hailey, 28 April 1926.

community that it made no effort to secure the return of Muslims on the party ticket.[41] Of the thirty-nine Muslim members elected, only one was a Swarajist, and the other thirty-eight pledged themselves to work the constitution in the interests of the community. In the Bengal Legislative Council, the days of sympathy with the Congress were over.[42]

The Reforms in Punjab: the government's role

Though the Muslim community in Bengal was made more homogeneous by the government's subtle use of political patronage, it remained a tool in the government's hands. The government of Bengal was not enamoured of the Bengali Muslim; he merely served as a useful counterweight to the power of the Swarajists. Abdur Rahim was the architect of Muslim unity; but the plans he drew up were only adopted by the government because it was in its own interest. Even after 1927, therefore, the same political necessity which had forced Das to bid for the support of the Muslims forced the Muslims to adjust their political programme to the wishes of the government bloc. Such was not the case in the Punjab. The Punjab Muslims were a vital element in the government's administrative and military strategy; they started off with a better share of the seats in the council; and they succeeded from the beginning in making more use of the Reforms.

In the Punjab before 1920 the political activity that did take place was confined to the large towns and particularly those of the Lahore and Jullundur divisions.[43] The most important centre was Lahore, the capital of the province, a town of over 280,000 inhabitants. Second in importance was Amritsar, one of the most important commercial centres of North India; and in the third rank stood Sialkot, Jullundur, Ferozepur, Ludhiana and Hoshiarpur. When the most advanced

[41] Gordon, op.cit., pp. 297-8.

[42] For an account of Abdur Rahim's activities in 1925 and 1926, see Broomfield, op.cit., pp. 269-81.

[43] Before 1920 the Punjab had a reputation for political inactivity. A letter to the *Tribune* at the height of the Home Rule movement complained that 'the Punjab and the Punjabis, despite their boasted matter of factness, are indolently dozing over their affairs as if it were no business or concern of theirs to keep pace with the rest of their countrymen in the race for the political goal of Self-Government for India. The valorous and practical Punjabis are, alas, showing themselves to be Tennyson's veritable lotus-eaters.' (*Tribune*, 25 May 1917).

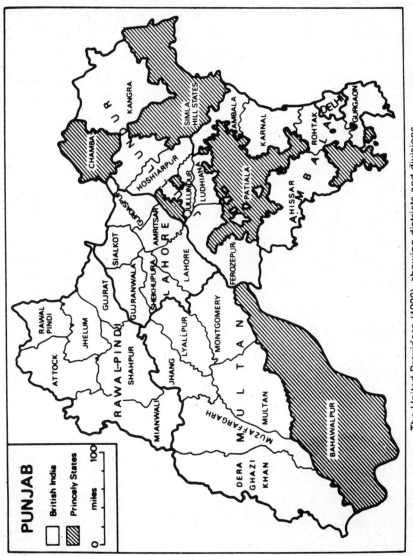

The United Provinces (1920), showing districts and divisions

political organization in the Punjab, the Punjab Provincial Conference,[44] met Montagu in 1917, it consisted chiefly of Hindu and Muslim lawyers, merchants and industrialists of these cities; and what was true of this deputation was also true of the active communal organizations, the two branches of the Muslim League and the Hindu Sabha.[45] After 1920, however, as a result of the Montagu-Chelmsford Reforms, the Old World was called into play to redress the balance of the New: power was transferred to the rural areas and the urban centres of the Central Punjab ceased to be the focus for provincial politics. Where the Muslim community was concerned, this shift in the balance of power was particularly significant. The majority of urban Muslims, as is shown by Tables 4a and 4b, was concentrated in the districts east of Lahore, whereas the majority of rural Muslims was concentrated in the districts to the west. After 1920, therefore, the focus of Muslim politics shifted from Central to Western Punjab. Of the thirty-four seats allocated to Muslim representation under the Montagu-Chelmsford Reforms, only four went to the urban areas of the Lahore, Jullundur and Ambala divisions, whereas twenty-nine were allocated to the rural areas, and twenty-three to rural areas of the Muslim majority districts west of Lahore.

TABLE 4A

Distribution of Muslim population in the Punjab

Division	Total	Muslims	Urban	Muslims
Ambala	3,826,615	1,006,159	452,975	183,863
Jullundur	4,181,898	1,369,648	350,788	171,504
Lahore	4,977,441	2,848,800	773,214	425,310
Rawalpindi	3,460,710	2,973,371	335,008	196,188
Multan	4,218,360	3,246,343	300,207	166,241
Total	20,685,024	11,444,321	2,212,191	1,142,108

[44] The Punjab Provincial Conference contained representatives of the Punjab Provincial Congress, the Hindu Sabha and the more advanced branch of the Muslim League. It withered away when these organizations came to frame their detailed Reform proposals.

[45] Montagu papers, 35: Deputations from the Punjab to the Secretary of State.

TABLE 4b

Towns over 50,000 in the Punjab

Division	Number	Towns	Total	Muslims
Ambala	1	Ambala	76,326	·31,448
Jullundur	3	Jullundur	71,008	42,261
		Ludhiana	51,880	30,921
		Ferozepur	54,351	
Lahore	3	Lahore	281,781	149,044
		Amritsar	160,218	71,180
		Sialkot	70,619	44,846
Rawalpindi	1	Rawalpindi	101,142	47,653
Multan	1	Multan	84,806	55,864

Sources: Punjab Census 1921, part 2, Tables I, V, VI, pp. 2-3, 22-6, 30.

The Muslim community of West Punjab was a far more homogeneous community than the Muslim community of Eastern and Northern Bengal. Table 5 shows the number of Muslims, Hindus and Sikhs paying over twenty rupees land revenue and over 500 rupees land revenue in the Rawalpindi, Multan and Lahore divisions in 1918. It demonstrates firstly that west of Lahore the Muslims were the main landholding community and secondly that they also possessed a majority of the largest estates in all districts except the Sialkot district. In districts opened up by irrigation projects, notably Gujranwala, Lyallpur and Montgomery, they shared this pre-eminence with the Sikhs,[46] but further west, in the districts where the Muslims formed more than eighty per cent of the population, their pre-eminence was unqualified. In those districts, as is demonstrated by reference to Griffin's *Chiefs and Families of Note in the Punjab,* the Muslims provided not only the bulk of the agriculturalists but also the most firmly established social leadership. Except in the Rawalpindi, Jhelum and Gujrat districts, where Muslim tribes possessed an influence which is not made apparent by a mere counting of heads, every family of note in these districts was a Muslim family.[47]

[46] Table 5 also makes clear, however, that the Muslims were recruited in overwhelmingly superior numbers as crown tenants in Montgomery, Lyallpur, Jhang and Shahpur.

[47] Sir Lepel Griffin, *Chiefs and Families of Note in the Punjab* (rev. edn. Lahore 1940), vol. ii, pp. 165-466.

By comparision with Bengal, therefore, the Muslim majority community of Punjab possessed a well-entrenched landed leadership; and for this reason, if for no other, it had a favoured position in the political thinking of the Raj.

The relations between the Muslim landed leadership and the Raj fell under two related heads, the first administrative and the second military. Recruitment to the services in the Punjab was, if anything, more geared to the preservation of the old landed aristocracy than elsewhere in India. In the United Provinces tried loyalty to the Raj was a very important criterion in the recruitment process but with the spread of education, educational qualifications were required even of the scions of landed houses. In the Punjab, however, the administration showed a much more pronounced bias towards the landed classes and a determination to maintain their position at all costs. This was shown by the regulations for recruitment to the services laid down in the late nineteenth century[48] but it became most apparent in 1900 when the Punjab Government passed the Land Alienation Act to prevent indebted landlords from losing their property to the urban moneylender. From that time forward a distinction was drawn between agricultural and non-agricultural tribes and those unfortunate enough to fall into the second category suffered severe discrimination. They could not purchase land in their own right and those of them who practised moneylending were restricted in their ability to foreclose on their debts.

One of the main reasons why the Punjab government alone amongst the various provincial governments took such strong measures was because it relied very heavily on the landed interest in the recruitment of soldiers for the Army. The Muslims of West Punjab had played an important role in the annexation of the province, and both the Muslims and the Sikhs provided the forces which enabled the government to put down the Mutiny of 1857. In the aftermath of the Mutiny, therefore, the Punjab became the main recruiting area for the Indian Army, and acquired a reputation as the 'Sword Arm of India'. The extent to which the government relied on Punjabi soldiers could be demonstrated in the later nineteenth century by reference to the part they played in the Afghan Wars. At that time fear of Russian expansion was the guiding prin-

---

[48] *Proceedings of the Public Services Commission* (Calcutta 1887), vol. i, *Proceedings relating to the Punjab*, pp. 49-59.

TABLE 5

Landholding in the Lahore, Rawalpindi and Multan division

Showing land revenue payments of tenants by Community

District	Over 500 rupees			Over 20 rupees					
	Muslim (CT)	Hindu (CT)	Sikh (CT)	Muslim	CT	Hindu	CT	Sikh	CT
Lahore	19 (2)	11	24	3,001	419	614	44	7,261	605
Amritsar	4	10	26	2,475	0	517	0	13,158	0
Gurdaspur	6	50	16	6,074	0	4,639	0	8,054	0
Sialkot	7	8	10	9,124	0	5,815	0	4,166	0
Gujranwala	119 (4)	51 (1)	90 (7)	11,864	867	2,810	80	6,692	1,057
Gujrat	8	3	2 (1)	8,471	511	508	13	208	62
Shahpur	128 (34)	23 (8)	11 (7)	8,531	4,212	658	190	183	887
Jhelum	19	2	1	4,395	33	267	2	105	1
Rawalpindi	3	0	3	3,222	1	139	0	176	0
Attock	45	0	1	4,557	6	165	2	87	2
Mianwali	33	3	0	2,427	4	293	1	8	1

District	Over 500 rupees			Over 20 rupees					
	Muslim	Hindu	Sikh	Muslim	CT	Hindu	CT	Sikh	CT
Montgomery	21 (12)	11 (3)	19(10)	2,492	3,979	840	383	898	761
Lyallpur	195 (32)	68 (3)	175 (3)	19,982	7,881	1,167	119	13,839	478
Jhang	85 (38)	6 (1)	1	6,603	4,280	859	159	87	25
Multan	95 (20)	46	4	6,583	1,499	2,577	134	263	375
Muzafargarh	39 (1)	11	0	4,205	6	1,725	1	7	0
Dera Ghazi Khan	16 (2)	3	0	1,773	97	922	8	0	0
Total for 3 divisions	842(155)	306(16)	383(28)	106,139	23,795	24,675	1,036	55,192	4,254
Total for Punjab	939(155)	511(16)	439(28)	134,549	23,824	90,601	1,144	92,088	4,255

(CT) = Crown Tenant:

Source: IOR/L/Parl./409B: Proceedings of the Reforms Committee (Franchise), Proposals of the Punjab Government, pp. 156-67.

ciple of Indian military strategy, and the location of the Punjab astride the route from Central Asia made a strong Punjab essential for India's defence. The most eloquent proof of government reliance on the Punjabi soldier, however, is provided by the statistics for recruitment to the Army during the First World War. Out of a total of 683,149 combatant troops recruited in India between August 1914 and November 1918, 349,688 came from the Punjab.[49]

The government's reliance on the Punjab in its recruitment to the Army was essentially a reliance on the rural Punjab. The urban classes made a very poor response to the government's exhortations to enlist and they became increasingly a subject for government derision as the War progressed.[50] Even amongst the rural classes, however, there was a significant difference in the degree of commitment from one area to another. Of the 250,000 soldiers recruited up till April 1918, the lion's share had been provided by three main communities, the Muslims of West Punjab, the Jat Sikhs of Central Punjab and the Hindu Jats of the Ambala division. The first community provided 98,000 combatant troops, the second 65,000 and the third 22,000. The finest record, however, belonged to the Muslim majority districts of the Rawalpindi division. From Rawalpindi and Jhelum over thirty per cent of the manhood of the district went to the War; in Attock the figure was sixteen per cent, in Gujrat thirteen per cent and in Shahpur ten per cent. These five districts were amongst the eight most heavily recruited districts in the entire Punjab, the other three being Ludhiana and Amritsar, the two main Sikh recruitment areas, which sent fourteen and eleven per cent respectively, and Rohtak, the main Hindu Jat recruitment area which sent fifteen per cent.[51]

The degree of favour shown by the Punjab government to the

---

[49] *India's contribution to the Great War*, published by authority of the Government of India (Calcutta 1923), appendix C, p. 276.

[50] In the Spring of 1918 O'Dwyer informed the Viceroy that the urban areas had only produced 250 recruits for the Indian Defence Force. He described the strained feelings which existed between the urban and martial classes as a result of the failure of the first group to make sufficient sacrifices during the War, and he argued that any increase in taxation should be borne by those who had not sent their manpower to the front line. Chelmsford papers (IOL MSS Eur. E 264) 20: O'Dwyer to Chelmsford, 12 April and 6 May 1918.

[51] J.P. Thompson papers (IOL MSS Eur. F 137) Box File 4: Speech by O'Dwyer in the Punjab Legislative Council, 26 April 1918.

landed interest was made clear by the Lieutenant Governor, Sir Michael O'Dwyer, in a characteristically blunt speech delivered to the Imperial Council in September 1917. At a time when the government of India was endeavouring to convince the urban politicians of the Presidencies and the United Provinces of its good faith where the prospects of Reform were concerned, O'Dwyer threw out a derisive challenge to the urban classes and spelt out the special relationship between the Raj and the landed interest which the Punjab government had been at pains to develop. Speaking against a resolution introduced by Sardar Sundar Singh Majithia in favour of the assimilation of the legislative and administrative system in the Punjab to that of the province of Bihar and Orissa, O'Dwyer explained that the Punjab government relied on two main classes, the landed aristocracy and the mass of peasant proprietors, and gave his opinion that these classes were not interested in political reform:

The political and administrative reforms already discussed and others that may follow in due course [he said] will appeal primarily to the educated urban class which is in the best position to appreciate and profit by them: but they will leave the vast majority of the two classes in question cold.

O'Dwyer then went on to answer the question posed by Sundar Singh as to what the Government proposed to do to reward these classes:

I am glad to think [he said] that we have already a good record on the credit side. The great improvement in the pay, pensions and allowances of the Indian army has already given a powerful stimulus to the fighting classes, the earmarking of 180,000 acres of colony land for allotment to men who have rendered distinguished services in the field is a further encouragement, while the recent announcement in regard to the grant of Commissions will specially appeal to the landed gentry.

Next, after casting aspersions on the courage of the urban classes and hinting at future legislation to regulate usury, he laid stress on the importance of the Land Alienation Act.

It is to it [he said] that we owe the fact that we are appealing today not to be a sullen, discontented and half-expropriated peasantry, eager perhaps for a change which might restore them to their own, but to a loyal and contented body of men who realise that the

Government has stood and still stands between them and ruin and who consequently rally in their tens of thousands to its support.

But [he continued] we have not only done what legislative and administrative measures could do to maintain the zemindars in possession of their paternal acres, we have also relieved congestion and increased their prosperity by opening up to them several millions of acres in the great canal colonies. In allotting those lands we have invariably given them priority seeking not so much the profit of the Government as the advantage of the rural population.

In the older colonies we have allowed the colonists who came in as Government tenants to purchase for Rs 12-8-0 per acre, or even less, land which they could sell next day for Rs 200 to Rs 300 per acre; and even in the more recent colonies they are allowed to purchase the proprietory right, which has a present average value of Rs 250 per acre, for a sum which must not exceed Rs 100 per acre—the payment being spread over 30 years.

Again, take the question of land revenue settlements. The Punjab government has long accepted it as a principle of revenue administration that the peasant proprietors, especially in those districts from which the Indian army is largely drawn, shall receive special favour in assessment. The re-assessment of all the rich districts of the Central Punjab has been completed within the last 5 or 6 years and I am in a position to say that Government has rarely imposed a demand above half of the half net rental which is supposed to be the standard of assessment in the Province. At the same time, where agricultural conditions are fairly stable and fully developed it has raised the terms of settlement from 20 to 30 years. The result of this leniency is to appreciate enormously the value of proprietory rights which 50 years ago sold at from 5 to 10 times but now sell at an average of 170 times the land revenue demand, a figure which excites the envy and admiration of other provinces, even those under permanent settlement.

All these things are done in the interests of our zemindars and especially of those tribes and classes which enlist so freely in the Indian Army.[52]

In O'Dwyer's view these tangible rewards were a substitute for political reform. Like most Punjab civilians he was extremely conservative in his political inclinations[53] and this was made abundantly clear when his Government put forward its franchise proposals. The Montagu-Chelmsford Report had laid down that each

[52] *ILC Debates*, 1917-18, 13 Sept. 1917, pp. 233-4.

[53] For the views of leading Punjab civilians on the Montagu-Chelmsford Report, see IOR/L/Parl./409A: Enclosure to the Punjab government's letter no. 19351 of 5 Nov. 1918.

council should contain a minimum of fifty members and that thirty per cent should be nominated; the Punjab government proposed a council of fifty-one members with a thirty-three per cent nominated element. The most striking evidence of the government's conservatism, however, lay in its proposals for the distribution of urban and rural seats and in its recommendations concerning the franchise. Where the distribution of rural and urban seats was concerned, the government showed a strong bias towards the rural areas. Of the thirty-four elected members, twenty-five were to be allocated to the rural areas, ten to the Muslims, six to the Hindus, five to the large landowners and four to the Sikhs, and only six to the urban areas, three to the Muslims and three to the Hindus. And where the franchise was concerned, the desire to obtain a conservative electorate in both the rural areas and the towns was very apparent. In the rural areas the government proposed that the payment of fifty rupees land revenue should be the main voting qualification. This qualification was twice as high as that proposed by other governments and would have made the Punjab electorate by far the smallest in India. It also proposed quite unashamedly that in each village the officially appointed *lambardar* should be given the vote, a proposal which made the 65,327 *lambardars* a substantial element in the total rural electorate of 161,610.[54] Finally, it prevented the urban politicians from standing in rural constituencies, even if they possessed land in those constituencies, by laying down that candidates for rural seats must fulfil a three-year residence requirement; and it restricted the influence of the small-town politician in rural politics by excluding all towns with a population of over 5,000 from the rural constituencies.[55] In the urban areas the government restricted the number of urban seats to a bare minimum and proposed extremely high voting qualifications. To vote in urban elections it was necessary either to pay income tax, or to possess immovable property to the value of 10,000 rupees, or to occupy premises valued at

[54] The most amazing proposal of all was put forward by one 'Jullundur Smith'. He had an ingenious scheme for running English candidates for all the rural constituencies and believed they would get in everywhere. J.P. Thompson papers, Diary, 20 August 1918.

[55] This proposal contrasted markedly with the practice in the United Provinces where even Jhansi, a town of over 60,000 inhabitants, was included within a rural area.

20,000 rupees. These stipulations restricted the vote to three per cent of the urban population.[56]

In making these proposals the Punjab government made clear its suspicions of the urban politician and its reliance on the rural areas. It justified the allocation of five special seats to the landed gentry in terms of their importance for the administrative services and for the Army and, while stressing their lack of English education and their aristocratic reluctance to tout for votes amongst their social inferiors, it clearly saw them as a useful counterweight to more radical politicians. 'Their representatives', ran its proposals, 'will form a valuable steadying influence in the council chamber where their practical experience and conservative tendencies should prove a healthy check on the impatient idealism of middle class politicians.'[57] A similar calculation was also evident in the government's acceptance of separate representation for the Sikhs, a measure it justified in terms of their share of the land and their military importance;[58] and in its desire to secure adequate representation for the Army interest, not only by nomination but also through the rural electorates: 'Retired military men', it believed, 'would form an element in the electorate whose intelligence has been sharpened by contact with the outside world and has moreover been subjected to the wholesome influence of regular discipline.'[59] Finally, in acceding to the Muslim demand for separate representation, it was clearly endeavouring to restrict the influence of the educated and moneyed Hindu middle class. Not only did it fear that within a joint electorate this class would dominate the urban seats; it also feared that it would have an influence in rural elections because of its economic power. In a joint electorate, moreover, the Hindus would form a larger proportion of the electorate than they did of the population. For all these reasons, separate electorates were held to be essential.

. . . the Lieutenant Governor calculates [ran the proposals] that assuming the Sikhs to be given special electorates of their own and the other two communities to compete in general rural and urban electorates coterminous with Revenue divisions, the Mahommedans

---

[56] IOR/L/Parl./409B; Franchise proposals of the Punjab government, pp. 147-205.
[57] IOR/L/Parl./409B: Franchise proposals of the Punjab government, pp. 149-50.
[58] Ibid., p. 148.
[59] Ibid., pp. 150-1.

could not count on obtaining more than 9 out of 16 rural seats and 2 out of 6 urban seats, or 11 in all against 11 Hindus though they outnumber the Hindus by 70%.... This calculation is based on a view favourable to the Mahommedans but the result would certainly not satisfy their expectations.[60]

As a result of the Franchise Committee report, the recommendations of the government of India and the decision of the Joint Select Committee, these proposals were subsequently modified. The Punjab government was obliged to accept a larger council and a larger electorate than the one it had originally proposed. The council was increased to ninety-four members and the rural and urban franchises were lowered, the first to include those who paid twenty-five rupees land revenue and the second to include those possessing immovable property to the value of 4,000 rupees. Where the main features of the earlier proposals were concerned, however, no substantial changes took place and as a result of the terms of the final constitution, urban educated politicians were deprived of any real share of political power.

In the demands of the main urban political associations, the Punjab Provincial Congress Committee, the Hindu Sabha and the two branches of the Muslim League, the main emphasis had been on the enfranchisement of the urban areas. The Congress Committee in a memorandum drawn up in March 1920 had demanded that thirty per cent of the elected seats should be given to the urban areas, sixteen seats in a council of eighty-seven or twenty in a council of 100.[61] The Hindu Sabha had demanded eighteen seats for the urban areas and three seats for the University in a council of 100.[62] The more advanced branch of the Muslim League had demanded a council of 125 members, eighty per cent being elected and six urban seats being created for every ten rural seats.[63] All these demands were disregarded. Only ten seats were allocated to the urban areas; the urban franchise was not lowered to the level demanded by the urban politicians;[64] and the three-year residence

[60] Ibid., p. 148.

[61] GI Reforms Office, Franchise B, May 1920, nos. 129-34.

[62] IOR/L/Parl./409B: The Reforms Committee (Franchise), p. 226.

[63] Ibid., pp. 218-9.

[64] The Punjab Provincial Congress Committee wanted the urban vote to be given to those possessing property valued at 3,000 rupees. The government was not prepared

requirement, against which the urban educated protested, was increased by one year to keep urban influences out of rural politics for the second council as well as the first.[65] The most important feature of the final constitution, however, was its provisions with regard to the military vote. In its first constitution the Punjab government proposed to enfranchise only retired and pensioned Indian military officers above the rank of *jemadar,* estimating their number at 2,000 and opposing the enfranchisement of lower ranks 'for fear of enfranchising too large an electorate'.[66] By July 1920, however, as a result of a pressure group in the House of Commons under the leadership of Sir Charles Yate,[67] Montagu had agreed, contrary to the wishes of the government of India that the vote should be given to the ex-sepoy,[68] admitting in a speech to the House in the same month that this concession would add 200,000 soldiers to the Punjab electorate.[69] In the final constitution, therefore, despite the opinion of the Joint Select Committee that 'this might mean that soldiers in the Punjab would have a preponderating voice in elections,'[70] the Punjab soldier was enfranchised and the military vote became a very substantial element in the electorate. It cannot be claimed that this particular concession was desired by the Punjab government itself but its effect certainly was to strengthen the government's hand under the new constitution. Calculations based on the government's own figures suggest that nearly forty per cent of the rural electorate had served in the Army and over fifty per cent had derived direct benefit from Government

to accept that such a person compared well with the rural voter who paid 25 rupees land revenue.

[65] GI Reforms Office, Franchise A, Sept. 1920, nos. 133-80: C.J. Hallifax, Punjab Reforms Commissioner, to S.P. O'Donnell, 23 March 1920.

[66] IOR/L/Parl./409B: The Reforms Committee (Franchise), p. 208, H.D. Craik, called and examined.

[67] Sir Charles Yate served in the Indian political service from 1868 to 1904. He spent most of his time in North-West India and Afghanistan. His last post was as Agent to the Governor-General in Baluchistan. Between 1910 and 1924, he was MP for the Melton division of Leics.

[68] IOR/L/P and J (R)/6/881/1920: Mr Montagu to Sir Charles Yate, 22 July 1920.

[69] *House of Commons Debates (Hansard),* vol. 132, Friday 23 July 1920, cols. 869-74.

[70] This was Sir James Meston's verdict on the Joint Select Committee decision. See GI Reforms Office, Deposit, April 1920, no. 5: Proceedings of the Governors' Conference on the Reforms, 23 Jan. 1920, p. 1.

patronage.[71] Those returned to the council after 1920, therefore, were men heavily committed to the maintenance of the Punjab military machine. It was these men who formed the government, and it was the classes recruited to the Army that derived most benefit from the power which had been devolved.

The Reforms in Punjab: beneficiaries and policies

The men who benefited most from the Reforms were the Muslim interests represented by the Punjab Muslim Association, and the Sikh and Hindu Jat interests represented by the Punjab Zemindar Central Association. The similarity between the arguments used by Umar Hayat Khan Tiwana,[72] the leader of the agriculturalist Muslim lobby, and those put forward by the government itself, is a remarkable feature of the Punjab debate on the Reforms and it must be taken as a measure of the dependence of the government on men of Umar Hayat's class in the maintenance of the Punjab military machine. His demands for special representation for landholders,[73] if not his demand for a second chamber,[74] were accepted and enforced. His wariness of the trading class and his desire to see its influence over the rural voter curtailed by constitutional provisions was met by the government's insistence on a residence requirement for rural candidates.[75] His demand that the discharged

[71] The total rural electorate at the 1920 elections was 379,409. Of these 168,714 paid land revenue over 25 rupees, 38,000 were *lambardars* not included in this category, 5,500 were payers of income tax and 9,610 were *zaildars*, jaghirdars, non-official members of district boards, presidents of co-operative societies, registered graduates and civil pensioners. The total electorate excluding soldiers amounted to 216,324. On these calculations 163,085 had the right to vote on account of their military services to Government. The figures on which these calculations are based can be found in the Franchise proposals of the Punjab government (IOR/L/Parl./409B, pp. 151-3, 156-67) and in the Electoral Returns for the 1920 election (GI Reforms Office, Franchise B, March 1921, nos. 34-99).

[72] Umar Hayat was recognized by the administration as 'probably the most influential individual in the Punjab' (see GI Reforms Office, General, Deposit, Dec. 1919, no. 12: Note by H.D. Craik, 8 July 1919). For a history of the Mitha Tiwana family and of Umar Hayat's own career, see Griffin, op.cit., vol. ii, pp. 191-208.

[73] IOR/L/Parl./409B: The Reforms Committee (Franchise), p. 236: Proposals of the Punjab Muslim Association.

[74] GI Reforms Office, Franchise A, Sept. 1920, nos. 133-80, appendix iii.

[75] GI Reforms Office, General, Deposit, Dec. 1919, no. 12: Memorandum by Umar Hayat, July 1919.

soldier should be given the vote was ultimately accepted by the Secretary of State, and though his request that the military classes should be given their own representatives[76] was not accepted, men representing those interests were returned in very large numbers from the rural electorates. Finally, the political programme which he put forward, the main item of which was the stoppage of recruitment to government service of non-zemindars 'till equilibrium is restored and the aggrieved class of zemindars has got its rightful share',[77] was later to be implemented by the Muslim agriculturalist party.

A similar emphasis on the rights of the zemindars and the military classes was evident in the Reform proposals of the Punjab Zemindar Central Association,[78] and the comprehensive programme put forward by the Association was also to be significant for the future. The Association demanded government action, firstly to improve the lot of the agriculturalists and secondly to give them greater control of their own affairs. The detailed programme included, under the first head, demands for free and compulsory primary-school education, agricultural and technical education, a sixty-year land revenue settlement, subsidized irrigation, the expansion of cooperative credit, improved pay for the Indian Army, adequate representation of peasant proprietors in the legislatures, and recruitment of personnel for the Agricultural, Revenue, Canal, Police and Registration departments 'mainly from the agricultural classes'. Under the second head, demands were made that the village should be made the main unit for local self-government; that every village should have a panchayat elected by the people with powers to raise local taxes; that sanitary, educational and policing arrangements should be placed in the hands of the panchayat; and that District and Municipal Boards should be made wholly elective and freed from official control. The government noted that these demands were 'more radical in some respects than even the Congress scheme' and concluded that the programme was the product of befuddled agriculturalist thinking.[79] Under the Reformed constitution, how-

---

[76] GI Reforms Office, General, Deposit, Dec. 1919, No. 12: Memorandum by Umar Hayat Khan Tiwana, July 1919.

[77] Ibid.

[78] For the personnel of the deputation and the text of the programme, see Montagu papers, 35.

[79] See Montagu papers, 35: Note by the Punjab government.

ever, a large number of these demands were implemented as part of the agriculturalist party programme.

The Muslims who dominated the Punjab council under the Montagu-Chelmsford Reforms were those represented by the Punjab Muslim Association; and a large number of them were from 'families of note' who had been involved in recruitment during the War. Umar Hayat Khan Tiwana served first in the Council of State from 1920 to 1929 and then on the Secretary of State's Council during the crucial period when the 1935 Act was being framed.[80] Syed Mehdi Shah of Gojra was elected for Lyallpur South in 1920.[81] Makhdum Syed Rajan Shah of Multan sat in the Central Assembly from 1920 to 1936, and his nephew, Syed Mahommed Raza Shah, sat in the Punjab council for West Multan during the same period.[82] Raja Mahommed Akbar of Jhelum was elected to the provincial council in 1920 for West Punjab towns.[83] Captain Ajab Khan, one of the leading members of the military lobby, was nominated to the Central Assembly in 1923.[84] Captain Mumtaz Mahommed Khan Tiwana, the younger brother of Nawab Malik Mubariz Khan Tiwana,[85] was returned from Shahpur West in 1923, and Mahommed Hayat Qureshi was elected from the same seat in 1926 and 1930. Malik Khan Mahommed Khan was the member for Sheikhupura from 1923 to 1930. Karam Ilahi, a leading member of the Chatha family, was returned from Gujranwala in 1920 and his second cousin, Riasat Ali, was elected from the same constituency in 1930.[86] All these men appeared before Montagu in the Punjab Muslim Association deputation.

Other leading Muslims in the legislative council after 1920 were also of a similar origin. Ahmed Yar Khan Daultana, who was elected

[80] Griffin, op.cit., vol. ii, pp. 207-8. His son, Khizr Hayat, became the second Premier of the autonomous Punjab in 1942.

[81] Mehdi Shah was recommended for the OBE in 1918 for his services to recruiting. He was largely responsible for an offer of 20 lakhs made to the government by the Lyallpur zemindars. Chelmsford papers, 21: O'Dwyer to Chelmsford, 2 Sept. 1918.

[82] For the history of the Jilani family of Multan, see Griffin, *op.cit.*, pp. 395-7.

[83] Mahommed Akbar was the chief of the Chib Rajputs of Jhelum (*ibid.*, vol. ii, pp. 243-5).

[84] For an instance of Ajab Khan's lobbying, see Chelmsford papers, 20: Ajab Khan to Chelmsford, 11 Jan. 1918.

[85] Mubariz Khan was the head of the Mundial Tiwana family of Shahpur (Griffin, op.cit., vol. ii, pp. 218-20). He was awarded the CBE for his services during the War.

[86] Griffin, op.cit., vol. ii, pp.120-3.

from East Multan in 1920 and 1926 and from the Moslim landholders constituency in 1930, had an estate of 45,000 acres in that district.[87] Alan Khan, the member for Dera Ghazi Khan from 1920 to 1923, came from the well known Drishak family.[88] Sardar Jamal Khan who represented the Baluch tumandars throughout the period of the Montagu-Chelmsford Reforms was President of the Chiefs' Jirga in that district after the death of Sir Behram Khan in 1923.[89] Chaudhuri Fazl Ali, who represented Gujrat West from 1920 to 1923 and Gujrat East from 1923 to 1936, was one of the leading landowners of the district.[90] Firoz Khan Noon, who represented Shahpur West from 1920 to 1923 and Shahpur East from 1926 to 1936 and who became Minister for Local Self-Government in 1927 and Minister for Education in 1931, came from the Noon family of Mitha Tiwana, a related branch of Umar Hayat's clan.[91] Karimullah Khan and his brother Nawab Major Talib Mehdi Khan, who were elected from Jhelum in 1920 and 1926 respectively, were both senior members of the Darapur branch of the Janjuah tribe.[92] Mahommed Abdullah Khan, elected from Muzaffagarh in 1920 and 1923, was one of the main zemindars of that district.[93] Mahommed Saifullah, the member for Mianwali from 1920 to 1930, came from the wellknown Isakhel family,[94] and Khan Sahib Malik Muzaffar Khan, who succeeded him, was the eldest son of the chieftain of the Bhachar tribe.[95] K.B.

[87] Purushotamdas Thakurdas papers (Nehru Memorial Museum, New Delhi) 362: Thakurdas to NR and Company Limited, Bombay, 25 July 1946. Daultana met Thakurdas at Murree in the summer of 1946 and asked for his help in setting up a cotton-ginning factory on his estate.

[88] Griffin, op.cit., vol. ii.

[89] Ibid., vol. ii, pp. 417-21. For an account of Dera Ghazi Khan in the early years of the twentieth century, see Sir Malcolm Darling, *Apprentice to Power* (London 1966), pp. 45-132.

[90] Griffin, op. cit., vol. ii, pp. 188-90. Fazl Ali provided 1,500 recruits during the War and was awarded the MBE.

[91] Firoz Khan Non was educated at Wadham College, Oxford. He was subsequently Indian High Commissioner in London (1936) and Chief Minister in the post-Partition Punjab Government (1953), Ibid., vol. ii, pp. 232-5; see also Firoz Khan Noon, *From Memory* (Lahore 1966).

[92] Griffin, op.cit., vol. ii pp. 262-5. Almost all the men in this family had served in the Army.

[93] Ibid., vol. ii, pp. 401-2.

[94] Ibid., vol. ii, p. 346.

[95] Ibid., vol. ii, p. 357.

Malik Mahommed Amin of Shamsabad, the member for Attock from 1926 to 1936, was the head of the Awan tribe and was awarded the OBE for his services to recruiting.[96] Finally, Sikunder Hayat Khan, who was elected from Attock in 1920 and 1923 and from the Punjab landholders constituency in 1926, and who became Revenue member in 1929, Acting Governor in 1932 and the first Premier of the autonomous Punjab in 1937, came from a zemindar family of Wah with great military and administrative traditions. His grandfather had marched with Nicholson to Delhi in 1857 and he himself had been commissioned during the War. His brother, Liaquat Hayat, began life in the police service and was responsible for detecting the leaders of the Ghadr Conspiracy. He later became Prime Minister of Patiala. His cousin, Muzaffar Khan, after a distinguished service in the Political Department, became Director of Information in the Punjab Government in 1924, Reforms Commissioner in 1929 and Revenue member in 1935.[97] This was the only family to rival the influence of the Tiwanas in the period between 1920 and 1947.

In the period after 1920, these Muslim zemindars formed the backbone of the agriculturalist party. But they worked very closely with the agriculturalists of other communities and particularly with the Hindu Jats of the Ambala division. The two main leaders of the Hindu Jats were Chaudhuri Lal Chand and .Chaudhuri Chothu Ram, both of Rohtak. In 1919, Lal Chand had been associated with Umar Hayat, and with Gujjan Singh of Ludhiana[98] in an effort to produce a united front of rural and military Muslims, Sikhs and Hindus at the time of the Joint Select Comittee,[99] and in 1920, together with Syed Mehdi Shah, Mirza Ikramullah, Captain Bhagowal

[96] Ibid., vol. ii, pp. 322-6. In recommending Mahommed Amin for the OBE, O'Dwyer informed Chelmsford that Attock had provided 14,000 men for the Army and that a 'very large proportion' had come from 'his Awan tribe'. (Chelmsford papers, 21: O'Dwyer to Chelmsford, 2 Sept. 1918).

[97] Griffin, op.cit., vol. ii, pp. 332-6. Sikunder Hayat himself was educated at Aligarh and University College, London. In the Aligarh junior school, he, the Nawab of Chhatari and Khwaja Nazimuddin shared the same dormitory. Much later they were to work together in all-India Muslim politics.

[98] Gujjan Singh was a Jat pleader of Ludhiana. He contributed 64,000 rupees to the War effort and produced 104 recruits in his own name. He was awarded the CBE in 1918. See Chelmsford papers, 21: O'Dwyer to Chelmsford, 2 Sept. 1918.

[99] GI Reforms Office, General, Deposit, Dec. 1919, 12: Telegram, Umar Hayat Khan Tiwana to the Secretary, Home Department, Government of India, 10 July 1919.

Singh and Sonah Lal, he had served on the Punjab Reforms Advisory Committee, which had produced a report criticizing the government's revised proposals for including towns under 10,000 in the rural electorates.[100] Both he and Chothu Ram had been members of the Punjab Zemindar Central Association, and both had performed huge services during the War as recruiting agents for the government. Lal Chand's 'tactful working and personal influence' were held to have been 'a great factor' in the recruitment of 20,000 Jats from Rohtak district, and he was recommended for the OBE in 1918.[101] Chothu Ram was awarded the title of *Rai Sahib* for his recruiting work.

Of the two, Chothu Ram was the earthier character. Like all those involved in the war effort, he was at pains to stress the contribution of his community and to demand that it should be given politicial rewards. Yet he was more concerned than most with practical questions. A man with a following amongst both Jat Sikhs and Hindus, and something of a guru for the small numbers of those communities who were slowly receiving education, he was a perennial wearer of khaddar and one of the earliest advocates of rural uplift. He possessed the Jat's fulsome loathing of the bania, and when the Provincial Congress Committee showed a bias in favour of the urban areas in its Reform proposals, he made plain his annoyance, though he himself was at that time President of the Rohtak District Congress.

The Punjab Provincial Congress Committee [he wrote] has adopted a distinctly sectarian attitude in its memorandum, has wholly identified itself with the urban and commercial classes and deals with the rights and the claims of the rural population as if the latter formed no part of the Indian nation and should be content with such crumbs of political rights and privileges as their urban—shall I say—masters might be pleased to throw over to them.[102]

In the same memorandum, moreover, he showed clearly that if he had to choose between the Muslim agriculturalist and the urban Hindu his sympathies lay with the first:

While the general urban population of Jullundur town has received a suspiciously generous treatment, the poor rural Mahommedan

[100] GI Reforms Office, Franchise B. May 1920, nos. 129-34, pp. 29-31.

[101] Chelmsford papers, 21: O'Dwyer to Chelmsford, 2 Sept. 1918.

[102] GI Reforms Office, Franchise B, May 1920, nos. 129-34, pp. 36-9: Memorandum by Chothu Ram, 10 May 1920.

population of that district seems to have been entirely lost sight of....Am I to suppose that 3,16,148 Mahommedans living in the rural tracts of the Jullundur district will go without any representation in the new council?

In this lay the seeds of the future agriculturalist combination in the council. Lal Chand, who had been associated with Umar Hayat in in 1919, was appointed Minister of Agriculture in 1924, and when he was unseated as a result of an election petition in the same year,[103] it was Chothu Ram who took his place.[104] From that year onwards, Chothu Ram became a key member of the government, and throughout the 1920s and 1930s he worked closely with the Muslim agriculturalists to implement a political programme favouring the rural areas.

If the agriculturalists benefited most from the Reforms, however, the architect of agriculturalist policy was Mian Fazli Husain, a man of strictly urban origins whose political record before 1920 made him a thoroughly unlikely candidate for the job. Though he claimed Rajput descent, and possessed a small estate in Gurdaspur district, his was essentially a 'service' family. His grandfather had served in the Sikh armies, his father had risen to the rank of District Judge, and he himself was a Cambridge graduate with a lucrative practice at the Lahore Bar.[105] In the years before 1920, like many leading lawyers, he had been a member of the Congress, and had been elected to the Morley-Minto Council from the Punjab University. This in itself was a measure of his acceptability to Hindu opinion because Hindu graduates far outnumbered Muslim graduates and he could not have been elected without their support. His political attitudes at that time were considered 'advanced' and he

---

[103] Hailey papers, 6A: Sir Malcolm Hailey to. Sir Malcolm Seton, 17 July 1924. 'I deeply regret', wrote Hailey, 'the result of the election petition in regard to my minister Lal Chand. He was a very good fellow and though a Hindu had the support of the agriculturalist party; he was therefore able to work with the agricultural Mahommedans who form a practical majority in the council. I shall be at very great difficulty in replacing him.'

[104] Chothu Ram stood for the South-East Rohtak seat in 1920 and was defeated. Returned in 1923 from the same seat, he was appointed Minister of Agriculture in Sept. 1924. Hailey was sorry that he could not appoint a more distinguished man but Chothu Ram was ultimately to disappoint his critics.

[105] For an account of Fazli Husain's family background, his early life at Cambridge, Sialkot and Lahore, and his political activities before 1920, see Azim Husain, *Fazli Husain, a political biography* (Bombay 1946), pp. 1-129.

was one of the government's most prominent critics. He supported the Lucknow Pact and heartily concurred in the censure of Mahommed Shafi, the Punjab Muslim League President, who opposed it.[106] He dissociated himself from the Shafi League, formed a separate League of his own, and while the Reforms were being framed, he and his colleagues worked closely with the Congress. He appeared before Montagu as a member of the Punjab Provincial Conference deputation, and in the franchise proposals which his League laid before the Southborough Committee his desire for substantial urban representation and his opposition to residence requirements for rural seats are clearly stated.[107] He was not, it is true, unaware of the importance of representing Muslim opinion. He had played a leading role in the foundation of Islamia College, Lahore,[108] and the constitutional demands of his League were heavily laced with demands for communal concessions.[109] Yet considering his Congress sympathies, his urban bias and, more particularly, the fate of other urban Muslim politicians after 1920, his survival requires explanation.

For most urban Muslim politicians, whether of Shafi's League or Fazli Husain's League, the terms of the Montagu-Chelmsford constitution spelt political eclipse. Even before the Franchise Committee visited the Punjab, Shafi and his associates had given up hope of playing an important provincial role and had come to see their future in all-India politics. By September 1918, Shafi was working assiduously to secure a place on the Viceroy's council,[110] and in the franchise proposals of his League, significantly reborn as the All India Muslim Association, there is a strong emphasis on the distribution of seats at the Centre.[111] Nor were these calculations misconceived. None of those who appeared with Shafi before Montagu was to be elected to the provincial council between 1920

---

[106] Mahommed Shafi was an Arain lawyer with one of the largest practices in Lahore. His grandfather had been an artillery commander in the Sikh armies. He himself was the leading urban Muslim collaborator of the Raj in the years before 1920. An interesting insight into Shafi's social and political circle is provided by his daughter, Jehanara Begum Shahnawaz, in her autobiography, *Father and Daughter* (Lahore 1971).
[107] IOR/L/Parl./409B, p. 218.
[108] Azim Husain, op. cit., p. 78.
[109] Montagu papers, 35.
[110] J.P. Thomson papers: Diary, 14 Sept. 1918.
[111] IOR/L/Parl./409B, pp. 216-17.

and 1936, and it was at the all-India level that they were to exercise what little political influence remained to them. Shafi himself was appointed to the Viceroy's council in 1919 on the resignation of Sir Sankaran Nair,[112] and two of his colleagues were elected to the Central Legislative Assembly, Mian Abdul Hai from the East Punjab Muslim constituency in 1923 and 1926 and Mian Ghulam Bari from the West Central Punjab Muslim constituency in 1923.[113] Fazli Husain's colleagues shared the same fate as Shafi and his colleagues. Except for Fazli Husain himself, the leading members of his group, Mirza Yakub Beg, Pir Tajuddin, Malik Barkat Ali and Khalifa Shujauddin, played no role either in the Central Assembly or in the provincial council during the Montagu-Chelmsford Reforms.[114] Like their Congress counterparts they were deprived of a constitutional role by the terms of the Reforms and though some of those with whom they were more loosely associated, men like Dr Kitchlew, Aga Mohammed Safdar and Ataullah Shah, became involved in the Khilafat movement, even this proved only a temporary panacea. Once the movement was over, they too were condemned to the wilderness. There were, of course, a number of exceptions. Sheikh Abdul Quadir and Chaudhuri Shahabuddin, both politicians of similar origins, played an important role in the Muslim agriculturalist party. Both acted as President of the Punjab council and Sheikh Abdul Quadir was Minister for Education and Revenue Member during Fazli Husain's absence from the province. Yet for these and a handful like them, a constitutional role was only possible insofar as they were prepared to work with the agriculturalist Muslims, and to that extent it involved a change of political direction.

Considering the fate of his colleagues, Fazli Husain's emergence as the architect of agriculturalist policy must be considered largely fortuitous. Though there are suggestions that he had some zemindar

[112] Chelmsford considered that Shafi had 'no moral backbone' and only appointed him when Ibrahim Rahimtoolah refused to serve. He proved, however, to be of very material help to Government. See Chelmsford papers, 5: Chelmsford to Montagu, 28 May, 18 July and 20 Sept. 1918.

[113] Another colleague, K.B. Mian Mahommed Khan, stood against Nawab Ibrahim Ali Khan of Kunjpura for the East Punjab Muslim constituency in 1920.

[114] Malik Barkat ali, the most important of these men, was to become the main supporter of the Muslim League in the Punjab in the period immediately after the introduction of provincial autonomy. See Rafiq Afzal, *Malik Barkat Ali, His Life and Writings* (Lahore 1969).

support even before the first council met,[115] his main springboard to fame and fortune was his appointment as a minister in 1921. Like most politicians of the moderate school, he had broken with the Congress in 1920 when Gandhi's policies were approved. But though at this point his political future looked very bleak, he benefited from the government's desire to appoint liberal ministers as a means of disarming the forces of non-co-operation.[116] As a result of this policy, he and Lala Harkishen Lal were appointed ministers in the Punjab, and C.Y. Chintamani and Jagat Narayan Mullah in the United Provinces. Unlike most politicians appointed at that time, however, Fazli Husain consolidated his position. Chintamani and Jagat Narayan proved too independent to work well with government, and Harkishen Lal could not command a sufficiently large following. All three failed to be reappointed after the second election in 1923. Fazli Husain, on the other hand, became the leader of the Muslim bloc in the Punjab council and was reappointed Minister for Education and Local Self-Government in 1924.[117] By contrast with the fate of his colleagues, therefore, as a minister no less than as an urban politician, Fazli Husain's success was remarkable.

Fazli Husain always maintained that his success was due to the implementation of Congress policy. 'What did I do as a Minister?' he asked a Unionist gathering in 1930. 'Nothing-more than carrying out the Congress programme that had been initiated before the Reforms. I venture to assure the members of the party that they have done more in the Punjab in carrying out the Congress programme than has been done in any other part of India'.[118] In one respect he was right. The Congress had talked a good deal of the

---

[115] Fazli Husain was elected to the first two councils from the Muslim landholders' constituency.

[116] Fazli said later of his appointment as a minister that 'although from one point of view that time may be considered as unfavourable to the starting of responsible government, at the same time, from another point of view, it was not altogether unsuitable. We were really received by the Government with open arms.' See Mihr collection (Research Society of Pakistan, Lahore): Fazli Husain, 'Our Political Programme', a speech delivered in 1930 before leaving the Punjab to join the Viceroy's Executive Council.

[117] For Governors' comments on the strengths and weakness of these Ministers, see Reading papers (IOL/Mss/Eur. E 238) 25: Morris to Reading, 2 May and 15 July 1923, and Maclagan to Reading, 30 Aug. 1923.

[118] Mihr collection, 87:Fazli Husain, 'Our Political Programme.'

need to improve the condition of the people, and Fazli Husain's policy had been to aid the backward sections of society. 'The principle that I stand by', he told the Punjab council in March 1923, 'is the principle of helping the backward community, irrespective of their religion, be they Muslim, Hindu or Sikh.'[119] Nor was this mere propaganda. The legislation which he introduced in his first period of office to decrease official control of District and Municipal Boards and to establish largely autonomous panchayats and small-town administrations was strictly in accordance with the demands put forward by the Jat Zemindar Association in the pre-Reform period. The introduction of compulsory primary-school education and the building of dispensaries, high schools and intermediate colleges in the rural areas did not only benefit the Muslims.[120] Other communities also benefited, and on occasion their needs were supported even in the face of urban Muslim opposition.[121] Moreover, between 1926 and 1930, when Fazli Husain was Revenue Member, whilst resisting strident appeals by zemindars for large-scale reductions in land-revenue assessments and water rates, he did his best to persuade both Hailey and de Montmorency to keep the zemindars of all communities contented.[122] Like government itself, he relied on the support of those rural classes which were recruited to the Army, and in order to maintain the position of his party these men had to be appeased.

Many of his policies, however, were more exclusively to the advantage of the Muslims. In November 1921, he laid it down that places at the Lahore Medical College and at Government College, Lahore, should be distributed amongst Hindus, Muslims and Sikhs

[119] *PLC Debates*, vol. iv, 15 March 1923, p. 1318.

[120] No definitive analysis of the distribution of political patronage in the Punjab under the Montagu-Chelmsford Reforms has yet been published. But statistics on the introduction of compulsory primary education suggest that the Hindu Jats secured very favourable treatment. Another pointer to this conclusion is the increase in the number of Fazli's Hindu Jat supporters in the Punjab council after the 1923 elections. See *Indian Statuory Commission*, vol. x, *Memorandum Submitted by the Government of the Punjab* (London 1930), pp. 122 and 132; also GI Home Public 953/1924, p. 225.

[121] A motion for the establishment of a committee to report on the educational needs of zemindars was supported by all the rural Muslims, all the Sikh members and the Hindu Jats of the Ambala division but it was opposed by all the urban Hindus and by Mohorram Ali Chishti, the Muslim member for Lahore city. See *PLC Debates*, vol. ii, 25 Oct. 1921, pp. 374-5.

[122] Mihr collection, 87: Fazli Husain, 'Our Political Programme'.

TABLE 6

Muslims in the Punjab Educational and Medical Services, 1921

	Total	Muslims	Muslims %
Punjab Educational Service	74	19	25.7
Subordinate Educational Service	32	7	21.9
District Inspectors	30	11	36.7
Headmasters	40	11	27.5
Civil Surgeons	9	2	22.2
Assistant Surgeons	227	34	15.0
Sub-Assistant Surgeons	603	132	21.8
Clerks	87	18	20.7

Source: PLC Debates, vol. ii, 4 Nov. 1921, p. 509: Answers to Questions 1077 and 1078.

in the ratio 40:40:20. This was of undoubted benefit to the Muslims. They had formed only 15.2 per cent of Government College admissions in 1917-18[123] and their share of Medical College places was probably much lower.[124] Similar orders were also issued with regard to recruitment to the medical and educational services; and with similar effects, as Table 6 shows.[125] It is significant, however, that Fazli made no attempt to persuade government to apply the same quota system to the Muslim-dominated police force. In 1922, the Muslims formed forty-eight per cent of the permanent police force, fifty per cent of the temporary force. and seventy-five per

[123]*PLC Debates,* vol. iii, 10 Jan. 1922, p. 66. Answer to question 1176.

[124] Of 65 pupils who passed the first examination in Medicine in 1917, six were Muslims, and of 45 who passed the second, four were Muslims. (*Tribune,* 31 May and 3 June 1917). The B.A. results for Punjab and Delhi also told the same story. Muslims numbered five out of 34 successful candidates at St Stephen's College, Delhi; five out of 33 at Khalsa College, Amritsar; four out of 94 at Dayal Singh College, Lahore; six out of 63 at Government College, Lahore; 13 out of 71 at Foreman Christian College, Lahore; and 26 out of 26 at Islamia College Lahore. Out of a total of 411 successful candidates, 59 or 14.3 per cent were Muslims. (*Tribune,* 7 June 1917).

[125] Those who lost most heavily as a result of these orders were the urban Hindus. In 1921, in the Medical service, 66 per cent of the assistant surgeons, sub-assistant surgeons and clerks were Hindus, and in the Educational services, Hindus held 56.3 per cent of the posts in the provincial service and 51.8 per cent in the subordinate service. See *PLC Debates,* vol. ii, 4 Nov. 1921, p. 509; *Punjab Civil List 1922* (Lahore 1922), pp. 188-210.

cent of the officiating force, and the implementation of such a quota would have undermined his position with his Muslim followers.[126] The same concern for communal advantage also lay behind the terms of the Municipal Amendment Act of 1923. Between 1917 and 1920 the Punjab Government itself had greatly increased the number of municipalities which possessed communal electorates and the percentage of Muslim seats rose from forty to forty-four per cent during those years. As a result of Fazli's Bill, however, the Muslims improved their position still further. The Bill itself redistributed seats where communal electorates already existed and redrew electoral boundaries where joint electorates were still in operation. The criterion for this redistribution of power was the mean difference between voting strength and population strength and as such it was calculated to benefit the numerically preponderant Muslim community at the expense of the educationally and economically superior Hindu community. The statistics for the changes which took place, however, do not give an entirely clear picture of the impact of the legislation. In the forty-one municipalities where joint electorates had previously existed, the balance of power remained unchanged in thirty-three cases, and the redrawing of electoral boundries benefited the non-Muslims in two cases and the Muslims in one case. Where election was introduced for the first time, six municipalities were given non-Muslim majorities and only two Muslim majorities. In the most important municipalities, however, where communal electorates already existed, the Muslims did derive the greatest benefit. In eighteen out of thirty-eight of these municipalities the Muslims gained seats, whereas the non-Muslims gained seats in only five; and in seven municipalities, including Lahore and Ambala, the Muslims gained majorities or equalities, whereas the non-Muslims gained majorities in only two. Where municipal power was most substantial, therefore, the Muslims benefited most, and by 1930 their share of the total number of municipal seats had risen from forty-four to forty-nine per cent.[127] The reality of power in the Punjab council was made very clear

---

[126] It is also significant that British officials, while supporting Fazli's efforts in other departments, rejected an urban Hindu demand to this effect in 1922. See *PLC Debates,* vol. iii, 10 Jan. 1922, pp. 61-2.

[127] *Indian Statutory Commisssion (ISC),* vol. x (London 1930), p. 141.

in March 1923 when Raja Narendra Nath,[128] the leader of the urban Hindu bloc, moved for a cut in Fazli Husain's salary as a protest against his policies. He complained that insufficient weightage had been given to minorities in the Panchayat Act, the Municipal Act and the District Board Act. And he alleged that the effect of the policy of communal representation in the services was to replace competent Hindus by incompetent Muslims.[129] Against both these charges Fazli Husain defended himself most eloquently. He showed that he had supported many of his policies even before he became a minister, and he defended the policy of reservation both by reference to individual cases and in terms of his general desire to aid the backward. With regard to his local-government legislation, moreover, he held that he had implemented one principle throughout the province and that whilst Muslims had gained in the west, Hindus had gained in the east.[130] The voting on Raja Narendra Nath's motion, however, was very instructive. Apart from Lala Harkishen Lal and Sundar Singh Majithia, both of whom held official posts, the only non-Muslim to support Fazli Husain was L.K. Rallia Ram, a nominated Christian. Twenty-three Sikhs and Hindus supported Narendra Nath's motion and forty-seven Muslims and British officials opposed it. It was defeated by twenty-three votes to fifty. In the last resort, therefore, even Fazli's Hindu Jat supporters were reluctant to side with him in a confrontation with the Hindu and Sikh blocs.[131] It was the Muslim bloc on which he ultimately relied and, because this bloc was the most substantial bloc working the Reforms, it was the Muslims who obtained the maximum amount of official support. After 1920, therefore, the Muslim interest in the Punjab grew and prospered, and Fazli's party was soon the most powerful Muslim constitutional party in the subcontinent.

---

[128] For the history of Narendra Nath's family and his own career, see Griffin, op.cit., vol. i, pp. 271-80. Though he came from one of Lahore's most respected families and possessed 'an inherited sympathy with the big landlords', Narendra Nath was recognized as the leader of the urban Hindus throughout the 1920s and 30s. This was a measure of their dependence on the protection of the Raj after 1920.

[129] *PLC Debates*, vol. iv, 13 March 1923, pp. 1274-7.

[130] *PLC Debates*, vol. iv, 15 March, 1923, pp. 1313-20.

[131] Chaudhuri Bans Gopal, Chaudhuri Lajpat Rai and Chaudhuri Ghasi Ram voted against Fazli Husain. Chaudhuri Lal Chand and Chaudhuri Daya Ram abstained (ibid., vol iv, p. 1320).

CHAPTER 2

The Growth of Communalism and the Polarization of Politics

From the point of view of Hindu-Muslim relations, the period after the introduction of the Reforms stands out in stark contrast with the period which preceded it. During the War years, the Muslim League and the Congress worked together for constitutional reform, and after the War, Gandhi and the Ali brothers joined forces to preserve the Khilafat and to gain Swaraj. After the introduction of the Reforms, however, and particularly after the subsidence of the Khilafat and non-co-operation movements, communal unity gave way to communal antagonism, the fraternization of 1919 seemed an aberration, and many parts of North India were plunged into scenes of bloodshed and strife which were to have no parallel until Partition itself. Nor was this development merely of temporary significance. On the contrary, because it polarized relations between the two communities in the crucial period before the Montagu-Chelmsford constitution was reviewed, it had far-reaching implications for the future of the subcontinent. This chapter will attempt to explain, therefore, why communalism became so rampant and how it affected the chances of political agreement between the two communities at the all-India level.

It is not possible within the scope of this study to investigate the causes of communal tension on an all-India scale. Yet, as Table 7 shows, except in 1926, when the statistics were adversely affected by three bouts of intensive rioting at Calcutta, over fifty per cent of those dead or injured between 1923 and 1927, and a considerably higher proportion in the first two years, were victims of riots in the Punjab, the United Provinces and the two administrations most closely connected with them, the Frontier and Delhi. This survey will deal, therefore, with the communal situation in those two provinces, the one a Muslim majority province and the other a Muslim minority province. The experience of Muslims in these provinces was not identical with that of Muslims elsewhere, but insofar as the growth of communalism related to the constitutional

status of the community the evidence from these two provinces is of
more general significance.

TABLE 7

Deaths and injuries in communal disturbances by province 1923-1927

Province	1923		1924		1925		1926		1927	
	D.	I.	D.	I.	D.	I.	D.	I.	D.	I.
Frontier	0	0	36	145	0	0	0	0	0	0
Punjab	1	83	0	0	0	35	17	90	39	289
U.P.	14	335	19	312	6	182	1	21	39	384
Delhi	0	0	16	150	1	56	4	114	3	79
Bombay and Sind	0	0	0	20	2	115	1	49	10	320
B and O	0	0	1	34	0	0	2	34	14	84
Bengal	0	0	0	6	1	9	151	1,490	22	50
CP	2	18	14	91	3	40	0	7	20	173
Madras	0	0	0	0	0	0	0	0	1	7
Grand Total	17	436	86	758	13	337	176	2,207	148	1,386
Punjab/Delhi Frontier/U.P.	15	418	70	607	7	273	22	233	81	752

Source: ISC, vol. iv (London 1930), memoranda submitted by the government of India
and the India Office, pp. 108-20.

Communalism in the United Provinces

The growth of communal antagonism in the United Provinces may
be dated from the inception of the *shuddhi* campaign directed by
the Arya Samaj against the Malkana Rajputs of Agra in 1923. This
is a verdict explicitly supported by a U.P. government survey of
1925[1] and it is borne out by the fortnightly reports of 1923 itself.
Concern was expressed in March that the communal situation in
Agra might get out of hand; by early April, the controversy had
spread to the Muttra and Aligarh districts; by the end of May,
incidents had been reported in Etawah, Fatehgarh, Saharanpur and
Mainpuri; and by the end of August, the western divisions of the
province were thoroughly inflamed. At the Moharram festival of

[1] GI Home Poll. 206/1926: Chief Secretary, U.P. Government, to Secretary, Government of India, Home Department, 2 Jan. 1925.

that month, communal antagonism was reported to have spread to the villages of Rohilkhund; and the District Magistrate of Bareilly informed the government that the utmost vigilance had been required to avert disorder.[2] Explicit evidence of the connection between this Arya Samaj campaign and the growth of communal rioting is not available. Yet the fact that those areas which were most inflamed by the campaign were the very ones where communal riots took place suggests that such a connection did exist. In 1923, the most serious outbreaks took place at Saharanpur, Shahjehanpur and Agra, and in 1924, apart from two riots at Allahabad and Lucknow, the main outbreaks took place at Muzaffarnagar, Hapur, Sambhal and Shahjehanpur.[3]

It is not the purpose of this survey to stigmatize the Arya Samaj. That was done by countless mob orators at the time. If any comment is necessary it is that the *shuddhi* movement was not unprovoked. In all probability, it was a Hindu reaction to the superior powers of mobilization demonstrated by the Muslims during the Khilafat movement. What is equally important, however, is that it appears to have been religious in origin. Swami Shraddhanand, one of its main instigators, had certainly played a prominent role in the scenes of fraternization in Delhi in 1919. But though many Hindu politicians had become disenchanted with Gandhi's policy of Hindu-Muslim unity after the Malabar disturbances of 1921, there is little evidence to suggest that any of them lent their wholehearted support to Shraddhanand in 1923. Malaviya, who was elected president of the revived Mahasabha which met at Benares in August, was outspoken in his support of *shuddhi* and offended many orthodox pandits by making them listen to the exhortations of a *chamar* from Nagpur.[4] But like Chintamani, who resigned his ministership in April 1923 and paid court to the Arya Samaj in the columns of the *Leader*,[5] he found it inexpedient to do more than flirt with the movement before the 1923 elections.

The reluctance of orthodox Hindu politicians to make political profit out of the *shuddhi* campaign was dictated by the national political situation. When Gandhi suspended non-co-operation after

[2] GI Home Poll 25/1923: United Provinces FR II March, I April, I May, II May, II June, II Aug.

[3] *ISC*, vol. iv, pp. 108-10.

[4] *Indian Annual Register (IAR) 1923*, vol. ii (Calcutta 1924), pp. 130-3 and 139.

[5] GI Home Poll. 25/1923: U.P. FR I June 1923.

the Chauri Chaura incident, Congress ranks became divided with regard to future policy. One faction led by Gandhi's lieutenants, Vallabhbhai Patel, Rajendra Prasad and Rajagopalacharya, advocated the continuation of non-co-operation outside the councils. Another, led by C.R. Das and Motilal Nehru, who formed the Congress-Khilafat Swaraj Party, advocated entering the councils with a view to bringing them to a standstill. This was the main debate in the Congress between April 1922 and September 1923, and Malaviya and Chintamani found themselves firmly on the side of Nehru and Das. They undoubtedly wished, as Chintamani's acceptance of a ministership demonstrates, to work the councils rather than to bring them to a standstill, but they were aware of the pressure of nationalist opinion and they worked on the principle that half a loaf was better than no bread at all.

This preference for the policy of Nehru and Das involved a compromise over communal questions. Both Nehru and Das, as the title of their party showed, were basing their council-entry programme on the same political alliance with the Khilafatists which Gandhi had fostered during the non-co-operation movement, and for Malaviya and Chintamani to have lent their wholehearted support to the Arya Samaj would have been to create communal divisions within the council-entry party at a time when it needed to be strengthened. A more important factor, however, was that Nehru and Das were in the ascendant. At the municipal elections of 1923 their Congress-Swaraj party had been voted into power at Lucknow. Allahabad, Benares, Kanpur, Aligarh and Bareilly; and in Allahabad, Malaviya and Chintamani's home town, Motilal's son, Jawaharlal, had been elected chairman of the Municipal Board.[6] Whilst Malaviya and Chintamani flirted with the Arya Samaj in the period before the 1923 elections, therefore, they showed themselves most anxious of all to come to terms with Nehru.[7] They knew how well-positioned he was and they feared for their survival if they did not keep on good terms with him.

Their anxiety to win their way into Nehru's favour, however, was not reciprocated. Nehru was anxious to keep them in hope but he had no intention of coming to terms with them. Indeed, before the

---

[6] GI Home Poll. 25/1923: U.P. FR II March and I April 1923.

[7] Ibid., U.P. FR I July, I Aug. and I Sept. 1923.

provincial election took place, he was confident of superseding Chintamani's Liberal Party completely.[8] As soon as the elections were over, however, it became clear that his party would not be able to bring the council to a standstill. Out of 100 elected seats, the Mahommedans and landholders won fifty-one, the Swarajists thirty-one, the Independents seven, and the Liberals, Progressives and Europeans four each.[9] Even with the support of all the other parties, therefore, the Swarajists were not strong enough to defeat the land-lord-Muslim combination. In January 1924, a motion of no-con-fidence in the government was defeated without official support,[10] and in March 1924, the only Budget demand to be rejected, the Land Revenue demand, was only rejected because the Swarajists obtained an accession of landlord support.[11] By the spring of 1924, therefore, it had become clear that the policy of non-co-operation within the U.P. Council would only be of limited success, and for those like Malaviya and Chintamani, who were anxious to use the Reforms for the advantage of the Hindu party, the time had come for a reappraisal of their political strategy.

To plot the connection between political ambitions at the provin-cial level and the growth of communal antagonism in the localities is too ambitious a project to receive detailed attention here. Not only is evidence of local disputes in poor supply but what is known of provincial political networks suggests that they were limited in influence, and poorly co-ordinated.[12] Whilst co-ordination was poor, however, local and provincial politicians did share common inter-ests. The same Swarajist party which had been returned to the provincial council had secured control of the largest municipalities in the previous municipal elections, and local control and provincial success were clearly interrelated. Any party endeavouring to under-mine the position of the Swarajists at the provincial level, therefore, would obviously encourage their opponents in the locality. More-

[8] Ibid., U.P. FR II Nov. 1923.

[9] GI Home Public 953/1924: Tgm Chief Secretary, U.P. Government, to Secretary, Government of India, Home Department, 22 Dec. 1923.

[10] GI Home Poll. 25/1924: U.P. FR II Jan. 1924.

[11] *Ibid.*, U.P. FR I March, 1924.

[12] See, for example, All India Congress Committee (AICC) papers (Nehru Memorial Museum and Library, New Delhi) 9/1925: Motilal Nehru to G.B. Pant, 15 Aug. 1925. In this letter, Nehru discloses that he had reliable agents in only thirteen districts outside Allahabad.

over, because the same political alliance of Hindus and Muslims had been successful in both spheres, both local and provincial networks could be undermined by the same methods. A wedge driven between Hindu and Muslim Swarajists in the locality was also a wedge driven between the two communities at the provincial level. Evidence for this sort of manipulation is not plentiful but the communal situation at Allahabad and Lucknow was watched with particular care by the authorities and the reports on the riots which took place in these two centres provide an interesting insight into the methods which were later to be used by the same politicians at the provincial level.

The evidence for the connection between political ambition and the stimulation of communal antagonism at Lucknow comes from very detailed reports on the situation in that city during and after the communal riot of September 1924. That riot, which broke out on 12 September over a dispute regarding the regulation of prayers in Aminabad park, led to two deaths and 163 injuries. It did not compare in magnitude with the Saharanpur or Allahabad riots of the same year but its political implications were nonetheless far-reaching. The political battle which raged round the *arti-namaz* controversy was to dominate local politics in Lucknow throughout the 1920s and 30s.[13]

The extent to which the politicians were responsible for provoking the riot is uncertain. Both Hindus and Muslims had said their prayers in the Aminabad park for many years, and the development which intensified religious feeling was the increasing Muslim attendance at evening prayers. Attempts to produce an amicable settlement failed and an order under section 144 had to be passed by the District Magistrate. This was followed shortly afterwards by an attack on a Muslim shop and from that point the riot spread.[14] The situation never got out of control but it was necessary to station two squadrons of cavalry in the troubled areas and it was some days before the situation returned to normal.

Though there is no direct evidence of political provocation, the

[13] For information on the working of the same political factors in 1927-28, see GUPGAD 503/1927.

[14] GUPGAD 479/1924: Cassels, Commissioner of Lucknow, to Lambert, Chief Secretary, U.P. Government, 13 Sept. 1924.

Commissioner laid the responsibility for the riot at the Hindu door.

As I read the events [he wrote] the Hindus have really been the aggressors. In January 1924, there was the incident of the Alambagh temples. The Hindus seized a very good opportunity presented to them by the mistake of the Railway and the Hindu Sabha asserted itself successfully in the eyes of the world. All no doubt part of the aggressive *shuddhi* and *sangathan* movements—both of them in their objects anathema to the orthodox Hindus but still used by these same orthodox Hindus for political purposes. Then came the Amethi incidents. In the building of one of the two temples in dispute a few months ago the Hindus were really the provocative party: though the Muslims gave themselves away by their desecration of the other temple. Blowing of *sankhs* by Hindus during the *tazia* procession may also have occurred. Then came the *Ram Dol* incidents at Amethi. Ruttledge made a concession to the Hindus. Thereupon the Muslims got up and threatened and were only held back by the troops being warned. Then the *Ram Dol* incidents in Lucknow cantonment carried through in the end by the Hindus with much blare and noise. Then at last the dispute about Muslim prayers and Hindu *puja* and the time for each. Hindu leaders would not agree. Hence an order under section 144. Then the Hindus held their meeting in a *dharamsala*. Inflammatory speeches no doubt: and then disorder got going, the Hindus starting it. The Muslims retaliated and won all along the line, the Hindus getting panic-stricken and sending continuous calls for assistance. Now panic is slowly disappearing and 'leaders' are re-emerging.[15]

This Hindu provocation was undoubtedly related to the political situation in the municipality. Even during the riot itself it was noted that Narayan Swami, a leading Hindu agitator, was living in the house of Raja Sir Rampal Singh, and this suggested to the officials that Rampal Singh's political ambitions were being furthered by the Swami's activities.[16] In the aftermath of the riot, however, more substantial evidence was forthcoming. The Hindu party unearthed a bye-law which forbade the use of the Aminabad park for any purposes except recreation, and Dr Laksmi Sahai, one of the Hindu party leaders, called for its enforcement at a meeting of the Municipal Board.[17] This was an attempt to divide the Hindu Swarajists from their Muslim colleagues, and the majority party, unwilling to

[15] GUPGAD 479/1924: Cassels to Lambert, 16 Sept. 1924.
[16] Ibid., Cassels to Lambert, 18 Sept. 1924.
[17] Ibid., Cassels to Lambert, 10 Nov. 1924.

see such a development, refused to accept the doctor's suggestion. This refusal, however, merely served to intensify the Hindu campaign against the Swarajists,[18] and communal relations deteriorated still further.

This intensification of communal feeling tended to obscure the political manipulation which lay behind it but it was clear to the Commissioner, as it was to Swarajists themselves, that 'party jealousy between Liberals and Swarajists amongst the Hindus has much to do with it.'[19] The most perspicacious comment on the affair, however, came from 'a Hindu', undoubtedly a Congressman, who wrote to the *Indian Daily Telegraph* on 8 November. The basic point, as far as he was concerned, was that 'the defeated members of the last Board are leading the present movement in almost every ward'.

In plain words there is little doubt that an electioneering campaign is surging behind the veil of *Arti* and *Namaz*. But nay, this is not yet the worst phase. Sermons are openly being preached against Swaraj and non-cooperation. The movement is being knowingly confused with personalities. Strange logic is being used in heaping all sorts of abuses upon Congressmen because Congressmen are thought to have failed in their duty at the last meeting of the Board. The *Amanists* of Lucknow are striving heart and soul to turn the Municipal Board into an arena for communal strife meaning thereby to kill two birds with one stone, i.e., exalting their position and aiming a death blow at the future hopes of Hindu-Muslim unity in this unfortunate city.[20]

Nor was this campaign unsuccessful. Mr Gwynne, the new District Magistrate, succeeded in December in persuading the two parties to agree to a settlement but feelings continued to be embittered and in the municipal elections of late 1925 every Swarajist lost his seat.[21]

Much the same sort of political analysis can be made of the communal situation at Allahabad. There Nehru and Malaviya confronted each other on their own home ground. Nehru's party had been victorious in the municipal elections of 1923, and Malaviya's party exploited religious passion as a means of displacing their oppo-

[18] Ibid. 'This has given offence to the militant Hindus, especially Dr. Kaiker, the Secretary of the Hindu Sabha, who is asking what the Hindu members are doing. The inevitable cry is sack the lot.'

[19] Ibid.

[20] *Indian Daily Telegraph*, 8 Nov. 1924 (enclosed GUPGAD 479/1924).

[21] GI Home Poll. 112/1925: U.P. FR I Dec. 1925.

nents. The first serious communal incident was the *Ram Lila* riot of 1924, which had its origins in the blowing of a *sankh* in front of the Colonelgunj mosque when the *azan* was being sounded. The bad feeling which this occasioned was further exacerbated by a provocative Hindu demonstration in front of the Jumma Musjid on the first day of *Dusehra* and, before that festival was over, Allahabad was rocked by a riot in which twelve were killed and over one hundred injured.[22] It cannot be claimed authoritatively that the Malaviyas were responsible for this riot but the circumstantial evidence against them is strong. They were the most virulent of all the Hindu groups in the city and it seems likely that the exclusion of Muslim musicians from the *Ram Lila* celebration was their work. This was a crucial predisposing cause of the riot. The part played by Muslim musicians in earlier celebrations had ensured that music was not played before mosques, and to the District Magistrate their exclusion seemed a clear indication that the Hindus intended to be provocative.[23] Nor was his judgement wrong, for the incidents which provoked the riot were of precisely this character. Further evidence against the Malaviyas is also provided by their behaviour once the riot was over. When Zahur Ahmed and Purushotamdas Tandon made a tour of the bazaars in an attempt to secure a return to normality they received assurances from the *mukhyas* of almost all the *mohallas* that the people were calm and that prospects were good. When they reached the Malaviya stronghold, however, they met with a very different reception:'...they were received with a volley of foul abuse by the Malaviyas and told that if he [Zahur Ahmed] and the other Mahommedans had not been in the company of Srijut Purushotamdas they would have killed them and been glad to get it done.'[24] The Malaviya family, indeed, did their best to prevent the restoration of normal relations. 'There are no signs of reconciliation', wrote the District Magistrate. 'Conversations between even respect-

[22] GUPGAD 613/1926: Crosthwaite, the District Magistrate, provided this information in a survey of *Ram Lila* troubles at Allahabad written for the Chief Secretary's benefit on 10 Oct. 1926.

[23] Ibid. Crosthwaite informed the Chief Secretary that Knox, the District Magistrate in 1924, had written in the DM's Confidential notebook: 'Muslims were not employed to play music in the procession this year for fear that they should stop playing of their own accord in front of mosques.'

[24] GUPGAD 520/1924: Knox, District Magistrate, to Alexander, Commissioner, Allahabad division, 9 Oct. 1924.

able members of the two communities generally end in recriminations and the Malaviya tribe is especially virulent.[25] Moreover when the Unity Conference called at Delhi after the Kohat riot offered prospects of peace at the national level, the local Hindu Sabha, of which the Malaviyas were the leading lights, lessened the chances of any benefit accruing to Allahabad by passing a resolution to the effect that it would not be bound by the conference's decisions.[26]

In all these reports from 1924 little mention is made of political ambitions but by the time of the *Ram Lila* in 1925 these ambitions had become a good deal more evident. The municipal elections were only a matter of weeks away and communal antagonism was clearly being aroused in order to secure the defeat of the Swarajists at the polls. The controversy of 1925 centred on the *Ram Lila* procession and the increasingly hoary question of music before mosques. The Hindus refused to guarantee that the procession would be over before the sunset prayers and they would not agree to stop the music if the procession was still in progress. The District Magistrate persuaded the Muslims to close fifteen out of the seventeen mosques on the route if the Hindus would guarantee to allow no music before the two remaining mosques, but the Hindus were not even prepared to accept this stipulation.[27] The District Magistrate was thus obliged to issue an order under section 144 and the Hindus responded to this order by calling off the *Ram Lila* altogether. No riot ensued, as it almost certainly would have done without the order, but the communal temperature rose and the relations between the two communities became increasingly polarized.

All the officials agreed that the Malaviyas were at the bottom of this incident. 'The Malaviya family have deliberately stirred up the Hindus and this has reacted on the Muslims', wrote Crosthwaite, the District Magistrate.[28]

Mr Crosthwaite [wrote the Commissioner] has been more than reasonable in his attitude to the Malaviya family and he had done

---

[25] Ibid., Knox to Alexander, 12 Oct. 1924.

[26] GUPGAD 520/1924: Alexander to Lambert, 19 Oct. 1924.

[27] GUPGAD 680/1925: Report by Crosthwaite on the proceedings of a joint Hindu-Mussulman committee held at the Collector's house on Saturday, 5 Sept. 1925.

[28] Ibid., Crosthwaite, District Magistrate, to Smith, Commissioner, 14 Sept. 1925.

all that any one could possibly do to avert strife but they are bent on extremes. I had a visit from them and they were clearly against any *modus vivendi*.[29]

Why were they against any *modus vivendi*?

To a very large extent [wrote the Commissioner] the whole movement has been political, with a view to its result on the coming elections. In addition to a display of their stalwart Hinduism, the Malaviya party evidently wanted a passage of arms with Government, and when they found that Crosthwaite refused to be bounced they decided to shirk the ultimate issue and have cancelled the processions. In my opinion they have come very badly out of the affair.[30]

Yet though the Commissioner saw the Malaviyas in a bad light he was the first to admit that their tactics had succeeded admirably in cowing their opponents.

A lamentable feature [he wrote in the same letter] is that out of all the well-known public men and prominent politicians among the Hindu community of Allahabad, not one has had the courage to stand up and point out the danger or folly of the attitude taken up by the Malaviya party.

Nor indeed were they likely to take up such a position when their electoral position was at stake. What was the value in being conciliatory to either the government or the Muslims when the community itself was up in arms against them? Yet though other Hindu leaders were cowed into silence, the Malaviyas were the main beneficiaries. Even at the time of the *Ram Lila* dispute the District Magistrate had been convinced that their motive was 'to show the Nehru family that they do not rule the Allahabad Hindus'[31] and in this ambition they amply succeeded. In the municipal elections of 1925, the Swarajists were almost totally eliminated and the Malaviya family resumed control of the Municipal Board.[32]

Malaviya's decision to turn to the exploitation of communal differences in 1924 and 1925 appears to have been as related to the provincial and national political situation as his reluctance to accept

[29] GUPGAD 680/1925: Smith, Commissioner, to Alexander, Chief Secretary, 14 Sept. 1925.

[30] Ibid., Smith to Alexander, 19 Sept. 1925.

[31] GI Home Poll. 112/1925: U.P. FR I Sept. 1925.

[32] Ibid., U.P. FR I Dec. 1925.

such a policy in the period before the 1923 elections. He was unable to act in support of his interests as long as his opponents were likely to acquire kudos in the localities by their efforts at the provincial and national level. Once it became clear that the Swarajists were unable to make any provincial gains, however, the time was ripe to move against them, first at the municipal level, because the municipal elections were to take place before the provincial elections, and next at the provincial level. It was always possible, of course, that they might redeem themselves at both these levels by a spectacular success at the national level. The possibility was not great—because the Raj was unlikely to give way to national pressure when the provincial situation was turning in its favour. But it was a sufficient argument for caution and it was only when the Swarajist initiative had failed demonstrably at the national level that Malaviya openly advocated a communalist platform outside his own municipality.

In the growth of communalism in the U.P. the part played by the Muslims was a secondary one. Their powers of mobilization may have sparked off the Arya Samaj campaign and that campaign in its turn did undoubtedly galvanize the maulvis into action. But what created a permanent state of communal tension in the province was not the evangelical zeal of Hindu and Muslim religious leaders but the political rivalries of the Swarajists and Liberals. The lurid pictures of an all-devouring Muslim leviathan conjured up by such intelligent men as Malaviya and Chintamani bore almost no relation to the Muslim position as a minority community with only thirty per cent of the elected representation in the council. They bore a great deal of relation, however, to the reality of power within the Hindu community itself. Such propaganda exercises must be seen, therefore, as a means of outmanoeuvring the Swarajists rather than as a response to a Muslim challenge. The implications for Muslim politics, however, were no less serious. It was one thing to set the communal bandwagon rolling downhill: it was quite another to arrest its progress in full motion.

Communalism in the Punjab

Communal rioting in the Punjab was never as extensive as in the United Provinces. Until 1926 fewer people were killed or injured, and even after 1926 those riots that did take place were largely confined to the urban centres. There was a serious riot at Multan during Moharram in 1922, a further riot in the same city in April 1923 and another at the same festival in 1927. Amritsar witnessed two riots in April and May 1923, Panipat two riots in July 1923 and August 1925, Rawalpindi a major communal outbreak in June 1926, and Lahore a mammoth conflagration in May 1927. Outside these centres, however, no serious riot took place and only two other riots, in Ludhiana and Gurgaon, receive any official mention.[33]

The number of towns affected by riots, however, provides little indication of the depths of communal tension. The Punjab, indeed, had the worst reputation for communalism of any province in India, and in the urban areas the relations between Hindus and Muslims became implacably hostile at a very early stage. When C.R. Das, Motilal Nehru, Sarojini Naidu, Kalam Azad and Ajmal Khan visited the province in March 1923 in an effort to compose communal differences before the elections of that year, they found the communal situation virtually beyond hope: 'On our arrival here', ran their report, 'we found that the relations between the Hindus and Mussulmans, both educated and uneducated, were so greatly strained that each community had practically arrayed itself in an armed camp against the other.'[34] 'In fact', commented the government at the same time, 'it is generally conceded by Congress and Khilafat leaders alike that political life in the Punjab is stagnant and that for the present, at all events, Hindu-Muslim unity is out of the question.'[35] In assessing the reasons for this state of affairs, both the Congress and the government agreed that the *shuddhi* movement had been an important contributory factor, but they placed the main burden of responsibility on political manipulators.

The conclusion to which we have arrived [continued the Congress report] is that while it is true that almost the whole Hindu and Mussulman population of the Punjab is more or less affected, the reasons which apply to the so-called educated classes are entirely different from those which apply to the masses and we feel constrained to say that the latter have to no small extent been exploited by interested persons among the former for their own selfish purposes.

[33] *ISC*, vol. iv, pp. 108-10.
[34] AICC papers, 3/1923.
[35] GI Home Poll. 25/1923: Punjab FR I April 1923.

This was also the view of the Deputy Commissioner of Amritsar, who was faced with two communal riots shortly after the Congress report was completed. In his view there was no uncontrollable religious fanaticism or communal ill-will amongst the masses. Ill-will was confined to the upper middle class and to public men, and it was these elements who were responsible for introducing communal tension into the general population from above.[36] 'It is notorious', he wrote to the Commissioner of Lahore after the first riot in April, 'that excitement has deliberately been fanned by interested men of position, principally by prospective candidates at the next elections.'[37]

It is not possible within the scope of this study to investigate the individual rivalries which stimulated this sort of manipulation. It seems clear, however, that a political explanation such as has been given for the growth of communalism in the United Provinces will not fit the facts in the Punjab. There the conflict was not between two parties excluded from power by the structure of the constitution but between a Muslim majority working the Reforms and an urban Hindu minority suffering from the legislation introduced by the Muslim Minister for Education and Local Self-Government. It is, of course, difficult to lay the blame for the riots on Fazli Husain's ministerial activities but an examination of the effect on the life of the province of his most controversial piece of legislation, the Municipal Amendment Act of 1923, makes it clear that these activities did have a polarizing effect on communal relations.

The reconstitution of municipal committees which took place under the terms of the Municipal Amendment Act was chiefly to the benefit of the Muslims. No Hindu seats were lost but the provision of extra Muslim seats changed the balance of power in several municipalities and the resulting Hindu resentment was very great. As early as January 1923, the Hindus were reported to be suspicious of Fazli Husain's motives and opposed to the changes which he proposed.[38] By April, Hindu resignations were reported to be imminent and by August the whole province was affected. At Lahore, where the municipal boundary was extended to give the

[36] GI Home Poll. 25/1923: Punjab FR II May, 1923.
[37] GI Home Poll. 125/1923: Dunnett, Deputy Commissioner, Amritsar, to the Commissioner of Lahore, 18 April 1923.
[38] GI Home Poll. 25/1923: Punjab FR II Jan. 1923.

Muslims a majority, the Hindus resigned *en masse* early in June. Then followed a bitter press campaign against both Fazli Husain and Chaudhuri Shahabuddin and as the communal temperature rose the educated of each community maligned all that the other held sacred. The editor of the *Kesri* was prosecuted for alleging that the Prophet had been immoral; two Muslims were arrested for disparaging Hindu customs; and Zafar Ali, ever ready to boost his circulation by fanning the flames of dissension, urged the Muslims to take the law into their own hands.[39] Had it not been common knowledge that the Army was being held at the ready a riot would almost certainly have broken out. Even without a riot, however, Lahore had been divided into two hostile camps and communal relations elsewhere were soon similarly affected. In July, mass resignations followed at Ambala, where the Hindus had also been reduced to a minority, and at Ferozepur, where the motive was to demonstrate communal solidarity with the Lahore Hindus.[40] By August, these resignations had provoked others at Gujrat and Jhelum[41] and by October, as a result of the communal antagonism which had been aroused, there had also appeared two para-military organizations, the *Mahabir Dal* and the *Ali Gol.*[42] As a result of this one piece of legislation, therefore, the relations between the two communities were seriously affected. The use of executive powers provided by the Reforms provoked a backlash from urban Hindu interests, and from that point forward the process of deterioration assumed a momentum of its own.

That the origins of this communal tension were political is also shown by the fact that the urban Hindus sought a political solution to their difficulties. In March 1923, even before the Municipal Amendment Act had been passed, Narendra Nath had moved unsuccessfully for a reduction in Fazli Husain's salary as a protest against his communal policies.[43] When the Act was passed and took effect this opposition increased considerably. Loud demands were made that Fazli Husain should not be reappointed after the 1923 elections and when he was not only reappointed but given a

---

[39] Ibid., Punjab FR I June 1923.
[40] Ibid., Punjab FR I July 1923.
[41] GI Home Poll. 25/1923: Punjab FR I Aug. and I Sept. 1923.
[42] Ibid., Punjab FR I Oct. 1923.
[43] *PLC Progs.*, vol. iv, 13 March 1923, pp. 1274-7.

colleague from amongst the agriculturalist Hindus, the majority of Hindus and Sikhs boycotted the Governor's speech at the opening of the second council.[44] They did not confine themselves, however, merely to a policy of boycott. They also brought an electoral petition against the new Minister of Agriculture, Chaudhuri Lal Chand, and succeeded by this means not only in unseating him but also in reopening the whole question of how ministerial appointments were to be made. The urban Hindus argued that ministers should be appointed to represent communities and not parties and they requested the new Governor, Sir Malcolm Hailey, to appoint Narendra Nath, who had the support of a majority of Hindu members. When discussions between Fazli Husain and Narendra Nath proved disappointing, however, Hailey decided to reject Narendra Nath in favour of Chaudhuri Chothu Ram of Rohtak, another agriculturalist Hindu.[45] This decision further alienated the urban Hindus and communal tension continued to run high.

But the urban Hindus were in a political cul-de-sac. They could find no solace in the policies of the all-India Congress leadership, whom they suspected of a desire to win over the Punjabi Muslims, if necessary at their expense; they resented Gandhi's attacks on the Arya Samaj;[46] and particularly after the Kohat riot of September 1924, as a result of which large numbers of Hindus were obliged to flee the Frontier and to take refuge in Rawalpindi, they slowly began to reorder their political priorities. The first significant evidence of this trend came in December 1924, when Gandhi visited Lahore in an endeavour to improve communal relations. On that occasion, the urban Hindus stood sternly aloof from his efforts, and Hailey, who was watching the situation carefully from Government House, saw this as an indication of a change of heart:

It is generally felt by Punjab Hindus [he wrote to the Home Member] that Gandhi has been much too favourable to the Mahommedans, but local feeling goes somewhat further than this. It is clear that our Hindus are beginning to regret the fact that they have practically thrown the Mahommedans into the arms of Government and have begun to see that if they are to get protection as a minority it must be from Government and that they can hope for

[44] GI Home Poll. 25/1923: Punjab FR II Dec. 1923. This same policy of boycott was also extended to the municipal elections at Lahore and Ambala in March 1924.

[45] Hailey papers, 6B: Note by Hailey, 15 Sept. 1924.

[46] GI Home Poll. 25/1924: Punjab FR II June 1924.

little from the Mahommedans.[47]

This shift of political emphasis was formally approved by the Punjab
Hindu Sabha in January 1925, and Malaviya, who was already
opposing the Swarajists in the United Provinces, gave the new
policy his blessing.[48] Though they had changed their policy towards
government, however, they had done so only to improve their
chances of arriving at the same end. They still wished to secure a
ministership for their own party and to reduce the influence of
Fazli Husain. In a memorandum written in February 1925 on behalf
of the Hindu Sabha, Narendra Nath complained that Fazli Husain
had been given 'mere dummies' as colleagues; he lamented the fact
that the Hindu minority had been given no opportunity 'to modify,
if not to eradicate the evils caused by the administration of the
Mahommedan minister'; he called for the establishment of a convention whereby minorities would have some control over the
appointment of ministers; and he held that the first priority for the
following ten years was the eradication of the communal contagion
which dominated Punjabi life. This, in his view, was far more
important than the achievement of yet more political concessions.
Indeed the Hindu minority would not be prepared to agree to such
concessions until this work had been done: 'To introduce provincial
autonomy hedged around by communalism of all sorts', he wrote,
'is to sow the seed of the plant of self-government with the seed of a
pernicious creeper which will eventually destroy the plant.'[49] By
1925, therefore, the urban Hindus had not only identified the working of the political system as the cause of their communal difficulties;
they had also taken a firm stand against any further political concessions until those difficulties had been removed.

The government also saw the growth of communalism in political
terms, but it chose to cast itself, officially at least, in the role of
spectator. In a review of the working of the Reforms prepared for
the Reforms Enquiry Committee in August 1924, the Chief Secretary
wrote:

It is doubtful if the Mahommedans at large or the agricultural

---

[47] GI Home Poll. 37/1925: Sir Malcolm Hailey to Sir Alexander Muddiman, 11 Dec.
1924.

[48] GI Home Poll. 112/1925: Punjab FR I Jan. 1925.

[49] Hailey papers, 7B: Memorandum by Narendra Nath, 18 Feb. 1925.

community were yet entirely aware of the opportunities which the ballot box would give them for developing their own interests. Certainly the authors of the scheme cannot have foreseen the speed with which its working would drive the two main communities into open dissension and would develop a declared antagonism between the urban and rural interests.[50]

Yet having disclaimed any premeditated desire to produce such a state of affairs, the Chief Secretary held that the use of executive power by the majority for its own advantage was only to be expected.

That the Minister should attempt to secure definite opportunities to the community which constitutes his chief support in the council is not in itself unreasonable; it may indeed be admitted as one of the inevitable results of the Reforms scheme. His action again could be justified on its merits, for the community was backward in education and had not so far gained in the administration a representation at all commensurate with its numbers.[51]

This statement was a defence, not only of the Mahommedan minister but also of the British administration. The authors of the constitution had given the Muslim agriculturalists the largest share of seats in the council but they had not laid down that ministers should only be selected from the agriculturalist party. Indeed in 1920, Sir Edward Maclagan had in mind a policy of communal representation.[52] There are grounds for believing, therefore, that the appointment of an agriculturalist Hindu in 1924 was prompted by more than just a concern for constitutional niceties. Hailey justified Maclagan's appointment of Chaudhuri Lal Chand because it had been made on grounds 'more constitutionally correct' than the appointment of Lala Harkishen Lal in 1921, but when he himself appointed Chaudhuri Chothu Ram in September 1924 he was clearly motivated by his opposition to the Swarajist element amongst the supporters of Narendra Nath.[53] In part this was sound tactics. There was a possibility that Lajpat Rai, who was in Europe, would withdraw his support from Narendra Nath on his return, and in that case Narendra Nath, with only seven supporters of his own,

[50] *Reforms Enquiry Committee, Views of Local Governments on the Working of the Reforms.* (London 1925), *Cmd. 2362,* p. 197.

[51] *Reforms Enquiry Committee, Views of Local Governments...., Cmd. 2362,* pp. 200-1.

[52] Chelmsford papers, 25: Sir Edward Maclagan to Lord Chelmsford, 16 July 1920.

[53] Hailey papers, 6B: Note by Sir Malcolm Hailey, 15 Sept. 1924.

would scarcely be a better choice than Chothu Ram. When Hailey informed Sir Michael O'Dwyer of his choice however, he did not justify it on these tactical grounds but more bluntly in terms of his opposition to Swarajist ideology. 'To begin with', he wrote, 'I do not care to have in the Ministry a man who owes his support to the Swarajists.'[54] Seen in this light, the government's support for Fazli Husain appears more sinister. The Punjab administration could not make the Reforms work without Muslim support but it was obviously prepared to allow Hindu noses to be rubbed in the dirt in order to teach that community a lesson. Communalism, provided that it did not lead to a community's permanent alienation from government or to political chaos from which the opponents of the Raj might benefit, was an acceptable corrective to excessive nationalist zeal.

This is shown most clearly by the government's reaction to the change of policy of the Hindu Sabha in 1925. When it had become clear that the Swarajists were losing ground and that the body politic was being divided along communal lines, Hailey began to woo the urban Hindus with political concessions. When Fazli Husain returned from Delhi where he had officiated as a member of the Viceroy's council between August and November 1925, Hailey did not reappoint him to the Ministry of Education and Local Self-Government. He gave that Ministry instead to Chothu Ram; he gave Chothu Ram's ministry to Jogendra Singh, a Jat Sikh land-holder; and he promoted Fazli Husain to his own Executive Council as the Member for Land Revenue. This reshuffle was the first step towards a reconciliation with the urban Hindus and the reasons for Fazli Husain's promotion made a mockery of the constitutional arguments which had been advanced only a year before.

His appointment [Hailey wrote to Reading] would have some advantage in removing him from the sphere of transferred subjects, in which his position as a supporter of Muslim claims has brought him under general criticism from the Hindus. One is obliged to give to a Minister a certain latitude in regard to appointment and promotion of officials, control of grants to schools and local bodies and the like which one need not give to a Member.[55]

Hailey's reshuffle was calculated to limit Fazli Husain's activities

[54] Hailey papers, 6B: Sir Malcolm Hailey to Sir Michael O'Dwyer, 19 Sept. 1924.
[55] Hailey papers, 8B: Sir Malcolm Hailey to Lord Reading, 1 Dec. 1925.

and to encourage the urban Hindus to turn more wholeheartedly
to government. And this they soon began to do. In February 1926,
the Hindus of Ambala and Lahore were persuaded by Chothu Ram
to return to their respective Municipal Committees[56] and as the
1926 council election approached, though they campaigned along
unashamedly communal lines, they satisfied the government where
their attitude towards council-entry was concerned. Indeed the
government's reaction to the election results was indicative of its
general political outlook. Twenty-five Swarajist candidates had been
set up but only two had been returned and the government quickly
commented that this constituted 'an unmistakably adverse verdict
on the policy of non-co-operation'.[57] The stage was therefore set
for the appointment of an urban Hindu minister. Chothu Ram was
dropped as Minister for Education and Manohar Lal was appointed
in his place.

The arguments put forward by the government when Manohar
Lal was appointed, however, illustrate the complexity of the situation
in which it found itself. On the one hand, it disapproved of Swarajist
ideology and was prepared to take action which was likely to encourage communalism as a means of outmanoeuvring the Swarajist
party. On the other hand, the development of a communal ideology
amongst the Hindu minority was no permanent guarantee that it
would continue to look to government. Some form of political
concession to the Hindus was essential if they were not to feel
themselves permanently excluded from the political process. At
the same time, to make concessions to the Hindu minority involved
in some degree alienating the Muslim agriculturalist and, because
they were the strongest party in the council, the government could
not afford to let that happen. Hailey, therefore, decided to appoint
a third minister, in charge of Local Self-Government, from amongst
their ranks.

... even as it is [he wrote to Muddiman] there will be a good deal of
strain on their feelings and some charge that I am dropping them
after depending for three years on their support; the best that I
could do was to give them a Minister of a distinctly rural type.
Feroz Khan, who is a barrister, is also a representative of the 'county
families'.[58]

[56] Hailey papers, 9A: Chaudhuri Chothu Ram to Sir Malcolm Hailey, 7 Feb. 1926.
[57] GI Home Poll. 112/xii/1926: Punjab FR I Dec. 1926.
[58] Hailey papers, 10A: Sir Malcolm Hailey to Sir Alexander Muddiman, Jan. 1927.

Though there can be no doubt, therefore, that the government had supported what was in effect Muslim control of the transferred departments for political reasons during the second council, its capacity for manoeuvre was not what it had been before 1920. It could use its powers of appointment to ministerships as a corrective either to the nationalist zeal of the Hindus or to the communal zeal of the Muslims but it was obliged in the last resort to throw its weight behind the Muslim bloc. Though it could indulge, therefore, in any amount of sophisticated political jugglery in order to preserve its own position, it would not ultimately be capable of saving the Hindu minority from the subjection and discrimination which it feared.

Communalism and all-India Muslim politics

The effect of the communalization of provincial politics on the nature of all-India politics was not to be seen clearly until the Montagu-Chelmsford constitution was revised. Until that time, though many politicians pressed for immediate reform, the Raj's recalcitrance made it unnecessary for all parties to declare themselves. In particular, those who were enjoying the power provided by the Reforms had no reason to involve themselves prematurely in lobbying at the all-India level because they already had a share of their respective administrations and were preoccupied with the daily tasks of political consolidation. Whilst these vested interests did not participate openly in all-India politics, however, the pattern of politics produced by their activities soon influenced all-India politicians. From 1920 onwards they were the guy-ropes and pegs anchoring the Imperial balloon and no amount of hot air produced by all-India politicians at the Centre could raise the balloon whilst its was thus firmly anchored in the provinces. For an all-India confrontation with the Raj to be successful after 1920, therefore, it was not only necessary to outmanoeuvre the Raj; it was also necessary to outmanoeuvre the vested interests created in the provinces by the Montagu-Chelmsford Reforms.

In the early 1920s, the two Muslim political groups most involved in all-India politics were the Khilafatists and the Constitutionalists. Both these groups had been successful politically when they had advocated a policy of Hindu-Muslim unity and of co-operation with the Congress, and both were slowly obliged, as a result of the growth of communalism in the provinces, to veer away from this policy and to turn instead to the representation of provincial communal interests. In the second part of this chapter, the political activities of these groups in the period before the 1926 elections will be discussed. The relations of the Khilafatists with the Congress organization, however, will not receive detailed treatment. When the Khilafat movement collapsed, many Khilafatists turned to the pursuit of more local objectives and a study of their activities would pay few dividends. Even where Khilafatists remained involved in all-India politics, however, their relations with the Congress *per se* are less illuminating than their relations with their own colleagues. Even important figures like the Ali brothers had always been Khilafatists first and Congressmen second, and their control over their own organization was more important to them than their standing with the Congress. From the point of view of the measurement of the effect of the growth of communalism on the Khilafatist, therefore, it is more rewarding to study the activities of the Khilafat organization than to study the activities of individual Khilafatists within the Congress. By so doing, the trap of treating individual activities as significant in themselves is avoided and a clearer idea of the increasing isolation of the all-India politicians is obtained. Where the activities of the Constitutionalists are concerned, however, their relations with the Congress are of paramount importance. They were working, as they had done during the War years, for a devolution of power at the Centre, and co-operation with the Congress was essential to achieve that end. In a study of their activities, therefore, the effects of the growth of communalism not only on their own position but also on the Congress organization can be more accurately measured.

The fate of the Khilafatists

For the Khilafatists, the publication of the government's dispatch on the Turkish question in March 1922 was a watershed. The movement had derived much of its impetus from the fact that the British government was opposing the Turks at the Peace Conference and once it became clear that the government of India was representing the Indian Muslim position, non-co-operation seemed less justifiable. At that time, therefore, two of the main groups involved in the movement, the Bombay moderates and the ulema of North India, showed signs of a change of policy.

The moderates had been eclipsed politically as early as May 1920, and from that time forward, though they continued to render the movement invaluable financial assistance, political control had rested in the hands of the North Indian politicians and ulema. After March 1922, however, the dissociation of the moderates became complete. At a meeting of the Congress Working Committee at Ahmedabad on 17 and 18 March 1922, Mahommed Chothani, the President of the Central Khilafat Committee and the leader of the Bombay group, broke with the politicians over the attitude to be adopted to Montagu's resignation and drew upon himself the enmity of the North Indian faction.[59] Chothani, however, was not alone. Many of the most influential ulema were similarly affected by the same development. After the government's dispatch was published, Abdul Bari and Hasrat Mohani and many leading U.P. Khilafatists issued a manifesto urging Muslims to cease hostilities against the government,[60] and Abdul Bari, in a letter intended for the Viceroy's eye, declared that his opposition to the government had been solely with a view to preserving the Khilafat and that the government's changed attitude warranted a similar change on the part of the Muslims.[61] Most spectacular of all, however, was Hasrat Mohani's reaction. He had been the most virulent protagonist of independence for India and his activities had been curbed with difficulty by Gandhi at Ahmedabad in December 1921,[62] but by March 1922 he showed himself prepared to drop non-co-operation altogether[63]. By March 1922, therefore, those ulema who did remain politically active were not those who had led the movement from the beginning but the secondary leaders, men like Abdul Majid

---

[59] GI Home Poll. 501/1922.

[60] GI Home Poll. 501/1922: Mahommed Abdullah to Sir Mahommed Shafi, 15 March 1922.

[61] Ibid., Abdul Bari to Mahommed Abdullah, 15 March 1922.

[62] GI Home Poll. 461/1921.

[63] GI Home Poll. 501/1922: Mahommed Abdullah to Sir Mahommed Shafi, 15 March 1922.

Badauni, whose antipathy towards the Raj went deeper than their aversion to particular policies.

After March 1922, the movement began a rapid decline. Most of the leading politicians were in gaol, subscriptions began to fall off,[64] and though the government continued to be wary of any developments in Europe which might spark off a resumption of civil disobedience, it was gratified by the enhanced esteem in which it was held.[65] The only major revival of Muslim feeling took place in September and October when the British opposed the retaking of Smyrna and Eastern Thrace. At that time, a clash between British and Turkish forces seemed imminent and the Khilafatists organized a body of semi-military volunteers called the Angora legion.[66] Government fears were allayed, however, by British concessions to the Turks and the signing of an Armistice[67] and after that time the Angora legion ceased to be treated seriously. Finally, in November, the Turks themselves delivered the death-blow to the movement in India by abolishing the temporal powers of the Khalifa. This action went clean contrary to the demands of the Khilafat organization and though they rationalized the position as best they could it was a blow from which they never recovered.[68]

By the beginning of 1923, Khilafat activity had virtually come to an end.[69] The masses had lost interest; with few exceptions the ulema had dissociated themselves from the work of the Khilafat Committee; and the politicians, finding themselves to be leaders without a following, sharpened their knives for internecine war. The North Indian faction made public Chothani's embezzlement of 18 lakhs of Khilafat funds and preoccupied themselves with retrieving the money by the liquidation of his assets,[70] while Chothani's colleague, Khatri, the Treasurer of the Khilafat Committee, gave plentiful

[64] GI Home Poll. 741/1922: from March (and even earlier in some provinces) subscriptions were getting smaller and by July they were scarcely coming in at all.

[65] Reading papers (IOL MSS Eur. E 238) 5: Reading to Peel, 8 June and 5 Oct. 1922.

[66] GI Home Poll. 868/ii/1922.

[67] Bernard Lewis, *The Emergence of Modern Turkey* (London 1961), p. 249.

[68] IOR/L/P and J/6/6151/1922: a survey of Indian Muslim opinion on this question.

[69] GI Home Poll. 25/1923: Punjab FR I Jan. 1923; Bihar and Orissa FR II Jan. 1923; U.P. FR II Feb. 1923.

[70] The meetings of the Khilafat Committee at Muzafferabad on 25 April, at Bombay on 26 and 27 May, and at Bombay on 8 July were largely concerned with this issue. See GI Home Poll. 15/II, 15/III and 15/V/1923.

evidence to the Khilafat Accounts Enquiry Committee of the parasitical activities of the Ali brothers and Dr Mahmud.[71] Neither of these disclosures improved the public image of the leadership, and future efforts to raise funds were treated with justifiable cynicism. Yet though the Khilafatists were leaders without a following, they found themselves in an identical dilemma to that faced by their Congress counterparts. Were they to follow Gandhi and his lieutenants in the continued pursuit of non-co-operation outside the legislatures or were they to join the Congress-Swaraj-Khilafat party, under the leadership of C.R. Das and Motilal Nehru, in order to contest the elections and make the Reforms unworkable? Like the Congress, the Khilafat Committe was deeply divided over this issue and this added to its ineffectiveness.

The main protagonists of the 'no-change' party were the Ali brothers, Dr Kitchlew of Amritsar and Dr Mahmud of Patna. For the Ali brothers, the obstacles to a policy of council entry were the same as the obstacles to their participation in constitutional politics in the years before 1920. As individuals, they might have secured election to either the U.P. Council or the Central Assembly, yet they were too committed to non-constitutional activity to change their policy overnight, and too accustomed to straddling the subcontinent to confine themselves to being small cogs in a constitutional machine. For Dr Kitchlew, the existence of a zemindar party in the Punjab which despised his Kashmiri origins as much as he despised its consistent loyalism left him no alternative but to continue as a political activist, and for Dr Mahmud, habitual vacillation and an emotional attachment to Jawaharlal Nehru, himself a fervent no-changer, provided on this occasion, as on many others, a stumbling block to rational action. Lastly, in early 1923, when the Swaraj party was formed, all these men were in gaol and incapable for that

[71] GI Home Poll. 15/1923: The Khilafat Accounts Enquiry Committee Report. The Committee found that 50,000 rupees could not be accounted for. For a further lakh no satisfactory accounts were available. It discovered that Dr Mahmud had received 21,000 rupees for the publication of a book on *The Khilafat and England* and that only 1,600 rupees had been spent on the printing. It also discovered that most Khilafat officials travelled first class on the railways and that huge sums had been spent on taxis and entertainment. 'When the Secretary travels', ran the report, 'the cloud of bounty showers rupees on all sides, Muhajirs, deserving persons, newspapers, servants, are all fully satisfied from the fountain of generosity...'

reason of participating in the new political initiatives which were being taken.

The main protagonists of the Swarajist policy were the young men who had followed Mahommed Ali since their Aligarh days, Tassaduq Ahmed Khan Sherwani, Abdur Rahman Siddiqui, Chaudhuri Khaliquzzaman, Abdul Aziz Ansari, Khwaja Abdul Majid and Shuaib Qureshi. These men were secondary leaders; they were mostly from the United Provinces; and whether through disenchantment with the Turks produced by their activities as emissaries of the Khilafat Committee in Europe[72] or through a closer relationship with Motilal Nehru developed after the imprisonment of the Ali brothers, they supported a policy of council entry. Sherwani and Khaliquzzaman both served as secretaries of the Swaraj party from its inception in January 1923, and as they freed themselves from their Panislamic entanglements the others threw their weight behind these two men.

Somewhere between these two groups but progressively inclining to the second were Hakim Ajmal Khan, Dr Ansari and Kalam Azad. The role of Ajmal Khan and Ansari in the Khilafat movement had been strictly limited. They were men of caution, opposed to violence, reluctant to participate in mass politics and wary of the extremism of the Ali brothers and the *ulema*. At the height of the Khilafat movement they remained in the background and when they did emerge again after the imprisonment of the Ali brothers it was largely as a moderating influence, working hand-in-hand with Gandhi in an endeavour to co-ordinate the two movements under his leadership.[73] After the government's dispatch of February 1922, they continued to follow the same policy, urging both the *ulema*

---

[72] Shuaib Qureshi and Abdur Rahman Siddiqui were sent to university in England in 1919 but they gave up their studies to be Mahommed Ali's right-hand men in Switzerland. Shuaib returned to India and became the editor of *Young India* in Nov. 1921 and was imprisoned for his writings in June 1922. Siddiqui returned to Lausanne as an emissary of the Khilafat Committee in Oct. 1922 but his efforts to persuade the Kemalists to restore the temporal power of the Khalifa met with no success. See GI Home Poll. 60/1923 and 253/1924.

[73] See, for example, GI Home Poll. 137/1921: CID Report on the meetings of the Central Khilafat Committee and the *Jumiat ul Ulema i Hind* at Delhi on 21 and 22 Sept. 1921.

and the moderates, in the name of Hindu-Muslim unity, not to make any gesture of conciliation to the government.[74] Over the question of council entry, however, they differed. Both considered a return to civil disobedience the resort of desperate men,[75] but Ansari was more anxious than Ajmal Khan to keep both wings of the movement together. Ajmal Khan came out in favour of council entry in October 1922[76] but Ansari continued to favour the no-change party and worked to prevent party divisions from becoming deeper.[77]

After the defeat of council entry at Gaya, these differences increased. Ansari continued to support the no-changers; Ajmal Khan joined the Swarajist party and endeavoured to persuade the ulema, though with little success, to amend the *fatwa* passed in 1920 on this question.[78] In this he was aided by Kalam Azad, who had resigned from the Khilafat Committee in January 1923 when he saw that the Swarajist star was in the ascendant.[79] He had been obliged to admit by this stage that his hopes to become *Sheikh ul Hind* would not be fulfilled and he chose a broker's role instead.[80] These differences persisted until September 1923, when the Special Congress gave the green light to the Swarajists. After that time, Ansari ceased to support the no-changers and applied himself instead to the task of healing Hindu-Muslim divisions.

These differences over council entry did not entirely dominate the proceedings of the Khilafat Committee. Indeed, even after November 1922, it pursued Panislamist policies which were unani-

[74] GI Home Poll. 501/1922: Report on the Congress Working Committee meeting at Ahmedabad on 17 and 18 March 1922.

[75] After the revolutionary oratory of the Congress Committee meeting at Lucknow on 10 and 11 June 1922, Ansari and Ajmal Khan made plans to retire from political life. See GI Home Poll. 941/1922.

[76] Mahommed Ali papers (Jamia Millia Islamic Library, New Delhi): Statement by Ajmal Khan, 27 Oct. 1922.

[77] In Nov. 1922, for example, at the AICC meeting at Calcutta, Ansari opposed Nehru's motion in favour of council entry and took the lead in securing an adjournment of the discussion until the Gaya Congress in Dec. See AICC papers 8/1922, pp. 57 and 91.

[78] GI Home Poll. 25/1923: Delhi FR I Feb. 1923.

[79] Ibid., Bombay FR II Jan. 1923.

[80] For evidence of Azad's ambitions to become *Sheikh ul Hind*, see GI Home Poll. 180/1921: CID Report on the conference of Bihar ulema held at Patna on 25 and 26 June 1921.

mously supported by all factions. Reactions to the abolition of the
temporal and spiritual powers of the Khalifa and to Sharif Hussain's
bid for election to that office, all fall into this category. Not all
Panislamist issues, however, can be disentangled from Indian issues,
because particularly for the Ali brothers, the pursuit of Panislamist
policies was largely dictated by their need to maintain themselves
as credible Muslim leaders after the decline of non-co-operation.
Their advocacy of Panislamist activities, therefore, did not always
meet with widespread support. Indeed, it often brought them into
conflict with those Khilafatists who wished to use the Khilafat organization for purely Indian purposes.

In 1923, the main opposition within the Khilafat Committee to its
continuing preoccupation with Panislamic ventures came from the
Muslim Swarajists who had joined Nehru and Das in January. These
men had involved themselves in the U.P. municipal elections in
March, and Khaliquzzaman and Khwaja Abdul Majid had emerged
as the Chairmen of the Lucknow and Aligarh Municipal Boards.[81]
This involvement in Swarajist politics made them less sympathetic
to Panislamic activities. Their feeling was that the Khilafat organization should be used to strengthen the pro-change party, and this
feeling grew stronger as the battle between the no-changers and
pro-changers became more acute. One small indication of the
emergence of this feeling was provided at the Khilafat Committee
meeting at Muzafferabad in April 1923, when Khaliquzzaman and
Sherwani fought with Ansari over the allocation of 12,000 rupees to
Kalam Azad for propaganda in Persian and Arabic in the Khilafat
cause.[82] Matters got worse, however, after the Ali brothers were
released from gaol, for they proceeded to nail their colours firmly
to the Khilafat mast and to plan three deputations to the Middle
East. This escapist political thinking won them few friends among
the Swarajists, and at Coconada in December the differences between the two groups came to a head. Khaliquzzaman led the Swarajists in an attack on the Ali brothers' proposals for three deputations,
holding that one would be quite sufficient, and when this attack
failed, he, Shuaib Qureshi and Abdul Aziz Ansari refused to stand

[81] GI Home Poll, 25/1923: U.P. FR II March 1923.
[82] GI Home Poll. 15/ii/1923: CID Report on AIKC meeting at Muzafferabad, 25
April 1923.

for election as secretaries of the organization.[83] By this stage, the political rift between the Ali brothers and their former *chelas* was virtually complete.

But the Ali brothers were not only faced with opposition from their former followers. They also had to face a Muslim community throughout North India which was becoming less interested in the problems of Turkey and more preoccupied with the growth of communal tension in its own back yard. By June 1923, communal feeling in the U.P. was already intense, and on the eve of Mahommed Ali's release from prison, rumours were rife that he would respond to this situation by breaking with the Congress and by leading an anti-*shuddhi* campaign.[84] Consequently, when he turned a blind eye to these developments and plunged himself into Middle East affairs, there was much disappointment and opinion hardened against him. The Moradabad Municipal Board decided in July by the casting vote of the Chairman not to present him with an address,[85] and though the Aligarh and Lucknow Boards did so in September and October he met with a very poor reception in both places. At Lucknow, where he campaigned for the freedom of the *Jazirat ul Arab,* he only collected fifty rupees for his projected deputations, and at Jhansi, whither he proceeded the following day, he was 'so chagrined' by his reception at the railway station 'that friends had some difficulty in persuading him to proceed to the city to receive the address.'[86] By the end of 1923, therefore, it had become clear that the fortunes of the Ali brothers were in decline. The Panislamic questions with which they were concerning themselves were only of peripheral appeal to the masses, and it was not to be long before the rise of communal antagonism in the provinces began to erode their control of the Khilafat organization.

In 1924, after their successes in the elections, the Swarajists took less interest in the affairs of the Khilafat Committee, and the main opposition to the Ali brothers came from the Punjabi Khilafatists under the leadership of Dr Kitchlew. His Amritsar Khilafat party

---

[83] GI Home Poll. 253/1924: CID Report on the Khilafat conference at Coconada, 26 Dec. 1923. Dr Mahmud, who had become depressed at the poor response to his Khilafat tours, also refused to stand.

[84] GI Home Poll. 25/1923: U.P. FR II June 1923.

[85] Ibid., U.P. FR II July 1923.

[86] Ibid., U.P. FR II Oct. 1923.

had sided with the no-changers in the debate over council entry, but as communal tension increased, Kitchlew was obliged to become more communal himself. Even in 1923 there had been a split in the Punjab Khilafat Committee over the *shuddhi* movement,[87] but at that stage Kitchlew had worked hard to reduce communal tension[88] and to revive non-co-operation by forming a united front with the Akalis.[89] What he lost by these endeavours, however, was considerably greater than what he gained. The Muslims of Amritsar were offended by the introduction of Akalis into their mosques[90] and in the early months of 1924, in the face of waning support for his policies,[91] Kitchlew was obliged to give up his hopes of an alliance with the Akalis and to concentrate on constructive work amongst his own community.

The plans which he initially put forward were not of a communal character but his ambitions were clearly political and he met with opposition from both the Swarajists and the Panislamists on this score. The Swarajists did not relish the idea of mass mobilization: they were involved in constitutional opposition to the Raj and given the nature of the franchise, they were obliged to take into account the prejudices of the more established sections of the community. When Kitchlew's programme was debated by the Central Khilafat Committee at Delhi in June 1924, Khaliquzzaman emphasized the fact that 'most of the rich men, the landholders and the Shia community will not like to work on any organization founded under the Khilafat committee, and he suggested that the best plan would be 'the capturing of the Muslim League by the Khilafatists'. The Muslim League had a history behind it and any work done through it would carry more weight.[92] He pointed out, furthermore, that the Muslim League had appointed a committee to confer with other nationalist organizations and he said that it would be inadvisable to pre-empt the work of the League before it had been given a chance to prove itself. This advice was in line with Swarajist policy, and Kitchlew did not take exception to it. His differences with the Ali brothers,

[87] GI Home Poll. 25/1923: Punjab FR I May 1923.
[88] Ibid., Punjab FR I Sept. 1923.
[89] Ibid., Punjab FR II Sept. 1923.
[90] Ibid., Punjab FR II Nov. 1923.
[91] GI Home Poll. 25/1924: Punjab FR II Feb., II March and II April 1924.
[92] GI Home Poll. 167/1924: CID Report on the meeting of the CKC at Delhi on 24 and 25 June 1924.

however, were more fundamental. They were less opposed than the Swarajists to his plans for political mobilization[93] but they reacted strongly against two of his proposals which struck at their chances of political survival. Of the two, the proposal to convert the Jamia Millia into a school for propagandists was the less serious because the Delhi and U.P. Swarajists were as opposed to this as the Ali brothers. But his proposal for the transference of the Khilafat office from Bombay to Delhi met with the support of both these groups and placed the Ali brothers in a very threatened position. It amounted to a vote of censure on Panislamist politics and a demand for a Khilafat organization geared to the North Indian situation. The Ali brothers resisted it to the hilt, tempers rose on both sides, and they only escaped defeat by much blistering rhetoric and a thinly veiled attack on Ajmal Khan and Ansari which produced a characteristic plea for compromise from these two men.[94]

After this, Kitchlew became progressively more communal. By September 1924 he had offended not only Malaviya but also Das and Nehru by his advocacy of Muslim economic independence,[95] and though he still remained a member of the Congress he concentrated more on attacking Hindu communalists than on settling Hindu-Muslim differences. When Gandhi visited Lahore to improve communal relations in early December, neither Kitchlew nor Zafar Ali took any part in the proceedings[96] and when Kitchlew composed his presidential address for the Belgaum Khilafat conference he included virulent attacks on Malaviya and Lajpat Rai which provoked an uproar even after modification.[97] His disenchantment with the Congress was also shown by his refusal to attend the Belgaum session and the difficulty with which he was persuaded to meet Gandhi. By February 1925 he had begun a *tanzim* tour of Northern Punjab and was reported to be 'on the point of breaking

[93] Mahommed Ali accused Kitchlew of stealing his ideas, but though he had been reported in April to be 'contemplating the spending of his time in the propagation of Islam and the combating of the shuddhi movement...', he had produced no coherent plan of his own. See GI Home Poll 25/1924: Delhi FR I April 1924.

[94] GI Home Poll. 167/1924: CID Report on the meeting of the CKC at Delhi, 24 and 25 June 1924.

[95] GI Home Poll. 25/1924: Punajb FR I Sept. 1924.

[96] Ibid., Punjab FR I Dec. 1924.

[97] GI Home Poll. 167/III/1924: CID Report on the All India Khilafat Conference at Belgaum on 23 Dec. 1924.

with the Congress and joining the ordinary Muslim progressive party in the Punjab.[98]

Kitchlew's new strategy strengthened his position amongst the Amritsar Muslims, and in March 1925, amid much excitement, all his candidates were returned to the Municipal Board.[99] This success made it less essential for him to capture the Khilafat organization and he concentrated instead on setting up a new central organization for the *tanzim* movement. Even in this, however, he met with the opposition of the Ali brothers, and the all-India Muslim parties conference at Amritsar in July witnessed still more accusations and counter-accusations between the two parties. Once again a compromise was reached. But this time it was to no avail. Kitchlew had reached the end of his tether and he resigned the Presidency of the Khilafat organization at the same meeting.[100] He had come to the conclusion that the pursuit of non-co-operation was no longer a viable policy. He was thoroughly disenchanted with the Congress and he concentrated increasingly on *tanzim* and left the Ali brothers to stew in their own juice.

The plight of the Ali brothers was scarcely enviable. As early as August 1924, in the hope of a financial return from journalism, Mahommed Ali had considered reviving the *Comrade*. But though he received an initial offer of help from Shuaib Qureshi, he was ultimately disappointed[101] and it was not until November, following a donation of 10,000 rupees from Haji Abdullah Haroon, that the project got off the ground.[102] By October 1924, such was the financial plight of the Ali brothers that they were obliged to espouse sectional interests in order to survive: they began supporting Ibn Saud, the Wahabi king of Saudi Arabia, in his ambitions to take over the Hedjaz.[103] This provoked a Sunni backlash and ultimately alienated their old colleagues, Hasrat Mohani, Abdul Bari and Mushir Hussain Kidwai,[104] but so long as Ibn Saud and his Indian followers provided

[98] GI Home Poll. 112/1925: Punjab FR II Feb. 1925.

[99] Ibid., Punjab FR 1 March 1925.

[100] GI Home Poll. 112/1925: Punjab FR II July 1925.

[101] Mahommed Ali papers: Mahommed Ali to Shuaib Qureshi, 27 Aug. 1924.

[102] Ibid., Mahommed Ali to Haji Abdullah Haroon, 24 Oct. 1924; GI Home Poll. 25/1924: Bombay FR II Oct. and Delhi FR I Nov. 1924

[103] GI Home Poll. 1924: Bombay FR II Sept. 1924.

[104] C. Khaliquzzaman, *Pathway to Pakistan* (Lahore 1961), pp. 80-2; GI Home Poll. 112/1925: U.P. FR I May 1925 and I Nov. 1925; Punjab FR II Nov. 1925.

them with cash the Ali brothers refused to throw him over.[105] Like
Zafar Ali, however, who was also in Ibn Saud's pay, the Ali brothers
were placed in a difficult position when his troops desecrated the
Prophet's tomb at Medina in August 1925.[106] Shaukat did his best to
play down Wahabi excesses but he met with considerable opposition,
not least in Bombay, where Chothani took the opportunity to wreak
his revenge. On 28 September, on leaving the Juma Musjid, Shaukat
was met by Chothani at the head of a hostile mob and was only
saved from serious injury by the intervention of the Afghan
consul.[107]

This particular reversal of fortune was perhaps the most dramatic
from which the Ali brothers suffered, but it was not untypical, and
if they remained Panislamist politicians it was largely because they
had nowhere else to go. By May 1925, the *Comrade* had proved a
failure and Mahommed Ali had taken to the printing of seditious
articles in the hope of a cheap martyrdom. The Chief Commissioner
of Delhi informed the government of India that Mahommed Ali
was 'thoroughly discredited and almost penniless' and refused to
prosecute him in order to watch him flounder still further.[108] And
flounder he did. He went cap in hand to his former associates and
colleagues,[109] and having failed in almost all quarters he finally
secured a grant of 6,000 rupees from the deposed Maharaja of Nabha
to do propaganda for his restoration.[110] This acceptance of employment from a Sikh is perhaps the best illustration of his loss of credibility with his own community. By the end of 1925, the growth of

[105] By the summer of 1925 collections for Panislamic activities from traditional sources
had reached their nadir: Mahommed Ali collected 153 rupees on the Id day at Delhi in
April and two rupees from 400 people at the Juma Masjid, Aligarh, in June. In May,
however, he collected 12,000 rupees from the Delhi Wahabis, and by Sept., the Ali
brothers were considered Ibn Saud's chief paymasters in India. See GI Home Poll.
112/1925: Delhi FR II April and II May 1925; U.P. FR I June 1925; GI Home Poll.
99/xiv/1925: Deputy Commissioner, Lahore, to Chief Secretary, Punjab Government,
4 Sept. 1925.

[106] For an account of Zafar Ali's activities at this time, see GI Home Poll. 99/xiv/
1925.

[107] GI Home Poll. 112/1925: Bombay FR II Sept. 1925.

[108] GI Home Poll. 226/1925: Chief Commissioner, Delhi, to the Home Member,
Government of India, 14 May 1925.

[109] Mahommed Ali papers: Mahommed Ali to Ahmed Moola Dawood Madani, 11
July 1925; Mahommed Ali to the Editor of the *Daily Herald*, 30 July 1925.

[110] GI Home Poll. 112/1925: U.P. FR II Oct. 1925.

communalism in the provinces had made the Ali brothers look like prehistoric animals unable to adapt to a new environment.

The fate of the Constitutionalists

In the field of constitutional politics, the most notable politician to share the predicament of the Ali brothers was Mahommed Ali Jinnah. Jinnah had been a leading member of the nationalist movement before 1920 but he had been disappointed by the Reforms. Unlike his U.P. colleagues in the Muslim League, he had been ambitious for power at the Centre, and when Dyarchy was only introduced in the provinces he was obliged to reconcile himself to fighting the same old battles all over again in the new Legislative Assembly.[111] Nonetheless he showed no inclination to adopt non-constitutional methods of agitation. On the contrary, he sided with Gandhi at Amritsar in securing a qualified acceptance for the Reforms and he had every intention of working them with a view to securing their early revision.[112] In September 1920, however, when Gandhi stampeded the Congress into non-co-operation at Calcutta, this intention became politically irrelevant and Jinnah was obliged to rethink his policy. Where non-co-operation was concerned, he had no second thoughts. He condemned it unequivocally and he resigned from both the Home Rule League and the Congress on this issue.[113] It is noteworthy, however, that he did not stand for election to the Assembly in 1920. He was anxious for Reform at the Centre and the support of the Congress was essential for that purpose. He could not afford, therefore, to alienate Congress sympathy by working the Reforms when Congressmen were rejecting them. All he could do was to take a back seat until political conditions returned to normality.

While the non-co-operation movement was in progress, Jinnah performed a broker's role. In the summer of 1921, he visited England and lobbied there for a constitutional response to Gandhi's activities. He warned the British public of the dangers of driving

---

[111] For evidence of Jinnah's desire for power at the Centre, see *ILC Debates 1917-18,* 17 Sept. 1918, p. 135; *Joint Select Committee on the Government of India Bill,* vol. ii, Minutes of Evidence (London 1919), p. 212.

[112] IOR/L/P and J/6/1337/1920: CID Report for Upper India, 2 Jan. 1920.

[113] *The Times,* 3 Jan. 1921; GI Home Poll. Dec. 1920, D59: Bombay FR I Oct. 1920.

the Indian intelligentsia to rebellion and he suggested that if the Punjab wrong were righted and the constitution amended to allow for provincial autonomy and Dyarchy in the central government, India might be restored to an even keel.[114] It was an appeal which fell on deaf ears. The Secretary of State was anxious to reassure Indian opinion over the Jallianwalabagh tragedy but he would not revise the constitution and Jinnah returned to India empty-handed.[115]

He then tried to break non-co-operation, not by securing political concessions from the Raj but by driving a wedge between Hindu and Muslim non-co-operators. He set about discovering the terms on which the Khilafatists would cry halt, and like Shafi, who was also about the same business, he urged upon Reading 'a settlement of Turkish affairs which would restore Smyrna and Thrace to her, leaving the Hedjaz and Mesopotamia under the two present rulers, Hassan and Feisul'.[116] These terms were virtually identical to the ones subsequently enshrined in the famous government dispatch of February 1922. But before they could be acted upon, the All India Congress Committee declared in favour of civil disobedience, Gandhi and his Muslim supporters drew closer together, and the whole scheme was foiled.

Before the year was out, however, Jinnah was given one more chance of achieving the same end. The Prince of Wales landed at Bombay on 17 November 1921 to the accompaniment of a very serious riot. Gandhi, proclaiming that Swaraj stank in his nostrils, suspended the civil disobedience movement, and the government, which had long been urged to act against the extremists, saw its opportunity and struck. As was so often the case, however, the use of extraordinary powers to ban public meetings and imprison leading Congressmen provoked a backlash in Gandhi's favour. The very men who had called for action criticized the government for going too far[117] and the brokers seized their chance to profit from a buyers' market. Malaviya led a deputation to Lord Reading on 22 December;[118] Purushotamdas Thakurdas, through Ambalal Sara-

[114] *The Times,* 29 June 1921.
[115] Reading papers, 10: Tgm Reading to Montagu, 2 Nov. 1921.
[116] Ibid.
[117] Ibid., 3: Reading to Montagu, 15 Dec. 1921.
[118] IOR/L/P and J/6/7961/1921.

bhai, the Ahmedabad mill-owner, persuaded Gandhi to discuss terms for a truce with government;[119] and Jinnah, Malaviya and other moderates planned a meeting with Gandhi which took place in mid-January.[120] As it turned out, however, Gandhi was not interested in parleying with government. He did not wish to alienate moderate opinion by appearing to be uncompromising but he declined to discuss peace on the terms suggested by Jinnah and Malaviya. He persuaded them to raise their terms to a point at which they were unacceptable to government, and having brought them down on his side of the fence, he resumed civil disobedience with his position re-established.[121] Jinnah could only throw up his arms in exasperation and let Gandhi and the government fight it out.

Jinnah re-entered the political arena once Nehru and Das had committed themselves to council entry. In March 1923, in an effort to woo the Muslims away from the Khilafat Committee, he called a meeting of the Muslim League at Lucknow and invited his old friend, G.M. Bhurgri,[122] to deliver the presidential address. Bhurgri proceeded cautiously. He had no desire to offend the Khilafatists and he paid tribute to their activities. He condemned the British government for siding with the Greeks, he praised the achievements of Mustafa Kemal and he looked forward to the formation of a Federation of Oriental States. The burden of his song, however, was that non-co-operation had proved a failure, that the British Raj had come to stay and that the only feasible course of action was to work the Reforms and to press for the early appointment of the Statutory Commission. This was very much Jinnah's own view, but it was opposed tooth and nail by Ansari and his Khilafatist followers, and the two sides were so evenly balanced that no decision was forthcoming. A five-hour session of the Subjects Committee on 31 March resolved nothing and though Jinnah's motion for council entry was rejected by twelve votes to nine the following day this was only because Ansari contrived to have the vote taken during the lunch interval. Jinnah was confident that he would win in the

[119] Purushotamdas Thakurdas papers, 24: Ambalal Sarabhai to Thakurdas, 9 Jan. 1922.

[120] *The Indian Social Reformer*, 8 Jan. 1922.

[121] For an account of the meeting at Bombay at which Gandhi outmanoeuvred the moderates, see GI Home Poll. 461/1921.

[122] For a detailed account of Bhurgri's political history, see GI Home Poll. 66/1924, KW4.

open session but his confidence was not put to the test. After only two resolutions had been passed, Zahur Ahmed, a non-co-operating barrister from Allahabad, objected to the continuation of the proceedings on the grounds that there was not a quorum of *bona fide* members. This objection was sustained and the session was adjourned *sine die*. Jinnah had failed in his endeavours and it was to be over a year before the League met again.[123]

Jinnah only re-emerged as a significant political force after the 1923 elections. He was returned to the Assembly by the Muslims of Bombay city and he became the leader of the Independent party. In that capacity he co-operated with Nehru's Swarajist party, and together the two parties were known as the Nationalist party. Nonetheless Jinnah held the upper hand. There were 101 seats in the Assembly and the Swarajists had won only forty-one of them. Jinnah with a party of some seventeen members, held the balance between the Swarajists and the government.

From the beginning the two parties were separated by political ideology. Nehru's party was recruited chiefly outside the Presidencies, from those areas which had either co-operated wholeheartedly with Gandhi or seen the wisdom of compromising with him. Of its forty-one members, ten came from the United Provinces and Delhi, seven from Bihar and Orissa, five each from the Punjab and the Central Provinces, and two from Assam. Only twelve came from the Presidencies, five from Bengal, where Das had bowed to Gandhi, four from Bombay, and three from Madras.[124] Jinnah's party, on the other hand, was recruited almost entirely from the Presidencies, six of its seventeen members coming from Bombay, six from Madras, three from Bengal and only two from the United Provinces.[125] Unlike the Swarajists, the Independents had mostly

[123] Pirzada, op.cit., vol. i, pp. 566-74.

[124] Gordon, op.cit., Table 7, p. 182.

[125] The seventeen Independents were: Jinnah (Bombay city Mahommedan urban), G.M. Bhurgri (Sind Mahommedan rural), Purushotamdas Thakurdas (Indian Merchants' Chamber and Bureau, Bombay), Kasturbhai Lalji (Ahmedabad mill-owners), Sardar Mutalik (Sardars of the Deccan), Harchandrai Vishindas (Sind non-Mahommedan), K.K. Nambiyar (Madras landholders), Venkatapatiraju (Ganjam cum Vizagapatam), Ramchandra Rao (Godavari cum Kistna), Venkatarama Reddi (Guntur cum Nellore), Shanmukhan Chetty (Salem and Coimbatore cum North Arcot), Rama Iyengar (Ramnad and Madura cum Tinnevelly), B.C. Pal (Calcutta non-Mahommedan urban), K.C. Neogy (Dacca division), Ranglal Jajodia (Marwari Association), Madan Mohan Malaviya (Allahabad and Jhansi divisions) and Mahommed Yakub (Rohilkhund and Kumaon, Mahommedan rural).

opposed non-co-operation and several had contested the elections of 1920. If they could be identified with any political group at all, it was with the school of 'moderate' nationalism which had broken with the Congress over the acceptability of the Reforms. Though Jinnah was the President of the Muslim League, therefore, the differences between the two parties were political, not communal. Motilal Nehru, indeed, had more Muslim supporters than Jinnah. Of the forty-one Swarajists, eight were Muslims,[126] whereas of the seventeen Independents, only three were Muslims, and after the death of G.M. Bhurgri the number was reduced to two. The outcome of their co-operation, however, was of great importance for communal relations in North India. If Jinnah enabled Nehru to carry the day against the government and to obtain political concessions with which to pay off his supporters, the Swarajist-Khilafat alliance would be strengthened, but if Nehru, through Jinnah's recalcitrance, failed to carry the day, his opponents were poised and ready to exploit communal differences to destroy him. It was an awesome responsibility but Jinnah was not entirely aware of the burden which he carried. He had his eyes firmly fixed on the central government and he had his own notions of the best methods to achieve the political revision which he sought.

The initial period of co-operation was cordial enough. The ground was prepared by Das, Jayakar and Jinnah at Bombay after the Coconada Congress.[127] A National Demand, calling for provincial autonomy and responsibility in the central government, was subsequently approved by the Swarajist Executive at Lucknow,[128] and the two parties agreed to make this the basis of a joint political programme at Delhi on 3 February. On 18 February, Motilal Nehru moved this demand as an amendment to Diwan Bahadur Rangachariar's resolution calling for the early appointment of the Statutory Commission. It was supported by virtually all the elected

---

[126] Nehru's Muslim supporters were Sarfaraz Hussain Khan (Patna and Chota Nagpur cum Orissa), Shafi Daudi (Tirhut division), Nawab Ismail Khan (Meerut division), Yusuf Imam (U.P. Southern divisions), Khwaja Abdul Karim (Dacca division), Mahommed Kasim Ali (Chittagong division), Ahmed Ali Khan (Assam) and Samiullah Khan (Central Provinces). Syed Murtuza (South Madras) was elected as a Khilafatist, but subsequently joined the Swarajists. Biographies of these men ae to be found in GI Home Poll. 66/1924, GI Home Public 953/1924, and Gordon, op.cit., pp. 364-73.

[127] M.R. Jayakar, *The Story of My Life*, vol. ii (Bombay 1959), p. 182.

[128] AICC papers, 8/1924 and 31/1924.

Indian members of the Assembly and it was passed by a handsome majority. Even before Nehru moved his amendment, however, the Home Member's reply to Rangachariar's resolution had made it clear that the government of India was in no mood to make concessions. All manner of obstacles to advance were erected, not least the problem presented by the position of minorities and all that was offered ultimately was a departmental enquiry to remedy justifiable complaints within the terms of the Act itself.[129] The main hopes of the Swarajists, however, rested not with the government of India, but with the new Labour government in England. They had friends in the Labour party and they continued throughout the summer to expect a summons to a conference.[130]

The first response to the National Demand by the new Secretary of State, Lord Olivier, however, was distinctly disappointing. In a speech to the House of Lords on 26 February, he made it plain that he was not prepared to go any further than the government of India, and as Nehru was later to remark, this response was 'not only insufficient, but highly unsatisfactory and disappointing.'[131] When it came to pressing home this disappointment, however, the Swarajists and Independents were at loggerheads. Many Swarajists wished to reject the Budget in its entirety, but the Independents were not prepared to resort to such tactics and because their agreement was necessary for any policy to be successful they ultimately won the day. It was agreed that the first four heads should be rejected and that the rest of the Budget should be treated on its merits. This was the first instance of Jinnah using his advantage to modify Swarajist policy, but it was very clear from the statement which he made to the Assembly on 11 March that it was not to be the last. The whole tone of the speech suggests not only a desire to reassure the government as to the reasonableness of the Nationalist position but also an ambition to bring the Swarajists under his own more constitutional umbrella.

...the Nationalist party [he said] is a party which is formed to work in this Assembly and nothing more; and in this Assembly we stand

---

[129] *ILA Debates*, vol. iv, part i, 18 Feb. 1924, pp. 355-66.
[130] See speech by Nehru, *ILA Debates*, vol. iv, part ii, 19 Feb. 1924, p. 783; report of speech by Jinnah at Hindu College, Delhi, GI Home Poll. 25/124: Delhi FR II March 1924; B.R. Nanda, *The Nehrus* (London 1965), pp. 230-3.
[131] *ILA Debates*, vol. iv, part ii, 10 March 1924, p. 1382.

to pursue a policy and a programme of a constitutional character. We shall pursue that policy and that programme until the last stages of the constitutional struggle are exhausted. There is no idea in the mind of the Nationalist party to resort to civil disobedience. There is no idea in the mind of the Nationalist party that we want revolution. There is no idea in the mind of the Nationalist party that we are going to carry on the campaign of non-payment of taxes.[132]

In Reading's view, Jinnah was making a bid for leadership[133] and his activities over the next three months do not belie that impression.

He first attempted to achieve this ambition by direct methods. After the Assembly session ended, he returned to Bombay and held almost daily conferences with Nehru, Jayakar, Purushotamdas Thakurdas and V.J. Patel with a view to producing a new, inclusive, constitutional party. Gandhi also participated in a number of these discussions, as did Das on his arrival from Bengal.[134] Ultimately, however, Jinnah's efforts foundered on the rock of internal Congress differences. Nehru and Das were under pressure from Gandhi and, though they did not bow before him, they were too wary of his antics to ally openly with men who repudiated his creed. It was only after the promulgation of the Bengal ordinance in October 1924, when Gandhi agreed to suspend non-co-operation and to place the Swarajists in charge of the Congress organization, that Jinnah's ambitions stood any chance of being fulfilled and by then new obstacles had been thrown into his path.

Jinnah's other *ballon d'essai,* the revival of the Muslim League, had more ominous consequences. When Jinnah called the Council of the League at Delhi on 16 March and persuaded his colleagues to agree to a session at Lahore,[135] he was undoubtedly motivated by a desire to strengthen the chances of a government response to the National Demand. The choice of Lahore was not fortuitous. The Punjab was the only province where the Muslims were working the Reforms for their own advantage, and the Punjabi Muslims were the most likely to support a policy of constitutional advance. Such a demand, coming from the premier Muslim political organization, would be a complete answer to the argument that communal differences were an obstacle to advance, and Jinnah, as the man who

[132] Ibid., 11 March 1924, pp. 1443-4.
[133] Reading papers, 7: Reading to Olivier, 13 March 1924.
[134] Jayakar, op.cit., vol. ii, p. 264.
[135] Shafi Daudi papers, Diary, 16 March 1924.

had secured Muslim support for this purpose, would also add to his own political stature. So it must have seemed. But the reality was different. Fazli Husain was keen on provincial autonomy, but he was wary of selling his support too cheaply and he made sure that he was in a position of overwhelming strength at the League meeting.[136] This preparation paid dividends; and when the main resolution defining the Muslim position emerged from the Subjects Committee it was an almost entirely Punjabi affair. It looked forward to a Federal Government at the Centre, 'the functions of the Central Government being confined to such matters as are of general or common concern'; it demanded that no measure of territorial redistribution should affect Muslim majorities in Punjab, Bengal and the Frontier; and it made scant provision for the position of minorities. Representation was to be by population,

except that very small minorities may be given representation in excess of their numerical proportion in those cases in which they would remain entirely unrepresented in the absence of such exceptional treatment, subject, however, to the essential proviso that no majority should be reduced to a minority or even to an equality.

This last clause was a direct product of the Punjabi situation, the stress on 'very small minorities' being calculated to exclude the Hindus and the Sikhs, and the proviso itself to improve the position of the Muslims at their expense. As such it was resented by the minority-province Muslims, and particularly by those working the Reforms, and an amendment eliminating the reference to 'very small minorities' and replacing it with a demand for 'adequate and effective representation for minorities in every province' was moved by Dr Ziauddin Ahmed and carried by one hundred and twenty-six votes to eighty-three. This amendment was supported by the Punjabi agriculturalists, suggesting that their original resolution had reflected parochialism but not prejudice, but it was vociferously opposed by the Khilafatists and notably by Ghazi Abdur Rahman of Lyallpur, Chaudhuri Khaliquzzaman and Mahommed Ali. These were the men who had worked closest with the Congress and they saw that these terms would not be accepted by that body. It had become clear when Dr Ansari and Lala Laipat Rai tried to formulate their National Pact that even separate electorates had ceased to be

[136] Fazli Husain papers; Fazli Husain to Amir Din, 24 Nov. 1932.

universally accepted,[137] and a communal majority by separate electorates had already been rejected by the Congress at Coconada.[138] If
the League were to demand this concession again without giving
any compensation in the minority provinces, the result would be a
foregone conclusion.[139] Nonetheless, by the passage of the amendment, the League did demand just that, and Jinnah emerged from
the Lahore session, not only armed with a declaration in favour of a
complete overhaul of the Government of India Act, but committed
to securing an improvement on the Lucknow Pact as a precondition
for united action. He did not shirk this responsibility but even his
powers of persuasion ultimately proved insufficient.[140]

Within a week of the Lahore session, Nehru and Jinnah were
invited to sit as non-official members on the Reforms Enquiry
Committee, an extended version of the departmental enquiry promised by Hailey in February.[141] Nehru would have liked to accept
this invitation but opposition from the Swarajist Executive obliged
him to turn it down.[142] Jinnah, being less subject to external pressure, accepted with alacrity. It gave him an ideal opportunity to
pursue his ambitions for Reform, to explore the views of others,
and where necessary to convert them to his point of view. His
questions to witnesses suggest three main preoccupations. He seeks
firstly to show that Dyarchy has failed and that the constitution
needs overhauling; secondly to counter the argument that communal
tension is an obstacle to advance; and thirdly, to discover terms on
which a new Lucknow Pact might be devised. His path was not
smooth, however, for he met with considerable opposition from the
Chairman, Sir Alexander Muddiman, who was also the Home Member,

[137] Ansari and Lajpat Rai had failed to agree about separate electorates. Dr Ansari
wanted them extended to municipalities and local boards. Lajpat Rai not only disagreed with this but desired their abolition throughout the system after a fixed time.
When the Pact was circulated for opinion, most Hindus agreed with Lajpat Rai and
most Muslims with Ansari. See AICC papers, 25/1924.

[138] Mahommed Ali, as President of the Coconada Congress, had done his best to get
the Bengal Pact passed, but he had been defeated by the efforts of Lajpat Rai and
Malaviya. See GI Home Poll. 152/1924.

[139] Khaliquzzaman, op.cit. p. 77.

[140] For an account of the League session at Lahore, see Pirzada, *op.cit.*, vol. i,
pp. 575-82.

[141] The other non-officials invited were Sir Tej Bahadur Sapru, Sir Sivaswamy Iyer,
Dr Paranjpye, Sir Arthur Froom and the Maharaja of Burdwan.

[142] IOR/L/PO/278: Tgm. Viceroy (Home) to Secretary of State, 3 June 1924.

and from Sir Mahommed Shafi, the Law Member, who had been put on the committee to represent the communal point of view.[143] As at Lahore, Jinnah obtained the greatest co-operation from the Punjabi Muslims. They were anxious for Reforms and willing to minimize the significance of communal tension in order to achieve it. Furthermore they had already come to an understanding with Jinnah and based their position on the resolution passed by the League.[144] Malik Barkat Ali, who represented the Punjab Muslim League before the committee, was the best witness Jinnah could have hoped for. He condemned Dyarchy unequivocally; he gave his opinion that communalism was restricted to the large towns and inspired by disputes over loaves and fishes; he held that these disputes would be easier to handle with provincial autonomy; he supported the view that separate electorates did not necessarily imply communal politics; and he expressed his willingness to accept a Muslim majority in the Punjab of only one per cent.[145] This evidence was of very material assistance to the Nationalist cause and it figured prominently in the committee's Minority Report.[146]

Jinnah also received support from three U.P. Muslims, Maulvi Mahommed Yakub, a member of his own party, Syed Raza Ali, a member of the Council of State, and Professor Shafaat Ahmed, a member of the U.P. Legislative Council. Mahommed Yakub was the most outspoken. He held it 'a malicious subversion of facts to say that the Mussulmans are not in favour of responsible government' and he opposed the argument that communal discord was an obstacle to political advance. He admitted, however, that he was 'more keen for an extension of democratic powers in the Central Government than in the provinces'.[147] As an all-India politician he wished for responsibility at the Centre, but as a Muslim from a minority

---

[143] Ibid., Tgm. Viceroy (Home) to Secretary of State, 26 May 1924.

[144] See memoranda by Pir Tajuddin and Malik Barkat Ali, *Reforms Enquiry Committee*, Appendix 5, *Written Evidence* (London 1925), pp. 374-80; also memorandum by Fazli Husain and Chaudhuri Lal Chand, 21 May 1924, *Reforms Enquiry Committee, Views of Local Governments on the Working of the Reforms* (London 1925), *Cmd.2362*, pp. 211-13.

[145] *Reforms Enquiry Committee*, Appendix 6, *Oral Evidence*, part i (London 1925): Barkat Ali called and examined, 20 Aug. 1924, pp. 411-20 and 426-9.

[146] *Reforms Enquiry Committee, Report* (London 1925), *Cmd.2360*, pp. 150-1 and 177.

[147] *Reforms Enquiry Committee*, Appendix 5, *Written Evidence* (London 1925), pp. 270-3.

province he had his scruples about provincial autonomy. The same dichotomy was also noticeable in the evidence of Raza Ali. He was less bold than Mahommed Yakub with regard to the central government, holding that Dyarchy, though unpopular, would be a more sensible beginning than complete responsibility, but more sceptical about provincial autonomy, declaring quite openly that communal tension was an obstacle to further devolution.[148] Shafaat Ahmed's views were less precise. On the one hand, he held that full advantage had not been taken of the opportunities afforded by the Act; on the other, that it would be possible even within the terms of the Act to abolish dyarchy and to introduce responsibility at the Centre. Did he wish for the overhaul of the Act? It is not clear. He did demand, however, that Muslim representation should be increased both in the provinces and at the Centre, and as this appeared to be an escalation of the League demand made at Lahore, Jinnah was anxious to clarify the position.[149] Shafaat agreed almost immediately, however, that the minority-province Muslims were satisfied with the Lucknow Pact, and Jinnah proceeded no further.[150]

The main opposition to a renegotiated settlement with the Congress came from the Bengali Muslims. Fazlul Haq and A.K. Ghuznavi, both ministers whose salaries had been refused by the Swarajists, and Nawab Ali Chaudhuri, who was to suffer the same fate in 1925, were all of the opinion that Dyarchy was a necessary training ground for full responsible government and that it should run for the entire statutory period.[151] They undoubtedly had hopes of a Muslim majority in the Bengal Council but with half of their co-religionists voting for Das their first priority was to disrupt Das's alliance and to regain control of their own community. They were prepared, therefore, to play up communal differences as an argument against concessions, and Jinnah, in his examination of Bengali Muslim witnesses was on a much more difficult wicket. He and Shafi were at cross-purposes and their clashes over Sir Abdur Rahim's evidence

---

[148] Ibid., pp. 264-9.

[149] This demand was also supported by a public meeting at Agra under the Presidency of Dr Ziauddin Ahmed. See *ibid.*, pp. 324-9.

[150] *Reforms Enquiry Committee*, Appendix 6, *Oral Evidence*, part ii (London 1925): Shafaat Ahmed called and examined, 30 Aug. 1924, pp. 122-5.

[151] *Reforms Enquiry Committee*, Appendix 5, *Written Evidence:* memoranda by Fazlul Haq, A.K. Ghuznavi and Nawab Ali Chaudhuri, pp. 207-9, 210-11, 217-21.

provided one of the most heated sessions of the entire committee. Abdur Rahim ultimately agreed that the Lucknow Pact, though unsatisfactory, did provide a basis for renegotiation, but he would not adopt a flexible attitude towards the size of the Bengali Muslim majority, and he was aided and abetted by both Shafi and Muddiman. Jinnah was prepared to accept a majority by separate electorates but he wanted leeway for negotiation and he sought Rahim's approval for a scheme to give weightage to the Hindus on the basis of their voting strength. This, however, was not forthcoming. While Jinnah was questioning Rahim, Shafi interrupted him to elicit the view that population was the principle criterion, Muddiman hurried him along, and ultimately Rahim himself refused to budge from fifty-six per cent.[152] If any revision of the Lucknow Pact were to be attempted, it was plain by this stage that among the Muslims, the Bengalis were the biggest obstacle to success.

When the work of the Reforms Enquiry Committee was completed, Jinnah, Sapru, Sivaswamy Iyer and Paranjpye refused to sign the Majority Report and produced a Minority Report instead. In that report, they condemned Dyarchy unequivocally and they demanded the introduction of provincial autonomy and responsibility in the central government. They used the evidence of Barkat Ali to show that communal tension was a phenomenon of restricted importance; they quoted the Muslim League resolution to prove that the Muslims were not opposed to advance; and, whilst admitting that the Bengali Muslims were of a different view, they held that even they would be satisfied if their majority was recognized. '...the correct interpretation of their attitude', they said, 'is that if the conditions mentioned above are fulfilled and no majority is reduced to a minority in any province, they will agree to political advance.'[153] Their chief concern, however, was for advance at the Centre, and they showed some anxiety lest the Government should cheat them of their prize, as in 1920, by conceding the demands of the provinces whilst leaving the Central Government untouched. They therefore invoked the spectre of centrifugalism as an argument for simultaneous advance:

...with provincial governments fully responsible to their legislatures

[152] *Reforms Enquiry Committee*, Appendix 6, *Oral Evidence*, part ii: Abdur Rahim called and examined, 23 Oct. 1924, pp. 415-16 and 419-22.

[153] *Reforms Enquiry Committee*, *Report* (London 1925), *Cmd. 2360*, p. 179.

and the Central Government irresponsible in the last resort, the control of various kinds which it is desired to be continued in the Central Government will be more difficult to enforce and the centrifugal tendency observed in many Federal states and especially marked in the history of India will manifest itself more and more making stable Government unworkable.[154]

This was perhaps the first time that Partition had been foreshadowed in constitutional terms and it provides a very significant marker on the road to that destination. In the short term the argument was specious, for while British control was retained at the Centre, there was no such danger. But it was based on an anxiety which proved well-founded. In 1935, only provincial autonomy was conceded, and in the absence of an Indian government to replace the Raj, the transfer of power eventually took place in conditions which maximized the leverage of the provinces. All this was only seen hazily in 1924, but that it was seen at all shows how strong provincial interests had become. Between the millstone of provincialism and that of the Raj, the *pukka* all-India politician was being ground to a fine powder.

On 3 December 1924, when the Reforms Enquiry Committee Report was signed, Jinnah's ambitions looked capable of fulfilment. The government, by its promulgation of the Bengal Ordinance, had provided a real spur to unity; Gandhi, by his suspension of non-co-operation, had paved the way for a new accession of strength to the Congress; and already, on 21 November, an all-parties conference had met at Bombay and set up a representative committee to devise a united front against the government.

Nonetheless, Jinnah was wary of taking part in unity discussions on other people's terms. Strictly speaking, the suspension of non-co-operation enabled him to rejoin the Congress. But when he considered attending the Belgaum session he found himself in two minds. 'He is apparently of the view', Venkatapatiraju wrote to Purushotamdas Thakurdas, 'that we need not bother ourselves outside the Assembly. My point is that to carry any influence in the Assembly we should have public support.'[155] This was a crucial

154 Ibid., p. 172.
155 Purushotamdas Thakurdas papers, 40: Venkatapatiraju to Thakurdas, 12 Nov. 1924.

difference not only between Venkatapatiraju and Jinnah, but more importantly, between Jinnah and the Swarajists. Jinnah wanted the Swarajists to adopt purely constitutional methods but he had no desire to fight their battles for them. His own position, both as leader of the Independents and as President of the Muslim League, was already secure, and he did not wish to compromise his chances of negotiating with the Congress as an equal by becoming a party to its decisions. The same considerations also affected his participation in the all-parties conference. He only agreed to sit on Gandhi's Unity Committee providing its decisions were not taken by vote. Decisions by majority implied differences of opinion and he was only prepared to subscribe to an agreement which was voluntarily adopted by all parties.[156]

Jinnah was saving himself for negotiations with the Congress. But Mahommed Ali, as Congress President, had already put a number of spokes in his wheel. Jinnah's self-importance, his fine clothes and his precise manner of speech had long been a subject for Mahommed Ali's satire, but by the middle of 1924, with Panislamist enthusiasm at low ebb, Jinnah was no longer just good material for the gossip column of the *Comrade*. If Mahommed Ali had any chance of re-establishing himself as a political leader it was as a purveyor of Hindu-Muslim unity, and Jinnah's efforts to revive the League and to renegotiate the Lucknow Pact provoked a jealous response for that reason. Mahommed Ali opposed the revival of the League;[157] he attended it only to object to the resolution on communal safeguards; and when the session was over, he turned with a new zeal to the promotion of communal harmony.[158] Jinnah was not unduly perturbed so long as Mahommed Ali confined himself to pouring oil on troubled waters: within the League his opposition was manageable and the reduction of communal tension was a desirable end in itself. But he was considerably inconvenienced when Mahommed Ali stopped playing peace-maker and

[156] *Indian Quarterly Register,* 1924, vol. ii, p. 190.
[157] GI Home Poll. 25/1924: Bombay FR II May 1924.
[158] Both Mahommed Ali and Gandhi saw the pursuit of Hindu-Muslim unity as a means of retrieving their political pre-eminence and they worked closely together. In August, they attempted to mediate between the two communities at Delhi after a riot at *Bakr-Id,* and in September, Mahommed Ali was chairman of the reception committee at the Unity conference called during Gandhi's penitential fast after the Kohat riot.

started playing politician.

During the Lahore League, a committee had been appointed to formulate a consitution in consultation with other organizations. This was Jinnah's brainchild and he had great hopes of it.[159] When it made overtures to the Congress, however, it was unceremoniously snubbed. This was the first instance of Mahommed Ali's activities influencing the relations between the two organizations and it prevented the holding of a joint session at Belgaum.

Some of the members of the council [Mushir Hussain Kidwai wrote to Motilal Nehru] were so ruffled by the contemptuous treatment with which the Secretary of the Congress treated the request of the Muslim League constitution committee. . . that it rejected the suggestion of holding the session at the same place where the Congress is going to be held.[160]

More significant still, however, was the attempt made by Gandhi and the Ali brothers to solve the communal tangle in the Punjab by political means. Early in December they visited Lahore and offered the Muslims proportionate representation in the legislatures and services in exchange for the abolition of separate electorates.[161] This offer was both an affront to the League's claim to represent the Muslims and a clear indication of Congress unwillingness to accept the terms laid down at Lahore. It was not ultimately accepted but it showed the way the wind was blowing.[162]

Though relations between the League and the Congress had become testy, both Jinnah and the Swarajists remained anxious for a settlement. When Motilal learned that the League had decided to hold its session at Bombay, he urged Jinnah to change the venue to Belgaum, and, Jinnah, though he claimed it was too late to do so, did postpone the meeting for several days to allow for Congress attendance.[163] At the League itself, the President, Syed Raza Ali,

---

[159] See *Reforms Enquiry Committee*, Appendix 6, *Oral Evidence*, part i: Barkat Ali examined by Jinnah, pp. 426-7.

[160] AICC papers, 37/1925: Kidwai to Nehru, 5 Dec. 1924. The Congress Secretary during Mahommed Ali's presidency was Motilal's son, Jawaharlal.

[161] GI Home Poll. 37/1925: Sir Malcolm Hailey to Sir Alexander Muddiman, 11 Dec. 1924.

[162] Fazli Husain did enter into correspondence with Gandhi but duscussions broke down over separate electorates. See *Collected Works of Gandhi* (*CWG*), vol. xxvi, p. 215: Gandhi to Fazli Husain, 2 March 1925.

[163] AICC papers, 37/1925: Motilal Nehru to Mushir Hussain Kidwai, 8 Dec. 1924.

warned his audience against a merger with the Congress.[164] But Jinnah, whilst acknowledging the differences which had emerged over separate electorates, renewed his plea for an attempt at a settlement.[165] Nor was he unsuccessful. The constitution committee appointed at Lahore was refashioned to accommodate a significantly larger Congress Muslim element, and presumably as a result of Gandhi's intervention, this new committee was subsequently co-opted bodily on to the Unity Committee of the all-parties conference.[166] All this shows that hope was not yet dead.

The main obstacle to a settlement came from the communalist Hindus of the Punjab and the United Provinces. Lajpat Rai, the Punjabi Swarajist leader, was slowly being alienated from the national leadership, and like Malaviya and Chintamani, who had already begun to break Nehru's alliance with the U.P. Muslims in the municipalities, he found the communal war-cry a useful means of consolidating his political position. For both these parties a policy of concession to the Muslims was incompatible with the exploitation of communal fears for political ends, and for the Punjabi party in particular there was the added danger that such concessions would involve their permanent subordination to a Muslim majority by separate electorates.

The most vociferous of these communalists was Lajpat Rai. Between 26 November and 17 December 1924, he published thirteen articles in the *Tribune* criticizing Muslim insistence on absolute rights, stigmatizing Jinnah as a recruit to the communalist Muslim party and condemning communal electorates in the most provocative terms. He told his readers that communal electorates, once accepted, would not be abolished without civil war; that to accept them was to divide the country into Hindu India and Muslim India; and that as the Punjabi Muslims were unwilling to grant weightage to minorities it would be better to partition the Punjab, and if necessary Bengal, and to establish a federation of autonomous Hindu and Muslim states.[167] At the same time, in a circular to prominent Hindus of all provinces, he condemned the Congress for its

---

[164] Pirzada, op.cit., vol. ii (Karachi 1970), p. 17.
[165] *Indian Quarterly Register*, 1924, vol. ii, p. 481.
[166] Mahommed Ali papers: Syed Zahur Ahmed to Mahommed Ali, 12 Jan. 1925.
[167] *Lala Lajpat Rai, His Writings and Speeches*, ed. V.C. Joshi, vol. ii (Delhi 1966), pp. 175-8 and 210-14.

part in the Lucknow Pact and urged them to make the Hindu Mahasabha their political mouthpiece.[168] This call to arms met with a ready response at Belgaum where the Mahasabha's activities took a distinctly political turn for the first time. A committee was appointed to formulate Hindu opinion on the communal question, and its composition was ominous for the future. Amongst others, it consisted of Lajpat Rai, Raja Narendra Nath, Chintamani, Raja Sir Rampal Singh, Jairamdas Daulatram of Sind and, most ominously of all, Nehru's Swarajist allies from the Central Provinces, B.S. Moonji and N.C. Kelkar.[169]

It was these Mahasabhites who frustrated the chances of a new Lucknow Pact when the all-parties conference reconvened at Delhi on 23 January 1925. During the preliminary consultations, when Jinnah urged the committee to attend first to Hindu-Muslim differences, the Mahasabhites did not actually oppose a new settlement. They feigned ignorance of Muslim demands and having first preempted Jinnah's position by condemning both communal representation and the Lucknow Pact they claimed that there was no point in discussing the question until the Muslims laid their cards on the table. It became obvious the following day, however, that this position was mere camouflage. Jinnah's speech demanding recognition for Muslim majorities in Bengal and the Punjab was followed by an uncompromising harangue from Lajpat Rai and there was some danger of the committee being disrupted. This danger was averted by the acceptance of Mrs Besant's proposal for the establishment of two committees, one to formulate a scheme for Swaraj and the other to solve the communal question, but no sooner had the second committee started work than Chintamani announced that its decisions would not be acceptable to the Hindus until they had been endorsed by the Mahasabha. Both Jinnah and Nehru objected to this condition and it was eventually withdrawn at Gandhi's insistence, but the relations between Hindus and Muslims within the committee became steadily worse and on 26 January Hakim Ajmal Khan had to propose an adjournment to allow for the removal of misunderstandings. These misunderstandings, however, were too substantial to be removed and after a further five-minute session on 28 January the committee was adjourned for a month. That in effect

---

[168] Purushotamdas Thakurdas papers, 40: Circular letter, dated 13 Dec. 1924.
[169] *Indian Quarterly Register*, 1924, vol. ii, pp. 485-8.

marked the end of it. It met briefly on 28 February and 1 March but on both occasions the attendance was too poor for any profitable discussions. After the January session, even Jinnah had ceased to take any real interest in it, and apart from Swami Shradhanand, the attendance was confined to Gandhi, Motilal Nehru, the Ali brothers and a few Assembly politicians.[170]

The Mahasabhites, having achieved their purpose, stayed well away. But it was significant for the future that they were able to hold the Congress to ransom. Nehru and Gandhi, though keen for a settlement, were not prepared to make concessions in the face of Mahasabha opposition. They chose instead to leave well alone. In a communiqué issued at Delhi on 2 March, they informed the public that there was no likelihood of a settlement; and three days later in Bombay, Gandhi told reporters that he intended to put the Hindu-Muslim problem on one side. It was an insoluble riddle and he had no alternative but to wait on God for its solution.[171]

After the failure of the all-parties conference, the division between Nehru and Jinnah definitely widened. Nehru, faced with the political machinations of the Mahasabha, became more obstructionist in the Assembly, whereas Jinnah, despite his sense of disappointment, refused to lend support to what he considered wrecking tactics. In the spring of 1925 the two men began to disagree publicly, and the united front against government collapsed. Jinnah thwarted the Swarajists in their attempt to throw out both the Railway Budget and the Finance Bill, and they in their turn made him the butt of prolonged attacks during both these debates. The speeches of Vithalbhai Patel were largely devoted to criticism of Jinnah,[172] and Jamnadas Mehta, in the debate on the Finance Bill, even accused him of being 'the leader of communal strife in this country'.[173] This was a stray allegation from a personal enemy and Jinnah repudiated it with some heat.[174] Moreover, the fact that it was not made in this form by either Patel or Nehru suggests that it did not ring true. Nonetheless, though Jinnah could not legitimately be accused of

[170] AICC papers, G72/1925; *Indian Quarterly Register,* 1925, vol. i, pp. 66-7.

[171] *CWG,* vol. xxvi, pp. 232-4.

[172] *ILA Debates,* vol. 5, part ii, 25 Feb. 1925, pp. 1504-10; *ILA Debates,* vol. 5, part ii, 16 March 1925, pp. 2422-41.

[173] Ibid., 16 March 1925, p. 2462.

[174] Ibid., p. 2478.

stirring up communal strife, he had undertaken to secure better
terms for the majority-province Muslims and having failed in that
endeavour he could not both be true to his Muslim clients and
support the Swarajists unreservedly. There is no explicit evidence
that he modified his position as a result of the all-parties conference
but the likelihood remains very strong.

However, this was only one side of the story. Jinnah had been
anxious for a settlement to strengthen his hand in the debate on the
Muddiman report,[175] and though no settlement was forthcoming he
continued to press the government to allow the report to be debated.[176]
As Lord Reading was about to visit England to confer with the new
Secretary of State, however, the government decided to postpone
the debate until his return. Both Jinnah and Nehru condemned
this decision, and a vote was carried against the government on this
issue.[177] Jinnah, however, continued to coax the government with
offers of co-operation, whereas Nehru adopted a derisive attitude
towards government promises. The response of the new Secretary
of State, Nehru told the Assembly, could easily be predicted. Butler,
Sly, Wheeler, Vincent and Blackett would all be in London at the
same time as the Viceroy and they would effectively quash any
proposals for advance. The House had been gagged over the
Reforms Enquiry Committee Report, and its effect on Government
policy was about as great as the squeaking of a rat in an Honourable
Member's bedroom.[178] Though the two men disagreed publicly,
however, privately they appear to have seen each other as comple-
mentary elements in the same endeavour. Nehru was the stick;
Jinnah the carrot. 'Please do not allow yourself to be disturbed',
Nehru wrote to Purushotamdas Thakurdas, 'until you come to the
end of the chapter. Do not for a moment think that we are creating
an impassable gulf between ourselves. We can afford to fight like
Kilkenny cats and still be friends.'[179]

[175] Indian Quarterly Register, 1925, vol. i, p. 73.

[176] Birkenhead papers (IOL MSS Eur. D 703) 1: Reading to Birkenhead, 19 Feb.
1925.

[177] The political situation was debated when the demand for the expenses of the
Viceroy's Executive Council was put to the Assembly. See *ILA Debates*, vol. 5, part iii,
14 March 1925, pp. 2344-404.

[178] Ibid., pp. 2346-7.

[179] Purushotamdas Thakurdas papers, 40: Motilal Nehru to Thakurdas, 27 April
1925. See also Broomfield, *op.cit.*, pp. 263-6. These sources suggest that both Nehru
and Das hoped that Reading's visit to England would result in an honourable peace.

As it turned out, Nehru's derisive utterances were more apt than his private hopes. Reading visited England not to discuss political reform but to devise a formula for pouring cold water on nationalist aspirations. He had viewed the Muddiman Committee merely as an expedient for holding the situation in check,[180] and contrary to Jinnah's expectations he had been thoroughly unimpressed with the policy of rational protest.[181] In 1924, with a Labour government in office and the Nationalists in control of the Assembly, he had shown distinct signs of strain; in 1925, with a Conservative government in office and Jinnah and Nehru at loggerheads, he was strengthened in his determination to stand firm.[182]

On 7 July, in the House of Lords, Lord Birkenhead put paid to hopes of immediate reform. He did not entirely rule out the possibility of an early statutory commission but he made it plain that no concession could be expected until Indian leaders had co-operated in the working of the Reforms.[183] This speech was a turning-point for the politics of confrontation. Until that time, Nehru's leadership and Swarajist tactics had been unchallenged and a victory at the all-India level seemed possible. Afterwards, both were rejected, and many provincial battalions withdrew from the battle and made overtures to the enemy. Consequently, Nehru was obliged to cease front-line operations and to take up the task of quelling rebellion amongst his own forces. To do that successfully, however, he eventually had to quit the legislature and to resume non-co-operation.

But the most crestfallen politician was Jinnah. It was his policy which had suffered a reverse and when the Muddiman Report was eventually debated his patience for once gave way to a mood of unrestrained exasperation :

I again here ask the Government, I ask Lord Birkenhead, I ask Lord Reading, what is your answer to those men who have cooperated with you? None. Your answer to me as one who has not non-

---

[180] Birkenhead papers, 1: Reading to Birkenhead, 26 March 1925.

[181] Reading had considered the Muddiman Committee valuable precisely because it was likely to split the Swarajists and the Independents. See Reading papers, 7: Reading to Olivier, 17 April and 22 May 1924.

[182] See Reading papers, 7: Reading to Olivier, 13 March, 17 April, 13 Aug., 18 Sept. and 28 Oct. 1924; also Birkenhead papers, 1: Reading to Birkenhead, 12 Feb. 26 Feb. and 19 March 1925.

[183] *Indian Quarterly Register*, 1925, vol. i, pp. 337-47.

cooperated with you is this: 'Will you bring a section of the politically minded people, who happen to be the largest political party,
will you bring them down to their knees? Will you bring Pandit
Motilal Nehru to bow before the throne at Viceregal Lodge and
say: 'Sir, I am humble, I crawl before you, and will you now graciously be pleased to give me a Royal Commission?" Is that what you
want? What has Pandit Motilal Nehru been doing in this Assembly?
Has he not been cooperating with you? I want to know what more
you want, and may I know what evidence, what proof, documentary
or oral, do you want me to produce or adduce that the responsible
leaders are willing to cooperate with you? Have you no eyes, have
you no ears, have you no brains?[184]

This was the speech of a man who had fought and lost an important
battle. Unlike Nehru, Jinnah could find no solace in non-co-operation.
All he could do was to take up Birkenhead's challenge and work the
Reforms for what they were worth. He had already pursued this
policy on a small scale in Bombay[185] and he proceeded to advocate
it on a national scale. In July, he made overtures to Jayakar, the
Bombay Swarajist, and in November he also tried to form a party
with discontented Congressmen from the Central Provinces.[186] Yet
the further he moved towards Congress dissidents, the further he
moved away from the most powerful elements in the League. This
was a paradox which could not be resolved. To support Nehru was
to support a policy of non-co-operation and Hindu-Muslim Unity:
to support his opponents was to support a policy of co-operation and
Hindu-Muslim antagonism. Jinnah could not have his cake and
eat it. He escaped to Europe in 1926 as a member of the Skeen
Committee and he did not become prominent again until after the
1926 elections.

Communalism and the Congress: the 1926 elections

After Birkenhead's announcement, the confrontation with the Raj
ceased to hold the centre of the stage and its place was taken by a
conflict between Nehru and his opponents. Opposition to Nehru
came from two main sources; firstly from his own allies in the Central

---

[184] *ILA Debates*, vol. 6, part ii, 8 Sept. 1925, pp. 940-1.
[185] Purushotamdas Thakurdas papers, 40: Jinnah to Thakurdas, circular letter, 22
May 1925; M.R. Jayakar, op.cit., vol. ii, pp. 558-60.
[186] Jayakar, op.cit., vol. ii, pp. 590-1 and 705-6.

Provinces and Bombay, and in particular from the Tilakite Congress organizations in Maharashtra, C.P. (Marathi) and Berar; and secondly from the communal Hindus of the Punjab and the U.P. and their allies in Sind, C.P. (Hindi), Bihar and Orissa, and Bengal. The main point at issue was office-acceptance. Nehru had built his all-India organization on the rejection of the Reforms and a demand that the constitution be completely overhauled. Yet having failed to budge the British, he had to face a demand that the Reforms be worked for what they were worth. This had been Tilak's advice to his followers in the Deccan in 1920 and though they had bowed first to Gandhi and then to Nehru they now sought to implement that advice. In early October, Tambe, a Swarajist leader in Berar, flouted party discipline and accepted office. Nehru condemned his action only to find it being compared to his own in accepting a seat on the Skeen Committee; and before the year was out, despite efforts to patch up differences, a full-scale revolt had taken place.[187] At the same time, in North India, Malaviya's activities had become more overtly political. In August, the working committee of the Mahasabha decided to set up candidates for the forthcoming elections if other candidates were inimical to Hindu interests,[188] and in September, Malaviya began to give all-India importance to the issue of music before mosques. On 5 September, his relative, Pandit Rama Kant Malaviya, told a joint Hindu-Muslim meeting at the Collector's house at Allahabad that local Hindus could not agree to stop music before mosques until there was an all-India settlement[189] and on 21 September, Malaviya himself saw the Home Member in this connection.[190] Malaviya was slower than the Maharashtrians to come out in favour of responsive co-operation but this escalation of communal issues from the local level to the all-India level was an indication of his rising political ambition.

Both these groups clashed jointly with Nehru at the Kanpur Congress. Nehru proposed a resolution reaffirming the faith of the Congress in civil disobedience, insisting on non-acceptance of office as the party programme for the 1926 elections, and calling for a

[187] See Nanda, op.cit., pp. 263-5.

[188] AICC papers, G 47/1926: Pandit Dev Ratan Sharma to Motilal Nehru, 29 April 1926.

[189] GUPGAD 680/1925: Note by Crosthwaite, Collector of Allahabad, enclosed with Smith to Alexander, 7 Sept. 1925.

[190] GI Home Poll. 368/1925: Note by Sir Alexander Muddiman, 21 Sept. 1925.

withdrawal of Swarajists from the legislatures if the National Demand
had not been met by February 1926. Malaviya proposed an amendment urging the Congress to work the Reforms to the best possible
advantage, replacing the National demand of February 1924 with
the less extreme demand of September 1925, and deleting all
reference to civil disobedience and resignation.[191] Malaviya was
supported by Jayakar, the leader of the Bombay Swarajists, Kelkar,
Tilak's lieutenant at Poona, Aney, the party leader in Berar, and
Moonji, the key man at Nagpur, but Nehru ultimately carried the
day.[192] Nonetheless, the scene was set for a substantial political battle
in the crucial months before the 1926 elections.

The Mahasabhites and the Maharashtrians were fighting a political
battle but they were using communal weapons. Malaviya had already found communal war-cries useful for dividing Nehru from
his Muslim supporters in the U.P. municipalities; and in the Central
Provinces and Bombay, though the Muslims were less of an obstacle
to office-acceptance, the same cries of Hindu unity served to rally
support for the Brahmin party and to divert attention from the
growing non-Brahmin challenge both in local self-government and
in the services. The battle between Nehru and his opponents,
therefore, was not only significant for the political future of the
Congress but also for the chances of Hindu-Muslim unity at the all-
India level. The crucial factor was Nehru's ability to cope with the
opposition which now faced him. Would he be able to defeat the
forces of communalism or would he be obliged to compromise with
them in order to survive?

The central plank in Nehru's platform — non-acceptance of office —
was dictated by his concern to preserve a strong national opposition
to the Raj. Unlike in 1937, when the Congress possessed majorities
in eight provinces and could take office without compromising its
national position, in 1926 the Congress possessed only one strong
majority, in the Central Provinces, and one shaky one, in Bengal.
Elsewhere, with the communal temperature running high and alliances with Muslim members virtually out of the question, office-acceptance involved not only compromising the Congress creed in order
to ally with other parties but also co-operating with the Raj itself. It

[191] For the demand of Sept. 1925, see *ILA Debates,* vol. 6, part ii, 7 Sept. 1925,
pp. 854-5.
[192] *Indian Quarterly Register,* 1925, vol. ii, pp. 331-40.

involved, in short, the end of the Congress as a disciplined national opposition party and the transformation of the national confrontation into a number of fragmentary provincial confrontations. Moreover, in the U.P., Nehru's own political base, it was tantamount to capitulation to Malaviya. Thus both for personal and national reasons, office-acceptance had to be resisted.

Nonetheless, the trend towards office-acceptance had to be balanced against the need to preserve the Congress as a comprehensive political organization: Nehru did not proceed recklessly when the allegiance of entire Congress provinces was at stake. If the Swarajists of Maharashtra, C.P. (Marathi) and Berar were totally alienated, the Congress would be virtually unrepresented in those provinces and Nehru thus strove manfully to discover common ground between his own position and that of his former allies. Between October 1925, when Tambe accepted office, and May 1926, when the Sabarmati Pact became a dead letter, he held innumerable meetings and wrote endless letters cajoling and encouraging the Maharashtrians to stand by the Swarajist creed until after the 1926 elections. Indeed he was prepared to hold out hopes of office-acceptance after the elections as an incentive for continued allegiance.[193] It was only when these negotiations broke down irretrievably that he disaffiliated the committees in question and appointed fresh ones to take their place.[194]

Nehru's efforts to retain the allegiance of the Bombay and C.P. Swarajists illustrate the working of a principle which had important repercussions for Hindu-Muslim unity when applied to the Punjab and Bengal. The Punjab Congress was divided into two main factions, the first led by Lajpat Rai and closely associated with the Hindu Sabha, and the second led by Dr Satyapal and Girdharilal and based on a cross-communal alliance of Hindus, Muslims and Sikhs. Lajpat Rai was the leading Punjabi Swarajist,[195] but after his return from Europe in 1924 his activities had become increasingly communal. He had campaigned against the Congress leadership on the Mahasabha platform; he had repudiated the Lucknow Pact and he had demanded the abolition of separate electorates. Had Nehru put the

---

[193] AICC papers, 21/1926: Motilal Nehru to M.S. Aney, 7 Jan. 1926.

[194] See Gordon, op.cit., pp. 261 and 264-6.

[195] Lajpat Rai was returned to the Assembly as a Swarajist at a by-election in Dec. 1925. See V.C. Joshi, op.cit., vol i, pp. xlix-l.

secular image of the Congress first, he would have withdrawn his support from Lajpat Rai and backed Satyapal and Girdharilal instead. This he did not do. Indeed so long as Lajpat Rai toed the party line on office-acceptance, Nehru did nothing to offend him. He realized that relations between the communities in the Punjab were thoroughly polarized and that the Congress stood little chance of success without an electoral adjustment with the Hindu Sabha.[196] Consequently even when Satyapal and Girdharilal succeeded in reaching an agreement with the Khilafatists whereby joint electorates would be accepted after six years, he ignored their appeals and showed signs of sacrificing them to Lajpat Rai.[197] When both factions put forward nominations for the 1926 elections, the working committee approved only those names which appeared on both lists, and left all others to be discussed with Lajpat Rai himself.[198] It was only in September when Lajpat Rai ceased opposing office-acceptance and joined Malaviya in opposing the Congress that Nehru threw his weight behind Satyapal.[199] In order to secure better Congress representation, he was obviously willing to back a communally oriented party, providing it did not err on office-acceptance, in preference to a more secular party with less chance of success.

A similar situation also obtained in Bengal where the death of Das exacerbated internal divisions within the Congress organization. As a result of Gandhi's intervention, Das's mantle fell first on J.M. Sen Gupta, a native of Chittagong with a following in the Northern and Eastern divisions. Sen Gupta continued Das's policy, particularly with regard to the Bengal Pact, but he met with intense opposition, notably from the *Karmi Sangh*, a Congress workers party with revolutionary sympathies. The *Karmi Sangh* derived much of its ideological impetus from Hindu mythology and, encouraged by Malaviya and G.D. Birla, it sought by hook or by crook to secure the Pact's abrogation. The Pact was first rescinded on 22 May 1926, after Sen Gupta had adjourned a stormy meeting for fear of defeat; it was then reinstated on 13 June, in the presence of Sarojini Naidu and Kalam Azad; and finally, it was quietly dropped by Sen Gupta

---

[196] AICC papers, G 47/1926: K. Santanam to Nehru, 6 April 1926.

[197] AICC papers, G 57(ii)/1926: Girdharilal to Motilal Nehru, 11 June 1926; Girdharilal to Sarojini Naidu, 30 June 1926.

[198] AICC papers, G 57 (iii)/1926: Rangaswami Iyengar to Nehru, 14 July 1926.

[199] AICC papers, G 57(v)/1926: Rangaswami Iyengar to Nehru, 20 Oct. 1926.

himself as the price of an electoral alliance with the *Karmi*. Where Das's Muslim alliance was concerned, the working committee was not impassive. Yet a note written by Nehru at the height of the Bengal dispute shows that beyond sending Sarojini Naidu to Calcutta it was a virtually powerless spectator:

I do hope that all parties will join to save the Congress. If they do not, we can only do our duty and leave it to the party in power to carry out the Congress resolutions as best they can. If this party turns hostile to the Congress nothing can save it and we must submit to the inevitable.[200]

Faced with a choice between no representation in Bengal and a party of communal inclinations, the Congress inevitably chose the communal party; and it did not cease to support Sen Gupta even after he had dropped the Pact and alienated his Muslim supporters.[201]

Nehru also wooed the Mahasabha. In a statement read in his absence to the Hindu Mahasabha at Delhi on 15 March 1926, Nehru urged the Sabha to join the Congress rather than start a separate political organization of its own.[202] Moreover, even when this advice was disregarded, and the Mahasabha both confirmed its decision to set up candidates where necessary and demanded that all political parties should allow free voting on communal questions, Nehru continued to be conciliatory. He took his stand not on the need to protect minorities but on the demands of party discipline, and as in his dealings with the Maharashtrians, he encouraged the Mahasabhites to remain in the Congress in the hope of securing a victory for their policy when the elections results were out.[203] Nehru also showed distinct signs of flexibility where separate electorates were concerned. The working committee laid down that no Congressman could move a resolution for the abolition of separate electorates until there was general agreement between the Hindu and Muslim members of the legislatures in question, but it conceded a free vote for Congressmen on motions introduced by non-Con-

[200] AICC papers, G 57(iii)/1926: Note by Nehru on the situation in Bengal, 27 June 1926.
[201] For a fuller discussion of the Bengal dispute, see Gordon, op.cit., pp. 270-6; also *Indian Quarterly Register,* 1926, vol. i, pp. 65-100.
[202] *Indian Quarterly Register,* 1926, vol. i, pp. 407-8.
[203] AICC papers, 24/1926: Nehru to Dev Ratan Sharma, 22 May 1926.

gressman and this was a clear loophole for the Mahasabha.[204] It also attempted to secure from Lord Irwin, the new Viceroy, through the offices of Vithalbhai Patel, a guarantee that there would be no further extension of communal electorates to local self-government.[205] This was a cardinal plank in Lajpat Rai's platform and it shows how anxious Nehru was to keep him happy.

But it was Nehru's attitude towards Reforms for the Frontier which caused most suspicion amongst his Muslim followers. The Muslim League had supported Reforms for the Frontier from May 1924,[206] but the Mahasabha had never been sympathetic towards the idea, and after the Kohat riot of September 1924, its opposition intensified. Lajpat Rai played on Hindu fears of an Afghan invasion both at the all-parties conference in January 1925[207] and as President of the Mahasabha in April,[208] and faced with these divided counsels, the Congress remained silent. Matters came to a head in February 1926, however, when Syed Murtuza, a Swarajist from Madras, drew first place in a ballot to move a resolution on this question in the Assembly. The ballot took place on 1 February, and on 9 February, allegedly at Lajpat Rai's instigation, Nehru called a Swarajist meeting and opposed the moving of the resolution, firstly on the technical ground that the Executive had not been given twelve hours notice, and secondly on the political ground that the Swarajist party could not support the introduction of Dyarchy on the Frontier whilst condemning it elsewhere. All four of the Swarajist Muslims at the meeting wished the resolution to be moved, if necessary by a non-Swarajist, but Nehru remained adamant and the meeting was adjourned. The following day, owing to a secession of Muslim support, the Swarajists failed to prevent the consideration of a Government Bill to amend the Criminal Procedure Code,[209] and

---

[204] AICC papers, 57(ii)/1926: Nehru to Rangaswami Iyengar, 25 June 1926. Mahommed Ali objected to this decision but he was overruled.

[205] Halifax papers (IOL MSS Eur. C 152) 2: Irwin to Birkenhead, 8 July 1926.

[206] See Pirzada, op.cit., vol. i, p. 580, and vol. ii, pp. 26 and 70.

[207] AICC papers, G 72/1925.

[208] *Indian Quarterly Register,* 1925, vol. i, pp. 379-80.

[209] The resolution to consider the Bill was carried by 52 votes to 45. Five Swarajists (Syed Murtuza, Shafi Daudi, Yusuf Imam, Nawab Ismail and Khwaja Abdul Karim) and three other likely Muslim supporters (Mahommed Yakub, Sadiq Hassan and Mahmood Schamnad) did not vote. See *ILA Debates,* vol. 7, part ii, 10 Feb. 1926, p. 1081.

efforts were then made to produce a compromise. Nehru produced a formula to the effect that the Reforms demanded by the Assembly in February 1924 and September 1925 were intended for the people of India as a whole, including the inhabitants of the Frontier, but though this was acceptable as a bare minimum to the Frontier Muslims, it was made unacceptable at a party meeting on 15 February by the addition, on Lajpat Rai's insistence, of the clause, 'subject to such redistribution of provinces as may be found necessary'. This addition gave rise to the suspicion that Congress was only prepared to support Reforms for the Frontier at the cost of the Frontier's independence, and this suspicion was strengthened when Nehru made amalgamation with the Punjab a party question. At that point Syed Murtuza and Shafi Daudi resigned from the party, Syed Murtuza proceeded to move his original resolution, and the scene was set for a party split along communal lines in the Assembly. Nehru ultimately avoided that contingency by revising his original order and instructing the party to remain neutral,[210] but he did nothing further to reassure his Muslim supporters and the whole matter was eventually debated in the press.

Syed Murtuza's charge against Nehru was that he had sacrificed the Frontier Muslims in order to gain Lajpat Rai's support in the 1926 elections:

I was driven to the conclusion [he wrote] that a considerable part of the Hindu opposition to the extension of the Reforms to the Frontier province was based on considerations that are not provincial but are imported into these discussions from other provinces of India, and in particular from the Punjab. In no other province are the Hindus in such a small minority as in the Frontier and being in most provinces in large majorities...the most communally minded Hindu can pose as a Nationalist and pretend that he asks for the abolition of communal representation and of separate electorates only because their existence is incompatible with nationalism...If the Frontier province remains a separate province and also secures the Reforms this pose of Nationalism cannot possibly be maintained any longer. One need not be a prophet to predict that the moment the Reforms are granted...the Hindu minority, which is as insignificant as our own in my own province, will begin to clamour as vociferously as the most nervous or the most greedy Mussulman seeking adequate and effective separate communal representation....

---

210 On 16 Feb., the debate was adjourned on a government motion, and when it resumed on 18 March, the Swarajist walk-out had already taken place.

This is the reason why the Punjab Hindus and their Hindu supporters of other provinces brought pressure to bear on the leader of the Swaraj party, who is openly and obviously in need of their support against Pandit Madan Mohan Malaviya and the Hindus Sabhas at his back....[211]

Nehru did not attempt to refute this charge in detail: he merely re-affirmed his personal opposition to all forms of communalism.[212] Yet, as Shafi Daudi pointed out in reply to Nehru's statement, there was a difference between personal ideology and political practice:

I have not charged him, nor has any other Mussulman, so far as I know, with 'positive hostility to Musulman interest' as he has stated. But what I, and all Mussulmans with whom I had occasion to talk over the matter, do charge him with is his weak surrender to those who are universally credited with 'positive hostility to Musulman interest.' He is not himself communally biassed and he will never find me hesitating to admit his lifelong freedom from that kind of communalism, but it is not true that he has been fighting against that vice. It is his failure to fight that vice when that fight was most necessary in the interests of the country and of the Swaraj party itself that is our charge against him. Freedom from a vice in one's person is one thing and fighting against that vice in others is quite another thing.[213]

In the United Provinces, Nehru faced not the secession of an entire Congress organization but a challenge to his own control of the party machine. Malaviya was supporting office-acceptance, maximizing his contacts with Hindu landlords and using a communal platform as a means of rallying support. He had already defeated Nehru's Swarajist alliance in the 1925 municipal elections,[214] and from the Spring of 1926 he began to use the same methods for provincial ends.[215] Nehru did not want an outright battle with

---

[211] *The Frontier Question in the Assembly, being the statements of Pandit Motilal Nehru, MLA, Maulvi Shafi Daudi, MLA, and Syed Murtuza, MLA* (Comrade Press, Delhi 1926), pp. 26-7.

[212] Ibid., p. 36.

[213] Ibid., p. 40.

[214] GI Home Poll. 25/1924: U.P. FR I Dec. 1925.

[215] See GUPGAD 246 and 613/1926, and GI Home Poll. 112/iv/1926: U.P. FR I June, I July, II Aug. and I Sept. 1926. The chief issue was music before mosques. Malaviya attempted to secure a general ruling from the government: the government stuck rigidly to precedent and custom. Riots took place both at the *Id* and the *Ram Lila.*

Malaviya: he realized the implications of Malaviya's activities for communal relations and he knew that with the aid of Birla's lakhs Malaviya would be in a strong position. Nonetheless, though he wanted a compromise, he was not prepared to compromise on Malaviya's terms, and after September, when negotiations broke down, an outright battle took place.[216] In that battle, Malaviya used every communal device available. Nehru was accused of being a beef-eater; the Congress was stigmatized as a prostitute of Muslim India; and such was the communal hatred aroused that Nehru afterwards considered retiring from public life in disgust.[217] Yet though his every personal sentiment revolted against Malaviya's tactics, Nehru could not ignore the atmosphere which those tactics created.

An indication of the depth of communal tension and its political implications is provided by a letter from the Secretary of the Delhi PCC to the Congress President, Sarojini Naidu:

You know [he wrote] that Delhi is the one place in the whole of India where we have got joint electorates; and during the coming elections the question of having joint electorates all round in future will be put to the test here. The Muslim and Hindu votes are in ratio of 1 to 2 and the PCC Delhi has put up Mr Asaf Ali, bar at law, as their candidate for the Assembly. It has to be admitted that Mr Asaf Ali's work and his sacrifice during the noncooperation have been of a very high order. And if judged impartially the choice of the PCC Delhi in this respect cannot be questioned.

It is a matter of very great regret, if not of positive shame, that the Hindus of Delhi do not realise the importance and significance of the Delhi elections, and swayed by communal currents are determined upon putting up Hindu candidates on communal tickets. . . . The result is a foregone conclusion; the Muslim candidate fails simply because he is a Muslim. *And quite naturally this incident would furnish a very strong illustration, to be quoted in and out of season by all those who swear by separate electorates all round.*[218] [original italics].

Elsewhere, Nehru had to campaign within a solely Hindu electorate, and with communal feeling running high he was obliged to recruit

---

[216] See AICC papers, G 57(iv)/1926: Tgm, Nehru to Rangaswami Iyengar, 5 Sept. 1926 and draft reply. The negotiations broke down because Nehru and Iyengar, primarily for reasons of party discipline, were not prepared to concede free voting on communal questions.

[217] *A Bunch of Old Letters, written mostly to Jawaharlal Nehru and some written by him* (Bombay 1960), pp. 51-3: Motilal to Jawaharlal, Dec. 1926.

[218] AICC papers, G 52(i)/1926: Shankar Lal to Sarojini Naidu, 22 Aug. 1926.

candidates who would fare well in that political atmosphere. At Jhansi, the Swarajist candidate would gladly have stood as Malaviya's nominee and did in fact receive his blessing. 'Men like Pandit Bhagwat Narayan Bhargava and Jhanni Lal Pande are not Swarajists in the old sense,' commented the government, 'and in voting for them the majority of people have no idea of a vote subversive of Government. All parties are in the end opposition parties. The only difference is that the Swarajist party will be a better organised opposition.'[219] Another comment on Nehru's campaign is provided by his attempt, even before negotiations with Malaviya broke down, to capture the U.P. Hindu Sabha,[220] and by his willingness, once the campaign was under way, to exploit orthodox Hindu opposition to Malaviya as a means of disarming his communal appeal.[221] Recourse to such tactics did not imply that Nehru had become more communal in his personal outlook, yet in recognizing the necessity of combating Malaviya with his own weapons, he inevitably increased his reliance on communal forces. Indeed, in Rohilkhund, such was the impression created by Swarajist tactics that it was commonly thought the two men would join hands after the election.[222]

Though Nehru made considerable concessions to communal feeling, the election results were disastrous for his party. In both the U.P. and the Punjab, the Swarajists lost seats to the communalists. In the U.P., from thirty-one members in 1923, they were reduced to sixteen members in 1926. Nehru was thoroughly routed by Malaviya in Oudh, and without Pant's activities in the west the result would have been even more disappointing. In the Punjab, the party lost six seats, only two of Nehru's nominees being elected compared with nine of Lajpat Rai's. In the Central Provinces, the Congress lost its hold over the council. From a strength of thirty-five in 1923, the party was reduced to seventeen members in 1926. The Res-

[219] GI Home Poll. 112/X/1926: U.P. FRII Oct. 1926.

[220] AICC papers, 13/1926: Sitla Sahai to Motilal Nehru, 13 July, 20 July, 23 July, 27 July and 4 Aug. 1926.

[221] See, for example, AICC papers, 10/1926: Tgm Motilal Nehru to the manager, *Aj*, Benares, 26 Nov. 1926: 'Print immediately 5000 copies manifesto of sanyasis Benares published in recent issue of *Aj* against Malaviya's party and send by special messenger to Nandkumar Sahai Vakil Sivan.'

[222] GI Home Poll. 112/X/1926: U.P. FR I Nov. 1926.

ponsivists won nine seats and Malaviya's Independent Congress party ten. Both these parties accepted office, and salaries were voted by 55 votes to 16 on 11 January 1927.[223] In Bombay, the party lost thirteen seats and was reduced to a strength of twelve, and in Bengal, though it retained its original size, largely by an amalgamation of Hindu Swarajists and Independents, it lost all its Muslim support and failed to prevent the formation of a ministry.[224] The only bright spots were Madras and Bihar. In Madras, from a strength of ten in 1923, largely by absorbing liberal defectors and followers of Mrs Besant, the party secured the return of forty-seven members in 1926. As in Bengal, however, it achieved success at the cost of its connections with non-co-operation. In Bihar, one of the strongholds of non-co-operation, only eight Swarajists had been returned in 1923, but in 1926, following the conversion of Rajendra Prasad, the number increased to thirty-five. In the Assembly, the size of the party was not greatly altered but it ceased to be dominated by the United Provinces. Of thirty-eight members, eleven came from Madras and nine from Bihar and Orissa. Only five came from the U.P., four from Bengal, three each from Bombay and the Punjab, two from Assam and one from the Central Provinces.

The loss of support amongst Muslims was even greater. In the Central Provinces, where the Swarajists had possessed one Muslim follower in the local council and sent one to the Assembly, no Muslim was returned to either legislature in 1926. In Bengal, relations between the Congress and the Muslims were so bad that no Muslim stood on the Congress ticket. There had been fifteen Muslim Swarajists in 1923: there was none in 1926. In the Punjab, no Muslim stood on the Congress ticket in 1923 and none stood in 1926. Even those Khilafatists who sympathized with the Congress realized that to do so would be self-defeating whilst separate electorates persisted.[225] In the United Provinces, where eleven Muslims had been nominated and four returned in 1923, only six were nominated and only one returned in 1926. Of the original eleven only one was renominated, Maulvi Zahuruddin, the member

[223] IOR/L/P & J/6/267/1927: Secretary, GI Home (Public) to Secretary, Public and Judicial Department, India Oiffice, 20 Jan. 1927.

[224] In Bengal, ministerial salaries were voted by 94 votes to 38 on 17 Jan. 1927. See *Bengal Legislative Council Progs.*, vol. 24, pp. 51-2.

[225] AICC papers, 47/1926: K. Santanam to Nehru, 6 April 1926.

for Bareilly and Shahjehanpur cum Moradabad, and he was the only one returned. Not only had Muslim support decreased: there had been a virtually complete change of personnel. Indeed the indications are that Nehru concentrated on supporting Independent candidates in the hope that they would join the party once elected.[226] Only in Bihar was this dreary picture relieved, chiefly as a result of Shafi Daudi's activities. Despite his differences with Nehru over the Frontier question, Shafi Daudi campaigned vigorously for the Swarajists and prevented Muslim Congressmen from being alienated by Malaviya's activities. On 6 October, he wrote to Nehru from Monghyr:

As to running about in 3rd class and in bullock carts and wading through kneedeep waters to approach the influential voters in the interior, you will hardly find another example except in Bihar.
We had to struggle hard for want of funds when came Malaviyaji to Patna and opened up the strings of his purse and carried away some of our zealous but avaricious Hindu workers. Mussulmans were seen to be anxious to follow the example of their Hindu brethren but could not succeed in creating disruption in Muslim workers' ranks and the proposed party fell through. Now the Mussulman candidates are being opposed by Government men or men of pro-Government tendencies but in their individual capacity.[227]

Ultimately fourteen Swarajist Muslims stood for eighteen seats and six were returned. These were almost the only Muslims returned to provincial councils on the Congress ticket throughout North India.[228]

In the Central Assembly, of the eight Swarajist Muslims returned in 1923, only three were returned in 1926. The two Bengalis and the Assamese did not stand, nor did the C.P. Muslim, Samiullah Khan of Nagpur. Of the other four, Shafi Daudi, Sarfaraz Hussain Khan and Yusuf Imam were returned again on the Swarajist ticket,

[226] Halfiz Mahommed Ibrahim, who was returned from Bijnor, got the best of both worlds. He was not only supported by Nehru, unofficially, but also by the pro-government elements. He undertook to support the Swarajists after his election. He utilized the same tactic, though with more dramatic consequences, in 1937. See AICC papers 21/1926: Nehru to the Rani Sahiba of Dhampur, 24 Oct. 1926; Abdul Latif to Nehru, 30 Nov. 1926.

[227] AICC papers, 21/1926: Shafi Daudi to Nehru, 6 Oct. 1926.

[228] Apart from four Muslims returned on the Swarajist ticket in Madras, the only others elected to local councils were two Khojas in Bombay and Maulvi Zahuruddin in the U.P.

while Nawab Ismail Khan got back as an Independent.[229] Syed Murtuza, a Khilafatist in 1923, was returned as a Swarajist in 1926. The only new blood came from Bihar and the U.P. From Bihar, Maulvi Badiuzzaman was returned by the Bhagalpur Muslims, and from the U.P., Tassaduq Sherwani from the Cities and Rafi Ahmed Kidwai from Oudh. Both Sherwani and Kidwai, however, were close friends of the Nehru family,[230] and their election was not an indication of a mass following in the U.P. Indeed, the narrower Assembly franchise may well have worked in their favour: their colleague, Khaliquzzaman, who stood for the U.P. Council from the Lucknow, Unao, and Hardoi constituency, was soundly defeated by the Raja of Salempur.[231]

When Nehru contemplated these results[232] with the Gauhati Congress in prospect he was profoundly discouraged:

The Malaviya-Lala gang [he wrote to his son] aided by Birla's money are making frantic efforts to capture the Congress. They will probably succeed as no counter effort is possible from our side. I shall probably make a public declaration after the Congress and with it resign my seat in the Assembly though I am still acclaimed as the leader of the strongest party in the country. We can do no possible good in the Assembly or the Councils with our present numbers and the kind of men we have.[233]

As it turned out, such despondency was unwarranted. The Malaviya-Lala gang did not make a bid for power at Gauhati: Nehru's leadership was confirmed and all Swarajist motions were carried by large majorities. Nonetheless, where Congress relations with the Muslims were concerned, the Gauhati Congress produced an incident which augured ill for the future. If the Congress had retained any Muslim support at all, it was because it had not repudiated separate electorates, yet at Gauhati fifty-four members, including not only communalists like Gauri Shanker Misra and M.S. Aney,

---

[229] Nawab Ismail had disagreed with Nehru's 'walk-out' policy as early as Oct. 1925. AICC papers, 9/1925: Motilal Nehru to Nawab Ismail Khan, 2 Oct. 1925.

[230] Kidwai was Motilal's Secretary and Sherwani was a close friend of Jawaharlal's from their Cambridge days.

[231]See Khaliquzzaman, op. cit., pp. 87-8.

[232]Except where otherwise acknowledged, the foregoing anylysis of election results is based on information contained in Gordon, op. cit., pp. 181-2, 291-312 and appendices i to ix, pp. 321-79.

[233] *A Bunch of Old Letters*, p. 52: *Motilal to Jawaharlal, 2 Dec. 1926.*

but also progressive Congressmen close to Nehru like Sitla Sahai and Narendra Dev, proposed a resolution for the abolition of separate electorates.[234] This resolution was overruled as a result of pressure from Nehru and Gandhi but the time was not far off when Nehru would have to take a stand on this issue in order to retain the support of even his closest followers.

---

[234] AICC papers, 20/1926: I am indebted to Mrs Jolly of the Nehru Memorial Museum for the translation of a number of Hindi signatures.

CHAPTER 3

The Emergence of Punjabi Dominance

In the treatment of all-India politics, whether from the point of view of the Congress party or the Muslim League, it is customary, whilst dealing with the period of operation of the Montagu-Chelmsford Reforms, to pay considerably less attention to the period between 1920 and 1927 than to that between 1927 and 1935. Such a concentration of attention appears to be governed less by explicit choice than by the nature of the material available. In the first period not only is material a good deal less plentiful; it is also more intractable. The non-co-operation movement very often obscures the importance of the new constitution, and concentration on the Swaraj party at the all-India level gives only a limited insight into the all-India politician's dilemma. In the second period, on the other hand, the constitution itself is being revised and the various procedural stages make for a wealth of evidence and documentation. Political loyalties become explicit; provincial interests emerge on to the all-India stage; and conflict both between the government and the Congress and between the Congress and the Muslims becomes intensified. For all these reasons, the second period provides a more obvious subject for study than the first. It is the contention of this book, however, that the seeds of this dramatic conflict were sown during the first period; that the constitution itself fostered the political developments of the later years; and that the result of the battle between centrifugalism and centripetalism might have been predicted in 1926. If the second period receives less detailed treatment than the first, therefore, it is not because its importance is underestimated but because attention is being paid less to the events themselves than to their place within the context of politics already delineated.

The Montagu-Chelmsford Constitution produced two main trends in all-India politics, a centrifugal trend and a communal trend. Between 1923 and 1927, every all-India confrontation with the Raj was beset by provincial pressures, and the lesson which the all-india

politician learnt during these years was that he either had to bow
before these pressures or to bow out of politics altogether. Particularly after 1925, the Congress Swaraj party resembled a Colossus
doing the splits, one leg planted at the Centre, the other pulled ever
nearer to the provincial periphery; and the Muslim League and the
Khilafat Committee, though possessed of fewer organizational
resources, displayed similar tendencies, as may be demonstrated by
reference to the careers of the Ali brothers and of Jinnah. Of a piece
with this centrifugal trend was a trend towards communal polarization.
Because separate electorates were continued, the introduction of
ministerial responsibility set the two communities at each other's
throats. Either one community effectively dominated the transferred
departments to the detriment of the other, as in the Punjab, or
politically depressed sections of a majority community exploited
communal feeling for their own regeneration, as in the United
Provinces. In either case, the result was the same : Hindu was
divided from Muslim at the provincial level, and all-India politics
soon came to be affected.

In the battle between the forces of centrifugalism and centripetalism, the government was not a disinterested party. In 1920 it had
not only resisted devolution of power at the Centre: it had also
endeavoured to devolve power to the provinces in such a way as to
reproduce within the conciliar sphere the collaborative system which
already worked well in the sphere of administration. In effect it
sought the cooperation of provincial interest groups in maintaining
the *status quo*. In exchange for an extension of their provincial
privileges, these interests were to acquiesce in continued British
control at the Centre: 'The Raj hath given and the Raj may give
more: Blessed be the name of the Raj.' In 1918, these decisions were
based more on instinct than on sinister calculation. Even the demand for provincial responsibility had only just been voiced and
the government of India was in a position of overwhelming strength.
By 1928, however, the non-co-operation movement had produced a
considerable change in the political atmosphere. Dominion status
was a widely recognized ambition and the government of India was
much more sensitive to challenges to its authority. Furthermore,
the working of the Reforms had reinforced the wisdom of the decisions taken ten years previously. In the provinces, devolution of
power had produced staunch allies in the Punjab and Madras;

workable combinations of Hindu and Muslim landlords in the United Provinces, Bihar and Orissa, and Bombay; and even in Bengal and the Central Provinces, the Swaraj party had only succeeded in bringing the Reforms to a standstill for the duration of one council session. In the Central Assembly, on the other hand, the government had constantly been in difficulties, and even though the Legislature had no power over the Executive, without the Council of State even the pretence of democracy could not have been maintained. By 1928, therefore, what had begun as an instinctive reaction to all-India pressure had hardened into a deliberate policy: in response to challenges to its authority at the Centre, the Raj was to rely increasingly on the provinces.

This reliance on the provinces involved maximum reliance on the Muslims. There were, it is true, other important interests—the non-Brahmins of Madras and the various landlord parties of U.P., Bihar and Orissa and Bombay—yet from the all-India point of view, the Muslims formed the most coherent group. Not only did they form majorities in the Punjab and Bengal: they also formed important minorities in U.P., Bihar and Orissa, C.P. and Bombay. Moreover, where the reform of the constitution was concerned, all Muslim groups had good reason to combine. Given the prevailing atmosphere of communal antagonism, the inauguration of provincial autonomy threatened to subject the minority-province Muslim to a communal Hindu majority; and in the majority provinces, because of the backwardness of the community educationally and economically, the concession of provincial autonomy was less important than the terms under which it was introduced. For these reasons, in both Muslim minority and majority provinces, separate electorates were held to be essential for the maintenance of the Muslim position. And because only the government was prepared to make such a political concession, almost all provincial Muslim groups found themselves in the government camp. Finally, where the majority-province Muslims were concerned, there was the additional fear of Hindu control at the Centre. This added to the community of interest between these Muslims and the Raj: the continuation of British control at the Centre was a small price to pay for a free hand in one's own province.

Pride of place amongst the Muslims belonged to the Muslims of the Punjab. Fazli Husain's Unionist party was the most substantial provincial party in India and no other party was better placed to benefit from provincial autonomy. Provincial ambitions were thus strongest in the Punjab, and during the crucial years of constitutional revision, owing to their superior political leverage, it was the Punjabi Muslims who played the leading role in Muslim politics. Even the U.P. Muslims, who habitually prided themselves on their sophistication and despised the Punjabi for his lack of it, were obliged to recognize the facts of the situation:

The eyes of your brethren in other parts of India [a leading U.P. politician told a Lahore audience in 1929] are directed towards the Punjab at this critical juncture. . . . They ask their Punjabi brethren: 'Are you willing and able to undertake the task of keeping Muslim India effectively organised and united in order that it may play a part in the rearrangement of the Indian constitution which is in consonance with its historical past and glorious culture?[1]'

And of course they were. Yet whilst the Government's reliance on the Muslims increased with the intensity of the challenge it faced from the Congress, the same officials who sought to use the Muslims as a counterweight to Congress were unwilling to allow them to encroach beyond a certain point on what they considered their own preserves. Much depended, therefore, on how the Muslims played their cards. And in the period between 1927 and 1935, that is tantamount to saying, how Fazli Husain played his cards, for during those years the bulk of the responsibility fell on his shoulders. Between 1927 and 1930, as Revenue Member of the Punjab government, he exercised his influence for the most part privately, through such lieutenants as Firoz Khan Noon, Sikunder Hayat, Chaudhuri Zafrullah and Ahmed Yar Khan Daultana, but after 1930, when he became a member of the Viceroy's Council, his became a key voice in the counsels of the government of India. Between 1930 and 1936, his political vision was a crucial factor in the process of constitutional reform, and his success or failure in achieving his objectives was to influence the future of the subcontinent as a whole.

The four proposals of March 1927

The first significant development in all-India politics after the 1926

---

[1] Mihr collection, 223: Shafaat Ahmed Khan's presidential address to the 8th Punjab Educational Conference, Lahore, 11 Oct. 1929.

elections was an offer by a conference of Muslims which met at Delhi on 20 March 1927 to give up separate electorates if four proposals were accepted. These proposals were as follows: the separation of Sind from Bombay; Reforms for the Frontier and Baluchistan; representation by population in the Punjab and Bengal; and thirty-three per cent for the Muslims in the Central Legislature. No such offer had previously been made by so representative a gathering, and the evidence suggests that Jinnah was the moving spirit behind it. Even for Jinnah, however, it marked something of a *volte-face*. In 1916, he had accepted that separate electorates were indispensable so long as the Muslims demanded them; and his career in the mid-1920s suggests that he saw the wisdom of sticking by the demands of the League. Why then did he put forward a proposal which he must have known would be rejected by provincial opinion?

The reason lies in the changed balance of power within the Central Assembly after the 1926 elections. The elections took place in an atmosphere of communal antagonism and Jinnah's Independent party suffered most. In the previous Assembly, Jinnah had held the balance between the Congress and the Government: in the new one, he was a leader without a following. 'There is a touch of humour', reported one unsympathetic correspondent, 'about the position of Mr M.A. Jinnah, who in the last Assembly led the Independents. It seem unlikely that there will be any such party this session..'..[2] If Jinnah was to continue to play an important role in the Assembly, therefore, it was essential for him to discover a new following, and even before the Assembly met, the same correspondent reported that he was fishing for the leadership of the Muslim group. The father-figure of the group, Sir Abdul Quaiyum, however, was not an easy fish to land, and Jinnah's subsequent behaviour suggests that no agreement was reached. He continued to judge all legislation on its merits, supporting the government over the Steel Protection Bill but opposing it over the Currency Bill, whereas the Muslim bloc, under Quaiyum's leadership, voted solidly for the government and so thwarted the ambitions of the Swaraj party and the Nationalist party.[3] The obvious lesson to be

---

[2] *The Times*, 20 Jan. 1927.

[3] The government had worked hard to secure this accession of Muslim support, notably by their part in the election of Mahommed Yakub as Deputy President. See

learnt from this situation was not lost on the Congress. It was already divided, and without Muslim support it was likely to become ineffective. As the session closed, therefore, the Congress President, Srinivasa Iyengar, made an appeal to Muslim members to join his party in pressing for political reform.[4] It was in response to this appeal that the conference of 20 March was called.

What makes it doubly clear that the four proposals were a response to Central Assembly conditions is the fact that of twenty-nine Muslims who attended the conference sixteen were members of the Central Assembly and two were members of the Council of State.[5] No member of a provincial legislature attended; and the remaining Muslims were either Congressmen, Panislamists or all-India constitutional politicians. It is also noteworthy that the terms themselves make no provision for the continuation of weightage in the minority provinces despite the fact that almost all those present were either from minority provinces or from minority divisions of majority provinces.[6] This suggests that the four proposals were a new political initiative by politicians who had little chance of power in their own provinces. The first group might be termed 'Independents' pure and simple: Jinnah, Mahommed Yakub (though he had become more pro-government since his election as Deputy President of the Assembly), and the Raja of Mahmudabad. The second was a group of Swarajists who had come to adopt a more independent stance: Shafi Daudi and Shah Mahommed Zubair from Bihar, Syed Murtuza and Nawab Ismail. The third was a group of urban politicians from the Muslim majority provinces: Sir Mahommed Shafi and his son-in-law, Shah Nawaz, whose political base was in east and central Punjab, and Abdullah Suhrawardy, Calcutta's original Young Turk. Shafi and Shah Nawaz had no chance of political power in their own province while the Maliks of Shahpur were

Halifax papers, 3: Irwin to Birkenhead, 3 Feb. 1927; also *ILA Debates,* 3rd Assembly 1st session, vol. i. 31 Jan. 1927. pp. 301-3. For the voting list on the Steel Industry Protection Bill, see ibid., vol. i. 21 Feb. 1927, p. 1114; for the vote on the ratio during the Currency Bill debate, see ibid., vol. ii. pp. 1894-5.

4 *Indian Quarterly Register,* 1927, vol. i, pp. 32-3.

5IOR/L/P and J/6/1197/1927: Indian News Agency tgm. 20 March. 1927.

6Apart from the Frontiersmen, there were only three Muslims present from Muslim majority areas: Raja Ghazanfar Ali of Jhelum. Sardar Mahommed Nawaz Khan, who represented the Punjab landholders, and Anwar ul Azim of Dacca. All were members of the Assembly.

running the show, and Suhrawardy, after jumping from Das's pocket
into Rahim's pocket and back again, had decided in 1926 that Central Assembly politics might be more to his liking. A fourth group
consisted of Mahommed Ali, Dr Ansari and Abdur Rahman
Siddiqui. Mahommed Ali was uncomfortable in the Congres; and
Ansari and Siddiqui, though less uncomfortable, saw the urgency
of the communal situation. Lastly, there were the Frontiersmen, Sir
Abdul Quaiyum and Abdul Aziz. Like the Sindhis, they were possessed of a grievance which gave them a ready reason to join a new
confrontation and the promise of Reforms for the Frontier was
enough to sweep them into the net.

Even more significant than the terms themselves, however, was
the response to them, for, as the Viceroy anticipated, whatever
Jinnah's original intentions (and these were by no means clear at
the time), the result of his initiative was to 'widen rather than diminish the breach between the two communities.'[7] The response, indeed, did no more than illustrate two recurring features of the all-
India political scene, the importance of provincial Muslim opinion
and the reluctance of the Mahasabha to accept any terms which did
not amount to total submission.

On 23 March, certain Hindu legislators, under Malaviya's presidency, gave the first indication of the communal Hindu response
to the terms. They snatched at the concession over separate electorates. They turned the demand regarding representation by
population in the Punjab and Bengal into a demand for the abolition of weightage in Muslim minority provinces. And they declared,
regarding the Frontier and Sind, that the time was not ripe for the
discussion of such questions.[8] It did not augur well for the future.
On 29 March, seeing the way things were going, Jinnah issued a
statement to the press making it clear that the four proposals had to
be accepted or rejected *in toto*.[9] But this did not improve the situation. Indeed, when the Mahasabha met at Patna on 16 April, Jinnah's
own statement was used as an excuse for not discussing the offer at
all. The same meeting did not fail to express its opinion, however,
that consideration of the proposals by the Congress would be premature and harmful, and it made its position doubly clear by de-

---

[7] Halifax papers, 3: Irwin to Birkenhead, 24 March 1927.
[8] *Indian Statutory Comission*, vol. iv (London 1930),p. 169.
[9] *Indian Quarterly Register*, 1927, vol. i, pp. 36-7.

manding new discussions on the basis of joint electorates and a uniform franchise. Reservation of seats was only to be for a prescribed period and reservation by population was only one of several alternatives. Voting strength and taxation, criteria which particularly favoured the Hindus of the Punjab and Bengal, were also to be considered.[10] This response suggests that the Mahasabha was not interested in coming to terms at all.

The provincial Muslim response was not much better. By the end of April, the Muslims of the U.P. and Madras councils had condemned the offer, and by the middle of May, similar sentiments had been expressed by representative gatherings in the Punjab, Bengal and Bihar. At a meeting at Lahore on 1 May, the Punjab Muslim League, under the presidency of Sir Mahommed Shafi, whilst acknowledging the good faith of the Muslims who had made the original offer, condemned the Hindu press and political organizations for showing it such scant courtesy. The four proposals, it was said, were virtually the same as those put forward by Mr Kelkar at the Kanpur Mahasabha in 1925, and the fact that they had been rejected by the same organization at Patna was taken as an indication of the grasping mentality of the communal Hindu politician.[11] Seven days later, at Barisal, Sir Abdur Rahim presided over a meeting of the Bengal Provincial Muslim Conference which came to the same conclusions. Had conditions been more peaceful, he said, the Muslims might have been more inclined to accept joint electorates, but given the state of communal tension, negotiations were unlikely to be productive.[12]

The provinces were vetoing Jinnah's all-India initiative, and several supporters of the original offer began to change their minds. In the aftermath of the Delhi conference, for example, Sir Mahommed Shafi received a flood of abusive and threatening letters, not only from the Punjab but from all parts of India, and it was these letters, quite as much as the Mahasabha response, which produced his *volte-face* at Lahore.[13] Another man who had second

[10]*Indian Quarterly Register,* 1927, vol. i, pp. 422-3: Proceedings of the All Indian Hindu Mahasabha at Patna, 16-18 April 1927, Resn no. xvi.

[11] IOR/L/P and J/6/1442/1927: Resolutions of the Punjab Muslim League meeting at Lahore on 1 May, enclosed in GI. Home Public dispatch 74/1927, 26 May 1927.

[12] *Indian Quarterly Register,* 1927, vol. i, pp. 432-3.

[13] Halifax papers, 3: Irwin to Birkenhead, 26 May 1927.

thoughts was Sir Abdul Quaiyum. In his case, however, it seems likely that official pressure was partly responsible. He may well have been told that the Frontier would get Reforms more quickly if it backed the official horse.[14] Two men who did stand by the proposals were Shafi Daudi and Sir Ali Imam. They convened a special meeting at Patna on 8 May, and put forward their case with some passion. The opposition of Sir Mahommed Fakhuruddin and the Bihari Muslim rural interest, however, was too substantial to be overcome.[15] By the middle of May, the proposals had been rejected by every important provincial group.

Unlike in 1925, the Congress did not hide behind the Mahasabha. The day after the proposals were announced, the working committee welcomed the Muslim initiative and set up a subcommittee to examine its implications. This subcommittee, consisting of Srinivasa Iyengar, Motilal Nehru, Sarojini Naidu nad Mahommed Ali, was clearly sympathetic towards the Muslims, and it recommended that the Congress accept the proposals. Indeed two additional concessions were also recommended, the first guaranteeing liberty of conscience, and the second giving minorities the right to veto legislation affecting their community by a seventy-five per cent vote.[16] The AICC which met at Bombay on 15 May, however, was less easily convinced than the members of the subcommittee. Jayakar, Moonje and Kelkar were not initially prepared to accept the proposals regarding Sind and the Frontier, and what came to be known as the Delhi-Bombay compromise was only adopted when two of Jayakar's amendments had been carried. Reforms for the Frontier became conditional on the provision of a suitable judiciary, and the separation of Sind conditional on the separation of Andhra. Neither of these conditions militated against the spirit of the four proposals, however, and both Dr Ansari and Mahommed Ali were happy to accept them[17]

But though the Congress accepted the proposals, they never became a landmark to rival the Lucknow Pact, largely because the political will necessary for a new confrontation was singularly lack-

[14] Ibid., Irwin to Birkenhead, 11 and 19 May 1927. In the second letter, Irwin confesses to Birkenhead that some members of his council are keen for an extension of Reforms to the Frontier before the Statutory Commission is appointed, partly ...to build a dyke against the Statutory Commission . . . and partly in order to please Muslim opinion for general purposes'.

[15] *Indian Quarterly Register,* 1927, vol. i, pp. 39-40.

[16] Ibid., 1927, vol. i, pp. 14-21.

[17] Ibid.

ing. The Congress put itself in a favourable light by accepting the Muslim offer but it did very little more. Jinnah was the only politician to use the Congress resolution in an attempt to consolidate his position and even he realized that paper agreements would not alter provincial opinion. When he visited Lahore in June, he not only advocated the acceptance of the Delhi-Bombay compromise: he also claimed that as a result of his influence with the Government of India, Reforms would be granted to the Frontier.[18] This was an appeal based not on reason but on power, and though the claim was false, as Muddiman hastened to inform Hailey,[19] it touched on the essential factor in the situation. To make an agreement was one thing: to implement it quite another. And where implementation was concerned, the government had the satisfaction of knowing that its position was supreme. As Muddiman put it, while commenting on a draft dispatch relating to these events: 'It is a case of manoeuvring for a political position and as usual the Muslims will be out manoeuvred but neither side can deliver the goods even if they wished to do so.'[20]

The appointment of the Statutory Commission

The divisions of Indian political life demonstrated by the various reactions to Jinnah's initiative were undoubtedly a source of confidence to the government. It was in a stronger position than it had been for many years, and its strength was on the increase. At the provincial level, Hindu was divided from Muslim, and at the all-India level, not only was cooperation both between Gandhi and the Ali brothers and between Nehru and Jinnah virtually a thing of the past: Swarajist was also set against Mahasabhite and the confrontation with the Raj had all but broken down. Indeed all the evidence suggests that the government's main opponents, the Swarajist leaders, recognized the weakness of their position and were searching for a good excuse to give up non-co-operation.[21]

[18] Hailey papers, 10B: Sir Malcolm Hailey to Sir Alexander Muddiman, 13 June 1927.

[19] Ibid., Muddiman to Hailey, 15 June 1927.

[20] GI Home Poll. 6/1927: Note by Muddiman, 24 May 1927.

[21] Halifax papers, 3: Irwin to Birkenhead, 6 Jan., 3 Feb., 24 Aug., 31 Aug. and 29 Sept. 1927. On 2 Feb., discussions actually took place between Muddiman, Nehru, Rangaswami Iyengar and Srinivasa Iyengar about how the government could help to extricate the Swarajists from this situation.

In such circumstances, the government made a serious miscalculation in appointing an entirely Parliamentary Statutory Commission. This was the one development calculated to lift the entire conflict between government and its all-India opponents from the political to the racial plane and to reunite those who were slowly being divided from each other. And this is precisely what happened. A large body of Indian opinion was alienated, opposition was intensified, demands sharpened and, as Irwin himself anticipated in a rare moment of insight, the game on each side was thrown 'very much into the hands of the extremists both in India and out of it.'[22] What is surprising is that the government did not realize the wisdom of making some concession to Indian *amour-propre*. The entire course of politics after the collapse of non-cooperation serves to show that the working of the Reforms in the provinces was making a successful confrontation with the Raj more and more difficult. The appointment of Indians to the Statutory Commission, particularly as selection would have been the government's prerogative, was only likely to reinforce the divisions which had already become apparent. At best, it would have produced a salutary change in the relations between the Congress and the Raj; at worst, merely a minority report. Why, then, did the government make such a Himalayan blunder? The answer lies in the origin of the advice on which the Viceroy based his decision.

When Lord Irwin arrived in New Delhi in April 1926, raw and untutored in Indian problems, he fell under the influence of Sir Malcolm Hailey, the Governor of the Punjab. By his own admission, Hailey was one of his chief advisers,[23] and his private secretary, whom he inherited from Lord Reading, was Geoffrey de Montmorency, one of Hailey's greatest friends and closest colleagues.[24] There are grounds for believing, therefore, that Irwin was introduced to India in his first months as Viceroy with the help of a Punjabi guidebook. It was Hailey and de Montmorency who ad-

[22] Ibid., Irwin to Birkenhead, 26 May 1927.

[23] Irwin subsequently admitted that he had 'relied greatly' on Hailey's advice 'from the time I first landed in India'. See Frederick, 2nd Earl of Birkenhead, *F.E.* (London 1965), pp. 323-4.

[24] De Montmorency had served as Hailey's assistant when Hailey was Chief Commissioner of Delhi. He was appointed private secretary to Lord Reading when Hailey was Finance Member of the Viceroy's Council. In 1928, he was to succeed him as Governor of the Punjab.

vised him in the appointment of the Statutory Commission and it was this first step which set the scene for what followed. Moreover, though Irwin later differed with Hailey over broad outlines of government policy, he continued to rely on his advice where recruitment to the government of India secretariat was concerned. Apart from de Montmorency, a number of other Punjab civilians held key posts at this time. James Dunnett, who served in the Home Department from 1926 to 1930, first as Joint Secretary and then as Additional Secretary, was appointed Reforms Commissioner in 1930 and held the post throughout the period of constitutional revision. A man of very outstanding intelligence, his part in reshaping the constitution has yet to receive proper attention. In 1929, when a Muslim was required for the Secretary of State's Council, it was Malik Sir Umar Hayat Khan Tiwana, the most influential agriculturalist Muslim in the Punjab, who was appointed. In 1930, when a new Muslim member was needed on the Viceroy's Council, it was Fazli Husain who received the summons. And in 1931, when the government of India wanted a competent man to manage the administrative difficulties produced by the Gandhi-Irwin Pact, it was Herbert Emerson, the man whom Hailey had used to win Sikh support for government legislation on the Gurdwaras, who was appointed Home Secretary. The Punjab had long been considered the sword-arm of India, but from the early 1920s, as a result of Hailey's influence, it also became the soul in the machine.

This reliance on Punjabi personnel was not mere favouritism: between 1909 and 1937, with the possible exception of Sir Reginald Craddock, there was no government of India official to compare with Hailey, de Montmorency, Emerson or Dunnett: their clarity of mind and political shrewdness were in a class of their own. Yet such reliance did have important implications: it involved accepting Punjabi ideas and managing all-India politics from the Punjabi point of view. What did this imply in detail? At the simplest level, the Punjab civilian had three main characteristics: firstly, contempt for the political classes; secondly, a political vision that was essentially communal in outlook—the belief that the government could maintain its prestige by holding the balance between the two communities; and thirdly, a distinctive *esprit de corps* which separated him from other civilians elsewhere. Because of the importance of the Punjab as a recruiting ground for the Army, genuine loyalty to the

Crown still existed amongst large sections of the community, and the growth of Indian political ambitions had yet to sap civilian morale. If Indian politics were to go the way of Bengal, therefore, the Punjab civilian wished to have nothing to do with it. What he wanted—and here his ambitions coincided with those of the Punjabi Muslims—was continued British control at the Centre and the freest possible hand in his own province. These three characteristics, through the influence of Hailey and his men in the secretariat, were to have a very extensive influence on the government of India's attitude to Reform.

The Statutory Commission took the form it did almost exclusively as a result of Hailey's advice. On 19 August 1926, in reply to a suggestion by Birkenhead that Indians should be appointed to the Commission, Irwin confessed to grave doubts as to the wisdom of such a step. The danger, he said, was that the Commission would become unwieldy and that two reports would be produced, one of which could well have been written beforehand.[25] These grave doubts may well have been sown by Hailey. In a letter written to Lord Irwin on 20 August, in which he referred to an earlier discussion, Hailey reaffirmed his preference for a Parliamentary Commission: 'If the Commission is to include Indian politicians, then it must be representative of all communities, and it will be impossible to expect from it a clear view on such questions as communal representation'. This stress on the importance of communal divisions was a reflection of Hailey's experience of Punjabi politics. There, communal polarization had reached such a point that all communities understood the dangers of boycott:

I have some feeling [Hailey wrote in the same letter] that Indians themselves, divided as they are at present on communal lines, would prefer a Commission composed as I suggest. At the moment, the communal question is even more important than the form which political advance may take.[26]

Undeterred by this advice, in March 1927, Birkenhead again pressed for the appointment of Indians. Irwin forwarded his letter to Hailey for comment, and Hailey replied along much the same lines as before. If Indians were to be appointed, the Commission

---

[25] Halifax papers, 2: Irwin to Birkenhead, 19 Aug. 1926.
[26] Hailey papers, 9 C: Hailey to George Cunningham (Private Secretary to the Viceroy), 20 Aug. 1926.

would have to be representative. But if it were representative, it would not be unanimous, and if it were not unanimous, Parliament would not be satisfied. Openmindedness was essential: hence the need to exclude all experienced civilians and politicians.[27] This letter was submitted by Irwin to Birkenhead on 19 May.[28]

By May, however, Irwin was beginning to have second thoughts. On 7 May, in a letter to Hailey, whilst adhering to the principle of a Parliamentary Commission, he suggested either that Indians should be associated with the Commission as adjutors or that the Commission report should be submitted to a joint committee of the Central Assembly and the Council of State.[29] On 21 May, Hailey and de Montmorency discussed this question, and the following day, de Montmorency replied on Hailey's behalf. The letter gives away more than Hailey's earlier epistles: it is clear that the main fear of the Punjab civilians was that all-India politicians would secure the lion's share of Indian representation.

The men chosen will be too deeply imbued with the All India politician point of view. The provinces already feel that the All India politician does not represent the real interests of the people of a province, and is too apt to attach himself to parties in and outside the Central Legislature with labels which have no true meaning and no reality as far as the living issues are concerned. The provinces, on the other hand, have had more practical experience of representative institutions. They are anchored to facts. They know or think they know what they want. They are more likely to know what will work.[30]

And the corollary of this view was that there should not be one body of adjutors but several, indeed one for each province as well as one for the Central Legislature.[31]

For Irwin, the value of Indian adjutors was that they would lessen the chances of boycott. And to that extent, Hailey's acceptance of the principle involved, was clearly welcome. Yet fears of boycott still persisted,[32] and by the end of May Irwin was again considering putting Indians on the Commission. He wrote to both Hailey and

---

[27] Hailey papers, 10A: Hailey to Irwin, 23 April 1927.
[28] Halifax papers, 3: Irwin to Birkenhead, 19 May 1927.
[29] Hailey papers, 10A; Irwin to Hailey, 7 May 1927.
[30] Ibid., de Montmorency to Irwin, 22 May 1927.
[31] This suggestion was ultimately adopted by the government of India.
[32] Halifax papers, 3: Irwin to Birkenhead, 26 May 1927.

Birkenhead on this score and even suggested personnel on the Indian side.[33] Once again, however, he was steered away from this suggestion by Hailey and de Montmorency. At the same time that he was voicing his fears of boycott to the Secretary of State, Hailey, de Montmorency and Muddiman were putting forward 'their very definite view...that as things are today a general boycott is in the highest degree improbable.'[34] A certain number of Irwin's advisers, notably Sir Mahommed Habibullah, the Muslim member of his council, took another view. They pointed out the unwisdom of giving the Swarajists a racial grievance at the very moment when they found themselves in an unprofitable cul-de-sac.[35] But this advice was ignored. Throughout that summer at Simla, whilst Irwin paced Viceregal Lodge making his decision, it was Hailey, only a stone's throw away at Barnes Court, whose advice carried most weight.

Hailey's position was one of reliance first on the provinces and second on the Muslims. In his advice to the Viceroy, whether with regard to the composition of the Statutory Commission or the various other expedients put forward as means of satisfying Indian opinion, he continually stressed the unreasonableness, the unpracticality and the unrepresentative status of the all-India leaders, and he made sure that the coincidence between his own views and those of the Punjabi Muslims was well-known to the Viceroy. He appears to have established a close working relationship with Firoz Khan Noon, his Minister for Local self-Government, and both in the corridors of the government of India and in the councils of the Muslim League, Firoz worked assiduously to secure the triumph of the Punjabi point of view. At the end of August, Irwin informed Birkenhead that 'Hailey's Muslims' had definitely come out for a Parliamentary Commission,[36] and a month later, in an interview with Firoz Khan Noon, he heard the same news himself at first hand:

---

[33] Hailey papers, 10A: Note by Lord Irwin, forwarded by George Cunningham to Hailey, 24 May 1927: Halifax papers, 3: Irwin to Birkenhead, 2 June 1927. No names were suggested to Birkenhead, but to Hailey, Irwin suggested Motilal Nehru, Fazli Husain, C.P.,Ramaswami Iyer and Sir Chunilal Mehta. In addition, there were to be 'three good Englishmen', one official and one non-official. The Indians would have been in a minority of one.

[34] Halifax papers, 3. Irwin to Birkenhead, 26 May 1927.

[35] Ibid., Irwin to Birkenhead, 2 June 1927.

[36] Ibid. Irwin in Birkenhead, 24 Aug. 1927.

The upshot of his conversation [he reportea to Birkenhead] was that communal electorates were as vital to Mussulmans as they had ever been, and that on this point there was, as I have already said, substantial unanimity of opinion in Moslem circles. They were anxious as to the influence that might be exerted against their views by what they considered to be mugwump politicians like Jinnah, Mahmudabad, Ali Imam etc., and had been considering very anxiously how best to forestall this danger in connection with the Statutory Commission. He insisted that in this matter all Hindus were unanimous in their desire to get rid of communal electorates, and therefore any Hindus who might be placed on a Mixed Commission would be advocates in this sense.For this reason, it was of the utmost importance to them that,if there were to be any Moslems at all on the Commission,the Moslems to be placed on it should be men about whose staunchness on this vital question from the Moslem point of view there could be no doubt. The only two names he mentioned as names in whom the whole Moslem community would have confidence on this issue were Fazli Husain and Abdur Rahim. Unless these two men could be appointed on the Commission, he was charged by all his Moslem friends to tell me that they would definitely prefer a Parliamentary Commission with no Indians at all.[37]

By degrees, therefore, Irwin's doubts and worries were calmed down and Birkenhead's own suggestions rejected by the Viceroy on the basis of civilian knowledge and experience. By July 1927, the question was no longer in doubt. Simon had accepted the chairmanship of the Commission,[38] and attention was being paid more to the preparations for its announcement than to the form it should take. Such features as the interview with Firoz were used, not as arguments for one sort of Commission or another, but as evidence that the decision to appoint a Parliamentary Commission was meeting with Indian approval. By July, despite a good deal of dillydallying, Irwin had swallowed the Punjabi bait, and by October, in letting the Secretary of State know about his plans for the Commission, he was putting forward the very strategy which Hailey himself had advocated. He told Birkenhead that the government would be able to rely on three main sources of support, firstly the Muslims, secondly the provinces and thirdly the liberals.[39] Except with regard to the liberals, whose position the government never fully appreciated,

[37] Ibid., Irwin to Birkenhead, 29 Sept. 1927.
[38] Irwin approved Simon's appointment in a letter to Birkenhead on 14 July.
[39] Halifax papers, 3: Irwin to Birkenhead, 5 Oct. 1927.

this was an accurate prediction of future developments. But whereas this strategy was appropriate to the conditions in the Punjab, where the majority community was cooperating with the government and where the minorities could not afford for that reason to boycott the Commission, it was less defensible elsewhere. In other provinces, where divisions between communities did not work so effectively to the government's advantage, it was to provoke a confrontation with Indian opinion which put a very severe strain on the government's credibility and resources.

The Punjabi breakaway

The announcement of the all-white Commission led to a considerable strengthening of national feeling. Lord Irwin had seen Congress leaders before the announcement was made and had reported to Birkenhead that they were not very happy at the prospect.[40] But it was only when the news became public that the real depth of Indian feeling could be gauged. 'The shouting at present', he wrote to Birkenhead on 16 November, 'is rather louder and more uncompromising than I had perhaps anticipated.'[41] It was a typical case of understatement. On 10 November, Dr Ansari, who had just been elected Congress President, issued a statement enjoining all Congressmen to boycott the Commission completely.[43] On 16 November, to the surprise of both government and Congress, Sir Abdur Rahim presided over a boycott meeting at Calcutta.[43] And on 18 November, Fazli Husain, just returned from representing India at the League of Nations, told reporters that he opposed the Parliamentary commission and would support a Mus..m League boycott providing the Hindu Mahasabha came out for the same policy.[44] In all probability this was simply political manoeuvring; the threat to withdraw Muslim support from Government was to be used to good effect on a number of occasions in the future. Yet these manoeuvrings added to government's anxiety. Only a fortnight after the announcement had been made, the calculations behind Irwin's decision looked unsound.

Where all-India Muslim politics was concerned, the effect of the

[40] Ibid., Irwin to Birkenhead, 3 Nov. 1927.
[41] Ibid., Irwin to Birkenhead, 16 Nov. 1927.
[42] *Indian Quarterly Register, 1927,*vol, ii, p. 14.
[43] Ibid., p. 15.
[44]*Indian Daily Mail,* 1927; *The Herald,* 19 Nov. 1927 (enclosed, Hailey papers, 11 B).

announcement was to force politicians like Jinnah and the Ali brothers back into the mainstream of nationalist protest. The exclusion
of Indians boded ill for the chances of any substantial devolution at
the Centre, and all those interested in such a development consequently closed their ranks. Jinnah was particularly active at this
time. He did not actually come out for a policy of complete boycott
because he hoped that Indian appeals would produce a change of
personnel on the Commission.[45] But he worked hard to produce a
united national front. Before the parliamentary debate on the Viceroy's announcement, he organized a telegram of protest and circulated all important leaders for permission to add their signatures[46]. And when the Parliamentary debate produced no
change, he organised a joint meeting of all political organizations
at Bombay on 12 December.[47] Mahommed Ali was less active but
inclined to the same view. He favoured holding a joint session of
the Congress and the League at Madras and he wired his brother,
Shaukat, to get Jinnah to make the necessary arrangements.[48]

These tendencies to unity were encouraged by the Congress. Dr
Ansari, the President, wrote to all prominent Indian politicians,
Hindu and Muslim, co-operator and non-co-operator, urging them
to use the opportunity provided to reunite nationalist forces. Reactions to the Commission had convinced him that divisions in the
body politic were merely over matters of detail: on matters of principle they were all virtually unanimous.[49] He received a number of
encouraging replies, some from unexpected sources. Hassan Imam
and the Raja of Mahmudabad supported boycott, Mahommed
Yakub agreed that 'a large number of Muslims should attend the
Congress,' and Abdur Rahim, though unprepared to meet other
leaders on the Congress platform, wished to make plans for concerted action. Only Hafiz Hidayat Hussain of Kanpur indulged in

---

[45] See Halifax papers, 3: Irwin to Birkenhead, 9 Nov., 1927.

[46] Mahommed Ali papers: Jinnah to Mahommed Ali, 11 Nov. 1927; Purushotamdas
Thakurdas papers: Thakurdas to Birla, 16 Nov. 1927.

[47] Mahommed Ali papers: Jinnah to Mahommed Ali, 20 Nov,; Purushotamdas
Thakurdas papers; Malaviya to Thakurdas, 7 Dec. 1927. Jinnah was also instrumental
in organizing a protest meeting of Bombay politicians on 3 Dec. at the Sir Cowasji
Jehangir Hall.

[48] AICC papers, G64/1926-8: Mahommed Ali to Srinivasa Iyengar, 21 Nov. 1927.

[49] Ansari papers (Jamia Millia Islamia, New Delhi): circular letter, 1 Dec. 1927.

outspoken criticism.[50] Moreover, if the composition of Ansari's personal entourage for the Madras Congress is any indication of his success, his efforts certainly bore fruit. It included Mahommed Ali, Shaukat Ali, Shuaib Qureshi, Abdur Rahman Siddiqui, Chaudhuri Khaliquzzaman, Abdul Aziz Ansari, Farid ul Haq Ansari and Dr Zakir Hussain.[51] The politicians of the old Delhi—Aligarh axis had been brought together again.

But if Panislamists, Congressmen and Constitutionalists were drawing closer together, the seeds of division within the Muslim League had already been sown. Whatever Fazli Husain may have told reporters at Bombay, there had never been any question of the Punjabi Muslims boycotting the Commission. Indeed, even before it was announced, preparations had been made at Lahore to ensure it a prompt and favourable reception. A preliminary meeting of Muslim leaders was held on 6 November. The editors of important newspapers were canvassed and a consensus in favour of co-operation was obtained. Firoz Khan Noon had a long session with Sir Mahommed Shafi, Sir Abdul Quadir and Abdullah Yusuf Ali, and reported to the Governor that matters were 'likely to take a correct course'[52] This prediction proved accurate. On 13 November, only five days after the Commission was announced, the Punjab Muslim League met officially and voted for co-operation by twenty-two votes to four. The only opponents of the resolution were Dr Kitchlew, Zafar Ali, Malik Barkat Ali and Ghulam Mohiuddin.[53] Thus even before Jinnah sent off his protest telegram to the Secretary of State, the Punjabi Muslims had fulfilled the government's expectations. They had placed themselves in the forefront of the battle against boycott, and made a confrontation with Jinnah and his followers inevitable.

Ever since Jinnah's March initiative, the Punjabis had been suspicious of his intentions. At the beginning of October, when the Muslim League Council met at Simla, they had prevented him from holding the annual session at Madras for fear that he might secure a

[50] Ibid., Mahommed Yakub to Dr Ansari, 7 Dec. 1927; Hassan Imam to Dr Ansari, 7 Dec. 1927; Raja of Mahmudabad to Dr Ansari, undated; Abdur Rahim to Dr Ansari, 7 Dec. 1927; Hafiz Hidayat Hussain to Dr Ansari, 12 Dec. 1927.

[51] Ibid. Dr Ansari to Secretary,Reception Commitee, Madras Congress, 9 Dec. 1927.

[52] Hailey papers, 11B: Firoz Khan Noon to Hailey, 6 Nov. 1927.

[53] Ibid., Firoz Khan Noon to Hailey, 13 Nov. 1927. See also Mahommed Rafiq Afzal, *Malik Barkat Ali, his Life and Writings* (Lahore 1969), part i, pp. 19-20.

verdict in favour of the Delhi-Bombay compromise. They made it plain, as did the U.P. contingent, that the League must be held in North India. Fazli Husain, then in London, received the news direct from the Governor: 'It was clear', he wrote, 'that the advocates of the joint electorate were outnumbered. I fancy as a result that we shall certainly have a meeting at Lahore instead of Madras.'[54] But though Jinnah had been warned, he was disinclined to submit. He gave up the idea of a joint session with the Congress but he did not settle for Lahore. Instead, he began to lobby in favour of Calcutta. This choice did not initially meet with Punjabi objections. 'The political views of the Muslims of the two provinces coincide', Firoz Khan Noon wrote to Hailey, 'and a collection of all-India Muslims may unite the scattered forces of Muslim politicians in Bengal.[55]' After Abdur Rahim had joined the boycott camp, however, Calcutta seemed a good deal less suitable. Because the Punjabis had voted for co-operation, it was of vital importance to them that the All India Muslim League should be held in a province where their policy would be approved. They therefore viewed the League Council meeting at Delhi on 20 November with some concern. If they were not to become isolated, it was essential that they emerge from that meeting with agreement that the League should be held at Lahore.

Thanks to the preparations made by Firoz Khan Noon, the Muslim League Council at Delhi was a triumph for the Punjabis. In the face of opposition from Jinnah and the Ali brothers, a verdict was recorded in favour of Lahore, with Sir Mahommed Shafi as President. It seemed as if a major tragedy had been averted.[56] For Jinnah, however, a Lahore meeting was as unsatisfactory as a Calcutta meeting was for the Punjabis, and if he was not to lose his representative status, it was essential that the decision be reversed. Mahommed Yakub, his Assembly colleague, agreed wholeheartedly. He encouraged Dr Kitchlew, the Secretary, to call another meeting of the council, and he urged Dr Ansari to use his influence to secure a majority for Calcutta, with the Aga Khan as President.[57] As a result, on 11 December, the council met again. Twentythree

[54] Hailey papers, 11B: Hailey to Fazli Husain, 6 Oct. 1927.
[55] Ibid., Firoz Khan Noon to Hailey, 2 Nov. 1927.
[56] Ibid., Hailey to Irwin 23 Nov. 1927.
[57] Ansari papers: Mahommed Yakub to Dr Ansari, 7 Dec. 1927.

people attended, and Firoz Khan Noon and his followers were in fact in a majority. On this occasion, however, absentee votes swung the decision in Jinnah's favour. By eightyfour votes (seventyfour absentees) to fiftyfour (fortyone absentees), the previous decision was reversed. It was decided that the session should be held at Calcutta.[58] But though Jinnah had won, it was a Pyrrhic victory. Firoz Khan Noon, Sir Mahommed Iqbal, Hasrat Mohani and a number of Firoz Khan's Punjabi followers left the meeting in disgust: the time had come for the Punjabis to strike out on their own.

As a result of the clash at Delhi, there were two Muslim Leagues in 1927, one at Lahore and one at Calcutta. Sir Mahommed Shafi, who had been elected President at both council meetings, presided over the Lahore session, and Maulvi Mahommed Yakub presided at Calcutta. Predictably, the Lahore resolutions followed those passed by the Punjab Muslim League on 13 November. The main resolution advocated a settlement between Muslim and non-Muslim communities 'with a view to the joint preparation of a draft constitution for India ... for presenting the same before the Statutory Commission or the British parliament or both'. Several others reiterated demands for the separation of Sind, the introduction of Reforms in the Frontier and Baluchistan and the concession of majority rights to the Punjabi and Bengali Muslims. More significant than the resolutions, however, was the consolidation of U.P. and Punjab Muslims which the session produced. The more vocal Punjabi leaders, Sir Mahommed Shafi, Sir Mahommed Iqbal, Sir Zulfiquar Ali Khan, Mian Shah Nawaz and Chaudhuri Zafrullah were supported by a number of important U.P. Muslim politicians, notably Shafaat Ahmed Khan, Mahommed Yamin Khan, Masudul Hassan, Shaikh Abdullah and Hasrat Mohani, and this co-operation, which was also evident in the selection of new office-bearers, foreshadowed the alliance between these two provinces in the All India Muslim Conference.[59]

The likelihood of a Punjabi breakaway had been inherent in the pattern of power introduced by the Montagu-Chelmsford Reforms. As early as 1924, when the League met at Lahore, it was clear that the Punjabis were the strongest provincial faction. Though supported vocally by many U.P. politicians, the demands put forward on that occasion had displayed a very distinct Punjabi bias and their rejection

[58] *Indian Quarterly Register*, 1927, vol. ii, p. 438.
[59] See Pirzada, op. cit., vol. ii. 128-38.

by the all-parties conference of 1925 showed clearly enough how forces were likely to be divided when the time for constitutional revision arrived. All that happened after the Delhi Muslim League Council meeting of 11 December was that the implicit became explicit. As a result of the clash between provincial and all-India interests, the Punjabis decided to cut themselves adrift from their co-religionists elsewhere and to stake out a claim for themselves less in relation to the subcontinent as a whole and more in relation to the Muslim North-West. Sir Malcolm Hailey narrated this change of mood to Sir Arthur Hirtzel, Permanent Secretary at the India Office, in a letter which shows how far this separatist trend had progressed:

They see that they can never have quite the same interests as Muslims in the provinces with large Hindu majorities and they seriously think of breaking away from the All India Muslim League and starting a Federation of their own. This will seek to embrace the Punjab, parts of the U.P., the North West Frontier, Baluchistan and Sind; it is part of the programme to secure Sind for the Punjab and to give up to Delhi some of our Hindu districts in the South East of the province. they openly say that this in itself is only a preparation for a larger Federation which shall embrace Afghanistan and perhaps Persia.

This was far-reaching enough. But, to complete the picture, Hailey made plain also the very significant attitude of the Punjabis to their brethren inBengal: 'You will notice that the dream of the future to which I had alluded does not include Bengal. For the moment, the Northern India Moslem has given up his coreligionist in Bengal as hopeless and seems to expect no assistance from Bengal in the cause of Islam'[60] Twenty years before the creation of Pakistan and forty-five years before the creation of Bangladesh, these were prophetic insights.

The Nehru report: end of the road for Hindu-Muslim unity

For those Muslims interested in agreement at the all-India level, the Punjabi breakaway did not mark the end of the road. Indeed for a further year they tried to produce an agreement to which all parties could happily subscribe. Their endeavours, however, only serve to illustrate the working of the factors already outlined — the obstructionism of the Mahasabha, the inhibiting effect of communal pressure

---

[60] Hailey papers, 11B: Sir Malcolm Hailey to Sir Arthur Hirtzel, 15 Dec. 1927.

on the Congress leadership and the unwillingness of provincial Muslim opinion to come to the conference table because co-operation with government seemed likely to pay higher dividends.

Those who attended Jinnah's League at Calcutta in December 1927 were essentially the same people who had attended his meeting at Delhi in March. Apart from Jinnah himself, the Independents were represented by Sir Ali Imam and Maulvi Mahommed Yakub, and the Congress-Swaraj-Khilafatist group by Shafi Daudi, Syed Murtuza, Kalam Azad, the Ali brothers, Chaudhuri Khaliquzzaman and other members of the consolidated Delhi-Aligarh axis. Two groups had by then defected, the Frontiersmen (Sir Abdul Quaiyum and Syed Abdul Aziz) and the urban constitutionalists from the majority provinces (Sir Mahommed Shafi, Mian Shah Nawaz and Dr Suhrawardy). But the place of the second group had been taken by a number of other urban politicians from the same provinces, chiefly Khilafatists. The Punjab was represented by the four men who had dissented from the Punjab Muslim League resolution of 13 November — Dr Kitchlew, Zafar Ali, Barkat Ali and Ghulam Mohiuddin — and Bengal by a less homogeneous group, including Congressmen like Maulana Akram Khan and former Swarajists like Tamizuddin Ahmed.[61]

The Congressmen and Khilafatists met first at Madras, where the annual sessions of their two organizations produced two developments reminiscent of the palmier days of non-co-operation. The first was the Independence resolution passed by the Congress at the instigation of Jawaharlal Nehru. This did not have any immediate impact on politics. Indeed, many Congress politicians quickly repudiated it.[62] But it did provide a powerful indication of the racial animus provoked by the Statutory Commission, and in the long run it was to be important.[63] The second was a concession, albeit temporary, by Malaviya, to the Congress school which favoured Hindu-Muslim unity. Malaviya had not been present at Bombay in May, and his absence, together with that of Lajpat Rai who was in Europe, was taken, at least in government circles, as an indication of the unaccept-

[61] For an account of the Calcutta League, see Pirzada, *op.cit.*, vol. ii, pp. 107-27.

[62] See *A Bunch of Old Letters...*, pp. 57-8: Gandhi to Jawaharlal Nehru, 4 Jan, 1928; also Nanda, *op. cit.*, pp. 295-8.

[63] Subhas Bose believed the resolution to be the 'logical fulfilment' of continuing demands by the youthful element in the Congress for a more extremist ideology. See *The Indian Struggle 1920-42* (London 1964), pp. 145-6.

ability of the Delhi-Bombay compromise to the communal Hindus of North India.[64] At Madras, however, Malaviya was subjected to immense pressure, both private and public, to make him agree to the Bombay proposals, and this pressure succeeded.[65] He endorsed the Bombay proposals and the AICC resolutions passed at Calcutta in October concerning cowslaughter and music before mosques; and he also subscribed to a resolution empowering the Congress working committee to convene an all-parties conference for the purpose of formulating a Swaraj constitution. These developments generated some hope that the communal question might be nearer solution. Mahommed Ali, for example, looked forward at the Congress session to the day when Muslims would turn not to government but to Malaviya for protection. Srinivasa Iyengar, for his part, announced that the day of perfect nationalism was not far off.[66] However this optimism turned out to be unwarranted. For even before the Madras session began, the Bombay and Calcutta resolutions had provoked a Hindu backlash. In December, letters and telegrams had poured into the Congress office, from Punjab, Bihar and Bengal, criticizing the Calcutta resolution permitting cowslaughter, and from Sind, opposing the Bombay terms for separation.[67] Malaviya had chosen to step down, but others were waiting in the wings to take his place.

At the Muslim League at Calcutta, the question of a declaration in favour of Independence was never officially raised, and this was a comment both on the schizophrenia of the Khilafatists and the ascendancy of the Independents—Jinnah, Ali Imam and Mahommed Yakub. These last three men dominated the session, Jinnah as the permanent President, Yakub as the session President and Ali Imam as the mover of the boycott resolution. Their position was a pragmatic one. They were not outside the mainstream of constitutional politics and they were consequently disinclined to declare for Independence, or even for unconditional boycott. This indeed had been their policy from the beginning. When the Commission was first announced, Jinnah had made a point of not committing himself to boycott irretrievably. He had added his voice to the general chorus of

[64] GI Home Poll. 6/1927: GI Home Department Dispatch 74/1927, to Secretary of State, 26 May 1927.

[65] See speech by Sarojini Naidu, moving the Madras resolution on communal unity, Indian Quarterly Register, 1927, vol. ii, pp. 408-9; also Khaliquzzaman, *op. cit.*, p. 90.

[66]*Indian Quarterly Register* 1927. vol. ii, pp. 409-11.

[67] See AICC papers, G 64 (1926—28).

condemnation but he had kept in close touch with the Viceroy, pressing him continually to alter the arrangements which had been made. He told him in mid-December, for example, that if he, Chimanlal Setalvad and Sapru were allowed to sit with the Commission and to cross-examine witnesses, he would in fact declare for co-operation. He was only supporting boycott, he said, for fear of being supplanted by men of a less compromising disposition.[68] Similar sentiments were also voiced by Ali Imam. He told the League gathering that he was only supporting boycott because he had no alternative: 'We were called partners. We were told of a change in the angle of vision. Our blood and mixed in the battlefields of Flanders. I frankly tell you I fully believed in a change in the angle of vision but I have been disillusioned'.[69] Like Jinnah, however, Ali Imam belonged to a category of Muslims who would be satisfied with the Commission if Indians were appointed, and such being the leadership of the Calcutta League, it was not surprising that the boycott resolution was of a general umbrella type. It accommodated all shades of opinion and left plenty of room for manoeuvre.

The Calcutta League organizers also laid great stress on communal unity. But it became clear during the proceedings that Jinnah's four proposals would not be swallowed hook, line and sinker, even in Bengal. Maulvi Mujib ur Rahman, the Chairman of the Reception Committee and a leading Congressman, told his audience that separate electorates were 'the corner-stone of Muslim politics' and should not be given up.[70] Moreover, when Wahid Hussain of Chittagong supported joint electorates because of his experience in that municipality, he was quickly told that there were only two such cases in the whole of Bengal. Elsewhere, said his critics, joint electorates were not to the Muslim advantage.[71] Consequently, where the four proposals were concerned, though the League leaders remained anxious to cement their alliance with the Congress, they were obliged to tighten their negotiating position. The League resolution on this question made it plain that only *when* the Frontier had received the Reforms and Sind had actually been constituted a separate province would separate electorates be given up.[72] It was

---

[68]Halifax papers, 3: Irwin to Birkenhead, 16 and 22 Dec. 1927.
[69] Pirzada, op. cit., vol, ii, p. 115.
[70] Ibid., p. 109.
[71] Ibid., p. 122.
[72] Ibid., p. 118-21.

the first of series of retreats which were to culminate in Jinnah's fourteen proposals of March 1929; and what Jinnah himself said about it suggests that he was beginning to lose hope :

We have got a majority in this house, but shall we be able to carry the majority in the country? Nothing will please me more, but at the same time, it will be fair to say that I am not sure that I am satisfied that the majority of Mussulmans throughout the country are in favour of it. That remains to be decided ....[73]

Despite this cautiousness, the League leaders did pass a resolution accepting the Congress invitation to an all-parties conference at Delhi, and they set up a sub-committee for that purpose, urging it to safeguard Muslim interests in its transactions.[74] When the conference convened on 12 February, however, it became apparent that agreement would not be easy. Malaviya, who was increasingly under suspicion for being too much in the Congress pocket,[75] was deprived of the limelight by Moonji, who effectively tore up the Delhi-Bombay compromise by refusing to agree either to the separation of Sind or the reservation of seats for majorities.[76] Jinnah met this intransigence with a reiteration of the terms of the League's Calcutta session and a deadlock ensued. On 5 March, when the Muslim League Council met to discuss these developments, it determined to stand firm, and when the conference reconvened three days later the position soon became critical. No appeals seemed capable of shifting the Mahasabha, and the Congress leaders refused to commit themselves to one side or the other, even though the Mahasabha was defying Congress resolutions. Instead they chose to shelve the main problems by appointing committees to examine them in detail, one to discover whether it was financially feasible to separate Sind from Bombay and the other to examine proportional representation as a means of safeguarding Muslim majorities.[77] From Jinnah's point of view, this was extremely unsatisfactory. His League was already very isolated and it began to appear

[73] Ibid. p. 123.

[74] Ibid., p. 119.

[75] Halifax papers, 4: Irwin to Birkenhead, 23 Feb. 1928.

[76] *Statement Exhibiting the Moral and Material Progress and Condition of India during the year 1927-28* (London 1929), pp. 24-5.

[77] For the early history of the all-parties conference, see *All Parties Conference 1928, Report of the Committee* (Allahabad 1929), p. 21-2; Khaliquzzaman, op. cit., pp. 93-4; Motilal Nehru papers (Nehru Memorial Museum, New Delhi): Motilal to Tej Bahadur Sapru, 26 Feb. 1928.

as if he had taken a stand for boycott at the expense of his entire political following. So back he went to the Viceroy's House and urged Irwin once more to make a change in the arrangements for the Statutory Commission.[78] Either appoint a mixed Commission, he said, or failing that, a body of Indian Commissioners with twin powers and responsibilities. Not surprisingly, his appeals were disregarded. Irwin saw that Jinnah's influence was on the wane and he had no intention of conciliating him. So what was Jinnah to do? He had failed to get a seat on the Commission and he had also failed to find a platform for boycott which would command even minimal Muslim approval. If he participated further in the all-parties conference he was merely inviting political humiliation. The only sensible alternative was retreat. On 17 March, he withdrew the Muslim League delegation from the conference and by May he was in England licking his wounds.

The withdrawal of the League and Jinnah's departure for Europe had a depressing effect on the all-parties conference. For most Congressmen, Jinnah was 'the only man to deliver the goods on behalf of the Muslim League'.[79] 'Jinnah's absence from the country is most unfortunate', wrote Motilal Nehru. 'I can think of no other responsible Muslim to take his place.'[80] Srinivasa Iyengar, Sarojini Naidu and Shanmukhan Chetty, all advocated postponing the conference till Jinnah returned from Europe in August,[81] and Motilal himself, fearing that the next session might even undo some of the work done at Delhi, inclined to a similar view.[82] Others, however, believing that the conference had degenerated into a slanging match between extremists, felt it useless to wait on Jinnah, or even on the subcommittees set up in March. 'We must decide', Shuaib Qureshi wrote to Dr Ansari, 'to stand by the Congress resolution [passed at Madras] which is based on or embodying the Delhi proposals ..., hold the conference ... adopt the Congress resolution and shape the programme of political activities on that basis.'[83] Jawaharlal showed a similar

[78] Halifax papers, 4: Irwin to Birkenhead, 8 and 15 March 1928.

[79] AICC papers, G 60: Ansari to Jawaharlal Nehru, 29 March 1928.

[80] Purushotamdas Thakurdas papers, 40: Motilal to Thakurdas, 28 April 1928.

[81] Ansari papers: Tgm Srinivasa Iyengar to Ansari, 5 May 1928; Shuaib Qureshi to Ansari, 7 May 1928.

[82] Ibid., Thakurdas to Ansari, 3 May 1928; Purushotamadas Thakurdas papers, 40: Motilal to Thakurdas, 28 April 1929.

[83] Ansari papers: Shuaib Qureshi to Ansari, 7 May 1928.

impatience,[84] though he was less bothered about adhering to the Congress resolution. At a time when his father's faith in settlement by conference was on the wane, he appears to have seized the initiative and to have pressed Motilal into actions which had the effect of alienating the Muslims still further. In a letter written in his capacity as Secretary to other members of the Congress working committee, the younger Nehru said the idea of postponing the all-parties conference had been firmly rejected. It was better, he said, to face the trouble and overcome it than to shirk the issue. What the President had decided, he said, was that the Congress must pursue its own programme despite all defections:

In the main [he continued] this programme will be naturally based on [the] resolution of the Congress but of course it is open to the Committee to make such alterations in it without going [against] the Congress mandate as it desires to do. We have seen, for instance, the All India Liberal Federation, the Home Rule League, the South India Liberal Federation, Bengal Liberal League, and various other organisation [are in sub] stantial agreement. It should not be difficult if we have the support of most of the organisations [mentioned to win over the] conference to any reasonable plan which pr[ovides something] for all interests.[85]

Even for Congress Muslims, Nehru was advocating a distressing amount of flexibility, and his seizure of the initiative at this time did not augur well for the future of communal unity.

At the meeting called at Bombay on 19 May, Dr Ansari, the conference President, had bad news for his listeners. His endeavours to persuade Muslim League members to attend in an individual capacity had in most cases been fruitless,[86] and the sub-committees set up at Delhi had not produced their reports. The conference decided, nonetheless, 'that a small committee, viewing the communal problem as a whole in relation to the constitution, might succeed in finding a way out'.[87] Motilal Nehru was appointed Chairman and there were nine other members, Shuaib Qureshi and Sir Ali Imam to represent the Muslims, M.R. Jayakar and M.S. Aney for the Mahasabha, Sardar

[84] See, for example, Syed Mahmud papers (Nehru Memorial Museum, New Delhi): Jawaharlal to Syed Mahmud, 17 March 1928.

[85] AICC papers, G 63: circular letter, 3 May 1928 (motheaten).

[86] See Ansari papers: Nawab Ismail Khan to Ansari, 10 May 1928: Mahommed Yakub to Ansari, 9 May 1928.

[87] *All Parties Conference 1928, Report*, p. 23.

Mangal Singh for the Sikhs, G.R. Pradhan for the non-Brahmins, T.B. Sapru, the liberal leader, N.M. Joshi, the trade unionist, and Subhas Chandra Bose from Bengal. Of these, Jayakar took no part at all, and Sir Ali Imam,[88] N.M. Joshi, G.R. Pradhan and Subhas Bose only made limited contributions. The bulk of the work fell on five men, Motilal Nehru, Shuaib Qureshi, Mangal Singh, Aney and Sapru, though Jawaharlal Nehru also attended many of the later and more important meetings.

Between 5 June and 22 June, the committee met for several hours each day in Motilal's house at Allahabad. It made good progress on the general outlines of the constitution but the communal question remained intractable. After a number of deadlocks, Nehru persuaded Mangal Singh and Aney to accept the separation of Sind and equal status for the Frontier, but even then Shuaib Qureshi remained adamant about reservation for majorities, and ultimately Sapru supported him. In the hope of extricating the committee from this impasse, Nehru then called on Ansari, who suggested tailoring the franchise to give each community a voting strength commensurate with its population.[89] On 22 June, however, this suggestion was also rejected and dissentient reports seemed inevitable. Nehru and a close circle of colleagues decided nonetheless to make one further attempt to secure a unanimous report. They called a final meeting at Allahabad on 6 and 7 July and issued additional invitations, chiefly to Mahasabhites and nationalist Muslims.[90]

On 7 July, somewhat surprisingly, this conference adopted a compromise formula, subject to a note by Sardar Mangal Singh. According to this formula, all members of the conference were opposed to reservation of seats, whether for majorities or minorities. 'But', it went on, 'if this recommendation is not accepted and an agreement can be arrived at only on the population basis, we recommend that

---

[88] As a former Prime Minister of Hyderabad, Ali Imam was keeping out of British Indian politics to avoid prejudicing the Nizam's demand for the restoration of the Berars. The report gives 'ill health' as the main reason for his non-attendance, but there is no mention of ill-health in a letter from Nehru urging him to attend the important meeting of 6 July. See Ali Imam papers (Karachi University Library): Ali Imam to the Nizam, 5 Jan. 1928: Motilal to Ali Imam, 28 June 1928.

[89] AICC papers, AP 2/1928; Minutes of 18th sitting, 22 June.

[90] For details of the progress of these discussions, see AICC papers, AP 2/1928; Mahommed Ali papers (a fuller record); and Motilal Nehru papers: Motilal to Gandhi, 27 June 1928.

such reservation be made for majorities or minorities without any weightage and with a clear provision that it shall automatically cease at the expiry of 10 years, or earlier by consent of the parties concerned.'[91] Far from really solving the problem, this formula merely pandered to all interests without deciding anything. Some accepted it as a statement of principle, while others only supported the principle because they were confident that it would never form the basis of an agreement. Those who fell into this second group subsequently discovered, however, that they had made a serious miscalculation, for by this stage, the committee organizers were more concerned to produce a unanimous report than an agreement which would secure wider acceptance.

On 20 July, in the middle of drafting his report, Motilal wrote a letter to members of the committee which indirectly put a new interpretation on the formula of 7 July.[92] The bulk of the letter referred to a meeting of the committee on 8 July at which the previous day's formula had been modified to allow for reservation of seats according to population for minorities in the Central Legislature and the provinces.[93] Nehru pointed out that these changes had been intended to refer only to Muslim minorities and he wanted permission to make this clear in his report. Both the length of the letter and some of its arguments, however, suggest that he had other intentions as well. There was no need, he said, to make any provision for the Sikhs, for they only wanted reservation if other communities in Punjab were granted reservation. This was the first argument to make Muslims feel uncomfortable for it appeared to close the door on the second part of the original formula. The second was to be found in his conclusion.

We have already arrived at a common understanding to do away with separate electorates, reservation of seats for Muslim majorities and weightage for other minorities, the three greatest obstacles in the way of our political advancement. We should not risk this great

---

[91] All Parties Conference 1928, Report, p. 50. In his note, Sardar Mangal Singh expressed his opposition to reservation for majorities 'under all circumstances'. If this was found to be the only basis for agreement, he gave notice that the Sikhs would require weightage 'far in excess of their numerical strength'.

[92] Ansari papers: circular letter from Motilal to members of the all-parties conference committee, 20 July 1928.

[93] For the 'official' account of these meetings, see Note on the Informal Conference and After, *All Parties Conference 1928, Report*, pp. 125-6.

achievement by taking a narrow view on the question of Muslim minorities in the provincial councils.

Couched in these terms, this argument seems to be an appeal for compassion towards minority-province Muslims. In effect, however, it required all those who had attended the conference of 7 July to modify their position. They had not agreed to do away with reservation of seats for Muslim majorities. They had merely declared their opposition to reservation, whilst making provision for it in both majority and minority provinces if its abolition was not generally accepted. This, at any rate, was the view of Shuaib Qureshi, who, on receiving Motilal's letter, complained that the original agreement had been altered.[94] Motilal did not accept this, and Sherwani supported Motilal, but Shuaib continued to be dissatisfied and when Motilal's interpretation was enshrined in the report, Shuaib wrote a minute of dissent.

In his minute of dissent, Shuaib does not refer in detail to the proceedings of the Nehru committee. Instead, he harks back to the Congress resolutions passed at Bombay and Madras in May and December 1927.

Is it open to Congress [he asks] to denounce an agreement while the other party to it, the League, stands by it and specially when it has driven one section of it out of its fold on that particular issue? I maintain that it is too late in the day for political explorers to equip expeditions to pick holes in the agreement.

There was an obvious reason for Shuaib's reversion to the *status quo ante:* he was anxious to secure for Muslim majorities in Punjab and Bengal those concessions which had been granted both by Congress and Mahasabha in 1927 but retracted by the Nehru committee following its meeting on 7 July. This is clear both from the fact that he devotes a substantial part of his minute to justifying reservation for majorities and from his willingness to limit such reservations to a period of ten

---

[94] At the informal conference of 8 July, Shuaib Qureshi had been alone in objecting to the decision to allow reservation of seats for minority province Muslims. He probably feared then that this concession would undermine the second part of the formula agreed the day before. For evidence of Shuaib's indignation on receiving Nehru's letter, see Khaliquzzaman, op. cit., pp. 94-6. Khaliq's memory of these events is faulty in detail. Both he and Shuaib were present on 8 May, and he supported reservation for minorities.

years, the precise stipulation of the second part of the 7 July formula.[95] Shuaib had obviously voted for that formula in the confidence that abolition would not be accepted when the all-parties conference considered the report, and he clearly considered himself the victim of a political manoeuvre when the whole matter was prejudged by other members of the committee before the conference met.

The circumstances in which the Nehru committee took this direction suggest that Jawaharlal was chiefly responsible. During the committee itself, though not officially a member, he had played a part in several of the more important sessions,[96] and after the meetings of 6 and 7 July, by his father's own admission, he was one of the chief architects of the report.[97] Sapru was responsible for the sections on the Indian states and on Dominion Status and responsible government,[98] but Motilal wrote the sections dealing with the communal question and Jawaharlal prepared much of this material himself.[99] It is admitted in the report, for example, that Jawaharlal was responsible for the statistical tables on Punjab and Bengal, which were collated after 7 July and designed specifically to show that Muslims of those provinces would be better off without reservation.[100] It also seems likely, however, from the tone of the report on this issue, that Jawaharlal actually wrote this part himself. The determination of the author to face the problem and solve it, his condemnation of communal organizations for not wanting to change the existing structure of society, and his faith that in a free India political parties would be formed on an economic basis, all smack strongly of Jawaharlal and not his father.[101]

Supporting evidence for this interpretation is also provided by

[95]Shuaib Qureshi, confidential minute on the draft constitution prepared by the Nehru committee (copy provided by Syed Sharifuddin Pirzada).

[96]It is indicative of Jawaharlal's influence that Shuaib Qureshi dissuaded Khaliquzzaman from staying with him when in Allahabad for the meetings of 6 and 7 July. See Khaliquzzaman, op. cit., p. 94.

[97] *A Bunch of Old Letters*, p. 60-1: Motilal to Gandhi, 11 July 1928, 'The members have all gone to their respective homes, leaving Jawahar and myself to prepare the report and we are now hard at work at it.'

[98] Nanda, *op.cit.*, pp. 289-90.

[99] *A Bunch of Old Letters*, p. 65: Motilal to Gandhi, 19 July 1928. 'Jawaharlal has left copious notes for me but points not foreseen by him or me are arising at every step as I dictate the report.'

[100]*All Parties Conference 1928, Report*, pp. 43-4, appendices A and B, p. 137-53.

[101] Ibid., pp. 48-9.

Motilal's depressed state of mind. Before the meetings of 6 and 7 July, he had confided to Gandhi that he had no hopes of a successful boycott of the Simon Commission and only slender ones of a productive conclusion to his committee's endeavours. Indeed such were his feelings that he had already agreed to visit Canada in the autumn and had no intention of changing his mind unless a unanimous report materialised.[102] After the meeting of 7 July, this mood does not appear to have changed. He informed Gandhi that some kind of unanimity had been achieved. It was sufficient to stand by at the all-parties conference and he had therefore cancelled his passage to Canada. But it was neither complete nor of a genuine type; nor was it sufficient to make him yield to Gandhi's suggestion that he should become Congress President. In his view, the first choice was Vallabhbhai Patel, and failing him, Jawaharlal. 'Our race', he wrote, 'is fast dying out and the struggle will sooner or later have to be continued by men of Jawahar's type. The sooner they begin the better.' 'As for myself,' he continued, 'I feel I have lost much of the confidence I had in myself and am more or less a spent force.'[103]

It was in these circumstances that the younger Nehru acquired the ascendancy over his father and pressed him into a brittle defiance of the political system which he had tried so hard to work. How this actually happened is perhaps more a subject for the psychologist than for the historian. Suffice it to say, however, that just six days after describing himself as a spent force, Motilal was displaying a significant change of mood. He told Purushotamdas Thakurdas that he was 'entirely wrong' in thinking that the committee would not be unanimous. 'I like your way of putting it', he wrote, 'when you say that it is disconcerting to find that I have differed from men like Ansari and Shuaib Qureshi, instead of saying that it is unfortunate that Dr Ansari and Shuaib Qureshi should differ from a man like me. How could they dare?'[104] The political implications of this change of mood are made clear in another letter written shortly afterwards to Sen Gupta and Bose in Bengal. In this letter, Nehru again refuses to accept the Congress Presidency. 'My own opinion,' he writes, 'is that the occasion requires a strong go-ahead party in the country prepared to go the whole hog at all costs and that this party should have the further direction of the campaign in its own

[102]Motilal Nehru papers: Motilal to Gandhi, 27 June 1928.
[103]*A Bunch of Old Letters*, pp. 60-1: Motilal to Gandhi, 11 July 1928.
[104]Purshotamadas Thakurdas papers, 71: Motilal to Thakurdas, 17 July 1928.

hands. A quiet climb down from Independence to Dominion Status will bring the Congress into ridicule.'[105] Such was, of course, the logic of the situation, for as Nehru had always known, communal harmony did not only depend on satisfying Shuaib Qureshi. It also depended on the virtually impossible task of winning over those provincial Muslim interests who had never taken part in any national discussions and who, even as the Nehru committee was doing its work, were voting one by one to co-operate with the Simon Commission. Granted, however, that the younger Nehru's impatience of all-parties conferences and his desire (in the words of the report) to get going were justifiable,[106] the method of settling the communal issue employed by the committee nonetheless marked a very serious break with Congress tradition. In effect, it had given up negotiating and begun steamrolling instead.

The emergence of the All India Muslim Conference

The Nehru report was first published on 21 August, and it immediately aroused tremendous interest. Even before the all-parties conference met, a second edition had to be run off, and by the end of September, 12,000 copies had reached the market. The constitution which the report put forward was the most coherent and radical ever framed by a group of Indian politicians, and though its communal provisions have since received most attention, its political provisions were equally controversial and undoubtedly contributed to the welter of communal dissension in which it was soon submerged. All departments of the Central government, including Defence, Finance and relations with the States, were to be transferred to the control of a responsible Indian legislature, and though Dominion Status was the goal, it was demanded as the next immediate step in India's political evolution. The Central Government was to consist of a Governor-General appointed by the King, a Prime Minister appointed by the Governor-General, and six Ministers, appointed by the Governor-General on the Prime Minister's advice. The appointment of a provincial government was to follow a similar pattern. In both cases, Cabinets were to be jointly responsible to their respective legislatures, and the powers of both Governor-

[105]*A Bunch of Old Letters*, p. 64: Motilal to Bose and Sen Gupta, 19 July 1928.
[106]*All Parties Committee 1928, report*, p. 49.

General and Governor reduced to a bare minimum. The lower house of the central legislature and all provincial legislatures were to be elected on an adult franchise. There was also to be a Supreme Court, a Committee for Defence, and a Public Services Commission. Relations between the central government and the provincial governments were not discussed in detail. But it is clear from the schedules of subjects under their charge the the national government was to be of a unitary rather than a federal type, with residuary powers in the hands of the central government. This was subsequently to be a bone of contention with many opponents of the Congress point of view. In the communal sphere, the report recommended the abolition of separate electorates and of weightage for minorities, and it also rejected the Muslim demand for reservation for majorities and for thirty-three per cent at the Centre. Only those Muslims from the North-West had reason to be pleased, for the separation of Sind was supported, as was equal status for the Frontier.

The all-parties conference to consider the report was convened at Lucknow on 28 August. The Raja of Mahmudabad, Sarojini Naidu and Dr Ansari, all urged the Nehrus to postpone it so that Jinnah could attend,[107] but though they secured a token postponement of one day,[108] the indications are that the Nehrus were not anxious to be conciliatory. All 'religious' bodies, including two influential Sikh organizations, the Akali Dal and the Siromani Gurdwara Prabhandhak Committee. were excluded,[109] and the attendance was kept down to about a hundred people.[110] Special passes were issued for the press, and at least one prominent journalist, Syed Habib Shah of the Lahore *Siyasat,* was kept out of the meeting.[111] Such being the case, it was not surprising that the meeting produced a happy result. On 30 August,

---

[107]Jawaharlal Nehru papers (Nehru Memorial Museum, New Delhi): Dr Ansari to Jawaharlal, 27 July 1928; AICC papers, 2/1928: Sarojini Naidu to Motilal, 26 July 1928; Dr Ansari to Motilal, 25 July 1928; Raja Mahmudabad to Motilal, 23 July 1928.

[108]AICC papers, 2/1928:, Motilal to Sarojini Naidu, 28 July 1928.

[109] Ibid., Jawaharlal to Secretary, All India Aryan League, 21 Aug. 1928.

[110]Ibid., Jawaharlal to Mohanlal Saxena, 3 Aug. 1928. When Saxena asked for a list of persons to be accommodated, Jawaharlal told him it would be impossible to provide one. They were only expecting a hundred people and names would not be known till the last minute.

[111] Firoz Khan Noon, *Dominion Status or Autonomous Province?* (Lahore 1928), p.ii.

it was unanimously agreed that 'simultaneously with the establishment of a constitution in accordance with the Nehru committee's report', Sind should be constituted a separate province, provided that it was found to be financially self-supporting, or failing that, provided that a majority of the inhabitants favoured the scheme. And on the following day, amid much public enthusiasm, the Punjab Khilafatists and Lajpat Rai's party agreed to accept joint electorates without reservation of seats, provided that the franchise was based on adult suffrage and that the question could be reconsidered after ten years. Several other amendments were also passed, including one giving Baluchistan the same treatment as the Frontier, and the conference concluded with a resolution adopting the report in principle and reappointing Nehru's committee with powers of co-option to give its recommendations the shape of a Parliamentary Bill.[112]

As the various agreements were reached, the only murmur of dissent came from Shaukat Ali, who fell out with the Punjabi Khilafatists over the abolition of reservation for majorities, stating that the Central Khilafat Committee still stood by its original resolution on this question.[113] This provoked an angry response from the Punjabis, who held that they had been authorized to come to an agreement on the majority provinces and that therefore the agreement had the blessing of the entire organization.[114] Strictly speaking, the Punjabis were right, for after a nine-hour meeting, the Central Khilafat Committee had agreed to delegate powers for this purpose.[115] The length of time taken to reach this decision, however, suggests that many concurred reluctantly, and amongst them, undoubtedly, was Shaukat Ali. For him, as for his brother, the secession of the Punjabi and Bengali Khilafatists was a bitter blow. Even by 1925, their standing with their own community had been very much in decline, and if Congress now struck bargains independently with different Khilafat factions, their only remaining political asset, control of the all-India organization, would also be in jeopardy. Following the Lucknow conference, therefore, Shaukat girded up his loins for action. He broke with Motilal Nehru, denouncing him for making concessions

---

[112]*All Parties Conference 1928, Report,* p. 159-68: summary of proceedings of Lucknow Conference.

[113]This was precisely the same question over which Shuaib Qureshi had quarrelled with Motilal.

[114] *All Parties Conference 1928, Report,* p. 164-5.

[115]*Searchlight,* 29 Aug. 1928.

to the Mahasabha, and he also broke with the Muslims who supported Motilal, chief among whom was Ansari, denouncing them as Congress stooges.[116]

Shaukat Ali's repudiation of the Nehru report was a considerable embarrassment to Congress. But a more serious challenge to the report came from those provincial forces on whom the government had relied from the beginning. In the government's view, these interests were the key to the success of the Statutory Commission, and as early as March, even before Nehru's committee was appointed, the Viceroy had been confident that they would come round.[117] As might have been expected, the province which took the lead was Hailey's Punjab. On 14 March, the Punjab Legislative Council voted without a division to appoint a committee to co-operate with the Commission, and on 11 May the committee was set up.[118] Other provinces responded more slowly, but despite early setbacks in the Central Provinces, Madras and the U.P.,[119] these also fulfilled the Viceroy's expectations. By the time the Nehru report was published, three other provinces had voted for co-operation (Assam on 3 April, Bengal on 10 July and Bombay on 3 August) and soon afterwards, Bihar and Orissa, U.P. and Madras followed suit. In this process the Muslims played a crucial part. The earliest councils to vote for co-operation were those with the largest Muslim membership (Punjab, Bengal and Assam),[120] and the last ones, those with the smallest (Madras, U.P. and Bihar and Orissa). Even in the minority provinces, however, it was Muslim co-operation with nominated and official members which enabled the government to carry its point,[121] and only in the Central Provinces,

[116] GI Home Poll. File 1/1928: FR Delhi I Sept; Shaukat Ali papers: Shaukat Ali to Mahommed Ali, 13 Oct. 1928.

[117] Halifax papers. 4: Irwin to Birkenhead, 8 March 1928.

[118] *PLC progs.*, vol. xi, pp. 716-59. In anticipation of this success, Hailey was recommended for the GCIE in February.

[119] The C.P. Council voted against co-operation on 20 Jan., the Madras Council on 24 Jan., and the U.P. Council on 25 Feb.

[120] In the Bengal Council, 72 voted for co-operation (including 32 Muslims) and 50 against (including two Muslims). In the Assam Council, 31 voted for co-operation (including 10 Muslims) and 15 against (no Muslims). See *Bengal LC Progs.*, vol. 29, pp. 181-2; *Assam LC Progs.*, vol. viii, pp. 256-75.

[121] In the U.P., the precise extent of government reliance on the Muslims cannot be quantified because the opposition walked out. In Bihar and Orissa, where a committee was appointed by a majority of six, 19 Muslims supported government and four opposed it.

where the constitution did not provide for government rule by means of such combinations, was no co-operating committee ever elected.

Those who already found themselves in the separatist lobby could look to leadership chiefly from two sources, the Punjab and the United Provinces. In the Punjab, it was Fazli Husain's Unionist party which gave the lead, and in the U.P. a group of Muslim members of the Legislative Council, chiefly from the western divisions of the province, who were co-ordinated by Professor Shafaat Ahmed Khan of Allahabad University and financed by Sir Mahommed Yusuf, the Minister of Local Self-Government. The views of the first group are most succinctly expressed in the majority report of the Punjab Legislative Council co-operating committee set up in May 1928 under the chairmanship of Sikunder Hayat Khan,[122] and those of the second in the *Representation of the Muslims of the United Provinces (India) to the Indian Statutory Commission.*[123]

In many respects, the views of these two groups were diametrically opposed to each other. The Unionist party in the Punjab was confident that any further devolution of power at the provincial level would be to its advantage, and Sikunder's committee reflected this confidence in the outlines of its scheme. It suggested that the Muslims be given a majority of one seat by separate electorates in a house of 165,[124] and it sought to minimise the importance of communal tension in order to secure the widest and most unfettered devolution possible.[125] Within the provincial council, it proposed to abolish the official element, special constituencies and nominated seats,[126] and it rejected anything

[122]*Indian Statutory Commission* vol. iii, *Reports of the Committees appointed by the provincial legislative councils to cooperate with the Indian Statutory Commission* (London 1930), *Cmd. 3572*, pp. 389-508. In the foreword to the Punjab report, it is acknowledged that its preparation was largely Sikunder's work. Zafrullah, Owen Roberts and Chothu Ram praise his efforts to reconcile 'conflicting claims'. But the Hindu and Sikh representatives, Gokul Chand Narang, Raja Narendra Nath and Sardar Ujjal Singh, all submit notes of dissent.

[123]This representation was dispatched to the Simon Commission in July 1928. Besides Shafaat, the main contributors were Sheikh Zahur Ahmed, the Secretary; Hafiz Hidayat Hussain, who wrote the sections on the provincial government and the judiciary; and K.B. Masud ul Hassan, a former Chairman of the Moradabad Muncipal Board, who advised on local government affairs. Nawab Yusuf's financial support is acknowleded in the preface.

[124]*ISC*, vol. iii, p. 418.

[125]Ibid., pp. 397-400.

[126] Ibid. pp. 408, 418, 420.

but the most elementary safeguards for minorities and vested interests. It was not in favour of a second chamber, it was not prepared to allow reservation of Cabinet posts for minorities and it proposed to make the High Court and the provincial services the responsibility of the provincial government.[127] The U.P. Muslims, on the other hand, fearing that in the prevailing communal atmosphere of their province a further devolution of power would merely usher in 'a Brahmin or a Kayasth domination',[128] declared their opposition to all forms of provincial advance if their position was not safeguarded. They favoured a continuation of Dyarchy, with Law and Order and Revenue remaining reserved subjects.[129] They were opposed to the abolition of the nominated element and special constituencies.[130] They demanded a second chamber and they required that thirty three per cent of all Cabinet posts should be allocated to their community. These U.P. Muslim demands were, in fact, the most far-reaching ever put forward by a minority community. They also demanded separate electorates with weightage at every level of government, effective representation on all autonomous institutions created by the legislatures, safeguards for Urdu, adequate safeguards for the exercise of Muslim religious rights, due allocation of grants in aid by government and local bodies, and a share of the services according to their representative proportion in any given body.[131] In short, no body of demands further removed from those of the Punjab Unionists could possibly have been envisaged.

Outside the sphere of provincial devolution, however, the two groups shared similar views. Not only did they both support the separation of Sind, reforms for the Frontier and Baluchistan, a thirty-three per cent Muslim share in the Central Legislature and the

[127]Ibid., pp. 421-3, 439. The report particularly condemned the existing Punjab government practice of appointing ministers to represent communal interests. If adopted, it said, such a practice 'would cut at the very roots of the principle of responsible government. It is inconceivable that a Cabinet constituted on the lines suggested would survive even a day.'

[128]*Representation of the Muslims of the United Provinces (India) to the Indian Statutory Commission* (Allahabad 1928). p. 149.

[129]Ibid., p. 16.

[130]Ibid., p. 12. They proposed that in a council of 200, non-Muslims should account for 100 seats, Muslims for 50, nominated officials and non-officials for 30, and special interests for 20.

[131] Ibid., pp. 16-18, 284.

continuation of separate electorates;[132] they also showed a common opposition to control of the central government by the majority community, though for different reasons in each case. The Unionists were not opposed in principle to full responsible government at the Centre, though for fifteen or twenty years they envisaged some form of Dyarchy. It was their considered opinion, however, that any further advance at the Centre should follow and not precede or synchronise with the establishment of autonomy in the provinces.[133] This was a clear indication of their suspicion of central government control, which was also evident in their rejection of a unitary system of government at the national level. 'In our opinion,' they said, 'the adoption of the proposal that the central government should be vested with unlimited powers of interference with and control over the provincial governments would mean merely the substitution of one oligarchy for another.'[134] What they wanted (and here they were supported by the official members of the Punjab government, Hailey and de Montmorency), was a federal system in which power would devolve directly from Parliament to the provinces and not from Parliament to the provinces through the central government.[135] In their scheme, the central government was to be confined to those spheres of activity which were specifically allocated to it, and residuary powers were to rest with the provinces. This stipulation, which had been made in embryo at the Lahore League of 1924, was to assume great importance as the revision of the constitution progressed.

The U.P. Muslims adopted a very different attitude. The Unionists envisaged the establishment of responsible government at the Centre, and made provision in their recommendations to restrict such a government's control over the provinces. The U.P. Muslims, on the other hand, were scarcely prepared to envisage such a development. In their view, the existence of communal mistrust was a sufficient reason for the maintenance of the *status quo:*

We are of the opinion that the relationship between the Governor-

---

[132]*ISC,* vol. iii, pp. 407, 411-13, 418-19, 434; *Representation of the Muslims of the United Provinces,* pp. 11,18,137.

[133]*ISC,* vol. iii, pp. 432-3.

[134]Ibid., p. 430.

[135]Ibid., p. 430-1. Hailey and de Montmorency had made this suggestion in a memorandum submitted to the Statutory Commission in 1928. See *ISC* vol. x (London 1930), part iii, p. 26.

General and his Executive Council which now subsists be maintained. ... We feel that a strong central government, which is able and willing to pursue a policy that is not coloured by communal, racial, local, provincial or economic prejudices is necessary at the present juncture, and is essential in a country where conflict of interest necessitates absolute impartiality and prompt action.[136]

The U.P. Muslims wanted a strong central government—and this involved vesting residuary powers at the Centre—because they envisaged the continuance of British control. In the words of Masud ul Hassan, they wanted 'fundamental safeguards which nobody in India can touch,'[137] and this was only possible if the British Parliament retained the right to interfere in the provinces on behalf of the minorities. 'We are strongly opposed', wrote Shafaat Ahmed, to vesting the Central Government with the power of amending any constitution that is granted to it by the British parliament'.[138] In their different ways, therefore, both the Unionists and the U.P. Muslims were opposed to what Jinnah and the Congress were campaigning for. Neither wanted to be subjected to a national government at the Centre.

Among the Muslims of these two groups, the publication of the Nehru report did not produce any major changes of political orientation. Most of them had always believed that they would get a better hearing from government than from Congress, and before the report was published, most of them had already decided to co-operate with the Simon Commission.[139] As had been the case with the publication of the Congress-League scheme in 1916, however, the Nehru report immediately made the running politically, and forced even those politicians who were opposed to Congress to define their attitudes to the political future which it outlined. For both the U.P. separatists and the Punjab Unionists, the report posed the question: 'What is your attitude to the prospect of an effective British withdrawal from the central government'?

Among the Unionists, the most systematic response came from

---

[136] *Representation of the Muslims of the United Provinces,* p. 135.

[137] Ibid., P. 132.

[138] Ibid., p. 134.

[139] An exception was Sheikh Habibullah, a member of the U.P. council, who confessed that the report had made him a supporter of co-operation. He was alienated, however, not so much by the report's communal provisions as by its 'absurd' proposals for the franchise and by its failure to provide special representation for landlords. See *UPLC Progs.,* vol. xxxix, no. 2,18 Sept. 1928, pp. 173-4.

Firoz Khan Noon, the Minister for Local Self-Government, who in October 1928, published a pamphlet with the significant title *Dominion Status* or *Autonomous Provinces*. This pamphlet, which, in the author's words, was 'nothing short of the Nehru Committee's report shorn of its Hindu clothes and centralisation structure and placed into Muslim garb and shaped into a provincial figure', provides a powerful indication of the increasing importance of Centre-Province relations in determining attitudes towards Reform. 'Why do Muslims fear over-centralisation?' asked Firoz. 'It is because in the Central legislature the Hindus will always be in an overwhelming majority and if they have the power to legislate for the provinces also, then the Muslim majorities in Bengal, Punjab, North West Frontier Province, Sind and Baluchistan will be entirely imaginary.'[140] Firoz's answer was to draw up a constitution in which the powers of the central government were even more severely restricted than in the proposals of the Sikunder Committee. Complete responsibility was rejected in favour of a form of Dyarchy. Of nine ministers, four were to be nominated and irremovable by vote (Ministers for Foreign Affairs, Political Relations, Defence and Law), and of the five elected ministers, who were to hold office on the basis of joint responsibility, two were always to be Muslims, and the representation of other minorities was to be encouraged in the Governor-General's Instrument of Instructions.[141] The same restrictions were also applied to the Executive and Judiciary. Officers of the all-India and provincial services, and of the Defence services, were to be paid from a consolidated fund over which the legislatures were to have no control,[142] and the Governor-General was to be empowered 'to enforce representation of all classes and communities of His Majesty's subjects in all departments of the Central Government.'[143] High Court judges were to be appointed by Governors on the advice of their Cabinets,[144] and in the Supreme Court, thirtythree per cent of the judges were to be Muslim and 'there must always be some Europeans....'[145] In effect, the proposals were designed to prevent the majority community from exercising any real power.

In the U.P., where Muslim demands for all manner of separate

[140]Firoz Khan Noon, *Dominion Status or Autonomous Provinces* (Lahore 1928), p.v.
[141]Ibid., pp. 10-11.
[142]Ibid., p. 14
[143]Ibid., P. 11.
[144]Ibid., p. 18.
[145]Ibid., p. 15.

representation had met with a hammer blow from Nehru and his colleagues, those who had been responsible for the Statutory Commission Memorandum convened an all-parties Muslim conference at Kanpur on 4 November. Hafiz Hidayat Hussain, Masud ul Hassan and Sheikh Zahur Ahmed, all three of them important contributors to the memorandum, now figured prominently on the platform and reiterated the demands which they had earlier submitted to the Commission. By November 1928, however, one additional and more extreme demand had emerged—for a fifty per cent share in the provincial government. This demand, which appears initially to be just another indication of Muslim nervousness, may well have been the result of a change of attitude towards the prospect of a national government at the Centre. Hafiz Hidayat Hussain, the Chairman of the Reception Committee, told his audience that the Nehru report's greatest drawback was that it concentrated power in the central government where Muslims would always remain in a minority. The solution, he said, was a federal system of government which would provide for provinces where the Muslim majority could retaliate the treatment [*sic*] meted out to their community in the Hindu provinces.[146] This statement reflects a considerable change in perspective since the submission of U.P. Muslim memorandum to Simon, and it suggests that Nehru's recommendations had forced Hidayat Hussain and his friends to face the question: 'How are we to protect ourselves if we cannot rely on the Raj'? It suggests, moreover, that their answer to this question was to put their faith in a system of 'retaliation', which depended for its effectiveness on a maximum degree of provincial autonomy for the majority-province Muslims. By November, therefore, the political future of the U.P. Muslims was seen to be far more interlocked with that of their Punjabi co-religionists than had been the case in July.

The Kanpur conference was also significant because it witnessed an important accession of strength to the minority-province separatists from those 'nationalist' Muslims who had been alienated by the Nehru report. The President of the session was no less a person than Shaukat Ali, who now established himself in the separatist camp. In the future he was to make occasional forays into 'nationalist' politics, drawn by his personal indications and his lengthy acquaintance with Congress

---

[146] For an account of the Muslim meeting at Kanpur, *see Indian Quarterly Register*, 1928, vol. ii, pp. 421-5.

leaders. Yet just as the constraints of the system had forced him into the separatist camp, so they continued to keep him there. The same was also true of his brother, Mahommed, who following his return from Europe in October, took up an identical position. Not only did he support the demands of the U.P. Muslims for safeguards: he also campaigned for a loose federation with maximum provincial autonomy. At the Bihar all-parties Muslim conference early in December, he condemned the Nehru report for favouring the Hindu Mahasabha. 'Even in the provinces where Muslims had a majority,' he said, 'the Nehru report was so planned as to counteract the influence of that Muslim majority by having too dominant a central government at Delhi.'[147] It was not to be long before he was to find himself on the same platform as Fazli Husain and Sir Mahommed Shafi.

The Congress response to these developments was to support those Muslims who subscribed to the Nehru report—the Delhi group under Dr Ansari's leadership, including Asaf Ali and Dr Zakir Hussain, the Bengalis, with whom Abul Kalam Azad was the chief Congress link, and the Punjabi Khilafatists led by Zafar Ali, Dr Kitchlew, Mahommed Alam and Habib ur Rahman. Congress support was given chiefly in cash, and for this purpose collections were made both in Bombay and Calcutta. In the first three weeks of October, 25,000 rupees were collected, 16,000 coming through G.D. Birla, and the rest, with the exception of 1,000 rupees each from Sir Ali Imam and the AICC, from Bombay and Ahmedabad. Of this, 5,000 rupees went to Abul Kalam Azad, 3,000 to Lajpat Rai and 1,000 to Sardar Mangal Singh. Most of the rest went to pay Rafi Ahmed Kidwai's salary and expenses and for editions of the Nehru report in various Indian languages.[148] The success of the campaign was limited, particularly in Delhi, where Dr Ansari, despite help from the Punjab, found himself severely taxed both on the platform and in the press by Shaukat Ali.[149] But in the Punjab and Bengal, where Jinnah's League had set

[147]*Indian Quarterly Register, 1928, vol. ii, p. 426.*

[148]Shaukat Ali wrote to his brother about this campaign: 'Hindus want to kill the Muslim opposition [to the Nehru report] by sheer force or propaganda. Birla and others have subscribed 1½ lakhs for this purpose. Abul Kalam, as usual, will get a share of the loot.... Zafar Ali is also hovering about for carrion.' See Shaukat Ali papers: Shaukat to Mahommed, 13 Oct. 1928. For details of the all-parties conference fund, see AICC papers, 16/1928

[149]GI Home Poll.,File I/1928: Delhi FR I Sept, I and II Oct. 1928.

up 'nationalist' branches in December 1927,[150] it was sufficient for resolutions supporting the Nehru report to be passed by both these bodies, and by November, Motilal was clearly basing the success of his propaganda operation on the continued adherence of these two provinces.[151]

The most important personality in Motilal's calculations, however, was Mahommed Ali Jinnah, who returned to India some months later than expected as a result of his wife's illness in Paris. If Jinnah could be won over, the Nehru report would acquire added prestige, and Motilal therefore deputed Purushotamdas Thakurdas to 'rope in Jinnah' before Shaukat Ali got to him.

So much depends on Jinnah [he wrote] that I have a mind to go to Bombay to receive him. If I have the necessary funds within the next few days I hope to create a strong opinion amongst the Mussulmans to greet Jinnah on his arrival. Therefore please lose no time to raise as much money as you can for this great enterprise.[152]

When Jinnah arrived, however, he did not immediately proclaim his support for Nehru's recommendations but characteristically chose to sound out Muslim opinion first. Nehru, who wrote to him from Ahmedabad the day after he arrived, urged him to attend the all-parties committee meeting at Delhi on 5 November, assuring him that members of the committee were not representatives of the organizations to which they belonged and that his presence would not commit the Muslim League to any decision reached. All such decisions, he said, would be open to alteration at the all-parties convention at Calcutta on 17 December.[153] But Jinnah was too experienced a politician to put his head in such a noose. He was not

[150]The new Punjab Muslim League was chiefly composed of the Khilafatists who came to agreement with Nehru's committee at Lucknow. See Rafiq Afzal, *Malik Barkat Ali, His Life and Writings* (Lahore 1969), part i, pp. 22-3. Also GI Home Poll., File 1/1928: Punjab FR I Sept. 1928.

[151]The outlines of this policy had already been formed in Sept., when Nehru told Mrs Besant that the most effective answer to the minority province Muslims who championed the rights of the majority provinces 'would be that the Punjab and Bengal have accepted the Lucknow resolutions and do not need the other provinces to champion their cause'. But by Nov., after the Punjab and Bengal Muslim Leagues had passed their resolutions, Nehru could write to Gandhi that Punjab and Bengal were 'the only two provinces that matter. . . The provinces where the Muslims are in minorities have really no say in the matter'. See *A Bunch of Old Letters*, p. 65-9: Motilal to Mrs Besant, 30 Sept. 1928; Motilal Nehru papers: Motilal to Gandhi, 24 Nov. 1928.

[152]Purushotamdas Thakurdas papers, 71: Motilal to Thakurdas, 20 Sept. 1928.

[153]Ibid: Motilal to Jinnah, 28 Oct. 1928.

prepared to attend any all-parties conference until he knew his brief,
and though he sent Nehru a letter to be read out at the Delhi meeting,
he waited to see what would happen at the Muslim League council
meeting which he had called at Lucknow on 11 November.[154]

The Lucknow Muslim League council meeting was less conclusive
than Jinnah would have liked. Three different schools were present
(the Independents, the Congress Muslims and the U.P. separatists)
and no decision was reached by a substantial majority. A resolution
thanking the Nehru committee for its report (but not committing the
League to accepting its provisions) was carried by only four votes,
and the Raja of Mahmudabad was elected President of the annual
session by a majority of two.[155] From Jinnah's point of view, this
absence of unanimity made it impolitic for him to open negotiations
with the Congress. He ensured that the two organizations met in the
same city but he was not prepared to attend the all-parties convention
until a full session of the League had met. This attitude forced him
into disagreement with Motilal who wished the League to meet after
the convention so that it could ratify its decisions. Jinnah was adamant,
however, that authorization to attend the convention could not come
from the council alone; and he also held that subsequent ratification
by the League would not be necessary if adequate authorization was
forthcoming in the first place. This difference of opinion caused
some ill-feeling between the two men and the air was only cleared
when Sir Ali Imam helped them to come to a compromise. The all-
parties convention was to begin on 22 December, as Nehru had planned,
but its open session was to be held on 27 and 28 December, to allow
the League to send accredited representatives. The open session of
the Congress was to start on the 29th.[156]

Before the League met at Calcutta, a powerful section of support
had seceded from it. This was the Khilafat section which had repudiated

[154] Ibid., Thakurdas to Motilal, 30 Oct. 1928. Thakurdas tells Nehru that Jinnah 'does
not wish to prejudice the prospect of bringing the two sides together by joining your
committee at this stage before he has roped in his side (*sic*)'. But he obviously feels
uneasy for he adds: 'I wish that you could have come to Bombay instead of returning to
Allahabad...'

[155] GI Home Poll, File 1/1928: U.P. FR I Nov. 1928.

[156] AICC papers, AP 35/1928: Confidential note by Motilal Nehru on the timing of
the Congress, League and all-parties convention at Calcutta, 14 Nov.; Motilal Nehru
papers: Motilal to Gandhi, 24 Nov. 1928. Motilal told Gandhi that Jinnah's 'game' was
to postpone ratification. This would mean a protracted controversy in 1929 and it
would be impossible 'to keep the Muslims in hand all this time'.

the Nehru report—Shaukat Ali, Mahommed Ali, Shafi Daudi, Hasrat Mohani, Azad Sobhani and a section of the *Jumiat ul Ulema i Hind* under the leadership of Mufti Kifayatullah. The confrontation between these men and the 'nationalist' Khilafatists, which had been on the cards since the Lucknow session of the all-parties conference, came to a head during the Christmas week. By that stage, Punjabi and Bengali opposition had convinced the Ali brothers that bold tactics were necessary to retain control of the organization. Mahommed Ali and H.S. Suhrawardy, the Calcutta Khilafat leader, broke up the Bengal Provincial Khilafat Committee meeting and overruled the election of delegates from the districts to the annual session. Instead, quite unconstitutionally, they enrolled their own delegates from Calcutta itself.[157] The Ali brothers also succeeded in banning the attendance of North West Frontier delegates elected by the Punjab Khilafat Committee, and they outraged the Bihar delegation, led by Shah Mahommed Zubair and Dr Mahmud, by siding with Shafi Daudi's rival organization.[158] These tactics gave them a majority in the annual session but only at the cost of a split in the party. Dr Ansari and his followers broke with the Ali brothers and called their bluff by electing their own delegation to the all-parties convention. The Ali brothers responded by withdrawing from the convention entirely.[159]

The Muslim League meeting at Calcutta was attended by Jinnah, the Raja of Mahmudabad and Sir Ali Imam, the old Independent trio, and by Ansari's Khilafatists. The session began with a note of warning from the Chairman of the reception committee, Maulvi Abdul Karim, who argued that some form of special representation was essential for the protection of Muslim interests, and it continued with a plea for 'sweet reasonableness' by the Raja, who made a strong case for Dominion Status rather than Independence and urged his audience to elect a delegation to the all-parties convention to settle outstanding communal issues on that basis 'in the spirit of broad-mindedness.'[160] On the second day, following a meeting of the

[157]*Indian Quarterly Register,* 1928, vol. ii, pp. 406-8.

[158]*Proceedings of the All Parties National Convention* (Allahabad 1929) pp. 124-8: statement made on behalf of the Hon'ble Shah Mahommed Zubair and other members of the Central Khilafat Committee. Of the 45 Muslims who withdrew from the C.K.C., 28 came from Punjab.

[159]*Proceedings of the All Parties National Convention,* pp. 128-32: letter from the Secretary, CKC (Shaukat Ali), to the President of 'the so-called all parties convention' (Ansari).

[160]Pirzada, op.cit., vol. ii, pp. 139-43.

Subjects Committee on the previous afternoon, Mr. M.C. Chagla, Jinnah's disciple and friend, proposed a delegation to the all-parties convention consisting of twenty persons, ten of whom had seceded from the Khilafat Committee with Dr. Ansari. Haji Abdullah Haroon, the Karachi businessman, objected that the delegation only consisted of members of one party but he was called 'toady' by Zafar Ali and no major changes were made. Two additional delegates were added, however, to give representation to the Frontier and Assam.[161]

The same afternoon, these Muslim League and Khilafat delegates met a sub-committee of the all-parties convention. The demands which they put forward had not been discussed at the open session of either organization, and it is therefore difficult to decide who was responsible for which demand and whether both organizations subscribed to all of them. They were put forward jointly by Jinnah and T.A.K. Sherwani, however, and it must be assumed that they decided to stand together. The demands were as folows:[162]

1. That one-third of the elected representatives of both the Houses of the Central Legislature should be Mussulmans.
2. That in the Punjab and Bengal, in the event of adult suffrage not being established, there should be reservation of seats for the Mussulmans on the population basis for ten years subject to a re-examination after that period, but they shall have no right to contest additional seats.
3. (a) That residuary powers should be left to the provinces and should not rest with the Central Legislature.
   (b) That clause 13A embodied in the Supplementary report be deleted.
   (c) That the division of subjects in the Schedule I and II be revised.
4. That the constitution shall not be amended or altered unless the amendment or alteration is passed first by both the Houses of Parliament separately by a majority of four-fifths of those present and then by both the Houses in a joint sitting by a majority of four-fifths.
5. Article V—Communal representation. . . . . Delete the words 'Simultaneously with the establishment of Government under this constitution.
6. Embody the Pact regarding Communal representation in Punjab in full in the Nehru report.

161 Ibid., pp. 145-8.
162*Proceedings of the All Parties National Convention,* pp. 76-8.

In all probability, Jinnah was responsible for the demand for thirty-three per cent at the Centre. This had been one of his four proposals in March 1927 and he had every reason to stick to it rigorously, because his Muslim followers in the Central Assembly, and particularly those from the minority provinces, had been very critical of the Nehru report on precisely this point.[163] Jinnah's insistence, in defence of this demand, that the extra seats should be distributed to give weightage to the minority provinces, is probably a reflection of his awareness of this situation.[164] Such men as Nawab Ismail Khan, Mahommed Yakub, Sarfaraz Hussain Khan, Abdul Matin Chaudhuri and Fazl Ibrahimtoolah, were all members of the Legislative Assembly from the minority provinces, as were Shafi Daudi and Syed Murtuza, both former Swarajists who were in the process of taking up a more central position. Nor is it impossible that Sherwani subscribed to similar views, for it was he who raised the question of reservation of seats for minorities both in the provinces and at the Centre during the Nehru committee proceedings, and he himself had been a member of the Central Assembly since the 1926 election. Similar 'Central Assembly' considerations may also have been influential in the framing of the demand relating to Sind, which was designed to allow it to achieve separate status before the Nehru constitution was implemented. The fact that Haji Abdullah Haroon, the wealthy businessman, was both a member of the Assembly and the foremost protagonist of separation cannot be overlooked. At least three of the demands, however, appear to have come chiefly from the Punjab Khilafatists. This group had clearly been put out when the Nehru committee supplementary report made no reference to adult suffrage as a precondition for the introduction of joint electorates in their province.[165] This had been agreed at Lucknow and they wanted that agreement to be incorporated into the Nehru report in full.[166] The demand that reservation of seats should

---

[163] In his letter to Gandhi of 24 Nov., in which he discussed Jinnah's attitude towards the all parties convention, Motilal attributes Jinnach's prevarication to Central Assembly considerations. '...the Muslim members of the Assembly belonging to Jinnah's party... are one and all bitterly opposed to the Report and the Lucknow decisions. All told they number 8 or 9 and with the addition of Sir Purushotamadas constitute the whole of Jinnah's party. In his anxiety to keep his hold on these people, Jinnah is playing into their hands.'

[164]*Proceedings of the All Parties National Convention*, pp. 79-80.

[165]*All Parties Conference 1928, Supplementary Report of the Committee* (Allahabad 1928), p. 50.

[166]*Proceedings of the All Parties National Convention*, pp. 80-1.

be on a population basis if adult suffrage was not introduced also seems likely to have come from them, though Jinnah may have prompted them to be realistic. Finally, the demand that residuary powers should rest in the provinces certainly did come from them, as it was put forward first in a letter from Ansari's Khilafat faction to the all parties convention.[167] Jinnah, for his part, supported this demand, but more out of necessity than of choice. Being intent on ministerial power at the Centre, he did not wish the Centre's powers to be eroded before he could enjoy them, and he only bowed to the Punjabi Khilafatists, as they had bowed before public opinion in their own province, because he had no alternative.

The reception given to these demands by the all-parties convention sub-committee could have been safely predicted after a perusal of its personnel. Of its thirty-seven members, eleven were Hindus, Sikhs and Christians of the Punjab, one was a leading opponent of the separation of Sind, and six were leading lights of the Hindu Mahasabha.[168] The demand for thirty-three per cent at the Centre was supported by Gandhi and by Sapru, but opposed by the Hindu Mahasabha and the Sikhs. The demand that residuary powers should rest with the provinces was opposed by both the Mahasabha and the Liberal Federation, though both Sapru and Chintamani were prepared to re-examine the schedules of subjects. Neither Gandhi nor Motilal Nehru intervened during the discussion of this most important point. The demand for reservation on a population basis in Bengal and Punjab if adult suffrage was not adopted was skirted by means of the formula: 'We do not contemplate any such contingency.' The demand regarding Sind was rejected on the grounds that it involved altering the agreement reached at Lucknow.[169] In the open session, Jinnah tried to change the verdict of the committee. He told his audience that the modifications required were fair and reasonable; that no country had succeeded in establishing its independence without making provision for its minorities; and that a Hindu-Muslim settlement was essential for the political progress of the country.[170] Yet though

[167] Ibid., p. 127: statement on behalf of the Hon. Shah Mahommed Zubair and other members of the CKC.

[168] Ibid. pp. 73-4. Members of the sub-committee included Malaviya, Moonji, Jayakar, Aney, Chintamani, Harbilas Sarda and Gulshan Rai.

[169] Ibid., pp. 76-7; Ansari papers: a note in pencil headed 'Modifications in the Nehru report', setting out the reactions of the various groups within the sub-committee.

[170] *Proceedings of the All Parties National Convention* pp. 78-82.

he was supported by Dr Sapru, he met with a highly reasoned opposition from Jayakar, who told the convention that Jinnah only represented a small minority of Muslims and that it was not worthwile making concessions because it would make no difference to the Muslim community as a whole. Besides, he said, Jinnah was on their side anyway, and would do his best to bring the Muslim League with him.[171] Jinnah's reply shows how clearly he realized the isolation of his position:

It is essential that you must get not only the Muslim League but the Musulmans of India and here I am not speaking as a Musulman but as an Indian. And it is my desire to see that we get seven crores of Musulmans to march along with us in the struggle for freedom. Would you be content if I were to say, I am with you? Do you want or do you not want Muslim India to go along with you?[172]

It was a good question. But Jayakar had already answered it. The convention rejected Jinnah's offer and brought him to 'the parting of the ways'.

The circumstances responsible for forcing Jinnah into the wilderness were extremely complex. They went far beyond the individual attitudes of Mahasabha politicians. They reflected the working of the political system itself. In the early 1920s, though the forces of provincialism did occasionally impinge on the all-India scene, the real conflict of interest between the 'nationalist' politician and the provincial politician working the Reforms was obscured by the absence of points of friction. Only when the Montagu-Chelmsford Reforms come under the hammer does this conflict of interest become explicit; and the fascination of studying this period is that one can observe political reactions as the constraints of the system make themselves felt. Jinnah's main difficulty was that he had no solid political base. He was a 'consultative' politician in an age of political responsibility. Consequently, however sincere his 'nationalism', he could only survive by acting as a broker between Muslim politicians in the provinces and his Congress colleagues at the Centre. He was not himself engaged in provincial politics. He merely attempted to fashion the provincial clay at his disposal into a shape suited to his all-India purposes. His task, however, was like that of a sculptor required to work in materials which constantly change their texture. As the provinces threw up new provincial

[171]Ibid. pp. 86-92.
[172]Ibid., p. 93.

demands, so, ineluctably, Jinnah was obliged to change his political objectives. In 1927, he put forward four proposals; in 1928, they became six; and in 1929, fourteen.

Ultimately, negotiation between Jinnah and the Congress was no longer productive. Jinnah was looking over his shoulder at the provinces so much that he was no longer actively engaged in the same battle as the Congress. He was not prepared to accede to the Congress programme merely as an individual. He wanted to take a large body of Muslims with him. Yet those Muslims whose activities forced Jinnah to alter his all-India negotiating position were the provincial opponents of the very men who swelled the ranks of the Congress. Here was the heart of Jinnah's dilemma. It had ceased to be possible to occupy a central position in Indian politics. One either had to be in the Congress camp or the Muslim camp. It was this logic which ultimately turned Jinnah into the *Quaid i Azam* of Pakistan.

But Jinnah's discomfiture at Calcutta was not the end of the story. Just as the rise of provincial Muslim separatism had cut the ground from under the feet of the 'all-India' politician, so was the Calcutta convention followed by the emergence of the All India Muslim Conference. Just as those Congressmen favouring 'Independence' and non-co-operation were beginning to replace the Nehrus and Saprus so the Muslims of the various legislatures gathered at Delhi to declare their allegiance to the King Emperor and their respect for constitutional norms. The Indian body politic was being divided, government and Muslims on one side, Hindus on the other, and as the Congress embarked on the road to Dandi, the beneficiaries of the system rallied to its defence.

The idea of a conference of Muslim legislators was first mooted by the Aga Khan in December 1927.[173] But it was not taken up enthusiastically until after the publication of the Nehru report, at which stage certain of Jinnah's colleagues in the Central Assembly, notably Sir Mahommed Yakub and Mr Fazl Rahimtoolah, brought the scheme

---

[173] GI Home Poll. 32/12/1927: Bombay FR II Dec. 1927, appendix B. In a manifesto issued in that month, the Aga Khan appealed to all Muslim members of the central and provincial legislatures: 'I urge them with all the force at my command to meet and constitute a permanent Muslim governing political body which shall absorb into itself the political activities of the community as a whole and also finally absorb such antiquated political bodies as at present exist.... The need for an authoritative body of this character is great at a time when our constitution is in the melting pot.'

to fruition.[174] They invited members of the legislatures and other prominent men to a conference at Delhi on 31 December and they persuaded the Aga Khan to deliver the presidential address. The reasons for their initiative have already been touched on in discussing Jinnah's own dilemma. The Nehru report had made it clear that Muslims in the Central Assembly could no longer maintain an 'Independent' position. By advocating joint electorates and abolishing weightage it had reduced Muslim representation in the minority provinces and made it almost certain that minority-province Muslim representation in the Central Assembly would also be reduced. These were sufficient reasons for such men to want to make common cause with their provincial colleagues. Those who responded most readily to their invitation, however, were either those who were highly organized already, the Punjab Unionists under the leadership of Firoz Khan Noon and the U.P. Muslims under Shafaat Ahmed Khan and Hafiz Hidayat Hussain, or those who had become disillusioned with the politics of confrontation once it became clear that Jinnah's negotiations with the Congress would be fruitless — the Frontiersmen, the Punjabi and Bengali urban constitutionalists, the minority-province Khilafatists and Sindhis. The appearance of all these different schools on the same platform was the most remarkable feature of the first meeting of the Conference. That Mahommed Ali should sit beside Sir Mahommed Shafi, whom he had so often derided as a government stooge, and that the Aga Khan should be cheered by Azad Sobhani, whose vitriolic speeches at Kanpur in 1913 had forced him to wash his hands of the Muslim League, were amongst the most delicious ironies of the Montagu-Chelmsford Reforms.

The terms put forward by the All India Muslim Conference were a combination of Unionist and U.P. Muslim demands:

1. Federal system with complete autonomy and residuary powers vested in the constituent states.
2. No bill to be passed if ¾ of the affected community is against it.
3. Separate electorates to be retained until Muslims decide to give them up.

[174]See K.K. Aziz, *The All India Muslim Conference, 1928-35, a Documentary Record* (Karachi 1972), pp. 44-7: Statement on the origins of the Conference by Fazl Rahimtoolah, the Secretary; see also GI Home Poll., File 1/1928: Delhi FR I Oct. 1928. This second source attributes a leading role to Mahommed Yakub.

4.   Fair Muslim share in the cabinets of provinces and the Centre.

5.   Where Muslims constitute a majority of the population, their ascendancy may not be undermined by electoral reorganisation.

6.   Where Muslims were in a minority, they shall have no less representation than they do at present.

7.   33% representation in the Central Legislature.

8.   Separation of Sind.

9.   Reforms in the North-West Frontier Province and Baluchistan.

10. Same safeguards for Hindu minorities in Muslim provinces as for Muslim minorities in Hindu majority ones.

11. Adequate share for Muslims in the services.

12. Safeguards for the protection of Muslim culture and education, language, religion and personal law.

13. No change in the constitution except with the assent of the federal legislatures.

Of these demands, (1) and (5) clearly came from the Unionists, whereas (2), (4), (6), (11), (12) and (13) came from the U.P. Muslims. (3), (7), (8) and (9) were commonly demanded by both groups, (7) gaining added urgency as a result of the presence of several 'all-India' groups. As the Unionists contemplated having a free hand in the Punjab, it is not surprising that only two of the demands can be attributed to them. It is significant, however, that their first demand became the first demand of the Muslim Conference, and that it was given an even higher place than the demand for the continuance of separate electorates. It is also significant that the U.P. Muslim demands, though covering the same ground as those put forward at Kanpur, were shorn of the hysterical percentages which were a feature of that occasion and given a more balanced and deliberate look. Both these facts show clearly which faction was in the driving seat. In the difficult years of constitutional revision which lay ahead, it was the Punjabis who drove the Muslim Indian bus and the other provinces who sat behind.

CHAPTER 4

The Muslim Conference
and the Reforms

By the end of 1928, with the formation of the All India Muslim
Conference at Delhi, the main Muslim negotiating position for the
complex constitutional negotiations which were to follow had been
established:

The principles which we had enunciated [wrote the Aga Khan] were
to be our guiding light henceforward in all our encounters with British
or Hindu representatives and negotiators, with the Government of
India or with the Congress party, in every discussion of schemes of
Reform or new projects for the administration of the country . . . If
India's political and constitutional evolution could be likened to a
protracted and hard fought chess contest (the analogy is imperfect, I
know, for there were always at least three players in the game), then
it may be said that the board had now been set for an especially
crucial game, the pieces were all in place, and there was a considerable lull while everyone thought out his next move.[1]

In this hard-fought contest, as the Aga Khan's analogy implies, the
All India Muslim Conference found itself on the government's side
and the Congress found itself on the other. Those politicians who
dominated the Conference were chiefly men who had worked the
Reforms and realized the importance of co-operating with the British
in order to secure the concessions they required. Those who
dominated the Congress were men who had given up hope of persuading the government to allow them a share of power by constitutional
means. The Conference worked by pressurizing the government
from within. The Congress embarked on a policy of non-constitutional agitation.

The government had its firmest ties with the organizers of the
Conference. It had relied principally on their support in planning
its strategy for the Statutory Commission, and this reliance did not
diminish in the constitutional negotiations which were to follow.
However the Government could not rule India on the backs of the

---

[1]*The Memoirs of the Aga Khan: World Enough and Time* (London 1954) p. 210.

Muslims, and as Congress influence increased, so did the government's need to be conciliatory. It may not have thought it possible to win over the Jawaharlal Nehrus and the Subhas Boses, but it could not afford to alienate the bulk of educated Hindu opinion, for under those conditions no constitution would be workable. For these reasons, even in 1929, Irwin attempted to persuade Congress to take part in the process of constitutional reform, first by the offer of a round-table conference, and subsequently, on the eve of the Lahore Congress, by a meeting with Gandhi, Motilal Nehru, Sapru and Jinnah. Yet despite these efforts, the one-year ultimatum issued at Calcutta became the Independence resolution passed at Lahore. Congress initiated a boycott of the councils and of the round table conference; and in April 1930, with Gandhi's march to Dandi, the civil disobedience movement began. At first, the government tried to kill the movement with kindness, but when this proved ineffective, the gloves came off. Congress leaders were imprisoned and government began to rule by ordinance. As the revision of the constitution proceeded, however, the government's tough posture in India was found to be increasingly at odds with the need for Congress involvement in the constitution-making process. The importance of Congress had been made apparent by the success of civil disobedience; it commanded not a little respect in Labour circles in England; and in the aftermath of the first round-table conference, the government was obliged to turn once more to conciliation. In March 1931, the Gandhi-Irwin Pact was signed: the government suspended rule by ordinance and released its political prisoners, and in exchange the Congress agreed to accept Dominion Status as its goal, to give up civil disobedience and to attend the second round-table conference.

From the point of view of the Muslim Conference, the most disturbing feature of these developments was that they coincided with the main phase of negotiations regarding the future constitution. The Conference was not a homogeneous body. It consisted of a very large number of Muslim interests, all of which considered it worthwhile at the end of 1928 to group together. They all felt at that stage that they were more likely to get what they wanted from government than from Congress. But as Congress prestige rose, and as government's slow and grudging plans for Reform unfolded themselves, it became an open question for many of these interests whether their original decision had been the correct one. Might not alliance with Congress produce a better deal for the Frontier? Might not Sind be separated at an earlier date? Might not the Bengali Muslims enjoy a greater share of power on Congress terms? This kind of reassessment threatened to weaken the Conference, to undermine its right to speak for the Muslims of the subcontinent as a whole, indeed to jeopardize the Muslim claim for special treatment everywhere.

For the Conference organizers, therefore, being on the government's side of the chessboard did not guarantee favourable treatment. Their alliance with government was subject to the same pressures as the government's confrontation with the Congress, and in order to maintain the credibility of the Conference, they had got to provide their supporters with a better deal than they were promised by other political organisations; and not in the future but as frustration came to a head. This task required great political skill, a high degree of organization, and above all the ability to force the government — and not only the government of India but the British government as well — into concessions which they were very often reluctant to make.

The Muslim Conference: leadership, support and resources

The chief architect of Conference policy during this period was Mian Fazli Husain, the founder of the Punjab Unionist party, who in 1930 was appointed member of the Viceroy's Council with special responsibility for Education, Health and Lands. Fazli's elevation to the Council at this time was certainly not fortuitous. It was a recognition both of his rare political gifts and of the paramount importance of Punjab Muslim support for the government's political strategy. Yet in picking Fazli, the Raj had not obtained a sleeping partner. He knew his own value to government[2] and he was not afraid to sell his support at a high price.

Throughout the period of constitutional reform, Fazli worked at two distinct but related levels. The first was as a member of the Viceroy's

---

[2]An interesting example of Fazli's confidence on this point is provided by his difference with Hailey over the appointment of the Simon Commission. When the Commission was first announced, Fazli was representing India at the League of Nations. But on his return to Bombay, he told a correspondent of the *Herald* that he objected to the exclusion of Indians and would advocate boycott by the Muslims if the Hindu Mahasabha also supported boycott. When Hailey pulled him up for this, Fazli immediately offered his resignation, and Hailey climbed down. See Hailey papers, 11B: Hailey to Fazli, 24 Nov. and 7 Dec. 1927; Fazli to Hailey, 6 Dec. 1927.

Council, cogently putting forward his views, both in minutes and in personal meetings with other councillors, and the second was as the co-ordinator of Conference activity in the country as a whole. In the first capacity, he made sure that the Muslim point of view never went by default in the council, and in the second that he was never short of a credible sanction outside the council when he met with opposition from his colleagues. For both these roles he was well endowed. He always prepared his brief thoroughly; he made his points directly and well, both on paper and in person; he understood the value of persuasion and organization; and he had a very excellent sense of when to compromise and when to stand firm.

But in keeping the Muslim Conference together, Fazli was dealing with a very mixed bag. Firstly, and most importantly, there were the provincial interests, those who had worked the Reforms in the provinecs, chiefly the Muslim landlords, whose degree of organization varied enormously from province to province. Where the two majority provinces were concerned, Fazli was chiefly interested in securing a better deal for the Punjab, and though his colleagues and followers in the Punjab council were not averse to quarrelling among themselves, he could generally rely on them to back him up. Firoz Khan Noon, Sikunder Hayat, Ahmed Yar Khan Daultana and Nawab Muzaffar Khan—these men knew how to organize the press, they had a virtual majority in the legislature, they had the sympathetic ear of government, and they had an overwhelming interest in keeping the Unionist party together until provincial autonomy had been granted on their terms. In Bengal, on the other hand, though the prospect of provincial autonomy put a premium on united action, the divisions within the community made it difficult to achieve. Abdur Rahim's party was organized separately from Fazlul Haq's, whilst the Nawabs of Dacca and Mymensingh maintained their distance from both. Fazli does not appear to have been on close terms with Sir Abdur Rahim. He had no contacts with Fazlul Haq. If he had any allies, it was the Nawabi party—Nazimuddin, A.H. Ghuznavi and Syed Abdul Hafiz. But though he did his best to cajole them into action, he found them generally unresponsive. On the whole, Fazli expected little from the Bengalis:

The masses have hardly any feeling except one of misery, now approaching the verge of exasperation. The middle class Muslims go their own way trying to make some sort of living.... As regards the upper educated people, their very position has made them intensely selfish, trying to gain something from both sides. It is perhaps uncharitable but it is not altogether incorrect'.[3]

Amongst the minority provinces, there were similar discrepancies. The most organised was the United Provinces, where the Nawab of Chhatari, Sir Mahommed Yusuf, the Raja of Salempur, Dr Shafaat Ahmed Khan, Sir Mahommed Yakub and Hafiz Hidayat Hussain all realized the need to keep the community united under the Conference banner. They may not have relished an alliance with the Punjabis but it made sound tactical sense. It was advocated vociferously by Shafaat Ahmed, Shafi's relation, and no less effectively behind the scenes by the Governor of the province, that most eminent of Punjabis, Sir Malcolm Hailey. In Bihar, the Conference possessed one of its most energetic workers, Maulana Shafi Daudi, who in 1928 was elected working secretary of the entire organization. But though Daudi was ably assisted at Patna by Zamiruddin Ahmed, his impact in Bihar was limited. Coming from north of the river, he did not find an open welcome in the salons of Patna and Bankipore, and even in the service of a wider cause, the barriers of parochialism did not come down. In Bihar, as in the other minority provinces, the Central Provinces, Madras and Bombay, the Conference relied chiefly on the passive support of local interests. In all these provinces, almost all Muslim members of council subscribed to the Conference,[4] but they did not throw up any provincial leaders of all-India stature. They relied on their case being put forward by the North Indians. For Fazli Husain, this passivity had its dangers, for where support was passive, inroads into Muslim unity could more easily be made. He made sure, therefore, that the demands of the minority provinces, like the demands of the Bengalis, were kept in the forefront of the Conference programme. Throughout the period of constitutional revision, in all public negotiations, whether with government or with other political parties, he insisted that the demands of the minority provinces and of the Bengalis be settled first. He made the Punjab the sheepdog of Muslim India and pushed the more timid brethren into the front line.[5]

[3] See Fazli Husain papers: undated note 'Bengal and its problems'.

[4] See *List of Members of the Working Committee, the Executive Board and the General Body of the All India Muslim Conference* (Patna 1932).

[5] See, for example, Fazli Husain papers: Fazli Husain to Iqbal, 30 May 1931; Fazli Husain to the Nawab of Chhatari, 5 Sept. 1931.

A second group of importance consisted of the urban constitutionalists—men like Jinnah, Shafi, Shah Nawaz and Abdullah
Suhrawardy, who had been thwarted in their political ambitions by
the nature of the Montagu-Chelmsford Reforms and who had
attempted in the late 1920s to do a deal with the Congress at the all-
India level in order to improve their own position. These men had
been forced to take sides with their provincial brethren by the growth
of communalism in the provinces and the subsequent polarization of
all-India politics. But their ambitions remained distinct, particularly
with regard to devolution at the Centre, and they were less sturdy
than the provincial interests in their support for separate electorates.[6]

Thirdly, there were the minority-province Khilafatists, men like
the Ali brothers, Hasrat Mohani and Azad Sobhani, whose importance
had declined with the abolition of the Khilafat and whose increasingly
fragile relationship with the Congress was disrupted by the Nehru
report. Like the urban constitutionalists, these men had gravitated
towards the Conference. But they sat uncomfortably on the same
platform as Firoz Khan Noon and the Nawab of Chhatari. Not only
were their political methods different—sometimes embarrassingly
different—but also, by dint of their previous association with such
Congress Muslims as Ansari, Khaliquzzaman and Sherwani, they
possessed a sympathy for the 'nationalist' school which made them
unreliable allies. There was always the danger that they would repudiate the Conference programme in some new all-India agreement
with the Congress.

Lastly, there were the Frontiersmen and the Sindhis. In both these
areas, the fact that no concessions had been made to the political
ambitions of the inhabitants meant that those who favoured a policy

---

[6]Jinnah did not attend the Muslim Conference at Delhi in Dec. 1928, but in March
1929, after a meeting with Conference representatives, he drew up his famous 14 points,
which were virtually identical to the Conference demands of 1 Jan. 1929. Technically
he remained open to negotiation on the question of electorates, providing the 14 points
were accepted. But if Motilal Nehru is to be believed, such an offer did not belong to
the realm of practical politics: 'He is simply trying to reinstate himself with his followers',
he wrote to Gandhi in Aug. 1929, 'by making preposterous demands.... I am quite clear
in my own mind that the only way to reach a compromise with the truly nationalist
Muslims is to ignore Mr. Jinnah and the Ali brothers altogether.' See Motilal Nehru
papers: Nehru to Gandhi, 14 Aug. 1929. I am indebted to Mr V.C. Joshi of the Nehru
Memorial Museum for this reference.

of quiet, firm pressure within the system were easily outrun in the race for popular support. Even before Fazli was appointed to the Viceroy's Council, the Pathans of Peshawar and Mardan had worsted the administration, and had embarrassed the Conference by openly declaring their allegiance to the Congress; and in Sind, though matters had not yet come to a head, those who were in the vanguard of the separation movement were already showing signs of impatience. Such men as Haji Abdullah Haroon, the Memon merchant prince, and Sheikh Abdul Majid Sindhi, Mahommed Ali's old Khilafat colleague, were not committed to the Conference irretrievably and if the Conference wanted to retain their support it had to deliver the goods faster than its opponents.

What advantages-beyond his personal ability did Fazli Husain possess in keeping these interests together? Within the Imperial machine, his main advantage was the presence of officials who understood and sympathized with his point of view. Hailey and de Montmorency, the Governors of the U.P. and the Punjab, Herbert Emerson, the Home Secretary, and James Dunnett, the Reforms Commissioner, were all Punjab civilians, men who saw the essentials of the Indian problem from the same viewpoint. They were not always responsive to Fazli's opinions. Dunnett was often too 'original'[7] particularly where the issue of central responsibility was concerned; Hailey and de Montmorency were disinclined to give away as much as Fazli wanted in the Punjab. But in the last resort, they realized that they and Fazli stood or fell together, and in Fazli's dealings with the government of India that was a considerable advantage.

Outside the Council, Fazli was poorly served. Unlike the Congress, the Conference did not have the backing of wealthy industrialists. There were no Birlas, no Ambalal Sarabhais, no Jamnalal Bajajes. Nobody contributed in lakhs. The nearest equivalent was Haji Abdullah Haroon and he was a small man by comparison. The Conference was backed primarily by the princely states and the landed interest. The Nizam of Hyderabad made at least one substantial donation.[8] The Nawabs of Bhopal and Rampur were more regular supporters.[9] The Aga Khan gave generously and regularly; and

[7] Fazli Husain papers, Diary, 21 May 1930: 'Dunnett is inclined to be original, while I wish him to be only imitative.'

[8] Ibid., Sir Akbar Hydari, Prime Minister of Hyderabad, to Fazli Husain, 29 July 1931.

[9] Interview with Syed Hussain Imam of Gaya, Karachi, April 1970.

202 Prelude to Partition

paid out bonuses when his horses won the Derby.[10] In the U.P., the Raja of Salempur rose to political prominence by financing the Conference. According to one source, he gave more money to the Conference than anybody except the Aga Khan.[11] In the Punjab, Firoz Khan Noon organized collections amongst the Unionists. but for the most part, the Conference was financed by small monthly subscriptions.[12] It had no substantial reserves. The money was spent as it was collected, and the working secretary, Shafi Daudi finished his association with the Conference deeply in debt.[13]

Partly as a result of these financial problems, the Conference did not have a newspaper to match the big Congress organs. There was no *Tribune*, no *Leader*, no *Hindu*. To reach that kind of audience, it had to rely on the sympathy of the British-owned papers, the *Civil and Military Gazette*, the *Pioneer*, the *Statesman*, the *Madras Mail* and the *Times of India*. But there were a number of lesser local papers, both in English and Urdu, which served the Conference well. In the Punjab, there was the *Muslim Outlook* which had been founded by Shafi, Abdul Quadir and Fazli Husain in 1924; there was *Siyasat*, edited by Syed Habib Shah: and there was the more distinctly pro-Unionist paper, *Inquilab*, edited by Ghulam Rasool Mihr. In the U.P., there was Hafiz ur Rahman's *Aligarh Mail;* there was the Allahabad *Star;* and there was Abdullah Khan's *Hamdam*, which the Government assisted by the establishment of a special post office.[14] At Delhi, there was *Millat*. In Bihar, there was Shafi Daudi's *Ittehad*. But what the Conference lacked was an efficient news agency to ensure that its position was reported without bias in the British press. In 1931, efforts were made to remedy this defect, but the five lakhs required for the project do not appear to have been collected.[15]

[10]Fazli Husain papers, Shafi Daudi to Fazli Husain, 17 Aug. 1931; see also Azim Husain, *Fazli Husain, a political Biography* (Bombay 1946), p. 312.

[11]Fazli Husain papers: Mushir Hussain Kidwai to Fazli Husain, 18 May 1930.

[12]Ibid., circular letter to Fazli Husain requesting 30-rupee subscription of the month of July 1931, enclosed, Shafi Daudi to Fazli Husain, 17 Aug. 1931.

[13]Ibid. By Aug. 1931, Daudi had loaned nearly 1,500 rupees to the Conference to keep the central office running. See also Shafi Daudi papers: Shafi Daudi to his bank manager, 3 March, 1939 (Nehru Memorial Museum, New Delhi).

[14]Fazli Husain papers: Abdullah Khan to Fazli Husain, 4 Dec. 1932.

[15]For a discussion of the Muslim Conference and the press, see Fazli Husain papers: Fazli to the Raja of Salempur, 3 May 1931. See also Mihr collection, 454: Progs. of the All India Muslim Conference Working Committee, Lahore, 24 May 1931, resolution 1.

Fazli's main advantage was a thoroughly conscientious Conference working secretary, Maulana Shafi Daudi, a man of great experience in many different political spheres, in local, provincial and national politics. As a former Khilafatist, Daudi was well acquainted with the politics of religion; as a non-co-operator, he had learnt how to give a programme mass appeal; as Motilal's lieutenant in Bihar, he had acquired the techniques of provincial organization; as a member of the Central Assembly, he was well aware of what was at stake in all-India terms; as a national politician, he had innumerable contacts in many different provinces. For all these reasons, he was an ideal man for the job. He may not have spoken very good English, and a certain class of Muslim has neglected to give him his due for this reason,[16] but he was an extremely devoted and selfless worker in the Conference cause and to him undoubtedly goes much of the credit for the success of the organization.

From his newspaper office at Bankipore, the *Quaumi* press, Daudi corresponded with Muslim leaders throughout India. He was responsible for much of the Conference publicity; for the organization of deputations to the Viceroy; for the running of the Executive Board; for sending telegrams to Britain during all stages of the process of constitutional reform; for relations with the press; for the collection of subscriptions; for touring on behalf of the Conference in Bihar, U.P. and Bengal; and for trouble-shooting in difficult areas, in Alwar and on the Frontier. In short, he did the work of several men, and for nearly five years was scarcely ever at home[17] With this man, Fazli Husain had what has been described as 'a perfect liaison'[18]; and thanks to this liaison the Muslim Conference became the organizational arm of his work in the council. When the government appeared to be making too many concessions to Congress or too few to the Muslim community, it was Shafi Daudi on whom Fazli relied for a public statement, a Conference resolution or a deputation in support of his point of view. But even with Shafi Daudi, Fazli had his problems, for as an old Khilafatist and non-co-operator, he was inclined to favour agitation when the going was rough.

[16]See, for example, Mahommed Mujib, *The Indian Muslims* (London 1967), p. 443. Rafi Ahmed Kidwai apparently poked fun at Daudi on these grounds.

[17]Shafi Daudi's diary, though reticent like the man himself, tells its own tale of endless travelling, meetings and organization. I am indebted to his son Mr. Ata ur Rahman Daudi of Muzaffurpur, for translating many passages into English.

[18]Interview with Syed Hussain Imam of Gaya, Karachi, April 1970.

The Simon Commission report and the Government of India dispatch

The Muslim Conference met its first serious challenge with the publication of the Simon Commission report in May 1930. Already by that stage, the report had been deprived of any degree of finality by the Viceroy's offer of a round-table conference, but the fact that the Commission had been appointed by Parliament, the co-operation which it had received from the provincial wings of the Conference, and the enormous amount of work which had gone into producing its report, all gave it a degree of authority which, in view of its findings, was highly dangerous to Conference interests.

From the Unionist point of view, the report was not an unadulterated disaster. It put greater powers into the hands of the Governor than Fazli would have liked, but it did concede a full measure of provincial autonomy. There were to be no official ministers, there was to be joint responsibility, and all government departments were to be transferred.[19] Nor did the report subject the provinces to a responsible centre. It rejected the idea of an immediate federation of British Indian provinces, instead introducing a proposal for an all-Indian federation of British India and the States at some future, unspecified date.[20] This was clearly to be a very conservative body, designed primarily to uphold British control at the Centre, and it was only to be brought into being once the new provincial governments had established themselves. '...the nature of the constituents themselves', ran the report, 'has a great influence on the form which federation takes.' This recommendation was very much to Fazli's liking, for it was tantamount to giving the provinces a veto on the form of the federal government. Moreover, it was clear, as the report admitted, that such a federation, consisting of both autocratic and democratic governments, would only be possible if 'the greatest possible internal freedom' was given to each of the constituent units.[21] This was also to Fazli's liking.

But the merits of the report stopped there. In the first place, the writers of the report did not think that the existing provinces were ideal units for federation. They made 'a definite recommendation for reviewing, and if possible for resettling the provincial boundaries

[19]*Report of the Indian Statutory Commission* vol. ii, *Recommendations Cmd. 3569*, presented to Parliament, May 1930, pp. 16-17, 33-4. 44-8.
[20]Ibid., pp. 9-14.
[21]Ibid., pp. 18-19.

of India at as early a date as possible.'[22] Muslim majorities were not
mentioned specifically but the possibility of redistribution affecting
those majorities was not ruled out. Nor was the separation of Sind
granted in principle. There would first have to be 'a close and detailed
enquiry into the financial consequences which would follow such a
step.'[23] This was not heartening news for the Sindhis. The Frontier's
demand for equal status was also neglected. 'The inherent right of a
man to smoke a cigarette', said the report, 'must necessarily be curtailed
if he lives in a powder magazine.' The military importance of the
Frontier made it necessary that 'executive responsibilities should, as
at present, rest with the Chief Commissioner'. The Commission
recommended the formation of an irresponsible legislature along
the lines of the Morley-Minto Reforms.[24] In Baluchistan, the report
envisaged no change at all. The authors believed that the demand
for representative institutions of a western type did not come from
the Baluch but had been foisted on them from outside.[25]

The report also displayed an unsympathetic attitude towards separate
representation. In the light of the virtually unanimous recommendations of all provincial governments and provincial committees, it
grudgingly admitted that in default of a new agreement between
Hindus and Muslims, 'Mahommedan voters should not be deprived
of this special protection until a substantial majority of Muslim
representatives in the provincial legislatures declare themselves in
favour of a change.' But it did not confine itself to recommending a
continuation of the same system of separate communal electorates.
It examined a number of alternatives, including proportional representation, and ultimately recommended a scheme of its own whereby
Muslims would be returned by a system of reservation within joint
electorates provided that they polled forty percent of the votes of
their own community.[26] In the Central Legislature, moreover, it
recommended the abolition of separate representation and the
introduction of a system of indirect election by proportional representation, calculating, though with what validity is uncertain, that the

[22]Ibid., p. 16.
[23]Ibid. p. 25. In the meantime, as a palliative, the Commission recommended the
establishment of a special legislative committee within the Bombay Council.
[24]Ibid., p. 103.
[25]Ibid., p. 106.
[26]Ibid., pp. 60-3.

Muslims would win thirty per cent of the seats by this method.[27] The report's biggest bombshell, however, was its hostility to the Muslim demand for majorities by separate electorates in Punjab and Bengal. The Commission approached this question from the standpoint of the Lucknow Pact. As regards weightage for the minority provinces, it agreed that it should not be withdrawn without the consent of the Muslims. But it was not prepared to countenance majorities by separate electorates for the Punjab and Bengal at the same time:

It would be unfair that Mahommedans should retain the very considerable weightage they now enjoy in the six provinces, and that there should at the same time be imposed, in the face of Hindu and Sikh opposition, a definite Muslim majority in the Punjab and Bengal, unalterable by any appeal to the electorate.

In so many words, the authors laid down that if the Punjabis and Bengalis wanted majorities they would have to fight for them within joint electorates.[28]

The Muslim response to the publication of the report was one of annoyance and exasperation. The Conference supporters had taken no part in the non-co-operation movement—Muslims in general had held aloof from it—and their support for government had been an important factor in the preservation of law and order. But they appeared to be getting nothing for their pains; indeed to many of them, the Simon Commission report seemed like an open invitation to throw in their lot with the Congress. This was particularly the case at Lahore, where the Conference organizers had difficulty restraining their supporters. Nawab Muzaffar Khan, the Unionist party trouble-shooter, held meetings both with the publicists and the politicians to try to reverse the trend towards despair. But he had a hard row to hoe.[29] The editors of the *Inquilab, Siyasat, Muslim Outlook,* and other Muslim papers told him frankly that the scheme of provincial autonomy suggested by the report was entirely unsatisfactory. They alleged that the report 'had practically established Hindu Raj, under British protection, in all provinces throughout India, including the

[27]Ibid. pp. 118-21.

[28]Ibid., pp. 71-2.

[29]The following account of Nawab Muzaffar's meetings with Muslim politicians and journalists at Lahore is based on his secret note, which was forwarded by the Punjab Government Chief Secretary to Herbert Emerson, Government of India Home Secretary, on 4 July 1930 (GI Home Poll., 346/1930).

two provinces of Bengal and Punjab where the Muslims were in a majority'. 'What was the use of the Commission and its long enquiry', they asked, 'if they had to settle the question themselves with the Hindus?' Dr Iqbal, Chaudhuri Afzal Haq and Malik Barkat Ali were no less scathing. According to Iqbal:

A death blow had been struck at the Muslim majority in the Punjab. He was for starting a very strong and effective agitation against the report and was prepared for every sacrifice. Chaudhuri Afzal Haq was of the same view and said that he and other Congressites like Alam, Zafar Ali and Abdul Qadir Qasuri were all for the Muslim majority in the Punjab. They would like to make a common cause, go to [the] villages and set up an unprecedented agitation.

Muzaffar did his best to reassure them. He drew particular attention to the Commission's federal scheme 'which prevented Hindus becoming powerful in the Central Government', to its concession that separate electorates should continue while the Muslims wanted them, and to the 'inclination of the Commission' regarding the demands of the Sindhis and Frontiersmen. But he had difficulty meeting their point that the Muslim position in the Punjab was in jeopardy; indeed, he was of the same opinion himself:

Up till now the Muslim majority in the Punjab has been maintained with the help of official votes. If the Simon suggestions are followed and the official element removed, the present strength of the Muslims will be gone and they will be at the mercy of the Hindus. I personally would prefer hundred times real British Raj to this sort of self-government.

As a temporary expedient to win over the discontented, he suggested that Iqbal be given a seat on the round-table conference, but he made it clear that more drastic measures were required if a situation, 'neither in the interests of the Muslims nor of the British Government' was to be avoided.[30]

On 5 July 1930 at Simla, the Executive Board of the Muslim

[30]Prominent Bengali Muslims were no less displeased. Sir Abdur Rahim complained that the advance outlined by the report was unsatisfactory. Communal divisions had been used at every stage as an argument against making substantial concessions. No real effort had been made to provide a viable framework for Federation, nor to deal with the question of Defence. 'It is now for the Mussulmans of Bengal to consider seriously', he said, 'whether they should or should not discard separate electorates and take their chance in a common electorate according to the extended franchise.' See *Indian Annual Register*, 1930, vol. ii, pp. 351-54.

Conference passed detailed resolutions on the report. While appreciating the fact that the future constitution was to be organized on a federal basis and that the provinces were to be given a substantial degree of autonomy, the Board described the report as 'unacceptable to the Mussulmans of India' and 'retrograde and reactionary in spirit'. It demanded that the community be guaranteed 'a clear majority in Bengal and Punjab', that Sind be separated, that the Frontier and Baluchistan be given equal status, that the community be guaranteed 'adequate and effective representation in the cabinets and public services of the country', that election to the Federal Assembly be by separate electorates, that the army and navy be speedily Indianized and that an element of responsibility be introduced in the federal government.[31] The meeting was most notable, however, for the spirit of defiance lent to its proceedings by the President, Maulana Shaukat Ali:

> The Maulana said that they would wait for four or five months for their demands to be conceded after which he and his workers would not keep to non-violence. The Maulana said that they got too involved these days in section 144 and the Indian penal code. They had lost their historical sense, the kind of sense which Bacha Saqqao showed in capturing Kabul with 27 horsemen....[32]

With such plentiful evidence of Muslim disillusionment, Fazli had a strong hand to play in dealing with his colleagues in the council. His basic argument was that the Indian Muslims 'would prefer the present position and no political advance to the political advance outlined in the Simon report.'[33] In other words, if government was to press forward with its plans for Reform (and by 1930 it had very little alternative), it would have to make more substantial concessions to the Muslims. In general terms, the government acknowledged this necessity. It was too committed to the Muslims to alienate them, and if concessions had to be made to retain their support, it was prepared in the last resort to make them. This attitude gave Fazli considerable

---

[31]Mihr collection, 454: *Resolutions of the All India Muslim Conference, the Executive Board and the Working Committee, from September 1929 to March 1932.* The demand for an element of responsibility at the Centre reflects the presence of all-India politicians on the Executive Board. One of the difficulties faced by those provincial politicians who dominated the Conference was in keeping these men under control.

[32]For an account of the Simla meeting, see *Indian Annual Register,* 1930, vol. ii, pp. 325-8.

[33]Halifax papers, 6: Note by Fazli Husain, enclosed, Irwin to Wedgwood Benn, 28 Aug. 1930.

powers of leverage within the council, and a study of the formulation of the government's response to the Simon proposals, the government of India dispatch of 20 September 1930, illustrates how he was able to use this leverage to improve the Muslim position.

Even before the Simon Commission report was published, Fazli realized the importance for the Conference of winning over the Frontier Muslims. But the mutiny of the Gurhwalis at Peshawar in April and the subsequent imposition of martial law made his task difficult. Members of council believed that the primary need was to restore government prestige and they were not initially receptive to his suggestions for Reform. By degrees, however, he won them over to his point of view. Early in May, he made initial approaches to Haig, the acting Home Member, and to Schuster, the Finance Member, and finding them sympathetic, put up a note for Haig to lay before the Viceroy.[34] After this, the council appears to have listened carefully to Fazli's advice. They appointed a Muslim High Court Judge to the enquiry committee set up to investigate the Peshawar troubles,[35] and they allowed Fazli to organize two deputations, one to the Governor of the Punjab and the other to the Viceroy, so that government could publicly reassure the Muslims, both with regard to the position on the Frontier and to the position of the community as a whole under the reformed constitution.[36]

In his plans for Reform, however, Fazli got most support from Howell, the Foreign Secretary, and Emerson, the Home Secretary. Howell believed that the Frontier administration had been culpably inefficient and considered a new deal necessary to improve government's image.[37] Emerson agreed with Howell. In his view, the introduction of Reforms was 'by far the most promising method of providing a rallying post for the well-disposed'. Emerson's main point, however, was that the Frontier question had an important bearing on government's relations with the Muslims generally:

In the older provinces, Mahommedans have the majority in the Punjab and Bengal only, and in both these provinces the majority is a small one. Hence they naturally wish to strengthen their position *vis a vis* the Hindus by bringing within the orbit of the Reforms the N.W.F.P

[34]Fazli Husain papers: Diary, 6 and 8 May 1930.
[35]Ibid., Diary, 14 May 1930.
[36]Ibid. Diary, 31 May 1930 and 4 June 1930.
[37]GI Home Poll, 206/1930: Note by Howell, 24 May 1930.

where their community is in an overwhelming majority. Not only do they feel that there is insufficient reason for withholding the Reforms but they believe that ultimate self-government in the N.W.F.P. will be of great value to them in the future political game. The movement for constitutional reform in that province has therefore received a strong and perfectly legitimate impetus from outside with the result that it is impracticable to regard the problem as a parochial one[38]

By the beginning of June, the Viceroy had agreed to let Fazli go to the Frontier to see the situation for himself,[39] and on his return he wrote a memorandum making a strong case for Reform. It was not possible, he said, for the Frontier to continue any longer with a different scheme of government from all the other provinces. The Frontier people were aware that the Punjabis had benefited from the Reforms — particularly in the field of education and local self-government — and from the other side of the Frontier, reports were also filtering into the Peshawar bazaars about the 'socialist and democratic' measures being carried out in the Soviet Union. Already, he said, the Frontier people, and particularly the educated, were feeling a sense of inferiority, not only *vis-a-vis* the Europeans, but also *vis-a-vis* the Punjabis, and it was highly desirable that Reforms should be granted promptly and their co-operation enlisted in uplift work before they became 'thoroughly discontented, disgusted and disappointed.'[40] These views carried weight within the council, and a sub-committee was set up under Fazli's presidency, to draft a new constitution. This constitution gave the Frontier a unitary system of government, a legislature with a majority of elected members, and two responsible ministers. The Chief Commissioner still retained considerable powers (forty-nine per cent of the seats were to be filled by nomination) but the constitution conformed in type with those of other provinces, a point on which Fazli insisted, and it contained within itself the seeds of future liberalization. During the drafting of the government of India dispatch, Fazli piloted this scheme through the council, and persuaded his colleagues to finance the province's anticipated deficit by means of a central subvention.[41] But he continued to feel that a more liberal constitution was necessary if the atmosphere in the province was to

[38]Ibid., Note by Emerson, 26 May 1930.
[39]Fazli Husain papers: Diary, 30 June 1930.
[40]Ibid. Memorandum on Reforms for the Frontier, 5 July 1930.
[41]GI Reforms Office, 67/v/1930: Minutes of informal discussion in council on the government of India's proposals for Reform, 12th meeting, 19 July 1930.

be changed, and during the first round-table conference he tried to improve the scheme by bringing pressure to bear on the government in Britain. In a brief to Sir Mahommed Shafi, one of the Muslim delegates to the Conference, he wrote:

It is up to you to get this province into line with other provinces if you can, or at all events, to get the very best for the province. The important point concerning this matter is that if that province is not given a really good constitution, it will always be ready to play into the hands of the Congress and therefore the position of the Indian Mussulmans will be very much weakened. Political wisdom lies in doing the province well, and I trust British statesmanship will not fail to grasp this point.[42]

Once he had improved the position on the Frontier, Fazli endeavoured to get the council to make a decision in principle on the separation of Sind. He submitted to the Viceroy a pamphlet by Mahommed Ayub Khuhro in favour of separation,[43] and at Irwin's instigation, Haig examined the question in some detail. Haig came to the conclusion that there was 'a strong prima facie case in favour of separation'. He held that Sind was quite distinct from the rest of Bombay presidency, geographically, racially, linguistically and administratively, and he recommended that separation should be carried out if it really was a practical proposition. On that point, however, he held that there was no evidence on which to make a decision. He considered that the Bombay government had based its case against separation on poorly analysed statistics and he recommended that the whole matter should be examined by a special committee.[44] Sir George Schuster, the Finance Member, agreed. The existence within the territory of Sind of the vast Sukkur Barrage Irrigation Scheme, for the Bombay government one of the principle arguments against separation, was for Schuster an argument in its favour. He had a poor opinion of the Bombay Finance Department and felt certain that 'full advantage will not be taken of this project, the success or failure of which may have results which affect the whole of India, so long as it remains under the Bombay Government.' For financial reasons, therefore, he was prepared to support separation, providing that the government of India's interest in the Barrage

---

[42]Fazli Husain papers: Fazli to Shafi, 1 Dec. 1930.
[43]GI Reforms Office, 126/1930: Note by Fazli Husain, 23 Aug. 1930.
[44]Ibid., Note by Haig, 27 Aug. 1930.

could be recognized.[45] With the exception of Birdwood, the Commander in Chief, who had a scheme of his own for amalgamating Sind and the Punjab, other members of council followed Haig and Schuster, and the result was that the government of India dispatch was modified to provide for a speedy enquiry into the financial aspects of separation.[46] The government recommended that the enquiry should be completed within six months, and that a decision on separation should be taken on the basis of its findings. This was a considerable improvement on Simon's recommendation for a Boundary Commission, which, as Fazli pointed out, was 'next door to shelving the question.'[47]

But Fazli's most strenuous efforts were devoted to securing the Muslim position in the majority provinces, and more especially in the Punjab. He pursued this objective in two ways: firstly, by working for maximum provincial autonomy on terms which were favourable to Muslim control; and secondly, by working for a central government which would exercise minimum control over the provinces.

In the pursuit of maximum provincial autonomy, Fazli argued strongly against vesting the Governor with unspecified powers of 'supervision, direction and control'. He dissented from the view supported in the government of India dispatch that the Governor should have a discretionary power to appoint an official minister,[48] and he also opposed giving the Governor overriding powers, even in the interests of 'safety and tranquillity' and 'the protection of minorities'.

'Safety and tranquillity' will not do because it has been argued often enough that 'safety and tranquillity may be endangered by wrong action in almost any department.... I am quite clear that what is needed is specification of the departments in which overriding powers of the Governor are desired to be secured.[49]

Similarly, with regard to the protection of minorities, he pointed out that they were not only interested in questions of religion and

[45]Ibid., Note by Schuster, 2 Sept. 1930.

[46]Ibid. Note by W.H. Lewis, Assistant Reforms Commissioner, 6 Sept. 1930. See also *Government of India Dispatch on Proposals for Constitutional Reform, 20 September 1930,* presented to Parliament, Nov. 1930, *Cmd. 3700,* pp. 16-17.

[47]Ibid., Note by Fazli Husain, 23 Aug. 1930.

[48]GI Reforms Office, 67/v/1930: Minutes of informal discussion in council on government proposals for Reform, 21st Meeting, 3 Sept. 1930: see also *Government of India Dispatch,* p. 38.

[49]GI Reforms Office, 67/x/1930: Note by Fazli Husain, 18 Aug. 1930.

culture, but also in representation in local bodies and services. In both these spheres, he argued, overriding powers would involve 'a very serious encroachment on the responsibility of the ministry to the legislature'.[50]

At the same time, he endeavoured to secure for the Muslims of Punjab and Bengal a majority of seats by separate electorates. This was a difficult task. There were some Governors, in all probability Hailey and de Montmorency, who believed that 'political considerations' might require that the Muslims be given majorities in these two provinces while retaining their weightage in the minority provinces.[51] But most members of council were more circumspect. To show public approval for a system which put minorities at the mercy of an unalterable communal majority was likely to make government a number of powerful enemies and to be a source of incessant agitation. Moreover, it was so obviously 'undemocratic' that it would certainly not meet with parliamentary approval in Britain.[52]

Fazli's main argument was that the Simon Commission had done a great injustice to the majority provinces by making its recommendations on the basis of the Lucknow Pact. That understanding had been repudiated both by the Congress and by the Conference and formed no basis for a discussion of the problem. Recognition of Muslim majorities in Punjab and Bengal should not be made dependent on the surrendering of weightage in the minority provinces. The question

[50]Ibid. Fazli's views on these questions show how far his interests were removed from those of the minority-province Muslims. He made no effort to support statutory safeguards for minorities in cabinets and services, even though the Muslim Conference was putting this demand forward vociferously on their behalf. Indeed, he appears to have argued against statutory representation in Cabinets, and to have concurred with the general council view that for the services a negative formula was the best answer. It is clear that in his scheme of provincial autonomy, the minority would have to accept the arbitration of the majority. In his view, even giving the Governor overriding powers would be an insufficient guarantee: 'Personally', he wrote, 'I think the Governor will not be able to do much, for the reason, among others, that he would not consider it worth his while to pick a quarrel with his Cabinet for the sake of any minority.' See Minutes of informal discussion.., loc. cit., 3rd meeting, 27 June, 1930; Fazli Husain papers: Fazli Husain to Mahommed Shafi, 1 Dec. 1930.

[51]GI Reforms Office, 65R/1930 (Secret): Proceedings of the Governors' Conference, 1st meeting, 21 July 1930.

[52]GI Reforms Office, 67/x/1930: Minutes of informal discussion in council, 1st meeting, 25 June 1930.

of Muslim representation in Punjab and Bengal should be treated
on its own merits and not from an all-India point of view. Fazli appears
to have carried the day on this issue. It was recognized that 'the Muslims
both in the United Provinces and in Bihar and Orissa would react
sharply against any decision to deprive them of their present
weightage'[53] and no attempt was made to do so. But where the granting
of a communal majority to the Punjabis and Bengalis was concerned,
Fazli found his colleagues far less tractable. They were prepared to
concede separate electorates so long as majority-province Muslims
desired them, but they were very reluctant to make precise recommendations regarding the distribution of seats. Indeed, they were inclined
to postpone consideration of the problem until the 1931 census was
published.

Fazli made it plain that this was not satisfactory to Muslim opinion.
Whatever the figures for the 1931 census might be, he said, the main
question was whether the issue should be decided on a population
basis, or on the basis of voting strength or some other criterion:

Muslims attach a great deal of importance to an expression of opinion
on this matter. The Simon Commission has practically decided that
distribution on population basis should not decide the matter, but it
has not decided whether a bare majority should to given to Muslims
or not. The draft also shelves this question. The way it will strike the
Indian Mussulmans is that the Labour Government has been believed
to have expressed itself in the past against Muslim claims; and,
therefore, if neither the Commission nor the Government of India
support their claim, they cannot expect the Labour Government to
support them. The alternative is that the Muslims in these two provinces
should rely on their own strength, work toward the lowering of the
franchise (against which the draft has expressed dissent from the
view of the Commission) and abandon their present attitude in Indian
politics.[54]

This was strong talk. But Fazli backed it up with two suggestions for
solving the question which were designed to meet the 'technical' objection
to a communal majority. The first provided for a small number of
nominated seats and the second for a small number of special
constituencies. The Muslims were to be given a virtual majority of
the elected seats and to pick up the extra votes they needed from
nominated or special members: 'It should be noted', he wrote, 'that

[53]Proceedings of the Governors' Conference loc. cit. 1st meeting, 21 July 1930.
[54]GI Reforms Office, 67/X/1930: Note by Fazli Husain, 1 Sept. 1930.

where special constituencies exist and the number of electorates which the Muslims have is less than half the total number of seats, it is not open to the criticism that a communal majority has been set up.[55]

At a result of Fazli's pressure, the council was persuaded to modify its draft dispatch. 'It was decided that Council might definitely express an opinion that they would not consider it right to penalise Muslim majorities in the Punjab and Bengal because of weightage given to that community elsewhere.'[56] This was an important concession. But the council went further. Though they did not recommend Fazli's scheme for solving the problem, they did recommend a scheme put forward by the Punjab government which was very similar in principle. In that scheme, the Muslims were to have sixty-six seats out of 134, and the balance of power was to lie with two Europeans. Fazli would obviously have liked the Muslims to be more self-reliant. But he was not dissatisfied. The Punjab scheme gave the Muslims a virtual majority by separate electorates and it was an offer which might be improved in subsequent negotiations.[57]

Fazli fought his most difficult battle, however, over the relations between the provinces and the Centre. He anticipated that the Muslims would secure control of the Punjab under the reformed constitution and he wished to exercise that control free of central interference. But on this question, he met with determined opposition within the government of India. In the strategy of the Raj, the devolution of power to the provinces under the Montagu-Chelmsford constitution had worked as a successful counterweight to the nationalist challenge at the Centre. But with provincial autonomy about to be introduced, a new danger emerged, which Dunnett, the Reforms Commissioner, labelled 'extreme provincialism'. Dunnett argued that if provincial autonomy was introduced without any change at the Centre there was a danger of the government of India falling to the provinces.[58]

---

[55]Ibid.

[56]Minutes of informal discussion in council, loc. cit., 20th meeting, 2 Sept. 1930.

[57]*Government of India Dispatch*, p. 28: 'The scheme satisfies neither the Muslim, nor the Hindu, nor the Sikh members of the government, but in our view merits consideration.'

[58]It was on this question that Dunnett found the Simon Commission report most unsatisfactory. 'One of the greatest failures of the report is its blindness to the dependence of central administration in almost all departments on provincial co-operation. A system of self-sufficient federal agencies is impossible. This is one reason why there cannot be full responsibility in the provinces and full irresponsibility at the Centre.' GI Reforms Office, 67/vi/1930: Note by Dunnett, 10 July 1930.

It is difficult to examine this question independently of the challenge which the Raj was facing from the Congress. Some members of council felt that a concession at the Centre should be made as a positive response to that challenge. The Viceroy himself was of this view, and amongst the Indian members, the case for responsibility at the Centre was put forward very strenuously by Sir Joseph Bhore, the Member for Industry and Labour. Moreover, those who took the opposite view, the advocates of 'extreme provincialism', the Punjab and Madras governments and the Punjab Unionist party, who argued that the Raj should stand fast at the Centre, these interests were equally influenced in the formation of their political views by the likelihood of Congress domination at the Centre. Dunnett's contribution, however, was to point out that what was at stake was not who should control the central government but whether there should be a central government at all. Dunnett argued that it would be unwise to appease Muslim fears of a Hindu Centre if the price was loss of British control over the provinces.

The question first came up when the Simon report's recommendations for the central government were being discussed. The council agreed that 'it would not be right to commit the future and that to try to develop the Centre along the same lines as the provinces might be a serious political mistake'. But though they agreed with the report's long-term recommendations for an all-India Federation, they felt that dealing with the central government over the interim period presented difficulties, and they recommended that 'the constitutional problem of British India should be considered on its own merits'.[59] The main question was: how was the central government to ensure compliance with its wishes in the period between the establishment of provincial autonomy and the eventual establishment of the all-India Federation? In a note on the scope of the central government's powers of supervision, direction and control, Dunnett argued that these powers would be more effective if they were exercised, at least to some extent, in association with the Central Legislature. He considered it impracticable to place them solely in the hands of the agents of the Crown, and he argued that it would be better 'to give the Centre powers so obviously effective that their exercise will be obviated by their mere existence than to require the Centre to fall back on the Secretary of State for the assertion of its legislative

[59] GI Reforms Office, 67/v/1930: Minutes of informal discussion in council on Government proposals for Reform, 5th meeting, 2 July 1930.

authority'.[60] This note produced a very strong counter-attack from Fazli Husain. He informed the council 'that unless the Assembly were wholly excluded from the use of this power, provincial opinion would reject any reforms'. In his view, 'the provincial electorate would derive its sovereignty from Parliament and it would be inappropriate that the Assembly should be set up in a position to dominate the provinces'.[61] But though his point was taken, Dunnett's argument clearly carried more weight. It was recognized that the central government did require a measure of popular support in its dealings with the provinces, and as an initial step the council decided not to exclude the Assembly from an interest either in the supervision of central subjects or in the raising of loans for provincial purposes.[62]

The chasm widened when discussion turned to the question of introducing responsibility in the Central Executive. The Viceroy favoured a unitary scheme because this would ensure legislative support for unpopular measures.[63] But Sir George Schuster was rigorously opposed to the transfer of Finance, at least until a Reserve Bank had been set up, and it was generally recognized that the India Office would not stand for it.[64] On these grounds, the unitary scheme was talked out almost as soon as it was suggested, and when Sir Joseph Bhore reintroduced it, complete with official advisers on the Egyptian model, it met with the same fate.[65]

Fazli's view was that no change should be made at the Centre until the provinces had established themselves.[66] But once a decision had been made in principle that certain subjects should be transferred, he endeavoured to limit them to the bare minimum. He was prepared to see the transfer of those subjects which already fell within the portfolios of the three Indian members of council, but he strongly rejected Dunnett's contention that if some form of Dyarchy was introduced, the Home portfolio should also be transferred:

[60]GI Reforms Office, 67/vi/1930: Note by Dunnett, 10 July 1930.

[61]Minutes of informal discussion in council...,loc. cit., 11th meeting, 18 July 1930.

[62]Ibid.

[63]Ibid., 13th meeting, 28 July 1930.

[64]Ibid., 13th and 17th meetings, 28 July and 16 Aug. 1930.

[65]Ibid., 17th and 18th meetings, 16 and 18 Aug. 1930.

[66]In a note of 18 Aug. 1930, Fazli associated himself with those provincial ministers who felt that 'the proposed provincial autonomy should have a chance for the next ten years or so to get established before an all grasping Central Legislature begins to encroach upon them'. GI Reforms office, 67/x/1930.

Provincial Governments would prefer being under an irresponsible Home Department at the Centre .... An irresponsible Home Department cannot set itself against the responsible Home Department in the province; but a responsible Home Department at the Centre can claim to represent the Legislature, and through the Legislature, the country, quite as much as, if not to a larger extent than the provincial government. Again there is a tendency in all deliberative bodies of an all Indian nature to kill provincial bodies. That is the reason why the All India Congress Committee prospers; while the provincial Congress Committees, are except in a few cases, inert; and, in some cases, not even alive.[67]

The nature of Fazli's argument against the transfer of the Home Department suggests that Dunnett's reasoning was sound. But Fazli's colleagues preferred the devil they knew. Feelings in favour of responsibility in the Central Executive were tempered by the likelihood of a Congress majority in the Central Legislature. Dunnett himself estimated that if the Congress entered the provincial councils to the full extent of its strength it could be expected 'to establish a very strong position in the three presidencies, Bihar and Orissa, the Central Provinces, and possibly Assam, and to be far from negligible in the United Provinces'. And on these grounds, he argued against Simon's recommendation for indirect election to the Assembly. Such a system, he said, would throw power into the hands of the dominant provincial caucus and would probably 'put Congress in a dominating position in the Legislative Assembly threatening the power of the Central Government'.

We may have to lay our plans with a Congress which will capture and work the provincial constitutions, but will retain their creed of Independence and seek to destroy the Central Constitution from within. Indirect elections will help them. Independence should be a clear-cut issue and the best safeguard against it is direct election.[68]

But if Congress could capture the provincial councils, would it have difficulty capturing the Assembly, even if there were direct election? The use of such arguments encouraged parsimony. Fazli's colleagues decided it would be better to retain control of the Home Department. Sir James Crerar, the Home Member, argued that 'all those activities ... which are effectively related to law and order must remain in official hands',[69] and it was decided ultimately that 'the close connection

[67] Ibid.
[68] GI Reforms Office, 67/vi/1930: Note by Dunnett, 30 July 1930.
[69] GI Reforms Office, 67/v/1930: Minutes of informal discussion in council.. 17th meeting, 16 Aug. 1930.

of this problem with internal security and defence' made it impossible to state conditions for its transference :

In the search for some source of definition of what those conditions might be it was suggested that the transfer of Home Affairs at the Centre must necessarily depend more or less directly on the success or failure of the transfer in the provinces of Law and Order to responsible Ministers.[70]

But though Fazli scored a notable victory over Dunnett on this question, he remained apprehensive that the form of Dyarchy suggested by the government would be considered transitional and encourage agitation :

Sir Fazli Husain expressed his personal opinion that the scheme put up by the Government of India would mean, within the next ten years, either the surrender of the whole position, or a going-back on the Reforms entirely. It might be more graceful to make the surrender now and to give over all departments to popular control.... If this was more than British opinion would concede, then in his opinion, the alternative was to stand fast at the Centre.[71]

On this issue, Fazli was not appeased. In its dispatch on the Reforms, the government of India recommended that the functions of the central government should be divided into three categories: those like Defence, Foreign Relations, Financial Stability and Responsibility for Peace and Tranquillity, over which Parliament should continue to exercise control; those like Taxation, Commercial Policy and Railways, over which it would need to exercise occasional control; and those like General Economic Development, Labour, Posts, Telegraphs, Communications, Customs, Education, Health, Agriculture and Social Reform, over which it could safely relinquish control to the Indian Legislature.[72] These last subjects were to be transferred to elected members of the legislature who would hold office within a unitary form of government and who would be *responsive* to the legislature (but not *responsible* to it) in certain specified areas.[73] It was to be the most diluted form of Dyarchy, but in that the door had opened even a crack, Fazli continued to be fearful, and it was only when this scheme for a British Indian Federation was replaced at the first round-table

[70]Ibid. 18th meeting, 18 Aug. 1930.
[71]Ibid., 23 rd meeting, 5 Sept. 1930.
[72]*Government of India Dispatch,* pp. 14-15.
[73]Ibid., pp. 106-11.

conference by a new scheme for an all-India Federation involving
the Princes that these fears subsided.

The first round-table conference: the Liberal challenge fails

With the beginning of the first round-table conference, the constitution-
making process entered a new and important phase. The focus of
political attention shifted from India to Britain, and all those claims
which had previously been argued before the government of India
were subjected to direct British government arbitration. This had a
profound impact on Indian politics. It subjected the claims of the
government's allies to fresh discussion in a new environment and it
gave to those dissatisfied with the *status quo* the hope that they might
obtain in London what they had been denied in New Delhi. Behind
the scenes, of course, the government of India continued to exercise
considerable influence. But with claims and counterclaims now being
made in London, outward and visible signs of support became more
necessary. Public relations became a vital aspect of any party's
programme, and with the civil disobedience movement raging in
India and demonstrating to the British government that the Congress
did have mass support, it soon became necessary for parties opposed
to the Congress to develop sanctions of their own.

For Fazli Husain, one of the main problems was a shortage of
qualified personnel to put the Muslim Conference case effectively in
these new surroundings. Men like Jinnah, and even Shafi, were
chiefly interested in responsibility at the Centre, and the danger
was that the provincial Muslim case would go by default. 'Frankly',
Fazli wrote to Sir Malcolm Hailey, 'I do not like the idea of Jinnah
doing all the talking and of there being no-one strongminded enough
to make a protest in case Jinnah starts expressing his views when
those views are not the acceptable Indian Muslim view.'[74] But finding such people presented problems, for Jinnah and Shafi were
among the most fluent lawyers in India. They were well acquainted
with political debate at the highest level and they would make a
good showing in London. Fazli's main counterbalance to these men
was Zafrullah Khan, an Ahmadi whom he had brought into politics
in the face of much orthodox criticism. Zafrullah was an advocate
of exceptional ability, Fazli's successor in the government of India,

[74]Fazli Husain papers: Fazli Husain to Hailey, 10 May 1930: also Azim Husain, op.
cit., pp. 250-1.

and subsequently Pakistan's Foreign Minister and the President of the International Court of Justice at the Hague. But even Zafrullah could not hold the fort alone. So Fazli persuaded Hailey to allow Shafaat Ahmed to go from the United Provinces. He recognized Shafaat's shortcomings: he was inclined to spoil a point by pushing it too far and he was obsessed with constitutional safeguards for minorities.[75] But he was by far the keenest U.P. Muslim both in debate and organization, and he also had the advantage of a special relationship with Shafi which might be useful to Fazli in keeping Shafi under control. Hailey had originally favoured Hafiz Hidayat Hussain, whom he believed to command more 'all round support in point of character'. But under pressure from Fazli he conceded that Shafaat would provide 'a somewhat effective counteraction to Jinnah', and the two men ultimately agreed that Shafaat should go with the Nawab of Chhatari.[76]

But despite these precautions, the round-table conference gave Fazli an uneasy time, and for the very reasons which he had anticipated. The conflict between those politicians intent on securing all-India concessions and those whose future lay in the consolidation of provincial gains had never come to a head in India. Both groups had lobbied the government of India independently, and in its assessment of their representativeness, the government had thrown its weight behind the provinces. In London, however, both groups gathered round the same table, and put their cases to a new arbiter, the Labour government. The pressures for a settlement were strongest on the all-India politicians. The Hindu 'liberals' who gathered in London — men like Sapru, Sethna, Sastri and Setalvad — all realized that the continuation of non-co-operation posed a serious threat to their political future, and they were anxious to return to India with positive proof of their effectiveness as an inducement to Congress to return to the conciliar fold.[77] Their main aim was to achieve a measure of responsibility at the Centre, and in furtherance of this aim they put forward the idea of a Federation of British India and the princely states. They

[75]Shafaat had written a lengthy note on this question as a member of the U.P. co-operating committee. See *ISC*, vol. iii, pp. 281-381.

[76]Fazli Husain papers; Hailey to Fazli, 24 May 1930; Fazli to Hailey, 29 May 1930.

[77]For an account of the Liberal strategy at this time, see D.A. Low, 'Sir Tej Bahadur Sapru and the first round table conference' in D.A. Low,(ed.), *Soundings in Modern Asian History* (London 1968), pp. 294-329; also Sir Chimanlal Setalvad, *Recollections and Reflections, an Autobiography* (Bombay 1947), p. 357 *et seq.*

knew how reluctant all British political parties were to part with the reality of political power, and the Federal idea offered the most credible means of reassuring them that devolution at the Centre was feasible without surrendering to the 'Independence' school. In order to set the seal on the idea, however, the communal question had to be settled, and to this end they adopted a generous attitude to Muslim demands. This, in its turn, acted as a spur to Muslim involvement in negotiations on this question. Such men as Jinnah and Shafi were equally anxious to rehabilitate themselves as national leaders, and the atmosphere of the conference—the sympathetic impression created by Ramsay Macdonald, the feeling that far-reaching concessions were possible, and the absence of pressure from their Indian followers—encouraged a similar spirit of generosity on their side. For those whose interest lay in the provinces, however, this quest for all-India agreement had distinct dangers, and this was particularly so for the Punjabi Muslims, who were seeking very specific concessions in the face of well-organized Hindu and Sikh opposition. The Hindus, represented by Narendra Nath, and the Sikhs, represented by Sardar Ujjal Singh and Sardar Sampuran Singh, were strongly opposed to subordination to a communal Muslim majority, and in the Mahasabha leaders, Moonji and Jayakar, they had firm allies. The danger of the Punjabi Muslims being sacrificed to 'national' advantage were consequently very real, and all the more so in view of the historical sympathy of the Labour party for the 'national' school.

In the initial stages of the Conference, when discussions were proceeding informally, the Muslim delegation, under the leadership of the Aga Khan, appears to have worked cohesively and to have stuck rigidly to the Muslim Conference demands. The Hindus showed every desire to win over the Muslims, being prepared, according to one report, 'to concede the substance of Jinnah's 14 points, except that they are sticky on the subject of residuary powers and relations between the Centre and the provinces'.[78] But the Muslims showed no inclination to compromise,[79] and the Hindu party then became split between the Liberals, led by Sapru, who were prepared to pay a high price for a settlement in order to push through their demand for Federation, and the Mahasabhites, led by Jayakar and Moonji, who were not prepared to surrender important points without knowing what they would receive in return.[80] By the middle of November,

[78] GI Reforms Office, 173/1930R: W.H. Lewis to Dunnett, 31 Oct. 1930.

[79] Ibid., V.P. Menon to Dunnett, 7 Nov. 1930.

[80] GI Reforms Office 147/1930R: Tgm Secretary of State to Viceroy, Reforms Office (Haig to Dunnett), 13 Nov. 1930.

however, even Sapru's negotiations had become deadlocked over the question of electorates;[81] and though differences of opinion over the allocation of residuary powers and Muslim representation at the Centre continued to be explored, the situation did not materially improve over the next three weeks.[82]

At this stage, the Prime Minister himself intervened, and negotiations were resumed under his chairmanship, first in London and subsequently at Chequers. During these negotiations, the Punjab clearly emerged as the main stumbling block to an agreement. The Punjab Muslims demanded a majority by separate electorates. The Sikhs and Hindus held that such a concession was undemocratic. Ramsay Macdonald, for his part, inclined to favour the minorities. He told the Muslims that it would be impossible to talk of democracy 'if all the seats were fixed and reserved', and he suggested a scheme of his own 'reserving in a mixed electorate 80% of the seats and leaving 20% to go to anyone.'[83] This was well received by Moonji, Narendra Nath and Jayakar, but it was opposed by Mahommed Ali; and ultimately he was supported by Sapru. Mahommed Ali told the Prime Minister that he was prepared to discuss a solution 'on the basis of a mixed electorate' but he was adamant that the Muslim majority in the Punjab should be recognized. The Hindus, however, were not prepared to make this concession and the talks broke up.

For Fazli Hussain, observing these developments from India, the attitude of the Prime Minister, the willingness of Mahommed Ali to consider a solution based on joint electorates, and the continued quest for an agreement by both Hindu and Muslim Liberals,[84] were all subjects of intense concern. On 21 December, he wrote in his diary: 'The Muslim position at the round table conference is deteriorating and I must do something to put it right. I cannot let my life's work be spoiled. I must think hard and plan out a course of action

[81]Ibid., Tgm Secretary of State to Viceroy, Reforms Office (Haig to Dunnett), 18 Nov. 1930.

[82]Ibid. V.P. Menon to Dunnett, 5 Dec. 1930. In Menon's view, the Muslims were less anxious to compromise than the Liberals. They knew, he said, 'that their political position is not a stake and in the event of the failure of the Conference, the Government is bound to protect their interests'.

[83]This account of the negotiations at Chequers is based on Mahommed Ali's letter to Nawab Ismail Khan, 19 Dec. 1930 (Mahommed Ali papers).

[84]Negotiations between Hindu and Muslim Liberals were still in progress when the Minorities Committee was first convened on 23 Dec. See GI Reforms Office, 147/1930R: Tgm Secretary of State to Viceroy, Reforms Office (Haig to Dunnett), 23 Dec. 1930.

which will answer the purpose.'[85] Fazli attributed most of the trouble on the British side to the Labour party and its 'theories', and on the Indian side, to Bhopal, Shafi, Fazlul Haq, Sultan Ahmed and Jinnah. What he feared most was that the Muslims would give up separate electorates in order to strengthen the case for devolution at the Centre, and that as a result, the Punjab would be relegated 'to the position of a backward province tied to the chariot wheels of Hindu India.'[86]

Now, who will benefit more by responsibility being introduced at the Centre at this stage, Hindus or Muslims? Undoubtedly the Hindus. Therefore who should be anxious to settle communal differences in order to secure the promised gain? Naturally, the Hindus. Then why should Muslims, who are politically, educationally and economically weaker in the country, pretend that by ousting the British power from India, and by introducing responsibility, they stand to gain so much that for it they are prepared to sacrifice communal interests? .. Is the Indian Muslim community to be ruined by the Muslim delegates to the Round Table Conference?[87]

But Fazli did not only remonstrate with individuals. He organized the press in India, he arranged for an emergency meeting of the Muslim Conference working committee,[88] and he put pressure on the Viceroy to make it clear to the authorities in England that any discussion on the basis of joint electorates did not have the support of the community. In a very strong note to the Viceroy's Secretary, he deplored the Labour government's insistence that the Muslims should not have a majority, and he made it plain that the Muslims of Punjab and Bengal considered it 'an act of treachery on the part of the Government in as much as the Government encouraged the Muslims to oppose the civil disobedience movement and for their pains are now siding with the Hindus'.

As a matter of fact [he wrote] if separate electorates were taken away, I and with me a large number of Muslims will feel called upon to try our luck in the political reconstruction of India through the Congress rather than submit to gradual obliteration through the proposed reformed constitution.'[89]

[85]Fazli Husain papers: Diary, 21 Dec. 1930.

[86]Ibid., Fazli Husain to Sikunder Hayat Khan, 26 Dec. 1930 and 12 Jan. 1931.

[87]Ibid., Fazli Husain to Shafaat Ahmed, 20 Dec. 1930, quoted in Azim Husain, *op, cit.,* pp. 255-6.

[88]This meeting took place at Lucknow on 21 Dec.

[89]Fazli Husain papers: Fazli Husain to George Cunningham, 23 Dec. 1930.

At the same time, in the Secretary of State's Council, the Punjabi Muslim case was being pressed by the Muslim member, Umar Hayat Khan Tiwana. In a note which emphasized the military importance of Muslim support for government, Umar Hayat gave his opinion that the Punjabis had a very special claim to consideration.[90] In his view, weightage was of little avail to minority-province Muslims 'because they would remain in a minority in any case'. In Bengal, 'voting Mahommedans' were in a majority, but 'such a class could not help the British Empire or India with a single recruit...' In Sind, 'those who were recruited and sent to Karachi for training, deserted and tracked back on foot to their homes... The only province of significance for the Mahommedans is the Punjab.' Even within the Punjab, however, Umar Hayat made important distinctions. The two Punjabi Muslim representatives at the round-table conference, Shafi and Zafrullah, came from the Sikh Punjab:

One has got half a dozen near relations as barristers who cannot say a word against the High Court or the Hindus.... If they are boycotted by them, they will starve, as they have got no other income to fall back upon; while the other barrister from Sialkot is not a proper Mahommedan as he belongs to the Ahmedia sect.

The only significant class of Muslims were those from the West Punjab, and particularly those from the Rawalpindi division:

It is the Rawalpindi division which is full of soldiers which predominate in the Army; and they are the people who have served the Government since Punjab was annexed. They fought on the side of the Government during the Sikh wars and were instrumental in suppressing the Mutiny. My home is in the middle of this division .... I am the biggest landed proprietor in the province and even the children know my name. I know the feelings of the inhabitants of this tract in particular and other Mahommedans in general.

In this very representative capacity, Umar Hayat proceeded to criticize the influence of the Hindu moneylender, which he held responsible for the indebtedness of the Muslim agriculturalist, and the ascendancy of the Hindu money-lending class within the Punjab High Court, which he alleged had undermined the privileged position given to the agricultural classes by the Land Alienation Act.

---

[90] IOR/L/PO 48: Confidential note by Umar Hayat Khan Tiwana. The note is not dated, but it was seen by Wedgwood Benn on 22 (? Dec.).

Whole of Mahommedan Punjab is sick of all this and there have been periodical outbursts when the agricultural Mahommedans have burnt the houses of the moneylenders along with their account books .... So the only remedy for the Mahommedan agriculturalists is firstly, separate electorates, so that they may be able to send their representatives who do not belong to this class; and secondly, that they have a clear majority to safeguard their interests and get certain amendments passed to some Acts which were originally passed for their salvation and have since been misinterpreted.

Within the minorities subcommittee, the Muslims did initially stick to separate electorates: Shafi's speech of 1 January 1931 was very strong on this point.[91] But only five days later, Shafi went back on this position and offered to accept joint electorates on the basis of Mahommed Ali's formula,[92] provided that the Punjabis and Bengalis got representation according to population, and the minority-province Muslims retained their weightage.[93] Shafi clearly had hopes that this offer would be accepted, because it was virtually identical to a solution proposed earlier by Sir Chimanlal Setalvad. On this occasion, however, Moonji dominated the proceedings. If the Hindus were generous enough to agree to Muslim demands, he said, they would be reduced to a minority in almost every province in India. The Muslims had no right to special treatment, either on account of their historical importance, or because of the part they played in the existing Imperial machine. Historically, there was no continuity between the mass of the Muslims and the Moghuls. They were merely Hindus converted to Islam. And if they did play an important part in the Army, it was only because of the recruitment policy of the Raj. When pressed, Moonji agreed that the minorities might be given weightage, but he rejected Mahommed Ali's formula, which he held to be a form of separatism, and he refused to accept the principle that representation in Punjab and Bengal should be according to population.[94] In this, he was supported by the Punjabi Hindus and Sikhs; and on these grounds Shafi's suggestion was talked out. On 14 January, however,

---

[91] *Round Table Conference, First Session, Proceedings of the Sub-Committees,* (London 1931), part ii, p. 102.

[92] According to Mahommed Ali's formula, for a Muslim candidate to be returned, he had to obtain at least 40 per cent of his votes from his own community, and 10 per cent from other communities.

[93] *Round Table Conference, First Session, Proceedings of the Sub-Committees,* part ii, pp. 115-16.

[94] Ibid., pp. 116-21.

when discussion was resumed, Shafi made yet another attempt to produce a settlement; this time by offering terms very similar to those suggested in the government of India dispatch. The Punjabi Muslims were to be given forty-nine per cent by separate electorates, and the Bengali Muslims forty-six per cent; and both were to have the opportunity to increase this percentage by contesting special constituencies. Neither the Sikhs nor the Punjabi Hindus showed much interest in this offer. But both Moonji and Ramsay Macdonald thought it worth pursuing, and the committee was adjourned so that discussions could be resumed in private.[95] During these discussions, differences were fined down to a matter of one seat in a house of 134. But even then the Sikhs refused to budge, and it is difficult to avoid the conclusion that this one seat had a strong symbolic significance.[96] Despite Fazli's efforts to strengthen Muslim determination in London, it was in reality the polarization of political feeling in India which prevented the conference from coming to an agreement.

In the aftermath of the deadlock, the Muslim delegation dissociated itself from all previous conference discussions on the constitutional question. Participation in such discussions, Fazlul Haq told the conference, had been conditional on the settlement of the communal question, and in the absence of such a settlement, the Muslims were not prepared to see any changes in the constitution whatsoever.[97] This was an understandable bargaining position. But though the Muslims had not got what they wanted in the minorities sub-committee, they had no reason to be displeased with the work of the other committees. The Provincial Constitution Committee had accepted the recommendations of the government of India's dispatch, almost without alteration. All subjects were to be transferred, and there was to be joint responsibility and a unitary executive. Only where the powers of the Governor were concerned, were the delegates dissatisfied.[98] The Sind and Frontier Committees also produced satisfactory

[95]Ibid., pp. 127-9.

[96]During the proceedings of the conference, Sampuran Singh referred to 'letters flooding into London from the Punjab'. If Muslim government was introduced, he said, 'there might be a civil war and we might be annihilated and washed off the face of the earth'. Ibid., p.86. Other observers testify to the reluctance of the Sikh delegates to come to terms for fear of retribution on their return to Punjab. See Jehanara Begum Shah Nawaz, op. cit., pp. 113-14; Interview, Sir Francis Mudie, Dundee, July 1969.

[97]*Round Table Conference*, first session, Proceedings (London 1931) *Cmd 3778*, p. 245.

[98]Ibid., pp. 301-4.

results. The Sind Committee, while reserving judgement on the financial aspects of separation, recommended that the principle should be accepted.[99] And the Frontier Committee even went beyond the government's dispatch, suggesting a council with a larger elected element.[100]

For Fazli, however, it was the work of the Federal Structure Committee which proved most satisfactory. On the eve of the conference, when the All India Federation scheme was first published in London, Fazli had welcomed it:

> Personally, I am for it [he wrote in his diary], because it means movement towards Federation and the British Government will supply the power at the Centre, so that disruptive tendencies have no chance of success .... It really comes to Dyarchy and nothing else and only means decentralisation, greater autonomy for provinces and less scope for parliamentary interference. British public don't know enough to see change of these laws.[101]

This essentially provincial view of the likely impact of the Federal idea proved even truer than Fazli could have imagined. With Sapru at the helm, the idea was launched at the first plenary session of the conference of 17 November, and as arranged on board the *Viceroy of India* as the various delegates travelled to England, it met with a cordial reception from both the Muslims and the Princes. British parliamentarians responded less rapidly, but before long, even the Conservatives had heralded the idea as the answer to India's constitutional dilemma, and had agreed to the introduction of central responsibility if an all-India Federation was set up.[102] As negotiations proceeded upon the form of the Federation, however, it became apparent that the princes and the politicians had very different aims. Whereas the politicians had supported Federation to pave the way for central responsibility, the princes had seen it chiefly as a mechanism for restricting central government interference in the states. Some feared that the powers of paramountcy might be exercised by a responsible British Indian Centre and wished to influence the shape of the Central Executive. Others feared an extension of influence by

[99]Ibid., pp. 412-13.
[100]Ibid., pp. 378-80.
[101]Fazli Husain papers: Diary, 14 and 15 Nov, 1930.
[102]A detailed account of the acceptance of the Federal Idea by the British political parties is to be found in R.J. Moore. *The Making of India's Paper Federation 1927-35,* in Philips and Wainwright, *The Partition of India: Policies and Perspectives, 1935-47* (London 1970).

the Imperial power itself. Both these fears were assuaged by the adoption of the all-India federal idea. But once advance at the Centre had been made dependent on the establishment of such a Federation, the princes found themselves in possession of an even more valuable bargaining counter — a virtual veto on constitutional advance. And once that situation developed, their enthusiasm for federation began to wane. Firstly, when it became plain that the politicians were not prepared to grant them any special position in the lower house of the legislature, they began to talk less of acceding to the Federation as an order, and more of the rights of individual princes to decide the question for themselves.[103] And secondly, on the very important procedural point of how the Federation was to be formed, they declared themselves unwilling to federate with a unified British India. They were only prepared, they said, to federate with a British Indian Federation.[104] Whilst they had acquired a veto on the form of the central goverment, therefore, the formation of that government depended no less than before on the settlement of the British Indian issue. In short, a policy had been initiated which could only serve to hamper the eventual development of a responsible centre. Where Fazli Husain was concerned, however, the emergence of this problem was very welcome, for it made it likely that the first stage in the reform of the existing constitution would be the establishment of provincial autonomy unfettered by responsible central control. This prize, for which Fazli had campaigned unsuccessfully during the drafting of the government of India dispatch, was now delivered into his hands as a result of Liberal ambition and princely manoeuvre.

The Gandhi-Irwin Pact and after: a disturbing diplomatic interlude

At the closure of the first round-table conference, the Prime Minister, Ramsay Macdonald, announced that the government was prepared to accept devolution of power at the Centre if a legislature could be constituted on a Federal basis. This was a powerful bargaining counter for the Liberals — even though the communal problem had not been settled — and they returned to India intent on using it to lever the

[103]Round Table Conference, First Session, Proceedings of the Sub-Committees, part i, pp. 46-7: Speeches to the Federal Structure Sub-committee by the Maharajah of Bikaner and the Nawab of Bhopal, 5 Dec. 1930.

[104]Ibid., pp. 17 and 48: Speeches by the Nawab of Bhopal (2 Dec. 1930) and by Sir Akbar Hydari, the Prime Minister of Hyderabad (5 Dec. 1930).

Congress into the constitution-making process. In this, they were assisted by the government of India, which released the leading members of Congress so that they could reconsider their position in the light of the progress made in London. There then followed a fortnight of hectic negotiations and consultations, first between Congress and the Liberals, and then between Gandhi and the Viceroy, and the result was the Delhi Pact of 5 March 1931. The government agreed to suspend rule by ordinance and to release its political prisoners, and Congress agreed to suspend civil disobedience, to accept Dominion Status as its objective, and to attend the second round-table conference.

It would be wrong, however, to mistake the process of conciliation for the prospect of agreement. Though the government of India wished to recapture the middle ground of Indian politics and was prepared to make concessions to get Congress back into the constitution-making process, it was still firmly committed to its provincial allies and well aware of the importance of keeping them on its side. Similarly, though Congress did not wish to appear totally inflexible to those who were deciding India's future in London, it had little hope of achieving its objectives at a conference attended by those it was committed to supplanting. The reasons which had provoked the civil disobedience movement still held good; and it was primarily in order to convince British opinion of the validity of their respective interpretations of Indian politics that the two sides came together.

As soon as the Pact had been signed, however, it appeared that Congress had gained a good deal more than the government. The Viceroy may have been astonished 'that Gandhi should have been so far persuaded to come in line',[105] but the message which reached the villages was that Congress had won a great victory and that *Ram Raj* was just round the corner. Before the Pact was signed, the government had virtually brought civil disobedience to an end by the use of extraordinary powers. But with the suspension of those powers and the relaxation of administrative control, the way was clear for the reassertion of Congress influence. It was an opportunity which many leading Congressmen seized with both hands. In a circular to local Congress committees written on 10 March, Jawaharlal Nehru indicated that he saw the Pact as 'a truce only and no final peace'. 'That peace can only come', he wrote, 'when we have gained our objective in its

[105]Halifax papers, 6: Irwin to Wedgwood Benn, 9 March. 1931.

entirety.' In the meantime, Congressmen were to establish definite centres of work and strengthen Congress organization in the rural areas so that they could meet 'any contigency that might arise'.[106] In Jawaharlal's own district, moreover, even the truce was not being observed.

Just before the truce [wrote the Collector of Allahabad], things were improving and rent was beginning to come in; and it looked as if the no-rent campaign was shortly to be broken. The release of the prisoners, however, had an extremely bad effect. They went back to their villages proclaiming their victory—and victory for the tenant means non-payment of rent. Rental payments fell off at once and have got steadily worse ....The Congress undertook effectively to discontinue the no-rent campaign. But actually, they have effectively continued it.[107]

The government's apparent capitulation to the Congress inevitably raised questions about its capacity to protect its friends. In the Punjab, as far north as Jhelum, Muslims began debating whether a Congress government would repeal the Land Alienation Act.[108] In Bengal, the prospect of civil war between Congress and government left the Muslims uncertain as to how to safeguard their own position.[109] And in the U.P., where the re-assertion of Congress authority was most marked, fuel was added to the fires of suspicion by an outbreak of very serious communal rioting. At Benares, on 11 February, a Muslim shopkeeper, returning home after a clash with Congress pickets, was murdered in a narrow lane near the bazaar. This incident was followed by a riot in which three died and seventy-seven were injured. The position grew worse after the Gandhi-Irwin Pact, when Congress policy appears to have assumed a more communal guise, particularly in Allahabad and Muttra.[110] But it deteriorated irretrievably on 24 March at Kanpur, when a riot broke out in which ninety-nine Muslims and forty-nine Hindus lost their lives; 500 houses, forty-two temples

[106]GI Home Poll. 33/xi/1931: AICC circular no. 12, 10 March, 1931.

[107]Ibid., R.F. Mudie to Commissioner, Allahabad Division, 25 March 1931.

[108]GI home Poll. 5/45/1931 Extract from tour report of officers of the third batallion, the Baluch regiment, Camp Jhelum, 21 March, 1931. For a full account of the nervousness produced among the Muslims in the Punjab, see GI Home Poll. 33/vii/1931: de Montmorency to Emerson, 13 May 1931.

[109]Ibid., Reid to Emerson, 11 May 1931.

[110]See GI Home Poll. 33/xi/1931: Marsh Smith's confidential report on the rural areas of Allahabad district, 28 March 1931; Collector of Muttra to Commissioner of Agra, 27 March 1931.

and eighteen mosques were burnt or damaged; and whole areas of the city were reduced to smouldering wreckage.[114] As at Benares, this incident was sparked off by Congress attempts to enforce a hartal on Muslim shopkeepers, on this occasion as a sign of mourning at the execution of Bhagat Singh, but as a result of administrative negligence, the riot was not contained at the crucial time, and the results were disastrous. A Commission of Enquiry was immediately set up, and this eventually showed that individual Hindus and Muslims had made heroic efforts to save members of the other community from the outrages of the mob.[112] But even the death of so prominent a Congressman as Ganesh Shankar Vidyarthi, who was killed by a Hindu mob while protecting his Muslim neighbours, did little to modify the traumatic effect of this riot on the North Indian Muslim psyche. Never before in living memory had a riot of such proportions taken place, and Muslims were quick to reach the conclusion that they were experiencing the first fruits of the Congress victory. 'The riots in the U.P. have been simply dreadful...', Shafaat Ahmed wrote to Jinnah. 'The Hindus are so puffed up with what they call their victory over the British Government that they wish to dispose of the Muslims like so much cucumber.'[113]

The Muslim Conference response to these developments was to become more strident in its demands. A special session of the organization, held on 5 April at Delhi, was highly critical of both Congress and government, and many of the demands first voiced at Delhi in 1928 were pushed even further. Moving the first resolution, Zahur Ahmed of Allahabad condemned 'the so-called non-violence of the Congress satyagrahis' as being 'little short of an unclean political stratagem adopted in the face of the superior organised force of the state and cast off in dealings between the communities'.

This Conference [ran the resolution] warns the Governments in England and this country that their spineless handling of the situation due to their continued pandering to the Congress will create a condition of things in India which will spell the complete ruin of this unfortunate country.

The U.P. Muslims were undoubtedly worried; and they reacted as

---

[111]The *Leader* of 18 April 1931 carries pictures of the devastation.

[112]See GI Home Poll. 215/1931: a copy of the report and details of the government's action upon it.

[113]Mukhtar Masood, ed., *Eye Witnesses of History, a Collection of Letters Addressed to Quaid-i-Azam* (Karachi 1968), p.66: Shafaat Ahmed Khan to Jinnah, 26 March 1931.

worried men. On the one hand they rattled the sabre: 'Why not test our metal today?', asked Zahur Ahmed. On the other, they called for further safeguards. In addition to demands made on previous occasions, they demanded for the first time that fundamental rights should be made justiciable, that Muslims should be subject 'only to their own personal law in all matters related to religious observance', and that no government should at any time have the power to alter this law. These were significant developments. All three demands demonstrate the anxiety of the minority-province Muslims at the prospect of Congress rule, and the last two illustrate a growing convergence of political and religious themes.[114]

Hand in hand with these resolutions went others designed to maximize provincial autonomy. In part, these were sponsored by the minority-province Muslims. For as their future appeared more insecure, so the hostage' argument grew in strength. Many of them thought that a strong Punjab was their best guarantee of even-handed treatment within their own provinces; and such men were apprehensive lest the ascendancy of Gandhi deprive them of this protective shield.

The feeling among Muslims here [wrote one such politician] is that Gandhi will support the demand for Unitary Government. If this is done, the Muslim provinces will be like clay in the hands of the potter. The Hindu majority in the Centre and the Hindu government will make short work of the Punjab and Sind.[115]

Those most apprehensive at such a development, however, were the Punjabis themselves, for they stood to be deprived not of a protective shield but of the chief prize for which they had been working—provincial autonomy. Significantly, therefore, their terms for joining an all-India Federation are raised at this time. Not only do they demand that the provinces should enter such a Federation as sovereign units on virtually the same terms as the states. They also demand that there shall be no change in the Federal constitution unless all the constituent units agree.[116] The most striking indication of this change of mood, however, was a proposal put forward by Firoz Khan Noon for the provincialization of the Army. This was not embodied in a

[114]Mihr Collection, 254: Resolution of the All India Muslim Conference, New Delhi, 5 April 1931; *The Leader*, 8 April 1931.
[115]Mukhtar Masood, op. cit., pp. 66-7: Shafaat Ahmed Khan to Jinnah, 26 March 1931.
[116]*The Leader*, 8 April 1931.

formal resolution, though it was much ventilated in Delhi when the Conference met.

If the Army were at a later stage handed over to Indian control [Firoz told the Viceroy] it would be at the beck and call of the Hindus. What then would happen, he asked, if communal disorders started? His solution was that the control of the Army should pass not to the Centre but to the provinces.[117]

The Viceroy told Firoz that such a proposal was impracticable; and Firoz is reported to have agreed. But while it was not formally advocated, it illustrates the strength of the centrifugal forces at work. The Punjab Unionist party, which was heavily dependent on the soldier's vote and heavily involved in recruitment for the Army, was beginning to see devolution at the Centre as a threat not only to its political interests, but also to its privileged position within the Imperial military machine.

At the same time, however, just as the government had made conciliatory gestures to the Congress, so the Congress began to make conciliatory gestures to the Muslims. By the terms of the Delhi Pact, Gandhi had committed himself to attending the round-table conference, and he realized that his position would be enormously strengthened if he arrived in London as the purveyor of a united demand. No sooner was the pact signed, therefore, than he began to say that it would be useless to go to London without a settlement of the communal question, and even that he would be prepared to give the Muslims all they wanted as the price of agreement.[118] As in his negotiations with Irwin, however, it may be doubted whether Gandhi ever thought agreement possible on the basic constitutional issues. The Congress decision to start non-co-operation had itself been an acknowledgement that a joint demand by both communities was no longer a feasible method of securing political reform; and the movement itself had done nothing to change this estimate of the situation. The Congress had strengthened its position and made it imperative for government to take it into account. But Muslim support for non-co-operation had been negligible; and Muslims working the Reforms had been alienated still further.

Gandhi's conciliatory gestures to the Muslims are best seen as part of his diplomatic tussle with the government of India. The government

[117]Halifax papers, 6: Irwin to Wedgwood Benn, 2 April 1931.

[118]GI Home Poll. 136/1931: Williamson's note on the Karachi session of the Congress, 7 April 1931.

wanted to shoehorn him into the company of those whose claims the Congress had consistently refused to recognize. Congress wanted to lend weight to its claim to represent the Indian people as a whole. On both sides, the important thing was not actually to make concessions but to appear willing to do so. It was noticeable, for example, that there was no sign of Gandhi's 'blank cheque' when he and Vallabhbhai Patel met members of the Muslim Conference working committee at Delhi early in April. As in London, negotiations became deadlocked over the question of electorates.[119] But Gandhi did not even make concessions on points on which Conference Muslims and Nationalist Muslims were in agreement. Rather he used the fact that differences existed within the Conference, and between the Conference and the Nationalist Muslims, as a reason for making no concessions at all. If a settlement was to be 'frankly based on communalism', he said, then there must be unanimity. 'My own personal position is quite clear. It is that of full surrender to any unanimously expressed wish of the Mussulmans and Sikhs. I would like the Hindus to see the beauty of this solution. It can only come out of the consciousness of moral strength.'[120]

Gandhi might also have added: 'and out of an understanding of the divided nature of Indian politics'. For as Emerson made clear during discussions with Gandhi in May, if Reform had to wait for communal agreement, there never would be any Reform. Moreover, even if Gandhi took that view, Government could not accept it.

Government had often been accused of Machiavellian methods, and if it adopted the line taken by Mr Gandhi, there would be an immediate outcry accompanied by political agitation on an intense scale. This must therefore be ruled out, and Government must pursue the policy of constitutional advance even if no agreed settlement were reached. Why should Mr Gandhi take in this matter a more reactionary attitude than Government?[121]

The answer was simple: for diplomatic reasons. Gandhi knew that with or without agreement Reform would come, and despite his insistence that the Indians should settle the communal question themselves, he also knew that the government would eventually have

[119]*The Leader*, 6 April 1931.
[120]Ibid., 8 April 1931.
[121]GI Home Poll. 33/ix/1931: Note by Emerson on his talks with Gandhi, 13-16 May 1931.

to settle it. Indeed, by May, he was himself suggesting that Lord Irwin should be asked to arbitrate.[122] The real 'beauty' of his 'solution' was that it preserved the Congress claim to represent India as a whole without involving it in negotiations with other parties to find a settlement. If Congress were to shut the door on negotiations, it would suffer diplomatically in London. But if it actually got involved in negotiations, it would divide its own supporters and lose the momentum which it had already generated. Gandhi's formula was an attempt to get the best of both worlds.

Even so, there were Muslims both within the Conference and the Congress who were prepared to try their hands at a settlement. The Conference Khilafatists had been reluctant converts to the Conference platform, and when the faith of their leaders in government promises appeared ill-founded, as it did after the Gandhi-Irwin Pact, it was natural for them to doubt the wisdom of their conversion. Would it not be better, they asked themselves, to try again for a settlement with the Congress? The urban constitutionalists of Punjab asked themselves the same question. Shafi's efforts at the round-table conference had not won him any popularity among the Unionists.[123] But their ascendancy in 1920 had not benefited him; and the same logic which had made him a party to Jinnah's four proposals in 1927 continued to make him sympathetic to the prospect of a negotiated settlement. To some extent, Iqbal fell into the same category. True, by the time of his speech to the Allahabad Muslim League in 1930, his spiritual and cultural ideology had acquired a distinct territorial dimension.[124] But Iqbal was an urban Muslim of Kashmiri descent and as yet his ideology appealed only to a restricted audience within Punjab—the Arains, the Kashmiris, the urban intelligentsia and the products of Islamia college. He had little in common with the bulk of the Unionists and he was prepared to consider a settlement with Congress if it secured advantages to his class. Unlike Shafi, however, Iqbal was amenable to Fazli Husain's influence, and this was to be an important factor in the negotiations ahead.[125]

[122]Ibid.

[123]See Halifax papers, 6: de Montmorency to Irwin, 6 Feb. 1931, enclosed, Irwin to Wedgwood Benn, 16 Feb. 1931.

[124]See Pirzada, op. cit., vol. ii, p. 153-71.

[125]Iqbal and Fazli Husain both had links with Sialkot. They had also studied in the same class at Government College, Lahore. For an interesting account of Fazli Husain's efforts to 'help' Iqbal, see Azim Husain, op. cit., pp. 318-21.

Those keenest for a settlement, however, were the Congress Muslims —Ansari, Khaliquzzaman and Sherwani. For these men, the period after the Calcutta convention had been difficult. They had refused to be browbeaten by the Ali brothers, and they had continued to work within the Congress. But the Lahore session of 1929 had left them very disillusioned. The Nehru report, over which they had broken with so many of their friends, had been thrown into the Ravi, and the Congress had decided that negotiations for a communal settlement would have to be suspended until *purna swaraj* was achieved. This was distinctly unpalatable to them. *Swaraj* was to be achieved by civil disobedience, a movement in which the Muslims were not likely to figure prominently, and even if it were achieved by that method, it was unlikely that it would result in a communal settlement to their advantage. Consequently, early in 1930, Ansari, Khaliquzzaman and Sherwani resigned their various offices in the Congress, remaining only four anna members;[126] and Sherwani even made attempts to come to terms with the Muslim League.[127] These attitudes softened when government began to deal firmly with Congress. At that stage, Ansari broke his silence and denounced the Government's 'black and tan' methods;[128] and Khaliquzzaman even served for a while, though somewhat half-heartedly, as Congress dictator.[129] But throughout this period their underlying aim was to get Congress back to conciliar politics, and they welcomed the Gandhi-Irwin Pact for this reason.[130]

These Congress Muslims took the lead in proposing terms for a settlement at a well-attended meeting of nationalist Muslims at Lucknow on 18 and 19 April. They offered a provision to protect Muslim culture, language, education and religion; a guarantee that appointments to

[126]The conflict of loyalties and of political interpretation brought to a head by the Lahore Congress is best seen in Ansari's letter to Gandhi of 13 Feb., and in Motilal's reply to Ansari of 17 Feb. 1930 (Ansari papers: Jamia Millia Islamia, New Delhi). See also Khaliquzzaman, op. cit., p. 104.

[127]Ansari papers: Sherwani to Ansari, 3 March 1930.

[128]Ibid., undated draft of Ansari's letter to the press (July? 1930).

[129]Khaliquzzaman, op. cit., p. 107; Halifax papers, 6: Irwin to Wedgwood Benn, 30 Oct. 1930.

[130]Ansari continued to favour a conciliar policy until his death in 1936. In 1934, he and Dr B.C. Roy were amongst the first to call for the return of Congress to the legislatures. This nationalist Muslim preference for conciliar politics is a significant indicator of the extent to which they relied, consciously or unconsciously, on British arbitration in their hopes of a fair deal.

the services would be according to a minimum standard of efficiency with no community being allowed to predominate; a promise of separation for Sind and of equal status for the Frontier and Baluchistan; and a Federal constitution in which residuary powers would reside with the provinces. On the question of electorates, however, they remained adamant. Ali Imam, the President, confessed to a feeling of remorse for his part in the drafting of the Simla manifesto of 1906. Separate electorates, he said, had poisoned the relations between the communities and should be abolished. If they could not stand on their own feet, why not frankly say that they depended on the British and that they did not want freedom? Ansari was less outspoken. The Nationalist Muslims recognized, he said, that the Muslim demand for safeguards was genuine, and he promised that they would 'do their best to press all such genuine demands and secure their acceptance by all concerned'. But Ansari, too, refused to countenance separate electorates. The measure and method of representation in the Federal and provincial legislatures should be settled, he said, on the basis of joint electorates and adult suffrage. And he suggested that a round-table conference of Muslim organizations be convened for this purpose.[131]

For the organizers of the Muslim Conference, this initiative was potentially very dangerous. For if members of the Conference became involved in discussing such terms, existing Conference demands would appear questionable. Fazli Husain did his best to close Conference ranks on this issue. Adult suffrage was not practical politics, he told Mushir Hussain Kidwai, and to consider joint electorates on such terms was merely to give away a substantial advantage without being sure of any substantial return. The first essential was to secure Congress acceptance of the Conference demands for continued weightage in the minority provinces and for the recognition of Muslim majorities in Bengal and Punjab. If these demands were accepted in principle, he said, then discussion might be started on the question of electorates. In the meantime, the best policy was to stick to separate electorates and to show no inclination to give them up unilaterally.[132] For the same reasons, Fazli also dissuaded Iqbal from calling a meeting of the Muslim Conference to consider the nationalist Muslim offer There was no need for further meetings, he told him, because the

[131]*The Leader,* 19, 20, 22 and 23 April 1931.

[132]Fazli Husain papers: Fazli Husain to Mushir Hussain Kidwai, 27 April 1931.

Muslim Conference programme was already decided. Any meetings to discuss the programmes of other organizations, he said, would be likely to impair the representative standing of the Conference itself. The point to emphasize was that there was almost no difference between the demands of the nationalists and of the Conference. The Punjab press, he said, should be urged to make the most of this.[133] Fazli also discouraged Iqbal from considering certain other terms for settlement which were being canvassed in Lahore by Sir Mahommed Shafi. Fazli told Iqbal that these terms fell short of the Conference demands and should not be put forward by the Conference Muslims themselves. Shafi's terms were almost identical to those put forward in the government of India's dispatch, and the Conference had nothing to gain by offering to accept what the government had already recommended. If the Hindus chose to make such an offer, it would be up to the Muslims to consider it. But it was not up to the Muslims to make offers themselves.[134]

But despite this advice, Iqbal, Shafi, Shaukat Ali and Nawab Ismail met Ansari, Khaliquzzaman and Sherwani at Bhopal in the middle of May to see if they could reach a compromise. During the two days they spent together, discussion appears to have been thorough and long. But no definite agreement emerged; only two sets of suggestions regarding the introduction of joint electorates on which both sides agreed to consult their individual organizations. Ansari's suggestions, which were the more radical, were designed to commit the Muslims to some form of joint electorate, at least for an experimental period, either by introducing them first partially and then more substantially, or by alternating them with separate electorates and providing for a referendum once the trial period was over.[135] Shafi's suggestions were to have a less immediate impact. One provided for the introduction of joint electorates with adult suffrage after ten years, though with the provision that they could be introduced earlier if a majority of Muslim councillors so desired. The other provided for five years of separate electorates with a referendum on joint electorates at the beginning of the fifth year. But even Shafi's suggestions failed to meet with Fazli's approval. He told Iqbal that the first committed the

133Ibid., Fazli Husain to Sir Mahommed Iqbal, 30 April 1931.
134Fazli Husain papers: Fazli Husain to Sir Mahommed Iqbal, 1 May 1931.
135*The Leader*, 25 June 1931: Statement by Dr Ansari on the breakdown of negotiations.

community irreversibly to joint electorates, albeit after ten years, and so gave away their main bargaining counter, while the second did not make it clear who was to take part in the referendum.

The only position which Muslims can take up is that the first election under the new constitution be held on the basis of separate electorates and that it should be open to Muslim members of any legislature to pass a resolution by a majority that the next election be held through joint electorates and that in future that shall be acted upon.[136]

With a little help from Firoz Khan Noon, who arrived in Lahore at Fazli's instigation to assist with the drafting of a Conference response,[137] this advice appears to have been taken. At a meeting of the Conference working committee at Shafi's house on 25 May, a formula very similar to Fazli's was agreed upon,[138] and when this was put to a meeting with the Nationalists at New Delhi on 19 June, it effectively brought negotiations to an end.[139]

After the breakdown of negotiations, Ansari became far more critical of the the Conference, seeking to undermine its all-India position by a direct appeal to the Muslims of Bengal. This was shrewd tactics. For the Muslim Conference was dominated by Punjabi and U.P. Muslims, and despite the adherence of the Nawabi party and a section of the Calcutta intelligentsia, the problems of Bengal had never received priority. At the round-table conference, for example, when Shafi put forward his second offer of terms for a settlement, it was noticeable that the Bengalis were to get the poorer deal — forty-six per cent compared with forty-nine per cent for the Punjabis. At a Muslim Nationalist meeting at Faridpur on 27 June, Ansari made the most of these indications of neglect. He denounced the Conference leadership — 'the benighted knights of Bengal and the Punjab' — and he told his audience that adherence to the Conference was likely to place the Bengali Muslims in a permanent position of inferiority. It was time, he said, that the Muslims of India returned their verdict on the futility of separate electorates. The Bengali Muslims had been successful under joint electorates in local elections and they could make the same impact on provincial

---

[136]Fazli Husain papers: Fazli Husain to Iqbal, 14 May 1931.

[137]Ibid., Fazli to Shafi Daudi, 16 May 1931.

[138]Ibid., Fazli to Iqbal, 30 May 1931.

[139]*The Leader*, 25 June 1931: Statements by Dr Ansari and Shafi Daudi on the breakdown of negotiations.

elections if only they developed the will to work and the courage to be independent. At the same time, Ansari put forward more detailed terms for an all-India settlement. These terms, he claimed, had been part of the original package, but had not been divulged at Lucknow for fear of prejudicing negotiations. They included reservation of seats for minorities of less than twentyfive per cent (and weightage for Muslim minorities if others also received it); reservation according to population in Punjab and Bengal if adult suffrage was not introduced; an embargo on constitutional change unless eighty per cent of both federal Houses approved it; and thirty-three per cent at the Centre. No more far-reaching terms had ever been put forward by a nationalist Muslim organization.[140]

But even to these terms, the Congress response fell short of 'full surrender'. At Bombay in the second week of July, after a lengthy but fruitless attempt to win Shaukat Ali's support for an agreement based on joint electorates,[141] the working committee adopted proposals which only improved marginally on the Nehru report.[142] It accepted joint electorates and adult suffrage, with reservation for minorities of less than twenty-five per cent. It agreed to equal status for the Frontier and Baluchistan. It accepted the need for a convention to safeguard Muslim rights in cabinets, and for a special provision to protect Muslim personal law It also agreed that population should be reflected in the legislatures if adult suffrage was not introduced. But it only adopted the other Faridpur proposals subject to qualification. Sind was to be separated 'if the Sindhis will bear the financial burden'. Residuary powers were to rest with the provinces 'unless it is found to be against the best interests of India'.[143] And two of Ansari's proposals were rejected — the first for thirty-three per cent at the Centre, and the second making changes in the Federal constitution dependent on eighty per cent approval by both houses.

The Muslim Conference was not impressed. At Allahabad on 9 August, the Executive Board ruled that the Congress resolutions, far from solving the communal question, sought to deprive the Muslims of almost all their safeguards without offering them any advantage

---

[140]*The Leader*, 29 June 1931; *Indian Annual Register*, 1931, vol. ii, pp. 311-16.
[141] *The Leader*, 11 and 12 July 1931.
[142]Ibid., 15 July 1931.
[143]Jawaharlal Nehru believed it was. See Syed Mahmud papers: Jawaharlal to Syed Mahmud, 30 April 1931. 'About the residuary powers vesting in the provinces, I do not agree. This is bound to encourage provincialism and this is even now a bane of India.'

in return. They were to sacrifice separate electorates and weightage in minority provinces. But they were not even assured of majorities in Punjab and Bengal. The question of Sind's separation, already ceded in principle in London, had been reopened. And the demand that residuary powers should rest with the units of the all-India Federation had been 'qualified by a condition which makes that recognition unreal as well as changeable'.[144]

Hostility increased when Gandhi tried to take Ali Imam and Ansari to London with him as Congress nominees. This seemed a deliberate attempt to undermine the Conference claim to speak for the Muslims as a whole, and it brought home the dangers of the parleys which had taken place earlier. In Fazli's view, Gandhi was out to get 'the position of dictator' and did not mind too much how he went about it. 'This is to be the reality', Fazli wrote to Lord Irwin, 'but he is ready to clothe this reality in the apparel of negotiation, discussion, argumentation, controversy, anything you like.'[145] The Muslims had said that they wanted safeguards. What was the Congress reply?

To confuse the issues, to indulge in irrelevance and to begin to talk of Muslim demands, and then begin to talk of Congress Muslims, of Dr. Ansari and so on. These are all devices with which Hindus as well as Muslims are quite familiar. Gandhi's insistence upon Dr. Ansari's inclusion and his parading readiness for complete surrender in case complete Muslim unity is forthcoming have nothing new about them. They are the very old devices which the Congress, Gandhi and the Indian Hindus have been condemning in the British Government and the British statesmen. They are doing now exactly what they alleged Lord Birkenhead was doing—asking for complete unanimity and resorting to the well known principle of Divide and Rule.[146]

But despite the fears generated by the activities of the Congress— fears which led to talk of boycotting the round-table conference[147] and which gave Fazli the necessary leverage to secure the exclusion of

[144]Mihr collection, 254: Resolutions passed by the Conference Executive Board, 9 Aug. 1931.

[145]Fazli Husain papers: Fazli to Lord Irwin, 24 Aug. 1931. Though Lord Irwin was succeeded as Viceroy by Lord Willingdon in April 1931, Fazli Husain continued to correspond with him in England.

[146]Ibid., Fazli to Maswood Ahmed, Syed Abdul Hafiz, and Syed Hussain Imam, 1 Oct. 1931.

[147]See Ibid., Fazli to Shafi Daudi, 31 July 1931. Shafi Daudi canvassed round-table delegates about the possibility of boycott. But Fazli advised caution.

Ansari from Gandhi's party[148]—the round table conference did not produce many surprises. For with Gandhi refusing to take part in discussions on the communal question except as a mediator, the situation was only marginally different from what it had been in 1930. As on the previous occasion, the Hindu Liberals found members of the Muslim delegation who were prepared to come to terms. But once again the Punjab proved an insuperable barrier to general agreement. The Muslims wanted a statutory majority, in fact if not in name, but neither the Sikhs nor the Hindus were prepared to accept it, and the Sikhs took the lead in resisting it by demanding terms for themselves which were so plainly unjust to the Hindus that they could not be accepted. If Begum Shah Nawaz is to be believed, however, there was a time, after the Muslims and Liberals had agreed among themselves, when a settlement did seem possible. Shafi ordered sweets and drinks and 'with joy and happiness', the Muslim delegates assembled in the Aga Khan's rooms at the Ritz to celebrate the great occasion. But the party failed to start. For the chief guest, Gandhi, who had gone to secure the agreement of the Sikhs and the Mahasabha, came back without it. Gandhi said: 'Gentlemen, I am sorry to report that I have failed in my efforts for settlement. The Sikhs and the Mahasabhites are not prepared to accept the terms devised by us.' 'There was a hush in the room', recalls Begum Shah Nawaz,'...and most of us felt like shedding bitter tears.' Shafi, however, had an alternative proposal. He said to Gandhi: 'Let us, the Muslims and the Congress come to a settlement tonight on those very terms.' Gandhi replied: 'Shafi, I know my limitations and I cannot do it.' And so the party broke up, Shafi and his daughter returned home, 'and when we reached our flat, Father broke down completely and fainted.'[149]

Gandhi's refusal to commit himself to terms which the Mahasabha and Sikhs would not accept was part and parcel of the same policy which he had enunciated in India in the summer. He was prepared to be a mediator, but he was not prepared to take sides. Publicly, this

[148]Ibid., Note by Fazli Husain on Secretary of State's telegram of 13 June 1931. Fazli also tried to get Sir Ali Imam excluded. But his arguments were not accepted. Ali Imam was not a member of Congress, and he was ultimately selected to replace Mahmudabad. Mahmudabad had been invited to the first session but ill-health kept him in India. He died on 23 May 1931. See Ibid., Fazli Husain to Eric Mieville, 27 July 1931.

[149]Jehanara Begum op. cit., pp. 127-31.

was explained in ideological terms. The nature of the Congress position as the representative of the people precluded it from being party to an agreement. All the Congress could do was to accept what was acceptable to all the other parties. As in so much of Gandhi's politics, however, ideology and political self-interest went hand in hand. Gandhi knew the power of the communal appeal, and he knew what it would mean for Congress if he committed himself publicly to stand against communal Hindu demands. Within the existing electoral system, until such time as it became clear what concessions were forthcoming, it could only mean a communal backlash and loss of support. It was far better to let government make the decisions and bear the unpopularity that they would bring. And so, having been through the ordeal of negotiations with the other delegates, Gandhi put the ball firmly back into the government's court. In the Minorities Sub-Committee, he confessed himself saddened and humiliated by his failure to produce a settlement. But he attributed it to the fact that the delegation had been selected by the government.[150] The argument, in short, moves back into a well-worn groove. The government was demanding communal agreement as the price of discussing political concession. But agreement would only be possible if the government first agreed to make the concessions. 'If we knew in a definite manner that we are going to get the thing we wanted', he said, 'we should hesitate fifty times before we threw it away in a sinful wrangle.' The Congress would accept any agreement accepted by all the parties. But in the meanwhile it was incumbent on the government not to hold up constitutional progress. For there would be no progress at all if unanimity was demanded, whereas 'the iceberg of communal difference will melt under the warmth of the sun of freedom'.

Not long after the round-table conference ended, the Congress resumed civil disobedience. It was part of the logic of the situation. Despite the outward show of conciliation, the polarization of political forces at the provincial level, which by 1928 had divided Indian politics into communal camps, had remained in essence unchanged. For a brief period, after the Gandhi-Irwin Pact, both Congress and government adopted more flexible positions for the sake of the political public in Britain. But this was merely war by other means, a diplomatic interlude which lapsed into war again when the diplomacy was over.

[150]*Indian Round Table Conference, Second Session, Proceedings of the Federal Structure Committee and Minorities Committee* (London 1931), p. 530.

Who won the diplomatic contest? In India, before the round-table conference, Congress undoubtedly gained more. But in London, the advantage lay with the government. It succeeded in making Congress look like one force among many, and this strengthened its hand in Britain when the next period of repression began. For the government's allies, however, and particularly for the Muslims, this was a disturbing period. It was difficult for the leaders of the Muslim Conference, let alone the rank and file, to distinguish between appearances and reality, and as government conciliated Congress, and Congress prestige rose, there seemed a real possibility that Conference interests would be sacrificed. As Congress and Government played out their various roles, therefore, the Muslim Conference began to adopt a more independent position. This had been apparent before the round-table conference, when fears that government would give way to Congress provoked talk of boycott; and when the round-table conference did nothing to safeguard the Muslim position, this trend became more marked. Though the government had won a position of strength *vis-a-vis* the Congress, therefore, in the same process it had impaired the confidence of its most important allies. In the absence of a communal settlement, it had obtained the responsibility for deciding the issue itself. But the Muslims were no longer sure that the decision would be in their favour, and as the Communal Award approached, they became increasingly belligerent.

The Communal Award: a triumph for Muslim provincialism

One of the chief factors accounting for Muslim belligerence was the fear that central responsibility would be conceded on terms favouring the Congress. In June 1931, commenting to Irwin on the negotiations which had taken place at Bhopal, Fazli Husain gave his opinion that Congress unwillingness to safeguard the Muslim position was based on its confidence that central responsibility was assured. According to Fazli, the Congress argued as follows: 'If we let the Muslims have weightage and majorities now under separate electorates, we shall not be able to get rid of them later, but if the British Government imposes them on us, we shall be justified in throwing them overboard at the earliest possible opportunity.'[151] As the second round-table conference approached, this fear of central responsibility on Congress

[151]Fazli Husain papers: Fazli to Irwin, 8 June 1931.

terms prompted the Conference to insist that the Minorities Committee should meet before the Federal Structure Committee.[152] The Conference was not prepared, it said, to discuss central responsibility until after the Muslim position had been safeguarded — or, in other words, until the forces of Muslim provincialism had been fortified against that very contingency. 'As you can well understand', the Aga Khan wrote to Sir Sam Hoare, 'this central responsibility is a leap in the dark, and before my people are ready to put their necks in the noose, they must know whether it can be tightened or not.'[153]

On this point, the round-table conference did little to reassure them. No communal settlement was reached and no safeguards were provided. Indeed the willingness of Muslim delegates to negotiate with Gandhi on terms inferior to Conference demands, and their participation in the work of the Federal Structure Committee contrary to Conference injunctions, caused considerable uneasiness.[154] The fact that Jinnah and Shafi had been prepared to discuss vital issues relating to the powers of the central government, and their declaration at the close of the committee's proceedings that 'the better mind of India' would not be satisfied unless provincial autonomy and central responsibility were introduced simultaneously,[155] appeared to have given the Muslim case away.

At the Conference itself, the Aga Khan did his best to counter the effects of these developments by the formation of a 'Minorities Pact' between the Muslims, the Anglo-Indians, the Indian Christians, the Europeans and the Depressed Classes.[156] This Pact, which was inspired by Fazli Husain and the Punjabis,[157] united the majorities in Bengal and Punjab with the minorities in other provinces and made it more difficult, particularly by its generous treatment of the Depressed Classes, for the government to throw over the Muslims. The government estimated that the organizations subscribing to the Pact rep-

[152]Mihr collection 454: Progs. of Muslim Conference Executive Board, Allahabad, 9 Aug. 1931, resolution 4; Progs. of Muslim Conference Working Committee, Simla, 13 Sep. 1931, resolution 3.

[153]IOR/L/PO 48: Aga Khan to Hoare, 30 Aug. 1931.

[154]Mihr collection 454: Progs. of Muslim Conference Working Committee, Delhi, 18 Nov. 1931, resolutions 1 and 2.

[155]*Indian Round Table Conference, Proceedings of the Federal Structure Committee and Minorities Committee*, pp. 464-5. Jinnah also made a final plea for the construction of a British Indian Federation.

[156]Ibid., appendix iii, pp. 550-5.

[157]Fazli Husain papers: Fazli to Alma Latifi, 6 Oct. 1931.

resented 120 million people, and with Congress resuming civil disobedience, it had no wish to lose this substantial body of support.[158]

The Aga Khan also materially assisted the Conference by securing the exclusion of Shafi and Sultan Ahmed from the work of the committees set up to continue the work of the round-table conference. He told Hoare that they had a leg in the Hindu Liberal camp and he appealed to him 'in the name of the large, loyal, law-abiding Muslim population ... to get the proper kind of men nominated at this time of life and death'.[159] For the main committee—the Consultative Committee—he suggested Shafaat Ahmed, Zafrullah and Hafiz Hidayat Hussain. The government appointed Shafaat, Zafrullah and A.H. Ghuznavi. This strengthened Conference powers of leverage in the difficult months ahead.

But in India, Conference supporters were no longer satisfied with manoeuvres. They were impatient for results. When Haji Abdullah Haroon, acting on instructions from the Aga Khan, attempted to organize a deputation to the Viceroy to elicit a reassuring statement of the government's position, he met with a poor response, even from leading members of the working committee. Iqbal, the President elect, confessed that while in London, he had been 'very pessimistic about Muslim demands'. But he did not feel that another deputation was the answer. He preferred to reserve his views for expression on the Conference platform.[160] Nawab Ismail felt even more strongly. In his view, the policy of the Conference was counterproductive, and he resigned his membership.

The indifference displayed by the British Government to Muslim demands convinces me that we can gain nothing by supporting the Government at this stage .... The Conference is at present dominated by persons who fight shy of exercising any compulsion on the Government for the acceptance of Muslim demands.[161]

Nor was Ismail Khan an isolated individual. Others who shared his views, notably the old Khilafat faction, were already beginning to pressurize the dominant interests. A resolution of the working

[158]IOR/L/PO 48: Cabinet Minute RTC (31) 11, 9 Nov. 1931.

[159]Ibid., Aga Khan to Hoare, 17 Dec. 1931; Note by Hoare, 19 Dec. 1931.

[160]*Haji Sir Abdoola Haroon*, a biography by Alhaj Mian Ahmad Shafi of Lahore (Karachi, n.d.), pp. 99-100: Iqbal to Haroon, 16 Jan. 1932.

[161]Ibid., pp. 97-8: Nawab Ismail to Haroon, 14 Jan. 1932.

committee, held at Delhi on 4 January, mentioned the possibility of 'political crisis'. It noted 'the general tendency of the Muslim public to take active part in the political struggle', and it considered it 'absolutely necessary to decide as soon as possible ... the proper course of action for the grave contingency which has now arisen'.[162] On 31 January, again at Delhi, the same committee moved one stage further towards non-co-operation. A resolution was brought forward calling upon Muslim members of the round-table conference to non-co-operate with the committees set up by it. This resolution was only kept in abeyance 'after a long discussion'. But the Khilafat faction was reluctant to accept the decision, and Hazrat Mohani and Ghulam Rasool Mihr dissented.[163]

This spirit of defiance was intensified by two developments in India. The first was the emergence of a confrontation between the Maharaja of Kashmir and his Muslim subjects, and the second was the harsh treatment meted out to Ghaffar Khan and the Redshirts when the government reimposed rule by ordinance to combat the resumption of civil disobedience.

Kashmiri Muslim opposition to the Maharaja first attracted attention in British India in July 1931.[164] But it intensified considerably in September, when a number of demonstrations in the Kashmir valley were put down with considerable brutality.[165] Resentment was greatest in the urban areas of Central and Eastern Punjab, where many Kashmiri Muslims had settled, but within a matter of weeks the Kashmir issue was causing concern as far away as Bengal.[166] An All India Kashmir Committee was set up, supported by Sir Mahommed Iqbal and the Quadiani Ahmadis; and the old Punjab Khilafat Committee, by this stage refurbished as the *Majlis-i-Ahrar-i-Islam,* began sending *jathas* across the border into Kashmir. The main demand of these pressure groups was that the government should take over the state, institute

---

[162]Mihr collection 454: Progs. of Muslim Conference Working Committee, Delhi, 4 Jan. 1932, resolution 2.

[163]Ibid., Progs. of Muslim Conference Working Committee, Delhi, 31 Jan. 1932.

[164]See Rafiq Afzal, *Malik Barkat Ali, His Life and Writings,* part i, pp. 30-2.

[165]For a summary of the Middleton Enquiry into these disturbances, see Indian Annual Register, 1932, i, pp. 472-4.

[166]In London in November, Fazlul Haq received telegrams from Bengal urging him to withdraw from the round-table conference if Kashmir Muslim grievances were not remedied. See IOR/L/PO 48: Transcript of the deputation which met the permanent secretary at the India Office, 9 Nov. 1931.

enquiries, and if necessary, depose the Maharaja. But the government did not accede to this demand and so drew upon itself the anger of the Muslim community. By the end of 1931, the Muslim Conference had become a vehicle for the expression of this anger. Partly, this was because Conference organizers felt a genuine sympathy for the Kashmiri Muslims; partly because they realized the importance of keeping the *Ahrars* under the Conference umbrella. These urban activists had a value to the Conference as the shock troops of the politics of Reform, and if they were not appeased, there was a danger that they might secede from the Muslim camp and regroup with the Congress. In large measure, however, the agitation was encouraged because it offered a means of increasing pressure on Government to satisfy Muslim demands in the constitutional field. In November 1931, the New Viceroy, Lord Willingdon, told the Secretary of State that 'the Mahommedan community — I am rather afraid with the support and approval of my Mahommedan Honourable Colleague — are keeping up the agitation . . .until they see whether they get satisfactory terms as a result of your discussions in London.'[167]

The reimposition of rule by ordinance in the Frontier provoked a similar response. A Conference resolution was passed sympathizing with the Frontier Muslims in their distress, and Shafi Daudi and Maulana Mazharuddin were deputed to visit the province to see the situation for themselves.[168] The main fear was that the Redshirts would be thrown further into the arms of the Congress at a time when the imminence of a new constitution offered hopes that the Frontier would draw into line with the rest of Muslim India.[169] As the same resolution put it: 'The sudden promulgation of the terrible ordinances ...[will] have no other effect than to banish the idea of cooperation with the Government in the general mass of the people.' The government of India did not wish to alienate the Conference and the way was cleared for the mission. It was arranged that Daudi and Mazharuddin should meet the Governor, the Inspector-General of Police, and other officials, and that they should be free to go wherever they pleased. But the result of the mission was not to the government's liking. The government had hoped that its hand would be strengthened

---

[167]Templewood papers (IOL MSS Eur. E 240) 5: Willingdon to Hoare, 22 Nov. 1931.

[168]Mihr collection 454: Progs. of Muslim Conference Working Committee, Delhi, 4 Jan. 1932, resolution 1.

[169]Fazli Husain papers: Diary, 3 Jan. 1932. At this time, Fazli was leading a delegation to South Africa. He returned to India on 26 Feb.

against Muslim criticism. But Daudi and Mazharuddin came to the conclusion that the Ordinance should be repealed, that Frontier officials responsible for acts of repression should be transferred, and that internees not convicted of acts of violence should be released.[170] Both before and after the mission, moreover, the two men were in regular contact with prominent Congress ulema and with the Ahrars,[171] and this prompted fears that a common front might be produced between Muslim activists in both organizations.[172] These fears were increased when the Conference called on Muslims to observe 'Frontier Day' on 5 February, and the government had to issue special instructions to prevent any unnecessary confrontations from taking place.[173]

Such being the Muslim mood, it was not surprising that the committees set up to continue the work of the round-table conference met with difficulties. Willingdon smoothed over Muslim doubts about participating in the Consultative Committee late in January,[174] but even though they served, they refused to discuss any question relating to devolution of power at the Centre unless Muslim demands were met. By the end of February, this effectively brought the Committee's work to a halt, and Willingdon had no alternative but to adjourn its proceedings.[175] The other committees were similarly affected. The Franchise Committee did not actually have to stop work. But, as Lord Lothian, its chairman, confided to Hoare, this was only because the communal question did not come within its brief. 'If would have torn my committee to pieces', he said, 'if I had admitted it.'[176] Even Lord Eustace Percy's Federal Finance Committee found it difficult to make helpful recommendations because of the fluidity of the situation. 'Eustace Percy tells me', Willingdon confided to an old friend, 'that they have collected all their facts and don't know what the devil to do with them. And that is much what we all feel.'[177]

---

[170]Mihr collection 454: Progs. of Muslim Conference Working Committee, Delhi 31 Jan. 1932, resolution 5.

[171]Shafi Daudi papers: Diary, 4-20 Jan. 1932.

[172]GI Home Poll. 123/1932: Note by Howell, 15 Jan 1932; circular letter to all local governments, 16 Jan. 1932.

[173] GI Home Poll. 14/ix/1932: Circular letter to all local governments, 1 Feb. 1932.

[174]Templewood papers, 5: Willingdon to Hoare, 25 Jan. 1932.

[175]Ibid., Willingdon to Hoare, 22 Feb. and 6 March 1932.

[176]IOR/L/PO/ 48: Lothian to Hoare, 4 March 1932.

[177]Harcourt Butler papers (IOL MSS Eur. F 116) 54: Willingdon to Harcourt Butler, 14 Feb. 1932.

By this stage, Willingdon was seriously worried: delay was encouraging dissaffection, and the government was running short of allies. The Princes showed no signs of coming into Federation,[178] and the problem of running the central government without British Indian allies, which Dunnett had elucidated during the drafting of the government of India dispatch, was turning him into 'a sort of Mussolini'.[179] The Budget of November 1931 and the various ordinances to deal with the Congress were all rejected by the Assembly and had to be certified. Willingdon called it 'a hopelessly Gilbertian state of things'.[180] 'How on earth Edwin Montagu ever got himself to put forward, and Parliament to pass, such a strange form of legislative life, I really fail to understand.'[181] But what was the answer? Again in line with Dunnett's original analysis, Willingdon considered that the only practical solution was to strengthen the central government by introducing a greater degree of responsibility. This is a constant theme of his correspondence with Hoare from November 1931 to March 1932. Indeed, when Hoare wrote to him in January that the all-India Federation must come first, Willingdon replied that this was the best way of forcing every all-India politician into the Congress.[182] Both from the point of view of reassuring the all-India politician, and in order to force the Princes to be more realistic, Willingdon considered that determination to press on with a British Indian Federation was the best method of procedure. If necessary, he said, he would come home to explain the idea personally to the Conservatives.[183] But the idea was rejected outright. The Conservatives had only agreed to concede responsibility at the Centre if the Princes were brought in, and Hoare knew that any talk of a British Indian Federation would provoke a full-scale revolt in the party at Westminster.

Willingdon does not in the least realise [he wrote to Lothian] the almost insuperable difficulty of the kind of piecemeal proposals that he and his Council have been making. I go constantly on worrying him with the urgent necessity of getting something out of the Princes.

[178]Templewood papers, 5: Willingdon to Hoare, 1 Feb. 1932.

[179]Ibid., Willingdon to Hoare, 20 Dec. 1931.

[180]Ibid., Willingdon to Hoare, 1 Feb. 1932.

[181]Ibid., Willingdon to Hoare, 17 Jan. 1932.

[182]Ibid., Willingdon to Hoare, 8 Feb. 1932.

[183]Ibid., Willingdon to Hoare, 22 Feb. and 14 March 1932.

On no account must the Princes be allowed to give a negative to All-India Federation ... If they say 'No', all the fat in the world will be in the fire here. Nine out of ten members of the House of Commons will then go straight back to unadulterated Simon Report.[184]

If Willingdon's efforts to strengthen the Centre illustrate one side of the Imperial dilemma, his determination to win back Muslim support illustrates the other. The government had encouraged provincialism to offset challenges to its authority at the Centre. But in the process it had become dependent on provincial allies. By March 1932, Fazli-Husain had the Raj over a barrel, and the Viceroy was crying for help. Early that month, when Willingdon met the Muslim members of the Consultative Committee and other Conference leaders in deputation, and learnt from them of the prospect of non-co-operation, he speedily relayed his fears to the India Office:

These gentlemen are most anxious to support us, but are seriously disturbed at the unsettled frame of mind of their followers and are doubtful if they can control them. Many influences are at work and very important decisions are likely to be reached at the Muslim Conference to be held at Lahore on 21 March. It is very desirable that a decision as to whether HMG now accept responsibility for settling communal problems should be arrived at with as little delay as possible.[185]

But the British government was reluctant to accept the responsibility for making any decision, let alone the kind of decision which Willingdon envisaged—a 'hookum' which would take the whole question out of the sphere of controversy. Hoare told Willingdon that any decision by the British government would have to be essentially 'provisional' in character, in line with the Prime Minister's speech at the close of the round-table conference. It should be open to revision if Indian political parties came to an agreement of their own.[186] This attitude conflicted markedly with Willingdon's desire for a statement of intention to quieten Muslim fears. Ultimately, however, Willingdon did score a minor victory. The British government was persuaded to publish a statement in which it accepted responsibility for making the decision and promised to discharge it without unavoidable delay. Willingdon was delighted. The statement

[184]Lothian papers (Scottish Record Office, Edinburgh) GD 40/17/152: Hoare to Lothian, 3 March 1932.

[185]IOR/L/PO 48: Tgm Viceroy to Secretary of State, 9 March 1932.

[186]IOR/L/PO 48: Tgm Secretary of State to Viceroy, 14 March 1932.

was in time for the Lahore session of the Conference and it averted an open breach between the government and its allies.

Even so, the Lahore session of the Conference was far from being a gathering of loyalists. Indeed, in his presidential address, Iqbal encouraged members of the audience to put their religion and culture before their citizenship of India. The British government, he said, could no longer be relied on to hold the balance impartially between the communities. Hindus and Muslims were being driven indirectly 'into a kind of civil war'. The situation was one in which every community would have to look to its own strength. The Muslims must not be found wanting. Mussolini's maxim was: 'He who has steel has bread. Iqbal modified it: 'He who is steel has everything.'[187] The Conference resolutions reflected the same spirit. The main one, which dealt with the constitutional question, expressed dissatisfaction with the round-table conference and declared that the organization could take no further part in the process of Reform. The British government's undertaking was welcomed. But a decision was demanded 'at the earliest opportunity', so that the community could know where it stood. In the meantime, the working committee was to draw up a programme of direct action, branches were to be established in all parts of the country, and volunteers enrolled and prepared to make 'all possible sacrifices'. The government was given till the end of June to announce its decision. Failing that, the Executive Board was to meet to launch the direct action programme.[188] This threat hung over Willingdon as he pushed the British government into making out a programme for Reform. He realized the dangers of delay and he asked for an early decision. If it could be made by July, he told Hoare, 'it would have an enormously good effect here, and I think would completely satisfy the Muslims, who have given us until the beginning of July for a decision to be made'.[189] By this stage, the Muslims were making the running.

The British government accepted that the matter would have to be settled. No further constitutional progress was possible without a

[187]*Indian Annual Register*, 1932, i, pp. 301-8.
[188]Mihr collection, 455: Resolutions passed at the Lahore session of the All-India Muslim Conference (Delhi 1932). Another resolution, proposed by Shafi Daudi and seconded by Ahmed Yar Khan Daultana, demanded the immediate introduction of provincial autonomy 'while details of the Federation scheme are being explored and worked out'.
[189]Templewood papers, 5: Willingdon to Hoare, 1 May 1932.

settlement, and constitutional progress was essential, for as Hoare told the Cabinet: 'We cannot go on indefinitely ruling by Ordinances'.[190] But the task was unenviable in the extreme. For whatever was decided, the Raj was bound to be weaker. The constitution itself had set up a tension between centrifugal and centripetal forces which could only be resolved to the Raj's disadvantage. Between the all-parties conference of 1925 and the round-table conference of 1931, Indian politicians of both communities had tried unsuccessfully to reach agreement. Now the Raj was forced to tackle the problem itself. Was Muslim provincialism to be encouraged further? Or was the trend already established to be reversed? In many ways, the decision had already been made. Strengthening the Centre had been rejected. The only alternative was to strengthen the provinces. It was a victory for the strategy of the Punjab civilians.

The main problem was representation in Punjab and Bengal, and the main question : how far should the Muslims be strengthened? It was uncertainty on this point, Hoare told his Cabinet colleagues, which more than anything else was holding up the evolution of a new constitution.[191] In making detailed recommendations to decide the issue, Hoare was guided by the government of India dispatch. He had accepted it as a basis for settlement in November 1931, and in March 1932, when pressing his colleagues for a decision early in the summer, he relied on statistics drawn up on that earlier occasion. In the Punjab, he favoured giving the Muslims 48.8 per cent by separate electorates, to be made up to fifty-one per cent from the special constituencies. This was the device originally recommended by Fazli Husain and Hoare preferred it to the official Punjab scheme which would have left the balance of power with two Europeans. 'In the Punjab...', he wrote, 'I myself do not think it is any good talking of less than 51%.' Whether the Muslims got a majority or not depended on how generously the Sikhs were treated. But Hoare believed the Sikhs incapable of satisfaction, and he favoured giving them only eighteen per cent to make the Muslim majority possible. In Bengal on the other hand, Hoare's recommendations were to leave the Muslims in a very definite minority. Special electorates were to continue to

[190]IOR/L/PO 48: Secret Cabinet Minute, C.I. 32 (2), 11 March 1932.

[191]Ibid., Hoare opposed extending the range of the Award beyond representation in the legislatures. To do so, he believed, would be to abandon the concept of evolving a constitution by free mutual discussion.

account for twenty per cent of the seats (though Hoare admitted that the Minorities Pact might make it difficult to keep this figure so high), and the rest were to be divided among the communities according to population. This would give the Muslims 41.4 per cent and the Hindus 40.4 per cent. The balance of power was to be held by the Europeans. Both in the majority provinces and in the minority provinces, Hoare recommended that separate electorates should continue, and in the minority provinces, Muslims were to continue to enjoy the same weightage. It was also anticipated that separate representation would be extended to the Depressed Classes 'from among the seats allotted to the non-Muslims or Hindus'.[192]

The provincial governments were in broad agreement with these suggestions, though in many cases they voiced fears which reflected the political uncertainties of the Raj's position. Sykes, the governor of Bombay, would have preferred the decision to be included in the final bill. In his view, an early decision made it likely that the prospective Federation would be ruined by the establishment of 'a congerie of provincially autonomous governments'. But he recognized the necessity for it, and he thought if it favoured the minorities, they might organize on the government's side.[193] The governor of the Central Provinces agreed that the Muslims should continue to enjoy separate electorates. But as the head of a province where Muslim support for government had been insufficient to prevent serious disruption, he warned against building too much on the existing strategy. The support of the Muslims had secured 'certain temporary advantages, but it raised their hopes unduly, consolidated the Hindus against us and made suspect our impartiality'.[194] In the Punjab, Hoare's suggestions were accepted with fewer qualifications. But even there, increasing militancy among the Sikhs was causing concern, and de Montmorency suggested that the range of the decision should be extended to include minority representation in Cabinets. If the Sikhs and Hindus were satisfied on this question, it might offset the effect of a decision in favour of the Muslims.[195] Hailey, the Governor of the U.P., the original architect of government strategy, appears to have felt by this stage that the government of India was inclined to go too far in buying off the

[192]Ibid.

[193]IOR/L/PO 48: Sykes to Willingdon, 11 April 1932.

[194]Templewood papers, 65: Extracts from Governor's letters on the communal problem.

[195]IOR/L/PO 49: de Montmorency to Willingdon, 29 April 1932.

Muslims, and for this reason he welcomed Hoare's decision to limit
the range of the decision to representation in the legislatures. He did
not undervalue Muslim support, but he warned against making
wholesale concessions in their favour. This would force all the Hindus
into non-co-operation and it would leave the Muslims with nothing
to agitate for. This was also the view of the Chief Commissioner of
Delhi. As to the effect of the decision, Hailey believed it would
depend on whether the Punjabi and Bengali Muslims were satisfied.
But the Punjab was the crucial province. 'So far as our local opinion
is concerned', he wrote, 'Muslims appear to attach less importance to
a statutory majority in Bengal than in the case of Punjab.'[196]

But it was over Bengal that the main conflict of opinion arose.
Anderson, the new Governor, recommended that the Muslims should
have 44.4 per cent and the Hindus 42.8 per cent.[197] This was in line
with Hoare's own recommendations, merely taking into account the
number of seats conceded by the Europeans in the Minorities Pact.
But Willingdon, who was under pressure from Fazli Husain, considered this unsatisfactory from the all-India point of view. Fazli told
Willingdon that if the Bengali Muslims did not get their majority,
there was a danger that they would go over to Congress, and in order
to offset the effect of such a development, he urged him to increase
Muslim representation throughout the minority provinces—by three
seats in Madras, two in the Central Provinces, and by one seat in
both U.P. and Bihar and Orissa. 'The loss of a Muslim majority in
Bengal is a very important matter and I want to use all these palliatives
so as to keep politics undisturbed.'[198] These views forced the council's
arm. On 14 June, the government of India recommended that
Anderson's offer be revised. The Bengali Muslims should get 48.4
per cent and the Hindus only 39.2 per cent.[199] Hoare objected. Such
a concession was unfair to the Hindus. But Willingdon remained
adamant.

Do please visualise the political situation out here. The Congress
are against us, the Moderates are not cooperating, and remember
that these two bodies are nearly all Hindus ... The Muslims, who, on

[196]IOR/L/PO 48: Hailey to Willingdon, 7 April 1932.

[197] IOR/L/PO 49: Tgm Anderson to Hoare, 7 June 1932.

[198]Fazli Husain papers: Fazli Husain to Eric Mieville, Private Secretary to Viceroy
14 June 1932. In this letter, Fazli expands on views put forward the previous day at a
meeting of council.

[199]IOR/L/Po 49: Tgm Willingdon to Hoare, 14 June 1932.

the whole, have generally supported Government, are, with the Princes, at present on our side. But if you give them less than de Montmorency proposes for Punjab and I propose for Bengal, I am quite certain that they will non-cooperate too. You may say that in Bengal, you must consider the Governor's views. My answer is that he is only looking at Bengal ... and that I have to look at the country as a whole .... What we propose is, I think, fair and equitable. Anything else would spell disaster and I can only add that if owing to your decision I lost their support as well, I should probably have to ask you to send out someone else to take up the role of Akbar....[200]

Under this pressure, the British government gave way. On 4 August, the Cabinet agreed to the Viceroy's terms, and on 16 August, the Communal Award was published.

The publication of the Award was a crucial event in the history of Muslim separatism. For it gave to the Muslims of Punjab and Bengal the possibility of dominance in their own provinces. This was the objective for which Fazli had worked throughout the period of constitutional reform, and in August 1932 his efforts were crowned with success. From the beginning, he had realized that only the British government would give him the substance of this concession, and he had successfully prevented others from surrendering this demand in negotiations with other bodies. This policy paid off handsomely. The government was made to pay the full price for the support on which it had come to rely.

But the Communal Award was not only significant because it made Muslim control possible in two substantial Indian provinces. It was also significant for the future of the government of India. The Award was the price the Imperial power had to pay for continued control at the Centre. But the Muslims who triumphed by the Award were not enamoured of any other kind of Centre but a British Centre. As the constitutional negotiations proceeded and the central responsibility issue was increasingly discussed, Conference demands became more and more separatist in their orientation. By March 1932, the Aga Khan was telling the Secretary of State that the community's survival depended not only on the substance of the fourteen points but also on 'the permanence of the real authority of the Imperial crown throughout India'.[201] By the same date, moreover, for Fazli Hussain, the architect of Conference policy, even the all-India Federation no

[200]Templewood papers, 5: Willingdon to Hoare, 10 July 1932.
[201]IOR/L/PO 48: Aga Khan to Hoare, memorandum 2 March 1932.

longer offered the prospect of security. Late in February, on his return from South Africa, Fazli landed at Porbander, Gandhi's birthplace, in the princely state of Rajkot. He was greeted by a Congress demonstration and by shouts of 'British Government *Murdabad*' and '*Inquilab Zindabad*'.

What struck me [he wrote in his diary] was that in an Indian State, which are believed to be so non-political, there should be so much agitation of an anti-British character. It appears that whenever a town is practically Hindu, anti-British feeling is very strong, and the fact that it is an Indian state makes no difference. The longer Federation is put off the better for the country as a whole.[202]

Whilst the Communal Award had made continued Imperial control possible, therefore, it had also fortified the Punjabi and Bengali Muslims against any other kind of centre. In terms of the structure of the system of Imperial control, this was a crucial milestone on the road to Pakistan.

[202]Fazli Husain papers: Diary, 26 Feb. 1932.

Conclusion

The period of operation of the Montagu-Chelmsford constitution produced developments of great significance for the future of Muslim India. It was during this period that political interests were consolidated around communal issues, and that Muslim attitudes were framed both towards the emergence of provincial autonomy and towards the eventual withdrawal of Imperial control. These attitudes, though subsequently developed and refined under the impact of provincial autonomy, continued to govern Muslim thinking in the remaining years of Empire.

In existing studies of Partition, the period from 1937 to 1947 commands more attention. It was then that the Pakistan movement gathered momentum and that the Muslim League began to command a substantial mass following. It was only then—though there were rumblings earlier—that the political and religious themes of modern Pakistan fused together. But though the ideology of Muslim separatism emerged more strongly later, the structure of power within the community created during these years remained in essence unchanged. Though the Pakistan movement initially obtained more adherents in the minority provinces, it was only when the League had captured Bengal and Punjab that Pakistan became a possibility; and when the lines of Partition were drawn and the Imperial power withdrew, it was chiefly the Muslims of those provinces who found themselves on the Pakistani side of the line. Hitherto, studies of the later years have seen the conversion of Bengal and Punjab as a reluctant concession to the demands of a 'national' movement. This study suggests that it may be valuable to re-examine those years from a more purely provincial point of view. To those provincial interests which campaigned from the late 1920s against the introduction of a responsible government at New Delhi, the Pakistan movement offered a chance to create a centre of their own.

Within Pakistan, it was the Punjab which emerged as the dominant provincial interest, and the military machine created by the British, and manned chiefly by Punjabis. which was to loom large in the political complexion of the state. This was also foreshadowed in the period under study. It was at this time that the Raj transformed its military alliance with the Punjabi Muslims into an electoral alliance, and that the Punjabi Muslims, from a consolidated base in their own province, assumed the political leadership of Muslim India. It was also in these years, as a result of Punjab civilian advice, that the Raj adopted a strategy for dealing with the growth of nationalism which made it heavily dependent on Punjabi Muslim support. By the end of this period, moreover, it had already paid a significant price for it. By the terms of the Communal Award, the Punjabi Muslims were granted the prize for which they had been campaigning—control of their own province under the new constitution. Finally, as the Montagu-Chelmsford constitution was being revised, it was the Punjabis who took the lead in working against responsible government at the Centre. From as early as 1928, their inclination was to pull out of British India and develop a relationship with the Crown, and under their leadership this attitude was adopted by the All India Muslim Conference. This also was to be significant for the future.

In the consolidation of political interests around communal issues, the Imperial power played an important role. By treating the Muslims as a separate group, it divided them from other Indians. By granting them separate electorates, it institutionalized that division. This was one of the most crucial factors in the development of communal politics. Muslim politicians did not have to appeal to non-Muslims; non-Muslims did not have to appeal to Muslims. This made it very difficult for a genuine Indian nationalism to emerge. In the years before 1920, cross-communal alliances did take place in the interests of Reform at the provincial level. But after 1920, with the introduction of Dyarchy, communal antagonism became a permanent feature of provincial politics, and the formation of all-India cross-communal alliances became first difficult and then impossible. In this period, the effects of the working of separate electorates were compounded by the balancing of communal interests within provincial councils. By the end of the 1920s, all-India Muslim politics had become in essence the sum of the politics of Muslim provincialism, and the all-India Muslim politician without a provincial base had either to withdraw from politics or to submit to these forces. Jinnah's retirement to England provides the most striking example of the working of these constraints. The alliance of the main Khilafat faction with the forces of Muslim provincialism provides another.

In the years after 1920, Congress efforts to abolish separate electorates reflect the working of these factors. Separate electorates provided the government with communal allies, and in many provinces enabled it to run the system of control without Congress co-operation. Consequently, the Congress could not condone their continuance without jeopardizing its coherence as an all-India organization. This was part of the logic of the working of the system. For Muslim interests in most provinces, the way forward was by accepting the government's categories and working the system. For the Congress, it was by opposing those categories and rejecting the system. When government resisted devolution at the Centre in 1920, the Congress strengthened its own centre. When separate electorates began to work effectively to the government's advantage, the Congress campaigned for their abolition. Where the Raj exploited the particular, the Congress built on the general, and where strategies were reversed, so were reactions. But Congress itself was affected by the developments it refused to condone. As the main opposition party, it relied on the support of those excluded from the rewards of the existing system, and with political relations in the provinces polarized along communal lines, the sources of opposition were also affected. In this situation, the Congress as a conciliar party came to depend increasingly on communal Hindu support, and in those circumstances, an all-India communal settlement was no longer possible.

By the end of the 1920s, all-India politics had become deadlocked, and the Congress had no alternative but to broaden and extend its popular appeal. By this stage even the most constitutional Congressman realized that it was no good opposing the system on its own terms. The only way forward was to challenge the social and economic forces which the constitution had been designed to reinforce. It was at this time that the Congress began to work systematically in the countryside and to bracket the landlord with the government.

By this stage, however, Muslim provincialism was in the ascendant, and the new orientation of Congress policy only added a fresh dimension of uneasiness to an already tense communal situation. The majority-province Muslims had little to fear from an extension of the franchise or from a broadening and deepening of political mobilization, but for them 'Congress' already meant 'Hindu', and Congress control at the Centre threatened to limit their capacity for manoeuvre. In the minority provinces, and particularly in the United Provinces, Muslims had a great deal to fear, because their social and economic importance, which had made them so valuable to the system of control, was brought under fire. For these reasons, by the early 1930s, for both majority and minority-province Muslims, the political future lay in co-operation at the all-India level. By this stage, an important section of U.P. Muslims had accepted the need for a strong Punjab, and Muslim politics had assumed a distinct centrifugal tendency. As the Congress began to undermine the foundations of the Raj, the Muslims began to leave by the back door.

The Imperial answer to this dilemma was the All India Federation. It was never wholly approved in New Delhi, and it was accepted in Britain for reasons which had more to do with British political problems than with the reality of power in the subcontinent. But by 1931 it had become the cornerstone of a new Imperial strategy. The theory was that with the bulk of the politically active Hindu community against continued British control at the Centre, the only way forward was by the construction of a new Centre as a rallying point for the well-disposed. Within the British Indian context, even the united support of the Muslims was inadequate for this purpose. But it was hoped that by bringing in the Princes, a stable Centre might be possible. This turned out to be a bankrupt notion. In the first place, even if the Princes had come in, the areas of common concern would necessarily have been extremely limited, and the provinces would have exercised very substantial powers of leverage against the Centre. This was a point continually stressed by the Reforms Commissioner but it was never fully appreciated in London. More importantly, however, the acceptance of the idea of an all-India Centre did not solve the vital problem of how British India was to be governed in the interim. Indeed in many ways it made it more acute, for it increased pressure on the Raj from those who would lose by its inauguration. In the short term, of course, there were expedients. Until 1937, the Raj still held control of all the vital departments not only at the Centre but also in the provinces, and by an act of will it could continue to exercise control through its administrative and military machine. But with provincial autonomy in the offing, this was no long-term solution. Politically, even by 1932, the Raj had become a victim of its own system of control.

The system of control which the Imperial power built up in India reflected the nature of the Imperial presence. For a few thousand

Europeans to rule the vast subcontinent, it was necessary to build on the existing social and political structure; to recognize the realities of power and influence in Indian India. More than this, it was necessary to categorize and to classify; to organize Indian society, albeit largely on its own terms, so that the Imperial system was subsumed and validated by Indian society at large. From the man who waited in the Collector's office, sitting or standing according to status, to the nine or eleven-gun Raja or Nawab, Indians were separated from each other and given a place in the hierarchy of Empire.

Until electoral institutions were introduced and political responsibility devolved to Indian hands, this system worked satisfactorily. True, it was cumbrous, often long-winded; but it was not inflexible, and however slowly it worked, it was capable of modification and adjustment to meet changing realities. With the introduction of electoral institutions, however, a chink appeared in the armour of autocracy; for however restricted the franchise, electoral institutions offered to the opponents of the Imperial system an opportunity to secure by organization what they could not achieve by deputation and petition.

The Raj itself attempted to contain such developments by constitutional manipulation It attempted within the conciliar sphere to reproduce the system of control which had served it well outside it. In the days of consultative politics, representation was by interest. In the days of political responsibility, the same system continued. The rural areas were favoured; the Muslims were given separate electorates; seats were allotted to special interests; and the Depressed Classes were granted the same privileges, though they subsequently gave them up. But these expedients failed to provide the Raj with a viable means of control. Political realities began to change too fast. As the localities were drawn into the orbit of provincial politics, and the provinces into the orbit of national politics, categories broadened and the Raj's capacity for manoeuvre was seriously reduced. By the time the Montagu-Chelmsford constitution was revised, the management of Indian politics was no longer conducted at the local level. It was no longer a question of district officials, with the authority of the Imperial system behind them, balancing the claims of Hindu and Muslim in some village or district town. The Raj was called to balance the U.P. Muslims against the U.P. Hindus, the Punjabi Muslims against the Punjabi Hindus, and ultimately, the Muslims of India against the Hindus of India.

The working of the electoral system forced the Raj to the wall. Imperialism and Democracy were incompatible bedfellows. In Britain, political reform strengthened the existing social and economic system by absorbing and accommodating its political opponents. In India, no such absorption was possible. The Europeans who ruled the Empire were themselves a socially and culturally discrete community, meeting and working with Indians only on their own terms. In the days of autocracy, this was their strength. In the days of electoral politics, it became their undoing. With each stage of devolution, Indian was set against Indian, caste against caste, community against community. But as each area of government and administration was ceded to Indian control, it was followed by demands for more concessions. Ultimately, even the Raj's closest allies were only allies for a purpose.

In 1947, the Raj withdrew, ceding its dominant position to those who had triumphed in the electoral arena. But the final act of devolution was also a final act of division. It was the system which won in the end.

Glossary

Alim	A Muslim religious scholar; pl. ulema.
Ahmadi	A follower of Ghulam Ahmed of Qadian, a nineteenth-century religious leader whose followers have been declared non-Muslims in Pakistan.
Anjuman	Association.
Arain	A caste of market-gardeners from Central Punjab.
Arti	A ceremony, involving the lighting of a flame and the singing of songs, associated with Hindu prayers.
Arya Samaj	A reformist Hindu sect founded by Dayananda Saraswati.
Azan	Summons to Muslim prayer.
Bania	A caste of Hindu moneylenders.
Chamar	A Hindu of low caste whose business is working in hides and leather.
Chela	Disciple, pupil.
Crore	Ten million, a hundred lakhs.
Dar ul Harb	A country under a government that does not recognize Muslim law.
Dar ul Islam	A country under a government which recognizes Muslim law.
Dharamsala	A charitable institution provided as a rest place for Hindu pilgrims.
Dusehra	A ten-day Hindu festival, held in October and dedicated to the worship of Rama.
Goonda	A hooligan or thug.
Gurdwara	A Sikh temple.
Haj	The Muslim pilgrimage to Mecca.
Haji	One who has performed the Haj.
Hakim	A Muslim physician.
Haram	Forbidden, prohibited.
Hartal	A strike.
Hijrat	Migration or departure from one's own country, One of the options enjoined upon Muslims under a government which does not recognize Muslim law. Originally the name given to the flight of the Prophet Mahommed from Mecca to Medina which marks the beginning of the Muslim era.
Hookum	An order.
Jamaat or Jamiat	Association, organization, party.
Jat	A caste of peasant farmers found in Eastern Punjab and Western U.P.
Jatha	An organized band or group.

Jihad	A holy war waged by Muslims against unbelievers.
Kayasth	A caste of Hindu scribes or accountants, found mainly in U.P.
Khaddar	Homespun cloth.
Khoja	A Muslim sect, originally from Western India.
Kotwal	The chief police officer for a city or town.
Lakh	One hundred thousand.
Lambardar	A village headman in Punjab.
Majlis	An assembly.
Maulana	A title given to eminent Muslim religious scholars.
Maulvi	A Muslim teacher or learned man.
Mofussil	Country districts, particularly in Bengal.
Mohalla	A quarter of a town or city.
Moharram	The first month of the Muslim calendar, of which the first ten days are specially dedicated to the memory of Hussain, the grandson of the Prophet, who was martyred at Kerbela.
Mukhya	A village headman.
Mulla	Originally a judge or magistrate; more colloquially used for a Muslim schoolmaster or village priest.
Naib Tehsildar	Assistant Tehsildar, a land Revenue official in charge of part of a tehsil.
Namaz	Prayer, obligatory for Muslims five times a day.
Nawab	A noble, title denoting nobility.
Pargannah	A subdivision of a district, particularly in Bengal.
Pukka	Real, genuine.
Puja	Ritual of Hindu worship.
Rais	A gentleman of respectable position.
Raiyat	Cultivator, farmer, peasant, tenant.
Raja	Originally a King or Prince; awarded as a title of rank by the Government of India.
Rajput	Warrior caste from Rajputana.
Ram	One of the ten Avatars.
Ram Dol	Krishna's cradle, which is taken in procession to celebrate his birthday.
Ram Lila	A Hindu religious festival, culminating in Dusehra.
Ram Raj	A Hindu utopia.
Sabha	An association (usually Hindu).
Sangathan	Organization; one plank of an Arya Samaj campaign to revitalize Hindu society.
Sankh	A conch shell blown at Hindu prayers.
Satyagraha	Commitment to the truth force, the use of moral pressure for political purposes as pioneered by Gandhi.
Shia	A major sect of Islam, which regards the first three Caliphs as usurpers and recognizes Ali, the son-in-law of the Prophet, as the only rightful Caliph.

Shuddhi	A movement for the purification of Hindu society and the reconversion of Muslims.
Sunni	The main sect of Islam; a follower of the Prophet and the first four Caliphs.
Swadeshi	Made at home; a movement to support Indian industry.
Swaraj	Freedom, self-government.
Tabligh	The preaching of Islam.
Taluqdar	A landed aristocrat in Oudh.
Tanzim	Organization; the name given to a reform movement among the Indian Muslims.
Tazia	A float taken in procession by Shia Muslims during Moharram.
Tehsil	Subdivision of a district, in the charge of a tehsildar.
Vakil	A lawyer or pleader.
Wahabi	A puritanical sect of Islam founded by the Arabian reformer, Sheikh Abdul Wahab.
Zemindar	A landowner.

Bibliography

UNPUBLISHED SOURCES

OFFICIAL

Records of the Government of India, Home Department, Political and Public branches, National Archives of India, New Delhi.

Records of the Government of India, Reforms Office.

Records of the Government of the United Provinces, General Administration Department, U.P. Government Secretariat, Lucknow.

India Office Records, Public and Judicial Department.

India Office Records, Parliamentary Department.

India Office Records, Private Office papers.

UNOFFICIAL

1. Collections of papers

Ali Imam papers, Karachi University Library.

All India Congress Committee papers, Nehru Memorial Museum and Library, New Delhi.

Ansari papers, Jamia Millia Islamia, New Delhi.

Birkenhead papers, IOL MSS Eur. D 703.

Chelmsford papers, IOL MSS Eur. E 264.

Fazli Husain papers, by courtesy of Mr. Azim Husain.

Gandhi papers, Gandhi Smarak Nidhi, Delhi (microfilm copy, Trinity College, Cambridge).

Hailey papers, IOL MSS Eur. E 220.

Halifax papers, IOL MSS Eur. C 152.

Harcourt Butler papers, IOL MSS Eur. F 116.

Lothian papers, Scottish Record Office, Edinburgh.

Mahommed Ali papers, Jamia Millia Islamia, New Delhi.

Meston papers, IOL MSS Eur. F 136.

Montagu papers, IOL MSS Eur. D 523.

Nehru papers, Nehru Memorial Museum and Library.

Purushotamdas Thakurdas papers, Nehru Memorial Museum and Library.

Reading papers, IOL MSS Eur. E 238

Shafi Daudi papers, by courtesy Mr Ata ur Rahman Daudi, Muzaffarpur.

Shaukat Ali papers, Jamia Millia Islamia, New Delhi.

Shuaib Qureshi's minute of dissent to the Nehru report, by courtesy of Syed Sharifuddin Pirzada.

Syed Mahmud papers, Nehru Memorial Museum and Library.

Templewood papers, IOL MSS Eur. E 240.

Thompson papers, IOL MSS Eur. F 137.

2. *Interviews*

Azim Husain, Berne, April 1969.

Sir James Penny, Oxford, June 1969.

Sir Francis Mudie, Dundee, July 1969.

The Nawab of Chhatari, New Delhi, September 1969.

Syed Mahommed Jaffri (formerly Sub-Editor of *Hamdard*), Delhi, September 1969.

Aruna Asaf Ali, New Delhi, November 1969.

Ata ur Rahman Daudi (son of Shafi Daudi), Muzaffarpur, January 1970.

Lady Imam, Bankipore, January 1970.

Zamiruddin Ahmed (Assistant Secretary of the Muslim Conference), Patna, January 1970.

Dr Azimuddin Ahmed (son of Sir Sultan Ahmed), Patna, January 1970.

The Maharajkumar of Mahmudabad, Lucknow, February 1970.

General Habibullah, Lucknow, February 1970.

K.L. Gauba, New Delhi, March 1970.

Sardar Shaukat Hayat, Lahore, March 1970.

Mazhar Ali Khan, Lahore, March 1970.

Begum Shah Nawaz, Lahore, March 1970.

Malik Lal Khan, Lahore, March 1970.

Begum Viquarunissa Noon, Lahore, March 1970.

Ghulam Rasool Mihr, Lahore, March 1970.

Dr Niaz Ahmed, Lahore, March 1970.

Malik Shaukat Ali (son of Malik Barkat Ali), Lahore, March 1970.

Chaudhuri Khaliquzzaman, Karachi, April 1970.

Syed Hussain Imam of Gaya, Karachi, April 1970.

Lady Haroon, Karachi, April 1970.

G.M. Madeni, Karachi, April 1970.

Nawab Siddiq Ali Khan, Karachi, April 1970.

M.A.H. Ispahani, Karachi, April 1970.

Syed Hamza Ali (son of Syed Raza Ali), Karachi, 1970.

Mahommed Ali Chaiwallah (Jinnah's solicitor), Bombay, September 1970.

Akbar Peerbhoy, Bombay, September 1970.

Rasoolbhai Rangoonwallah, Bombay, September 1970.

Fazl Rahimtoolah, Bombay, September 1970.

3. *Unpublished theses and dissertations*

Bayly, C.A. 'The development of political organisation in the Allahabad locality 1880-1925', unpublished D.Phil. thesis, Oxford, 1970.

Gordon, R.A. 'Aspects in the history of the Indian National Congress, with special reference to the Swarajya party, 1919-1927', D. Phil. thesis, Oxford, 1970.

Reeves, P.D. 'The Landlords: response to political change in the United Provinces of Agra and Oudh, India, 1921-31, Ph.D. thesis, Australian National University, 1963 (microfilm copy in the India office Library).

Robinson, F.C.R. 'The two nations', fellowship dissertation, Trinity College, Cambridge, 1969.

PUBLISHED SOURCES

OFFICIAL

U.P. District Gazetteers.
Punjab District Gazetteers.
British Parliamentary Debates.
Proceedings of the Imperial Legislative Council (1909-20).
Proceedings of the Imperial Legislative Assembly (1921-36).
Proceedings of the U.P. Legislative Council (1909-36).
Proceedings of the Punjab Legislative Council (1921-36).
Proceedings of the Bombay Legislative Council (1921-36).
Proceedings of the Bihar and Orissa Legislative Council (1921-36).
Proceedings of the Assam Legislative Council (1921-36).
Proceedings of the Bengal Legislative Council (1921-36).
Census of India (1901, 1911, 1921, 1931).
India Office List (1900-35).
Punjab Civil List (1920-35).
United Provinces Civil List (1920-35).
Moral and Material Progress of India (1908-9 to 1934-5), from 1929-30 published as *'India in...'.*
India's Contribution to the Great War (Calcutta 1923).
Report of the Public Services Commission 1886-7, with appendices (Calcutta 1888).
Report of the Royal Commission on the Public Services in India, vols. 1-20 (London 1913-1917).
Ritchie, J.A. *The Progress of Education in India 1917-22* (Calcutta 1923).
Littlehailes, R. *The Progress of Education in India 1922-27* (Calcutta 1929).

Parliamentary Papers and HMSO publications

Cmd. *4635* (1909). Progress of Education in India, Fifth Quinquennial Report, 1902-1907.
Cmd. *7485* (1914). Progress of Education in India, Sixth Quinquennial Report, 1907-1912.
Cmd. *9109* (1918). Report on Indian Constitutional Reforms (Montagu-Chelmsford report).
Cmd. *9190* (1918). Report of the Indian Sedition Committee (Rowlatt Committee report).
Cmd. *256* (1919). Progress of Education in India, Seventh Quinquennial Report, 1912-1917.
H.C. 203 (1919). Joint Select Committee on the Government of India Bill, Vol. i, Report vol. ii, Minutes of Evidence.
Cmd. *681* (1920). Report of the Committee Appointed to Investigate Disturbances in thePunjab (Hunter Committee report).
Cmd. *1251* (1921). Return Showing the Results of Elections in India.
Cmd. *2154* (1924). Return Showing the Results of Elections in India.
Cmd. *2360* (1925). Reforms Enquiry Committee (Muddiman Committee) Report.
Cmd. *2361* (1925). Views of the Local Governments on the Working of the Reforms, 1923.

Cmd. 2362 (1925). Views of the Local Governments on the Working of the Reforms, 1924: Reforms Enquiry Committee, appendix 5, Written Evidence (London 1925); Reforms Enquiry Committee, appendix 6, parts i and ii (London 1925). 1925.

Cmd. 2923 (1927). Return Showing the Results of Elections in India.

Cmd. 2986 (1927). Indian Statutory Commission. Statement Published on 8 November 1927 by the Governor-General in India.

Cmd. 3302 (1928-29). Report of the Indian States Committee.

Cmd. 3451 (1929). Report of the Indian Central Committee.

Cmd. 3525 (1930). Supplementary Note by Dr. A. Suhrawardy to the Report of the Indian Central Committee.

Cmd. 3568 (1930). Report of the Indian Statutory Commission (Simon Commission), vol. i, Survey.

Cmd. 3569 (1930). Report of the Indian Statutory Commission, vol. ii, Recommendations.

Cmd. 3572 (1930). Indian Statutory Commission, vol. iii, Reports of the Committees Appointed by the Provincial Legislative Councils to Co-operate with the Indian Statutory Commission.

Report of the Indian Statutory Commission, vols. iv-xiv. Memoranda Submitted by the government of India and the India Office and by provincial Governments (London 1930).

Cmd. 3700 (1930). Government of India Despatch on Proposals for Constitutional Reform.

Cmd. 3738 (1931). Proceedings of the Indian Round Table Conference, First Session.

Cmd 3891 (1931). Cawnpore Riot Enquiry Commission Report.

Cmd. 3922 (1931). Return Showing the Results of Elections in India.

Cmd. 3997 (1932). Proceedings of the Indian Round Table Conference, Second Session.

Indian Round Table Conference, Second Session: proceedings of the Federal Structure Committee and the Minorities Committee (London 1932).

Cmd. 4086 (1932). Report of the Indian Franchise Committee.

Cmd. 4147 (1932). East India (Constitutional reforms): Communal Decision.

Cmd. 4238 (1933). Reports and Proceedings of the Indian Round Table Conference, Third Session.

UNOFFICIAL

1. *Material published by Indian political organizations*
Annual Reports of the Indian National Congress.

All Parties Conference 1928, Report of the Committee Appointed by the Conference to Determine the Principles of the Constitution for India (Allahabad 1929)

Proceedings of the All Parties National Convention (Allahabad 1929).

All Parties Conference 1928, Supplementary Report of the Committee (Allahabad 1928).

Representation of the Muslims of the United Provinces (India) to the Indian Statutory Commission (Allahabad 1928).

Speeches Delivered at the Chashi given by Ch. Chothu Ram to meet Sir Fazli Husain (Lahore. 1932).

For information on the Muslim League, I have relied on S.S. Pirzada's *Foundations of Pakistan, All India Muslim League Documents, 1906-47*, 2 vols, (Karachi 1969-70).

For the Muslim Conference, there is K.K. Aziz's *All India Muslim Conference, a Documentary Record* (Karachi 1972), but I have chiefly relied on the material available in the Mihr collection at the Research Society of Pakistan, Lahore.

Presidential Address (by the Aga Khan) to the Muslim Conference, Delhi, December 1928 (Bombay 1928).

Report of the All India Muslim Conference, Lucknow (Aligarh 1930).

Presidential Address by Sir Mahommed Iqbal, All India Muslim Conference, Lahore, March 1932 (Lahore 1932).

Resolutions of the All India Muslim Conference, the Executive Board and the Working Committee, from January 1929 to March 1932 (Lahore 1932).

Resolutions Passed at the Lahore Session of the All India Muslim Conference, March 1932 (Delhi 1932).

List of Members of the Working Committee, the Executive Board, the General Body of the All India Muslim Conference Elected on 24 August 1932 (Patna 1932).

Resolutions Passed at the Special Session of the All India Muslim Conference, Calcutta, December 1932 (Calcutta 1932).

Copies of Letters to Maulana Mahommed Shafee Daoodi, 1932 (? Patna 1932).

Prominent Men Elected by the Working Committee of the All Indian Muslim Conference (?Patna 1932).

Speech by Sir Fazli Husain at the Opening of the Punjab Unionist Party Headquarters (Lahore 1936).

2. Newspapers, journals, periodicals and annuals

Bombay Chronicle.
Civil and Military Gazette (Lahore).
Comrade (Delhi).
Indian Annual Register 1923-32 (Calcutta), published as the *Indian Quarterly Register 1924-29.*
Indian Daily Telegraph (Lucknow).
Indian Social Reformer.
The Leader (Allahabad).
Moslem Outlook (Lahore).
Pioneer (Allahabad).
Searchlight (Patna).
The Times (London).
Times of India (Bombay).
Tribune (Lahore).

3. Articles

Barrier, N.G. 'The Arya Samaj and Congress Politics in the Punjab 1894-1908'. *Journal of Asian Studies (JAS)*, xxvi, no. 3 (May 1967), pp. 363-79.

Bayly, C.A. 'Local Control in Indian Towns: the Case of Allahabad, 1880-1920' *Modern Asian Studies (MAS)*, 5 (1971), pp. 289-311.

Brass, P.R. 'Muslim Separatism in the United Provinces: Social Context and political Strategy before Partition', *Economic and Political Weekly*, v, nos. 3, 4 and 5 (annual number 1970), pp. 167-86.

Danzig, R. 'The Announcement of August 20th, 1917', *JAS*, xxviii, no. 1 (November 1968), pp. 19-37.

Gopal krishna. 'The Development of the Indian National Congress as a Mass Organisation', *JAS*, xxv, no. 3 (May 1966), pp. 413-30.

Gordon, R.A. 'The Hindu Mahasabha, and the' Indian National Congress 1915-26, (MAS), 9,2, (1975).

Heeger, G.A. 'The Growth of the Congress Movement in Punjab, 1920-1940', *JAS*, xxxi, no. 1 (Nov. 1972), pp. 39-51.

Islam, Zafar ul and Jensen, R. 'Indian Muslims in the Public Services 1871-1915, *Journal of the Asiatic Society of Pakistan*, iv (1964), pp. 85-93.

Jones, K.W. 'Communalism in the Punjab: the Arya Samaj Contribution', *JAS*, xxviii, no. 1 (Nov. 1968), pp. 39-54.

Minault, G, and Lelyveld,D, The Campaign for a Muslim University 1898-1920, *Modern Asian Studies*, 8,2 (1974), pp. 145-189.

Moore, R.J. 'The Demission of Empire in South Asia: Some Perspectives', *Journal of Imperial and Commonwealth History*, xx no. 1 (Oct. 1973), pp. 79-94.

Owen, H.F. 'Negotiating the Lucknow Pact', *JAS*, xxxi, no. 3 (May 1972), pp. 561-87.

Robinson, F.C.R. 'Consultation and Control: the United Provinces' Government and its Allies, 1860-1906', *MAS, 5 (1971), pp. 313-36.*

Rothermund, D. 'Constitutional Reform versus National Agitation in India 1900-1950', *JAS*, xxi, no. 4 (Aug. 1962), pp. 505-22.

4. Printed books and pamphlets

Afzal, M. Rafiq (ed.). *Selected Speeches and Statements of Quaid-i-Azam Mahommed Ali Jinnah* (1911-34 and 1947-48) (Lahore 1966).

— — — — — — — — — — — —. *Malik Barkat Ali, His Life and Writings* (Lahore 1969).

Aga Khan. *Memoirs, World Enough and Time* (London 1954).

Ahmed, Aziz. *Studies in Islamic Culture in the Indian Environment* (Oxford 1964).

— — — — — —. *Islamic Modrnism in India and Pakistan* (London 1967).

Ahmed, Jamal Mahommed. *The Intellectual Origins of Egyptian Nationalism* (London 1968).

Ahmed, Nafis. *An Economic Geography of East Pakistan* (2nd edn, Oxford 1968).

Ahmed, Shafaat. *Presidential Address to the Punjab Muslim Educational Conference* (Allahabad 1929).

Allana, G. *Quaid-i-Azam Jinnah, the Story of a Nation* (Lahore 1967).

Ambedkar, B.R. *Pakistan or the Partition of India* (Bombay 1946).

Azad. Maulana Abul Kalam, *India Wins Freedom* (Calcutta 1959).

Aziz, K.K. *Britain and Modern India, 1857-1947* (London 1963).

— — — .*The Making of Pakistan, a Study in Nationalism* (London 1967).

— — — . *The All India Muslim Conference 1928-1935, a Documentary Record* (Karachi 1972).

Banerjea, S.N. *A Nation in Making, Being Reminiscences of Fifty Years of Public Life* (London 1925).

Barrier, N.G. *The Punjab Alienation of Land Bill of 1900* (Durham, North Carolina 1966).

— — — — —(ed). Roots of Communal Politics (Delhi 1976)

Bayly, C.A., *The Local Roots of Indian Nationalism. Allahabad 1880-1920* (Oxford 1975)

Beteille, A. *Castes: Old and New. Eassays in Social Status and Social Stratification* (Bombay 1969).

Bhatnagar, S.K. *History of M.A.O. College, Aligarh* (New Delhi 1969).

Binder, L. *Religion and Politics in Pakistan* (Berkeley 1961).

Birkenhead, 2nd earl of. *F.E., the Life of F. E. Smith, First Earl of Birkenhead, by His Son* (London 1965).

Birla, G.D. *In the Shadow of the Mahatma: a Personal Memoir* (Bombay 1953).

Bolitho, Hector. *Jinnah: Creator of Pakistan* (London 1954).

Bose, S.C. *The Indian Struggle 1920-42* (London 1964).

Brass, P.R. *Language, Religion and Politics in North India* (Cambridge 1974).

Brecher, Michael, *Nehru; a Political Biography* (London 1959).

Broomfield, J.H. *Elite Conflict in a Plural Society, 20th Century Bengal* (Berkeley and Los Angeles 1968).

Brown, J.M. *Gandhi's Rise to Power: Indian Politics 1915-22* (Cambridge 1972).

Butler, Sir Spencer Harcourt. *India Insistent* (London 1931).

Callard, K. *Pakistan, a Political Study* (London 1968).

Chaudhuri, N.C. *The Autobiography of an Unknown Indian* (London 1951).

Chintamani, C.Y. *Indian Politics since the Mutiny* (London 1939).

Chirol, V. *Indian Unrest* (London 1910).

————. *India* (London 1926).

Chopra, P.N. *Rafi Ahmed Kidwai* (Agra 1959).

Coatman, J. *Years of Destiny: India 1926-32* (London 1932).

Coupland, R. *The Indian Problem 1833-1935* (Oxford 1968).

Dani, Ahmed Hassan. *Peshawar, Historic City of the Frontier* (Peshawar 1969).

Darling, Sir M.L. *The Punjab Peasant in Prosperity and Debt* (3rd ed, Oxford 1932).

—————.*Wisdom and Waste in the Punjab Village* (Oxford 1934)

————————.*Apprentice to Power, India 1904-1908* (London 1966).

Das, M.N. *India under Morley and Minto* (London 1964).

Desai, A.R. *Social Background to Indian Nationalism* (Bombay 1948).

Dichter, David, *The North West Frontier of Pakistan, a Study in Regional Geography* (Oxford) 1967).

Dwarkadas, Kanji, *Ruttie Jinnah. The Story of a Great Friendship* (Bombay 1962).

————————.*India's Fight for Freedom 1913-1937, an Eye-witness Story* (Bombay 1966).

Dumont, L.C.J. *Religion, Politics and History in India: Collected Papers in Indian Sociology* (Paris 1970).

Dungen, P.H.M. van den. *The Punjab Tradition: Influence and Authority in 19th-century India* (London 1972).

Farquhar, J.N. *Modern Religious Movements in India* (London 1929).

Faruqui, Zia ul Hassan. *The Deoband School and the Demand for Pakistan* (London 1963).

The Frontier Question in the Assembly, being the Statements of Pandit Motilal Nehru, Maulvi Shafi Daudi and Syed Murtuza (Delhi 1926).

Frykenberg, R.E. *Land Control and Social Structure in Indian History* (Madison, Wisconsin 1969).

Gallagher, J., Johnson, G. and Seal, A. (eds.). *Locality, Province and Nation, Essays on Indian Politics 1870-1940* (Cambridge 1973).

Gandhi, M.K. *Communal Unity* (Ahmedabad 1949).

————— .*An Autobiography, the Story of My Experiments with Truth,* translated from Gujerati by Mahadev Desai (London 1966).

————— .*Collected Works of Gandhi,* vols. xiii-xlvi (Ahmedabad 1964-71).

Gopal, Ram. *Indian Muslims, a Political History, 1858-1947* (Bombay 1959).

Gopal, S. *British Policy in India, 1858-1905* (Cambridge 1905).

——— .*The Viceroyalty of Lord Irwin* (Oxford 1957).

Griffin, Sir Lepel. *Chiefs and Families of Note in the Punjab,* Vols. i-iii (rev., Lahore 1940).

Gwyer, M. and Appadorai, A. (eds.). *Speeches and Documents on the Indian Constitution, 1921-47,* vols. i-ii (London ·1957).

Halifax, Earl of. *Fulness of Days* (London 1957).

Hamid, A. *A Brief Survey of Muslim Separatism in India* (London 1968).

Hardinge, Lord. *My Indian Years 1910-1916* (London 1948).

Hardy, P. *The Muslims of British India* (Cambridge 1972).

Hayat, Abul. *Mussulmans of Bengal* (Calcutta 1966).

Heimsath, C.H. *Indian Nationalism and Hindu Social Reform* (Princeton 1964).

Hodson, H.V. *The Great Divide, Britain-India-Pakistan* (London 1969).

Husain, Azim. *Fazli Husain, a Political Biography* (Bombay 1946).

Husain, Sir Fazli, *Our Political Programme* (Lahore 1930).

Hussain, Mahmud and others (ed.)*A History of the Freedom Movement,* vols. ii-iv (Karachi 1961-70).

Hussain, Syed Abid. *Indian Culture* (Bombay 1963).

Ibbetson, Sir Denzil. *Punjab Castes* (A Punjab Government reprint, Delhi 1970).

Ikram, S.M. *Modern Muslim India and the Birth of Pakistan* (Lahore 1965).

Ikramullah, Begum Shaista. *From Purdah to Parliament* (London 1963).

Iqbal. Afzal (ed.) *Select Speeches and Writings of Maulana Mahommed Ali,* First edition (Lahore 1944) Second edition, vols. i-ii (Lahore 1963).

————————— *My Life: a Fragment, an Autobiographical Sketch of Maulana Mahommed Ali* (Lahore 1946).

Ismail, Sir Mahommed. *My Public Life* (London 1954).

Ispahani, M.A.H. *Quaid-i-Azam Jinnah as I Knew Him* (Karachi 1967).

Jambunathan, M.R. (ed.). *Swami Shraddhanand, an Autobiography* (Bombay 1961).

Jayakar, M.R. *The Story of My Life,* vol. i (Bombay 1958); vol. ii (Bombay 1959).

Johnson, G. *Provincial Politics and Indian Nationalism: Bombay and the Indian National Congress 1880-1915* (Cambridge 1974).

Joshi, V.C. (ed.)*Lala Lajpat Rai, His Writing and Speeches,* vols. i-ii (Delhi 1966).

Kabir, H. *Muslim Politics, 1906-42* (Calcutta 1943).

Karim, Maulvi Abdul. *Letters on Hindu-Muslim Pact* (Calcutta 1924).

Khaliquzzaman, Chaudhuri. *Pathway to Pakistan* (Lahore 1961).

Kidwai, Mushir Hussain. *Swaraj and How to Obtain it* (Lucknow 1924).

———————— *Panislamism and Bolshevism* (London 1938).

Kumar, R. (ed.)*Essays on Gandhian Politics, the Rowlatt Satyagraha of 1919* (Oxford 1971).

Lambrick, H.T. *Sind, a General Introduction* (Hyderabad 1964).

Lawrence, W.R. *The Valley of Kashmir* (reprint, Srinagar 1967).

Leach, E. and Mukherjee, S.N. (eds.). *Elites in South Asia* (Cambridge 1970).

Lewis, B. *The Emergence of Modern Turkey* (London 1961).

Low, D.A. (ed.) *Soundings in Modern South Asian History* (London 1968).

— — — — — —. (ed). *Congress and the Raj* (London 1977).

Lytton, Lord. *Pandits and Elephants* (London 1942).

Malik, Hafiz. *Muslim Nationalism in India and Pakistan* (Washington 1963).

Masood. Mukhtar (ed.). *Eye-witnesses of History, A collection of Letters Addressed to Quaid-i-Azam* (Karachi 1968).

Mayo, Katherine. *Mother India* (London 1927).

Mehrotra, S.R. *India and the Commonwealth 1885-1929* (London 1965).

— — — — — — —.*The Emergence of the Indian National Congress (London 1971).*

Mehta, A. and Patwardhan, A. *The Communal Triangle in India* (Allahabad 1942)

Mehtar, M.A. *Whys of the Great Indian Conflict* (Lahore 1947).

Meston, Lord. *Nationhood for India* (London 1931).

Minto, Mary, Countess of. *India, Minto and Morley, 1905-1910* (London 1934).

Montagu, Edwin Samuel. *My Indian Diary* (London 1930).

Moon, Sir Penderel. *Divide and Quit* (London 1961).

Mujeeb, Mahommed. *The Indian Muslims* (London 1967).

Mukherjee, S.N. (ed.). *The Movement for National Freedom in India,* St Anthony's papers, no. 18 (Oxford 1966).

Naidu, Sarojini. *Mahommed Ali Jinnah, an Ambassador of Unity: His Speeches and Writings 1912-1917* (Madras 1917).

Nanda, B.R. *Mahatma Gandhi* (London 1958).

— — — — — —.*The Nehrus, Motilal and Jawaharlal* (London 1965).

Nehru, J. *An Autobiography, with Musings on Recent Events in India* (London 1936).

— — — —.*The Discovery of India* (London 1946).

— — — — *A Bunch of Old Letters, Written Mostly to Jawaharlal Nehru and Some Written by Him* (London 1960).

Noman, Mahommed.*Muslim India* (Allahabad 1942).

Noon, Firoz Khan. *Dominion Status or Autonomous Provinces?* (Lahore 1928).

— — — — — —. *From Memory* (Lahore 1966).

O'Dwyer, Sir Michael.*India as I Knew it 1885-1925* (London 1925).

Pandey, G, *The Ascendancy of the Congress in Uttar Pradesh 1926—34* (Delhi 1978).

Parikh, Narhari, D. *Sardar Vallabhai Patel,* vol. i (Ahmedabad 1953); vol. ii (Ahmedabd 1956)

Patel, G.I. *Vithalbhai Patel, Life and Times,* vol. i-ii (Bombay 1950).

Philips, C.H. (ed.) *Politics and Society in India* (London 1963).

— — — — — — — — —.*The Evolution of India and Pakistan 1857-1947, Select Documents* (London 1964).

Philips, C.H. and Wainwright, M.D. (eds.) *The Partition of India, Policies and Perspectives 1935-1947* (London 1970).

Pirzada, Syed Sharifuddin (ed.) *Foundations of Pakistan, All India Muslim League Documents, 1906-47,* vol. i (Karachi 1969); vol. ii (Karachi 1970).

Prasad, Rajendra. *India Divided* (Bombay 1947).

— — — — — — *Autobiography* (Bombay 1957).

Rahman, Matiur. *From Consultation to Confrontation, A study of the Muslim League in British Indian politics, 1906-1912* (London 1970).

Rashiduzzaman, M. *The Central Legislature in British India, 1921-47* (Dacca 1965).

Reed, Sir Stanley. *The India I Knew, 1897-1947* (London 1952).

Reid, Sir Robert. *Years of Change in Bengal and Assam* (London 1966).

Robinson, F.C.R., *Separatism among Indian Muslims. The politics of the United Provinces Muslims 1860–1923* (Cambridge 1974).

Ronaldshay, Lord. *India, a Bird's Eye View* (London 1924).

— — — — — — —.*'Essayez'* (London 1956).

Saiyid, Matlub ul Hassan. *Mahommed Ali Jinnah, a Political Study* (Lahore 1945).

Sampurnanand. *Memories and Reflections* (Bombay 1962).

Sarda, Harbilas. *Recollections and Reminiscences* (Ajmer 1951).

Sarkar, S. *The Swadeshi movement in Bengal, 1903-1908* (New Delhi 1973)

Sayeed, Khalid bin. *Pakistan, the Formative Phase, 1857-1948* (2nd ed. London 1968).

Schuster, Sir George, and Wint, Guy. *India and Democracy* (London 1941).

Seal, Anil, *The Emergence of Indian Nationalism, Competition and Collaboration in the later Nineteenth Century* (Cambridge 1968).

Sen, N.B. *Punjab's Eminent Hindus* (Lahore 1943).

Setalvad, Sir Chimanlal. *Recollections and Reflections, an Autobiography* (Bombay 1947).

Shafi, Alhaj Mian Ahmed. *Haji Abdullah Haroon, a Biography* (Karachi, n.d.)

Shafi, Sir Mahommed. *Some Important Indian Problems* (Lahore 1930).

Shah Nawaz, Jehanara Begum. *Father and Daughter* (Lahore 1971).

Siddiqui, N.H. *Landlords of Agra and Avadh* (Allahabad and Lucknow 1950).

Sitaramayya, P. *The History of the Indian National Congress*, vols. i-ii (Bombay 1946-47).

Smith, W.C. *Modern Islam in India* (Lahore 1954).

Tandon, Prakash. *Punjabi Century, 1857-1947* (London 1963).

Tara Chand, Dr. *Influence of Islam on Indian Culture* (Allahabad 1963).

Taylor, A.J.P. *English History 1914-1945* (Oxford 1965).

Templewood, Lord. *Nine Troubled years* (London 1954).

Tendulkar, D.G. *Abdul Gaffar Khan* (New Delhi 1967).

Tinker. H. *The Foundations of Local Self-Government in India Pakistan and Burma* (London 1954).

Tomlinson, B.R. *The Indian National Congress and the Raj, 1929–42* (London 1976).

Trevaskis, H.K. *The End of an Era: Memories of the British Raj in India, 1905-1928* (Shoreham on Sea 1973).

Tyabji, H.B. *Badruddin Tyabji: a Biography* (Bombay 1952).

Wasti, Syed Razi. *Lord Minto and the Indian Nationalist Movement 1905-10* (Oxford 1964).

Zakaria, Rafiq. *Rise of Muslims in Indian Politics* (Bombay 1970).

Index

Abdul Aziz, Syed 147, 163
Abdul Bari, Maulana 23-5, 95, 104
Abdul Karim, Maulvi 43, 187
Abdul Majid Budauni 96
Abdul Majid, Khwaja 98, 100
Abdul Majid, Nawab 38
Abdul Majid Sindhi, Sheikh 201
Abdul Matin Chaudhuri 189
Abdullah Khan, Editor of *Hamdam* 202
Abdullah Khan, Mahommed 62
Abdullah, Sheikh 38, 161
Abdullah Yusuf Ali 159
Abdur Rahim, Sir 42, 45-6, 116, 117, 148, 156-60, 198
Abul Kalam Azad, Maulana 85, 98-9, 100, 130, 163, 184
Afghanistan 27, 162
Afghan Wars 51
Afzal Haq, Chaudhuri 207
Aga Khan 22, 160, 192-3, 194-5, 201-2, 222, 246-7, 257
Agra 16, 17, 31, 37, 74, 75
Ahmadiya sect 220, 225, 248
Ahmedabad 95, 108, 184, 185
Ahrars 248-50
Ajab Khan, Capt. 61
Ajmal Khan, Hakim 23, 85, 98-9, 122
Akram Khan, Maulana 163
Alam, Dr Mahommed 184, 207
Ali brothers 22-9, 73, 84, 97, 98, 100-6, 120, 123, 142, 158, 160, 163, 176, 183-4, 187, 200, 237; *see also* Mahommed Ali, Shaukat Ali, and Khilafat movement
Ali Imam, Sir 15, 39, 149, 156, 163-5, 168-9, 184, 186, 187, 238, 242, 243
Aligarh 14, 15, 23, 31, 37, 74, 76, 100, 101, 202
Aligarh college, university 14, 22, 24

All India Muslim Conference, *see* Muslim Conference
All India Muslim League, *see* Muslim League
All parties conference, at Bombay (1924) 1:8-19; at Delhi (1925) 121-3, 162; at Delhi (1928) 166; at Lucknow (1928) 175-6; and the Nehru report 168-75, 176-7, 181-90
All parties convention (1928) 190-1
Allahabad 16, 18, 24, 31, 38, 75, 76, 78, 80-3, 169, 202, 236, 242
Allan Khan 62
Ambala 47, 48, 52, 63, 87, 92
Amir Hassan Khan, Chaudhuri 37
Amritsar 46, 48-50, 85, 86, 101-2
Aney, M.S. 128, 139, 168, 169, 190
Angora Legion 96
Anjuman-i-Khuddam-i-Kaaba 24
Ansari, Abdul Aziz 98, 100-1, 147, 159
Ansari, Farid ul Haq 159
Ansari, Dr M.A. 23, 24, 98-9, 103, 108, 113, 147, 149, 157, 158, 167, 168, 169, 173, 175, 177, 184, 187, 188, 200, 237, 238, 239, 240-1, 242-3
Army, *see* Indian army
Arya Samaj 74-5, 85-6, 101, 102
Asaf Ali 135, 184
Assam 8, 34, 109, 137, 177, 188, 218
Azad Sobhani 187, 193, 200

Badiuzzaman, Maulvi 139
Badre Alam, Shah 38
Balkan Wars 22-3
Baluchistan 58, 162; and the demand for Reforms 145, 161, 176, 179, 182, 194, 205, 208, 238, 241
Bangladesh 162
Bareilly 16, 31, 37, 75, 76, 138

Barkat Ali, Malik 67, 115, 117, 159, 163, 207
Bhagat Singh 232
Benares 18, 31, 75, 76, 231
Bengal 118; and Congress 42-6, 109, 127, 128, 130-1, 137, 142-3, 164, 173-4, 185, 218, 240-1; and Muslim politics 8-9, 11, 12, 40-6, 116-17, 143, 160, 162, 165, 176, 184, 187, 198-9, 203, 224-6, 231, 240-1, 246, 248, 259; and Reforms 33-4, 41-6, 116-17, 142-3, 177; riots, 45, 73-4
Bengal Pact (1923) 43-4, 130
Besant, Dr Annie 122, 137
Bhopal state 239, 245
Bhopal, Nawab of 201, 224, 229
Bhore, Sir Joseph 216-17
Bhurgri, G.M. 108, 110
Bihar and Orissa 53; and Congress 109, 127, 137, 138, 139, 164, 218; and Muslim politics 8, 12, 36, 143, 148, 149, 184, 187, 199, 202, 203, 214; and Reforms 33-4, 142, 177, 256; riots 25, 74
Birla, G.D. 184
Birkenhead, Lord (Secretary of State) 125-6, 152-7, 242
Bombay city 107, 110, 112, 123, 149, 158, 168, 184, 241; and Khilafat movement 24-6, 103, 105; Muslim League sessions 19, 120-1
Bombay Presidency, and Congress 109, 127, 128, 129, 137, 218; and Muslim politics 8-9, 11-12, 36, 143, 199; and Reforms 33-4, 142-3, 177, 255; and separation of Sind 211-12; riots 74, 107
Bose, Subhas Chandra 169, 173, 196
British government, and Communal Award 253-8, and Khilafat movement 24, 28, 94, 96; and Reforms in India, 11-12, 107, 111, 124-5, 153-7, 197, 214, 216, 245, 247, 251-2
British Parliament 11, 58, 125, 180-1, 204, 217, 219, 228, 251
Butler, Sir Harcourt 14, 39

Calcutta 11, 25, 28, 41, 45, 73, 106, 131, 160-3, 184-92
Central Legislature 6, 39, 67, 93, 106, 143, 154, 251; Nehru-Jinnah co-operation 109-12, 123-6; 1926 elections 137-9; and Nehru report, 170, 174-5; and central responsibility 6, 117-18, 142, 180-4, 216-19; *see also* Muslim demands
Centre-province relations, *see* Constitutional Reform
Central Provinces, and Congress 109, 122, 126-9, 136-8, 218; and Muslim politics 8, 12, 143, 199, 256; and Reforms 33-4, 177-8, 255; riots 74
Chagla, M.C. 188
Chelmsford, Lord (Viceroy) 61, 63, 64, 67
Chetty, Shanmukhan 167
Chhatari, Nawab of 37, 199, 200, 221
Chintamani, C.Y. 68, 75, 76-7, 84, 121, 122, 190
Chothani, Mahommed 95, 96, 105
Chothu Ram, Sir 63-5, 88, 90-2, 178
Civil Disobedience 196, 230-1, 234, 237, 244, 247
Communal Award 253-8, 260
Communal riots 73-4 (with table); in Bihar 25; at Calcutta 45; at Kohat 82, 88, 132; in Punjab 84-5; in U.P.: at Lucknow 78-80, at Allahabad, 80-3, at Kanpur 231-2
Communalism 1, 17-21, 260-2; its increase after 1920 73-4; in U.P. 74-84, in Punjab 84-93; and all-India Muslim politics 93-126; and the Congress 126-40
Comrade, The 23-4, 104-5, 119
Congress, Indian National 2, 6, 10, 73, 75-6, 106, 107, 112, 114, 118, 141, 146, 173-4, 186, 201, 211, 213, 216, 218, 256, 258; and the Government of India 6, 195-6, 261-2; and Muslim League 14, 15, 19-20, 24-5, 73, 113-14, 119-20, 121, 158, 160, 163, 167, 168, 185-6, 190-2; and Reforms 21, 31-2, 157, 195-6; and Khilafatists 22, 23, 25-8, 76, 94, 95, 97-

101, 103-4, 130, 137, 163, 164, 176-7, 184, 186-7, 200, 236; in U.P., 31, 77-84; in Bengal 42-6, 130-1; in Punjab 57, 85, 88, 120, 129-30, 132-4; and communalism 85, 88, 129-36; and nationalist Muslims 121, 167, 169, 200, 207, 235, 237-8, 239-41, 242-3; and Hindu Mahasabha 121-3, 127-8, 131-2, 147-8, 149, 162-4, 166, 190-1, 243-4; and Muslims 146, 149-50, 158-9, 167-72, 177, 181, 231-2, 234-5, 241, 243; and Nehru report 167-77, 181, 184-91, 192-3; and Muslim Conference 195, 196, 197, 203, 224, 232, 235, 238, 242, 245; and the Gandhi-Irwin Pact 230-2, 234; and the round table conference 242-4; *see also* Non-cooperation and Civil Disobedience

Congress Swaraj party 42, 98-9, 100, 141-2; in Bengal 42-6; in Punjab 92; in U.P. 77-8, 79-80, 84; in Central Legislature 94, 109-12, 114, 118-19, 120, 123-6, 128, 132-4, 150; and office acceptance 126-7, 128-9, 136-7; and 1926 elections 136-9

Conservative party 125, 251

Constitutional Reform, and political development 3-6; Indian and British · experience compared 11-12; and separate electorates 13-14, 260-1; and communalism 17-19, 73-140, 260-1; bias against urban areas: in U.P. 30-2, 36-7, 39; in Punjab 52-3, 55-8, 66-7; distribution of seats in councils 32-5; favours landed class, 35-8, 59-65; centre-province relations, 106-7, 110, 115-18, 180-4, 201, 204, 207, 212-13, 215-22, 224, 228-9, 245-6, 251, 257, 260, 262; provincial autonomy, 107, 113, 115-18, 178-80, 204, 208, 212-13, 215-20, 227, 229, 233, 246, 262; residuary powers 113, 175, 180-1, 188, 190, 193, 222-3, 238, 241, 242

Cowslaughter 43, 164

Craddock, Sir Reginald 152

Crerar, Sir James 218

Dacca division 9, 41, 42

Dacca, Nawab of 198

Dandi 192, 196

Das, C.R. 42-6, 76, 85, 100, 110, 112, 130

Daulatram, Jairamdas 122

Daultana, Ahmed Yar Khan 61-2, 144, 198

Delhi, 8, 75, 82, 102, 103, 109, 110, 131, 145, 151, 160-3, 184, 185, 193, 195, 202, 248, 256; Delhi-Aligarh axis 23, 159; all parties conference (1925) 122-3; Delhi-Bombay compromise 149-50, 166; riots 25, 73-4

Dominion Status 142, 172, 174, 182, 187, 196, 230

Dunnett, Sir James 152, 201, 215-19, 251, 262

Dyarchy 30, 43-4, 106-7, 114-17, 132, 142, 179, 180, 182, 217, 219, 260

East India Company 9

Education, and nationalism 10; and Muslims 11-12, 14, 16-17, 22, 45, 69-70

Emerson, Sir Herbert 152, 201, 209-10, 235

Fakhuruddin, Sir Mahommed 149

Fazl Ali, Chaudhuri 62

Fazl Ibrahimtoolah 189, 192

Fazli Husain 65-6, 91, 113, 143-4, 152, 156, 157, 159, 160, 236, 245-6, 249, 252; as Punjab minister 67-72, 86-8; as architect of Muslim Conference policy 197-203; reaction to Simon Commission report . 204-6; and Government of India response 208-20; and first round table conference 220-4; welcomes all-India Federation scheme 228-9; opposes joint electorates 238-40; and Gandhi 242; and the Communal Award 254-8

Fazlul Haq 44, 116, 198. 224. 227

Fazlur Rahman Khan 38

Federal Finance Committee 250

Federal Structure Committee 228-9, 246

Federation 121; favoured by Muslims 113, 162, 180, 183, 193, 238; opposed by Nehru report 175; of British India and princely states, proposed by Simon 204; and central responsibility in British India 216-17, 219-20, 262; and the princes, 221, 228-9, 251-2, 257-8

First World War 15, 21, 23-5, 52, 61-4

Four proposals (1927) 144-5; and reaction 146-7

Franchise committee (1919) 21, 37, 57, 66

Franchise committee (1932) 250

Frontier, *see* North West Frontier Province

Gandhi, M.K. 88, 95, 103, 112, 118-19, 120, 130, 140, 173, 190, 196; and Khilafat movement 22, 25-9; suspends non-cooperation 75-6, 97, 106-8; and all parties conference (1925) 122-3; and Gandhi-Irwin Pact 229-36; and round table conference 242-5

Gandhi-Irwin Pact 152, 196; 229-36

Ghaffar Khan, Khan Abdul 248

Ghulam Rasool Mihr 202, 206, 248

Ghuznavi A. H. 198, 247

Ghuznavi A.K. 116

Girdharilal 129-30

Government of India, its contribution to nationalism 2; introduces electoral institutions 3-6, 11-13; and Congress 6, 141-2, 195-6, 244-5, 260-2; reliance on landed class 6-10, 30-1, 37-9, 41, 59-65; civil service recruitment 7-8, 10, 51; and Muslims 7-9, 13-14, 36-41, 44-6, 51, 61-3, 92-3, 143-4, 155, 161-2, 259-60; and all-India opposition 9-11, 35-6, 93, 117-18, 141-4, 191-2; and Montagu-Chelmsford reforms 30-6, 141-4; military recruitment 51-4; role of Punjab civilians 151-3, 201, 254, 260; *see also* Central Legislature

Habib Shah, Syed 175, 202, 206

Habibullah, Sir Mahommed 155

Habibullah, Sheikh 38, 181

Habib-ur-Rahman 184

Hafiz, Syed Abdul 198

Haig, Sir Harry 209, 211, 212

Hailey, Sir Malcolm 150, 162, 177, 180, 199, 201, 213, 220-1, 255-6; reshuffles Punjab cabinet 90-3; and the appointment of the Statutory Commission 151-7

Haroon, Haji Sir Abdullah, 104, 188, 189, 200, 247

Harkishen Lal, Lala 68

Hasrat Mohani 95, 104, 161, 187, 200, 248

Hassan Imam 15, 158

Hidayat Hussain, Hafiz 38-9, 158, **178**, 183, 193, 199, 221, 247

Hijrat movement 26, 27

Hindu Jats, and the Army 52, 59; and the Reforms 63-5, 72; *see also* Chothu Ram

Hindu Mahasabha 75, 121-3, 127-8, 131-2, 133-4, 147-8, 149, 166, 190-1, 222, 226-7, 243-4; *see also under* Punjab and U.P.

Hirtzel, Sir Arthur 162

Hoare, Sir Samuel (Secretary of State) 246, 247, 250, 251, 254-5, 256

Howell, Sir Evelyn 209

Hunter report 27

Hyderabad, Nizam of 9, 39, 169, 201

Imperialism, and nationalism 1-3; and democracy 263-4

Imperial system of control, *see* Government of India

Inayat Ali Khan, Kunwar 37

Independence 1, 163, 164, 174, 187, 192, 196, 218, 222

Independent party, in the Central Legislature 109-11, 119, 123-5, 145; in Muslim politics 146, 163, 164, 186, 187

Indian Army 28, 60, 152-3, 209, 226; and Punjab Muslims 9, 61-3, 182, 225-6, 233-4, 259-60; recruitment in Punjab 51-4; and the Punjab electorate 56, 58-

60; and communal troubles 78, 87; and the Skeen committee 126, 127
Indian Statutory Commission 108, 110, 125; appointment 150-7; reactions 157-61, 164-5, 174, 177-8; report published 204-6; Government of India response 208-20
Iqbal, Sir Mahommed 161, 207, 236, 238-9, 247-8, 253
Irwin, Lord (Viceroy) 132, 167, 177, 196, 210, 216, 217, 224, 234, 242; and appointment of Statutory Commission 151-7; and Gandhi-Irwin Pact 230-2
Islamia College, Lahore 66, 236
Ismail Khan, Nawab 110, 138, 146, 189, 239, 247
Iyengar, Srinivasa 146, 149, 164, 167
Iyer, Sivaswamy 117

Jamshed Ali Khan, Kunwar 37
Jallianwalabagh tragedy 107
Jamal Khan, Sardar 62
Jamia Millia 103
Jats, *see* Hindu Jats
Jayakar, M.R. 110, 112, 128, 149, 156, 168, 191, 222-3
Jehangirabad, Raja of 38
Jinnah, M.A. 19, 106-26, 150, 181, 184, 200, 232; and all-India politics 15, 39, 117-18, 142, 191-2, 220, 260; opposes non-cooperation 106-8; revives Muslim League (1923) 108-9; as leader of Independent party 109-12, 119, 123-5, 145; and Lahore League (1924) 112-14; and Reforms Enquiry Committee 114-18, 124-6; and four proposals (1927) 144-50; opposes Statutory Commission 156, 158, 164-5, 167; and League session at Calcutta (1927) 159-61, 163-6; (1928) 187-8; and all parties conference (1928) 166-7, 175, 185-91; forced into wilderness 191-2; and first round table conference 220-2, 224, 246
Jogendra Singh, Sardar 91
Joint electorates 18, 56, 71, 120, 135, 145,

165, 188-9, 193, 206, 223-4, 226, 238-40
Joshi, N.M. 169
Jullundur 46-8, 64-5

Kanpur 31, 38, 76, 183, 194, 231-2
Karachi 225
Karam Ilahi 61
Karimullah Khan 62
Kashmir 24, 97, 236, 248-9
Kelkar N.C. 122, 128, 148, 149
Khaliquzzaman, Chaudhuri 24, 98, 100, 102, 104, 113, 139, 159, 163, 200, 237, 239
Khan Mahommed Khan, Malik 61
Khilafat Committee, Central 26-7, 42, 95, 97, 99, 100-4, 176
Khilafat movement 21-9, 75, 94-6, 98, 107; alliance with Gandhi 25-9; and Khilafat accounts enquiry committee 96-7
Khilafatists 93-4, 95-7, 146, 158-9, 164, 186-7, 200, 203, 236, 260; in Bengal 42, 176, 187; in Punjab 67, 101-4, 130, 163, 176, 184. 187, 189-90, 248; and Congress 76, 94, 95, 97-101, 103-4, 130, 137, 163, 164, 176-7, 184, 186-7, 200, 236; and Muslim League 102, 107, 108-9, 113, 119, 158, 186-90
Khuhro, M.A. 211
Kidwai, Mushir Hussain 23, 104, 120, 238
Kidwai, Rafi Ahmed 139, 184
Kifayatullah, Mufti 187
Kitchlew, Dr Saifuddin 67, 97, 159, 160, 163, 184; and relations with Ali brothers 101-5
Kohat 82, 88, 132

Labour Party 111, 196, 214
Lahore 46-50, 65-71, 88, 148, 150, 206, 237; municipal politics 71, 86-7, 92; Gandhi visits 88, 103, 120; League sessions (1924) 112-14; (1927) 160-1
Lajpat Rai, Lala 90, 103, 121-2, 129-30, 132, 139, 163, 176, 184
Lal Chand, Chaudhuri 63-4, 65, 88, 90
Landed class, its role in Imperial system

7-9; under Morley-Minto Reforms 12-13; and Muslim demand for separate electorates 14; under Montagu-Chelmsford Reforms 30-2, 36-40, 41-2, 45-6, 48-65, 92

Liaquat Hayat Khan, 63

Liberal Federation, All India 156, 168, 169, 190; at round table conference 221, 226, 228-9, 230, 243

Lothian, Lord 250

Lucknow 18, 31, 76, 100-1, 108, 110, 175, 186-7, 237; as Muslim League headquarters 14-16; riots 75, 78-80

Lucknow Pact 20, 25, 41, 66, 119, 129, 149; and Montagu Chelmsford Reforms 31-3; and Reforms Enquiry Committee 114-17; and Simon Commission report 206, 213

Macdonald, Ramsay 222, 223, 227, 229

Maclagan, Sir Edward 90

Madras Presidency, Muslim politics 8-9, 11-12, 143, 148, 160, 199, 256; Reforms 33-4, 142, 177; riots 74; central representation 109, 137; Congress politics 163, 218

Mahboob Ali Khan, Hakim 37

Mahmud, Dr Syed 97, 187

Mahmudabad, Maharaja of 15, 38, 39, 146, 156, 158, 175, 186, 187, 243

Mohammed Akbar, Raja 61

Mahommed Ali, Maulana 98, 101, 104-5, 113, 147, 149, 158, 159, 164, 187, 193; and Khilafat movement 22-9; as Congress president 119-20; and round table conference 223, 226; *see also* Ali brothers

Mahommed Amin, K.B. Malik 63

Mahommmed Ubedar Rehman Khan 37

Majithia, Sardar Sundar Singh 53, 72

Malaviya, Pandit Madan Mohan 75-7, 89, 103, 107-8, 109, 121, 127-8, 130, 147, 163-4, 166, 190; and rivalry with Motilal Nehru 80-4, 134-7, 138-9

Mangal Singh, Sardar 168-70, 174

Manohar Lal, Sir 92

Masud ul Hassan 161, 178, 181, 183

Mazharuddin, Maulana 249-50

Mazhar ul Haq, 15, 19, 39

Meerut 16, 18, 31, 37

Mehdi Shah, Syed 61

Mehta, Jamnadas 123

Minorities Pact 246-7

Misra, Pandit Gauri Shankar 139

Mohiuddin, Ghulam 159, 163

Mohsin ul Mulk 14

Montagu, Edwin (Secretary of State) 20, 24, 31, 58, 61, 66, 251

Montagu-Chelmsford Reforms, and political development 5-6; and changing structure of all-India politics 30-6, 141-2; and Muslim politics 36-41, 41-6, 54-72; and development of communalism 73-4; in U.P. 74-84; in Punjab 85-93; and Reforms Enquiry Committee 89-90, 117-18, 125; *see also* Indian Statutory Commission

Montmorency, Sir Geoffrey de 151-2, 154-5, 180, 201, 213, 255-6

Moonji, B.S. 122, 128, 149, 166, 190, 222-3, 226-7

Moradabad 16, 101, 138

Morley-Minto Reforms 4-6, 30-1, 205; Imperial strategy and electoral response 11-21

Muddiman, Sir Alexander 114-15, 117, 124-5, 150, 155

Mujib ur Rahman, Maulvi 165

Multan 48-50, 61, 62, 85

Municipal politics, in U.P. 15, 17-20, 76-83, 100, 121, 134; in Punjab 71-2, 86-7, 92

Murtaza, Syed 110, 132-4, 139, 146, 163, 189

Muslims, *see under* province and organization

Muslim Conference, All India 161, 192-4, 195-258, 260; leadership, support and resources 197-203; reaction to the Simon Commission report 204-20; and the first round table conference 220-9; and the Gandhi-Irwin Pact

229-45, and the Communal Award 245-58

Muslim demands, assured majorities in Bengal and Punjab, 113, 115, 117, 122, 147-8, 161, 166, 169-72, 175, 178-9, 182, 188, 190, 194, 204-8, 213-15, 222-3, 226-7, 232-4, 238, 241-3, 254-5; Minority safeguards 113, 116, 169-71, 175, 180, 193, 194, 206, 214, 233, 238, 241, 255; 33% representation in the Central Legislature, 145, 175, 179, 188-9, 190, 194, 223, 241; *see also* Baluchistan, Constitutional Reform, Federation, North West Frontier Province, Separate electorates and Sind

Muslim League, All India 2, 14, 22, 23, 117, 132, 141, 193, 259; relations with Congress 14, 15, 19-20, 24-5, 73, 113, 119-20, 121, 158, 163, 167, 168, 185-6, 190-2; Jinnah's role 15, 19, 106, 108-9, 112-14, 117, 119-20, 121, 158, 159-61, 163, 164-6, 185-92; and Montagu-Chelmsford Reforms 31-2, 36-9, 73, 141-2; relations with Khilafatists 102, 107, 108-9, 113, 119, 158, 186-90; and Simon Commission 108, 157, 159, 161, 164-5, 166; and Nehru report 185-6; and all parties convention (1928) 187-91; Sessions: Agra (1913) 19; Bombay (1915) 19; Lucknow (1916) 20; Calcutta (1917) 25; Lucknow (1923) 108-9; Lahore (1924) 112-14, 117, 119, 180; Bombay (1925) 120-1; Lahore (1927) 159-61; Calcutta (1927) 160-1, 163, 164-6; Calcutta (1928) 187-8; Allahabad (1930) 236

Mutiny, 9, 51, 63, 225

Muzaffar Khan, K.S. Malik 62

Muzaffar Khan, Nawab 63, 198, 206, 207, 210

Nabiullah, Syed 15-16

Nagpur 28

Naidu, Sarojini 85, 130-1, 135, 149, 167, 175

Narayan, Swami 79

Narendra Dev 140

Narendra Nath, Raja 72, 87-9, 90, 122, 178, 222-3

Nationalism, and Imperialism 16; and educational development 10-11

Nawab Ali Chaudhuri 116

Nazimuddin, Khwaja Sir 198

Nehru committee, *see* all parties conference

Nehru, Pandit Jawaharlal 76, 97, 120-1, 139-40, 163, 164, 167-9, 175, 196, 230-1, 241; and the Nehru report 172-4

Nehru, Pandit Motilal 76, 85, 97, 98, 114, 120, 122, 131, 167, 168, 170, 175-6, 185-6, 190, 196; rivalry with Malaviya 80-4, 134-9; leads Swaraj party in Central Assembly 109-12, 123-6, 136-9; opposes office acceptance 126-9; and Reforms for the Frontier 132-4; and communalism 134-6; chairs Nehru committee 168-74

Non-cooperation 25, 26-8, 39, 68, 73, 75-6, 95, 97, 106, 107, 110, 112, 118, 126, 141-2, 150

Noon, Sir Firoz Khan 62, 92, 144, 151, 155-6, 159, 160-1, 182, 193, 198, 202, 233-4, 240

North West Frontier Province 12, 73-4, 82, 88, 162, 188, 200-1, 209-11, 249-50; and the demand for Reforms 113-14, 132-4, 145, 147, 149, 150, 161, 162, 165, 175, 179, 182, 194, 205, 209, 227-8, 238, 241

Pakistan 1, 22, 192, 258, 259

Panislamism 21-9, 99-100

Paranjpye, Dr 117

Partition 1, 118, 259, 264

Patel, Vallabhbhai 76, 235

Patel, Vithalbhai 112, 123, 132

Patna 138, 147-9, 199

Peshawar 201, 209, 210

Pirpur, Raja of 38

Pradhan, G.R. 169

Press 23, 45, 75, 80, 87, 104, 105, 121, 148, 157, 159, 175, 184, 206-7; and the Muslim Conference 202-3

Princes 201, 220-2, 228-9, 251-2, 257, 262
Provincial autonomy, *see* Constitutional reform
Punjab, and Reforms 4, 33-4, 40-1, 46-72, 89-93, 142-4, 178-81, 259-60, 263; Muslim League politics 47, 57, 66-7, 112-14, 115, 148, 157, 159-62, 163; urban Hindu politics 47, 57, 72, 86-9, 121-2, 130, 133-4, 148; Congress politics 57, 85, 88, 92, 120, 129-30, 132-4, 136, 164; Khilafat politics 67, 101-4, 130, 163, 176-7, 184, 187, 189-90, 248; municipal politics 71-2, 86-7, 92; communal riots 73-4, 84-5; communalism 84-93, 129-30; *see also* Hindu Jats, Sikhs, and Indian army
Punjab Land Alienation Act 51, 53-4, 225, 231
Punjab Legislative council, 33-4, 46, 54-9, 61-72, 136, 142-3, 177, 178-81
Punjab Municipal Amendment Act (1923) 71, 86-7
Punjab Muslim Association 59, 61-3
Punjab Muslims and Imperial system 9; educational development 11-12, 69-70; emergence as leaders of Muslim India 40-1, 141-94; and Montagu-Chelmsford constitution 40-1, 46, 50-1, 55, 56, 61-3, 65-72, 89-93, 178-84, 259-60, 263; and Reforms Enquiry committee 89-90, 115; and Central Assembly politics 109, 137; and Indian Statutory Commission 155-7, 206-7; and Nehru report 181-2; and Government of India dispatch 213-15; and round table conference 221-7, 243; and Gandhi Irwin Pact 231; and Communal Award 254-7; and Pakistan 258-60
Punjab provincial conference 47
Punjab Unionist party, origins in agriculturalist co-operation 59-65; Fazli Husain's policies 67-72, 86-7; and government 90-3, 143-4, 201; and Statutory Commission 155-7, 159, 177-81, 201-5; and Nehru report 181-2; and formation of Muslim Conference

193-4, 197-8; and Indian army 225, 233-4
Punjab Zemindar Central Association 59, 61, 64, 69

Qadir, Sir Abdul 67, 159
Qaiyum, Sir Abdul 145, 147, 149, 163
Qasuri, Abdul Qadir 207
Qureshi, Mahommed Hayat 61
Qureshi, Shuaib 98, 104, 159, 167-9; dissents from Nehru report 171-3

Rajagopalacharya 76
Rajan Shah, Makhdoom Syed 61
Rajendra Prasad, 76
Rampal Singh, Raja Sir 79, 122
Rampur, Nawab of 201
Rawalpindi 47-9, 50, 85, 88, 225
Raza Ali, Syed 16-17, 36, 39, 115-16, 120-1
Raza Shah, Syed Mahommed 61
Reading Lord (Viceroy) 107, 112, 124-5, 151
Reforms Enquiry Committee (Muddiman committee) 89, 114-17, 118, 124-5
Residuary powers, *see* Constitutional Reform
Riasat Ali, 61
Riots, *see* Communal riots
Rohilkhund 16, 18, 75, 136
Round table conference, first 196, 204, 220-9; second 230; and Congress overtures to Muslims 234-42; search for communal agreement in London 242-6; formation of Minorities Pact 246-7
Rowlatt Act satyagraha 25

Sahai, Lakshmi 79
Sahai, Sitla 140
Saifullah, Mahommed 62
Salempur, Raja of 38, 139, 199, 202
Samiullah Beg, Mirza 15, 16, 39
Samiullah Khan 110, 138
Sampuran Singh, Sardar 222
Sangathan movement 79
Sapru, Sir Tej Bahadur 20, 117, 165,

169, 172, 190-1, 221-3, 228
Sarfaraz Hussain Khan 110, 138, 189
Sastri Srinivas 221
Satyapal, Dr S. 129-30
Schuster, Sir George 209-12, 217
Sen Gupta, J.M. 130-1, 173
Separate electorates 19, 56, 71, 115, 121,
   135, 142, 145, 147, 200, 238-40, 260-1;
   granted to Muslims 13-14; to Sikhs
   56; Congress seeks their abolition
   113-14, 120, 131-2, 140, 238, 245, 261;
   Muslims favour their retention 143,
   165, 180, 193, 214-15, 224; rejected by
   Nehru report 175, 188; maintained by
   Simon report 205; discussed at round
   table.conference 223-4
Setalvad, Sir Chimanlal 165, 221, 226
Sethna, Sir Phirozeshah 221
Shafaat Ahmed Khan, Dr 38, 115-16, 144,
   161, 178, 181, 193, 199, 221, 232, 247
Shafi Daudi, Maulana 110, 116-17, 133-4,
   138, 146, 149, 163, 187, 189, 199, 200,
   202-3, 220, 226-7, 236, 242, 249-50
Shafi, Sir Mahommed 66, 67, 107, 115-
   17, 146, 148, 159, 160-1, 163, 193, 200,
   211, 220-7, 236, 239, 240, 243, 246-7
Shah Nawaz, Jehanara Begum 243
Shah Nawaz, Mahommed 146, 161, 163,
   200
Shahabuddin, Chaudhuri 67, 87
Shahid Hussain, Lt Sheikh 38
Shaukat Ali, Maulana 22, 24, 105, 158,
   159, 183-4, 185-7, 208, 239, 241;
   repudiates Nehru report 176-7; *see
   aslo* Ali brothers
Sherwani, T.A.K. 98, 100, 139, 171, 188-
   9, 200, 237, 239
Shraddhanand, Swami 75, 123
Shuddhi campaign, in Punjab 85, 101,
   102; in U.P. 74-5, 79
Sialkot 46, 48, 225
Siddiqui, Abdur Rahman 98, 147, 159
Sikhs 102, 105, 129, 152; and
   landownership 48, 49, 50; and the
   Army 51-2; and the Reforms 55-7, 59,
   63-4, 69, 72, 88, 91, 113; and the Nehru
   report 169-70, 175, 190; and the round

table conferences 222-3, 225-7, 243,
   254, 255
Sikunder Hayat Khan 63, 144, 178, 198
Simla deputation 23, 95-6, 98, 238
Simon, Sir John 156
Simon Commission, *see* Indian
   Statutory Commission
Sind 24, 74, 127, 162, 182, 233; and the
   demand for separation 145, 147, 149,
   161-2, 164, 165, 166, 175, 176, 179, 189,
   190, 194, 200-1, 205, 208, 211-12, 227-
   8, 238, 241-2
Skeen committee 126, 127
Southborough committee, *see*
   Franchise committee
Soviet Union 210
Sultan Ahmed, Sir 224, 227
Suhrawardy, Dr Abdullah 42-3, 44, 146,
   163, 200
Suhrawardy, Hussain Shahid 42-3, 45,
   187
Syed Ahmed, Sir 14, 17
Swaraj party, *see* Congress Swaraj party

Tajuddin, Pir 67
Talib Mehdi Khan, Nawab Major 62
Tambe, S. 127, 129
Tamizuddin Ahmed 163
Tandon, Purushotamdas 81
Tanzim movement 103, 104
Thakurdas, Sir Purushotamdas 107,
   112, 118, 124, 173, 185
Tilak, B.G. 127-8
Tiwana, Nawab Sir Umar Hayat Khan
   59-60, 61-2, 65, 152, 225-6
Tiwana, Nawab Malik Mubariz Khan
   61
Turkey, and the Khilafat movement 21-
   9, 95-6, 101, 107

Ujjal Singh, Sardar 178, 222
Ulema 23, 27, 95-6, 98, 250
Unionist party, *see* Punjab Unionist
   party
United Provinces, and Morley-Minto.
   Reforms 12-20; Municipal politics
   15, 17-20, 76-83, 100, 121, 134;

communalism 18-19, 74-84; Hindu politics 20, 77, 79, 80-2, 121, 136; Congress politics 31, 77-84, 134-8; and Montagu-Chelmsford Reforms 31-4, 36-40, 74-84, 142-3; communal riots 73-4, 78-9, 81, 231-2; Liberal politics 77, 80, 84

United Provinces Legislative Council 16-17, 33-4, 37-40, 77, 136, 148, 177

United Provinces Muslims, and Imperial system 8, 263; education 11-12; and Morley-Minto Reforms 12-20; and Montagu-Chelmsford Reforms 36-40, 84, 142-4; and Central Assembly politics 39, 109-10, 137-9; and Reforms Enquiry Committee 115-16; and Indian Statutory Commission 178-81; and Nehru report 181-4; and Muslim Conference 161-2, 193-4, 199; and round table conference 221; and Gandhi-Irwin Pact 231-3; and Communal Award 256

Unity Committee (1924) 119-21

Urdu 179

Venkatapatiraju 118-19

Vidyarthi, Ganesh Shankar 232

Wahid Hussain 165

Wales, Prince of 107

Wazir Hassan 15, 36-7, 39

Willingdon, Lord (Viceroy) 250-8

Yakub, Sir Mahommed 39, 115-16, 145-6, 158, 160-1, 163, 164, 189, 192, 199

Yamin Khan, Sir Mohammed 161

Yate, Sir Charles 58

Yusuf, Nawab Sir Mahommed 38, 40, 178, 199

Yusuf Imam 110, 138

Zafar Ali, Maulana 87, 103, 105, 159, 163, 184, 188, 207

Zafrullah Khan, Sir Mahommed 144, 161, 178, 220-1, 225, 247

Zahur Ahmed, Sheikh 81, 109, 178, 183, 232-3

Zahuruddin, Maulvi 137-8

Zakir Hussain, Dr 159, 184

Zamiruddin Ahmed 199

Ziauddin Ahmed, Dr 38, 113

Zubair, Shah Mahommed 146, 187

Zulfiquar Ali Khan, Sir 161

Contents

Preface	v
Abbreviations	x
Acknowledgements	xii
1 Elections and the Congress in Office: April 1936 to September 1939	1
2 India and the War: September 1939 to December 1941	45
3 Provincial and All India Politics: Currents and Cross-Currents—December 1941 to April 1945	71
4 The Success of the Muslim League—June 1945 to March 1946	118
5 The Cabinet Mission: March to July 1946	142
6 Negotiations for The Interim Government and Direct Action	179
7 Prelude to Partition: November 1946 to February 1947	203
8 Divide and Quit	217
Conclusions	236
List of Important Persons	253
Bibliography	257
Index	265

Preface

The origins of the partition of India have been traced to the medieval period of Indian history, so it might well be asked why 1936 is chosen as the starting point for this book One reason is that there is insufficient evidence on social relations during the medieval era to establish whether or not two nations were innate in that society, and there is little point in repeating the controversies surrounding the material that does exist. Secondly, some aspects of communal politics in India before 1935 have been discussed recently, among others, by R. J. Moore, Mushir-ul-Hasan, Gail Minault, and David Page.[1] Moore's latest book, *Escape from Empire* dealt with British policy between 1945–7, while M. N. Das's *Partition and Independence of India*[2] concentrated on the Mountbatten viceroyalty. There are, therefore, many gaps in our knowledge of the interplay of British, Congress and Muslim League strategies after 1936 which culminated in partition, which this book attempts to fill; and, both in scope and in terms of the questions raised, it differs from many earlier works on the communal problem and the partition of India. 1936 is also a useful starting point as it furnishes the immediate background to the coalition controversy between the Congress and the League in the UP in 1937, regarded by many as a milestone on the road to partition. One of the questions raised by this book is why agreement eluded the Congress and Muslim League to the point of civil war. Was it because of irreconcilable political differences between them? What alternatives did the Congress, which did not want partition, have which might have enabled it to defeat the League's claim for a sovereign Pakistan?

If it cannot be proved whether there were 'always' two nations in India, but only majority and minority communities, then at what point in time did the religious minority become a nation? Did the

---

[1] R.J. Moore, *The Crisis of Indian Unity 1917–1940* (Oxford, 1974); M. Hasan, *Nationalism and Communalism in Indian Politics* (New Delhi, 1979); G. Minault, *The Khilafat Movement* (Delhi, 1982); D. Page, *Prelude to Partition* (Delhi, 1982).
[2] R. J. Moore, *Escape from Empire* (Oxford, 1983); M.N. Das, *Partition and Independence of India* (New Delhi, 1982).

introduction of separate electorates and responsible government bring about this transformation? Or did the demand for a sovereign Muslim state in March 1940 express the aspirations of an historic nation struggling to be born? Above all did Jinnah owe his standing in all India politics to the interests and tactics of the British or to grass-roots support?

Many questions relate to British policy and tactics. The Labour government's directive to the Cabinet Mission in March 1946 stressed that power would only be transferred to Indians if they agreed to a settlement which would safeguard British economic and military interests in India. But in Feburary 1947, the Labour government announced that it would wind up the Raj by June 1948, even if no agreement had emerged. Less than four months later, Lord Mountbatten announced that the British would transfer power on 15 August 1947, suggesting that much happened during this interval which persuaded the British to bring forward the date for terminating the empire by almost one year. Also, the British have often claimed that they had to partition because the Indian parties failed to agree. But until the early 1940s the differences between them had been a pretext for the British to reject the Congress demand for independence. The British had earlier regarded the Congress–League rift as the bulwark of their rule. Why then did they divide and quit in 1947, when these differences were exacerbated?

Mountbatten has said that he would not have agreed to partition if he had known that Jinnah would be dead 'in X months'.[3] But for all Jinnah's obduracy, people do not get what they want simply because they ask for it—someone is usually willing to give it to them or is unable to stop them. Having demanded a sovereign Pakistan in March 1940, would Jinnah have accepted anything less? If so, on what terms? The high-handedness of the Congress and the 'divide and rule' policy of the British have both been blamed for the partition of India. While it is not our intention to whitewash either the British or the Congress, the question does arise whether they and the League dealt with each other at cross-purposes, and whether Jinnah's insistence on a sovereign Pakistan must account for its realization as much as the failure of the Congress and British to persuade him to join the Constituent Assembly for a united India. These

[3] L.Collins and D. Lapierre, *Mountbatten and the Partition of India Vol. 1, 22 March–15 August, 1947* (New Delhi, 1982) p. 39.

are some of the questions which this book will attempt to answer.

As the main question posed by this book is what led to the partition of India in August 1947, I have concentrated on those developments which, in my opinion, provide the most answers, and some explanation is probably needed about the emphasis given to certain issues. For example, the League's election campaign in the Punjab and its attempt to gain power in that province between 1944–7 are given more weight than, say, its election campaign in Bengal, because the possibility of an intercommunal coalition in the Punjab posed the greatest threat, in the eyes of the League, to the emergence of Pakistan. In Bengal, the League ministry had been able to cultivate grass-roots support during the war; the greatest electoral battles were not fought in this province in 1945–6. Again, the discussions between Mountbatten and the British cabinet in May 1947 are not detailed, partly because they merit separate treatment, partly because the emphasis is on why the British accepted the principle of partition and not on the technicalities of the transfer of power. For the same reasons, the slender possibility of a united Bengal receiving independence in 1947 is not discussed in depth; nor is the problem of the princely states.[4]

Finally, I would like to clarify my usage of some of the terms used in this book, especially where they comprised the categories used by the authors of the sources consulted. With evidence from British, Congress, League[5] and Mahasabha sources, I have often had to sort out what each of them meant by labels such as 'communal', 'problem of minorities', 'Hindu-Muslim problem', etc. I have used 'communalism' and 'communal problem' to describe thinking in terms of religious identity. I do not use 'Hindu-Muslim problem' except when quoting from sources, because, until 1946–7, there is little

---

[4] See ibid; some of these issues have been discussed in V.P. Menon's *The Story of the Integration of the Indian States* (1956); and *The Transfer of Power in India* (Madras paperback, 1968); W.H. Morris-Jones, 'The Transfer of Power, 1947: A View from the Sidelines', *Modern Asian Studies*, 16, 1, 1982, pp. 1–32; R.J. Moore, *Escape from Empire*; official documents have been published in *TOP*, vols. 10–12.

[5] At the time of writing, Indian scholars do not have access to Muslim League papers. But fairly good accounts of League attitudes and politics can be gleaned from newspapers, four of which espoused the cause of the League. These were *Dawn*, started in 1942 by Jinnah himself; the *Eastern Times* of Lahore, the *Star of India* and the *Morning News* of Calcutta, which was edited by a leading member of the Calcutta and Bengal Leagues. Reports of British officials and Congress leaders have also been helpful.

evidence of the communities being at *all* levels. One of the reasons why it can be used is because the Muslim League claimed to have established a Muslim homeland on the subcontinent in 1947. But is India the homeland of Hindus only? Also, the term 'Hindu-Muslim problem' tends to assume that Hindus and Muslims are homogenous entities: their religious affiliation marks them off from other groups socially, economically, culturally, politically. In a sense this is true—a person may identify himself as a Hindu, Muslim, Sikh, Christian or whatever. Merely by doing so, he does not create a social or political problem. The problem arises when a unified 'Hindu or 'Muslim' religious, political, social or economic consciousness is assumed (usually without evidence); which leaves no room for political and other intellectual differences within a particular community. According to this scheme of things, there cannot be Congress Hindus, Mahasabha Hindus, Communist Hindus, anti-Congress Hindus; nor can we have Muslim League or non-Muslim League Muslims. Indeed, as the Muslim League claimed, 'Muslims' were only those who supported it.

One should also distinguish between a community as a religious minority or majority—the census figures tell us that—and a political majority, which owes its position to its political platform and the amount of support it receives from voters for its political programme. For example, we can see that Muslims were a religious majority in the NWFP in 1937, but the Muslim League was a political minority. This distinction is vital when we discuss Indian or Pakistani nationalism.

Generally speaking, the British helped to confuse issues by labelling the Congress as Hindu, and *loyalist* Muslim opposition to it as 'Muslim' opposition to a Hindu Congress. Loyalist Hindu opposition to the Congress was ignored by the British, presumably because it may have been politically inexpedient for them. Talking about political division, both the League and the Hindu Mahasabha thought the economic programmes of the Congress were too radical in the 1930s. Both wanted a continuing long-term British presence in India, while the Congress had started talking about complete independence, involving the severance of all ties with the British Crown after 1930.

The term, 'problem of minorities' raises the question why the divide occurred largely between Hindus and Muslims in 1947; and to a lesser extent between Sikhs and Muslims—and not say, between

Hindus and Christians or Christians and Muslims. 'Problem of minorities' has also been used most often in a political context. We find that Muslims were the only minority to whom the British gave guarantees about their political position in British-sponsored constitutions on the ground that they would be able to safeguard their religious, cultural, social and economic interests. Similar guarantees were never given to other minorities. The question is why, and the answers would probably tell us at least as much about British perceptions of Indian society and politics and of their interests and tactics in India as about the 'problem of minorities'.[6]

The 'problem of minorities' is misleading because it refers only to Muslims at the all India level, leaving out Sikhs, Christians and other minorities, and even the Hindu minorities in the Muslim majority provinces. This last observation could explain why the Congress had 'Minorities Departments' in the Muslim minority provinces but not in the Muslim majority provinces—which may have been a psychological stumbling block to their ability to make a bid for Muslim support in the provinces which were to form the backbone of Pakistan. In fact, this categorization is probably the reason why scholars have only discussed 'Hindu-Muslim' differences and have not attempted to explain why, in the face of similar differences between say, Hindus and Christians or Christians and Sikhs, no politico-communal conflict emerged between these communities; why the Muslims were the only minority to whom the British gave constitutional guarantees.

---

[6] Some of these points are discussed more fully in Anita Inder Singh, 'Nehru and the Communal Problem, 1936–1939', (unpublished M. Phil dissertation submitted to Jawaharalal Nehru University, 1976), chapter 1; and my 'Decolonization in India; The Statement of 20 February 1947', *International History Review* May, 1984.

Abbreviations

AICC	All India Congress Committee
AIML	All India Muslim League
BDC	Bhulabhai Desai Correspondence
BSRC	B. Shiva Rao Correspondence
CC	Cunningham Correspondence
CP	Central Provinces and Berar
Correspondence	S.S. Pirzada, *Leaders' Correspondence with Mr. Jinnah* (Bombay, 1944).
CWC	Congress Working Committee
DC	Deputy Commissioner
FR	Fortnightly Report
GHQ	General Headquarters
HC	Haig Correspondence
HMG	His Majesty's Government
HP	Home Political (Internal) Department
ICS	Indian Civil Service
IAR	*Indian Annual Register*
INA	Indian National Army
LC	Linlithgow Correspondence
KPP	Krishak Praja Party
MGC	Mahatma Gandhi Correspondence
MLA	Member of Legislative Assembly
MLPB	Muslim League Parliamentary Board
MLWC	Muslim League Working Committee
NAP	National Agriculturist Party
NC	Nehru Correspondence
NDC	National Defence Council
NWFP	North-West Frontier Province
PC	Durga Das, (ed.) *Sardar Patel Correspondence, 1945–50* (10 vols., Ahmadabad, 197–4).
PCC	Pradesh Congress Committee
PTC	Purshottamadas Thakurdas Correspondence

Pirpur Report: Report of the Inquiry Committee appointed by the Council of the All India Muslim League to inquire into

Muslim Grievances in Congress Provinces (November 1938).

Pirzada, *Documents*: S.S. Pirzada (ed.) *Foundations of Pakistan: All India Muslim League Documents*, Vol. 2 (Karachi, 1970).

RPC   Rajendra Prasad Correspondence

SW   S. Gopal (ed.), *Selected Works of Jawaharlal Nehru* (12 vols., New Delhi, 1972–79)

(T)   Telegram

TBSC   T.B. Sapru Correspondence

TOP   P.N.S. Mansergh (ed.), *The Transfer of Power* (9 vols., HMSO, 1970–80)

UP   United Provinces

UPML   United Provinces Muslim League

VCO   Viceroy's Commissioned Officer

ZC   Zetland Collection

Acknowledgements

This book is based largely on my Oxford D.Phil thesis. Grants from the Oxford Graduate Studies Committee, the Bartle Frere and Radhakrishnan Memorial Funds, helped me to complete the thesis. I wish to thank my supervisor, Professor Ronald Robinson, who helped me to say what I wanted to say. I have found extremely useful the advice of my examiners, Professor Nicholas Mansergh and Sir Penderel Moon. Professor Thomas Metcalf, Professor W.H. Morris Jones, Professor Bipan Chandra, Mr Richard Symonds, Mr W.H. Saumarez-Smith, Mr Henry Taylor, Mr Arthur Williams and Dr Tapan Raychaudhuri have all read the manuscript and have made many valuable suggestions. Professor Sarvepalli Gopal has given me the most generous encouragement thoughout the period of the writing of this book. For moral support, without which this book could not have been written, I am grateful to my mother, Vanita and Asoke Mukerji—and very special thanks to Amrita and Ranjan Kapur.

CHAPTER 1

Elections and the Congress in Office

April 1936 to September 1939

'Minorities means a combination of things. It may be that a minority has a different religion from the other citizens of a country. Their language may be different, their race may be different, their culture may be different, and the combination of all these various elements—religion, culture, race, language, arts, music and so forth makes the minority a separate entity in the State, and that separate entity as an entity wants safeguards. Surely, therefore, we must face this question as a political problem'.

MUHAMMAD ALI JINNAH, 1935.[1]

'It is, after all, a side issue, and it can have no real meaning in the larger scheme of things'.

JAWAHARLAL NEHRU, 1936.[2]

These two statements, made by the men who led the main all-India parties in the elections of 1936 and who played a leading role in the negotiations for the transfer of power in 1946–7, indicate their very different approaches to the communal problem, which influenced decisively the British decision to transfer power to two successor states in 1947. In 1947, what for Nehru and his colleagues in the Congress had always been the real issue—the achievement of independence by India—was settled. But it was accompanied by the partition of India on a religious basis which was the antithesis of the secular Indian nationalism on which the Congress had always prided itself, and which suggested that, the 'side issue' of 1936 had become inextricably woven with the main issue in 1947. It was not

[1] Jamil-ud-din Ahmad (ed.), *Speeches and Writings of Mr. Jinnah*, vol. 1, 6th edn. (Lahore, 1960), pp. 5–6.
[2] Presidential address to the Lucknow Congress, 12 April 1936; hereafter referred to as Lucknow, S. Gopal (ed.), *Selected Works of Jawaharlal Nehru* (New Delhi, 1975), hereafter referred to as *SW*, vol. 7, p. 190.

before 1940 that Jinnah demanded a separate Muslim state. One of the arguments of this book is that the League's position—after the elections—induced its demand for Pakistan. It is these developments between 1937 and 1939 that we shall try to analyse in this chapter.

Elections to the provincial legislature under the Government of India Act of 1935 occupied the attention of all political parties in 1936. An electorate of some 36 million, as compared to an electorate of 7 million in 1920, and representing 30 per cent of the adult population,[3] would elect 1585 representatives to the provincial legislatures. The Act of 1935 was the first constitutional measure introduced by the British in India which envisaged that the parties winning a majority of seats in the legislatures would form ministries which would function on the basis of joint and collective responsibility.[4]

Both the Congress and the League were dissatisfied with the Act and held that it did not go far enough to satisfy the political aspirations of Indians. Nehru had described the act as 'a charter of bondage',[5] and a Congress resolution of 1936 stated that the future constitution of India could only be framed by a Constituent Assembly based on adult franchise.[6] The League had criticized the Federal part of the Act as 'most reactionary', but decided to work the provincial part 'for what it is worth'.[7] It was expected that the Congress would sweep the polls in the Hindu majority provinces, and the League, or other parties led by Muslim leaders, would win in the Muslim majority provinces. Their opposition to the federal part of the Act would be counterbalanced by the presence of the 115 Princely States which would join the federation in accordance with the federal part of the Act.[8]

In spite of their opposition to the Act, both Congress and the League decided to contest the provincial elections, if only to make use of the election campaign to spread their respective messages to the electorate.

[3] *Indian Franchise Committee Report*, vol. 1 (Calcutta, 1932), p. 33.

[4] *Government of India Act* (New Delhi, 1936).

[5] M. Gwyer and A. Appadorai (eds), *Speeches and Documents on the Indian Constitution 1921–47*, vol. 1 (Oxford, 1957), p. 386.

[6] Ibid., p. 385.   [7] Ibid., pp. 384–5.

[8] For the politics behind the making of the Act of 1935, see R. J. Moore, *The Crisis of Indian Unity, 1917–40* (Oxford, 1970).

In 1936, there appeared to be some reason for Nehru's optimism on the communal problem. The Hindu Mahasabha, the leading Hindu communal organization, had no influence among the Hindu masses, and had been dismissed by Congress leaders as politically irrelevant.[9] On the Muslim side, Jinnah, then the most outstanding Muslim leader at the all India level, had expressed willingness to 'forget the Communal Award and to apply our mind to larger questions affecting India'.[10]

Jinnah's own position in Indian politics was far from secure. In 1931, he had exiled himself to England after being ignored by Congress, the British, and most sections of Muslim political opinion.[11] An invitation from Liaqat Ali Khan, a prominent Muslim Leaguer from the UP, to return to India and to 'put new life into the Muslim League and save it',[12] had resulted in his attempt, in 1936, to organize the League for elections to the provincial legislatures.

The League had been more or less defunct since 1920. In 1927, its total membership was 1330. Between 1931 and 1933 its annual expenditure did not exceed Rs 3,000. Decisions of the Council of the Muslim League were taken by a very small minority, with only 10 out of its 310 members forming a quorum. Since the central office of the League was situated in Delhi, Leaguers from provinces far away from Delhi hardly ever attended party meetings.[13]

The League's popular appeal was negligible. Part of the reason for this lay in the social conservatism of its members. Wealth, social position and education determined entry into the League. Between 1924 and 1926, only 7 out of 144 resolutions passed had touched upon

[9] Anita Singh, 'Nehru and the Communal Problem, 1936–1939', unpublished M. Phil Thesis submitted to Jawaharlal Nehru University, 1976, p. 103.

[10] *Bombay Chronicle*, 3 April 1936.

[11] Jinnah himself admitted that in 1931, 'Muslims were unhappy with me because of my views regarding joint electorates. My Hindu friends were angry with me because of the fourteen points that I advocated . . . The British Parliamentarians were also resentful because I had characterized the Round Table Conference itself as a fraud'. Quoted in K. B. Sayeed, *Pakistan: the Formative Phase* (London, 1968), p. 291.

[12] Hector Bolitho, *Jinnah Creator of Pakistan* (London, 1954), p. 105.

[13] This paragraph is based largely on C. Khaliquzzaman, *Pathway to Pakistan*, (Lahore, 1961), pp. 137–8; K.B. Sayeed, *Pakistan the Formative Phase*, pp. 176–7, and Z. H. Zaidi (ed.), *Introduction to M. A. Jinnah-Ispahani Correspondence 1936–48* (Karachi, 1976), pp. 10–14, and Z. H. Zaidi, 'Aspects of the Development of Muslim League Policy' in C. H. Philips and M. D. Wainwright (eds.), *The Partition of India* (London, 1970), p. 246.

social and economic problems. The last time these issues had been debated was in 1928.[14] The League had never contested elections on an all-India basis,[15] and the extent of support for it in the Muslim majority provinces was doubtful. It could only provide a rallying point for Muslims at the all-India level on questions such as representation in the services and in legislatures; and when these had been settled, as, for example, in the Communal Award of 1932, the League appeared to have little to offer Muslims in the provinces.[16]

The Act of 1919 had introduced responsible government in the provinces. This set the scene for the emergence of parties and politicians whose base and horizons were essentially provincial, and whose political alliances cut across communal divisions.[17] They had, therefore, little interest in Jinnah's all-India Muslim politics.

In the Punjab, for example, Fazli Husain, whose Unionist party had governed the province since 1920, believed that Muslims, whose majority in the province was only marginal, could not achieve anything without the cooperation of the Hindu and Sikh minorities. The need for Hindu and Sikh support partly determined the intercommunal character of the Unionist party, which represented agrarian interests in the Punjab.[18]

Jinnah received, then, a crushing rebuff when he asked Fazli Husain to join the Muslim League Parliamentary Board in 1936. Jinnah was told of

'the advisability of keeping his finger out of the Punjab pie . . . we cannot possibly allow "provincial autonomy" to be tampered with in any sphere, and by anybody, be he a nominee of the powers who have given this autonomy or a President of the Muslim League or any other association or body.'[19]

In Bengal, an opportunity for Muslim unity arose when Hindus in Calcutta started an agitation against the Communal Award in August 1936. The Award had given Muslims 48.6 per cent of the

[14] Zaidi, Introduction to *Jinnah-Ispahani Correspondence*, pp. 13–14.

[15] Zaidi, 'Muslim League Policy', p. 253.

[16] Zaidi, Introduction to *Jinnah-Ispahani Correspondence*, pp. 13–15.

[17] On the effects of the Act of 1919 see D. Page, *Prelude to Partition: The Indian Muslims and the Imperial System of Control 1920–1932* (New Delhi, 1982).

[18] Ibid and Azim Husain, *Fazli Husain* (Bombay, 1946).

[19] Sikander Hyat Khan to Fazli Husain, 1 May 1935, Fazli Husain papers, quoted in Zaidi, Introduction to *Jinnah–Ispahani Correspondence*, p. 16.

seats in the legislature, and the British had envisaged that landlords would support them and raise their majority to 51.4 per cent. Hindus alleged that they had not been represented in proportion to their population in the province, while Muslims had been allowed weightage in all Muslim minority provinces. But a cleavage soon arose between the parties which had united against the Hindus. The United Muslim Party had been started by the Nawab of Dacca to contest the provincial elections and it represented big landlords, lawyers and businessmen. It could not make common cause with the Krishak Proja Party of Fazlul Huq, which had been founded as the Nikil Banga Proja Samity in 1929,[20] and which espoused the interests of poor peasants and small landowners. As the majority of poor peasants in Bengal were Muslims, Huq could claim that his party represented the Muslim majority of Bengal. But the intercommunal character of his political alliances can be seen by his maintenance of links with Hindu and Congress leaders even while he was Vice-President of the Bengal Provincial Muslim League.[21]

Jinnah initially managed to bring together the United Muslim Party and the KPP. But Huq walked out of the agreement because Leaguers refused to accept his demand that they also join the KPP and incorporate in the League's election manifesto a promise to abolish the Permanent Settlement in Bengal. The big *zamindars* of Dacca's United Muslim Party would not agree to this, so Jinnah brushed aside Huq's proposals as not being 'practical politics'. But the final break between Huq and Jinnah seems to have been caused by Huq's opposition to the nomination of 4 non-Bengali businessmen to the Muslim League Parliamentary Board.[22]

In Bihar, the United Muslim and Ahrar parties could not sink personal differences and unite with the League. In the Central Provinces and Madras, disagreements about the nomination of candidates proved the stumbling block in the way of Muslim unity. In Sind, leaders of the Azad Muslim Party did not want their initiative in provincial matters to be fettered by an all India parliamentary board. So, personal and provincial rivalries prevented the formation of a single Muslim party in most provinces.[23]

[20] Shila Sen, *Muslim Politics in Bengal, 1937–1947* (New Delhi, 1976), pp. 74–5.
[21] Zaidi, Introduction to *Jinnah–Ispahani Correspondence*, pp. 8–9.
[22] Ibid., p. 22 and Sen, *Muslim Politics*, pp. 76–8.
[23] Zaidi, *Muslim Politics*, pp. 248–9.

It was in the United Provinces, with the Muslim Unity Board, that Jinnah was able, eventually, to make an alliance. The Board had been formed at the time of the Unity Conference of 1933, when representatives of two leading Muslim organizations, the Muslim Conference and the Nationalist Muslims, led by Khaliquzzaman, agreed to form a joint front to promote the political interests of Muslims.[24] The Board seems to have had little sympathy with the Muslim League, against whom some of its own candidates successfully contested for Muslim seats in the Central Legislature in the elections of 1934.[25]

The success achieved by the Unity Board in the elections—it won a third of the Muslim seats in the Legislature[26]—probably explains Jinnah's eagerness to reach a settlement with it. Why the Unity Board responded so enthusiastically to Jinnah's call for Muslim unity is not so easily discernible. Perhaps, as Sir Harry Haig, the Governor, wrote, it was because the name of the Muslim League carried considerable influence in the UP.[27] Khaliquzzaman, who skilfully balanced himself between three parties, does not give a very satisfactory account of the events which prompted him and other leaders of the Unity Board to respond to Jinnah's appeal. He simply says that the Board was at first willing to consider a Congress request to put up Muslim candidates to contest the Muslim League and the National Agriculturist Party[28] in the coming elections. Later, however, one of the leaders of the Unity Board, Ahmad Said, seemed to be in agreement with Jinnah on what is vaguely described as 'the future policy of Muslims', and felt that Jinnah was 'prepared to go very far' to satisfy the Board.[29]

Jinnah and the leaders of the Unity Board appeared to agree that the Muslim League 'consisted mostly of big landlords, title-holders and selfish people, who looked to their class and personal interests more than to communal and national interests and who had always

---

[24] For an account of the circumstances leading to the formation of the Unity Board, see Khaliquzzaman, _Pathway to Pakistan_ (Lahore, 1961), pp. 117–20.

[25] Ibid., p. 130.   [26] Ibid., p. 142.

[27] Haig to Linlithgow, 21 May 1936, _HC_, vol. 5.

[28] The formation of the NAP was encouraged by Sir Malcolm Hailey, Governor of the UP, to counterpoise the Congress. See P.D. Reeves, 'Landlords and Party Politics in the United Provinces 1934–1937', in D.A. Low (ed.) _Soundings in Modern South Asian History_ (London, 1968), pp. 261–82.

[29] Khaliquzzaman, _Pathway to Pakistan_, pp. 140–1.

been ready to sacrifice them to suit British policy.' Jinnah wished to purify and revive the League. In this connection, he intended to ask the League to give him a mandate to form a parliamentary board for the purposes of the forthcoming elections. He promised the Unity Board a majority on the parliamentary board, and stressed the need for a united Muslim front. One difference remained between the Unity Board and the Muslim League. The Unity Board was committed to the goal of independence; the Muslim League was not. Jinnah reassured the Unity Board. 'When I give you a majority in the Parliamentary Board you can do everything'.[30]

It was against this background that the twenty-fourth session of the Muslim League opened at Bombay on 11 April 1936. The two hundred delegates who assembled there sought primarily the 'all-round uplift of the Muslims.[31] From the outset, dissimilarities between the League and the Congress on political issues were evident. Whatever the differences between Nehru and his colleagues on the Congress Working Committee, they were all agreed on one point— the winning of independence by India. But Syed Wazir Hasan, far from taking an anti-imperialist stand in his presidential address to the Muslim League, spoke of 'the fortunate connection between India and the British Crown'. He defined 'ultimate object of the constitutional advancement of the Muslims of India' as 'the attainment of responsible government for our mother-land'. *Swaraj, purna swaraj*, 'self-government', 'complete independence', 'responsible government', 'substance of independence', and Dominion Status, were to be, among other things, 'under the aegis . . . of the Crown of the Emperor of India'.[32] A resolution passed at this session of the Muslim League did not demand independence: it referred to 'India's most cherished goal of complete responsible government'.[33]

The election manifestoes of the Congress[34] and the League[35] further reflected the differences in their objectives and ideals. The manifesto of the League was vaguely worded, and was characterized by an absence of commitment on any issue. It made a show of concern for the religious rights of Muslims, which it professed to

[30] Ibid., p. 141.
[31] S.S. Pirzada, (ed.) *Foundations of Pakistan: All-India Muslim League Documents*, vol. 2 (Karachi, 1970), p. 235.
[32] Ibid., pp. 241, 248–9.   [33] Ibid., p. 261.
[34] The Congress Election Manifesto, 22 August, 1936, *SW*, vol. 7, pp. 459–64.
[35] Khaliquzzaman, *Pathway to Pakistan*, p. 417.

protect. It asked for the repeal of all repressive laws, reduction in the cost of administration and military expenditure, and called for the social, educational and economic uplift of the rural population.

The Congress manifesto, drafted by Nehru, rejected the new constitution 'in its entirety', while the Muslim League manifesto made no mention of it. The manifesto of the League also made no reference to the future political development of India. Independence was not demanded, and, it was clear that the Muslim League did not desire the severance of the British connection. It is, in fact, significant that one of the reasons for the failure of negotiations between Jinnah and the Ahrars, who had a radical social programme, was Jinnah's refusal to promise them that a demand for independence would be made in the election manifesto of the Muslim League.[36]

The Congress manifesto reflected the growing mass support for the organization, and stressed the crucial role to be played by the masses in the struggle for freedom.[37] The Muslim League manifesto merely asked for the creation of 'a healthy public opinion and general political consciousness throughout the country'. In this connection, it should be noted that the Muslim League, in its session at Bombay, had rejected a proposal to reduce the membership fee from one rupee to four annas.[38]

It seems rather strange that British officials in 1936, and many writers since then,[39] thought that the social and economic objectives of the Congress and the League were similar. British officials thought that the manifesto of the League was as socialistic as that of the Congress! Haig in fact considered the NAP as a counterpoise to both the Congress and the Muslim League in the UP.[40] The election manifesto of the League resembled not the Congress manifesto, but the manifestoes of the National Agricultural Parties of Agra and Oudh, whose formation had been encouraged by the British in 1934

[36] M. Noman, *Muslim India: The Rise and Growth of the All-Indian Moslem League* (Allahabad, 1942), p. 329. On the Ahrars, see also P. Hardy, *The Muslims of British India* (Cambridge, 1972), p. 216.

[37] *SW*, vol. 7, p. 460.   [38] *IAR*, 1936, vol. 1, p. 295.

[39] See, for example, FR for Punjab for first half of June, 1936, HP File No. 18/6/36; S. Gopal, *Jawaharlal Nehru: A Biography*, vol. 1, 1889–1947 (London, 1975), p. 223; S.R. Mehrotra, 'The Congress and the Partition of India,' in Philips & Wainwright (eds), *Partition of India*, p. 193.

[40] Haig to Linlithgow, 29 October 1936, *HC*, vol. 112.

to counter what they regarded as the political, and social radicalism of the Congress.[41]

As the provincial elections approached, Nehru reiterated in his presidential address to the Faizpur Congress in December 1936 the struggle against imperialism, the issues of social and economic freedom, the demand for a Constituent Assembly, his hostility to the Indian States system, and the need for greater mass participation in the Congress.[42] The address emphasised his belief that the contest in India was 'between two forces—the Congress as representing the will to freedom of the nation, and the British Government in India and its supporters who oppose this urge and try to suppress it.'[43]

Jinnah did not agree. There was a third party in India, he sharply informed Nehru, and that was the Muslims' Party;[44] revealing a vital difference in his attitude to political questions from Nehru's. For Nehru, the issue was that of independence. 'He who is for it must be with the Congress and if he talks in terms of communalism he is not keen on independence'.[45] Jinnah's sole aim was to establish the Muslim League as the only representative of Muslim affairs and to maintain it as such in the forefront of Indian politics.

Nehru's reply to Jinnah revealed his disdain for the political and long-term role a communal organization such as the League could play on the Indian political scene. He expressed unhappiness over Jinnah's reference to a 'third party', for, as he saw it, between British imperialism and Indian nationalism Jinnah would have Muslims remain as a political group apart, apparently playing off one against

[41] The election manifesto of the NAP of Agra: 'To devise means for peace, prosperity and good government of the country; to adopt all constitutional means in order to promote self-government in India; to create a healthy public opinion; to protect and advance by all constitutional means the interests of the people generally and of the agricultural population particularly in these provinces; to help and advance the political, social, educational and economic uplift of the province; to encourage industries and cottage and agricultural industries particularly; . . . to regulate exchange policy in the interests of the country; to reduce expenditure and effect substantial economy in every branch of the government administration'. The manifesto of the NAP of Oudh also called for 'the relief of agricultural indebtedness' and 'the reduction of the burden of taxation'. See P.D. Reeves, 'Landlords and Party Politics', pp. 292–3.

[42] Presidential address to the Faizpur Congress, 27 December 1936, *SW*, vol. 7, pp. 598–614.

[43] 'Line up with the Congress', 18 September 1936, Ibid., p. 468.

[44] *Bombay Chronicle*, 4 January 1937.

[45] 'Line up with the Congress', *SW*, vol. 7, pp. 468–9.

the other, and seeking communal advantage even at the cost of the larger public good.[46] This was 'communalism raised to the nth power'. Nehru explained, with a patient sarcasm, the unacceptability of the 'logical conclusion' of Jinnah's statement—'that in no department of public activity must non-Muslims have anything to do with Muslim affairs'.[47] He ridiculed the 'new test of orthodoxy' being enunciated by Jinnah—that Muslims were 'only those who follow Mr Jinnah and the Muslim League'.[48]

Nehru decried the communal philosophy of the League, as he pointed out that 'real issues', pertaining to economic and political problems, could not be considered communally.[49] He attached no significance to 'third parties', 'middle and undecided groups', for, in the long run, they had no role to play. The Congress represented Indian nationalism 'and is thus charged with a historic destiny'.[50]

Nehru was contemptuous of the indifference of the League to the question of independence, and of its distance from the masses. 'It represents a group of Muslims no doubt, highly estimable persons but functioning in the higher regions of the upper middle classes and having no contacts with the Muslim masses and few even with the lower middle class'.[51] He welcomed cooperation with the League, but only on the basis of anti-imperialism and the good of the masses. He ruled out pacts between handfuls of upper class people which ignored the interests of the masses.[52]

Jinnah chafed under Nehru's derisive view of the Muslim League even as he attacked what he regarded as Nehru's claim to be the 'sole custodian of the masses'. With a sarcasm that matched that of Nehru, he challenged the Congress claim that it was a national organization and defended the communal character of the League. 'The League does not believe in assuming a non-communal label with a few adventurers or credulous persons belonging to other communities thrown in and who have no backing of their people, and thus pass off as the only party entitled to speak and act on behalf of the whole of India'.[53]

Jinnah's stand on political and economic questions was also revealed. He asserted that the Muslim League would maintain a sepa-

---

[46] 'The Congress and Muslims,' 10 January 1937, *Eighteen Months in India*, hereafter referred to as *EMII* (Allahabad, 1938), p. 152.

[47] Ibid., pp. 150–1.   [48] Ibid., p. 151.

[49] Ibid., p. 152.   [50] Ibid., p. 153.   [51] Ibid., p. 154.

[52] Ibid., pp. 155–6.   [53] *Leader*, 23 January 1937.

rate identity; and he made a show of the League's importance, gratuitously laying down the terms under which the League would cooperate with any party in the struggle for freedom. The Muslim League 'is prepared to join hands with any progressive party in the fight for the country's freedom, but to achieve this the question of minorities must be settled satisfactorily'. Jinnah expressed his disagreement with 'certain methods and means to which the Congress stands pledged.' He informed Nehru that 'Even a large bulk of patriotic and nationalistic Hindus are not members of the Congress. Because they do not believe in the Congress methods'.[54]

The British had the most interest in the electoral fortunes of the Congress, which they regarded as a test of its strength against them. Even as they predicted a Congress victory in most provinces,[55] British officials discussed the possibility of an opposition to it, especially in view of the emphasis on independence and economic reform in its election manifesto. In the UP, the British were supporting the National Agriculturist Party against the Congress; Linlithgow hoped that Nehru's expounding of his radical economic theories would consolidate the Right throughout India for the purpose of the elections.[56] It is interesting, in view of the fact that both the Congress and the British sought the hand of the Muslim League only three years later, that there are only the most cursory references—or none at all—to the election campaign of the League in official reports, and, at this time, the British do not seem to have envisaged its emergence as an opposition of any significance. Perhaps it was because the League was considered similar to the Congress in its socialistic tendencies—and Jinnah the arch enemy of the Raj![57]—and, of course, the League had not been able to consolidate its position, as the leading Muslim organization, especially in the Muslim-majority provinces.

The elections revealed the strength of the Congress as an all India force. The Congress contested 1161 seats in the general constituencies and won 716, securing a clear majority in six out of the eleven

---

[54] Ibid.

[55] See, for example, Brabourne to Linlithgow, 13 November 1936; Keane to Linlithgow, 28 October 1936; Sifton to Linlithgow, 3 November 1936; Hyde Gowan to Linlithgow, 10 November 1936; *LC*, vol. 112.

[56] Linlithgow to Zetland, 27 August 1936, Ibid., vol. 3.

[57] Raja of Mahmudabad, 'Some Memories', in Philips and Wainwright (eds), *Partition of India*, p. 384.

provinces of British India. It emerged as the largest single party in three other provinces. The extent of the success of the Congress confounded most political pundits,[58] and one British official could only remark, somewhat grudgingly, that it remained to be seen whether the Congress would actually fulfil its promises.[59] Officials unanimously attributed the victory of the Congress to the absence of any organized opposition against it, [60] the attraction of the names of Gandhi and Nehru,[61] and 'wild promises' of the reduction of rent.[62] The enormous extent of the new franchise was regarded as a great advantage to the Congress, especially in Bihar and in the UP, where Congress election propaganda had been directed more against landlords than against the British.[63] Here the Congress defeated, often in straight fights, big landlords who were thought to have exercised exceptionally great influence over their tenants,[64] and whom the British had hoped would be able to check any rising tide of Congress fortunes. In the NWFP also, the Congress defeated the Khans—the great feudal landowners—usually by very big margins.[65]

The Congress fared best in the UP, where it captured 133 out of 288 seats in the Legislative Assembly. It was in a position to form governments in Bihar, where it won 95 out of 152 seats; in Bombay, where it secured 88 out of 175; in the CP, where it emerged victo-

[58] See, for example, FR for Assam for first half of January 1937; FR for Orissa for second half of January 1937; HP file no. 18/2/37; and FR for UP for first half of February 1937, HP file no. 18/2/37; Anderson to Linlithgow, 8 February 1937, *LC*, vol. 112.

[59] Haig to Linlithgow, 13 February 1937, *LC*, vol. 112.

[60] FR for Bihar for first half of February 1937, HP file no. 18/2/37; Keane to Linlithgow, 15 December 1936; Anderson to Linlithgow, 3 December 1936; Hyde Gowan to Linlithgow, 10 November 1936; Sifton to Linlithgow, 9 February 1937; all these letters to Linlithgow in *LC*, vol. 112.

[61] See, for example, FR for UP for first half of February 1937; FR for Bihar for second half of February 1937; HP file no. 18/2/37.

[62] Haig to Linlithgow, 9 February 1937, *LC*, vol. 112; FR for Assam for second half of January 1937, HP file no. 18/1/37; and FR for Bihar for first half of February 1937, HP file no. 18/2/37.

[63] Griffith to Linlithgow, 9 November 1936; Haig to Linlithgow, 26 January and 4 February 1937; *LC*, vol. 112; FR for Assam for first half of January 1937, HP file no. 18/1/37; FR for Bihar for first half of February 1937; HP file no. 18/2/37.

[64] Haig to Linlithgow, 13 February 1937; *LC*, vol. 112; and FR HP file no. 18/2/87 for Bihar for first half of February 1937.

[65] Griffith to Linlithgow, 22 February 1937, *LC*, vol. 112.

rious winning 71 out of 112 seats; in Madras and Orissa, where i: obtained 150 out of 215 and 36 out of 60 seats respectively in the Legislative Assemblies. The Congress routed the Hindu Mahasabha in the UP and in the Punjab, and disabled it politically.

Handicapped during its election campaign by a shortage of Muslim workers,[66] the Congress achievement with Muslim seats was somewhat less remarkable. It contested only 56 out of the 482 Muslim seats in British India, and won 28. It did not secure a single Muslim seat in the UP, Bengal and in the Punjab. It did not contest any Muslim seats in Sind, Bombay, Bihar and the UP, and failed to win any Muslim seat in Bengal, the CP and the Punjab. Its greatest successes with Muslim seats were achieved in Madras where it obtained 4, and in the NWFP, where it won 15.

The success of the Congress in the NWFP was only one indication that its overall failure in Muslim constituencies did not necessarily reflect communal trends. The Muslim League fared very badly in the Muslim majority provinces and was not in a position to form a government in any of them. Of the 117 seats allotted to Muslims in Bengal it won 38. In the Punjab it contested 7 and obtained only 2 out of 84 Muslim seats; and in Sind it won only 3 out of 33 Muslim seats. Its inability to put up a sufficient number of Muslim candidates in these provinces showed that it lacked a popular base in the Muslim majority provinces. The fact that an intercommunal party based on the agrarian interests of all communities won a majority in the Punjab showed that communal questions did not play a decisive part in the elections. The same could be said of Bengal, where the success of the Congress and the KPP pointed to the popularity of radical economic programmes.[67] Taking into account the rout of the Hindu Mahasabha in the general constituencies at the hands of the Congress, and the lack of success of the League in the Muslim majority provinces, it can be concluded, then, that communal questions did not play a major role in the elections of 1937.

The election results proved that neither the Congress nor the League could claim to represent Muslims. But the success of the Congress in the general constituencies showed its popularity on the all India level; for the Muslim League, the future did not appear very promising as it had failed to capture a majority of the Muslim

[66] G.B. Pant to Rajendra Prasad, 21 January 1937, *RPC* File II/37, Col. 1, reel 5.
[67] FR for Bengal for first half of February 1937, HP file no. 18/1/37.

votes; and more significantly, it was not in a position to form a government on its own in any province. This realization lay behind the almost conciliatory posture taken up by Jinnah after the elections. He therefore expressed the League's willingness to cooperate 'with any group or party if the basic principles are determined by common consent.'[68]

Jinnah, however, was never the man to humble himself, or, as he put it later, 'to bow our head before Anand Bhawan'.[69] It was characteristic of him to declare that 'Minus verbiage and slogans there is no substantial difference between the policy of the Muslim League and the Congress', refer to 'fundamental differences' between them, and to dissuade Muslims from signing the pledge of another party 'for the sake of ministers',[70] all in the same breath. Jinnah's position in March 1937 was an unenviable one. Not only had the Muslim League failed to capture a majority of Muslim votes; there were few signs of the Muslim unity which Jinnah had tried to build up since 1934, as provincial Muslim leaders of the League were showing no interest in a united Muslim front, and some Leaguers were even suggesting that it would be better if the Congress and the Muslim League could reach some sort of understanding.[71] Jinnah, therefore, had to reconcile his personal antagonism towards the Congress with the conciliatory mood of the League towards it, as well as of the need of the League to cooperate with it, without appearing to be confessing the League's weakness and swallowing his pride. This is illustrated by a statement in which he said that there was no difference between the Congress and the 'Moslems' except that the latter stood for the establishment of the rights of the minority community, while at the same time he attacked Congress propaganda which, he said, had no other object than capturing votes.

Jinnah's statements anticipated a Congress decision on the question of office acceptance.[72] Much to the dismay of Nehru and the radicals in the Congress, the AICC, on 18 March 1937, voted, by 127 votes to 70, in favour of acceptance of office by the Congress, subject to the condition that Governors of provinces would not use the special powers vested in them by Section 93 of the Government of India Act. The AICC decision provided Jinnah with an oppor-

---

[68] *Leader*, 1 March 1937.   [69] *Leader*, 12 May 1937.
[70] *Leader*, 15 March 1937.   [71] *Leader*, 16 March 1937.
[72] See, for example, *Bombay Chronicle*, 19 March 1937. Also Gopal, *Nehru*, pp. 217–19; Tomlinson, *Congress and the Raj* (London, 1976), pp. 62–3.

tunity to renew his offer of cooperation with congress ministries. Jinnah now highlighted points of agreement between the League and the Congress.

'I congratulate the right wing of the Congress leaders for having carried the Congress with them. They have adopted the formula which practically is the same as was adopted by the All-India Moslem League on April 12, 1936, namely, that in the present conditions we should utilize the constitution for what it is worth . . . . Now struggling as we are for national self-government, perhaps it will be easier for the All-India Muslim League parties to cooperate with other progressive parties as the Congress is also lined up.'

Characteristically, however, Jinnah scoffed at Congress attempts to gain assurances that the Governors would not use their special powers of interference. Any such assurance, said Jinnah, would be futile as the Governor was the ultimate authority in the province according to the Instrument of Accession of the Act. 'It may, however, appeal to the imagination of some people that the Congress has laid down something novel'.

Jinnah skilfully veiled his apprehension about the future of the League as he persisted in upholding its separate identity. He exhorted Muslims to rally round the Muslim League banner. [73] It was not possible for Muslims and Hindus to merge their identities; and while it was most feasible for them to march together towards the goal of freedom, he did not want Muslims to do this to please every particular person or organization. He did not want them to be camp followers but to be in the vanguard.[74]

Nehru was not inclined to respond sympathetically to Jinnah's call, and his terms, for cooperation, especially at a time when he felt confident that the Congress itself could win over the Muslim masses on the basis of economic issues. Nor was he dismayed that the Congress had won only a fraction of the Muslim seats in the elections. During the election campaign the Congress had found a willing response from the Muslim masses 'and a desire to line up with our freedom movement'. Until now the Congress had not made much effort to work among the Muslim masses, and it was essential that the Congress take 'full advantage of this new interest and awakening', and make 'a special effort' to enrol more Muslim members, 'so that our struggle for freedom may become even more broadbased than it is, and the Muslim masses should take the prominent part in

[73] *Leader*, 22 March 1937.   [74] *Leader*, 24 March 1937.

it which is their due.'[75] The Congress was not interested in pacts with a few persons representing communal organisations, 'with no common political background, meeting together and discussing and quarrelling.'[76] Clearly, Nehru, whether or not he saw the motives behind Jinnah's cautious overtures to the Congress, turned them down.

'It is remarkable that Jinnah and Shaukat Ali have worked themselves in a mad fury just because we have decided to work among the masses'.[77] The inception of the Congress Muslim mass contact programme, and Nehru's declaration that the Congress hoped to rouse the Muslim masses in its favour could hardly have been welcomed by a communal organization such as the League. Whatever Nehru may have said to the contrary,[78] this could only mean that the success of the programme would lead to the rout of the Muslim League as a political organization. To Jinnah, it must have seemed an insult, added to the injury, that not only was the Congress indifferent to the idea of cooperating with the Muslim League, but also that it was inaugurating a campaign, the very success of which would spell the political extinction of the League. The very reasons which made Nehru confident of its success roused Jinnah's fears. The appeal of Congress programmes to voters had been proved in the elections. If, as Nehru himself admitted, the Congress had not been very successful in winning Muslim seats, the League had not fared very well either. It had obtained only 4.8 per cent of the Muslim vote, and won only 43 out of 272 Muslim seats in the Muslim majority areas.[79] So far, it had also failed to enlist the support of Sikandar Hyat Khan and Fazlul Huq, whose parties were leading ministries in the Punjab and Bengal respectively. Not only had the League fared badly in the elections; it could not even count on successful parties led by Muslim leaders.

The implications of the Congress Muslim Mass Contact programme being quite clear, Jinnah's sharp reaction to its inauguration was not surprising. He regretted that Nehru should have found a solution which would produce more bitterness and frustrate the object that every nationalist had at heart.[80] To Jinnah, the Congress

---

[75] *Leader*, 3 April 1937.
[76] 'The Congress and Muslims,' 4 April 1937, *EMII*, p. 161.
[77] K.M. Ashraf to S.A. Brelvi, 23 April 1937, AICC file G-68, 1937, p. 137.
[78] Nehru to Ismail Khan, 5 February 1938, *NC*, vol. 39.
[79] Calculated from election returns of 1937.   [80] *Leader*, 22 April 1937.

attempt 'under the guise of establishing mass contact with the Musalmans, is calculated to divide and weaken and break the Musalmans, and is an effort to detach them from their accredited leaders'.[81]

Jinnah's consternation was not eased by the attempts being made by some members of the Muslim League parliamentary board in the UP for cooperation between the Congress and the League in the province. Discussions between G.B. Pant and Khaliquzzaman, leader of the provincial MLPB, started almost as soon as the elections were over, and were encouraged by 'the amicable manner' in which the elections had been fought by both the Congress and the League.[82] For during the elections there had not been much conflict between the two parties, and in some places they had cooperated against the National Agriculturist Party. The Congress had supported the Muslim League candidate, where there was no Congress Muslim candidate, 'if he was not an obvious reactionary'.[83]

Uncertainty prevailed in Muslim League ranks in the UP after the elections. Some Muslim Leaguers were sympathetic to the 'interim' government headed by Chhatari,[84] while Khaliquzzaman spurned an offer to join it. Pant reportedly offered the League two seats in a possible Congress ministry[85] and earned Nehru's displeasure.[86] At a time when he stressed the need for unity and discipline among Congress legislative parties,[87] the Congress objectives of independence and mass betterment,[88] Nehru was not inclined to support moves for pacts with communal organizations which had no common political and economic policy, were dominated by reactionaries, and looked to the British for favours.[89] Nehru thus rebuffed the overtures of the League for a Congress-League ministry, even as he chided Congressmen who talked 'in terms of pacts and compromises with Muslims or other religious groups'.[90]

[81] Pirzada, *Documents*, p. 270.

[82] Khaliquzzaman, *Pathway to Pakistan*, p. 153; see also note by Donaldson dated 14 August 1940, Reforms Office file 89/40-R; referred to hereafter as Donaldson.

[83] Nehru to Rajendra Prasad, 21 July 1937, *NC*, vol. 85, and Donaldson.

[84] Chhatari was invited by the British to form an 'interim' government in the UP following the Congress refusal to form a ministry in the province because it had not received an assurance from the Governor that he would not interfere in the working of the ministry.

[85] Haig to Linlithgow, 7 April 1937, *HC*, vol. 17A.

[86] Nehru to Pant, 30 March 1937, AICC file E-1, 1936–1937, p. 7.

[87] *EMII*, p. 126.   [88] Ibid., p. 157.   [89] Ibid., p. 160.   [90] Ibid., p. 157.

The negotiations between Pant and Khaliquzzaman did not get off to a very promising start. On 2 April Pant informed Nehru that he had received no definite response to a suggestion made by him that nationalist Muslims join the Congress actively both inside and outside the legislature.[91]

Meanwhile, the manoeuvres of Khaliquzzaman for a Congress-League settlement on the one hand; the announcement of the Congress Muslim mass contact programme on the other, created some consternation in the UP Muslim League. Many provincial Leaguers were alarmed at the political implications of the Congress programme, and it was believed that a majority of them were not likely to support Khaliquzzaman's overtures to the Congress. Even as Khaliquzzaman wavered between taking the risk of being defeated in the Muslim League[92] and fulfilling his ambition of securing a ministerial post in a Congress government, a majority of the members of the UP Muslim League appeared willing to take a lead from Jinnah.[93] Jinnah now made open his opposition to Khaliquzzaman's flirtation with the Congress. '. . . I want to make it clear,' he admonished Khaliquzzaman, 'that it will be useless for any individual or individuals to effectively carry the Muslims behind them if any settlement is arrived at with a particular group or even . . . with the whole province. I say that it is a pity that these roundabout efforts are being made. The only object of it can be to create some differences between Mussalmans.'[94]

Jinnah's warning went home. On 7 May, at a meeting of the UP Muslim League at which he was also present, it was decided that the Muslim League would not merge with the Congress or lose its independence either inside or outside the legislature. Khaliquzzaman was asked to make it plain to the Congress that Muslim Leaguers would not accept Congress decisions on matters affecting the Communal Award.[95] A resolution was passed which emphasized the differences in the aims of the Congress and the League. It said that the Muslim League party in the legislature could not and should not join the Congress in its policy of wrecking the Constitution.[96] The

[91] Pant to Nehru, *NC*, 2 April 1937, vol. 79.
[92] Haig to Linlithgow, 23 April 1937, *HC*, vol. 17A.
[93] Haig to Linlithgow, 7 May 1937, Ibid.
[94] *Leader*, 10 May 1937.   [95] *Bombay Chronicle*, 8 May 1937.
[96] *Leader*, 10 May 1937.

resolution was considered a personal triumph for Jinnah: Khali-quzzaman accepted the situation.[97]

The animosity displayed by the Muslim League towards the Congress on the occasion of the Bundelkhand by-election symbolised 'the alarm that has been caused among the Muslims generally by the Congress attempts to capture the Muslim masses', the strong feeling among them 'that if the community is to retain its individuality, no efforts must be spared in resisting the attempts of the Congress to absorb them'.[98] The existence of such feeling showed how a political conflict with the League could be construed as an attack on Muslims as a community. In June 1937, the seat of the constituency of Jhansi-Hamirpur-Orai in Bundelkhand fell vacant owing to the death of its holder, K.B. Habibullah, who had belonged to the Muslim League. Both the Congress and the League put up their own candidates—Nisar Ahmed Sherwani and Rafiuddin respectively—to contest the by-election for the seat. For the League, it was a question of survival. For, in spite of Jinnah's call for Muslim unity, there were signs of restlessness within the ranks of the Muslim League over its policies. Syed Wazir Hasan, who had presided over the Muslim League session in April 1936, now appealed to Muslims to join the fight for independence led by the Congress.[99] On the eve of the by-election, A.H. Qureshi and Hakim Riazuddin, two Vice-Presidents of the Jhansi Muslim League, resigned from their posts and advised Muslims not to join the League.[100]

Jinnah now demonstrated his strategy for survival. On 30 June 1937, a statement, allegedly written by him, appeared in the Urdu newspaper *Khilafat*, which made a frankly communal appeal to the Muslim voter.

'My only object in organising the Muslim League, and the Muslim League Parliamentary Board, and putting forward the programme for the "Nazm" (Organization) of Musalmans . . . is that Mussalmans should unite among themselves as they have been ordered to do by God and his Prophet . . . Thank God our efforts are proving fruitful. Our success and progress is becoming an eye-sore to the enemies of Islam. They want to frighten and bully us. Their putting up a candidate for the by-election from Bundelkhand in opposition to the Muslim League is also one of such efforts.'

[97] Haig to Linlithgow, 8 May 1937, *HC*, vol. 17A.
[98] Haig to Linlithgow, 24 May 1937, Ibid.
[99] *Bombay Chronicle*, 12 June 1937.
[100] *Bombay Chronicle*, 26 June 1937.

The appeal exhorted Muslims to vote for Rafiuddin 'so that it will mean a crushing reply to the non-Muslim organisation and in future it will not dare to interfere in the affairs of Musalmans . . . . I assure you in my capacity as the President of the Muslim League and the Muslim League Parliamentary Board, that God willing the Shariat Islami, special rights of Musalmans, their culture and their language will be saved from the interference of outsiders'.[101]

Jinnah denied authorship of the statement[102] but it is significant that he did not condemn the exploitation of religious sentiment for political ends. Meanwhile, Shaukat Ali raised the cry of 'Islam in danger'. Exhorting Muslims to vote for Rafiuddin, Shaukat Ali said, 'Do it in the name of Islam, in the name of religion and its honour'.[103]

Nehru was astounded at the tactics of the League—'this is communalism in excelsis'[104]—even as he was determined that the Congress must face the challenge with all its strength.[105]

But even as Nehru urged that the Congress should approach the Muslim electorate in Bundelkhand 'on economic lines', and not compete with the Muslim League on its own ground,[106] Sherwani asked him to arrange for visits of prominent ulema to help him in his election campaign,[107] and a disapproving Nehru noted that Sherwani thought 'too much of the Maulvi type of individuals'.[108] For some Congress workers in Bundelkhand, appearances were everything. One of them requested that only Muslim volunteers be sent to campaign for Sherwani, 'and, if possible, with all the outward signs of a "Muslim" (I mean beards etc.)'.[109]

The Muslim League emerged victorious at Bundelkhand. Rafiuddin secured 4,700 votes; Sherwani obtained 2,000. The success of the Muslim League was a personal triumph for Jinnah. But its real significance lay in the nature of the League's challenge to the Congress. Bribery and the cry of 'religion in danger' contributed to its

[101] *Bombay Chronicle*, 2 July 1937.
[102] *Bombay Chronicle*, 2 July 1937.
[103] NC, part II, file 114, p. 8, from extract entitled 'Maulana Shokat Ali Sahib,' pp. 6–8.
[104] *Bombay Chronicle*, 1 July 1937.
[105] Nehru to Kidwai, 1 July 1937, AICC file G-61, 1937, p. 213.
[106] Nehru to Sherwani, 3 July 1937, Ibid., p. 105.
[107] Sherwani to Nehru, 2 July 1937, Ibid., pp. 161–2.
[108] Nehru to M.L. Saxena, 23 June 1937, Ibid., p. 247.
[109] Asst. Secy., UPCC, to R.A. Kidwai, 6 July 1937, Ibid., p. 157.

victory. Congress propaganda started only two days before the election and was entirely political and economic. So Congress leaders were not disheartened by the party's defeat at Bundelkhand and were satisfied that when the Muslim peasant was asked why he was voting for the Congress, 'he confessed frankly that he did so because he expected the Congress to reduce his rent.'[110]

Even as the battle for Bundelkhand was on, Khaliquzzaman and Ismail Khan approached Pant with the question of seats in a possible Congress ministry in the UP. On learning of this at the beginning of July, Maulana Azad met Khaliquzzaman who told him that he would give him a blank cheque provided he and Ismail were included in a ministry. Azad looked suspiciously on this move, and he and other members of the Congress Working Committee disliked the bargaining for seats in the ministry. They were wary of taking in two persons 'who, from the Congress point of view, were weak,' who had been fighting the Congress and who only seemed interested in the spoils of office, at the cost of Muslims who had always been staunch supporters of the Congress. Yet the Congress Working Committee were willing to consider the proposal as it held out the possibility of the winding up of the Muslim League in the UP and its absorption in the Congress; which would undoubtedly clear the political field of communal troubles. It would also 'knock over the British Government which relied so much on these troubles'.

At a time when the need for organizational unity and discipline appeared to be of paramount importance to Congress leaders, stringent conditions were offered to the UP Muslim League parliamentary group, and it was decided that Khaliquzzaman and Ismail would be taken into a Congress ministry only if they accepted all of them.[111] The Congress expected Muslim Leaguers to abide by decisions taken by the Congress party both inside and outside the legislature, and called for the dissolution of the Muslim League Parliamentary Board in the UP. Thereafter, the Muslim League would support Congress candidates during by-elections. Members of the League would also be bound by any Congress decision to resign from the legislature or from the ministry.[112]

Khaliquzzaman writes that he rejected the terms, which, to him,

---

[110] Nehru to Prasad, 21 July 1937, *NC*, vol. 85.
[111] Ibid.   [112] Khaliquzzaman, *Pathway to Pakistan*, p. 161.

meant signing 'the death warrant' of the provincial Muslim League Parliamentary Board as well as of the Muslim League organization.[113] According to Nehru, however, he agreed to all the conditions except two: the winding up of the Parliamentary Board and the agreement not to set up separate candidates at by-elections; and said that he personally would agree to even these two conditions but that he did not have the authority to do so. Azad then informed him that he could not give him a final answer.

Meanwhile, Nehru felt 'very uncomfortable and was instinctively repelled by all this talk on an opportunistic basis'. He also feared that any settlement with the League would be temporary. The Congress Working Committee insisted that the League should accept all the conditions. Khaliquzzaman then promised to ask the Muslim League Executive to consider the question of by-elections. But now, Nehru did not encourage him at all.[114]

Khaliquzzaman writes that a few days later, on 24 July, Azad presented him with a modified version of the conditions laid down by the Congress for a coalition. Khaliquzzaman then demanded that 'the Muslim League Party members in the UP Assembly will be free to vote in accordance with their conscience, on communal matters', which would include religion, religious ceremonies, languages, culture, services, etc.[115] The Congress refused to accept such a provision, as it would have given the League a communal veto on many matters, and the possibility of a Congress–League coalition in the UP ended.

According to Maulana Azad, the negotiations foundered when Nehru, with his 'theoretical bias', turned down Khaliquzzaman's proposal to include both himself and Ismail Khan in the UP ministry.[116] But Nehru does not seem to have been directly involved in the negotiations, or even been fully informed of all that had taken place since March, until the beginning of July.[117] In any case, as Nehru himself pointed out, he alone was not responsible for the final decision. G.B. Pant, Rafi Ahmad Kidwai[118] and Azad,[119]

---

[113] Ibid., p. 161.
[114] Nehru to Prasad, 21 July 1937, *NC*, vol. 85.
[115] Khaliquzzaman, *Pathway to Pakistan*, pp. 162–3.
[116] M.A.K. Azad, *India Wins Freedom*, (New York, 1960) pp. 187–8.
[117] Nehru to Prasad, 21 July 1937, *NC*, vol. 85.
[118] *The Hindu*, 8 February 1959.
[119] Azad had opposed a Congress–League pact even in March. (Nehru to Abdul

among others, were also instrumental in arriving at the decision not to form a coalition with the League. From Wardha, Gandhi signalled his approval of the terms of the Congress offer to the League.[120] There was also no necessity for the Congress to form a coalition with any party as it had a clear majority in the UP. It was, in fact, the League which got valuable assistance from the Congress in the election: the direct benefits of the electoral understanding went to the League.[121]

'A ministry,' wrote Nehru to Jinnah in April 1938, 'must have a definite political and economic programme and. policy.'[122] Such a basis for a coalition did not exist between the Congress and the Muslim League. The League, like its Hindu counterpart, the Hindu Mahasabha, was strictly a communal organization, more interested in claiming special privileges from the British, with whom it avoided any conflict. The Congress, on the other hand, was irrevocably opposed to British imperialism. The Congress was also interested in agrarian reform and feared that the League, which was largely a representative of the big zamindars of the UP, would stymie its attempts in that direction.[123] The Muslim League did, in fact, oppose the Tenancy Bill which was introduced by Pant's ministry in 1938.[124] How an economic problem could be given a communal colouring was illustrated by Khaliquzzaman's statement before the Cabinet Mission in 1946 that to strike at the zamindari in the UP was to strike at the root of Muslim existence.[125]

The conduct of Muslim Leaguers, including Khaliquzzaman and Ismail,[126] was at variance with their professed desire for a coalition.

Walli, 30 March 1937, AICC file G-5 (KW) (i), 1937, p. 139.) It is clear (Nehru to Prasad, 21 July 1937) that he was a party to the final decision not to form a coalition with the Muslim League.

[120] Nehru, 22 July 1937, *NC*, vol. 25.   [121] Donaldson.

[122] Nehru to Jinnah, 6 April 1938, Pirzada, *Correspondence*, p. 1124.

[123] *The Hindu*, 8 February 1959.

[124] Papers relating to the Muslim League and the UP Tenancy Act, *NC*, part II, file 55.

[125] Meeting between Cabinet Delegation, Wavell, Ismail, Chundrigar, Raufshah and Khaliquzzaman on 8 April 1946, P.N.S. Mansergh (ed.) *The Transfer of Power 1942–1947*, hereafter referred to as *TOP*, vol. 7 (H.M.S.O., 1977) p. 166.

[126] Khaliquzzaman seems to have been a party to what was probably a communal appeal, which greatly dismayed Nehru. (Nehru to Khaliquzzaman, 27 June 1937, *NC*, vol. 39). Ismail has made an appeal to Muslim voters which was very similar to Jinnah's. 'I hope the Muslims now fully realize the political exigency of nominating

Jinnah opposed, all along, Khaliquzzaman's efforts to bring the negotiations to a successful conclusion. Khaliquzzaman himself vacillated between the prospect of a ministerial future and his anxiety not to lose influence in the Muslim League; and he eventually chose to abide by the dictates of Jinnah. Throughout the negotiations, he was also insistent that he would not collaborate in the ministry with Congress Muslims.[127] The differences in the aims of the Congress and the Muslim League, the fact that at no time did the League give the Congress an assurance that it would cooperate fully with it, justified the Congress decision not to form a coalition with the League.[128] Jinnah's opposition to the negotiations between provincial Leaguers and the Congress showed that the failure could not have been the reason behind his call for a sovereign Muslim state in March 1940.

The main significance of the failure of the negotiations for a Congress–League coalition in the UP was that it provided the Muslim League with excellent propaganda material to 'expose' the 'Hindu' bias of the Congress. Disagreements with the League on political and economic issues were made to imply that the Congress was biased against Muslims as a community. Jinnah alleged that the Congress had, 'by their words, deeds and programme shown, more and more, that the Musalmans cannot expect any justice or fair play at their hands. Wherever they were in a majority and wherever it

---

their own candidate to the legislatures . . . The League Parliamentary Board has been formed with a view to choose candidate (sic) for the legislature, who will safeguard the political and religious rights of the Muslims besides their culture and language. I hope you also realize the gravity of the situation with which we are faced in Bundelkhand. A non-Muslim organization has set up a nominee against the chosen representative of a Muslim organization . . . the victory of the former will falsify the Muslim right to choose their own representative and our community, in result, may face the gravest consequences . . . Therefore I appeal to you to call a halt to the intervention of the non-Muslim organization in our problems by electing the representative of the Muslim League'. *The Hindustan Times*, 30 June 1937.

[127] Donaldson.

[128] Interestingly, Haig correctly prophesized the outcome of the negotiations for a coalition between the Congress and the League in February 1937. 'There are rumours that the Congress will make considerable efforts to win over the whole of the Muslim League group, realising that if they do this and thus split the Muslims seriously, they will render the whole opposition ineffective . . . Nevertheless, it seems doubtful whether for the Ministry they will pass over the handful of genuine Congress Muslims in favour of those who are clearly not in real sympathy with the Congress aims.' Haig to Linlithgow, 17 February 1937, *HC*, vol. 16.

suited them, they refused to co-operate with the Muslim League parties and demanded unconditional surrender and the signing of their pledges'.[129]

Jinnah's presidential address to the Muslim League in October 1937 was, in fact, a declaration of war against the Congress. His political strategy was starting to crystallize. It consisted of attacking the Congress, and of equating Congress governments with 'Hindu' Raj. Jinnah alleged that the Congress was 'pursuing a policy which is exclusively Hindu', that it was imposing Hindi, *Bande Mataram* and the national flag on 'all and sundry'. By identifying the Congress with the majority community, Jinnah sought to create Muslim apprehensions against the Congress. 'On the very threshold of what little power and responsibility is given, the majority community have clearly shown their hand: that Hindustan is for the Hindus'.[130] The failure of the negotiations was depicted, not as the consequence of the absence of a common political programme between the Congress and the League, but as an example of the Congress' conception of nationalism, which, as the Pirpur Report alleged later, was based on 'the establishment of a national state of the majority community in which other nationalities and communities have only secondary rights'.[131] It was made to appear that the 'sectarianism' of the Congress, and not the League's own lack of popular support, was responsible for the fact that it had been 'deprived' of political power in the provinces, even as Jinnah acknowledged that the Congress leadership did not have a very high opinion of the Muslim League. 'No settlement with the majority is possible, as no Hindu leader speaking with any authority shows any concern or genuine desire for it'.[132]

Even as he railed against the Congress, Jinnah tacitly confessed the political inefficacy of the League, as he urged Muslims to 'develop power and strength' till they were 'fully organized, and have acquired that power and strength which must come from the solidarity and the unity of people'.[133] The Muslim League now seemed to have realized the importance of building up mass support. Provincial branches of the League were reorganized, and the membership fee was lowered from one rupee to two annas.[134] A comprehensive socio-economic programme was also framed. The program-

[129] Pirzada, *Documents*, p. 267.   [130] Ibid., pp. 267–8.
[131] *Pirpur Report*, p. 2.   [132] Pirzada, *Documents*, p. 269.
[133] Ibid., p. 269.   [134] Zaidi, 'Muslim League Policy'. p. 259.

me included the fixation of working hours and minimum wages for factory workers, the reduction of rural and urban debts, the promotion of indigenous industries, and the advancement of primary, secondary and university education.[135]

But 'power' and 'strength' could not be built up until Jinnah had gained a foothold in the Muslim majority provinces. His ability to achieve this depended on the position of provincial Muslim politicians, rather than on the strength of any communal sentiment. In Bengal, no single party had obtained a majority in the elections. As leader of the largest single group, Fazlul Huq had some difficulty in forming a ministry. The provincial Congress was willing to form a coalition with him,[136] but the Congress High Command called a halt to the negotiations because of Huq's refusal to promise that his government would release political prisoners. Huq then turned to an assortment of groups—the Hindu Nationalist Group, the Europeans and the Scheduled Castes—for support. The family of his old adversary, the Nawab of Dacca, was given three posts in the ministry.[137]

The accommodation with Dacca and his group lost Huq the support of a radical group in the KPP, led by Nausher Ali and Shamsuddin, who crossed the floor of the House. Deserted by a section of his own followers, Huq now made overtures to the League, which was the largest single Muslim group in the Assembly. Declaring that 'no problem . . . relating to the administration of India can be solved without the League,'[138] he successfully wooed Jinnah in order to ensure the support of the provincial League for his ministry. At the Lucknow session of the League, he rounded on the Congress in terms that would have done credit to Jinnah himself. Acceptance of Congress offers, said Huq, would have meant signing 'with my own hands the death warrant of Islam.' Coalition with the Congress could only be 'on such terms as amount to the virtual effacement of the Muslims as a separate political entity.'[139]

But the strains were never far from the surface in this political marriage of convenience. Ispahani, one of Jinnah's most loyal lieutenants in Bengal, complained that the moment the ministry was

---

[135] Pirzada, *Documents*, p. 280.

[136] John Gallagher, 'The Congress in Bengal: The Period of Decline 1930–1939,' *Modern Asian Studies*, 7, 7, 1973, p. 643.

[137] Zaidi, Introduction to *Jinnah–Ispahani Correspondence*, p. 26.

[138] *IAR*, 1938, vol. 1, p. 377.   [139] Ibid., p. 386.

formed, 'the League was shelved. No meeting of the League Board or Party, no League Whips, leaders or other office bearers.'[140] Yet Jinnah himself believed that he could only strengthen his hand through compromise and patience. He had no intention of throwing away the gains his alliance with Huq had brought him.

'You must not mix up the aims we have with the achievements. The aims are not achieved immediately they are laid down. But I think, on the whole, Bengal has done well and we must be thankful for small mercies. As you go on, of course with patience and tact, things are bound to develop and improve more and more in accordance with our ideals and aims'.[141]

Why Sikander Hyat Khan joined up with Jinnah at the Lucknow session of the League is not quite certain. Sikander himself was known to have little sympathy with the 'virulent communalism' of the League. But sympathy for the League of a section of Muslim Unionists, caused by their alarm that the Congress would have no regard for the 'position of Muslims' in a federal government, persuaded Sikander, in the interests of maintaining unity within the party, to join the Muslim League.[142] It is also possible that Sikander saw the growing strength of the Congress as a threat to his own political interests. Ahmad Yar Khan Daulatana, Chief Secretary of the Unionist Party, said that Congress attempts to organize a Muslim Mass Contact Campaign in the Punjab would open a fresh chapter of communal controversy,[143] as it would attack one of the bases of Unionist strength.

The path to an understanding with Unionists was not a smooth one for Jinnah. Sikander wanted the Unionists to control the League's parliamentary board in the Punjab and also the finances of the League.[144] Whether he achieved this objective is not known, but it was not until April 1938 that Muslim Unionists actually signed the membership forms of the League.[145] The understanding appears to have been that Jinnah would not interfere in provincial politics, while he would speak for Muslims at the all India level.[146]

---

[140] Ispahani to Jinnah, 23 July 1937, *Jinnah–Ispahani Correspondence*, p. 83.

[141] Jinnah to Ispahani, 4 April 1937, Ibid., p. 81.

[142] P. Moon, *Divide and Quit*, p. 17.   [143] *Bombay Chronicle*, 8 May 1937.

[144] Iqbal to Jinnah, 10 November 1939, G. Allana, *Pakistan Movement: Historic Documents*, 2nd edition (Lahore, 1968), pp. 148–9.

[145] Emerson to Linlithgow, 12 April 1938, *LC*, vol. 86.

[146] Emerson to Linlithgow, 21 October 1937, *LC*, vol. 113.

The NWFP remained a Congress province; Allah Baksh would not subscribe to the communalism of the League in Sind; but the arrangements with Huq and Sikander enabled Jinnah to assert that 'The All-India Muslim League has now come to live and play its just part in the world of Indian politics; and the sooner this is realized and reckoned with, the better it will be for all interests concerned.' Jinnah, however, remained aware that the League was not in a position to bargain on its own terms with the Congress.

> 'An honourable settlement can only be achieved between equals; and unless the two parties learn to respect and fear each other, there is no solid ground for any settlement. Offers of peace by the weaker party always mean a confession of weakness, and an invitation to aggression . . . Politics means power and not relying only on cries of justice or fairplay or goodwill.'[147]

Jinnah did not appear to be interested in any compromise with the Congress, as he emphasised the political differences between it and the League. He criticized yet again the economic programmes of the Congress. 'All the talk of hunger and poverty is intended to lead the people towards socialistic and communistic ideas, for which India is far from prepared'. The Congress demand for a Constituent Assembly was scathingly described as 'the height of all ignorance'.[148] Jinnah could not bring himself to visualize a situation where the British might leave India, leaving behind political authority in the hands of the Congress. He revealed what was to develop into regular strategy later: to wait for the Congress to express an opinion first; even to throw a challenge about the course of action he might take, without stating his own intentions at all. The British were talking about the inauguration of Federation. What, enquired Jinnah, was the Congress going to do? without himself revealing the League's position.

What infuriated Jinnah was the indifference of the Congress to the League. He was, in fact, looking for a way to bring the Congress High Command 'to its senses'; and he challenged Nehru to come and sit with the Muslims in order to formulate a constructive, practical and ameliorative programme which would give immediate relief to the poor.[149] Fazlul Huq, who had by now joined the League, alleged that the Congress press had given distorted accounts of his

---

[147] Pirzada, *Documents*, p. 280.　　　[148] Ibid., p. 270.
[149] *Bombay Chronicle*, 27 December 1937.

activities on a tour of Eastern Bengal simply because he was a Muslim, and threatened to use 'a stern rod' on those who preached communalism and disturbed the peace of the country.[150]

If the leadership of the Muslim League had been looking for the best way to influence Congress leaders so that they would attach some importance to the League as a political organization, the statements of Jinnah and Huq accomplished the purpose. Both Gandhi and Nehru were roused not only to take up Jinnah's challenge, but also to initiate correspondence with him on communal matters; and, in a way, accorded the League the status it sought—as spokesman of the Muslims. 'I had no desire whatever to carry on a controversy,' wrote Nehru to Ismail Khan, 'but in view of Mr. Jinnah's "Challenge" to me, I had to say something in reply'.[151]

For his part, Gandhi doubted that he could do anything to bring the Congress and the League together, after Jinnah's declaration of war against the Congress at the Lucknow session of the Muslim League.[152] Jinnah's reply to Gandhi made no bones about what he wanted. 'We have reached a stage when no doubt should be left'. The Congress should recognize the League as the authoritative and representative organization of Muslims, and Gandhi should negotiate on behalf of the Congress and the Hindus. 'It is only on this basis that we can proceed further and further and devise a machinery of approach'.[153] Gandhi turned down the suggestion, saying that he could represent neither the Congress nor the Hindus.[154]

Knowing of Gandhi's reaction by 8 March, it is unlikely that Jinnah was serious in making the same demand of Nehru on 17 March,[155] or indeed, that any of his points for discussion with Nehru had any purpose behind them at all. 'Obviously the Muslim League is an important communal organization and we deal with it as such,' replied Nehru. But there were Muslims in the Congress, in trade and peasant unions, and in zamindar associations, which had both Hindu and Muslim members. There were also special Muslim organizations such as the Jamiat-ul-ulema and the Ahrars. Moreov-

---

[150] *IAR*, 1937, vol. 2, pp. 466–7.
[151] Nehru to Ismail, 2 January 3938, *NC*, vol. 39.
[152] Gandhi to Jinnah, 3 February 1938, *IAR*, 1938, vol. 1, p. 360.
[153] Jinnah to Gandhi, 3 March 1938, Ibid., p. 361.
[154] Gandhi to Jinnah, 8 March 1938, Ibid., p. 362. Also *Harijan*, 30 April 1938.
[155] Jinnah to Nehru, 17 March 1938, Pirzada, *Correspondence*, p. 99.

er, Nehru felt that the importance of organizations depended on their inherent strength and not on outside recognition.

Jinnah's suggestion that the two leaders discuss the Fourteen Points lacked substance.[156] The Fourteen Points, as Nehru rightly remarked, 'were somewhat out of date'. Many of their provisions had already been effected; others required constitutional changes which were beyond the competence of the Congress.[157]

Guarantees for Muslims in the services and protection of their rights, were minor constitutional changes, and any case the Congress wanted to do away 'completely with the present constitution and replace it by another for a free India.'[158]

Nehru assured Jinnah that the Congress was not trying to impose Hindi or to injure Urdu. Referring to his article, 'The Question of Language,' he told Jinnah that the Congress wanted to introduce Hindustani, which could be written in either the Urdu or the Devanagri script.[159] On the Communal Award, Nehru reiterated that the Congress sought alterations only on the basis of mutual consent of the parties concerned. 'I do not understand how any one can take objection to this attitude and policy.' But he emphasised that the Award was anti-national. 'If we think in terms of independence, we cannot possibly fit in this Award with it.'[160]

Nehru did not take very seriously Jinnah's demand for coalition ministries. A ministry must have a definite political and economic policy. Any other kind of ministry would be a disjointed and ineffective body, with no clear mind or direction. 'What seems to me far more important', continued Nehru, 'is more basic understanding of each other'—implying that such an understanding did not exist at that moment—'bringing with it the desire to co-operate together.' Any cooperation must be based on independence and the interests of the masses.

What prompted Congress leaders to seek an understanding with the Muslim League was their desire to strengthen the nationalist front against Federation,[161] and their fear that an unreconciled Jin-

---

[156] Jinnah to Nehru, 17 March 1938, Ibid., pp. 113–15.
[157] Nehru to Jinnah, 3 April 1938, Ibid., p. 115.
[158] Ibid., p. 113–14.
[159] Ibid., p. 120.
[160] Ibid., p. 115.
[161] P. Sitarammaya, *The History of the Indian National Congress*, vol. 2, 1935–1947, (Bombay, 1947), p. 74.

nah might not sympathize with them and might even try to thwart their effort.[162] The intensification of communal bitterness in public life also troubled them, and it is interesting that communal friction was increasing even as the correspondence between Jinnah and Gandhi and Nehru continued. Communal tension prevailed in many cities including Nagpur, Lahore, Benares, Jubbulpore and Allahabad during the last fortnight of March, and April 1938.[163] Official sources held the League responsible for the tense communal situation,[164] and pointed out that it reflected the strained relations between the Congress and the League.[165]

The anxiety of Congress leaders to reach an understanding with the Muslim League did not diminish, and, even as Jinnah's correspondence with Nehru came to an end, he was due to meet Gandhi at the end of April 1938. Jinnah was thinking of capitalizing on the eagerness of Congress leaders for a settlement, and had admitted that the strong communal tone of his speeches to the League on 17 April had been calculated at securing some tactical advantage in his approaching conversations with Gandhi.[166]

Jinnah, however, overestimated the chances of getting Congress leaders to agree to his main demand—recognition of the Muslim League as the sole representative of the Muslims. His talks with Gandhi failed on this score. Subhas Chandra Bose, who had become president of the Congress in February 1938, then continued the discussions, and turned down Jinnah's demand on the ground that the Congress could not give up its national character.[167] Congress leaders, including Bose, Azad, Prasad, Patel and Gandhi informed Jinnah that they favoured an amicable settlement of the communal question, but there could be no infringement of Congress programmes and policies.[168] As it turned out, the discussions between Jinnah and Bose never progressed beyond the stage of 'the examination of credentials'.[169] On 5 June, Jinnah informed Bose that the Execu-

[162] Survey of secret information relating to Congress attitude towards Federation, Enclosure 8; Linlithgow to Zetland, 6 April 1938, ZC, vol. 15.

[163] *Bombay Chronicle*, 17, 18 March 1938.

[164] FRs for UP for first and second half of March; also for Bihar, CP, March, 1938; HP file no. 18/3/38.

[165] Linlithgow to Zetland, 27 March 1938, ZC, vol. 15.

[166] Linlithgow to Zetland, 27 April 1938, ZC, vol. 15.

[167] Bose to Jinnah, 14 May 1938, Pirzada, *Correspondence*, p. 62.

[168] *Bombay Chronicle*, 13 May 1938,

[169] Linlithgow to Zetland, 24 May 1938, ZC, vol. 15.

tive Council of the Muslim League had passed a resolution which reiterated that the Congress must recognize the League as the only representative body of Muslims in India. Also, the Congress could not invite representatives of other Muslim organizations to participate in any talks that might take place.[170]

Bose rejected the proposals once more, saying that it would be 'not only impossible, but improper' for the Congress to agree that the League was the sole representative of Muslims.[171] The correspondence between Jinnah and Bose continued in this vein until October.[172] On 16 December, the Congress Working Committee finally rejected the demand and also stated that it was not in a position to do anything further in the direction of starting negotiations with the League with a view to arriving at a settlement of the Hindu-Muslim question.[173] On the same day the Working Committee passed a resolution which defined the Hindu Mahasabha and the Muslim League as communal organizations, and forbade any Congress member from belonging to either of them and the Congress simultaneously.[174]

If, by the close of 1938, it was clear to Jinnah that the Congress would never accept his claim to represent all Muslims, he had to create an atmosphere which would dissuade Muslims from sympathizing with it. His main political weapon since 1937 had been attacks on the Congress, and he had to give some substance to them. This the League attempted in the Pirpur Report, which was published in November 1938.

Perhaps the greatest significance of the assumption of office by the Congress was the opportunity which it provided the Muslim League to stir up Muslim opinion against the alleged communal bias of Congress governments. The League did not challenge the Congress on political issues publicly to any great extent, perhaps because the election had proved the appeal of the Congress stand on these issues. Instead, the League sought to embarrass Congress governments, by alleging that Congress governments were either incapable or unwilling to safeguard the religious and cultural rights of

---

[170] Jinnah to Bose, 5 June 1938, Pirzada, *Correspondence*, pp. 64–5.
[171] Bose to Jinnah, 25 July 1938, Ibid., p. 66.
[172] Jinnah to Bose, 10 October 1938, Ibid., pp. 69–74.
[173] *National Herald*, 17 December 1938.
[174] *Bombay Chronicle*, 16 December 1938.

Muslims, and had no intention of fulfilling the assurances made to minorities in the Karachi Resolution of 1931.

There was little justification for the charge that Congress governments discriminated against Muslims. The allegations stemmed from the failure of the Congress and the League to resolve differences on political issues. But in a situation where ideological differences often took on a religious colouring, the accusations levelled against Congress governments put Congress leaders very much on the defensive. As the majority of Indians were Hindus by religion, the Congress, a broad nationalist front which represented the majority of Indians, regardless of class or creed, knew that it often appeared representative of Hindus only. The defensive reactions of Congress leaders to these allegations shows how easily propaganda builds up into myths, which are then accepted as facts on the basis of which policies are formulated—keeping in mind, of course, the political context.

The inquiry conducted by the Pirpur Committee into Muslim grievances in Congress provinces contended that with the acceptance of office by the Congress, Muslims were being discriminated against not only by Congress officials and workers, but also that 'People of a particular community were encouraged to believe that the government was not theirs'.[175]

Congress governments were in fact accused of deliberately engaging in actions, or of formulating policies, that offended the religious sentiments of Muslims. Among the issues raised by the Pirpur Report were the singing of *Bande Mataram* and the hoisting of the Congress flag in public places, attacks on the religious right of Muslims to slaughter cows, and the suppression of the Urdu language by Congress governments. A resolution passed by the League was quoted which contended that *Bande Mataram* was 'positively anti-Islamic and idolatrous in its inspiration and ideas . . .'.[176] The tricolour was described as 'purely a party flag and nothing more . . . the foisting of the so-called national flag on the unwilling minorities' was 'an expression of the narrow communalism of the majority community'. The flag should represent the 'true feelings and sentiments of the Muslim community' merely in showing of the Muslim colour was not of much significance. The implication was, of course, that Hindus, Hindu communalism and Congress govern-

[175] *Pirpur Report*, p. 15.   [176] Ibid., p. 17.

ments were all synonymous. Hindus in educational institutions had been encouraged 'to ignore the feelings of the Muslims,' and they lost no opportunity to offend Muslim sentiments.[177]

'The question of cow slaughter has been one of the causes of conflict between the Hindus and Muslims of India.'[178] Muslims were said to have been intimidated to give up cow sacrifice and the eating of beef. Action had been organized to prevent the sale of cows to Muslims, and Hindus had resorted to violent measures to do this. It was also alleged that some Congress governments had refused to grant licences to Muslim butchers for selling beef.[179] Such action was being taken 'in the name of law and order and on the false ground that the Muslims did not prove the custom to sacrifice cow or that they proposed to kill cows openly or that it was a nuisance in the eyes of some people . . .'.[180] This was looked on as deliberate discrimination against the religious rights of Muslims. 'Muslims have been enjoined by their religion to prevent idol worship and other idolatrous practices. Will the Government abolish or restrict idol-worship and prohibit public exhibition of idols in processions in the name of law and order, if some Muslims object to it or form an unlawful assembly to secure their object?'[181] It was also alleged that Gandhi's emphasis on cow protection, and his advocacy of charkha, showed an apprehension that Congress Raj was Hindu Raj and offended the religious sentiments of Muslims.

Congress governments were also accused of discrimination against Urdu and of trying to impose Hindi on Muslims. Muslims, it was implied, spoke only Urdu, and the imparting of education in vernaculars would lead to their cultural degeneration and would also place Muslim students at a disadvantage in competition with boys of other communities, 'who are fortunate enough to receive their education in their own mother tongue'.[182] Some Congress governments were not opening Urdu schools where there was a demand for them, or were not giving grants to them, or were abolishing Urdu classes in schools.[183] The Vidya Mandir Scheme introduced in the Wardha scheme of education was criticized on the ground that the word Mandir, connoting idol worship, went against the grain of Islamic tenets and was repulsive to a Muslim.[184] Mus-

---

[177] Ibid., p. 35.   [178] Ibid., p. 20.   [179] Ibid., pp. 20–1.
[180] Ibid., pp. 41–2.   [181] Ibid., p. 43.   [182] Ibid., p. 29.
[183] Ibid., pp. 51–2.   [184] Ibid., p. 54.

lims were also said to be placed at a disadvantage because Urdu, while allowed in courts officially was discouraged unofficially by officers.

Departmental examinations were held in Hindi in Bihar but not in Urdu; municipal committees in the Central Provinces did not entertain applications in Urdu. It was alleged that in one district in the CP which had been converted into a Compulsory Education area, the government had provided for expenditure with the express condition that the medium of instruction would be only Hindi.[185]

The Pirpur Report tried to 'expose' the highhandedness and hostility of Hindus as a community towards Muslims and alleged that Congress workers and officials either connived with Hindu mobs who tried to prevent Muslims from exercising their religious and cultural rights, or were simply incapable of protecting the rights of Muslims. One instance cited in the Report said that Muslim butchers at Badri village near Ballia had made arrangements to buy some two thousand cattle, when 'a large crowd of about a thousand well-armed Hindus attacked the butchers . . . and beat them mercilessly, thus rendering the butchers unfit to protect their cattle. The assaulters took away all the cattle forcibly from the butchers' possession'.[186] Again, in the village of Khairatia in Bihar, 'some trouble arose when the sugarcane of one Muslim peasant was being cut. Hindus assembled near the field and a crowd of many thousands attacked the Muslims, who were overpowered. They fled for their lives and some of them took shelter in their houses and some in a mosque. The Hindu rioters, who came from neighbouring villages, started looting and setting fire to the Muslim houses. Even the mosque was not spared by the Hindus who attacked the Muslims there with spears, *lathis*, and brick-bats. A number of Muslims were injured and many had spear wounds . . .'.[187]

Hindus were also accused of hindering processions on occasion of festivals celebrated by Muslims. Hindus placed obstacles in the way of Muslims carrying tazias.[188] Cow sacrifice was sometimes prevented on the festival of Bakrid;[189] Hindus would not let Muslims call *Azan*;[190] Hindus would play music before mosques and the Muslims, being in a very small minority, would have to yield.[191]

[185] Ibid., p. 40, 520.   [186] Ibid., p. 68.   [187] Ibid., pp. 46–7.
[188] Ibid., pp. 57, 63–4, 70, 72–3.   [189] Ibid., p. 38.
[190] Ibid., p. 48.   [191] Ibid., p. 63.

The government would give them no protection. In most of the cases cited in the Report, it was implied, if not definitely stated, that the number of Muslims killed or injured in communal riots exceeded that of the Hindus.[192]

Thus the Pirpur Report sought to embarrass Congress governments and also to instil in Muslims the fear that under 'Hindu' Raj they would always be a weak, powerless, and oppressed community.

The underlying cause behind the allegations made by the Muslim League against Congress governments was, as official British opinion quickly perceived, that it did not have effective political power. Administratively, it was felt that the League had little to complain of

'except that they do not have the general political influence, and the pull in petty local matters, that the supporters of the Ministry have. In essence the grievance is not a religious one, though it assumes an intensely communal form. It is political, and is due to the fact that the community is in opposition. It would largely cease to exist if the Muslim League had a share in the Government'.[193]

Official British opinion discounted the charges of atrocities and prejudice of Congress governments against Muslims. Linlithgow felt that 'proof of specific instances is not easily forthcoming . . .'.[194]

Sir Maurice Hallett, Governor of Bihar, said that he did not know of any case in which government or local officials had failed to take action against aggressors in communal riots. Muslims whom Hallett had met had 'admitted their inability to bring any charges of anti-Muslim prejudice against Government'.[195] It is worth remembering that in 1937, 58.69 per cent of ICS officers were British. In January 1940, the British held 64.8 per cent of the posts in the Indian Police Service.[196] It is difficult to believe that deliberate ill-treatment of Muslims would have gone on unnoticed and unrecorded by British officials in their confidential correspondence.

British officials infact supported the Congress view that the League was fomenting communal trouble in Congress-governed

[192] Ibid., pp. 71, 76, 77, 80.
[193] Haig to Linlithgow, 10 May 1939 and 3 June 1939, *HC*, vol. 6.
[194] Linlithgow to Zetland, 28 March 1939, *ZC*, vol. 17.
[195] Hallett to Linlithgow, 8 May 1939, *LC*, vol. 46.
[196] Home Establishments file no. 50/37, Home Establishments file no. 42/40.

provinces.[197] Sometimes issues of a very trivial nature could spark off a communal controversy, and, the case of Bihar showed that an indecisive government did not help matters. The Bihar ministry was reluctant to make any clear pronouncement on communal policy, which resulted in a piquant situation. The Muslim League in Bhagalpur took advantage of a suggestion in the provincial Legislative Assembly that custom should be the guiding principle regarding processions before mosques and the right to slaughter cows. A certain Hindu took out an idol in procession as he had done for many years. But he changed his residence and the procession was necessarily taken along a different route. There was therefore a departure from custom and the Muslims protested vigorously. The idol awaited the return journey while the Ministry 'are scratching their heads as to how they will deal with the situation.' The incident was trivial in itself but it was symptomatic of the desire of the Muslim League to embarrass the government at any cost. The indecisiveness of the Ministry created a near riot situation. The District Magistrate tried to mediate, but his influence was undermined by the circumstance that the Prime Minister himself had been listening to representations from both sides. The following year, the District Magistrate of Bhagalpur prohibited processions. This time, the Hindu Mahasabha protested and threatened satyagraha and the Prime Minister vacillated on the issue, for if the procession was allowed, the League would have a charge against the Ministry 'who are put in the difficult position of having to offend either Hindus or Muslims!'[198]

Opposition to the flag and Bande Mataram manifested itself soon after Congress ministries assumed office on September 1937. Congress leaders were quick to realize that the opposition was gaining strength, 'partly because of the thoughtless and inopportune action of our workers and sympathizers at certain places'.[199] But Congress governments usually dealt promptly with the situation. In Madras, the Prime Minister requested that the singing of Bande Mataram before assembly sessions be discontinued because of bad feeling stir-

[197] FRs for UP for July and September 1938, HP file nos. 18/7 and 18/9/38; FRs for Bihar for August and September 1938, HP file nos. 18/8 and 18/9/38.

[198] Stewart to Brabourne, 9 August 1938, 7 September 1938; *LC*, vol. 45, Hallett to Linlithgow, 5 August 1939, Ibid., vol. 46.

[199] Prasad to Patel, 28 September 1937, *RPC*, file II/37.

red up among Muslims.[200] By February 1938, agitation over the flag in Bihar was reported to be decreasing 'because Congress see clearly that it offends the Muslims and do not wish to press this issue.'[201] The official secret information report on Congress ministries had this to say on the flag and Bande Mataram at the end of 1938: 'Little is now heard of the exhibition of the Congress flag or the singing of Bande Mataram, except as a standing grievance of anti-Congress organizations'.[202] Congress ministries obviously moved fast to remove any causes of grievance.

Nevertheless, the Congress Working Committee was anxious to put the record straight. The Working Committee had already recommended in October 1937 that only the first two stanzas of the song Bande Mataram could be sung.[203] But in January 1939, the Committee decided, obviously in a defensive reaction to the Pirpur Report, that 'In regard to the Flag and to Bandemataram . . . we should avoid making this a matter of controversy as for (sic) as possible . . .'.[204]

The Congress Working Committee had also suggested that legal rights to cow slaughter as well as to music before mosques should be recognised and given effect to unless there was definite custom to the contrary. Nehru suggested that decisions on such matters should be taken after negotiations with the Muslim League, as 'it would be better than if a one-sided announcement was made. In a one-sided announcement that part which favoured one party would be accepted while the other party would be rejected'.[205]

British officials supported the Congress view that the Muslim League was often responsible for communal violence. 'Finding themselves unable to effect much by parliamentary methods, they are inevitably tempted to create unrest and disturbance outside the

[200] Erksine to Linlithgow, 7 March 1938, *EC*, vol. 13. See also FR for Madras for first half of March 1938, HP file no. 18/3/38.

[201] Hallett to Hubback, 8 February 1938, *LC*, vol. 34.

[202] *Quarterly Survey of Political and Constitutional Position of the British in India*, No. 6, p. 35, *LC*, vol. 142.

[203] Nehru to Jinnah, 6 April 1938, Pirzada, *Correspondence*, p. 119. The statement made by the CWC said that the first two stanzas were 'a living and inseparable part of our national movement . . . There is nothing in the stanzas to which any one can take exception.' *IAR*, 1937, vol. 2, p. 327.

[204] Draft Note by Gandhi on Hindu-Muslim Relations, AICC file no. G–34, 1939, pp. 65–9.

[205] Nehru to Pant, 16 January 1939, *NC*, vol. 79.

legislature, and there is no doubt that the Muslim League have set themselves quite deliberately to this policy.'[206] But Congress governments often hesitated to take action against the League for instigating communal violence—sometimes because of a seemingly intrinsic tendency to vacillate, as in the case of the Bihar government[207]—but more often because every effort on the part of governments to curb communalism 'is immediately represented as a breach of the elementary right of free speech and our Governments are fighting shy of strong measures.'[208] It was a forebearing Pant who informed Nehru in February 1938 that 'it will not be possible . . . to ignore their [the Muslim League's] activities of this type *any longer*.'[209] (Emphasis mine).

Congress leaders sought the cooperation of the League in resolving communal issues because they were aware that they did not enjoy much Muslim support, and because they recognized the psychological effect the League's propaganda could have on Muslims. This implies that they were anxious to conciliate, not the League, but the average Muslim voter. There is no evidence to suggest that any Congress leader between 1937 and 1939 was willing to accept the two major demands of the League—the recognition of its status as the 'sole' representative of Muslims, and the disbandment of the Congress Muslim Mass Contact Programme. The programme was started by Nehru, and many comments on it by other Congress leaders are not available, but there does not appear to be any evidence of disagreement over the aims of the programme within the Congress.[210]

There is, however, no doubt that the inception of the Programme contributed to an atmosphere of communal bitterness. It was because the success of the Programme would have spelt the defeat of the League that it roused Jinnah's ire. It was also natural that the campaign would stir some communal acrimony, as the League would turn to communal propaganda to counteract it.[211] But that

---

[206] Haig to Linlithgow, 23 October 1938, *HC*, vol. 2A.

[207] Hallett to Linlithgow, 7 April 1939, *LC*, vol. 46.

[208] AICC file no. G–32, 1938, p. 34.

[209] Pant to Nehru, 11 February 1938, *NC*, vol. 79.

[210] But see Gandhi's defence of the programme, Gandhi to Bashir Ahmad, 30 September 1937, *CWG*, vol. 66, p. 182.

[211] See, for example, FRs for Bihar and Bombay for first half of April 1937; Sind and CP for first half of May 1937; HP file nos. 18/4 and 18/5/37; FR for Sind for second half of May 1938, HP file no. 18/5/38.

did not mean that the Programme should never have been started. What was wrong with it was that it was carried out in a half hearted manner. It was 'totally unorganized. Except for the enrolment campaign of primary members, I do not think any other effort was made to come into direct contact with Muslims in large numbers'.[212] Consequently, it did not make much of a headway in any province. Instead, it left behind a residue of communal acrimony—the negative effect of the programme—without achieving the positive objective of winning Muslim mass support for the Congress.

The inception of the Muslim Mass Contact Programme had shown that the Congress recognized that it lacked a base among Muslims and considered it politically important to win their support. Why the programme was allowed to fizzle out by the summer of 1939, then, is something of a mystery. Why did the leadership not take more interest in the campaign? Was it because it was too involved in problems of party discipline and organization and the working of the Congress ministries? Was their implicit belief, that all Indians would eventually unite against the British, responsible for the lack of attention Congress leaders paid to the Muslim Mass Contact Programme? Whatever the reason, there can be no doubt that, in the long run, the failure of the campaign was an important factor in limiting the chances of the Congress in securing an undivided India.

The absence of prejudice against Muslims by Congress governments did not mean that communal elements were altogether absent from the organization. A Congress worker reported that an Arya Samaj preacher had become president of the Tehsil Congress Committee at Balrampur, and was advocating *shuddhi* and Hindu-Muslim unity simultaneously. Obviously it was felt that there would be 'great conflict, collision and mis-representation', if both things continued side by side.[213]

Communal prejudice and social reaction among Congressmen in Sind were reported to be alienating Muslims from the Congress in the province. Congress MLAs in Sind, who represented the trading and educated classes among the Hindus, 'cast away congress (sic) principles and programme (sic) to the winds, by obstructing and

[212] AICC file no. G-32, 1938, p. 15.
[213] Letter from Ambika Charan, 4 April 1937, AICC file no. P-20, p. 657.

sometimes even nipping in the bud legislation which aims at ame-
liorating (sic) the condition of Muslim masses in Sind who are
mainly agriculturists and are weighed down by poverty and
debts . . . As long as the congress (sic) is confined to the Urban Hindus, and acts as a cheap edition of the Hindu Mahasabha, there is no
very bright future for congress (sic) amongst the downtrodden and
ignorant muslim (sic) peasantry of Sind.'[214]

It was only in December 1938 that the Congress Working Committee passed a resolution defining the Muslim League and Hindu
Mahasabha as communal organizations.[215] Congress workers themselves were often confused about the relationship between the Congress and the Mahasabha. The Bengal PCC reported that they were
receiving enquiries from District Congress Committees if executives of Congress organizations could be members of the Hindu
Mahasabha simultaneously. 'In our belief, Congress Organisation
will suffer very much in prestige and hold over the masses, if Congress members be allowed to be members of the Hindu Mahasabha
Organisations.[216] Prior to the passing of the resolution in December
1938, a Congress worker from Sylhet pointed that no specific
organizations were mentioned as communal. 'If you think that the
Hindu Mahasabha is such an organisation public opinion must
assert itself and prevent the election of a member of Hindu Sabha to
Congress Committee'.[217] There does not seem to be evidence of disciplinary action taken against communal elements within the Congress. They deepened its Hindu religious hues; and must have dam-
pened Muslim enthusiasm for the organization.

The Congress attitude to tenancy legislation in Bengal and Bihar,
somewhat conservative in contrast to its policy in the UP, also provided Muslim Leaguers with an opportunity to accuse the Congress
of insincerity and communal prejudice. A supporter of the League
wrote that Congressmen had opposed the Tenancy Bill in Bengal
because 'most of the landlords there are Hindus and the peasants
Muslims. But in the UP they insist on an ill-conceived and

---

[214] Report on Communal Riots in Sukkur town submitted to the Congress
Working Committee by Abdul Qayyum, AICC file no. 1, 1939–1940, p. 18.

[215] *Bombay Chronicle*, 16 December 1939.

[216] Letter from Ashrafuddin Ahmad, Secretary, BPCC, to General Secretary,
AICC, 16 August 1938, AICC file no. P-5, 1938, pp. 131–3.

[217] Letter from Acting Office Secretary to Secretary, Habiganj Sub-divisional
Congress Committee, AICC file no. G-32, p. 33.

crooked tenancy law to persecute the landlords, no matter whether it would do real good to peasants or not, for the Muslims have some share in the land ownership . . . . But in Bihar, where Hindu land-lords are strong, the Congress readily entered in a compromise with them over the tenancy question.'[218]

There seems little to substantiate these allegations. Local conditions and the overall—somewhat contradictory—attitude of the Congress to tenancy legislation were the main factors which determined the stand taken up by provincial Congress organizations. The UP tenancy bill of 1939 was not as radical as it has been made out to be,[219] and, prior to the introduction of the bill in the legislature, Congressmen were generally using their influence to induce tenants to pay up their rents and to maintain harmonious relations with zamindars.[220] The Bihar ministry was embarrassed by kisan agitation in the province, but the Bihar Tenancy Bill did not go 'as far as the demands of the Kisan Sabha.'[221] The Congress legislative party in Bengal remained 'neutral' in the debate on the Tenancy Amendment Bill which was introduced by the Huq ministry in October 1937—which was given a communal colouring in a province where the majority of cultivators were Muslims. Sarat Chandra Bose, leader of the Congress legislative party said that while the Congress did not look upon the rights of landlords as something which could not be touched, it discouraged any attempt on the part of a section of the people to describe another section as exploiters.[222]

In the NWFP, the Congress made the most of its opportunities to consolidate its position. Through intensive propaganda and a number of popular measures, the Congress had become, by January 1938, 'practically unassailable in the rural areas.' The Congress ministry introduced several measures which ended the monopoly

---

[218] Jamil-ud-din Ahmad, 'Is India One Nation?' (1941) quoted by K.N. Chaudhuri, 'Economic Problems and Indian Independence,' in Philips and Wainwright (eds.), *Partition of India*, pp. 308–9.

[219] G. Pandey, 'Rural Base for Congress 1920–1940' in D.A. Low (ed.) *Congress and the Raj* (London, 1977), pp. 217–18.

[220] FRs for UP for first half of September and second half of October 1937. HP file no. 18/9 and 18/10/37 respectively.

[221] Prasad to Nehru, 23 November 1937, *RPC*, file I/37; and Max Harcourt, 'Kisan Populism and Revolution in Rural India: the 1942 Disturbances in Bihar and East United Provinces,' in Low (ed.), *Congress and the Raj*, pp. 304ff. See also Patel to Prasad, 4 December 1937, *RPC*, file II/37.

[222] *IAR*, 1937, vol. 2, p. 142.

the Khans had enjoyed for centuries, by abolishing the posts of Naubati chaukidari and zaildari, and by throwing open to election the post of Lambardari.[223]

In the Punjab, the Congress remained neutral in the voting on the Alienation of Land (Third Amendment) Bill, which was introduced by the Unionist Ministry in June 1938. The bill sought to place agriculturist moneylenders under the same disabilities as non-agriculturists in respect of permanent acquisition of land in settlement of debts. Agriculturists of all communities supported the bill, while the Hindu non-agricultural and moneylending classes protested against it. The Congress Working Committee asked the Congress parliamentary party to support the measure and Azad reminded them of their duty to give full and unstinted support to all legislation likely to ameliorate the condition of the masses. Non-agriculturist members of the Congress were unhappy over these instructions, for the party, though realizing the necessity for not alienating the agriculturists, was at the same time loath to lose the support of the commercial and non-agriculturist classes who financed it.[224] The strategy of provincial Congress leaders was to accuse the Unionists of deliberately causing a split between agriculturists and non-agriculturists, a strategy which only led to the Congress losing further ground in the rural areas.[225]

If, by the beginning of 1939, it was clear that the Congress had yet to win the support of the Muslim masses, it was also evident that Jinnah had still to find a political vantage point. His parleys with the Congress in 1938 combined with attacks on Congress ministries kept him on the political horizon, but they also revealed the weakness of his position, the fact that his only weapon against the Congress was negative and somewhat unconstructive. The alliances with Huq and Sikander prevailed uneasily, as Huq flirted, off and on, with the Congress and the breakaway branch of the KPP.[226] Sikander's recognition of Jinnah's position as leader of Muslims at the all India level did not imply any unquestioning obedience to him. In July 1939, he was at odds with him over the question of Muslim

[223] NWFP Governor's Report dated 10 and 24 January 1938, *LC*, vol. 72. See also Summary of events in NWFP, March 1937–February 1946, *CC*, vol. 17.

[224] FR for Punjab for first half of July 1938 and supplement to FR, and FR for second half of July 1938, HP file no. 18/7/38.

[225] FR for Punjab for first half of August 1938; HP file no. 18/8/38.

[226] See, for example, Sen, *Muslim Politics*, p. 121.

League support to the British in the event of a war.[227] In Sind, Jinnah had failed, time and again, to persuade the ruling Azad Muslim Party to accept the communal policy of the League; to overthrow the ministry because provincial Muslim Leaguers remained unable to sink their differences against Allah Baksh.[228] Dominated by indolent and unpopular feudal landlords in the NWFP, the League earned the nickname, 'Motor League,' because its members reportedly spent most of their time driving to tea parties![229] Except in Bengal, where it had organized some district level branches to counteract the Muslim Mass Contact Programme of the Congress,[230] the constructive work of the League was negligible, and the few feeble and ineffective appeals to the Muslims of Lucknow to end the Shia-Sunni controversy were an example of its lack of real influence over Muslims.[231]

It is obvious, then, that the alienation of Muslims from the Congress had obviously not united them or made them into supporters of the League by 1939. The politicization of electorates since 1937 had not necessarily resulted in success for communal parties like the League. This observation is important if we are to avoid one of the pitfalls of the Whig interpretation of history—of judging the past from hindsight and concluding that anti-Congress feeling had made Muslims a nation by 1939.

---

[227] Haig to Linlithgow, 1 July 1939, *HC*, vol. 2A.

[228] See for example, FR for Sind for first half of October 1938, HP file no. 18/10/38; Graham to Linlithgow, 9 January 1939, L/P & J/5/254. See also Graham to Linlithgow, 2 March 1938, Ibid.

[229] Entry for 23 May 1938, Cunningham diaries, vol. 3, *CC*. See also Cunningham to Linlithgow, 26 May 1938, *LC*, vol. 72.

[230] Sen, *Muslim Politics*, pp. 123–5.

[231] See, for example, Jinnah to Ispahani, 20 April 1939, *Jinnah–Ispahani Correspondence*, pp. 49–50. Also *Quarterly Survey of the Political and Constitutional Position of the British in India*, no. 8, p. 32, *LC* vol. 143.

CHAPTER 2

India and the War
September 1939 to December 1941

On 3 September 1939, a new chapter in Indian politics opened. The Viceroy announced India's entry into the war without consulting political parties, legislatures or provincial ministries.[1] Linlithgow's overriding objective was to turn India into a war base, and to provide men and money;[2] and he regarded the problem of winning the cooperation of Indian parties for the war effort to be one of 'particular urgency'.[3] The Viceroy admitted that those in the Central Legislature as it stood did 'not necessarily' contain the men who were most representative of public opinion. His Executive Council would also have to be strengthened with more non-officials.[4] He attached the greatest importance to winning the support of Gandhi and Nehru, because of their popular appeal,[5] for the war effort. As late as May 1941 Linlithgow wrote home to Amery:

'... I should myself regard it as unjustified in the light of all the teachings of history to try to proscribe or to ignore a great political party which represents unquestionably the spearhead of nationalism in this country ... I have often wondered what is in the Mahatma's mind. Of course, he has been an intolerable nuisance since the beginning of the war. On the other hand, I do not believe that he wants our enemies to win this war ... what he is really concerned to do is to maintain his nuisance, and his bargaining value at as high a level as possible, with a view to the post-war discussions ... his desire is to keep the pot simmering but not boiling'.[6]

The other, more pressing, reason for seeking the cooperation of political parties for the war effort was to expand the numbers and to preserve the loyalty of the army, the ultimate bulwark of the

---

[1] Reginald Coupland, *The Indian Problem* (Oxford, 1944), p. 212.

[2] Linlithgow's report of his conversation with W. Philips, President Roosevelt's personal representative, 19 February 1943, *TOP*, vol. 3, p. 689.

[3] Linlithgow to Zetland, 31 August 1939, ZC, vol. 18.

[4] Linlithgow to Zetland, 5 September 1939, Ibid.

[5] Linlithgow to Zetland, 5 September and 4 October 1939, Ibid.

[6] Linlithgow to Amery, 15 May 1941, *LC*, vol. 10.

Empire. Hence the Viceroy began talks with Indian leaders to probe their terms for supporting the British. The attitude of Gandhi, who said that he contemplated the present struggle 'With an English heart,' 'could not have been better.' Throughout the talks, Linlithgow was 'profoundly moved' by Gandhi's sympathy for England; and he hoped that Gandhi would be able to 'keep things on the right line' at the CWC meeting on 14 September, especially on the matter of defence liaison.[7]

Linlithgow knew that Indian parties would require political concessions in return for their support of the war effort.[8] Jinnah hoped to extract from the Viceroy a promise that the British would jettison the idea of federation. The working of provincial autonomy had shown how 'Hindus' would behave if they were in a majority, and the Congress ministries should be turned out 'at once.'[9]

Linlithgow, however, saw no reason to give up the idea of federation and majority rule altogether. Jinnah's hold over the provincial Muslim Leagues was insecure; and his demand was probably a tactic to keep the Muslim League in tow, especially as Sikander Hyat Khan and Fazlul Huq had already promised the British unconditional support for the war effort against his wishes, and his disposition to bargain.[10] Jinnah's leadership was under fire from radicals in the League, Ispahani, for example, voiced 'their utmost regret and disappointment that you are gradually drifting more and more into the arms of the reactionaries and "jee hoozoors" [yes men].' Sikander had challenged the 'potency of the Muslim League . . . you as President . . . had chosen to keep silent . . . is it not time that you take stock of the whole situation and put your foot down with firmness?'[11]

As a 'public man who had to think of his followers,'[12] Jinnah had to tread a path which would preserve unity as well as his own authority within the League. He now placed his cards on the table. 'If . . . Britain wants to prosecute this war successfully, it must take Muslim India into its confidence through its accredited

---

[7] Linlithgow to Zetland, 5 September 1939 and Enclosure on his talks with Gandhi on 4 September 1939, ZC, vol. 18.

[8] Linlithgow to Zetland, 24 August 1939, Ibid.

[9] Linlithgow to Zetland, 5 September 1939, Ibid.

[10] Ibid.

[11] Ispahani to Jinnah, 12 December 1939, Zaidi, *Jinnah–Ispahani Correspondence*, p. 133. See also Raghunandan Saran to Nehru, 24 October 1939, *NC*, Vol. 84.

[12] Linlithgow to Zetland, 5 September 1939, ZC, vol. 18.

organization—the All-India Muslim League . . . Muslims want justice and fair play.'[13]

Coming as it did after a combative Congress resolution,[14] Jinnah's statement seemed to the Viceroy 'not on the whole unsatisfactory'.[15] While avoiding the impression of meddling in the politics of the Muslim community, Linlithgow's endeavour 'obviously must be to do all that I can to get *all* sections of the Muslim community into line behind us.'[16]

In the Congress Working Committee, Gandhi was alone in suggesting unconditional support for the British on a non-violent basis.[17] The Congress resolved on 14 September 1939, that the issue of war and peace 'must be decided by the Indian people, and no outside authority can impose this decision upon them, nor can the Indian people permit their resources to be exploited for imperialist ends.' The British government was invited 'to declare in unequivocal terms what their war aims are in regard to democracy and imperialism and the new world order that is envisaged; in particular, how these aims are going to apply to India and . . . be given effect to in the present.'[18]

In response to the Congress demand for a declaration of British war aims, Linlithgow thought the British should reiterate 'that we are not concerned with the form of government of particular countries; that what we are concerned to ensure and achieve is in the first place the restoration of good faith and of confidence in dealings between nations: in the second place the discharge of our treaty obligations.'[19] If the Congress was going to show itself 'entirely intransigent,' and if it became clear that Congress ministries would continue in office only 'at the price of promises or immediate concessions which you [Amery] and I are not in a position to make, it may appear expedient to call an all-parties conference, at which the

[13] *Times of India*, 9 September 1939.

[14] *IAR*, 1939, vol. 2, p. 261.

[15] Linlithgow to Haig, 8 September 1939, *LC*, vol. 102. See also Linlithgow to Zetland, 7 September 1939, Ibid., vol. 8.

[16] Linlithgow to Lumley, 9 September 1939, Ibid., vol. 53, and Linlithgow to Haig, 8 September 1939, Ibid., vol. 102.

[17] *Harijan*, 23 September 1939. See also Sitaramayya, *History of the Indian National Congress*, vol. 2, pp. 130–5.

[18] Congress Resolution on India and the War, J. Nehru, *The Unity of India* (New York, 1942), pp. 410–14.

[19] Linlithgow to Zetland, 18 September 1939, *ZC*, vol. 18.

hollowness of the Congress claim to speak for India would very soon be exposed.'[20] So, although Gandhi told him that what was needed was a declaration 'of a satisfying kind, rather than a great deal in the field of action,' the Viceroy told him that there was no prospect of amending the Act of 1935 at that stage. 'I added that it was not a question of fighting for democracy . . . to which I did not think that His Majesty's Government had ever committed themselves in the slightest degree'.[21] A consultative liaison group could be set up—and the British cabinet only agreed to this slight concession after Linlithgow had assured them that such a Committee would have no chance at all to entrench itself too deeply in the machinery of government.[22]

Nevertheless, Linlithgow still hoped to woo the Congress into cooperation with the war effort. They were after all the largest and most important party in British India and were responsible for the governments of nine provinces, and the British should be ready to turn to their advantage such readiness as the Congress Right might show to work with them. Linlithgow regarded the 'nuisance value of Congress, if they turn against us, as very substantial . . . Commander-in-Chief agrees with me, that they have it in their power in that event largely to cripple our capacity to exert our maximum strength in the war'. So it was worthwhile to take some risk to secure the support of the Congress.[23]

In the light of the Congress attitude, meanwhile, the Muslim League resolution of 18 September had given the Viceroy what he badly needed to resist Congress demands. The League offered its support for the war effort if the Viceroy would take its leaders into confidence and accept the League as 'the only organisation that can speak on behalf of Muslim India.'[24] In contrast to Congress, the League was not interested in an independent, united and democratic India: it resolved that such a system was 'totally unsuited to the genius of the peoples of this country which is composed of various nationalities and does not constitute a national state.'[25]

[20] Linlithgow to Zetland, 21 September 1939, Ibid.
[21] Linlithgow to Zetland, 27 September 1939; Enclosure containing note of interview between Viceroy and Gandhi on 26 September 1939, *LC*, vol. 8. See also Enclosure to Linlithgow to Zetland, 4 October 1939, Ibid.
[22] CAB 67/1, W.P. (G) (39) 24 Secretary of State to Viceroy, 27 September 1939.
[23] Viceroy to Secretary of State, (T) 11 October 1939, *ZC*, vol. 26.
[24] *National Herald*, 19 September 1939.
[25] *National Herald*, 20 September 1939.

If the League's resolution was aimed at frustrating a possible settlement between the Congress and the British, it succeeded. Zetland decided that the British could not meet Congress demands, and, in the present situation, they should avoid offering them any concession which might antagonize the League.[26]

Although most Congress leaders were put off by the Muslim League resolution, in an attempt to draw the League into a united nationalist front, they offered an impartial enquiry into Muslim grievances against their ministries. Jinnah's rejection of this olive branch seemed to some Congress leaders to have 'practically barred the door' to any settlement.[27] Nevertheless, mindful of the need for unity among Indian parties at this time, Nehru and Azad still hoped to bring Jinnah to terms, and were willing to discuss any Congress-League differences with him.[28] At the Nehru-Jinnah talks between 16 and 18 October 1939, it was obvious that the real difference between the two men lay in their attitude to the British. Jinnah wanted the Congress to give up its anti-imperialist policy. According to Nehru, 'On no account did he [Jinnah] countenance any action on our part which might lead to a conflict with British Government (sic) . . . under the circumstances he felt that unless this matter was cleared up, other important questions did not arise'.[29]

Meanwhile, Linlithgow was frustrated both with the political deadlock and with the British government's failure to define their political objectives—'that is, if H.M.G. know what their political objectives are.'[30] He knew that the statement which he had been authorized to issue would not satisfy the Congress.[31] The Viceroy stated that, for the time being, the British would not define their war aims, but they would be willing to consult with representatives of different communities, parties and interests in India and with the Indian princes to discuss constitutional reforms for India after the war. The Viceroy added that representatives of minorities had urged most strongly on him the necessity of a clear assurance that full weight would be given to their views and interests in any modifica-

---

[26] Memorandum by Zetland on India and the War dated 25 September 1939, War Cabinet W.P. (G) (39) 21, *ZC*, vol. 26.

[27] Prasad to Azad, 13 October 1939, *RPC*, file no. XIV/40.

[28] Nehru to Prasad, 16 and 17 October 1939, Ibid., file no. 3–C/39.

[29] Nehru to Zakir Husain, 25 November 1939, *NC*, vol. 104.

[30] Viceroy to Secretary of State, (T), 11 October 1939, *ZC*, vol. 26.

[31] Linlithgow to Prasad, 16 October 1939, *RPC*, file no. 2–P/39. See also Linlithgow to Zetland, 16 October 1939, *LC*, vol. 8.

tions that might be contemplated. This assurance the Viceroy readily gave.[32]

The statement fell far short of Congress demands, and there was little hope of winning the party's cooperation in the war effort. Rajendra Prasad regretted that 'a great opportunity has been missed.'[33]

Jinnah hastened to make political capital out of the Viceroy's statement, exaggerating the strength of his position. The MLWC claimed that the British Government had 'emphatically repudiated the unfounded claim of the Congress that they alone represent all India . . .'. Referring to Linlithgow's assurance that the British would not ignore representatives of minorities, the resolution noted with satisfaction, though, as British officials acknowledged,[34] not very accurately, 'that his (sic) Majesty's Government recognise the fact that the All-India Muslim League alone truly represents the Muslims of India and can speak on their behalf . . .'. Accordingly, the Working Committee empowered Jinnah, as President of the League, to assure Britain of Muslim support and cooperation during the war.[35]

Linlithgow was relieved at the Muslim League resolution, while noting that it would be wrong to assume 'that the present Moslem attitude will long persist. Their platform is essentially anti-national and anti-democratic, and I feel sure their younger leaders will soon grow restive about a policy so utterly sterile. I therefore do not regard Moslem support as something upon which, by itself, we can safely afford to build any long term policy.' Linlithgow's feelings about the Congress remained ambivalent. 'It would be much easier to deal with the situation that confronts us had the Congress claims not been pitched so high.'[36]

A few days later, after the League had resolved that the 'entire problem of India's future constitution . . . be considered "de novo",'[37] Linlithgow concluded that the safeguards for Muslims which were demanded by the League were 'quite incompatible'

[32] *National Herald*, 18 October 1939.

[33] Prasad to Linlithgow, 18 October 1939, *RPC*, file no. 2–P/39.

[34] (This assumption seems a large one). *Quarterly Survey of the Political and Constitutional Position of the British in India*, no. 7, p. 25, *LC*, vol. 143.

[35] *National Herald*, 23 October 1939.

[36] Viceroy to Secretary of State (T), 24 October 1939, *ZC*, vol. 26. See also Linlithgow to Zetland, 22 October 1939, Ibid., vol. 18.

[37] *National Herald*, 26 October 1939.

with any relaxation of British control over India.[38] Congress leaders accused the British of using Congress–League differences as an excuse to avoid political advance.[39] Zetland's speech in the House of Lords on 18 October had been a pointer to British policy in the days to come.[40] Linlithgow later agreed that the policy of the League could be criticized as 'the sole, or most important' obstacle to the achievement of Indian independence,[41] while Jinnah himself admitted that his attitude was exposing him to a very formidable indictment—that he was a supporter of imperialism.[42]

Samuel Hoare's speech in the House of Commons on 28 October ensured that the political stalemate would persist. Partly conciliatory, partly admonitory, he pointed to the absence of unity amongst Indians themselves as the main obstacle to Dominion Status. The Congress, he insisted, should join the Viceroy's consultative committee. The alternative was non-cooperation, which would lead to civil disobedience, to breaches of law and order and repression.[43] For the Congress, Rajendra Prasad concluded that Hoare's speech 'has not carried anything further . . . there does not seem to be any intention of parting with the power (sic) at present to any extent and making definite promise (sic) of doing so at the end of the war.' There was thus 'no point of contact.'[44] As a result, on 30 October 1939, the CWC ordered the Congress ministries to resign.

The Congress decision to withdraw from office deprived Jinnah and the League of their chief weapon of attack against it—the Muslim grievances against Congress ministries. On the other hand, Linlithgow was now all the more dependent on the League as a counterpoise to the Congress. Dismayed by the Congress attitude to the war effort, the Viceroy shaped his policy in an attempt to attract both the Congress and the League into his Council, while discouraging them from uniting against the British.[45] On 1 November, at a meeting with Jinnah, Prasad and Gandhi, he placed a veto on political advance in Jinnah's hands by stipulating that

---

[38] Viceroy to Secretary of State, (T), 22 October 1939, ZC, vol. 26.
[39] *National Herald*, 26 October 1939.
[40] *Times of India*, 20 October 1939.
[41] Linlithgow to Zetland, 28 November 1939, *LC*, vol. 13.
[42] Linlithgow to Zetland, 16 January 1940, Ibid., vol. 9.
[43] *Times of India*, 30 October 1939.
[44] Prasad to B. Shiva Rao, 28 October 1939, *RPC* file no. 2–P/39.
[45] CAB 67/2 W.P. (G) (39) 53. Viceroy to Secretary of State, 22 October 1939.

there could be no agreement about the centre unless the two parties came to an agreement about the provinces.[46] No such agreement was possible in November 1939. The Congress would not contemplate any coalition with Jinnah unless he clarified his position on the Viceroy's broadcast of 18 October.[47]

Congress leaders, of course, were dismayed that Linlithgow was encouraging the pretensions of the League to put off the question of independence, but decided that there was little use in talking further to Jinnah. While he could rely on the British so much, the Congress could do nothing to satisfy him. Jinnah would exploit the situation to ask for even more than the British were willing to give or guarantee. Therefore, Congress leaders inferred, there would be no limit to his demands.

Linlithgow was gratified at Jinnah's refusal to support the Congress demand for a declaration of British war aims. Summing up the British position, the Viceroy observed that had the British been confronted with a joint demand, 'the strain upon me and upon H.M.G. would have been very great indeed.' At the same time, Linlithgow was aware of the intrinsic weakness of Jinnah's political position. 'I thought . . . I could claim to have vested interest in his position, and I had been asking myself how far that position was intrinsically sound. But I was bound to confess that I did not like it.' The 'eroding effect of nationalism' on Jinnah's platform was likely to be swift and serious.[48] Jinnah was also unreliable, and Linlithgow had feared 'a *volte face* of the most drastic character at the shortest notice' during their discussions with Gandhi. Jinnah's demands were exorbitant, and there was no case for abandoning federation and the principle of majority rule altogether. But the wise course would be to give him brief and reassuring replies, 'and to give even fuller weight than we may have done in the past in such public statements as you and I may have to make on Indian policy generally'.[49] Apparently, the Viceroy did not think much of the chances of Muslim political communalism standing up against Congress nationalism at the end of 1939.

[46] Note of interview between Viceroy, Prasad, Gandhi and Jinnah on 1 November 1939; enclosed in Linlithgow to Zetland, 2 November 1939, *LC*, vol. 8.
[47] Ibid.
[48] Note of interview between Linlithgow and Jinnah on 4 November 1939; Enclosure no. 2 of Linlithgow to Zetland, 6 November 1939, *LC*, vol. 8.
[49] Linlithgow to Zetland, 5 November 1939, Ibid.

Jinnah's refusal to support the Congress demand for independence had indeed weakened his position. With the Congress out of the way, the League had to find a new course of action. Jinnah could not openly support the British, for he would not have been able to carry the League with him. The Congress would not discuss provincial matters with him except on the basis of a British declaration, which was not forthcoming. So Jinnah would have to wait for political developments.

So Jinnah adopted a strategy to keep anti-Congress feeling high He called on Muslims to observe 22 December as 'the day of deliverance and thanksgiving as a mark of relief that the Congress Governments have at last ceased to function.'[50] The call surprised many of his own party, for Muslims in the NWFP and Bengal thought that he had fallen back on a low form of politicking.[51] Deliverance Day itself passed off quietly in most places, and 'fell very flat' in the Muslim majority provinces of Sind and the NWFP;[52] but naturally it infuriated Congress leaders. 'There is a limit even to political falsehood and indecency but all limits have been passed', wrote Nehru. 'I do not see how I can even meet Jinnah now.'[53]

In December 1939, Huq published a series of articles in the League press,[54] and in January 1940, the Bihar Muslim League brought out a report on the grievances of Muslims in Bihar under Congress ministries,[55] on lines similar to those of the Pirpur Report of 1938. In reply the Congress suggested an inquiry into the charges by a federal judge, which Jinnah refused. An impartial inquiry perhaps would have deprived the allegations of their propaganda value for the League. Instead he asked for a Royal Commission to investigate the charges, knowing that the Congress would not agree,

[50] Quoted in Bolitho, *Jinnah Creator of Pakistan*, p. 124.

[51] Entries for 12 and 16 December 1939, Cunningham Diaries, vol. 3, *CC*. See also Ispahani to Jinnah, 12 December 1939, Zaidi, *Jinnah-Ispahani Correspondence*, p. 132.

[52] FRs for Punjab, UP, CP, Sind and NWFP for second half of December 1939, HP file no. 18/12/39. See also NWFP Governor's Report date 23 December 1939, *LC*, vol. 74.

[53] Nehru to Mahadev Desai, 9 December 1939, *NC*, vol. 17.

[54] Published as *Muslim Sufferings Under Congress Rule*. A copy is available in L/I/628.

[55] *All-India Muslim League (Bihar Province) Publicity Committee: Report . . . on some Grievances of the Muslims 1938–9*, President S.M. Shareef. (Shareef Report) (Patna, 1940).

as it would have implied acquiescence in British intervention in Indian affairs.[56]

The Viceroy saw little substance in Jinnah's charges, but, as he had commented earlier, 'the existence of the atmosphere is the thing that matters and the thing to which we have to give weight in formulating our policy and reaching our conclusions.'[57] British officials maintained a deliberate silence about their opinion of the League's exaggerated charges against Congress ministries, while Sir Hugh O'Neill, Under Secretary of State for India, announced in the Commons that no inquiry would be held into the allegations as no purpose would be served by it. Jinnah replied that O'Neill's statement had imposed 'an additional task upon us.' The charges against Congress ministries must be investigated in order to prevent a recurrence in future.[58] By repeating his demand for an enquiry, Jinnah, with some help from the British, kept alive 'Muslim sufferings' under Congress rule.

Evidently Jinnah did not want a settlement with Congress. When Linlithgow asked him if he would be able to settle with Congress if the British assured him that no constitutional departure would be made without the approval of the League, he replied, ' "But what have you to lose if no agreement is reached?" '[59] And so the political *impasse* continued. The British had no intention of giving way to Congress demands, and noted the disparity between the personal friendliness of Congress leaders and their politically tough attitude.[60] Both Linlithgow and Whitehall stood firm. The Act of 1935 had been passed not to terminate the Empire but to preserve it. The War Cabinet turned down Zetland's proposal for any concessions to Congress, insisting that talk of independence within the Empire' should be avoided in favour of 'autonomous communities within the Empire.' Such terminology was less likely to imply the right of secession from the Empire. So long as the Congress and League remained divided, the Viceroy could mark time and wait until the pieces on the political chess-board had taken their place.[61]

---

[56] *Bombay Chronicle*, 16 December 1939.

[57] Linlithgow to Zetland, 28 November 1939, *LC*, vol. 13.

[58] *National Herald*, 26 and 29 January 1940.

[59] Linlithgow to Zetland, 16 January 1940, *LC*, vol. 9.

[60] *Quarterly Survey of the Political and Constitutional Position of the British in India*, no. 9, p. 25.

[61] See R.J. Moore, *Churchill Cripps and India, 1939–45*, (Oxford, 1979), p. 26. See, for example, Linlithgow to Zetland, 18 December 1939, *LC*, vol. 8.

While the British ruled by ordinance, introduced press censorship, and rounded up Congressmen in many places, the Congress Working Committee, meeting at Patna on 1 March 1940, discussed the possibility of civil disobedience as soon as organization permitted and circumstances demanded. The Ramgarh Congress on 20 March reaffirmed the Patna resolution. Freedom could not exist within the orbit of British rule, and the Congress could not be a party to the war without British guarantees for a Constituent Assembly based on adult suffrage and independence. For Congress, there could be no solution to the communal problem except through the Constituent Assembly, where the rights of minorities would be protected by agreement between the representatives of various communities.[62]

The political stalemate was also worrying Jinnah. His platform of blank negation was wearing out, for the Congress resolutions at Patna and Ramgarh were passed in spite of League hostility and its intensification of communal tension over the last three months. Even Linlithgow was tiring of Jinnah's tactics and had advised him to formulate constructive suggestions for a political settlement. Jinnah sulked at the British refusal to break with Gandhi,[63] and warned Linlithgow 'not to sell the pass behind their [League's] backs.'[64] In Bengal, Huq was engaged in one of his intermittent flirtations with the Congress;[65] and in the NWFP, the possibility of an intercommunal ministry appeared imminent.[66] Muslim Leaguers themselves were urging Jinnah to define the party's goals;[67] some even suggested a Congress–League pact.[68] There was, then, not much sign of a solid Muslim political front in the early months of 1940.

Against this background, on 23 March 1940, the Muslim League passed its celebrated 'Pakistan' resolution at Lahore. It declared that no constitutional plan would be acceptable to Muslims unless

'geographically contiguous units are demarcated into regions which should be so constituted, with such territorial readjustments as may be necessary, that the areas in which the Muslims are numerically in a

[62] *IAR*, 1940, vol. 1, p. 218.
[63] Viceroy to Secretary of State, (T), 6 February 1940, *LC*, vol. 19.
[64] Linlithgow to Zetland, (T), 16 March 1940, *LC*, vol. 74.
[65] Herbert to Linlithgow, 2/3 January and 6 February 1940, Ibid., vol. 40.
[66] Entry for 13 February 1940, Cunningham Diaries, vol. 4, *CC*.
[67] *National Herald*, 20 February 1940.
[68] *National Herald*, 26 February 1940.

majority, as in the North-Western and Eastern zones of India, should be grouped to constitute Independent States in which the constituent units shall be autonomous and sovereign.'[69]

Although this was the first time that any Muslim party had adopted 'Pakistan' for a policy, the idea was not entirely new. The notion of a Muslim homeland in north-west and north-east India was made possible, not by the fact that the majority of Indian Muslims lived in the Muslim provinces—indeed, more than 60 per cent lived in the Muslim minority provinces—but because of what has been described as an 'accident of geography'[70]: that there happened to be four provinces in which Muslims were in a majority. Without these Muslim majority areas, communalism would have existed in India but it seems inconceivable that any section of Muslims would have been able to demand any kind of "homeland." The Aga Khan and Muhammad Iqbal were among the first to moot the idea of a Muslim homeland, and the term "Pakistan" was coined by Chaudhury Rahmat Ali, a student at Cambridge, in 1933. In the summer of 1939, Sikander Hyat Khan had published a scheme for the loosest of federations, with regional or zonal legislatures to deal with common subjects. In January 1940, Dr. Abdul Latif of Hyderabad had outlined a plan for a minimal federation of homogeneous cultural zones.[71] In March 1939, Khaliquzzaman had discussed the possibility of partition with Zetland[72] and in September Jinnah had suggested it to Linlithgow as a political alternative to federation.[73] In February 1940, Aurangzeb Khan, provincial League leader in the NWFP, told Cunningham that the League proposed to press for a Muslim homeland in the northwest and northeast of India in direct units with the Crown.[74] On 4 March, Jinnah told Edward Benthall, Finance Member in the Viceroy's Executive, that Muslims would not be safe without partition,[75] and twelve days later, he told Linlithgow that if the British could not resolve the political deadlock,

[69] Pirzada, *Documents*, p. 341.

[70] S.R. Mehrotra, 'The Congress and the Partition of India,' in Philips and Wainwright (eds.), *Partition of India*, p. 201.

[71] For these partition schemes see Gwyer and Appadorai, *Speeches and Documents on the Indian Constitution*, vol. 2, pp. 435–65.

[72] Khaliquzzaman, *Pathway to Pakistan*, pp. 205–8.

[73] Note of interview between Linlithgow and Jinnah on 4 September 1939; Enclosure 2, Linlithgow to Zetland, 5 September 1939, ZC, vol. 18.

[74] Entry for 13 February 1940, Cunningham Diaries, vol. 4, CC.

[75] Entry for 4 March 1940, Benthall Diaries, *Benthall Collection*.

the League would have no option but to fall back on some form of partition.[76]

That Jinnah envisaged a sovereign Pakistan was clear from his assertion at Lahore, that 'The problem in India is not of an intercommunal character, but manifestly of an international one and must be treated as such.'[77] By international, as Professor Mansergh points out, he meant literally as between nations.[78] The demand for a sovereign Pakistan answered both Linlithgow's criticism that he was unconstructive, and the indictment that he was not supporting the Congress demand because he was on the imperial side. It has often been argued that Jinnah's call for a sovereign Pakistan was simply a ploy to secure the League a vantage point at the centre. But even if the demand was mere tactics, the tactics must have been aimed at achieving something or preventing something. Prevention would surely be of a Congress–British agreement bypassing the Muslim League. In that case, Jinnah, as we have seen, preferred the prevalence of the differences between them and the maintenance of the status quo, that is, the continuation of the Raj. On the other hand, if he wanted to achieve something, why not a sovereign Pakistan? The League's weak position in the provinces need not have put him off from making the demand; he might get more popular support for an idea which promised Muslims salvation from imagined 'Hindu' domination. The League's poor position in the Muslim majority provinces probably introduced the element of calculation in the demand. A man of Jinnah's political shrewdness and dialectical skill might have calculated that, from political expediency, the British would not reject the possibility of Pakistan, because the very existence of the idea would help them to repudiate the Congress demand for independence.

Jinnah calculated correctly. On 23 March 1940, Linlithgow wrote that the British should mark time. To the Viceroy, the Lahore resolution was the answer to Patna and Ramgarh, showing 'how deep is the gulf and how little the prospect of these two parties getting together in the present circumstances.'[79] On 9 April, the War

---

[76] Viceroy to Secretary of State, (T), 16 March 1940, *LC*, vol. 19.

[77] Pirzada, *Documents*, p. 337.

[78] Mansergh, *Prelude to Partition*, p. 27.

[79] Linlithgow to Lumley, 23 March 1940, *LC*, vol. 54, and Linlithgow to Herbert, 28 March 1940, R/3/2/14. See also Viceroy to Secretary of State, (T), 6 April 1940, *LC*, vol. 19.

Cabinet decided that the Lahore resolution had 'complicated' the situation, and that it was difficult for the Viceroy to announce any positive policy.[80] On 18 April, Zetland stated in the House of Lords that agreement among Indian communities was essential if the vision of a united India was to become a reality, and added that the British could not force a constitution on the Muslims.[81] This statement could only be interpreted as an indication that partition would henceforth be one of the options to be kept open by the British in India. Indeed, on 8 April, Linlithgow had cautioned Zetland against overemphasizing the unacceptability of the Pakistan scheme—'it would be politically unfortunate'—and it 'might be pressed' after the war.[82]

Many Muslim politicians, as Linlithgow himself observed, were 'unhappy' about the Lahore resolution.[83] No Muslim minister in Sind favoured it;[84] and Allah Baksh, the erstwhile Premier of Sind, described it as 'harmful and fantastic.'[85] The interest the resolution aroused in the NWFP can be gauged from the fact that neither Cunningham nor the Chief Secretary mentioned it in their reports in March or April 1940. In Bengal, Fazlul Huq, who moved the resolution at Lahore, was talking, only a month later, of working for a united India.[86]

These reactions of Muslim politicians from the Muslim majority provinces suggest that the call for Pakistan was not an expression of the political aspirations of a solid Muslim communal nationality from below, but those of Jinnah and his all India Committee from above. Nevertheless, the evidence does leave open the possibility that from Jinnah's point of view the demand for Pakistan was required as a tactic to gain more cooperation from, and control over, Muslim provincial politicians, whether within or without the League, by appealing to and arousing Muslim communal sentiment.

The sharp reactions of Congress, Hindu Mahasabha and Sikh leaders to the Pakistan resolution, along with the calculated silence

[80] War Cabinet W.P. (G) (40) 96, Memorandum by Zetland, 9 April 1940, ZC, vol. 26.

[81] *Times of India*, 20 April 1940.

[82] Viceroy to Secretary of State, (T), 8 April 1940, *LC*, vol. 19.

[83] Viceroy to Secretary of State, (T), 6 April 1940, *LC*, vol. 19.

[84] Graham to Linlithgow, 9 April 1940, L/P&J/5/256.

[85] *Tribune*, 28 April 1940.

[86] *Tribune*, 29 April 1940.

of the British on the subject, gave more substance to the demand for Pakistan than perhaps it deserved. Rajagopalachari described the two-nation theory as 'a mischievous concept . . . that threatens to lead India into destruction.'[87] Hindu Mahasabha leaders conjured up—prophetically—visions of civil war;[88] Satyamurti accused Jinnah of wanting on a smaller scale what Hitler wanted in Europe.[89] Nehru declared that the Congress would not have anything to do with the 'mad scheme' of the Muslim League and ruled out the possibility of any settlement or negotiations.[90] Gandhi expressed the emotion of Indian nationalism with an idealism which was defined by his understanding of his religion: 'I am proud of being a Hindu, but I have never gone to anybody as a Hindu to secure Hindu-Muslim unity. My Hinduism demands no pacts.'[91] 'Partition means a patent untruth. My whole soul rebels against the idea that Hinduism and Islam represent two antagonistic cultures and doctrines. To assent to such a doctrine is for me a denial of God. For I believe with my whole soul that the God of the Quran is also the God of Gita . . . I must rebel against the idea that millions who were Hindus the other day changed their nationality on adopting Islam as their religion.'[92]

And so the Lahore resolution, until now the dream of theorists, was put forward by an important political organization as a serious aim, and it altered the complexion of Indian politics. Its practicability for the time being was irrelevant, and it was given some substance by the sharp reactions of its opponents. It hoisted the banner of Muslim separation, at least partly because the British chose to ignore nationalist Muslim opinion, and dealt only with Jinnah 'on the Muslim side'.[93]

Its political ramifications on the provincial as well as all India level ensured that the Pakistan resolution could not be ignored. It stirred the politics of the Punjab partly because it gave Jinnah a foothold in the province and partly because of the uncertain future it held out for the Sikhs, who were a minority in every district of the province which was their homeland. Behind his silence on the Lahore resolution lay Sikander's political debt to Jinnah. On 28 February, his Unionist ministry had banned the carrying of arms

[87] *Bombay Chronicle*, 27 March 1940.   [88] *Tribune*, 25 March 1940.
[89] *Tribune*, 26 March 1940.   [90] *Tribune*, 14 April 1940.
[91] *Harijan*, 30 March 1940.   [92] *Harijan*, 13 April 1940.
[93] Linlithgow to Amery, 14 May 1940, *LC*, vol. 9.

under the Defence of India Act and the police had fired on the Khaksars, a semi-military organization of Muslims, who had defied the ban. On the eve of the Muslim League session at Lahore, Sikander's Muslim opponents in the Unionist party demanded an enquiry into the police firing and urged removal of the ban on the Khaksars. Banners proclaiming "Sikander murdabad" [death to Sikander] were hoisted near the entrance to the hall where the session was to be held. Sikander was indebted to Jinnah for shelving discussion of the issue at the open session of the League: Jinnah thus avoided a clash between a government headed by a Muslim and a Muslim organization, safeguarded the position of the Punjab ministry, but also maintained the unity of the League in a very difficult situation, and increased his influence over Leaguers in the Punjab.[94]

So Sikander was safe for the time being, but he was in no position to oppose the Pakistan resolution, although he knew that it would place his intercommunal coalition under a strain. The first sign of restiveness within the coalition came from Sikander's Sikh colleagues, the Khalsa Nationalist Party. The exact nature of Pakistan had been left undefined at Lahore. The Lahore resolution promised that 'adequate, effective and mandatory safeguards should be specifically provided in the constitution for minorities . . . for the protection of their religious, cultural, economic, political, administrative and other rights and interests in consultation with them'[95], without spelling out the least idea of what would be considered adequate and effective. As the League had dismissed similar assurances to Muslims, Tara Singh could well argue that if Muslims could not trust the Hindu majority they should also presume that the Sikhs could not trust the Muslim majority in the Punjab.[96] If, as the Raja of Mahmudabad had suggested at Lahore, Pakistan was to be an Islamic state, based on the *Sharia*,[97] the Sikhs had reason to be alarmed.

After giving up all hope of agreement with the League, the majority of the CWC persuaded Gandhi that the Congress must embark on civil disobedience. Action was necessary to avoid demoralization in Congress ranks; the problem of civil disobedience against a back-

[94] *Quarterly Survey of the Political and Constitutional Position of the British in India*, no. 11, pp. 11–12 and 26; Craik to Linlithgow, 31 March 1940 and 8 April 1940, *LC*, vol. 89.

[95] Pirzada, *Documents*, p. 341.

[96] *Times of India*, 25 March 1940.

[97] Pirzada, *Documents*, p. 342.

ground of communal tension had been known even at the time of the passing of Patna and Ramgarh resolutions.[98]

By the end of April 1940, the British felt prepared to cope with civil disobedience. Reginald Maxwell, the Home Member, however, advised Linlithgow to resolve the political stalemate, otherwise even moderate opinion would veer round to the Congress.[99] Linlithgow remained satisfied with the Congress–League rift. Jinnah would continue to blow hot and cold, but he would not obstruct any constitutional initiative made by the British, and they could look in general for the help of the Muslim League.[100]

So Linlithgow was understandably dismayed when neither the Congress nor League allowed their members to join the War Committees and the Civic Guards, the formation of which he announced on 5 June. War Committees would be set up in every district to organize people and to disseminate official information. The Civic Guards were organized from volunteers to help the regular police maintain order.[101] Both the Congress and League, however, decided to set up their own organizations for civil defence, and the Viceroy considered yet again the possibility of making a move 'at the right moment' which would bring the two parties into the Executive Council.[102] With the fall of France on 27 June 1940, Linlithgow confessed that he was willing to reconsider his attitude about not appearing to take sides, if the League was willing to enter the Executive Council and the Congress remained intransigent.[103] Jinnah was anxious 'above all things' to get into the administration, but refused to lift the ban on Muslim Leaguers serving in the War Committees—they would only be allowed to go into civil defence organizations set up by the government if and when his party came into the Executive Council.[104]

There were good reasons for the Viceroy to want the Congress and the League—or at least the latter—in his Council at this time. The German invasions of Holland and Belgium on 10 May, and the

[98] *IAR*, 1940, vol. 1, pp. 228ff. See also AICC file no. G-32, 1940.

[99] Maxwell to Laithwaite, 25 April 1940, HP file no. 3/13/40, p. 3.

[100] See, for example, Viceroy to Secretary of State, (T), 28 June and 1 July 1940, *LC*, vol. 19.

[101] *Times of India*, 6 June 1940.

[102] Viceroy to Secretary of State, (T), 10 June 1940, *LC*, vol. 19.

[103] Linlithgow to Amery, 27 June 1940, Ibid., vol. 9.

[104] Viceroy to Secretary of State, (T), 28 June 1940, Ibid., vol. 19.

British withdrawal from Dunkirk on 27 May, exposed Britain to a possible German attack. England faced the Axis singlehanded, and this fact was at least partly responsible for a changed role for India in the Imperial defence machine. India was of vital importance because of her resources, her manpower and the economic potential east of Suez. On 21 May Defence Plan of India "A" was issued by the Commander-in-Chief, ordering the immediate expansion of the Indian Army by six divisions;[105] on 24 May the development of aircraft production in India, so far refused, was recommended by the Government of India;[106] and on 7 June, Linlithgow launched his plan for pooling the resources and production of member countries of the British Empire in the Indian Ocean with India as its 'natural' centre,[107] a plan which was to result in the creation of the "Eastern Group Supply Council." On 27 June, Parliament passed the India and Burma Emergency Provisions Act providing 'in the event of a complete breakdown of communications with the United Kingdom' for the Governor General to take over the powers normally exercised by the Secretary of State. 'I am quite clear that the point has been reached in the prosecution of the war at which it is unsound and unsatisfactory and likely to prove increasingly difficult in terms of public reaction, that we should continue at the Centre to handle matters through an entirely bureaucratic government,' wrote Linlithgow to Amery on 1 July.[108]

In these circumstances, the CWC made another offer on 3 July. If the British would acknowledge that the complete independence of India was the only solution to the political deadlock, the Congress would join a provisional National Government, formed of representatives of all parties. Only such a government, Congress claimed, would be able to organize effectively the material and moral resources of India for defence.[109] The Working Committee disagreed with Gandhi's emphasis on non-violent cooperation. 'We know that arms and ammunitions have not been able to save the freedom

---

[105] Memorandum by Amery for War Cabinet, W.P. (G) (40) 137 and 139, 23 and 24 May 1940, CAB 67/7. See also S.N. Prasad, *Expansion of the Armed Forces and Defence Organisation 1939–45* (Calcutta, 1956), pp. 58ff.

[106] Private Secretary to Viceroy to Private Secretary to Secretary of State, 24 May 1940, L/E/8/1711.

[107] Linlithgow to Amery, 30 May, 1940, *LC*, vol. 9.

[108] Linlithgow to Amery, (T), 1 July 1940, Ibid., vol. 19.

[109] See AICC file no. G-32/KW-1, Part I, 1940, pp. 31–43.

of France, Holland, Belgium and Norway but we also know that human nature . . . is not prepared to give up force . . . Mahatma Gandhi has to give the message of non-violence to the world and, therefore, it is his duty to propagate it, but we have to consider our position as the representatives of the Indian Nation meeting in the Indian National Congress. The Indian National Congress is a political organization pledged to win the political independence of the country. It is not an institution for organizing world peace.' Gandhi would go his own way, but the Congress would co-ordinate its activities with him whenever possible.[110]

The British Cabinet, however, frowned on the Viceroy's proposal for a British constitutional initiative, especially as the Congress and League had yet to reconcile their differences.[111] An indignant Churchill, seeing the correspondence between the Viceroy and the Secretary of State for the first time,[112] rejected Linlithgow's suggestion that the cabinet promise in advance to frame at the conclusion of the war, a constitution to which representatives of the principal Indian parties would agree. It was also quite impossible to pledge in advance the attitude of a future parliament, and to fix a date for India to achieve Dominion Status. The cabinet agreed merely to an enlarged Executive Council and the setting up of a War Advisory Committee.[113]

This was the background to the "August Offer", which the Congress turned down even as it was published in the press. There was no suggestion of a National Government and therefore no scope for further discussion.[114] Even Rajagopalachari, who had framed the Poona Congress resolution for a National Government, was one of the first to reject the Offer.[115]

The League was apparently satisfied with the British stipulation in the August Offer of consultation with the minorities in any future constitutional discussions, and its assurance that they would not transfer their 'responsibilities' to any government whose au-

[110] *IAR*, 1940, vol. 2, pp. 193–4.
[111] Viceroy to Prime Minister, (T), 18 July 1940 and Prime Minister to Viceroy, (T), 16 July 1940, PREM 4/47/1.
[112] Prime Minister to Viceroy, 26 July 1940, Ibid.
[113] Prime Minister to Viceroy, 28 July 1940, Ibid.
[114] See Linlithgow to Azad, 4 August 1940 and Azad to Linlithgow, (T), 8 and 10 August 1940; AICC file no. G-1, Part 1, 1940-1941.
[115] *IAR*, 1940, vol. 2, pp. 196ff.

thority 'is directly denied by large and powerful elements in India's national life.' This meant that the British would ignore the Congress demand for independence. The demand for a sovereign Pakistan had served at least one of Jinnah's aims: to ensure that the League was not ignored in any settlement between the Congress and the British. Not surprisingly, the MLWC now allowed Leaguers to join war committees. Probably this also signified a concession to loyalists like Sikander and Huq, who had earlier defied Jinnah's orders banning Leaguers from serving on war committees. But the British had not accepted Pakistan; nor had they accepted the League's claim to be treated as an equal of the Congress in any constitutional discussions. So the League rejected the August Offer on the ground that it had not been offered 'equal partnership' at the centre and in the provinces in return for cooperation with the war effort. The logic of the League's claim to parity and recognition by the British as the 'sole' representative of Muslims demonstrated the seriousness of Jinnah's call for a sovereign Muslim state. Concession of parity by the British would mean their acceptance of the Muslim claim to nationhood, the League the equal of the Congress, with an equal claim to the spoils of a transfer of power. Conversely, if the British accepted the contention that Muslims were a nation, they must accord them parity. This logic rationalized Jinnah's persuasion of his working committee to reject the August Offer. The majority of the MLWC wanted to accept it, but deferred to Jinnah's warning that full cooperation would mean that the entire burden of responsibility for protecting the Indian empire, crushing the Congress, supplying men and money and running the administration would fall on the League. If the Congress decided to cooperate, the British would reject the Pakistan scheme. So he counselled patience with a view to extracting as many concessions as possible.[116] That Jinnah's word prevailed points to his ability to get his way, responsible in no small measure for is hold over the all-India Muslim League.

'It is lamentable that we should have to await in this way on Jinnah's vanity, but it cannot of course be helped,' wrote Linlithgow to Amery on 5 September. His demand that the League should be taken into full and equal partnership with the British in the running of the country was absurd. At the same time, it was important to

---

[116] This account is based on FR for Bombay for first half of September 1940, HP file no. 18/9/40; and Pirzada, *Documents*, p. 403.

hold the League together, 'and in those circumstances there is nothing for it but to be patient with Jinnah.'[117] But there was no response from Jinnah, who dashed Linlithgow's hopes of his full cooperation, and by October, the offer had been put into cold storage.[118]

With the Congress embarking on its individual civil disobedience campaign, and with no further British initiative, Jinnah found the political stalemate worrying, perhaps because there was nothing for him to reject and so keep himself in the limelight, especially at a time when the League was in trouble in the Muslim majority provinces. The call for Pakistan seems to have done little to strengthen his control over provincial Leaguers. In Sind, the League's coalition ministry headed by Mir Bunde Ali Khan broke up when Allah Baksh and two Hindu ministers resigned; and the League was out of office in March 1941.[119]

In the Punjab, Sikander had defied Jinnah's ban on Muslim Leaguers joining War Committees, while his personal antipathy to Pakistan and the need to reassure his Hindu and Sikh colleagues had brought him out against Pakistan in February 1941. Unity alone could bring freedom, declared Sikander. The Punjab had no use for Pakistan or any separatist scheme. His ministry announced plans to promote communal harmony by organizing lectures on the subject, subsidizing newspapers sympathetic to the idea, and organizing common birthday celebrations for the founders of different religions.[120] He and other Muslim Unionists stayed away from Jinnah's meetings in Lahore on 1 and 2 March;[121] and he also did not attend the Muslim League Conference in Madras in April 1941.[122] Embarrassed by Jinnah's continued advocacy of Pakistan, Sikander proposed to resign from the MLWC; but the idea did not suit Linlithgow. He instructed Henry Craik, Governor of the Punjab, to persuade Sikander discreetly not to resign from the Working Committee, for two significant reasons. First, Muslim Leaguers in the

---

[117] Linlithgow to Amery, 5 September 1940, *LC*, vol. 9.
[118] Linlithgow to Amery, 8 October 1940, Ibid.
[119] Graham to Linlithgow, 3 March 1941, Ibid., vol. 97.
[120] *Times of India*, 4 February, 5 March 1941.
[121] Craik to Linlithgow, 4 March 1941, *LC*, vol. 90. FR for Punjab for first half of March 1941, HP file no. 18/3/41.
[122] Extract from FR of Central Intelligence Officer, Madras, dated 22 April 1941, HP file no. 4/8/41.

Punjab who were opposed to Sikander might try to overthrow his Unionist ministry on the Pakistan issue. Linlithgow wanted Sikander to stay on as Prime Minister of the Punjab, because of his successful organization of the provincial war effort. If Sikander were hounded out by extreme Muslim elements, it 'would be a bad thing from the Punjab point of view.[123] Secondly, the Viceroy did not want a split in the Muslim League. He had taken great pains to get Sikander to drop his negotiations with the Congress in the summer of 1940.[124] In March 1941, when the individual civil disobedience campaign was in progress, a split in the League could only encourage the Congress. In Linlithgow's policy, it was 'very important' to maintain the League a 'a solid political entity,' able to speak on behalf of Muslim opinion in India. Jinnah was 'the one man' who had succeeded in unifying the Muslims over the last forty years and whose control over them appeared at the moment to be effective.[125] Sikander eventually decided not to resign from the MLWC, as this might have lost him the support of some Muslim Unionists in favour of Pakistan. Linlithgow was satisfied. For, as he confessed later, 'I do not want to be left with only one side in this business organized'.[126] In this instance also, Jinnah's call for Pakistan had divided him from the most influential Muslim leader in the Punjab, though it had attracted the support of others whom Sikander feared. Ironically, however, though Sikander needed Jinnah, and to a lesser extent Jinnah needed Sikander, the Viceroy needed them both; and it was he in this case who worked most effectively to preserve unity within the Muslim League.

The deep division between Jinnah and provincial Leaguers was illustrated again in June 1941, when the Viceroy invited Sikander, Huq and Saadullah, among others, to serve on the National Defence Council. He intended to secure their acceptance before Jinnah got wind of the invitations. Once they had entered the NDC, he doubted whether Jinnah would quarrel with them.[127] The Muslim Prime Ministers agreed to serve on the NDC. Jinnah said nothing

---

[123] Viceroy to Governor of Punjab, (T), 1 March 1941, *LC*, vol. 90. See also Linlithgow to Amery, 1 March 1941, Ibid., vol. 10.

[124] P. Moon, 'May God Be With You Always,' *The Round Table*, July 1971, p. 418.

[125] Linlithgow to Amery, 15 May 1941, *LC*, vol. 10.

[126] Linlithgow to Amery, 8 September 1941, Ibid., vol. 10.

[127] Linlithgow to Reid, 19 June 1941, Ibid., vol. 34.

until he found out that the Viceroy had made the tactical error of inviting the provincial Premiers not as Premiers but as representatives of the Muslim community. Then Jinnah claimed that the invitations should have been issued through the League as it was the 'sole' representative of Muslims.'[128]

Jinnah drew the attention of the League Prime Ministers to his circular of June 1940, which barred Muslim Leaguers from joining war committees. At first, the Premiers stood up to him. Saadullah, Prime Minister of Assam, made it clear to Jinnah that he was already on provincial war committees and his government was committed to the prosecution of the war.[129] He threatened Jinnah that if he had to resign from NDC or from the League, it would be the end of his ministry and a setback to the League in Assam.[130] But he took shelter behind Sikander. Sikander wavered but felt that his position would remain secure in the Punjab even if he fell out with Jinnah. According to Linlithgow,

'Jinnah sent for Sikander at Bombay and told him that he had decisive evidence that I had invited him to serve as a Muslim representative and not qua Prime Minister. There seems to have followed an amusing scene; for Sikander asked to be shown the evidence, and Jinnah, after a great deal of searching around the room and turning up papers, expressed his regret that he could not lay his hand on it. Sikander holding his ground, Miss Jinnah was called to pursue the search, but she was equally unsuccessful. Sikander was still holding his ground, the missing document was produced and Sikander was told that this was the answer and that he had better go away and think about it. Later in the evening two members of the League (quite obviously on Jinnah's instructions) called on him to say that they had seen Lumley's letter and that Sikander must give way.'[131]

At the meeting of the Muslim League Council next morning, Sikander told someone present who said to him ' "you seem to be in the position of an accused" ', ' "I am not an accused, I am a convict!" ' (sic).[132] On 25 August, he resigned from the NDC.

Saadullah returned to Assam and submitted his resignation from the NDC, while Huq struggled to maintain his Premiership in Ben-

---

[128] Lumley to Jinnah, 20 July 1941 and Jinnah to Lumley, 21 July 1941, Ibid., vol 55. See also Linlithgow to Amery, 30 August 1941, Ibid., vol. 10.

[129] Reid to Linlithgow, 29 July 1941, Ibid., vol. 34.

[130] Reid to Linlithgow, Ibid.

[131] Linlithgow to Amery, 30 August 1941, *LC*, vol. 10.

[132] Linlithgow to Amery, 1 September 1941, Ibid.

gal. His alliance with the League in 1937 had been made at the expense of the support of radicals in the KPP, who deserted him when he joined hands with their old adversaries. The League's support enabled him to maintain his Premiership, but it had also meant that he was in a minority in the Bengal Provincial League.[133] A political maverick, Huq was restive with League attempts to dictate to him, and had, on more than one occasion, roused their ire because of his flirtation with the Congress and the Mahasabha. In September 1939, he had come out in support of the war effort, which had further estranged him from many provincial Muslim Leaguers, and, in June 1940, he had defied Jinnah's directive that Leaguers must not join War Committees.

Jinnah had not taken disciplinary action against Huq because he had been joined by other provincial Leaguers, including Nazimuddin and Suhrawardy, who said they would not support any action against Huq.[134] Wanting to avoid a split in the League, Jinnah did nothing.[135]

Ispahani and his friends called on Jinnah to take action against Huq when he joined the NDC in August 1941.[136] Huq then came out with a lengthy manifesto attacking Jinnah:

'. . . Principles of democracy and autonomy in All India Muslim League are being subordinated to arbitrary wishes of a single individual who seeks to rule as omnipotent authority over destiny of 33 millions in Bengal who occupy key position in Indian Muslim Politics'.

At the same time, he played safe and announced his resignation from the NDC![137]

Even as Huq's enemies in the provincial league organized mass demonstrations against him in several towns,[138] Jinnah made up his mind to remove Huq from the MLWC. Huq's attack on his authority could not be ignored. But he did not want to take action against him unless he was certain that the provincial League would support it. On 26 September 1941, he wrote to Ispahani:

[133] Sen, *Muslim Politics*, p. 98.
[134] Governor of Bengal to Viceroy, (T), 31 July 1941, *LC*, vol. 41.
[135] Zaidi, Introduction to *Jinnah–Ispahani Correspondence*, p. 38.
[136] Ispahani to Jinnah, 6 September 1941, *Jinnah–Ispahani Correspondence*, pp. 176–7.
[137] Huq to Liaqat Ali Khan, 8 September 1941, HP file no. 17/4/41.
[138] Herbert to Linlithgow, 21 September and 1 October 1941, *LC*, vol. 41.

'In my opinion he is a source of danger to the vital interests of not only the Musalmans of Bengal but of the whole of India. It is humiliating for the Musalmans to acknowledge a man of this type to be one of their leaders. The whole world is laughing at this issue. It is entirely up to you all in Bengal to stand united and put an end to this agony.'[139]

Jinnah was anxious to avoid what Herbert, the Governor of Bengal described as 'the onus of splitting the Bengal Muslims' being put on him.[140]

Provincial Leaguers, including Nazimuddin and Suhrawardy, were keen to avoid a break with Húq, and on 20 October 1941, the Bengal League passed a motion of confidence in him.[141] On 16 November Jinnah accepted Huq's explanation for joining the NDC although Huq had not withdrawn the letter attacking him. Ispahani and his friends were now spoiling for a fight with Huq and withdrew support from his ministry. They were joined by Nazimuddin and Suhrawardy, who had been given, interestingly enough, the tacit assurance by the governor that they would be asked to form a ministry in case Huq lost his majority in the legislature.[142]

But as Pearl Harbour fell, and allied fortunes reached their lowest ebb, Herbert seems to have had second thoughts. He was apprehensive that a League ministry which excluded Hindus would not be able to inspire support for the war effort amongst a sizeable section of the population in Bengal. Moreover, there was no guarantee that the League would work wholeheartedly for the war effort.[143] So he decided to allow Huq to form a ministry with the breakaway Bose Congress group and the Mahasabha. This gave Jinnah and the MLWC an opportunity to accuse Huq of betraying Muslims, and Huq was expelled from the League in December 1941.

These episodes illustrated first, that the Viceroy's need to maintain the League as a counterpoise to the Congress at the all India level did not necessarily mean that he or provincial officials wanted it in power in Muslim majority provinces. Linlithgow himself, as we have seen, did not want the League in power in the Punjab because

[139] Jinnah to Ispahani, 26 September 1941, Zaidi, *Jinnah–Ispahani Correspondence*, p. 188.

[140] Herbert to Linlithgow, 21 October 1941, L/P & J/5/134.

[141] Zaidi, Introduction to *Jinnah-Ispahani Correspondence*, p. 41.

[142] Copy of letter from Nazimuddin to Jinnah, 14 December 1941, HP file no. 232/41.

[143] Governor of Bengal to Viceroy, (T), 9 December 1941, R/3/1/30.

he feared that they would throw a spanner in the successful organization of the war effort in the province. Thus the Viceroy himself could follow different policies towards the League at the all India and provincial levels.

Secondly, it was clear that Jinnah could ultimately emerge the winner in any trial of strength with provincial Leaguers at the all India level, and could threaten them at the provincial level: nevertheless, his direct influence on Muslim provincial politics depended on tactical opportunities of exploiting rivalry between factions.

It was also obvious that it mattered less to Linlithgow that Jinnah was not cooperating fully with the war effort than that he was opposing the Congress. The Viceroy was surprised and dismayed that Jinnah could put up 'as stiff a show' against the League Prime Ministers on the NDC issue,[144] but saw no point in calling what he regarded as Jinnah's bluff. The League was the only counterpoise to the Congress at the all India level. There was no platform at this level on the Muslim side in opposition to Jinnah. Saadullah and Haroon were too small on the all India level, Huq was emotionally uncertain, and Sikander had no backbone. 'I am not averse to a little tiger shooting', concluded the Viceroy, 'but I attach a good deal of importance to my companions being staunch before I embark on sport of that kind.'[145]

[144] Linlithgow to Herbert, 25 August 1941, R/3/2/46.
[145] Linlithgow to Amery, 1 September 1941, *LC*, vol. 10.

CHAPTER 3

Provincial and All India Politics:
Currents and Cross-Currents—December
1941 to April 1945

The Cripps Mission and Its Aftermath

The attack on Pearl Harbour on 6 December 1941 inspired the British to consider a fresh political initiative in India to attract a greater measure of popular support for the war effort. Pressure came from India, the USA, China and the UK,[1] and Whitehall was confronted with the task of showing its allies that it was making constitutional moves to end the political deadlock in India. Whitehall could not have been heartened by reports from some provinces that anti-British feeling was becoming more widespread.[2] But neither Whitehall nor Linlithgow were interested in offering the political advance which Congress demanded at Bardoli at the end of 1941.

Frustrated by the political *impasse*, the Congress Right discussed the possibility of returning to office in November 1941. Rajagopalachari and Bhulabhai Desai, who had no confidence in *satyagraha*, wanted the Congress to resume parliamentary activities. But they did not want Gandhi to leave the Congress or to abstain from supporting their suggestions, as they would then have 'real trouble' in controlling their 'leftist colleagues.'[3] Rajagopalachari wanted the Congress to give the government an inkling of the party's desire to return to office and to cooperate with the war effort so that the government could make an offer.[4] Nehru, however, was impatient with the talk of negotiations with the British. 'With whom are we going to negotiate—with an Empire which is crumbling to dust?'[5] Gandhi

---

[1] M.S. Venkataramani and G. Srivastava, *Quit India: The American Response to the 1942 Struggle* (New Delhi, 1979), pp. 72 and 33–61.

[2] See, for example, Lumley to Linlithgow, 7 February 1942, *TOP*, vol. 1, p. 130; and Hallett to Linlithgow, 10 February 1942, Ibid., p. 147.

[3] Sapru to B. Shiva Rao, 13 November 1941, *BSRC*.

[4] G.D. Birla to P. Thakurdas, 8 November 1941, *PTC*, file no. 239, p. 179.

[5] Shiva Rao to Sapru, 26 January 1942, *BSRC*.

was not prepared to budge an inch from the stand he had taken. 'The Congress represents the spirit of resistance of a certain pattern.'[6] He was confident that he had Nehru's support and with this could defeat any proposition that the Congress should return to office.[7] Rajagopalachari, however, was prepared to have it out with Nehru. When Shiva Rao told him that Nehru, being 'a man of strong convictions,' would turn down any move that was intended to get the Congress into office again, Rajagopalachari 'corrected me over the word "convictions" and said I had better use "strong opinions."'[8] At Bardoli, Rajagopalachari persuaded the Congress Working Committee to set aside Gandhi and to ignore Nehru and to offer the cooperation of a free India in defence of the country on a national basis. Civil disobedience seemed to him to have served its purpose; the people were exhausted and unless the Congress did something definite in this crisis its cause would suffer. Wisdom lay in making as much political progress as possible during the war.

British officials failed to perceive the sincerity of the desire of the Congress Right to cooperate with the war effort and to return to office. Roger Lumley, the Governor of Bombay, for example, regarded Bardoli as an attempt by the Congress Right to paper over the cracks in the party. The Congress had not softened its stand. Bardoli was merely intended to make it appear realistic and generous. If the British failed to respond, '"arrogant imperialism"' would again have banged on the door. Bardoli made nothing easier for the British: they could not expect anything from the Congress except 'interminable manoeuvring for position and hard bargaining.'[9] Amery surmised that it was 'nonsense' to say that Bardoli meant that the Congress had 'opened the door to co-operation, the need for our meeting them half-way by some initiative, and all the rest of it.'[10] Linlithgow thought it 'important not to let ourselves be hypnotised by Rajagopalachariar and his appearance of reasonableness and plausibility.' He was endeavouring to concentrate the spotlight on himself and to obscure 'the very significant dissident strains' that had emerged in the discussions at the AICC.[11]

[6] Gandhi to Jayakar, 9 November 1941, *MRJC*, file no. 276, p. 369.

[7] Note from D. Pilditch to R. Tottenham, 19 November 1941, HP file no. 4/8/41, p. 47.

[8] Sapru to Jayakar, 11 December 1941, *TBSC*, vol. 10.

[9] Lumley to Linlithgow, 1 January 1942, *TOP*, vol. 1, pp. 2–3.

[10] Amery to Linlithgow, 5 January 1942, Ibid., p. 9.

[11] Linlithgow to Amery, (T), 21 January 1942, Ibid., p. 45.

Jinnah and the Muslim League, ever fearful that the British would respond to the overtures of the Congress Right, reminded them that the League could not be ignored,[12] and assured them of the League's opposition to the Bardoli resolution.[13]

The British smugly concluded that Jinnah's stand precluded the possibility of any surrender to the Congress.[14] The War Cabinet simply wanted to sit pat. Churchill argued that bringing a hostile political element into the defence machine would paralyse action,[15] conveniently forgetting that the Congress was not hostile to the war effort as such, but to their exclusion from any responsibility for it. Merely picking and choosing friendly Indians would do 'no serious harm,' but would 'not in any way' meet the political demands. The Indian liberals, though plausible, 'have never been able to deliver the goods. The Indian troops are fighting splendidly, but their allegiance is to the King Emperor.'[16] Amery had convinced himself that 'there is no further interim constitutional advance that we can make.'[17] The Viceroy made no bones about what he stood for.

'India and Burma have no natural association with the Empire,' [he wrote to Amery] 'from which they are alien by race, history and religion, and for which as such neither of them have any natural affection, and both are in the Empire because they are conquered countries which had been brought there by force, kept there by our controls, and which hitherto it has suited to remain under our protection.'

So the British must not relinquish power 'beyond a certain point.'[18] There could not have been a better summing up of British intentions in India at this time.

How much power were the British prepared to part with? Pressure from the USA, the Congress Right, and, at the beginning of February 1942 from Attlee, the Lord Privy Seal, induced Churchill to propound 'the great scheme.' It left the crucial executive and legislative position in India untouched, while it gave the proposed Defence of India Council 'some interesting sugar plums' in the shape of democratic representation in it and at the Peace Conference. It would fulfil British pledges to bring Indian parties together on the

[12] Muslim League Nagpur Resolution, 27 December 1941, Ibid., pp. 884–6.
[13] Lumley to Linlithgow, 15 January 1942, Ibid., pp. 26–9.
[14] Lumley to Linlithgow, 1 January 1942, Ibid., p. 3.
[15] Churchill to Attlee, (T), 7 January 1942, Ibid., p. 14.
[16] Ibid.   [17] Memorandum by Amery, 28 January 1942, Ibid., p. 90.
[18] Linlithgow to Amery, (T), 21 January 1942, Ibid., p. 49.

constitutional issue by offering to accept this body as the future constitution-making body. Neither the Congress nor the League were expected to accept the proposals. The Congress would turn it down as it did not offer India immediate self-government, while Jinnah would be suspicious of any body in which Muslims were represented in proportion to population and in which he might not be actual leader of Muslims. But the failure of the effort would not discredit the War Cabinet; it would show 'our goodwill and only expose the unreasonableness of Indian parties.'[19] However, the scheme was eventually put into cold storage because Linlithgow strongly opposed giving the proposed Defence of India Council any constitution-making powers. Communal rivalries, he argued, would throw defence into disarray and would interfere with the conduct of the war, gravely damage 'our power of resistance to the Japanese invasion.'[20]

A draft declaration by Whitehall remained necessary, if only to convince its allies of its liberal intentions in India. So any talk of transferring power to Indians would be qualified by the requirement that the Congress and League must agree. The British would not coerce minorities into a political system against their will.[21] Even the possibility of accepting "Pakistan" was considered, inspite of Linlithgow's confession that he had no idea of the popularity of the idea of Pakistan; and the strength of the League had not yet been tested. He did not know what Jinnah meant by it and he would not ask him to define it because he was sure that Jinnah would come up 'with something pretty woolly and general.' He did not think that there was anything to justify the demand for Pakistan in terms of the League's allegations against Congress ministries.

Jinnah had made clear in his presidential address to the League in April 1941 that Pakistan would have 'the status of an independent nation and an independent State in this Subcontinent.'[22] He emphasized his definition of Pakistan when he told British officials that he 'preferred to talk of a co-national or a coalition government, rather than a national government.'[23] But Muslim Leaguers the Reforms Commissioner had met—and they included Nazimuddin, Ismail

[19] Amery to Linlithgow, 8 February 1942, Ibid., pp. 137–9.

[20] Linlithgow to Amery, 13 and 16 February 1942, (T), Ibid., pp. 166–8 ard 178 respectively.

[21] Speech by Amery on 4 February 1942, Ibid., p. 230, fn. 5.

[22] Pirzada, *Documents*, p. 362.

[23] Lumley to Linlithgow, 15 January 1942, *TOP*, vol. 1, p. 29.

Khan and Abdul Matin—'interpreted Pakistan as consistent with a federation of India for common purposes like defence, provided the Hindu–Muslim elements therein stood on equal terms.'[24] Abdul Hamid Khan, who chaired the League's session in Madras in April 1941, had defined Pakistan as 'the establishment of independent and separate Muslim States with a confederating outlook,' a vision which would 'not run counter to the idea of India's political unity, nor does it mean the vivisection of India, since the basis of Pakistan has existed all the time in this country.'[25] From the NWFP, Cunningham reported that educated Muslims wanted safeguards for their community, but that it was 'very difficult to get any constructively helpful ideas out of them.'[26] From Sind, Dow reported that most people who called themselves Muslim Leaguers knew or cared very little about the League's policy or affairs, and are 'actuated almost entirely by opposition to Allah Baksh and his Hindu supporters. There are hardly more than half a dozen Muslim Leaguers in Sind who have any contacts with Leaguers outside the province.'[27] The view of many educated Muslims in the Punjab that independence must not place them at the mercy of Hindus[28] gave credence to Hodson's observation that one of the reasons Muslims he had met would not repudiate Pakistan was that they did not want to impair Muslim solidarity. Their fear of 'Hindu' domination did not, however, necessarily mean that they favoured the creation of a sovereign Pakistan. The idea of Hindus and Muslims as two nations, even within a federation, had emotional appeal for Muslims, even if its content had not been very consciously thought out, because it put both communities on an equal footing—*nations* negotiated as equals. "Safeguards" defined their status as *minorities*; safeguards would improve but not alter their position as a minority, 'a Cinderella with trade-union rights and a radio in the kitchen but still below stairs.' The two-nation theory therefore transmuted the ideology of "minorities", and may well, as Hodson discerned, have been more fundamental to the present thought of educated Muslims than the Pakistan theory, which transmuted the ideology of "safeguards."[29]

---

[24] Annexure to Linlithgow to Amery, 23–7 January 1942, Ibid., p. 66.

[25] Pirzada, *Documents*, p. 356.

[26] Cunningham to Linlithgow, 22 March 1942, *TOP*, vol. 1, p. 457.

[27] Dow to Linlithgow, 22 March 1942, Ibid., p. 459.

[28] Glancy to Linlithgow, (T), 4 March 1942, Ibid., p. 321.

[29] Annexure to Linlithgow to Amery, 23–7 January 1942, Ibid., pp. 66–7.

The fall of Rangoon on 21 February, and that of Singapore on 8 March 1942, spurred Whitehall to make a show of working for political change in India. But the British, Churchill informed Roosevelt, could not renege on their obligations to the Muslims or the Princes.[30] Amery admitted that it could be argued that the League was being given a blackmailing veto on political advance.[31] But this charge could be averted. The British would say that no province could be coerced into joining the federation. That would meet Jinnah 'in principle.' On the other hand, the Congress would feel that the British were not holding back freedom, and would be given a strong incentive to settle with the Muslim majority provinces.[32]

The draft declaration Cripps brought to India envisaged the granting of Dominion Status to India, leaving the Dominion free to remain in or to secede from the Commonwealth. Elections to provincial legislatures would be held after the war. The Lower Houses would then act as a single electoral college and elect the constitution-making body by proportional representation. The constitution framed by it would be accepted by the British subject to the right of any province that was unwilling to accept the new constitution to secede from the Union. The British government would be prepared to agree to a new constitution framed by the seceding provinces.[33]

Jinnah pointed out to Cripps that in a Constituent Assembly elected by proportional representation, Muslims would have only 25 per cent of the votes, and would not be able to vote against joining the Union. Cripps assured him that if less than 60 per cent of the provincial legislature voted in favour of accession, the minority would have the right to call for a plebiscite of the adult male population of the province, the verdict of which would be implemented by the British government.[34] Thus a simple majority vote in a plebiscite could turn the balance in favour of Pakistan.

According to Cripps, Jinnah was 'rather surprised' in the distance the British offer went to meet the Pakistan case and did not raise any serious objection to it.[35] But the provision for provinces to opt out of the federation does not seem to have encouraged the League to

[30] Churchill to Roosevelt, 4 March 1942, Ibid., pp. 309–10.

[31] Amery to Churchill, 25 February 1942, Ibid., p. 240.

[32] Amery to Linlithgow, (T), 22 February 1942, Ibid., p. 223.

[33] Draft Declaration, Ibid., pp. 314–15.

[34] Note by Cripps on interview with Jinnah on 25 March 1942, Ibid., pp. 480–81. See also Cripps to Azad, 2 April 1942, Ibid., p. 610.

[35] Note by Cripps on interview with Jinnah on 25 March 1942, Ibid., pp. 480–81.

settle with the Congress. It is worth noting that, after Cripps had discussed his formula with Jinnah, a proposal by Sikander Hyat Khan for a Congress–League *rapprochement* was brushed aside at a MLWC meeting.[36] By giving the provinces the right to opt out of the federation, Whitehall was creating the sort of political climate that must have confirmed Jinnah's belief that as the British held power, they would transfer or confer it: so why should he go out of his way to reach a settlement with the Congress?[37]

The Cripps formula thus made provision for partition before the transfer of power took place. In one stroke, the British overthrew the act of 1935 as a basis for a post-war constitutional settlement. Cripps' visit to India also made clear, for the first time, that the British envisaged that the main parties involved in the transfer of power would be the Congress and the Muslim League: the principle of partition had in fact been incorporated into the Cripps proposals in recognition of the League's demand for Pakistan.

These points were confirmed by the clarification given by Cripps to Sikh leaders, that the position of the Sikhs in the new constitution would be decided by agreement between the Congress and the League: that Sikh fears about their position would not stop the British from agreeing to a constitution which had been accepted by those two parties. Cripps tried to console the Sikhs by telling them that the Congress, in order to enlarge its majority in the Constituent Assembly, would try to win over the Sikhs by making the most ample provision for them in the new constitution, which might even entail the sub-division of the Punjab into two provinces or the setting up within the province, of a semi-autonomous district for the Sikhs on the Soviet model. Similarly, although the Muslims would be able to obtain a narrow majority in a plebiscite to secede from the Union, they would be anxious to increase that majority as much as possible, both in order to make certain of a majority and also to have a favourable atmosphere for setting up the second new Dominion. Cripps 'promised' Akali leaders that he would mention to Jinnah their demand for a special vote for Sikhs to decide whether they would join the first or second union.[38] There is no evidence in

---

[36] Note by D. Pilditch, Intelligence Bureau, Home Department, dated 28 March 1942, HP file no. 221/42, p. 18.

[37] K.B. Sayeed, *Pakistan: The Formative Phase*, p. 187.

[38] Note by Cripps on interviews with a number of Sikhs, 27 March 1942, *TOP*, vol. 1, pp. 496–7, and with the Sikh delegation, 31 March 1942, Ibid., p. 581.

Cripps' own notes that he did in fact raise the point with Jinnah; nor did it ever come up for discussion in the War Cabinet. But it was obvious that Cripps—and Whitehall and Linlithgow—thought that Jinnah was the man who counted in coming to a decision about the Punjab, and that his role in the transfer of power was already being taken for granted by them.

'One permanent effect', to quote R.F. Mudie, Chief Secretary to the UP government, 'of the British Government's offer will probably be an increase in estrangement between the two major communities. Pakistan has advanced one stage further.'[39] Communal tension was indeed intensified in many provinces, as communal organizations began to organize local defence volunteers to safeguard their communities, ostensibly for purposes of defence. The UP League Defence Committee had 'for its sole object' the defence of Muslims against attacks by Hindus.[40] In Bihar, the committee appointed by the League to organize a Muslim Protection Scheme urged Muslims to organize to oppose Hindu aggression in the event of a deterioration in the war situation. Muslim League Defence Committees weaned away Muslims from non-party defence committees set up by the Congress.[41] In the Punjab, the Sikhs were relieved at the failure of the Cripps Mission. But Glancy feared internal unrest, as Muslims and Sikhs became increasingly suspicious of one another.[42] The Akalis, League, Hindu Mahasabha, RSS, and Khaksars all had plans to raise volunteer communal organizations. The Akalis talked of plans to arm the Sikh community and to organize them on a semi-military basis for self-preservation. The Congress deprecated the formation of a communal volunteer corps and stressed the need for Indians to unite against British imperialism. But faction fights within the provincial Congress kept its influence at a low ebb.[43] From the NWFP, Cunningham reported that Hindus had been 'thoroughly alarmed' by the conditional offer of Pakistan, and 'I have heard more talk than usual lately of the necessity for Hindus to establish themselves on a strong footing in the Army. Indeed, Hindu and Sikh officers have been heard talking in terms of complete independence and Hindu *raj* in India.' Muslims

[39] FR for UP for first half of April 1942, HP file no. 18/4/42.
[40] FR for UP for second half of April 1942, Ibid.
[41] FR for Bihar for second half of April 1942, Ibid.
[42] Glancy to Linlithgow, 1 May 1942, *TOP*, vol. 2, p. 7.
[43] FR for Punjab for second half of April 1942, HP file no. 18/4/42.

believed that their interests were identical with those of the British, and they had some idea of the British coming to a separate agreement with the League. Hindus also hinted apprehensively at this.[44]

Sikh fears were not eased by Rajagopalachari's formula to end the Congress–League deadlock. There was frustration in Congress circles with the failure of the Cripps mission, and Gandhi renewed talk of civil disobedience. Almost singlehandedly, Rajagopalachari, believing that an end to Congress–League differences was the necessary precursor to any constitutional settlement, pushed through the Congress legislative party in Madras two resolutions, one in favour of conceding Pakistan and the other calling on the provincial Congress to enter office again. He resigned from the Congress Working Committee to introduce the first resolution at the AICC session in Allahabad on 23 April. The AICC turned down the resolution by 120 votes to 15,[45] and Gandhi chided Rajagopalachari. 'He yields the right of secession now to buy unity in the hope of keeping away the Japanese. I consider the vivisection of India to be a sin ... '[46] If Rajagopalachari really thought the League was interested in settling differences with the Congress, 'Why don't you go now to Q A and discuss the whole thing with him.?'[47] But despite Rajagopalachari's defeat in the AICC, the acceptance of the principle of Pakistan by a leading Congressman kept it in the air and intensified communal tension.

The Rajagopalachari scheme came as a shock to the Sikhs, who felt that further reliance on the Congess was useless. Sikh leaders fell back on a counter demand for changes in the boundaries of the Punjab which would provide for Sikh autonomy between Delhi and Lahore.[48] Let down, as they saw it, by the Congress, in spite of their support to the organization since 1920, the Akalis now sought to improve relations with the British, who controlled India, and the Unionist Muslims, who headed the Punjab ministry. Interested in maintaining their position in the army, and persuaded by an Indian

[44] Cunningham to Linlithgow, 23 April 1942, *TOP*, vol. 1, p. 833.

[45] P. Sitaramayya, *History of the Indian National Congress 1935–1947*, vol. 2, p. 336.

[46] *Harijan*, 24 May 1942, See also *Harijan*, 31 May 1942 and 7 June 1942.

[47] Gandhi to Rajagopalachari, 3 June 1942, *MGC*, Serial no. 2087. Gandhi often referred to Jinnah as "QA"—the abbreviation for "Qaid-i-Azam"—as Jinnah was often called.

[48] Weekly Summary no. 28, 15 May 1942, L/WS/1/1433, p. 33.

Army officer, Major Short, a section of the Sikh leadership now sought to improve their relationship with Sikander and the Muslim Unionists as the best way of safeguarding their position in the Punjab. Their dislike of Pakistan made some Muslim Unionists receptive to the idea of strengthening their coalition with Akali support.

Division of the Punjab was opposed to the interests of all three communities in the province. 'At first sight the distribution of population in the Punjab as it then existed might appear not unfavourable to partition.' The western districts were predominantly Muslim, the eastern predominantly non-Muslim; and it might therefore have seemed 'easy and natural' to divide the province into two roughly equal parts by a line drawn between Amritsar and Lahore. But the population of the Punjab was so intermingled that, wherever the line was drawn, 'large numbers of all three communities would find themselves on the wrong side of it'. The Lahore division, for example, had a Muslim majority, but it included a great part of the Sikh "Holy Land" and economic interests which were largely non-Muslim. Partition would destroy the Punjab economically. British Punjab was what Sir Evan Jenkins described as 'an artificial creation of Irrigation Engineers', consisting of a large network of canals, which had enabled large areas of desert to be converted into flourishing colonies, and on which the prosperity of the province rested. A line drawn between Amritsar and Lahore would mean that the non-Muslim state would inherit the colony districts which were the joint creation of all Punjabis over half a century.[49]

Pakistan according to the conception of extremist Muslims included the whole of the Punjab. For the Sikhs, division would leave two million of them, with all their colony lands as well as some important Sikh shrines, on the Pakistan side. 'To a small community of only six million such a division might well be fatal.' The prospect of a disruption of the Punjab, which the demand for Pakistan seemed to portend, made natural the coming together of Unionists and Akalis. Even if, at worst, the latter were compelled to translate into reality their nominal adherence to the idea of Pakistan, a Unionist–Akali alliance was likely to prevent the division of the province between two sovereign states and lead to an offer to the Sikhs of special rights and privileges.[50] This was the logic behind the

[49] This paragraph is based on Moon, *Divide and Quit*, pp. 34–5, and enclosure to Jenkins to Wavell, 7 March 1947, *TOP*, vol. 9, pp. 880–1.

[50] Moon, *Divide and Quit*, pp. 35–7.

Sikander–Baldev pact of June 1942. The terms of the pact included the extension of facilities for the provision of *jhatka* meat to all government institutions where separate kitchens could be provided; the introduction, as soon as possible, of *Gurmukhi* as a second language in schools where an adequate number of students desired it, and the establishment of a convention that in matters which exclusively concerned a particular community the members of that community alone would exercise voting power in the Assembly, and the maintenance of Sikh representation in the provincial services at 20 per cent. Sikh claims for representation in the Executive Council would be supported by the Unionists.[51]

Though most sections of Sikhs were satisfied with the Sikander–Baldev pact, it left unanswered what was for them the crucial question of their future political status. With the British incorporating the principle of partition in the Cripps plan, and with a section of the Congress apparently accepting it as well, Pakistan loomed threateningly on the political horizons of the Sikhs. So far, the Sikhs had not received any assurances about their future from either the British, Congress or League—all three seemed to treat them as if they were of little or no political consequence. In Sikh eyes, the demand for Pakistan would remain 'a demand for civil war', as Tara Singh put it.[52]

Sikander's alliance with a section of the Sikhs, as well as his own discomfiture with the Pakistan theory, induced him to outline in July 1942 a proposal which would satisfy the political aspirations of the Sikhs and Muslims and also show up the impractability of Pakistan. In the absence of a majority of three-quarters of the members of the Punjab Legislative Assembly voting in favour of either accession or non-accession to the Indian federation, the Muslim community should by means of a referendum be given an opportunity to decide on non-accession, and that, if they so decided, the non-Muslim population should by a similar referendum be accorded the right to cut themselves adrift from the province as constituted at present. If it actually came to the point of deciding to cut themselves adrift, this would mean, assuming that the unit covered was a district, that

---

[51] FR for Punjab for first half of June 1942, HP file no. 18/6/42. '*Jhatka*' can be translated literally as 'a sudden jerk'. Thus *Jhatka* meat would mean that the head of the animal must be cut off with a single stroke; the meat of such an animal alone is lawful for Sikhs.

[52] *IAR*, 1942, vol. 2, pp. 299–300.

Ambala division and a large part of Jullundur division and also Amritsar district would cease to belong to the Punjab. If a smaller unit such as a *tehsil* was taken, at least a very large part of the areas mentioned and possibly certain others would disappear from the province.[53]

According to Glancy, Sikander's position was that he had succeeded in bringing about a *rapprochement* with the Sikhs; he had in mind proposals to placate the urban population over the Sales Tax Act;[54] and the 'only other remaining menace which he fears as being likely to impede the war effort in the Punjab is the Pakistan controversy.' He felt his formula would lay it to rest until the war was over. If the Viceroy had no objection, Sikander would consult Muslim Unionists and Sikh members of the coalition, and then put the formula before the party as a whole. If the reactions were favourable, the provincial assembly would be invited to pass a resolution endorsing the scheme.[55]

Both Glancy and Linlithgow doubted that the plan would show up the weakness of the Pakistan theory. It would also offend Jinnah. With the Congress threatening 'total rebellion', Linlithgow had no desire to offend him. The British could not stop any individual from making assumptions about their future policy. But the formal position would be that Glancy could not encourage his Prime Minister 'to promote a plan which makes unjustifiable assumptions as to the future policy of His Majesty's Government,' and it was 'equally not possible' for the Governor to tell his Prime Minister not to propose such a plan, '*outside the provincial sphere though it may be.*' Glancy could only give Sikander 'friendly advice' to save him from error.[56] Sikander's weakness was that he would not do anything without the permission of the British; so he shelved his proposals, while Pakistan disturbed the atmosphere of the Punjab so long as the possibility of its realization existed.

---

[53] Glancy to Linlithgow, 10 July 1942, *LC*, vol. 91.
[54] The Sales Tax Act, IV of 1941, imposed a levy on annual turnover in excess of Rs. 5,000 per annum. The measure aroused strong opposition from shopkeepers, and in February 1942, it was amended, so that the Punjab General Sales Tax Amendment Act, III of 1942, raised the exemption limit from Rs. 5,000 to Rs. 10,000 per annum.
[55] Glancy to Linlithgow, 10 July 1942, *LC*, vol. 91.
[56] Linlithgow to Glancy, 17 July 1942, Ibid. (Emphasis mine)

The Quit India Movement—August 1942–March 1943

On the all India front, British officials sensed the frustration among most sections of Indian political opinion—barring the Sikhs and the Mahasabha—with the failure of the Cripps Mission;[57] and Linlithgow favoured the inclusion of more non-officials in the Executive Council to relieve the atmosphere of bitterness.[58] For the moment, however, he was satisfied that the Congress lacked direction; that it was 'now in a more difficult position than they had even been in; we had reduced them to pulp and destroyed the national spirit'.[59] But his complacency was shortlived. By the middle of May 1942, reports of preparations for a mass movement were coming in from many provinces[60] and Linlithgow showed signs of discomfiture at the 'indecently outspoken' tone of Gandhi's writings in *Harijan*.[61] The Congress Working Committee resolution of 13 July[62] left no doubt about the intentions of its leadership. 'There is no room-... for withdrawal, for negotiation', explained Gandhi, 'either they recognize India's independence or they don't .... There is no question of one more chance. After all it is an open rebellion.'[63]

Jinnah's reaction was predictable. He accused the Congress of aiming to establish Hindu *raj* 'under the aegis of the British bayonet, thereby placing the Muslims and other minorities at the mercy of the Congress *raj*.'[64] Jinnah's perennial fear was that the British would be pressurized by the Congress into accepting its terms, leaving the League in the cold.[65]

For all that he was not surprised by Jinnah's interpretation of the Congress resolution, Gandhi was, nevertheless, emotionally wounded by it. 'How can you expect me to approach QA after his performance,' he wrote to Rajagopalachari. 'Will he not be right in showing me the door if I dared to go to him. I should certainly re-

[57] See, for example, Lumley to Linlithgow, 1 May 1942; Twynam to Linlithgow, 1 May 1942; Stewart to Linlithgow, 3 May 1942; Hallett to Linlithgow, 4 May 1942; Clow to Linlithgow, 9 May 1942, *TOP*, vol. 2, pp. 2, 3, 19, 25, 55 respectively.

[58] Linlithgow to Governors, 30 April 1942, *TOP*, vol. 2, p. 1.

[59] Linlithgow to Amery, 25 May 1942, Ibid., p. 123. See also Amery to Linlithgow, 27 May 1942, Ibid., p. 141.

[60] FRs for Bengal, Bihar, UP, CP, Bombay—from April to July 1942, HP file nos. 18/4 to 18/7/42.

[61] Linlithgow to Amery, 18 May 1942, *TOP*, vol. 2, p. 102.

[62] Quoted in Sitaramayya, *Indian National Congress*, vol. 2, pp. 340–2.

[63] *Statesman*, 15 July 1942.   [64] *Statesman*, 1 August 1942.

[65] See, for example, *Statesman*, 3 July 1942.

fuse to see a person whom I thoroughly distrust and discredit. Supposing he is great and good enough to see me, what am I to say to him?'[66] He did not think Jinnah wanted a settlement with the Congress. Otherwise, why had he not accepted Azad's offer that representatives of the Congress and the League 'should put their heads together and never part until they have reached a settlement. Is there any flaw or want of sincerity in this offer?'[67]

The British cabinet reacted to the Congress resolution with indignation. 'What I feel', wrote Amery, 'is that Congress has definitely shown its hand as claiming to be an authority parallel to the Government of India and entitled to tell the public to defy the authority of the latter'. The challenge must be taken up. If the War Cabinet hesitated, Amery had 'no doubt that they will not be able to stand up to the two of us together ... This is a time when a fire brigade cannot wait to ring up headquarters, but must turn the hose on the flames at once'.[68]

But Amery need not have worried. The war cabinet authorized Linlithgow to take decisive action whenever it seemed necessary.[69] The Government of India would strike when the AICC ratified the resolution.[70] Yet Linlithgow would have preferred public opinion to counteract Gandhi and the Congress.[71] Governors, however, had no success in persuading influential provincial politicians to speak out against the Congress. Fazlul Huq airily told Herbert that he did not think civil disobedience would succeed in Bengal; that the League and the Mahasabha would be enough to deal with it. He was reluctant to issue any statement or to carry out any propaganda against Gandhi, on the ground that his present relations with Jinnah made it difficult to identify himself with statements which Jinnah had issued.[72] Jogendra Singh, who had recently joined the Executive Council, was not expected to be 'as outspoken as one would like',

---

[66] Gandhi to Rajagopalachari, 1 August 1942, *MGC*, Serial no. 2093.

[67] *Harijan*, 26 July 1942.

[68] Amery to Linlithgow, 13 July 1942, *TOP*, vol. 2, pp. 380–1.

[69] War Cabinet W.M. (42) 91st Conclusions, Minutes 8–9, 13 July 1942, Ibid, p. 378.

[70] Government of India Home Department to Secretary of State, 3 August 1942, Ibid., pp. 535–6.

[71] See, for example, Linlithgow to Lumley, (T), 16 July 1942; and Linlithgow to Herbert, (T), 16 July 1942; Linlithgow to Glancy, 16 July 1942, Ibid., pp. 395–6, 396, 398 respectively.

[72] Herbert to Linlithgow, 23 July 1942, Ibid., pp. 439–40.

for he took his cue from the Akalis, who, sailing as usual in two boats, were represented in the Unionist ministry and in the Viceroy's Executive but had not severed their connection with the Congress.[73]

Even as they discussed the administrative measures to be taken in the event of a civil disobedience movement, British officials were sceptical whether Gandhi would really launch one. There had been very few signs of preparations for a no-tax or no-rent movement, or of interference with civil and military establishments. 'Lack of any real eagerness' for this latest assault on the British *raj* by Congress was very noticeable throughout the country, noted intelligence officials. This, coupled with 'the apparent lack of preparation', cast 'an air of unreality' over the whole movement, and raised doubts as to whether it was not all 'a piece of bluff on the part of Gandhi'.[74]

Only a month later, Linlithgow informed Churchill: 'I am engaged here in meeting by far the most serious rebellion since that of 1857, the gravity and extent of which we have so far concealed from the world for reasons of military security'.[75] The British reacted to the ratification of the Congress Working Committee resolution by the AICC on 8 August by arresting Congress leaders on the morning of 9 August, in the expectation that the arrests would finish off any contemplated movement.[76] They were, therefore, understandably taken aback when, three days later, the leaderless and unorganized supporters of the Congress rose in revolt in various parts of the country. Intelligence sources held that the disturbances 'represent the spontaneous reaction to the arrest of popular leaders . . . there is no indication of any real coordination of effort.' There was nothing new which had not been tried in previous campaigns, 'except perhaps that the sense of frustration leading to racial animosity is more marked'.[77]

The events of 1942 showed the depth of the national will. In August and September, the British used 57 batallions to crush the rebellion, twenty-four of which had to be withdrawn from field formations under training.[78] The administration broke down com-

[73] Glancy to Linlithgow, 18 July 1942, Ibid., p. 409.

[74] Weekly Summary no. 39, 31 July 1942, L/WS/1/1433, p. 63.

[75] Linlithgow to Churchill, 31 August 1942, *TOP*, vol. 2, p. 853.

[76] Government of India Home Department to Secretary of State, 3 August 1942, Ibid., p. 536.

[77] Weekly Summary no. 41, 14 August 1942, L/WS/1/1433, p. 71.

[78] John Connell, *Wavell: Supreme Commander* (London, 1969), p. 230.

pletely in most of North-Central Bihar and Eastern UP, and the Fortnightly Reports from Bihar for August could not be sent to Delhi because of a breakdown of communications.[79] Railways were blocked or dismantled, telegraph wires were cut, certain railway stations in Orissa could not be declared protected areas because forces were not available to protect them.[80] The Whipping Act was revived in Bombay, and a concerned war cabinet was told that it would be used very sparingly; that the introduction of whipping, 'which might better be termed corporal punishment, is a minor detail in a serious situation.'[81]

By the beginning of 1943, the movement was suppressed, but the administration did not come out of it unscathed. The British knew that Indians did not identify with the war effort, and it was difficult to cultivate a spirit of war-mindedness among the masses 'when the spirit of self-sacrifice and personal identification with the war effort is weak among the educated classes, and even among members of the European business community and some officials.'[82] Nor was it 'particularly bracing', as Herbert wrote, 'for sorely-tried police officers to read in the Press that Jawaharlal Nehru and his friends are extremely well and enjoying a game of Badminton.'[83]

The long-term problem was the British intention to leave India 'at no very remote date'. Indian officials were opportunistic: they had remained staunch during the Quit India movement, but they looked to their future rulers, 'whoever they may be,' and shared with 'a large part of the human race a desire to be on the winning side.'[84] In Bihar, for example, where the movement resulted in a major administrative breakdown, government officials 'as a class' did not relish being cited as opponents of the Congress. They claimed to be, as was the British Civil Service, outside politics. 'No doubt the exponents of this view are looking to the future when Congress adminis-

[79] FR for UP for the first half of August 1942, HP file no. 18/8/42. See also Max Harcourt, 'Kisan populism and revolution in rural India', in D.A. Low (ed.) *Congress and the Raj*, p. 316.

[80] Minutes of Home Department Meeting held at 3 p.m. on 28 August 1942 in Additional Secretary's room, HP file no. 3/17/42, p. 22.

[81] Lumley to Linlithgow, 14 August 1942, *TOP*, vol. 2, p. 700.

[82] Some reflections on official propaganda, by H.V. Hodson, Reforms Commissioner, dated 26 August 1942; Reforms Office file no. 143/42-R.

[83] Herbert to Linlithgow, 8 October 1942, L/P&J/5/149.

[84] Maxwell to Laithwaite, 24 October 1942; *TOP*, vol. 3, pp. 156–8.

trations will again be in power.'[85] Hindu officials, in any case, had Congress sympathies; while Muslim officials thought that Pakistan held out good prospects for them.[86] The uncertain loyalties of Indian officials were already beginning to stir the foundations of the Raj.

Jinnah described the movement as 'a most dangerous mass movement' intended to force Congress demands "at the point of the bayonet," which, if conceded, would mean the sacrifice of all other interests, particularly those of Moslem in India'. He appealed to Muslims 'to keep completely aloof' from the movement, and to the Hindu public 'to stop this internecine civil war before it is too late.'[87]

Provincial Muslim Leaguers followed Jinnah's lead,[88] even as the Muslim League Working Committee made another overture to the British. The League would negotiate 'with any party on a footing of equality' to set up a provisional Government of India in order to mobilize the resources of the country for the defence of India. 'If the Muslim masses are to be roused to intensify the war effort it is only possible provided they are assured that it will lead to the realization of Pakistan.' The League called on the British, 'without further delay,' to make an 'unequivocal' declaration guaranteeing the right of self-determination with a pledge to abide by the verdict of a plebiscite of Muslims.[89] Jinnah declared that the words "any party" in the resolution meant any recognized party 'which is able to deliver the goods', and called on the British to give the League half the seats in the Executive Council.[90]

Jinnah and provincial Muslim Leaguers concentrated on using their influence to keep Muslims away from the Quit India movement. The League devoted much attention to getting Muslims exempted from collective fines imposed on villagers in areas where sabotage had taken place.[91] In the NWFP, however, many Muslims appeared willing to follow the Congress lead, and anti-Congress propaganda had to be built up 'by pretty intensive propaganda' by

[85] Stewart to Linlithgow, 19 September 1942, L/P&J/5/178.
[86] Note by Conran Smith dated 19 October 1942, *TOP*, vol. 3, pp. 160–1.
[87] *Statesman*, 10 August 1942.
[88] E.g. *Morning News*, 15 August 1942, *Eastern Times*, 17 August 1942.
[89] *Statesman*, 21 August 1942.
[90] *Morning News*, 21 August 1942.
[91] *Morning News*, 1, 8 September 1942.

ulema organized by British officials.[92] But there was evidence of Muslim complicity in Baramati town in Bombay;[93] in the CP and Berar Muslims were generally exempted from collective fines but individual liability was enforced.[94] The League and its followers held aloof from the movement in Bihar—but so did the Mahasabha—but there were cases of arrests of Muslims because of participation in lawlessness.[95] Muslims, 'like other people, for instance the big landholders of Bihar, generally took no part in opposition to Hindu law-breaking.'[96] In Bengal, Herbert was apprehensive of an 'increasing lack of support for Government in this all-important question of law and order, and even in the war effort, in quarters where we generally expect it.

'At a recent meeting of the Provincial League Working Committee, the view was advanced that the "neutrality" towards the war effort forced upon the League by the attitude of the British Government might be regarded as an asset to Muslims in the event of a successful Japanese invasion! . . . I am concerned at the grave possibility of our losing throughout India the support of even those whom we have hitherto regarded, if not as our friends, as the enemies of our enemies.'[97]

In Bihar and Assam, Muslims protested against their being included in collective responsibility schemes for safeguarding communications.[98] Muslim League circles in Patna were agitated over the question of lighting restrictions as they affected arrangements for Moharrum processions.[99] Assam officials were concerned that 'protest has been aroused among non-Muslims at the use of assistance to check subversive activity, rather than Muslims protesting at the serious hardship which had been caused by that activity.'[100] Muslims joined in prayers for Gandhi's life when he

[92] Cunningham to Linlithgow, 28 September 1942, *TOP*, vol. 3, p. 56. On organization of ulema by NWFP government since August 1939, see *CC*, vol. 19.

[93] FR for Bombay for the first half of September 1942, HP file no. 18/9/42.

[94] FR for CP and Berar for the first half of September, Ibid.

[95] FR for Bihar for the first half of September, Ibid.

[96] *Quarterly Survey of the Political and Constitutional Position of the British in India*, no. 21, *LC*, vol. 145.

[97] Herbert to Linlithgow, 6 November 1942, *TOP*, vol. 3, p. 211.

[98] FR for Bihar for the first half of November and December and FR for Assam for the first half of October 1942. HP file nos. 18/10, 18/11 and 18/12/42.

[99] FR for Bihar for the first half of January 1943. HP file no. 18/1/43.

[100] FR for Assam for the second half of November 1942 and Clow to Linlithgow, 17 November 1942, HP file no. 18/11/42.

undertook his fast in February 1943 'until Mr. Jinnah's statement in reply to the invitation to attend the All-Parties Conference came and stopped them from joining in'![101]

One of the most remarkable features of the Quit India movement is the absence of any communal incident or disorder. In report after report, notes Hutchins, the entry under 'Communal' was the single phrase, '"Nothing to Report."'[102] If the aloofness of the Muslim community at large was one of the most noticeable characteristics of the movement, 'the almost complete absence of Hindu aggression against Muslims remains a remarkable fact.'[103] On the question of fines, there was no doubt that 'Muslims . . . held aloof from any acts of commission,' but there were many cases in which 'they did not do all they could in their power to help the authorities and were thereby equally guilty of acts of omission with other communities.'[104] Reports from provinces indicate that officials had difficulty in obtaining evidence against saboteurs, either because of sympathy with the Congress or apathy.[105] In the sources consulted, except for two instances in the Midnapore district in Bengal,[106] I have not come across a single instance of Muslims giving evidence against saboteurs, most of whom, presumably, were Hindus. So, if the Quit India movement demonstrated for the first time since 1937 that the Congress did not have a hold over Muslims, except perhaps in the NWFP, the absence of reports of Muslim cooperation with British officials in tracking down saboteurs and rebels suggests that they collaborated with neither the Congress nor the British.

The Akali reaction to the Quit India movement was to allow a limited number of followers to offer token civil disobedience while Tara Singh exhorted his followers to support the British. The Akali Conference at Vahilla Kalhan in Lyallpur district on 26 and 27 September 1942 passed a resolution which called for the independence of India and an end to the political deadlock. The resolution represented a compromise between the Kartar Singh faction who

[101] FR for Bihar for the second half of February 1943. HP file no. 18/2/43.

[102] F. Hutchins, *Spontaneous Revolution* (Harvard, 1971), p. 228.

[103] *Quarterly Survey of the Political and Constitutional Position of the British in India*, no. 21, *LC*, vol. 145.

[104] P.D. Barran to R. Tottenham, 6 November 1942, HP file no. 3/46/42, p. 9.

[105] E.g. FR for Bombay for the first half of December 1942; FR for Bengal for the first half of January 1943; FR for Bihar for the second half of February 1943, HP file nos. 18/12/42, 18/1 and 18/2/43.

[106] FR for Bengal for the first half of September 1942, HP file no. 18/9/42.

wished to avoid any reference to the Congress and the pro-
Congress faction who wanted the Dal to pledge unequivocal
support for the Congress.[107] The Akalis wished to maintain the
position of the Sikhs in the Army; and they thought that the best
way of doing so was to support the British. They were also aware of
the political advantage of being associated with the Punjab government and at the Centre. So Tara Singh's conception of the role of a
leader was, in the words of Glancy, 'a resolute refusal to give a lead
in any definite direction.' The attitude was understandable in view
of Sikh fears of their future, for they could not rely on anyone. The
British had not granted them any favours unconditionally. 'We have
taken steps to point out to him and his friends that any continuance
of this form of response to the favours which the Sikhs have received from Government must make it increasingly difficult for
those who sympathise with the community to espouse their
cause.'[108]

The Muslim League Ministries and Jinnah—August 1942 to March 1945

With the Congress and its sympathizers engaged in civil disobedience on a scale which had shaken the very foundations of Empire,
Linlithgow advised Governors to explore the possibilities of forming non-Congress ministries in their provinces, in view of their
'propaganda value.'[109] The basic principle, then, behind the reconstruction of ministries in Assam, Sind, NWFP and Bengal, was that,
wherever possible, a counterpoise to the Congress should be built
up in the provinces. To the extent that British policy resulted in the
formation of League ministries in the Muslim majority provinces,
they were responsible for the enhanced stature of the League, and
the growth of the idea of Pakistan.

How much control did Jinnah exercise over provincial League
ministries, and what evidence was there of support for a sovereign
Pakistan in the Muslim majority provinces? These are among the
questions which we shall try to answer.

The arrests of Congress MLAs in Assam led to the fall of the
coalition ministry which had existed since 1937, and Mohammad

[107] FR for Punjab for the second half of September 1942, Ibid.
[108] Glancy to Linlithgow, 21 August 1942, L/P&J/245.
[109] Linlithgow to Amery, (T), 16 August 1942, *TOP*, vol. 2, p. 731.

Saadullah formed a new coalition with other parties represented in the legislature.[110] In Sind, Allah Baksh was dismissed by Dow, on instructions from Linlithgow, because he had renounced his titles. Linlithgow had earlier been critical of the half-hearted manner in which Allah Baksh's ministry was carrying out the war effort, and the renunciation of his titles, which the Viceroy regarded as being inconsistent with his oath of office, gave Linlithgow an opportunity to dispose of him.[111] The way was now open for G.H. Hidayatullah to form a ministry.

Provincial Leaguers decided to join Hidayatullah's ministry against the wishes of Jinnah, who urged them not to enter a government in which they were not the dominant element. The provincial League passed a resolution asking Jinnah to abstain from giving instructions on provincial matters of which he did not know much, and supported the decision of the League Assembly party to join the ministry.[112] A new turn was given to ministerial politics when Hidayatullah decided to join the League. He stated that his Hindu colleagues were being pressurized by the Congress, and in view of this and in the interests of his community, he had decided to join the League. Hidayatullah's decision surprised everyone, including provincial Leaguers, who had not been told of his intentions.[113] The rationale behind his joining the League could have been his apprehension that Hindu ministers and their supporters might eventually walk out on him: in that event, he could best assure his future prospects of retaining the Premiership by lining up with the League.

The League extended its organization in Sind while it held power. By March 1943, nearly 30,000 members had been enrolled in the Thar Pakkar district alone.[114] Whether this was done by the provincial League of its own accord or under instructions from the all-India body, is not known. It is possible that the provincial League took the initiative itself to strengthen its base against its Muslim opponents in Allah Baksh's Azad Muslim Party. For, if both parties resorted to communal propaganda, as they did during the by-

[110] FR for Assam for the first half of September 1942, HP file no. 18/9/42.

[111] Viceroy to Governor of Sind, (T), 26 September 1942, *LC*, vol. 98.

[112] Dow to Linlithgow, 22 October 1942, L/P&J/5/258. See also *Eastern Times*, 25 October and 10 November 1942.

[113] Dow to Linlithgow, 5 November 1942, L/P&J/5/258.

[114] FR for Sind for first half of March 1943, HP file no. 18/3/43.

election in Shikarpur,[115] the party which had the broader political base would be more likely to consolidate its position in the province.

In the NWFP, divisions in the provincial League had discouraged Cunningham from installing a League ministry. The detention of eight of the twenty-one Congress legislators had reduced the party's majority in the assembly, but Cunningham turned down a suggestion from Feroze Khan Noon, a member of the Viceroy's Council, that the League could win the support of non-Congress MLAs. 'The balance between the Congress and the non-Congress in the assembly is so delicate that this would almost certainly mean a defeat for the ministry', he informed Linlithgow on 28 September 1942.[116] It was not until April 1943 that the League was able to form a ministry. Aurangzeb Khan wanted to form an intercommunal ministry, and solicited the support of the Akalis and the Mahasabha. The Akalis debated whether their interests would be served better by cooperation with the League or by joining 'nationalist' elements in the opposition. A statement by V.D. Savarkar, the Mahasabha leader, that where the formation of a Muslim League ministry was inevitable, Hindus and Sikhs might enter into a coalition with the League to further their interests,[117] coupled with the refusal of Khan Saheb to guarantee a seat for the Akalis in a future Congress ministry, induced Ajit Singh to accept a portfolio in Aurangzeb's cabinet. The Akalis joined the coalition on the understanding that the question of Pakistan would not be raised during the tenure of the ministry.[118] The Mahasabha withdrew from the coalition following Aurangzeb's refusal to concede the speakership of the House to Mehr Chand Khanna; and Aurangzeb's ministry came to be known as the League–Akali coalition. The ministry never acquired the support of more than 19 of the 43 members in the Assembly.[119]

Bengal provided an illustration of a Muslim League ministry being brought into power almost solely by the inclination and action of the governor. Since the start of the Quit India movement, Herbert had expressed dissatisfaction with the conduct of the Huq

[115] Dow to Wavell, 3 November and 22 November 1943, L/P&J/5/260.

[116] Cunningham to Linlithgow, 28 September 1942, *TOP*, vol. 3, pp. 55–6.

[117] FR for NWFP for first half of May 1943, HP file no. 18/3/43.

[118] A.K. Gupta, *Northwest Frontier Province and the Freedom Struggle, 1932–1947* (New Delhi, 1979), p. 133–4.   [119] Ibid., p. 135.

ministry in all matters relating to the war effort. His coalition with the Bose section of the Congress produced, in Herbert's opinion, a situation 'in which local officers are deterred from exercising firmness and initiative in dealing with disturbances.' Herbert thought that the dismissal of the ministry was 'increasingly called for consideration'.[120] It was not that Herbert had any great faith in the advantages of a League ministry. This alternative would be 'little better, as its main concern would be to find more and better jobs for Muslims'.[121] The circumstances of Huq's dismissal in April 1943 are best explained by Herbert himself. The Governor thought that the ministry was already tottering, that it could only maintain itself 'by pandering to the wishes of those whose votes kept it in existence'. A motion of no-confidence was to be moved in the assembly on 29 March. 'I felt, perhaps wrongly,' that yet another debate on such a motion resulting in the fall of the Ministry would further embitter the relations between parties to an extent which would make negotiations for a Ministry of all the parties quite impossible. 'If, on the other hand, Huq wanted to scrape through the session . . . he would have continued his tricks . . . . Further, it would . . . have been exceedingly difficult for me to dismiss Huq despite his numerous acts of misconduct.'

Huq had announced publicly several times that he would resign if such an action would facilitate the formation of an all-parties ministry. Herbert felt that 'Huq's promise to resign, openly expressed in the Assembly, was an opportunity not to be neglected; and I must admit that I urged him pretty firmly to honour it, though "compulsion" is quite unfair description'.[122]

Huq did not intend to resign when he came to see Herbert on 28 March,

> 'but . . . at some stage in the interview he decided that it might be to his advantage to do so if he subsequently played his cards well. This . . . he succeeded in doing. He signed a draft letter of resignation prepared, not for his signature, but merely as a model, so that he could say that he was "framed" by the Governor; he undertook to see the Budget through the next day, thus allaying my mind until it was too late; and he asked for the announcement of his resignation to be postponed in order that he might spring it himself, wreck the budget and claim universal sympathy'.[123]

[120] Herbert to Linlithgow, 8 October 1942, L/P&J/5/149.
[121] Herbert to Linlithgow, 11 January 1943, Ibid.
[122] Herbert to Linlithgow, 7 April 1943, L/P&J/5/150.   [123] Ibid.

When the House met on the 29th, Huq stated that he had been made to resign by the Governor. The speaker then announced that the ministry did not exist and adjourned the assembly for a fortnight. On the 31st, Herbert proclaimed Section 93. 'I do feel that I have (shall I say?) blundered into the right solution in spite of all the political disadvantages,' concluded Herbert.[124]

Section 93 was proclaimed while Huq still had a majority. He had won a division by 10 votes only on the previous day. But they were the votes of the Congress. 'The position was that he was in the hands of the party in sympathy with the disturbances which are prejudicing our war effort'.[125]

Linlithgow was 'uneasy' at the manner of Huq's dismissal, and also at the prospects of a Muslim League ministry in Bengal. The criticism in the press had been embarrassing to the government, and 'Jinnah if he wants to' might try to make the formation of any administration impossible 'save on his own terms which might be quite unpalatable so far as we are concerned.'[126] The Viceroy had no alternative but to approve of Section 93, but he informed Herbert that he would not approve of any League ministry unless it was supported by a 'suitable majority' in the legislature. 'Nor should you commit yourself to commission Nazimuddin in light (sic) of his investigations to form a Ministry without prior reference to me.'[127] Clearly, Linlithgow had little faith in Herbert's ability to handle the ministerial crisis in Bengal. In his view, it was a mistake to put Huq in a position to suggest that his resignation was based on a letter, the draft of which had been prepared in Government House. He could not, he wrote to Amery, 'imagine a greater folly'.[128]

Nazimuddin formed a ministry with the support of the 25 Europeans in the Bengal legislature, who had, until now, always supported Huq. They openly said that they would oppose any new Huq ministry because they were 'disgusted' with his misgovernment and corruption. The new ministry contained no Muslim who was not a member of the Muslim League. Nazimuddin failed to get the support of the Congress Bose group, which had supported Huq,

---

[124] Ibid.   [125] Governor of Bengal to Viceroy, (T), 31 March 1943, *LC*, vol. 43.
[126] Viceroy to Governor of Bengal, (T), 30 March 1943, R/3/2/84.
[127] Viceroy to Governor of Bengal, (T), 31 March 1943, Ibid.
[128] Linlithgow to Amery, 2 April 1943, *TOP*, vol. 3, p. 875; and Linlithgow to Herbert, 11 April 1943, R/3/2/46.

and the Mahasabha. Nazimuddin promised to 'take every possible measure to advance the war effort.'[129]

Nazimuddin's expression of support for the war effort was probably made against Jinnah's wishes.[130] Yet Jinnah would not, or could not take any action against Nazimuddin, presumably because he did not want to fritter away the prestige the League had acquired by forming a ministry in Bengal. There does not seem to be much evidence of Jinnah's increasing control over the League ministries. It was not until December 1943 that Jinnah appointed a Committee of Action, consisting of 5 to 7 members, 'to prepare and organize the Muslims all over India to meet all contingencies, resist the imposition of an all-India Federation or any other constitution for the United India, and prepare them for the coming struggle for the achievement of Pakistan'. The Committee of Action would control and direct the activities of the provincial Leagues.[131]

How much control was actually exercised by the Committee of Action is difficult to say. When the Committee visited the NWFP in June 1944, it was surprised and dismayed to find that no organizational work had been attempted in the province.[132] This suggests that contacts between the Committee and the provincial League were almost non-existent; and that the provincial League had not carried out the Committee's instructions, assuming that they had been given.

Jinnah himself does not appear to have been very interested in provincial politics. Ispahani wanted him to advise Nazimuddin on the selection of personnel for his ministry in April 1943.[133] But much to Ispahani's disappointment, Jinnah expressed his preference

'that Sir Nazimuddin and you people there should settle the personnel of the Ministry, and I hope that you will do it in a manner which will be most creditable to the Party, the Bengal Muslims and Muslim India as a whole . . . I, therefore, think that I should not go to Calcutta, nor is it really necessary.'[134]

[129] Herbert to Linlithgow, 19 April 1943, *LC*, vol. 53; see also FR for Bengal for second half of April 1943, HP file no. 18/4/43.

[130] Jinnah to Ispahani, 9 April 1943, *Jinnah–Ispahani Correspondence*, p. 347.

[131] K.B. Sayeed, *Pakistan: The Formative Phase*, p. 190.

[132] NWFP Governor's Report dated 24 June 1944, *CC*, vol. 16.

[133] Ispahani to Jinnah, 13 April 1943, and 15 April 1943; Zaidi (ed.) *Jinnah–Ispahani Correspondence*, pp. 353 and 355.

[134] Jinnah to Ispahani, 15 April 1943, Ibid., p. 357.

Again, Jinnah turned down an appeal by Muslim Leaguers in the Punjab to visit the province and to sort out their problems with the Unionists. He merely expressed the hope that if the ministry and the League would work together 'these little ripples that you see on the surface will disappear'.[135] Jinnah did exert himself—albeit unsuccessfully—in Sind in February 1945. A dispute arose between G.M. Syed, President of the provincial Muslim League and Hidayatullah, and Syed withdrew support and supported a cut motion against the ministry. Jinnah pointed out to him that only the Hindus would benefit from the quarrel between two Muslim leaders.[136] Hidayatullah was now ready to take in Maula Baksh, brother of Allah Baksh, into his ministry and to coalesce with his Azad Muslim party. Jinnah's efforts to persuade Hidayatullah to drop Maula Baksh were of no avail. Hidayatullah regarded as interference by Jinnah the suggestion that he should either get Baksh to sign the League's pledge or drop him. Hidayatullah was still a member of the League, but he defied a directive from the provincial League to drop Baksh.[137] Dependent on Maula Baksh, he now accepted a suggestion by him that he release Congress MLAs. The Congress legislative party agreed to support Hidayatullah in return for the release of their MLAs. For the time being then, the League was out of power in Sind, having been replaced by the Azad Muslim party and the Congress. It also lost prestige as it lost two by-elections in the province to the Azad Muslim party in March.[138] The events of February and March 1945 clearly demonstrated that Jinnah's hold over the Sind League was extremely uncertain; and that when openly defied, he could do very little unless he was sure of his following in the provincial League.

Jinnah's apparent lack of interest in the provincial politics of the Punjab and Bengal in 1943, as compared with his attempts to interfere in Sind in 1942 and in 1945, suggests that his primary aim was to maintain his position and prestige as leader of all Muslims at the all-India level. Coalitions with non-League Muslims in the pro-

[135] Jinnah to Amjad Ali, 8 May 1943, S. Jafri (ed.) *Qaid-e-Azam Jinnah's Correspondence with Punjab Muslim Leaders* (Lahore, 1977), p. 14.

[136] *Statesman*, 13, 22, 25 February, 1 March 1945.

[137] *Statesman*, 9 and 12 March 1945, 15 March and 27 March 1945. See also Wavell to Amery, 21 February 1945, *TOP*, vol. 5, p. 286, and Memorandum by Amery, 5 April 1945, Ibid., pp. 830–2.

[138] See for example, Dow to Wavell, 22 January 1945, L/P&J/5/261.

vinces would detract from the League's claim to represent *all* Muslims, and this could be why he tried to put his foot down whenever Leaguers attempted to line up with non-League Muslims. In the CP, for example, he would not allow the provincial League leader to enter into a coalition with any non-League Muslims, and Rauf Shah seems to have given way tohim.[139] Where the League had not coalesced with non-League Muslims, as in the NWFP and Bengal, he does not seem to have paid much attention to provincial Leagues.

The Unionist–League Tussle—November 1942 to June 1944

It was in the Punjab that Jinnah launched a unique campaign to establish a League ministry in a province. His visit to the Punjab in November 1942 rippled the surface of Punjab politics, disturbing the Unionist coalition by his advocacy of Pakistan and his reference to the Sikhs as a 'sub-nationality'. The main points made by him in his speeches were that the League had made enormous strides in recent years towards attaining the goal of Pakistan; the Quit India movement aimed at establishing Hindu domination over India; the British should acknowledge the right of Muslims to self-determination and promise to give effect to the verdict of a Muslim plebiscite. He ridiculed the view that 'sub-national' groups should be given the same right of self-determination as the Muslims. The 'Hindu-Muslim question is an all India one, but the Muslim-Sikh question is between Pakistan and the Sikhs.' This statement created the impression that he was opposed to the Sikander formula; an impression which was not wholly dispelled by his subsequent assertion that he had no knowledge of this formula and had never referred to it.[140]

Embarrassed by Jinnah's statement, yet afraid to risk his position among Muslim Unionists by an open rupture with Jinnah, Sikander proclaimed that he saw eye to eye with the 'champion of Pakistan'—thus shaking the foundations of his alliance with Baldev Singh and widening the communal cleavage in the Punjab.[141] The Sikhs, whose political horizons were essentially provincial, were

[139] Twynam to Linlithgow, 12/14 July 1943, *LC*, vol. 64.

[140] FR for Punjab for second half of November 1942, HP file no. 18/11/42. See also *Morning News*, 17 November 1942.

[141] Glancy to Linlithgow, 28 November 1942, *LC*, vol. 91.

caught between their wish to confine discussion on the communal problem to 'local men' and the uncomfortable knowledge that the League, 'by including the Punjab within the scheme of things for Pakistan, has made our problem an all India one.' Pakistan would mean the annihilation of the Sikhs.[142] Simultaneously, the Akalis negotiated with Jinnah, leading Hindus to accuse them of deserting the Hindu-Sikh front against Pakistan. The negotiations with Jinnah broke down because of Jinnah's unwillingness to agree to a readjustment of the provincial boundaries, while the Akalis made it clear that the Sikhs were not prepared to live under Muslim rule unconditionally. The failure of the negotiations between the Sikhs and Jinnah led to recriminations within the Unionist coalition, with the Sikhs accusing Sikander of not honouring his pact with Baldev Singh and of Muslim bias.[143]

It is interesting to look at the extent of support for the League in the Punjab at this time. Punjab officials noted that Jinnah's meetings had attracted large audiences of between ten to thirty thousand persons and had given the Pakistan movement a fillip, but doubted whether the effect of his visit to the province would be lasting. The League's influence in the Punjab was mainly confined to the urban classes; few of the provincial leaders commanded any widespread support; much of the interest attached to reports of current political speeches was artificially stimulated by the press and died down as soon as another topic presented itself for discussion. Jinnah voiced the determination of Muslims not to submit to the rule of the Hindu majority at the *all-India* level, but in the Punjab, most Muslims were with the Unionists.[144]

These comments were corroborated by the *Eastern Times*, a paper sympathetic to the League in the Punjab. An editorial lamented that the number of persons on the rolls of the League was very small, and that no sustained effort had been made to remedy the situation. Jinnah's meeting at Lahore was described as 'a badly managed affair'. Some volunteers seemed more interested 'in watching the *tamasha* (fun) than in doing their job', and it was obvious that they were never trained for any such work. This was because the Lahore City Muslim League was itself a non-entity, and had made no effort to organize primary Leagues in the city. 'And how has the

[142] *Tribune*, 10 December 1942.

[143] *Tribune*, 17 December 1942.

[144] FR for Punjab for second half of November 1942, HP file no. 18/11/42.

City Muslim League come into existence without Primary Leagues? The Lahore City Muslim League is a clique, whose main purpose seems to be to enable certain men to pose as President, Vice-President, etc., and remain in the public eye'. The city League had presented a purse of Rs. 3000 to Jinnah; a city like Lahore 'could have easily presented ten times that sum.'[145]

The death of Sikander Hyat Khan in December 1942 was a blow to his party and to the British, who acknowledged that they owed the success of the war effort in the Punjab to him.[146] Sikander had maintained political stability in the province—Punjab was probably the only Muslim majority province which had escaped internecine conflicts and frequent changes of ministries since the outbreak of the war. Jinnah failed in his attempt to have a say in the selection of a new leader of the Unionist party, and therefore, of the Punjab. Khizar Hyat Khan Tiwana, son of Sir Umar Hyat Tiwana, was one of the biggest landowners in the Punjab. His loyalty to the British dated from 1919, when he had lent 150 horses to the British to control the non-cooperation movement in Amritsar. He had served in the ministries of Fazli Husain and Sikander, and he was chosen as the new leader of the Unionists. A motion of confidence, moved by Chhotu Ram, the Revenue Minister, at the meeting of the Unionist party, was seconded by Mamdot, president of the Punjab Muslim League. Earlier, Muslim Unionists had unanimously passed a vote of confidence in Khizar.[147]

Linlithgow doubted Khizar's ability to stand up to Jinnah, but he thought that Glancy, who had become Governor of the Punjab in 1942, was 'now well in the saddle' and in a position to give him a great deal of assistance.[148] The Viceroy was probably implying that Jinnah should not be allowed to disturb the war effort in the Punjab. Linlithgow did not make clear whether he would have encouraged Khizar to break with Jinnah, if necessary, thus reversing his policy of using influence with Sikander in 1941—especially as the Congress leaders were now in jail and the Quit India movement had been brought under control; and the need for Muslim unity, under Jinnah's leadership, may not have appeared so urgent. Linlithgow had regarded Jinnah as unreliable and uncooperative as the Con-

---

[145]*Eastern Times*, 29 November 1942.
[146] Linlithgow to Amery, 28 December 1942, *TOP*, vol. 3, p. 431.
[147] *Statesman*, 24 January 1943.
[148] Linlithgow to Amery, 11 January 1943, *LC*, vol. 12.

gress in the matter of supporting the war effort, and was apprehensive that Jinnah, always out to extract the most favourable political bargain—in this case from the British—might hamper the war effort in the Punjab if he managed to tighten his hold over the Unionist ministry, or actually establish a Muslim League ministry in the province. Linlithgow feared that the break up of the tenuous alliance between the Muslim and non-Muslim ministers would lead to purely communal politics in the Punjab, which in turn would create instability in the province. The Sikhs already appeared nervous; non-Muslim officials might be anxious. Therefore, Glancy must make it clear that he would use his special powers to prevent the fall of the Unionist ministry.[149]

Somewhat on the defensive against Jinnah, Khizar managed, nevertheless, to hold his own. At a meeting of the all-India Muslim League in Delhi in March 1943, Khizar acknowledged the general leadership of Jinnah and affirmed his adherence to the Sikander–Jinnah pact, but a resolution advocating more active interference by the League in the Punjab was withdrawn. Khizar, however, failed to prevent the setting up of a separate League party in the Punjab—he said it already existed under the terms of the Sikander–Jinnah pact—and promised, however vaguely, that he would work for the uplift of the League in the province in accordance with the terms of the pact. But Khizar would remain leader of the provincial League.[150]

On the warpath with Khizar, Jinnah now alleged that Glancy had violated constitutional procedure by failing to consult the Muslim League before taking steps for the appointment of a Prime Minister and was 'disagreeably surprised' when Khizar drew his attention to the Governor's Instrument of Instructions.[151]

The tussle between the League and Khizar continued. Mamdot and Jinnah told Khizar that the Unionist ministry should be redesignated 'Muslim League coalition.' Khizar retorted that he intended to abide by the Sikander–Jinnah pact and to maintain the name 'Unionist'. He pointed out that he himself had been elected to the assembly on the Unionist ticket. Jinnah was 'much incensed'. But he realized that he could not go further as he did not have a majority in the provincial assembly. So he instructed Mamdot to come to a satisfactory agreement with Khizar. The weakness of Jin-

[149] Linlithgow to Glancy, 1 February 1943, Ibid., vol. 92.
[150] *Statesman*, 5 and 8 March 1943; and *Tribune*, 8 March 1943.
[151] Glancy to Linlithgow, 14 March 1943, *TOP*, vol. 3, p. 809.

nah's position on Unionist–League relations in the Punjab was also illustrated by his failure to force a decision that the constitution of the provincial League should be determined by the all-India Muslim League so as to remove any inconsistency with the constitution of the all-India body.[152]

It was Wavell's appreciative reference in February 1944 to the geographical unity of India, and his praise for the 'conspicuous success' which had characterized the working of the intercommunal Unionist ministry which roused Jinnah's ire against Khizar.

> 'On the main problem of Indian unity', said Wavell, 'the difference between the Hindu and Muslim, I can only say this. You cannot alter geography. From the point of view of defence, of relations with the outside world, of many internal and external economic problems, India is a natural unit . . . That two communities and even two nations can make arrangements to live together in spite of differing cultures or religions, history provides many examples . . . . Coalition government by Indians for Indians is not an impossible ideal. It is being carried out at the Centre without friction; it has been carried on for nearly seven years with conspicuous success in the Punjab. Thanks to the leadership of men of good sense, goodwill, and good courage, the affairs of that Province have prospered with the minimum of communal friction; they have administered their Province in the interests of the Province, but also with regard to the interests of India and of the war effort of the United Nations, to which the Punjab has made so striking a contribution.'[153]

Ministerial circles in the Punjab welcomed Wavell's reference to the harmonious working of the Unionist majority—they thought it would strengthen their position for the future. Jinnah now showed his displeasure with Wavell. He summoned Mamdot to Delhi on the eve of the budget session of the Central assembly. In the assembly itself, the League joined the Congress in defeating cut motions on the railway budget. Liaqat Ali Khan was cheered by Congress benches when he stated that Britain was fighting the war for interests other than India's.[154]

The League's war with the Unionists was now under way. Daultana, then General Secretary of the Punjab Muslim League, outlined an ambitious mass contact programme to mobilize Muslims against the British and the Hindus.[155] In discussions with Muslim Leaguers,

---

[152] *Statesman*, 29 March 1943.
[153] *Legislative Assembly Debates*, 1944, vol. 1, pp. 342–3.
[154] *Statesman*, 21 and 28 February 1944.
[155] *Statesman*, 20 March 1944.

Jinnah reportedly emphasized that the Unionist party should be liquidated.[156] Leaguers alleged that Muslim Unionist ministers were ignoring the interests of their community, whose position in every department of the provincial government was deplorable. The creed of the Unionist party was Dominion Status and a united, democratic federal constitution 'for India as a whole.' Its policies reflected the interests of only one class—the zamindars—whereas the League was 'the people's party and the custodian and trustee of all interests and classes that constitute the Muslim nation.' Its 'fundamental and basic principles' were therefore 'quite different' from those of the Unionist Party.[157]

Jinnah returned to Lahore in April 1944. He was preaching Pakistan as the panacea for all ills, but avoided any reasoned explanation 'of where it begins and ends and what benefits it will confer. He might make an ideal leader of a Demolition Squad', mused Glancy, 'but anything in the way of constructive suggestion seems foreign to his nature'. His attempts to woo Chhotu Ram and Baldev Singh had met with little success. Many rural Muslim MLAs resented his dictatorial attitude and went so far as to threaten resignation from the League.[158]

Khizar, however, was assailed by grave misgivings, according to Glancy. He had told Glancy that 'he is thinking seriously of giving way to Jinnah's demand'.

> 'He says that the Unionist Party exists only in name, it has no funds and practically nothing in the way of organization, and its disappearance would cause little regret . . . He believes that there will be only two parties of any importance in India in the near future—the Congress and the Muslim League: if he defies Jinnah and persuades his staunch adherents to adopt this course, he fears that in a comparatively short time they will all be relegated to political oblivion.'

Khizar kept 'harping on the bitter experiences' of what occurred after World War I: 'those in the Punjab who had fought for the Empire found themselves ousted by traitors and non-cooperators while the British Government stood by and acquiesced.' Khizar wanted an "order" from Glancy that he should stand up to Jinnah in the interests of the war effort: 'tell him that I consider it to be his duty as a loyal subject to act in the manner suggested.' Glancy told

---

[156] *Statesman*, 23 March 1944.
[157] *Statesman*, 5 April 1944.
[158] Glancy to Wavell, 6 April 1944, L/P&J/5/247.

Khizar that he could not issue any such "order": he could only tell him 'as a friend' that 'he will have no peace hereafter, nor will he be serving the interests of the Province or of India or of Muslims or of the Empire if he gives way to Jinnah and places himself in his power'.[159]

Wavell favoured the encouragement given by Glancy to Khizar to stand up to Jinnah.[160] Wanting to help Khizar, Glancy discerned that he could take action against one of his ministers, Shaukat Hyat Khan, the son of Sikander, who appeared to be flirting with the League. Shaukat, observed Glancy, 'by his betrayal of his leader and his colleagues . . . has richly earned his removal.' But it would be better to avoid removing him on political grounds and there were other reasons which entitled him to dismissal. Shaukat had dismissed a lady inspectress of schools ostensibly for corruption but actually because she reportedly offended one of his subordinates. Eight different charges, mainly concerned with corruption, were made against her. Not one was proved. At the cabinet meeting Glancy intervened and dismissed Shaukat on the ground that his colleagues had lost confidence in him. Glancy admitted that 'I do not altogether like this course of action, but larger issues are at stake—the tranquility of the Province and the continuance of the war effort'.[161]

Shaukat's dismissal from the Unionist ministry added a new element to the Unionist–League rift for Shaukat claimed that he resigned a week before his dismissal on this issue. His ejection became an all India issue at the Sialkot session of the League in May 1944, when Jinnah demanded an explanation from Khizar and Glancy, and alleged not altogether unjustifiably, that Shaukat had been dismissed for his sympathy with the League. At Sialkot, Jinnah denied that there had ever been a pact between him and Sikander. There was, he said, only 'a record of what Sikander had said he would carry out.' Khizar's attitude was childish, and Jinnah wanted 'to kill the very name "Unionist" and see its funeral.'[162]

Hindu and Sikh Unionist ministers, joining the fray, refused to

---

[159] Glancy to Wavell, 14 April 1944, *TOP*, vol. 4, pp. 880–2.

[160] Wavell to Glancy, 15 April 1944, Ibid., p. 882, and Wavell to Amery, 18 April 1944, Ibid., p. 898.

[161] Glancy to Wavell, 24 April 1944, Ibid., pp. 922–5.

[162] *Statesman*, 30 April and 1 May 1944. See also FR for Punjab for second half of April 1944, HP file no. 18/4/44.

accept a League coalition and suggested that it could only be part of an all-India settlement. Jinnah described their proposal as 'preposterous'. Choosing to misinterpret their suggestion, he stated that an all-India understanding could not be achieved 'with only 3 non-Muslim Ministers in the Punjab.' Together they represented only 20 out of 175 MLAs in the provincial assembly. There could be no settlement with them on Pakistan, which was an all-India question.[163] While reaffirming his faith in Pakistan—Muslim right to self-determination—Khizar said that he could not accept a demand involving the all-India League's interference in provincial affairs. If he did so he would be guilty of a breach of promise to the other communities represented in his coalition.[164] Earlier, Khizar had defended his dual adherence to a communal party like the League and the intercommunal Unionist party, but Jinnah had argued that 'for a Muslim to adhere to the Unionist Party as well as to the Muslim League was like keeping a mistress in addition to a wife. To this Khizar adroitly responded that being a Muslim himself he was entitled to have two wives, if he wished to do so.'[165]

It was against this background that the Muslim League Committee of Action charged Khizar with having acted in contravention of the constitution and rules of the League, rendering him liable to expulsion. It was evident from his statement of 27 April that he did not either approve or believe in the formation and organization of communal parties, while the aim of the all-India Muslim League 'is to organize and consolidate the position of the Muslims as a separate nation both inside and outside the legislatures under the control, discipline and supervision of the All-India Muslim League and its provincial branches.' Khizar's rejection of the League's authority in provincial matters was 'fundamentally in opposition' to the rules and constitution of the League. His first allegiance was evidently to the Unionist party and 'allegiance to the League, if at all, is only a secondary one.' It was the declared policy of the all-India Muslim League that 'a member of the Muslim League organization cannot owe allegiance or belong to any political party except the Muslim League.'[166]

Denying the existence of the Sikander-Jinnah pact once more, the

[163] *Statesman*, 2 and 3 May 1944.
[164] *Statesman*, 28 April 1944.
[165] Glancy to Wavell, 21 April 1944, *TOP*, vol. 4, pp. 906–7.
[166] *Statesman*, 5 May 1944.

League's Working Committee declared that the Unionist label 'was a pretence for keeping down the Mussalmans and making them subservient to the dominant Hindu group'.[167] And so a communal rationale was given to Khizar's expulsion from the League, even as 26 Muslim Unionists joined the Punjab provincial Muslim League. The League now announced that its organization would be strengthened and extended. Five organizing secretaries would be appointed in each of the five divisions of the Punjab.[168] Divisional workers would complete a tour of the province by the end of June. In July they would hold large meetings at *tehsil* headquarters followed by district conferences at short intervals. 'At this stage we will need speakers of all India fame.'[169] One League worker reported to Jinnah that he visited mosques at prayer time on Fridays and explained the programme of the League to Muslims. 'Three times a week I lead a deputation to leading wards and mohallas in the city and enrol members in large numbers.'[170]

That the majority of Muslim Unionists remained with Khizar in May 1944 indicated that the extreme form of Pakistan defined by Jinnah held little appeal for them. The League's lack of support in the Punjab legislature was also evident from a province-wide campaign it started in December 1944 to enrol new recruits for the legislative party.[171] Why even some Muslim Unionists went along with the League in 1944 is hard to gauge. In some cases, the deserters appear to have been individuals who, for one reason or other, were disenchanted with the Unionist ministry.[172] Mamdot's personal wealth may have made provincial Leaguers eager to have him on their side: for his part, as a rather simple and not very strong character, he may have been lured by the possibility of holding the Presidentship of the Punjab League or enticed by promises of power in the future.[173] Other Unionists may have simply responded to the call of Pakistan.

[167] *Statesman*, 29 May 1944.

[168] FR for Punjab for second half of November 1944, HP file no. 18/11/44.

[169] Daultana to Jinnah, 31 May 1944, *Qaid-e-Azam Jinnah s Correspondence with Punjab Muslim Leaders*, p. 249.

[170] Rashid Ali Khan to Jinnah, 4 July 1944, Ibid., p. 336.

[171] *Civil and Military Gazette*, 31 December 1944.

[172] As suggested by Glancy to Wavell, 6 April 1944, L/P&J/5/247.

[173] This was suggested by Mr. Henry Taylor, then D.C. Ferozepur. Interview with author on 23 February 1981.

There is little sound evidence that most Leaguers were thinking of a sovereign Pakistan in 1944. Ispahani could only tell Casey that the Muslims did not want to be under Hindu domination. Muslim writers in Bengal thought East Pakistan would promote Bengali language and culture.

> 'Religion and culture are not the same thing. Religion transgresses the geographical boundary but "tamaddun" (culture) cannot go beyond the geographical boundary . . . Here only lies the difference between Purba-Pakistan and Pakistan. For this reason the people of Purba-Pakistan are a different nation from the people of the other provinces of India and from the "religious brothers" of Pakistan.'[174]

Nazimuddin, then heading the League ministry in Bengal, thought that East Pakistan should include Bengal (less the Burdwan division), all of Assam, and a part of Purnea district in north-west Bengal. A centre that had always been controlled by Bombay, UP and Madras had worked against the interests of Bengal. It was for this reason, together with the intolerance towards Muslims that the Congress governments had displayed, that Bengal Leaguers found attractive the idea of a sovereign state in northeast India separated from the rest of India. Apparently Nazimuddin was thinking of an independent East Bengal.[175] On another occasion, Nazimuddin told Twynam, the governor of the CP, that the League insisted on the principle of self-determination, but that this principle would not necessarily involve complete severance from Hindustan.[176] The manifesto brought out by the Bengal provincial League in 1944 emphasized the link between Pakistan and East Bengal. It did not say that Pakistan would be an Islamic state, but it looked forward to a revival of the law of the *Shariat* and the culture of East Bengal. It defined the League's objectives to establish equal opportunities for all, irrespective of creed, caste or class; the right to education, the nationalization of the jute industry and the elimination of 'vested interests.'[177]

The manifesto of the Punjab Muslim League[178] promised to safeguard the religious, cultural and spiritual traditions of Muslims. It

---

[174] Quoted in Sen, *Muslim Politics*, p. 179. I have corrected some grammatical errors in Sen's (?) translation of the passage.

[175] Casey to Wavell, 11 September 1944, *TOP*, vol. 5, pp. 29–30.

[176] Twynam to Wavell, 9 October 1944, Ibid., p. 95.

[177] Sen, *Muslim Politics*, pp. 184–5.

[178] *Civil and Military Gazette*, 8 November 1944.

was intended to appeal to the small landed proprietor, who formed the bulk of the agrarian classes in the Punjab. Agricultural development would be based on the welfare of smaller zamindars, peasants and landless agriculturalists. Agricultural debts would be wiped out; and cheap credit facilities provided by the state. Taxation would be increased on big landlords. Non-Muslim minorities would be allowed to organize education in accordance with their religious and cultural traditions.

But the minorities would not have been lured into Pakistan by the League's hymn of hate against them, especially against Hindus. The Zamindar League was described as 'a substitute for the *Shudhi* movement';[179] League propaganda took the line that Islam was in danger. Another theme of the speeches delivered was that Pakistan would mean the revival of the Caliphate.[180] Pakistan, then, clearly meant all things to all Muslims.

It is interesting that, while the League held power in the NWFP from 1943–1945, the provincial legislature, in which almost 75 per cent of the seats were reserved for Muslims,[181] never passed a resolution in favour of Pakistan. As for the Muslim minority provinces, most Leaguers appear to have thought of Pakistan as a bargaining point, and an indication of Muslim opposition to Hindu raj. Most of them would have been satisfied with 50:50 representation for the Congress and the League at the centre and coalitions in the provinces.[182] The dislike or fear of Hindu domination of Muslims, did not, therefore, necessarily mean that they wanted a sovereign Pakistan.

Congress and the League—March 1943 to March 1945

Of the Pakistan of Jinnah's conception there had never been any doubt. In March 1943 he urged Leaguers to 'remove from your mind any idea of some form of loose federation. There is no such thing as loose federation. When there is a central government and provincial governments, they [Central Government] will go on

---

[179] *Civil and Military Gazette*, 23 November 1944. On the revival of the *Zamindara League*, see editorial, 'The Zamindara League', *Eastern Times*, 7 November 1944.

[180] *Civil and Military Gazette*, 3 December 1944.

[181] A.K. Gupta, *NWFP Legislature in the Freedom Struggle*, p. 146.

[182] Note by Porter (undated), R/3/2/54. The note was probably written around the end of November 1944.

tightening, tightening and tightening until you are pulverized with regard to your powers as units.'[183] The League's muscular reaction to Wavell's reference to the geographical unity of India was actuated by the party's apprehension that the British would renege on Cripps's offer of self-determination for minorities. The League wanted an advance on that offer. Khaliquzzaman's thesis in April 1944 was that the Congress would, eventually, accept any British award, even if it were made without their consent—they had done so in 1909, 1932 and 1935. 'That is what Jinnah is playing for.' Therefore Jinnah would no longer accept the Cripps offer with its provision for a preliminary National Government at the centre. The League's reliance on the British was underlined by Khaliquzzaman's assertion that British rule must be 'retained for many years'; once they declared for Pakistan, administrative problems would be raised and the 'unreality' of the Congress demand for independence exposed.[184] The inference is that the League could not publicly ask for the retention of the Raj for fear of exposing itself to Congress charges of servility to the British. But both its political conservatism and the Muslim fears of Hindu domination that it represented; the desire and expectation that a sovereign Pakistan would be created under the British aegis and guaranteed by them were inextricably interwoven, and although their separate threads can be picked out, their combination would render impossible any agreement with the Congress on the basis of a united independent India. So it is not surprising that Jinnah negotiated with Gandhi on the basis of a sovereign Pakistan in September 1944.

Gandhi and Rajagopalachari helped to restore Jinnah's prestige at the all-India level by political initiatives which conceded the principle of Pakistan. The origins of the Gandhi–Jinnah talks in July 1944 lay in a formula which was presented by Rajagopalachari to Gandhi in March 1943, when Gandhi was still under detention. The formula reflected Rajagopalachari's belief that an agreement with Jinnah was a necessary precursor to the establishment of a National Government at the centre, no matter how obdurate Jinnah might be. 'I could easily give a grand fight to Jinnah now and demolish him in his own organization', he wrote to Devdas Gandhi on 29 November 1942, 'but even Hercules is no match for two. Had the British Government not been there, the whole thing would have been different.

---

[183] Pirzada, *Documents*, p. 427.
[184] Enclosure to Mudie to Jenkins, 14 April 1944, *TOP*, vol. 4, pp. 878–9.

We should clench our teeth and choose our opponent.'[185] Rajagopalachari argued that 'Pakistan is not so dreadful.' The Punjab and Bengal were already under Pakistan. His proposals aimed at bringing a
majority of Hindus in these two provinces under one Hindu fold
and only contiguous districts of those provinces in which Muslims
were in a majority would be given the right of self-determination.
His formula would not throw the Sikhs to the wolves. They would
be better off in a free India and a strong force on the side of the
Hindus.[186]

In April 1944, Rajagopalachari presented his formula to Jinnah in
the hope that it would bring about 'a final settlement of the most
unfortunate impasse we are in.'[187] Jinnah replied that he could not
accept the formula, but he would place it before his Working Committee. This would have served no purpose, so Rajagopalachari ended the correspondence on 8 July.[188]

Gandhi put forward the formula to Jinnah after his release from
prison in May 1944. The terms of the formula were as follows.
When the war ended, a commission would demarcate the "contiguous districts" in North West and East India having an absolute
majority. In the areas thus demarcated, a plebiscite of the adult
population would be taken. If the majority voted 'for a separate
sovereign state, it would be given effect to, but border districts
would have the option to join one of the new states. In the event of
separation, mutual agreements would be entered into for safeguarding defence, commerce and communications. These terms would be
binding when the British transferred full power to India.[189]

The formula clearly conceded the principle of Pakistan, and
embodied Rajagopalachari's belief that this would satisfy the Muslims and that they would, in time, cease to want Pakistan.[190] Provincial Muslim Leaguers and Muslim League papers were jubilant that
Gandhi had accepted Pakistan in principle.[191] Congressmen were

[185] Rajagopalachari to Devdas Gandhi, 29 November 1942, *MGC*, serial no. 2032.
[186] *Statesman*, 13 January 1943.
[187] Rajagopalachari to Jinnah, 8 April 1944, *IAR*, 1944, vol. 2, p. 129.
[188] Jinnah to Rajagopalachari, 2 July 1944, Ibid., p. 130; and Rajagopalachari to
Jinnah, 4 July 1944, Ibid.
[189] See Jinnah to Gandhi, 10 September 1944; Gandhi to Jinnah, 11 September
1944, Ibid, pp. 135–7.
[190] See Wavell to Amery, 11 July 1944, *TOP*, vol. 4, pp. 1077–9.
[191] E.g. *Eastern Times*, 10 July 1944, FRs for Punjab for second half of July and
first half of August 1944, HP file nos. 18/7 and 18/8/44.

surprised and did not know what to make of Gandhi's attitude.[192] The Sikhs, the Mahasabha and the Unionists were alarmed that the success of the Gandhi–Jinnah parleys would prejudice their position in the Punjab.[193]

The Rajagopalachari formula was probably an attempt to get Jinnah out into the open about Pakistan. Until then, the only attempt at a definition of Pakistan had been made in the Lahore resolution of 1940, and it was considered even by the British to be an obscure definition.[194]

It is unlikely that Gandhi ever thought that Jinnah would accept the formula. For, as Jinnah pointed out, demarcation of boundaries on the lines suggested would relegate 11 districts in the Punjab and the same number in Bengal to Hindustan. Karachi and Dacca would be the only ports left to Pakistan. Gandhi had also not said how the new constitution would be framed and the provisional government formed.[195]

Gandhi replied that the constitution would be framed by the provisional government or an authority set up by it after the British withdrawal. The independence contemplated was 'of the whole of India as it stands.' The Boundary Commission would also be appointed by the provisional government. Absolute majority meant a clear majority over non-Muslim elements in the Muslim majority province. Power would be transferred by the British to the provisional government.[196]

For Jinnah, however, 'the only solution of India's problem was to accept the division of India into Pakistan and Hindustan.'[197] He said it was clear that Gandhi did not accept that Muslims were a separate nation, and that they had the inherent right of self-determination; he did not accept that 'they alone are entitled to exercise this right of theirs for self-determination.'[198]

Gandhi rejoined that Muslims could not be a separate nation 'by reason of acceptance of Islam. Will the two nations become one if

[192] FRs for UP, Bombay, Bengal and Punjab for second half of July and first half of August 1944, HP file nos. 18/7 and 18/8/44.

[193] FRs for Punjab for July 1944, HP file no. 18/7/44.

[194] Note by Jenkins, 23 July 1945, R/3/1/105.

[195] Jinnah to Gandhi, 10 September 1944.

[196] Gandhi to Jinnah, 15 September 1944, *IAR*, 1944, vol. 2, p. 141.

[197] Jinnah to Gandhi, 11 September 1944, Ibid., p. 137.

[198] Jinnah to Gandhi, 25 September 1944, Ibid., p. 147.

the whole of India accepted Islam?' The majority of Muslims in India, were, after all, converts to Islam.[199]

Gandhi later said that the outlines of any scheme of interim government were never discussed by him and Jinnah. His impression was that Jinnah wanted 'two independent sovereign states with no connection between them except by treaty'. Gandhi accepted a division of India 'as between members of the same family and therefore reserving for partnership things of common interest. But Qaid-e-Azam would have nothing short of the two nations theory and therefore complete dissolution amounting to full sovereignty in the first instance. It was just here that we split.'[200]

Jinnah had pointed to the unrepresentative character of Gandhi at the start of the negotiations. British officials wondered why he went to talk to Gandhi in the first place.[201] According to Gandhi, he declared Gandhi to be unrepresentative, but 'he insisted . . . that if I first accepted the Pakistan of his conception, he could then discuss other things with me even though I was but an individual.'[202]

Wavell could not believe that Jinnah, as 'a highly intelligent man, is sincere about the "two nations theory".' His refusal to answer the awkward questions raised by Gandhi showed that he had not thought out the implications of Pakistan, or that he would not disclose them.[203] Sir Evan Jenkins, then Private Secretary to the Viceroy, later observed that the Gandhi–Jinnah talks clarified the Lahore resolution only to the extent of showing that, in Jinnah's mind, Pakistan 'consists initially of Sind, Baluchistan, the NWFP and Punjab, Bengal and Assam; and that the question of their sovereignty is to be decided by Muslims resident in them without reference to wishes of other inhabitants.' This was 'not really a definition' of Pakistan in any case. 'Does Jinnah . . . really mean that, because in Eastern and parts of Central Bengal the Muslims are in an absolute majority, a Muslim vote alone is to transfer Calcutta to a Muslim sovereign state?'[204]

The breakdown of the Gandhi–Jinnah talks pleased only the Un-

---

[199] Gandhi to Jinnah, 15 September 1944, Ibid., p. 140.
[200] Gandhi to Sapru, 26 February 1945, *TBSC*, vol. 6.
[201] *Quarterly Survey of the Political and Constitutional Position of the British in India*, no. 29, L/WS/1/1433.
[202] Gandhi to Sapru, 26 February 1945, *TBSC*, vol. 6.
[203] Wavell to Amery, 3 October 1944, *TOP*, vol. 5, p. 75.
[204] Note by Jenkins, 23 July 1945, R/3/1/105, pp. 34–5.

ionists, the Sikhs and the Mahasabha. Provincial Leaguers were disappointed, but pleased at Gandhi's concession of the principle of Pakistan.[205] Gandhi himself may not have expected anything from the talks, for he went 'in hope but without expectation. So if I return empty handed, I shall not be disappointed.'[206] But by inviting Jinnah soon after the latter's failure to bring the Unionists to heel, and by letting Jinnah thus occupy in the talks 'the dominating position of one who spurns what is offered him and of whom favours are sought', Gandhi helped Jinnah to recover the prestige he had lost in the Punjab.[207]

On the all-India front, it was Wavell who was now considering a political initiative. Since August 1942, the British had concentrated on suppressing the Quit India movement, and there had been no inclination, either by Whitehall or Linlithgow, to make any move in India. Since his arrival in India in October 1943, Wavell had pleaded with Whitehall for 'a change of spirit' on the British side; a declaration by the British government that it had a definite intention to give India self-government as soon as possible.[208] Churchill, however, appeared to be the main stumbling-block in the way of political advance in India. According to Amery, he 'passionately' hoped that any solution involving the fulfilment of British pledges 'can somehow still be prevented.' Whenever the question of India cropped up in the Cabinet, ministers would be 'over borne by the Prime Minister's vehemence.'[209] Wavell himself favoured a settlement with the Congress Right and an understanding with the League. The Right were restive with Gandhi's obstructionist policies, and if Rajagopalachari was offered a seat in the government, the Right could be weaned away from Gandhi. Some 'inclination of the ear' to the League's demands might prove the 'shortest way of bringing about a more reasonable frame of mind in the Congress High Command, and so paving the way towards ending the deadlock.' Once Gandhi understood that the British would not be frightened out of the principle of self-determination for the Muslim

---

[205] FR for Punjab for first half of October 1944, HP file no. 18/10/44.

[206] Gandhi to Sapru, 8 September 1944, *TBSC*, vol. 6.

[207] *Quarterly Survey of the Political and Constitutional Position of the British in India*, no. 29, L/WS/1/1433.

[208] See, for example, Wavell to Amery, (T), 26 October 1944, *TOP*, vol. 5, pp. 68–9, and 140.

[209] Amery to Wavell, 16 August 1944, *TOP*, vol. 4, p. 1206.

areas, a more reasonable approach could be expected from the Congress. Such a policy has its long-term implications as well. The Cripps offer envisaged not only a settlement between the League and the Congress 'but also the negotiation of a treaty between H.M.G. and the proposed Constituent Assembly' which would make provision for the safeguarding of Britain's interests as a world power and for a winding up of British control on terms 'which will be just and equitable'. If the Congress remained in its present frame of mind, it would oppose all proposals for treaty provisions essential to British interests and world security 'as incompatible with the word "Independence".'

Wavell welcomed the news that the Congress Right was interested in an agreement with Jinnah and hoped to form a national government.[210] K.M. Munshi, ex-Premier of Bombay, suggested to Jenkins the establishment of a centre to discuss constitutional details.[211] Reports that Liaqat Ali Khan was keen to come to an agreement gave heart to the Congress Right. Gandhi would not discourage them. Writing with his approval, Syed Mahmud, a Congress Muslim from Bihar, asked Bhulabhai Desai, leader of the Congress in the Central Assembly, to meet Liaqat.[212]

Desai met Wavell on 15 November 1944, and told him that the British should take the initiative, which nᵉ d not include any constitutional change during the war. This fitted in with Wavell's own ideas, and he wanted to visit London to discuss the prospects of a British move with the cabinet. But the war cabinet did not respond,[213] and a frustrated Wavell wrote at the end of his first year in office: 'I have found H.M.G.'s attitude to India negligent, hostile and contemptuous to a degree I had not anticipated, or I think I might have done more.'[214]

Encouraged by his talks with Wavell, Desai met Liaqat Ali Khan who said that a Congress–League coalition at the centre was not only desirable but possible. Later, Desai gathered from him that he had mentioned the matter to Jinnah.[215] In the first week of January

[210] See Wavell's appreciation of the Indian Political Situation, February 1944, Ibid., pp. 884–93.

[211] Wavell to Amery, 15 November 1944, *TOP*, vol. 5, p. 206.

[212] Syed Mahmud to Desai, 18 November 1944, *Syed Mahmud Collection*.

[213] Wavell to Amery, 23 November 1944, *TOP*, vol. 5, enclosure: pp. 230–1. See, for example, Amery to Wavell, 14 December 1944, Ibid., p. 303.

[214] Wavell, *Journal*, entry for 20 October 1944, p. 93.

[215] Pyarelal, *Mahatma Gandhi, the Last Phase*, vol. 1, p. 103.

1945, Desai met Gandhi at Sevagram. Gandhi was against a return to office by the Congress, but he knew that many Congressmen desired it. So he encouraged Desai to go ahead.[216] The British and the public never ascertained whether Desai's proposals had the support of Gandhi. There is, however, a copy of the proposals in Desai's handwriting, with alterations in Gandhi's handwriting in pencil—in the papers of Desai.[217]

Desai hoped that a successful coalition at the centre with the League might induce them to give up Pakistan. The terms of the Desai–Liaqat pact were that the Congress and the League would join the interim government at the centre. Each party would have 40 per cent of the seats, and 20 per cent would be reserved for minorities. The government would work under the act of 1935, though the Viceroy should not use his powers to enforce a measure not passed by the legislature. The first task of the interim government would be to release the arrested members of the Congress Working Committee. If the coalition was formed at the centre, the next step would be to form coalitions in the provinces.[218] A copy of the Desai–Liaqat Pact, carrying the initials of the two leaders, is also in the Desai papers.

The release of the Congress Working Committee was not made a preliminary condition of the signing of the pact, as Desai explained to Wavell, because the Working Committee would wreck the negotiations, but once the coalition government had started functioning at the centre and in the provinces the Committee would accept the *fait accompli*.[219] But Gandhi always doubted the *bona fides* of Jinnah and Liaqat. Their public denial of any knowledge of the pact shocked him, and he warned Desai not to go ahead without the approval of the Congress Working Committee. 'Jinnah says one thing and Liaqat repeats it', he wrote to Desai on 24 January. 'I am letting you know what I see from this distance. I fear what I see.'[220]

Wavell believed that Gandhi knew of the proposals, for he held that Desai was 'an important and experienced politician' who would not go ahead without being sure of his ground. He considered the proposals to be 'undoubtedly important' and moderate, and wanted the war cabinet to accept them.[221] Mudie thought that the proposals

---

[216] Ibid.   [217] Diaries, *BDC*, file no. 7.   [218] Ibid.

[219] V.P. Menon to Jenkins, 27 January 1945, *TOP*, vol. 5, p. 476.

[220] Gandhi to Desai, 13 February 1945, *BDC*.

[221] Wavell to Amery, (T), 14 January 1945, *TOP*, vol. 5, pp. 400–2.

'were exactly what we have been working for. The move has come from the Congress and the League. So there can be no question of H.E.'s receiving a rebuff'. The initiative had been taken by the leaders of the Congress and the League in the Legislative Assembly. 'It is definitely right wing and gives an opportunity, which may never occur again, of splitting the Congress.'[222]

Churchill, however, demanded an explanation for 'this new, sudden departure'.[223] Could Desai deliver the goods, and would the interim government support the war effort? Would the Quit India movement be withdrawn? The cabinet suggested that Jenkins, rather than Wavell, should meeet Desai. 'In other words, they felt that the bridge should be further tested by a sagacious but lighter weight quadruped before my lord the elephant himself puts even a portion of his weight on an uncertain structure.'[224]

But Wavell had already arranged to meet Desai on 20 January, and was satisfied by his explanations. The Viceroy would have the final say in deciding the portfolios: the only change would be that he would consult party leaders before making any appointment. Desai told him that the new councillors would not take orders from Jinnah or Gandhi and said that 'he never contemplated outside control of the Centre. He was against any immediate attempt by the provisional government to promote a long-term solution, until the atmosphere seemed more favourable'.[225] There was no further reaction from the war cabinet.

Despite his denials, British officials in India were certain that Jinnah knew about the Desai–Liaqat pact. Wavell instructed Colvill₵ the Governor of Bombay, to ascertain whether Jinnah thought Desai's proposals were worth pursuing and whether he would be willing to discuss them with the Viceroy and Desai.[226] Jinnah was emphatic that there had been no 'authorized discussion' between Liaqat and Desai. Then he said that Colville's communicating the points in Wavell's letter 'was the first approach to him in the matter'. He said '"this conversation is the starting point"'. He agreed to meet Wavell in Delhi and to call a meeting of his Working Committee immediately.[227]

[222] Mudie to Jenkins, 15 January 1945, Ibid., p. 403.
[223] Minute by Churchill, 16 January 1945, Ibid., p. 404.
[224] Amery to Wavell, 18 January 1945, Ibid., p. 419.
[225] Wavell to Amery, (T), 20 January 1945, Ibid., pp. 423–5.
[226] Wavell to Amery, 22 February 1945, Ibid., p. 596.
[227] Colville to Wavell, 24 February 1945, Ibid., pp. 607–8.

Jinnah tried to commit Jenkins 'to negotiations with him and through him to the League Committee as though the proposals came from me and not from Desai, and Desai were not directly concerned.'[228] After meeting him on 26 March, Wavell's impression was that Jinnah's disclaimer of all knowledge of the pact was 'an obvious falsehood I am sure . . . He is playing his usual slippery game in fact.'[229] Jinnah's tactics were probably inspired by Desai's offer of parity with the Congress at the centre. But his mistrust of the Congress was echoed in his desire that the *British* present the proposals, for he probably believed that once they put them down on paper, they would stand by what would then be a British offer. Having made the overtures in the first place, the Congress would accept an identical British one, and the concept of parity would at once be formalized and institutionalized. But the stalling tactics of the war cabinet deprived Jinnah of any British reed to lean on; this, coupled with his inability to trust Congress *bona fides*, was the main reason why the Desai–Liaqat pact come to nothing, despite the reported interest of many Leaguers in taking office under its terms.[230] The point is important and discounts the oft-made contention that the Congress was never prepared to compromise.

Jinnah's interest in the Desai–Liaqat pact was perhaps also stirred by the difficulties most League ministries were finding themselves in by February 1945. The release of Congress MLAs in the NWFP led to the defeat of the League ministry and the return of the Congress to office. In Sind, as we have seen, Hidayatullah had defied Jinnah and coalesced with Maula Baksh's Azad Muslim party. In Assam, Saadullah had been obliged to turn to the Congress for support to preserve his position. The Congress had acted on Gandhi's advice to act as they thought best in the light of the local circumstances. Nazimuddin's ministry was defeated in the Bengal legislature by a snap vote on 28 March, and the assembly had been prorogued by the Speaker. Intrigues within the ministry and the provincial League meant that the Governor did not know on whom to rely to form a new government, so he had imposed Section 93. In the Punjab, the Unionists had won a by-election against the

---

[228] Jenkins to Symington, 25 February 1945, Ibid., p. 616.

[229] Wavell, *Journal*, entry for 26 February 1945, p. 114.

[230] *Statesman*, 23 January 1945; Hallett to Colville, 27 March 1945, *TOP*, vol. 5, pp. 749–51.

League.[231] With the League more or less off the political map of India, participation in a government at the centre would have given it a much-needed, tangible gain at the all-India level.

The enhancement of the League's prestige between 1942 and 1945 owed much to the British and the Congress. For tactical reasons, the British recognized the League's claim to speak for Muslims at the all-India level. The Cripps offer went far to concede the right of cession to the Muslim majority provinces, and so gave some substance to the possibility of Pakistan. In Sind and in Bengal, the League came into power as a result of official reactions to the ministries which were governing in those provinces until October 1942 and March 1943 respectively. However, as their support for the Unionists against Jinnah showed, the British did not necessarily want the League to govern all the Muslim majority provinces: what mattered most to them was the success of the war effort.

Like the British, Congress leaders gave recognition to the principle of Pakistan in 1942 and in 1944, regardless of Jinnah's position in the Muslim majority provinces. They thus undoubtedly gave substance to the demand for Pakistan, and indirectly built up the stature of the League at the all-India level.

There is some evidence that the League's call for Pakistan strengthened its appeal to Muslim popular sentiment, but it did not necessarily strengthen its hold over provincial Leaguers or Muslim groups, who were often not committed to the sovereign Pakistan of Jinnah's definition, but were interested in provincial power. The provincial Leagues relied on Jinnah to some extent to look after their interests with the Viceroy against the Congress at the all-India level, but retained autonomy in the provinces; and Jinnah found it difficult to assert control over them. With Pakistan as a slogan the all-India League was a party which depended for support at the provincial level on bargains with Muslim leaders who either rejected this aim or whose overriding interests lay chiefly in intercommunal parties or coalitions. The solidification of Muslim opinion against the Congress during the war had not, then, necessarily resulted in the solidification of the Muslim political community in favour of a sovereign Pakistan by April 1945.

[231] Memorandum by Amery, 5 April 1945; Wavell to Amery, 20 March 1945, *TOP*, vol. 5, pp. 830–2, 712 respectively; NWFP Governor's report, 23 March 1945, *CC*, vol. 16; FRs for Sind for February and March 1945, HP file nos. 18/2 and 18/3/45.

CHAPTER 4

The Success of the Muslim League:

June 1945 to March 1946

The Simla Conference June–July 1945

Since October 1944, Wavell had urged Whitehall to allow him to include representatives of leading Indian parties in his Executive Council. An official administration, he argued, could not cope efficiently with post-war economic and political problems; nor would it enjoy the popular support necessary to mobilize India's resources for a successful offensive against Japan. But it was not before May 1945 that Whitehall reluctantly agreed that Wavell call a conference of Indian leaders at Simla the following month.[1]

On 15 June 1945, Wavell announced that he would invite Indian leaders to discuss the formation of a new Executive Council which would be 'more representative' of organized political opinion. The reconstituted Council would continue the war against Japan; tackle problems of post-war development until a new and permanent constitution could be agreed upon.[2]

Knowledge of an impending British initiative aroused widespread interest in India. The Congress Right welcomed Wavell's announcement of the Simla Conference as 'the fulfilment of our joint prayers and efforts'.[3] Their unstinted support to the war effort raised hopes among the Unionists that at least one of their number would be represented in the Executive Council among the Muslim members. Glancy encouraged their expectations, for they had 'from the very beginning' of the war consistently and unconditionally supported the war effort, while the Muslim League has at the best remained neutral'.[4] Wavell assured Glancy that he had no intention of hand-

[1] For Wavell's account of his discussions with the Cabinet, see his *Journal*, pp. 118–135.

[2] *Statesman*, 15 June 1945.

[3] Rajagopalachari to Sapru, 15 June 1945, *TBSC*, vol. 20.

[4] Glancy to Colville, 4 May 1945, L/P&J/5/248, p. 84. Colville sent Glancy's letter

ing over the interim government to any one party. An interim government of the kind proposed might prove a useful step towards inducing Muslims to abandon the objective of Pakistan.

Though Gandhi protested against the provision for parity between 'Caste Hindus' and Muslims in the proposed new Council, the Congress Working Committee, whose release from prison was announced by Wavell in his broadcast on 15 June, authorized Azad to accept the Viceroy's invitation to come to Simla.[5] Congressmen were instructed[6] that they were attending the conference on the understanding that the suggested arrangements were on 'an interim and temporary basis only, and especially in regard to communal parity'. The principle of such parity was 'an evil when and if accepted in the Centre and cannot be extended to the Provinces'. While communal parity in the limited and temporary sense could be agreed to, Congress would not accept the right of the League to nominate all the Muslim members of the new government, and would nominate individuals belonging to all communities. The continued ban on the AICC was described as 'an obstacle in our way and must be regarded as coercion'. The congress would also seek clarification from the Viceroy on the withdrawal of Indian troops from South-East Asia after the end of the war with Japan.

These points were raised by Azad and Gandhi when the Conference opened on 25 June. Wavell agreed that the Congress could nominate Muslims and Scheduled Castes, 'but said the principle of parity must be maintained'.[7]

Jinnah displayed a persecution complex, fearing that the Muslims would always be in a minority in the new Council because the other minorities, for example, the Sikhs and the Scheduled Castes, would always vote with the Hindus, and that the Viceroy would be reluctant to use his veto. Wavell tried to reassure him. 'I said I doubted his assumption' and pointed out that the Viceroy and Commander-

---

to Amery and asked him to draw Wavell's attention to it. Wavell was at that time having discussions with the British cabinet in London. A note in the margin said that Wavell had seen Glancy's letter. Colville to Amery, 7 May 1945, L/P&J/5/248, p. 83.

[5] Azad to Viceroy, (T), 21 June 1945, AICC file, G-26, 1945–6, p. 45.

[6] Confidential Note containing Instructions to Congressmen attending the Simla Conference, 25 June 1945, AICC file, p. 52, G-58. An undated, probably earlier, note, simply titled 'Memorandum' is almost identical to the Instructions of 25 June, and can be found in AICC file no. 41, 1945.

[7] Wavell to Amery, (T), 25 June 1945, *TOP*, vol. 5, pp. 1151–4.

in-Chief would ensure fair play for Muslims. Jinnah proposed that if a majority of Muslims were opposed to any decision, it should not go by vote and claimed that the League had the right to nominate all Muslim members to the Council. Wavell would not accept this and further told him that he also had it in mind to nominate a Unionist Muslim. Jinnah reacted sharply to the proposal of Unionists representing Muslims.

The wrangle over credentials continued when Wavell stated that there was nothing in the proposals to brand the Congress as a communal organization. Jinnah interjected here that the Congress represented only Hindus, a statement to which Dr Khan Sahib took vehement objection. Wavell concluded that Congress represented its members and both Congress and Jinnah accepted this.[8]

The main problem at Simla was, of course, the method of selecting new members of the Executive Council.[9] In the light of Jinnah's claims, Wavell circulated a statement of matters to be decided by the Conference.[10] The statement was divided into two parts. Part A was for settlement between the parties and the Viceroy representing the British government. It committed the parties to the tasks set out in the Viceroy's broadcast on 15 June, the selection of men of ability to the Council, with all portfolios, except that of the Commander-in-Chief, going to Indians. The new government would work under the existing constitution. All parties agreed to these points. On point (iv) of the statement, which provided for communal parity, Azad reiterated the Congress view that members of the Council should be appointed not on a communal but on a political basis. Part B of the statement was for agreement between the parties themselves. If all parties agreed to Part A, they would decide on the strength and composition of the Executive Council by parties and for communities and the method by which panels of names would be submitted to the Viceroy to enable him to make his recommendations to the British Government. Delegates wanted to have private discussions on this part of the statement, and the Conference adjourned till the next day.[11]

When the Conference met the next morning, Jinnah maintained a

[8] Wavell to Amery, (T), 25 June 1945, *TOP*, vol. 5, pp. 1155–6.

[9] Wavell to Amery, 25 June 1945, Ibid., p. 1157.

[10] Wavell to Amery, (T), 26 June 1945, Ibid., pp. 1162–4. Also Wavell to Amery, (T), 26 June 1945, Ibid., pp. 1164–5.

[11] Wavell to Amery, (T), 26 June 1945, Ibid., p. 1165.

rigid attitude and refused to see Azad. The Congress reiterated that they would not accept the League's demand for the exclusion of Congress Muslims. Khizar, meanwhile, was apprehensive that the Congress and the League would strike a bargain which would include the substitution of a Congress–League ministry for the Unionist ministry in the Punjab. The proposals would be 'disastrous' for the Punjab if a Punjabi Muslim independent of the League were not included in the Council. Khizar's fear reflected the likelihood that a League–Congress settlement at the Centre would change the balance of power in the provinces.

The critical point of the Conference had now been reached, and, for Wavell, the main stumbling-block was the attitude of Jinnah, that is, his claim to nominate all Muslim members.[12] The attitude of the Congress 'so far has been conciliatory and reasonable'. Wavell did not expect trouble from the Sikhs and Depressed Classes.[13] When the Conference met on 29 June, it was clear that the parties had failed to agree. So Wavell decided to take the initiative himself, and asked the parties to submit lists of their nominees for the Executive Council. The Congress agreed to submit a list which would include members of all communities. The Viceroy agreed to a suggestion by Khizar that the lists should be submitted secretly to him. Jinnah said he would consult his Working Committee, and Wavell feared that he 'may decline to submit a list at all'.[14]

Reports from the provinces suggested that Jinnah was under pressure from Muslim Leaguers not to break up the Conference. Saadullah and Nazimuddin were dependent on Congress support; Liaqat was anxious to take office.[15] In the NWFP, 50 per cent of educated Muslims did not think Jinnah had the right to nominate all Muslims. Aurangzeb was discredited and with him the local Muslim League. In the Punjab, some Muslim Leaguers were keen on a Congress–League settlement and the Unionists had recently defeated the League in a by-election in the constituency of Dera Ghazi Khan.[16] By winning the by-election from Shikarpur, where he had lost to the League's candidate only a year earlier, Maula Baksh had turned the tables on the League in Sind. Dow described the

[12] Wavell to Amery, (T), 27 June 1945, Ibid., pp. 1165–6.
[13] Ibid., p. 1167.
[14] Wavell to Amery, (T), 29 June 1945, Ibid., pp. 1171–3.
[15] Wavell to Amery, 1 July 1945, Ibid., p. 1182.
[16] *Statesman*, 3 July 1945.

League's hold over Sind Muslims as 'tenuous', and thought that Hidayatullah would require little persuasion to break away from the League.[17] Jinnah's position within the party was weakened by the fact that the League did not have a majority in any province, and all provincial Leagues were riven by dissensions. "Pakistan", had, until now, failed to unite provincial Muslim leaders. Jinnah, therefore, was under great pressure from other Leaguers. He told Wavell more than once, ' "I am at the end of my tether; I ask you not to wreck the League." '

Jinnah finally refused to submit a list, on the ground that Wavell had not accepted his right to nominate all Muslim members to the Executive Council.[18] But Wavell did not want the Conference to break down 'before every possible effort has been made'. He proposed to send Amery his own list of nominees for approval. He would then show the list to Jinnah and other party leaders. If either the League or the Congress or both rejected the list he would close the Conference and disclose the names put forward by him in a broadcast.[19]

In the Cabinet, Amery supported the course of action suggested by Wavell. But other members raised objections. Simon said that Wavell's proposal was not in accordance with the original plan, according to which the parties were supposed to submit lists. Now one of the principal parties had refused to put forward any names but the Viceroy proposed to go ahead with a list of his own. Grigg thought that leaving out the League would mean that the British 'risked losing our friends without getting any security that the resultant arrangements would in fact be workable.' The Cabinet knew that the Congress had submitted a list of names, but wanted to 'avoid a situation in which the Muslim League could be held up as the one obstacle to progress.'[20] The Cabinet wanted Wavell to persuade Jinnah once again. If the latter did not agree the Cabinet wanted Wavell to report back.[21] The Cabinet were 'afraid of the whole onus of failure being thrown on Muslims'.[22] In fact, Simon,

[17] Dow to Wavell, (T), 2 July 1945, *TOP*, vol. 5, p. 1191; and *Statesman*, 3 July 1945.

[18] Jinnah to Wavell, 9 July 1945, *TOP*, vol. 5, p. 1213; note by Wavell, 8 July 1945, Ibid p. 1208.

[19] Wavell to Amery, 9 July 1945, *TOP*, vol. 5, p. 1214.

[20] Cabinet C.M. (45) 13th Conclusions, minute 9, Ibid., p. 1222.

[21] Amery to Wavell, (T), 10 July 1945, Ibid., pp. 1223–4.

[22] Amery to Wavell, 10 July 1945, (T), Ibid., p. 1224.

Grigg and Butler all wanted the proposals to break down: Grigg felt that Amery was only concerned in selling four hundred million Indians 'to a handful of greedy Hindu industrialists.'[23] This provoked Wavell to point out that given British undertakings to India 'I do not see how we can now take a high moral line and say that we will hand over only to people of whose motives we approve.' The League and the Congress were the most important parties, and 'I do not see how we can disregard either or both of them any more than you could disregard the Conservative and Labour Parties at home'.[24]

Jinnah emerged victorious at Simla. On 11 July, Wavell showed him his list. It was rejected by Jinnah although Wavell had gone as far as he could to meet Jinnah 'even at the risk of alienating Congress by excluding Nationalist Muslims who are particularly disliked by the League'.[25] Wavell included the names of 4 Muslim Leaguers and a Unionist Muslim. But Jinnah refused even to discuss the names unless he could be given the absolute right to select all Muslims and some guarantee that any decision which the Muslims opposed in the Council could only be passed by a two-thirds majority—in fact a kind of communal veto. Wavell told him these conditions were entirely unacceptable.[26]

Wavell decided to close the conference. The Cabinet did not want his provisional list to leak out,[27] so he could not show his list to other leaders as he had wanted to. He would simply tell them its communal and party composition and say that the League felt unable to accept them. At the last meeting of the conference on 14 July, Jinnah claimed parity inside the Council *with all other parties combined. If he really meant this*', commented Wavell, 'it shows that he had never at any time an intention of accepting the offer, and it is difficult to see why he came to Simla at all.'[28]

Congress leaders were understandably bitter at Wavell's decision to close the conference. Within a week of their release from prison and able to cope with strenuous work only with difficulty, they had

[23] Amery to Wavell, (T), 11 July 1945, Ibid., pp. 1228–9.
[24] Wavell to Amery, 22 July 1945, Ibid., pp. 1290–1.
[25] Wavell to Amery, (T), 11 July 1945, Ibid., pp. 1224–6.
[26] Ibid.
[27] Cabinet C.M. (45) 14th conclusions, Minute 5, 12 July 1945, Ibid., p. 1235.
[28] Wavell, *Journal*, entry for 14 July 1945, p. 155. Italics in original. Also Wavell to Amery, (T), 14 July 1945, *TOP*, vol. 5, pp. 1247–8.

accepted Wavell's invitation to Simla. They had submitted their list to Wavell, but he had never shown them his and given them an opportunity to express an opinion on it. In his interview with Azad, Wavell had not raised any objection to any name on the Congress list. Jinnah's refusal to submit a list was for the Viceroy sufficient ground to wind up the conference. 'The Working Committee found themselves helpless in the face of this extraordinary attitude of the Viceroy . . . The Conference as a whole had no say in the matter at any stage'.[29] In Congress eyes, the conference could not have succeeded so long as the British gave 'one party the power to veto all effort'. The Congress Working Committee never learned that the directive not to embarrass Jinnah came from the war cabinet. Gandhi did not deny that Wavell had made an honest attempt to break the political deadlock, but his pithy comment on the Viceroy's ending the conference was that ' "An honest attempt should have ended honestly".'[30]

As in the case of the Desai–Liaqat Pact of January 1945, it is significant that the Congress accepted the principle of parity as a temporary expedient to get into a coalition government, with the Act of 1935 still holding sway. Not even the British accepted the League's claim to a monopoly of the Muslim nominations to the executive council. But the war cabinet destroyed their own initiative partly because they were averse to any political liberalization—Churchill had agreed to it because he was advised of its inevitable failure[31]— partly because their dislike of the Congress was at once too intense and petty to allow that party to wear a halo. To say that Jinnah's demand killed Wavell's attempts to reconstruct the executive council[32] implies that the British had no possibility of salvaging their efforts to ease the political stalemate. The options *were* discussed by them; they considered Jinnah's claims unfounded and wrong, but they chose to let him get away with it.

As for Jinnah, it is doubtful that he ever wanted a settlement.

[29] Draft letter from Azad to Wavell, 14 July 1945, AICC file no. G-58, 1945–6, pp. 30–1. The letter was not sent, but it reveals the frustration and disappointment of Congress leaders.

[30] Quoted by Pyarelal, *Mahatma Gandhi: The Last Phase*, vol. 1, part 1, p. 132. Pyarelal was Gandhi's personal secretary and one of his closest companions.

[31] Cabinet meetings, 31 May and 8 June 1945, CAB 65/33.

[32] R. J. Moore, 'Jinnah and the Pakistan Demand', *Modern Asian Studies*, 17, 4, 1983, p. 550.

Khaliquzzaman and Nazimuddin told Francis Mudie, the Home Member, that Jinnah was anxious to get out of the whole thing. Quite apart from his right to nominate, he was afraid that if the League came into a central government they might have to take action that would prejudice their Pakistan demand.[33] Jinnah's obduracy was received with mixed feelings in different quarters. In the UP and the NWFP, the League thought its action had been welcomed. Many educated Muslims and the Sind and the Punjab Leagues were disappointed at the breakdown.[34]

The Elections of 1945–6

The elections in Britain in July 1945 brought the Labour party into power. Congress circles expected quick action from the new government,[35] but Labour's desire to settle the Indian problem did not necessarily mean that they were in any hurry to end the empire. It did, however, accept the recommendation of a Governors' Conference held in Delhi on 1–2 August that elections to the provincial and central legislatures should be held in the coming winter: the Governors agreed unanimously that an official government could not solve post-war problems.[36] On 21 August Wavell announced that the elections would take place. What gave the elections immense significance was Attlee's statement in Parliament on 11 September; that the 'broad definition of British policy contained in the Declaration of 1942 . . . stands in all its fullness and purpose'. Wavell would undertake discussions with new representatives in the provincial legislatures to ascertain whether it was acceptable or whether some alternative or modified scheme would be preferable. Their election would be followed by positive steps to set up a constituent assembly which would frame a new constitution.[37] Obviously, the imminence of the British departure was clear to all parties and sections of public opinion, though the British government had not fixed a date for it, or even declared it to be an immediate aim of policy.

[33] Enclosure to Mudie to Jenkins, 16–17 July 1945, *TOP*, vol. 5, p. 1269.

[34] Dow to Wavell, 17 July 1945, L/P&J/5/261;FR for Punjab for first half of July, HP file no. 18/7/45.

[35] Government of India, Information and Broadcasting Department to Secretary of State (T), 1 August 1945, *TOP*, vol. 6, p. 1.

[36] Governors' Conference, 1–2 August 1945, Ibid., pp. 3–4 and 23.

[37] Pethick-Lawrence to Wavell, (T), 18 September 1945, Ibid., pp. 270–1.

If the Cripps offer stood as the basis of British policy, it meant that the right of provinces to opt out of an Indian Union stood with it. For Jinnah, it was necessary, if he had any hope of achieving a sovereign Pakistan, to get a majority in the legislatures in the Muslim majority provinces. Wavell knew that Jinnah attached 'more importance to the number of seats the League can win both in the Central Assembly and in the Provincial Assemblies than to the ability of the League to form Ministries in the Muslim majority provinces'.[38] The League must also win the support of the Muslim masses, especially in the Punjab and Bengal, where a plebiscite might eventually be necessary to decide the case for Pakistan. Thus, the 'immediate and paramount issues' before Jinnah were Pakistan and to make good the League's claim to represent the Muslims of India.[39]

Jinnah's task was not easy. The League organization in most places was poor; the leaders were mostly men of some social standing and did not bother themselves with mass contacts and local committees.[40] Mamdot, for example, had not allowed mass contact committees on his estate.[41] In the NWFP, the League was divided and lacked funds. Aurangzeb stood discredited because of the corrupt methods he had used to retain himself in power. In Sind, the provincial League was riven by factions. In Bengal, the tussle between Nazimuddin and Suhrawardy culminated in the former not being given the League ticket for the elections.[42]

Nevertheless, Jinnah appears to have been able to assert his authority over the provincial Leagues. The Central Parliamentary Board of the League had the final say in the selection of candidates for the provincial and central legislatures.[43] In Sind, G.M. Syed's

[38] Wavell to Pethick-Lawrence, 5 November 1945.

[39] *Dawn*, 31 August 1945. Jinnah must have taken Attlee's statement at its face value: he could not have known of the reasons behind it. For the discussions which led to Attlee's statement, see Cabinet India and Burma Committee meetings on 29 August 1945, *TOP*, vol. 6, pp. 173–80; 31 August 1945, Ibid., pp. 188–90; 3 September 1945, Ibid., pp. 202–209; and 6 September 1945, Ibid., pp. 225–30.

[40] Wavell to Amery, 12 August 1945, *TOP*, vol. 6. p. 59.

[41] Khan Rab Nawaz Khan to Jinnah, 25 March 1943, *Jinnah papers*, quoted by I.A. Talbot, 'The 1946 Punjab Elections', *Modern Asian Studies*, 14, 1, 1980, p. 68.

[42] Cunningham to Wavell, 9 October 1945, L/P&J/5/222; Dow to Wavell, 20 September 1945, L/P&J/5/261; Casey to Wavell, 10 September 1945, R/3/2/56.

[43] *Quarterly Survey of the Political and Constitutional Position of the British in India*, nos. 34 and 35, L/WS/1/1559.

group were not given any tickets, which stirred them to put up their own candidates against Jinnah's in every constituency.[44] Jinnah got his way in the Punjab as well. The provincial League was divided; and most provincial Leaguers did not want Firoz Khan Noon, who had resigned from the Viceroy's executive in October to contest the elections in the Punjab, to stand as the League's candidate for Rawalpindi. They regarded him as an outsider and were afraid that he would take the credit for the League's success in the Punjab. That he was nevertheless allowed to contest from Rawalpindi at Jinnah's bidding[45] points to the increasing authority Jinnah had come to exercise over the provincial League since the break with Khizar in June 1944.

That the AIML was able for the first time to have the final say in the selection of candidates suggests that it was expanding its own organization instead of relying entirely on provincial Muslim Leagues or parties; and that it also had its own provincial machinery. In the Punjab, for example, the League's Committee of Action had started propaganda to popularize the party even before Khizar's expulsion from it. Permanent paid workers were employed to carry out propaganda in the rural areas, and a centre was set up in Lahore to train volunteers and to employ members of the Punjab Muslim Students Federation during their vacations. The Committee of Action moved its office to Lahore in May 1944 and Liaqat Ali Khan, then General Secretary of the League, supervised the organization of propaganda, which included preaching in mosques. The stake the AIML had in the province is illustrated by the fact that it donated half the money for the party's activities in the Punjab; the rest was raised by the provincial League.[46] It was when Jinnah had his own machinery in the provinces, that "Pakistan" was popularized. It could be used to brand provincial Muslim politicians who were lukewarm or opposed to it as traitors to Islam, and it could suggest that the League was the only party offering a guarantee of political

---

[44] *Statesman*, 3, 5 and 9 January 1946 and 1 February 1946. That the majority of Syed's candidates were defeated was a personal triumph for Jinnah.

[45] Firoz Khan Noon, *From Memory* (Lahore, 1966), pp. 184–90.

[46] This account is based on FR for Punjab for first and second half of May 1944, HP file no. 18/5/44, and Glancy to Wavell, 8 May 1944, *TOP*, vol. 4, pp. 953–6. On the organization, powers and functions of the MLWC, Committee of Action and Central Parliamentary Board, see K.B. Sayeed, *Pakistan: The Formative Phase*, pp. 184–196.

security and opportunity at the all-India level; where decisions on the political future of India would be taken.

In the Punjab, the brunt of the League's attack was directed against the Unionists. The party had ruled the province since 1920, and had successfully countered the influence of both the Congress and the Muslim League. It was not easy for the League to fight through the maze of power and influence that the Unionists had built up in the last twenty odd years. Writing in *Dawn* on 2 September, a League sympatizer observed that panchayat officers in most cases were nominees or relatives of Unionist MLAs. The Unionists represented the jagirdars, honorary magistrates and government grantees. Therefore, the bureaucracy and aristocracy were dependent on each other, and their influence over the peasants had been demonstrated in the elections of 1937, The success of the League would not come

> 'by working in the top strata of the Punjab Muslims alone . . . the
> League should work from the bottom upwards. The villager must be
> contracted (sic) by mass propaganda . . . the Congress was successful
> in the U.P. not because it won over the landlords but . . . because it
> made the peasantry class conscious.'[47]

It was in this tactic that the cry for Pakistan could be made most effective. The Punjab League's election manifesto was believed to have been drawn up by G. Adhikari, a Communist leader, and touched up by Jinnah.[48] In December 1944, Muslim Leaguers in the province were being told to associate with Communists to draw on their supporters.[49] Since 1944, the Communists themselves had decided to infiltrate the Congress, League and the Akalis and were working among the Muslim masses with "Pakistan" as their slogan, which may be taken as an indication of its popular appeal. The Communist contribution to the League's victory in the elections cannot yet be ascertained from the material available. Not that their part in drawing up the League's manifesto implies any significant Communist or radical influence within the League. Landlords were the largest single group within the provincial and all India Leagues, though a struggle between them and more radical elements may

---

[47] 'Need for All-Out Effort in the Punjab', by 'A Punjab Peasant', *Dawn*, 2 September 1945.

[48] FR for Punjab for second half of November 1944, HP file no. 18/11/44 and *Civil and Military Gazette*, 8 November 1944.

[49] FR for Punjab for first half of December 1944, HP file no. 18/12/44.

have been taking place in the party.[50] But if the manifesto was drawn up by them with Jinnah's knowledge, it shows the lengths to which he was prepared to go to win the majority of Muslim votes in the Punjab and to oust the Unionists.

The Unionists—and their British supporters—were attacked on any pretext which presented itself. The Unionist decision not to contest any seat for the Central Assembly gave rise to the League's argument that if the central elections were beyond their scope of work, their demand for a seat in the Viceroy's executive was also not within their sphere of action. *Dawn* editorialized about

'the disreputable caucus known as the Unionist Ministry of the Punjab. That reactionary junta who has long fattened on the ignorance of the Punjab masses and traded on the latter's dread of the bureaucracy ... Most shamefully servile of all Indian Ministries, the Khizr Cabinet had learned to depend upon the support of permanent officials through whom it bestowed patronage for its own nefarious political and personal ends.'[51]

Wavell's favourable reference to the Unionists even induced Jinnah to proclaim: 'When we fight for Pakistan we are fighting against the British and not against the Hindus.'[52] Muslim Leaguers alleged official interference in favour of the Unionists and the provincial League passed a resolution demanding the dismissal of the ministry and the 'liquidation' of bureaucratic machinery. Glancy declined a demand by the provincial League to issue a communique assuring voters that the provincial election would be entirely free from official interference.[53] This only intensified attacks on the Unionists and the British by the Muslim League.

Evidence of official interference and pressure comes from both League and British sources. Campaigning in Mamdot's constituency, a League worker asked Jinnah for one lakh rupees from the League's central fund as official pressure was 'too much'.[54] The British Deputy Commissioner in Attock wrote to his parents that Khizar was sympathetic to his application for leave.

[50] Sayeed, *Pakistan: The Formative Phase*, p. 207; and W.C. Smith, *The Muslim League*, 1942–1943 (Lahore, 1945), pp 25–6.

[51] *Dawn*, 2 December 1945.   [52] *Dawn*, 29 December 1945.

[53] *Civil and Military Gazette*, 11 December 1945.

[54] Amiruddin to Jinnah, 28 January 1946. S. Jafri, (ed.) *Qaid-e-Azam Jinnah's Correspondence with Punjab Muslim Leaders*, pp. 37–8.

'Actually, certain interested parties—which I think includes the Premier—want me to get out of Attock as I am not prepared to swing the Elections for the Unionist Party (which is the party in power).'[55]

Again, the Deputy Commissioner of Lyallpur reported that 'nearly 80 per cent' of the subordinate Muslim staff, both revenue and District Board had active League sympathies and a large number of them had been used as instruments by the League for submitting false and forged applications of Muslim League voters. Official interference inspite of Government instructions regarding neutrality in the matter 'is largely on the side of the League rather than the Unionist Party.'[56] As it turned out, the League achieved its greatest victories in constituencies where it had made the strongest allegations about official interference.[57] Earlier, Glancy expressed the view that the Unionists suffered 'at least as much' as any other party from the activities of officials who were not impartial.[58]

The defection of 30 Muslim Unionists to the League since 1944 made the League's task easier, but it did not imply a walkover for the League in the provincial elections. The ex-Unionists included Daultana, Mamdot, and Ghazanfar Ali, all big landlords. At the beginning of October 1945, Major Mumtaz Tiwana, the biggest Tiwana landowner and one of the pillars of the Tiwana tribe, joined the League.[59] He was followed by Firoz Khan Noon, who resigned from the Viceroy's Council to work for the League and to counter the influence of Khizar, who was his cousin.[60] Families were divided—would Muslims vote for Khizar or Mumtaz? And who would win when two candidates of great social and religious influence were pitted against each other—for example, Mustafa Shah Jilani and his Unionist opponent, Makhdum Murid Husain Qureshi? The Qureshis claimed descent from the Muslim saint Bahauddin, the hereditary guardian of the shrines of Bahauddin, who was said to have descended lineally from Hasham, the grandfather of the Prophet. One of his brothers was a *Sajjad Nashin*; Murid Husain himself was President of the *Zamindara* League. The Jilanis came from Jilan in Persia, had enjoyed a grant of

[55] Allan Arthur to his parents, 15 October 1945, *Allan Arthur Papers*.
[56] Glancy to Wavell, 1 December 1945, L/P&J/5/248.
[57] Glancy to Wavell, 28 February 1946, L/P&J/5/249.
[58] Glancy to Wavell, 2 February 1946, Ibid.
[59] *Statesman*, 4 October 1945.
[60] F.K. Noon, *From Memory*, p. 184.

Rs. 12,500 from the Mughals, and were regarded as one of the most influential families in Multan.[61] Mamdot was opposed by Mohammad Ghulam Sarwar, who belonged to an important landowning family of Ferozepur district, and was also a *pir*. The influence of Daultana in Multan was offset by Major Ashiq Husain, regarded by his followers as a hereditary saint. With many men of influence pitted as candidates against each other, social influence could not have been the decisive factor in the League's win in the Punjab in 1946. It may have counted where a candidate of influence was set up against one with less influence or a political unknown. But it must also be remembered that the Punjab was not a province of many big landlords—most of the landed classes in the province comprised of small peasant proprietors. It was to them the League had addressed its appeal since November 1944. But it was not before November 1945 that the provincial League set up branches in *tehsils*.[62] The League's entry into the villages, then, occurred at a very late stage; only three months before the polling for the provincial elections took place in the Punjab.

Even so, the organization of the League was much better than that of the Unionists. The calm in the Unionist headquarters in Lahore was explained by the secretary of the Unionist Party thus:

> 'We are a rural party . . . . We do not believe in public meetings . . . . Our men go to villages and talk to local notables who wield influence over voters. They explain to them the work we have done and the benefits our legislation has conferred on peasants. Villagers, we know, will follow them.'

His remarks accounted for the difference in the propaganda technique of the two parties. The League held forty to fifty meetings a day all over the province. The Unionist Party's average was 'not even one a day'.[63] Almost a statement a day was issued from the League office in Lahore, criticizing the government or explaining their stand on one thing or another. Ghazanfar Ali used to preside over a daily round table conference with a European cartoonist and a number of journalists working for the League.

It was in the countryside that the issue was to be decided, for only 12 of the 85 Muslim seats were allotted to the urban areas. The game

[61] L. Griffin, *Chiefs and Families of Note in the Punjab*, vol. 2 (Lahore, 1940), pp. 374–9 and 396–7.

[62] FR for Punjab for first half of November 1945, HP file no. 18/11/45.

[63] *Statesman*, 24 November 1945.

was tough; at the beginning of February 1946, the League and the Unionists were reportedly running neck and neck in the villages.[64] In some constituencies a voter was alleged to be richer by almost half a year's income if he pledged his vote. It was estimated that over 15 *crores* had changed hands during the elections, which were certainly not a poor man's show. In some constituencies they cost 7 to 10 *lakhs* of rupees. There were cases of whole villages pledging themselves to the highest bidder.[65] Paper, petrol and transport played an exceptionally important part in the Punjab elections, and prices of buses soared. Most of the 100 trucks ordered by the League in December 1945[66] were used in the Punjab to cart their potential voters from distant villages to polling booths. The *Statesman* commented that the success or failure of a candidate could depend on his ability to provide transport. 'This is particularly true of rural areas where promise of a joyride is all the price one need pay for a voter.'[67]

Students, politicians, and *ulema* carried out religious propaganda for the League. Politicians would often preach in mosques after the Friday prayers.[68] Students had earlier campaigned against Unionists who had cooperated with the National Defence Council in 1941.[69] Aligarh Muslim University started a special election training camp for students in August 1945,[70] and more than one thousand students worked for the League in the Punjab and Sind alone. Student leaders were in constant touch with Jinnah.[71] Their youthful idealism may have made them more reliable than some party politicians as propagandists for the League. Ali Ahmad Faziel, a League worker writing in *Dawn*, was especially keen that college students be trained as party workers in different areas. The League would provide at least one trained worker for every 1000 voters; therefore at least 800 chief workers would have to be trained, and every constituency was to have 'at least' 12 such workers. A minimum of six of these workers should belong to the constituency in which they would campaign for the League, and in addition an equal number of outside workers.

---

[64] *Civil and Military Gazette*, 4 February 1946.
[65] *Civil and Military Gazette*, 8 February 1946.
[66] *Dawn*, 21 December 1945.   [67] *Statesman*, 18 December 1945.
[68] *Dawn*, 2 October 1945.
[69] K.B. Sayeed, *Pakistan: The Formative Phase*, p. 290.
[70] *Dawn*, 30 August 1945.
[71] Sayeed, *Pakistan: The Formative Phase*, p. 290.

The headquarters of the constituency would act as the link between the provincial committees and individual field workers. They would be assisted in everyday affairs by the League's National Guard. Muslim League newspapers put students in the 'vanguard' of the League's election campaign in the Punjab. Daultana declared that in many districts in Multan division, student workers had been able to turn the tide in favour of the League.[72]

Now that the League was expanding its organization into the countryside, it was able to exploit the religious appeal of Pakistan effectively, and its propaganda was based on the identification of Pakistan with Islam. For example, Firoz Khan Noon openly preached that a vote cast for the League was a vote in favour of the Prophet.[73] Omar Ali Siddiqi, leader of the Aligarh Election Delegation to the Punjab declared that 'the battle of the Karbala is going to be fought again in this land of the five rivers.'[74] A poster issued in Urdu over the signature of Raja Khair Mehdi Khan, the League candidate in Jhelum district, asked Muslims to choose between 'Din' and 'Dunya'; in the 'battle of righteousness and falsehood.'

Din	*Dunya*
On one side is your belief in the Almighty and your conscience	On the other side you are offered squares and *jagirs*
Righteousness and faithfulness are on one side	The other side has to offer *Lambardaris* and *Zaildaris*
One side is the rightful cause	On the other is *Sufedposhi*
One side has Pakistan for you	The other has *Kufristan* (reign of infidels)
On the one side is the problem of saving Muslims from slavery of Hindus	As opposed to this there is only the consideration of personal prestige of one man
On one side you have to bring together all those who recite the *Kalima* (the basis of Islam)	On the other is Baldev Singh and Khizar Hyat

[72] *Dawn*, 4 January 1946.
[73] Glancy to Wavell, 27 December 1945, L/P&J/5/248.
[74] *Dawn*, 19 December 1945.

On the one side is the consideration of the unity and brotherhood of all Muslims	On the other side is the *Danda* (big stick) of bureaucracy and terror of officialdom
On the one side are the lovers of Muslim League and Pakistan	On the other are the admirers of Congress and Unionists
On the one side is the honour of the Green Banner	On the other is the Government of Khizar Ministry

. . . for the sake of your religion, you have now to decide in the light of your strength of faith, to vote for . . .'[75]

Ulema from the UP, Punjab, Bengal and Sind and local *pirs* threatened Muslims with excommunication; which included a refusal to allow their dead to be buried in Muslim graveyards and a threat to debar them from joining in mass Muslim prayers, if they did not vote for the League. Those who opposed the League were denounced as infidels, and copies of the Holy Quran were carried around 'as an emblem peculiar to the Muslim league'.[76]

The religious appeal of Pakistan was admitted by Khizar when he declared that the Unionists were for Pakistan; that Muslims would be voting for Pakistan whether they voted for a Muslim League candidate or a Muslim Unionist.[77] The banners flown on the election camps of the Unionists and League were an identical green, bearing the Muslim legend of the Crescent.[78] Khizar was on the defensive and lacked conviction in adding that intercommunal cooperation was necessary in the Punjab. The Unionists argued that the crucial electoral issue for voters was *not* Pakistan, to which the Unionists were already committed; the choice was

'between chaos, disorder and communal bitterness on the one side, which is the only prospect held out by the Muslim League group, and a stable and efficient administration offered by the Unionists in the interests of the masses to which the majority of the Muslims of the province belong.'[79]

[75] Translation enclosed in Glancy to Wavell, 28 February 1946, L/P&J/5/249. I have italicized some non-English terms.

[76] Glancy to Wavell, 27 December 1945, L/P&J/5/248. See also Glancy to Wavell, 16 January and 2 February 1946, L/P&J/5/249.

[77] *Statesman*, 28 October 1945.

[78] *Civil and Military Gazette*, 8 February 1946.

[79] *Statesman*, 28 October 1945.

The election manifesto of the Unionist Party stressed the economic achievements of the ministry including the reduction of the agricultural debt by two *crores* of rupees. Provincial autonomy, complete independence, free and compulsory primary education for the poor, a reduction in military expenditure were the party's aims.[80] But the economic achievements of the Unionists seem to have had little influence on the Punjabi Muslim voter in 1946.

That Khizar's Pakistan, implying intercommunal cooperation, was rejected so decisively by the Muslim voter points to the success of the communal propaganda of the League and to the appeal of a communal Pakistan for Muslims. But though the cry for Pakistan had now become the most successful means of politicizing the Muslim masses, it is by no means clear what they understood by it. Statements by Punjab Leaguers based precisely on Jinnah's definition of Pakistan as a sovereign state[81] are hard to find, as are statements opposed to it or even a discussion on Pakistan as part of a federation. To most Leaguers in 1945–6, Pakistan appears to have stood for some sort of general salvation from Hindu domination and symbolized and Islamic revival in India.

What counted most in the League's victory in the Punjab in 1945–6? The great effort it made; the fact that for the first time the League's organization had reached down to contact the Muslim voter, partly accounted for its win. The appeal was essentially religious and attempted to convince Muslims of the benefits of Pakistan. Propagandists were directed when they visited a village to: 'Find out its social problems and difficulties to tell them [the villagers] that the main cause of their problems was the Unionists [and] give them the solution—Pakistan'.[82] Soldiers were told that the Unionists had not done anything for them after the war.[83] For the students who campaigned for the League, Pakistan held out the promise of the resurgence of Islam—'our aim is essentially to reorientate Islam in the modern world, purge our ranks of the reactionary Muslim Church and to free ourselves from economic and political bondage'.[84] This seemed a far cry from the assurance given by Jin-

[80] *Civil and Military Gazette*, 29 November 1945.

[81] See, for example, Jinnah's reply to Patel in *Statesman*, 19 November 1945.

[82] Translation of pamphlet issued by the election board of the Punjab Muslim Students Federation, quoted by Talbot, 'The 1946 Punjab Elections'. *Modern Asian Studies*, 14, 1, 1980, p. 75.

[83] *Statesman*, 10 November 1945.   [84] *Dawn*, 4 December 1945.

nah to the Pir of Manki Sharif in November 1945 that Pakistan would be based on the laws of the Quran in which the sharjat would be established,[85] but it showed that Pakistan could mean, as it was intended to mean, all things to all men. S.E. Abbott, then Secretary to Khizar, attributed the League's victory to the Muslim belief in the inevitability of Pakistan.[86] The League had presented the elections as a plebiscite for Pakistan.[87] The claim had not been contradicted by the British, who would actually transfer or confer power. To that extent, their silence on the subject also contributed to the League's victory.

In Bengal, the League's influence in urban areas had been rising since its coalition with Huq in 1937. After provincial Leaguers fell out with Huq in 1941, they had organized demonstrations against him in several towns of the province. The popularity of the League in urban Bengal was evident by 1944, when Huq's Muslim candidates lost every seat in the elections to the Calcutta Corporation to the League. Radical Leaguers like Suhrawardy built up a base among Muslim labour during the League's tenure in power from 1943–5. Involved in ministerial politicking, Huq had gradually lost the rural base which had swept him into power in 1937.[88] In 1946, Bengal League candidates were personally selected by Suhrawardy and approved of by Jinnah. "Pakistan" as Bengal Leaguers presented it to their voters would consist of an autonomous Bengal and Assam, and would lead to prosperity for backward Muslims. At a Bengal League conference, Liaqat Ali Khan promised the abolition of *zamindari* without compensation—a promise which could have only won the League support of the poor Muslim peasantry of Bengal.[89] But were Bengal Leaguers thinking of the sovereign Pakistan of Jinnah's conception? It seems unlikely. Ispahani, one of Jinnah's most loyal lieutenants in Bengal, told the Governor in January 1946 that Muslims needed opportunities for self-advancement, administratively and otherwise, and Casey's 'definite

[85] Sayeed, *Pakistan: The Formative Phase*, p. 208.

[86] Letter to author, 15 February 1981.

[87] Wavell to Pethick-Lawrence, 22 October 1945, *TOP*, vol. 6, p. 377. For Pethick-Lawrence's reasons for not clarifying Whitehall's stand on the League's propaganda, see his letter to Wavell, 9 November 1945, Ibid., pp. 466–7.

[88] This paragraph is based on Sen, *Muslim Politics*, p. 127ff. See also Ispahani to Jinnah, 8 January 1942, 14 January 1942, 16 June 1942, *Jinnah–Ispahani Correspondence*, pp. 234–5, 235–7, 276 respectively.

[89] Sen, *Muslim Politics*, pp. 196–7.

impression' was that adequate safeguards would be acceptable to the Muslims. Ispahani said he realized very well that the day of small states was past, and that if the British imposed an interim govern-ment of India, which had adequate safeguards for the Muslims, it would be accepted.[90]

The League's success in Bengal and Sind can be partly accounted for by the fact that it did not face any serious, organized opposition in these provinces. Huq's party was in disarray; in Sind, no Muslim stood on the Congress ticket as this would have been fatal for any chances of victory.[91] The Congress lacked the money and organiza-tion required to contest Muslim seats in every province. The release of Congress prisoners less than three months before the elections added to their difficulties and large amounts of money were needed in the Muslim majority provinces, especially in the Punjab and Ben-gal, which, for the Congress, 'held the key position' in the election. But it was in these two provinces that the provincial Congress groups were riven by factions, and organizational work never really got under way.[92] Congress strategy in Muslim constituencies some-times confounded its own supporters. For example, in Sind the Congress negotiated with the League for a coalition, even as it was fighting the League in other provinces. Azad's offer to the League of a coalition in Sind 'came as a great surprise' to Congressmen in the Punjab. Anti-League Muslims 'cannot understand these things, nor can the rest of us'.[93] The Congress allied with Nationalist Mus-lims, Ahrars, Momins—indeed, with any anti-League Muslim par-ty. It carried out propaganda for Nationalist Muslims, and the League and the Congress vied with each other in the virulence of their appeals to religious loyalty. The Congress used Muslim di-vines in the UP and Bengal. League ministries during the war were condemned as the stronghold of the British.[94] In Bengal, National-ist Muslims alleged that one of the 'wonders' of the League ministry during the war was the 'man-made famine' of 1943.[95] To this the

[90] Entry in Casey's Diary, 2 January 1946, *TOP*, vol. 6, p. 732.

[91] FR for Sind for second half of December 1945, HP file no.-18/12/45.

[92] Azad to Patel, 21 October 1945, Patel to Prafulla Ghosh, 26 October 1945, *PC*, vol. 2, pp. 24–5 and 122 respectively.

[93] B.S. Gilani to Patel, 10 February 1946, Ibid., pp. 301–2.

[94] See, for example, *Hindustan Standard*, 11 February 1946.

[95] *Amrita Bazar Patrika*, 29 November 1945, and 3 December 1945; *National Herald*, 26 February 1945.

League reported that Hindus, who were in a majority in the Viceroy's executive council, had refused to send food to Bengal and were therefore responsible for the famine.[96] League newspapers published reports of Hindu volunteers donning Turkish caps while campaigning for Nationalist Muslims.[97]

The League, however, had the whip-hand in Muslim religious propaganda against the Congress. The *Morning News* in Calcutta claimed that the *Jamiat-ul-ulema-i-Hind*, which campaigned for the Congress was working for *Hindiat*, while the *Jammat-i-Islami*, which supported the League, stood for the *Islamiat*.[98] The *Jammat-i-Islami* accused the *Jamiat-ul-ulema-i-Hind* of making a distinction between religious and secular matters.

> 'They remembered the prayer, but they forgot the chain of armour donned by the Prophet Muhammad when he went forth to fight the unequal battle with the infidels . . . They misled the Muslims to the unworthy tenets of *ahimsa*.'[99]

Its attempts to outdo the League in religious propaganda, without having a widespread popular base among Muslims, profited Congress little, and only contributed to the atmosphere of communal bitterness.

Only in the NWFP was the Congress successful in both Hindu and Muslim constituencies. Here, in spite of defections from the Congress to the League before the elections, the Congress was the better organized party. Aurangzeb stood discredited because of the undignified methods he had used to remain in power and was not even given a League ticket. Although the Congress and their Red Shirt allies used the religious appeal (the tri-colour was marked with the *Kalima*),[100] it was not this alone that won the election for the Congress. The Congress was successful in representing the League as a catspaw of the British. It appealed to the less well-to-do, over whom the Khans were losing their hold. Moreover, the provincial League was disorganized, and it was only on 10 December that a Committee of Action was set up. The fact that Mamdot was

[96] Congress worker (name illegible) to Sadiq Ali, 5 December 1945, AICC file no. P-24, 1945–1946, p. 28.

[97] *Morning News*, 30 November 1945.

[98] *Morning News*, 25 October 1945.

[99] *Morning News*, 28 October 1945.

[100] *Star of India*, 28 February 1946.

appointed as its convenor[101] suggests that the League found it difficult to get a reliable man from the province to head the committee. All candidates in the NWFP attached importance to personal contacts with voters and visited individual houses or mohallas. Election officials reported a growing sense of political discipline in canvassing, addressing and organizing mass meetings. Appeals to tribal and sectional loyalties were made, but they may not have made much difference in a province where a Khan only had to declare his loyalty to the League, and his relatives would support the Congress. They would also give their tenants a free running, and it was 'a tenantry which had been primed that they would be allowed to take over the Land belonging to the Khan if the Congress came to power.'[102] The election saw a fight more on ideological than on personal grounds.[103] The League's charge that the Congress was using office to win votes was balanced by the fact that most Muslim officials had League sympathies, and even some British officers and their wives campaigned for the League.[104] Pakistan did not have much appeal for the Pathans, because, according to Cunningham, they did not think they would be dominated by the Hindus or anyone else![105]

Nevertheless, the League did not fare so badly in the province, contesting all 33 Muslim seats and winning 15. It also won the special seats reserved for landholders, none of which was contested by the Congress. The Congress won 19 Muslim seats and lost 8. Anti-League parties secured 58.75 per cent of the total Muslim vote.[106] The extent of the League's success in Muslim constituencies in 1945–6 can be gauged from the fact that it won 76 per cent of the total Muslim vote in India—a very far cry indeed from the 4.8 per cent it had obtained in 1937! Its achievements in the Punjab were remarkable: it defeated, and unseated, 57 Unionists in Muhammadan rural constituencies; the Congress in 9 rural constituencies; and swept the Ahrars from 5 urban seats. The Unionists defeated the League in only 11 rural constituencies. With a total of 62 wins in ru-

[101] *Dawn*, 11 December 1945.

[102] Caroe to Wavell, 8 May 1946, L/P&J/5/223.

[103] *Report on the General Elections to the Central Legislative Assembly and the NWFP Legislative Assembly* (Peshawar, 1946), p. 10.

[104] A. Ghaffar Khan, *My Life and Struggle* (Delhi, 1969), p. 175.

[105] Cunningham to Wavell, 27 February 1946, *TOP*, vol. 6, p. 1086.

[106] Nehru to Wavell, 8 May 1946, Reforms Office file no. 70/46/R, 1946.

ral areas, all 9 urban seats and both the women's seats, the League chalked up 73 seats in the Punjab legislature, and polled 65.10 per cent of the votes polled in Muslim constituencies.

In Bengal, it did even better, obtaining 83.6 per cent of the Muslim votes polled. The Krishak Praja party secured only 5.3 per cent, and the *Jamiat-ul-ulema* and Nationalist Muslims, both supported by the Congress, won 1.2 and 0.2 per cent of the Muslim votes polled.

The NWFP was the only province where the League failed to secure a majority of Muslim votes: anti-League parties obtained more than 58 per cent of the votes polled. Nevertheless, of the extent of the League's victory, and its appeal to Muslims, there was no doubt. The gains of the League clearly represented a turning of many Muslims from essentially provincial concerns to rally behind the only Muslim party which would take care of their interests at the all-India level, in the bargaining for the spoils of the transfer of power. The League's success also represented a solidification and politicization of the Muslim religious community, a rallying to "Pakistan", but whether that meant the victory of Jinnah's conception of a sovereign state can perhaps be questioned.

With the election results out, there arose the question of the formation of governments in the provinces. In Bengal and Sind, the League had enough seats to form ministries, but in the Punjab it needed the support of 10 more members to obtain a majority in the legislature. Here the League offered 3 portfolios to the Sikhs if they would enter a Muslim League coalition.[107] But Pakistan was the stumbling-block. The Sikhs objected to the League's insistence on Pakistan, to which the Muslim League leaders replied that the ministry came under the Act of 1935 and that all India issues did not come into question. The Sikhs retorted that there was no all India issue for them.[108] Negotiations between the League and the Congress failed because the League refused to enter into a coalition with any non-League Muslim group.[109] This was in contrast to the years before 1945, when the AIML had not always been able to prevent provincial Leagues from coalescing with non-League Muslim parties. Jinnah's authority was now apparently sufficient to prevent such coalitions. Every candidate for the elections had been selected

---

[107] *Statesman*, 26 February 1946.
[108] *Civil and Military Gazette*, 28 February 1946.
[109] *Statesman*, 6 and 9 March 1946.

with his approval; their victory was therefore a personal triumph for him.[110]

On 7 March, the Congress, Akalis and the Unionists formed the Punjab Coalition Party, under the leadership of Khizar. The strength of the Coalition worked out to at least 10 more than that of the League. Glancy accordingly called on Khizar as leader of the coalition to form a ministry, despite the contention of Muslim League leaders that they represented the largest individual party.

Deprived of constitutional power, the League organized demonstrations against the Ministry. Muslim students were directed by provincial League leaders to demonstrate before Khizar's residence in Lahore. Communal feeling had been strengthened by an election fought on the slogan of Pakistan; and Congress leaders advised Hindu students not to start counter-demonstrations,[111] while the League demanded Glancy's dismissal. Local Muslim Leaguers were directed 'to organize the Muslim masses to prepare them for the struggle that lies ahead. Khizar Quisling Ministry . . . is an insult to the determined will of the Mussalmans and a blot on the fair name of this Province'.[112] The Congress was condemned for joining the Unionists whom it had formerly derided as reactionaries.[113] A coalition which included so small a percentage of Muslims was a strange anomaly in the Province, especially when the party which commanded a majority of the Muslim votes found no place in the government. It did not augur well for the future.

[110] See note by 'F.M.', *TOP*, vol. 6, pp. 767–8.

[111] *Statesman*, 10 March 1946.

[112] *Eastern Times*, 13 March 1946.

[113] *Eastern Times*, 13 March 1946. On this paragraph see also Glancy to Wavell, 15 March 1946, L/P&J/5/249.

CHAPTER 5

The Cabinet Mission:
March to July 1946

If, as some scholars have suggested, the emergence of Pakistan as a sovereign state through the partition of 1947 was the inevitable result of the politicization of two intrinsic 'nations', the question of how and when that politicization occurred to make that inevitable arises. In the case of the Muslim community in the majority provinces the first essential for such a development was their unification behind the AIML, capable of focussing their political weight at the central negotiating table. In Chapter 4 a case has been made for thinking that this prerequisite was not achieved until 1945, and then the imminence of the British relinquishment of central authority appears to have contributed much to confirm the League's claim to speak for the Muslim community as a whole. But was the consolidation of the League's claim a superficial product of momentary crisis rather than a fundamental and lasting political unification of Muslim communalism? Carried to its logical extreme, such a view would suggest that Jinnah and the League adopted "Pakistan" as a mere political slogan which would draw Muslim religious sentiment behind the League's candidates and align Muslim provincial leaders and parties into conformity with its central directorate. It is, however, argued in this thesis that Jinnah and the League intended the claim to a sovereign Pakistan to be more than a bargaining lever to extract the greatest possible constitutional concessions for the Muslim community from both the British and Congress in an eventual Indian federation; and that at Simla in 1946 Jinnah played this tactic so that both the other parties had to concede Pakistan before, or when, power was transferred to Indians. It is, therefore, necessary to review the negotiations with the Cabinet mission in some detail in order to test the seriousness of purpose with which Jinnah contended for a sovereign Pakistan.

Pakistan was the issue which dominated all discussion on the political future of India at the Governors conference held in August 1945 to discuss the political fallout from Simla. Most Governors held that Jinnah should be asked to define Pakistan. His intransigence at Simla had raised his popularity among Muslims. Glancy warned that Pakistan, in its crude form, was a potent political slogan and might well carry the day. If Pakistan became an imminent reality, there would be civil war in the Punjab.[1] The election propaganda of the League in the Punjab had taken the line that 'these elections will decide whether there is to be Pakistan or not, and that if the League win in the Pakistan provinces no further vote by the legislature or plebiscite will be needed'.[2] Significantly, at least one Governor, Clow, was of the view that the British themselves had contributed to the growth of the Pakistan idea because they had given recognition to it in the constitutional proposals of 1942 without ever asking Jinnah what he meant by it.[3] Jinnah's demand at Simla that the League must be given parity with all other parties combined made it difficult for the British to make any constitutional advance without first accepting Pakistan. But, as Evan Jenkins, then Private Secretary to the Viceroy, observed, he had never defined it; and the Rajagopalachari formula had failed in its attempt to bring Jinnah out into the open. 'It failed', concluded Jenkins, 'and I do not think that any other attempt is likely to succeed at present'.[4] Wavell's wry comment on Jenkins' note was that it would 'obviously be difficult to bring Jinnah into the open over this, but we may have to try some day'.[5] Now, in October 1945, he favoured a clarification of the British stand on Pakistan. 'We clearly could not agree to permit any Province to stand out of the new constitution, or to secede at a later stage, on the result of elections to the Provincial Assembly or of a purely Muslim plebiscite'.[6] Of course, it would not be easy for the British to make such a declaration: with the present Congress attitude, the British should avoid any action which would turn the League against the Government as well.[7] The British had to balance against the advantage of reassuring the minorities the disadvantage of alienating the Muslim League. Although the denial of the claim for a Muslim plebiscite would annoy Jinnah,

---

[1] Glancy to Wavell, 16 August 1945, L/P&J/5/248.
[2] Wavell to Pethick-Lawrence, 22 October 1945, *TOP*, vol. 6, pp. 337–8.
[3] Enclosure to Clow to Colville, 23 August 1945, Ibid., p. 149.
[4] Note by Evan Jenkins, 23 July 1945, R/3/1/105, pp. 34–5.
[5] Handwritten note by Wavell on Jenkins' note above.
[6] Wavell to Pethick-Lawrence, 22 October 1945, *TOP*, vol. 6, p. 377.
[7] Menon to Abell, 20 November 1945, R/3/1/105, p. 119.

'it is fairer to Jinnah to deny it now than to let him assume its validity throughout the elections and tell him afterwards that we are quite unable to accept it.'[8]

Faced with the prospect of making a declaration about an issue on which it would be difficult to please either party, Pethick-Lawrence was unable even to justify a renewal of the Cripps proposals. The British, he argued, had never said they accepted Jinnah's assumption. It would be better if the British said nothing in favour of the Cripps plan as one of the parties might then refuse to enter into negotiations. The British could consider alternatives to it—for example, the right of smaller areas of a province to opt out.[9] The British Cabinet decided that the Viceroy could tell Jinnah that if Muslims insisted on self-determination in 'genuinely' Muslim areas this would be conceded. But there would be 'no question' of compelling large non-Muslim populations to remain in Pakistan against their will.[10] Pethick-Lawrence also put aside the right of provinces to opt out of an Indian union if 60 per cent of the population voted to do so in a plebiscite, as the balance of Hindu and Sikh votes would probably turn the verdict against Pakistan.[11] Pethick-Lawrence's apparent attempt at keeping all options open disclosed his desire to avoid taking a stand on any issue; indeed, the Labour government had very little idea of what constitutional settlement they could obtain in India. The British could not give up the idea either of a union government or Pakistan. They could announce that the principle of Pakistan would only be recognized after attempts to form a single constitution-making body had failed. Alternatively, they could say that no progress could be made on the basis of a union government; that if the Muslims insisted on self-determination in 'genuine' Muslim areas this would be conceded, but large non-Muslim areas would not be forced to stay in Pakistan against their will.[12] How Muslims and non-Muslims would give expression to their wishes he did not say.

Much has been made of the Labour party's commitment to Indian independence. However, a closer look at Labour's imperial attitude reveals a woolliness and illusions about decolonization which

[8] Note by Jenkins, 22 October 1945, R/3/1/105, p. 104A.
[9] Pethick-Lawrence to Wavell, 9 November 1945, *TOP*, vol. 6, pp. 466–7.
[10] Cabinet India and Burma Committee meeting, 14 January 1946, Ibid., p. 787.
[11] Note by Pethick-Lawrence, 14 February 1946, Ibid., pp. 978–9.
[12] Ibid., pp. 980–2.

blurred a commitment to empire which was as strong as that of the Conservatives. Redolent of Amery in 1943, Bevin had favoured marriages between British soldiers training in different parts of the Commonwealth and local women.[13] Attlee's desire, in January 1942, to do for India what Lord Durham did for Canada did not manifest an interest in Indian independence, for Durham only wanted to consolidate the empire by concession and reform.[14] As late as 1945, Attlee shared with the Conservatives a horror of self-government for Indians. His talks with Nehru and Krishna Menon in 1938 did not include discussion of the terms of any treaty between an Indian constituent assembly and the British, otherwise their strongly differing attitudes to any treaty provisions would have been revealed at that stage. The British knew that the Congress would never agree to foreign bases on Indian soil, while the Labour party subscribed to a widely held official British idea that a transfer of power should be conditional upon satisfactory arrangements to safeguard British economic and military interests in India. It would, of course, have been unrealistic to expect the British not to conceive the prospects the loss of empire would have on their international position. As Deputy Prime Minister in the war cabinet, Attlee asked the India Office in January 1945 to investigate how British troops could be kept on Indian soil once India received dominion status. Evidently he was contemplating treating India on a different footing from other dominions, for in those countries British troops had marched out as soon as dominion status was given.[15] Independent Labour opinion shared the dominant official desire for defence arrangements with an independent India, while Bevin's speech to the pre-election Labour party conference in May 1945 reconciled socialist revolution with empire:

'You will have to form a government which is at the centre of a great Empire and Commonwealth of Nations, which touches all parts of the world, and which will have to deal . . . with every race and with every difficulty, and everyone of them has a different outlook upon

[13] C. Thorne, *Allies of a Kind* (London, 1978), pp. 708–9, V. Rothwell, *Britain and the Cold War 1941–1947* (London, 1982), p. 224: See also N. Mansergh, *The Commonwealth Experience* (London, 1969), p. 402.

[14] Mansergh, *The Commonwealth Experience*, p. 38.

[15] Thorne, *Allies*, p. 640. War Cabinet India Committee paper 1(45)5, 9 January 1945, *TOP*, vol. 5, p. 381.

life . . . . Revolutions do not change geography and revolutions do not change geographical need.[16]

Following the assumption of office by the Labour party in August 1945, the priority accorded to defence emanated from the top: Attlee was Minister of Defence until December 1946. On 14 January 1946, the cabinet decided that the pledge of independence in the Cripps offer was 'not a blank cheque but had been conditional on a scheme being devised on which all parties agreed.'

> 'We had a moral responsibility not to hand over the country to Indians without being satisfied that the succession governments were fully aware of the military and economic problems which a self-governing India would have to face and that they had concerted reasonable plans to meet them . . . It was agreed that the risk . . . was that in effect we set ourselves up as the sole judge of what solution was reasonable both economically and from the defence aspect. If no solution was reached which we could regard as reasonable, logically we should continue governing India even if it involved rebellion which would have to be suppressed by British troops.'[17]

Labour's commitment to the maintenance of British power was understandably greater than its so-called commitment to Indian independence.[18] British interests were paramount; the political decision to transfer power rested on the strategical premise that Indian security required that India remain in the Commonwealth.[19] The logical conclusion of this idea should have been that if Indian security had dictated that she leave the Commonwealth, the British would not have taken any decision to transfer power! Official thinking on India's participation in imperial defence seems to have taken the line that Britain might be weakened by war; India might receive dominion status or even independence; but with India in the Commonwealth, Britain could preserve her global primacy. It has been observed that the awareness that British manpower and economic resources were barely adequate for a world role only reinforced

[16] For example, *New Statesman and Nation*, 22 March 1946, p. 149; Labour Party *Report of the Annual Conference 1945*, p. 115, quoted in P.S. Gupta, *Imperialism and the British Labour Movement 1914–1964* (London, 1975), p. 281.

[17] Cabinet India and Burma Committee meeting, 14 January 1946, *TOP*, vol. 6, pp. 788–9.

[18] As suggested, among others, by V. Brittain, *Pethick-Lawrence* (London, 1963), p. 134; and H. Tinker, *Experiment with Freedom* (Oxford, 1967), pp. 33–4.

[19] Cabinet Far Eastern Planning Committee Paper GEN 77/94, *TOP*, vol. 6, pp. 780–1.

British determination 'to reconstruct solid foundations for permanent Great Power Status'.[20] Labour's offer of independence to India
was, then, conditioned by the effort to preserve *Pax Britannica*.

From August 1945 onwards, the British were also concerned over
the problem of law and order. The large crowds which enthusiastically greeted political prisoners on their release from jail, the inflammatory speeches of Congress leaders against the bureaucracy,
had a demoralizing effect on British officials.[21] Nehru justified his
speeches by saying that he did not see how violence could be
avoided, if legitimate aims could not otherwise be attained, However, Wavell noted that Nehru's attitude was 'quiet and friendly
throughout', even though 'he seems to me to have reached the state
of mind of a fanatic'.[22] The fact was that Congress leaders distrusted
the British especially after their experience at Simla.[23] Gandhi
admitted that Nehru's speeches were 'hot', but only if the British
had no intention to part with power.[24]

The question of the loyalty of Indians in the armed forces and
Civil Service also concerned the British keenly. Auchinleck felt that
if they were honest about leaving India, there could be no justification for reinforcing the British garrison in the country save at the request of an Indian government.[25] Both he and Wavell were against
trying the loyalty of Indian troops too highly in an attempt to rep-
ress their own countrymen, and advised Whitehall against using Indian troops in Indonesia. Being imbued with nationalist ideas they
might not wish to suppress freedom movements elsewhere.[26]

Popular unrest at the trial of three INA officers on the charge of
waging war against the King led to demonstrations and riots in
Bombay, Calcutta and Delhi from November to February 1946.
British officials did not know what the policy of the government

---

[20] Rothwell, *Britain and the Cold War* p. 3. For a fuller discussion of these points,
see Anita Inder Singh, 'Imperial Defence and the Transfer of Power in India, 1946–
1947', *International History Review*, November 1982, pp. 568–88.

[21] For example, Colville to Wavell, 2 November 1945; Dow to Wavell, 3
November 1945; Wavell to Pethick-Lawrence, 16 November 1945, *TOP*, vol. 6, pp.
429–30, 437–8, 488 respectively.

[22] Enclosure to Wavell to Pethick-Lawrence, 4 November 1945, Ibid., pp. 440–1.

[23] Casey to Wavell, 2 December 1945, Ibid., p. 589.

[24] Gandhi to Jenkins, 13 November 1945, Ibid., p. 481.

[25] Auchinleck to Viceroy, 22 August 1945; John Connell, *Auchinleck*, p. 792.

[26] Ibid., pp. 823–4; and Wavell to Pethick-Lawrence, 17 October 1945, *TOP*, vol.
6, p. 360.

was, and the authority of the government was being undermined.[27] The three INA men, in Nehru's words, 'became symbols of India fighting for her independence . . . The trial dramatised . . . the old contest: England versus India'.[28] Official intelligence reports noted that the situation in respect of the INA is one which warrants disquiet. There has seldom been a matter which has attracted so much Indian public interest and, it is safe to say, sympathy'. The Congress had led the outcry, but the Sikhs, who had great influence in the rural areas of Central Punjab, were organizing daily meetings where demands on behalf of the INA were voiced.[29] Muslim soldiers belonging to the INA were campaigning for the League in the elections.[30] The League, probably moved by considerations of expediency, had decided to defend Muslim officers of the INA, and the trial of Muslims was expected to make their effect on the Muslim public and the League alike. INA weeks and days were being organized in towns and villages. It was clear that sympathy for the INA 'is not the monopoly of those who are ordinarily against Government. It is equally clear that this particular brand of sympathy cuts across communal barriers . . . In many cases officers of the INA belong to influential families'.[31] There were also indications that 'majority opinion' in the Indian Armed Forces was in favour of leniency. So 'abstract justice must to some extent give way to expediency'.[32] The policy would be revised and only those accused of murder and brutality would be brought to trial, and in future the charge of waging war against the king would be dropped.[33] Auchinleck, with his knowledge of the men he had commanded, wrote that the pleasure and relief which followed the commutation of the sentences on the three officers were born of the conviction that confirmation of the sentences would have resulted in violent internal conflict.

[27] FR for Bengal for second half of January 1946, HP file no. 18/1/46.

[28] Nehru, quoted in Connell, *Auchinleck*, p. 810.

[29] Note prepared by Intelligence Bureau, enclosed in Government of India, Home Department to Secretary, Political Department, India Office, 20 November 1945, *TOP*, vol. 6, pp. 512–13, referred to hereafter as Intelligence Bureau note.

[30] *Star of India*, 28 January 1946.

[31] Intelligence Bureau note, *TOP*, vol. 6, pp. 513–4.

[32] Governor General (War Department) to Secretary of State, Ibid., p. 572.

[33] Auchinleck to Wavell, 22 January 1946, and Wavell to Auchinleck, 23 January 1946, quoted in Connell, *Auchinleck*, pp. 812–13.

'This feeling does not ... spring universally from the idea that the convicted officers were trying to rid India of the British and therefore, to be applauded, whatever crimes they might commit, but from a generally genuine feeling that they were patriots and nationalists and that, even if they were misled they should be treated with clemency, as true sons of India. In this connexion, it should be remembered ... that *every* Indian worthy of the name is today a "Nationalist", though this does not mean that he is necessarily "anti-British" .... It is no use shutting one's eyes to the fact that any Indian officer worth his salt is a "Nationalist".'[34]

With political and economic unrest on the rise, a conciliatory gesture was needed to placate Indian opinion, and the result was the Labour government's decision to send the cabinet mission to India.[35] But even as the cabinet decided to send a ministerial team to discuss the transfer of power, it had not, as we have seen, ruled out repression as a political alternative if that proved necessary to secure British interests. Earlier, the cabinet had considered a suggestion by Auchinleck to increase the size of the British garrison in India. Indian opposition to such a move was anticipated, and was sought to be countered with the deception tactic that the troops were really in India for a short spell of training before they left for Indonesia![36] But in February 1946, two things led the Labour government to change its mind. First, on 4 February, the Chiefs of Staff reported that British troops could not be moved from the Middle or Far East without seriously disrupting the British position in those areas. At home, demobilization was apace, and the shortage of manpower was 'forcing' the Cabinet Defence Committee to make reductions with the result that 'we are now left with an irreducible minimum in all areas where our commitments continue'.[37]

The crumbling imperial military base was signalled further by the mutinies of the Royal Indian Air Force and Royal Indian Navy in January and February 1946. The mutinies came without any warning to the British. Although the Air Force mutiny was quickly suppressed, in the naval mutiny the strikers captured twenty British

[34] Ibid., pp. 945 and 949.

[35] India and Burma Committee meetings on 19 November 1945 and 14 January 1946, CAB 134/341 and 342 respectively; Pethick-Lawrence to Wavell, 21 November 1945 and cabinet paper, 22 November 1945, *TOP*, vol. 6, pp. 516–17 and 522–3 respectively; cabinet meeting, 22 January 1946, CAB 128/5.

[36] Auchinleck to Chiefs of Staff, 22 December 1945 and 18 January 1946. Cabinet Defence Committee meeting, 11 Jan. 1946, *TOP*, vol. 6.

[37] Alanbrooke to Auchinleck, (T), 4 February 1946, L/WS/1/1008, Ibid., p. 120.

ships in Bombay[38] and in Karachi, they retaliated with the ships' guns after British troops opened fire.[39] Congress, League, and occasionally Communist flags flew side by side in Bombay, where industrial labour also joined the strike.[40] Congress and League leaders did not incite the mutineers—they used their influence to bring the strikes to an end.[41] But racial sentiment was now very strong, and with the loyalty of the armed forces in doubt, the British now thought of constitutional expedients to avert violence.

This, then, was the background to the Cabinet Mission, which arrived in India on 14 March 1946. Its aim, as described by Attlee, was to get machinery set up for framing the constitutional structure in which Indians will have 'full control of their own destiny and the formation of a new interim government'.[42]

The Mission noted that their administrative weakness did not make it possible for the British to face the situation 'with the same confidence as in the past owing to doubt whether the forces behind law and order' were reliable. 'They felt this lack of confidence for the first time'. If the negotiations failed and the armed forces had to be called in, they must be certain that they 'will not be handed over to those whom they have had to suppress'. Although it would be difficult to give any set undertaking of support, it would be necessary if their support was to be obtained. 'The general conclusion from this was that negotiations must succeed and we must refuse to permit a breakdown'.[43] Nor could the British impose a solution. For 'the hookum principle . . . ceases to apply if the authority issuing the hookum is forthwith going to step down from the gadi'.[44]

The consequences of a failure of negotiations seized much of the attention of British officials in India and in the India Office. They realized that an attempt by the Congress to paralyse communications and the administration would be successful, even if the police and armed forces remained loyal. In any case, the services would be

---

[38] *Statesman*, 20 February 1946.　　[39] *Statesman*, 22 February 1946.

[40] *Times of India*, 23 February 1946.

[41] Mudie to Wavell, 27 February 1946, L/P&J/5/252. See also Colville to Wavell, 27 February 1946, L/P&J/5/167.

[42] Cabinet delegation to Cabinet Office, (T), 25 March 1946, *TOP*, vol. 7, p. 6.

[43] Note of meeting between Cabinet delegation and Viceroy's Executive Council on 26 March 1946, Ibid., p. 7.

[44] Croft to Monteath, 1 April 1946, Ibid., pp. 73–4.

unlikely to remain 100 per cent staunch. Some sections of the Air Force, Navy and Signals units might mutiny. There were chances of a mutiny by the police as well. For their part, British officers were weary and depressed. Indian officers were naturally looking over their shoulders and ahead. Communal antagonism was developing among them and over wide areas they would fail to stand up to a severe test.[45]

The British favoured a transfer of power to a united India, which would keep the army undivided, and be of the greatest advantage to them strategically. In considering the military implications of their future policy with regard to India, they had to bear in mind that in any future war their strategic requirements in India were that they should be in a position to have recourse to her industrial and man-power potential and to use her territory for operational and administrative bases. It was therefore important that India should be secure from external aggression and internal disorder. For defence purposes, 'it is essential' that she should remain a single unit.[46] Neither the League nor the Congress was told about these intentions. Partition would destroy the homogeneity of the Indian army and would be resorted to 'if the only alternative is complete failure and consequent chaos'. If it had to be adopted, 'every effort should be made to obtain agreement for some form of central defence council to be set up which will include not only Pakistan, Hindustan and the Indian States, but also Burma and Ceylon'.[47] The British were, however, anxious that both parties accept a settlement. The Congress might not want to stay in the Commonwealth at all; Pakistan, if formed, could remain in it, but would be economically and militarily unviable.[48] If the Congress alone made a settlement with the British, the British would be bound to support the Congress in dealing with any Muslim disturbances which eventuated.[49] With a British decision on Palestine which favoured the Jews in the offing, the British would have to cope with trouble from Muslims in

[45] Enclosure to Thorne to Abell, 5 April 1946, Ibid., pp. 150-1; Enclosure to Auchinleck to General Mayne, 3 May 1946, Ibid., pp. 407-8.

[46] Defence Committee Paper dated 12 June 1946, Ibid., pp. 889-90.

[47] Attlee to Cabinet delegation, (T), 13 April 1946, Ibid., pp. 260-1.

[48] Note by Abell discussed by Mission and Wavell on 16 May 1946, Ibid., pp. 568-9.

[49] Note by Croft and Turnbull, enclosed with Minutes by Croft, Turnbull and Pethick-Lawrence, 25 April 1946, Ibid., pp. 336-7.

India and in the Middle East, and this would pose 'a very grave threat to the defence system of the Commonwealth'. It would also defeat plans for a Middle East Security system. If there was no agreement between the Congress and League the British would have to produce a settlement. Allowing the Congress alone to join the interim government would mean that the British would get involved in the suppression of Muslims. This situation the British wished to avoid, for the Muslims had supported them during the war and wished to preserve their association with the Commonwealth.[50] The British could range themselves behind Pakistan, leaving Hindustan free to work out her own destiny as she pleased. This course of action would also avoid a situation in which the British would find themselves staying on in Hindustan and suppressing Hindus.[51] The political logicality of a withdrawal into Pakistan did not appeal to British defence chiefs. Pakistan would be in two halves, and the forces needed to defend it would be as great as those needed to defend India. Pakistan had insufficient resources for defence, the cost of which would fall on Britain. An alliance with Pakistan might push the Congress into a defence treaty with the USSR, and the British position in Pakistan and in Europe could be endangered. The British would also have to contend with minorities in Pakistan, who might act as a fifth column.[52] So if repression was difficult, scuttle humiliating, Pakistan economically and militarily unviable, the only alternative left was that the negotiations for a transfer of power to an undivided India must succeed. It was the only basis on which the British could hope to secure their long-term aim of maintaining India within the imperial security system; and therefore made every effort to achieve it.

When the Mission arrived in India, there were reports of rising communal tension from all provinces, and forebodings of civil war from the Punjab, where the Sikhs, especially, feared Muslim domination in any form of Pakistan.[53] In the NWFP, Muslim League volunteers had started carrying spears in their processions.[54]

[50] Note by Croft and Turnbull, Ibid., p. 337.

[51] Meeting between cabinet delegation and Wavell on 15 May 1946, Ibid., pp. 563–4.

[52] Note by Abell discussed by cabinet delegation and Wavell on 16 May 1946, Ibid., p. 569. In writing these two paragraphs, chronology has been sacrificed for coherence—also to avoid subsequent repetition of the points discussed.

[53] Jenkins to Wavell, 15 April 1946, Ibid., p. 272.

[54] FR for NWFP for second half of March 1946, HP file no. 18/3/46.

Even as the League negotiated with the British and the Congress, Liaqat Ali Khan talked of ' "Pakistan or death" ',[55] and Firoz Khan Noon proudly proclaimed: 'If we find that we have to fight Great Britian (sic) for placing us under one Central Government of Hindu Raj, then the havoc which the Muslims will play will put to shame what Jenghiz Khan and Halaku did'.[56] In the Punjab, Sind and NWFP, the Muslim League National Guards were being reinforced and Shaukat Hyat Khan called on Muslim ex-military personnel to enlist in the force.[57] All Commissioners in the UP reported deteriorating communal relations. There were also tendencies for labour disputes to take on the colour of inter-communal strife. The Sind government discerned the sinister role of the RSS 'in every recent violent communal incident',[58] and the RSS declared its creed to be Hindustan only for the Hindus.[59] The effect of RSS propaganda brought to the notice of Muslims can be imagined: 'Trust not a Muslim. A Muslim is a *goonda* incarnate. Muslims are our eternal enemies . . . Strengthen your ranks so that after 5 or 6 years when your strength reaches sufficient proportions you may be able to swoop down upon Muslims and free the country of these "mlechhas." . . . Every Hindu must keep daggers and spears at his home and carry a sharp knife with him'.[60]

From the start of the negotiations, Wavell thought that Cripps and Pethick-Lawrence paid too much deference to Congress leaders and their wishes. He thought that the first interview with Gandhi was 'a deplorable affair', with Pethick-Lawrence displaying 'his usual sloppy benevolence to this malevolent' politician. The interview closed with a little speech by the Secretary of State expressing 'penitence' for 'Britain's misdeeds in the past!' The Viceroy was 'horrified' at the deference shown to Gandhi; 'when he expressed a wish for a glass of water, the Secretary was sent to fetch it himself, instead of sending for a chaprassi; and when it did not come at once Cripps hustled off himself to see about it'. Gandhi, in Wavell's eyes,

[55] *Civil and Military Gazette*, 26 March 1946.

[56] *Eastern Times*, 11 April 1946.

[57] *Eastern Times*, 11, 16 and 29 May 1946; *Star of India*, 25 April 1946.

[58] FR for Sind for first half of May 1946, HP file no. 18/5/46.

[59] Letter to Secretary, AICC, from Tula Singh. AICC file no. G-60, 1945–1946, pp. 37–8.

[60] *Star of India*, 11 May 1946, *Goonda* is a bad character. *Mlechha* means foreigner.

was a 'remarkable old man, certainly, and the most formidable of the three opponents who have detached portions of the British Empire in recent years: Zaghlul and de Valera being the other two. But he is a very tough politician and not a saint'.[61]

Interviews with Jinnah and other Muslim Leaguers revealed their fear that, in spite of their electoral success, the party would be left out in the cold by the British and the Congress; their inability to define Pakistan; their expectation that the British would unfold a settlement,[62] which they would accept or reject. All Muslim Leaguers broke down under Cripps' cross-examination of the practical implications of Pakistan. Jinnah, in Wavell's words, 'talked for one hour on the history of India (largely fanciful) and the cultural differences between Hindu and Muslim (also somewhat fanciful)'.[63] The other Leaguers could adduce no real argument, except perhaps 'vague phrases' such as balance of power, prestige, psychological effect, but 'a good deal of hate' against Hindus.[64] Such were the men for whom Wavell confessed to having sympathy; whom he and Alexander thought should not be let down.[65]

The cabinet delegation's opinion of the definition of Pakistan by Leaguers probably reflected the official British dislike of the Pakistan solution, for Jinnah had made clear to them and to the parliamentary delegation which visited India in January 1946 the essential elements in the League's demand for Pakistan. Jinnah had emphasized parity, which underlined Muslim nationhood; the League would never enter a coalition government, the possibility of which had existed only during the war. 'All that is finished', he told the editor of the *Statesman* on 31 January 1946.[66] The League would never agree to a coalition government being set up even as an interim measure as it would relegate the demand for Pakistan to the background.[67] He dismissed as 'complete humbug' the Congress offer to serve under his leadership in an interim government. The

---

[61] Wavell, *Journal*, p. 236.

[62] Note by Cripps, 30 March 1946, *TOP*, vol. 7, pp. 59–60. Entries for 4 and 17 April 1946, Alexander diaries, Churchill College, Cambridge.

[63] Wavell, *Journal*, p. 237.

[64] Ibid., p. 240; Alexander diaries, entry for 2 April 1946.

[65] Wavell, *Journal*, p. 368; Alexander diaries, entry for 20 June 1946.

[66] Attlee to India Committee, 3 February 1946; note by Rankin on Woodrow Wyatt's talk with Jinnah on 8 January 1946, *TOP*, vol. 6, pp. 876–7, 798–9 respectively.

[67] *Hindustan Standard*, 30 January 1946.

Congress, he said, had ·always insisted that such a government should be responsible to a legislature which meant that it would be 'quickly overthrown'. It would not work at all. 'We should be fighting like Kilkenny cats all the time'. The League would never enter a constituent assembly for a united India; any attempt to impose one would be resisted, if necessary, by force. Jinnah's promise of good neighbourliness to India only underlined his determination to achieve a sovereign Pakistan. Relations with India would be purely diplomatic, without any common currency, armed forces, transport. For him, division of the armed forces was the crux of the matter. After the British transferred power, Pakistan would remain within the Commonwealth with a British Governor-General and would encourage British investment.[68] Jinnah's reliance on the British both before and after the transfer of power was an essential element in the demand for a sovereign Pakistan. He was, after all, aware that the Congress would not agree to British supervision of the constituent assembly, dominion status for India and alliances between India and any power bloc.[69] At one level, then, the future Pakistan's dependence on the British would win their support for it against the Congress, which sought the termination of the Raj. Assuming that the Congress got its way on Indian non-alignment, the British, with Pakistan in the Commonwealth, would be able to keep a foothold on the subcontinent, which would simultaneously be a military guarantee for Pakistan against Indian or other aggression. Between a Pakistan dependent on British help for its defence and a non-aligned India there could hardly be a common military policy; hence the question of having a common army, whether or not under British command, would not arise. The League demanded a full Pakistan; its "inability" to define the boundaries of which was rationalized by the realization that any definition would circumscribe that demand, whereas if they did not "define" it they might even get the maximum they wanted. If the British gave an award they would enforce it; and it would be accepted by the Con-

[68] Attlee to India Committee, 3 February 1946; note on Wyatt's interview with Jinnah, 8 January 1946; Wavell to Pethick-Lawrence, 29 January 1946, *TOP*, vol. 6, pp. 875–8, 798–9, 862 respectively; also Wyatt's memorandum, 29 March 1946, note by Cripps, 30 March 1946, *TOP*, vol. 7, pp. 54, 59–60 respectively.

[69] Among the many statements by Nehru on these points, see the reports in *National Herald*, 5 March 1946; confidential note for AICC by Nehru, 15 March 1946, Nehru papers; *Hindustan Times*, 6 April 1946.

gress. For the League and Jinnah, the British held the balance between them and the Congress.

Congress leaders stressed immediate rather than long-term demands. Gandhi demanded abolition of the salt tax, the release of political prisoners and the dismissal of Ambedkar from the government.[70] On behalf of the CWC, Azad wrote that the Congress would proceed on the basis of independence, and that the future constitution would have to be dealt with by a constitution making body. Before a constitution making body was set up, there must be an interim government which must be in charge of all subsequent stages, itself setting up the constitution making body as well as conducting the administration of the country. Members of the interim government should be chosen by the provinces—11 out of 15 members could be provincial representatives; four representatives of the minorities could be chosen by the legislature or the provincial governments. The Congress envisaged a federation in which fully autonomous provinces would have residuary powers. In accordance with the Cripps plan of 1942, no areas would be compelled to join the federation. The League must allow a plebiscite of the total population in the Muslim majority provinces, and the states must attend the constitution making body. Owing to the exigencies of the moment, the Congress was prepared to give up its earlier demand for a constitution making body elected on the widest possible franchise. Instead, provincial legislatures could act as a federal college to choose a constitution making body, and the federal college would vote together and not in provincial compartments.[71]

The Congress proposals were inspired by Gandhi's faith that the cabinet mission was sincerely desirous of transferring power 'but wanted a face saving device for Jinnah'. Gandhi said that the reference to self-determination in the Congress formula referred 'only to matters like Municipal Government'. Jayakar pointed out the difficulties against accepting such an interpretation to which Gandhi replied that 'matters would be cleared up at the right time.'[72] Patel held that Nehru had 'incautiously' gone on laying the clause on self-determination, but he was clear that

---

[70] Note of interview between cabinet delegation and Gandhi, *TOP*, vol. 7, p. 117.

[71] Note of interview between cabinet delegation, Wavell and Azad on 3 April 1946, Ibid., pp. 111–13.

[72] Note by M.R. Jayakar, 6 April, 1946, *MRJC*.

'the formula cannot be interpreted in any way more liberally than the interpretation given to it in the Congress Resolution of 1942, i.e., that it only confined full provincial freedom to remain out so as to enjoy full control over internal (?) affairs, under the control of the Governor General. His interpretation in other words was the same as Gandhi's on the previous evening . . . If the Constitution framed as a result of discussion was not favourable to certain Muslim areas & if plebiscite was favourable, they would be permitted to remain out on the footing with Residuary powers enjoyed by them under the Governor General. . . . Talking of Jinnah's threat of bloodshed he laughed it out and said Congress could control the situation by persuasion if not by force, . . .[73]

Having ascertained the views of the Indian parties, the mission accepted Cripps' view that there could be no agreement on the constitution of the Interim Government until a broad agreement had been reached upon 'the fundamental question of whether there shall be one India only in the future, or two or more Indias'.[74] Cripps concluded that there were only two possible solutions which stood any chance of acceptance by the Indians. Scheme A envisaged an Indian Union which would consist of three principal parts—the Hindu majority provinces, the Muslim majority provinces, and the Indian States. The Union Government would control such subjects as Defence, Foreign Affairs and Communications. A wider range of optional powers might, by agreement, either be exercised by provinces cooperating as groups, and thereby constituting a third tier, or be transferred to the centre. Scheme B provided for two Indias, Hindustan and Pakistan, to either of which the States could federate. The boundaries of Pakistan would be determined on the principle that the Muslim majority districts would have a right to form a separate and sovereign state, with a defensive and offensive treaty of alliance between the two Indias. They would, however, have no common executive and therefore no common control of defence or foreign policy.[75]

Attlee agreed with the Mission that Scheme A would be preferable: Pakistan would be weak and would be strengthened only in so far as it could rely upon its treaty with Hindustan. Without defensive agreement with India, no scheme of defence would be of any

[73] Note by Jayakar on interview with Patel, 7 April 1946, Ibid.

[74] Memorandum by Cripps, undated but probably around 8 April 1946, *TOP*, vol. 7, p. 174.

[75] Ibid., pp. 175–6.

value.[76] Scheme B would destroy the homogeneity of the Indian army. Even if all were acting in common for the defence of India, co-operation would be far from easy unless all acknowledged a central directing authority.[77]

The Mission now tried to get the parties to agree to one of the alternatives set out by Cripps. They decided to tell Jinnah that they did not believe that the *full* claim for Pakistan had any chance of acceptance or could be supported by them.[78] On 16 April, Jinnah was told that he could not reasonably hope to receive both the whole of the territory, much of it inhabited by non-Muslims, which he claimed and the full measure of sovereignty which he said was essential. If the full territories were insisted upon then some element of sovereignty must be relinquished if there were to be a reasonable prospect of agreement. If, on the other hand, full sovereignty was desired, then the claims to the non-Muslim territories could not be conceded.[79] Jinnah was then asked whether he would be willing to discuss a possible constitution on the basis of Scheme A.[80]

'I have never seen a man with such a mind twisting and turning to avoid as far as possible direct answers', wrote A.V. Alexander, who was friendly to the League's view point.

> 'I came to the conclusion that he [Jinnah] is playing this game, which is one of life and death for millions of people, very largely from the point of view of scoring a triumph in a legal negotiation by first making large demands and secondly insisting that he should make no offer reducing that demand but should wait for the other side always to say how much they would advance towards granting that demand.'[81]

Characteristically, Jinnah said that the Congress should make a statement first. Confronted with Pethick-Lawrence's admonition that 'if the Delegation gave an award in the Muslim League's favour and then Great Britain withdrew her troops, the Muslims would be exposed to grave dangers', Jinnah's reaction suggests that, inspite of his success at the polls, he was relying on the continuing presence of

[76] Cabinet Meeting on 11 April 1946, Ibid., pp. 229–30.

[77] Attlee to cabinet delegation and Wavell, (T), 13 April 1946, Ibid., p. 260.

[78] Meeting between cabinet delegation and Viceroy on 13 April 1946, Ibid., pp. 251–2.

[79] Note of interview between cabinet delegation and Jinnah on 16 April 1946, Ibid., p. 281.

[80] Ibid., pp. 281–3.

[81] Entry for 16 April 1946, *Alexander Diaries.*

the British in India. He said that 'he was 100% in favour of agreement but what if there were no agreement. The situation was unprecedented. The British Government was asking the Indian people to take self-government and the Indians were unable to do so'. But he could make no alternative suggestion. He said that it was Congress which should say what it wanted. He thought he had little to lose in a setback and left it to the British to produce a settlement.[82]

When it became clear that Jinnah had not accepted either scheme, the Mission thought they would have to propound the basis of settlement themselves.[83] Cripps held that a Pakistan confined to Muslim districts alone was not acceptable to the League and would be impracticable; and there was no justification for including large non-Muslim areas in Pakistan. He concluded that 'there is no practicable scheme whereby the Muslim-majority areas can be brought together to form an independent Sovereign State wholly separated from the rest of India'. Nor would a separate Pakistan state solve the communal difficulties.[84] Nevertheless, Muslims desired some practical form of self-government. There should, therefore, come into being a three-tier constitutional arrangement, the bottom tier of which would comprise the provinces and States which expressed a desire to join Hindustan or Pakistan. At the top would be a Union of India embracing both Pakistan and Hindustan.

The Mission decided to discuss the proposals with Jinnah first; and to warn him that 'it was the last suggestion' which the Delegation had to make in the hope of promoting agreement between the parties and that 'unless Mr. Jinnah had some positive proposition to make the Delegation would have to deal with the Congress and do what they could for the Muslim Community'.[85]

Jinnah agreed to put the proposals before his Working Committee if they were accepted by the Congress. The Mission were now encouraged to put Plan A before the Congress, as Gandhi's main objection to Pakistan was to it having sovereignty and 'now it appeared that Mr. Jinnah was for the first time prepared to consider

[82] Note of interview between cabinet delegation and Jinnah, 16 April 1946, *TOP*, vol. 7, pp. 284–5.

[83] Cabinet delegation to Attlee, (T), 18 April 1946, Ibid., p. 314.

[84] Memorandum by Cripps, 18 April 1946, Ibid., p. 305.

[85] Meeting of cabinet delegation and Wavell, 24 April 1946, Ibid., p. 324.

something less than a sovereign Pakistan'.[86] Azad himself raised the question of the three-tier constitution when he met Cripps on 26 April. He thought he could get the Working Committee to agree to a single federation which could be broken down into two parts legislating separately for optional subjects.[87]

With both Azad and Jinnah willing to negotiate on the basis of the three-tier solution, the Mission now invited them to nominate 4 representatives each to meet the Delegation and the Viceroy.[88] Azad raised objections to Pethick-Lawrence's reference to 'predominantly Hindu and predominantly Muslim provinces'. The Congress had never agreed to such a division. It however recognized that there might be provinces which wished to delegate to the Central Government subjects in the optional list, while others might agree to delegate only compulsory subjects like Foreign Affairs, Defence and Communications. Also, the Cabinet Delegation had left no choice to a province in the matter of joining or not joining a group. There might be provinces which did not wish to join any particular group. The Congress Working Committee agreed to the provinces having full powers for all remaining subjects as well as the residuary powers, but it 'should be open to any Province to exercise its option to have more common subjects with the Federal Union'.[89]

Jinnah blew hot and cold as usual. He accepted the invitation to Simla to discuss proposals which envisaged, in the final analysis, an Indian Union; but he enclosed a copy of a resolution passed by the Subjects Committee of the all India Muslim League Legislators Convention on 9 April. The resolution stated that 'the Muslim Nation will never submit to any constitution for a United India and will never participate in any single constitution-making machinery set up for the purpose'.[90]

To both Azad and Jinnah, Pethick-Lawrence replied that their objections would be discussed at the Conference, for the British had never considered that acceptance by Congress and the Muslim League of their invitation 'would imply as a preliminary condition full approv-

---

[86] Meeting of cabinet delegation and Wavell, 26 April 1946, Ibid., p. 342.

[87] Meeting between Cripps and Azad, 26 April 1946, Ibid., p. 345.

[88] Pethick-Lawrence to Azad and Jinnah, 27 April 1946, Ibid., p. 352.

[89] Azad to Pethick-Lawrence, 28 April 1946, Ibid., p. 357.

[90] Jinnah to Pethick-Lawrence, 29 April 1946, Ibid., pp. 371–2. Muslim Convention resolution, Ibid., p. 373.

al by them of the terms set out in my letter'. The terms were a 'proposed basis for a settlement'.[91]

Jinnah began the proceedings at Simla by refusing to shake hands with Azad and Ghaffar Khan.[92] His vagueness on many points was probably due to his deliberately unconstructive attitude. He suggested that the foreign policy of the Union should be decided by consultation 'as between members of the Commonwealth'; to which Cripps reminded him that 'there was no common Foreign Policy of the Commonwealth'. Pethick-Lawrence raised the point that even if the Centre had a limited field, there must be someone responsible for the common army and he must have a popular mandate—how could he be responsible to two legislatures that might have different policies? Jinnah answered that 'the executive could settle all these matters and he was definitely against a Union Legislature'. He did not suggest how the executive should proceed. When Nehru agreed with Wavell that a Union Court would be necessary to deal with disputes between the units, and might also deal with fundamental rights as included in the Constitution, Jinnah's reaction was that, on the assumption that there would be no communal trouble once the Union was set up, 'there was no need of a Court'.[93] After some time, he said that if there was to be a Union Legislature its members should be elected in equal numbers by group legislatures.

The Congress was against group legislatures and executives. This would mean 'a sub-federation, if not something more and we have already told you that we do not accept this'. It would result in creating three layers of executive and legislative bodies, an arrangement which would be cumbersome, static and disjointed, leading to continuous friction. 'We are not aware of any such arrangement in any country'.[94] Wavell assured Nehru that the scheme 'was designed to get over a psychological difficulty. It was not claimed to be ideal from the administrative point of view'. The Congress, said Nehru, would exercise no compulsion on units to stay in an all India federa-

[91] Pethick-Lawrence to Azad and Jinnah, 29 April 1946, Ibid., pp. 374 and 375 respectively.

[92] Pethick-Lawrence to Attlee, 5 May 1946, Ibid., p. 431; and Alexander diaries, entry for 5 May 1946.

[93] Simla proceedings on 5 May 1946, *TOP*, vol. 7, pp. 429 and 430.

[94] Azad to Pethick-Lawrence, 6 May 1946, *TOP*, vol. 7, p. 434.

tion. But it was against splitting up India; the Union of India, 'even if the list was short, must be strong and organic'. He appealed to the League to come into the constitution-making body on the assurance that there would be no compulsion.[95]

Jinnah declined the invitation but he said that if groups could have their own legislature and executive, the League would accept the Union subject to argument about its machinery. Nehru pointed out that Jinnah had accepted no feature of the Union. The Union without a legislature would be 'futile and entirely unacceptable'.[96]

In the afternoon, Jinnah expressed himself against one constitution making body, and said that the constitution should not be for more than five years in the first instance. Alexander told him that this was 'too short'. 15 years would be more appropriate. The Congress was justifiably suspicious about Jinnah's intentions. Patel seized upon Jinnah's statement: 'there we have it now; what he has been after all the time'[97]—implying that in the long run, Jinnah would never be interested in a Union.

The Delegation now decided to present points which were intended as a compromise to the Congress and the Muslim League. There would be a Union government and legislature dealing with Foreign Affairs, Defence, Communications, fundamental rights and having the powers to raise finances for these subjects. All remaining powers would be vested in the provinces. Groups of provinces would be formed and such groups would determine the provincial subjects which they desired to take in common. The groups could set up their own executive and legislatures. The Union legislature would be composed of equal proportions from the Muslim and Hindu majority provinces, 'whether or not these or any of them' formed themselves into groups, together with representatives of the States. The Union and Group constitutions would contain a provision whereby any province could by a majority vote of its legislative assembly review the terms of the constitution every 10 years. The constitution making body would include representatives from each Provincial assembly in proportion to the strengths of the various parties in the assembly on the basis of one-tenth of their numbers. The Constituent Assembly would be divided into three sections

---

[95] Simla proceedings, 6 May 1946, Ibid., pp. 436–7; and Alexander diaries, entry for 6 May 1946.

[96] Ibid., p. 437.

[97] Wavell, *Journal*, p. 259; Alexander diaries, entry for 6 May 1946.

representing Hindu and Muslim majority provinces and the States. The Hindu and Muslim groups would meet separately to decide the provincial constitutions for their group, and if they so wished, the group constitution. When these had been settled, it would be open to any province to opt out of the group. Thereafter the three bodies would meet together to settle the Union constitution.

These points were communicated to Jinnah and Azad for comment.[98] Jinnah saw Congress inspiration behind the new formula, especially on grouping. He protested that the meeting had adjourned for the Mission to consider further the matters arising out of the Congress rejection of a Union government vested with powers to deal with only three subjects and grouping. New proposals had now been made, and 'By whom they are suggested, it is not made clear.' The League would never agree to one constitution making body or to the proposed method of forming the Constituent Assembly. Jinnah wanted not one Constituent Assembly but three, which would meet together only for the purpose of deciding the Constitution of the Union Government.[99]

The Congress delegates wanted a declaration from the Mission that acceptance of the terms for negotiation would not make them binding on either party; and that the Constituent Assembly would be free to throw out any items and to add or to amend the suggestions before it. The difficulty about parity between six Hindu majority provinces and five Muslim majority provinces was 'insurmountable.' the Muslim majority provinces represented nine crores of the population as against over nineteen crores of the Hindu majority provinces. Azad pointed out that the proposals limited the discretion of the Constituent Assembly. Two or three constitutions might emerge for separate groups, joined together by 'a flimsy common super structure left to the mercy of the three disjointed groups'. There was also compulsion in the early stages for a province to join a particular group—'why should the Frontier Province which is clearly a Congress Province, be compelled to join any group hostile to the Congress?'[100]

When the conference met again on 9 May, Nehru suggested that the Congress and League could sit together with an umpire accepted by both parties, whose decision would be final. Jinnah agreed to sit

[98] Turnbull to Azad and Jinnah, 8 May 1946, Ibid., pp. 462–3.
[99] Interview between Wyatt and Jinnah on 9 May 1946, Ibid., pp. 475–6.
[100] Azad to Pethick-Lawrence, 9 May 1946, Ibid., pp. 476–7.

with Nehru and 'consider whether this proposal could be accepted and, if so, who the umpire would be'.[101] But on 11 May, Jinnah said he had not agreed to anything or to an umpire. If there was to be arbitration the first question which would arise would be the partition of India. The matter had been settled at the elections and it was 'inconceivable' that it should ever be the subject of arbitration'.[102]

With the Congress and League unable to reach any agreement, inspite of some concessions to both sides, the Mission now decided that the time had come for them to make their own statement, which had been in preparation for some time. The League and the Congress were shown copies of the statement before it was published on 16 May. An account of the conversations between the British, Congress and League is important, for they contained the seeds of future bickering between all three parties. Cripps and Pethick-Lawrence told the representatives of the League, which included Liaqat Ali Khan, Ismail Khan and Abdur Rab Nishtar, that 'sections of the constitution-making body would meet to decide the character of the provincial constitutions within the Group, and the Group constitution. The decision would be taken by representatives of the Provinces within the section'. If a province, such as the NWFP, refused to come into the meetings of the sections of which it was a part, 'the sections would . . . proceed without those representatives'. Cripps told Rab Nishtar that each section of the constitution-making body would be entitled to frame the constitution for the provinces within it whether they attended or not, and also to determine whether there should be a group and what the group subjects would be, 'subject only to the right of a Province to opt out after the constitution had been framed'. The option, said Cripps, would be exercisable 'after the whole picture including the Union Constitution had been completed'.[103] This, of course, meant that grouping in practice would not be voluntary at all. Cripps said that the statement was not negotiable and that it was intended to go ahead with convening the Constituent Assembly on the basis of it. The only alterations which could be considered would be those agreed upon by the two main parties. The League representatives

---

[101] Simla proceedings, 9 May 1946, Ibid., p. 490; Alexander diaries, entry for 9 May 1946.

[102] Simla proceedings, 11 May 1946, *TOP*, vol. 7, p. 508.

[103] Meeting between Pethick-Lawrence, Cripps and members of the League on 16 May 1946, Ibid., p. 577.

wanted a copy of the note of the explanations which they had been given. It was agreed that Rab Nishtar might see the note of the meeting and take notes from it 'but these would not have the status of an official record.'[104] Pethick-Lawrence told Liaqat that 'it would require a majority of each of the major communities' in the Constituent Assembly to depart from the basic provisions set out in the Statement. Cripps said that the League could 'cease to participate' in the Assembly if it failed to comply with the basic provisions. Sovereignty 'would not be given until the constitution had been framed'. An Act of Parliament to set up the new constitution 'would not be appropriate'. He thought that 'all that would be necessary' was an act of cession by the Crown to the constitution-making body or to the new Government.[105]

As the notes taken by Rab Nishtar would not constitute an official record, the passage on the sovereignty of the Constituent Assembly was excluded from the official record of the meeting. Rab Nishtar 'did not fail to notice this omission when he saw the notes and commented on it to me . . . there is no doubt that this question of sovereignty is an important one to the Muslims and they will have taken careful note of what was said'.[106]

Somewhat different assurances were given by Wavell to Nehru and Azad when they discussed the Statement on 16 May. The Viceroy told them that the Constituent Assembly 'might be regarded as a sovereign body, for the purpose of constitution-making, and that when agreement was reached it would remain for Parliament to repeal the Government of India Act, 1935, and for formal steps of recognition to be taken'.[107] Wavell also told them that the Interim Government 'must be under the existing constitution'.[108]

This was the background to the Statement of 16 May. Gandhi asked Cripps and Pethick-Lawrence whether the procedure laid down for the Constituent Assembly was subject to alteration by a majority of votes, and also by a majority of both of the major communities voting. Cripps said that 'there was in fact on a strict interpretation nothing in paragraph 19(vii) making it clear that the majority of each of the two major communities was required for

[104] Ibid., p. 579.   [105] Ibid., pp. 579–80.
[106] Addendum, Turnbull to Abell, 22 May 1946, Ibid., p. 580.
[107] Meeting between Wavell and Azad and Nehru on 16 May 1946, Ibid., pp. 581–2.
[108] Ibid., p. 581.

such a decision unless it were held to be a decision which raised a major communal issue'.[109] Indeed, the said paragraph read:

> 'In the Union Constituent Assembly resolutions varying the provisions of paragraph 15 above or raising any major communal issue shall require a majority of the representatives present and voting of each of the two major communities.'[110]

The Congress understood that the Constituent Assembly would be a sovereign body for the purpose of drafting the constitution as well as for entering into any treaty with the British government. It would be open to the Assembly 'to vary in any way it likes the recommendations and the procedure suggested by the Cabinet Delegation.'[111] The statement had not said anything about either of these points; Wavell had assured Nehru and Azad that the assembly would be a sovereign body for the purposes of constitution-making.

Azad raised valid questions about grouping. Paragraph 15 (5) of the Statement read that 'Provinces should be free to form Groups with executives and legislatures, and each Group could determine the Provincial subjects to be taken in common'.[112] But clause (3) of the same paragraph stated that 'All subjects other than the Union subjects and all residuary powers should vest in the Provinces'.[113] However, paragraph 19 said that provincial representatives would divide up into the three sections, and these sections would proceed 'to settle the Provincial Constitutions for the Provinces included in each section, and shall also decide whether any Group Constitution shall be set up for those Provinces and, if so, with what provincial subjects the Group should deal'.[114] The Congress discerned a basic discrepancy in these provisions. The basic provision gave full autonomy to a province to do what it liked and subsequently there appeared to be a certain compulsion in the matter which infringed that autonomy. It was true that a province could opt out later if it wanted to. But it was not clear how a province or its representatives could be compelled to do something which they did not want to do. A provincial assembly could give its mandate to its representatives not to enter any group or a particular group or section. Also, the Punjab would dominate Section B and Bengal Section C. It was

[109] Meeting between cabinet delegation and Wavell on 18 May 1946, Ibid., p. 616.
[110] 16 May statement, Ibid., pp. 589–90.
[111] Azad to Pethick-Lawrence, 19 May 1946, Ibid., p. 639.
[112] 16 May statement, Ibid., p. 587.
[113] Ibid., p. 587.   [114] Ibid., p. 589.

conceivable that this dominating province might frame a constitution against the wishes of Sind or the NWFP; it might even lay down rules nullifying the provision for a province to opt out of the group.[115] Azad was told that once the Constituent Assembly had been formed, 'there is naturally no intention to interfere with its discretion or to question its decisions.' When the Constituent Assembly had completed its labours the British government would recommend to Parliament such action as would be necessary for the cession of sovereignty to the Indian people, 'subject only to two provisos . . . namely, adequate provision for the protection of minorities and willingness to conclude a treaty to cover matters arising out of the transfer of power'. For these reasons independence could not precede the new constitution.[116]

The status of the Interim Government cropped up again in correspondence between Congress leaders and the Mission. 'Has the cry "Independence in fact" no foundation?' asked Gandhi.[117] Wavell subsequently wrote to Azad that the spirit in which the Government was worked would be of much greater importance than any formal document and guarantees: 'if you are prepared to trust me, we shall be able to co-operate in a manner which will give India a sense of freedom from external control' as soon as possible. The British government would treat the Interim government 'with the same close consultation and consideration as a Dominion Government'. It was his intention 'faithfully to carry out' the undertaking in the Statement that the interim government would be given the greatest possible freedom in the day-to-day administration of the country.[118] This letter was important, for it was on the basis of the assurances given by Wavell that the Congress subsequently agreed to enter the interim government.

Jinnah protested at the Statement's preference for a united India; the provision for one constitution-making body and for union finances; and the absence of parity between Hindu and Muslim majority provinces in the Union executive and legislature.[119] On the question of parity, Wavell pointed to the alternative safeguards

[115] Azad to Pethick-Lawrence, 20 May 1946, Ibid., p. 640.
[116] Pethick-Lawrence to Azad, 22 May 1946, Ibid., pp. 659–60.
[117] Gandhi to Pethick-Lawrence, 22 May 1946. Also Azad to Wavell, 25 May 1946, Nehru to Wavell, 25 May 1946, Ibid., pp. 660, 690–2, 693–4 respectively.
[118] Wavell to Azad, 30 May 1946, Ibid., p. 738.
[119] Statement by Jinnah on 22 May 1946, Ibid., pp. 663–9.

provided and had urged that the Muslim League could hardly expect to receive parity in an Indian Union. Jinnah asked Wavell what would happen if Congress rejected the proposals and the League accepted them. Wavell said 'he could not give any guarantee but speaking personally he thought that if the Muslim League accepted them they would not lose by it and that His Majesty's Government would go on with constitution-making on the lines they had proposed as far as possible in the circumstances.' Jinnah asked whether the Muslim League would in such circumstances be invited to join the Interim Government and be given their due proportion of the portfolios. The Viceroy had said that 'he thought that he could guarantee that the Muslim League would have a share in it'. Jinnah wanted a written assurance on these points as it would help him with his Working Committee.[120] Jinnah was shown the text of two verbal assurances which were to be given to him. No written assurance could be given, but Wavell could give him 'on behalf of the Delegation, my personal assurance that we do not propose to make any discrimination in the treatment of either party; and that we shall go ahead with the plan laid down in our statement so far as circumstances permit, if either party accepts . . .'[121] This, and a similar assurance by Cripps, were shown to Jinnah and, according to Wavell, 'he seemed satisfied'.[122]

Some sources suggest that initially, many Leaguers were shocked at the absence of parity between the Congress and the League at the centre, and wanted Jinnah to reject the Plan.[123] Others noted that the League was not in a position to launch civil disobedience, and they advocated that the prudent strategy would be to work up the Plan up to the group stage, while refusing to submit to a centre that did not accord them parity. If the Congress did not accomodate them at the centre, the League could withdraw from the constituent assembly and resist the imposition of an unwanted centre.[124] The evidence of both Khaliquzzaman and Chaudhuri Muhammad Ali is that Wavell's assurances of 3 and 4 June that the British would form a government without the Congress if that party rejected the Mission Plan 'played a decisive role in determining the final attitude

---

[120] Meeting between cabinet delegation and Wavell on 3 June 1946, Ibid., p. 784.

[121] Verbal assurance given by Wavell to Jinnah on 3 June 1946, Ibid., p. 785.

[122] Assurance by Cripps to Jinnah, Ibid., p. 786. See also Wavell to Abell, 3 June 1946, p. 785.

[123] Note by Wyatt, 25 May 1946, Ibid., pp. 684–5.

[124] Moore, *Escape from Empire*, pp. 121–4.

of the Muslim League leaders'. Many Leaguers, including Jinnah, feared that the Congress would use its majority in the constituent assembly to break the Plan.[125] Jinnah's own inclination seems to have been to accept the Plan. He reportedly told the Muslim League council that the Plan conceded the substance of Pakistan and provided a machinery for achieving a fully sovereign state in ten years. Rejection would mean that the League had given up constitutional methods and had become a revolutionary body: why shed blood when they could achieve their goal by peaceful methods? Groups would have power on all subjects except defence, communications and foreign affairs. Defence would remain in British hands until the new constitution was enforced.[126] Jinnah evidently envisaged a long drawn out process of constitution making, a British presence until it was complete, and British enforcement of their interpretation of the Mission Plan. He was, after all, aware of disagreement with the Congress both on grouping and on parity; it is hard to see how he and the Congress would have ever agreed on the British having the last word on the constitution.

According to M.A.H. Ispahani, Jinnah was requested by his working committee to take a decision on the Mission Plan. The general consensus in the committee was that if the League turned down the proposals, they would be drawing on themselves the onus of failure. They accepted in the hope 'that it would ultimately result in the establishment of a complete, sovereign Pakistan'. But Jinnah was unsure that he had taken the right decision and on consideration 'he would rather have rejected the proposal'.

> 'But it was too late ... All that he could do was to hope that the Congress would either reject the proposal or ask for such amendments or put such interpretation on it as would vitiate their acceptance of it.'[127]

The issue of parity provided him with his first occasion to find fault with the Congress and the British. Jinnah said he would only enter the Interim Government on the basis of parity with the Congress, and asserted that Wavell had assured him on 3 June, before he

[125] Khaliquzzaman, *Pathway to Pakistan* p. 362 and C.M. Ali, *The Emergence of Pakistan* pp. 59, 60, 69.

[126] *Star of India*, 7 June 1946.

[127] M.A.H. Ispahani, *Qaid-e-Azam Jinnah As I Knew Him* (2nd edition, Karachi, 1966, pp. 168–9); League resolution, *TOP*, vol. 7, p. 839.

met the League Working Committee that portfolios would be distributed on the 5:5:2 ratio. This was 'one of the most important
considerations' which weighed with the Working Committee.[128]
According to Woodrow Wyatt, 'Jinnah *did* promise the Muslim
League Council and Working Committee that he would not go into
an Interim Government without parity'.[129] Wavell thought that the
British must adhere to the 5:5:2 ratio as the most helpful basis of
settlement. But he had given Jinnah no assurance that he would get
it. However, the Congress reiterated its opposition to parity. 'What
was proposed now was not Hindu/Muslim parity, but Muslim
League and Congress parity. This cut out all the non-League
Muslims'.[130]

The Mission tried to discuss alternatives to parity: Pethick-
Lawrence even suggested that 'we were not committed to parity and
he was not able to see why we should necessarily have it.'[131] The
next day, Cripps said he had met Jinnah who seemed willing to discuss portfolios and had agreed not to discuss parity. So Wavell
wrote to Nehru and Jinnah asking them to discuss personnel for the
new Interim Government.[132] Jinnah replied tha the League had
accepted the May 16 statement on the basis of parity. Also, there
would be no point in discussing portfolios until the Congress had
given their decision on the Statement.[133] Pethick-Lawrence secured
Attlee's agreement to a proposal made by the Delegation on 3 June
that if the Congress refused to come in, while the League agreed, the
latter would be invited to go on with their won constitution
making. The centre would have Muslim League representatives and
representatives of minorities with seats reserved for the Congress
but held temporarily by officials or non-Congress Hindus.[134] But
Pethick-Lawrence said 'he would not like to be committed to asking
Jinnah to form the Government'.[135]

[128] Jinnah to Wavell, 8 June 1946, Ibid., p. 839.
[129] Interview between Wyatt and Jinnah, 11 June 1980, Ibid., p. 867. Italics in
original.
[130] Meeting between cabinet delegation and Azad and Nehru on 10 June 1946,
Ibid., p. 855. See also note of Wyatt's interview with Gandhi on 10 June 1946, Ibid.,
pp. 857–8.
[131] Meeting between cabinet delegation and Wavell, 11 June 1946, Ibid., p. 862.
[132] Wavell to Nehru and Jinnah, 12 June 1946, Ibid., p. 877.
[133] Jinnah to Wavell, 12 June 1946, Ibid., p. 885.
[134] Cabinet delegation and Wavell to Attlee, 3 June 1946, para. 4 (b), Ibid., p. 789.
[135] Meeting between cabinet delegation and Wavell on 14 June 1946, Ibid., p. 918.

Nehru gave Wavell a list of his nominees for the interim government on 13 June. The list included 5 Congress, 4 Muslim League, 1 Congress Scheduled Caste, 1 Congress woman, 1 independent Muslim and 3 other minority representatives. Wavell said the League would never agree to the list and suggested that he would meet Jinnah. Both Nehru and Jinnah appeared willing to consider a 5:5:3 basis, with the Scheduled Caste outside Congress.[136] If no agreement could be reached, the Mission would make a statement, setting out its own proposals for the formation of an interim government.[137]

The Statement of 16 June contemplated an interim government composed of 6 Congress representatives, all of them Hindus and including one Scheduled Caste, 5 Muslim Leaguers, 1 Sikh, a Parsi and a Christian. This composition was not meant to be taken as a precedent for the solution of the communal question, but was intended as 'an expedient' to solve the present difficulty.[138] Paragraph 8 of the statement, however, promised if both parties or either of them proved unwilling to join in the setting up of a coalition Government 'on the above lines, it is the intention of the Viceroy to proceed with the formation of an interim Government which will be as representative as possible of those willing to accept the Statement of May 16'[139] Differing interpretations of this provision by the British and the Muslim League were to culminate in the League's call for "Direct Action" on 29 June.

Jinnah claimed that though the Viceroy had not promised him parity with the Congress in the interim government, 'he had conducted the discussion on the basis of parity' and that it was on this basis that he had agreed to come in. Pethick-Lawrence said he 'quite understood his position' and it was true that the Viceroy was endeavouring to construct an Interim Government on the basis of parity, but he had not found it possible to do so. 'Accordingly, if Mr. Jinnah had given a promise on this basis to take part in the Government he was released from this promise when the basis was changed'.[140] Jinnah said nothing more on this point.

[136] Meeting between cabinet delegation and Wavell on 13 June 1946, Ibid., pp. 913–14.

[137] 16 June statement, Ibid., pp. 954–5.

[138] Ibid., p. 954.   [139] Ibid., p. 955.

[140] Meeting between Jinnah, Alexander and Pethick-Lawrence on 17 June 1946, Ibid., p. 960.

Wavell now assured Jinnah, against the wishes of Pethick-Lawrence, that the names of those invited to join the interim government in the Statement of 16 June 'cannot be regarded as final', but that 'no change in principle will be made in the statement without the consent of two major parties.' He also promised that the 'proportion of members by communities will not be changed without the agreement of the two major parties'.[141] This assurance by the Viceroy was to further complicate the chances of agreement, for the Congress had decided that they would nominate a Muslim out of their own quota. They had in mind Zakir Husain, who, as the British recognized, 'is not known to have any definite political affiliations, but had been associated with Mahatma Gandhi as an expert on education'.[142]

Jinnah now published his correspondence with Wavell in the press, and provoked the Congress to refuse to enter the interim government because of the assurances given by the Viceroy to him. Within the Mission, even Alexander agreed that the British could not accept the principle that the League could have a monopoly of appointing Muslims. The Delegation failed to persuade the Congress leaders not to include a Muslim in their own quota.[143] The Congress Working Committee decided not to enter the Interim Government, but added, while reiterating their objections to the Statement of 16 May, 'we accept your proposals and are prepared to work them with a view to achieve our objective'.[144] In effect, Congress would accept the long-term plan, with reservations.

Wavell thought that the Congress had outmanoeuvred the British because of their ability to 'twist words', in formally accepting the 16 May statement.[145] The British had hoped that their threat to form an interim government of one party if the other party rejected their long-term plan would compel both to accept it and join the interim government, but this tactic had resulted in both parties accepting

[141] Wavell to Jinnah, 20 June 1946, paras. 5 (i) and (iv), Ibid., p. 989. This was sent in reply to Jinnah's letter of 19 June 1946, Ibid., pp. 974–7.

[142] Draft Cabinet paper, on instructions to be given to Viceroy regarding resumption of negotiations for Interim Government, para. 8, by Pethick-Lawrence, July 1946, L/P&J/10/73.

[143] Meeting between cabinet delegation and Congress members on 23 June 1946, Ibid., pp. 1012–15.

[144] Azad to Wavell, 25 June 1946, Ibid., p. 1036.

[145] Note by Wavell, 25 June 1946, Ibid., pp. 1038–9.

the plan with conflicting reservations. Since Congress had not accepted the interim proposals, the Mission decided to tell Jinnah that new negotiations for an Interim Government would be stated after a while; and that Jinnah would be told that 'we could not support his objection' to the Congress including a Muslim in their own quota.[146]

Accordingly, Jinnah was informed that Azad's letter of 25 June constituted acceptance of the long-term plan, though Wavell pointed out that 'the Delegation had said in their Statement of May 25th that they did not accept the Congress interpretation'. In reply to Jinnah's charge that the reservations made by the Congress 'were most vital and broke the whole thing', Pethick-Lawrence said that 'the Muslim League reservations were quite as fundamental'.[147] When Jinnah charged the Delegation with departing from the 16 June statement, Pethick-Lawrence told him that 'the Delegation were not asking for Mr. Jinnah's opinion of their conduct'. Alexander tried to console Jinnah by telling him that he appreciated his sacrifices, but requested him to use his influence with the League Working Committee and to come into the interim government on the basis of their acceptance of the 16 May statement. On 29 June, the Cabinet Delegation returned to Britain.

British officials now debated the basis on which the League and the Congress should be called in to form the interim government. Penderel Moon suggested that the 6:5:1 basis could be adhered to.

> 'If, for any reason, including the non-co-operation of either of the major parties, it is impossible to form a Coalition Government ... then the Congress as the largest single party should be called upon to form a Government; *but the intention of doing this should not be disclosed*, except possibly at the last moment to Jinnah. ... If we had the courage to recognize the Congress' right to include a nationalist Muslim in their quota of representatives, the League would *not* have refused to co-operate. The League could not possibly go into the wilderness on the ground that an extra Muslim was being included in the Government in place of a Caste Hindu. The League is relatively weak and quite unused to fighting. If it decides to fight it will fight on strong ground and not on an absurdity.'[148]

'Of course what prevented us from doing that which Moon refers to in last para', commented Pethick-Lawrence, 'was the pledges

---

[146] Meeting between cabinet delegation and Wavell on 25 June 1946, Ibid., p. 1044.
[147] Ibid., p. 1045.
[148] Note by Penderel Moon, 29 June 1946, L/P&J/10/73, p. 341.

we gave Jinnah in the ill-advised letter of Viceroy to Jinnah on 20 June para 5(1) and (4) . . . to which I was at that time strongly opposed'.[149] Turnbull was also in general agreement with Moon. Pethick-Lawrence, drawing up instructions for the Viceroy in consultation with the cabinet, firmly believed that 'it is unreasonable of Jinnah to demand that all the Muslim members should be nominees of the Muslim League in view of the fact that the Muslim League achieved only 76% of the Muslim votes'. If the principle was repudiated, the Congress 'may be prepared not to press for the actual inclusion of a Congress Muslim'. The Viceroy should make it plain to Jinnah that 'we cannot support his claim' that all the Muslims should be nominated by the Muslim League, but that the British agreed with him that a majority of both communities would be required for raising a major communal issue. He should, at the same time, urge upon Nehru the 'essential importance' of Congress not pressing their claim to the inclusion of a Congress Muslim. If the League refused to come in, the Congress would be asked to form the Government, though the Viceroy would oppose it.[150] Wavell favoured the 6:5:3 ratio for the formation of the interim government, to which the cabinet agreed.[151]

Jinnah felt let down by the British. He had assumed that the Congress would not be allowed to join the interim government because of its conditional acceptance of the 16 May statement and its rejection of the statement of 16 June. On 6 July, he wrote to Attlee that the delegation's handling of the negotiations had

> 'impaired the honour of the British Government and have shaken the confidence of Muslim India and shattered their hopes for an honourable and peaceful settlement. They allowed themselves to play in the hands of the Congress. . . . I . . . trust that the British Government will still avoid compelling the Muslims to shed their blood, for, your surrender to the Congress at the sacrifice of the Muslims can only result in that direction.'[152]

A series of statements by Congress leaders against grouping and their assertion that they were not bound by anything except their decision to join the Constituent Assembly, combined with the si-

[149] Handwritten note by Pethick-Lawrence, undated but probably around beginning July, Ibid., p. 339.

[150] Note by Pethick-Lawrence, July 1946, Ibid., pp. 320–3.

[151] Cabinet Meeting on 18 July 1946, Ibid., p. 220.

[152] Jinnah to Attlee, 6 July 1946, Ibid., pp. 200–2.

lence of the British, heightened the apprehensions of the League.[153]
Dawn commented that if Attlee and his colleagues indicated in Parliament that their silence hitherto,

> in face of Congress leaders' bragging to treat their Statement of 16 May as a scrap of paper, has been due to extreme patience and not cowardice, and if they restate that there shall be no departure from the fundamental basis of that Statement, Muslims would still be willing to play their part honourably and peacefully, provided that such a restatement by the British Government is logically followed up by such action in respect of the setting up of an Interim Government also.'[154]

Pethick-Lawrence's reply to Lord Simon in the House of Lords raised the League up in arms. Simon enquired whether the British government regarded it as 'being quite open' to the Constituent Assembly to frame a constitution 'which squares with Government's framework, or have they a wider ambit than that, so that they can propose something of a different kind? The Secretary of State replied:

> 'I think it would be quite impossible for me to give direct, specific, definite answers as to the precise position of that body . . . The object of setting up the Constituent Assembly is to give Indians the power to make their own Constitution. The only reason we intervened at all was that it was necessary to get both major Parties into the body so that there should be certain understanding between them as to the basis of a new government.'[155]

In the Commons, Cripps stated that the Indian parties were 'at perfect liberty to advance their own views on what should or should not be the basis of a future Constitution'.[156]

Accusing the British of appeasing the Congress, the League rejected on 29 July the 16 May statement, 'due to the intransigence of the Congress on one hand, and the breach of faith with the Muslims by the British Government on the other'. The Congress was bent upon setting up 'Caste Hindu Raj in India with the connivance of the British'. The Council of the League called on Muslims to resort to 'Direct Action to achieve Pakistan . . . to get rid of the present British slavery and the contemplated future Caste-Hindu domina-

---

[153] Statements by Azad, Patel and Nehru between 6–10 July 1946, *TOP*, vol. 8, p. 517.

[154] *Dawn*, 17 July 1946.

[155] *TOP*, vol. 8, p. 516.   [156] Ibid., pp. 516–7.

tion'. As a protest against 'their deep resentment of the attitude of the British', the League called upon Muslims to renounce the titles 'conferred upon them by the alien Government.'[157]

Nehru has often received most of the blame for the passing of the Direct Action resolution by the League. Azad wrote that the League would have come into the Constituent Assembly had it not been for Nehru's press statement of 10 July, which he describes as 'one of those unfortunate events which changed the course of history'.[158] But Nehru, along with other Congress leaders, had expressed himself against grouping throughout the negotiations with the cabinet mission. Azad himself upheld the Congress view that 'there should be no compulsion in the matter of grouping' on 6 July.[159]

Nehru also thought that once the parties entered the constituent assembly, discussion of the political, social and economic problems facing the whole of India would relegate grouping to the background.[160] In any case, Nehru envisaged that grouping would fail on its merits because Section A would oppose it; the NWFP would not join Group B; provincial jealousies would work against grouping, as the NWFP and Sind would not like Punjabi domination.[161] This assumption was not unreasonable: Khizar had expressed similar views to the cabinet delegation in April.[162] But if Nehru expected grouping to collapse *sui generis*, it could hardly have been the *leitmotif* of his statement, or the idea seizing his mind. In fact, the sovereignty of the constituent assembly was at the core of many of Nehru's statements around the beginning of July,[163] and it is difficult to understand why his press interview of 10 July has been singled out by his contemporaries and historians as the *casus belli* of the League's call for direct action. On 10 July, he merely reaffirmed what he had said earlier: that the constituent assembly must be a sovereign body. Nehru's remarks were clearly aimed at the British:

[157] League resolution of 29 July, Ibid., pp. 138–9.

[158] Azad, *India Wins Freedom*, p. 181.

[159] Statement by Azad, 6 July 1946, *TOP*, vol. 8, p. 517.

[160] See, for example, Nehru's note of 10 July 1946, *SW*, vol. 15, pp. 248–9.

[161] Press interview, 10 July 1946, Ibid., pp. 242–3.

[162] Meeting between cabinet delegation and Khizar on 5 April 1946, *TOP*, vol. 7, p. 148.

[163] Nehru's editorial in *National Herald*, 3 July 1946; speech at Jhansi, 4 July 1946; 7 July 1946, *SW*, vol. 15, pp. 233, 234–5, 236–8 respectively.

'When the Congress stated that the constituent assembly was to be a sovereign body, the Cabinet Mission's reply was more or less "yes", subject to two considerations: first, a proper arrangement for the minorities, and secondly, a treaty between India and England. I wish the Mission had stated that both these matters were not controversial. It is obvious that the minorities question has to be settled satisfactorily. It is also obvious that if there is any kind of peaceful changeover in India, it is bound to result in some kind of a treaty with Britain.

What exactly the treaty will be I cannot say. But if the British Government presume to tell us that they are going to hold anything in India, because they do not agree either in regard to the minorities or in regard to the treaty, we shall not accept that position . . . if there is the slightest attempt at imposition, we shall have no treaty.

In regard to the minorities . . . we . . . accept no outsiders' interference in it—certainly not the British Government's—and, therefore, these two limiting factors to the sovereignty of the constituent assembly are not acceptable to us.

The only limitation on the party's action would be its anxiety to carry the work of the constituent assembly to successful conclusion. It does not make the slightest difference what the Cabinet Mission thinks or does in the matter.'[164]

The point was reiterated by him on several occasions after 10 July.[165]

Jinnah took exception to the absence of any assurance from Cripps and Pethick-Lawrence that the British would insist on the working of the constituent assembly as laid down in the 16 May statement. He and other Leaguers made this very clear to the British after the passing of the direct action resolution on 29 July 1946.[166] Even moderate Leaguers like Nazimuddin lamented that the 'British have let us down'.[167] All this only underlined the essential political division between the League and Congress: what for the Congress implied British dictation to the constituent assembly was, for the League, a British guarantee against Congress domination. British assurances to the League on grouping would have no value if they were not backed up by a guarantee of British responsibility for the procedure of the constituent assembly. But not only were the

[164] Press interview, 10 July 1946, Ibid., pp. 242–3.
[165] Nehru's editorial in *National Herald*, 16 July 1946; speech on 20 July 1946; press interview, 29 July 1946; speech, 1 August 1946, Ibid., pp. 255–6, 260–1, 273–4, 276–7 respectively.
[166] Wavell to Pethick-Lawrence, (T), 27 August 1946; note by Wavell, 16 September 1946; undated note by Mudie, *TOP*, pp. 311, 525, 212–13 respectively.
[167] *Morning News*, 5 August 1946. See also *Morning News* editorial, 31 July 1946.

British unwilling to proceed without the Congress; they seemed to be reneging their assurances on the status and procedure of the constituent assembly, while their rejection of parity at the centre implied that they had not acquiesced in the logic of the two nation theory. Differences with the Congress had prevailed on all these points throughout the negotiations with the cabinet mission; it was the realization that they might, in the end, get nothing from the British which proved the catalyst for the League's call for direct action.

CHAPTER 6

Negotiations for The Interim Government and Direct Action

Discussing the 'novel and serious situation' created by the League's call for Direct Action, the British cabinet advised Wavell that they must not lose the initiative and that it was 'impossible' to allow Jinnah's non-cooperation to hold up progress in the formation of an interim government. The Viceroy was instructed to see Jinnah as soon as possible and to press him to allow Muslim Leaguers to join the interim government. The British could not allow themselves to get into a situation in which both Congress and the League were in opposition and the government had to be carried on by officials indefinitely.[1] The decision to proceed without the League was 'undoubtedly a grave one' but there was 'no practicable alternative'. That Whitehall was prepared to go a considerable distance away from the assurances it had given the League on 16 May is illustrated by Pethick-Lawrence's suggestion that if the Constituent Assembly met without the League 'there appears to be nothing short of the May 16 Statement which would make it necessary for the Provincial representatives to meet in sections.' Paragraph 19 of the statement which laid down this procedure could be varied if a majority of both communities were in agreement. 'As a majority of the Muslim representatives would, in the absence of the Muslim League, be pro-Congress Muslims, such a decision is not impossible. The result would be that the Provincial constitutions of the Muslim Provinces would be framed by a predominantly Hindu body and the possibility of Groups being formed would be very faint indeed.' But the British must not disguise the fact that if the Muslims (Muslim League) were to resort to violence 'we should inevitably be involved in supporting a predominantly Congress Government in putting down the disturbances.'[2] Political considerations can make for the strangest bedfellows.

[1] Secretary of State to Viceroy, (T. 14078), 31 July 1946, L/P&J/10/73, p. 136.
[2] Cabinet Paper C.P. (46) 315, Memorandum by Secretary of State, 31 July 1946, Ibid., pp. 121–6.

Wavell was thinking of extricating the British from a situation in which they were being castigated by Jinnah for letting him down, and, to that extent, indirectly bore the responsibility for the League's refusal to join the interim government. The onus of getting Jinnah in could be thrown on the Congress. The British had 'some chance of using the present situation to good effect if we can put responsibility for satisfying League on Congress'.[3] Wavell also did not take seriously Jinnah's call for Direct Action. He did not expect Jinnah to ask Muslim League ministries to resign. Jinnah, in his opinion, had few lieutenants who would be willing or able to run a mass movement. Also, Jinnah had given no indication that he would start a mass movement.[4]

The cabinet agreed with Wavell that the best tactics would be to call Nehru to make proposals for the formation of the interim government and to secure the agreement of the Congress Working Committee before any details were discussed. If the Working Committee agreed the Viceroy would stress the need for a coalition with the League.[5] So, on 6 August, Wavell invited Nehru, as Congress President, to submit proposals for an interim government on the basis of his letter of 30 May. Nehru was asked to discuss the proposals with Jinnah as a coalition would be the most effective form of government. The Congress Working Committee gave its approval for the Congress to enter the interim government. The Congress would approach the League for cooperation, though they did not expect it in view of their recent resolutions and statements. If cooperation was denied, then 'we shall be prepared to go ahead without it'.[6]

There was in fact little indication that the League would enter the government. Replying to Wavell's invitation of 22 July, Jinnah now argued that in making the proportions 6:5:3 the basis of the new government, the British were reneging on their earlier promises to form a government on the 5:5:3 and 5:5:4 basis in order to appease the Congress.[7] Wavell reminded him that the 6:5:3 basis was

[3] Viceroy to Secretary of State, (T 1587-S), 1 August 1946, Ibid., p. 118.

[4] Viceroy to Secretary of State, (T 1587-S), 1 August 1946, p. 118.

[5] Viceroy to Secretary of State, (T 1609-S), 4 August 1946, and Secretary of State to Viceroy, (T 14197), 2 August 1946, Ibid., pp. 102 and 103 respectively.

[6] CWC Resolution, 10 August 1946, Ibid., p. 217 and Nehru to Wavell, 10 August 1946, Ibid., p. 218.

[7] Jinnah to Wavell, 31 July 1946, Ibid., p. 156.

accepted by the Working Committee of the League in its resolution of 25 June.[8] The League's attitude was echoed in an editorial in *Dawn* on 14 August, which threatened that the moment 'a Hindu Government is set up without the consent and collaboration of Moslems the first shot of aggression will have been fired against them and that will be the signal for Muslims to do or die.'[9]

What the League intended by Direct Action is unclear. Jinnah himself refused to comment—'I am not going to discuss ethics'.[10] Liaqat Ali khan described it as 'action against the law'.[11] Most provincial Leagues called for peaceful demonstrations, and on 16 August itself, Jinnah enjoined upon Muslims 'to carry out the instructions and abide by them strictly and conduct themselves peacefully and in a disciplined manner'. An advertisement in Muslim League papers on 16 August read:

'Today is Direct Action Day
Today Muslims of India dedicate anew their lives and all
they possess to the cause of freedom
Today let every Muslim swear in the name of Allah to resist aggression
Direct Action is now their only course
Because they offered peace but peace was spurned
They honoured their word but were betrayed
They claimed Liberty but are offered Thraldom
Now Might alone can secure their Right'.[12]

Direct Action turned violent only in Calcutta. There were many portents of its nature in Calcutta. The *Morning News*, published from Calcutta and whose editor, Akram Khan, was a member of the Calcutta and Bengal Muslim Leagues, asserted in an editorial on 5 August that Muslims 'do not believe in the cant of non-violence.'[13] The conservative landlord Nazimuddin, often at odds with Suhrawardy and his labour supporters, threatened: 'There are a hundred and one ways in which we can create difficulties, specially when we are not restricted to non-violence. The Muslim population of Bengal know very well what "Direct Action" would mean so we need not bother to give them any lead'.[14] Muslims, according to *Dawn's*

[8] Wavell to Jinnah, 8 August 1946, Ibid., p. 203.
[9] *Dawn*, 14 August 1946.
[10] *Morning News*, 2 August 1946.   [11] *Morning News*, 2 August 1946.
[12] *Dawn, Eastern Times, Morning News*, 16 August 1946.
[13] *Morning News*, 5 August 1946.   [14] *Morning News*, 11 August 1946.

Calcutta correspondent, had 'no faith in non-violence and they are neither hypocrites that they would preach non-violence in words and practice violence in action'.[15] From 10 August Muslim goondas from outside Calcutta armed with sticks, spears and daggers began to appear in the slum areas of the city.[16] A pamphlet written by S.M. Usman, the League mayor of Calcutta proclaimed:

> 'In the month of Ramzan the first open war between Islam and *Kafirs* started and the Mussulmans got the permission to wage Jehad . . . and Islam secured a splendid victory . . . . According to wishes of God, the All-India Muslim League has chosen this sacred month for launching this Jehad for achieving Pakistan . . . . We Muslims have had the crown and have ruled. Do not lose heart, be ready and take swords . . . . Oh *Kafir*! your doom is not far and the general massacre will come.'[17]

On 16 August, the *Star of India* and the *Morning News* advised their readers that the pamphlet was available from the local Muslim League office. Suhrawardy himself did not rule out communal violence. That the Bengal government expected it is illustrated by the fact that troops were confined to barracks on the morning of 16 August.[18]

Europeans were the only groups which emerged unscathed on Direct Action Day in Calcutta.[19] There was in fact considerable evidence that Direct Action would be aimed at Hindus. Earlier in the month, Khurho had told Mudie that it would be 'directed not so much at the British as at the Hindus'.[20] Gazdar, a Muslim League leader from Sind, declared that the Congress was out to crush the League by turning British guns and police bayonets on Muslims. 'I warn them that they will have to pay for Muslim lives thus lost in Hindu blood with compound interest'.[21] An editorial in the *Morning News* advised Muslims that 'any molestation or attempted molestation of British men or women, be they civilian or military, is

[15] *Dawn*, 12 August 1946.

[16] *Report of the Commissioners of Police on the Disturbances of 16–20 August* (Calcutta, 1946), quoted in Richard Lambert, 'Hindu-Muslim Riots', unpublished Ph.D. dissertation presented to University of Pennsylvania, 1951, p. 170.

[17] Extract from Muslim League pamphlet, *Let Pakistan Speak for Herself* (Calcutta, 1946), quoted in Sen, *Muslim Politics*, p. 213. See also Lambert, 'Hindu-Muslim Riots', p. 237.

[18] Burrows to Wavell, 22 August 1946, *TOP*, vol. 8, p. 295.

[19] Ibid., p. 302.   [20] Undated note by Mudie, Ibid., p. 213.

[21] *Morning News*, 12 August 1946.

not only against the Bombay resolutions, but also against the spirit and letter of Islam'.[22] The editorial did not express any similar sentiment in favour of Hindus. The Spens Enquiry Commission enquired of Brigadier Thomas Binny, on the general staff of the Eastern Command: '"Had anybody, European or otherwise, any doubt in his mind that this was going to be an attempt against the Hindus?"' Binny answered, '"No."'[23] Official reports from Bengal had warned of the 'potential danger of communal clashes' on 16 August. They also took note of the Hindu feeling that Direct Action would be directed against them in particular. Non-Muslims, except Christians and Europeans, expected and were ready to face violence. Hindu leaders in Calcutta contributed to the atmosphere of hate and violence by calling on Hindu workers to abstain from the hartal organized by the League; to resist it by force if necessary.[24] A prominent Sikh leader in Calcutta declared that 'if rioting did start, the Sikhs would back the Congress and between them they would give the Muslims a good thrashing'.[25] That Hindus were well prepared for violence is indicated by their ready retaliation of attacks by Muslim League processionists as they passed Hindu localities on the morning of 16 August,[26] and the fact that there were eventually more Muslim than Hindu casualties in Calcutta.

Suhrawardy, as Chief Minister and Home Minister, declared 16 August a public holiday with the approval of the Governor. Burrows mentioned the point to Wavell on 8 August. The idea was to minimize the risk of communal conflict on the 16th.[27] Reports of scuffles began to reach police headquarters even before 6 a.m. on the 16th. Some of the early incidents occurred when Hindu shopkeepers refused to comply with demands by Muslim League processionists to close down their shops.[28] Stabbing, arson and looting started early in the day. There were cases of the police participating in the looting; for the rest, they did nothing.[29] The situation became so serious by the afternoon that at 2.40 p.m. the Chief Secretary rang up Burrows' secretary to say that he supported the request of

---

[22] *Morning News*, 16 August 1946.

[23] Thomas Binny, Staff HQ Eastern Command in Spens Commission Report, quoted by Lambert, 'Hindu-Muslims Riots', p. 172.

[24] Tuker, *While Memory Serves* (London, 1950), pp. 156–7.

[25] Ibid., p. 156.   [26] Burrows to Wavell, 22 August 1946, *TOP*, vol. 8, p. 296.

[27] Ibid., p. 294.   [28] Ibid., p. 296.

[29] Lambert, 'Hindu-Muslim Riots', p. 178.

the Commissioner of Police that the army should be called in at once. Burrows agreed 'on my own responsibility' to their being called in without delay. For the moment, however, troops were not used, because the Governor, on a tour of the city, formed the impression, which he did not detail, 'that the situation was not as bad as I had expected to find it.'[30]

At 4 p.m. Suhrawardy and other League leaders addressed a meeting of Muslims—numbering between 30,000 to 100,000—at the Ochterlony Monument. The Special Branch of Police, by what Burrows described as 'a culpable omission', sent only one Urdu shorthand reporter to the meeting, so that 'no transcript of the Chief Minister's speech is available'. But the Central Intelligence Officer and a reliable reporter deputed by the military authorities agreed on 'one most mischievous statement (not reported at all by the Calcutta Police whose report reached us first). The version in the former's report is:– "He had seen to police and military arrangements who would not interfere". The version in the latter's is:– "He had been able to restrain the military and police". The audience interpreted this as an invitation to disorder; and many of the listeners started attacking Hindus and looting Hindu shops as soon as they left the meeting.[31]

There is no doubt of the complicity of Suhrawardy and the provincial League in the incidents in Calcutta. Days before the rioting, coupons bearing the Chief Minister's signature were issued for the use of Muslim League lorries. Elaborate preparations were made for first aid stations and mobile units by the League for the 16th. The *Statesman* commented:

> 'Some of those disrupting the city's peace were privileged. The bands of ruffians rushing about in lorries, stopping to assault and attack and generally spreading fear and confusion found the conveyances they wanted. On a day when no one else could get transport for their lawful occasions, these men had all they wanted; it is not a ridiculous assumption that they had been provided for in advance.'[32]

S.G. Taylor, then Inspector General of police in Bengal, recollects:

> 'The Chief Minister's own attitude during the rioting was reprehensible to a degree. During the height of the disturbances he drove round Calcutta with the local Army Commander to asses (sic) the situation.

[30] Burrows to Wavell, 22 August 1946, *TOP*, vol. 8, p. 296.
[31] Ibid., pp. 296–7.   [32] *Statesman*, 18 August 1946.

As they drove the Army Commander said: "This is all extraordinary; in the Army Hindus and Mohamedans live and work very happily together." To this the Chief Minister replied: "We shall soon put an end to all that." '

Suhrawardy also ordered Taylor to tell the police superintendent in the 24 Parganas district to release all Muslims who had been arrested in connection with the rioting. Taylor retorted that he had no authority to give such an order, and that such orders were illegal. ' "Very well then" said the Chief Minister, "you will tell the Superintendent of the Police that if he has occasion to arrest any Mohamedans in the future he will arrest at least as many Hindus!" '[33]

One of the great controversies about the Calcutta riots centres around the role of Sir Frederick Burrows, the Governor of Bengal. Section 52(1) of the Act of 1935 gave the Governor the special responsibility to prevent 'any grave menace to the peace of the province or any part thereof'. But law and order was not a discretionary matter under the constitution, and the Governor was to 'exercise his individual judgement' as to the action to be taken in the carrying out of his special responsibilities.[34]

Burrows himself wrote that in handling the situation, particularly at the outset, 'I had always to consider the susceptibilities of my Ministry. The dual personality of Suhrawardy, as Chief Minister (in charge of the Home portfolio) and as the most influential member of the Muslim League in Bengal, was a constant embarrassment'.[35] As 'slippery as a basket of eels', Suhrawardy combined a reputation as a labour leader backed by the *goondas* of Calcutta with one of being a ladies' man, who, wearing a white sharkskin suit, frequented the club, "The 300", in the city, and had 'all the Western vices'.[36]

Nevertheless, it is not difficult to see why Burrows was charged by the Congress and Hindus for conniving with the League ministry on 16 August. Suhrawardy spent a great deal of time in the Control Room, often attended by some of his supporters. This made it

---

[33] S.G. Taylor, 'Bengal 1942 to the takeover in 1947,' *S.G. Taylor papers.* Taylor was then Inspector General of Police in Bengal.

[34] *Government of India Act, 1935,* pp. 35–7.

[35] Burrows to Wavell, 22 August 1946, *TOP,* vol. 8, p. 303.

[36] I owe this personal account of Suhrawardy to Mr. W.H. Saumarez Smith, then Deputy Secretary to the Governor of Bengal. Interview with author on 31 October 1980.

difficult for the Police Commissioner, who was handling the situation, to give clear decisions. It was not the function of the minister to direct detailed operations, but the position was delicate as the Police Commissioner 'could not insist' on the extrusion from the Control Room of the Minister responsible for law and order. Short of a direct order from Burrows, there was no way of preventing the Chief Minister from visiting the Control Room whenever he liked; and the Governor was not prepared to give such an order, 'as it would clearly have indicated complete lack of faith in him'. A curfew was imposed on Calcutta only at 9 p.m. It was to last till 4 a.m. Stabbing, looting and arson continued, so the army patrolled some streets. Burrows' tour of the city on the 17th, which was undertaken at about 11 a.m. 'convinced me' that earlier reports had erred on the side of under-estimation. 'I observed very great damage to property and streets littered with corpses. I can honestly say that parts of the city on Saturday morning were as bad as anything I saw when I was with the Guards on the Somme'. It was then that Burrows decided, after consulting with the acting Area Commander, the Chief Secretary and the Police Commissioner, that a military operation would be staged in the area worst affected. The operation began at 3.30 p.m., and it was not until 6.30 p.m. that order was restored in the Bow Bazar area. Reinforcements were called in, and by 20 August, the situation showed a marked improvement.[37]

Why were troops used so late, especially as the police strength in Calcutta—250 with another 250 in reserve—was, to quote S.G. Taylor's understatement, 'quite inadequate to deal with a disaster of this magnitude', and their complicity in the disturbances, either by way of participating in them or being reluctant to open fire, was in no doubt at a very early stage?[38] Brigadier Binny held that troops, if deployed or employed in proper time 'Not only would have been but were sufficient' to prevent or quell the riot.[39] This corroborates Taylor's view. In disturbances which saw the loss of 10,000 lives, when corpses were piling up on the streets even as Burrows toured the city and were beginning to block Calcutta's drainage system, his tardiness in using the army did him no credit, and laid him open to the charge of partiality towards his ministry; and of complacency because there was not 'a single case of any attack on a European or

[37] Burrows to Wavell, 22 August 1946, *TOP*, vol. 8, pp. 217–18, 302.
[38] S.G. Taylor, 'Bengal 1942–1947', *S.G. Taylor papers*.
[39] Spens Commission Report, quoted by Lambert, 'Hindu-Muslims Riots'. p. 179.

even an Anglo-Indian as such'.[40] General Roy Bucher, the Army Commander, recorded that the Bengal government remained inactive even after the army had taken charge. 'Neither then, nor afterwards, did one member of that Government give me any real assistance in bringing order out of disorder'.[41] The ministry was not dismissed, inspite of an assurance by Cripps to Nehru that it would be in any contingency such as this.[42]

Burrows' admission that he did not go into Section 93 because he would not have been able to cope with any agitation by the League, which might then ensue, raises the question of the capacity of the administration to deal with large-scale disorders. Direct Action day in Calcutta resulted in 10,000 deaths, yet only one prosecution was carried out. The only thing which prevented a complete collapse of the administration, according to Burrows, was the three battalions of British troops.[43] Once called in, troops were able to restore order easily—it is this which leads to criticism of Burrows for not calling them in earlier.

Direct Action day passed off peacefully in other provinces, including Sind, which was also governed by a League ministry which had declared 16 August a public holiday. Mudie had also chided his ministers for incitement to violence.[44] In Jorhat in Assam, the communal complexion of an imposing League procession was 'somewhat marred by the fact that it was accompanied by a band comprised mainly of Hindus led by a Chinaman and giving an indifferent rendering of "The British Grenadiers" '.[45]

Jinnah condemned the violence in Calcutta, and declared that the Bengal Provincial League would take action—whatever that might mean—against those who had broken instructions and participated in violence.[46] But as the Congress joined the interim government, he and his lieutenants continued to incite violence. Declaring a *jihad* against the British and the Congress, Ghulam Ali Khan, minister for Law and Order in Sind, proclaimed that anyone opposing Muslims

---

[40] Burrows to Wavell, 22 August 1946, *TOP*, vol. 8, p. 302.

[41] General Sir Roy Bucher to Nehru, 13 November 1954, *NC*, quoted by Gopal, *Nehru*, vol. 1, p. 330.

[42] Patel to Cripps, 19 October 1946, *Patel Correspondence*, vol. 3, pp. 131–2.

[43] Burrows to Wavell, *TOP*, vol. 8, p. 303.

[44] Minutes of Conference with Governors of Bengal, UP, Punjab, Sind and NWFP, Ibid., pp. 206–7.

[45] Bourne to Wavell, 23 August 1946, Ibid., p. 305.

[46] *Dawn*, 19 August 1946.

in the pursuit of Pakistan 'shall be destroyed and exterminated.'[47] Mamdot announced the League's intention to use 'all methods worthy of an aroused nation . . . Now we have burst our bonds. Now we are determined to stake our all in the Jehad to achieve freedom for Islam in India'.[48] Even as direct action was brought under control in Calcutta, Jinnah's rhetoric—that the inauguration of the interim government would result in 'unprecedented and disastrous consequences'—was dangerous precisely because it did not define the limits or nature of Direct Action.

Direct Action by the League was a new factor for the British to contend with. The British had earlier worked on the assumption that the Congress would be hostile and the League friendly. 'That is certainly not the present position', observed Pethick-Lawrence. 'Jinnah is not only angry with us but is threatening open rebellion. Even if we agree that he was provoked and was perhaps not handled in the best way (which I admit), we cannot ignore his present attitude. He does not even suggest to us a policy which would provide a settlement except the barren slogan of Pakistan. Congress is, at any rate for the moment, friendly'. Whitehall did not know what to do. The situation changed from day to day, and any "ultimate policy" decided on this week would almost certainly by force of events prove to be all wrong next week or the week after.[49]

Wavell remained anxious to get the League into the interim government, for he held that communal violence could not be otherwise halted.[50] But Gandhi and Nehru would not accept grouping in the face of the League's intransigence and the instigated violence in Calcutta. Nor would Congress give up its right to include a non-League Muslim in its own quota.[51] Wavell took their reaction as justification for Jinnah's doubts about Congress; as 'convincing evidence' that Congress always meant to use their position in the Interim Government to destroy the grouping scheme which was the one effective safeguard for the Muslims.[52] There was little condemnation of the political methods which had resulted in the loss of

[47] *Sind Observer*, 3 August 1946, enclosed in letter from Choitram P. Gidwani, President, Sind PCC, 10 August 1946, AICC-file no. G-36, 1946, p. 51.

[48] *Dawn*, 22 August 1946.

[49] Pethick-Lawrence to Wavell, 19 August 1946, *TOP*, vol. 8, p. 263.

[50] Viceroy to Secretary of State, 27 August 1946, (T 1791–S), L/P&J/10/75, p. 401

[51] Gandhi to Wavell, 28 August 1946, and Nehru to Wavell, 19 August 1946, Ibid., pp. 322 and 259 respectively.

[52] Viceroy to Secretary of State (T 1804–S), 28 August 1946, Ibid., p. 398.

hundreds of lives; only a warning that the League would continue to employ such methods if the British did not confirm their promises to the League on grouping.[53] Wavell did not want the British to go ahead with the Constituent Assembly if the Congress failed to accept grouping.[54]

The cabinet disagreed with Wavell's interpretation of the attitudes of Gandhi and Nehru. Pethick-Lawrence also pointed out that the formation of the constituent assembly had been publicly announced: not calling it would be represented as a breach of faith.[55]

Wavell himself was not very consistent on the question of procedure. In his broadcast on 24 August, he accepted the Congress view that any dispute over paragraph 15 of the 16 May Statement could be referred to the Federal Court.[56] But in a letter to Nehru on 28 August, he suggested that the Congress accept grouping as laid down in the Statement as distinguished from the legal interpretation which could be put on it by the Federal Court.[57] '*This approach is new*', pointed out Nehru. The Calcutta occurrences had taken place 'before your broadcast in which you have referred to the Federal Court deciding questions of interpretation'.[58]

The inconsistencies in British attitudes stemmed from the 16 May statement itself, and their acceptance of resolutions which stated contradictory aims of the Congress and the League. The British accepted Azad's letter of 25 June as an acceptance by the Congress of the Statement. The Congress had 'throughout openly held' that they accepted the statement subject to paragraph 15(5)— '"Provinces should be free to form groups and each group could determine the provincial subjects to be taken in common"'. This overrode the subsequent provision that representatives of provinces would meet in sections '"which shall proceed to settle certain constitutions of the Provinces included in each section, and shall also decide whether any group constitution shall be set up for those Provinces, and if so with what provincial subjects the group shall

[53] Ibid., and Wavell to Pethick-Lawrence, 28 August 1946, *TOP*, vol. 8, p. 314.

[54] Viceroy to Secretary of State (T 1791-S), 27 August 1946, *TOP*, vol. 8, p. 311.

[55] Secretary of State to Viceroy, (T 15817), 28 August 1946, L/P&J/10/75, p. 390; and Secretary of State to Viceroy (T 15940), Ibid., p. 368.

[56] Text of Wavell's broadcast on 24 August 1946, *TOP*, vol. 8, pp. 306–7.

[57] Wavell to Nehru, 28 August 1946, R/3/1/117, p. 147.

[58] Nehru to Wavell, 28 August 1946, *TOP*, vol. 8, p. 327. Emphasis mine.

deal" '. The Congress had never moved from this position: the Congress resolution of 10 August reiterated it. Azad's letter of 25 June accepted the British proposals '*with a view to achieve our objective* (which, incidentally, is the avoidance of groups).' The League, on the other hand, did accept the scheme although the basic paragraph 15 contained as its first feature the establishment of a Union.[59] Here Monteath erred. The League accepted the 16 May statement

> 'inasmuch as the basis and the foundation of Pakistan are inherent in the Mission's plan by virtue of the compulsory grouping of the six Muslim Provinces in Sections B and C, [the League] is willing to cooperate with the constitution-making machinery proposed in the scheme outlined by the Mission *in the hope that it would ultimately result in the establishment of a complete sovereign Pakistan, and in the consummation of the goal of independence for the major nations, Muslims and Hindus*'.[60]

The British persisted stubbornly in the wishful thinking that the League was not serious about Pakistan perhaps because it was at odds with the official conception of their future role in India.

The inauguration of the interim government on 2 September was greeted with threats of direct action by the League. Jinnah saw a division of India as the only alternative to it,[61] and there were reports of the organization of direct action from many Muslim majority provinces. The Punjab Provincial League called on all able-bodied Muslims to enlist in the National Guard.[62] Abdulla Haroon was appointed dictator to organize direct action in Sind, and Muslims in the Punjab and NWFP were instructed not to buy anything from Hindu shopkeepers.[63] Jinnah declared that India was on the brink of civil war. Suhrawardy warned that 'the prospects before us are not merely gloomy but just cannot bear contemplation'.[64] Ghazanfar Ali thought Muslims should prepare for direct action rather than indulge in speculation about the outcome of the Jinnah-Wavell parleys,[65] and to wait for the 'final signal for a tremendous struggle for the establishment of Free Pakistan'.[66] The League's Committee of Action defined Direct action as a *jihad* against the enemies of Islam in India.[67]

[59] Notes by Turnbull and Monteath, 30 and 31 August 1946 respectively, L/P&J/5/10/75, pp. 362–4. Emphasis in original.
[60] *TOP*, vol. 7, pp. 837–8.　　[61] *Dawn*, 28 August 1946.
[62] *Dawn*, 5 September 1946.　　[63] *Dawn*, 5 and 8 September 1946.
[64] *Dawn*, 13 September 1946.　　[65] *Eastern Times*, 20 September 1946.
[66] *Eastern Times*, 22 September 1946.　　[67] *Eastern Times*, 26 September 1946.

The Congress now tried to go some way in satisfying Jinnah. In a broadcast on 7 September, Nehru stated that the Congress would enter sections, which would then consider the formation of groups.[68] Describing this as a step in 'the right direction', Wavell now wanted to put to the Congress a formula which would make clear that the League would get 'what the Mission wanted by their Statement of 16th May to give them'. Wavell preferred to lose the cooperation of the Congress at the centre and in the provinces 'than go ahead with constitution making on a one-party basis and in a way which the Mission never intended'.[69] He believed that Jinnah now wanted a settlement. This had been indicated by Suhrawardy, and Jinnah had stated that he would accept an invitation by the British government to start a new series of conferences on an equal footing with other negotiators.[70] Of course, the Congress would have to be told of the assurances on grouping which were given to the League on 16 May.[71]

Even as Jinnah stalled on entering the interim government, in spite of the willingness of the Congress to implement the basic principle of the 16 May statement, Wavell continued to urge on the Labour government the need for a breakdown plan. The unprecedented savagery and extent of the communal violence led Wavell to contend on 7 September, and again on 23 and 30 October, that on administrative grounds, the British could not govern India for more than eighteen months. They should therefore be ready to withdraw by March 1948, though Wavell visualized a breakdown as early as January 1947. For Wavell, the "administrative grounds" could be found only partly in the uncertain allegiance of Indians in the civil and armed services to the Raj, for the question was whether loyalist services alone could decisively suppress widespread unrest. Indeed it was in the administrative inability to crush such unrest that the crux of the administrative weakness of the British lay. The increasing Indianization of the services during the war had promp-

[68] *National Herald*, 8 September 1946.

[69] Wavell to Pethick-Lawrence (T 1889-S), 9 September 1946, *TOP*, vol. 8, pp. 470–1.

[70] Wavell to Pethick-Lawrence (T 1895-S), 9 September 1946, Ibid., p. 474; and Wavell to Pethick-Lawrence (T 1897-S), 10 September 1946, Ibid., p. 476.

[71] Viceroy to Secretary of State (T1910-S), 11 September 1946, Ibid., p. 489. See also Secretary of State to Viceroy (T 16574), 11 September 1946, and Turnbull to Monteath and Pethick-Lawrence, 11 September 1946, Ibid., pp. 490–1 and 490 respectively.

ted Wavell to advise the war cabinet to widen political liberalization between 1943–5, but he had not counselled winding up the Raj. It was the deepening political and communal rift, combined with labour unrest, which added a new dimension to the crumbling administrative and military foundations of the Raj after August 1946, especially as it held out the spectre of a sweeping anti-British wave. While Wavell worried about holding responsibility without power,[72] the cabinet pinned their hopes on successful negotiations. The cabinet's reasons for doing so were apparent in the *manner* in which ministers discussed the withdrawal proposals: in each case they pointed to their probable consequences before considering the accuracy of Wavell's estimate of the situation. There is no evidence in cabinet minutes to suggest a willing and long thoughtout British departure from India. The effect of withdrawal on Britain's international prestige weighed most with the Labour government in rejecting Wavell's suggestion to fix a terminal date for the Raj. To leave India before a constitution had been framed would be regarded by the world as an act of weakness and it would seriously undermine Britain's international position. The Chiefs of Staff had advised the essentiality of keeping India in the Commonwealth defence system; and India's cooperation was 'especially necessary' for the maintenance of Britain's strategic position in the Middle and Far East. Only an amicable transfer of power would make this possible. Above all, the British must avoid a situation in which they had to withdraw under 'circumstances of ignomy after there had been widespread riots and attacks on Europeans. It must be clear that we were going freely and not under compulsion'.[73]

To what extent did the Labour government agree with Wavell's appraisal of the administrative machine? On 5 June the cabinet delegation confessed that it was 'extremely weak'. On 23 September, Pethick-Lawrence agreed that it was deteriorating, but that there was no danger of a breakdown. The Viceroy's proposals, if carried out, would lead to a breakdown. The cabinet's anxiety to avoid a breakdown was reflected by their endorsement of A.V. Alexander's

---

[72] Enclosure by Wavell to Pethick-Lawrence, 8 September 1946, *TOP*, vol. 8, pp. 455–9.
[73] Record of meeting at 10 Downing Street on 23 September 1946, Ibid., pp. 570; cabinet meeting, 5 June 1946, *TOP*, vol. 7, pp. 812–19; Pethick-Lawrence to Wavell, 25 November 1946, *TOP*, vol. 9, pp. 170–1. Chronology has been sacrificed for coherence in this paragraph.

suggestion to strengthen the administration by recruiting additional Europeans on the basis that they would be guaranteed at least fifteen years' service in India or in the Colonial or Foreign Services if they were not required in India for the whole of that period.[74] The proposal was eventually shelved because Wavell warned that it would intensify Indian suspicions of British intentions. It would also have little practical value as the British would face a crisis in India in 1947 or 1948, while the recruits would not have completed training before 1950.[75] In November, Attlee ruled out the re-establishment of British rule for another fifteen years as neither the administrative nor military machine was capable of sustaining it.[76] So the cabinet concurred with Wavell that the administration was shaky, and that the British would not be able to crush a mass revolt. But because they wished to avoid scuttle, ministers did not share his pessimism that it was inevitable. At any rate, they wanted to pursue negotiations until failure became a certainty. In other words, they were reluctant to tell parliament that they expected a breakdown and could do nothing about it.

Wavell was apprehensive of what the British would do if the League embarked on direct action. 'If we allow the Muslims to enter on direct action without making it clear that we have *not* made an alliance with the Congress against the League and do not propose to hold the British forces available for internal security duties for more than a very short time, we shall be accepting a very heavy responsibility'.[77] The British government must decide its policy.

Whitehall did not want to take responsibility for the implementation of the Mission plan. The British could not make a statement that sections could decide their own procedure. Jinnah would then ask for a statement on others 'and we shall be led a considerable distance on the road of laying down in detail' the procedure of the Constituent Assembly.[78]

The tussle between the Congress and the League on the issue of a Nationalist Muslim continued, until Wavell told Jinnah that he

[74] Ibid.

[75] Wavell to Pethick-Lawrence, 23 October 1946, *TOP*, vol. 8, p. 794.

[76] Undated note by Attlee, *TOP*, vol. 9, p. 68. Also Pethick-Lawrence to Wavell, 25 November 1946, Ibid., pp. 170–1.

[77] Wavell to Pethick-Lawrence, 24 September 1946, L/P&J/10/75, p. 160. Emphasis in original.

[78] Secretary of State to Viceroy (T 17341), 25 September 1946, L/P&J/10/75, p. 197.

could not press the Congress further on the issue. Jinnah said nothing about this but said that he must be able to show his Working Committee other gains, for example, the safeguard against being outvoted on major communal issues, the Vice Presidency of the Executive Council, and minorities. Wavell's impression was that the matter of the Vice President was 'obviously one to which Jinnah attached most importance, from the psychological point of view'. On minorities Wavell assured him that no representative would be appointed without the concurrence of the Congress and the League.[79] On the question of a convention on major communal issues that no decision should be taken if either Hindus or Muslims were opposed, Wavell agreed with the Congress that 'it would be fatal to allow major communal issues to be decided by vote in the cabinet'. The efficiency and prestige of the Interim Government would depend on ensuring that differences were resolved in advance of cabinet meetings by friendly discussions. 'A Coalition Government either works by a process of mutual adjustments or does not work at all'. Wavell asked the league to reconsider the resolution of 29 June and to accept the long-term plan of the Mission's formula, that is, to enter the Constituent Assembly.[80] Probably to counter the inclusion of a Nationalist Muslim in the Congress quota, the League nominated a Scheduled Caste representative in its own quota.[81] To this the Congress raised no objection.[82] On 13 October, Jinnah communicated to Wavell the League's decision to enter the interim government.[83]

Why the League entered the Interim Government is not easy to ascertain. Wavell and Pethick-Lawrence had been satisfied that the Congress had 'put their best men' into the government;[84] Wavell expressed his disappointment with the names Jinnah put forward.[85] Nehru considered the inclusion of men of low calibre and standing such as Rab Nishtar and Ghazanfar Ali as indicative of the League's insincerity in making the government a success.[86] Ghazanfar Ali

---

[79] Viceroy to Secretary of State (T 2025-S), 26 September 1946, L/P&J/10/75, pp. 186–7, and Viceroy to Secretary of State (T 2085-S), 2 October 1946, Ibid., p. 151.

[80] Wavell to Jinnah, 4 October 1946, *TOP*, vol. 8, pp. 654–5.

[81] Viceroy to Secretary of State (T 2160-S), 14 October 1946, L/P&J/10/75, p. 122.

[82] Viceroy to Secretary of State (T 2170-S), 15 October 1946, Ibid., p. 115.

[83] Jinnah to Wavell, 13 October 1946, *TOP*, vol. 8, pp. 709–10.

[84] Pethick-Lawrence to Wavell, 28 August 1946, Ibid., p. 333.

[85] Note by Wavell, 16 October 1946, Ibid., pp. 739–40.

[86] Nehru to Wavell, 15 October 1946, Ibid., p. 735.

seemingly justified the Calcutta riots by saying that they showed Muslims would not submit to any government that did not include their representatives. The Interim Government 'is one of the fronts of the direct action campaign and we shall most scrupulously carry out the orders of Mr. Jinnah on any front that he orders us'.[87] There was not let down in its attacks on the Congress; in the organization of the League's National Guards in many provinces, or any inclination to defuse the atmosphere of communal tension.[88] Liaqat admitted to Abell that the League could only retain its popularity by a policy of 'opposition' and communal propaganda.[89]

The League's entry into the Interim Government did not bring about the expected lull in communal violence. Even as the League joined the government, there occurred in the districts of Noahkhali and Tippera in East Bengal one of the worst communal riots ever seen in india, all the more brutal, because, like the communal killings in Bihar, and in the Punjab in March 1947, they were organized.

Of this there was no doubt in Noahkhali and Tippera. There was evidence of organization behind all aspects of the trouble, which included murder, rape, conversions and forced marriages. The method of attack was consistent. First, a Muslim group approached a Hindu house and told the family that if their wealth was given to this group, they would be protected from other Muslims. Upon the departure of this group, another Muslim group would arrive and tell the Hindus that the only way to escape with their lives was to accept conversion to Islam. Local Maulvis travelled with the second group to perform the conversions. Hindus who resisted were murdered, as were those with influence in the district. A third group would complete the looting and set fire to the Hindu houses. The Hindus who had been forcibly converted were given white caps with *"Pakistan zindabad"* written on them, so that they would be protected from further attacks.[90] Officials found local Muslims sympathetic to the forced conversions,[91] and some were shown the caps which the con-

[87] *Eastern Times*, 9 October 1946.

[88] See, for example, Wylie to Wavell, 14 November 1946, *TOP*, vol. 9, pp. 70–1, FR for UP for first half of November 1946, HP file no. 18/11/46.

[89] Abell to Scott, 16 November 1946, *TOP*, vol. 9, p. 84.

[90] Tuker, *While Memory Serves*, p. 174. Pyarelal, *Mahatma Gandhi: The Last Phase*, vol. 1, part 1, pp. 280–1.

[91] Governor of Bengal to Viceroy (T 2656-S), 22 October 1946, HP file no. 5/55/46.

verted Hindus were made to wear after the conversions had taken place.[92]

Hindu women were raped, their conch shells were broken and their caste marks were erased from their foreheads.

> '"Outside goondas do not loot things of everyday use such as clothes, foodstuffs etc." [observed Kripalani, General Secretary of the Congress]. "They don't drive away cattle . . . Outside goondas are . . . not interested in forcible conversions and marriages. They don't take pirs and maulvis with them to perform conversion ceremonies." '[93]

The performance of the Bengal government was reprehensible. Burrows was on holiday in Darjeeling when the trouble started on 10 October, and his first report to Wavell was dated 16 October from Darjeeling. This was sent in response to a request from Wavell, who had been asked by Congress leaders for a report on the communal incidents.[94] The trouble was organized by a local landlord, Ghulam Sarwar, an ex-Congressman, who had recently joined the League.[95] Suhrawardy stated that the League had nothing to do with the disturbances, and local Leaguers did help to restore order.[96] But the League ministry put pressure on the police to withdraw all criminal cases connected with the rioting. These included murder, rioting, arson, dacoity and in a few cases, rape.[97]

The Bengal ministry's attitude to refugees also left its intentions in doubt. It left district officers in the dark as to the broad policy and details of refugee relief. It relied on "Volunteers", who one British official described as 'young men of the excitable student type' to shepherd and advise the refugees, and appointed junior Muslim officers to important supervisory jobs in Calcutta, but left district officers to arrange food and accommodation for the refugees. No information was given as to how long the refugees should be accommodated or if an attempt should be made to get them away from Muslim areas. The only interpretation that seemed

[92] Pyarelal, *Mahatma Gandhi: The Last Phase*, vol. 1, part 1, p. 299. See also Lambert, 'Hindu-Muslim Riots', p. 244.

[93] Statement by J.B. Kripalani, 29 October 1946, quoted in Lambert, 'Hindu-Muslim Riots', p. 184.

[94] Wavell to Burrows, (T), 15 October 1946, *TOP*, vol. 8, p. 729; and Patel to Burrows, 19 October 1946, Ibid., p. 750. See also *Statesman*, 18 October 1946.

[95] *Morning News*, 26 September 1946.

[96] Governor of Bengal to Viceroy (T 291), HP file no. 5/55/46, pp. 32–3.

[97] M.O. Carter, 'Trouble in 1946' *M.O. Carter papers*, pp. 10ff.

possible was that the Bengal . . . ministry was privately sponsoring a kind of transfer of the population in an effort to create "cells" of Muslim resistance, over the heads of its own officers'.[98]

The League's central leadership did not issue any statement condemning the events in Bengal. A plea by Burrows to members of the Interim Government who visited the province to issue such a statement met with a negative response from the League leaders. Liaqat Ali Khan said 'it would probably be better to have such a statement issued by prominent Muslim religious leaders. I said that I appreciated that, but . . . a statement by political leaders would also be of immense advantage. Patel agreed with me. Nishtar said nothing'.[99] Wavell drew attention to speeches made by Liaqat and Ghazanfar Ali which clearly incited to violence. Jinnah only referred to 'what was happening in other parts of India'.[100]

The reorganization of the Muslim League National Guards in October 1946 raises questions about the intentions of the central leadership of the League. Ex-military Muslim personnel had been invited to join the Guards since the end of the war, and many reports show that they were involved in the organization of the riots in Noahkhali,[101] and later in the Punjab. On 1 October 1946, the Guards were reorganized so that the control of Presidents of provincial Leagues over them was withdrawn. The whole organization was given a 'wholly military' character, as opposed to its earlier political cum military character, and was put 'so to speak on a war footing'. The *Salar-i-Ala* was to be appointed by the Committee of Action of the League, and he would appoint provincial *salars* in consultation with the Committee.[102] They pledged to strive for the achievement of Pakistan. Whether the National Guards acted on their own in East Bengal, or whether they were carrying out the orders of the Committee of Action, remains unanswered.

As news of Noahkhali spilled over into Bihar and the UP, these two Hindu-majority provinces witnessed the worst communal vio-

[98] J.M.G. Bell, 'Note on recent experiences in Bengal', *J.M.G. Bell papers*, file 3, item 4.

[99] Burrows to Wavell, 4 November 1946, *TOP*, vol. 9, pp. 5–6.

[100] Note by Wavell on discussion with Jinnah, 22 October 1946, *TOP*, vol. 8, p. 762.

[101] FR for Bengal for first and second half of October 1946, HP file no. 18/10/46.

[102] Note by E.J. Beveridge, 8 November 1946, on the Muslim League National Guards—HP file no. 28/4/46. See also *Star of India*, 14 October 1946.

lence since the beginning of British rule in India. Hindu refugees carried tales of conversions, rapes, the burning of Hindu houses. Propaganda by the Hindu Mahasabha in Bihar added fuel to the desire for revenge. *Searchlight* and the *Indian Nation*, edited by a Hindu landlord, the Maharaja of Darbhanga, put out particularly scurrilous writing after the Noahkhali massacres. *Searchlight* carried reports of *goonda raj* in East Bengal even as the League joined, the interim government. The League was attempting to establish Islam by the sword. 'Gone are the days when Hindus . . . proved helpless before successive hordes of invaders.'[103]

The trouble began in Patna with a hartal by Hindus to observe 25 October as Noahkhali Day, which led to an outbreak of rioting. On 26 October, Hindus from villages north of Chapra invaded Muslim *tolas* and killed 20 Muslims. The situation was brought under control by the evening, but the next day rioting spread through eastern and southeastern parts of Jehanabad subdivision in Gaya district and into the western part of Monghyr district. There was evidence of organization of massacres of Muslims in Bihar. Marwari businessmen of Calcutta were believed to have organized them in retaliation for Direct Action day in Calcutta. But it is not possible to detect the hand of a single party in the organization of the violence.[104] Some evidence against the RSS in the UP riots comes from Congress workers.[105]

The Congress ministry in Bihar and Congress leaders in the interim government reacted swiftly to the events in the province. Police opened fire in the Patna and Saran districts on 23 occasions by 31 October. Dow testified that the ministry 'were . . . insistent during the early days of the rioting that the military should shoot to kill larger numbers of the mobs, which generally dispersed, however great their number, as soon as firing was resorted to'.[106] Nehru's threatened bombing of the affected areas—leading to an outcry by the Mahasabha and some resentment among Hindus about the

---

[103] *Searchlight*, editorial, 21 October 1946.

[104] Dow's reports and the fortnightly reports do not mention any party. This is corroborated by Tuker. Nehru believed it was organized by Marwari businessmen and Hindu landlords. Nehru to Gandhi, 3 October 1946, *NC*.

[105] Statement by Mridula Sarabhai, General Secretary AICC, 13 November 1946, and statement by Shah Nawaz Khan, 13 November 1946, AICC file no. 20, pp. 1–6 and 9–11 respectively.

[106] Dow to Wavell, 22/23 November 1946, *TOP*, vol. 9, p. 149.

alleged ruthlessness with which Hindu mobs were suppressed while Muslim mobs in Bengal were apparently given a free hand.[107]

The attitude of Congress leaders provides a contrast to that of the League, over the riots in both Bengal and Bihar. Kripalani expressed shame that his co-religionists had been betrayed into reprisals.[108] Gandhi's judgement—justified—was that Bihar had disgraced India even as Bengal had done.[109] Wavell, no great admirer of Nehru, praised the work done by him in Patna and Calcutta as having done good, which did 'considerable credit to his courage and energy'.[110] There was evidence of the Congress leaders' concern for Muslims harmed in the violence.[111]

Jinnah's reaction lent credence to the view that he was not interested in a united, independent India. If the League and the Congress did not agree on division, 'What happens is what you see . . . [112] From 10–14 November, *Dawn* carried provocative epitaphs in black-bordered 'boxes' on the Muslims killed in the riots. The first of these read:

> "Think only of the martyrs of Bihar that they died for Islam. Clustering around the throne of God they must be saying: our Lord! they killed us because we worshipped you. Because we followed your Prophet. Think also this that their souls are watching. Let the blood of those that are dead cleanse the hearts of those that are living. Let it wash their weakness away: make them strong, united, invincible."[113]

The League's attitude to relief work was obstructive. It discouraged Muslim refugees from returning to their villages and encouraged them to leave the province. Muslim League 'helpers' in relief camps concentrated on circulating political manifestoes. Hearing of Dow's tour of the relief camps on 1 November, they arranged demonstrations and processions, and were 'ghoulish enough to dig up the bones and skulls of buried victims and strew them in my path in order to demonstrate the callous neglect of my ministry'. This was carried on under the authority of Firoz Khan Noon.[114] That orders for arranging mass transfers of the population came from Jinnah is

[107] FRs for UP and Bengal for first half of November 1946, HP file no. 18/11/46.
[108] *Searchlight*, 7 November 1946.   [109] *Searchlight*, 8 November 1946.
[110] Wavell to Pethick-Lawrence, 13 November 1946, *TOP*, vol. 9, p. 56.
[111] See, for example, Gandhi to Syed Mahmud, 22 January 1946, (in Hindi), *Syed Mahmud papers*.
[112] *Searchlight*, 16 November 1946.
[113] *Dawn*, 10 November 1946. (Original in Capitals.)
[114] Dow to Colville, 10/11 December 1946, L/P&J/5/181.

suggested by Dow's report that both Noon and Nazimuddin realized that it was impracticable to arrange mass transfers of the population, 'but their efforts cannot have much effect so long as Jinnah remains intransigent and openly advocates the movement'.[115] Jinnah's attitude could also account for the fact that Hindus were not encouraged to return to their homes in Eastern Bengal after the Noahkhali violence.[116]

Whatever the ministry may have done by way of firm and effective action in Bihar, the province produced, until June 1947, the largest 'butcher's bill'. Some 20,000 Muslims are estimated to have lost their lives. This raises the question of the ability of the administration in both Bengal and Bihar. In Bengal, Burrows held that there was adequate warning for the authorities to have taken action, but that they failed to do so.[117] On a visit to Calcutta and Noahkhali, Wavell was unconvinced by attempts by the Deputy Inspector General of Police to defend his men against accusations of communal violence and lack of energy. In Chandpur they gave a 'not very convincing' account of why arrests had not been made earlier. 'I cannot believe', concluded Wavell, 'that the district officials had not a considerable amount of warning which ought to have put them on their guard; and when trouble did break out the measures taken seem to have been quite ineffective. The failure to send information more quickly to superior authorities seems to have been inexplicabe'.[118] Tuker gives only one instance of a provincial official in Bihar having known about the Bihar riots in advance.[119] That officials could not be relied upon was illustrated again in the UP, where police did not check people carrying spears, or mounted horsemen who were really destructive gangs, even when Congress workers drew attention to them.[120] The communal sympathies of the District Magistrate of Chittagong had been noted by British officials as early as Direct Action day.[121]

[115] Ibid.

[116] J.M.G. Bell, 'Note on recent experiences in Bengal', *J.M.G. Bell papers*, file 3, item 4.

[117] Burrows to Secretary of State, 18 November 1946, L/P&J/5/153.

[118] Wavell to Pethick-Lawrence, 5 November 1946, *TOP*, vol. 9, pp. 17–18.

[119] Tuker, *While Memory Serves*, p. 181.

[120] Statements by M. Sarabhai and Shah Nawaz Khan on 13 November 1946, AICC file no. 20, pp. 1–6 and 9–11 respectively.

[121] See also J.M.G. Bell, 'Note on recent experiences in Bengal', Bell papers, file 3, item 4.

Another aspect of the administrative problems involved in bringing the riots under control and in carrying out relief work is illustrated by the problem of bad communications and inadequate staff in Bihar, which had a population of 40 million but the same budget as Sind, which had a population of 4.5 million. With a population nearly ten times that of Sind it had only 50 per cent more police than in Sind where they were 'admittedly insufficient.'[122] In January 1946, Bihar had a permanent strength of 13,500 unarmed police, 5,000 armed police and 1,500 military police. This was then considered adequate for the '*normal* needs' of the province. At the same time 3 battalions of internal defence troops were located at Calcutta for use in Bengal, Bihar, Assam and Orissa with a population of over 100 million. The Bihar government had warned the Home Department of the Government of India that these troops were inadequate in a country 'which, even assuming there is a peaceful political settlement seems likely to be torn by communal strife, agrarian uprisings and labour trouble. . . .'[123]

Administrative inadequacy was illustrated when Dow visited the Mishouri district where 60 deaths had occurred. He found no motorable road to it and the only way to get there was by train up to a point and then walk. The road to another village was barely accessible by jeep, and it took an hour to get there. The village itself was off the road and had to be reached by walking through paddy fields. From the 1st November, when 200 Muslims had been massacred there, until the 27th, when Dow visited it himself, nobody had visited it on behalf of the government. 'There was simply no staff, high or low, who could be expected to do it except by neglecting some other duty equally or more important'. Dow did not specify what these might have been. It would be weeks before any police investigation could begin. If the police concentrated on prosecution, they would be diverted from ordinary administration of law and order.[124]

With an administration that was both inadequate and to some extent unreliable, and unable to suppress communal violence except with military help; with an increasing awareness that the adminis-

[122] Dow to Colville, 10/11 December 1946, *TOP*, vol. 9, pp. 328–9.

[123] Secret letter from J. Bowstead, Chief Secretary, Bihar Political Department to Secretary, Government of India, 22 January 1946, Home Police file no. 174/32/45. Emphasis in original.

[124] Dow to Colville, 10/11 December 1946, *TOP*, vol. 9, pp. 329–30.

tration was weak, if not broken down already, with communal passions rising even as news spread of atrocities committed on both communities, partition appeared inevitable by the end of 1946. Developments on the constitutional front confirmed this assumption, despite hopes by both Congress and the British that it could still be avoided.

CHAPTER 7

Prelude to Partition:
November 1946 to February 1947

Between November 1946 and February 1947, the League's attitude to the Interim Government, its attempt to overthrow by force the Unionist ministry in Punjab, its refusal to enter the Constituent Assembly and to accept the Cabinet Mission plan of 16 May 1946—all signified its intent to achieve Pakistan. During these months it also became clear that it would attain its objective as the British were bending over backwards to attract it into the Constituent Assembly, by making concessions to it and ignoring its incitements to violence. The hope of attaining independence for India as soon as possible made the Congress yield to the League and the British, and by remaining the Interim Government, it was caught in a maze of negotiations in which only Jinnah seemed to know where he was going; and the British, as arbiters between the League and Congress, were equally consistent in quickly putting aside old promises, but all the same making new ones in the fond hope that partition could be avoided. If not they still hoped their interests could be safeguarded.

The League never intended the interim government to work as its success would have weakened the case for Pakistan. Liaqat Ali Khan considered it a coalition only in the sense that it contained representatives to two parties; it was 'not a combination in the full sense'.[1] Jinnah also did not regard it as a coalition but only as containing two groups.[2] Indeed, the Interim Government was probably unique in that each party met separately before a cabinet meeting and there functioned in opposition to each other. In this they were not discouraged by Wavell, who saw members belonging to both parties separately, and regarded Congress complaints against the behaviour of the League as inspired by their pique that the League did not recognize Nehru as *de facto* Prime Minister.[3] As the League, un-

[1] Indian Conference in London, 4 December 1946, *TOP*, vol. 9, p. 264.
[2] *Dawn*, 15 November 1946.
[3] Indian Conference in London, 4 December 1946, *TOP*, vol. 9, p. 253.

like the Congress, wanted the Viceroy to retain his special powers, both Wavell and Whitehall were not displeased by differences between the two parties on this issue.[4]

The British believed that 'interference' by the interim government in provincial matters, especially in Muslim majority provinces, would further alienate the League and lessen the chances of its entering the government and the Constituent Assembly. So Wavell did not allow the cabinet to discuss the riots in Bengal and Bihar on the ground that they were a provincial matter.[5] In Sind, a League government which had lost its majority in the legislature was allowed to continue in office until fresh elections were held in November 1946. The constitutional course of calling on the Congress leader in the assembly, who could have commanded a majority, was not resorted to, because Jinnah would not have stood for a Congress government in a Muslim majority province.[6] Mudie allegedly tried to persuade Europeans to support the League and advised the League to offer more portfolios so as to attract waverers and their supporters.[7] Privately, Wavell did not have much faith in Mudie's judgment. But he defended his conduct. 'If what I consider a racket and a public scandal has your approval', rejoined an indignant Nehru, 'then it is obvious that our standards and sense of values differ considerably'.[8]

In the NWFP, the League organized demonstrations when Nehru, whose portfolio included tribal relations, visited the tribal areas. The Mullah of Manki was allowed to carry out religious propaganda among the tribes, and Nehru was lucky not to have been killed on his tour. The governor, Sir Olaf Caroe, made no effort to restrain the Mullah and the League. 'I think that in the circumstances, and given the fact that Nehru's tour was obviously intended to push the Congress cause, it would have been wrong to put active restraint against the League's propagandists going into tribal territory, and an attempt to do so would certainly have led to disturbances.'[9]

[4] Pethick-Lawrence to Attlee, 1 June 1946, PREM 8/247/1946.

[5] Wavell to Pethick-Lawrence, (T), 26 October 1946, *TOP*, vol. 8, p. 825.

[6] Wavell to Pethick-Lawrence, (T), 6 September 1946; Note by Turnbull and Monteath, 7 September 1946; Pethick-Lawrence to Wavell, (T), 8 September 1946, Ibid., pp. 429, 445 and 466 respectively.

[7] Nehru to Wavell, 5 September 1946, Ibid., p. 421.

[8] Nehru to Wavell, 23 September 1946, Ibid., p. 569.

[9] Caroe to Wavell, 23 October 1946, Ibid., p. 787.

To have to work with the League in the Interim Government was, then, no easy task for the Congress; and with the constitutional restrictions, imposed readily by Wavell, on the Interim Government 'interfering' in provincial matters, and with communal violence spreading in Bengal, the Congress was unhappy and frustrated with its position:

> 'Indeed I have come seriously to think whether it serves any useful purpose for me to be in the Interim Government if an important part of India sinks to barbarism or something much worse . . . . What is the good of our forming the Interim Government of India if all that we can do is to watch helplessly and do nothing else when thousands of people are being butchered and subjected to infinitely worse treatment?'[10]

In yet another attempt to cajole the League into the Constituent Assembly, the Labour government, in December 1946, invited representatives of the Congress, the League and the Sikhs to London for fresh discussions. At the same time, the Statement of 16 May was referred to Lord Jowitt, the Lord Chancellor, for a decision on the correct interpretation of paragraphs 15 and 19 of the statement.[11] Jowitt upheld the Mission's interpretation that provincial representatives would form sections, and that the sections—not the individual provinces—would settle provincial constitutions. The sections would also decide whether and to what extent a group constitution should be set up for any province.[12] In a new statement on 6 December, the Labour government announced that its intention had always been that the grouping decision should be taken by simple majority vote in sections. On other questions in the statement which might come up for interpretation, the Federal Court would be asked to decide matters of interpretation and the British government 'will accept such decision so that the procedure both in the Union Constituent Assembly and in the Sections may accord with the Cabinet Mission's Plan'. The Congress was requested to accept the statement so that the League might reconsider its attitude and enter the Constituent Assembly.[13]

Jinnah saw Pakistan being presented to him. Taking aside Baldev

[10] Nehru to Wavell, 15 October 1946, Ibid., pp. 732–3.

[11] Pethick-Lawrence to Lord Jowitt, 29 November 1946, L/P&J/10/111, pp. 100–4.

[12] Jowitt to Pethick-Lawrence, 2 December 1946, Ibid., pp. 47–8.

[13] Statement of 6 December 1946, *TOP*, vol. 9, pp. 295–6.

Singh, the Sikh representative at the London Conference, he offered him any guarantees the Sikhs might require. 'Baldev Singh, you see this matchbox. Even if Pakistan of this size is offered to me I will gladly accept it, but it is here that I need your collaboration. If you persuade the Sikhs to join hands with the Muslim League we will have a glorious Pakistan, the gates of which will be near about Delhi if not in Delhi itself.'[14] As Pethick-Lawrence had earlier perceived, what Jinnah wanted was not an assurance of the intentions of the Cabinet Mission but a guarantee that they would be enforced by the British. He replied to the Statement of 6 December that unless H.M.G. could guarantee that there would be a constitution on the lines recommended by the Cabinet Mission, details about the procedure of the Constituent Assembly were of no interest to him.[15] He would also not accept any decision of the Federal Court which went against him. He promised to call a meeting of his Council to consider that 6 December statement, but gave no assurance that he would ask them to reaccept the Statement of 16 May. The Congress protested that the British should have made their real intentions clear long ago. The Cabinet Mission had accepted the Congress interpretation of the 16 May statement and had told them that there would be no further amendment or change. The 6 December statement created a new situation for the Congress.[16]

On 9 December the Constituent Assembly opened without the League and without any communal incident. Gandhi opposed its meeting without the League, for such a Constituent Assembly was being held without agreement among Indians themselves, and under cover of British arms.[17] Nehru and Patel had reasons to disagree with Gandhi. In December the Assembly passed a resolution that India would be a sovereign, secular republic. The two leaders persuaded an indignant AICC to accept the Statement of 6 December

---

[14] Baldev Singh to Nehru, 18 September 1955, *NC*, quoted by Gopal, *Nehru*, vol. 1, p. 338.

[15] Secretary of State to Viceroy (T20252), 18 November 1946, L/P&J/10/76, pp. 293–4. See also Indian Conference in London, 4 December 1946, *TOP*, vol. 9, pp. 252–3.

[16] Indian Conference in London, 5 & 6 December 1946, L/P&J/10/111, pp. 60–1, 46–8. See also note of conversation between Jinnah and Wyatt on 9 December 1946; CAB 127/136. On Congress reaction, see also note of interview between Colville and Patel on 10 December 1946, L/P&J/10/76, pp. 59–61.

[17] Confidential notes by Gandhi dated 4 and 17 December 1946, AICC file no. 71, 1946–7, pp. 60 and 61 respectively.

to keep the Constituent Assembly alive. For the significant point about the Constituent Assembly was that it could not be dissolved by the British except by force. It was a weapon with which independence could be achieved. If the Congress rejected it, the British might withdraw the Mission Plan and give the League Pakistan.[18] The Assembly could not, in any case, function without the League or impose a constitution on unwilling provinces. Acceptance of the 6 December statement was 'definitely a climb-down on the part of the Congress but for the good of the people of India principles have sometimes to be swalloed for the sake of expediency'.[19] It appears that Congress leaders thought that Jinnah and the League would enter the Constituent Assembly if they accepted the 6 December statement, which would create some sort of Pakistan within a federation. An unsigned note, probably by J.B. Kripalani, then Congress president, suggests that the Congress favoured accepting the Mission plan with the joint interpretation of it between themselves and Jinnah. Assam, NWFP and Baluchistan would probably secede from Groups B and C, which would frame what group constitutions they could 'inspite of the seceders'. If the British set up or recognized another Constituent Assembly, they would 'damn themselves for ever'. They were duty bound to leave India 'when' a constitution was framed in accordance with the Mission Plan. This was not playing into Jinnah's hands.

The Assembly would frame a constitution for the whole of India and the constitution would contain a specific clause showing in what way boycotters could avail of the constitution.[20] The note is important, because it shows that the Congress had strong hopes that their acceptance of the 6 December statement would bring the League into the Constituent Assembly, and a constitution for a united India would emerge. The confidence of the Congress is suggested by the phrase that the British were 'bound *when* a constitution is framed'; 'if' would have reflected uncertainty.

Even as the Congress debated the 6 December statement, the Labour government had realized the full import of Jinnah's refusal to enter the Constituent Assembly, and the real reason for it—their reluctance to guarantee the procedure of the Constituent Assembly.

[18] *Statesman*, 7 January 1947. *National Herald*, 7 January 1947.
[19] Confidential AICC note, 29 December 1946, probably by Kripalani, AICC file no. G-66, 1946–1947, pp. 149–50.
[20] Ibid.

As the Constituent Assembly met on 9 December, the 'pressure of events' was leading to Pakistan.[21] A withdrawal announcement might still echo of scuttle, but the minutes of the India and Burma Committee meeting on 31 December 1946 are worth quoting, for they show how Labour ministers transformed the political alternative they had hitherto construed as defeat into a moral and political triumph.

'The general feeling of the Cabinet was that withdrawal from India need not appear to be forced upon us by our weakness nor to be the first step in the dissolution of the Empire. On the contrary this action *must be shown to be* the logical conclusion, which we welcomed, of a policy followed by successive Governments for many years . . . . There was, therefore, no occasion to excuse our withdrawal: *we should rather claim credit* for terminating British rule in India and transferring our responsibilities to the representatives of the Indian people.'[22]

But Attlee's heart was not in the announcement, and even as the cabinet decided that the withdrawal statement would be made soon after the British parliament met on 21 January 1947,[23] he was looking for a way out of it. The Congress resolution of 6 January 1947 accepting the 6 December statement obviously renewed his hopes that the League might enter the Constituent Assembly, and a political breakdown avoided. On 8 January, the cabinet decided against making any announcement with a view to overcoming the League's refusal to enter the Constituent Assembly.[24]

But there was no sign of the League entering the assembly. Liaqat Ali Khan said that the Congress resolution of 6 January did not constitute 'true acceptance' of the Mission Plan,[25] and Muslim Leaguers continued their diatribe against the interim government and the Congress. The activities of the League's National Guards increased communal tension in many provinces,[26] and in Sind, Mudie had to tell his League ministers that there was no point in a

---

[21] India and Burma Committee meetings on 11 and 17 December 1946, CAB 134/342.

[22] Confidential annex to Cabinet C.M. (46) 108th conclusions, 31 December 1946, CAB 128/8.

[23] India and Burma Committee meeting on 20 December 1946 CAB 134/343.

[24] India and Burma Committee meeting on 8 January 1947, CAB 134/342.

[25] Wavell's note on interview with Liaqat Ali Khan, 7 January 1947, *TOP*, vol. 9, p. 481.

[26] See, for example, *Eastern Times*, 2 January 1947, *Dawn*, 5, 10 and 15 January 1947.

Muslim League private army fighting the police of a League administration.[27] On 31 January 1947, the Working Committee of the Muslim League decided that it would remain outside the assembly; that the proceedings of the present assembly were illegal and that it should be dissolved. The Council of the League would therefore not meet to reconsider the Direct Action resolution.

That Jinnah was largely responsible for the resolution was suggested by Mudie's comment that provincial Leaguers in Sind would go by what Jinnah said on an all-India matter;[28] and Wavell himself perceived that other Leaguers would not go against Jinnah.[29] The refusal to withdraw the direct action resolution meant that the League was in opposition to the Cabinet Mission Plan, including the Interim Government formed under that plan and of which it was a member.

The intentions of the League were now made clear in the Punjab. The communal situation had been worsening in the Punjab since October 1946, so that by 29 November, Jenkins had to use his discretionary powers under section 89 of the Act of 1935 to promulgate the Punjab Public Safety Ordinance.[30] Khizar himself was shocked by the deterioration in communal relations coming in the wake of communal riots in Bengal, Bihar and the UP, and on 24 January 1947, he passed with the approval of Jenkins, an ordinance banning the RSS and the Muslim League National Guards under the Criminal Law Amendment Act.[31] Such declarations were always followed by routine searches of party offices. The searches passed off without incident except in Lahore where Muslim Leaguers who had obstructed the police had to be arrested under Section 353 of the Indian Penal Code. They refused to apply for bail. The arrests were followed by disturbances in Lahore on 25 and 26 January. On 25 January, 15 MLAs defied the ban on processions and meetings in two separate batches and also had to be arrested.[32] The League alleged that the ban on the National Guards was an attack on the Muslim League. Ghazanfar Ali, still a member of the Interim Gov-

---

[27] Mudie to Wavell, 22 January 1947, L/P&J/5/263.

[28] Mudie to Wavell, 8 January 1947, Ibid., p. 489.

[29] Wavell to Pethick-Lawrence, 14 January 1947, Ibid., p. 502.

[30] Jenkins to Wavell, 30 November 1946, Ibid., p. 229.

[31] Jenkins to Pethick-Lawrence, 26 January 1947, Ibid., pp 556–7; *Eastern Times*, 25 January 1947.

[32] Jenkins to Pethick-Lawrence, (T), 26 January 1947, *TOP*, vol. 9, p. 556.

ernment, warned that the Punjab Ministry's action could endanger the peace of the province 'to an extent which cannot be foreseen'.[33] Jinnah expressed 'shock' at the ban on the National Guards and the arrests of provincial League leaders. If there was 'one more mad and inimical action against the Muslim League' by the Punjab government, the reaction all over India would be 'terrific'. He appealed to the Viceroy to intervene and 'save the situation which may otherwise take a very serious turn for which the entire responsibility will rest with the Viceroy and His Majesty's Government'.[34]

Jenkins pointed out that the National Guards had a written constitution of their own and a commander with military titles. They were a party army on the same lines as Hitler's Brown Shirts. All National Guards were presumably members of the League but the converse was not true.[35] There was no need for a similar ban on Congress volunteers as they were not an organized body in the Punjab. The *Akali Jathas* had existed for many years. They were formed *ad hoc* and were not active. The INA was not worth banning from a communal point of view.[36]

Khizar withdrew the ban on 27 January to show that he was not biased against the League as a party. But the demonstrations did not stop. Hartals, meetings and processions were organized in many cities and were most successful in Multan, Lahore, Gujrat and Jullundur.[37] Processionists would shout slogans such as '*Khizar Wizarat murdabad*'.[38] Those taking part in the demonstrations were usually politicians and their wives, and Muslims in rural areas belonging to the poorer classes. The agitation had the sympathy of most Muslims, official and non-official. The processionists made it clear that their aim was to establish Pakistan.[39] Jenkins believed— and Nazimuddin confirmed this—that the aim of the demonstrators was to overthrow Khizar's government by force. The searches on the 24th gave them a starting point. There was evidence that an agitation would have started on 8 February.[40] According to Jenkins,

---

[33] *Eastern Times*, 26 January 1947.
[34] *Eastern Times*, 29 January 1947.
[35] Jenkins to Pethick-Lawrence, (T), 26 January 1947, *TOP*, vol. 9, p. 557.
[36] Jenkins to Wavell, 28 January 1947, Ibid., p. 570.
[37] See for example, *Eastern Times*, 29 January 1947; *Statesman*, 28 January 1947.
[38] *Civil and Military Gazette*, 28 January 1947.
[39] Jenkins to Wavell, 8 February 1947, *TOP*, vol. 9, p. 654.
[40] Jenkins to Wavell, 15 February and 28 February 1947, L/P&J/5/250.

the main grievance of the League was its failure to form a ministry after winning a majority in the provincial elections of 1946. He thought there might be some truth in the allegation made by Leaguers that they were being victimized by officials, but equally there was evidence of many officials using their influence in favour of the League during the election campaign, and most Muslim officials appeared to sympathize with the League's agitation in the Punjab. It was also likely that Khizar was not conferring on Leaguers rewards such as *jagirs* because of their political hostility. But this was more a question of witholding benefits than of interfering in legitimate rights.[41]

Provincial Leaguers boasted that there had been no communal incidents during the demonstrations, and that this indicated Hindu and Sikh support for them. But this was probably due to the tendency of other communities to abstain from attacks on a government in which they were represented. Restrictions on the press, the exemplary conduct of Sikh leaders who restrained their followers, also prevented the non-Muslim minorities from organizing counter-demonstrations which could have easily degenerated into communal violence. But Hindus and Sikhs were fearful of the Pakistan that the demonstrators clamoured for, especially as the League would give them no assurance about its meaning; and the widespread belief that Muslim Raj was round the corner had a deplorable effect on communal feeling.[42]

Jinnah gave his blessings to the agitation.[43] Liaqat expected the Punjab ministry to fall as a result of the League's show of force. It was an example, he said, of what the League could do all over India although 'I couldn't guarantee that it would always remain non-violent'.[44] The despatch of a batch of National Guards from Bihar under their provincial commander to the Punjab to defy the Public Safety Ordinance[45] could suggest the connivance of the central leadership of the League in the agitation in the Punjab. In any case, the activities of the National Guard must have been known to the leadership, and may well have taken place in accordance with its instructions.

[41] Jenkins to Wavell, 15 February 1947, *TOP*, vol. 9, pp. 721–2.
[42] Jenkins to Wavell, 28 February 1947, L/P&J/5/250.
[43] Jinnah to Mamdot, 23 February 1947, S. Jafri (ed.) *Qaid-e-Azam Jinnah's Correspondence with Punjab Muslim Leaders*, pp. 233–7.
[44] *Eastern Times*, 2 February 1947.   [45] HP file no. 33/9/47, p. 94.

Wavell did not reprimand the League for the Punjab demonstrations. The British simply did not know what to do. Compliance with the Mission Plan would mean acquiescing to the Congress demand to remove the League from the interim government. But the British would then be placed in the uncomfortable position of lining up with the Congress against the League. Having earlier acknowledged the validity of a Constituent Assembly, which included only the Congress,[46] the cabinet now contended that an assembly without the League could not be regarded as conforming to the Mission Plan. But it would not be 'practical politics' to disregard it altogether as the Congress might then start civil disobedience,[47] which would plunge the British into the confrontation they had tried to avoid for a year. With the League in active opposition to the Mission Plan as well as the British, political breakdown loomed large. There was only one card to be played, and on 5 February the cabinet decided to issue a withdrawal statement as a 'last attempt' to bring to the Indian parties the 'realities' of the situation. Overturning its earlier objections to Wavell's proposals, the cabinet now justified an announcement on the very grounds on which Wavell had been dismissed.[48] On 11 February, Mountbatten's insistence that Attlee fix a terminal date for the Raj clinched the issue, and two days later, Attlee informed the cabinet that he was 'satisfied' that no announcement would be effective unless the British specified a time limit.[49]

On 20 February 1947, the British announced on the first and penultimate occasion the date for a final transfer of authority to Indians. Urged on a vacillating Labour government as a consequence of the weakness of the British administrative machine by Wavell, and then, after December 1946 by Mountbatten, who made it a condition of the acceptance of his appointment as Viceroy,[50] it

---

[46] Downing Street meeting, 23 September 1946, L/P&J/10/45.

[47] India and Burma Committee meeting, 5 February 1947, CAB 134/343. For the developments leading to Wavell's dismissal, See Moore, *Escape from Empire*, pp. 202–14.

[48] Confidential annex to cabinet meeting on 13 February 1947, CAB 128/11, and my 'Decolonization in India: The Statement of 20 February 1947', *International History Review*, May 1984, pp. 191–209.

[49] Ibid., and undated note by Mountbatten, (probably around 11 February 1947), *TOP*, vol. 9, p. 674.

[50] Wavell to Pethick-Lawrence, 3 February 1947; Mountbatten to Attlee, 7 January 1947; Attlee to Mountbatten, 16 January 1947; Mountbatten to Cripps, 26 January 1947, Ibid., pp. 595–602, 483, 506, 553 respectively.

was fixed for 30 June 1948. The statement expressed the hope that the Indian parties would work out a constitution by then. If not, the British government would consider 'to whom the powers of the Central Government . . . should be handed over . . . whether as a whole to some form of Central Government . . . or in some areas to the existing Provincial Governments, or in such other way as may seem most reasonable and in the best interests of the Indian people'.[51]

There remained only the need to formulate a strategy to justify the statement in parliament. Mountbatten's insistence may have been the immediate occasion for fixing a terminal date for the Raj, but there was no doubt about the underlying reasons for doing so. The historical and rhetorical part of the statement, confided Attlee to Mountbatten, was needed to keep the opposition in Britain quiet. Accordingly,

> 'While nothing should be said which would suggest that *we are not in a position to prevent Indian parties from seizing power themselves*; it should be pointed out that the problem of transferring power into Indian hands has been exhaustively discussed and progressively effected . . . there must be some date beyond which British administration cannot be continued: that the advice from reasonable authorities in India is that British rule could not be maintained on its existing basis after 1948.'[52]

In the Commons debate on 5 March 1947, Cripps rhetorically posed the question whether, in the absence of agreement between Indians, 'could we have been in any way able to discharge our responsibilities after that later date?' Yet, as Henry Raikes, the Conservative MP from Liverpool, discerned, Cripps had said that one alternative was to fix a terminal date, the other was to carry on for some years. It was impracticable to go on. 'Thus in effect he did not put up any alternative. In effect, he merely said bluntly that there is no possible alternative other than to run out of India, irrespective of to whom we hand over, in the course of the next 16 months.'[53] Henry Raikes's interpretation was confirmed by Wavell's summing up of the advantages to the British of an early withdrawal:

---

[51] Statement of 20 February 1947, Ibid., pp. 773–5.
[52] Annex to India and Burma Committee meeting on 24 February 1947, L/P&J/10/77. Emphasis mine.
[53] *Hansard*, vol. 434, 1947, cols. 504–9, 541.

'We should . . .thus avoid being responsible for, and probably involved in, any widespread breakdown of law and order which may result from the communal situation or from labour troubles induced by revolutionary teaching or economic conditions. *The worst danger for us* is an anti-European movement which might result in the killing of some of our nationals, and of our having to carry out an ignominous forced withdrawal, instead of leaving in our own time and voluntarily.'[54]

As yet another attempt to get the League into the Constituent Assembly, the statement was a conspicuous failure. Even as the Congress hailed it as 'a courageous document'[55] Jinnah declared that the League would 'not yield an inch' in its demand for Pakistan and that the existing Constituent Assembly was dead.[56] Other Leaguers talked of a transfer of power to two sovereign states.[57] An editorial in *Dawn* welcomed the Statement of 20 February but criticized the British government for

'fighting shy of saying clear things clearly. They might as well have stated categorically that agreements would be entered into with the Congress for the Hindu majority areas and with the Muslim League for the Muslim majority areas. If paragraph 13 has any meaning this is the only manner in which agreements for the transfer of power can be successfully negotiated.'[58]

In the Punjab, the League started a new direct action movement, stopping trains, hauling down Congress flags and the Union Jack from public buildings and using violence in some towns, including Amritsar, Lahore, Multan and Jullundur.[59] Seeking to end the agitation as he believed that the Statement of 20 February had made the Unionist ministry politically irrelevant, Khizar tried to reach an agreement with provincial Leaguers. The terms were approved of or dictated by Jinnah. The ban on carrying arms and wearing uniforms would remain, but private armies could be maintained as a right. Direct action by the opposition was a legitimate weapon against a constitutional government, and special powers would not be used to prevent outbreaks of violence.[60]

[54] Wavell to King George VI, 24 February 1947, *TOP*, vol. 9, p. 809.
[55] Wavell to Pethick-Lawrence, 22 February 1947, Ibid., p. 785.
[56] *Civil and Military Gazette*, 25 February 1947.
[57] Abell to Harris, (T), 25 February 1947, *TOP*, vol. 9, p. 813.
[58] *Dawn*, 21 February 1947.
[59] Jenkins to Pethick-Lawrence, 25 February 1947, *TOP*, vol. 9, p. 814.
[60] Jenkins to Wavell, 28 February 1947, L/P&J/5/250, pp. 78ff.

Dawn described a new movement in the Punjab as 'imminent', for

> 'nothing short of Punjab's sovereign independence. The vast army of Punjabis who will have had training and gained valuable experience in this non-violent struggle may soon be called out to launch a new one. That may well require new techniques, with harsher things than the lathi, the tear gas, and the prison cell awaiting the fighters at the end of their day's work.'[61]

The League also started direct action in the NWFP. Its propaganda suggested that it would achieve Pakistan by shedding blood.[62] The Bengal Muslim League started sending volunteers to Assam.[63] The League's aim was apparently to capture power in the Punjab, NWFP and Assam by force. The Statement of 20 February gave the parties no incentive to come to an agreement, for it promised power either to the centre or to the provinces. If the League could capture power in these provinces it would get Pakistan as of right. Interestingly, Pethick-Lawrence expressed satisfaction at the agreement between Khizar and the League in the Punjab. 'If the Punjab Muslims are, in the last resort, with the League then I think it is really better that fact should be exposed . . . The League have so much to gain by getting into office in the Punjab that I should think the Sikhs could get pretty good terms from them, and if a Muslim League/Sikh coalition does emerge the problems of handing over to more than one authority, if we are driven to that, will be a great deal simplified.'[64]

But the League made no attempt to assuage the fears of the Hindus and Sikhs about the nature of Pakistan, presumably because it intended to use force. The British had always turned a blind eye to its intransigence, partly because they welcomed Congress and League differences on many issues, partly because of their belief that the Congress was out to dominate everybody else, that Jinnah only sought 'justice' for Muslims, that they could not transfer pow-

---

[61] *Dawn*, 25 February 1947.

[62] Caroe to Wavell, 22 February 1947, L/P&J/5/224. Fortnightly reports for NWFP for first and second half March 1947, HP file no. 18/3/47.

[63] FR for Bengal for first half of March 1947, HP file no. 18/3/47, FR for Assam for first half of March 1947, and Clow to Wavell, 3 April 1947, L/P&J/5/140, FR for NWFP for second half of March 1947, L/P&J/5/224. See also *Eastern Times*, 12 March 1947.

[64] Secretary of State to Viceroy, 27 February 1947, R/3/1/105, p. 108a.

er to only one party; and partly because it was in their own interest to transfer power to an undivided India. The fixing of a terminal date for the *Raj* in the 20 February statement, far from leading to an agreement between the League and Congress, proved the signal for an attempt to carve out Pakistan by direct action by the League.

CHAPTER 8

Divide and Quit

The League celebrated 2 March as 'Victory Day' following the settlement with Khizar. On the same day Khizar announced the resignation of his government because he felt that the Statement of 20
February obliterated the boundaries between the central and provincial spheres of administration and made it incumbent on him to
leave the field clear for the League to come to an agreement with
other parties. A coalition which included the League was essential
for the communal safety of the Punjab, and the League would not
negotiate with the minorities as long as the Unionists acted as a buf-
fer between them and the Hindus and Sikhs.[1] Khizar's resignation
symbolized the capitulation of one of the greatest bastions of intercommunal provincialism to the political weight of the League at the
Centre.

Khizar's resignation shocked his non-Muslim colleagues, who
immediately declared that they would not cooperate with a Muslim
League government.[2] The Panthic Party passed a resolution opposing the establishment of a Muslim League government, 'so long as
its object is Pakistan or Muslim domination of the Punjab, the
homeland of the Sikhs'. As he came out of the party meeting, Tara
Singh brandished his kirpan and shouted, *'Pakistan murdabad!'*[3]
(Death to Pakistan).

The attitude of provincial Congress and Sikh leaders was provocative and hysterical. But it was explicable because the League's
attitude during its agitation against the Khizar coalition was one of
arrogance towards the minorities and it had never given them any
indication of what Pakistan meant or what it might offer them in return for support. The League, as Jenkins pointed out, had also set a
foreboding precedent by overthrowing a popular ministry by force,
and, after the announcement of 20 February, had made every suggestion that it would capture the Punjab by any means.[4]

[1] Governor of Punjab to Viceroy, (T), 3 March 1947, R/3/1/89, p. 4. See also
Jenkins to Wavell, 3 March 1947, Ibid., p. 5.
[2] Jenkins to Wavell, 3 March 1947, Ibid.
[3] *Civil and Military Gazette*, 4 March 1947.
[4] Note by Jenkins dated 16 April 1947, file no. R/3/1/90, pp. 12–13.

On 4 March Hindu and Sikh students took out a procession through the main part of Lahore shouting '*Pakistan Murdabad*', '*Jinnah Murdabad*'[5] and according to *Dawn*, '*Allaho-Akbar murdabad*'.[6] Rioting broke out in Lahore and Multan, and Khizar resigned as caretaker Prime Minister, chiefly because his ministry could not control the situation.[7]

The provincial Muslim League leader, the Nawab of Mamdot, was unable to form a government. Jenkins was suspicious of his claim to have the support of 10 Unionists, including Khizar, and asked him to produce a complete list of his supporters. The claim proved false, so the next day, Jenkins decided to go into Section 93 under the 1935 Act until Mamdot could form a ministry.[8] Mamdot stalled in keeping his appointment with the Governor, and asked him to accept his assertion that the League would command a majority in the legislature. But without evidence that he did in fact have a majority, Jenkins would not let him form a government. The installation of such a ministry would 'be a fraud' on the constitution and the Instrument of Instructions. 'I should simply be inviting one of the Parties to . . . communal conflict to assume charge of it without even satisfying myself of its Parliamentary competence to do so.'[9]

Jenkins' reluctance to allow a League ministry was strengthened by reports of attacks on non-Muslims which were being carried out in the name of the League in several districts of the Punjab, including Rawalpindi, Attock, Multan and Chakwal. Following the provocative speeches made by Hindu and Sikh Leaders on 3 March, he had expected, at the most, rioting in one or two towns. 'What shocked the non-Muslims of the Punjab, and most of the officials, was the savage outbreak of rioting in the Rawalpindi Division and the Multan district.'[10] The rioting was on a scale never seen before in British India, and was characterized by extreme and sadistic vio-

---

[5] *Statesman*, 6 March 1947, and Note by General Messervy, enclosed in *Auchinleck* to Abell, 22 March 1947, *TOP*, vol. 9, p. 1005.

[6] *Dawn*, 14 March 1947.

[7] FR for Punjab for the first half of March 1947, L/P&J/5/250, and *Civil and Military Gazette*, 6 March 1947.

[8] Mamdot to Jenkins, 5 March 1947, R/3/1/176, p. 19; and Jenkins to Mamdot, 5 March 1947, Ibid.

[9] Governor of Punjab to Viceroy, 5 March 1947, (T 28-G), Ibid., pp. 21–2.

[10] Note by Jenkins of interview with Mamdot and Daultana on 29 March 1947, Ibid., p. 165.

lence. In the rural areas large Muslim mobs banded together from several villages to destroy, loot and kill Sikhs and Hindus. Women and children were hacked or beaten to death and burned alive. There were a number of cases of forcible conversions and forced marriages.[11] In Rawalpindi the attacks were directed against the Sikhs. By 8 March Hindus and Sikhs were being evacuated from Muslim majority districts including Attock, Mianwali, Gujrat.[12]

Officials had no doubt that the attacks on non-Muslims were planned and aimed at exterminating the Hindu and Sikh population. One element of planning was evident from the fact that Muslims would hoist white flags on their houses and then invite Muslim mobs from the neighbouring villages to attack the property not so marked. Hindus and Sikhs were invited to join peace committees and subsequently murdered.[13] Ex-soldiers and pensioners, including VCOs and Honorary Commissioned officers, led the attacks in many areas.[14] That hand grenades, tommy guns and rifles were frequently employed suggested that military deserters and demobilized soldiers played a leading role. The three districts worst affected—Rawalpindi, Mianwali and Attock sent up the greatest number of recruits during the war.[15]

Jenkins discounted the charge that officials had failed to do their duty.[16] There is, however, no reason to accept these denials unquestioningly, simply because the allegations were usually made by Indians. A personal friend of Attlee saw police stand aside in Rawalpindi as Muslims massacred Sikhs.[17] Penderel Moon recollects that not a shot was fired by the police as the two principal bazaars in Amritsar were destroyed and looting went on in almost every part of the city. In Multan many private houses of Hindus were set on fire and 'the inmates had the choice of perishing in the flames or

[11] Note by Messervy, *TOP*, vol. 9, p. 1006.

[12] *Eastern Times*, 18 March 1947.

[13] See Note by Messervy, *TOP*, vol. 9, p. 1006; Jenkins to Wavell, 17 March 1947, R/3/1/89, p. 141; Statement by A.A. Macdonald, Home Secretary, Punjab, in *Civil and Military Gazette*, 11 March 1947.

[14] Jenkins to Wavell, 17 March 1947, R/3/1/89, p. 132; also Auchinleck to Abell, 8 April 1947, R/3/1/176, p. 136.

[15] Letter from Mr. Arthur Williams to author, 22 March 1981, and *Statesman*, 23 March 1947.

[16] Memorandum by Jenkins, enclosed in Jenkins to Mountbatten, 4 August 1947, R/3/1/89, pp. 234–5.

[17] Col. Reginald Schoenberg to Attlee, 11 May 1947, *Attlee Papers*, Box 7.

running the gauntlet of a murderous mob awaiting them below.'[18] The district magistrate of Siria village was informed at 6 p.m. that the village was on fire. Yet it was not until 10 p.m. that he decided to visit the village which lay at a ten minute drive from his headquarters.[19] However, the allegation that districts headed by British officials came out worse in the rioting cannot be substantiated. In Rawalpindi, the Divisional Commissioner, the DIG Police, the Deputy Commissioner and the Superintendent of Police were all British. The Deputy Commissioners of Attock and Jhelum were both Indian when the trouble began, and they had a British and an Indian Superintendent of Police respectively. In Lahore Division, the Commissioner was Indian; the DIG police, the Deputy Commissioner and senior police officers were all British.[20]

The task of the administration was not made easier by the attitude of provincial party leaders. First, there was the complacency of Leaguers. Ghazanfar Ali, still a member of the interim government and perhaps acting under Jinnah's instructions, denied that the League had anything to do with the disturbances in Rawalpindi and suggested to Jenkins that a League ministry be put into power. He also expressed concern that the new Central Powers ordinance, which gave the army more powers to control disturbances, might turn popular feeling against the army.

'I was exasperated by Raja Ghazanfar Ali's complacency [wrote Jenkins] and dealt with him rather roughly. I said he did not appear to realize that what had happened in Rawalpindi, Attock and the Chakwal Sub-Division was a general massacre of the most beastly kind . . . . The massacre had been conducted in the name of the Muslim League and senior Military officers thought that it had been carefully planned and organized.'[21]

The League, Jenkins told Firoz Khan Noon, must realize that 'a brutal massacre had been conducted in their name.' The remedy lay in a recognition of the facts and the expression of repentance in some practical form; the League must realize it had never made any attempt to maintain peace or to win over the minorities.[22]

[18] Moon, *Divide and Quit*, pp. 78, 79–81.
[19] Cutting from *Hindustan Times*, undated, HP file no. 33/11/47, p. 97.
[20] Memorandum by Jenkins, enclosed in Jenkins to Mountbatten, 4 August 1947, file no. R/3/1/89, pp. 22, 27–8.
[21] Note by Jenkins of interview with Ghazanfar Ali, 20 March 1947, R/3/1/76.
[22] Note by Jenkins on interview with Noon, 24 March 1947, Ibid.

Meanwhile, Mamdot remained unable to form a ministry. Nor did the League make any attempt to win over the Hindu and Sikh minorities in the Punjab. Some Sikh leaders expressed willingness to discuss an arrangement if the League made an open effort to stop the outrages at Rawalpindi and Multan, and obtained authority from their high command to negotiate freely with other parties in the Punjab.[23] But Mamdot could give no indication of Jinnah's attitude.[24] Jinnah's attitude was clear by his declaration that the League ought to be allowed to form a ministry.[25] Both Wavell and Jenkins thought Mamdot was acting under Jinnah's instructions and Jenkins believed that the League's attitude was intelligible only on the assumption that it believed that if it came to power it could seize and hold the Punjab by force.[26] By May both Jinnah and Liaqat Ali Khan were 'most bitter' that the League had not been allowed to form a ministry in the Punjab.[27]

An inference at the intentions of the central leadership of the League can be drawn by its support for direct action in the NWFP and Assam. On 21 February a large League procession formed in Peshawar city, overpowered the police and broke into the Congress Premier's house. Police had eventually to resort to firing. Communal trouble spread to the rural areas around Peshawar and in Hazara district there were forcible conversions of Sikhs, and burning of gurdwaras.[28] The movement had Jinnah's blessings.[29] Meanwhile, Muslim League National Guards carried out 'direct action' and incited Muslims to violence in Assam.[30]

The part played by the National Guards in the Punjab, the NWFP and Assam, and earlier in the UP and Bengal, raises once again the question of how far their activities were directed by the central leadership of the League itself. Discussing their role in Bengal, J.D. Tyson, then Secretary to the Governor of Bengal, observed

---

[23] Governor of Punjab to Viceroy, (T), 11 March 1947, R/3/1/89, p. 99.

[24] Governor of Punjab to Viceroy, 13 March 1947 (T 43-G), file no. R/3/1/89, p. 105.

[25] *Civil and Military Gazette*, 14 March 1947 and *Eastern Times*, 14 March 1947.

[26] Note by Abell (?), 8 March 1947, R/3/1/89, p. 51; and Viceroy to Governor of Punjab, (T), 8 March 1947, Ibid., p. 54; Jenkins to Mountbatten, 15 May 1947, Ibid., p. 205.

[27] Viceroy to Governor of Punjab, 5 May 1947, Ibid., p. 195.

[28] Caroe to Wavell, (T), 13 March 1947, *TOP*, vol. 9, pp. 930–1.

[29] FR for NWFP for first half of May 1947, L/P&J/5/224.

[30] Clow to Mountbatten, 3 April 1947, L/P&J/5/140.

that the Guards were organized on an all-India basis and were not subject to the ministry 'or even the party in Bengal' (or indeed of any provincial party).[31] Commenting on the communal massacres in the Punjab, *Dawn* admitted that 'here and there Muslims may have overstepped the limits of self-defence and indulged in disproportionate retaliation.' But people who threatened Muslims and who were now blaming them 'because events have belied their expectations, betray cowardice of a very low order'![32]

Jenkins often implied that the League was responsible for the massacres of the Hindus and Sikhs.[33] Probably quoting official sources, the *Times* reported on 17 March 1947 that the 'chief offenders were said to have been the Muslim League National Guards'.[34] If these beliefs were well-founded, then the question is what the League hoped to accomplish. Initially the disturbances were aimed at ousting Khizar's ministry, and the League must have thought it would then be able to form a government. At another level, Jenkins thought that the massacres were a response to the Congress resolution calling for the partition of the Punjab. Both these explanations imply that the League wanted to take over the whole province before June 1948, under the terms of the 20 February statement, and that it believed that it would hold the Punjab by force.[35] This could also explain why the Sikhs formed the main target of the League's National Guards—some brutish, mindless notion of wiping out the obstacle (Sikhs) to achieve the end (Pakistan) probably prevailed. Jenkins discounted the League's claim to form a ministry and introduced Section 93 as it did not have a legislative majority; and Leaguers from Jinnah and Liaqat Ali Khan downwards alleged that Muslims were being persecuted by officials trying to restore order—an allegation that Jenkins dismissed, as intelligence reports made it clear that the Muslim majority, acting in

---

[31] Note by J.D. Tyson, 18 April 1947, and Burrows to Mountbatten, 22 April 1947, R/3/2/59A, pp. 48 and 41–2 respectively.

[32] *Dawn*, 20 March 1947.

[33] Governor of Punjab to Viceroy, (T 35-G), 8 March 1947, R/3/1/89, p. 56; Notes by Jenkins of interviews with Noon on 24 March 1947, with Mamdot and Daultana on 29 March 1947, with Mamdot and Shaukat Hyat Khan on 16 May 1947, R/3/1/176, pp. 55, 63–5, 205, 163 respectively; and Jenkins to Mountbatten, 14 May 1947, R/3/1/89, p. 198.

[34] *Times*, 17 March 1947.

[35] Governor of Punjab to Viceroy, 15 May 1947, R/3/1/89, p. 205.

the name of the Muslim League, had been the aggressors.[36] Jenkins was convinced that one of the aims of the organized violence, which continued after 3 June 1947, was simply to discredit his administration. Two days before the transfer of power, he wrote to Mountbatten:

'Many of the Leaguers are remarkably smug. They say that as soon as the British leave peace will be restored. It has long been rumoured that Daultana and the like intended to make as much trouble as possible during the last few weeks before the transfer of power so as to discredit the British regime. If this is so, it does not seem to have been appreciated that if all Muslim outrages stop in Lahore on the morning of 15th August, it will for practical purposes be clear that the local butchery was organized by the leaders themselves.'[37]

The communal violence demonstrated the impotence of the Raj in maintaining law and order. The decline in the performance of the services had become obvious during the League's agitation in January and February 1947 when they took no action against Leaguers who defied the ban on processions and meetings. British officers, uncertain of their future allegedly told Indians who came to them for help to go to their future rulers, the Congress and the League![38] That the police were infected by communalism was illustrated not only by the reluctance of Muslim administrators against Muslim mobs but also by the fact that police weeded out for corruption in Amritsar resigned and joined the Muslim League.[39] A few days before the transfer of power, the situation worsened in Amritsar and Lahore as the Hindu Superintendent of Police in Amritsar disarmed the Muslim Police, and, according to a British report, Sikh and Hindu police declined to protect the Muslims from attacks by their co-religionists.[40] Already by June 1947, Jenkins had concluded:

[36] Governor of Punjab to Viceroy, 8 March 1947, (T 35-G); Jenkins to Wavell, 17 March 1947; Jenkins to Mountbatten, 4 August 1947; R/3/1/89, pp. 56, 131 ff., 221 respectively. See also Note by Jenkins of interview with F.K. Noon, 24 March 1947; and with Liaqat Ali Khan on 26 May 1947, R/3/1/176, pp. 55, 185 respectively; and Liaqat Ali Khan to Mountbatten, 15 April 1947 and Jenkins' note of 16 April 1947, R/3/1/90, pp. 5–10, 12–6 respectively.

[37] Jenkins to Mountbatten, 13 August 1947, L/P&J/5/250, p. 6.

[38] Statement by J.P. Narain, 21 March 1947, HP file no. 33/11/47.

[39] Jenkins to Mountbatten, 25 June 1947, R/3/1/176, p. 212.

[40] Memorandum by Minister of State for Commonwealth Relations, 3 September 1947, to India and Burma Committee, CAB 13/346.

'So far as the services are concerned, we are going through a very difficult period, with some men yearning to leave India, others trying to please new masters, and others again upset and apprehensive. The old administrative machine is rapidly falling to pieces.'[41]

Jenkins probably faced the toughest task that any provincial government had faced until March 1947. In the past communal violence had seldom occurred in two places simultaneously. The administration had been able to concentrate its resources and to come down very heavily on each outbreak as it occurred.

But when outbreaks were widespread, it was impossible to make reinforcements at all points and district officers and military commanders were left to deal with each situation as it occurred. Only five days after the outbreak of rioting in Lahore, the Army Commander told Jenkins that if trouble developed in the rural areas of a large number of districts 'it would be virtually uncontrollable'. The administration had little experience of large-scale disturbances in rural areas with bad communications. Conditions in many of the villages were unknown, since they were approachable only by bridle-path or tracks. The average rural police station had a strength of only a dozen men, to deal with some 100 villages scattered over an area of 100 square miles.[42] About 20,000 troops were used to suppress the violence during March 1947, and on 15 April, Jenkins asked Mountbatten for 60,000 more 'if partition were to be avoided'.[43] A month later, he was informed that no more troops were available for the Punjab, as the British expected disorder in other parts of India following an official announcement in June.[44] Jenkins' reason for not accepting Nehru's suggestion to introduce martial law in the Punjab was revealing: troops were not the answer to 'cloak and dagger' activities; martial law might well fail, and troops would be exposed to the same communal attacks as the police.[45]

The British acknowledged that they did not possess the power to stem the violence; writing retrospectively in September 1948,

[41] Jenkins to Mountbatten, 15 June 1947, L/P&J/5/250, p. 32.
[42] Jenkins to Wavell, 9 March 1947, R/3/1/89, pp. 22, 27–8.
[43] Jenkins to Mountbatten, 15 April 1947, Ibid.
[44] Governor of Punjab to Viceroy, 22 May 1947, and Viceroy to Governor of Punjab, (T 1155-S), 24 May 1947, R/3/1/90, pp. 57, 90.
[45] Jenkins to Mountbatten, 24 June 1947, R/3/1/176, p. 207.

Mountbatten believed that it was 'precisely' in those cases 'where there had been failure to curb movements of violence by sufficiently strong and quick use of armed force, that the massacres had spread'.[46] The communal frenzy was 'without parallel' in any other province in India, and 'nothing which the Governor or his officials had it in their power to do could have altered these fundamentals and removed the sense of insecurity to which they gave rise'.[47] By the beginning of May 1947, Hindus had started retaliatory attacks on Muslims in Eastern Punjab. In the Gurgaon district, six companies of troops were inadequate to deal with a disturbed area of 1000 square miles. Arson ruled the roost in Lahore and Amritsar, and on 27 June, Mountbatten admitted that they would 'soon be burnt to the ground'.[48] The Sikhs, who had faced the brunt of the attack in Rawalpindi, had lost faith in the administration.[49] Those who had suffered could not know what the problems of the administration were. The only fact obvious to them was that the *sarkar* had not been able to defend themselves—in other words, to take the law into their own hands. There were reports of Hindus and Sikhs organizing private armies. The prospects of vengeance being waged on Muslims induced the provincial League to set up a Muslim Central Vigilance Committee in Lahore, with sub-committees all over the province. *Janbazees*—persons ready to sacrifice themselves in their comunity's cause—were being enrolled: they would play the role of storm troopers.[50] By May, the communities had settled down to the 'maximum amount of damage to one another while exposing the minimum expanse of surface to the troops and police'. The police could do little against burning, stabbing and bombing by individuals.[51] Indeed, over a greater part of northern India, in an

[46] Mountbatten's *Secret Report of the Last Viceroyalty, 22 March–15 August 1947* (London, 1948), PREM 8/1002, p. 61.

[47] Memorandum by Minister of State for Commonwealth Relations, 3 September 1947, CAB 134/346.

[48] S.E. Abbott-Abell, 10 June 1947, (T) R/3/1/90, p. 153, and Viceroy's personal report no. 10, 27 June 1947, *TOP*, vol. 11, p. 680.

[49] *Civil and Military Gazette*, 25 March 1947; *Statesman*, 16 March 1947, note by Jenkins on interview with Tara Singh, 19 May 1947, R/3/1/176, p. 168.

[50] FR for Punjab for second half of April 1947, received by Central Intelligence Officer, Lahore, R/3/1/90, pp. 28–9.

[51] Jenkins to Mountbatten, 31 May 1947, L/P&J/5/250, pp. 38ff., Jenkins to Mountbatten, 4 August 1947, R/3/1/89, p. 221.

area bound by Peshawar, Calcutta, Bombay and the Central Provinces, communal clashes were reported daily by the first week of April.[52] Civil war was inevitable. As Jenkins wrote on 4 August 1947: 'Nor can all the King's horses and all the King's men prevent—though they may be able to punish—conflict between communities interlocked in villages over wide areas of country'.[53]

Having experienced the attitude of the League in the Interim Government, the Congress had, by February 1947, despaired of achieving an independent united India. The Congress would not press the British for an immediate announcement on the dismissal of the League from the Interim Government but the issue would have to be faced in the near future. Attlee's statement meant that the Mission Plan would continue to apply only if the League entered the Constituent Assembly. If not, other consequences would follow.[54] Nehru was thinking of the partition of Bengal and the Punjab if the Mission Plan ultimately failed.[55] With the League's intentions made clear in the Punjab after 3 March, the Congress Working Committee passed on 9 March a resolution calling for the partition of the Punjab. It was not easy for the Congress to contemplate such a course but it was preferable to an attempt by either party to impose its will on the other. Large non-Muslim minorities could not be coerced into joining Pakistan any more than Muslims could be made to join the union.[56]

However, the British still hoped that Jinnah would come round. Instructed by Attlee to do his best to secure a united India within the Commonwealth and the imperial defence system,[57] Mountbatten, who, on his own admission, was 'governing by personality',[58] wanted, by April, to announce a quick decision in favour of Pakistan so that it would fail on its merits. The problem would be to reveal the limits of Pakistan so that the League could revert to a unified India with honour. He presented the draft of his "Balkan Plan" to the Governors' Conference on 15 April. This envisaged the trans-

[52] *Times*, 9 April 1947.
[53] Jenkins to Mountbatten, 4 August 1947, R/3/1/89, p. 221.
[54] Nehru to Wavell, 24 February 1947, L/P&J/10/77.
[55] Wavell to Pethick-Lawrence, (T), 22 February 1947, *TOP*, vol. 9, p. 785.
[56] Nehru to Wavell, 9 March 1947, Ibid., p. 898 and enclosure, Ibid., pp. 899–900.
[57] Attlee to Mountbatten, 18 March 1947, L/P&J/10/78, pp. 44ff.
[58] Mountbatten's interview with S. Gopal, 28 May 1970, quoted in Gopal, *Nehru*, vol. 1, p. 342.

fer of power to provinces, or to such confederations of provinces as might decide to group together, before the actual transfer of power.[59]

Jinnah made it clear that he would not reaccept the Mission Plan, —' "You must carry out a surgical operation; cut India and its army firmly in half and give me the half that belongs to the Muslim League" '. Mountbatten felt that a decision on Pakistan would have to be taken within a month. Though he used every argument Jinnah gave in favour of Pakistan against partition, or against dividing Bengal and the Punjab, Mountbatten failed to bring him round. Jinnah's arguments grew increasingly futile and he ended up by saying, ' "If you persist in chasing me with your ruthless logic we shall get nowhere".' Mountbatten concluded that Jinnah was 'a psychopathic case; in fact until I had met him I would not have thought it possible that a man with such a complete lack of administrative knowledge or sense of responsibility could achieve or hold . . . so powerful a position.'[60] Mountbatten warned Jinnah that he would have to choose between the Cabinet Mission Plan which would give him the five provinces of Pakistan with autonomy and a very weak centre and a very moth-eaten Pakistan, the eastern and north-western parts of which would be economically unsound, and which would still depend for its defence on arrangements with India. Jinnah replied, ' "I do not care how little you give me as long as you give it to me completely." ' He would ask for dominion status for Pakistan within the empire.[61]

Jinnah made clear his opposition to any suggestion that a political settlement might be based on the Mission Plan and that the League might enter the Constituent Assembly at every stage of his discussions with Mountbatten.[62] The League's intentions were underlined by the insistence of Jinnah and Liaqat Ali Khan that the British Indian army should be divided. Liaqat expressed the League's opposition to the reorganization of the armed forces on the basis of a united India: the division of India, he told Mountbatten, implied the division of the armed forces to serve Hindustan and Pakistan.[63] Jin-

[59] Governors' Conference, 15 April 1947, L/P&J/10/79, pp. 474, 473.

[60] Viceroy's personal report no. 3, 17 April 1947, L/P&J/10/79, pp. 488–9.

[61] Ibid., p. 490.

[62] Viceroy's personal reports of 9 and 17 April 1947, Ibid, pp. 506 ff. and 486 ff. respectively.

[63] Ibid. and Liaqat Ali Khan to Mountbatten, 7 April 1947, Ibid., pp. 498–9.

nah opposed the move to partition Bengal and the Punjab,[64] as he wanted the full provinces to be included in Pakistan, but Mountbatten believed that he would not seriously contest the need for partition.

Jinnah now pressed the Viceroy to end Governor's rule in the Punjab. He claimed that Mamdot had the support of 93 MLAs and a majority in the provincial legislature. Mountbatten told him that Governor's rule would not be lifted until a decision had been taken by the British government, as the Sikhs were so bitter about atrocities committed by Muslims that they would never accept a one party government by the League. Jinnah then suggestedthat Mamdot should be allowed to see the Viceroy on his own, and he would telephone Mamdot not to see Jenkins again until the Governor had met Mountbatten in Rawalpindi.[65] Jinnah's move, as Jenkins discerned, was intended to increase the importance of the League and to transfer direct control of the Punjab from the Governor to the Viceroy. Jenkins stood his ground. He did not object to a meeting between Mamdot and Mountbatten, but 'there can be no question' of a joint interview between the Viceroy, Mamdot and himself. Mamdot was only a provincial party leader and any procedure adopted for him would have to be available to all party leaders. There was no need to depart from the established constitutional practice in this matter.[66] On 28 April, when Mamdot reiterated his claim to form a ministry, Jenkins told him that he did not think that a communal ministry, whether Muslim or non-Muslim, would have any chance of succeeding in the Punjab.[67] 'The real point is that once any large section of the population declines to recognize a parliamentary majority, a revolutionary situation supervenes and constitutional government in the ordinary sense becomes impossible.' Whether or not this was sufficient on constitutional grounds for refusing to go out of section 93, there was the 'practical point' that it would be 'foolish' to permit the formation of a ministry when an important

---

[64] Viceroy to Secretary of State (T 21-SC), 8 May 1947, Ibid., pp. 354, 355. Note by Jinnah, received on 17 May 1947, Ibid., pp. 167–8.

[65] Mountbatten's note of interview with Jinnah on 26 April 1947, and Viceroy to Governor of Punjab (T 902-S), 26 April 1947, Ibid., pp. 172, 171 respectively.

[66] Governor of Punjab to Private Secretary to Viceroy (T 84-G), 28 April 1947, Ibid., p. 176.

[67] Governor of Punjab to Private Secretary to Viceroy (T 86-G), 28 April 1947, Ibid., pp. 177–9.

announcement about the future of India was imminent. A section 93 proclamation could be revoked at any time; but it was arguable that the governor was entitled to demand more than 'a mere capacity' to comply with the technical requirements of the Act of 1935.[68] The Unionist coalition forced out by the League had a larger majority than that now claimed by the League.[69] The League continued to be complacent and had made no approach to the Sikhs. Their attitude was that 'Muslims are entitled to rule' the whole of the Punjab and that 'when this is admitted they will be good enough to treat the non-Muslims with generosity'.[70]

With the administrative machine collapsing, with the knowledge that the League would not enter the Constituent Assembly under the Mission Plan, Mountbatten concluded, by the middle of April 1947, that partition was inevitable, and that the Punjab and Bengal would have to be divided. Mountbatten himself did not believe that non-Muslim minorities could be coerced into Pakistan;[71] nor would the Congress have ever agreed to such a proposal. The Congress had suggested the partition of Bengal and the Punjab as early as March 1947, and on 28 April, Rajendra Prasad, president of the Constituent Assembly, reiterated that no constitution would be forced upon any part of India. This would not mean the division of India, 'but a division of some provinces'. For this the Congress would be prepared and a constitution based on such a division might have to be drawn up.[72] In May, non-Muslim MLAs in the Punjab and Bengal legislative assemblies passed resolutions calling for the partition of their provinces.[73] Mountbatten discussed his proposals for the partitioning of Bengal and the Punjab with Patel and Nehru, and on 3 June, when he announced the British government's plan for a transfer of power to Indians, he had already secured the consent of those two leaders to the proposal that MLAs in those provinces would vote to decide whether or not their respective provinces should be partitioned.[74]

---

[68] Jenkins to Mountbatten, 30 April 1947, Ibid., pp. 182ff.

[69] Draft of letter from Jenkins to Mamdot, 7 May 1947, Ibid., pp. 188ff.

[70] Jenkins to Mountbatten, 30 April 1947, L/P&J/5/250.

[71] Viceroy's personal report no. 3, 17 April 1947, L/P&J/10/79, pp. 486 ff.

[72] V.P. Menon, *The Transfer of Power* (paperback, Madras, 1968) p. 360.

[73] Ibid. and *Statesman*, 7 May 1947.

[74] See, for example, note by Nehru, 16 May 1947; Nehru to Mountbatten 17 and 20 May 1947, L/P&J/10/79.

Patel and Nehru faced criticism in the AICC for committing the Congress to partition without consulting the party. They in turn pointed to the difficulty of consulting the AICC at every stage of the negotiations, and said that their stand flowed out of the resolutions passed by the AICC itself since1942—that no part of India could be coerced into accepting a constitution against its will. Gandhi opposed partition as a moral failure, but said he would not hinder the Congress Working Committee.[75]

The reasons which led the CWC to propose the partition of Bengal and the Punjab in March, and to accept it by June 1947, were summed up by J.B. Kripalani. Their visits to riot-affected areas in Bengal, Bihar and the Punjab 'were a succession of shocks, one greater than the other.' It was not only that the innocent had been massacred; 'our respective religions were degraded'. Each community had vied with the other in the worst orgies of communal violence. The decision to accept partition had been taken out of fear that things might get worse. Gandhi's non-violence had not been able to tackle the problem on a mass scale. Non-violence was not stopping communal riots in the Punjab. 'There are no definite steps, as in non-violent non-cooperation, that lead to the desired goal.'[76] For the Congress then, partition and the communal violence which accompanied it were a sad finale to a movement which had prided itself on secularism and non-violence—a noble way to achieve a noble end.[77] Even as he fasted for peace in June 1947, Gandhi was filled with foreboding that the disillusion was not over, that the killing would go on.

Ever since their release from prison in July 1945, Congress leaders had stressed the necessity to reorganize and revitalize the party organization so that it could channel popular social and political unrest along constructive lines. But the cabinet mission's offer of independence sooner rather than later induced the Congress leadership to concentrate on the negotiations for the transfer of power, since they believed that only an independent government would have the will to tackle the problems facing India. The involvement in the negotiations, coming as it did so soon after the Congress leaders's term in prison after August 1942, took its toll of organizational

[75] AICC meetings on 1 and 2 June 1947, AICC file no. G-30, 1946–1948, pp. 101–2 respectively.

[76] AICC file no. G-47, part 1, 1946–1947, pp. 168–71.

[77] J. Nehru, *Autobiography* (Indian edition, 1962), p. 73.

work, and in August 1946, Nehru reiterated that the Congress had lost its vitality. The links between the central, provincial and local committees must be tightened up; a labour department would have to be set up to study and to suggest solutions for the increasing social unrest; a special department would be established to deal with the work of the Constituent Assembly.

Nehru had hoped that the entry of the Congress into the Interim Government would open the opportunity to carry out Congress programmes and would relegate communal differences to the background by concentrating on economic issues as 'the real issues faced by all communities together'. But the Congress-League division had dominated the Interim Government, it was reflected in the savage communal violence in Noahkhali, Saran and Garmukhteswar; and Congress leaders had more or less despaired of working together with the League in any government. Yet they remained optimistic, and the British announcement of 20 February 1947 was welcomed by them for giving Indians yet another chance to unite and work for independence. At the same time, they knew that the League might never enter the Constitutent Assembly. With the British departure assured by June 1948, and with partition imminent, they insisted that Hindu and Sikh minorities in the Muslim majority provinces must not be submerged into Pakistan, any more than the Muslim minorities wished to be subjected to the all·India majority. The Rawalpindi massacres broke the last straw on the camel's back, and on 7 March 1947, the Congress Working Committee called for the partition of the Punjab and Bengal.

The Congress accepted the partition plan first, because it was based on the premise of a united India. Knowing of Mountbatten's preference for an undivided India, and also because they believed that India would be at a disadvantage if she left the Commonwealth and Pakistan stayed in, they agreed to temporary dominion status and invited him to act as Governor-General of India until June 1948. Partition and an early transfer of power were seen by them as the best check on the growing communal violence. The British seemed unable to end it; and in the NWFP, the Governor actually seemed to be encouraging the League's campaign to overthrow the Congress ministry. Far better that the Raj were wound up: once the new governments took over administrative problems the old bitterness would fade away and unity might still be realized. Kripalani hoped that once Pakistan was established, 'its government would have enough sense of reality not to discredit themselves by unfair treatment of the minorities'. Until now the Muslim League had held that its interest was to create an atmosphere of conflict and strife. Now its interest would 'obviously' be to create order, for any spirit of lawlessness would, sooner or later, be turned against its own minorities. Minorities in Pakistan should therefore not emigrate out of panic. 'They should wait and watch and not lose faith in their own strength, in the potential sanity of the Pakistan Government and in the ultimate unity of India which can never be permanently destroyed'.[78]

With partition almost a *fait accompli* by the end of May, there remained only the need to fix the date for the transfer of power. Mountbatten himself favoured an early transfer: the Congress might then join the Commonwealth; the Indian parties could get acquainted with administrative problems; the communal violence would, hopefully, be checked with a settlement at the centre, and the decline of the administrative machine stemmed.[79] Both Alan Campbell-Johnson and H.V. Hodson have said that the choice of 15 August 1947 as the date of the transfer of power occurred to Mountbatten at his press conference on 4 June 1947.[80] But in a letter to Lord Listowel, who had replaced Pethick-Lawrence as Secretary of State for India in April 1947, on 3 June, Mountbatten clearly stated that he wanted the British to wind up the Raj on 15 August 1947.[81] It is obvious, then, that by 3 June the Viceroy had already thought of 15 August as 'the appointed day'. Two illustrations will show that civil war was foreseen by the British, and that administrative reasons weighed most with Mountbatten in fixing the date. Immediately after the outbreak of rioting in Lahore on 4 March, Jenkins had warned Wavell that until June 1948, order could be maintained in the Punjab whether under a communal ministry or Section

---

[78] This account has been based on Nehru's note to presidents and secretaries of PCCs, *National Herald*, 1 July 1946; notes for AICC, 6 August 1946, AICC file no. 69 (Part 2), 1946, pp. 1–7 and 67–9. Also see, J.B. Kripalani to A.A. Chowdhury, 13 May 1947, AICC file no. CL-8/1946–1947, pp. 111–17; Kripalani to Lala Duni Chand, 14 May 1947, AICC file CL-9/1946–1947; press statement by Kripalani, 18 June 1947, AICC file G-47 (part 1) 1946–1947, pp. 158–9.

[79] Viceroy to Secretary of State, (T 1284-S), 3 June 1947.

[80] Alan Campbell-Johnson, *Mission with Mountbatten* (London, 1951), p. 109; H.V. Hodson, *The Great Divide* (London, 1969), pp. 319–20.

[81] Viceroy to Secretary of State, (T 1284-S), 3 June 1947, PREM 8/541/part X.

93 'only by use of force'. Under a communal ministry British officers and the Indian army would be used to conquer the Punjab for
'the community in power'; under Section 93 the administration
would have 'limited tenure and would hand over to chaos'.[82] A year
after the transfer of power, Mountbatten affirmed that

'... the main factor was the period during which it was likely to be
possible to keep the existing Interim Government functioning. Indications were daily growing that it was going to be a task of the
utmost difficulty to prevent one side or the other resigning if the
Government was kept in being for another month or so at the outside. The chaos which would follow such resignations, which were
... likely to prejudice the successful implementation of the whole
plan, was easy to imagine ... The August transfer of power was inherent in the Partition solution quite apart from any introduction of
Dominion Status.'[83]

As partition and the transfer of power had been dictated by political and administrative exigency, 'contrary to expectations', no
provision for formal treaties with the new dominions had been
made. Any question of making a conditional transfer of power had
vanished with the Statement of 20 February 1947, and British officials were uncomfortably aware that if no defence agreement with
India eventuated, Commonwealth defence would be in jeopardy.[84]
Meanwhile, the Labour government hoped for defence arrangements with at least Pakistan, and conjured up another sort of "divide and rule" tactic. The cabinet rejected a request from Gandhi for
a British assurance that they would not have differential agreements
with India and Pakistan. Lord Listowel observed that one of the
main Congress objections to partition had been its fear that Pakistan
would fortify itself with British, American or other outside assistance, and this fear had induced the Congress to accept temporary
dominion status. The British would prefer to have similar defence
arrangements with both India and Pakistan if the Commonwealth
provided the nexus between the two:

[82] Governor of Punjab to Viceroy (T 28-G), 5 March 1947, R/3/1/176, pp. 21–2.
[83] Mountbatten's *Secret Report of the Last Viceroyalty, 22 March–15 August 1947*
(London, 1948), pp. 90, 172.
[84] Secretary of State to Viceroy (T), 3 July 1947, L/P&J/10/21, p. 35; Stapleton to
Monteath, 13 June 1947, L/P&J/10/21, p. 3; Cabinet Official Committee on
Commonwealth Relations, 8 August 1947, CAB 134/117.

'But we feel that we should be very careful not to say that we shall not in any circumstances have closer relations with Pakistan than with India . . . The best hope of getting an effective relationship with the Congress derives from their fear that if they do not play up we shall have differential and better relationships with Pakistan and possibly with non-acceding Indian States. The probability is that this is the strongest bargaining point we have with the Congress . . . We feel that we should be very ill-advised to throw it away.'[85]

Here was the old game in a new setting: by maintaining the differences, the British hoped to bring about cooperation between India and Pakistan under their aegis. Imperialism still assumed that any means would achieve the desired end.

The League alone got what it wanted: a sovereign Pakistan. Jinnah's delight at the statement of 3 June was 'unconcealed'.[86] Before the Congress decision to accept temporary dominion status for India, the League had wanted Mountbatten as Governor-General of Pakistan, but once Jinnah knew that India would join the Commonwealth, he was silent on the subject. On 4 July he told Mountbatten that he wanted to be Governor-General of Pakistan himself, and that his Prime Minister would do what he said. '"In my position it is I who will give the advice and others will act on it."' Mountbatten warned him that the decision might cost him several crores of rupees in assets, but Jinnah remained unmoved. Mountbatten knew that the Congress had agreed to dominion status to facilitate a smooth transfer of power and not to be at a disadvantage if Pakistan joined the Commonwealth; they had also invited him to serve as Governor-General of India until June 1948 because of his own preference for a united India. Mountbatten himself had never wanted to stay with only one side as Governor-General. But he realized that Jinnah had got his way until the very end. 'I fear [wrote Mountbatten] that I have unintentionally led Nehru and all the Congress leaders up the garden path and that they will never forgive me for allowing Jinnah once more to have his own way'.[87] That Jinnah could not be persuaded against taking up the Governor-Generalship

[85] Listowel to Mountbatten, 27 June 1947, L/P&J/10/99, p. 3.

[86] Viceroy to Secretary of State, (T 1277-S), 3 June 1947, PREM 8/541/part X.

[87] Viceroy's personal report no. 11, 11 July 1947, L P&J/10/81, pp. 51–2. Attlee favoured Mountbatten's accepting the Congress invitation because it was 'a great boost for Britain, and for the Commonwealth . . . If Mountbatten *had* left India, it would have looked like a victory for that twister, Jinnah!' Quoted in Kenneth Harris, *Attlee* (London, 1982), p. 384.

of Pakistan ruled out any hope of eventual unity between the two dominions and signalled that India and Pakistan would be what he had always intended—two sovereign nations, having no links with each other except by treaty.

Conclusions

From the Statement of 3 June 1947 to 15 August 1947, the date chosen by Mountbatten for the British to transfer power to Indians, only a vote of the legislative assemblies of the Muslim majority provinces—and in the NWFP, of a plebiscite—remained to decide whether India would be partitioned. Non-Muslim MLAs in Bengal decided by 58 to 21 votes that the province should be partitioned, and that it should join the existing Constituent Assembly. Muslim MLAs decided by 106 to 35 votes against partitioning the province. Paragraph 6 of the 3 June statement laid down that if a simple majority of either part of the Legislative Assembly decided in favour of partition, the province would be divided. Hence, the vote of the non-Muslim MLAs decided the issue of partition in Bengal. In the Punjab, the vote of non-Muslim MLAs also decided that the province was to be partitioned. The Sind Legislative Assembly decided by 30 votes to 20 to join a new Constituent Assembly. The boycott of the referendum in the NWFP by the provincial Congress contributed to the League winning 50.49 per cent of the votes cast for Pakistan. It had a walkover in the province.

Mountbatten asserted that the British decision to partition was based on the will of the Indian people, as expressed by their representatives in the legislatures of the Muslim majority provinces; but did this expression of the 'will of the people' imply that the communal differences between Hindus and Muslims had made partition inevitable? To establish such inevitability would surely require a remarkably Whig interpretation not only of the partition of India, but of several centuries of India's history. Although a sense of social division in religious terms was pervasive in Indian society, Hindus and Muslims belonging to the same class or locality often had more in common with each other than with their co-religionists in other sections of society. The religious distinctions existed along with, and cut across, tribal, class and caste divisions. The question to be confronted is when and how religious feeling came to be 'politicized' to the point where partition became inevitable.

The answer to this question may be sought not only in the emergence of the Muslim League with its demand for a sovereign Muslim state from March 1940 and its mobilization of Muslim provincial support, but also in British and Congress tactics which contributed to the rise of the League and the solidification of its communal support. And the circumstances of a declining empire may have contributed as much to Muslim political unification as the League's appeals to the nationalism supposedly inherent in Muslim religious communalism.

Historiography offers a variety of suggestions for answering the question, each identifying some element within it. One of these traces back the roots of partition to the Congress refusal to admit League representatives to a share in ministerial power in the UP in 1937. Had they done so, it is argued, the League might not have opted for Pakistan three years later. Admittedly, the failure of the negotiations embittered the provincial Leaguers, but it never turned them into supporters of a sovereign Pakistan. Nor did it drive Jinnah to that extremity as he had opposed the negotiations between the Congress and the UPML throughout. Another suggestion stresses the British contribution made by way of communal representation, provincial responsible government and the extension of franchise to the politicization of communities along religious lines. However, while these institutional innovations promoted political feeling along religious lines, they showed little sign before 1945, of producing widespread Muslim support for the central leadership of the League in the Muslim majority provinces. Moreover, the needs of responsible government often dictated entry into inter-communal alliances, even in Muslim majority provinces. In 1944, in fact, Jinnah's League appeared in danger of political defeat in the Punjab, where it found itself at odds with a major Muslim leader who believed in intercommunal politics. And though Huq in Bengal and Sikander Hyat Khan in the Punjab appeared to adhere nominally to the League in all India matters, Jinnah found them utterly intractable when it came to representing the League's policies at the provincial level.

Of the political unification of Muslims before the war there is little evidence; and the lack of it explains Jinnah's fear that the British would introduce the scheme of federation provided for in the Act of 1935. Given the weakness of the League in the Muslim majority provinces, it would have been left high and dry at the all India level if federation had been implemented.

It was the outbreak of war in September 1939 which 'saved' the League. Even as Linlithgow put federation into cold storage for the duration of the war, Jinnah set out to exploit the British need for the support of the Indian parties for the war effort. At first, he feared that the exigencies of wartime would drive the British into concessions to the Congress, in which the League would be ignored; and he did what he could to prevent such a settlement. The League's resolutions of September and October 1939 declared that India was not a national state; that federation must be jettisoned and the political future negotiated *de novo* with the Muslim 'nation' through its accredited organization the Muslim League. If the League's resolutions of September–October 1939 were calculated to forestall a settlement between Linlithgow and the Congress, they succeeded in their aim. They helped the Viceroy to reject Congress demands for a promise of independence in return for its cooperation with the war effort. The League provided the British with a pretext to tell the Congress that the demand for independence must be weighed against the objections of minorities. But there was more to Jinnah's tactics than diplomacy. On the one hand, Sikander and Huq had come out in support of the war effort; on the other, radicals in the League were urging him to line up in an anti-imperialistic front with the Congress. Jinnah's call for 'Deliverance Day' fell flat in most provinces; and his reliance on the British to allow the League to veto the Congress demand for independence exposed him to the indictment that he was a supporter of imperialism. Unable to suggest any alternative path of constitutional advance to the scheme of federation which he had rejected, Jinnah's stance appeared entirely negative and unconstructive even to Linlithgow. In such circumstances, the demand for Pakistan as a sovereign state served to rebuff the Viceroy's criticism and the charge that in opposing the demand for independence, he was the servant of imperialism. It was not that he was opposed to freedom for Indians, explained Jinnah at Lahore in March 1940, but he must have freedom for Muslims. They would not tolerate domination by the British or by the Congress.

But more than that, the dramatic evocation of a Muslim nation of the future at Lahore might serve to hoist the League out of its political doldrums; for example, in reminding Muslim provincial leaders absorbed in their various provincial interests of the need for unity at the all India level; and that that unity was essential to preserve Muslim interests in the future; or in reminding Muslim voters of grievances, real or imagined, that they might have accumulated against Congress ministries between 1937–9, such as discrimination against Muslims in government service, the imposition of Hindi or the lack of protection for Muslims during communal disturbances. In proclaiming the demand for Pakistan, the League might have expected to reap the political dividends of communal religious sentiment. The slogan of Pakistan tended to identify Congress, in Muslim eyes, with 'Hindustan', and probably contributed to the fact that few Muslims joined the Quit India movement in 1942.

The importance of Jinnah's presidential address at Lahore lay in his assertion that the Indian problem was not an intercommunal but an international one—as between two nations. From that time onwards, Jinnah consistently defined Pakistan in terms of a sovereign state. Evidently, most Muslim politicians did not subscribe to his particular definition at that time or even later. Sir Muhammad Yusuf, for example, who chaired the AIML session in April 1942, saw Pakistan as 'an immeasurable dynamic and potential value for the creation of a united India on the basis of treaties in cooperation with the British government'.[1] Fazlul Huq moved the Pakistan resolution at Lahore, yet soon attacked Jinnah for preaching separatism and was expelled from the League in December 1941. The Unionists paid some lip service to the idea of Pakistan, which they disliked, but Sikander never broke with the League, partly because he seldom seems to have done anything without the permission of the British and was persuaded by Linlithgow in 1940 and 1942 not to come out into open opposition to Jinnah. For the Viceroy was concerned to sustain Sikander for the sake of the Punjab war effort and to sustain Jinnah for the sake of a semblance of Muslim opposition to the Congress at a time when the Congress was engaged in civil disobedience. Linlithgow himself could find, at the beginning of 1942, no genuine enthusiasm for Pakistan among Muslim Leaguers whom he had met, and concluded that they would be content with Pakistan within some sort of a federation. He inferred that whatever the League meant by the term, most Muslims took it as a symbol of a vague resolve against 'Hindu domination', which rarely implied a positive commitment to creating a sovereign state of Pakistan.

In the absence of any conclusive support for Pakistan in the Mus-

---

[1] Pirzada, *Documents*, p. 379.

lim majority provinces, it is difficult to see how Amery and Linlithgow decided, soon after March 1940, that there could be no return
to the Act of 1935 as the basis for a political settlement in the future,
because 'Muslims' would never accept it. Reading through their de-
spatches, one finds them critical of Jinnah's inability to define the
content of Pakistan. On examining its economic and military implications, they found it impracticable and concluded that an intelligent man like Jinnah could not be serious about it. That they were
not willing to take his demand for Pakistan as a sovereign state
seriously is shown by the fact that they considered his demand for
parity with the Congress in the Executive Council absurdly preten-
tious. In insisting on parity, Jinnah was claiming equality of political weight with the Congress; for *nations* negotiated as equals. In refusing to concede parity, the British made it clear that they considered the League to be no more than a *political and religious
minority*.

By the beginning of 1942, nevertheless, the necessities of the war
combined with American anti-imperialist pressure were compelling
the British to open the question of constitutional advance which
they had intended to shelve during the war. Almost fortuitously,
the Cripps plan offered provinces a right to opt out of a future Indian Union before the final transfer of power and to form a separate
union if they wished to do so. The British thus opened the way to
partition before the transfer of power. They appear to have had no
constructive reason for doing so, other than to justify their rejection
of Congress demands. But whatever their reasons, they had incidentally encouraged Jinnah's League to anticipate that, when power
had to be transferred after the war, Pakistan would be in sight,
whereas hitherto its prospect had been visionary. The Cripps offer
gave plausibility to the Lahore resolution and strengthened the
popular appeal of the League in the Muslim majority provinces;
except that at the time, the League had neither the provincial organization, nor, more important, the majorities in the provincial legislatures to take advantage of the Cripps offer.

If, as Cripps promised, Pakistan could come into being simply by
a majority vote in the legislatures of the Muslim majority provinces,
then the next step for Jinnah was to create a greater following there.
But he does not appear to have had much success in his efforts to
draw provincial Muslim legislative parties and ministries in those
provinces into the League's fold after the Cripps offer than he had

had previously. More than that, there is no strong evidence of the League organizing among the Muslim masses in the rural areas of these provinces until the election campaign of 1945–6. Provincial Leagues resisted his efforts to dictate to them, and the Muslim League's Committee of Action was unpleasantly surprised to find, in June 1944, that in the NWFP, the Muslim League was only a misnomer for party functions and had undertaken no organizational work. It was only in Bengal, where, because of the provincial League's tactic of undermining Huq's support among the poor peasants, that the League's propaganda was carried out in rural areas, while Suhrawardy's radical brand of politics made it popular in urban areas. Within the League, no one challenged Jinnah's stand on all India issues. When they differed with him, for example, in July 1944, over the desirability of a Congress-League settlement, Jinnah's threat to resign as President of the League silenced them. Provincial Leaguers appear to have paid little attention to him in provincial matters, while they gave him a comparatively free hand at the all India level.

Considering the tenuous relationship of the League to various provincial leaders, the variety and ambiguity of their different understandings of, and reactions to, the Lahore resolution, it does not appear that Jinnah's call for a sovereign Pakistan welled up from an emergent Muslim nation from below. The possibility is that the demand was proclaimed from above, and so it held no great significance or effect on the divisions among Muslims politicians in the majority provinces before 1945–6.

If this is so, it is surprising that both the British and the Congress, during the war, should have given Jinnah the position of a contender for the spoils of power at the all India level, regardless of his weakness in the provinces. A strong case can be made for thinking that the British deliberately built up his prestige at the all India level for their war purposes, though at the provincial level they subordinated this objective to the prime necessity of operating the war machine with maximum efficiency. In any event, British officialdom traditionally calculated their 'collaboration equation' in Indian politics in terms of loyal and disloyal elements, of 'Muslim' and 'Hindu'.[2] It suited Linlithgow, as we have seen, to accept Jinnah's claim to speak for all Muslims at the centre from 1939 onwards, to

[2] Anita Singh, 'Nehru and the Communal Problem', pp. 13ff.

justify rejection of the Congress demand for independence. The prestige thus acquired from the British helped make Jinnah's League the only plausible representative of Muslims at the all India level. To an extent British recognition compelled the Congress to recognize Jinnah's claim, though its aim of winning the League into a united anti-imperialist front pointed in the same direction. For instance, Rajagopalachari since 1940 had urged the Congress to accept the idea of Pakistan within a federation with a view to winning Jinnah's cooperation against the British, even though Jinnah was not interested in a settlement with the Congress. After turning a deaf ear to Rajagopalachari's pleas for four years, Gandhi himself entered, in September 1944, into discussions with Jinnah for the same purpose. The talks took place soon after Jinnah's setback in the Punjab at the hands of the Unionists, so they allowed Jinnah to adopt the position of one who spurned what had been offered, and so contributed to his standing and prestige with Muslims. But there was more than a desire for publicity behind Jinnah's talking to the Congress. At a time when the League ministries were battling for survival in other Muslim majority provinces, Jinnah was under considerable pressure from provincial Leagues to talk to Gandhi. Punjab Leaguers wanted him to work out a settlement with the Congress at the centre so that the two parties could then join hands to throw out the Unionist ministry. By entering into negotiations not likely to succeed—for he must have known that Gandhi would never offer him a sovereign Pakistan—Jinnah satisfied his followers that he had done his best to protect Muslim interests and maintained his prestige at the all India level. As it was the first time that the two leaders had met since 1939, Gandhi's apparent acceptance of the principle of Pakistan— that is, of Pakistan within a federation—was taken as a symbolic victory for Jinnah not only by the British and Muslim Leaguers, but also by many Congressmen who were bewildered at Gandhi's stance.

It was however at Simla that the British consolidated Jinnah's monopoly of Muslim representation at the centre in allowing his demand to nominate all Muslims to the Executive Council to break up the conference, instead of going ahead without him. The Congress had agreed to work the proposals. At that time Jinnah was under great pressure from provincial Leagues to join the Executive Council with the Congress, especially as the League considered entry in the Viceroy's Council as the only chance of maintaining themselves in the political limelight. Apparently even at this time Jinnah's demand for a sovereign Pakistan had not turned the balance of power in Muslim provincial politics in its favour. For all these reasons, it seems unlikely that Jinnah would have been able to stand exposure of his obduracy to the world, had the British stood firm. However, he was 'saved' by Whitehall's directive in July 1945 that the world 'should not come to know that his intransigence had led to the break up of the conference. The League, after all, had been, if not their friend, the enemy of their arch enemy the Congress, and it would not do to put the Congress in a favourable light. The result of Whitehall's decision was that Jinnah, by refusing anything less than parity at Simla, brought the British to a point, by March 1946, where they would offer him the possibility of a sovereign Pakistan if negotiations with the Congress on the basis of a united India were to fail.

But Pakistan was still not inevitable. The elections of 1945–6 provided the League's opponents with an opportunity to defeat it, but they failed to rise to the occasion. In the Punjab, the Unionists relied largely on influence to win mass support. The League, on the other hand, greatly extended its party organization, and organized mass meetings, student volunteers and ulema; it offered Pakistan as the panacea for all Muslim grievances. The League won 76 per cent of the Muslim vote in the elections, which offered the first convincing evidence of its support among Muslims in the majority provinces. The League triumphed by calling on Muslims to unite politically and avert the danger of Hindu domination and win 'Pakistan' in one sense or another. The result of the elections represented a great stride forward in the political unification and solidification of the Muslim community, but the extent of this unification need not be exaggerated into a communal mandate for a sovereign Pakistan. It has been shown that even among League politicians, let alone those who voted for them, 'Pakistan' meant all things to all men. It is not unlikely that the effects of peace, bringing the British departure into close prospect, rallied a majority of the Muslim community to the League. If a British departure was imminent, the competing interests of all Muslim provincial politicians, indeed of the entire Muslim community, could no longer be secured at the provincial level. All now depended on the negotiations proceeding at the centre. It seems probable that the circumstances of peace dictated the swing of Muslim provincial leaders behind the all India League in

244 The Origins of the Partition of India

1945–6, rather than any positive decision in favour of partition and a sovereign Pakistan.

Though the League's victory in Muslim constituencies in 1945–6 might be recorded as a mandate in some senses, it certainly did not make a sovereign Pakistan inevitable. That depended on how the British would work out the mechanics of the transfer of power in negotiation not only with the League but also with the Congress. The expression of widespread Muslim support for it in the elections did not lessen British opposition to Pakistan, any more than the absence of widespread Muslim support for it before the elections had prevented them from incorporating the principle of partition in the Cripps offer of 1942. Until 1945, the British had worked on the assumption that the empire must survive; and Pakistan had been a useful counterpoise to the Congress demand for independence. But by March 1946, the British announced that the Cabinet Mission would negotiate with Indian parties the basis on which power could be transferred to Indians, and they preferred to transfer power to a united India. No long term British decision to wind up empire by any date existed; there is no evidence to substantiate the Whiggish theory that it was 'always' on the cards, especially after the introduction of provincial self-government in 1919. The constitutional reforms of 1919 and 1935 were aimed at preserving, not terminating empire; the British offer of independence in 1946 was taken in the interests of maintaining the concreteness of their imperial power. This lay at the core of British opposition to Pakistan and their presumption that an agreement between the Indian parties would not for them be a sufficient condition for transferring power—that would depend on whether the agreement catered for their military concerns. This secret but overriding calculation influenced British tactics during the negotiations for the transfer of power in 1946–7 which rules out any labelling of Labour policy as one of an unforced voluntary withdrawal from India.

A complex set of circumstances led to the British announcement of 22 March 1946. One was their realization that their ability to enforce law and order had greatly diminished. The war and the non-cooperation of the Congress and the League had made evident to them the precariousness of their position in India. Despite their breaking the Quit India movement by early 1943, they confessed their inability to deal with large-scale disturbances in future. The loyalty of Indians at all levels of the administration could not be taken for granted. After November 1945, when Indian members of the ICS and armed forces showed sympathy with the rising wave of anti-imperialist sentiment, it was obvious that the civil and military services were not staunch bulwarks of the Raj. The air force and naval mutinies in January and February 1946 respectively confirmed the split in the military base of the empire. Britain's own post-war domestic and international commitments made impossible the trying out of the only alternative method of reviving the administration—the recruitment of more British citizens to the ICS and armed forces—assuming that Whitehall went in for all out repression and that it would have succeeded. So when the Cabinet Mission came to India in March 1946, it worked on the premise that the negotiations must succeed, preferably on the basis of an undivided India.

But a transfer of power to a united India was not an end in itself for the British, as it was for the Congress. The reason why the British were against Pakistan was their desire to keep an undivided, independent India within the imperial security system and to use India's army and economic resources for military purposes. The possibility that the Congress might object to such arrangements had made Wavell envisage, in February 1944, that British military interests must be guaranteed by treaty *before* the transfer of power took place. The way to counteract Congress objections would be to let the threat of Pakistan hang over the heads of Congress so that they would be obliged to give the British the military facilities they wanted.

The British wanted both the Congress and the League to agree to a plan for a transfer of power to a united India. But the opposition they expected from the Congress, not only with regard to their long term aims, but also in respect of the Viceroy's special powers, made them want to keep the League as a counterpoise to the Congress. In other words, the British wanted the two parties to agree on how to make the Mission Plan work in the British interest, and not to agree on how to work against them. One of the conclusions to their attitude that could be taken was of the League working for partition, the Congress against it, the British against it but somehow hoping or thinking that the League's hostility to the Congress would make it more pliable to their intentions—this would mean that the League would work against partition! There is no evidence that the British thought out the logical implications of their tactics. They probab' tried to please both parties so that both would enter the Constituent Assembly for an undivided India—where the British would have the last word and get the concessions they wanted—otherwise they would not transfer power.

The Mission Plan of 16 May 1946 provided that Hindu and Muslim majority provinces would form separate groups, and that groups would frame constitutions for their provinces. That this form of grouping could have been avoided in the first instance is suggested by the opinion of, for example, Khizar, that provincial rivalries would militate against the successful working of grouping.[3] The NWFP was in any case a Congress province, and would have preferred a provision for provinces to decide whether they should join a particular group, instead of being pushed into one from the very outset.

Grouping was then a major step on the road to Pakistan. Their obsession with using the League as a counterpoise to the Congress also made the British rule out any alternative which would have given the League less influence in the Interim Government. Azad's suggestion that provinces, not parties, should nominate members to the Interim Government was turned down by the Mission as an example of the diabolical cleverness of the Congress. Under this arrangement, the Congress would have got 8, the League 2 and the Unionists 1, seats in the Interim Government. With provincial tendencies raising their head even in the Muslim majority provinces at that time, it is not inconceivable that Suhrawardy, for example, would not have lined up with Jinnah as a matter of course— Suhrawardy was working with the Bengal Congress for a united Bengal in March 1947.

Perhaps because some provincial Leaguers suggested that Pakistan within a federation would be quite acceptable; perhaps because neither Jinnah nor any other Leaguer could define the content of Pakistan; perhaps because an undivided India favoured the British interest;—for one or more of these reasons the British concluded that Pakistan within a federation would be accepted by the League. But Jinnah had made it very clear to the Mission that he would accept nothing less than a sovereign Pakistan. Even as the negotiations were in progress, he declared before a convention of League legislators in Delhi on 16 April 1946, that the 'idea of a single consti-

[3] *TOP*, vol. 7, p. 148.

tutional body has then no place, and we shall never accept it, for it means our consent to proceed on the basis of a united India, which is impossible . . .'[4] The British ignored, or did not note, the reason behind the League's acceptance of the Mission Plan;[5] and happily concluded that a spirit of compromise had got the better of Jinnah's intransigence.

But there lay a rub. Jinnah and the League accepted the 16 May statement after an assurance given by Pethick-Lawrence and Cripps to members of the Working Committee on 16 May that it was the intention of the Mission that sections would determine the constitutions of their provinces. Sovereignty would not be transferred until the new constitution had been framed. Jinnah's suspicions were therefore roused when the British accepted, a little later, a Congress resolution accepting the 16 May statement with the intention of working *against* grouping in the Constituent Assembly the asserting that no one would dictate to the Assembly what it should nor should not do. Cripps and Pethick-Lawrence stated in Parliament on 17 July that the British aim was *only* to get the parties into the Constituent Assembly. Taken with British ignoring League's demand for parity, and its refusal to form a government without the Congress; these statements put Jinnah up in arms. Accusing the British of bad faith, the League passed, on 29 July, a resolution rescinding its earlier acceptance of the 16 May statement and calling on Muslims to resort to Direct Action—dangerous in its implications because it was never defined.

Could the British have gone ahead with only the Congress in the Interim Government? The alternative was considered by Whitehall, but raised the uncomfortable question whether the British would be prepared to back the Congress in suppressing a possible mass movement organized by the League. Then there was Wavell's attitude. A man who had always disliked and mistrusted the Congress to an extent that he preferred to have no government at all than one which included only the Congress, simply refused to govern without the League. What may have seemed politically logical to the men in Whitehall was, for the man on the spot, psychologically impossible.

Wavell's belief that the League would come into the Constituent Assembly if only the British would clarify their intentions on grouping, was the sort of self-deception that can only be explained

---

[4] Pirzada, *Documents*, p. 508.   [5] *TOP*, vol. 7, pp. 837–8.

by his intense dislike of the Congress. He never upbraided Leaguers for preaching violence even as they sat in his government; he justified and backed up their refusal to work as a team with the Congress. Neither he nor Whitehall ever faced squarely the possibility that Jinnah was intent on a sovereign Pakistan; and their need of the League as a counterpoise to the Congress in the Interim Government made them rule out the possibility of going ahead without it.

The contradiction in British thinking was also evident from the concern of both Wavell and Whitehall that the Viceroy's veto should not be abolished. The veto, they thought, would be needed to protect the services and to prevent the Congress from interfering in the Muslim majority provinces while it sat in the interim government. But if the Viceroy would not have the *power* to do anything against the wishes of the majority of his Executive, preserving the veto served no purpose except to create a barrier between him and the Congress. Of what use would the veto have been if the Congress had resigned from the Interim Government and started mass civil disobedience, which, fearing their inability to control, Wavell suggested that the British withdraw from India by 1 January 1947?

The final question is why mass feeling got out of hand. Communal temperature had remained fairly high, especially in the Punjab, after the Cripps mission. But the Punjab remained free from internecine disturbances during the war. Communal propaganda by the League reached a peak during the elections of 1945–6 and was kept up while the negotiations between the Cabinet Mission and the Indian parties were in progress. There are reports of the League, Akalis and the RSS organizing private armies. There is no mention of provincial action against them, or of the Congress trying to counteract them, so that communal propaganda had a free hand at the time.

Was it the mere prospect of Pakistan or Hindustan which roused mass feeling? It would depend on what they meant. In March 1947, Jenkins believed that the Sikhs could have reached a settlement with the provincial League had it not been for the fact that the latter were taking orders from Jinnah. The League had concentrated on getting Pakistan without ever telling the minorities what their position in it would be. If Pakistan was going to be an Islamic state, as Jinnah himself had suggested on occasion, Hindus and Sikhs would not walk willingly into it. Jinnah's refusal to define the content of Pakistan, and the prospect that he might get it, made the Hindus and

Sikhs quite delirious. Muslims, on the other hand, could not have been greatly enamoured of Hindustan, as stories of 'atrocities' committed on them under Congress rule remained in circulation; and the League carried out its anti-Congress propaganda through the war years, uninterrupted by any party, least of all by the Congress, most of whose leaders were in jail during that time.

Direct Action in Calcutta and Noahkhali, in the organization of which the League ministry connived, provided the spark which lit the fires of civil war. Rape, forced marriages, conversions—the fact that the atrocities had been committed on a fairly large scale before the disturbances could be brought under control—meant that stories and rumours spread like wildfire, arousing the deepest hatred and the fiercest desire for revenge; and stirred Hindus into waging the most bloody and brutal vengeance on Muslims in Bihar and the UP. *This was the breaking point.* A handful of riots in a few cities would not have led to it. But atrocities committed on a mass scale could not be forgotten on either side, and they lent the most sinister definition to Pakistan or Hindustan. As thousands of people lost their lives and as hundreds of refugees fled from their homes, the impression was created in the public mind that the *sarkar* was incapable of doing its job and that it was therefore incumbent on them to be able to defend themselves—in other words, to take the law into their own hands. All these factors came to a head in the Punjab in March 1947, where the outbreak of communal violence simultaneously in several districts meant that the police and the military could only deal with a few areas at a time: there were large areas which were affected by the disturbances but over which no action would be taken. Civil war was on its way.

Would the disturbances have stopped if the League (the AIML) had entered the Constituent Assembly? It is difficult to answer this question. With mass hatred aroused to an extreme, it might not have been possible, given the administrative limitations. The communal disturbances exposed not only the political abyss that separated the Congress from the Muslim League but also the essential weaknesses of Congress strategy. The political division between the Congress and League lay in the latter's wish that any political settlement must be guaranteed by the British, whereas the Congress worked British-sponsored constitutions to free India from imperialist rule. The schism had its roots in the 1920s and 1930s and never changed in its essentials; and it was the reason why Jinnah never accepted the

Congress offer of parity, forwarded by Bhulabhai Desai, in January–February 1945. It was not merely that the League's demand for a sovereign Pakistan was unacceptable to the Congress; but also its desire that it should be awarded by the British and to have post-independence military ties with them. The League's logic was simple. For, if the Congress majority could swallow up the League in a constituent assembly, what except a British guarantee could forestall Congress tactics against Pakistan in the assembly and subsequently protect a sovereign Pakistan from the aggressive designs of a Congress-led India? The League's dependence on the British after 1940 was actuated by its intention first, to achieve a sovereign Pakistan under their aegis, then to enlist their military umbrella for its survival.

Both the British and Congress discerned the meaning behind the League–Congress rift, but each for their own reasons, shied away from its extreme implications, taking refuge in the argument that Pakistan was unviable and that the League could not be serious about it—that it was only a ploy with which to secure a vantage point at the centre. So the British did their best to prevent a Congress–League agreement until 1945—then, assuming that the League, as a political minority, would be ever amenable to their wishes, tried to bring it into a united India while offering it the possibility of achieving the sovereign Pakistan that it demanded. A distinction can be made between their dislike of the Pakistan solution, and the contribution of their tactics to its materialisation: their short-term tactics worked against the achievement of their own long-term aims. The Congress found Jinnah intractable; it conceived the weapon of Muslim mass support against the League in 1937 but never sharpened it, partly because of an idealistic naivete that all Indians would eventually unite against the British, partly because its use of mass sanctions and non-cooperation was more of a temporary tactic in its long-run strategy of compromise-pressure-compromise.[6] In 1940, Nehru observed that Congress ministries had made insufficient progress towards implementing their social and economic programmes,[7] but he did not relate the effects of this inadequacy on a definitive solution to the communal problem. In 1945–7, his

[6] For an elucidation of the compromise-pressure-compromise strategy, see Bipan Chandra, 'The Indian Capitalist Class and Imperialism before 1947', in his *Nationalism and Colonialism in Modern India* (New Delhi, 1979), pp. 144–170.

[7] Nehru, *Autobiography*, pp. 603–4.

view that Pakistan should not succeed because it was the medievalistic, anti-democratic idea of a politically reactionary organization[8] seemed to gloss over the possibility and the fact that such ideas do succeed, often with mass support. Not having fully developed mass organization even for the anti-imperialist struggle, the Congress could not have done it to resolve an issue to which it accorded secondary priority. Jinnah's success in the elections of 1945–6 signified his realization of the necessity of mass backing for a political line; the Congress rout in the Muslim constituencies meant that it could override Pakistan or divide and rule machinations only in negotiations—in which the British acted as arbiters. In March 1946, the Congress coalesced with one of the greatest of loyalists—Khizar Hyat Khan Tiwana and his Unionist party—proving that Pakistan had become one of foremost issues of the day. Criticizing *divide et impera*, the Congress contradictorily joined the British-sponsored Interim Government in September 1946. In 1946, even more than in 1937, the acceptance of office by the Congress was its greatest tactical mistake as it made the party the focus of popular Muslim discontent, even hatred, which eventually burst into civil war.

Yet the fact remains of Jinnah's insistence on a sovereign Pakistan—at the very least, of his lack of interest in a settlement with the Congress unless it was backed up by the British. What agreement was possible with a leader who declared, even as communal massacres spread through the Punjab in March 1947, that the British had 'deliberately fostered' the idea of a united India as 'part of machinations for destruction and bloodshed in the country after their departure'?[9] Between March and May 1947, Jinnah's efforts at the centre to persuade Mountbatten to allow a League ministry in the Punjab symbolized his keenness to obtain the whole province for the League before June 1948. Gandhi alone discerned that Jinnah would not be wooed into a united India, but he had no answer to prevent the realization of a sovereign Pakistan. Jinnah achieved a sovereign Pakistan partly because he knew where he was going, while the 'muddling through' tactics of the British and the Congress were no match for his melange of obduracy, dialectical skill and deliberate, dogged negation of anything less than a sovereign Pakistan.

[8] See, for example, *National Herald*, 8 February, 4 April, 16 July 1946; *Hindustan Times* 30 August 1945.
[9] *The Times*, 28 March 1947.

In any case, given his blend of vanity, ambition, idealism and principle—and all these qualities have been attributed to him, with the emphasis depending on the perceptions of admirers or critics—it is difficult to see how he would have agreed to a united, secular India in which he would have had to play a likely second fiddle to Gandhi and Nehru. In the end, he left the British with the choice of scuttle or allowing the League to capture the NWFP and the Punjab by force—both alternatives reflecting their administrative impotence. Always underestimating the seriousness of the call for a sovereign Pakistan, neither the British nor the Congress formulated a strategy to challenge or to resist it. In August 1947, the Muslim League was the only party to achieve what it wanted. There was no possibility of the British securing any military treaties with India as the price for transferring power, and they faced the prospect of losing their whole eastern empire. Lord Dufferin's warning of 1887 that British attempts to 'divide and rule' would recoil on them rang true in 1947[10]. India paid a heavy price for the achievement of freedom, a consequence of the fact that communal forces were not defeated, nor unity totally achieved.

[10] Dufferin to Cross, 4 January 1887, Cross papers, vol. 22, p. 5.

List of Important Persons

Only the most important positions held by the prominent persons in this book are mentioned below.

ALEXANDER, A. V., First Earl Alexander of Hillsborough, Labour M.P. 1935–50; First Lord of the Admiralty 1940–5 and 1945–6; member of Cabinet Mission to India 1946.

AMERY, Leo, Secretary of State for India 1940–5.

ATTLEE, C. R., First Earl. Opposition leader 1935–40; Lord Privy Seal 1940–2; Deputy Prime Minister 1942–5; Prime Minister 1945–51.

AUCHINLECK, Field Marshal Sir Claude, Commander-in-Chief India 1941 and 1943–7; Commander-in-Chief Middle East 1941–2; Supreme Commander in India and Pakistan 1947.

AZAD, M. A. K., Congress President 1940–6.

BAKSH, Allah, Leader of Sind United Party 1937; Prime Minister of Sind at various times during 1937–42.

BALDEV SINGH, Minister in Punjab 1942–6; member of interim government 1946–7.

BOSE, Sarat Chandra, Leader of Congress Parliamentary Party in Bengal 1937–9; fell out with Congress in 1946 when he formed the Socialist Party.

BOSE, Subhas Chandra, Congress President 1938–9; organized Indian National Army 1942.

BURROWS, Sir Frederick, Governor of Bengal 1946–7.

CAROE, Sir Olaf, Foreign Secretary to Government of India 1939–45; Governor of NWFP 1946–7.

CASEY, Baron R. G., Governor of Bengal 1944–6.

CHHATARI, Nawab Hafiz Ahmad Said Khan, Leader of NAP in UP; Prime Minister of Hyderabad 1941.

COLVILLE, Sir John, Governor of Bombay 1943–7.

CRIPPS, Sir Stafford, Member of war cabinet and deputed by it to India in 1942; Minister of Aircraft Production 1942–5; President of Board of Trade 1945–7; member of cabinet mission to India.

CUNNINGHAM, Sir George, Governor of NWFP 1937–46.

DAULATANA, Mian Mumtaz, Unionist who joined Muslim League in 1943; General Secretary, Punjab Provincial League 1944–7.

DESAI, Bhulabhai, Member of Central Legislative Assembly, one of the authors of Desai-Liaqat Pact of 1945; defended INA men in 1945.

DOW, Sir Hugh, Governor of Sind 1941–6; Governor of Bihar 1946–7.

EMERSON, Sir Herbert, Governor of Punjab 1933–8.

GANDHI, Mahatma, the father of the Indian nation; made personal efforts to promote communal harmony in 1946–7 and only reluctantly accepted partition.

GLANCY, Sir Bertrand, Political Adviser to the Crown Representative 1939–41; Governor of Punjab 1941–6.

HAIG, Sir Harry, Governor of UP 1934–9.

HALLETT, Sir Maurice, Governor of Bihar 1937–9; Governor of UP 1939–45.

HASAN, Syed Wazir, Muslim League President 1936; joined Congress 1937.

HERBERT, Sir John, Governor of Bengal, 1939–43.

HIDAYATULLAH, Sir G. H., Premier of Sind 1937–8, 1942–7.

HUQ, Fazlul, KPP President in 1936; joined Muslim League 1937; Prime Minister of Bengal 1937–43.

HUSAIN, Fazli, Prime Minister of Punjab at the time of his death in 1936; founder of the Unionist Party.

ISPAHANI, M. A. H., prominent Bengal Muslim Leaguer and on its Working Committee 1936–47.

JENKINS, Sir Evan, Private Secretary to Viceroy 1943–5; Governor of Punjab 1946–7.

JINNAH, Muhammad Ali, reorganized Muslim League after 1934, President of League after that date; under his leadership the Muslim League won the independent state of Pakistan in 1947.

KHALIQUZZAMAN, Choudhury, prominent Muslim Leaguer and one of the leading figures in the coalition controversy in UP in 1937; on MLWC 1945–7.

KHAN, Aurangzeb, Prime Minister of NWFP 1943–5.

KHAN, Liaqat Ali, Muslim League General Secretary 1937–47.

KHAN, Muhammad Ismail, with Khaliquzzaman was one of the leading figures in UP coalition controversy in 1937; on MLWC 1945–7.

KHAN, Raja Ghazanfar Ali, member Punjab Legislative Assembly 1937–45; member Interim Government 1946–7.

KHAN SAHIB, Prime Minister of NWFP 1937–9 and 1945–7.

KHAN, Sikander Hyat, Unionist Party leader after 1936, Prime Minister of Punjab 1937–42.

KHUHRO, M. A., MLWC member 1942; Minister Public Works Department in Sind 1946–7.

KRIPALANI, J. B., General Secretary of Congress 1934–46 and President in 1946.

LINLITHGOW, Second Marquis of, Viceroy and Governor-General of India, 1936–43.

LISTOWEL, 5th Earl of, Secretary of State for India April–August 1947.

LUMLEY, Sir Roger, Governor of Bombay 1937–43.

MAMDOT, Nawab of, President, Punjab Provincial League 1942–7.

MIEVILLE, Sir Eric, Assistant Private Secretary to King George VI 1937–45; member of Lord Mountbatten's staff in India 1947.

MONTEATH, Sir David, Permanent Under Secretary of State for India and Burma from 1942.

MOUNTBATTEN of Burma, First Earl, Chief of Combined Operations 1942–3; Supreme Allied Commander South East Asia 1943–6; Viceroy of India March–August 1947.

MUDIE, Sir Francis, Chief Secretary to UP government 1939–44; member Viceroy's Executive Council 1944–5; Governor of Sind 1946–7.

NAZIMUDDIN, Khwaja, Prime Minister of Bengal 1942–5.

NEHRU, Jawaharlal, Congress President 1936–7; member CWC 1936–47; played leading role in negotiations for transfer of power in 1946–7.

NISHTAR, Abdur Rab, Minister of Finance in NWFP 1943–5; on MLWC 1945–6; member of Interim Government 1946–7.

NOON, Firoz Khan, in Viceroy's Executive Council 1941–5, leading Punjab Muslim Leaguer.

PANT, G. B., Congress Prime Minister of UP 1937–9.

PATEL, Sardar Vallabhai, leading Congressman and member of Interim Government 1946–7.

PETHICK-LAWRENCE, First Baron, Secretary of State for India 1945–7; member of Cabinet Mission to India 1946.

PRASAD, Rajendra, Congress President 1939 and 1947; President of Constitutent Assembly 1946–50.

RAJAGOPALACHARI, C., Congress Prime Minister of Madras 1937–9.

SAADULLAH, Muhammad, Chief Minister of Assam 1937–8, 1939–41 and 1942–6.

SYED, G. M., President Sind Muslim League 1938; nominated to MLWC 1941; expelled from League 1946.

SUHRAWARDY, H. S., Muslim League minister in Bengal 1937–45 and Chief Minister 1946–7.

TARA SINGH, prominent Akali leader for four decades; led movement for Azad Punjab in the forties.

TIWANA, Malik Khizar Hyat Khan, Prime Minister of the Punjab 1943–7; expelled from League in 1944, formed coalition with Congress and Akalis 1946–7; resigned after British government's announcement of 20 February 1947.

TWYNAM, Sir Henry, Governor of CP and Berar 1940–6.

WAVELL, Sir Archibald, later First Earl, Commander-in-Chief Middle East 1939–41; Commander-in-Chief India 1941–3; Viceroy of India 1943–7.

WYLIE, Sir Francis, Political Adviser to Crown Representative 1940–1 and 1943–5; Governor of UP 1945–7.

ZETLAND, Second Marquis of, Secretary of State for India 1935–40.

Bibliography

On a subject on which the reading list is seemingly endless, I have included in this bibliography only those sources which I found especially useful or stimulating.

UNPUBLISHED SOURCES

Private Papers

Bodleian Library, Oxford
    Attlee papers

India Office Library and Records, London
Allan Arthur	Mss. Eur. D.943
Viscount Cross	Mss. Eur. E.243
Sir George Cunningham	Mss. Eur. D.670
Sir John Erksine	Mss. Eur. D.596
Sir Harry Haig	Mss. Eur. F.115
Sir Maurice Hallett	Mss. Eur. E.251
Lord Linlithgow	Mss. Eur. F.125
Sir Robert Reid	Mss. Eur. E.278
Lord Zetland	Mss. Eur. D.609

Centre of South Asian Studies, Cambridge
    J.M.G. Bell
    E.C. Benthall
    M.O. Carter
    H.J. Frampton
    O.M. Martin
    I.M. Stephens
    S.G. Taylor

Churchill College, Cambridge

    A.V. Alexander

Gandhi Smarak Sangrahalaya, New Delhi
    Mahatma Gandhi

National Archives of India, New Delhi
    M.R. Jayakar
    Rajendra Prasad

Nehru Memorial Museum and Library, New Delhi
    Bhulabhai Desai
    Syed Mahmud
    Jawaharlal Nehru
    T.B. Sapru (Microfilm)
    B. Shiva Rao
    Purshottamadas Thakurdas

Government Records
India Office Library and Records, London
    L/E
    L/I
    L/P & J/5
    L/P & J/10
    L/WS/1
    R/3/1
    R/3/2

National Archives of India
    Home Establishments Department
    Home Police Department
    Home Political (Internal) Department
    Reforms Office

Public Records Office, London
    CAB 127
    CAB 134
    PREM 1/216/1937
    PREM 1/414/1939
    PREM 4/47/1
    PREM 8

Party Papers
Nehru Memorial Museum and Library, New Delhi
    All-India Congress Committee
    Hindu Mahasabha

PUBLISHED SOURCES

Cmd. 3568 (1930) *Report of Indian Statutory Commission*, Vol. 1.
Report of Indian Statutory Commission, Vols. IV-XIV (HMSO, 1930).
Cmd. 3778 (1932) *Proceedings of Indian Round Table Conference, Second Session*, 7 September 1931–1 December 1931.
Cmd. 4086 (1932) *Report of the Indian Franchise Committee*.
Cmd. 4147 (1931–2) *Communal Decision*
Government of India Act, 1935 (Delhi, 1936).
Census of India 1941 (Delhi, 1942).
Constitutional Relations between Britain and India: The Transfer of Power

1942–7, Vols. I–IX. Editor-in-Chief, N. Mansergh (HMSO, 1970–80).

Bengal Legislative Assembly Debates 1937–46.

Central Assembly Debates 1944.

NWFP Legislative Assembly Debates 1937–46.

Punjab Legislative Assembly Debates 1937–46.

Sind Legislative Assembly Debates 1937–46.

Ahmad, Jamiluddin, *Speeches and Writings of Mr. Jinnah*, Vol. 1, 6th edn. (Lahore, 1960).

Collected Works of Mahatma Gandhi (75 vols. 1958–79).

Durga Das (ed.) *Sardar Patel Correspondence 1945–50* (10 vols., Ahmedabad, 1971–74).

S. Gopal (ed.) *Selected Works of Jawaharalal Nehru* (12 vols., New Delhi, 1972–79).

Gwyer, M. and Appadorai, A. (eds.) *Speeches and Documents on the Indian Constitution 1921–47* (2 vols., Oxford, 1957).

Indian Annual Register

Jafri, S.S. (ed.) *Qaid-e-Azam Jinnah's Correspondence with Punjab Muslim Leaders* (Lahore, 1977).

Pirzada, S.S., *Foundations of Pakistan: All-India Muslim League Documents: 1906–1947*, vols. I (1906–23) and II (1924–47), (Karachi, 1970).

Moon, P. (ed.) *Wavell: The Viceroy's Journal* (Oxford, 1973).

Report of the Inquiry Committee Appointed by the All-India Muslim League to inquire into Muslim Grievances in Congress Provinces (November, 1938).

Zaidi, Z.H. (ed.) *M.A. Jinnah-Ispahani Correspondence 1936–1948* (Karachi, 1976).

Newspapers

Amrita Bazaar Patrika
The Bombay Chronicle
Civil and Military Gazette
Dawn
The Eastern Times
Harijan
The Hindu •
Hindustan Standard
The Hindustan Times
The Leader
Morning News
National Herald
Searchlight
Star of India
The Statesman
The Times of India
The Tribune

Secondary Sources

Ahmad, Aziz, *Studies in Islamic Culture in the Indian Environment* (Oxford, 1964).
———, *Islamic Modernism in India and Pakistan 1857–1864* (Oxford, 1967).
Ali, C.M., *The Emergence of Pakistan* (New York, 1967).
Ambedkar, B.R., *Pakistan or Partition of India* (Bombay, 1946).
Amery, L., *My Political Life* (4 vols., London 1953–5).
Ashraf, K.M., *Life and Conditions of the People of Hindustan* (2nd edition, New Delhi, 1970).
Attlee, C.R., *As It Happened* (London, 1954).
Azad, M.A.K., *Indian Wins Freedom* (New York, 1960).
Aziz, K.K., *The Making of Pakistan: A Study in Nationalism* (London, 1967).
Birla, G.D., *In the Shadow of the Mahatma* (Bombay, 1953).
Bolitho, Hector, *Jinnah: Creator of Pakistan* (London, 1954).
Brass, Paul R., *Language, Religion and Politics in North India* (Cambridge, 1974).
Brittain, V., *Pethick–Lawrence* (London, 1963)
Broomfield, J.H., *Elite Conflict in a Plural Society* (University of California, 1968).
Campbell-Johnson, Alan, *Mission with Mountbatten* (London, 1951).
Chopra, P.N. (ed.) *Quit India Movement: British Secret Report* (New Delhi, 1976).
Collins, L., Lapierre, D., *Mountbatten and the Partition of India*, vol. 1 (New Delhi, 1982).
Connell, John, *Auchinleck* (London, 1959).
Connell, John, *Wavell: Supreme Commander* (London, 1969).
Coupland, R., *The Cripps Mission* (Oxford 1942).
Coupland, Reginald, *The Indian Problem* (Oxford, 1944).
Dalton, Hugh, *High Tide and After* (London, 1962).
Das, Durga, *India from Curzon to Nehru and After* (London, 1969).
Das, M.N., *Indian Under Morley and Minto* (London, 1964).
Das, M.N., *Partition and Independence of India* (New Delhi, 1982).
Dixit, P., *Communalism: A Struggle for Power* (New Delhi, 1974).
Durrani, F.H. Khan, *The Meaning of Pakistan* (Lahore, 1944).
El Hamza, *Pakistan: A Nation* (Lahore, 1942).
Faruqi, Zia-ul-Hasan, *The Deoband School and the Demand for Pakistan* (Bombay, 1963).
Ghosh, S., *Gandhi's Emissary* (London, 1967).
Glendevon, Lord, *The Viceroy at Bay* (London, 1971).
Gopal, Madan, *Sir Chhotu Ram: A Political Biography* (Delhi, 1977).
Gopal, Ram, *Indian Muslims—A Political History (1858–1947)* (Bombay, 1959).
Gopal, S., *Jawaharalal Nehru: A Biography*, vol. I: 1889–1947 (Indian Edition, Oxford University Press, 1976).

Grewal, J.S., *Muslim Rule in India: The Assessments of British Historians* (Oxford, 1970).

Griffin, Lepel, *Chiefs and Families of Note in the Punjab*, 2 vols. (Lahore, 1940).

Gupta, A.K., *North-West Frontier Province and the Freedom Struggle 1932–47* (New Delhi, 1979).

Gupta, P.S., *Imperialism and the British Labour Movement 1914–1964* (London, 1975).

Hardy, P., *The Muslims of British India* (Cambridge, 1972).

Hasan, M., *Nationalism and Communalism in Indian Politics* (New Delhi, 1979).

Hodson, H.V., *The Great Divide* (London, 1969).

Husain, Azim, *Fazli Husain* (Bombay, 1946).

Hutchins, F.G., *Spontaneous Revolution* (Delhi, 1971).

Ismay, Lord, *Memoirs* (London, 1960).

Ispahani, M.A.H., *Qaid-e-Azam Jinnah As I Knew Him* (Karachi, 1966).

Jones, K.W., *Arya Dharm* (Berkeley, 1976).

Kaura, Uma, *Muslims and Indian Nationalism: The Emergence of the Demand for India's Partition 1928–40* (New Delhi, 1977).

Khaliquzzaman, C., *Pathway to Pakistan* (Lahore, 1961).

Khosla, G.D., *Stern Reckoning* (New Delhi, 1949).

Krishna, K.B., *The Problem of Minorities* (London, 1939).

Low, D.A. (ed.) *Soundings in Modern South Asia History* (London, 1968).

Low, D.A., (ed.) *Congress and the Raj* (London, 1977).

Lumby, E.W.R., *The Transfer of Power in India 1945–47* (London, 1954).

Madan, T.N. (ed.) *Muslim Communities of South Asia* (New Delhi, 1976).

Malik, Hafeez, *Moslem Nationalism in India and Pakistan* (Washington, 1963).

Mansergh, P.N.S., *The Commonwealth Experience* (London, 1969).

Mansergh, P.N.S., *Prelude to Partition: Concepts and Aims in Ireland and India* (Cambridge, 1978).

Mehta, A. and Patwardhan, A., *The Communal Triangle in India* (Allahabad, 1942).

Menon, V.P., *The Transfer of Power in India* (Paperback, Madras, 1968).

Minault, G., *The Khilafat Movement* (Delhi, 1982).

Molesworth, G.N., *Curfew on Olympus* (London, 1965).

Moon, Penderel, *Divide and Quit* (London, 1961).

Moore, R.J., *The Crisis of Indian Unity 1971–1940* (Oxford, 1974).

———, *Churchill, Cripps, and India 1939–1945* (Oxford, 1979).

———, *Escape from Empire* (Oxford, 1983).

Mountbatten, Lord, *Reflections on the Transfer of Power and Jawaharlal Nehru* (Cambridge, 1968).

Mujeeb, M., *The Indian Muslims* (London, 1967).

Nanda, B.R., *Mahatma Gandhi* (London, 1958).

Nehru, J., *Eighteen Months in India* (Allahabad, 1938).

———, *An Autobiography* (New Delhi, 1962).

———, *The Discovery of India* (Bombay, 1969).

Noman, M., *Muslim India: The Rise and Growth of the All-Indian Moslem League* (Allahabad, 1942).

Noon, Firoz Khan, *From Memory* (Lahore, 1966).

Page, David, *Prelude to Partition* (Oxford 1982).

Philips, C.H. and Wainwright, M.D., (ed.) *The Partition of India* (London, 1970).

Prasad, Rajendra, *India Divided* (Bombay, 1946).

Pyarelal, *Mahatma Gandhi: The Last Phase, vols. 1 and 2* (Ahmedabad, 1956–8).

Rothwell, V., *Britain and the Cold War 1941–1947* (London, 1982).

Saiyid, M.H., *Mohammad Ali Jinnah: A Political Study* (reprint of 2nd edition, Lahore, 1962).

Sayeed, K.B., *Pakistan: The Formative Phase 1857–1948* (2nd edition, London, 1968).

Sen, Shila, *Muslim Politics in Bengal 1937–1947* (New Delhi, 1976).

Sitaramayya, P., *History of the Indian National Congress, Vols. 1 and 2* (Bombay, 1947).

Smith, W.C., *The Muslim League 1942–45* (Lahore, 1945).

———, *Modern Islam in India* (Lahore, 1946).

Taylor, D. and Yapp, M. (eds.) *Political Identity in South Asia* (London, 1979).

Thapar, R. (ed.) *Communalism and the Writing of Indian History* (New Delhi, 1969).

———, *The Past and Prejudice* (New Delhi, 1975).

Thorne, C., *Allies of a Kind* (London, 1978).

Tomlinson, B.R., *The Indian National Congress and the Raj 1929–1942* (London, 1976).

———, *The Political Economy of the Raj 1914–1947* (London, 1979).

Thursby, G.R., *Hindu-Muslim Relations in British India: A Study of Controversy, Conflict, and Communal Movements in Northern India 1923–1928* (Leiden, 1975).

Tinker, H., *Experiment with Freedom* (Oxford, 1967).

Tuker, F., *While Memory Serves* (London, 1950).

Venkataramani M.S., and Shrivastava, B.K., *Quit India: The American Response to the 1942 Struggle* (New Delhi, 1979).

Wingate, R., *Lord Ismay* (London, 1970).

Zetland, Lord, *Essayez* (London, 1956).

Articles

Baxter, C., 'Union or Partition: Some Aspects of Politics in Punjab 1936–45', in L.Ziring el al., *Pakistan: The Long View* (Duke Univestity, 1977), pp. 40–69.

Brass, Paul R., 'Muslim Separatism in the United Provinces: Social Context and Political Strategy before Partition', *Economic and Political Weekly*, Annual Number, January 1970, pp. 167–86.

Chandra, Bipan, 'Secularism: Retrospect and Prospect', *Secular Democracy*, February 1973.

Chandra, Satish, 'Jizyah and the State in India During the 17th Century',

Journal of the Economic and Political and Social History of the Orient, Vol. 12, 1969, pp. 322–40.

Chatterjee, P., 'Bengal Politics and the Muslim Masses, 1920–1947', *Journal of Commonwealth and Comparative politics,* 1982, pp. 25–41.

Freitag, Sandra B., ' "Natural Leaders", Adminstrators and Social Control: Communal Riots in the United Provinces 1870–1925', *South Asia* (September, 1978), vol. 1, No. 2, pp. 27–41.

Gallagher, J., 'The Congress in Bengal: The Period of Decline 1930–39', *Modern Asian Studies,* 7, 7, 1973.

Gupta, P.S., 'The British Raj and the Communal Question Sept. 1939–Jan. 1940', *Indian History Congress Proceedings 1973,* vol. II, pp. 56–9.

Inder Singh, A., 'Imperial Defence and the Transfer of Power in India, 1946–1947', *International History Review,* November 1982, pp. 568–88.

Inder Singh, A., 'Decolonization in India: The Statement of 20 February 1947', *International History Review,* May 1984.

Listowel, Lord, 'The Whitehall Dimension and the Transfer of Power', *Indo-British Review,* vol. 7, nos. 3 and 4, pp. 22–31.

Low, D.A., 'The Indian Schism', *Journal of Commonwealth Political Studies,* vol. IX, No. 2 July 1971, pp. 158–67.

McPherson, Kenneth, 'The Muslims of Madras and Calcutta: Agitational Politics in the Early 1920s', *South Asia,* December 1975, pp. 32–47.

Moon, P., 'May God Be With You Always', *The Round Table,* July 1971.

Moore, R.J., 'The Mystery of the Cripps Mission', *Journal of Commonwealth Political Studies,* vol. XI, No. 3, November 1973, pp. 195–213.

Moore, R.J., 'Mountbatten, India, and the Commonwealth', *Journal of Commonwealth and Comparative Politics,* 1981, pp. 5–43

Moore, R.J., 'Jinnah and the Pakistan Demand', *Modern Asian Studies,* 17, 4, 1983, pp. 529–61.

Morris-Jones, W.H., 'The Transfer of Power, 1947: A View from the Sideline', *Modern Asian Studies,* 16, 1, 1982, pp. 1–32.

Oren, Stephen, 'The Sikhs, Congress, and the Unionists in British Punjab', *Modern Asian Studies,* 8, 3, 1974, pp. 397–418.

Potter, David, 'Manpower Shortage and the End of Colonialism', *Modern Asian Studies,* 7, 1, 1973, pp. 47–73.

Talbot, I.A., 'The 1946 Punjab Elections', *Modern Asian Studies,* 14, 1, 1980, pp. 56–91.

Tinker, H., 'Jawaharlal Nehru at Simla May 1947', *Modern Asian Studies,* October, 1970.

Tomlinson, B.R., 'Indian and the British Empire, 1935–1947', *Indian Economic and Social History Review,* vol. XIII, No. 3., pp. 323–351.

Oral Evidence

Interviews with:

W.H. Saumarez-Smith
Arthur Williams
Henry Taylor
S.E. Abbott

Unpublished theses

Lambert, Richard, 'Hindu-Muslim Riots', Unpublished Sociology Dissertation submitted to University of Pennsylvania for Ph.D. degree, Philadelphia, 1951.

Singh, Anita I., 'Nehru and the Communal Problem 1936–1939', Unpublished M.Phil dissertation submitted to Jawaharlal Nehru University, New Delhi, 1976.

Index

Abell, George, 195
Abbott, S.E., 136
Adhikari, G., 128
Administrative exigency, 85–7, 147, 149–51, 186–7, 191–3, 199–202, 219–20, 223–6, 228–9, 232–3, 244–5, 248–9, 252
Ahrars, 5, 8, 29, 137, 139
Akalis, 77–9, 85, 89–90, 98, 128, 141, 210, 248
Alexander, A.V., 158, 162, 172, 173, 192
Ali, Chaudhuri Muhammad, 168
Ali, Chaudhury Rahmat, 56
Ali, Ghazanfar, 130, 194–5, 197, 209, 220
Ali, Shaukat, 16, 20
Amery, Leo, 45, 47, 62, 64, 72, 73, 76, 84, 94, 112, 122, 123, 143, 240
Armed Forces: division of, 147–9; nationalism in, 227
Assam, 67, 88, 90, 111, 116, 136, 187, 207, 215, 221
Attlee, Clement, 1st Earl, 73, 125, 145, 146, 150, 157, 170, 174, 175, 193, 208, 212, 213, 219, 226
Auchinleck, Field-Marshal Sir Claude, on nationalism in the Indian army, 147–9;
August Offer, 63–5
Azad, Maulana Abul Kalam, 21, 22, 31, 43, 44, 49, 84, 119, 120, 121, 124, 137, 156, 160, 161, 163, 165, 166–7, 173, 176, 189–90
Azad Muslim Party, 5, 44, 91, 96, 116

Bahauddin, 130
Baksh, Allah, 28, 44, 58, 75, 91, 96
Baksh, Maula, 96, 116, 121
Baldev Singh, 81, 98, 102, 133, 205–6
Baluchistan, 111, 207

Bardoli Resolution, 71, 72, 73
Bengal, 4–5, 13, 16, 26, 41, 42, 44, 53, 55, 58, 67–9, 88, 89, 90, 91–4, 97, 106, 111, 116, 117, 126, 134, 136, 137–8, 140, 181–5, 195–7, 198–201, 204, 205, 209, 221, 226, 228, 229, 230, 231, 236, 241, 246
Benthall, Sir Edward, 56
Bevin, Ernest, 145–6
Bihar, 5, 12, 35, 36, 37, 41, 42, 86, 113, 195, 198–201, 204, 211, 230
Binny, Brigadier Thomas, 183, 186
Bombay, 7, 12, 13, 86, 88, 106, 225
Bose, Sarat Chandra, 42
Bose, Subhas Chandra, 31–2
British, seek to counterpoise Congress, 8–9, 11, 50–1, 52, 54, 57–8, 59, 63–6, 69–70, 73–4, 112–13, 122, 124, 203–4, 238, 239–40, 241–3, 245; and constitutional initiatives, 63, 71, 72–4, 76; and civil disobedience, 84–5; and united India; 151–2, 245–6; reluctant to withdraw, 191–3; reluctant to implement Cabinet Mission Plan, 193, 207–8; withdrawal announcement, 207–8, 212–14, 215–16; and conditional transfer of power, 233–4; see also Cabinet Mission, Linlithgow, Pakistan, Wavell
Bucher, General Sir Roy, 187
Bundelkhand bye-election, 19–21
Burma, 151
Burrows, Sir Frederick, 183–7, 196, 197, 200
Butler, R.A., 1st Baron, 123

Cabinet Mission, 142 ff; Indian parties and, 154ff; alternative schemes, 157–8
Cabinet Mission Plan, grouping and, 162–3, 164, 166–7, 174–5, 246;

Cabinet Mission Plan, (*Contd.*)
British assurances to Indian parties on, 164–6;
Indian parties and, 165ff; interim government and 167–8, 169–74;
League accepts, 168–9, 246–7; parity and 169–70;
Congress accepts, 172
League rescinds acceptance of, 174–8;
British inplementation of, 175, 189, 205, 212
Campbell-Johnson, Alan, 232
Caroe, Sir Olaf, 204
Casey, Richard Gardiner, 106, 136
Central Provinces, 12, 13, 35, 97, 106, 225
Chhatari, Nawab of, 17
Churchill, Sir Winston, 63, 73, 76, 85, 112, 115, 124
Civic Guards, 61
Clow, Sir Andrew, 143
Colville, Sir John 115
Communal Award, 3, 4, 18, 30
Communalism, and Indian society, 236
Communal tension, 31, 78, 152–3
Communal violence, in Calcutta, 181–7; in East Bengal, Bihar, and UP, 195–202; in Punjab, 218–20, 223–6, 248–9
Communists, 128
Constituent Assembly, and Cripps offer, 76; and Mission Plan, 163–7; sovereignty of, 164–5, 174–8; League refusal to enter, 193, 203, 205–8, 209, 212, 229, 246–7
Congress, Indian National, elections of 1936–7, 7–8, 11–14; differences with League, 14ff, 23, 48–9, 58–9, 63–4; seeks to accommodate League, 30–1, 38–9, 49; wants declaration of British war aims, 47–8, 62; Patna and Ramgarh resolutions of, 55, 57, 61; and civil disobedience, 55, 60–1, 65, 83, 84; and Simla Conference, 118, 119–24; elections of 1945–6, 137–9, 251; and Cabinet Mission, 156–7, 160ff, 189–90; enters interim government,

187; with League in interim government, 204–5; accepts 6 December 1946 Statement, 208; accepts partition, 226, 229, 230–2
Craik, Sir Henry, 65
Cripps, Sir Stafford, 76ff, 153, 154, 157, 158, 159, 160, 161, 164–5, 168, 170, 175, 177, 213, 247
Cripps offer, Indian parties and 76–7, 78–9, 156; communal tension and 78–9; Pakistan and 81, 108, 117, 144, 240–1, 244; British policy and 113, 125, 126, 144, 146, 149, 157
Cunningham, Sir George, 56, 58, 75, 92, 139

Darbhanga, Maharaja of, 198
Daultana, Mian Mumtaz, 101, 130, 223
Dawn, 128, 129, 175, 181, 199, 214, 215, 218, 222
Desai, Bhulabhai, 71, 113–16, 249
Desai-Liaqat Pact, 114, 115, 124
de Valera, 154
Direct Action, 175–6; 181, 187, 188–9
Dow, Sir Hugh, 75, 91, 121, 191, 198, 199–201
Dufferin and Ava, 1st Marquess of, 252
Durham, 1st Earl of, 145

Eastern Times 98
Elections, 1936–7, 2, 11–13; 1945–6, 126ff, 135–40, 243; *see also* Congress, Jinnah, Muslim League, Pakistan, Unionists

Faizpur Congress, 9

Gandhi, Mahatma, 12, 23, 34, 39n, 45, 46, 47, 48, 51, 52, 55, 59, 60, 62, 88, 147; differences with Jinnah and League, 29–31, 83–4, 108–12, 188–9, 242; and civil disobedience, 71–2, 83, 84; and Pakistan, 79; and Desai-Liaqat Pact, 114; and Simla Conference, 119; and Cabinet Mission, 156, 159, 165, 167, 172; and Constituent Assembly, 206; and partition, 230

Glancy, Sir Bertrand, 82, 90, 99, 100, 102–3, 118, 129, 130, 141, 143
Government of India Act 1919, 4, 240, 244
Government of India Act 1935, 2, 54, 77, 140, 165, 185, 237, 240
Grigg, Sir P.J., 122, 123

Habibullah, K.B., 19
Haig, Sir Harry, 6, 8, 24n, 36
Hallett, Sir Maurice, 36
Haroon, Sir Abdullah, 70, 190
Hasan, Syed Wazir, 7, 19
Herbert, Sir John, 69, 84, 86, 88; dismissal of Huq ministry, 92–4
Hidayatullah, G.H., 9, 91, 96, 122
Hitler, Adolf, 59
Hoare, Sir Samuel, 51
Hodson, H.V., 75, 232
Huq, Fazlul, 5, 16, 26–7, 28–9, 43, 46, 53, 55, 58, 66–9, 70, 84, 92–4, 136, 137, 237, 239
Husain, Ashiq, 131
Husain, Fazli, 4, 99
Husain, Zakir, 172

Indian Nation, 198
Indonesia, 149
Iqbal, Muhammad, 56
Interim Government, Cabinet Mission and 152, 165, 167–8, 169–70, 172–8; League attitude to, 168–70, 174, 194–5, 203–4, 231, 247; negotiations for 172–8
INA trials, 147–8
Ispahani, M.A.H., 26, 46, 68, 95, 106, 136, 137, 169

Jammat-i-Islami, 138
Jamiat-ul-ulema-i-Hind, 29, 138, 140
Jayakar, M.R., 156
Jenkins, Sir Evan, 80, 111, 115, 116, 143, 209–10; against League ministry in Punjab, 217–18, 220–3, 228–9; on communal violence and Punjab administration 219–26, 232–3
Jilani, Mustafa Shah, 130

Jinnah, Muhammad Ali, differences with Congress leaders, 1, 2, 9–11, 14ff, 24–5, 28–32, 46, 47–53, 64, 73, 83, 87, 89, 109–12; and Pakistan, 2, 57, 59, 74–5, 107–8, 110–11, 142, 143, 154–6, 227–8, 251–2; and Communal Award, 3; and provincial Muslim politics, 4–7, 26–7, 117; post-election attitude to Congress, 14ff, 25ff; against coalition, 18–19, 24; attitude on outbreak of second world war, 46–7; does not want a settlement with Congress, 54, 57, 77; and Unionists, 59–60, 97–107, and August offer, 64; and League premiers, 66–70, 84, 90–1, 95–7, 238–9; and Cripps offer, 76–8; and Desai-Liaqat pact, 113, 115–16, at Simla Conference, 119–25; elections of 1945–6, 126ff; and Cabinet Mission, 158ff; unprepared for independence, 158–9; and interim government, 179ff, 203; and communal voilence, 187, 199; and implementation of Mission Plan, 206; and League attempts to overthrow unionists, 210–11, 214–15; wants League ministry in Punjab, 220, 221, 228; wants Governor-Generalship of Pakistan, 234
Jowitt, William Allen, 1st Baron, interpretation of Mission Plan, 205

Kartar Singh, 89
Khaksars, 60, 78
Khaliquzzaman, Chaudhury 6, 17–24, 56, 108, 125, 168
Khalsa Nationalist Party, 60
Khan, Aga, 56
Khan, Abdul Hamid, 75
Khan, Aurangzeb, 56, 92, 121, 126, 138
Khan, Ghaffar, 161
Khan, Ismail, 21, 23–4 and n, 29, 74–5, 164
Khan, Liaqat Ali, 3, 101, 113–16, 121, 127, 136, 153, 164, 165, 181, 197, 203, 208, 211, 221, 227
Khan, Mir Bunde Ali, 65

Khan Saheb, 92
Khan, Shaukat Hyat, 103, 153
Khanna, Mehr Chand, 92
Khan, Sikander Hyat, and League, 16, 27, 43–4, 46, 59–60, 65–6, 67–8, 70, 97–8, 237, 239; suggests rapprochement with Congress, p. 77; and Sikhs, 80, 81–2; death of, 99
Khilafat 19
Kidwai, Rafi Ahmad, 22
Kripalani, J.B., 196, 199, 207, 230, 231–2
Krishak Proja Party, 5, 13, 26, 43, 68

Labour party, and Indian independence, 125, 144–7; *see also* British policy
Lahore resolution, 55–6, 57–8, 59, 60, 110; *see also* Jinnah, Muslim League, Pakistan
Latif, Abdul, 56
Linlithgow, Victor Hope, 2nd Marquess of, seeks counterpoise to Congress, 11, 47–52, 56, 57–8, 61–2, 64–6, 69–70, 72, 73–4, 82, 90, 238, 240, 241–2; on League charges against Congress governments, 36, 54, 74; and outbreak of second world war, 45–6; wants Indian parties in his government, 45–6, 61–2, 63; considers Jinnah unconstructive, 55, 99–100; and Quit India movement, 83–5; and League ministries, 90–2; on dismissal of Huq, 94, assessment of Khizar Hyat Khan Tiwana, 99; *see also* British policy, Jinnah, Congress, Muslim League, Pakistan
Listowel, William Hare, 6th Earl of, 232; on post-partition arrangements, 233–4
Lumley, Sir Roger, 72

Madras, 13, 37, 75, 79
Mahasabha, Hindu, 3, 13, 23, 32, 41, 58, 59, 68, 69, 78, 83, 84, 92, 95, 112, 198
Mahmud, Syed, 113
Mahmudabad, Raja of, 60

Mamdot, Nawab Iftikhar Husain Khan of, 99, 101, 105, 126, 129, 130, 131, 138, 188, 218, 221, 228
Matin, Abdul, 75
Mansergh, P.N.S., 57 and n
Maxwell, Sir Reginald, 61
Menon, Krishna, 145
Momins, 137
Monteath, Sir David, 190
Moon, Sir Penderel, 66n, 173, 219
Morning News 181, 182
Mountbatten, Admiral of the Fleet, Earl, 212, 213, 228, 231; and Pakistan, 226–7; and partition, 229, 234–5, 236; and early transfer of power, 232
Mudie, Sir Francis, 78, 114–15, 125, 204, 208, 209, 251
Munshi, K.M., 113
Muslims, political unification of, 44, 55, 58, 117, 140, 237
Muslim Conference, 6
Muslim League, 1; and Pakistan, 2, 55, 125, 154, 237; organization of, 3–4, 6, 25–6, 91–2, 95, 98–9, 105, 117, 126–7, 241; and elections of 1936–7, 7–9, 13–14; differences with Congress, 7, 9–11, 14–16, 24–5, 46, 48, 50–1, 63–4, 73, 87; and Bundelkhand bye-election, 19–22; allegations against Congress governments, 32ff, 53; position in Muslim majority provinces, 43–4; and outbreak of second world war, 46–7, 48; and August offer, 63–4; wants British guarantees, 87, 108, 116, 177–8, 249–50; and provincial Muslim politics, 91–7, 131ff, 237; rescinds acceptance of Cabinet Mission Plan, 175–8, 247; and interim government, 179ff; and Direct Action, 181, 187–8, 199–200, 203–4; attempts to overthrow Unionist ministry, 203, 209–16; gets sovereign Pakistan, 234–5; 250–2
Muslim League National Guards, 153, 190, 208, 209–11; reorganization of, 197; part in communal violence, 221–2

Muslim Mass Contact Programme, 16–17, 18, 27, 39–40, 44, 250
Muslim Unity Board, 6
Mutinies, R.I.A.F. and R.I.N., 245–6

National Agriculturist Party, 6, 8–9 and n, 11, 17
Nationalist Muslims, 6, 123, 137, 138, 173, 193, 194
Nawab of Dacca, 5, 26
Nazimuddin, Khwaja, 68, 69, 74, 94–5, 106, 116, 121, 125, 126, 177, 181, 200
Nehru, Jawaharlal, 8, 12, 38, 39, 45, 70, 86, 145, 147; differences with Jinnah, 1, 9–11, 14–16, 23, 28, 49, 161, 188–9; on independence, 1, 9; attitude to coalitions, 17, 30; and Bundelkhand bye-election, 20–1; and coalition controversy, 21–2; and civil disobedience, 71–2; and INA trials, 148; and Cabinet Mission, 161–2, 163–4, 165, 166, 170, 171; and League's call for Direct Action, 176–7; and interim government, 180, 188, 189, 191, 193–203, 204–5; and communal violence, 198–9; and Constituent Assembly, 206; and partition, 226, 229, 230–1
Nikil Banga Proja Samity, 5
Nishtar, Rab, 164–5, 194, 197
Noon, Firoze Khan, 92, 127, 130, 133, 153, 199, 200, 220
North-West Frontier Province, 12, 13, 28, 42–3, 44, 53, 55, 58, 75, 78, 87, 89, 90, 92, 95, 97, 106, 107, 111, 116, 121, 125, 126, 138–40, 152, 153, 173, 190, 204, 207, 215, 221, 237, 241, 246

Orissa, 13, 86

Pakistan, demand for, 55–7; Muslim politicans and, 58–60, 74–5, 81–2, 105–7, 117; Congress and, 58–9, 108–11, 117, Sikhs and, 59–60, 81–2, 97–8, 140, 211, 217, 248–9; British policy and, 74, 117, 142–4, 151–2, 157–9, 241–2, 249–50; Cripps offer and, 76–8; League and sovereign, 117,

142, 154–5, 241, 246–7, 251–2; elections of 1945–6 and, 126, 127, 134–7, 139–41, 249–50; 'two nations' and, 142; League's desire for military guarantees and, 155, 250; grouping and, 246; 'inevitability' of and, 243–4; *see also*, British policy, Congress, Jinnah, Muslim League
Palestine, 151
Pant, G.B., 17, 18, 21, 22, 23, 39
Parity, August offer and 64; Desai-Liaqat pact and, 114, 116; Simla Conference and, 119, 123, 124; League and, 168–70, 180–1, 171, 240
Partition, Cripps Plan and, 77, 81; British and, 151–2, 226–7; Congress accepts, 226; Mountbatten decides on, 229; Punjab and Bengal assemblies for, 236; coalition controversy and, 237; absence of agreement and, 237, 251–2
Patel, Vallabhai, 31, 156–7, 162, 206, 229, 230
Pearl Harbour, 69, 71
Pethick-Lawrence, Frederick William, 1st Baron, 144, 153, 158, 159, 160, 161, 164–5, 170, 171, 188, 189, 192, 206, 215, 232, 236, 247
Pirpur Report, allegations against Congress ministries, 25, 32–6; British officials discount charges, 36–7, 38–9; Congress reaction to, 37–41
Prasad, Rajendra, 31, 50, 51, 229
Punjab, 4, 13, 16, 27, 43, 59, 60, 65–6, 69, 75, 77–8, 79, 80–2, 96, 97–107, 110, 111, 112, 116, 121, 125, 126, 127, 128–9, 131–5, 139–41, 143, 152, 153, 190, 195, 195, 209–14, 217ff, 243

Quit India Movement, 83, 92, 97, 115; administrative problems and, 85–7, 244–5; Muslims and, 87–9, 239; Akalis and, 89–90
Qureshi, A.H., 19
Qureshi, Makhdum Murid Husain, 130

Rafiuddin, 19, 20
Raikes, Henry, 213

Rajagopalachari, Chakravarti, 59, 63, 71, 72, 79–80, 83, 108–10, 112
Ram, Chhotu, 99, 102
Rangoon, 76
Rashtriya Sewak Sangh (R.S.S.), 78, 153, 198, 209
Riazuddin, Hakim, 19
Roosevelt, Franklin D., 76

Saadullah, Muhammad, 66, 67, 70, 90–1, 116, 121
Said, Ahmad, 6
Sarwar, Ghulam, 197
Sarwar, Muhammad Ghulam, 131
Satyamurti, 59
Savarkar, V.D., 92
Searchlight, 198
Sherwani, Nisar Ahmed, 19, 20
Shiva Rao, B., 72
Short, Major John, 80
Sikhs, and Pakistan, 58, 59–60, 77–8, 79–82, 97–8, 100, 103–4, 112, 152, 248; and Quit India Movement, 89–90; and Gandhi–Jinnah talks, 112; and Simla Conference, 119, 121; and communal violence, 183; and League agitation in Punjab, 217ff.
Simla Conference, 118–25, 147, 242–3
Simon, 1st Viscount, 122, 175
Sind, 5, 13, 28, 40–1, 44, 53, 58, 65, 75, 90, 91, 96, 111, 116, 117, 121, 122, 125, 126, 134, 137, 140, 153, 182, 187, 201, 204, 208, 209, 236
Singapore, 76
Smith, W.H. Saumarez, 185n
Spens Inquiry Commission, 183
Star of India, 182
Statement of 16 May 1946, *see* Cabinet Mission Plan
Statement of 16 June 1946, 171, 172,
Statement of 6 December 1946, 205; Indian parties and, 206–8
Statement of 20 February 1947, 212–14, 216, 217
Statesman, 132, 154, 184
Suhrawardy, H.S., 68, 69, 126, 136, 181, 182–5, 190, 191, 241, 246

Syed, G.M., 96, 126

Tara Singh, 60, 81, 89, 90, 217
Taylor, S.G., 184–5 and 185n, 186 and n.
Tiwana, Khizar Hyat Khan, becomes Punjab Premier, 99; and Muslim League, 100–5, 121, 127, 129, 141, 209–11, 214, 215; and Simla Conference, 121; and Pakistan, 134–5; elections of 1945–6, 129, 133, 134–6; and Mission Plan, 176, 246, 251; resigns, 217
Tiwana, Major Mumtaz, 130
Transfer of power, British conditions and, 244–6; *see also* British policy, partition
Tuker, General Sir Francis, 200 and n
Turnbull, Sir Frank, 174
Twynam, Sir Henry, 106
Tyson, J.D., 221

Unionists, 4, 27, 59–60, 65–6, 79, 80, 81–2, 85, 97ff, 111–12, 116–17, 118, 121, 123, 128, 129, 130, 131, 134–5, 139–41, 243, 251
Unity Board, 6–7
Unity Conference, 6
United Muslim Party, 5
United Provinces, 5, 6, 8, 11, 12, 17–18, 21, 22, 23, 41, 42, 44, 78, 86, 125, 135, 137, 153, 198, 200, 209

War Committees, 61
Wavell, Field Marshal, Earl, 108, 125, 232; and Unionists, 101, 103; and Gandhi-Jinnah talks, 111; favours official political initiative, 112–15, 118; and Simla Conference, 119–24; and Pakistan, 143–4; and Congress leaders, 147, 153, 161, 165, 167, 172, 247–8; opinion of Cabinet Delegation, 153; and Muslim League, 154, 167–8, 171–2, 173–4; attempts to get League into interim government, 179, 188, advises British withdrawal, 191–

3, 213–14; and communal violence, 196, 200; with Indian parties in interim government, 179, 188
Whipping Act, 86
Wyatt, Woodrow, 170

Yusuf, Muhammad, 239

Zaghlul, 154
Zetland, 2nd Marquess of, 49, 51, 54, 56, 58

Divide and Quit

An Eyewitness Account of the Partition of India

Penderel Moon

New Edition

Preface and Acknowledgements

When Penderel Moon died in 1987, he left a varied literary legacy. His longest and most comprehensive study of the history of relations between Britain and India, *The British Conquest and Dominion of India*, completed just before his death, remained unpublished and most of his other works were out of print. After his death, his nephews resolved to publish *The British Conquest* which appeared in 1989.

They also decided to attempt the republication of *Divide and Quit* for the 50th anniversary of India's Independence. *Divide and Quit* was, according to Moon, his best and most enduring work, and the decision to republish it was brought about with the encouragement of scholars of Indian history both in India and in Britain. They endorsed the importance of its contribution to the continuing study of independence and partition. It is this area of scholarly interest that has provided a context for a re-examination of *Divide and Quit* itself.

How have Moon's views on the politics of partition stood the test of time and the judgements of subsequent writers? How enduring is his account of the role of key individuals and how accurate is his assessment of the numbers killed in the conflicts arising during partition? What too, has been the legacy of the work of the man whose career in the Indian Civil Service was not without controversy and contradiction? He was an independent minded member of the Service with strong, and at times, idiosyncratic views. He was a long time advocate of Independence: he resigned on an issue of principle (prompting a leading article in *The Statesman*—'Moon eclipsed'—sadly missing from our records) and returned to the service of the Government of Independent India to serve longer than any other former British Indian Civil Servant.

During the preparation of this new edition, I have been constantly reminded that there are no historical truths: there is evidence and there is interpretation. There may never be definitive answers to the questions raised above, nor to the general question of the legacy of the British Raj or the work of Civil Servants such as my uncle.

This edition owes much to Ian Taylor, who went far beyond the call of duty in his sensitive and expert handling of the Moon estate. I am very grateful too, for the support and advice of David Blake of the British Library, Oriental and India Office Collections; Judith Brown of Balliol College, Oxford; Ian Talbot of The School of International Studies and Law at Coventry University; Robert Oakeshott; Tapan Raychaudhuri, Mark Tully; Ravi Dayal; Mary Clemmey and Gillian Wright; to Philip Mason and Mangat Rai for their personal recollections and advice; and to Chatto and Windus, publishers of the original edition, for their permission for offset rights.

I am also grateful to Dr Bhagwan Josh of the School of African and Oriental Studies in London for assistance and advice on further reading and to Camilla Westergaard for her patient and painstaking research, particularly into the photographs.

William Clarke

Sheffield 1997

Contents

List of Illustrations   vii

Introduction to *Divide and Quit*—Mark Tully   ix

Brief Biographies of Key Figures   1

Introduction   7

Text of *Divide and Quit*

    I The Genesis of Pakistan   11

    II The Punjab and Pakistan   29

    III The Cabinet Mission   42

    IV The Mountbatten Plan   65

    V The Punjab and Partition   71

    VI Bahawalpur State   97

    VII Journey across the Punjab   114

    VIII Outbreak of Disturbances in Bahawalpur State   124

    IX Restoring Order—I   143

    X Restoring Order—II   159

    XI Disturbances in Bahawalpur City   190

    XII Events in Rahim Yar Khan   225

    XIII Resettlement   247

    XIV Summing Up   261

    Note on Casualties   293

    XV Re-reading *Divide and Quit*—Tapan Raychaudhuri   294

    Bibliography   311

    Index   315

MAPS

1 The Punjab   89

2 Bahawalpur State   112–3

List of Illustrations

Frontispiece: Sir Penderel Moon dressed in Indian clothes after independence whilst he was Chief Commissioner for Himachal Pradesh, Simla, 1950. [The Estate of Sir Penderel Moon, original copyright with The Photo Studios, 24 Lajpatrai Road, Simla.]

1. *Jawaharlal Nehru and Mohammed Ali Jinnah taking a walk in the garden at the latter's residence;* May 1946. [By permission of the British Library, MS 134/2 (28).]

2. *Mahatma Gandhi and Mohammed Ali Jinnah leaving the latter's residence en route for Delhi for talks with the Viceroy;* November 1939. [Getty Images.]

3. *Lord and Lady Mountbatten with Mahatma Gandhi;* 1947. [Getty Images.]

4. *Sardar Baldev Singh, Minister of Punjab Government in New Delhi;* April 1946. [By permission of the British Library, MS 134/1(34).]

5. *His Highness The Nawab of Bahawalpur in his regalia;* 1924. [By permission of the British Library, MS 10/16 (1).]

6. *Sir Richard Crofton, Prime Minister of Bahawalpur with the Nawab (far left);* December 1942. [By permission of the British Library, MSS EUR F 138/60 (273).]

7. *Mountbatten discloses the Partition of India plan. From left to right, Jawaharlal Nehru, Lord Ismay, Lord Mountbatten, and Mohammed Jinnah;* June 1947. [Getty Images.]

8. *Bahawalpur station with refugees boarding a train;* 1947. [The Estate of Sir Penderel Moon.]

9. *Sir Penderel Moon taking tea with Rajendra Prasad, the first President of the Indian Republic, on the verandah of the Viceregal Lodge at Simla;* 1950. [The Estate of Sir Penderel Moon.]

10.   *The second Marquess of Linlithgow, Viceroy Designate of India, leaving
      his home in London with the Marchioness, en route to India;* April 1936.
      [Getty Images.]

11.   *The Cabinet Mission and Jinnah, from left to right, A.V. Alexander,
      Mohammed Jinnah, and Lord Pethick-Lawrence;* May 1946. [By
      permission of the British Library, MS 134/2 (25).]

12.   *A special train used to take Delhi Muslims to Pakistan;* 1947. [Getty
      Images.]

13   *Nehru moves the resolution for an independent Republic in the Constituent
      Assembly at New Delhi;* February 1947. [Getty Images.]

Introduction to Penderel Moon's
Divide and Quit
Mark Tully

J awaharlal Nehru once wrote, 'I have become a queer mixture of the East and the West, out of place everywhere, at home nowhere. I am a stranger and alien in the West. I cannot be of it. But in my own country also sometimes I have the feeling of an exile.' There were in the Indian Civil Service, or ICS, Britons, who after spending many years in India, still remained of the West, but were at the same time very much at home in the East. They were the men who founded and nurtured that extraordinary relationship between two such different countries, between ruler and ruled, which enabled Britain to leave India without bitterness. I can testify to that because in thirty years of living in Independent India, I have never once had an occasion to regret that I am British.

Penderel Moon has been described as one of the ablest men recruited to the ICS during the last days of the Raj. With his experience as an administrator in Punjab, his independent mind, his conviction that Indians must become independent, and his friendships with Indians, he had a unique ability to see both sides, or rather I should say all sides, of the tragedy which befell Punjab at partition. It is most appropriate that fifty years after partition *Divide and Quit*, Moon's analysis of the causes of the bloodshed in Punjab and his record of his own rule during those days, should be republished.

Moon as a young man was an unlikely person to become so closely involved in India, to care so passionately about a relationship with a foreign country, although there were family connections with India on his mother's side. He had, what was considered in those days, the best of all possible educations at Winchester, one of England's top public schools, and New College, Oxford. At Oxford he not only obtained a first but he was also elected to a fellowship of All Souls, an honour only awarded to the most outstanding graduates. He could therefore have pursued a career as an academic, a home civil servant, or a politician with every hope of rising to the very top. In 1929 he was appointed to the Indian Civil Service.

When Moon was himself asked why he had chosen India he replied, 'I was the victim of propaganda. When I was a schoolboy at Winchester someone came down to speak to the two top forms on India and the scope for service in India and painted a very idealistic picture of the sort of work to be done, and I didn't realise this was propaganda at the time; I realise it now, they were having difficulty in recruiting people to the ICS from the public schools— and I was caught.' Elsewhere, however, he wrote of the opportunity 'to see the final accomplishment of England's mission in India— namely, under her guidance and fostering care to bring India into the scale of free, independent nations.' Later in his life Moon wrote that although recruits to the ICS were given 'no specific indications' that power was to be transferred, on the voyage to India he discussed this with the other members of the ICS travelling with him and their general conclusion was that British rule would last another twenty-five years.

If it is strange that a young man with Moon's prospects should have chosen India, it is equally surprising that one of his greatest achievements should have been the understanding of India and Indians that he acquired. Indians are friendly, and tolerant, but they expect others to be so too. They particularly dislike arrogance, especially arrogant foreigners. In the great Hindu epic, the Ramayana, the sin or crime of the demon King Ravana was 'ahankar' or pride. But Moon appears to have had more than his fair share of conceit as a young man. His self confidence was apparently nurtured at home and this he demonstrated at the very beginning of his ICS career, when he wrote of his training for the service with contempt, describing it as 'an atrocious waste of time', and had the temerity to write and complain about it to the Secretary of State.

On the voyage out to India, Moon treated most of his fellow passengers with disdain. He wrote, 'The products of unknown schools that have not yet (learned) how to do justice to their new status.' But at the same time the voyage did give an indication of the way Moon's life was going to develop because he found the Indian members of the ICS returning on the ship 'quite intelligent', and said 'the most remarkable is exceedingly acute, and we have had such long, obscure arguments'.

But although Moon had a considerable opinion of himself, and could be something of a snob he also had great charm. An Indian ICS colleague, Mangat Rai, remembers him as 'an extraordinarily well organised and a good host, and an excellent guest'. In later life David Blake, who worked with Moon on a project to publish the India Office Documents 1942–7 found Moon to be 'a charming man to work for with a gift for stimulating and amusing conversation.'

Moon's early impressions of India did nothing to convince him that he had made the right choice of career. When he reached Punjab he was 'aghast at the flat, featureless character of the countryside and the constant wastes of sand and cactus bushes and other unattractive elements.' He was posted to Jullundur, one of the most intensely cultivated areas of Punjab, but even there Moon found 'those horrible "tibbas" or sand dunes, and cactus', and described the good soil as being 'only just a little bit removed from sand'. The Green revolution and irrigation have since changed the face of Punjab. Now the newcomer driving down the Grand Trunk Road from Delhi to Jullundur would be struck by the fertility of the soil. Early in the year a yellow sea of wheat and mustard stretches as far as the eye can see. Later it's emerald green rice and maize. Punjab is now the granary of an India which feeds a population that has more than doubled since Independence.

For all his early reservations about joining the ICS and his initial dislike of Punjab, Moon went on to make a considerable mark as a civil servant in that province. He continued throughout his career to value his Indian colleagues and to be critical of the tendency of the British to seek each other's company. Mangat Rai said Moon felt the service had been too aloof, and had failed because its officers had no relationship with the Indian middle classes. He was particularly contemptuous of those who treated Indians as second class. When asked about this attitude in an interview he explained, 'I would say it was a result of our easy and complete conquest of India which made us feel that we were superior to Indians, not only in military science, but in almost every way.'

Moon's reputation as an administrator was not just built on his formidable intellect. He was a man of action too, who believed in getting out and about, in seeing things for himself. He understood only too well that, as he put it, 'in India the mere issue of orders is not necessarily equivalent to their execution', and he did his best to ensure that his orders were executed. He was a great believer 'in getting right into the villages', and was critical of district officers who became 'mere babus or clerks sitting at headquarters'. He thought district officers should spend long hot days in the villages of Punjab.

Long before the dark days of August 1947 when Punjab was partitioned and brutal ethnic cleansing took place in both parts of the Province, Moon learnt that it was necessary to take firm action against communal violence. In 1938 he tried forty two members of a crowd who had stormed the railway station at Gujrat in Punjab and dragged Sikh passengers out of a train. He criticized the authorities in Amritsar for not opening fire during the riots in the Punjab in March 1947. Philip Mason told me a story of Moon during the partition massacres. Coming across an armed Sikh soldier robbing a dying or dead man, Moon who was unarmed and half the Sikh's size, walked up to the soldier, gave him a 'hard kick up the bottom' and ordered him back to his unit. The order was obeyed promptly. Mason went on to say, 'that seems to me entirely characteristic—complete fearlessness and confidence, and the assumption that he could give orders to anyone.'

Moon claimed to have chosen to serve in Punjab because it was 'the fashionable thing to do'. But he proved himself well-suited to that province where the civil service had a tradition of being action-orientated and dedicated to economic development, which was by no means a universal priority throughout British India. The tradition was founded by John Lawrence, the first Commissioner of Punjab after the state was incorporated in British India in 1849. His ideal officer was described by John Beames, posted to Punjab in the early days, as 'a hard active man in boots and breeches, who almost lived in the saddle, worked all day and nearly all night'. Moon was no philistine, but John Lawrence would have approved of his lifestyle. He was an outstanding horseman, he had a reputation for never allowing the extreme summer heat to interfere with his life in any way, and some say wore himself out through hard work. In the correspondence between the Governor of the Punjab and the Viceroy about Moon's resignation, Sir Bertrand wrote, 'the fact is that the strain of work and the loneliness of the life he leads have been too much for him'. That might not be a judgement that Moon would have accepted, and it does not seem to accord with the picture of a tough, resilient, self-confident civil servant we get from Moon's own writings and other sources, but it certainly indicates that his superiors thought he had lived up to the Punjab tradition of unceasing toil.

Although Moon was not allowed to accompany Sir Stafford Cripps and the Cabinet Mission, in 1946, Viscount Wavell, now Viceroy, invited him to return to India as Secretary to the Boards of Development and Planning. In April 1947, he became Revenue Minister in Bahawalpur, the only one of the larger princely states to be ruled by a Muslim Nawab and to have a predominately Muslim population. The second half of *Divide and Quit* is the record of the disturbances in Bahawalpur during the partition riots. It, too, shows Moon's extraordinary energy and his belief that the only way to curb communal violence was to reach the scene of the rioting as soon as possible, and take firm action. He was in the north eastern tip of the state, trying looters and preventing an outbreak of cholera among the refugees, when he heard that trouble had broken out in the capital, Bahawalpur. He immediately drove back and took charge of restoring order and evacuating the Hindu population.

Moon's career in the ICS came to a premature end because of his friendship with Indians. Like many young British officers in the ICS, he considered that the government of the second Marquess of Linlithgow was dragging its feet about Indian advancement towards self-government. In November 1942, he addressed to the Punjab Government a letter arguing that those imprisoned for preaching civil disobedience should receive better treatment. When he received an unsympathetic reply, explaining the critical war situation, he sent a copy of the government's letter, with his own acid comments, to a personal friend who was brother of Rajkumari Amrit Kaur, secretary to Gandhi. She was at the time in gaol. This letter was intercepted and Moon was in serious trouble. In his comments on the reply he had received from the government he had written, 'I experienced mingled feelings of astonishment and disgust. I was astonished because I did not think that the government would have the nerve to deal out to me such pitiful claptrap. It is (an) insult to one's intelligence, besides being a reflection on their own'. Not surprisingly this was regarded as a serious misdemeanour by his superiors, unacceptable even in good times but that much more so when, following the fall of Singapore, the Japanese advance to Burma's frontier with India, the enemy threat to British India was felt to be at its most acute. After conversations between Moon and the Governor of Punjab, Sir Bertrand Glancy, and correspondence between the Governor and the Viceroy, Lord Linlithgow, Moon agreed to resign from the service and return to Britain. That was at the beginning of 1943.

Moon had always been difficult for his seniors to handle. Philip Mason, Moon's contemporary in the ICS, remembers that not long after his arrival he made a 'sharp comment' on a senior colleague's judgement. Sir Evan Jenkins, the last Governor of Punjab, said Moon liked to 'bait' his superiors. But this must not be taken to mean that Moon was a rebel, always at war with his superiors. He did undoubtedly believe it was his right and his duty to make his views known when he felt mistakes were made. He was at times disdainful of his superiors, but they admired his work and regarded him very highly. In his correspondence with the Viceroy, Sir Bertrand Glancy wrote, 'Moon has done splendid work during his service'. Sir Evan Jenkins said, 'With ten men like Penderel you could easily govern the whole of India'. When Attlee sent the Cabinet Mission to India in a last ditch attempt to get the Congress and Muslim League to agree on a united independent India, Sir Stafford Cripps, a member of the Mission, wanted Moon to accompany them as an adviser. The India Office was not prepared to forgive Moon so soon.

There was, of course, a major difference between Moon and the founders of the Punjab Civil Service under John Lawrence. They believed they had a mission to fulfil. Obviously they did not question the work they did, the nature of the administration and the legal system that they established. Moon most certainly did. It is extraordinary that a man who had such doubts about almost everything the British had done in Punjab should have devoted himself wholeheartedly to his work as a civil servant. One might have thought that he would have resigned much earlier and made a new career, which would not have been difficult for a fellow of All Souls. When he was forced to resign he did tell the Governor of Punjab that he had been thinking of doing so 'for several years'.

Moon was particularly critical of the legal system that Britain established. In his novel *Strangers in India* (1944) he described the young ICS officer and 'myriads' of Indian magistrates who 'daily spent hours in their courts solemnly recording word for word the evidence of illiterate peasants, knowing full well that 90% of it was false'. He also pointed out that the unsuitability of the English legal system had been recognized as far back as the eighteenth century by Warren Hastings.

There are those who argue that the British did introduce the concept of the rule of law into India, and that this was a great boon. Undoubtedly the India the British found was a lawless place.

The Mughal Empire was in its death throes and rival warlords were fighting over its patrimony, but in their heyday the Mughals did have courts, and the rule of law was a fundamental part of ancient Indian thought. Surely it's presumptuous to assume that we needed to teach a civilization as old as that existed in India that there had to be laws. It could be said that we needed to revive respect for the law and reinstate a legal system, but then Moon would argue we should not have modelled the Indian courts and their procedures on our own. In particular he believed that the Evidence Act should be scrapped, that leaders of local communities should assess cases giving their views in public, and that petty cases should be tried by village councils or Panchayats.

Moon acknowledged that the British tolerated police torture as a means of extracting evidence and solving cases. He seemed to regard that as inevitable given the inadequacies of the legal system, in particular the pressure on the police to secure convictions, and the limitations placed on the courts by the Evidence Act. It prevented magistrates and judges from taking into consideration anything except the verbal evidence presented in court. Moon narrated to an interviewer an example of a case where he gave 'very lenient sentences' to police officers who had tortured a suspect. When asked why he had been lenient, he replied 'Because I considered the position was so natural and inevitable that police officers should resort to torture that I didn't think it fair to put them in prison for a really long time'. Unfortunately, very few senior officials in independent India seem to think anything can be done about torture in police stations.

One result of the legal system that Moon particularly deplored was the indebtedness of the peasants. He blamed this on those reforms which made the peasants owners of their land. Possession of land, he said, gave them a security to offer to money-lenders, and their ignorance allowed the moneylenders to charge excessive rates of interest. All too often the peasant would fall behind with his payments which gave the money-lender the opportunity to go to court. Then, 'the Civil Judge, hedged in by elaborate rules of evidence and procedure, dominated by the theory that a written constitution is sacred and must be obeyed down to the last letter even when one of the parties is illiterate—became a mere automaton for registering the moneylender's decrees and setting in motion a well-regulated machinery for the seizure of the debtor's person and property.'

Against Moon's view, it is clear that The Green Revolution has been far more successful in those parts of India where the British did grant land rights to the peasants, than in the areas where they had the misfortune to become vassals of avaricious landlords under Cornwallis' permanent settlement (which Moon certainly did not approve of either). This would seem to indicate that owning land did create a more enterprising peasantry. The land reforms introduced in the late 1970s and early 1980s, by the Communist Government in West Bengal where agriculture was until then very backward, have given even clearer evidence of what security of tenure can do for production. So perhaps it was not so much the land rights given to peasants in states like Punjab which were at fault, but the credit system. When Indira Gandhi nationalized the banks in 1969, their branches spread to the rural areas and an alternative source of credit to the extortionate moneylender became available. Although rural banking is far from free of corruption, and bank staff do all too often demand commissions on loans, nevertheless this along with other government credit schemes have undermined the moneylender.

Throughout his career in India, Moon was most concerned about economic problems. He told an interviewer, 'I felt that we the British Raj, couldn't tackle the main problems of India which [were] economic. ... I felt that a foreign power could not achieve the revolutionary steps which would be necessary to change Indian peasant life. ... This was one of my basic reasons for wanting the British Raj to come to an end.'

When the Raj did end Moon stayed on, serving as Chief Commissioner of Himachal Pradesh setting up the administration in the new state. After Himachal Pradesh he went to the Planning Commission in Delhi, where his concerns were entirely economic. In independent India he seems to have agreed with the basic thrust of Nehru's policies—economic planning, nationalization of what were seen as essential industries, agricultural co-operatives, all in an economy planned and controlled by the government.

What is perhaps strange is that with his long experience as a civil servant, he does not seem to have anticipated the bureaucratic nightmare that a controlled economy would produce in India. But then it is easy to be wise after the event, and to forget how widespread was the belief that governments could and should control economies. What alternative was there on offer at independence anyhow? Britain still owned a large swathe of Indian industry and financial institutions, and they were unlikely to make large new investments in an independent India. India's own private sector was too weak to make a very effective contribution to Nehru's understandable ambition to expand the economy as rapidly as possible.

Perhaps the most controversial of Moon's opinions was his view on democracy. In the conclusion to *Divide and Quit* he has written, 'I there was introduced into a vast country of illiterate peasants, belonging to diverse races and religions, and held together only by geography and common subjection to British rule, a system of government, which while it has served the English and some closely kindred people well enough, has elsewhere been—and doubtless will continue to be—a constant source of strife, disunity and disruption'. He also argued that once we decided India was eventually to become a democracy we should have handed over power rapidly. In this way he believed Hindu–Muslim feelings would not have been inflamed. He wrote, 'If therefore the British ever care to ask wherein lay their responsibility for the massacres and migrations of 1947, the answer may be succinctly given. It lay in their belief in the virtues of parliamentary democracy and their reluctance to part with power.'

Moon may be right in his belief that Britain should have hastened to hand over power after the First World War when, with the Montagu-Chelmsford reforms, we committed ourselves to establishing democracy in India. But again, it is difficult now to assess whether the political circumstances in Britain would have made that even thinkable, let alone possible.

Moon sometimes suggested that the autocratic rule of the Maharajas would have provided a better model than democracy for independent India. It is true that the achievements of the best of those rulers in education and in health services was better than anything provided elsewhere in British India. The Indian state of Kerala's figures for life expectancy and literacy buck the national average and are better than China's, and that is no small measure due to the enlightened policies pursued by the rulers of Travancore State before Independence. But for the most part the Maharajas did not present a very inspiring example of governance. Moon records that the bloodshed at partition was not sufficient cause to persuade his own employer, the Nawab of Bahawalpur, to return from his summer holiday in London.

The long reign of the Nehru-Gandhi family after Independence indicates that Moon was right when in the conclusion to *Strangers in*

India he wrote of 'the deep seated Indian respect for authority and for hereditary rights'. But did the record of the Indian Princes really justify his claim that 'a hereditary monarchy is a most valuable political institution and is not incompatible with a gradual change-over from an authoritarian to a democratic form of government'?

Many Indians took pride in the first fully democratic provincial governments elected as a result of the constitutional reforms introduced in the 1935 Government of India Act. Moon, on the other hand, was dismayed by the corruption and the political interference with the bureaucracy which occurred during the brief period after the 1937 elections when the Provinces of India were ruled by democratically elected governments. Political corruption and the misuse of the government machinery in every form has got worse not better as election has followed election in India.

A look at Asia today might seem to indicate that Moon was right, that autocracy is a better system than democracy for developing in countries. It is the countries of South East Asia, where democracy has not flourished—some to a lesser, some to a greater degree—that have modernized, and achieved very high ratios of economic growth. The former British India has remained firmly wedded to democracy; even military dictators in Pakistan and Bangladesh have always had to commit themselves to the restoration of democracy, and democracy has eventually been restored. Yet South Asia lags far behind the East, including communist China. But autocracy does not seem to be the answer for South Asia. Military rulers achieved little or nothing in Pakistan and Bangladesh, and Indira Gandhi's brief period of emergency rule in India can hardly be described as a success.

It is now widely believed that it's not democracy which has held back South Asia but the failure to provide adequate education and health services. The renowned Indian economist, Amartya Sen, has pointed out that India and China in the forties had 'similar levels of poverty and distress'. But now the figures for literacy, infant mortality, and life expectation are much better in China than India. This improvement in the quality of life, Sen believes, has made significant contributions to China's economic success. But Sen warns, 'The fact that India's record is terrible in some related fields (related to poverty and deprivation) does not provide a good reason to be tempted by the political authoritarianism to be found in China'.

In the end it seems to me two arguments exist against Moon's view that the British should not have introduced democracy into India, which are difficult to refute. The first was put to me by Philip Mason, who said, 'If we had tried to say to them, "Oh, democracy is all right for us but it's not for you", it would have been condescending and patronising, and they would not have liked it.' The second argument is the oft quoted remark of Churchill: 'It has been said that democracy is the worst form of Government except all those other forms that have been tried from time to time.' For all its failings democracy is clearly the form of government the people of India want, and no-one to my knowledge has proposed a system that would be any better. That does not of course mean that the present constitutional arrangements in India, the division of power between the centre, the states, the districts and the villages, is correctly balanced. It does not mean that the division of responsibilities between parliament, the bureaucracy and the judiciary is clear and enforceable. It certainly doesn't mean that the administration is efficient and reasonably honest.

Moon's belief that democracy was not right for India in no way meant that he thought Indians were not ready to rule themselves. In *Strangers in India* his leading character, the Senior Civil Servant, reflects, 'What rot people talk about Indians not being fit to govern themselves. A stock remark of ignorant English women. How little they know and what harm they do.' Moon believed it had been 'a colossal blunder' on the part of the British not to involve Indians much earlier and in much larger numbers in the administration. He consistently pointed out that the Raj would never have survived without the co-operation of Indians. That was the theme of his most substantial work, *The British Conquest and Dominion of India.*

The history of the last fifty years has shown that Moon was absolutely right in stressing that the institutions the British established in India were alien and unsuited to the native genius of that country. In the conclusion of *Strangers in India* he described them as 'inferior replicas of unsuitable English institutions'. Because India has given little or no thought to administrative reform, the Police and Civil Service still function on the British lines, those relics survive; indeed they have expanded, spreading like a weed and choking the growth of any new initiative. They are so corroded by corruption that they achieve little more than insuring their own survival. Even Rajiv Gandhi, when Prime Minister, admitted that only fifteen per cent of the money he allocated for rural development actually percolated down to the villages.

The legal system Moon criticized has survived too. The courts are so clogged with cases that most Indian jails are full of people awaiting trial, rather than those who have been convicted. The appetite for litigation, first encouraged by the British system, has not diminished. False witnesses abound. I remember reading of a Delhi magistrate who complained to the police prosecutor, 'I know that you bring paid witnesses before me every day, but do you have to bring the same ones each time?' Clever lawyers make a mockery of the courts by delaying procedures so that the rich and influential often escape justice.

There have been innovations in the legal system since Independence, and there have been some remarkable judges. The introduction of public interest litigation which allows anyone to bring an injustice to the notice of the Supreme Court has produced judgements which should have had a profound impact on social evils. In some cases they have been effective, but all too often the executive has failed to implement the Supreme Court's judgements.

The courts and the administration present a bleak picture of modern India, but it is not just the institutions which have survived. India itself has survived and has made slow but steady economic progress. It has also preserved freedom of speech, freedom of worship, freedom to form political parties and freedom to approach the courts, no mean achievements compared with so many post-colonial countries. What is frustrating is that with a people as talented as Indians are, in a country where their talents should be free to flourish, the report on the first fifty years has to be 'could have done much better'.

To what extent is the British Raj to blame? To the extent, I believe, that it is to be counted as a success too. Nowhere in the British or any other Empire of the nineteenth and twentieth century did such a close relationship grow between the rulers and the ruled. In the conclusion of *Strangers in India*, written at the time when Britain was still involved in complicated and often bitter negotiations on the future of India, Moon wrote, 'The world hears the angry invective of politicians. It forgets the numberless unrecorded friendships between Englishmen and Indians; it forgets over the length and breadth of India, English and Indian officials are working side by side, often in remote and lonely stations; it forgets the long and happy record of comradeship between Englishmen and Indians in the Indian army—a record creditable to both nations which only prejudice will deride. Anyone who has had personal experiences of these ties of emotion and sentiment will believe that they have not all been casual and purposeless, but are part of something larger, significant, and destined to endure.'

At the village level there was a relationship of trust between the Britons and the Indians. Villagers believed that the British Raj was the 'mai-bap', the all protecting and providing mother and father. Among the leaders of Indian society, even those who fought for Independence, there was a belief that Britain had much to teach them. Mahatma Gandhi once said, 'I have thankfully copied many things from (the English). Punctuality, reticence, public hygiene, independent thinking and exercise of judgement, and several other things I owe to my association with them.'

It was the best of the British rulers of India, men like Penderel Moon, who inspired that respect for Britain, who persuaded the Mahatma and countless others that they had much to learn from our civilization. But, through no fault of their own, they also left many Indians with the feeling that there was little or nothing that was good in their own civilization. The trouble with independent India is that it has still to learn the lesson that Moon himself tried to teach, that foreign ideas and foreign institutions have to be adapted to the ancient wisdom of India itself. Mahatma Gandhi also said, 'My Swaraj (self-rule) is to keep intact the genius of our civilisation. I want to write many new things but they must be written on Indian slate. I would gladly borrow from the West where I can return the amount with decent interest.' India has still, I believe, to rediscover itself. When it does, it will have much to teach us.

Biographies of Key Figures

'Mahatma' Gandhi (1869–1948):
Mohandas Gandhi went to London in 1888 to study law. Thereafter followed a period in South Africa, before he returned to India in 1915 and became active in Congress politics. Gandhi soon became a leader of the Indian National movement, and of the Congress in 1920. He advocated non co-operation and believed strongly in Hindu–Muslim unity. He resigned from the Congress in 1934 when the policy of civil disobedience was abandoned. However, at the outbreak of the war Congress demanded Independence as a condition for co-operation, and in 1940 he resumed the leadership. Here, he was instrumental in the rejection of the Cripps and Cabinet Missions. Imprisoned during the 'Quit India' movement and released again in 1944, he continued to campaign for Hindu–Muslim unity and against partition. He was assassinated in 1948.

Mohammed Ali Jinnah (1876–1948):
Born in Karachi, Jinnah studied law in London and returned to practice in Bombay, where he became a barrister at the Bombay High Court. Elected as Muslim representative of the Imperial Legislative Council in 1909, he joined the All-India Muslim League in 1913. He became President of the League in 1934. Initially a member and firm supporter of the Congress, Jinnah opposed Gandhi's policy of non co-operation and accordingly resigned from the Congress in 1920. From beginning his political career as an Indian rather than as a Muslim Nationalist, Jinnah came to lead the campaign for a separate Muslim State and briefly, before his death in August 1948, Jinnah became the first Governor General of Pakistan.

Jawaharlal Nehru (1889–1964):
Educated at Harrow, Cambridge and London, Nehru returned in 1912 to India where he began practising law. He was drawn to politics and to the Indian National Congress, becoming its President in 1929, 1936, 1937, 1946 and 1951–4. Imprisoned four times in the 1930s, again in 1940, and released for the last time in 1945, Nehru spent over three thousand days in British Indian prisons. Nehru remained a key figure in the negotiations concerning Indian Independence and the transfer of power. He became vice-president of the Executive Council of the Interim Government 1946–7 and the first Prime Minister of Independent India in 1947.

VICEROYS

Lord Linlithgow (1887–1952):

Viceroy from 1936–43. Linlithgow held a number of positions in British Conservative Governments between 1924–38. He was the Chairman of the Select Committee on Indian Constitutional Reform, and introduced provincial autonomy and the separation of Burma. Appointed Viceroy in 1936 Linlithgow's work from 1939 as Viceroy was increasingly dominated by the 'war effort'. He faced hostility and civil disobedience from the Congress and the advancement of the doctrine of a separate Muslim state from the Muslim League. He attempted to get agreement on help for the war effort, but was met with the 'Quit India' movement. He also faced the rejection of the Cripps Mission proposals in 1942. He retired in 1943.

Lord Wavell (1883–1950):

Viceroy between 1943–7. Wavell had a background as a military commander, having been Commander-in-Chief of the British Forces of the Middle East (1939–41), of India (1941–3) and Supreme Commander of the South West Pacific in 1942. His time as Viceroy was dominated by attempts to get agreement on the establishment of an interim government. The 1945 Simla Conference failed to reach an agreement on Muslim representation and the proposals of the Cabinet Mission sent in 1946 also failed to reach agreements. Wavell was dismissed as Viceroy in 1947 and replaced by Mountbatten.

Lord Mountbatten (1900–1979):

Viceroy from March to August 1947, Governor General of India from August 1947 to June 1948. Second cousin to the British King, Mountbatten had limited personal experience of India, although he had been Supreme Allied Commander for South East Asia from 1943–6. His brief from the Labour Government was to end the British administration within eighteen months. The date was brought forward, and Independence agreed in 1947. Unlike his predecessors, he was given a relatively free-hand in the details of his political dealings. His period as Viceroy concluded with Independence and finalized agreement for the separate Muslim State of Pakistan.

CABINET MISSION

A.V. Alexander (1885–1965):

A.V. Alexander had a background as a lay preacher and trade unionist before entering British politics in 1922. He became the First Lord of the Admiralty 1929–31, a post he also held in Churchill's wartime government 1940–5, and again in 1945–6. After 1945 he served in the British Labour Government. Although he came to India with Stafford Cripps and Lord Pethick-Lawrence as a member of the Cabinet Mission, he is generally seen to have made little contribution to the discussions.

Sir Stafford Cripps (1889–1952):
Educated at Winchester College and then University College London, he had a legal background before entering politics. Cripps was appointed Ambassador to Moscow in 1940 and recalled to join the War Cabinet in 1942, when he served both as Leader of the House of Commons and as Minister of Aircraft. Cripps visited India in 1939, and became convinced of the cause of Indian Independence. Appointed Lord Privy Seal in 1942, he returned to India, this time on behalf of the Government (the Cripps Mission). He was a prominent member of the 1946 Cabinet Mission.

Lord Pethick-Lawrence (1871–1961):
Educated at Eton and Cambridge, Pethick-Lawrence had a background in social work in east London. He was a supporter of the women's suffrage movement, and a conscientious objector during the 1914–18 war. He was elected to the British Parliament in 1923 as a Labour member, and became Secretary of State for India and Burma in the British Labour Government 1945–7. Nominally leader of the Cabinet Mission, he was a veteran of Anglo-Indian talks, having been present at the Round Table Conference of 1931.

IMPORTANT INDIAN FIGURES

Major Ashiq Hussain Qureshi:
A Muslim landowner and personal friend of Sir Penderel Moon, Ashiq Hussain had been a Minister in the Punjab Government in 1944–6. He was shot dead in July 1947 by a Muslim police constable who mistook him for a Hindu—an early sectarian shooting in Bahawalpur.

Malauna Abul Kalam Azad (1888–1958):
Azad became involved in politics in the early part of the century, with the aim of bringing Muslims into the Indian political struggle. He started the Muslim paper *Al Hilal* in 1912, and was a leader of the All-India Nationalist Muslim Party, founded in 1929. In the 1930s he was active in the civil disobedience movement. In 1937 he supervised the work of the provincial Congress ministers, and was Chief Adviser to the Congress high command on the 'Muslim minority problem'. He represented Congress during the 1942 Cripps Mission, the Simla conference, and the 1946 Cabinet Mission. Azad became President of the Congress from 1940–6, and then Education Minister in Nehru's Cabinet, 1947–58.

Nawab (Amir) of Bahawalpur
Captain Sir Sadiq Mohammed Khan Sahib Bahadur Abbasi the Muslim Nawab ruled the largely Muslim State of Bahawalpur in Punjab. Born in 1904, the Nawab received full ruling powers in 1927, after a long minority.

His actual power was restricted largely due to the effects of debts owed to the Government of India. The Nawab spent much of his time abroad. He assumed the title of 'Amir' in August 1947, to signify independent status for Bahawalpur, although the State acceded to Pakistan in October 1947.

Sardar Baldev Singh (1902–61):

Baldev Singh was elected to the Punjab Assembly in 1937. He was associated with the Akali party, and financed some of its ventures. The Sikander/Baldev Pact of 1942 was intended to ensure that the Akalis ceased their attacks on Sikander Hyat's government, and in return Baldev Singh was assured a place in the Punjab Cabinet. He became the Sikh member of the Interim Government in 1946, holding the defence portfolio, and the following year he became the first Defence Minister in the Independent India Government, a position he held until 1952.

Maulvi Faiz Ahmad:

Having been Revenue Officer for Bahawalpur State, Faiz Ahmad was promoted to Deputy Commissioner for the Rahim Yar Khan district and remained Deputy Commissioner for this district throughout the period of partition. He worked closely with Moon on the evacuation of Sikhs and Hindus from the State.

Gopal Krishna Gokhale (1866–1915):

Originally from western India, Gokhale was a University teacher in Bombay, before becoming a member of the Bombay Legislative Council in 1899. In 1902 he became a member of the Imperial Legislative Council. He founded the Servants of India Society, and was Leader of the Congress in 1905. He was known for his moderate politics, believing that India should become a self-governing colony or dominion through constitutional reforms, and strove for Hindu–Muslim Unity. He was a close associate of Mahatma Gandhi.

Nawab Mushtaq Ahmad Gurmani:

Gurmani was named by the Nawab of Bahawalpur as his Prime Minister in 1947, upon which appointment he assigned Penderel Moon as Revenue and Public Works Minister. He went on in 1949 to take charge of the separate Ministry of Kashmir Affairs.

Sir Syed Ahmad Khan (1817–98):

A nineteenth century Muslim Leader from Delhi, who supported the idea of a separate Muslim nation. He had entered the service of the East India Company at twenty-four, and at the time of the Indian mutiny in 1857 he was a senior judicial officer in Rohilkand. He went on in 1858 to write *The Causes of the Indian Revolt*, in which he identified the lack of understanding between the Muslims and the British as being the primary cause for the mutiny. In 1875 he founded the Aligarh Scientific Society and the Muhammadan Anglo-Oriental College, which later became

Aligarh University. He intended the college to enable Muslims to study the English language and culture alongside their own. He was a member of the Imperial Legislative Council from 1878–82.

Liaquat Ali Khan (1895–1951):

A barrister from a wealthy Muslim family in the United Provinces, educated at the Muhammadan Anglo-Oriental College in Aligarh and then at Oxford, Liaquat Ali Khan joined the Muslim League in 1923, becoming the League's General Secretary in 1937. He went on to become the Deputy Leader of the Muslim League Party in the Central Assembly (1941–7), and Finance Minister in the Interim Government (1946–7). He attended the 1946 Simla Conference as a representative of the Muslim League. A member of the Interim Government, Liaquat Ali Khan is often considered as being Jinnah's 'right-hand man', and indeed he became the first Prime Minister of Pakistan at partition in 1947—a position he held until his assassination in 1951.

Sir Sikander Hyat Khan (1892–1942):

From the prestigious Muslim family—the Hyats of Wah—he served as Revenue Minister of the Punjab Government from 1930–5. He was Deputy Governor of the Reserve Bank of India (1937–42), before being elected as the leader of the Unionist Party in Punjab and the Premier of Punjab. He remained the Premier until his sudden death in 1942, when he was succeeded by Khizar Hyat Tiwana. His main interests lay in securing the independence of Punjab, and in 1937 he signed the Sikander-Jinnah Pact which ensured his, and the Muslim Unionist's, co-operation with the Muslim League and Muslim League 'all-India' policy. In return he received a relatively free-hand in Punjab affairs.

R.K. Leghari:

Leghari was Superintendent of Bahawalpur Police at the time of partition. He worked closely with Penderel Moon to help restore order in the largely Muslim State after the arrival of injured Muslim refugees provoked retaliation against the Hindus in Bahawalpur. He also worked with Moon on the protection and then relocation of Sikhs and Hindus from Bahawalpur State.

V.P. Menon (1899–1966):

Educated in India, Menon worked for the Government of India from 1914, joining the Reforms office. He attended the 1931 Round Table Conference in London. He was Deputy Secretary to the Governor General from 1940–2, when he became Reforms Commissioner to the Government of India under Linlithgow, in which post he remained until 1947. He also held the post of Secretary to the Governor General from 1945–6. He played a key role in the transfer of power. From 1947–8 he was Secretary of the Government of India States Ministry, and in 1951 he became the Governor of Orissa.

Fazlur Rahman, Rao:
Assistant Settlement Officer for Bahawalpur State, Rahman worked under Moon at partition organizing the relocation of Hindus and Sikhs. Rahman later became a member of the first Cabinet as Minister for Interiors, Information and Education, and as Minister for Commerce.

Malik Sir Khizar Hyat Tiwana (1900–75):
Coming from the Noon-Tiwana family of Sargodha, Khizar entered politics in 1937. He went on to succeed Sikander Hyat Khan as the Premier of Punjab and as leader of the Unionist Party on the latter's death in 1942. As Premier, he resisted Jinnah's attempts to assert the Muslim League authority in the government of Punjab, and was expelled from the League in 1944. Faced with problems of loyalty for Muslims, Khizar agreed to head a coalition Government in 1946. Following more disputes with the Muslim League, Khizar was finally forced to submit his government's resignation in March 1947.

IMPORTANT BRITISH FIGURES

Clement Attlee (1883–1967):
Attlee had been Leader of the British Labour Party from 1935, he served as Deputy Prime Minister in Churchill's War Cabinet, and in 1945 he became Labour Prime Minister. He had been Chairman of the India Committee of the War Cabinet, and was responsible for the original idea of the 1942 Cripps Mission. In February 1947 he announced the intended British withdrawal from India and appointed Mountbatten as Viceroy.

Sir Henry Craik (1876–1955):
Educated at Eton and Oxford, Craik joined the ICS and served in various posts in the home department of the Government of India. He was a member of the Punjab Executive Council from 1930 to 1934 before becoming the Governor of Punjab in 1938. Craik was succeeded by Sir Bertrand Glancy in 1941. He was also the Home Member of the Viceroy Linlithgow's Executive Council from 1934–8 and the Political Adviser to the Viceroy from 1941–3.

Sir Richard Crofton (1891–1955):
Crofton entered the ICS in 1914. He held various posts such as Finance Secretary to the Government and Deputy Commissioner. He became the Commissioner of the Central Provinces in 1941. In 1942 Crofton became Prime Minister of Bahawalpur, a position he held until his retirement in 1947, when he was succeeded by Mushtaq Ahmad Gurmani.

Sir Bertrand Glancy (1882–1953):
Educated at Oxford, Glancy entered the ICS and served as Political Adviser to Linlithgow from 1938–41. He became the British Governor of Punjab in 1941. He was replaced as Governor in 1946 by Sir Evan Jenkins.

Introduction

T HE dawn of Indian independence was marred by massacres and migrations in the Punjab on a scale unparalleled in world history in time of peace. Within
the space of three or four months thousands were killed or died
of privation and millions were compelled to abandon for ever
their ancestral homes and to start life afresh in new surroundings. These melancholy events attracted attention at the time,
but they were so local in their effects that they have quickly
faded from the world's memory. Nor have India and Pakistan
been sorry that they should fall into oblivion. Yet though sordid
and discreditable in themselves—redeemed, if at all, not by
striking deeds of heroism (for the weaker party were everywhere driven like sheep to the slaughter), but only by the dumb,
patient endurance of the multitude—these large-scale massacres
and migrations were sufficiently unusual to deserve more
chronicling than is supplied by contemporary newspaper
articles or by second-hand propagandist compilations of atrocity stories. Yet this is virtually the only record of them that
has so far appeared.

In this book I have attempted, on the basis of my own recollections of these events, to throw a genuine, if limited, ray of
light on both their character and causes. The book falls into
two fairly distinct halves. The second half contains a detailed,
connected, and in places almost day-to-day account of the disturbances that occurred from the end of August 1947 onwards
in the State of Bahawalpur—a territory immediately adjacent
to the Punjab—and of the manner in which they were handled
or mishandled. There are incidental references to the disorders
and migrations that were simultaneously in progress throughout the Punjab, but no attempt has been made to give a comprehensive—and necessarily second-hand—account of these.
The narrative is confined almost entirely to my own limited but
first-hand experience of the troubles in Bahawalpur. Within
this narrow scope it is a faithful and authentic record of what

7

actually took place; and though Bahawalpur lay on the outer edge of the area of disturbance, the happenings there do, I believe, illustrate a good many aspects of the whole upheaval.

The earlier part of the book is in a somewhat different vein. It is concerned with the causes of the upheaval and traces political events in India and the Punjab from 1937 until their tragic dénouement ten years later. It is not a purely personal narrative, but it is not objective history. The story is told as it unfolded itself to me at the time, not as it would appear to the disinterested historian; and therefore only those events and those actions and reactions of political leaders receive notice which made a strong contemporary impression on my mind. While some of these are of unquestionable significance—for instance, the Cabinet Mission of 1946 which, being a decisive turning-point, has been treated in some detail—others, particularly the twists and turns of Punjab politics and personalities, loom large mainly because I had some special interest in or connection with them. They may contribute—I hope they will —to an understanding of the final tragedy in the Punjab, but they are petty and parochial in comparison with all-India events, some of which have received in these pages scant mention or none at all.

The earlier part of the book deals with large issues, the latter part with minor local episodes. Though widely different, the two are intimately connected, for all the individual incidents of the Bahawalpur disorders which are described in the second part flowed directly from the broad political decisions of which an account is given in the first. To me this connection was vividly clear at the time; to most of the individual sufferers it was only vaguely comprehensible. They knew in a general way that their misfortunes were the result of the departure of the British and the creation of Pakistan, but the reasons why these two things should cause the sudden disintegration of the social order in which they were living and plunge peaceful Bahawalpur almost overnight into a state of virtual civil war were beyond their powers of analysis. These results were certainly quite at variance with the predictions and proclaimed intentions of political leaders and official spokesmen.

When the clash came, my position in Bahawalpur was like that of a battalion commander in an obscure outlying sector

of the field of battle. But during part of the preceding ten years I had held a staff appointment which gave me an insight into the movement and massing of forces leading to the conflict in which I was subsequently involved. Thus, to change the metaphor, I ended by playing a small part in a tragedy the preparations for which I had long watched moving to their appointed but unpurposed end.

In composing this narrative, I had originally laid down for myself the principle of 'nothing extenuate, nor set down aught in malice'. I hope that I have nowhere departed from the second half of it; but it has not been possible to adhere rigidly in all places to the first, and I feel that in addition some extenuatory remarks of a general character are necessary. The narrative depicts mainly an ugly side of human nature and an uninformed reader might derive from it a very adverse impression of Punjabis in particular and of Indians and Pakistanis in general. But just as one does not judge a man from how he behaves when he is drunk or in a fit of rage, so a whole people should not be judged by what they do when temporarily in the grip of mass hysteria; and this was the condition of a large number of people in the Punjab in 1947.

I must add another word of caution. In most of this narrative Muslims are the villains and Hindus and Sikhs the victims. The unwary reader might half-unconsciously slip into thinking that this was the universal picture. But in East Punjab the roles were reversed and Sikhs and Hindus were there guilty of excesses against Muslims which equalled and, in my judgement, exceeded in scale and atrocity the outrages perpetrated by Muslims in West Pakistan. During the course of the disorders in Bahawalpur I continually had to remind myself of this in order to enter into the feelings of the Muslims by whom I was surrounded. The reader likewise, if he is to preserve a fair balance, should bear this in mind.

I am not myself conscious of any bias for or against any of the three communities except perhaps a sneaking sympathy for the Sikhs. All of them, however, will probably be displeased with some portions, at least, of what I have written. The Sikhs in particular are likely to repudiate my interpretation of their part in the tragedy, even though I have endeavoured to explain and partially excuse it. Members of the other two commu-

A*

nities will, I am afraid, resent criticism of persons who have become national heroes. But if one attempts to unravel the causes of the Punjab massacres, it is impossible to disguise these heroes' large, if unconscious, share of responsibility for what took place. If, therefore, I have dragged to light the errors and ill-timed utterances of revered leaders which, though remarked on at the time, have since been glossed over or conveniently forgotten, this is not done in any spirit of gratuitous disparagement but simply to bring out the true sequence of cause and effect. Furthermore, I recognize that, even if their responsibility for the Punjab massacres was considerable, they were acting in pursuit of ends and ideals which they and their followers may feel to have fully justified these heavy forfeits.

I

The Genesis of Pakistan

THE emergence of India as a free self-governing country
had been foreseen more than a hundred years before
1947. By the turn of the present century it had become
the avowed object of Indian nationalists, and by the end of
World War I it was recognized by British statesmen as the inevitable outcome of the British Raj. Pakistan, on the other hand,
was not thought of till about 1930;[1] three years later Muslim
leaders were describing it to the Joint Select Committee of the
British Parliament as 'only a students' scheme . . . chimerical
and impracticable'; and not until July 1946 could its emergence
as a separate State be deemed inevitable.

In retrospect it is perhaps less surprising that Pakistan came,
as it were, with such a rush at the end as that it was at the
beginning such a slow starter; for as far back as 1888 Sir Syed
Ahmad, the great Muslim leader of the nineteenth century,
had laid down the premises which lead naturally, perhaps even
necessarily, to the idea of Pakistan. India, he had said, is a
country 'inhabited by two different nations' and there would
necessarily be a struggle for power between them, if the English
were to leave India. 'Is it possible', he had asked, 'that under
these circumstances two nations—the Mohammadan and
Hindu—could sit on the same throne and remain equal in
power? Most certainly not. It is necessary that one of them
should conquer the other and thrust it down. To hope that both
could remain equal is to desire the impossible and the inconceivable.'

In the Victorian era the possibility of the English leaving
India did not arise. Sir Syed Ahmad knew that he was asking

[1] The first clear expression of the idea is to be found in an address to the
Muslim League in 1930 by Sir Mohammad Iqbal. He had mainly in mind
what is now West Pakistan. At a somewhat earlier date the partition of
India between Hindus and Muslims had been vaguely mooted.

and answering an academic question. His immediate practical concern was to show that a system of government by elected representatives—for which the newly-founded Indian National Congress was beginning to press—could not be safely adopted in India, for 'the larger community would totally override the interests of the smaller'. Yet in propounding the two nation theory and drawing attention so pointedly to the difficulties of majority rule in a country where the population is not homogeneous, he had not only put his finger on the main crux of the problem of Indian constitutional development, but also by implication had suggested a possible answer to it; for if two nations could not sit on the same throne, why should they not divide it?

This possible solution, so natural a corollary of Sir Syed Ahmad's premises, so obvious in the light of what has actually happened, remained for forty years neglected; not till the eight years of investigation and discussion that preceded the passing of the Government of India Act 1935 did it receive notice, and then only to be dismissed as chimerical.

Of course it was the Muslims alone who could have been expected to sponsor it. To the Hindu nationalists, who dominated Congress and led the movement for independence, the idea of dividing India was anathema. To the British, dimly conscious that the unification of India was one of the greatest achievements of their rule, it was not in the least attractive. Though the multi-racial Ottoman and Austrian empires had dissolved before their eyes, they clung to the notion that their own polyglot Indian empire should survive as a unity after they themselves had quitted the throne. The backwardness of the Muslims in the matter is not so easy to explain. In part it may be attributed to the fact that some of their most ardent leaders, including Jinnah himself, were for years in the ranks of Congress and, under the influence of the common urge to shake off the British yoke, accepted readily the assumption that they would somehow be able to agree to share the throne with their Hindu friends. In addition, the inherent difficulties of division helped to keep the idea in the background. Hindus and Muslims, though they did not intermarry, were closely intermingled and in many parts of India lived side by side. Division of the country would, therefore, necessarily leave large minorities in the new States so formed. Moreover the two regions in which Muslims were in a majority—the north-west and north-east of India—were widely separated, and to form a single State out of such disconnected territories seemed hardly possible. For this very reason the idea of Pakistan, as at first adumbrated, embraced only north-west India.

The Government of India Act of 1935 took no account of the Pakistan 'chimera'. With the full concurrence of Jinnah and the Muslim League, Muslim interests were sought to be protected by other means. The quasi-monopoly of political power which the Hindus' superior numbers would tend to give them was diminished by abandoning the old tradition of unitary government in favour of a federal form of constitution under which the Provinces would enjoy a large measure of autonomy; Sind was detached from Bombay and made a separate Province so that there would be four Muslim-majority Provinces[1] out of a total of eleven; the system of separate electorates for Muslims and 'weightage' was continued; and it was envisaged that the Native States would be included in the Federation and that their representatives would have a neutralizing influence at the Centre. With these arrangements the Muslims appeared to be content. Jinnah, it is true, described the federal part of the Act as 'fundamentally bad and totally unacceptable'. His objection to it, however, was not that it failed to protect Muslim interests adequately, but that it did not provide immediately for full responsible government at the centre, since defence and foreign affairs were reserved to the Governor-General and not entrusted to ministers responsible to the legislature. Jinnah was in fact voicing, though less stridently, the same complaint as the Hindu leaders of Congress. Nevertheless, he and the Muslim League and other Muslim political parties all acquiesced in the Act and were apparently willing to give it a trial.

This was the position on April 1st 1937 when the provincial part of the Act came into operation, establishing in the Provinces full responsible government subject only to certain 'safeguards'. The federal part was necessarily deferred, as it was only to come into force when a specific number of the Native States had acceded to the Federation, and none had as yet done

[1] Bengal, Punjab, Sind and the North-West Frontier Province.

so. Negotiations with their Rulers regarding the terms of their accession were still in progress and it was hoped that after a little time their doubts and hesitations would be overcome and the Federation would be duly inaugurated. There was a possibility that Congress might employ 'wrecking' tactics in order to wring more concessions from the British, but no hint or suspicion of serious obstruction from the Muslims.

Within the space of a single year the whole situation had radically altered. A profound change came over Muslim opinion, and there opened between the League and Congress a breach destined to grow ever wider and to lead inexorably to the partition of the country and the massacres of 1947. The British at first noticed these developments with mild complacency and did not exert themselves to heal the rift. Later when they woke up to the fearful consequences that might ensue, they made desperate but unavailing efforts to avert them.

There is no doubt that the leaders of Congress were responsible, though quite unwittingly, for this critical change in Muslim sentiment. In retrospect it seems as though a curse was laid on them at this time which compelled them over the next ten years invariably to act in such a way as to bring about exactly the opposite result to that which they intended. They passionately desired to preserve the unity of India. They consistently acted so as to make its partition certain.

Their first mistake, which may be regarded as the *fons et origo malorum*, was made in the summer of 1937. In the preceding cold weather elections had been held to the new Provincial Assemblies and both Congress and the Muslim League had contested them. In all the six Hindu-majority provinces Congress had been conspicuously successful; it had also done well in Assam, where it was the strongest single party; but in three out of the four Muslim-majority provinces, viz. Bengal, the Punjab and Sind, it had fared comparatively badly. The experience of the Muslim League had been curiously different. In the Muslim-majority provinces it still counted for very little and won remarkably few seats. In these provinces Muslims were either divided into warring factions or, where united, belonged to local parties with traditions and alignments of their own. Thus in the North-West Frontier Province the dominant

Muslim party, the Red Shirts, had long been in alliance with Congress. In the Punjab most Muslims belonged to the Unionist Party, a combination of Muslims, Sikhs and Hindus representing rural and agricultural as against urban and commercial interests. Such success as the League achieved was not in these Muslim-majority provinces but in those in which Muslims were in a minority and could never hope to form a government themselves. Probably its greatest strength was in the United Provinces where Mogul traditions still lingered and Muslims, though only about 16 per cent of the population, had succeeded in retaining a political importance disproportionate to their numbers.

Though Congress and the League had entered into no electoral pact, the League leaders had been careful to draft their election manifesto so as to be in broad accord with the Congress programme. Undoubtedly they fully expected that in some of the Hindu-majority provinces, and particularly in the United Provinces, they would be invited by Congress to form coalition Ministries. But in the summer of 1937 these expectations were rudely disappointed. With overwhelming majorities in the legislatures, Congress had no need for an alliance with the League. The representation of Muslims in the Ministries could be obtained by the appointment of Muslims from within the ranks of Congress.[1] So the League leaders of the United Provinces were plainly told that there would be no coalition and that if any of them were to find places in the Ministry, then the Muslim League Party in the Assembly must 'cease to function as a separate group', and all its members must become members of Congress and submit themselves to Congress party discipline and to the policy laid down by the Congress High Command. In other words Congress were prepared to share the throne only with Muslims who consented to merge themselves in a predominantly Hindu organization. They offered the League not partnership but absorption.

This proved to be a fatal error—the prime cause of the creation of Pakistan—but in the circumstances it was a very

[1] Congress, which always claimed that it represented all communities in India, had within its ranks a sprinkling of Muslims. In the elections Congress Muslims had contested fifty-eight of the 482 Muslim constituencies and won twenty-six.

natural one. There was nothing in parliamentary tradition requiring Congress on the morrow of victory to enter into a
coalition with another party; and a coalition with the League,
which the Congress leaders looked upon as a purely communal
organization, was particularly distasteful to them. They may
also well have thought that if in the U.P. the League could be
lured into dissolving itself it would soon disintegrate throughout the country, leaving no all-India Muslim party in existence,
but only isolated provincial groups. Moreover the idea of
absorption, of gathering all the Muslims into the Congress fold,
was typical of the Hindu habit of mind and the past history of
Hinduism. Nearly three centuries earlier had not the absorptive
capacity of Hinduism impressed the Mogul emperor, Aurangzeb, with the danger that in India Islam might lose its identity
and become a forgotten element in an all-embracing Hinduism?

The Muslim League leaders rejected the Congress ultimatum. They were outraged at the suggestion that they should
dissolve their political organization; rather than do this they
were prepared to run the risk of permanent banishment to the
political wilderness. Among the disappointed candidates for
office was Liaqat Ali Khan, a wealthy landowner of western
U.P. who in the coming years was to be Jinnah's principal
lieutenant. Jinnah himself, who before the elections had been
saying that there was no substantial difference between the
League and Congress, at once began to adopt a very different
tone. Previously, though he had often stressed that Muslims
must maintain their separate political organization and that it
was 'no use encouraging individual Muslims to come into the
fold of Congress', he had by no means been an out-and-out
communalist. He had been described in Congress circles as
'the ambassador of Hindu-Muslim unity' and had been more
notable as an anti-British nationalist than as a champion of
Islam. But Congress rather than the British now became his
enemy number one and he embarked on a bitter campaign of
vilification. 'Muslims', he said, 'can expect neither justice nor
fair play under Congress Government' and all hope of communal peace had been wrecked 'on the rocks of Congress
Fascism'.

The reaction was not confined to Muslim League circles and
the Muslims of the Muslim-minority provinces. Muslims all

over India, even in the Muslim-majority provinces, took alarm.
If the U.P. sample was to be the pattern of Congress's political
conduct, then what would be the position of Muslims when a
federal government for all-India came to be formed? There
would be no room on the throne of India save for Congress and
Congress stooges. Before the year was out the Muslim members
of the Unionist Party in the Punjab, under the leadership of
the Premier, Sir Sikander Hyat-Khan, had gone over *en bloc*
to the League, and the Muslim Premiers of Bengal and Assam
had also shown that they supported it. The adherence of the
Punjab Muslims was especially significant. In this province the
League had failed completely at the elections and almost all
the Muslim seats had gone to members of the Unionist Party,
Yet now Sir Sikander took all his Muslim followers into the
League camp. They remained members of the Unionist Party,
but they also became members of the Muslim League. Sir
Sikander was very far from being a bigoted Muslim and had
little sympathy with the virulent communalism hitherto displayed by Muslim leaguers in the Punjab. But there was now
a strong section of his own Muslim followers anxious to join
the League as the one party standing forth clearly to champion
Muslim rights; and he feared that in the changed atmosphere
of Muslim alarm and resentment this section might break away
and then draw others after them, leaving him more or less
isolated and powerless to mould or guide Muslim opinion in the
Punjab. To avoid such a dangerous split he decided to join
the League himself with all his Muslim supporters. Subsequent
events showed that his fears were by no means groundless.

The League was enormously strengthened by the accession
of the Punjab and Bengal Muslims, and Jinnah himself was
suddenly raised to an eminence which he had never enjoyed
before. Instead of being merely one of several Muslim leaders,
without real backing from any of the main centres of Muslim
population, he became from now onwards the undisputed
leader of Muslims all over India and acknowledged as such
even by the Premiers of the Punjab and Bengal.

The Congress leaders do not appear to have appreciated the
strong currents which they had set in motion, still less to have
perceived where they were likely to lead. So far from repairing
their original mistake and seeking to bridge the gulf that had

been created between them and the League—grown suddenly much more formidable—they made matters worse by launching, at Nehru's instance, a 'mass-contact' movement among the ordinary Muslims of the countryside. This was a signal to the League to bestir itself and also gave it its cue. Hitherto it had appealed mainly to middle and upper class Muslims and had not sought to enlist the support of the Muslim masses. But for a predominantly Hindu organization like the Congress to try to 'contact' Muslim peasants and artisans on a mass scale was an affront and a challenge which the League could not ignore. So before the 'mass-contact' movement of Congress had made much headway, the League itself turned towards the masses. It reduced the annual membership fee to two annas, began to extend its organization to the countryside and with the aid of unscrupulous propaganda to rouse Muslims of all classes to the danger of Hindu domination. This was an appeal to essentially the same basic nationalist sentiment as the Congress had been playing upon in its long struggle against British rule and it is somewhat strange that the Congress leaders did not foresee that by embarking on a 'mass-contact' movement among the Muslims they would impel the League to invoke this powerful sentiment against themselves. As a means of appealing to the Muslim masses it was far more effective than the Congress programme of social and agrarian reform.

The significance of what was happening did not come home to me till the summer of 1938, when, after several years' service in the districts, I was called up to Simla to act temporarily for six[1] months as Secretary to the Governor of the Punjab. I then became aware of the crucial change in Muslim opinion and began to have a dim presentiment of what it might portend. The Viceroy, Lord Linlithgow, was at that time laboriously attempting to coax the Princes into joining the proposed Federation. Possibly a Viceroy with something of the brilliance and personal magnetism of Lord Mountbatten might have succeeded in this difficult task; but it was quite beyond the scope of the more pedestrian talents of Lord Linlithgow and it never seemed probable that the Princes would yield to his methods of persuasion. It became clear to me, however, that while everyone was still agog to bring in the Princes, their

_____
[1] The six months became three and a half years.

reluctance to enter the Federation had already become of
secondary importance and that far more serious and significant
was the growing opposition of the Muslims. I realized this when
in July Sir Sikander asked me to help him with the 'editing'
of a pamphlet, written by him or under his direction, entitled
'Outline of a scheme of Indian Federation'. Sir Sikander was a
man of moderate and sober views; I was therefore much struck,
on reading through the draft, to find even this level-headed
statesman expressing the opinion that the federal proposals of
the 1935 Act were no longer acceptable and must be modified
so as to remove the misgivings not only of the Princes but also
of the minorities—that is, of course, primarily the Muslims.
The details of his federal scheme are not of any importance
now.[1] His main objectives, as disclosed in the pamphlet, were
to limit the authority of the Centre to the barest minimum and
to exclude the possibility of 'Congress Raj' by laying down
certain provisions regarding the composition of the Federal
Executive calculated to ensure a nice balance of interests.

The scheme appeared to me to have little chance of acceptance and to be in some respects impracticable; but Sir Sikander
was very keen to lay it before the public. When I asked him the
reason for this, he replied with a wry smile that unless positive
proposals such as his were put forward for consideration other
people would come out with 'something worse'. The 'something worse' to which he referred was the idea of Pakistan—
the 'chimerical and impracticable students' scheme' which, I
gathered from him, was now gaining a hold in League circles.

Hitherto I had hardly known the meaning of the term
'Pakistan'. I tried now to get to the bottom of it. The essence
of the idea was that India should be divided, and a separate
predominantly Muslim State created out of the Punjab, the
N.W.F.P., Sind, Kashmir and Baluchistan. This would be
Pakistan. What should happen to the rest of the Muslims in
India had not at this time been clearly thought out, but there
was an idea that a second predominantly Muslim State should
be created in the north-east out of the provinces of Bengal and
Assam. This would provide a division of the country between
Hindus and Muslims on a rough population basis. There would

[1] He envisaged a three-tiered constitution such as was later suggested by
the Cabinet Mission in 1946.

be large minorities in all the three States, but their presence in *all* of them might ensure their fair treatment. Furthermore it seemed probable that States whose populations had previously been so intimately associated would automatically enter into some kind of close alliance or confederation and never become to one another quite like foreign countries.

I was attracted by the idea. It seemed at first sight to offer a simple solution of the Hindu-Muslim problem and, now that the bogy of Hindu domination at the Centre had been raised, perhaps the only solution. Any system of safeguards and statutory coalitions was all very well on paper but difficult to work in practice. Sooner or later it was bound to break down. I assumed, all too readily, that the Punjab, where three communities (Muslim, Hindu and Sikh) were closely intermingled, spoke a common language, shared a common provincial pride and to some extent a common culture, would remain a unity and pass as a whole into Pakistan without the Hindus and Sikhs raising too much objection.

One day in October 1938 during a conversation with Sir Sikander I began talking to him rather enthusiastically about the merits of the Pakistan idea and suggested that it might after all be the best way of dealing with the communal problem. Sir Sikander, usually so calm and suave, after listening for a few minutes turned upon me, his eyes blazing with indignation, and took me to task in these words:

'How can you talk like this? You've been long enough in western Punjab to know the Muslims there. Surely you can see that Pakistan would be an invitation to them to cut the throat of every Hindu bania.'[1]

I put forward the hostage theory—there would be so many Muslims in Hindustan and so many Hindus in Pakistan that both sides would hesitate to harass their minorities for fear of reprisals. He brushed it aside. The Baluchis and Awans of West Punjab, he said, wouldn't care at all about the lives of Muslims in Hindustan. The hostage idea was a mere fancy. Both sides would kill their own hostages. 'I do hope', he went on, 'I won't hear you talk like this again. *Pakistan would mean a massacre.*'

His words, spoken with unusual intensity of feeling, made a

[1] Hindu trader or shopkeeper, usually also a moneylender.

deep impression on me. My original enthusiasm for Pakistan evaporated, and for the next eight years my hope was that it might somehow be avoided. Sir Sikander, on the other hand, in less than eighteen months subscribed to a resolution calling for its creation.

The Muslim League's slide towards Pakistan was exceedingly rapid. It had first taken alarm in the summer of 1937; a year later it had repudiated the federal scheme of the 1935 Act; by the beginning of 1939 it was considering other constitutional schemes; in September 1939 it declared that Muslim India was 'irrevocably opposed' to any federal objective. Finally in March 1940, at a session in Lahore, it passed what is known as the 'Pakistan Resolution' demanding in plain terms the partition of India and the grouping of regions in which Muslims were numerically in a majority, as in the north-western and north-eastern zones, into 'Independent States'.

The League's rapid and revolutionary change of outlook was very natural; for once faith in the possibility of partnership was shaken, partition was logically the only alternative.

Privately Jinnah told one or two people in Lahore that this Resolution was a 'tactical move'; and the fact that six years later he was ready to accept something less than absolute partition suggests that in 1940 he was not really irrevocably committed to it. In part, therefore, it may have been at this time a tactical move, designed to wring from Congress concessions which would make partnership more tolerable. Certainly the implications of the resolution and even the composition of the proposed 'Independent States' and their interrelations had not at this stage been fully thought out. Some of these matters were clarified later, but Jinnah was never keen to expound the exact nature of Pakistan, and right up till 1947 there was some doubt as to what he would accept as conforming sufficiently to his conceptions.

Sir Sikander was gravely embarrassed by this resolution. His own dislike of Pakistan—or Jinnistan as he irreverently called it—was well known. He had publicly stated that if Pakistan meant 'a Muslim Raj here and a Hindu Raj elsewhere', he would have nothing to do with it. He was the head of a Government and the leader of a political party which included in its ranks or among its habitual supporters Hindus and Sikhs as

well as Muslims. Inevitably on the Pakistan issue there was
serious division. Sikander's Muslim followers, as members of
the Muslim League, became formally committed to the demand
for Pakistan, whatever their private opinions might be;[1] while
his Hindu and Sikh supporters were wholly opposed to it. Sir
Sikander endeavoured privately to explain away the resolution
and to make out that it was not really the intention that the
States into which India was proposed to be divided should be
entirely independent of one another. But his interpretation of
the resolution became more and more difficult to reconcile
with Jinnah's public utterances.

In Bengal, as in the Punjab, the Muslim Premier, Fazl-ul-Haq,
had not yet in his heart accepted Pakistan, though publicly he
stood committed to it. Both he and Sir Sikander were in a false
position, but neither of them at this stage wished to risk a
break with Jinnah. Sir Sikander both now and right up to the
end of his life thought—and with good reason—that if he were
openly to oppose Jinnah, the Punjab Muslims would become
divided and he would lose his hold over them. So outwardly he
bowed to Jinnah, however much inwardly he might chafe.

It was all very well for Sir Sikander, Fazl-ul-Haq and perhaps
even Jinnah himself to have mental reservations about Pakistan,
but once the cry was raised, how would it be silenced? The term
was, no doubt, a vague one; but after the 1940 resolution it
rightly became synonymous in the popular mind with 'Muslim
Raj'—a State where Muslims would be supreme. To the Muslim
masses this held out an ill-defined but alluring prospect of
looting Hindus. With greater clarity of vision, ambitious politicians and civil servants, as also some professional men, perceived
that under a Muslim Raj, with the crippling if not the elimination of Hindu competition, they could rise to positions of power
and affluence unattainable in a single mixed Hindu-Muslim
State. Thus the cry for Pakistan appealed to and excited powerful appetites and individual hopes, and these, once aroused,
would not be readily assuaged.

'The thicket of the people will take furtive fire
From irresponsible catchwords of live ideas

[1] In March 1940 a considerable number, probably a majority, of Sir
Sikander's Muslim followers shared his antipathy to the idea of Pakistan.

Sudden as a gorse-bush from the smouldering end
Of any loiterer's match-splint, which, unless trodden out
Afore it spread, or quelled with wieldy threshing rods,
Will burn ten years of planting with all last year's ricks
And blacken a countryside.'

Responsible statesmen like Sir Sikander might foresee the
dangers inherent in raising the cry for Pakistan, but ostensibly
the League had accepted Pakistan as its goal—a goal which it
would be easy for demagogues to pursue to disaster, difficult
for statesmen to abandon or render innocuous.

The ominous trend of thought in League circles, of which the
1940 resolution was the overt sign, might have been checked if,
soon after the breach in 1937, the Congress leaders had made
positive efforts to conciliate Jinnah and his henchmen. But
for several reasons it was difficult, if not impossible, for them to
do so. Jinnah attacked Congress bitterly, accusing the average
Congressman of 'behaving and acting towards the Mussalmans
in a much worse manner than the British did towards Indians',
and letting loose a flood of malicious propaganda. Reports were
issued regarding the ill-treatment alleged to be meted out to
Muslims in various Congress Government Provinces, in which
mountains were made out of mole-hills and trivial communal
incidents of everyday occurrence painted in lurid colours so as
to inflame popular feeling. Smarting under these largely unjustified attacks the Congress leaders showed a good deal of
restraint, but they would have been more than human if they
had responded immediately with an olive branch.

There was also another obstacle to any rapprochement. Just
as Congress claimed to be the only body representing all communities and alone qualified therefore to speak for the whole
of India, so Jinnah now claimed that the League alone represented the Muslims of India and must be recognized as the only
body qualified to speak on their behalf. To Congress, which had
several prominent Muslims within its ranks—one of them,
Maulana Abul Kalam Azad, became President of Congress in
1940—this claim was unacceptable; and in one shape or another
it remained a stumbling block in the way of any settlement from
this time right up till the final calamitous end of Congress-
League relations.

Nevertheless in the summer of 1939 there were signs that Congress saw the need for a settlement and desired to reach one. Gandhi in June expressed the hope that British statesmen would revise the federal scheme embodied in the 1935 Act and 'try to placate all parties'. Congress spokesmen studiously refrained from criticism of the proposals embodied in Sikander's 'Outline Scheme' which was published in the first half of the year. Gandhi himself obtained six copies of it and during June and July he and Sikander were in communication with one another in the hope of finding some common ground.

But, despite these feelers, up till the outbreak of war there had been no effective reconciliation between Congress and the League; and when war came the gulf widened. Confused by Gandhi's pacifism and blinded by their own violent antipathy to British rule the Congress leaders in September 1939 were unable to view coolly the realities of the situation. To remove or even lighten the British yoke in time of war was impossible; but the days of British rule were obviously numbered and already the crucial problem was not how to get rid of the British but how to preserve the unity of the country when they had gone. Jinnah and the League had already appeared as a potential source of disruption. The threat to unity was quite evident even before the League's 1940 resolution. A united effort in the war might have averted it and paved the way for settlement thereafter. If Congress had been willing to co-operate and accept for the duration of the war the existing Constitution with its inevitable limitations, the moderate Muslim elements, still quite strong in the Punjab and Bengal and not yet wedded to extreme courses or completely under Jinnah's thumb, would have gladly joined hands with them in forming a government at the Centre and thus the foundations might have been laid for a government of a united and independent India when the war was over. Instead, Congress decided to stand aloof, co-operating with nobody and coming to terms neither with the British nor with Jinnah. In October 1939 the Congress Ministries in the Provinces were ordered to resign from office and this proved to be the prelude to retirement into jail. Jinnah was thus left with a clear field and he took full advantage of it.

From every point of view the Congress attitude was unfortunate except perhaps that of the successful prosecution of the war. But this was the aspect which at the time most impressed itself on the British. Congress 'co-operation', it was felt, would take the form of daily and exasperating obstruction to which 'non-co-operation' or even active hostility would be preferable. A section of British opinion was, therefore, not at all keen to have members of Congress in office during the war and secretly welcomed their departure soon after its outbreak. On short-term considerations there was much to be said for this view; and, whether deliberately or not, the Viceroy ensured that events would conform to it. It is conceivable that if on the out-break of war he had proclaimed in a few stirring words his belief that a war for freedom could only end in the freedom of India[1]—as in fact it did—the Congress would have been swung in favour of co-operation—in which case Jinnah would have had to co-operate too. But Lord Linlithgow did not adopt this course. After several weeks of discussion and cogitation he came out on October 17th with a dreary prosaic statement, renewing previous assurances that Dominion Status was the goal of British policy in India, but giving no indication when that goal was likely to be reached. It was so ill-calculated to appeal to Congress that cynics said it was purposely designed to ease them out of office. Five days later the Working Committee called on the Congress Ministries to resign.

The British disposition now was to leave Congress to stew in their own juice. From the point of view of preventing a widen-ing of the gulf between Congress and the League, this attitude was unwise. But even after the 'Pakistan' resolution had high-lighted the danger of drift, no active effort was made by the British to awaken Congress leaders to the imperative need of early reconciliation with the League, if Indian unity was to be preserved. In both camps, however, the more sober elements were profoundly disturbed by the 1940 resolution and, inde-pendently of their leaders, endeavoured to come to some under-standing. During the summer of 1940 Sir Sikander through various intermediaries got into touch with right-wing Congress

---

[1] A group of British officers in the Punjab privately urged this course, the most senior of them, Sir Malcolm Darling, approaching the Viceroy on the subject while the rest tackled the Viceroy's private secretary. Their suggestions were ridiculed.

leaders such as Rajagopalachari in the hope of reaching a
settlement. Though reluctant to break with Jinnah, Sikander
was ready in the last resort to do so and confident that he could
carry sufficient moderate leaguers with him, *provided that* he was
assured of Congress support. But it was found that such support
could not be counted upon, for even right-wing Congress
leaders wanted that as part of the plan of settlement the Viceroy's Executive Council should be reconstituted so as to give it
an almost exclusively non-official character and a far greater
degree of independence than the British were likely to concede
in time of war. Lord Linlithgow, when he got wind of these
pourparlers, was wholly discouraging and expressed the view
that Sikander would burn his fingers; so they petered out early
in 1941 without any result except perhaps that Sikander,
though still wholly averse to Pakistan, became less inclined
even than before to stand up to Jinnah.

A year later, when the Japanese seemed poised for an attack
on India, the British themselves did at last make a determined
effort to unite all parties in the common defence of the country.
Sir Stafford Cripps flew out to India in March 1942 with proposals both for an interim government and for a final constitutional settlement after the cessation of hostilities. His mission failed and with its failure went the last chance of bringing
the Congress and League together in a 'National Government'
for the prosecution of the war. Congress clung to the demand for
virtual independence forthwith, and settlement of all outstanding problems—including the Hindu-Muslim quarrel—
afterwards. The British proposals, while they amounted in
effect to the promise of Dominion Status immediately after the
war, with full liberty to secede from the Commonwealth, contemplated no major constitutional change while the war was
still in progress. It was mainly on this ground that Congress
rejected them. But Congress also complained that the proposals were 'a severe blow to the conception of Indian Unity'.
From the point of view of Hindu-Muslim relations this was
much their most significant aspect; for this was the first occasion on which the British publicly admitted the possibility of
Partition. The creation of 'Pakistan' was not accepted outright
—on this ground Jinnah in his turn rejected the proposals—
but the right of individual Provinces and Indian States to stay

out of the proposed Indian Union and form separate Unions of their own was acknowledged. This was a triumph for Jinnah. It put him in a very strong position, for if the Muslims of the Muslim-majority provinces stood behind him, he could now, with the right to stay out conceded, bargain for the terms on which those provinces would come in and the dream of Congress Raj over the whole of India would never come true. Even Muslims who did not want Pakistan were impressed by the importance of supporting Jinnah.

Gandhi was mainly responsible for the rejection by Congress of the Cripps proposals. Not content with this he came out soon after with the startling demand that the British should immediately quit India altogether, even if this meant leaving it to chaos and the Japanese. One prominent and courageous Congress leader—Rajagopalachari, the ex-premier of Madras and an old friend of Gandhi—now boldly made a stand. He had for some time been uneasy at the negative, unrealistic attitude of Congress both towards the British and the Muslims. He had favoured reaching a settlement on the basis of the Cripps offer, but had been overborne and Gandhi's views had prevailed. Appalled by the disastrous and irresponsible futility of the Gandhian policy, he now protested both publicly and privately against the 'quit India' demand, asserting that it would be a crime for the British to leave India at this juncture and that their withdrawal without simultaneous replacement by another government 'must involve the dissolution of the State and society itself'. This was plain common sense; but in the policy which he advocated towards Jinnah and the Muslims he showed more than common sense; he showed far-sighted statesmanship. In May 1942 he submitted to the All India Congress Committee a resolution recommending acquiescence in the principle of Pakistan. Statesmanship does not however commend itself to the many except after the event. He was heavily defeated, and soon afterwards, threatened with disciplinary action for his denunciation of Gandhi's 'quit India' policy, he resigned from Congress. Few now would deny that the Congress leaders would have done well to follow his advice. For in 1942 most of the leaguers, perhaps even Jinnah himself, did not in their hearts desire the partition of the country, and to have conceded Pakistan in principle would have smoothed the path for a settlement on other lines. But the voice of reason was disregarded and Congress, following blindly the promptings of Gandhi's own 'inner voice', launched in August 1942 the insensate 'quit India' rebellion. All leading Congressmen were immediately arrested and put in confinement. When nearly three years later, at the close of the war with Germany, they emerged once again, they found Jinnah as intractable as ever and considerably stronger. Almost all Muslims were arrayed behind him in a solid phalanx.

The Punjab and Pakistan

BEFORE the general story is carried forward, it is necessary to explain in more detail the implications for the Punjab of the demand for Pakistan and the reasons for Sikander's dislike of it. He had said to me that Pakistan would mean a massacre. He had referred specifically only to a massacre of Hindus by Muslims; but there was also the opposite danger of a massacre of Muslims by Hindus, and this not only in distant parts of India hardly known to me, where the Muslims were far outnumbered, but in the Punjab itself—a Muslim-majority province. In the province as a whole the Muslims constituted about 57 per cent of the population and in the west of it were markedly predominant, but east of Lahore both their numbers and their dominance fell away. Here the non-Muslim population did not consist merely, or mainly, of merchants, shopkeepers and clerks. In the districts immediately east of Lahore lay the homelands of the Sikhs—the vigorous but violent peasant stock that only 100 years before had held sway over most of the province; and in the south-east towards Delhi dwelt the Hindu Jats—a tough peasantry with martial traditions and racially akin to the Sikhs. Would all these turbulent folk meekly accept a Muslim Raj?

Here lay the crux of the Pakistan problem. According to the ideas of Jinnah and the Muslim League, the Punjab, being a Muslim-majority province, would be part of Pakistan. But if so, it would be necessary to square the Sikhs. For how could this robust and highly self-conscious community be incorporated in a Muslim State against their will? They would certainly resist it by force.

The Sikhs had an importance in the Punjab, and even in India as a whole, quite out of proportion to their numbers. Altogether there were only about six million of them. Even in the Punjab, where they were mainly concentrated, they constituted less than 20 per cent of the population and were not in an absolute majority in a single district. But they were an enterprising and relatively prosperous community. They held a disproportionately large share of the best land in the Punjab—in part a legacy from the days when they were its rulers, in part a result of their remarkable success as colonists of the new canal-irrigated lands in West Punjab. They had also acquired under British rule a privileged position in the army—no other community had such a high percentage of its members serving as soldiers.

Originally the Sikhs were simply a religious sect. Their subsequent emergence at the end of the seventeenth century as a distinct and militant community was a result of Muslim rule and oppression and may be regarded as one of the Hindu protests against the proselytizing zeal of the Mogul emperor Aurangzeb. The core of the community consists of peasants of the Jat tribe.[1] A certain number of Hindus of the urban commercial classes have grown beards and embraced Sikhism and some of these with their superior education and intellectual qualities have played an important part in the leadership of the Sikh community. But the typical Sikh is a sturdy 'Jat' peasant. It was through his toughness that under the stimulus of Muslim oppression the Sikhs developed into a distinct community, and through his fighting qualities that Maharajah Ranjit Singh, himself a Jat Sikh, founded and sustained a Sikh kingdom in the Punjab on the ruins of the Mogul empire.

Naturally with this background the Sikhs were deeply alarmed at Jinnah's plan for dividing India and forming an independent Muslim-dominated State—Pakistan—in which they and the whole of the Punjab would be included. Their reaction to it was the exact counterpart of the reaction of the Muslims to a Hindu-dominated India. Just as the Muslims, with their memories of the Mogul empire, were not prepared to see themselves condemned to a position of inferiority under a permanent Hindu majority, so the Sikhs, remembering that only 100 years before they had ruled the Punjab, were not prepared to become a tiny minority in a large Muslim State.

---

[1] The Jats were the predominant agricultural tribe of the Punjab as it existed before Partition. There are Muslim and Hindu Jats as well as Sikh Jats. They probably all have a common Scythian origin.

Moreover, just as the Muslims could use the threat of dividing India as a means of extracting concessions from the Hindu majority, so the Sikhs saw that they could use the threat of dividing the Punjab as a means of extracting concessions from the Muslims.

The crucial position held by the Sikhs, if Pakistan were to become a live issue, could not escape the notice of any Punjab civilian. It was particularly forced on my attention; for soon after the outbreak of war I became rather intimately concerned with Sikh affairs, and in 1941 I was appointed Deputy Commissioner[1] of the district of Amritsar. It lay in the heart of the Sikh country and the city of Amritsar itself, built round the Golden Temple, was the main religious and political centre of the Sikhs. Here were the headquarters of the Akalis,[2] the most powerful Sikh political party, representing an extreme form of Sikh nationalism with a strongly anti-British bias. They controlled the Golden Temple—and indeed most other Sikh shrines—and buzzed about the place like angry wasps.

A very senior British official told me that the Deputy Commissioner, Amritsar, ought to regard himself as British ambassador to the Sikhs. The practice of some of my predecessors had conformed to this conception. They had considered it their duty to keep themselves fully informed of the Sikh point of view on all important matters and to represent it to the Government as cogently as possible. With many great issues looming ahead it seemed very desirable that this tradition should be maintained. Inevitably, therefore, I had to try to establish friendly relations with Sikh political leaders and particularly with Master Tara Singh and other prominent Akalis. In this I was greatly assisted both by my predecessor and also by a military officer, Major Short, with whom I had been thrown into close contact since the middle of 1940.

[1] In the Punjab the head of a district was called the Deputy Commissioner.

[2] Akali means immortal. The Akalis (Immortals) were originally a famous regiment of Ranjit Singh. The term was revived during the movement after World War I for the liberation of Sikh shrines (gurdwaras) from the control of hereditary priests. Those who took part in this movement were described as Akalis. Since the priests' possession of the shrines (often very well endowed) was legal, the Government tended to support them and the movement quickly took an anti-Government turn.

Short was a 'dug-out' officer of the XIth Sikh regiment and a great Sikh enthusiast—destined over the next few years to plead their cause in vain. He had come to the Punjab in the summer of 1940 in consequence of a series of disquieting incidents among Sikh elements of the armed forces, which had culminated in April 1940 in the refusal of the Sikh squadron of the Central India Horse to embark at Bombay for the Middle East. A considerable flutter had been caused in Army Headquarters. There was some wild talk of disbanding all Sikh units; and, more seriously, a proposal was put forward to stop all further recruitment of Sikhs. The Punjab Government strongly opposed any such drastic step and a decision was wisely taken to try to restore the situation by more conciliatory methods. At Short's suggestion, he and a number of officers specially selected for their experience of Sikhs were deputed to probe and report on Sikh unrest in certain army units and in the principal Sikh districts. Later, a few officers, similarly picked, were posted in the main areas of Sikh recruitment and required to stimulate sustained and co-operative efforts by the civil and military authorities to allay Sikh disquiet and to induce a healthier attitude among the Sikhs towards the war and recruitment. Short was one of these civil liaison officers, as they were called, with his base at Lahore.

The Sikhs' favoured position in the army, with all that it meant in the way of pay and pensions in a land of chronic under-employment, was something that it was very much in their interest to retain. But if owing to the misconduct of Sikh troops or the disaffection of the Sikh population the recruitment of Sikhs was stopped or greatly reduced, that favoured position would be lost—and lost for ever; for in a free India, which was already in sight, neither of the two major communities, Hindu or Muslim, would have the slightest motive for restoring it. This was a danger which no Sikh could overlook; and it was not lost upon the Akalis. They were, however, in a rather difficult position. Hitherto their attitude had generally been anti-British and they formed along with the Congress the opposition to Sir Sikander's anglophile Unionist Government.[1] Most of their leaders had been to jail and had spent their lives in anti-

[1] A weaker Sikh group, the Khalsa National Party, representative of conservative and relatively pro-British Sikhs, supported the Unionists.

government agitation; indeed it was largely Akali influence that had unsettled the Sikhs and shaken the loyalty of the Sikh soldier. It was not easy, therefore, for them to perform a complete *volte-face* and openly advocate full collaboration with the Unionist Government and the British in the prosecution of the war. But in order to safeguard the position of the Sikh in the army some of them were inclined to modify their attitude of opposition. The danger of becoming isolated, unbefriended by either the Congress, Muslim League or the British, also began to dawn on them. In the jockeying for position in anticipation of the end of the British Raj, who except the British would support a minority community like the Sikhs?

Circumstances were, therefore, not unfavourable to a revival of Anglo-Sikh amity, and for facilitating this rapprochement Short at Lahore, covering also Amritsar and the central Punjab districts and with influential friends in the Sikh State of Patiala, was in a key position. His duties were not strictly political; but obviously, if he was to effect anything in the Sikh recruiting areas, he had to meet, converse with, and try to have an impact on Sikh political leaders. He threw himself into his work with enthusiasm and was soon accepted by leading Sikhs, and not least by the Akalis, as a friend and well-wisher. In addition he became intimate with Sir Sikander and other influential Punjabi Muslims and won the confidence of the Governor, Sir Henry Craik.

Short conceived his immediate and pressing task to be to rally the maximum Sikh support for Britain's war effort by restoring Anglo-Sikh amity and by inducing the largest possible measure of Sikh-Muslim amity in the Punjab. But he also viewed current Punjab affairs in the wider context of India's future, 'Settle the Sikh', he would say, 'and you settle India.' There was an element of truth in this exaggeration; for, as already explained, the Muslim-Sikh problem in the Punjab was a reproduction in microcosm—and in reverse—of the general Hindu-Muslim problem in India as a whole, and a political settlement in the Punjab acceptable to the Sikh minority, besides serving the immediate purposes of war, would contribute to the larger end of an all-India Hindu-Muslim settlement. With a true but ill-fated prescience Short worked for a Muslim-Sikh accord— which in political terms meant an alliance between the Unionists and the Akalis. His first efforts were repulsed, and this was not

B

surprising; for though the Akalis were in process of becoming rather less hostile to the British and so indirectly—but more unwillingly—less hostile to Sikander's pro-British Unionist Government, there was still much suspicion on both sides. To the Akalis Sikander's ostensible support of the demand for Pakistan seemed hard to reconcile with any genuine goodwill for the Sikhs. To Sikander the Akalis appeared insatiable; one concession, he felt, would only lead to the demand for another and nothing would win their permanent attachment.

But Short persevered and with good reason; for in face of the demand for Pakistan some kind of understanding between the Akalis and the Punjabi Muslims was essential, if first a dissipation of the Punjab's war effort and then a disastrous division of the province was to be avoided. Both sides knew that division was contrary to the interests of all Punjabis, whether Muslim, Sikh or Hindu. Both sides dreaded it. But if the demand for Pakistan was pressed it might become inescapable; for the Akalis were quite determined that the Sikhs should not become a helpless minority in an independent Muslim State. Rather than this they would face—indeed insist upon—division despite all its disadvantages not least to the Sikhs themselves.

At first sight the distribution of population in the Punjab as it then existed might appear not unfavourable to partition. The western districts were predominantly Muslim, the eastern predominantly non-Muslim. It might therefore seem easy and natural to divide the province into two roughly equal parts by a line drawn down the centre between the two principal cities of Lahore and Amritsar. But any such line would be geographically, ethnically and economically wholly artificial. Save for a few outlying districts the Punjab was a close-knit unity, and the population so intermingled, especially in the central districts, that wherever the line was drawn large numbers of all three communities would find themselves on the wrong side of it. Moreover, though differing in religion, the population in all parts of the province was drawn from the same racial stocks, spoke a common language and was very conscious of being Punjabi. Economically too the province was a unity. Its prosperity rested on an elaborate network of canals, spread right across it from east to west, which had enabled large tracts of desert to be converted into flourishing 'colonies'. People from all over the province had a stake in these colonies and had played a part in their development. A line drawn down the centre of the Punjab might serve well enough as a boundary between two provincial administrations both subordinate to the same central government; but if it were to be made a regular frontier between two separate, sovereign, independent States, it would at best cause enormous economic dislocation and hardship and at worst lead to serious disorders.

Sikander and the majority of the Punjabi Muslims, aware of the real facts of the situation, were utterly opposed to such an artificial division of the province. Even extremist Muslims, who were animated by narrow sectarian impulses rather than by broad feelings of provincial patriotism and regard for the general interest, wished such division to be avoided. Pakistan according to their conception included the whole of the Punjab. Its division on a population basis would mean the acceptance by them of a truncated Pakistan, with large numbers of their co-religionists left just on the wrong side of the frontier and with Hindustan in control of the headwaters of three[1] of the five Punjab rivers. They had, therefore, strong motives for wishing to keep the Punjab intact.

The Akalis for their part also looked at the matter from a narrow sectarian point of view and fully realized how damaging division would be to the Sikhs. On a strictly population basis the likely dividing line would leave two million of them, with all their valuable colony lands not to mention some important Sikh shrines, on the Pakistan side. To a small community of only six million such a division might well be fatal. The Akali leaders sought to comfort themselves with the hope that the line of division might be shifted westwards, even as far as the river Chenab, so that all the rich colony lands of the Lyallpur and Montgomery districts with their numerous Sikh peasantry would fall into East Punjab and be excluded from Pakistan. During my time at Amritsar one of them tried hard to coax me into conceding that this was a possibility and urged that, if it came to a division of the Punjab, the Sikhs' stake in the colony lands and the part they had played in developing them would have to be taken into account. I told him bluntly that such hopes were in my view illusory and that if Pakistan became

[1] The Sutlej, Beas and Ravi.

inevitable either it would include the whole of the Punjab or
the Punjab would be divided on a population basis by a line
down the middle. The Wagah Rest House, I said, would mark
the dividing line—this being a well-known canal inspection
bungalow near the Grand Trunk Road on the border of the
Lahore and Amritsar[1] districts. I did not manage to convince
him. He recurred to the subject more than three years later at
the time of the Cabinet Mission, and in one form or another this
illusory hope persisted to the very end.

But in 1942-3 the Akalis' main hope was that the threat of
Pakistan would not materialize. In the then prevailing mood
of Punjabi Muslims this hope seemed well-founded; but the
prospects of its realization would be greatly improved by a
political alliance between Unionists and Akalis. If the Muslim
and Sikh communities, as represented by these political parties,
stood firmly together, Pakistan would in all probability remain
an aspiration; for without the support of the Punjabi Muslims
it could not come into being. Even if, at worst, the latter were
compelled to translate into reality their nominal adherence to
the idea of Pakistan, a Unionist-Akali alliance was likely to
prevent the division of the province between two sovereign
States and lead to an offer to the Sikhs of special rights and
privileges which would make them feel that their community
had a more glorious future as part of Pakistan, supported by the
combined might of Muslims and Sikhs, than as an insignificant
fragment of Hinbu India.

The prospect, then, of a disruption of the Punjab, which the
demand for Pakistan seemed to portend, made natural and
possible the coming together of Unionists and Akalis; and to
well-wishers of the province an understanding between them
certainly seemed desirable. The death early in 1941 of Sir
Sunder Singh Majithia, the leader of the Khalsa National
Party and a prominent member of Sikander's Government,
provided the opportunity for some political realignment; but
it was not till a year later that through the prolonged efforts of
Major Short and a few others an agreement was reached between Unionists and Akalis known as the Sikander-Baldev
Singh pact. S. Baldev Singh, who though himself not an Akali

---

[1] The frontier post between India and Pakistan on the Grand Trunk road
is, in fact, at Wagah.

was known to be acceptable to the Akali Party, became the Sikh Minister in the Punjab Cabinet and the Akalis tacitly undertook to refrain at least from active opposition. The first fruits of this pact were seen in the Akalis' attitude towards Gandhi's rebellion in August 1942. Only a handful of them took part in it; the majority held aloof and did nothing to embarrass the Punjab Government.

'At present', I commented at the time, 'this pact cannot be regarded as more than a temporary truce. Its significance lies in its potentialities for the future. That a predominantly Muslim Government should have been able to come to terms, even temporarily, with a party of extreme Sikh nationalists is something to the good, and if the truce holds good for a few years it may develop into real understanding between the Unionist Government and the Akalis and bear fruit in the form of a far-reaching Sikh-Muslim compromise regarding the sharing of power in the Punjab. If such a compromise were effected, it would facilitate and perhaps give the clue to a similar solution of the all-India problem.'

A series of misfortunes and mistakes blasted the hopes thus cautiously expressed. The Unionist Party crumbled to pieces, and in consequence the Sikander-Baldev Singh pact instead of being the salvation of the province contributed to its undoing. Jinnah gained complete ascendancy over the Punjabi Muslims, crushing all opposition till there was none left to resist him or even to tell him the real truth about the Punjab. He himself knew no more of the Punjab than Neville Chamberlain did of Czechoslovakia.

This tragic history will be traced in later pages;[1] but the first misfortune occurred at the close of 1942. Suddenly one night without any warning Sikander had a heart attack and died. He was only fifty and his death was entirely unexpected.

Felix opportunitate mortis. I said this at the time and I still feel that it is true. He died at the height of his power and reputation and escaped a future which seemed to threaten both. The truth is that the demand for Pakistan had put him in a quandary from which there was no obvious way out. For nearly two years he had contrived to reconcile the irreconcilable—his own political beliefs, proclaimed by his leadership of the Unionist Party, and

[1] Chapter V.

his acceptance of the Pakistan resolution. But it is doubtful whether even he, with all his skill, could have succeeded much longer in explaining away the contradiction. He would have been compelled to choose between the risk of a break with Jinnah (and consequent defection of a powerful group of Punjabi Muslims) and the loss of all credit with his non-Muslim supporters.

Many of us had been critical of Sikander for his constant submission to Jinnah and unwillingness to stand up to him. He was aware of these criticisms and during a long talk with me, just before I went to Amritsar, defended himself against them with considerable feeling. He said that unless he walked warily and kept on the right side of Jinnah he would be swept away by a wave of fanaticism and, wherever he went, would be greeted by the Muslims with black flags. I was by no means wholly convinced by his arguments. I thought that he underrated the strength of his position in the Punjab and his hold on the Muslims, reinforced as it was in the case of many of the prominent Muslim politicians by ties of personal affection. Subsequent events suggest that his reading of the situation was more correct than mine.

There can be no doubt that if he had lived and nerved himself to defy Jinnah he would have had more chance than his successor of doing so without disaster. The probability is that he would never have taken the risk, but would have continued his temporizing policy and faced the loss of all credit with non-Muslims rather than hazard any defection amongst his Muslim followers. If so, he would at any rate have been a moderating influence on Jinnah during the critical months of 1946–7 and would hardly have allowed him to be driven into acceptance of the partition of the Punjab without making the smallest attempt to reach an understanding with the Sikhs. On either alternative, therefore, his death must be reckoned a great misfortune.

Sir Sikander's successor as leader of the Unionist Party and Premier of the Punjab was Sir Khizar Hyat Tiwana, the scion of a well-known family of West Punjab where he enjoyed much of the status of a feudal baron. He was a man of the highest courage—far more resolute than Sir Sikander—and a strong, attractive personality. But, having only entered politics in 1937, he did not have Sikander's experience and standing, nor was he endowed in the same degree with his diplomatic gifts and charm of manner.

Like Sikander he was at heart strongly opposed to the demand for Pakistan; but he was less willing than Sikander to compromise or to bow to Jinnah's dictation. Compromise was in fact becoming impossible, for Jinnah stood firmly by the demand that all the Muslim-majority provinces should be formed into Pakistan and repeatedly stated that this meant their complete severance from the rest of India with no link save such voluntary agreements as might be concluded between independent sovereign States. He also began to evince a desire to control the actions of the Punjab Government, claiming that as the Muslims, who constituted the majority of the Unionist Party, were also members of the League, the Punjab Government was a 'League' government and should submit to his directives as President of the League. To this Khizar demurred on the ground that his government was not a League government but a coalition government with Hindu and Sikh members.

Jinnah soon realized that in Khizar he had a tougher man to deal with than Sikander. He therefore set himself to undermine his position. There had always been among the Muslim Unionists a clique of communal extremists, out of sympathy with Sikander's moderate policies and wholehearted supporters of the demand for Pakistan. Sikander with his capacity for being all things to all men had contrived to keep them in check. They were however readily available to Jinnah for the intimidation of Khizar or, failing that, for rousing Muslim opinion against him and bringing about his downfall. Khizar was not, however, a man to be intimidated. He courageously resisted Jinnah's attempts to dictate to him till finally in the middle of 1944 there was an open rupture and he was expelled by Jinnah from the League. The Muslim members of the Unionist Party were now forced to choose between loyalty to Khizar and the Unionist Party and loyalty to Jinnah and the League. Thus there opened the rift in the Muslim ranks which Sikander had always dreaded and the Unionist Party, which had dominated Punjab politics for over twenty years and governed the province since 1937, began to disintegrate.

It suffered a grievous loss in January 1945 by the death of Sir Chhotu Ram, the leader of the Hindu Jats of south-eastern Punjab. For a generation he had been one of the main pillars of the Unionist Party. He was a forceful politician of great renown within the province and had considerable influence among some sections of the Muslims.

Khizar, though weakened by these developments, was not immediately brought down; most of the Muslims in the provincial assembly continued to support him. But there were ominous signs of the way the tide was flowing and of what might happen when a general election was held. Several well-known Punjabi Muslims of comparatively moderate views announced their adherence to the League rather than to the Unionist Party. Where these went others were bound to follow.

Thus by 1945 Jinnah's influence in the Punjab—the key province so far as Pakistan was concerned—was very much greater than it had been five years earlier when the 'Pakistan Resolution' was passed. He had not destroyed the Unionists, but he had made a breach in their ranks. Elsewhere too he had strengthened his position. In Bengal Fazl-ul-Haq, the Premier since 1937, had dared to defy him and had been overthrown in 1943. His successor, Khwaja Nazimuddin, was more amenable and a whole-hearted leaguer. In Sind and Assam there were League governments, and even in the North-West Frontier Province, the one Muslim province attached to the Congress, a League Ministry was formed during the absence in jail of Congress's allies, the Red Shirts, and the League established itself as a political force to be reckoned with.

Jinnah's relentless determination to eliminate all independent Muslim parties and to marshal all Muslims under his own leadership was well illustrated in the summer of 1945, when the Viceroy, Lord Wavell, on the termination of the war with Germany, made a fresh attempt to break the political deadlock. The members of the Congress Working Committee who were still in jail[1] were released and invited to a conference at Simla to consider proposals for an Interim Government, all the members of which, except the Viceroy and Commander-in-Chief, would be drawn from the principal Indian political parties. After the folly of the 'Quit India' rebellion Congress were in a

---

[1] Some had already been released on grounds of health.

chastened mood and ready to co-operate. But if the Interim Government was to be fruitful for the future, Jinnah's co-operation was also necessary, and Jinnah put forward demands which effectually wrecked the conference. The Muslims, he claimed, must not only have half the total number of seats in the government, but all the Muslim seats must be held by nominees of the League. There must be no Muslim stooges of Congress, like Maulana Abul Kalam Azad, nor possible Muslim 'Quislings', like Khizar or any other Punjabi Muslim belonging to the Unionist Party. On this demand that the League should nominate all the Muslims Jinnah was adamant. Lord Wavell had wanted to include a nominee of the Unionists, but Jinnah, who was bent on eliminating them altogether as a political force, would not hear of it. If we had acquiesced, he said afterwards, in the inclusion of non-League Muslims in the Muslim quota, 'we should have signed our death warrant'. It was over this issue that the conference broke down.

The Congress had once claimed to speak for the whole of India. The claim was invalid and they had been compelled to abate it. Jinnah now claimed to speak for all the Muslims of India. This claim was also invalid; but unlike Congress he was not compelled to abate it and soon he succeeded for all practical purposes in making it good.

The Cabinet Mission

A NEW Labour Government came into power in Great Britain at the end of July 1945. Despite other pre-occupations they were determined to give high priority to the settlement of the Indian problem. The failure of Lord Wavell's Simla Conference left the field clear for some fresh initiative, and the capitulation of Japan on August 14th made it necessary to think not merely of interim arrangements but of a final constitutional settlement. The Labour Government's first action was to order elections for the Central and Provincial Assemblies. Owing to the war these had not been held since early in 1937. It was announced by the Viceroy on August 21st that there would be fresh elections during the ensuing cold weather. Their result, so far as the Hindu population was concerned, was a foregone conclusion—there would be over-whelming support for Congress. But they would be a test of Jinnah's claim to speak for all the Muslims of India.

The British Labour Party had always been sympathetic towards India's struggle for freedom and several of its prominent members had been in fairly close touch with Gandhi, Nehru and other Congress leaders. There was therefore a natural tendency to incline to the Congress' view of things and a reluctance to regard Pakistan as a really serious and live proposition. Though the importance of Jinnah could not be ignored, his firm adherence to the demand for Pakistan was believed to be for bargaining purposes; and in any case, so long as he failed to win the allegiance of the Muslims of the Punjab and N.W.F.P., Pakistan could not come into being and the unity of India could be preserved. These were the hopes and beliefs of the Labour Government as the year 1945 drew to a close.

Early in the new year the realities began to be seen to be a little different. A parliamentary delegation visited India in January. Its members were considerably impressed by the solidity of Muslim opinion in favour of Pakistan and some of them felt doubtful whether Jinnah's demand for it could any longer be regarded as mere bluff. One of those who most stressed the strength of Muslim feeling behind Jinnah was Mr. Woodrow Wyatt, a Labour M.P. and therefore not to be suspected of anti-Congress bias. The correctness of his appreciation was confirmed by the results of the elections. In the Central Assembly the League had already captured all the Muslim seats. In the Provincial Assemblies it now won 446 out of a total of 495 Muslim seats. Its only failure was in the N.W.F.P., but this was of small significance compared with its smashing success in the Punjab. Here in 1937 it had utterly failed, securing only one of the Muslim seats in the Provincial Assembly while the Unionists captured all the rest. But now the tables were turned. The League won seventy-nine seats and Khizar and the Muslim Unionists were reduced to a mere handful of ten.[1] It was for all practical purposes the end of the Unionist Party. The cry of Pakistan, with its vague but alluring connotation for the Muslim masses, had proved irresistible. Jinnah's claim to speak for the Muslims had been triumphantly vindicated.

Obviously the prospects of avoiding partition had considerably worsened; but the British Government were not lightly to be deflected from their aim of preserving, while granting independence, the unity of India which British rule had achieved. They made now a last supreme effort to realize this aim, atoning thereby to some extent for former British complacency over the communal cleavage. It was not their fault that it did not succeed.

The leading figure in this British effort was Sir Stafford Cripps. In March 1946, almost exactly four years after his previous abortive mission, he flew out once again to India, accompanied this time by two other Cabinet Ministers—Mr. A. V. Alexander and Lord Pethick Lawrence. Among the members of his staff was Major Short, who had by this time returned to England. His inclusion in the party was a small but graceful gesture to the Sikhs, suggesting (quite erroneously as it proved) that their interests would be safeguarded.

[1] After several defections to the League subsequent to the declaration of the election results.

The task of this trio of Cabinet Ministers was twofold, to assist the Viceroy in bringing about agreement on the method of framing a constitution and to assist him in the formation of a new Executive Council, representative of the main Indian political parties, for carrying on the government while the constitution was being hammered out. These two things were at this stage more than ever interrelated, for without a broad measure of agreement about the future constitutional set-up it was impossible to bring Congress and the League together in an effective Executive Council.

The task was sufficiently daunting. Since the original Congress-League rupture in 1937 all attempts to reconcile their conflicting aims had been unavailing, and these aims were now more glaringly contradictory than ever before. Jinnah contended that there were two nations in India and that therefore there must be two national States. The Congress maintained the opposite. Between these opposing viewpoints there seemed little room for compromise; equally there was little disposition for it. Each side, being deeply distrustful of the other, preferred to cling to its own perfect solution and unrealizable ideal rather than risk yielding an advantage to the other by seeking for a middle way. Moreover, if any compromise formula were to be devised, each side knew that the other would stand on its letter rather than its spirit, and instead of looking to its broad intention would seek later to twist its interpretation to suit their own ends. There was, therefore, great wariness about agreeing to anything.

One hopeful feature was the growing awareness in India that the British Government really meant business. Though in some quarters there was still distrust of British intentions, the principal political leaders were becoming convinced of the sincerity of the Labour Government's proclaimed resolve to quit the scene and leave India to Indians. Power—and responsibility—were at last within their grasp, and this might be expected to induce a more reasonable and realistic attitude; for without agreement between the two major political parties, transfer of power could only lead to chaos and civil war.

The main hope of such agreement lay in the possibility that Jinnah would be persuaded to accept something less than he apparently demanded. What was it he really wanted? Nobody was quite sure. Ostensibly he claimed a sovereign independent Pakistan consisting of the whole of six provinces,[1] subject only to minor frontier adjustments. In 1944, at the instance of Rajagopalachari, Gandhi had offered him something less than this—a Pakistan consisting of those contiguous areas in the north-west and north-east of India in which Muslims were in a majority. On this principle Pakistan would be shorn of nearly all Assam and of large parts of the Punjab and Bengal. Jinnah, not content with a bundle of contiguous areas, had rejected outright this offer of what he called a 'moth-eaten' Pakistan. But how could he hope to get the Pakistan of his conception except by persuading the Sikhs and other sections of the non-Muslim population willingly to throw in their lot with Pakistan? Such persuasions were not necessarily foredoomed to failure. Yet he had so far made no attempt to conciliate or win them over.

All in all it seemed possible that he had not even now quite decided in his own mind what he wanted or how to get it, but believed that by uncompromisingly demanding a 'six province' Pakistan he would ultimately extort for the Muslims something which, if not Pakistan, would be better than a bundle of contiguous areas. A formula, therefore, had to be devised, which offered the semblance of a 'six province' Pakistan while preserving the essentials of unity.

The Cabinet Mission's arrival in Delhi coincided with the onset of the hot weather and the temperature steadily rose as they went through a round of preliminary interviews with representatives of the main political parties, the Indian States, the Sikhs, the scheduled castes, and, not least, with Gandhi. He established himself in considerable style and with due publicity in the 'harijan' quarter of New Delhi and, though claiming to speak only for himself, was available as a sort of universal counsellor to anyone who sought his advice. The Cabinet Mission specifically requested him to remain at hand and in touch with them during the whole progress of the negotiations.

Towards the end of April, after completing their round of interviews, the Mission took a short recess, expressing the hope that the main parties would themselves now come together and offer some agreed basis for framing a constitution. There was

[1] Punjab, Sind, Baluchistan, N.W.F.P., Bengal and Assam.

not the slightest prospect of any such thing occurring. Everyone knew that the Cabinet Mission would themselves have to propound their own scheme, and herein lay the only hope of finding a compromise. Several schemes had in fact been mooted during the course of the preliminary interviews and conversations. One of these, though not perhaps intrinsically the best, when adumbrated by Sir Stafford to Jinnah informally, seemed to awaken in that cold serpent-like figure a spark of interest, the scintilla of a positive response. Seeing the chance, Sir Stafford took it. The fundamental principles of this particular scheme were set down in writing and communicated on April 27th to both Congress and the League as a possible basis of agreement. Each was invited to send four negotiators to discuss them in the more temperate climate of Simla. These fundamental principles were as follows:

   (i) A Union Government to deal only with foreign affairs, defence and communications;

  (ii) two Groups of Provinces, one of the predominantly Hindu provinces and the other of the predominantly Muslim provinces, to deal with such of the remaining subjects as the provinces in the respective groups desired to be dealt with in common;

(iii) the Provincial Governments to deal with all other subjects and to have all the residuary sovereign rights;

(iv) the Indian States to take their appropriate place in this structure on terms to be negotiated with them.

Both sides accepted the invitation, but both made it clear that this did not imply agreement with the fundamental principles. Jinnah merely reiterated his demand for a 'six province' Pakistan and, as a corollary, the setting up of two separate constitution-making bodies. Congress specified straight away their main objection to the proposed scheme. 'We consider it wrong', they wrote, 'to form Groups of Provinces under the Federal Union and more so on religious or communal basis. Any sub-federation within the Federal Union would weaken the Federal Centre and would otherwise be wrong. . . . It would result in creating three layers of executive and legislative bodies, an arrangement which will be cumbrous, static and disjointed, leading to continuous friction.'

It will be seen that they objected to just those features of the scheme which carried the faint impression of Pakistan. They stuck to this objection to the bitter end.

The discussions in Simla, though comparatively cordial, led to no agreement, and it was left, therefore, to the Cabinet Mission and the Viceroy to rehash and elaborate the scheme in the light of the views expressed and to put it forward publicly as offering the best arrangement for providing a new constitution for an independent India. This they did in a carefully drafted statement issued on May 16th.

In this statement the proposal for 'a separate and fully independent sovereign State of Pakistan as claimed by the Muslim League' was considered and decisively rejected. It was pointed out that a Pakistan of six provinces, as demanded by the League, would not solve the problem of communal minorities since twenty million Muslims would still remain in India and there would be non-Muslim minorities in Pakistan amounting to 38 per cent of the population in the western part and 48 per cent in the eastern part. 'Nor can we see any justification', the statement went on, 'for including within a sovereign Pakistan those districts of the Punjab and of Bengal and Assam in which the population is predominantly non-Muslim. Every argument that can be used in favour of Pakistan can equally, in our view, be used in favour of the exclusion of the non-Muslim areas from Pakistan. This point would particularly affect the position of the Sikhs.'

The possibility of a smaller 'truncated' Pakistan confined to the Muslim majority areas alone was also considered. The reasons advanced for rejecting this are of melancholy interest in view of what subsequently took place. 'Such a Pakistan', it was stated, 'is regarded by the Muslim League as quite impracticable. We ourselves are also convinced that any solution which involves a radical partition of the Punjab and Bengal, as this would do, would be contrary to the wishes and interests of a very large proportion of the inhabitants of these Provinces. . . . Moreover, any division of the Punjab would of necessity divide the Sikhs, leaving substantial bodies of Sikhs on both sides of the boundary.'

Having rejected Pakistan, the Mission proceeded to expand and commend the scheme which had been discussed at Simla.

In elaborating it they attempted to meet the views of both parties, but basically it remained the same. A three-tiered constitution was envisaged consisting of a Union limited to foreign affairs, defence and communications, Groups of Provinces dealing with such subjects as might later be determined, and the individual Provinces themselves in which all residuary powers would vest. After an initial period of ten years it was to be open to any Province, by a majority vote of its legislature, to call for a reconsideration of the constitution.

The Mission's statement then went on to propose that such a constitution should be brought into being by means of a Constituent Assembly to be elected by the members of the provincial legislatures,[1] and that the Constituent Assembly should follow a certain procedure designed to meet Jinnah's objection to a single constitution-making body. It was proposed that after an initial full meeting of a formal character, the Assembly should divide up into three sections—Section A consisting of the representatives of the five Hindu-majority provinces; Section B of the representatives of the Punjab, N.W.F.P. and Sind, and Section C of the representatives of Bengal and Assam. These Sections would draw up constitutions for the Provinces included in each of them and would also decide whether a Group should be formed and if so with what subjects; but a Province would have the right to opt out of a Group by a vote of its legislature *after* the new constitutional arrangements had come into operation. Finally the Constituent Assembly would meet again as a whole to settle the Union Constitution.

The statement referred to the need, while the constitution-making proceeded, for an Interim Government in which all the portfolios would be held by Indian leaders having the confidence of the people. It was mentioned that the Viceroy had already started discussions to this end.

The statement was well received. It was recognized at once

---

[1] Each Province was to be allocated representatives proportionate to its population and this provincial allocation was to be divided in turn between the main communities in each Province in proportion to their population. For this purpose only three main communities were recognized, Muslim, Sikh and General, the latter including all persons who were not Muslims or Sikhs.

as a genuine and ingenious attempt to reconcile conflicting aims and as unmistakable evidence of the British Government's sincere desire to bring British rule in India to a peaceful end. Gandhi speaking at a prayer meeting on May 17th said that the Cabinet Mission had brought forth something of which they had every reason to be proud; and even ten days later, when doubts had begun to assail him, he still considered it 'the best document the British Government could have produced in the circumstances'. In spite of these encomiums it soon became clear that Gandhi and the Working Committee of Congress would scrutinize every line and comma of the statement before committing themselves to an acceptance of the proposals.

Jinnah was less enthusiastic. The statement had flatly rejected the idea of a sovereign, independent Pakistan, and this he could hardly be expected to applaud. But though outwardly more critical of the statement, he was really, as it proved, less inclined to cavil at it than Congress.

The largest volume of vocal opposition came from various minority groups who felt that their interests were not adequately safeguarded—and not least from the Sikhs. The crushing defeat of the Unionist Party in the Punjab elections early in the year had come as a severe shock to them. As a result of the Sikander-Baldev Singh pact they had felt fairly secure while the Unionist Party still represented the bulk of the Punjab Muslims; and they had fully expected that the Unionists would be victorious at the elections. But to their utter dismay a rabid Muslim League Party had come to the front with whom they saw no prospect of reaching an understanding; and now, according to the Cabinet Mission proposals, the Punjab itself would be swallowed up entire in a group of predominantly Muslim provinces which, if not the equivalent of Pakistan, might ultimately turn into it or prove to be as bad.

It was pointed out to them that as the Muslims were a bare majority of the population in the Punjab they would find it impossible to rule the province without Sikh support—the Sikhs would, in fact, hold the balance of power. The Muslim League Party in the Punjab might for the time being seem very hostile to them, but ultimately, like the Unionists, they would be compelled to woo them. By these and similar arguments Major Short and the Cabinet Mission tried to reassure them;

but they would not be comforted. They had got it into their heads that the Muslims were out 'to crush them' and more and more their thoughts were turning to the idea of partitioning the Punjab so that they might escape altogether the threat of Muslim domination. Early in May the Akali leader with whom I had discussed this possibility as far back as 1942[1] came to see me in Delhi where I was at that time working. He had somewhat moderated his previous ambitions. He realized, he said, that there was no hope of the dividing line being so far west as the river Chenab, but would not the river Ravi be a very reasonable boundary? I pointed out some of the objections —such a boundary would deprive Pakistan of Lahore and of the overwhelmingly Muslim districts of Montgomery and Multan and yet leave many Sikhs on the wrong side. He said that he contemplated some exchange of population. I replied that this could only be accomplished by force and I counselled him not to think of the partition of the Punjab while there was a reasonable chance of preserving the unity both of it and of India as a whole. It was obvious, however, that he would continue to think of it; for now that the Punjab Muslims had gone over *en masse* to the League he despaired of reaching any accommodation with them.

Gandhi, who had hitherto shown little sympathy for the Sikhs—he objected to the Akali leaders as 'communalists'— began now, perhaps not very wisely, to draw public attention to their fears. Commenting in his paper *Harijan* on the Mission's statement he wrote: 'Are the Sikhs, for whom the Punjab is the only home in India, to consider themselves, against their will, as part of the Section which takes in Sind, Baluchistan and the Frontier Province?' Certainly it seemed hard that willy-nilly they should be lumped with predominantly Muslim areas, but this was dictated by the actual facts of their geographical distribution. There was at the moment nothing which could be done for them without upsetting the whole of the Mission's delicately poised scheme. Their fears, if not their interests, had necessarily to be overlooked.

Meanwhile both the two major parties were examining the scheme, apparently with some disposition to accept it. Hopes of a settlement were enormously raised when on June 6th Jinnah, abandoning his usual negative attitude, got the Muslim League

---

[1] See page 35.

to pass a resolution accepting the scheme and agreeing to join the constitution-making body. The acceptance, it is true, was stated to be 'in the hope that it would ultimately result in the establishment of complete sovereign Pakistan', which still remained the unalterable objective of the Muslims in India. But the Mission's scheme, whatever ultimate prospects and potentialities it might hold, was a definite rejection of 'sovereign Pakistan'. To have induced Jinnah at last publicly to accept something substantially less than what he had hitherto invariably demanded was a considerable success.

Jinnah's acceptance of the scheme had been fairly prompt and was certainly genuine; but it would be wrong to conclude that he agreed to it with enthusiasm. He had many misgivings and hesitated a good deal before recommending it to the Council of the League. Nevertheless from the Muslim point of view it offered solid advantages. All the six provinces[1] which the League claimed to be the Muslim 'home-lands' were included intact, without any division, in Sections B and C of the proposed Constituent Assembly; and since in these two Sections taken as a whole (though not in all the individual provinces composing them) the Muslims were in a clear majority, they could reasonably hope to ensure by majority vote[2] that in the constitution-making process these provinces would be formed into Groups or sub-federations. These Groups, though tied to an all-India Union, would be so powerful in themselves that no Hindu-dominated Union Government would be able to ride rough-shod over them; and there was always the possibility of secession after ten years. Thus over the short term, the scheme adequately protected essential Muslim interests and over the long term did not preclude the ultimate emergence of a 'sovereign independent Pakistan' embracing all the provinces which the Muslims claimed. All Jinnah's previous negations, more particularly his rejection of the 'moth-eaten' Pakistan offered by Gandhi in 1944, seemed justified now by results.

But the prospects of agreement still hung in the balance.

---

[1] Including British Baluchistan which was not constitutionally a 'Province' like the others, but would necessarily go into Section B.

[2] The Cabinet Mission had assured Jinnah that decisions in the Sections would be by a majority vote of the representatives of the Provinces within the Section and that the voting would not be by Provinces.

The Congress Working Committee had not yet given their verdict on the scheme and perhaps Jinnah's acceptance of it made them wish to scan it all the more closely. They tried hard to gain acceptance for an interpretation of the scheme which would make it optional for the individual provinces to join the Sections in which they had been placed. Since the Muslim League did not command a majority in the Punjab, the N.W.F.P. and Assam, it could be expected that these Provinces would elect not to enter B and C Sections and thus the grouping desired by the League would be frustrated. The Mission, however, firmly rejected the interpretation of the scheme suggested by Congress. The grouping of provinces, they said, was an essential feature of the scheme. A Province could opt out of a Group by the vote of its new legislature only *after* the constitution had come into force.

Days passed and the Congress Working Committee gave no decision but withdrew to Mussouri for recess, taking Gandhi with them. Meanwhile the Viceroy's attempts to bring about agreement between the two parties over the formation of an Interim Government had run up against the usual difficulties. The League claimed 'parity' with Congress and the exclusive right to nominate Muslims. Congress rejected both these claims. It became clear that, as in the case of the constitutional problem, there was no prospect of negotiating an agreement between the parties and that the only course was for the Viceroy and the Mission to put forward their own proposals and hope that they would be accepted by both parties as a reasonable compromise. The Mission was also getting impatient to return home and desired to bring matters to a head. Accordingly on June 16th—before Congress had pronounced on the constitutional scheme—the Viceroy, in consultation with the members of the Mission, announced that further negotiations were being abandoned and that he had issued invitations to a named list of fourteen persons to serve as members of an Interim Government. These consisted of six Hindu members of Congress (including one member of the scheduled castes), five members of the Muslim League, one Sikh, one Parsee and one Indian Christian. Thus Jinnah's claim to parity with Congress and with the Hindus was rejected, but his desire to veto non-League Muslims was respected.

The announcement stated that if the invitations were accepted by the two major parties it was hoped to inaugurate the new Government about June 26th. There then followed as paragraph 8 the following passage, designed perhaps to put pressure on Congress who were still hesitating over the constitutional scheme:

'In the event of the two parties or either of them proving unwilling to join in the setting up of a Coalition Government on the above lines, it is the intention of the Viceroy to proceed with the formation of an Interim Government which will be as representative as possible of those willing to accept the statement of May 16th.'

Since the League had already expressed its willingness to accept the May 16th statement whereas Congress had not, this seemed to imply that the possibility of forming a predominantly League Government without the inclusion of any representatives of Congress was not ruled out. Whether the Viceroy and Cabinet Mission really thought this to be a practical possibility or were merely bluffing is not very clear. It is somewhat difficult to believe that the British Government would have consented to the hazardous experiment of governing the whole of India with the aid of only Muslims, Christians and Parsees. Yet Jinnah seems to have thought that they might.

For a few days there was no public reaction to the announcement by either of the two major parties. The members of the Congress Working Committee had not all reassembled in Delhi and Gandhi also was temporarily absent. There was, however, a growing feeling of optimism. It was known that the proposals were acceptable to Jinnah; but he did not intend to intimate this until after Congress had spoken. In Congress circles there was some desire to substitute a Congress Muslim for one of the Congress Hindus, but it was hoped that they would not press the point in view of Jinnah's strong objection. Both Jawaharlal Nehru and Sardar Vallabhai Patel were believed to be in favour of acceptance and the rumour spread that the Congress Working Committee were going to express their readiness to work both the long-term and the short-term plan. All the labours of the past twelve weeks—the endless discussions in the

sweltering heat, the skilful and patient elaboration of a plan
to suit all parties, the drafting and redrafting of statements and
formulas—seemed on the point of being richly rewarded. For
nine years Congress and the League had been engaged in
barren controversy and non-co-operation. Now both were being
successfully shepherded into a Coalition Government and into
a Constituent Assembly which would frame a constitution on
an agreed basis. A cartoon appeared in the *Hindustan Times*
showing the Mission packing up to go home under the caption,
'All's well that ends well'.

It seemed too good to be true. And it was; for Gandhi had
not been reckoned with. Once again at the critical moment he
arrived on the scene and intervened with decisive and disastrous
effect. Those who were inclined to acquiesce in the omission of
a Congress Muslim from the Interim Government were overborne. Congress, being a national party with a Muslim president, could not, in Gandhi's view, agree to such an omission
even as a temporary expedient and on the Viceroy's assurance
that it would not be a precedent. It involved a principle which
Congress could not give up. It mattered not that the principle
had ceased to have practical significance now that Jinnah had
won almost all the Muslims to his side. It mattered not that
insistence on it would infuriate Jinnah, whose co-operation
in any unitary form of government was essential, and would
disrupt, with unpredictable consequences, the delicate web of
negotiations spun by the Cabinet Mission. Such mundane and
common-sense considerations did not appeal to Gandhi.

When the news spread that Congress were going to reject
the proposals for an Interim Government the dismay in Cabinet
Mission circles was intense, and intense too the indignation
against Gandhi. It was he who had wrecked the Cripps Mission
in 1942. Now he had done it again! Under the first shock of
disappointment deliberate maleficence was attributed to him.
This, of course, was mistaken. His influence may have been
baleful, but it was not intended to be so. His advice may have
been unwise, unstatesmanlike and, from the point of view of
preserving India's unity, absolutely calamitous, but it was given
in good faith and with the best of motives. If he could have been
shown all the grim consequences that were to flow from it he
would perhaps have said, as he had said on a previous occasion,

that he had not the remotest idea of any such catastrophe resulting from it. Following the promptings of an inner voice he was all too often careless of consequences—until they overtook him. In this case they were to overtake him with a vengeance!

With the rejection of the short-term proposals by Congress the last chance of an agreement which might have averted partition was thrown away. This is clear now; but it was not fully apparent at the time; for hope revived when it became known that Congress, while rejecting the proposals for an Interim Government, had at last made up their minds to accept the long-term constitutional proposals. Something, at least, seemed to have been secured.

The acceptance when it came was qualified and ambiguous. It was conveyed in a long letter dated June 25th from the President, Maulana Abul Kalam Azad, to the Viceroy. 'We have pointed out', the letter ran, 'what in our opinion were the defects of the proposals. We also gave our interpretation of some of the provisions of the statement'—which the Mission had firmly repudiated. 'While adhering to our views we accept your proposals and are prepared to work them with a view to achieve our objective.'

This might mean—and could always, if necessary, be claimed to mean—that they accepted the proposals only on *their* interpretation of them. But the Mission in their distress and disappointment were prepared to clutch at any convenient straws. This ambiguous acceptance, if not too closely scanned, gave ground for hope and also got them out of an embarrassing dilemma; for in default of acceptance by Congress of the constitutional plan they would have been plainly bound, in accordance with paragraph 8 of the announcement of June 16th, to form an Interim Government omitting Congress representatives altogether. But now they could find a way of wriggling out of any awkward obligation to go ahead with the League alone. Treating, therefore, the Congress's decision as a real acceptance, they came out with a statement on June 26th expressing their happiness that 'constitution-making can now proceed with the consent of the two major parties'. The failure to form an Interim Government was, they said, regrettable; but, after a short interval, renewed efforts would be made by the Viceroy to bring such a Government into being 'in accordance with paragraph eight of the statement of June 16th'. They themselves would leave India on June 29th.

The few days before their departure were filled with acrimonious controversy. Jinnah, as soon as he knew that Congress had rejected the proposals for an Interim Government, had quickly got the Working Committee of the League to accept them. He then claimed, with some apparent justification, that the Viceroy was bound by paragraph 8 of the statement of June 16th to ignore the Congress and proceed at once to form a government with representatives of the League and of such other parties as were willing to join. The plea that as both major parties had accepted the statement of May 16th, negotiations for an Interim Government had to be taken up *de novo*, had been dishonestly 'concocted by the legalistic talents of the Cabinet Mission'. He roundly charged the Viceroy and the Mission with breach of faith and cuttingly observed 'Statesmen should not eat their words'.

So the Mission ended in disappointment, tinged with resentment; for it was to the accompaniment of Jinnah's taunts and reproaches that the three Cabinet Ministers took their departure. This public controversy belied the hopes expressed that constitution-making would go forward speedily in a spirit of accommodation. The real situation was truly mirrored not in Sir Stafford's cheerful smiles but in the woebegone face of Lord Pethick Lawrence as he stood at the airport waiting to emplane. Three months in the heat of India seemed to have aged him ten years.

Within a fortnight of the Mission's departure all that remained of their precarious card-house had collapsed in irretrievable ruin. Gandhi, by persuading the Working Committee to reject the interim proposals, had already knocked down half of it. Nehru now proceeded to demolish the rest. At a press conference on July 10th he said that Congress, in accepting the Cabinet Mission's long-term plan, 'have agreed to go into the Constituent Assembly and have agreed to nothing else . . . we have committed ourselves to no single matter to anybody'. Thus the basic structure of the constitution, including the strict limitation of federal subjects, and the procedure to be followed by the Constituent Assembly, all of which formed part of the

long-term proposals ostensibly accepted by Congress, had in
reality not been accepted at all. In regard to Grouping, which
the Mission had specifically stated to be an essential feature of
their plan, Nehru expressed the view that 'the big probability
is that . . . there will be no Grouping'. The reasons which he
gave showed complete disregard for the Cabinet Mission's
intentions as to the manner of voting in the Sections.[1] Con-
temptuously brushing the Mission aside he declared that what
they thought or intended did not enter into the matter at all!

Jinnah retorted at once, and with some justice, that Nehru's
interpretation of the acceptance as amounting to nothing more
than an agreement to go into the Constituent Assembly was a
'complete repudiation of the basic form upon which the long-
term scheme rests and all its fundamentals and terms and
obligations'. It was clear, he said, that the Congress's so-called
'acceptance' of the long-term plan had been from the outset
disingenuous—they had never intended to honour it. Since
this was their attitude, since they did not really intend to abide
by the plan or to work it in a spirit of compromise and co-
operation, but rather to use their majority in the Constituent
Assembly to enforce their own views, the Muslim League would
have to reconsider the situation.

This they did at the end of the month. At a meeting held in
Bombay they decided to withdraw their previous acceptance
of the long-term plan and to prepare a programme of 'direct
action' for the achievement of Pakistan to be launched as and
when necessary. 'This day', Jinnah announced, 'we bid good-
bye to constitutional methods.'

Nothing was now left of the Cabinet Mission's fragile edifice
and, try as he might over the next six months, Lord Wavell
was unable to reconstruct it. Congress could not be brought to
declare unequivocally their acceptance of the long-term proposals in the sense that the League understood them and the
Cabinet Mission had intended them; while Jinnah and the
League would be content with nothing less. There was thus no
agreed basis for constitution-making and hence no prospect of
co-operation. There had never in reality been any agreement at
all, but only the illusion of one.

The League's withdrawal of their acceptance of the long-

[1] See footnote on page 51.

term plan, though it meant that they would take no part in the Constituent Assembly, simplified in some ways the formation of an Interim Government. It was decided, though with a good deal of misgiving, to go ahead without them, and accordingly on August 6th the Viceroy wrote to Nehru—who had recently succeeded Azad as Congress President—inviting him to form a government. The invitation was accepted.

Before the new government had taken office or the names of its members had been announced, the first fruits of the Cabinet Mission's failure were being gathered. On August 16th, which the Muslim League celebrated as 'Direct Action Day', there was an appalling outbreak of rioting in Calcutta, lasting several days. According to official estimates about 5,000 persons were killed and 15,000 injured. Compared with what was to follow this holocaust was nothing extraordinary, but it made a deep impression at the time. People had not yet become hardened to mass slaughter.

There was widespread criticism of the Muslim League Government of Bengal and its Chief Minister, Mr. Suhrawardy. Against all advice they had declared 'Direct Action Day' a public holiday and, though warned of the likelihood of trouble, had apparently not taken adequate precautions. After the rioting had started, there was an unaccountable delay in imposing a curfew and calling in troops. The British Governor remained imperturbable but inactive. Charged under the Constitution of 1935 with a special responsibility for preventing any grave menace to the peace and tranquillity of the province, his duty seemed to require that he should intervene promptly to remedy the negligences of the Bengal Government and suppress these terrible disorders. He did not do so. During the next year this apparent example of supineness was to be copied by others in humbler stations.

In these riots the Muslims had been the aggressors; but after the first day or two the non-Muslim population, spear-headed by the Sikh taxi-drivers of Calcutta, retaliated vigorously, giving as good as they got, and in the end perhaps neither party could claim any very decided advantage. The disturbances, however, spread to East Bengal where the Muslims were in a considerable majority. Dacca was at first the centre of disorder, but in October there were serious outbreaks of Muslim hooliganism in the remoter districts of Noakhali and Tipperah. The killings were not on a vast scale, running into hundreds rather than thousands, but there was much destruction and pillage of Hindu property and abduction of Hindu women.

Numbers of Hindus, fleeing in terror from the affected areas, arrived in Bihar. Their tales of woe, luridly written up by the local press, so excited popular feeling that now in Bihar there was a massacre of Muslims by Hindus. Several thousands were killed, in many instances in peculiarly revolting and barbarous circumstances. There was no knowing where this chain reaction would end. 'We are not yet in the midst of civil war,' Gandhi declared, 'but we are nearing it.'

The Viceroy thought that the dangers of the situation would be lessened if the League could be brought into the Interim Government. He also had reason to believe that the League would once again accept the long-term proposals and enter the Constituent Assembly if Congress would unequivocally agree to grouping as contemplated in the statement of May 16th. He strove hard to bring the two parties to terms and his efforts seemed partially successful when in the middle of October Jinnah agreed that five nominees of the League should join the Government. They took office on October 26th.

Congress were not too satisfied with the new arrangements. They wanted to be assured that the League would rescind their Bombay resolution and enter the Constituent Assembly, and that the League representatives in the Interim Government would really co-operate with the other members and try to work as a team. On both points the Viceroy obtained from Jinnah qualified assurances, but the Congress felt that not much reliance could be placed on them.

The country at large, not fully aware of all the inner discords, hailed the League's entry into the Government with relief; and its immediate effects were tranquillizing. But it soon became apparent that Jinnah's assurances were of no value. The League had entered the Government not to co-operate with Congress but simply to prevent Congress from tightening its hold on the whole governmental machine at the League's expense. The Interim Government became in fact a dual government. There was, as Liaqat Ali Khan put it, 'a Congress bloc and a Muslim bloc, each functioning under

separate leadership'. Each began to attract to itself its own supporters from among the civil servants and to build up its own separate and exclusive empire. As a Coalition Government it was a
farce.

There was also no progress in regard to the League's
entry into the Constituent Assembly. It was originally intended
that this body should begin its work early in September but the
Viceroy had postponed summoning it owing to the League's
unwillingness to participate. Postponement could not, however,
go on indefinitely and the Viceroy, under considerable pressure from Congress, fixed December 9th for the first meeting.
Would the Muslim League delegates attend? Jinnah, despite
his assurances to the Viceroy, took no steps to call a meeting
of the Council of the League to reconsider the Bombay resolution and when urged to do so contended that such a course was
futile so long as the Congress themselves declined to accept unequivocally the statement of May 16th. He strongly advised
the Viceroy to postpone the Constituent Assembly *sine die*.
Invitations were, however, issued for December 9th; whereupon
Jinnah directed the Muslim League representatives not to attend.

In a desperate last-minute bid to bring about agreement
before the Constituent Assembly met, the British Prime Minister now invited the leaders of Congress and the League, and
Baldev Singh as representative of the Sikhs, to come to London
for discussions. The field of disagreement had by this time been
narrowed down, as Congress had reluctantly accepted that
provinces could not *ab initio* refuse to take part in the work of
the Sections in which they had been placed. The main point at
issue was whether in the Sections the voting was to be by provinces, as Congress contended, or by simple majority vote of
those present, as the League claimed and as the Cabinet
Mission had intended. No agreement was reached, but the
British Government issued a statement on December 6th upholding the latter interpretation and urging Congress to accept
it 'in order that the way may be open for the Muslim League to
reconsider their attitude'.

Congress responded. At the instance of Nehru and despite
considerable opposition the All-India Congress Committee
passed a resolution agreeing 'to advise action in accordance
with the interpretation of the British Government in regard to

the procedure to be followed in the sections'. There was a caveat to the effect that this must not involve any compulsion of a province and that the rights of the Sikhs in the Punjab would not be jeopardized. Nevertheless it was perhaps as near to a genuine acceptance of the original proposals of May 16th as could be expected.

Alas, second thoughts had come too late! If only Congress leaders had adopted this attitude in July instead of petulantly asserting that they had committed themselves to nothing and that the intentions of the Cabinet Mission and British Government were of no consequence, the Muslim League would have had no occasion to resile from their acceptance of the plan and all the discords, disorders and massacres of the past six months could have been avoided. But now the League had hardened their hearts. Convinced of Congress's fundamental insincerity, they were not prepared to swallow any caveats. Moreover, whatever the All-India Congress Committee might resolve, Gandhi had been talking in quite a different strain. Consulted by some Assam Congressmen on the subject of grouping he had said: 'I do not need a single minute to come to a decision. . . . If there is no clear guidance from the Congress Committee Assam should not go into Sections. It should lodge its protest and retire from the Constituent Assembly. . . . I have the same advice for the Sikhs.' With Gandhi tendering such advice the League could reasonably conclude that, on the strength of his authority, both the Hindus of Assam and the Sikhs of the Punjab would refuse to co-operate in the work of their respective Sections. In these circumstances the League decided that the qualifying clauses of the Congress resolution completely nullified their acceptance of the British Government's statement of December 6th. They therefore flatly declined to reconsider their own Bombay resolution.

A dangerous crisis was now approaching. The League representatives had been taken into the Interim Government on the understanding that the Bombay resolution would be rescinded and that the League delegates would attend the Constituent Assembly. It was now clear that the League would not carry out their part of the bargain. There was, therefore, a demand for the resignation of the League representatives from the Interim Government; and the Congress members soon made it plain that they would themselves resign if the League members were retained.

Either alternative was fraught with alarming possibilities. If the Congress members withdrew, the British, with League support, might have to hold down forcibly the whole of Hindu India. On the other hand the extrusion of the League representatives from the Central Government would be the signal for fresh communal disorders which might lead to a virtual state of civil war; for there was a danger now that the army and services would begin to take sides. The British Government would then be compelled either to restore order by British arms—and this would involve reassertion of British dominance for at least ten to fifteen years—or to scuttle ignominiously from an anarchic situation.

Physically the reassertion of British authority would not have been very difficult; but politically and psychologically it was quite impracticable—neither British opinion nor world opinion would have tolerated it or permitted the necessary measures to be taken. The Labour Government rightly ruled it out. But some fresh move had to be made. Drift and delay could only lead to chaos. So they took a bold decision. On February 20th the Prime Minister, Mr. Attlee, announced in the House of Commons that it was His Majesty's Government's 'definite intention to take the necessary steps to effect the transference of power to responsible Indian hands by a date not later than June 1948'. All parties were urged to sink their differences—it was no doubt hoped that the mere fixing of a date so close at hand would shock them into some kind of agreement—but lack of agreement would not cause any postponement of the date. If it appeared that by the date fixed a fully representative Constituent Assembly would not have worked out a constitution in accordance with the Cabinet Mission's proposals, His Majesty's Government would have to consider 'to whom the powers of the Central Government in British India should be handed over, on the due date, whether as a whole to some form of Central Government for British India, or in some areas to the existing Provincial Governments, or in such other way as may seem most reasonable and in the best interests of the Indian people'.

This announcement meant Partition, and Partition within

the next seventeen months. Whatever London might think, everyone in Delhi knew that the Cabinet Mission's proposals were as dead as mutton. No constitution would be framed on their basis; and owing to the Hindu-Muslim feud there would be no Central Government capable of exercising authority over the whole of British India to whom the powers of the existing Government of India could be transferred. The power which the British held would have to be divided in order to be demitted, as indeed Mr. Attlee's statement itself vaguely foreshadowed. The British Government and Gandhi might perhaps still delude themselves with the hope of a united independent India; but for others it had faded from sight. As Sir Syed Ahmad had foreseen years earlier, two nations— Muslim and Hindu—could not sit on the same throne.

Thus nine months of strenuous British endeavour to preserve unity had led only to the inevitability of Partition. This deplorable outcome is not attributable, as the foregoing account might suggest, simply or even mainly to Gandhi's ill-starred interventions or Nehru's fits of arrogant impatience. At critical moments they may have given an adverse turn to events and thereby occasioned a result which neither of them desired. But the reasons for the failure to agree on some form of united India lay deeper. The truth is that the aims and aspirations of the two communities, as expressed by those whom they acclaimed their leaders, were irreconcilable; and, as it turned out in the end, their professed aims were also their real ones. The Congress leaders wanted a strong united India; the League a divided or divisible one. The Congress aim had never been in doubt and accurately reflected the wishes of the Hindu community. The League's aim, only proclaimed in 1940, may not have reflected any real or rational wish of the Muslim multitude, but at least accorded with their blind impulses. Instinctively they had rallied to Jinnah, deserting other leaders; and Jinnah, whatever his original views, had by now, rightly or wrongly, come to regard 'a sovereign independent Pakistan', actual or at least permanently potential, as an indispensable Muslim need.

This deep difference of aim could not be bridged by a flimsy paper scheme, such as the Cabinet Mission had devised. Both parties, in so far as they accepted it at all, avowedly did so in order to achieve their own objectives—and these were contradictory. This being so, even if constitution-making had begun, it could hardly have got very far; and even if a constitution, such as the Cabinet Mission envisaged, had somehow come into being, it could hardly have worked for very long.

Jinnah at an early stage became convinced that the Congress would never tolerate the weak, easily divisible Union of India such as he desired. And it gradually dawned on the Congress leaders, especially after their experience of the attitude of the League representatives in the Interim Government, that the price which the League would exact for preserving unity would be too high. They would insist on strong States or groups of States with divergent interests and outlook and a weak Federal Centre which would be paralysed by its own internal communal divisions and quite incapable of tackling India's enormous problems of poverty, illiteracy and outmoded social customs. Rather than commit the whole country to this it would be better to lop some of the branches from the main trunk—to let Jinnah and the League take the areas which they could indisputably claim. This was the mood to which most of the Congress leaders had come by the beginning of 1947.

The labours of nine months were not, therefore, wholly in vain. They had at any rate brought home to everyone, except perhaps Gandhi, the necessity of Partition. But Partition was a major operation which, even if agreed to by the party leaders, was bound to entail much shedding of blood.

The Mountbatten Plan

I N the course of his statement of February 20th, Mr. Attlee
had announced that with 'the opening of a new and final
phase in India' there would be a change of Viceroy. Lord
Wavell, the silent, war-scarred, middle-class soldier, would give
place to Lord Mountbatten, charming, brilliant, aristocratic, and
a sailor. It was a change and a contrast and gave rise to some questioning. Lord Wavell had not resigned; he had been sacked. Why?

No clear answer was given. The rugged old veteran's honesty
and straightforwardness had not always endeared him to Congress circles and some members of the Labour Government,
ever more receptive of the Congress than the League point of
view, considered, perhaps unfairly, that he had developed a
League bias. In any case for this final phase qualities were
needed different from and perhaps more glittering than the
sterling virtues of Lord Wavell. In selecting Lord Mountbatten
to wind up British rule the Labour Government could hardly
have made a happier choice.

Lord Mountbatten reached Delhi on March 22nd. He had
received instructions to work for a Unitary Government for
India on the basis of the Cabinet Mission plan. Only if by
October 1947 he found that there was no prospect of reaching
a settlement on these lines was he expected to put forward alternative proposals for the transfer of power. Within a few days
he grasped that these instructions were out of date and that all
talk of a Unitary Government and the Cabinet Mission plan
was now vain. Some alternative plan had to be devised and
acted upon, not in leisurely fashion some six months later, but
forthwith; otherwise anarchy might set in before power and
authority could be transmitted to other hands.

The Central Government was by this time hopelessly divided
against itself with League and Congress Ministers openly working against each other. Communal rioting of unprecedented

severity had broken out early in March in the principal towns of the Punjab and had spread in some places to the rural areas. Soon the fires of frenzy were lapping over into the North-West Frontier Province. In parts of the country it seemed that law and order would break down altogether.

After one false start, which might have proved calamitous, Lord Mountbatten produced a plan for the partition of the country to which all the principal parties were willing to agree. He owed this plan to the knowledge and insight of his Reforms Secretary, Mr. V. P. Menon. His own tact and persuasiveness helped to secure its general acceptance. Its main outlines were communicated in strict secrecy to the party leaders in the middle of May and their concurrence in principle obtained. The British Government's approval was then sought and on June 3rd it was publicly announced and publicly accepted by Nehru, Jinnah and Baldev Singh.

In essence the plan was simple. The country was to be divided into two dominions, known as India and Pakistan; but Pakistan was to be of the truncated 'contiguous area' variety involving the partition of both the Punjab and Bengal, which Jinnah had hitherto always spurned. In order to give to this division of the country the seal of democratic approval diverse and somewhat complicated arrangements were to be made for recording the popular will in the Muslim-majority provinces. The issue to be put to them was whether they should join the existing Constituent Assembly or an altogether new Constituent Assembly which would frame a constitution for a separate dominion of Pakistan.[1]

[1] In Sind this issue was to be voted upon by the provincial legislature. In the North-West Frontier Province (where the pro-Congress 'Red Shirts' were in a majority in the legislature) it was to be decided by a referendum. In Bengal and the Punjab the Legislative Assemblies were first each to meet as a whole and vote on this issue on the assumption that the Province would not be divided. (It was expected that in each case the small Muslim majority would turn the scales in favour of joining a new Constituent Assembly.) Thereafter they were each to meet in two parts, one representing the Muslim-majority districts according to the 1941 census figures and the other the rest of the Province. These two parts would then vote separately on whether the Province should be partitioned. If either part by a simple majority voted for partition, then the Province would be divided. The two parts of the Legislative Assemblies would also decide on behalf of the areas which they represented whether to join India or Pakistan.

On the assumption that the voting in the Muslim-majority provinces would endorse the division of the country, arrangements were to be initiated as quickly as possible for dividing the armed forces and the administrative services and the assets and liabilities of the Central Government between the respective successor authorities and for carrying out a similar division in respect of the provinces of Bengal and the Punjab.

For the actual partition of these two provinces, in the event of Partition being decided upon, a Boundary Commission was to be set up. The Commission would be instructed to demarcate the boundaries of the two parts of Bengal and the Punjab on the basis of ascertaining the contiguous majority areas of Muslims and non-Muslims, and also *to take into account other factors*.

It was also proposed to anticipate the date for the transfer of power and to bring it forward from June 1948 to some date in 1947. At a press conference on June 4th Lord Mountbatten suggested that this might be August 15th.

The plan was acclaimed not only in India but throughout the world; and with all its defects and grim promise of bloodshed—the certainty of which those at the summit did not realize—it was perhaps the best that could be devised. Certainly no-one either then or later was able to suggest anything better. Yet only a year earlier the Cabinet Mission had given cogent arguments[1] against a settlement based on a 'truncated' Pakistan. They had pointed out that it was not in accord with Muslim wishes, that the radical partition of the Punjab and Bengal which it involved would be 'contrary to the wishes and interests of a very large proportion of the inhabitants of these Provinces' and that it would necessarily divide the Sikhs. No-one had controverted these arguments, but now all parties, including the Sikhs, acquiesced in this solution.

Of all the parties principally concerned the Congress perhaps had least difficulty in accepting the plan. Congress leaders realized that the mood of the Muslims was now so hostile that even if the British transferred the authority of the Centre to a purely Congress Government, their writ would simply not run in the extreme west and extreme east of the country where Muslims' predominated. To gain control of those areas force

[1] See page 47.

would have to be supplied from the Centre and this would mean civil war. Thus at the very outset of independence they would be plunged into squalid, fratricidal strife which might see most of them into their graves. They would have to say good-bye to all their cherished ambitions of building up a strong, united, progressive India, free from the shackles of an outworn social system and capable of playing a part in the councils of the world. Rather than this it was better to sever completely from Mother India those stubborn Muslim areas that disowned her. They were willing to pay this price provided Jinnah and the League were not permitted to carry away too much. The plan by providing for the partition of Bengal and the Punjab satisfied them on this score.

For Jinnah the plan was a bitter pill. He had always rejected a truncated Pakistan and only a few weeks earlier had described the proposal for the partition of Bengal and the Punjab as 'a sinister move actuated by spite and bitterness'. But he had to bow to facts and logic. Logically the very principle on which he demanded the division of India justified the partition of these two Muslim-majority provinces. Bound by this logic the British Government, he knew, would never be party to coercing large unwilling minorities into joining Pakistan. And he and the League had not the strength to coerce them; physically he could not possess himself of East Punjab and West Bengal unless the majority of the inhabitants willingly attached themselves to Pakistan. But why should they? The League had done absolutely nothing to make Pakistan appear attractive to them. On the contrary in Calcutta Suhrawardy's League Government had quite failed to prevent an onslaught on the Hindus and subsequently in East Bengal Hindus had been plundered and terrorized. In the Punjab the story had been much the same. The League, after its success in the provincial elections, made no effort to conciliate and reassure the Sikhs and declined even to discuss their future. Throughout 1946 they were cold-shouldered or reviled and later—as will shortly be narrated—they were murderously assaulted and held up to ridicule.

So by their inexplicable acts and omissions Jinnah and the League were debarred from getting by agreement the Pakistan of their conception; and they were not strong enough to seize it by force. Once or twice Jinnah raised the question of an exchange of population. If all the Muslims in India could be concentrated he could legitimately obtain the whole area which he coveted. But he did not press the suggestion and perhaps felt that it was impracticable and might even lead to his own discredit. For how would the populations be induced to move? What except brute force or overwhelming fear would drive non-Muslims to leave their ancestral homes in Bengal and the Punjab to make room for incoming Muslims? And would the lure of Pakistan be sufficient to impel Muslims from all over India to migrate to that doubtful El Dorado? Jinnah may have foreseen that his own people would be liable to repudiate the promised land.

Whatever may have been his reasons, Jinnah never made the planned exchange of population a live issue, and being by now deeply committed to Pakistan in some form he had perforce to accept it in such form as he could get it. As far back as November he had told Lord Wavell that the British should give the Muslims their own bit of country, however small it might be, and they would live there, if necessary on one meal a day! This tallied with the views of his political henchmen and of the ambitious Muslim civil servants who were secretly abetting them. To these men, avid of power, even a small dunghill was better than none at all.

For the Sikhs the plan meant division. They knew it, they accepted it and privily they had their own plans for meeting it. The hard choice before them had long been clear. They had to submit either to inclusion as a whole in Pakistan or to division between India and Pakistan through partition of the Punjab. They had chosen the latter.[1] They had long been thinking in terms of Partition and the recent conduct of the Muslims had strengthened their preference for it. Inevitably by such Partition they would be split and if the 'contiguous area' principle were to be rigidly applied all the canal colonies and about two million Sikhs would fall to Pakistan. But the Boundary Commission was also to take into account 'other factors' and the Sikhs clung to the hope that on the strength of these 'other

---

[1] Some of the Akalis had been canvassing the idea of an entirely separate Sikh State of 'Khalistan'. Since they were not in an absolute majority in even a single district no one could take this idea seriously; but in one guise or another it had some influence on Sikh thinking both in the coming months and in the coming years.

factors' the boundary might be shifted westwards so that they would not be split so badly. They were encouraged in this false hope by the ill-advised utterances of some British politicians.

For the British Government, as for everyone else, the plan was very much of a *pis aller*; but they could not dissent from what Congress, the League and the Sikhs were all ready to accept. They recognized that since agreement on the Cabinet Mission plan had proved unattainable, Partition was the inevitable alternative. Churchill on behalf of the Opposition gave assurances of support.

So with a quite unprecedented unanimity all set forth together on a path leading straight to mass slaughter. In Bengal this end was a dangerous[1] possibility, in the Punjab an absolute certainty. Fortunately for the peace of mind of those who led the way none of them, except Baldev Singh, knew much about the Punjab and so they did not realize what was coming. British officials of the Punjab were not in that happy position. They were aware of an impending calamity which they were powerless to avert.

[1] Disaster was averted in Bengal largely through the influence of Gandhi. The Muslim leaguer, Mr. Suhrawardy, also fell temporarily under his spell and became a peacemaker.

V

The Punjab and Partition

To understand the menacing situation in the Punjab and how it had arisen it is necessary to go back a little. It will be recalled that at the elections at the beginning of 1946 Khizar and the Unionist Party suffered a crushing defeat and the Muslim League emerged as the strongest single party with seventy-nine seats in a house of 175. But not having an absolute majority the League alone could not form a Ministry, and the extreme, uncompromising attitude which they had adopted during the elections precluded them for the time being from obtaining support from elsewhere. In the circumstances it was expected that the Governor would temporarily take over the administration under Section 93 of the Government of India Act until a stable Ministry could be formed. With time, patience and discreet promises of loaves and fishes the League would probably have succeeded in winning over a sufficient number of members to secure a majority. But a cardinal error was now made. Baldev Singh induced Khizar to head a Coalition Ministry supported by Congress Hindus, Akali Sikhs and his own nine Muslim followers. Khizar, by all accounts reluctantly and after much persuasion, agreed and the Governor, Sir Bertrand Glancy, passively accepted the arrangement.

From the public point of view it was a disaster; and for Khizar personally it was political suicide. In every Punjab Ministry since the first beginnings of provincial self-government the Muslims had played the leading part, as their numbers entitled them to do. Now for the first time, on the eve of independence, a predominantly non-Muslim Government was being installed in power. The Muslim League, fresh from their triumph at the elections and fully expecting to form a Ministry themselves, found themselves totally excluded by an undreamed of combination of Congress banias, Khizar and the Sikhs. Not only the League but the whole Muslim community felt outraged

71

and affronted. This unnatural and unholy alliance seemed
to have been designed, with the connivance of the British
Governor, simply to keep them from power. It was an example of just the thing that Jinnah always feared and that had
prompted the demand for Pakistan. In a united India the wily
Hindus would always succeed in this manner in attaching to
themselves a section of the Muslims and using them to defeat
the larger interests of the community. Khizar, despite his
past record and reputation, was now represented as a traitor,
clinging to power and office without regard for Muslim
interests.

Sore and resentful the Muslim League now had a real
grievance with which to inflame Muslim feeling. Communal
relations in the province, already bad, became still further embittered and the mere existence of the Coalition Government
made any sort of reconciliation impossible. If it had not been
formed and the League leaders had been left with some hope
of office, they would have been compelled, just in order to gain
it, to adopt a more conciliatory attitude to the minorities;
and once installed in power and made responsible for the peace
and well-being of the whole province, they would have
been less tempted than they were now deliberately to stir up
strife. As it was, there was no inducement to them to seek
the path of peace and come to terms with parties which,
they felt, had combined to defraud them of their just claim to
office.

It was amazing that the Governor acquiesced without the
slightest struggle in the formation of a Ministry so harmful to
the public interests. But it had become easy and fashionable in
these days to evade responsibility on the plea of constitutionalism. His apologists have certainly taken this plea and pointed
out that since Khizar was willing and able to form a Ministry,
he had no option, as a constitutional Governor, but to let him
do so. True, yet utterly removed from the real truth. For Khizar
was no stranger with whom it might be necessary for him to
stand on ceremony. From the day when he assumed office as
Governor in April 1941 he and Khizar had been in almost
daily contact. Though as a constitutional Governor he was
bound in the last resort to let Khizar form a Ministry if he so
insisted, there was nothing to preclude him from talking to

Khizar as man to man and throwing all the weight of his influence and advice against such a course. In view of Khizar's own hesitations a few words of discouragement from the Governor, who was known to be his well-wisher, must have turned the scale against it. But the words were not spoken. The Governor took the easy, strictly constitutional line of least resistance and left his successor, who took office a few weeks later, and the province at large to reap the consequences.

Ironically enough the Sikander-Baldev Singh pact, designed to bring the Sikh and Muslim communities closer together, was indirectly responsible for this lamentable political arrangement which was bound to drive them apart; for it was Baldev Singh's association with Khizar as a colleague in the Punjab Ministry that enabled this new ill-starred coalition to be formed. An alliance between the Akalis and Khizar was a boon to the Province so long as he stood at the head of a Unionist party which commanded the allegiance of most of the Muslims; but it could only be a curse when he had become a renegade at the head of a rump. Thus in the end the pact proved a snare.

Several of Khizar's friends, too late to prevent him from putting himself in a false position, were anxious that he should withdraw from it as quickly as possible. A senior British official urged him, soon after he had taken office, to resign straight away before he had hopelessly compromised himself in the eyes of his own community. I argued to the same effect with two of his henchmen, who visited Delhi in April, and the discussion went on until the small hours of the morning. I dwelt not only on the embitterment of communal feeling, but also on the irreparable damage to Khizar's own reputation which must result from his continuance in office. The Muslim community, I said, would never forgive him if he appeared to cling to power in defiance of Muslim interests and wishes. His party had been decisively defeated at the elections. However regrettable that might be from the point of view of the real interests both of the Muslims and the Punjab, the best course was to accept the defeat with patience and dignity and lie low for the time being. The ambitious and inexperienced young men who had come to the front as leaders of the League in the Punjab were bound to make a mess of things. After a few years the Muslim masses would turn back to Khizar with relief as a tried elder statesman,

C*

provided he did not now brand himself as a traitor in their eyes and so permanently antagonize them.

My arguments seemed to make some impression on his two supporters but did not convince them. They felt that the reins of power—one of them was a Minister in Khizar's new Government—should not be voluntarily surrendered. 'We have a "danda"[1] in our hand,' they kept repeating, 'and mustn't give it up'; and it was with these words that they finally parted from me.

But the 'danda' was in reality only a broken reed; for the Punjab police force was about 75 per cent Muslim and in the hands of a predominantly non-Muslim Government, confronted with a mass Muslim movement, could not be fully relied upon. Here was another fatal defect in the political arrangement that had been made in the Punjab. In times of stress and communal tension any Punjab Government not enjoying substantial Muslim backing was liable to find itself in a precarious position. Khizar's Government not only had no such backing but, relying largely on the support of Hindu banias, was itself a standing offence to the Muslims of the Punjab. In any show-down with the Muslim League Khizar's Government, so far from being able to wield a 'danda', would be impotent, unless it called in outside military aid and proclaimed martial law.

During the period of acute tension that followed the failure of the Cabinet Mission, Khizar's Government remained uneasily in the saddle. Though there were isolated communal incidents, there was no widespread outbreak of violence in the Punjab such as occurred in Bengal and Bihar. But this outward tranquillity deceived no-one. All the three major communities— Muslims, Hindus and Sikhs—were collecting arms and getting ready for open war. As the prospects of a Congress-League agreement for a united India receded, the certainty of violence in the Punjab increased. Towards the end of December the Executive Officer[2] of the Amritsar municipality was to be found busily repairing the municipal hose-pipes. When questioned on this unwonted activity he replied: 'The city will soon be in flames. I'm making such preparations as I can.' His fore-

---

[1] Stick.
[2] The late P. C. Bhandari.

sight was unerring, but the hose-pipes, even when repaired, were insufficient.

On 24th January 1947 Khizar's Government took a decisive but fatal step. Alarmed at the collection of arms by various private volunteer bodies, operating under the direction of political parties, they declared the Muslim League National Guards and the Rashtriya Swayam Sewak Sangh—an extreme and militant Hindu organization—unlawful bodies under the Criminal Law Amendment Act. Simultaneously the police raided the headquarters of the National Guards in Lahore and began a search of the premises.

The Muslim League leaders were quick to see their chance. About half a dozen of them hurried to the National Guards headquarters while the search was in progress and courted arrest by obstructing the police. They were taken into custody.

The fat was now in the fire. The Punjab Government had inadvertently offered a challenge to the League without the strength to go through with it. News of the arrest of the League leaders spread through the city like wild-fire. There were demonstrations by Muslim mobs and meetings in mosques to condemn the action of the Punjab Government. Most unwisely the Punjab Government had at an earlier date issued general orders prohibiting meetings and processions in all the principal towns of the province. Such general orders usually lead to trouble. Their enforcement often unnecessarily precipitates the very disturbances they are designed to avert, while their non-enforcement brings government into contempt. The Punjab Government had developed the bad habit of promulgating these general bans. The Muslim League took advantage of the mistake. On the day of the arrest of the League leaders Muslim demonstrations in Lahore had been half-heartedly broken up by the police. The next day the League decided systematically to defy the bans. The authorities, not daring to interfere and break up meetings and processions by force, contented themselves with making a few arrests and sought to ease the situation by appeasement. On the 26th the League leaders who had been arrested in Lahore were released and on the 28th the orders declaring the Muslim National Guards and the Rashtriya Swayam Sewak Sangh unlawful were rescinded. But for some inexplicable reason the Punjab Government, instead of completing their climb down by withdrawing the bans on meetings and processions, continued them in force and continued not to enforce them. So for the next few weeks Muslim mobs and gangs of Muslim students amused themselves, much to the exasperation of the other communities, with 'non-violent' defiance of the bans; while the police looked on and tried to mitigate this open flouting of authority by occasional arrests. The hooligan Muslim elements in the big cities perceived all too clearly the weakness of the Government; the forces of law and order, not too staunch in any case, became puzzled and doubtful of what was expected of them.

This dangerous farce went on till February 26th when the Punjab Government climbed down further and came to a compromise with the Muslim League. The ban on processions continued in force, but the ban on meetings was withdrawn and all those arrested in connection with the agitation were released. The League, on their side, agreed to discontinue the agitation. Thus with loss of prestige and grave weakening of the whole fabric of administration, Khizar's Government extricated itself from its contest with the League. The half-hearted attempt to promote communal peace by strong measures had primed the province for an explosion.

Perhaps Khizar guessed what was in store. In any case by this time he had had enough. The impotence of his Government had been starkly revealed, and on February 20th Mr. Attlee's announcement of the forthcoming withdrawal of British power had introduced a new factor. Now at last and too late Khizar realized that the onus of managing the affairs of the Punjab should be thrown on the party representing the majority community—the Muslim League. On March 3rd he submitted the resignation of his Cabinet.

The reasons which he gave to the public for resigning are instructive. He said that the decision announced by Mr. Attlee required that parties in the province 'should be brought face to face with realities'. He went on:

'It is now incumbent on me to leave the field clear for the Muslim League to come to such arrangements vis-à-vis the other parties as it might consider in the best interests of the Muslims and the Province. If I were now to continue to lead a Coalition in which the Muslim League is not represented, this might put in serious jeopardy such chances as might otherwise exist of a settlement being arrived at between the communities in the Province.'

But already all chances of a settlement had been not merely jeopardized but destroyed. If only he had grasped a year earlier the truth of what he now said the realities would not have been quite so grim and the League would have had more time to face them. He himself might even have been able to exercise a moderating and conciliatory influence, if he had not cut himself adrift from the main body of Muslims by his leadership of a non-Muslim coalition. As it was, he was nothing now to his own community. His very life was in danger from its members and he had to be heavily guarded.

With Khizar's resignation the pent-up excitement of the past weeks broke loose. Though there was little or no chance now of the League being able to form a Ministry, the Governor had to go through the motions of asking them to do so before himself assuming control of the administration. The mere rumour of a League Ministry was sufficient to evoke demonstrations by the minority communities. The ban on processions was still in force, but in spite of this on March 4th Bhim Sen Sachar, the Finance Minister in the outgoing Khizar Government, feeling perhaps that non-Muslims should have as much liberty to defy law as the Muslims had enjoyed in the past weeks, led a procession to the Assembly Chamber in Lahore where he proclaimed to a vast assembled multitude: 'I, as a member of the Government, hereby declare that you have every right to take out processions.' The Sikh leader, Master Tara Singh, raised the slogan 'Pakistan Murdabad'[1] and brandishing a sword shouted, 'Raj karega Khalsa, aqi rahe na koi'.[2]

This foolhardy bravado brought at once its own nemesis. It touched off violent communal rioting throughout the province in which Hindus and Sikhs were far the worst sufferers. The first outbreak took place in Lahore on March 4th immediately after Master Tara Singh's ill-timed vauntings. It was

---

[1] Down with (death to) Pakistan.

[2] The pure (Sikhs) will rule; no resister will remain. (A well-known saying of Guru Gobind Singh, the tenth and last Sikh Guru.)

followed in the next couple of days by rioting in Multan, Rawalpindi and Amritsar and minor disturbances in other towns. The Muslim mobs, after their weeks of 'non-violent' agitation, suddenly, as though on a preconcerted signal, came out in their true colours and with weapons in their hands and, in some places, steel helmets on their heads, indulged in murder, loot and arson on a scale never witnessed before in the Punjab during a hundred years of British rule. The minority communities fought back vigorously wherever they could.

The conflagration in Amritsar was particularly terrific. The two principal bazaars were burnt to the ground and several others partially destroyed. There was looting in practically every part of the city. So far as I have been able to ascertain, not a shot was fired by the police while this destruction was in progress. In Multan many private houses of Hindus were set on fire and the inmates had the choice of perishing in the flames or running the gauntlet of a murderous mob awaiting them below. Caught in this predicament a prominent Congress Muslim, who was staying with a Hindu friend, narrowly escaped with his life by exposing his person as evidence of his religion. His host was duly done to death.

In the north-west of the province (in the Rawalpindi and Attock districts) and in the Multan district in the south-west the trouble spread to the rural areas. Here the Muslims were in an overwhelming majority and the minority communities practically helpless. The Multan authorities acted vigorously and by arranging prompt dispatch of military forces to the affected areas brought the situation under control before more than about a hundred casualties had occurred. But in the Rawalpindi and Attock districts many villages and small towns were raided by armed gangs of Muslims with heavy loss of life and property, and it was more than a week before large-scale use of troops began to effect an improvement. The Sikhs[1] were especial targets of attack, their houses and their beards alike being set on fire. Many were killed, many fled, and refugees began to flock into Rawalpindi for temporary shelter.

[1] In this area the Sikhs were for the most part Hindus of the money-lending and shopkeeping classes, who had embraced Sikhism and grown beards, rather than peasant cultivators like the majority of the Sikhs in Central Punjab.

This foretaste of the blessings of Pakistan was hardly encouraging to the minority communities in West Punjab. Some
of them, especially the Sikhs in the north-west districts, began
to think that they were not wanted and had better seek homes
elsewhere. But the exodus of Hindus and Sikhs at this time from
West to East Punjab was surprisingly small. They were reluctant to read the signs of an impending revolution.

Many people have supposed that this outburst of communal
rioting in the Punjab followed as a sort of chain reaction from
the disturbances in Bihar in the previous autumn which themselves had been provoked by the earlier trouble in East Bengal.
This is a mistaken impression. The Punjab had long been brewing its own explosive mixture which had now blown up spon-
taneously. It required no outside fuse for its detonation.

The explosion had long been apprehended, but its severity[1]
and the failure in several places to deal with it promptly and
effectively came as a shock. Congress, and Hindus generally,
were loud in their criticism. It was pointed out, as though of
sinister significance, that British officers were in charge in the
very places where the riots were worst—the implication being
that they had themselves stirred up the trouble or were indifferent to its suppression. The first charge is absurd, and since
it was the Punjab practice to post British officers at the likely
communal storm-centres, it was only natural that when the
riots broke they should be in the thick of them. The charge of
indifference may have more substance. Of several British
officers the story was told that when appealed to by panic-
stricken Hindus for help and protection they referred the peti-
tioners to Gandhi, Nehru or Patel. Nor can it be denied that in a
number of places the handling of the trouble was irresolute—
in one or two deplorably so. There were several factors accounting for this. The one of most general application was the reluctance of the Muslim police to take really strong measures
against Muslim mobs. Under vigorous leadership, as in Multan,

[1] The casualties, as officially announced by the Punjab Government on
March 20th, had been 2,049 killed and 1,103 seriously injured. No less than
1,538 of the killed were said to be in rural areas. These figures were certainly
underestimates. A later estimate put the casualties from March up till the
beginning of August at 5,000 killed and 3,000 seriously injured. Most of these
casualties must have taken place in March when the disorders were at their
worst.

they might do their duty well, but for the most part they were half-hearted and occasionally even recalcitrant. This was not surprising. Communal feeling had risen so high in the province that the police were necessarily affected by it. Throughout February they had seen that the Government were themselves hesitant to order firm action against defiant Muslims. How could they now be expected to lay about them vigorously with lathis or shoot straight with rifles to break up riotous parties of their own co-religionists? Above all, if they did so, who would appreciate or reward their services? Certainly not the British, who were about to leave the country, still less the Muslim leaguers who would soon be masters of at least half the province.

Another factor was the depletion of the services by war-time demands and the grant of leave after the war. As a result the Punjab had been left with insufficient British officials of first-class quality to man all the key districts. At the critical moment men were holding posts for which they were not well-fitted either by temperament or experience. Many of them too were tired after long years of service without a break and dispirited at the prospect of their careers in India coming abruptly to an end. The suppression of a communal riot calls for a good deal of determination and energy from those at the head of the forces of law and order. Tired and dispirited men were not able to rise to the occasion.

One of the worst failures of the civil authorities was in Amritsar—that place of ill-omen for the British name. A generation earlier, when there had been a wave of lawlessness in the Punjab directed against the British, Brigadier-General Dyer had poured 1,650 rounds into a mob in Amritsar, killing 600–700 and wounding over 1,000; he had ceased firing only when his ammunition was exhausted. The episode had become the classic example of barbarous and excessive use of force. Now exactly the opposite mistake was made. For over twenty-four hours riotous mobs were allowed to rage through this great commercial city unchallenged and unchecked. The finest bazaars were burnt to the ground without a shot being fired to disperse the incendiaries. The young and comparatively inexperienced District Magistrate had available, besides the police, 144 men of the Inniskilling Fusiliers; but, like the Grand Old Duke of York,

'Who had ten thousand men
He marched them up to the top of a hill
And marched them down again',

he marched this force into the city and marched it out again without making any effective use of it at all. Apparently he thought that it was too weak and would be overpowered. He could perhaps hardly be expected to know that Dyer performed his exploit and cowed the city into abject submission with a force of ninety men.[1] Indians living in Amritsar, who had witnessed both events, noted the contrast and drew adverse conclusions. In defence of themselves and their own Raj the British had used unlimited force, but in defence of one Indian community against another they had appeared content to stand aside and do nothing. The Amritsar district was to be the scene of fearful bloodshed later in the year. The complete breakdown of authority in the city at this time prepared the way for it.

By the third week in March the disorders were beginning to subside, but they continued sporadically, especially in Amritsar and Lahore, for the remaining few months of British rule. Punjab society, interwoven of three distinct communities, had been rent from end to end and the whole system of ordered government shaken to its foundations. Doubtless it was this alarming situation in the Punjab that convinced Lord Mountbatten of the need for speed. In Bengal Gandhi's presence had to some extent allayed the passions that had been aroused; but he could perform no such miracle in the Punjab. With Muslims he had no influence and even with Sikhs not much, and his voice would not have been heeded. He rightly directed his attention to Bengal.

This then was the position in the Punjab when the plan for its partition was formulated. At the best of times, involving as it did the division of the Sikhs, it would have been fraught with danger. But when passions had been so furiously aroused, how could it be carried through peacefully? Even if Muslim attacks on minorities in West Punjab were not repeated, they were certain to be revenged. The Sikhs in particular were blazing with anger, and in their case insult had been added to injury.

[1] Fifty armed with rifles and forty with kukris.

It was customary in the Punjab to laugh at the Sikhs, more or less good-humouredly, for their supposed incapacity for much cerebration; but now their valour was also impugned and their complete discomfiture in the recent disturbances—they had been beaten up by the Muslims not only in north-west Punjab but also in the city of Amritsar—was widely commented upon in a satirical vein. Forgetting that in the actual city of Amritsar the Muslims were the largest single community and the Sikhs only a small minority, overlooking too the fact that in no place had the Muslim gangs come up against the hard core of the Sikh community—the peasant cultivators of central Punjab —officials who should have known better began to talk knowingly of the degeneracy of the Sikhs. They had grown rich and fat, it was said, in the Punjab colonies and had lost their former martial vigour. They could not now stand up to the hardier Muslims who had not been debauched by excessive prosperity. With the partition of the province they would be divided and that would probably be the end of them as a distinct community—and a good thing too. These were the sort of sentiments that were being freely expressed.

The Muslim League leaders did little even now to reassure the Sikhs or assuage their wounded feelings. Jinnah kept harping on the fact that by the partition of the Punjab they would be the worst sufferers. The Sikhs were themselves only too conscious of this, but partition seemed to them preferable to blind submission to Muslim rule, and Jinnah had not made the slightest effort to persuade them to the contrary. He had not even expressed regret for recent events in West Punjab, though they were hardly calculated to enhance the attractions of Pakistan for the minority communities. One of the Punjab League leaders, Shaukat Hyat-Khan (Sikander's son), seems to have felt the need for a more positive approach and in April made a statement assuring the Sikhs that under a Muslim League Coalition Government their legitimate rights would be fully considered and 'justice meted out to all freely and equally'. But generalities of this kind were quite insufficient to heal the gaping wounds or inspire confidence in Muslim intentions. How could they carry conviction when in north-west Punjab Sikhs had been murdered and pillaged and their beards set on fire by Muslim gangs with little interference from the Muslim police and little or no expression of regret by Muslim leaguers?

No-one who knew the Sikhs could believe for one moment that they would take lying down all the insults and injuries that they had received. They were bound to strike back when and where they felt themselves to be in the ascendancy and that too with a violence and ferocity which would far eclipse the Muslim outrages. What had been seen in the Punjab in March was only a curtain-raiser. The main tragedy was still to come.

After the March outbreaks I was deeply conscious of impending calamity. There seemed to me to be only one faint possibility of averting it and that was if an agreement could be reached between the League and the Akali leaders whereby the Sikhs would voluntarily take their place in Pakistan on defined terms acceptable and favourable to themselves. Although it was really *ab initio* futile, I now made an attempt to bring this about. I was at this time in Bahawalpur State, having moved there from Delhi early in April. An old Punjab friend, Mushtaq Ahmad Gurmani, had been selected by the Nawab of Bahawalpur to be his Prime Minister and at Gurmani's request I accompanied him there as Revenue and Public Works Minister. When we took over in Bahawalpur Lord Mountbatten's plan for the division of India had not yet been announced, but it was already obvious that some form of Pakistan would have to emerge and that in the process there was every prospect of a holocaust in the Punjab. We discussed the whole position many times. Gurmani had spent most of his life in Punjab politics and knew the conditions of the province intimately. Originally a Unionist, his sympathies had in recent years inclined towards the League, with some of whose leaders he was in close contact; but he was essentially a man of moderate balanced views and had no illusions about the fearful dangers now threatening the Punjab as the result of League policies. He bitterly complained that these dangers had never been properly brought home to Jinnah by the young politicians who instructed him on Punjab affairs. I expressed the view that, as things now stood, terrific bloodshed in the Punjab could only be averted if somehow the Sikhs were made to feel that they would be safe and secure in Pakistan and that there would be an honourable place for them there. After all that had passed it might be very difficult to convince them of this, but division between two separate national States would be so ruinous to them that they could hardly afford to reject out of hand any reasonable Muslim approaches. The question was whether the Muslims really wanted to have the Sikhs in Pakistan and were prepared to pay the necessary price. The Sikhs were, no doubt, a turbulent troublesome set of people, always making a nuisance of themselves; but with all their faults they were one of the finest stocks in India. Pakistan would be enormously strengthened if it embraced the whole of the Punjab and enjoyed the support of the whole Sikh community; and all the unknown hazards of dividing the Punjab between India and Pakistan would be avoided. It was worth making considerable concessions to the Sikhs to gain these advantages.

After several discussions with Gurmani on these lines I suggested to him that I should try to discover from the Akalis what guarantees and concessions they wanted for the Sikhs—I had a pretty good idea of what they would be—and that he should sound Jinnah and the League. He agreed to do so.

I wrote accordingly early in June, immediately after the Mountbatten Plan had been announced, to an Akali friend; and a few days later, at the suggestion of Major Short who was in England at the time, I followed it up with a letter to a mutual friend of ours—a Sikh who was not himself a politician or an Akali but who was in close touch with Baldev Singh. I put it to them that the Sikhs should now definitely decide to throw in their lot with their Muslim brethren in the Punjab and take their place in the new Dominion of Pakistan. Though this might be quite contrary to recent Sikh policy it was in accord with the real interests of the Sikh community which lay with northwest India rather than with Hindustan, and would also avert the terrible strife and bloodshed threatening in the Punjab. This was the time, I wrote, to reach a 'samjhota'[1] with the Muslims, for they knew the disadvantages of a 'truncated' Pakistan. There was no reason why the Sikhs should not secure from them:

(1) a separate unit of Eastern Punjab with a position in Pakistan equal to that of any other unit, e.g. Sind or Western Punjab;

[1] Agreement.

(2) special privileges for the Sikh minority in Western Punjab;

(3) special privileges for the Sikhs in Pakistan as a whole.

If the Sikhs took the course I suggested they would become the most important minority in Pakistan and it would be in the Muslims' own interests to make them happy, secure and contented.

The initial replies which I received were not encouraging. Both of my friends said that while they personally agreed with what I had written matters had gone too far and there was too much distrust of the Muslims for an agreement to be reached. They very rightly pointed out that the Muslim League had never themselves made any constructive approach and that there was no real indication that they would be willing to do so now. One of them also observed that there could be no guarantee that the Muslims, once they had got Pakistan, would abide by any agreement they might have made earlier.

I did not immediately give up hope and about ten days later, after some further interchange of correspondence, Major Short's friend wrote that Baldev Singh, who at first had been reported unresponsive, was now more favourably disposed to my suggestions.

Though I had no inkling of it at the time, I subsequently surmised that this change of attitude was occasioned by the failure of the Sikhs to get all they wanted from the Congress. They were really hankering after a quasi-autonomous East Punjab, shorn of the four Hindu districts in the south-east so that it would have more of a Sikh complexion. Congress were not at all agreeable to this; hence an inclination to try to get it from the Muslims. Short's friend gave me his own suggestions as to the possible basis of negotiations. He said that he was communicating them to Baldev Singh and thought that they would be acceptable to him. They were briefly as follows:

(1) There should be a separate unit of East Punjab from which the four south-eastern and predominantly Hindu districts would be excluded. (The four districts would have gone to India.)

(2) The East Punjab unit should have the right to secede from Pakistan.

(3) The authority of the Central Pakistan Government should be confined to defence, foreign affairs, communications, currency and economic planning and all other powers should vest in the provincial units.

(4) A three-fourths majority of Sikh legislators should be essential for any change in the constitution.

(5) The Sikhs should have at least a one-third share in the armed forces of Pakistan.

These were stiff terms, but except for the provision for secession Gurmani and I did not think them impossible as a basis for negotiation. At this stage—it was now nearing the end of June—I felt that it was worth writing to Lord Ismay, the Viceroy's Chief of Staff, and consulting him on the possibilities of a settlement on these lines. He replied that Baldev Singh had recently seen the Viceroy and told him that there was no sign of either of the major parties making any concession to the Sikhs. While he agreed that 'from the point of view of avoiding a row[1] in the Central Punjab' the best course was to promote a settlement between the Muslim League and the Sikhs, he very much doubted whether such a settlement would come about.

He was absolutely right, and in the next few days this amateurish attempt to produce a settlement collapsed ignominiously. It had been arranged that I should meet a prominent Akali leader in Lahore to discuss the suggestions which had been put forward as a basis for negotiations. I duly went to Lahore; but the Akali leader failed to turn up at the appointed rendezvous! It was obvious that he was not interested and had other policies in mind. Since he was, in my view, more influential in the determination of Sikh policy than even Baldev Singh, I considered his attitude decisive. But the Sikh friend who was in touch with Baldev Singh continued to entertain hopes and on July 9th wrote to me that Baldev Singh had sent a cable to Short asking him 'to come out and help smooth matters'.

I was glad that Short was coming to India, but I knew that it was too late 'to smooth matters' and that the whole position was utterly hopeless. If the Sikhs were lukewarm about a settlement, the Muslims were icy cold. A few days after my

[1] This rather mild expression perhaps indicated an unawareness of the magnitude of the disorders that were impending, *vide* page 94.

rebuff in Lahore I met Gurmani who had been away from Bahawalpur for some time. He told me that there was nothing doing for the Sikhs so far as Jinnah was concerned. He was resigned to a 'truncated' Pakistan and had said in effect to Gurmani that the Sikhs could go to the devil in their own way. It was they who had demanded the partition of the Punjab. They could now take the consequences.

This was quite consistent with his past attitude. At no stage had he attempted to placate the Sikhs and secure their acquiescence in Pakistan. He had given them veiled threats, but no promises. He had warned them that division of the Punjab would be injurious to them, but he had not encouraged them to believe that Pakistan would be pleasant. There were some British officials who considered that in this he was very wise. In their view the Sikhs, wherever they were, whether in India or Pakistan, would be a 'bloody nuisance'. Jinnah was well advised 'to steer clear of the bastards so far as he could'. With a 'truncated' Pakistan he was likely to get about two million of them. This was at any rate better than having the whole hornets' nest.

It is debatable whether this view was really in accord with the long-term interests of Pakistan; but since it tended to prevail in League circles a settlement with the Sikhs such as I had envisaged was out of the question. The whole idea was in a sense utopian. Possibly if such a settlement had been consistently worked for during the preceding year, it might have been achieved; but it could not be achieved at the last minute, especially after the March disturbances. Yet though at this late stage a settlement was impossible, I was convinced that nothing else could avert the horrors that were threatening the Punjab. Early in July, therefore, when my attempt had palpably failed, I resigned myself fatalistically to the coming disaster. At the beginning of the month the Punjab legislators had duly met, duly followed all the procedure laid down in the Mountbatten plan, and duly cast their votes so as to doom the Punjab to division, thousands of its inhabitants to death and millions of them to misery and ruin. The voice of the people had become a judgement of God.

It was easy to predict disaster but what was the exact form that it would take? The earliest forecast known to me, which roughly corresponded with the event, was made by the Senior

Superintendent of Police, Delhi, at the end of March. Asked for his opinion as to what would happen if, as already seemed probable, the Punjab was partitioned, he replied crudely but tersely:

'Once a line of division is drawn in the Punjab all Sikhs to the west of it and all Muslims to the east of it will have their – – – chopped off.'

This, though couched in general and figurative terms, conveyed a correct idea of what to expect. A more precise warning came to me in the second half of June from a humbler but more reliable source. This formed part of an episode which requires to be recorded at some length.

At the end of June a meeting was arranged in Lahore to consider what stand should be taken before the Boundary Commission on behalf of Pakistan and the West Punjab. Sir Mohammad Zafrullah Khan, who had held many high positions under the British but was at this time more or less a freelance, had been engaged as counsel by Pakistan and West Punjab interests. Bahawalpur State had also retained his services. We had put forward and established a claim to be heard by the Commission since we were vitally interested in the future control of the canal headworks at Ferozepur and Suleimanke both of which, according to the population figures, were likely to fall very near the dividing line.

Zafrullah came up by train from Karachi to Lahore, Gurmani and I joining him at Bahawalpur. It was a delicious sensation to step from the blazing afternoon heat of the Bahawalpur platform into the quiet cool of Zafrullah's air-conditioned compartment. We were living in exciting times and so naturally there was a good deal of lively conversation and speculation about the future. One remark of Zafrullah's particularly stuck in my mind. We were talking about the division of the Punjab and I had said that the instruction to the Boundary Commission to take into account 'other factors' was perhaps designed to soothe the Sikhs and lead them to think that in fixing the boundary weight would be given to their large interests in the colony lands of West Punjab. But if any real concession was to be made to them on this account, the boundary would have to be drawn west of Lahore instead of between Lahore and Amritsar. We must, therefore, I argued, seriously contemplate the possi-

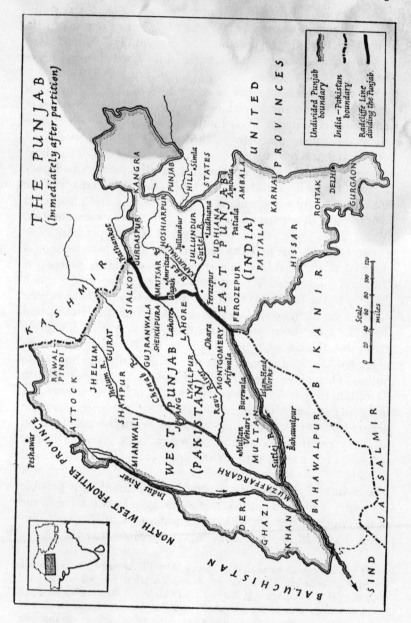

THE PUNJAB
(Immediately after partition)

Undivided Punjab boundary
India–Pakistan boundary
Radcliffe Line dividing the Punjab.

bility that Lahore would fall to India instead of to Pakistan.[1] Zafrullah was considerably roused by this line of reasoning. He warmly refuted the Sikh claims and said finally: 'Moon, if the British give Lahore to India the Muslims will never forgive them.'

We reached Lahore the next morning and after breakfast were collected by the Nawab of Mamdot and other members of the shadow Cabinet of West Punjab and taken to a large house where the meeting was to be held. We entered a good-sized room and found twenty to twenty-five persons already assembled there—nearly all of them prominent Muslim lawyers and politicians. On the floor and on a big table a number of maps of the Punjab were strewn about, variously coloured and chequered so as to show the distribution of the population by communities. We all fell to poring over these maps. It became plain in a few minutes that no-one had any very definite idea where we should claim that the dividing line should run—indeed, except for Gurmani and myself, no-one seemed to have given much thought to the matter or even to know the basic facts about the distribution of the population. The Sikhs and the Hindus had for some time been putting forward publicly the untenable claim that the river Chenab should be the boundary. Someone suggested that as a counterblast we should claim the line of the Sutlej. This claim was equally if not more untenable and Zafrullah in particular was averse to putting it forward. I think he felt that it would be unwise for us to suggest any wide departure from the line which would be given by consideration of the population figures, for if weight was given to 'other factors' they would tend to tell in favour of the Sikhs and Hindus.

The line of the river Beas was then discussed as a possible boundary. I pointed out that this would give Pakistan the whole of the Amritsar district, which was quite unjustified on a population basis. Moreover it was hardly credible that the city of

[1] It is of interest to recall that almost right up till August 15th there was a widespread belief in Hindu circles, based on what seemed to be good authority, that Lahore would fall to East Punjab and India. This mistaken belief was the cause of considerable pecuniary loss to Hindu families of Lahore, who wrongly supposed that all their movable property in that city would be quite safe.

Amritsar, the main centre of Sikh pilgrimage, would be handed over to Pakistan. I suggested that our best course was to press for a boundary based on Muslim- and non-Muslim-majority areas with such minor adjustments as might be to our advantage and which we could reasonably claim. I mentioned particularly the importance of getting control of the Ferozepur headworks and the headworks at Madhopur near Pathankot.[1] It was not quite clear whether on a population basis they would come to us or not.

I believe a decision was ultimately taken more or less on these lines, but at this point a dispute arose whether the distribution of the population had been correctly shown in the maps. A desultory discussion ensued and my interest and attention wandered. Glancing round the room, I was astonished to notice standing in a group of people near the window a young Muslim naib-tahsildar[2] who had served under me in Amritsar four years earlier. He was looking towards me, smiling rather shyly as though uncertain whether I would recognize and remember him. I may have shown some momentary hesitation as I could hardly believe that this very junior official would be present in this somewhat august gathering. He was a bright intelligent young man and had been rather a favourite of mine. I went up and greeted him with enthusiasm and the following dialogue ensued:

'What on earth are you doing here, Mohammad Ali?'

'Sir, a friend told me there might be quite an interesting meeting here, so I thought I'd come and see what was going on.'

'But how did you get in?'

'My friend brought me along and we just walked in. Nobody stopped us.'

I was rather staggered to find that what purported to be a high-level conference was being treated as an open public meeting. I had certainly never expected that a naib-tahsildar would be watching or assisting our deliberations. However I concluded that this casualness was just one of the signs of the changing times and turned to other topics.

---

[1] Both these headworks were assigned by the Radcliffe award to India. There was a strong rumour that the award in respect of the areas adjoining these headworks was altered at the last moment. A later age will perhaps learn what foundation, if any, there was for this report.

[2] A subordinate revenue official.

'Where are you posted nowadays?' I asked.

'In Amritsar, sir. I'm here in Lahore on a few days' casual leave.'

'Still in Amritsar! You've been there a very long time. Well, how's Amritsar?'

'Sir, it is awful. I can't tell you how awful it is.' He was almost quivering with suppressed excitement.

'Why, what's the matter? I thought that things had quietened down there now.'

'No doubt everything is quiet at the moment. But I tell you, sir, *the Sikhs are getting ready to kill us and drive us away.*'

'What do you mean?'

'Sir, the Sikhs are determined to kill or drive out all the Muslims from Amritsar district. They won't spare any of us.'

'When are they going to do this?'

'When they think the coast is clear. They're just awaiting their opportunity. I think myself, sir, that as soon as the line is drawn and the British leave, they'll attack us.'

I was not at all surprised at this information. I said: 'I can well believe that what you say is all quite true—indeed I suspected that the Sikhs were planning something of this kind. But I don't think there is anything that can be done about it.'

He agreed that nothing could be done. I told him that I was trying to arrange a 'samjhota' between the Akalis and the League leaders but that the chances of success were very slender, so in all probability the Sikhs of Amritsar would carry out their murderous plan. 'I hope you'll take care to get away in good time,' I said, 'and won't allow yourself to be killed!' He replied, 'Sir, it all depends on God.'

I have never seen or heard of him again, but the warning which he gave and the tense excitement with which he uttered it have remained imprinted on my memory. There was no-one better placed than he to judge the temper and intentions of the Sikhs of the Amritsar district. He had been there for five years, constantly touring round from village to village in the course of his ordinary duties. He knew the people through and through. I accepted what he said as correct.

With this definite warning about Amritsar it should have been possible to deduce fairly accurately what would happen in the Punjab a few weeks hence. I cannot claim that I did so.

I foresaw, of course, a terrific upheaval in the central districts which would have repercussions in the farthest corner of the province; but I quite failed to grasp the speed with which disturbances and displacements of population in the centre of the province would resolve themselves into a vast movement of mass migration, affecting not only the whole Punjab but adjoining areas as well. I envisaged a slower, more prolonged, more confused and chaotic agony.

Punjabis in general were strangely unprepared for what was coming. During May and June, I, like several other British officials, wrote to Hindu friends in West Punjab, pointing out that in Pakistan they could hardly expect the same secure enjoyment of life and property as they had been used to in the past and hinting that they should consider some rearrangement of their affairs. One of them took the hint and expressed gratitude to me afterwards. The rest clung obstinately to their ancestral homes and in the end escaped with little more than their lives. In this they were encouraged by official policy and by statements made by the leaders of Congress and the League and even by Master Tara Singh. Everywhere it was being preached that people should stay where they were and should not leave their homes.

The possibility of mass migrations did, however, cross some people's minds. At a conference on June 4th Lord Mountbatten was specifically asked whether he foresaw any mass transfer of population as a result of Partition. His reply was tantamount to a negative. A measure of transfer would come about, he said, 'in a natural way, that is to say people would just cross the boundary or the Government may take steps to transfer population'. Such minor marginal shifts near the boundary or planned transfer by government were very different from the uncontrollable mass migrations which were shortly destined to take place.

In furtherance of the advice to people not to leave their homes, assurances of protection to minority communities were freely given. Apart from the promises made by individual leaders a joint statement was issued on July 22nd by the spokesmen of the prospective Governments of India and Pakistan solemnly guaranteeing protection to all citizens. This guarantee, it was stated, 'implies that in no circumstances will violence be

tolerated in any form in either territory. The two Governments wish to emphasize that they are united in this determination.' These assurances were accepted at their face value with an amazing and pathetic credulity. In spite of all that had happened in March and the disturbed conditions which had prevailed thereafter in the cities of Lahore and Amritsar, most Punjabis allowed themselves to be lulled into a false sense of security. Disregarding their own inner forebodings they acted on the advice of the political leaders and the Government and remained where they were.

If Punjabis themselves were unduly sanguine about the future, it is not surprising that in official and political circles in Delhi there was no conception of the violence of the outbreak that was imminent. Their unawareness of what to expect has been candidly confessed by Mr. V. P. Menon.

'We had anticipated', he had written,[1] 'that there might be trouble in the border districts directly affected by the Partition, but we felt that the Boundary Force of mixed composition under Major-General Rees, an enormous and carefully picked body, would be able to cope with the situation. As for the rest, we had no reason to believe that the Governments concerned would not themselves be able to control any sporadic outbursts that might occur in their respective Dominions. We had the guarantee of the political leaders as set out in their joint statement of 22 July, as also the specific assurances in regard to the protection of minorities given by Jinnah in his address to the Constituent Assembly and in his broadcast to the people of Pakistan. It is true that the situation was full of fear and foreboding; but we had not expected to be so quickly and so thoroughly disillusioned.'

This passage reflects very faithfully the sentiments prevalent in Delhi at that time. Gurmani and I were both there for about a week during the last ten days of July—mainly in connection with the question of Bahawalpur's accession to Pakistan—and I had several talks with Menon himself and with other members of the Viceroy's staff. Cassandra-like I cried 'woe', but not too often or too loudly, since I could suggest no remedy and was convinced that nothing could now prevent catastrophe. It was no use therefore harping on it. I did however express my cer-

[1] *The Transfer of Power in India*, p. 417.

tainty that the Sikhs would turn upon the Muslims in East Punjab and take a fearful revenge for the March happenings. But in Delhi as elsewhere the idea had spread that the Sikhs were shadows of their former selves and that their comparative quiescence during the past few months in spite of so much provocation was evidence of their want of spirit. I could make little headway against these deep-seated delusions.

There was, I found, a remarkable faith in the projected Boundary Force. I could not share it. The Sikhs, I thought, were bound to attack the Muslims when they saw the chance. If the Boundary Force was really powerful and effective they would wait till it was withdrawn. If it was ineffective they would disregard it. On my way back from Delhi to Bahawalpur I happened to hear some views about this force from a young Sikh major who shared my compartment for part of the journey. He was himself about to join it, but was utterly sceptical of its capacity to maintain order. He thought that a large proportion of the troops would be infected by the communal virus and prove unreliable. He was also doubtful whether mechanized infantry would be able to operate effectively in the rural areas during the monsoon. I fully agreed with him in this. Cavalry alone could, in my view, check or suppress the widespread disorders in the villages which were likely to occur, and there were hardly any cavalry regiments in India which still had their horses. I was also impressed by the total inadequacy of the force in point of numbers. He told me that it would consist of two to three divisions. I reckoned that, with the rural areas ready to burst into flame and the prestige of government reduced to the lowest level by the failure to control the March disorders, Amritsar district alone would require one division and Lahore district, which is considerably larger, about two. Thus the whole Boundary Force would barely suffice for these two districts. Altogether there were twenty-nine districts in the Punjab, of which about eight in the centre were likely to be seriously affected and all the rest disturbed in a greater or lesser degree. A force of two to three divisions—or even of 50,000 men, which appears to have been its actual strength—could not possibly control the situation even if it were 100 per cent reliable. By the time I got back to Bahawalpur I had written off the Boundary Force completely.

During my stay in Delhi Major Short arrived from England in response to Baldev Singh's request to him to come out. He realized at once that the time had passed for thinking of a Sikh-Muslim rapprochement. All he could do for the Sikhs was to plead for drawing the dividing line in the Punjab sufficiently far to the west to bring some of the colony lands within India. With all my sympathy for the Sikhs I did not think that on merits this could be done. To include within India any of the Punjab colonies would mean shifting the line so far west that the city of Lahore and large tracts of country in which Muslims were in the majority would fall on the Indian side. The mere fact that the Sikhs had played a great part—as had also other communities—in developing the colonies could hardly justify such a material departure from the agreed principle for the partition of the country which was that it should be on the basis of contiguous Muslim-majority and non-Muslim-majority areas. On this basis the dividing line must necessarily fall between Lahore and Amritsar.

In various discussions in Delhi with Short and V. P. Menon I stuck to this view. Menon wanted to know whether by any juggling with the line the danger of disturbances in the Punjab could be diminished. I did not think so. I said that after all that had happened in March the Sikhs were bent on attacking the Muslims wherever they felt themselves to be superior and a shift of the line in their favour would not now deflect them. The Muslims, on the other hand, were not anxious to stir up fresh trouble, but if they were deprived of Lahore—and here I was probably influenced by what Zafrullah had said—they would be so incensed that without further provocation they would repeat the March outrages on a far bigger scale. The best course therefore and also the most just was to adhere strictly to the accepted principles for determining the boundary.

Short, who had to play an advocate's role, did not appear to be convinced; and when I left Delhi he was in a disconsolate mood, for there was really nothing he could do to help the Sikhs. Back in Bahawalpur I received about ten days later a laconic telegram from him: 'Your line has it.' This told me approximately where the line would run and gave the assurance that Lahore would come to Pakistan.

VI

Bahawalpur State

BAHAWALPUR, which was the seat allotted to me for witnessing the Punjab tragedy, was a Native State about the size of Denmark lying between the Punjab and Sind. On one side—the north-western—it was bounded continuously by rivers, first by the river Sutlej, then by the Panjnad (i.e. the combined waters of the five Punjab rivers) and finally by the Indus. The opposite, south-eastern boundary of the State ran for the most part through desert territory along the borders of the Rajputana States of Bikanir and Jaisalmir. At its south-western end the State marched with the Sukkur district of Sind and its extreme north-eastern tip just touched the Ferozepur district of what is now East Punjab.

Two-thirds of the State was desert and the remainder was only saved from being so by the rivers running along one side. The average annual rainfall being only about five inches, cultivation was impossible without irrigation which could only be provided by canals or by wells not far from the river banks where the subsoil water was fairly close to the surface. The inhabited agricultural zone of the State was, therefore, a narrow strip of territory, varying in width from five to thirty-five miles and running parallel to the rivers over a length of 300 miles. In the desert area only a sparse nomadic population of graziers was to be found.

The State, more or less in the form in which it existed in 1947, was founded by the ancestors of the present dynasty in the first half of the eighteenth century. They came from Sind but claimed descent ultimately from the Abbasid Caliphs of Baghdad. In 1833, in order to escape the attentions of Ranjit Singh, the Sikh ruler of the Punjab, the Nawab of Bahawalpur sought British protection and Bahawalpur joined the ranks of Native States over which the British exercised suzerainty. It was the only State of any consequence in India which had both a Muslim ruler and a predominantly Muslim population.

The total population in 1947 was between one and a half and two million, Muslims constituting about 83 per cent. In the preceding twenty-five years it had nearly doubled. This was a result of the Sutlej Valley Project which had extended irrigation and led to the immigration of colonists, principally from the Punjab, to settle on the newly-reclaimed land. Most of the colonists were Muslims but there was also among them a sprinkling of Sikhs, settled for the most part near the north-eastern border of the State. These Sikh colonists constituted the bulk of the Sikh population of the State which was at this time a little under 50,000. The Hindus numbered about 190,000. The majority of them had been established in the State for several generations, but among them also there were a good many recent immigrants—bankers, merchants, shopkeepers—who had bought sites in the new market towns that were springing up to serve an expanding agriculture. They were a somewhat floating population with their roots still elsewhere—mainly in the Punjab and Rajputana.

These recent immigrants, whether Muslim, Sikh or Hindu, tended to be more vigorous and enterprising than the indigenous inhabitants and by their drive and energy were bringing the State, which had previously been a rather stagnant backwater, into the full stream of progress. Their influx had aroused envy and apprehension in the minds of the original inhabitants. They felt that they were outmatched by these thrusting energetic stocks from the Punjab and would ultimately be outnumbered by them. The strong rivalry between the original inhabitants—the 'riasatis'[1] as they were called—and the 'non-riasatis' led to some measure of discrimination against the latter who were not treated in all respects as full citizens. The distinction cut across all communal divisions and in the day-to-day administration was a more obtrusive factor than they, since communal relations in the State were normally harmonious. It was also to prove of some significance in the ensuing disturbances. At the first sight of danger the 'non-riasatis' among the Hindus and Sikhs could slip away to their original homes, whereas for the 'riasatis'

---

[1] 'Riasat' was the word used to denote a 'Native State' and so 'riasati' meant the inhabitant of such a State.

departure from the State meant pulling up much deeper roots.

The Sutlej Valley Project, which had brought into the State all these immigrants, had substituted weir-controlled irrigation for the old 'inundation' canals which only ran four to five months in the year and were dependent on the natural rise and fall of the river. With the construction of four weirs or 'head-works', from which the new canals took off, at Ferozepur, Suleimanke, Pallah and Panjnad, irrigation on both banks of the river could be extended and made more assured, and the low winter supplies of water could be utilized so as to give perennial irrigation to some areas.[1]

The Project, which had been commenced in 1922 and finally completed about ten years later, had not fulfilled all the hopes entertained of it and Bahawalpur State in particular had suffered from its comparative failure. This had given rise to a good deal of controversy and in Bahawalpur to some not unjustified bitterness. From the very outset the Bahawalpur authorities had pointed out that the water available in the rivers had been over-estimated and that this miscalculation vitiated the whole Project in the form in which it had been put forward. They protested against it being undertaken unless substantially modified. They protested in vain. The Nawab was at that time a minor and the representatives of the Paramount Power were, therefore, under a special obligation to see that the interests of his State were fully safeguarded. This obligation was not discharged. Disregarding the protests of the Regency Council, recklessly accepting palpable over-estimates of the water supplies and gross under-estimates of the costs, the Paramount Power forced Bahawalpur into the Project without removing its defects.

It soon became apparent that the Bahawalpur authorities had been right. The supplies of water, it was found, were insufficient for the designed capacity of the canals; at the Suleimanke and Islam (Pallah) weirs in particular the shortage at the critical seasons of the year was serious and chronic. In the end large

[1] The total area which it was planned should ultimately receive irrigation, either perennial or non-perennial, was 5,108,000 acres (or nearly 8,000 square miles) of which 2,825,000 acres were in Bahawalpur, 1,942,000 in the Punjab and 34,000 in Bikanir State. The total cost of the Project was Rs 34 crores of which Bahawalpur's share was Rs 14 crores.

areas of land which it had been intended to bring under irrigation had to be given up. Miles of canals dug through the deserts of Bahawalpur were later abandoned, and rest-houses, built for the accommodation of canal officers but never occupied, crumbled away forlornly in a barren wilderness.

Even worse than this unproductive expenditure was the terrific shortfall in the receipts which the Project had been expected to yield. The inadequacy of the supplies of water for the canals quickly became known and adversely affected the prices at which land could be auctioned. On top of this came the collapse of agricultural prices in the thirties. Colony land in Bahawalpur became practically unsaleable; even in the Punjab the auctioning of land had to be greatly reduced. The effect on Bahawalpur's finances was very serious. To meet its share of the capital cost of the Project, which turned out to be nearly two and a half times the original estimates, the State had to borrow Rs 12 crores from the Government of India. By 1936 it had not been possible to make any repayment; even the interest charges had not been met in full and the debt had swollen to about Rs 14 crores. An agreement was then entered into for its liquidation by annual instalments over a period of fifty years ending in 1986.

Ultimately the war came to the rescue of Bahawalpur. After 1942 with the steep rise in agricultural prices and consequently of land values the position and prospects vastly improved. The debt began to be repaid much faster than seemed possible in 1936 and by the end of 1945 had been reduced to Rs 5 crores. But the financial difficulties and transactions which have been described had a profound effect on the whole organization of the State and consequently also on the position of the Nawab. Born in 1904, he had lost his father in 1907 and there had been a long minority. When in 1924 he was invested with ruling powers he found that in consequence of the borrowings for the Sutlej Valley Project the administration of his State was half-mortgaged to the Government of India, and soon seemed destined to remain so for most of his lifetime. To safeguard their loan the Government of India had contrived to secure a tight control over the affairs of the State by the appointment of their own nominees to key posts, and they showed no sign of relaxing it so long as any substantial part of the debt remained outstanding.

It cannot be supposed that the Nawab felt happy about the position. It meant that in practice he lost both in power and in wealth. Owing to the State's financial difficulties the amounts which could be officially allotted to him for his personal expenditure, though considerable, fell far short of his requirements, and owing to the Government of India's grip on the main branches of the administration, he could not easily, like other rulers whose financial powers were unfettered, obtain for himself a larger share of the revenues of the State. The army was in fact the only large department where he had a comparatively free hand. There were therefore perpetual disputes about money. Moreover since real responsibility for the State was in effect assumed by the Government of India instead of being made to rest fairly and squarely on the shoulders of the Nawab, his own interest in the State's administration was not as keen as it otherwise might have been.

These were defects for which the Paramount Power, through its failure to safeguard the Nawab's interests during his minority, was partly responsible. A more determined or more ill-natured man might have made more than he did of his grievances. But the people at large were not adversely affected. The State was on the whole quite well administered. The Nawab himself was much of the time away in England or elsewhere; and even when he was in residence, the fact that his palace was at Dera Nawab, a place connected with Bahawalpur by the only metalled road in the State but over thirty miles distant from it, made him rather remote and the transaction of official business with him a little difficult. Nevertheless he was by no means unpopular; and if the army accounts were never audited and if there were leakages from various minor departments, the mass of the people were no wiser and felt no worse. 'The unwelcome novelties of education and hygiene' were not, as yet, universally desired; nor did the people at large think ill of a ruler for wishing to spend more of the State revenues on himself than a civil servant would approve. In a State with which I was later associated I found that an enlightened ruler, the founder of many schools and other useful institutions, highly eulogized by Lord Curzon himself, held no greater place in popular memory and esteem than his successor who had to be deposed for drunkenness and riotous living, having squandered the

State's resources on merrymaking, fireworks and colourful debauches. Circuses have more appeal than uplift.

When Gurmani and I went to Bahawalpur in April 1947 the control of the Government of India was still in force and had behind it the sanction of over twenty years. It was exercised mainly and most directly in respect of the departments of Revenue, Colonization and Public Works. For years the Revenue Minister who was in charge of these branches of the administration had been a nominee of the Government of India[1]—generally a retired official from the Punjab. The Chief Engineer and at least one of the Superintending Engineers had likewise been British officials drawn from outside the State. There had also been British officials, generally borrowed from the Punjab, employed as Colonization Officers, and a Government of India official acted as Accountant-General for Development Expenditure. Thus in practice, if not in theory, effective control of these departments had been vested in outsiders in-instead of in the Nawab and natives of the State.

However necessary and however welcome to the colonists this arrangement may have been, it was not popular with educated 'riasatis'. But they had to endure it; and it had one good result—the efficiency of the Revenue and Public Works departments had been raised to a high level and in their general working and in the quality of their personnel they fell little short of the standards prevalent in the adjoining Punjab. The same could not be said of the other departments of the State which, except for the army, were starved of money and comparatively neglected.

During the past twenty-five years the normal practice in Bahawalpur had been to have a Muslim as Prime Minister and an Englishman as Revenue Minister; but Gurmani's immediate predecessor was an Englishman, Sir Richard Crofton, and mine a retired Muslim official from the North-West Frontier Province. With our appointments there was a reversion to the usual pattern. I could not fail to detect that court and official circles in Bahawalpur were not sorry to say good-bye to Crofton nor over-pleased at having to welcome me—another Englishman. I sensed a vague hostility such as I had never

[1] My own appointment as Revenue and Public Works Minister had to receive the Government of India's approval.

experienced in the Punjab. In part this sprang from the peculiar conditions of Bahawalpur which had long covertly nursed a tradition of anti-western, obscurantist and reactionary Islam. In part it was a manifestation of the general desire to see the last of the British now that the time had come for them to lay down their power.

Besides the Prime Minister and Revenue Minister there were three or four other Ministers, drawn from the ranks of State subjects, who held minor portfolios or Palace appointments. All the Ministers together formed a State Council or *kabina*, over meetings of which the Nawab himself occasionally presided. Since however all the important departments of the State, except the Military Department, were in the hands of the Prime Minister and Revenue Minister, the business transacted by the *kabina* was mainly of a formal character.

The Chief Engineer of the State at this time was according to established custom British—Mr. James Roy, a retired engineer from the Punjab who in his younger days had built the Panjnad headworks. One of the three Superintending Engineers under him, Mr. Duncan, was also British and lent to the State by the Punjab Government.

The Colonization Officers had been converted a few years earlier into Deputy Commissioners and put in charge not only of colony work but of all revenue work in the two districts into which the State was administratively divided.[1] For a time there had been two British officials holding these posts, but in 1947 only the Bahawalpur district was in charge of a Britisher —Mr. Oliver, an I.C.S. officer from the Punjab—and the Deputy Commissioner of the other district of Rahim Yar Khan was a promoted revenue officer of the State, Maulvi Faiz Ahmad.

On the revenue side one other official drawn from outside the State requires to be mentioned. This was the Settlement Commissioner, Khan Bahadur Nur Mohammad, a retired Deputy Commissioner from the Punjab and well-known both to Gurmani and myself. After over twenty years of the new irrigation system agriculture in the Bahawalpur district had become

---

[1] In the Punjab, Deputy Commissioners were also District Magistrates, but to avoid arrogating to outsiders too large powers this arrangement was not followed in Bahawalpur and revenue and magisterial functions were kept more or less separate.

established and Nur Mohammad with a large 'settlement' staff had been appointed to reassess the land revenue. The work was very nearly complete and there was talk of terminating his appointment; but we kept him on and later at the end of July, when with the general exodus of British officers from India Oliver wanted to leave, he temporarily took over the work of Deputy Commissioner in addition to his own duties.

Bahawalpur had both an army and a police force. The latter was sadly neglected. Crofton had done something to raise its standards and had recently appointed to command it a retired Punjab police officer of good reputation named Nur Hussain Shah. But the neglect of years could not be made good in a few months. As in many Native States, the police were neglected for the army which was the special preserve and plaything of the Nawab and under his own direct control. It consisted of three infantry battalions and some miscellaneous units. A certain number of the troops were recruited from Bahawalpur State itself, but the bulk of them were drawn from the martial classes of northern India—mainly Pathans from the North-West Frontier Province, though there were a few platoons of Gurkhas.

State Forces in India were generally commanded by a regular officer of the Indian Army seconded for the purpose. The Political Department would have liked such an arrangement in the case of Bahawalpur, but the Nawab preferred to have a commander entirely of his own choice. The man selected was J. H. Marden. He had seen service in World War I, but was not an officer of the Indian Army. By 1947 he had attained the rank of brigadier and had been in command for a good many years.

One battalion of the Bahawalpur Army had served in Malaya during the war as line of communication troops, but even before the Japanese attack there was trouble owing to dissensions among the officers and the Nawab had to go to Malaya to help set matters right. On the fall of Singapore an influential officer named Gilani, along with a portion of the battalion, joined the Indian National Army[1] and attained considerable prominence therein. Another officer, named Durrani, his enemy and rival, stoutly resisted all Japanese blandishments and was subjected by

[1] The force formed by the Japanese to fight against the British from Indian prisoners captured in Malaya and at Singapore.

them to ill-treatment and torture. At the end of the war Gilani, of whom more will be heard, was cashiered and Durrani was awarded the George Cross.

Bahawalpur, being a Muslim State and situated between Sind and the Punjab, seemed destined to be linked in some way or other with Pakistan. Theoretically, of course, with the departure of the British and the lapse of Paramountcy it would become completely independent. But in practice complete independence would be difficult to maintain, and an endeavour to assert it might unnecessarily irritate the Pakistani leaders with unfortunate consequences. It was known that Jinnah, unlike the Congress leaders, was not hostile to the Ruling Princes and had no plans for sweeping them away or even for curtailing their powers. There seemed, therefore, every prospect of reaching some arrangement with Pakistan whereby Bahawalpur State would remain completely autonomous in regard to its internal affairs and cede sovereignty to Pakistan only in respect of defence and foreign relations.

When Gurmani and I accepted appointments in Bahawalpur nothing had been decided about this—even the creation of Pakistan had not been formally announced—but we assumed that some arrangement on these lines would eventually be worked out. It would mean for the Nawab, both in theory and practice, more real independence than he had ever enjoyed under the British, and naturally he himself desired as much independence as he could safely assert. We felt that Pakistan, beset with many pressing problems and with all the instability of a new State and a new untried democracy, would have little time or disposition to interfere with our affairs, provided we kept them running along quietly and did not have to go to Pakistan cap in hand for money to meet our expenses or armed forces to quell disturbances.

After all the financial difficulties of the past twenty years the State seemed to us at this time to be well set on a course of steadily increasing prosperity. Revenues had trebled in the past six years and the back of the debt had at last been broken. The State produced large quantities of surplus foodgrains which with skilful management could be passed on to less fortunate parts of the country with great profit to the exchequer. Irrigation from the Panjnad weir—the last to be

D*

constructed—was proving much more satisfactory than from the earlier Suleimanke and Islam weirs and was beginning to bring considerable wealth to the Rahim Yar Khan district. Altogether it seemed that the State, unless confronted with some unexpected crisis, was capable of standing on its own legs in a position of semi-independence. There was, of course, the ominous shadow of the great storm gathering in the Punjab, but we hoped that Bahawalpur would only catch the tail-end of it and would remain a comparatively sheltered haven.

It was a bit disconcerting to find that despite the uncertainty of the times the Nawab insisted on going off for the summer to England where he had a house near Farnham in Surrey. He promised, however, to return if any big issues regarding the future of the State had to be decided. With the announcement in June that the date for the transfer of power was to be put forward to August 15th these issues could no longer be postponed. Accordingly when towards the end of July Lord Mountbatten called the Ruling Princes to Delhi to talk to them about the future of their States the Nawab flew back to India to attend the meeting.

Lord Mountbatten's object was to persuade all the rulers to 'accede' to one or other of the two new Dominions in respect of defence, external affairs and communications—in other words to subordinate themselves in some measure to India or Pakistan. Some of the bigger States had other ideas; they thought that they could successfully assert independent sovereignty. A plan had also been mooted—and had received some backing from the Political Department—for combining the States, or a large number of them, into a kind of third Dominion. Gurmani occasionally seemed attracted by the idea. It was not, in my view, a practical proposition; but a few of the larger States forming compact areas, for example the Rajputana States, might have successfully stood aloof both from India and Pakistan, if they had acted together in unison. Herein lay the only real chance of the survival of any of the States. Accession, more particularly to India—and most States for geographical reasons were precluded from acceding to Pakistan—could only mean speedy extinction, since the Congress Party, which would hold the reins of power in India, was bent on their liquidation. Nevertheless Lord Mountbatten, with a brilliant persuasiveness which could hardly have been excelled, induced them all, with the unfortunate exceptions of Kashmir and Hyderabad, to sign what proved to be their own death warrants on the assurance that this afforded them the best chance of survival.

I had assumed that Bahawalpur would quietly accede to Pakistan. Our discussions with Muslim League leaders in Lahore and our engagement of Pakistan's counsel, Zafrullah, to represent our interests also before the Boundary Commission clearly implied that this was our intention. I was astounded, therefore, when Gurmani informed me that the Nawab was being advised in certain quarters to accede to India. Gurmani himself seemed hardly less astonished and perplexed. The reason for this perverse advice was not far to seek. The Muslim League leaders had been offering tempting concessions to some of the Hindu rulers in the hope of inducing them to join Pakistan. In the case of the Maharajah of Jodhpur they very nearly succeeded. Some people thought that the Nawab might extract similar concessions from India if he agreed to accede to India instead of to Pakistan. These calculations were quite unfounded. The Congress leaders were not interested in enticing Bahawalpur into the Indian Union. Moreover, since Bahawalpur was a Muslim State with a Muslim ruler and lay right astride the rail and road communications between Karachi and Lahore, its accession to India would be a deadly blow to Pakistan and must produce a violent Muslim reaction. I told Gurmani that I thought the Nawab would be promptly assassinated if he attempted such a course, and that Gurmani had better warn him of this contingency. I do not know whether he did so, but in any case after a day or two all talk of acceding to India ended as the Nawab decided that Bahawalpur should in due course accede to Pakistan.[1] After attending the celebrations in Karachi on the inauguration of Pakistan he flew back to England.

Like me the people of Bahawalpur had assumed that the State would accede to Pakistan; they knew nothing of any other possibility. The majority of them, being Muslims, were well content with the prospect, and throughout most of the State even the minority communities had accepted it philosophically and without undue alarm. During the March dis-

[1] The instrument of accession was not actually signed till October 3rd 1947.

turbances in the Punjab perfect tranquillity had prevailed in Bahawalpur and there was a general disposition to believe that this would continue. Only at the north-east end of the State in the colony areas around Bahawalnagar, where there were many recent Hindu and Sikh immigrants and contact with the Punjab was closest, were there signs of uneasiness. The replacement of Crofton by a Muslim Prime Minister known to have Muslim League sympathies was the subject of comment and questioning. Would non-Muslim interests be safe in his hands? A trickle of Hindus began to leave the State and there was some underground propaganda designed to stimulate a greater exodus; for extremist Hindu circles entertained the notion that they could ruin Pakistan by depriving it *ab initio* of all the banking and commercial facilities and expertise which the Hindu community had hitherto provided. In order to spread alarm and afford a colourable pretext for an exodus—since Bahawalpur had remained entirely peaceful—some Hindus started petty cases of arson in their own houses—singeing a sofa, charring the leg of a wooden bedstead or burning up an old bit of matting—and then made out that Muslims had done it, that their lives and property were in danger and that they must leave at once for some place of greater security. A few actually locked up their houses and went away with their goods and chattels and family cow to their original homes.

In order to allay this unrest Gurmani himself paid a visit to Bahawalnagar in May. His genial expansive personality, persuasive speech and benevolent smile made an excellent impression. He gave assurances to the minority communities of full protection and quite dispelled any notion there might be that he was a bloodthirsty, bigoted Muslim. To inspire confidence he ordered some detachments of the Bahawalpur army to be sent to Bahawalnagar, Harunabad and other towns in that area. I was not too happy about this arrangement as I distrusted the discipline of the Bahawalpur troops, but the minority communities themselves welcomed it.

During the month of June I toured through this part of the State and found that previous fears had to a great extent disappeared. The Hindus were no longer talking of leaving and appeared to be quite reassured. Only the Sikhs were worried. Two or three deputations of Sikh colonists came to see me and asked, in effect, whether they should leave the State or whether it would be safe for them to stay. I was obliged to hedge. I could not advise them to leave as that would have been totally contrary to the general policy that was being followed. Yet I could not promise that they would be safe if they stayed; for, apart from the fact that as Revenue Minister I was not directly responsible for law and order, I did not feel certain that we would be able to protect them. So I simply said that I could see no danger to them at the moment and that therefore I could not understand how Sikhs, who were supposed to be brave people, could be thinking of running away. It was, however, up to them to decide. If they really felt that they were in danger despite appearances to the contrary, there was nothing to prevent them leaving.

They went away dissatisfied and I got the impression that unless I personally guaranteed their safety—which I was not prepared to do—they would decide to leave.

Throughout July the State remained absolutely calm; but in the Punjab there was some fresh deterioration in the situation, especially in Lahore and Amritsar. One incident that occurred at this time afforded us a lurid glimpse of the fanatical hatreds that had been aroused in those cities. Gurmani and I had a mutual friend named Major Ashiq Hussain Qureshi, a wealthy Muslim landowner and a man of some prominence in the Punjab—he had been a Minister in Khizar's Government in 1944–6. Late on the night of July 31st my telephone rang. Gurmani was at the other end and said: 'Ashiq has been shot dead in Lahore by a police constable.'

We only learnt the details of the incident later. They were certainly remarkable. It appears that as Ashiq Hussain was driving from the city to his house in one of the suburbs, an armed police constable signalled to him to stop. He did not see, or did not immediately obey, the signal and when finally he brought his car to a standstill an altercation took place between him and the constable and they parted with mutual abuse. About twenty minutes later Ashiq had occasion to return to the city by the same route. The same constable, with whom there was now a sub-inspector, signalled to him to stop. He did so and the sub-inspector came up and asked him why he had not obeyed the constable's signal on the previous occasion. He

replied that he had done so as soon as possible and started complaining of the constable's insolence; whereupon the constable lifted up the rifle which he was carrying and shot him
through the head. He was killed instantly and his brains
scattered over the seat of the car. The sub-inspector exclaimed:
'What a terrible thing you've done! Why, you might as well
have killed me! This is Ashiq Hussain.' The constable, who was
a Muslim, was taken aback at this and said in astonishment:
'Ashiq Hussain! I thought it was a Hindu.' He was arrested
and subsequently hanged.

This episode, confirming as tragically as it did how deeply
anti-Hindu Punjabi Muslims had by now become, came more
as a shock to me than anything that had previously occurred.

During the first half of August ripples from disturbances elsewhere began to reach Bahawalpur. Quite suddenly, without
notice or warning, 200–300 refugees arrived by train from Alwar
and Bharatpur—two small States south of Delhi—and deposited
themselves on a bit of open ground outside the city. They
claimed that they had been forcibly driven from their homes,
but there was no evidence of this and it appeared that they
had been impelled to leave more by fear of what might happen than by anything that had actually taken place. Their
arrival caused a mild stir in Bahawalpur city and various
Muslim organizations began to busy themselves with their
relief and to urge the Bahawalpur Government to make lavish
arrangements for their further entertainment. We were not at
all inclined to assume any responsibility for these uninvited
guests; and Gurmani told them that if they were seeking the
promised land of Pakistan they had come to the wrong place
and had better go on to Punjab or Sind. Gradually they drifted
away.

About the same time reports began to spread of renewed
disturbances in Lahore and Amritsar. No great notice was
taken of these reports in Bahawalpur, but a train outrage which
occurred on the evening of August 9th aroused a good deal of
excitement and indignation among sections of the Muslim
population. A number of the clerical staff of the new Pakistan
Government were due to pass through the State in a special
train carrying them from Delhi to Karachi, and preparations
had been made to cheer them on their way and offer them re-

freshments at Bahawalpur station. But before the train reached the borders of the State, it was derailed in the adjoining district of Ferozepur by the explosion of a bomb which Sikhs had placed on the railway track. Two or three passengers were killed and a number injured. A relief train had to be sent out from Bahawalnagar. This was one of the first train outrages and the first incident to make any noticeable impression on the Muslims of Bahawalpur.

We were still awaiting the public announcement of the Radcliffe award fixing the boundary line between East and West Punjab. I had expected the announcement to be made a day or two before August 15th and to be the signal for the storm to break in the Punjab, but it was delayed till August 17th. The Sikhs, however, did not wait for it. A few days earlier, as I was soon to learn, they had begun their long-meditated revenge.

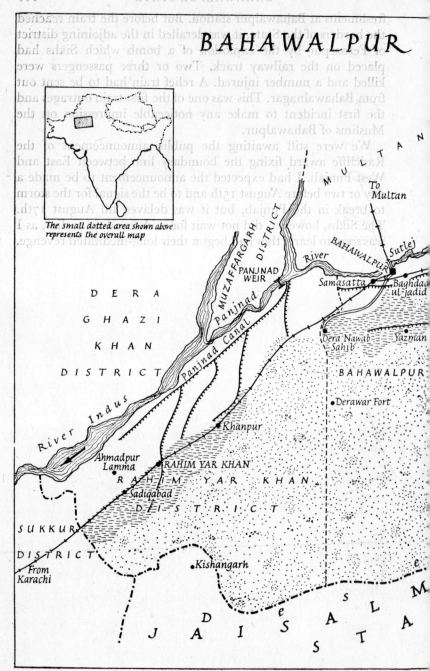

The small dotted area shown above represents the overall map

STATE

MONTGOMERY

DISTRICT

DISTRICT

To
Ferozepur

SULEIMANKE
WEIR

Sutlej

River   Minchinabad

Macleodganj Road

FEROZEPUR
DISTRICT

Hindumalkot

To
Bhatinda

Fordwah   Canal

Canal

ISLAM (PALLAH)
WEIR

Bahawalnagar

Karanpur

Sadiqia

Canal

Qaimpur

Chishtian

Dungabunga

Hasilpur

Khairpur

Harunabad

B   I   K   A   N   E   R

Lal Suhara

Fort
Marot

Fort
Abbas

Anupgarh

DISTRICT

S   t   a   t   e

B   I   K   A   N   E   R

**Key to symbols within
BAHAWALPUR STATE**

Old cultivated area

New colony area

Desert

State boundary

District boundary

Canals

Metalled road

Railways

Scale

0	20	40	60

miles

Journey Across the Punjab

I HAD been down in the heat all the summer and felt that I must have a break sometime in August. It was arranged that Gurmani, who during July and the first half of August had been a good deal out of the State in Simla, Karachi and elsewhere, should return to Bahawalpur by the middle of August and that I should then go up to Simla for a fortnight. I had thought that the conflagration that was about to sweep the Punjab might possibly miss Bahawalpur altogether, or at any rate would not spread to it till September, by which time I would be back in the State to give Gurmani any assistance that he might require. This was rather a bad miscalculation. The flames spread much faster than I had expected and may be said to have reached the eastern border of Bahawalpur by ·August 22nd. But a week earlier, when I set out on my journey to Lahore and Simla, the State was peaceful and undisturbed; and so were the immediately adjoining Punjab districts.

This drive across the Punjab to Simla and back again ten days later gave me a bird's-eye view of the conditions prevailing in the Province at this time. I started for Lahore early on the morning of August 15th, taking with me my driver and my bearer. There was nothing abnormal *en route* save that around Burewala (a town in the Multan district) individual Sikhs walking or bicycling on the roads were all wearing very large kirpans.[1] Somewhere near the boundary between the Montgomery and Lahore districts there was a military picket and a barrier across the road, but apart from this everything seemed normal and tranquil right up to the outskirts of Lahore itself.

About four to five miles from Lahore, as we approached the built-up area, we overtook a military lorry in the back of which

[1] A kirpan is a form of dagger or sword which every Sikh is supposed to carry.

there was a soldier with a rifle and two or three bloodstained corpses bumping about on the floor. A little farther on five or six men were lined up along the side of the road with their hands up and a soldier covering them with his rifle. Two hundred yards beyond there was a corpse lying on a charpoy. It now became noticeable that the road and the houses on either side of it were entirely deserted. On the other hand, through the gaps between the houses, peasants could be seen with their bullocks ploughing the fields a few hundred yards away, as though nothing had happened.

The Lawrence Gardens were full of troops; the Mall empty, every shop shut, and as silent as the grave. I made for the railway station to find out about trains to Simla. As I passed down Empress Road a fire engine was coping with a burning house, and to the left, from the city proper, numerous dense columns of smoke were rising into the air.

The railway station was in the hands of the military and barricaded off by barbed wire. I forced my way past the sentry and found Colonel Walker (whom I had known on the hunting-field eight to nine years earlier) established in a room off the main hall and apparently in charge. There was no sign of any station staff except two clerks in the inquiry office who returned inane answers to my questions about trains. They finally referred me to the head office in Empress Road. I reached the conclusion that no train was likely to leave for Simla that evening, but if one did, there would be few competitors for a seat in it apart from myself!

I then drove to Faletti's Hotel for lunch. As I got out of my car, a hand was stretched out to me from another car moving off and there was Jack Bennett, the Inspector-General of Police, driving off to the airfield to catch a plane home. He told me that Jenkins[1] had left earlier in the morning. The departure of the Governor and the Inspector-General of Police was the outward and visible symbol of the end of British rule. I could not help reflecting that we were leaving Lahore in the same state of turmoil and disorder as we had found it almost exactly a century earlier.

After lunch I went and had a chat with John Eustace, an old friend and exact contemporary who during the last few

[1] Sir Evan Jenkins, Governor of the Punjab 1946-47.

months had been working as Deputy Commissioner, Lahore. He had handed over charge the day before to a Muslim officer and was staying in the Under-Secretary's house at the Residency out towards the cantonments. While we talked a house on the opposite side of the road, belonging to a Hindu, was broken into by a band of Muslims and plundered. Eustace said that the Muslim police in Lahore were now openly taking sides with the rioters. Muslim police constables had been giving covering fire from roof-tops while Muslim mobs below broke into Sikh Gurdwaras.[1] He thought that the military were probably also unreliable and already taking sides. The recent recrudescence of trouble in Lahore was due to events in Amritsar district where, for the last ten days, armed gangs of Sikhs had been setting fire to Muslim villages and butchering the inhabitants.

He strongly urged me not to attempt to motor through to Simla unarmed, but, except for a shotgun for sporting purposes, I had never kept or carried arms in India and did not intend to do so now. During the troubled weeks in Bahawalpur that were to follow, I remained throughout unarmed and was, no doubt, all the better for it.

At about 7.0 p.m. I went to the station again to make further inquiries about trains to Simla. Twenty Sikh police constables were gathered together in a corner of the main entrance hall behind a barbed-wire barricade. Walker told me that they had sought his protection from the alleged violence of a Muslim mob and he had admitted them within his station stronghold. I walked on to the platform which was practically deserted, and, seeing a man coming along in stationmaster's uniform, went up and asked him if any train was going to Simla.

'Sir,' he said, 'I have just escaped from Moghulpura on an engine with some of my staff. We were attacked by 8,000 Sikhs; they have killed several hundred. I have been telephoning for help for thirteen hours.'

I did not attempt to get at the real facts underlying this exaggerated story, but, as he seemed rather distraught, I just popped him in my car and sent him to his home somewhere near Kashmiri Gate. While waiting for my car to return, I found out from somebody who seemed to know, that only one

[1] Gurdwara = Sikh temple.

train would leave Lahore that night and that would be for Quetta!

I now gave up all hope of getting to Simla by train. Earlier in the afternoon I had learnt that some five or six British officials, all well-known to me, who were due to sail from Bombay in about a week and had grown doubtful of the prospect of getting out of Lahore by train, had obtained a military lorry and a military escort to take them and their kit to Delhi. They were due to leave the next day and were very keen that I should accompany them as far as Ambala (from where I would have to turn off for Simla) as this would mean seats for two or three of them in a comfortable car instead of in a lorry. There was obviously nothing better to do. My car rather badly needed repairs and my plan had been to leave it at a garage in Lahore while I went on by train to Simla, picking it up again on my return. But no garage was open and no trains were running.

We left Lahore on the morning of August 16th at 6.15 a.m. and took the route via Ferozepur so as to avoid Amritsar, which was thought to be particularly dangerous. Besides two military lorries, there were several cars in the convoy. All the British officials, except myself, were leaving Lahore and the Punjab for good. It was a dismal exodus from a Province which we had governed with great success for one hundred years and which, perhaps more than any other Province, had liked us. But that Province itself was no more. It had been cut in two and its life and culture, as we had known them, were in the process of being destroyed for ever.

Except for terrific storms of rain, which made driving difficult, our journey was entirely uneventful and the military escort (as I had surmised) quite superfluous. At both Ludhiana and Ambala a curfew was in force, but nothing very serious seemed yet to have occurred at either of these places. From Ambala up to Simla everything was entirely normal.

Simla also was normal and full of summer residents, but buzzing with stories of ghastly happenings in Amritsar and Lahore. It was destined a few weeks later to be itself the scene of some disgraceful atrocities, but for the moment life flowed along smoothly. I was surprised to find several Hindus, who had large stakes in the West Punjab, apparently unperturbed by all that was going on. I lunched one day with one of them and, despite the fact that almost all his property and business interests were now in Pakistan, he was delightfully cheerful and sprightly. He had, however, taken the precaution a couple of years earlier of getting to know Jinnah and asking him to lunch. That lunch proved a good investment; he managed to salvage most of his Pakistan assets.

Another Hindu business man, a bulky benevolent old fellow whom I had known since my earliest days in the Punjab, I met one day on the Mall. Knowing that he had extensive mining and other interests in Western Punjab, I asked him how he felt about them.

'I've left them all to God,' he said.

'So then you're quite unaffected by all these events?' I questioned.

'Well,' he replied, 'I cannot claim to be quite unaffected, but, thanks to moral rearmament, I'm fifty to sixty per cent unaffected.'

In a very different mood was poor old Sir Manohar Lal. He had for many years been Finance Minister in the Punjab and was reputed, when at Cambridge, to have been one of Alfred Marshall's favourite pupils. Though by no means devoid of nationalist feelings—he had been arrested during the troubles of 1919—he was deeply steeped in English culture and English habits of thought and action. He prided himself on his mastery of the English language; on files he recorded the most polished notes in an exquisite handwriting. I met him, as so often in earlier years, going along the Mall in a rickshaw—a bit shaky, but much the same as ever. He stopped his rickshaw and, grasping me warmly by the hand, said:

'Tell me, Moon, for you're an intelligent man, tell me, why are you British leaving us like this?'

I replied, 'I think mainly because we feel that you no longer want us.'

'But surely you know that it's only a handful of Congress people who think like that. Just see what awful things are now happening in the Punjab; and there's going to be worse.'

I did my best to reassure him, saying that we were witnessing the birth pangs of two new nations and that after a while all would be well. But he was not to be comforted. The world which he had known was collapsing before him. He did not live to see very much of the New Order.

Day by day news from the Punjab seemed to get worse. Owing to censorship, reports were vague, but the disorder was clearly growing and spreading. I decided to curtail my stay in Simla. I wrote to Gurmani saying that I hoped to be back in Bahawalpur by the evening of the 25th. Many people told me that driving across East Punjab would be dangerous, especially with two Muslim servants. But it was infinitely safer than going by train. There was, in fact, no danger at all except possibly if one had a breakdown, and even then military patrols on the Grand Trunk Road would have afforded protection. I am glad to say that my servants neither showed nor, I think, felt the slightest alarm—indeed my bearer insisted that we should go by Amritsar, which was considered the more risky route, in order that we might pass through Jullundur, his native town. He rightly foresaw that this would be his last opportunity of seeing it.

The rains had been particularly heavy and great pools and sheets of water were standing in the fields and village tracks. I could not imagine how, in these conditions, the Boundary Force could hope to move about and keep order in the country-side. With their wheeled transport they would get bogged down immediately. Cavalry was the only answer, and there was no cavalry. So far as I could make out, the villages of the Eastern Punjab were just being allowed to run amuck as they pleased. From the Grand Trunk Road, particularly on the stretch from Ambala to Ludhiana, murderous-looking gangs of Sikhs, armed with guns and spears, could be seen prowling about or standing under the trees, often within fifty yards of the road itself. Military patrols in jeeps and trucks were passing up and down the road, yet taking not the slightest notice of these gangs, as though they were natural and normal features of the country-side. This was not at all my idea of how things should be done. I felt that gangs such as these should not be tolerated for one instant, but mercilessly shot down wherever they were seen.

The towns were all under curfew and had a curiously dere-lict appearance. At Ludhiana not a soul was visible and there was no sign of life at all, except two donkeys copulating in the middle of the road just near the clock tower. At Jullundur a few people were stirring, but many of the houses looked as though they had been plundered and the streets were strewn with litter. I asked my bearer whether he would like us to turn aside to have a look at his house, but seeing the condition of the town he shook his head and said, 'No; it's all been destroyed.'

At Amritsar we had to stop for petrol, our tank being almost empty. I thought I might have to try to obtain some from the Deputy Commissioner as all the petrol pumps seemed to be closed. However, at last we found one that was functioning. The Sikh serving it recognized me and was very obliging, but also very talkative. He was full of some alleged massacre of Sikhs by a Muslim battalion on the border, just beyond Atari. When I asked him about the massacres of Muslims by Sikhs that had occurred in the Amritsar district, he disclaimed all knowledge of them.

At Wagah, midway between Amritsar and Lahore, we had to cross the newly established frontier between India and Pakistan, but there were as yet no formalities and we drove across without, I think, even being stopped. Lahore was not burning as briskly as it had been ten days earlier and seemed generally in rather better shape, but all the shops in the Mall were still closed.

We stopped the night in Lahore and pushed on the next morinng down the Multan road. There were no armed bands roaming about the countryside as there were on the Indian side of the frontier and we struck nothing unusual till we had gone about seventy miles and reached Okara. Stopping at the outskirts of the town to get some petrol I was surprised to see Daultana, one of the Ministers of the newly formed West Punjab Government, sitting not far from the pump, surrounded by a group of men. It seemed a strange place to find a Minister. He came up to me and exchanged a few words and explained that there had been an 'incident' at Okara and he had come to inquire into it.

Ten miles farther on, as we rounded a bend in the road after crossing a canal, we almost ran into a bullock-cart, stranded in the middle of the road with the bullocks unyoked and standing to one side. We had to stop practically dead and then pull right over on to the side of the road, as the cart entirely blocked the metalled portion. As we did so, I noticed a man lying under the cart, and then two police constables suddenly appeared—they had been standing on the far side of the cart—and signalled us on. I felt a bit mystified and, looking back, saw one of the constables with his rifle raised to his shoulder aiming at the man under the cart. There was a crack —and the poor fellow was presumably finished off. This was to me a novel form of summary justice on the high road.

Along the outskirts of the town of Montgomery the road was completely blocked for about a mile by a string of bullock-carts laden with goods and chattels and paraphernalia of all kinds and halted under a fine avenue of trees. We had to get right off the road and drive along in the fields. Most of the men with the carts were Sikhs, but only low-caste Mazhabis or Labanas and not at all well-to-do. They were trekking towards India and had halted in the shade during the afternoon heat or perhaps even for the night. Some of them were pulling large chunks of bark off the trees to serve as fuel.[1] We were getting back again on to the road near the end of the column and I had alighted from the car to direct the driver over some rough ground, when someone recognized me as a former Deputy Commissioner of Multan and I was immediately surrounded by a throng of rather piteous-looking people clamouring for protection. I couldn't at first make out what from, as their column seemed in fairly good order; but they insisted that they were being looted and then, looking along the column on the side facing Montgomery, I saw that groups of men were helping themselves to bundles and packages from the carts and walking off across the fields towards the town carrying them on their heads. A few police constables were standing around, but doing nothing to prevent this. The Sikh refugees said that there were some military encamped on the other side of the town and begged me to go and ask them to give protection. I felt compelled to do so, but my efforts were entirely fruitless. I spent a long time searching for the military encampment, which was several miles away, only to find it empty except for one sepoy who said the troops had all gone out—he didn't know where.

I drove on again, making for the headworks at Pallah, where

[1] Great damage was done in this way to the trees along the routes followed by these columns of refugees. Rows of trees stripped of their bark became a common sight.

I would cross the river Sutlej into Bahawalpur State. I noticed that several chaks[1] near the roadside were deserted, but they didn't seem to have been plundered; the houses were quite intact and there were no signs of arson. Not far from Arifwala the road was again entirely blocked by bullock-carts evidently halted for the night, but the Sikhs with these were stalwart 'Jats' and evidently well-to-do. Their carts were large and well-built and the bullocks exceptionally fine. They had plenty of spears and I saw one or two guns. They seemed well able to look after themselves and to give as good as they got, if any-one dared to molest them. Altogether it was a much better organized and better equipped column than the one outside Montgomery.

It so happened that at this point there were quite deep ditches along either side of the road so I was unable to turn off into the fields to avoid the bullock-carts and was brought to a standstill. Almost immediately, however, a jathedar[2] came up, wearing the blue turban of an Akali, and ordered some of the men to fill up the ditch to enable me to cross into the fields. They did this quite quickly and also ran ahead and made a place for me to get back on to the road farther on. I asked the Jathedar why they were on the move like this. It was obvious, I said, that no-one had attacked them. They were all in fine fettle and apparently had been quite unmolested. Why then had they left their chaks and started on this trek? He replied, 'Hukum hai.' (It is an order.) I asked him, 'Whose order?' But to this he would give no clear reply, but just went on repeating, 'It is an order. We have received an order. We have to go to Hindustan.'

I had been somewhat delayed by these two road blocks and shortly afterwards I almost despaired of reaching Bahawalpur at all that night. There was a short stretch of unmetalled road which we had to traverse in order to get from the main road on to the canal bank leading to the Pallah headworks. A part of this had been flooded by a breach in a nearby distributary and here my car got hopelessly stuck when only about thirty yards from the canal bank. Though some villagers came to our help, no amount of pushing would move it and I thought that

[1] Colony villages.
[2] Leader of a 'Jatha' or band.

we were going to be marooned there for the night, when most opportunely a patrol of Mahratta Light Infantry belonging to the Boundary Force came along the canal bank in a jeep. They kindly gave me a tow and pulled my car out of the mud in no time. They said that there had been no disturbances in their area.

We reached Pallah at dusk and crossed the river to the Bahawalpur side. I asked the gatekeeper at the far end of the headworks if all was quiet. He said that there were reports of serious disturbances in Mailsi and Kahrore—two towns in the Multan district.

'But I suppose there's been no trouble this side?' I inquired hopefully.

'I believe, sir, there has been trouble in the State also,' he replied. 'A man came here a little while ago and said that Chishtian had been looted and several people killed.'

This was disquieting.

We had still more than sixty miles to do and drove on as fast as we could down the Bahawal Canal, reaching Bahawalpur at about 9.0 p.m. At my house there was a message to ring up the Prime Minister as soon as I arrived. I got through to him at once. He had been expecting me for some hours. He said that there were reports of disturbances at Bahawalnagar, but he had no details. Brigadier Marden was already there with a battalion of the Bahawalpur Army. He proposed himself to leave for Bahawalnagar the next morning and requested me to go with him. He thought that we might have to stay there several days.

I replied that I would gladly accompany him. I also told him that at Pallah I had heard a rumour of disturbances at Chishtian. Since this place lay on the route to Bahawalnagar we could look in there on our way.

My bearer and driver, without a murmur, got ready for an early start the next day.

VIII

Outbreak of Disturbances in Bahawalpur State

W E set out at about 7.0 a.m. while it was still fairly cool. I travelled with Gurmani in his car, my Buick following behind with his private secretary and with my personal assistant and our servants and chaprassis. In another car was the Commissioner of Police, Nur Hussain Shah, and a big burly Muslim in European clothes and a topi whom I had never seen before, but who turned out to be an ex-officer of the Bahawalpur State Forces. He was one of those who had joined the I.N.A.[1] Gurmani had apparently taken him under his wing in the last few days—whether to keep him out of mischief or because he thought he might genuinely be useful I was never quite able to determine. We also had with us a few other police officers, some police constables and a naik and several sepoys of the State Forces, and so altogether it was quite a procession of three to four big cars and a small truck which moved off along the main Bahawal Canal *en route* for Bahawalnagar.

The surface of most of the canal-bank roads in Bahawalpur was far from good, and the road along the Bahawal Canal was one of the worst. We could not, therefore, average more than 20–25 miles per hour. Still we travelled at a fair pace for the first twenty miles up to Lal Suhara where there is an important regulator and several branches take off from the main canal. Up to this point considerable stretches of the canal are lined with trees, which, besides affording shade, help to stabilize and compact the road. There is also fairly extensive cultivation on both banks, and so our route had been bounded by pleasant fields of ripening millets. But shortly after Lal Suhara the aspect of the country changes. A slight elevation of the land to the south

[1] The Indian National Army.

124

renders it uncommanded by the canal, and for about thirty miles cultivation and human habitations are almost entirely confined to the north bank—between the canal and the river Sutlej—and to the south one gazes out over a dreary grey desert, blotched with tibbas (sand-hills), and in places mottled with juniper and tamarisk scrub. The canal is practically tree-less and the road, which runs for the most part on the southern and desert bank, is correspondingly bad. We were proceeding slowly through this uninteresting terrain when, as we approached a bridge leading across the canal to a large village or townlet a little distance to the north, we suddenly saw on our right a group of about a dozen villagers bobbing up and down on a small sand-hill some thirty yards away. One of them in the middle was holding up a stick with a little green flag tied to the end. He seemed very pleased with the flag and was gazing up at it and shouting. The others were jiggering about round him. The whole thing gave the impression of being a very feeble and absurd pro-Pakistan or pro-Muslim demonstration staged for our benefit. Gurmani, with an expression of annoyance, told the driver to stop the car and we got out. In somewhat harsh terms we asked the villagers what the hell they thought they were doing. The man holding the flag grinned ingratiatingly and, pointing to the miserable bit of green cloth at the end of his stick, said, 'This is our flag. We now have Pakistan and Muslim Raj.' Gurmani was not very well pleased. He told the villagers that this sort of thing was not wanted and asked why they were fooling about at the edge of the desert instead of looking after their crops. By this time the Commissioner of Police had joined us and gone right up close to the knot of villagers and was eyeing them narrowly.

'These are Hindus,' he suddenly exclaimed, and, as we gaped astonishment, he grabbed hold of one of them saying, 'Look at this fellow; he's nothing but a Hindu shopkeeper. His ears are pierced. He's been wearing earrings.'

I was completely taken aback, and it was only after a few seconds that it dawned upon me that these were men who within the last day or two had accepted Islam, as it were, at the point of the sword. The new converts, to show their zeal for the Faith, started gabbling away at us bits of the Koran which they had hurriedly learnt up; but the Commissioner of Police quickly

put a stop to this nonsense and began asking them how they
had been driven to masquerade as Muslims. I was still somewhat incredulous and said, 'Surely they can't all be Hindus?'

Several of the villagers had by now unostentatiously separated
themselves from the main group and were beginning to walk
away. They were rounded up and brought back. The whole lot
were then examined individually and it was found that three
to four of them were Muslims and the rest Hindus. The Muslims
were detained for further interrogation and put into the truck.
I never discovered why they had brought their converts to
demonstrate near the canal road and thus needlessly got themselves into trouble.

The Hindus, after being consoled and reassured and finally
convinced that we did not mean to harm them, told us that they
belonged to the large village on the other side of the canal
and that it had been attacked and looted the previous day by
large mobs of Muslim peasants from the surrounding countryside. They had been compelled to embrace Islam in order to
save their lives. A good many Hindus had sought safety at the
police station.

Taking one of them as a guide, we got into our cars, crossed
the bridge and drove towards the village. The road was vile
and we had to make several detours to avoid getting stuck in
pools of water and mud. However, at last we reached the outskirts of the place, which turned out, in fact, to be a small town
called Khairpur with 5,000–6,000 inhabitants. It served as a
market-centre for a considerable tract of riverain country and so
had quite a large population of Hindu merchants, bankers and
shopkeepers, besides Muslim farmers and labourers. Skirting
along the edge of it, we made for the police station which was
situated outside to the west in a grove of trees.

A few Hindus were sitting about disconsolately under the
trees. Someone went and called the thanedar[1] who came running out of the police station in a flurry. He was voluble and, I
thought, rather jittery. He said that huge mobs from the nearby
riverain villages had assembled the day before to loot the Hindu
shops, but had been persuaded to disperse before much damage
was done. So far as he knew, there had been no casualties. I

---

[1] The officer in charge of a police station (thana), usually a sub-inspector
of police.

gathered that the Muslim inhabitants of Khairpur, so far from joining the looters, had been mainly instrumental in getting rid of them and protecting the Hindus. Possibly the conversion of some of them to Islam was one of the protective devices adopted for their benefit and to placate the raiders. The thanedar was, however, very much afraid that the place would be attacked again. He said that there was a party of Muslims within Khairpur who didn't like the pro-Hindu policy of the majority and wanted to call back the looters and join with them in the plunder. He requested very insistently to be supplied with arms. I asked where were the twelve rifles which ought to be available at the police station. He replied that they were no use and showed us some rusty old weapons of antique pattern, most of which had the bolt or some other essential part missing. Only two or three of them were capable of firing at all. In Bahawalpur, as in many other Indian States, the police were a depressed class, utterly neglected and despised, and all attention and funds were devoted to the army.

I soon found that Khairpur was typical of all the rural police stations in the State, and, indeed, that some of them had not a single rifle that would fire. The Commissioner of Police had done his best since joining the State service to improve the clothing and equipment of the force, but had not been able to get very far. The result was that the police, particularly in the rural areas, were quite unequipped to deal with the disturbed conditions that had now developed, even if they had the will to do so.

In view of the thanedar's apprehensions, which seemed not ill-founded, we decided to leave with him four of our escort of sepoys armed with modern rifles. Orders were also given for some rifles to be fetched from Bahawalpur for arming the police constables, though most of them had never been through their annual course of practice firing and could hardly be expected to use rifles effectively. Gurmani addressed some of the leading Muslim inhabitants in suitable terms, impressing on them their duty to help the thanedar and protect the lives and property of the Hindus—a duty which so far they seemed to have discharged quite well. The thanedar, in spite of the four armed sepoys and the hope of more rifles, still appeared rather worried, but we reassured him as best we could and got back again into our cars. We were, on the whole, very pleased both that nothing serious had so far occurred at Khairpur and also that we had been able to make timely arrangements for reinforcing the sub-inspector. These were, in actual fact, wholly inadequate.

We drove on along the canal bank for about ten miles till we came to another market town, similar in general character to Khairpur but a good deal smaller. Its name was Qaimpur. It was situated, like Khairpur, to the north of the canal, but at no very great distance from it—perhaps less than half a mile. We thought that we had better go and have a look at it and so once again we crossed over a bridge to the north bank of the canal, intending to drive along a rough unmetalled road which led to the place. But immediately beyond the far end of the bridge there was a great deal of muddy water and so, thinking that the cars would become bogged in it, we got out and began to walk. Between us and the outskirts of the town there was a stretch of open, flat, uncultivated ground. As we stepped on to it, we saw advancing towards us from the other side and heading for the bridge a party of twenty to thirty villagers, laden with bundles of clothes, quilts, boxes and packages of all kinds. I did not in the least tumble to the significance of what I saw, but the Commissioner of Police alerted us all by saying, 'They're probably looters!' When we met them we greeted them and asked where they were going. They said they were going to their homes.

'What is all this stuff you're carrying with you?'

'We've been shopping in the town.'

This was a palpable lie. The miscellaneous assortment of articles they were carrying, including odd bits of furniture, could not be the products of any normal shopping. They considerably outnumbered our party, but with the help of the sepoys and our other staff we arrested them before they could disembarrass themselves of their booty and run away. The Commissioner of Police arranged for them to be marched up under the guard of the sepoys to the police station at Qaimpur.

While all this was being put in train, some of us went on ahead to the townlet. On reaching the outskirts, we saw several people slipping out of the nearby houses and courtyards and running away—some of them dropping in their hurry the loot that they were carrying. I ran up a road after two of them, but the chase was hopeless and, after going about fifty yards, I had slackened pace, when a youth with a basket scooted out of a courtyard just ahead of me and made off up the road. I quickly overtook him and pounced upon him with great glee, quite delighted at my capture. I was, however, soon disappointed. The basket contained only some pots and pans and trumpery trinkets of little value and it was apparent that the lad was just a 'picker-up of unconsidered trifles' which others had left. An old man, who had also been scavenging in the wake of the main pillagers, now appeared and begged for mercy for his son. For the time being we put them both under arrest and took them with us to the police station. Later on we released them.

The police station was a ramshackle sort of building at the western edge of Qaimpur. Gurmani, whose weight and bulk unfitted him for our light-hearted diversions, had got there ahead of us in one of the cars which had found a way round the mud at the bridge. Near the police station there was a spacious mud-walled shed standing in an open compound and in this practically the whole Hindu population seemed to be crowded in a woeful condition of panic and lamentation. We learnt from the thanedar, who was remarkably cool and collected, that the town had been attacked early that morning by hordes of Muslims from the surrounding villages, and had been pretty thoroughly looted. We had just come in for the tail-end of the operation. Most of the looters had already left, laden with spoil, though there were still a few stragglers about. Since with his small force—most of the police rifles being as usual unserviceable—it had been impossible to ward off the attack, he had concentrated on saving the lives of the Hindus and, with the help of some Muslims of the place, had collected them in the large shed near the police station which had been placed at his disposal by its Muslim owner and became known to us as the 'Compound of Abdullah Shah'. He thought that he had been successful in saving most of them and that only one or two had been killed;[1] but their shops and houses had, no doubt, been broken into and plundered.

While we were still talking to him, there were loud shouts from close by. Some of our party had flushed several more

[1] The real number was seven.

looters who were to be seen making off as fast as they could across the fields. They were already 100–150 yards away, so there was no chance of catching them; but someone told two of the sepoys to open fire on them, whereupon they let off a number of rounds at quite a rapid rate, but without making the slightest attempt to take proper aim. This I soon found to be common form with the Bahawalpur troops, and on a later occasion some of them proudly claimed to have fired 657 rounds at a gang of Pathans without scoring a single hit, and expected me to applaud the performance. However, at this stage my knowledge of the Bahawalpur State Forces was derived mainly from hearsay rather than experience.

I was to learn a good deal more about them in the next few weeks.

The sepoys' futile fusillade was still in progress when there were more shouts from somewhere behind the police station and two more men were to be seen at no very great distance running away to the north. On the spur of the moment I dashed off in pursuit, followed by the Commissioner of Police (who must have been well over fifty), some constables and various others. Helter-skelter we went through the crops, scrambling over low mud walls, jumping watercourses and, I think, thoroughly enjoying ourselves, but without, perhaps, any very clear idea who we were pursuing and why. Our quarry at first ran straight on northwards as though they intended to leave Qaimpur altogether and were making for some village of their own elsewhere; but after a few hundred yards they bore round to the right in a semicircle parallel to the line of the town. I was steadily overhauling them when they turned sharply to the right down a track which crossed our path and led back into the town. I was afraid that in the maze of buildings I would lose them, but one of the constables behind had seen or anticipated their right turn and cut across to intercept them. Just where the track led into the town he suddenly appeared barring the way. One of them turned up an alley to the left and hid in a building where he was subsequently caught. The other, about fifteen yards ahead of me, ran full tilt into the arms of the constable. At exactly the same moment the Commissioner of Police from close behind me suddenly and for no ascertainable reason let off his revolver with a very loud bang—which surprised and startled me not a little. I never discovered what he was firing at or whether it was simply a *feu de joie*. Anyway, it made a very fitting end to the chase—like the huntsman blowing his horn over the kill.

It was past noon and, having stopped running, we at once became overwhelmingly conscious of the intense heat. We were all simply bathed in perspiration. As we sat panting and mopping our brows, we were opportunely relieved by a torrential shower of rain which, in a few seconds, drenched us to the skin but cooled us down. The rain fell so heavily for about ten minutes that it was with some difficulty that we picked our way with our two prisoners through the puddles and pools and slippery lanes of the town back to the police station.

The other prisoners, captured earlier near the bridge, had already arrived and were packed pretty tightly in the small police station lock-up. Gurmani was most indignant, indeed quite outraged, at the insolence of the villagers in attacking and looting Qaimpur, and loudly demanded that those we had caught should there and then, before any trial or investigation, be given a 'shoe-beating'—without prejudice, of course, to anything further that might be done to them later on. He was particularly insistent that the beating should be with shoes, presumably because this is attended as much with indignity as pain. I ought to have advised against such proceedings, for though it was appropriate and customary for a thanedar to give suspects a shoe-beating, it was hardly seemly for the Prime Minister and other high officers of the State to direct and supervise such operations. However, I kept silent and a batch of about ten of our prisoners were taken out of the lock-up and made to lie down prone in a line in the courtyard of the police station. A couple of constables then walked up and down the line whacking them in turn on the bottom with a shoe. Though they yowled and wriggled as if in great pain, the beating was really of a somewhat token character and could not, I thought, have any effect on these hardy yokels. If they were to be beaten at all, I should have liked it to be done much harder. Gurmani later on assured me that the moral effect of the indignity of a shoe-beating is very great, but I remained sceptical.

The Commissioner of Police very rightly disapproved of these proceedings and, not liking to speak to the Prime Minister himself, drew me aside, pointed out that they were not at all proper and urged me to request the Prime Minister to desist. I readily agreed, though I couldn't help wondering whether our steeplechase round the town, in which the Commissioner himself had taken such a lively part, had been altogether in order! Gurmani took the point as soon as I spoke to him. He announced tactfully that it was time for us to be getting along and directed that the men who were being shoe-beaten should be put back into the lock-up for the thanedar to deal with further at his leisure.

It was indeed high time for us to move, as we were still many miles from Bahawalnagar and the two new 'colony' towns of Hasilpur and Chishtian, which we would have to visit, lay ahead of us. The diversions to Khairpur and Qaimpur had been quite unexpected and had put us several hours behind our schedule.

The Qaimpur thanedar did not apprehend any further attack on the place as he thought the villagers had had their fill. He was rather anxious to get the Hindus off his hands and back into their own houses; but most of them were still so tearful and panic-stricken that we advised him not to press them to return just yet, but to let them remain on, as they wished, in the compound of Abdullah Shah under his immediate protection. We left with him two sepoys from our escort and said we would send him some more very soon.

It must be confessed that, as we journeyed on, Gurmani and I were in a mood of complacent self-congratulation. True, what we had seen and heard at Khairpur and Qaimpur was evidence of widespread lawlessness, but there had been few casualties—the number killed at Qaimpur was utterly insignificant compared to what we knew was going on in the East and West Punjab—and the prompt arrival on the spot of the highest officers of the State and our arrest at Qaimpur of a number of miscreants would, we flattered ourselves, have a very sobering effect. Moreover, more than half the State, from Bahawalpur south-west to the Sind border, was as yet absolutely tranquil and undisturbed. The trouble in the eastern part had only just begun and by vigorous action we should be able to nip the whole thing in the bud and show the Punjab, already the scene of a hideous holocaust, how to manage things! There were many advantages, we told ourselves, in a relatively small unit, such as Bahawalpur, in which it was possible for the members of the Government to get a direct personal grip of the whole situation.

Such were the consoling but deceptive thoughts that we exchanged as we drove on towards Hasilpur.

Our route required us to turn off from the Bahawal Canal some miles beyond Qaimpur and to travel for a little distance along a link road leading to the tail-end of the Fordwah Canal a few miles to the south. Once on this canal we could drive along it all the way to Bahawalnagar and beyond, if need be, to the headworks at Suleimanke at the extreme north-eastern corner of the State. This link road, which was maintained by the Irrigation Department, was of great administrative importance—and vital in the next few weeks—as it enabled one to go right from Bahawalpur city to the Bikanir border by canal bank—the only practicable way of covering the distance by car. These canal bank roads were kept for use by government officers and were not open to the general public or designed to carry heavy traffic.

The colony town of Hasilpur stands more or less at the edge of the desert near the tail of the Fordwah Canal. In the early days it had not prospered—indeed there was at one time an idea of abandoning it altogether—but in the last few years, with the agricultural prosperity and extension of cultivation brought by the war, it had come to life again. Excellent prices had been fetched for town sites at recent auctions and there was a demand for more. Altogether it was reckoned to be a growing and flourishing little market town with a bright future. It was, however, very far from being attractive in appearance. No trees or other vegetation had yet grown up; gaunt brick buildings rose starkly from the desert waste. The whole place was strewn with greyish sand and nasty heaps of sand lay scattered about even in the mandi[1] itself which had not yet been fully levelled and surfaced. In summer the burning heat was intense —I had stayed there myself in June—and there was not a scrap of shade. It says much for the hardiness and tenacity of the Hindu merchants of the Punjab that they were ready to settle down in these harsh surroundings and put their money into go-downs, shops and houses. They were now on the point of losing their whole investment.

[1] Market-place and hence used also of a town containing a market-place.

Being a colony town, Hasilpur was the headquarters of a number of revenue and colony officials, including two naib-tahsildars. There was also a police station with a sub-inspector in charge. We drove into the main bazaar, fully expecting some of these functionaries to be waiting to meet us. But there was not a soul to be seen. The bazaar was silent and deserted. We drove into the mandi and then out again and round the outside of the town, and at last we found someone who told us that the thanedar and all the Hindus had gone away to 'old' Hasilpur —a village lying about two miles to the north of the new town. I think neither of us had ever heard of its existence. We were shown the general direction in which it lay and were soon bumping along a sandy, sunken and twisty lane that was said to lead to it. I thought we were never going to reach it; and then, almost unexpectedly, we suddenly came upon it—a small but ancient village, rising up on a slight eminence, but concealed from view by big clumps of tall-growing reeds. Along its curving western side there was a belt, fifty to one hundred yards wide, of open sandy ground between the houses and the cultivated fields. Our road took us along this western side with the sandy belt on our left. As we drove along, I thought I saw well ahead of us some heaps of manure scattered about on this stretch of sand and nearer, though about seventy yards off and close to the edge of the fields, a couple of men seemed to be lying on the ground. I glanced towards Gurmani, murmuring, 'Why are those men lying over there?' and saw on his face a look of incredulous horror as he gazed out of the window of the car.

'They're corpses,' I exclaimed, answering my own question; and now, to my amazement, the heaps of manure took shape as heaps of human bodies. In twos and threes and sixes and tens, more and more came into view as we rounded the curve of the village, till at the north-western corner, close to the main entrance leading up into it, they lay 'Thick as autumnal leaves that strew the vale of Vallambrosa'. Men, women and children, there they were all jumbled up together, their arms and legs akimbo in all sorts of attitudes and postures, some of them so life-like that one could hardly believe that they were really dead. I was forcibly reminded of pictures that I had seen as a child of Napoleonic battlefields; and there was perhaps some reason for this in that all these people had in fact been shot down by rifle fire.

We got out of the car and walked slowly up into the village, too stunned to speak. We had heard reports of trouble at Bahawalnagar and Chishtian, but not a rumour of disturbances at Hasilpur, still less of such a massacre as this. It came, to me at least, as a staggering shock, sweeping away entirely, and for many days to come, the light-hearted and almost frivolous mood of the morning.

Near the top of the village, in a large two-storied building, we found the thanedar and a throng of women and children whose sobbing and whimpering swelled to a deafening crescendo of mingled grief and resentment as soon as they caught sight of us. It was hard to endure. In an open space outside there lay two or three wounded men under an ill-contrived awning of tattered sacking. One of them, almost stark naked, was literally covered with blood and an old woman was pathetically fanning his face and trying to keep the flies off him. We could do nothing to help.

Someone had noticed Brigadier Marden's car standing outside the village when we arrived, so we knew that he must be somewhere about the place. We were inquiring where he was when he himself appeared, dressed in uniform and carrying a tommy-gun. I did not at all like this last feature for in my opinion there was no reason for the commander of the troops to go about with anything more than a revolver. We commented on the hideous slaughter which Marden told us had only occurred that morning. He then said that at Bahawalnagar, from where he had just come, there had also been grave disturbances and heavy casualties. With a very serious face, he drew Gurmani aside and said he wanted to speak to him alone. I guessed at once what he was going to say and my guess was almost immediately confirmed for, in a few moments, Gurmani called me to where they were standing and said, 'Marden says the troops are unreliable.' This was a meiosis.

We did not stay very long at Hasilpur and I do not recall what, if anything, we did; I don't think anything useful. We were too dumbfounded. I tried cursorily to count the corpses as we left the village, but lost count at well over one hundred.[1] I was puzzled as to how such a terrific slaughter could have taken place, but I made no inquiries about it at this time—in fact I hardly spoke to the thanedar, though he was quite well known to me. Normally a bright, smart, cheerful little man, he was now subdued and seemingly overwhelmed by the disaster. Some days later, however, I did make inquiries and it will be convenient to set down at this point the outline of the story that was told to me subsequently. I cannot vouch for its accuracy as I never had leisure to probe into the matter deeply.

It appears that the thanedar suspected, or perhaps was warned, that the town of Hasilpur was going to be attacked. He decided that it would be impossible for him to defend the place and that his best course was to collect all the non-Muslim population in the small, compact and more easily defensible village of old Hasilpur. An additional reason for this course was that the police station was still located in the village. There were plans for a new one in the town, but it had not yet been constructed and only a makeshift office was maintained there. So the Hindus were evacuated from the town to the village. In due course, as at Khairpur and Qaimpur, bands of Muslim peasants began to gather round the place from all directions. The thanedar would have liked to parley with them and try to persuade them to go away; but among the population evacuated from the town was a fiery Sikh, armed with a rifle, who could not be restrained. Planting himself on the roof of a house, he opened fire on the marauders with considerable effect, killing or wounding several of them and dispersing the rest. Among those killed was one of their principal leaders, a well-known and popular badmash[2] of the locality.

The bands of rustics, though they may have had with them a few muzzle-loaders, were mostly armed only with lathis. They were not people of great courage or ferocity and, after meeting such a reception, they would probably not have dared to return by themselves and renew the attack. They were, however, much incensed at the loss of their leader and cast about for reinforcements. It so happened that there were encamped at the edge of the desert not far away a body of Pathans from the

---

[1] The actual number of Hindus and Sikhs killed at this place was about 350. A few Muslims, probably about six to twelve, were also killed.

[2] Bad character.

North-West Frontier. It was the regular custom for gangs of Pathans to come down into the Punjab, generally in the cold weather, to work on the roads and canals, returning after a few months to their own country with their earnings. They nearly always had with them unlicensed firearms which they kept concealed in bushes or buried in the earth somewhere near their camping-places. This gang near Hasilpur, who were either doing or expecting to do some work for the Irrigation Department, possessed several ·303 rifles. Their assistance was now invoked and was not refused. Pulling their weapons out of their hiding-places, the Pathans accompanied the peasants back to the village and, catching the people there unawares, mowed them down with rifle fire with the results already described.

This terrible incident at Hasilpur made us very anxious during the next few weeks to remove and keep away from the State all gangs of wandering Pathans.

We drove gloomily on to Chishtian—an important and well-established 'mandi' town—fearful of what we might find there. Several reports of disturbances had reached us, but Marden, who had passed the place in the morning, was comparatively reassuring. He proved correct. There had been a good deal of looting in the town and all the shops were shut, but the police, magistrates and revenue officials of the place seemed to be in quite good heart and assured us that their casualties had been few. Though they somewhat understated to us the numbers, subsequent inquiries showed that these did not in fact exceed a dozen. Compared with Hasilpur, Chishtian had got off very lightly.

I was rather pleased to notice among the crowd that met us a young Hindu tahsildar, named Gobind Baksh. He was employed on settlement work, and I had formed a high opinion of his ability. Somehow I had expected that, being a Hindu, he would be lying low at this time, as most of the Hindu officials were, but on the contrary he was well to the fore, seemed to be very little upset at what had taken place and not in the least alarmed for his own safety. He was wearing a fez—the common head-dress of urban Muslims in Bahawalpur[1]—which might be

---

[1] It was also the official head-dress in the State and I had to wear one when visiting the palace, and on ceremonial occasions. Many Hindus took to wearing a fez during those troubled times.

E*

supposed to offer him some protection. I was to learn later that he had more solid grounds for confidence.

We were still nearly thirty miles from Bahawalnagar and the day was drawing in. We did not therefore stay long at Chishtian but hurried on, reaching Bahawalnagar just after dark. We had been expected in the early afternoon and so were many hours late. There was a large group of officers awaiting us at the canal rest-house, morose and depressed.

Gurmani and I had settled in advance that immediately on arrival we would separately interview the principal officers one by one, and then meet together for dinner and compare notes. Dismissing therefore all but a few of the senior officers we sat down in different parts of the rest-house garden to hear what they had to say. I naturally gave most time to the Super-intendent of Police and the Sub-Divisional Magistrate. The latter was in a very excited state, stuttering and spluttering so as to be almost incoherent. He was bitterly indignant with the military who, he said, had, without authority, forcibly inter-fered, yet had done nothing to stop the rioting in the town. He had been brushed aside by these armed men who had even threatened him! I sympathized with him and tried to calm him down. He had spent most of his service as a judge and had no experience of riots. He had done his best but clearly had been ineffective; and I did not blame him, for even Leghari, the Superintendent of Police, a much more weighty and experi-enced man, had not been able to make head against the mili-tary.

Leghari was not very communicative, but I was able to obtain from him a rather better idea of what had actually taken place. He was a large, solid man and quite calm, but, like the magistrate, indignant with the military and very depressed. He told me that since August 22nd there had been unrest and excitement in the town, caused by the arrival of refugees from India with alarming tales of atrocities; but there was at first no outbreak of violence. He suspected some undesirable elements among the staff at the railway station of fomenting trouble, but he had nothing definite against them on which he could take action. On August 25th a train had arrived at about 1.0 p.m. crammed with refugees, some of them badly wounded. Large numbers of Muslims from the town, tipped off, he thought, by the railway staff, had come up to the station to meet this train. When the wounded, some of them women, alighted from it, displaying torn limbs and lacerated breasts, the crowd at the station got worked up into a frenzy and with one accord rushed madly from the station into the town and began murdering the Hindus and looting their shops. Leghari with his small force of police tried to restore order, but meantime the military appeared on the scene and, he said, 'They wouldn't let us do anything.' He repeated this phrase several times. I asked what the military had themselves done. 'Well,' he replied laconically with a grim but rather attractive smile, 'they didn't stop the rioting.'

I then inquired about the casualties. He would not commit himself to any precise figure; there were still, he said, a lot of corpses which had not been picked up; but he thought that the number killed must run to several hundred.[1] I asked how many of these were Muslims, this being, of course, a point of vital significance; for since it was the Muslims who were murdering and looting, the armed forces, if they had seriously attempted to restore order, must have shot a few of them. Leghari thought that only one or two Muslims had been killed. This was what I had expected, but it was really quite ridiculous. Marden alone with his tommy-gun could surely have done better! Riotous mobs provide quite easy targets. I felt more than ever that his parading about with a tommy-gun was not the most helpful gesture in the circumstances.

This was my feeling at the time. But on later reflection it occurred to me that if Marden had used his weapon effectively against the rioters, his own troops, in the existing state of religious and political hysteria, would probably have turned upon him and killed him; and to get killed was not really helpful. Marden, like others, was in a very difficult position, and things were perhaps not so simple and straightforward as they appeared to me then.

It need hardly be said that the military officers were on their part very indignant with the civil officials, especially the Sub-Divisional Magistrate, who, they alleged, would never give any order. There may well have been some truth in this.

After my talk with Leghari the general situation was fairly clear to me. The better part of a battalion of State Forces was

[1] The numbers, as finally ascertained, were 409 Hindus and one Muslim.

encamped at Bahawalnagar; there had been ample armed forces on the spot to control a town three or four times its size. But the civil authorities had been unable to control the military and the military officers had been unable or unwilling to control their own men or direct them to any useful ends; indeed the implication was that the military had themselves become wolves and descended on the fold of helpless Hindu sheep. My worst fears and suspicions were confirmed.

Before joining Gurmani for dinner, I had a few words with the Commissioner of Police. He too had been talking to the various local officials, and I was anxious to get his estimate of the situation. I knew him to be a brilliant officer. He had risen from the rank of sub-inspector and had far more experience of quelling disorders than any of the rest of us. I set great store by his advice. I found him disappointingly negative and very pessimistic. He said that the situation was quite unparalleled in his experience. The military were out of hand and the police were negligible. He had not been used to this in the Punjab and felt quite at sea. He bewailed the miserable inadequacy of the police in personnel, training, equipment and everything. He told me—as he had told me some months before—that he would never have come to Bahawalpur as Commissioner of Police if he had realized the shocking state of the police force. He thought we *might* be able to restore law and order, but appeared quite doubtful about this and somehow implied that I should have to see about it and that it would not be his concern. Altogether he had little constructive to offer; but he did say one very valuable and encouraging thing. After deploring the inefficiency[1] of the Bahawalpur police, he said, 'But I think Leghari is a good man. You can rely on him.' He was right.

It was nearly 10.0 p.m. when Gurmani and I sat down to dinner on the chabutra[2] outside the rest-house. After we had compared notes and agreed that the civil administration had broken down and that the military were out of hand, he asked me what I thought should be done. I said that I could only offer one suggestion, and didn't know if he would like it, and that was that I should be given powers of District Magistrate

---

[1] I would by no means wholly endorse his condemnation of them, though, of course, they were not up to Punjab standards.

[2] Raised platform or dais (to avoid snakes, etc.).

and should try to restore order. He replied that he was just going to request me to undertake this and that he would give me not only powers of District Magistrate but full powers of Government over the whole of the eastern half of the State, i.e. the Bahawalpur district. He, for his part, would go back to Bahawalpur and endeavour to preserve peace in the rest of the State which was, as yet, unaffected.

I said that powers of Government were not really necessary and that powers of District Magistrate would suffice. It was however essential that the military should be made clearly to understand that, acting as they supposedly were in aid of the civil power, they had to take directions from the magistracy; and this, if I took over the functions of District Magistrate, would ordinarily mean from me. They couldn't just go about doing as they liked, brushing aside magistrates and police, as they had in the past few days. They should, indeed, keep away from the public altogether and confine themselves to their own military exercises, unless a magistrate asked for their assistance and assigned to them some specific task in the maintenance of order. In carrying out that task, once assigned to them, they were their own masters; but it was not for them to intervene, until a magistrate called upon them. These were the principles embodied in the Code of Criminal Procedure, which was in force in the State, and if the military officers didn't know them, they must be made aware of them now. In the past they had not been accustomed to taking orders from anybody except the Nawab, but in the past they had probably not been called upon to quell civil disturbances. Now that they were acting in aid of the civil power, they would have to take orders from the District Magistrate.

I requested Gurmani to impress all this on the military officers; they were not likely to take it from anyone but him. If they were brought under control and duly accepted the position assigned to them by law, then I was reasonably confident, with the powers of District Magistrate, of restoring order in the affected area; but otherwise there was likely to be worse havoc.

Gurmani promised that the very next morning he would give the military officers a most serious talking to. After he had done so, he would return to Bahawalpur and leave me alone to get on with the job. He would concentrate his own energies on preventing trouble spreading to the other parts of the State. He insisted that I should have full powers of Government as well as of District Magistrate in the Bahawalpur district. Though these proved useful, enabling me to make appointments and do many other things quickly, I think I would have been better without them. I did not, however, refuse them.

Having reached these decisions, we went to bed.

IX

Restoring Order—I

T HE next morning Gurmani faithfully fulfilled his promise to speak to the military officers. I lay a good deal
of stress on this, not only because for the ending of bloodshed and the restoration of order in the eastern part of the State
it was of decisive importance, but also because it affords a
refutation of allegations, made later by many Hindus, that
Gurmani had engineered the attacks on them and 'conspired'
to drive them from the State. These base calumnies had no
foundation, except that Gurmani was a Muslim and a member
of the Muslim League; yet, once set going, they were readily
accepted and repeated as gospel truth. The facts are that Gurmani, with considerable moral courage, exerted himself to the
utmost to protect the Hindus. In the prevailing temper he, as a
Muslim, could have remained indifferent and allowed things
to go their own way without injury, and even with credit, to his
own reputation. Taking much pains to save Hindus was not
popular. But Gurmani did not adopt the easy course. He showed
throughout a determination to maintain in Bahawalpur the
standards of a civilized government. Though he may have made
some errors of judgement, as we all did during these times, he
remained steadfastly loyal to the oath of office, which we had
both taken and which he had himself prescribed, requiring us to
treat with impartial fairness every class, creed and individual
in the Nawab's dominions. At this critical moment the curbing
of the licence of the military was the biggest service he could
render to the non-Muslim sections of the Nawab's subjects.

India's past history afforded many examples of the miseries
inflicted by armed men when freed from the shackles of discipline and let loose among an unarmed population. Less than
a hundred and fifty years earlier, the Pindaris—broken remnants
of Mogul and Mahratta armies—had been roaming at large
through central India, pillaging and terrorizing peaceful village

143

folk, and it had required elaborate military operations (ending in a regular war) to put a stop to their depredations. Later, though on a smaller scale, the chronic indiscipline of the troops of the Nawab of Oudh had been a reason for the annexation of that State. Similarly the excesses of Sikh soldiery in the Punjab, immediately after the death of Ranjit Singh, had been partly responsible for the eventual intervention of the British in that province. It had been the claim of the British Raj to have rescued India in the past from this type of anarchy; now in northern India we seemed to be on the brink of sinking into it once again. Past history was coming alive before my very eyes. There were already appalling tales afloat of the atrocities perpetrated by the Sikh troops of Patiala. Would the Pathan troops in the Bahawalpur Army be any milder? They had clearly shaken off the shackles of discipline and had wrought serious havoc in Bahawalnagar. How much further would they go? And how could we restrain them?

Gurmani and I had no physical force at our immediate disposal to set against them and no force which we could quickly summon to our aid from elsewhere. Under the British regime the troops of a Native State, if they got a little out of hand, could be instantly overawed by the Government of India. But the British regime had ended and, so far as we were concerned, the Government of India was now a foreign government. The successor government for us was the Government of Pakistan, and this had had only twelve days of existence and its very survival seemed far from certain. Amid enormous difficulties, it was trying to establish itself in Karachi; its hands were full with the troubles in the Punjab, and at this juncture it had no time to give any thought to Bahawalpur—in fact, its relations with us were still of the haziest character.[1] We stood therefore alone and had to do the best we could unaided. Somehow we had to gain a moral ascendancy over the Bahawalpur Army so that, even in these abnormal times, they would respect us as the lawful Government of the day from whom it was natural and right that they should take orders. There was every temptation for them to do otherwise. All around the usual moral sanctions were breaking down and the Nawab, away in England, was not present to reinforce them. Gurmani and I were newcomers

[1] Bahawalpur State did not formally accede to Pakistan till October 3rd.

to the State. In the adjoining Punjab, ordered government seemed on the verge of collapse.

Gurmani's talk to the military officers was, therefore, of crucial significance. I do not know exactly what he said to them, but he talked to them for a long time and, to judge by results, with considerable effect. Reluctantly, and with some grumblings amongst themselves both against Gurmani and me, they came to heel. There were to be one or two more bad incidents, which probably the officers could not prevent, but on the whole this battalion of the State Forces took no further party in harrying and pillaging the non-Muslim population and co-operated with me steadily, though not enthusiastically, in measures for their protection. The battalion commander came to see me during the day and told me that Gurmani had impressed on them that they must carry out my instructions. He assured me that they would do as the Prime Minister had ordered. He hoped, however, that I would not make any unreasonable demands upon the troops. I said that I did not expect to have to press them very hard and hoped to use the police for most duties, only calling upon the military when absolutely necessary. I would in any case consult him and take him into my confidence regarding any tasks which I might wish to entrust to his men.

The battalion commander was true to his word, though the duty of safeguarding the lives and property of Hindus and Sikhs can hardly have been congenial to him. Across the border in East Punjab Muslims were being mercilessly slaughtered. What easier than to take revenge on the innocent Hindus and Sikhs in Bahawalpur? While the ordinary Muslim may have had no desire actually to kill them, he was naturally inclined to handle them roughly or at best to look with indifference at their sufferings. This was the general feeling, and the particular circumstances of the battalion commander were not favourable to his rising above it. For his home was in the East Punjab; several of his relatives had already been murdered there; others, including his parents, were in grievous danger. Though in his talks with me he to a great extent suppressed his feelings, anger and anxiety were dominant. To co-operate, therefore, in the effective protection of the Hindus in the State required of him a strong effort of will. This effort, not without difficulty, he made. He was a steady, competent officer, of somewhat phlegmatic temperament, and this was an advantage to him. Many of the Hindus of Bahawalnagar did not bear their misfortunes with much fortitude, and certainly not in silence. The noisy importunity with which they assailed those in authority was often very trying to the nerves and must have been particularly harassing to the battalion commander. He bore it with remarkably little irritation until Leghari and I were able to deflect it all on to ourselves. I am glad to say that a little later it was found possible to let him have a couple of military lorries with which he succeeded in rescuing from his home in East Punjab many of his relations and belongings.

While Gurmani was talking to the military officers, I went down to the town with Leghari. Our activities there were of a very prosaic nature, but it is perhaps worth giving a brief account of them as they were typical of what, with minor variations, we had to do in place after place and of what, no doubt, many others had to do all over the Punjab.

The first thing was to ensure the protection of the surviving Hindus. A large number of them were congregated in some big buildings belonging to a wealthy Muslim, who out of pure goodness of heart had given shelter to as many of them as he could. His co-religionists had so much respect for him that they had no inclination to molest those to whom he had given sanctuary. These, however, huddled together like roosting hens, were still in a miserable state of panic and begged me to evacuate them to India as quickly as possible. This I promised to do. Meanwhile I felt quite confident that they would be safe in the care of their benevolent protector.

Other Hindus we gathered together in defined areas which could easily be guarded. Leghari arranged for police guards and the military were withdrawn. I authorized him straight away to appoint special police constables, since the duties falling upon the police were far greater than the existing strength could cope with and we both wished to make the minimum calls upon the military.

A considerable number of injured Hindus had been admitted to the local hospital during the previous two days. The Muslim doctor in charge, who earlier had had to tend the wounded Muslims arriving from India, scarcely concealed his delight at the injuries to so many of the opposite community and openly

remarked that the sight had eased his mind. Though there was
no complaint that he had positively neglected his Hindu
patients, Leghari suggested that I should speak to him so as to
make sure that he was kept up to the mark. I did so as tactfully
as I could. He told me that he and his Muslim staff, whatever
their feelings might be, were attending to all alike without the
slightest discrimination. Despite his inward satisfaction at the
sufferings of the Hindus I do not think there was any serious
ground to complain of his treatment of them. If there were any
shortcomings, they were certainly nothing compared to what
was happening in a not so very distant district of East Punjab.
There the Hindu civil surgeon refused to admit injured Muslims
into the hospital and a number of them were left lying uncared
for in the road. When compelled at last by an officer of another
department to take them in, he deliberately neglected them and
they all died.

The town of Bahawalnagar was in an indescribable mess.
Many of the shops and houses had been ransacked and their
less valuable contents thrown indiscriminately into the streets
so that, apart from corpses, the whole place was littered with
broken furniture, paper, burst sacks of grain, broken glass,
garbage and rubbish of all kinds. The ordinary municipal services had entirely ceased to function and had to be started
again. Many of the subordinate staff were either gorged with
loot or stricken with fear. With some difficulty they were collected and, under a combination of threats and promises, they
proceeded to clean up the town at a fairly good speed.

Casualties among the Hindus and the herding together of the
rest in places of refuge had left many houses and shops deserted.
Some of the revenue and colony staff were turned on to locking,
numbering and registering these empty buildings and listing
their contents, if any. Already at this stage we foresaw that we
should soon be requiring them for allotment to incoming Muslim
refugees. I gave some general directions for framing proposals
for the assessment of their rent.

Another section of the revenue staff were deputed to the
market-place to secure and list the bags of grain that had not
been carried off by the looters. I attached great importance to
laying hands on as much grain as possible as I surmised that in a
few days' time we might have thousands of people to feed.

All this occupied me for the best part of the day.

Gurmani departed for Bahawalpur immediately after lunch, taking with him Marden and the Commissioner of Police. The ex-officer of the State Forces, who had joined the I.N.A., stayed behind for a few days. I think Gurmani's idea was that he would help to steady the troops. I had a long chat with him that evening. Although a Muslim, he had a liking for whisky and was prepared to consume it in considerable quantities. In an expansive moment he confided to me that he had been driven to join the I.N.A. simply by his craving for alcohol. I do not know whether this was really so, or was said to soften my judgement of his past conduct. But whatever may have been his conduct in the past, he was friendly and helpful now. He took a dim view of the behaviour of the Bahawalpur troops and, as a former officer of the State Army, was quite frank in his criticisms. He assured me, however, that Gurmani's talk to the officers had made a great impression on them, and that they would certainly now obey my orders. He also promised to assist me if I had any trouble with them.

There were quite a number of Hindu officials at Bahawalnagar in the Irrigation and Revenue Departments and I had to give up a good deal of time to their personal problems. I interviewed them—and many other people—during the afternoon and evening. Those in any sort of executive position—and these included two tahsildars and one executive engineer—were, through no fault of their own, wholly unable to carry on their duties; for they had lost all authority with their subordinates and with the public and could only move about under escort. The rest, who were mainly employed in clerical posts, were for the most part in such a state of trepidation as to be unfit for any sustained work. Thus, in effect, the whole Hindu staff in this area had to be written off and arrangements made to replace them. I told them not to worry about their official duties, but to take two weeks' leave and look after themselves and their families and that in the next few days I would try to send them under escort wherever they wanted to go. Many of them had their homes in the town of Bahawalpur and wished to get back there, but were justifiably afraid of travelling by train, alone and unguarded.

There was a marked contrast in the conduct of the two

tahsildars. The regular revenue tahsildar, in charge of the tahsil at Bahawalnagar, was a small but efficient little man. Though worried, he remained calm. He frankly admitted that he had become completely ineffective and was much relieved when I told him to take some leave and hand over to his assistant. Thereafter he never bothered me at all, though as an official of some consequence in the Revenue Department he was certainly entitled to special consideration from me.

The other tahsildar was engaged in settlement work and was very highly spoken of by the Settlement Officer, Nur Mohammad. Undoubtedly he was an able man, but the disorders in Bahawalnagar had quite unnerved him and reduced him to a quivering, but ubiquitous jelly. On the very evening of our arrival he approached me with a moan about his personal safety. Early the next morning, as I was setting out for the town, he turned up again with loud and voluble lament. He wanted to go back to Bahawalpur, to which I said there would be no objection, and I gave him a time to see me in the afternoon. In spite of this he kept on popping up during the morning with sobs and tears and uncontrolled importunity until at last I told him, as though he were a small child, that unless he went away, pulled himself together and stopped crying, I would not give him an interview at all. In the afternoon he came to see me in a quietened mood, looking like a fat and melancholy seal. All he wanted was an armed escort to take him back by train to Bahawalpur. This is what many other Hindu officials wanted and asked for in a decent and orderly manner. It was a reasonable request. But, of course, escorts could not ordinarily be provided for single individuals; a whole party had to be arranged and this necessarily took a little time. However, in a day or two an armed escort for a party of Hindus wishing to go to Bahawalpur was duly organized. He then refused to go! On the evening of the day on which he should have left and when I thought I was rid of him he turned up again, saying that he thought the escort might be unreliable and it was safer for him to remain in Bahawalnagar. I was so disgusted with him that I promptly suspended him for cowardice and left him to shift for himself.[1]

---

[1] Some time afterwards, at the request of Nur Mohammad, I reinstated him so as to enable him to draw his leave salary and he was evacuated to India along with other Hindus. It is perhaps of interest to record that

Besides the Hindu officials with their personal problems, there were many Muslim officials to be attended to. The officials of the Irrigation Department were in difficulty because heavy rains had breached several of the canal bank roads, severing *inter alia* our communications to the south with Harunabad, and labour gangs, on the plea of danger, were not forthcoming to repair them. The military had to be asked to provide escorts. Revenue officials reported that all the Sikh chaks, of which there were quite a number in this area, had been deserted. In the past few days the Sikh colonists, though for the most part quite unmolested, had gone across the border to Bikanir taking with them all that they could carry. But some stocks of grain and cattle had been left behind. What was to be done about them?

One of my most important visitors during the latter part of the day was the local thanedar. Under the guidance of Leghari, he had shown a good deal of initiative during the morning in shepherding the Hindus to convenient places of refuge and setting guards over them. He now told me that quite a lot of villagers from the neighbouring villages had taken part in the sack of Bahawalnagar and that, if he was given transport so that he could get to these villages quickly and carry out searches, he was sure that he could recover much stolen property and make a number of arrests. Other people would then voluntarily come forward and surrender part, at least, of their loot. I warmly welcomed the proposal and arrangements were made accordingly. I told the thanedar to arrest as many as he could and that I would try them summarily.

We had devoted the whole day (August 27th) to Bahawalnagar and it was urgently necessary for us to move around to other places which might be attacked at any moment and where the local authorities, unless stiffened physically and morally, would put up no effective resistance. So far as we knew, the wealthy colony town of Harunabad and the smaller town of Fort Abbas farther south were still intact. About Minchinabad, twenty-five miles away to the east—the abode of some very rich Hindus—and about Macleodganj Road, right on the

later, when I was in India, I was able to give both him and the other tahsildar good appointments in the newly-formed State of Himachal Pradesh, where they both did well.

frontier, there were conflicting stories. Some said that they had
both been looted; others that they were safe. Chishtian, though
already partially plundered, still had plenty to attract looters and
might be attacked again. The Hindus at Khairpur and Qaimpur were in danger and there were other Hindus scattered
about in villages whose position was even more precarious.
All these places claimed our immediate attention. But we could
not immediately reach them. Heavy rain had made all roads
impassable a few miles from Bahawalnagar. To travel by rail
was impracticable, unless we could arrange a special, as the
regular services were so infrequent that we should get marooned
at one place for a day and a night. A special could not be made
available till the 29th, so we had to spend another whole day
at Bahawalnagar. Though there was plenty to do there, the
delay was unfortunate.

During the next ten days Leghari and I spent most of the
hours of daylight touring up and down the eastern and most
disturbed part of the State. For the first three days we travelled
by special train; afterwards, when the roads had been reopened, we went by car. Everywhere we had to do more or less
the same, and so, before passing to any detailed account of
individual scenes and incidents, I will give a general description of our tasks and of our daily routine and also of the main
themes of our thoughts during these days.

Our principal tasks were:

  (i)   the collection and protection of the Hindus and the
        evacuation of those who wished to go to India,
 (ii)   the custody of their property, or whatever remained of
        it,
(iii)   the recovery of stolen property and abducted women
        and the arrest of as many offenders as possible,
 (iv)   the collection and safeguarding of stocks of grain,
and
  (v)   —more and more as the days passed—the feeding and
        settlement of incoming Muslim refugees.

Besides this, along all the length of the frontier with Bikanir
and to a depth of five to fifteen miles we had to devote much
time to calming and reassuring the Muslim inhabitants who
were, or professed to be, in mortal terror of attacks by Sikhs

from across the border. They seemed to think that an international frontier, as our boundary with Bikanir had now become, must necessarily involve incursions by hostile armies. The villages right on the border had mostly been evacuated. The Sikhs, who had been in occupation of some of them, had crossed over into Bikanir, while the Muslims, fleeing from dangers largely but perhaps not wholly imaginary, had betaken themselves to the west of the big Sadiqia Canal. This canal runs for about fifty miles parallel to and a few miles inside the border. All the bridges over it had at this time military pickets and so no Muslim to the west of it had any solid ground for fear. Yet many appeared to be in a panic and clamoured for military protection. Much of this alarm was, I believe, feigned; the rumour of a Sikh attack could be an excuse or cloak for assailing and plundering the Hindus. But some of it was probably genuine. I had little sympathy with such absurd fears and could hardly conceal my contempt for them—which was not the right approach; so I generally left it to Leghari to calm them, which he did in the most admirable manner. I can hear him now repeating in Punjabi to group after group in slow measured tones without the slightest trace of irritation:

'There is no danger at present. No Sikhs are coming. So go to your homes and sit down quietly there and do your ordinary work. We are in touch with the Bikanir Government and have our own soldiers on the frontier. If any Sikhs come, we will stop them and also warn you in good time.'

These unnecessary fears were only gradually dissipated; and it took weeks and the lavish provision of military protection to induce the Muslim peasants to cross the canal and settle down once again to cultivation on the east bank.

The heat during the day was at this time still pretty intense and Leghari and I, as we moved around, were glad to take advantage of the shade of a tree or building for our confabulations with those who came to meet us, even if it meant walking for some little distance. Standing in the full blaze of the sun for any length of time was apt to be very trying; but, apart from this, the heat caused us no inconvenience. We ate little or nothing during the day, but drank water from time to time. It was a strenuous but healthy existence.

I was still holding charge as Revenue and Public Works

Minister for the whole State and the work of this office had to be disposed of at night. I had telegraphed for some of my staff to come and join me at Bahawalnagar, including my invaluable Clerk of Court, Mir Ajmal Hassan. He and my personal assistant went through all the papers during the day and reduced the work to simple potted form, so that I was able to dispose of it with the minimum of trouble and the routine of administration continued unimpeded. This is what my personal assistant liked to describe as 'the work of government running on quietly in the hands of petty clerks'. It was a common condition in Bahawalpur—and perhaps elsewhere also. As the work of settling incoming refugees developed, Ajmal Hassan, who had previously been a tahsildar, was of immense assistance in drafting detailed orders about the allotment of land to them and the assessment of the rent of houses, shops, etc.

I am a great believer in the written word and have never been able to understand those who boast of managing affairs by word of mouth—preferably down the telephone—and despise the man who uses his pen. Their affairs, I conclude, must be very simple, for an organization with the wide ramifications of government cannot be controlled by feats of memory and word of mouth. Apart from this, in India the giving of verbal orders is too often a method of evading responsibility; for, if anything goes wrong, the giving of the orders can be denied. Anyhow, I made a special point at this time of putting in writing all the numerous directions which I gave. I did this either immediately on the spot or, if not practicable, as soon after as possible. Every evening on my return to Bahawalnagar, I notified my personal assistant of all the orders I had issued during the day and dictated those which had been too long or complicated to record on the spot or required further elaboration. I found that this was greatly appreciated as everyone not only knew exactly what to do, but had my undoubted authority for doing it. It also helped me to keep a check on the actual execution of orders, for a written order, unlike a verbal one, cannot easily be denied, evaded or forgotten. In India the mere issue of orders is not necessarily equivalent to their execution.

Something must be said of the background of our thoughts at this time. Most prominent and persistent was our absolute uncertainty whether we should succeed in restoring and main-

taining order. This gnawing anxiety amounted sometimes to the
fear that not only Bahawalpur, but the whole of northern India,
and with it Pakistan, might sink into utter and irretrievable
chaos from which there might ultimately emerge some kind
of war-lord administration on the Chinese model. Our sense
of isolation aggravated this fear. I had no wireless with me and
during the first twelve days of my stay in Bahawalnagar I
received no letters (except from within the State) and no newspapers and so was effectually cut off from the outside world.
Leghari used occasionally to gather some scraps of news from a
privately owned wireless-set in the town; but the news was all
bad and the rumours in circulation about what was happening
in the Punjab still worse. It was impossible to get any coherent
picture of the situation there; and perhaps ignorance was bliss;
for whereas in Bahawalpur we were in these days steadily
overcoming the disorders, in the Punjab they were reaching
their climax of horror.

It was largely this dread of chaos that made us run about
unceasingly from place to place and galvanize our subordinates
into activity in all directions. We felt that, so far as we could,
we must assert the authority of government in the most visible
and unmistakable manner and, by vigorous and decisive
action, show that we could stretch out our arm both fast and
far. All the while the military had to be held in check and kept
within their proper bounds; for potentially they were by far
the most dangerous source of anarchy. Yet we could not at
present dispense with their services. They were required to
provide escorts for trains; to accompany labour parties who
would not move without military protection; to patrol the
frontier and to provide pickets at bridges over the Sadiqia
Canal and at other places near the border—this was essential
if only to allay Muslim fears and satisfy Muslim opinion—and,
above all, to provide transport for the quick movement of police,
prisoners and stocks of grain, since the transport available to
the police was negligible.

As already mentioned, I had welcomed the proposal of the
thanedar, Bahawalnagar, to start making searches for looted
property in neighbouring villages. These were commenced on
August 28th and met with immediate success. Many arrests
were made and much stolen property recovered. A magistrate

and troops and police were dispatched the next day in a lorry to search more distant villages and, though their movements were hampered by rain, they returned with a good haul. Searches were also taken up in Bahawalnagar itself and similar operations set going elsewhere. As the Bahawalnagar thanedar had forecast, a good deal of looted property was voluntarily surrendered in the hope of thereby securing lenient treatment. In the course of these searches considerable quantities of gold and silver ornaments, plundered from the Hindus, were re-covered. These were listed and deposited in the sub-treasuries attached to the tahsils.

Some of the worst lawlessness had been shown by the riverain villages in the Khairpur-Qaimpur area. Gurmani arranged for troops from Bahawalpur to make a flag-march through this tract and a squad of police under an inspector was deputed to make searches, investigate offences and arrest all the known bad characters in these villages. On one village we clamped down punitive police. The main object of all these measures was to impress upon the rural population the continued existence of an effective government.

The fear of anarchy persisted for a considerable time. Right on in October, when everywhere the situation had greatly improved, one still wondered whether this might not be merely a lull before incursions of Pathans from the North-West Frontier or of Sikhs from the East Punjab produced a further storm and a final catastrophe. Another possible and alarming prospect was that Pakistan might be submerged altogether by an un-manageable flood of Mulism refugees from India. We could absorb, with perhaps not too much difficulty, the few millions of Muslims from East Punjab; but once the transfer of popula-tion had started where would it end? If all the Muslims not only from East Punjab but from the whole of Northern and Central India were driven into Pakistan, then Pakistan would be overwhelmed. Why should not India, out of sheer spite, deliberately hound her Muslim population across the frontier and so destroy the new-born State, the very existence of which was an offence to most Indians? These were apprehensions which had already crossed our minds by the end of August, and they did not diminish as week after week the tide of in-coming refugees rose higher.

In the light of after-events these fears may appear foolish and perhaps were so even at the time; but they were very real and not wholly without basis.

Allied to the fear of chaos was the fear of financial breakdown. Bahawalpur had no independent currency of its own and so no possibility of resorting, in an emergency, to the printing-press. An empty treasury had a real and not merely a symbolic significance. It meant literally that salaries could not be paid and other expenses met. Under the British regime some of the Native States were occasionally confronted with just this situation—something very like it had occurred at an earlier date in Bahawalpur itself—but the Paramount Power had always been there to step in, make temporary advances, take control of the finances and set them in order. Now the Paramount Power had gone.

The financial position of Bahawalpur was not at this time critical. With the successful development of the 'colony' areas during the war, there had been substantial surpluses of revenue over expenditure. These might be expected to continue and so ordinarily we should be able to pay our way quite comfortably. But a sudden unexpected drain on our resources could quickly bankrupt us; for we had no reserves. Every rupee of the past surpluses had been used by Sir Richard Crofton for repayment of the debt to the Government of India. He had left the State practically without debt, but practically without balances. We would have preferred larger balances even if these meant a larger debt—which might never have to be repaid.

The upheaval that was now taking place, involving *inter alia* the loss of all our Sikh colonists, the dislocation of agricultural markets, and the paralysis or disappearance of the Hindu trading community, was calculated to reduce substantially our ordinary revenues, while expenses would rise by leaps and bounds. The cost of suppressing the disturbances would be only a small item in the account; it was the liabilities likely to be thrown upon us by the incoming refugees from India that were frightening. These might be enormous. Up to a certain limit, destitute Muslims flocking in from India could be accommodated in the houses and on the lands of the outgoing Hindus and Sikhs, but even these might have to be fed for six to eight months till the spring harvest came round, while others would be like a millstone round our necks. Unless we managed things carefully, we should be broken financially and our Government would collapse through sheer lack of ways and means.

We could, of course, if hard pressed, turn to the Pakistan Government; but their own plight seemed in those days to be precarious; we could not count on them with certainty. Furthermore, if we went cap in hand to Pakistan, we should put ourselves at their mercy and enable them to assert the Paramountcy of the old British-Indian Government. The Nawab and Gurmani were anxious to avoid this and considered it both possible and desirable that Bahawalpur should maintain a quasi-independent existence. The former had on August 15th taken the title of Amir in place of that of Nawab, which carried the suggestion that Bahawalpur was now almost comparable with Afghanistan! We had agreed to accede to Pakistan only in respect of defence, external affairs and communications. It was not the intention that we should subordinate ourselves further or admit the right of Pakistan to interfere in the internal affairs of the State. But to maintain this position it was essential to remain solvent.

The whole operation, therefore, of quelling the disturbances and handling incoming Muslim refugees had to be made substantially self-financing. Ultimately this would involve limiting strictly the number of refugees that we would take. As will be seen, this was a point which we kept constantly in view. Immediately, it required that we should secure possession of the movables, and particularly stocks of grain, left behind by Hindus and not let them fall into the hands of looters; and that we should settle incoming refugees promptly, so that land and other assets did not lie idle and unproductive of revenue and so that the refugees themselves would quickly become self-supporting. For the collection of stocks of grain, both from the mandis and the villages, the staff of the Civil Supplies and Co-operative departments were mobilized, and excellent progress was made with this work from the very start. We also bought up considerable quantities of grain at low prices of Rs 5–7 per maund. The first effect of the disturbances was to make grain prices tumble in the State, for there were large offerings by Hindus who were contemplating flight, and looted stocks also quickly found their way into the market. Later we were able to resell some of our purchases at a profit. The net result was that

over the next four to five months we were able to feed thousands
of refugees at practically no cost to the State.

As regards the settlement of refugees, we had one very great
advantage. In addition to the ordinary revenue and colony
staff, there was ready to hand all the extra settlement staff who
were at that time engaged in the reassessment of land revenue
in the eastern part of the State. This work was immediately
suspended and the staff turned on to coping with refugees.
The Settlement Officer, Nur Mohammad, was at Bahawalpur—where later he was to play an invaluable part—but the
Assistant Settlement Officer, Rao Fazlur Rahman, and the rest
of the staff were all scattered about the eastern tahsils—exactly
where we wanted them. The outgoing Sikhs had left standing
crops which would soon be ripe. If allowed to remain untended
they would be carried off by neighbouring villagers or grazed
by their cattle. We were anxious to make them over at once to
refugees so that they could reap them in due course and thus
support themselves through the cold weather. Still more
important was it to get refugees settled on vacated lands and
furnished where necessary with bullock-ploughs and seed in
time to sow the 'rabi'[1] crop in October. If this were not done,
there would be loss of production and of revenue and the refugees would have to be supported by us for a whole year.

All these matters filled my mind and seemed to press upon
it with hardly less urgency than the task of restoring order and
shepherding the Hindus to safety. I discussed them with Rao
Fazlur Rahman and other revenue officers on the 28th and we
reached certain decisions regarding the principles and terms
on which temporary allotments were to be made. The main
point of entry for refugees at this time was Macleodganj Road.
It was resolved that Rao Fazlur Rahman should station himself at this place and, after preliminary screening, direct the
incoming refugees from there to the various deserted 'chaks'.
We could see at a glance from our records which were the
Sikh 'chaks' and what was their cultivable area.

Rao Fazlur Rahman was a forceful officer and began the work
the very next day with what proved to be an indefatigable zeal.

---

[1] There are two harvests in northern India, 'rabi' gathered about mid-
April and 'kharif' gathered about mid-October.

X

Restoring Order—II

MOST of the Hindus in Bahawalnagar were in a fever to get away to India and I had promised to evacuate them as soon as possible. We planned to make a beginning on the afternoon of the 29th. Leghari arranged with the railway authorities for a special train and the military were asked to furnish an escort. The distance to be covered was not great. Macleodganj Road, the last station in the State, was only forty miles from Bahawalnagar, and Hindumalkot, the first station in India, situated in the State of Bikanir, only five to six miles farther on.

But an unexpected difficulty now arose. Owing to the disturbances the through train service running from Samasatta —a junction a few miles south-west of the town of Bahawalnagar—right across the State, then through a small strip of Bikanir (in which Hindumalkot is situated) and so on into the Ferozepur district and to the junction of Bhatinda (in Patiala State), had been altogether discontinued, and within the last few days the running of any trains across the frontier between Macleodganj Road and Hindumalkot had become irregular and intermittent, though it had not ceased altogether. The engine drivers at Bahawalnagar now announced that they could not take a train beyond Macleodganj Road. They said that to proceed farther across the border into India and up to Hindumalkot was dangerous; they were likely to be fired at by Indian troops and killed. We pointed out that the train would have a military escort and that, in any case, Indian troops would not be likely to attack a train carrying Hindu refugees. But they were not satisfied. They alleged that there were thousands of Indian troops at Hindumalkot, and one romancer even claimed that guns were in position there.

These unreal fears were, of course, a mere pretence, invented so as to avoid having to assist Hindu refugees. Communal feeling was particularly rife among the Muslim employees of the railways and they were only too keen to make things as unpleasant and uncomfortable as possible for members of the opposite community. But I was not going to be imposed upon and was quite determined that the train should be taken on from Macleodganj Road right up to Hindumalkot. Between the two stations there was nothing but desert, traversed by a rough sandy track. It was impossible to expect terrified Hindus, with all their women and children and luggage, to make their way on foot in the blazing heat from one station to the other. Moreover once to admit that there was danger in proceeding to Hindumalkot might lead to an absolute break in our rail communications with India, and this would be attended with enormous inconvenience—even greater than I at that time foresaw.

Failing to convince the engine crew that there really were no Indian troops lying in wait for them at Hindumalkot, Leghari and I then said that we would accompany the train ourselves and travel with them on the engine. We would inform the stationmaster at Hindumalkot in advance by railway telephone that we were coming; but if, in spite of this, they still felt nervous, they could halt the train at the distance signal and Leghari and I would go forward on foot to reconnoitre. Sensing that we were determined and were, perhaps, making fools of them, they agreed to these terms.

Since now we had in any case to go to Macleodganj Road on the 29th, Leghari and I arranged that we should leave in our own special train in the morning, stop a few hours at Minchinabad on the way and also spend some hours at Macleodganj Road itself, where we would pick up the 'refugee special' in the afternoon and take it on to Hindumalkot. Rao Fazlur Rahman would accompany us to Macleodganj Road and remain on there to cope with the incoming refugees and to be in general magisterial charge of the whole area.

We were, however, also very anxious to secure the safety of Harunabad which, so far as we knew, was still unravished, but an alluring prize. Since we could not go there immediately ourselves, we decided to send there an Assistant Commissioner, along with some influential non-official Muslims in the hope that by mere persuasion they would be able to prevent any

outbreak. There is a branch line from Bahawalnagar to Harunabad and on to Fort Abbas, but at the best of times a train ran
only about twice a week and no train was available at the
moment. So the Assistant Commissioner and his party had to
try to make their way there by road. Owing to the heavy
rains, we were uncertain whether they would be able to get
through.

Leghari and I reached Minchinabad early on the morning of
the 29th. We found the Hindus in a state of great alarm and the
two senior officials—a First-Class Magistrate and an Inspector
of Police—pleased with themselves but distinctly nervous.
They were pleased with themselves because so far they had
succeeded in saving the town from any serious looting. A few
shops in one of the bazaars had been knocked about a bit by
some local 'toughs' but the damage was slight and the miscreants had been locked up. They were nervous because early
that very morning large bands of villagers had been seen moving
about at some distance from the town as though gathering for an
attack. We endeavoured to put heart into them. Though they
had controlled more or less successfully the rowdy element
within the town and we applauded them, probably excessively,
for this, the police seemed to be somewhat lacking in firmness
and resolution. We found that, despite the fact that they were
fearing an attack from outside, they had not taken the precaution of arresting all the known badmashes within the town. We
gave orders for them to be secured and locked up immediately.
We also looked to the police rifles. About half a dozen were
serviceable—a large number for a Bahawalpur police station—
and Leghari directed some more to be sent for from Bahawalnagar. I was, however, certain in my own mind that even six
rifles, if properly handled, would be more than sufficient to
ward off any possible attack. I told the Magistrate and the
Inspector of Police that, if any band of villagers approached the
town, they must fire upon them without hesitation and must
shoot to kill. We also instructed them to send some men round
to the surrounding villages and put it about that the police in
Minchinabad meant business and would use their rifles with
effect. This was not what the Magistrate and Inspector, left
to themselves, intended. Their idea was to fire a few shots into
the air and hope that the villagers would be scared away. I told

F

them that they must on no account do this, but must resign themselves to the possibility of killing two or three people. They assented and assured me that they would carry out my orders, but I came away with no full confidence that they would do so. To them shooting at Muslims was like shooting at one's own side. Everywhere one was confronted with this strong disinclination to use effective force against the aggressors.

Having served for three years in the adjoining district of Multan, I knew something of the Muslim peasantry of this part of the country. They are not given to violent crime or noted for boldness and ferocity. They have none of the reckless daring of the Muslim tribes of north-west Punjab, or of the fierce, savage passions of the Sikhs. I knew that a mere handful of armed men, if properly led and made to open fire with effect, could easily disperse thousands of Bahawalpuri villagers. But I began to despair of finding any reliable, armed men.

However, in the event the Minchinabad authorities acquitted themselves quite creditably. Late that afternoon bands of villagers again approached the town. They were fired upon, two or three were wounded and the rest dispersed. There was no further trouble at Minchinabad; but in the course of the next few weeks all the Hindus evacuated the place and migrated to India.

Leghari and I left Minchinabad at about 11.0 a.m. and went on to Macleodganj Road. Here we found a scene of great disorder. The place, it turned out, had been completely looted several days earlier. A number of Hindu and Sikh shopkeepers had been killed; the rest had all fled across the nearby border. The shops in the bazaar were deserted, many of them half-burnt; there was nothing in them but rubbish and fragments of smashed goods. In the small mandi all the godowns had been broken open and hardly a bag of grain was left. The municipal staff had disintegrated and next to nothing had yet been done to clear up the mess. On top of this, in the last few days Muslim refugees from the Ferozepur district of East Punjab had begun to pour in. They were squatting in masses outside the railway station and along the railway line in a most miserable condition; the accumulating filth was appalling; and they could get no supplies—there was only one Muslim shop in the town still functioning.

At the station there was a platoon of Bahawalpur troops under Lt. Babar, an enterprising but rather headstrong officer, and not in any way qualified to deal with the situation. The only surviving civil official was the thanedar. It was fortunate that we had brought Rao Fazlur Rahman with us to take general charge. The thanedar, though he had some valid excuses to offer, had made no serious attempt to prevent the looting of the town or to clean it up afterwards. He prided himself on having preserved the old village of Macleodganj, situated some four to five miles away, which was largely inhabited by rich Hindus and contained a number of very substantial brick houses. There must have been plenty to loot and I never really discovered how the thanedar had kept it completely unharmed.[1] It may have been luck; more probably some bargain had been struck.

A large number of the colony chaks in the region of Macleodganj Road had been inhabited by Sikh colonists who had abandoned their lands and migrated to Bikanir a week or ten days earlier. The Muslims in this area had also abandoned their lands and retired to the interior, thinking it too dangerous to be so near the frontier. It took weeks to persuade them to return and reoccupy them and sections of troops had to be dotted about at strategic points to give confidence. There was, no doubt, some ground to fear tip-and-run raids across the frontier, but the extent of the panic was very hard to understand. The Sikhs, who had so lately run away to Bikanir, would have perhaps been surprised to learn the terror that they now inspired.

Rao Fazlur Rahman settled down at once to screen the masses of Muslim refugees and direct them to abandoned chaks, thus relieving the congestion at the railway station. We gave him all the help we could, restocking the place with grain from elsewhere, and getting Muslim shopkeepers to come and open shops and bring in provisions and goods for sale. Slowly the place came to life again, but owing to the enormous numbers of refugees that continued to deposit themselves on the outskirts of this derelict and devastated little town it remained a headache for many weeks.

While we were at Macleodganj Road, Leghari got wind of a

---

[1] I did not actually visit this village till September 1st.

rather horrible incident that was reported to have occurred there a few days earlier, and of which later we received confirmation. Some twenty to thirty Hindus, who wanted to go through to Bhatinda or to other places in India, had arrived at Macleodganj at a time when the through service had been interrupted. The railway officials, however, told them that if they did not mind waiting a little while, they would arrange for an engine to take them all on to Hindumalkot. Their carriage was then pulled out of the station and shunted on to a siding some distance away and close to a canal. Here they waited with growing impatience, as the day was getting on, but they were assured from time to time that the engine which would take them on to Hindumalkot was just coming and that they need not worry. No engine came at all. At nightfall they were attacked, robbed and slaughtered. But at least one of them managed to escape. He jumped out of the railway carriage into the canal, swam across it and made his way in the darkness over the border into India. I received a letter from him two or three weeks later telling this grisly tale, of which Leghari had already heard vague rumours.

We immediately set investigations on foot. The facts were generally confirmed, and the complicity of the railway staff in the outrage was quite manifest. We obtained sufficient evidence to arrest one of them on a charge of conspiracy to murder and I kept him incarcerated for a good many weeks. But it was impossible to complete the investigations and put a case into court owing to the difficulty of securing the attendance of the survivor(s), now in India, for interrogation and identification of the suspects. So ultimately we had to release him. Being a believer in retributive punishment, I hoped that he had had some uneasy moments and serious qualms of fear during the period of his incarceration.

I have several times had occasion to mention the misbehaviour of the railway staff, and there were to be more instances of it. The fact is that, just as Muslim feeling and the demand for Pakistan were strongest in provinces like the U.P., where the Muslims were in a minority, so too bitterness against the Hindus was most acute in the services of the Central Government, where the Muslims were hopelessly outnumbered and always felt themselves to be suppressed, frustrated and unjustly deprived or tricked out of promotion by the wily Hindus. In the Provincial Services of the Punjab, where the Muslims could easily hold their own both in point of numbers and otherwise, there was much less of this bitterness. Bigoted officials existed on both sides, but in general the relations between the two communities in the Punjab Services were friendly. Certainly the Muslims had no cause to feel aggrieved on account of lack of opportunity or unfair discrimination; during the past fifteen to twenty years the boot had been on the other leg. Conditions were substantially the same in the State Services of Bahawalpur. In the Central Services and in all-India institutions like the Imperial Bank they were different. The Muslims were, or felt themselves to be, a helpless and oppressed minority.

After August 15th the Muslim staff of the railways lost no time in exhibiting their feelings. With Partition there had been a good deal of reshuffling of railway personnel and many Muslims had come from India to man the railways in Bahawalpur, replacing Hindus. At once they began hoisting the Pakistan flag on all the stations—much to the annoyance of Gurmani, since Bahawalpur State had a flag of its own—and painting all the engines with Pakistani slogans. At more than one place they were the direct cause of serious outrages against the Hindus, and initially they were often far from co-operative about measures for their evacuation. At a later date I drew up a memorandum, setting forth all their misdeeds and delinquencies in Bahawalpur, which Gurmani forwarded to the Railway Administration with a strongly worded covering letter. Being a keen patriot, he hated to see a Pakistan Service falling to such low levels of conduct and efficiency. The Pakistan Railway Authorities took the criticisms very well and deputed a high-ranking official to look into the complaints and improve the tone of the railway staff. But this was all many weeks later.

To return to August 29th. The 'refugee special' from Bahawalnagar reached Macleodganj at about 4.0 p.m. The brigade and cannon supposed to be waiting to repulse us at Hindumalkot had by now been quite forgotten. The driver of the train greeted us with a broad grin and, when reminded of the danger said to lie ahead of us, laughingly admitted that it was all humbug, for which a mischief-monger at Bahawalnagar had been responsible. There was no more talk of stopping to reconnoitre at the distance signal; but, for convenience, Leghari and I did go on ahead of the refugee train in our own special.

The young officer in charge of the Bahawalpur troops escorting the refugees had given deep thought to the military aspect of our expedition. He produced a little sketch map, showing the positions reported to have been taken up by the Indian forces at Hindumalkot, and explained to me how he proposed to deploy his own troops, if we met with a hostile reception. It was difficult for me to take all this seriously, but I believe I offered some criticisms of his proposed dispositions which he was good enough to accept.

During the next few weeks Hindumalkot was to be for many thousands of Hindus the goal of all their hopes, the gateway from the hell of Bahawalpur to the longed-for paradise of India. I trust that on reaching there they got some tranquillity of spirit; for they can have got very little else. Imagine a signal rising up from the desert, a small shed and a row of bare brick buildings a quarter of a mile away, and you have about the sum total of Hindumalkot. The Bikanir authorities certainly did what they could for the reception of refugees, but by its very nature Hindumalkot had little to offer in the way of creature comforts. There could hardly be a worse place at which to be decanted after a long, hot, exhausting journey in a tremendously overcrowded train.

But this is to anticipate. Our first trainload of Hindu refugees did not do badly. They had not had to travel far; they were crowded, but not packed in the train like sardines; and on arrival at Hindumalkot they were practically sole masters of its exiguous resources, since only a handful of refugees had come in previously on foot. Moreover arrangements had been made for another train to take them on, if they wished, to Bhatinda.

Indian troops were not much in evidence when we reached Hindumalkot; there appeared to be only a small detachment, perhaps two sections, posted there. Leghari and I were very politely received by the stationmaster who had raked out some subordinate official of the Bikanir State—probably a naib-tahsildar—to meet us. The latter was aghast to see the huge number of refugees we had brought with us and said he had nowhere to put them as the few buildings were already occupied. We told him that most of them would want to go on to Bhatinda, but we also warned him that we would be sending more in the next few days and asked him to inform the Bikanir Government of this so that they could make the necessary preparations to receive them.

We told the stationmaster that we wanted to run trains through to Hindumalkot regularly every day and so prevent a complete break in rail communications with India. We hoped that India would put no impediments in the way of this and that the Muslim personnel bringing the trains would be quite safe. The stationmaster gave us every assurance and settled further details regarding the reopening of traffic with railway officials whom we had brought with us for this purpose.

While we were chatting, about half a dozen refugees, who had reached Hindumalkot a few days earlier, came up to us and salaamed. They were shopkeepers from Macleodganj Road and I recognized one of them, a venerable Sikh with a white beard, as a prominent citizen of that place whom I had met before. We had just begun to inquire how they were, when this patriarchal figure lifted up his voice and in ringing tones poured forth at Leghari a torrent of impassioned reproaches. He spoke with a vehemence of feeling and a volume of sound unimaginable perhaps to anyone not familiar with the Sikhs. Leghari, he said, had assured them of protection, told them to remain at Macleodganj and that no harm would come to them. They had trusted and obeyed him; they had carried out all his orders, as they always did. How could they imagine that he would fail them and break all his promises? But he had deserted and abandoned them—left them to be mercilessly slaughtered and plundered by bands of Muslim hooligans. Their shops had all been burnt and looted; hundreds of them had been killed; his own nephew and other close relations had been murdered before his eyes. What had Leghari's police been doing all this while? Where was the thanedar? Where was Leghari himself? He had never come near them or paid the slightest heed to their cries. He had deceived them with false promises of protection. If they had not trusted in him, they could have all quietly slipped away from the place several weeks before, taking their valuables with them. As it was they had had to fly for their lives, leaving everything behind them. He himself, a leading citizen and member of the Committee, possessed now nothing at all. Here he was in this desert, completely destitute, without a tent or shed to shelter in, hardly able to get even water. It would have been better to die like his nephew than to live to endure all these miseries. This is what he had been brought to by trusting Leghari; this is what came of being loyal to the Government and helping the police. How did Leghari now have the face to come among them? Why was he inquiring about them when he had ruined them all?

On and on flowed the ceaseless stream of words. If he paused for a few seconds to draw breath, it was only to begin again in the same loud, deafening tones. Nothing would persuade him to stop or to realize that we were standing a yard and not a mile away from him.

Though I was not insensible to the sting of his reproaches, they did not touch me so nearly as Leghari, to whom they were directly addressed; for I had been careful never to give anyone any assurance of protection. I was thankful for my comparative immunity and wondered what might be the feelings of poor Leghari. Whatever they were, he gave no indication of them, but stood silent and impassive, apparently unmoved by the flood of eloquence and impervious to reproaches. He made no attempt to answer or excuse himself; he showed no trace of irritation.

The only way of ending the painful scene was to quit it. We had finished our business and the refugees had by now detrained; so, hastily saying good-bye, we climbed back into our special to return to Bahawalnagar. All the while the white-bearded Sikh continued to pour out his sorrows at the top of his voice and as the train steamed away he ran along babbling beside it till finally it gathered pace and he was left behind, still hurling his denunciations at us. His sufferings had temporarily unhinged his mind.

When we were clear of him, Leghari suddenly became communicative. He said that he had never experienced anything so painful in his life and that he had not known how to endure it. I said that I thought he had borne it very well, and had admired the way in which he had listened to those bitter reproaches without saying a word. He replied that as he felt they were justified there was nothing he could say and so he thought it best to remain silent.

It was dark when we finally got back to Bahawalnagar. Mixed news awaited us. We learnt with relief that the Assistant Commissioner and his party had got through to Harunabad —though with considerable difficulty—and that there had been no outbreak of violence there. They reported that most of the Hindus were peacefully leaving the place and proceeding by road across the border into Bikanir State, which was not many miles distant. When Leghari and I visited Harunabad a few days later, there were only about fifty Hindus left. Large stocks of food-grains in the mandi passed into our hands intact.

Similarly the Hindus in the small outlying town of Fort Abbas and the Sikhs settled in a number of chaks in that area all went over peacefully at this time to Bikanir without any casualties or looting. In this distant outpost it was the Muslims who were, or pretended to be, in a panic, alleging that the Sikhs, who had left, were going to come back and spring upon them suddenly from the desert. We had to send some troops down to Fort Abbas to reassure them.

To offset this good news from the Harunabad area there were two bits of bad news. A Hindu railway official—a permanent way inspector—and his two nephews had been murdered at a place called Dunga Bunga about fifteen miles away; and a number of Hindus had been slaughtered in the train from Samasatta which had reached Bahawalnagar that afternoon. So the killing was still going on. The second incident was particularly disquieting, since hitherto we had been immune from the frightful train massacres which had been a feature of the disturbances in the Punjab.

In both incidents railway personnel were probably involved. The Dunga Bunga murderers remained untraced, despite vigorous investigations, but there was strong suspicion that members of the railway staff at that place had instigated, if not perpetrated, the crime. As regards the train murders, there was a conspiracy of silence. They took place somewhere between Khairpur and Qaimpur. The train had stopped ostensibly because a signal was against it, and the signal was against it ostensibly for some good reason. In reality it was all prearranged. While the train was halted it was beset by villagers

F*

and most of the few Hindus in it were robbed and murdered. It was reported that some of the Muslim passengers had joined in the slaughter, but the facts were never fully ascertained.

It was now plainly quite unsafe for Hindu passengers to travel by train without escort and we let it be known that those who ventured to do so without authority from the Government did so at their own risk. Most of the Hindus were only too keenly alive to the dangers, but a week or so after this incident a Hindu railway official of Bahawalpur, trusting to the assurances of Muslim friends who were perhaps treacherous, entrained without authority with his whole family—in all about a dozen persons—hoping to get through to Hindumalkot and Bhatinda. The whole party came to grief. They were attacked *en route*, robbed and murdered. Some months later a chance ray of light was shed on this incident. In December a British brigadier serving in India, whom I had known ten years earlier, sent me a letter saying that he had been asked by the station-master of Ludhiana to inquire whether I could trace his niece, a little girl of eight, who belonged to Bahawalpur. Her parents and other relations had all been killed in a train coming from Bahawalpur; but it was not known what had happened to her, and whether she was alive or dead. The quest seemed pretty hopeless, but I asked the tahsildar of Bahawalpur to see if he could hear anything of her in the villages between Khairpur and Qaimpur. Within two days he had found her and we were able to send her safely to her uncle at Ludhiana. It appears that when her parents and relations were attacked, the train was brought to a halt, they were dragged out of it and she tumbled out after them. While they were being done to death by the side of the line, she crept into a field near by and hid herself in the crops. After the noise and shouting had subsided and the train had gone on and all seemed quiet, she crept out again. Two villagers still lingering at the scene spotted her. Though they had probably both been parties to the massacre, they shrank from taking the child's life in cold blood. Not knowing what to do with her and fearing to incriminate themselves if they surrendered her to the authorities, one of them took her to his home, looked after her and treated her kindly. Her presence was revealed to the tahsildar and she was handed over to him only on the express understanding that no action would be taken against any of the villagers for hiding her such a long time. Outwardly she was quite unharmed, and we were able to send her safely to her uncle at Ludhiana.

Leghari and I had already decided that, on return from Macleodganj Road, we must go down the line in the opposite direction. The attack on the train, showing that there was still much lawlessness in the Khairpur-Qaimpur area, made this all the more necessary. We set out very early the next morning (August 30th). Heavy rain had again fallen, so we travelled by special train, and, fearing that there might be a good deal of disorder to contend with, we took with us about a platoon of troops.

At Chishtian all was still quiet. A number of Hindus from outlying villages had sought refuge here; they seemed fairly contented and only a few of them expressed a wish to be evacuated to India. Among the officials who met us was the settlement tahsildar, Gobind Baksh.

'Are you quite all right, Gobind Baksh?' I inquired.

'Nur Mohammad, not Gobind Baksh,' came a chorus from the bystanders.

'Nur Mohammad, sir, if you please,' said Gobind Baksh himself. 'My name is Nur Mohammad, I'm no longer Gobind Baksh.'

We had met him as a Hindu on the 26th. Now four days later he was a Muslim with a Muslim name. I inquired whether he had taken the name of 'Nur Mohammad' after his superior, the Settlement Officer, and he replied that he had. I was delighted, as there was no-one more worthy of honour and imitation than K. B. Nur Mohammad. I congratulated him warmly on his choice of a new name and expressed the hope that he would live up to the reputation of his namesake.

Since Gobind Baksh, alias Nur Mohammad, was now obviously immune from all danger and, having been fully accepted as a Muslim, could act with effective authority, I at once invested him with the powers of a first-class magistrate and packed him off to Hasilpur to take charge of affairs there.

During these times of trouble there were many Hindus in Bahawalpur, including about half a dozen officials, who sought safety by temporarily embracing Islam, but Gobind Baksh is the only Hindu known personally to me whose conversion was

genuine and permanent and who has remained in West Pakistan as a regular citizen of that State. The fact is that he was
enamoured of a Muslim girl and, under her influence, he had
for some time been contemplating the adoption of the Muslim
faith. The outbreak of the disturbances afforded the occasion
for him to take the final plunge.

There was much for the new Nur Mohammad to do at
Hasilpur. Travelling on there from Chishtian, we found that
the police and Hindus had all left the ill-omened village of
'old Hasilpur' and were now concentrated in the 'colony'
town. Most of the corpses had been disposed of, but, on taking
a tally of the dead and the living, it had come to light that a
great many Hindu girls were missing. We deputed special staff
to make searches in the neighbourhood and within a week
sixty had been recovered. The military were asked to round up
all gangs of Pathans and to send them across the Sutlej into the
Punjab—a task which they successfully accomplished within the
next few days. The Hindus at Hasilpur almost without exception wanted to go to India and arrangements were made for
their evacuation to Hindumalkot.

The small town of Qaimpur is about two miles distant from
the station. We did not visit it on this occasion, as the thanedar,
who came to the station to meet us, said that all was well there,
save that the Hindus were still clustering in the compound of
Abdullah Shah and would not return to their own houses. But he
said that there were reports of trouble at Khairpur so we hurried
on there. On reaching Khairpur station, we were informed that
the place had already been looted and the bazaar burnt. We got
onto some ponies and rode over to the town which was about a
mile away. There was the usual scene of devastation and a
small sprinkling of corpses, most of them lying in the shops
and houses beneath charred beams and rafters. The main
attack had taken place on the 28th when, according to the
thanedar, the assailants were so numerous that even with the
small reinforcements we had given him he was powerless to
resist them. The looters had returned in smaller numbers on
the 29th—the day before our arrival—and had been beaten off
with one or two casualties, and eighty of them had been arrested.
This was the thanedar's story and he had certainly got eighty
men in custody whom we presumed to be looters. Whether they

really were, I never ascertained. However, for the present we
sent them all off to Derawar Fort, an ancient fortress in the
desert, where we had decided to confine all those arrested in
this area in connection with the disturbances.

Our arrival at Khairpur forestalled a third attack on the
place. Bands of looters had been gathering during the morning
for further pillage, but on learning that Leghari and I were
present they drew off and Khairpur was not molested again.

The number of Hindus killed in Khairpur was only about
twenty-five. The survivors, perhaps not without reason, were
terrified out of their wits, but had as yet formed no firm resolution whether to stay or to leave. On the whole their preference
appeared to be for staying, and this was not surprising as
Khairpur was an old town and most of the Hindu families
living in it had been settled there for generations. They were
attached to the place and deeply rooted in it—unlike the Hindus
in the colony towns who had come in from outside in the past
twenty years and still had their roots elsewhere. We were at
this time not at all anxious that these old Hindu subjects of the
State should leave, unless they themselves positively wished to
be evacuated to India, and so we threw our weight in favour of
their staying. In the hope of encouraging them, we left behind
two sections of the troops we had brought with us. Arrangements had also been made, as already mentioned, for some
troops from Bahawalpur to make a flag-march through the
area in order to restore confidence. We said that we ourselves
would visit them again in two or three days and see how they
felt then about staying or leaving.

We returned to Bahawalnagar with the impression that on
the whole they had been reassured and were content to remain.
The following day, when Leghari and I went to Harunabad
and Fort Abbas, it was Muslims rather than Hindus that we
had to reassure. The latter had left, or were leaving, peacefully
and in good order, but all along the border the Muslims were
in fear of imminent attack, as already described. So far as we
could make out, petty raids were being made across the border
by both sides, though naturally we heard more of the raids
made against us than of the raids by our people into Bikanir.
One of our military patrols on the Sadiqia Canal had recently
shot seven Sikhs who were alleged to have been looting a

deserted village. Such drastic action was probably unjustified, but I was not inclined to question it.

When we got back to Bahawalnagar from Harunabad late on the evening of August 31st, there was a message waiting for me from Sardar K. M. Pannikar, Prime Minister of Bikanir, to the effect that he and some of the State officials, along with Mr. V. P. Menon of the Government of India and Major Short, proposed to come over to see me the next morning at Bahawalnagar. He requested me to ensure that they would not be held up by any military or police picket on the road by which they would come.

I gave the necessary orders. In view of the disturbed state of the border and the growing streams of refugees flowing across it in both directions, I felt that discussions with the Bikanir authorities were most timely and would be very useful. As regards Menon and Short, I surmised that the Government of India, having heard of disturbances in Bahawalpur State, had sent them to spy out the land and report how things stood. Since all that had occurred appeared to me very shocking and disgraceful, I was not too keen to have to reveal it to the Government of India who might make capital out of it, and if Menon and Short had not been good friends of mine, I should have been very uneasy. I hoped, however, that I should be able to give them in confidence a true picture of the situation without unduly compromising either Bahawalpur or Pakistan.

Menon had previously been Reforms Commissioner to the Government of India and had played a crucial part in the negotiations and evolving of formulas which had preceded Partition and Independence. I did not know the exact position[1] now held by him, but I had an idea that he was Sardar Patel's right-hand man and I regarded him as Patel's representative. Short, I assumed, was a kind of liaison officer and had been sent on this expedition because he was an Englishman who knew both Gurmani and me well.

When the party arrived the next morning, I was delighted to find among them another old friend, Rai Bahadur Chuni Lal. Ten years earlier he had been Superintendent of Police in a district of which I was District Magistrate and we had worked together in the closest harmony and friendship. He was now

[1] He had just become Secretary to the Ministry of States.

Inspector-General of Police, Bikanir. I had forgotten this and it came to me as a most pleasant surprise and a good augury for our future relations with Bikanir.

Sardar Pannikar and his officials expressed much concern at the number of refugees that had flooded into Bikanir from Bahawalpur and wanted to know how many more were coming. I was able to assure them that almost all our Sikh colonists had already moved across into their State and that no more need be expected. I told them that we were in the process of evacuating urban Hindus from some of our colony towns and that they should be prepared in the next few days to receive several hundreds of them at Hindumalkot; but most of them, I said, would probably want to go on into the East Punjab and would not stay in Bikanir, unless they had originally come from there.

Sardar Pannikar complained that the Sikh colonists were being driven across the border in a destitute condition and were arriving in Bikanir stripped to the bone. I had to point out that this was not true. Except perhaps for two or three chaks near Macleodganj, the Sikh colonists had gone out quite unmolested and had taken with them everything that they could load on to their carts. Our Muslim colonists, so far from attacking them, had been more inclined to run away from them. I am glad to say that one of the Bikanir officials had the courage to speak up and told Sardar Pannikar that the reports given to him about the robbing of refugees had been much exaggerated.

I then referred to the raids that were going on across the border. So long as these continued, I said, it was difficult for us to withdraw our troops and so bring things back to normal. It was agreed that there should be further meetings of military and police officers to discuss these frontier problems. The Bikanir officials complained that several of their people had been shot at without warning on the border and killed or wounded. I did not deny that this might have happened for though no orders had been issued to the Bahawalpur troops to shoot without warning, it was not easy to control small detachments strung out over long distances. In the present circumstances, I said, we must assume, and let it be generally known, that anyone who poked his nose over the frontier without due authority did so at his own peril and should not, therefore, be surprised or annoyed if he got killed or wounded. Sardar Pannikar objected to this. I admitted that it should not be the normal rule, but I said that at the present time it applied and that, in any case, I must give clear warning that any Sikh who ventured across the border into our territory without authority was very likely to be killed and there was nothing I could do to prevent it.

After these general discussions I had some talk with Menon and Short alone. I took the former down to the town, which had by now been cleaned up and presented a fairly good appearance. Though we had been evacuating Hindus to Hindumalkot for the last three days, there were still two to three hundred of them in Bahawalnagar, mostly concentrated in the buildings provided as a sanctuary for them by the wealthy Muslim. I thought Menon ought to have a talk to them and satisfy himself that they were all right; so I introduced him to some of them and began talking away myself in Hindustani till I realized that he wasn't following and remembered that, being a South Indian, he knew no Punjabi and hardly any Hindustani. Thus I found myself, an Englishman, in the curious position of acting as an interpreter between an Indian and his fellow countrymen.

I explained to Menon and Short the situation in Bahawalpur and the measures we were taking to suppress the disorders. I was mildly optimistic regarding the future. I said that I thought the worst was over, that we should probably be able to keep the Rahim Yar Khan district tranquil, and that we might hope to escape further mass slaughters. I then came to the question of casualties. Those which had already occurred were, of course, to me very shocking, as in the old days we had felt great concern if only half a dozen were killed in a communal riot. Still I decided that I must give the true facts. Disgraceful though they might seem to me, they were probably less bad than the exaggerated tales reaching India. So place by place I told Menon the exact casualties as known to me. At that time they amounted in all to about one thousand. I felt rather apologetic about these, to me, high figures and may have shown a little diffidence in disclosing them. I said to Menon that I had no objection to his passing them on to Sardar Patel—and wrote them all down on a bit of paper for him—but I requested him not to give publicity to them or to use them officially. He made light of my anxiety.

'Don't worry,' he said, 'these figures are not very bad. You don't realize what is going on elsewhere. This State is a paradise compared with East Punjab.'[1]

He was so encouraging that I was considerably heartened. I had wanted to reassure *him* and through him to convey to Sardar Patel that we were doing our best to steady things in Bahawalpur; but the net result of his visit was to reassure me. It may not have been very proper to draw comfort from the misfortunes of others, but I did so. To know definitely—what I had, of course, surmised—that our plight was nothing like so bad as that of others was a stimulating tonic.

I was also pleased to note that both Menon and Short were very well impressed by Leghari.

Menon gave me some account of the difficulties in the East Punjab and bewailed the lack of experienced officers to cope with the disorders and with the mounting tide of refugees. He asked why I was not there and, in his impulsive way, suggested that I should immediately come over and help them. I pointed out that my hands were full and that I could not at such a critical moment desert my post in Bahawalpur. He agreed, but asked me to consider the matter when Bahawalpur had grown calmer. This conversation was the germ of my subsequent service in India.

Our visitors left at about noon and immediately afterwards Leghari and I set out again for Minchinabad and Macleodganj, travelling this time by car. We wanted to be sure that Minchinabad was still intact, but our main object was to confer with Rao Fazlur Rahman. In the past forty-eight hours Muslim refugees had been pouring into the State at Macleodganj Road in quite overwhelming numbers. Some of them were wounded and in an absolutely helpless condition and this was once again inflaming communal feelings. Two or three cases of cholera had

---

[1] At a later date, when the Government of India put out a propagandist statement that 70,000 Hindus had been killed in Bahawalpur State, we issued a contradiction and in the course of it quoted this remark of Mr. Menon. He then denied having made it. He may well have forgotten it and, in any case, in the circumstances of those times, he could hardly be blamed for disclaiming words used on the spur of the moment in the course of private conversation. But he did in fact use these very words. They were uttered in the presence of Major Short and were recorded by me in a report sent to Gurmani the same day.

been reported. The medical staff was quite insufficient and no anti-cholera serum was immediately available. Rao Fazlur Rahman was at his wits' end and was finding Lt. Babar an irritant rather than a help.

Lt. Babar, who was in command of the detachment of troops at Macleodganj Road, deserves a short paragraph to himself. He had been, I subsequently discovered, a lawyer in Peshawar and, not finding that very profitable, had joined the Bahawal-pur State Forces not long before this date. He was good com-pany and during our association I had some enjoyable rides with him in his jeep along the Sadiqia Canal. But he was impetuous and on so many occasions did not see eye to eye with Rao Faz-lur Rahman that I very soon had to ask for him to be removed. One of his most annoying habits was to arrest every Hindu he saw. It had been explained to him that he had no authority to make any arrest unless he was ordered to do so by a magistrate or saw someone actually committing an offence; but still he persisted and crowned his efforts by arresting a Hindu head constable of police who had been on leave and was trying to get back to duty at Jullundur. Lt. Babar seized him at the railway station, took away his belt, treated him in a humiliating manner and absolutely refused to release him until Leghari and I appeared on the scene and set him at liberty. I then told Lt. Babar that, if he did it again, I would arrest *him* and put him in the lock-up on charges of wrongful restraint and wrongful confinement. After this, he desisted.

On the whole Lt. Babar gave me more amusement than annoyance, but Rao Fazlur Rahman, manfully grappling from hour to hour with thousands of refugees, could not take his eccentricities quite so lightly. Strictly speaking there was no need for troops at Macleodganj, but we had to keep them there in deference to Muslim opinion and Muslim fears.

By midday on September 1st when Leghari and I started on our journey to Minchinabad and Macleodganj Road there was a long column of Muslim refugees strung out from the latter place almost up to Bahawalnagar. They were trudging slowly along the side of the Fordwah Canal (and making havoc of our canal road) with their bullock-carts, women and children and such of their simple chattels as they had been able to bring with them. We ran into the head of this column a few miles out of

Bahawalnagar. As we drove along, my heart sank at the vast numbers. We found that, besides those on the road, there was now a dense concentration of them at Minchinabad as well as at Macleodganj. Their condition varied. Some of them had sturdy bullocks and well-laden carts with plenty of bags of grain and did not themselves look at all done up by their march. Others seemed dead-beat and practically destitute. Most pathetic were those who had got stranded through their cart breaking down or one of their bullocks falling lame or dying. But at least now they were in a friendly country and could hope to obtain help. We stopped here and there, as we motored along, and tried to console them, advising them where they could best halt for the night and assuring them that we would allot them land. The great majority of them came from the Ferozepur district of the (East) Punjab. I was at a loss to understand why they had entered Bahawalpur instead of crossing the Sutlej into the (West) Punjab. They all said that Indian troops had scared them away from the road leading to the bridge over the river at Suleimanke and that they had therefore been compelled to turn aside into Bahawalpur. Some of them with connections in West Punjab still wanted to get there and were anxious to know where was the next crossing of the river. We had to direct them to the Pallah headworks—a good many miles distant.

I had scraped together all the revenue staff I could lay hands on and given them to Fazlur Rahman for refugee work, and we now had officers posted at all the principal centres both to allot land to cultivators and to allot shops and houses in the towns to urban refugees. But we were terribly short-handed, especially at Macleodganj itself. The only way in which we could supplement our resources was to recruit any trained revenue staff we could find among the incoming refugees. I authorized Fazlur Rahman to do this and we procured a few useful men, including one excellent naib-tahsildar.

A little cross-examination of the Medical Officer at Macleodganj showed that the reported cases of cholera at that place —more were reported from Minchinabad the next day—were likely to be false alarms. We sent for anti-cholera serum and staff from Bahawalpur and a large number of inoculations were carried out. But these were probably superfluous, and it is doubtful whether there had been any real case of cholera at all. Though there continued to be numerous alarms during the month of September, nothing came of any of them.

This huge wave of refugees from Ferozepur brought with it a man of some prominence in that district. He was a large landowner named Bagh Ali and had been a member of the Legislative Assembly of the old united Punjab. He arrived on foot at Macleodganj Road along with five thousand members of the Sakhera tribe, many of whom were his tenants. He had been trekking for a week and was clearly unaccustomed to such exertions. Clad in raiment by no means fine or clean, un-shaven, pinched and haggard, he presented a distressful appearance. One could hardly imagine that he was a wealthy Muslim landowner and an M.L.A. I had not met him before, but he was well-known to me by repute, for earlier in the year he had been the central figure in quite a celebrated scene in the Punjab Assembly. He had been one of the handful of Unionists supporting Sir Khizar Hyat who had been returned in the elections of 1945; but the Muslim League tried hard to win him over to their side and thought they had succeeded. One day there was a regular struggle for his body on the floor of the House, each party claiming him as their own and trying to drag him over to their benches. Sir Khizar had won this tussle and Bagh Ali had remained with him instead of going over to the League.

I reminded Bagh Ali of this incident. He said at once that his present tribulations were a just punishment from God for his failure to support the Muslim League. He feared that there were many more in store for him for, having offended the League, he could not expect to receive a warm welcome in Pakistan. He was quite uncertain whether he would be allotted any land in exchange for what he held in Ferozepur. He then told me that, in view of his previous opposition to the demand for Pakistan, he had left Ferozepur very much against his will, but had been compelled to quit by the Sub-Divisional Officer at Fazilka. This bit of information astonished and disturbed me. I knew that for the past three weeks the Sikhs had been deliberately driving Muslims out of the East Punjab, but this was the first intimation that Government officials were aiding and abetting their expulsion. If the Sub-Divisional Officer was acting under orders, where was this all going to end? We might

soon have the whole Muslim population of India thrust upon
us. We should then perforce have to turn out all our Hindu
population whom we were at that time still trying to retain
unharmed within the State. I sent a telegram to the Governor
of the East Punjab seeking clarification of his Government's
attitude, but received no reply. Many months afterwards I
learnt that a reply was sent, though it never got through to me,
in which the Governor explained that an agreement had just
been reached for an exchange of populations between East
and West Punjab. The actual date of this agreement was
September 2nd. Evidently the Sub-Divisional Officer, Fazilka,
acted in anticipation of it. I did not come to know of it till
some days later.

Bagh Ali also told me, like many others, that he and his
people had intended to cross the Sutlej into the West Punjab,
but had been forced aside into Bahawalpur because the road to
the bridge at the Suleimanke headworks was unsafe for refugees.
It was clear that unless this road was reopened we should continue to be inundated with refugees unable to pass over the
river into West Punjab. So I instructed Fazlur Rahman and
Lt. Babar to run up together to Suleimanke to reconnoitre and
also to report generally on the condition of the headworks,
about which I had begun to feel grave misgivings.

Bagh Ali was doubtful of the reception he would meet with
in West Punjab; he was also doubtful what our attitude towards
him would be. I guessed that, being quite worn out, he would be
thankful to end his wanderings and stay on in Bahawalpur now
that he had got there. But would we allot him land and permit
him to take up the position of a landlord with the tenants he
had brought with him cultivating under him? This was the
question that was agitating his mind, though he did not like to
put it to me directly. I decided that we were unlikely to get
better cultivators than these Sakheras from Ferozepur and
that from the State's point of view it would be a good bargain
to take Bagh Ali and his tenants with him. They had almost all
got their bullocks and implements with them, and since he was
a man of position and education he would relieve us of a lot
of trouble by himself looking after them and settling them on
the land. The tenants themselves were quite satisfied, indeed
delighted, with the idea. They felt for Bagh Ali a sort of feudal

loyalty, which was enhanced by the fact that he had stood by them in their troubles and himself led them out on foot from Ferozepur. So, in consultation with Fazlur Rahman, I allotted a large block of vacated land in the vicinity of Bahawalnagar to Bagh Ali and his tenants for one year in the first instance.

Gurmani was not very enthusiastic about this arrangement. Though there were plenty of big landlords of the old feudal type in the non-colony area of Bahawalpur, he did not like the idea of introducing any more. He may have thought that there would soon have to be far-reaching changes, sweeping away the old landlord-tenant relationship. I had myself felt for some years that a new pattern of agricultural society was required in India, superseding both landlords and tenants and peasant proprietors and based on the co-operative organization of the village. Nowhere had seemed more suitable for experiments on these lines than the new colony area of the Punjab; but none had been made. The present upheaval, with the uprooting of large sections of the population, might seem to afford in some ways an opportunity for change and the introduction of new patterns of rural society; yet I was convinced that to attempt anything of the kind at this time of crisis was wholly impracticable.[1] My view was that all those who came in from India should, so far as possible, be given exactly the same rights and status as they had enjoyed there. If landlords were to be abolished or rights in land curtailed, this should be done uniformly for all alike. Such changes should not be arbitrarily applied only to those unlucky ones who had been driven out of India and Pakistan.

These views were favourable to Bagh Ali!

It will be remembered that Leghari and I had promised on the 30th to revisit Khairpur in two or three days; so we spent the whole of September 2nd motoring along the route Chishtian, Hasilpur, Qaimpur and Khairpur, and, having thus approached so near to Bahawalpur, I went on and stopped the night there. At all places there were manifest signs of returning confidence and restoration of order. The recovery of stolen property and abducted women, the arrest of offenders and the collection of food-grains were going on apace. At Chishtian

---

[1] Though experiments were contemplated in some quarters, on neither side of the frontier was it found practicable to carry them into effect.

shops had reopened. At Qaimpur the Hindus were at last persuaded to leave the compound of Abdullah Shah and return to
their own homes. At Khairpur there was no longer talk of
evacuation to India; the Hindus had decided to remain.

In view of this general improvement I was somewhat perplexed at being approached in Bahawalpur itself by a deputation of Hindus who said that they felt unsafe and asked to be
evacuated to India. No incident of any kind had yet occurred
in or near the town of Bahawalpur. A good number of Hindus
from the rural areas had sought safety in the capital, but serious
disorders had stopped short around Khairpur. I was at pains to
ascertain from the Hindus whether they had any specific
grounds for alarm; but I could discover nothing other than
general fears and a vague uneasiness. I was not disposed to
encourage their thoughts of flight. To start evacuating Hindus
from the capital would make nonsense of our efforts to retain
and protect Hindus in Khairpur, Qaimpur and other places
eastwards. It could hardly fail to lead to a general exodus of
Hindus from the whole of the Bahawalpur district, if not from
the whole of the State.

I talked the matter over with Gurmani. He was emphatically
opposed to the idea of evacuation and said that only a small
section of the Hindu population wanted to leave. They were
recent comers, not deeply rooted in the State, and were trying
to spread alarm and despondency among the rest. He somewhat pooh-poohed their fears. He said that most of the Hindus
of the town, who were old 'riasatis' long settled in the State,
were feeling quite reasonably secure and had no thoughts of
moving.

All this chimed with my own views.

Except for this uneasiness among some of the Hindus everything appeared absolutely tranquil in the town of Bahawalpur.
Nominally, as District Magistrate of the Bahawalpur district,
I was also responsible for law and order in the town; but since
I had to be away in Bahawalnagar and Gurmani himself and
the Commissioner of Police were present on the spot, I had
tacitly assumed that they, with the help of the ordinary magistrates, would look after things there and only call me in if a
crisis arose and the District Magistrate's presence was required.
Gurmani rightly felt that there ought to be someone in the

town of Bahawalpur with the powers of Additional District Magistrate, but that none of the ordinary magistrates was of sufficient weight and experience to be invested with these powers. He therefore proposed that one of the judges of the High Court, a Muslim named Gilani who belonged to Bahawalpur and was much respected by the Hindu population, should temporarily be made Additional District Magistrate. I hardly knew Gilani and would have preferred to have the Settlement Officer, Nur Mohammad, who, though elderly, was an experienced District Magistrate. But Gurmani wanted to have a local man and so I agreed to the proposal.

A few days later, when I was once more back in Bahawalnagar, Major Short passed through the place on his way to Bahawalpur to see Gurmani with some message from the Government of India. I felt sure that while he was there some of the Hindus would approach him about evacuation. I thought that he ought to be informed in advance of our attitude; so I told him that we did not at present favour evacuation and requested him not to give any encouragement or even countenance to the idea without first discussing the matter with Gurmani. Short said that his instinct was to let the Hindus go if they wanted to. I had considerable respect for his instinct or, as he put it, for what his antennae told him; and his antennae in this instance did not err. But I had to point out that it was not just a question of letting Hindus go, but of positively providing for them to do so; for, since railway travel was now unsafe, none of them could leave unless we furnished escorts. Yet if we began furnishing escorts for Hindus wishing to leave the town of Bahawalpur, it would imply that we did not consider them safe there, and all of them would then wish, or feel compelled, to leave. We were thus in a dilemma.

Short was not wholly convinced by my arguments, but undertook to be wary in any talk he might have with Hindus until he had ascertained Gurmani's views. On his return journey he had a brief conversation with me. I gathered that, as I had expected, some Hindus had approached him, but that, in the light of his talks with Gurmani, he had dissuaded them from thinking of evacuation. On the whole he seemed to be satisfied that, in view of the improving situation throughout the State, the line which we were adopting was correct.

Back again at Bahawalnagar my main concern during the next ten days was the settlement of incoming refugees and the stabilization of the border. Anxiety about fresh communal outbreaks gradually diminished as days passed without further incident. We had one or two narrow shaves in Bahawalnagar itself, when Hindus were being sent off to Hindumalkot, passions having again been aroused by the arrival of wounded refugees from India. But from about the 6th there was a pause in the influx of refugees, and feelings subsided. Some troops of the Bahawalpur Army were, however, guilty at this time of a shocking atrocity. Fourteen Sikhs had been captured near the border and were being held at one of the military posts on the Sadiqia Canal for transference to police custody. It is not clear whether they had actually committed any offence. Most probably they were some of our own Sikh colonists returning just to fetch some more of their property. In any case it was for the police to investigate the offences, if any, of which they had been guilty, and the military had rightly notified the police and asked them to take over their prisoners. The police sent a guard; but it arrived in time to take over only corpses. All fourteen had been shot. I was intensely angry and so was Leghari. I insisted on the military holding an inquiry and some sort of rather perfunctory inquiry was held, but nothing much came of it. There was no desire, much less determination, to probe the matter to the bottom and to punish the guilty. The story was put forward that the Sikhs had attempted to escape and was readily accepted, though it did not account for the facts. The killing of Sikhs had now become a more or less legitimate form of blood sport.

I received about this time a report from Fazlur Rahman and Lt. Babar about the visit which, at my direction, they had paid to Suleimanke. They stated that there were hardly any Pakistan troops there, but large numbers of Dogra troops of the Indian Army were posted quite close to the headworks on the south side of the river. These had clashed with a party of Pakistan police and there had been an exchange of fire. It was probably this incident, or rumours of it, that had frightened the incoming refugees and deflected them into Bahawalpur. In accordance with their suggestions we posted detachments of Bahawalpur troops at strategic points near the southern approaches to the headworks so as to give confidence to the

Muslim refugees, who tended to be overawed by the Dogra troops, and to shepherd them over the bridge into the Punjab.

Fazlur Rahman gave an alarming account of the position at the headworks themselves. Muslim irrigation officers had recently arrived to take over charge, but were without subordinate staff, without communications and in a state of panic and helplessness. These headworks were vital to us, so I decided to go there myself, taking with me one of our superintending engineers—a Muslim officer whose headquarters were at Bahawalnagar.

At Suleimanke we found an executive engineer, an assistant engineer and one clerk, all newly arrived, in charge of the headworks and all their protective works, with no subordinate staff to assist them. The power-house was not working and telegraph and telephone wires had been cut. A platoon of Pakistan troops and a small party of police were stationed there, but they had no transport.

If through any accident or sabotage a breach was made in the protective embankments twelve miles long, it would be difficult, if not impossible, to repair the damage.

I now learnt to my amazement that, while the headworks themselves were in Pakistan, the frontier had been so drawn by Lord Radcliffe that most of the protective embankments on the south side were in Indian territory and were at the moment in the hands of Dogra troops. It seemed extraordinary that there had been no-one to impress upon Lord Radcliffe the importance of including the principal protective works in the same territory as the headworks. This could very easily have been done, as the area involved was uninhabited and, for the most part, uncultivated. I fondly imagined that this absurd error[1] would quickly be rectified. But it never was. We were destined very soon to feel the inconvenience of it.

It was essential to strengthen the hands of the Executive Engineer and we agreed to lend him immediately some of our own technical staff, for which he was very grateful. I also, at his request, sent him two sections of Bahawalpur troops along

---

[1] An exactly similar error was made at Ferozepur, save that there the headworks are in Indian territory and some of the protective embankments in Pakistan. Presumably Lord Radcliffe was never apprised of the relevant facts.

with a truck to assist in the protection of the headworks and to ensure the safe passage over the river of Muslim refugees.[1] These measures were useful at the time, but in the end proved inadequate.

By September 8th the general situation in the State had vastly improved and I reported to Gurmani as follows:

'No particular incident has been reported and, provided there are no alarms caused by marauding Sikhs from the Bikanir border, this area should now settle down once again after the recent disturbances. Minchinabad town has already resumed a more or less normal appearance and there are signs of some return of normal life at Hasilpur, Chishtian and Bahawalnagar.

'There has been no large fresh influx of refugees, but a considerable number are shuttling aimlessly to and fro by train from Macleodganj to Samasatta. . . .

'A meeting has been arranged for the 11th of September at Karanpur (Bikanir State) between officers of this State and of Bikanir to discuss repatriation of refugees and measures for preservation of peace along the border.'

Repatriation of refugees! It is strange to recall that at this time we were actually thinking in these terms. At Karanpur, after the official meeting, I met large numbers of Bahawalpur refugees who had collected there. While I made it clear to them that I saw no prospect of taking back any Sikhs, I expressed the hope that, if all went well, the Hindus would be able to return in one or two weeks' time. I genuinely thought so. I would not have been so optimistic if I had known fully what was going on elsewhere; for in the Punjab the disaster was still deepening and this was bound to affect us. But I could view only the Bahawalpur scene, and in Bahawalpur we seemed to be surmounting our troubles. I foresaw, of course, difficulties in reintroducing the Hindus when we had already taken in a good many Muslim refugees. But the number of refugees settled in the urban areas, to which the Hindus would mostly return, was as yet comparatively small. I thought it would be possible, with some temporary adjustments, to accommodate both them and

[1] The Bahawalpur troops were withdrawn about September 13th by which date the Pakistan troops at the headworks had been considerably reinforced.

the returning Hindus, while the Muslim cultivators settled in the lands vacated by the Sikhs could remain quite undisturbed. Within a week, these ideas had undergone a revolution.

The lull in the disturbances and in the arrival of refugees had enabled us to make good progress with the investigation of cases and the sorting out of offenders. The sub-jail at Bahawalnagar had become so overcrowded with prisoners awaiting trial that I had to have a jail delivery—releasing most of those who had been confined there before the disturbances began. Not finding at first any suitable magistrate to invest with summary powers, I myself tried summarily during the first week of September more than a hundred persons, produced before me by the thanedar, Bahawalnagar, from whom looted property had been recovered. Most of them confessed and I fined them Rs 10–20; but a few were fined more heavily and, so as not to make things too easy, I sent about half a dozen to jail for a month. The method of selecting the latter was somewhat arbitrary and would not have satisfied a High Court Judge! I was reminded of an incident recorded in the Hunter Commission's Report on the Punjab disturbances of 1919. The boys of some schools in the town of Kasur had taken part in the disorders and, at the suggestion of an English magistrate, the military officer who was administering martial law in the area had caused six of them to be flogged. Some members of the Commission were at pains to ascertain how the six boys subjected to flogging had been selected and the following passage occurs:

Q. Some schoolboys were flogged and you gave directions that the biggest six boys were to be selected for that purpose?
A. I said, generally speaking, take the six biggest.
Q. Do you think that a reasonable thing to do?
A. Yes, I think so, under certain conditions.
Q. It was a mere accident that a boy being big should invite on himself punishment.
A. It was his misfortune.
Q. His misfortune was that he was big?
A. Yes.

The conduct of the authorities, as revealed in this passage, had always struck me as a bit odd until in not dissimilar circumstances I found myself doing somewhat the same thing! The persons whom I sent to jail were selected on the strength of their appearance, demeanour and the advice of the thanedar.

Sometime on September 13th I received at Bahawalnagar a wire from Gurmani saying that some prisoners had attempted to break out of the jail at Bahawalpur and that they had not yet been brought under control. I deliberated whether I should straightaway go there. It looked a bit ugly that an attempted break-out of the jail had not been suppressed as soon as detected. But Gurmani had not asked me to come, he had got with him the Commissioner of Police, Gilani and various other officers, I was myself still fully occupied in the Bahawalnagar area and for me to run up to Bahawalpur, unasked, on the strength of an inconclusive report might seem rather meddlesome. I decided to wait. The next day there came a reassuring telegram—the disturbance in the jail had been quelled. On the 15th Leghari and I went first thing in the morning to Harunabad where cholera was reported to have broken out among the refugees. The Muslims of this place were, as usual, very fidgety about imaginary dangers from across the border. We were standing in the roadway about 11.0 a.m. talking to some of them about the precautions we had taken when someone remarked that there had now been trouble in Bahawalpur. I said that there had only been some disturbance in the jail and that this had been suppressed. But I was told that my information was out of date; there had been a recrudescence of the trouble and bloodshed in Bahawalpur; telegrams to this effect had reached Harunabad less than an hour earlier. Leghari sent for the thanedar who made inquiries at the post office and the canal office[1] and presently confirmed that such telegrams had been received and appeared to be authentic.

We at once got into the car and drove back to Bahawalnagar. Dropping Leghari there and picking up my personal assistant, I drove on to Bahawalpur, cursing myself for not having gone there on the 13th. Five minutes after I had left a wire was received from Gurmani asking me to come immediately.

---

[1] The Irrigation Department had a separate telegraphic system of their own.

XI

Disturbances in Bahawalpur City

THERE was an ominous hush over Bahawalpur when I reached it that evening—a hush that I had now learnt to associate with towns in which disturbances had taken place. I did not have to go through the city or close up to its walls in order to get to my house, but even from a distance I missed the faint hum and stir of its normal life and knew that it was dead.

I rang up Gurmani and in the course of conversation learnt that he had wired for me to come and so was expecting me. He asked me to come round to his house as soon as possible, and said he would call some of the senior officers for a meeting. As I was walking over, I met in the road one of the assistant secretaries. I did not know him well as he worked mainly for Gurmani. He had always struck me as a rather bigoted Muslim. I nodded a greeting, whereupon, to my surprise, he burst out with apparently genuine pleasure.

'Thank God, you've come, sir! We've all been waiting for you.'

'Waiting for me?' I queried. 'Why have you been waiting for me? I'm afraid I shan't be able to do anything. I've only this moment arrived and know nothing about the situation.'

'The Prime Minister will tell you the whole position. You'll be able to suggest something, I know. I've been saying it all along.'

I was a bit puzzled. The time was hardly opportune for conventional flattery, but if his words were more than this, then I was apparently expected to retrieve the situation. I had no clear idea what it was, still less how to deal with it.

I walked on to the Prime Minister's house and had a few minutes with him alone before the arrival of the officers whom he had summoned. He greeted me with his usual geniality, but at once began inveighing against the police and military who, he said, had completely let us down. The former, after mustering all their forces, had proved unequal to dealing with a small outbreak in the jail. Disturbances had spread to the city. He had called in the Bahawalpur Army. They had made more noise than the police, but had done no better. There had been indiscriminate firing and widespread looting. Both the mob and the military were out of control. A number of Hindus had been killed—he could not say how many—and it had become very difficult to protect them.

I was far from pleased to learn that the military had been called in. If the police were ineffective, they were at least submissive. The military were armed and in a dangerous mood. It was Bahawalnagar over again. Having regard to our experience there, it was, in my view, a mistake to have turned to the military at all for help in maintaining order in the city. If more armed force was deemed essential, then at most a platoon should have been called in. They could have been kept under strict observation and control and would have been ample to check the Bahawalpur mob, if they were prepared to use their arms effectively. If they were not, then a larger force would be no better, but rather worse. As it was, a whole battalion had been brought to the city.

I think I expressed to Gurmani some misgiving at the military having been called in, but he replied that the police had been utterly useless, so what else could he do? There was no point in pursuing the matter since I was myself to blame for not having come to Bahawalpur as soon as I heard that there was trouble there. Normally it would have been the duty of the District Magistrate to do so.

With the Bahawalpur soldiery already dominating the scene, I felt that the best course might be to try to extricate all the Hindus from the city straight away and send them off by rail to India, as some of them had requested us to do a fortnight earlier. (How foolish we had been not to accede to their request!) I threw out this suggestion to Gurmani who seemed not unfavourable to it, but we had no time to discuss it, as by now the officers who had been summoned had assembled and were ushered into the room.

There were among them several military officers—including, I think, Brigadier Marden—Gilani (the High Court Judge who was acting as Additional District Magistrate), my whisky-drinking friend of the I.N.A. and another man in civilian clothes whom I had never met before. He turned out to be Gilani of I.N.A. fame, a younger brother of the Judge. I was at a loss to know in what capacity he was present as he had been kicked out of the Bahawalpur Army and had now no official position in the State. He was a smooth, slick and obviously able man and took quite a prominent part in the subsequent discussion. He spoke sensibly and to the point, but in view of his past history his presence at this juncture at our deliberations was, to me, not very welcome and seemed even rather sinister. However, Gurmani had apparently thought that, owing to his reputed influence with the troops, it would be as well to keep him under his thumb and that he might be genuinely useful as a sort of liaison officer. He himself was said to be anxious to earn Gurmani's good opinion so as to facilitate his reinstatement in the Bahawalpur Army.

The Commissioner of Police was conspicuous by his absence. He made some excuse, but, as I subsequently learnt, he was thoroughly disgruntled. He complained to me later that the military had been called in and the police entirely superseded without any reference to him. If he had been consulted, he told me, he would never have advised such a course. The police were holding the situation at the time and there was every hope of their getting the better of it; but the intervention of the military had aggravated it and made it quite unmanageable. Since he had been unceremoniously thrust aside, he considered that his advice was no longer wanted and washed his hands of the whole affair. Gurmani was annoyed at his absence and I very much missed him, for he was the only really experienced police officer we had.

After some brief talk on the general situation, Gurmani mentioned my suggestion that the entire Hindu population should be immediately removed from the city and then evacuated to India. The suggestion seemed to commend itself to everyone present. But I had put it forward without any deep consideration and was not yet sure whether it was practicable. The whole Hindu population of the city could not be moved to India in one day. They had to be collected together in one or two places which could be easily guarded, and then sent off to

[1] See pages 104–5.

India in batches. What place could serve as a temporary
'keep'? In the city itself there were several Hindu shrines to
which were attached extensive outbuildings and courts, accessible only through one main entrance gate. These could accommodate several hundreds but not the fourteen to fifteen thousand at which the Hindu population was estimated. Various
alternatives were suggested, but it was quickly apparent that
only the new jail, at that time still under construction, would
serve the purpose. This was situated rather more than a mile
from the city and was reached by a rough track, in places deep
in sand. Only the outer wall had been completed. This enclosed
an extensive open space in which barracks, workshops and other
buildings would in due course be erected, but so far only a few
small sheds had been put up. Within the protection of this wall
the whole Hindu population could remain for a few days in
perfect safety and considerable, but not insupportable, discomfort. It was still warm enough at night to sleep outdoors, so
from this point of view the absence of buildings did not matter.
The most unpleasant feature would be the fierce heat of the
sun by day, as there was scarcely any shade. But this would not
kill them. The area being extensive, sanitation presented no
great problem; some primitive latrines could easily be put up
for the more fastidious. But was there any water? Nobody was
sure whether the water supply had yet been installed: so someone was sent to ring up the Public Works Department and find
out. After some delay we received an affirmative answer.

I still had considerable apprehensions about the whole
operation. Not knowing the temper of the city mob and of the
Bahawalpur troops, I could not gauge the danger of the
Hindus being attacked as they moved out of their houses in the
city and made their way to the new jail. The I.N.A. Gilani
assured me that the danger of this was negligible, and I saw
myself the next day that my fears had been exaggerated. The
Muslims were out for loot, not for blood. They were not inclined to kill, unless wantonly provoked or baulked of their
plunder. But on that first evening of my arrival in Bahawalpur
I had not been able to size this all up properly.

Since the new jail was more than a mile distant from the
city, many of the Hindus—the old and infirm, women and
children—would have to be transported there by lorry. We

G

could only rake together about ten lorries, including military vehicles, and some of them were doubtful starters; but we reckoned that, if we started promptly at about 9.00 a.m. we should just be able to complete the job by nightfall.

The Hindus would all have to be prepared for the move, especially if it was to start the very next morning. It was necessary to inform some of their leaders straight away of what was intended, so that word could be passed to all Hindu families that night that they would be expected to leave the city the next day. I was also anxious to get the reaction of Hindu representatives to our plan for their evacuation. Gurmani sent for the Hindu Minister, Dewan Fateh Chand, a tall, thin, grey-haired man whom I had always found a very pleasant colleague. He came in presently, very pale and nervous and with a haunting look of anxiety on his face. We put before him our plan and he seemed on the whole to approve of it. I specially questioned him whether, as it was already late, it would be possible to get the Hindus ready for a move—which would in fact be a final departure from their hearths and homes—by the next morning. He was hesitant about this and said that he would like to consult other members of his community. Somehow or other he then contacted several leading Hindus. Most of them were whole-heartedly in favour of the evacuation plan and considered it feasible. It was decided to proceed with it.

I think this decision was right and it was fortunate that we took it; but I myself certainly reached it on quite wrong premises. I was under the impression that the lives of the Hindus were in far more imminent danger than I found the next day to be the case. The city mob and the Bahawalpur Army were, as already stated, out for loot rather than blood. The removal of the Hindus from the city was, therefore, exactly what they wanted. It opened the field for loot and did away with resistance and obstruction. They had no special desire to wade through blood to get their plunder. They were conveniently relieved of this necessity. I had come to suspect this during the course of this first evening and I became convinced of it in the next two days. With fuller knowledge of all this (which fortunately at the critical moment I did not possess) I would probably not have advocated the drastic remedy of immediate and wholesale evacuation, but would have been tempted to try to restore order with the Hindus still in their houses. Such a course would have been at best futile, at worst fatal. It could have had no chance of success unless the Bahawalpur soldiery were first removed; and that was impossible. The disturbed state of the city afforded a plausible argument against any proposal for their immediate withdrawal, and in any case they had no intention of releasing their hold until they had secured and divided the spoils. The other battalion had sacked Bahawalnagar; Bahawalpur was their prize. Since the army wanted to share the loot rather than stop the looting, an attempt by an unarmed civil officer like myself to control the situation while they were present was doomed to failure. Either his orders would be unheeded, or, if he managed to cajole or dragoon a small party of them to take effective action against Muslim looters or himself seized a rifle and shot a few, then this, in the temper of the times, would have been the signal (as at Hasilpur) for a general massacre of Hindus in which he too would probably have succumbed.

Hindsight, therefore, confirms the somewhat panicky decision that we took, though not the grounds on which I, at least, at the time supported it.

The arrangements made or envisaged for the reception of the Hindus the next day at the new jail were of the sketchiest. There was nothing much that could be done that night, except to make sure that the water supply was working. This was done. I was hopefully counting on procuring grain from the mandi in the town and left this over till the morning. But it was essential to select at once someone to act as camp commandant and remain continuously at the jail after the arrival of the Hindus to keep order and see to their needs. No-one could be more fully relied upon to do this with efficiency and to the greatest comfort and contentment of the Hindus than the Settlement Officer, Nur Mohammad. But would he be willing to undertake such a thankless task?

Nur Mohammad was a retired officer of the Punjab Civil Service and a wonderful product of the Indo-British association. He combined the best of both the East and the West—a type all too little known to the outside world. To the charm, the exquisite courtesy and the piety of a cultured Muslim gentleman were joined the regular, methodical habits of business and

the sense of duty and responsibility derived from British training. Added to these were a first-rate intellect, a delightful sense
of humour and a natural benevolence—a combination of
qualities which made him one of the best and best beloved
officers of his day. Before retirement he had been a Deputy
Commissioner in the Punjab for a considerable time. Twelve
years earlier, when I was in Multan, he was in charge of an
adjoining district. I had known him ever since then.

'All Deputy Commissioners,' he used to say, 'have some
weakness. With some it is money, with others women, with
others love of power. My own weakness,' he would continue
with a chuckle, 'which I share with Mr. —— (naming a well-
known English I.C.S. officer) is simply love of popularity. An
amiable weakness, if you will, but a weakness none the less.
It makes you too soft; you can't say "No" to anyone.'

I felt that this amiable weakness and a touch of softness
would not come amiss in handling a mass of helpless, frightened,
friendless Hindus, rudely thrust out of their homes into the rigours
of a jail camp. He would pour balm and oil into their wounds,
whereas the general disposition was, in his own words, to rub
salt into them.

I requested him to take on the job. It was a good deal to
ask of an elderly Muslim nearing sixty. It would involve a day-
and-night vigil at the jail, roughing it in the open like the
Hindus themselves, and the strain of bearing patiently the ceaseless outpouring of their woes. I could see at once that he was
dismayed by my request and most reluctant to shoulder the
responsibility. But his sense of duty prevailed and, to my great
relief, he consented to do it.

He at once began questioning me about all our projected
arrangements and clearly felt doubtful whether the operation
was practicable. He was particularly concerned as to how we
could safely dispatch them to India by rail in view of the fearful train massacres that were occurring almost daily in the
Punjab. His fear was that, having moved them to the jail, we
might then find it impossible to send them on by rail and would
have them on our hands indefinitely in conditions which would
lead to the death of many of them through disease, under-
nourishment and exposure. I told him that I had already safely
dispatched large numbers of Hindus from Bahawalnagar and

Hasilpur to Hindumalkot and hoped to get them out from Bahawalpur along the same route. I reckoned that we should be able to send them all off in four to five days and that scratch arrangements for maintaining them in the jail would suffice for this short period. We had already verified that there was water installed there and I would requisition grain from the mandi. He said that the mandi had been looted and that he thought I would find nothing there. This was not encouraging, but I had plenty of stocks elsewhere and could, if necessary, bring them into Bahawalpur. There would be some delay, but a day's fast would not kill the Hindus.

He was not altogether satisfied with this for, as he pointed out, it would be very disgraceful to herd all the Hindus out of the city and into the jail and then for some time have nothing to give them to eat. He also drew attention to the absence of shade in the new jail and, during the next couple of days, complained about it repeatedly. There was no remedy for this and, having been continuously out in the sun for most of the past three weeks, I was perhaps not very sympathetic. I told him that the Hindus would get used to it and that, if necessary, they could get into the shade of the walls. The walls were burning hot and in the middle of the day cast no shade at all; so the latter suggestion was not very helpful. The former was more correct and the only real answer.

It was by now getting late. I ordered my bed to be made up just outside the main city gate so that I could be immediately available in case there was an uproar during the night. Marden also came and established himself there. The night was absolutely peaceful except for occasional stray rifle shots. I remarked to Marden on this casual unauthorized firing—a manifest symptom of indiscipline—but knew that in the circumstances it was not really possible for him to control his troops.

The evacuation of the Hindus from the city started the next morning, but by no means as early as we had intended. The lorries were late and the Hindus still later and it was not till about 11.0 a.m. that we got them moving out towards the jail in earnest. Until the lorries had blazed the trail, none of them would proceed to the jail on foot, but hung about just inside the main city gate at the bottom of the principal bazaar. Once, however, the lorries started plying there was soon a regular stream of pedestrians flowing out from the city gate to the new jail.

The city was in rather less disorder than I had been led to expect. Most of the Hindu shops in the main bazaar, running up from the city gate, and in the other principal bazaar which crossed it, had been wholly or partially looted, and there was the usual litter scattered about; but no sign of arson or wanton destruction of buildings. Farther on, the mandi had been thoroughly ransacked, as Nur Mohammed had warned me, and not much of value was left in it. There were some corpses lying about in the side streets and alleys, but in the main bazaars they had all been cleared away. Parties of Bahawalpur troops were stationed at cross roads and other focal points and a few were negligently patrolling the bazaars. Otherwise up till about 10.30 a.m. the streets were practically empty.

While waiting for the evacuation to begin, I did what I could to salvage some grain from the mandi and get it ground up and sent to the jail. There was a retired naib-tahsildar, a very honest, god-fearing but crusty old man, who, before the disturbances began, had been working under me in the Civil Supplies department. As soon as I could find him, I put him with some clerks in charge of the plundered mandi. He collected and guarded every grain like a dragon, scaring away would-be pilferers with flashing eyes, a fierce white beard and furious threatenings. But all that he could lay hands on fell far short of our needs.

Timidly and tardily the Hindus crept out of their houses and began gathering in the principal bazaars to board the lorries. There were no evident signs of danger and, as the day wore on, the bazaars became crowded with them waiting with bundles, suitcases and small trunks for places in the lorries, or making their way on foot towards the city gate. The evacuation was carried out fairly systematically, ward by ward. As soon as a ward was cleared, the looters quickly moved in and began ransacking the empty buildings. I surprised two sepoys in a deserted shop bending over some sacks and rummaging through their contents. They were so engrossed that they did not see or hear me approaching from behind until I gave one of them a hard kick up the bottom; whereupon they both snatched up their rifles and ran off clattering down the street.

But to stop this looting effectively was wholly impracticable, particularly as the officers of the Bahawalpur Army were conniving at it. A good many of them were to be seen lounging about a building just off one of the main bazaars which had been made a kind of advanced headquarters. Passing nearby this place in the middle of the afternoon, I saw a number of tin boxes and trunks strewn about the roadway. I asked a couple of military officers who were lolling at the door of their headquarters to get some of their men to clear these from the road and stack them all together on one side. (They were the property of Hindus and I intended later to have them carted to the jail so that they could be claimed by their owners.) The officers coolly replied that they could not do this without the orders of their C.O.! I did not stop to pick up a quarrel, but simply ignored their insolence. A little later I collected two or·three of my own men to do the job but by that time the boxes had all disappeared. The Bahawalpur Army had carried off their booty.

The movables which the Hindus left behind, because they could not carry them away, were perhaps legitimate spoils. Anyway one could hardly blame the ordinary Muslim for picking up what was his for the taking, whatever one might think about the propriety of officers claiming a share. But naturally, once this game had begun, almost everyone from the highest to the lowest desired to take part in it. A certain number obtained a kind of title to their gains. Outgoing Hindus entrusted their property, sometimes by written deed, to Muslim friends and acquaintances. These documents usually had no legal validity and were not recognized in respect of immovable property; but they afforded good practical cover to claims to movables. Some valuable furniture and carpets changed hands in this way.

By and large the contents of houses had to be left to their own fate. More important was to prevent the Hindus being relieved of such hand luggage as they were trying to carry away with them and as soon as I saw that their lives were not in imminent danger I devoted myself mainly to this. Military pickets and military escorts travelling on the lorries, not to mention casual Muslims in the streets, all tried to take their toll. I shuttled to and fro in my car between the city and the jail, endeavouring to check these exactions, and Nur Mohammed at the jail end imposed some restraint. But they went on. A small incident will serve as an illustration. On one of my visits to the jail in the late afternoon, a young lad of sixteen to seventeen complained to me that as he passed the military picket at the main city gate they had snatched away his suitcase. I told him to get into my car and took him with me back to the city gate. There was about a section of troops posted there under a jamadar. As soon as we alighted from the car, the young man espied his suitcase in a room leading off from one side of the gate.

'There it is,' he said and pointed it out to me lying on the floor amid some of the soldiers' kit-bags. I pushed my way into the room, picked up the suitcase and brought it out. The jamadar now appeared on the scene. I did not deem it politic to be angry with him or reprimand him, so I simply said in Hindustani,

'Jamadar sahib, this suitcase seems to have got in here by mistake.'

The jamadar saluted—a gesture which most of the Bahawalpur troops had by this time forgotten—and replied, 'No doubt it has, sir, for it isn't ours.'

'Very good, then, I'll take it away.' The jamadar saluted again and I got into my car with the suitcase and its owner and drove back to the jail.

On my return to the city, the same jamadar stopped me at the gate. He said that they had captured some Sikhs, about half a dozen I understood, and wanted to know what to do with them. I imagined that he had got them there at the gate and, knowing from experience how unsafe it was to leave Sikhs in the hands of the troops, I said immediately that he could make them over to me and I would see about their further custody. I asked him how and why they had captured them. He replied that the Sikhs had had revolvers and had been firing out of the windows of a building and had been captured with much difficulty. Still thinking that he had got them confined in one of the rooms adjoining the gate, I told him to bring them out. But he then said that he had already sent them away. Once again I was apprehensive until he explained that he had sent them over to his superior officers and pointed to a big school building about two hundred and fifty yards away which had been made the battalion headquarters. I was much relieved. I told him that that was quite all right and I would see about them later.

I hurried on into the city. It was getting late and if we were to evacuate all the Hindus by nightfall, we should have to hustle. There were now crowds of them waiting in the main bazaar and it did not seem possible to move them all in the short remaining period of daylight. The I.N.A. Gilani met me in the street and said that, as it was now impossible to get them all out that day, those belonging to a certain area should be allowed to take refuge in the precincts of the biggest of the Hindu shrines. I immediately agreed. A well-known Gosain presided over the shrine, a big fat fellow who used to be present on all ceremonial occasions to do a kind of public obeisance to the Nawab on behalf of the Hindu community. He was very anxious not to have to go to the jail camp, and assured me that there were ample stocks of food at the shrine—which proved to be the case.

It was about now that I heard a report that Marden had been wounded. It was said that earlier in the day he had been fired at from a building somewhere in the city and hit in the knee. No-one seemed to have any exact information about the incident.

Dusk drew on and the last lorries to ply that day moved down to the city gate. Quite a number of Hindus who had not been able to get places in them were still standing in the bazaar, laden with luggage. They asked me whether they should go back to their homes. I advised them to do so, as I thought it would be dangerous for them to try to walk to the jail in the gathering darkness, and I told them that we would transport them there the next day. Some women in the group said that their houses were some way off and that they did not feel equal to returning to them with all their luggage. They pointed to an entrance nearby, leading to a shrine with a lot of rambling buildings attached, and asked whether they should go in there. It seemed safe enough, as there was only one narrow entrance, so I told them they might do so.

I now repaired to Gurmani's house to report progress and to find out what had happened to Marden. It turned out that he really had been wounded in the knee. Gurmani was trying to

G*

get a skilled surgeon from Multan to come and extract the
bullet. Marden was hopping about on one leg, remarkably
cheerful, though probably in considerable pain. I never ascertained the exact circumstances in which he received this wound.
He simply told me at the time that he had been fired at from
a building—I presumed by one of the Sikhs whose capture had
been reported to me by the jamadar. The Hindus believed,
and believe to this day, that he was shot at by one of his own
men, but I don't think this was the case. He bore his wound
with fortitude, but was out of action for some time. This episode
led to a rumour in East Punjab that both Gurmani and I had
been killed.

I had all along been anxious to get the military withdrawn from the city as soon as possible. While, therefore,
a number of us were gathered at Gurmani's house and were
discussing arrangements for the next day, I tactfully suggested
that the troops were tired after two or three days' continuous
duty in the city and deserved to be brought out and given a
rest. I was pleasantly surprised to find this suggestion accepted
immediately by everyone present, including the I.N.A. Gilani.
It was agreed that the troops should be withdrawn the following afternoon, after evacuating the few remaining Hindus
during the morning.

This was more than I had dared to hope for, and the decision was later somewhat modified. The battalion commander
represented to Gurmani that he could not conveniently withdraw his troops so soon and they were eventually permitted to
remain in the city, with the Hindu property at their mercy,
for an extra twenty-four hours.

Nearly all of us who assembled at Gurmani's house that
evening believed that, apart from Marden's wound, the evacuation of the Hindus from the city had been successfully
accomplished without bloodshed. We informed Gurmani
accordingly. Unknown to most of us, a shocking crime was
being perpetrated at that very moment. There was a prominent
citizen of Bahawalpur, named Mehta Nand Kishore, who was
reputed to be very wealthy and had made himself conspicuous,
and perhaps obnoxious, by his staunch championship of Hindu
rights. On learning that the Hindus were to be evacuated from
the city, he had somehow contrived to arrange with the military

for a special lorry to transport him and his considerable baggage to the camp jail. Near the close of the day a special lorry
was duly provided and he and his goods were loaded into it and
driven off at nightfall with an escort towards the new jail. But
they never reached it. After going a short distance the lorry
turned aside and went down to the river. There he was murdered, his body consigned to the waters of the Sutlej, and his
goods divided among his supposed protectors.

The weight of this and of another as yet unknown tragedy
did not oppress me that evening. My thoughts were all of the
future and of the problems of transporting the Hindus safely
from the jail camp to the railway station and thence by train
to Hindumalkot.

The principal railway station of Bahawalpur was on the
main line from Karachi to Lahore, a little less than a mile from
the city. But the shortest route to India, and the only one which
we could use, was the branch line from Samasatta to Hindumalkot and on to Bhatinda. This line passed south of Bahawalpur and there was a small station on it called Baghdad-ul-jadid
about three miles from the city. This was the station at which
the Hindus would have to entrain. But how were we to get
them there? The one train in the day, which we had arranged
should run as a 'refugee special', passed through at 9.20 a.m.
With our exiguous supply of lorries, which, owing to break-
downs, was diminishing rather than increasing, we should not
be able to move appreciable numbers to the station by that
early hour.

Then there was the question of an escort. One train had
already been attacked on this line and Hindus butchered. We
should have to send an escort of troops to repel possible attacks.
But would the Bahawalpur troops be reliable? Or would they
precipitate a massacre?

The feeding of the refugees in the jail camp had also not been
ensured. Nur Mohammad had told me during the afternoon
that he wanted to discuss with me this and other matters connected with the camp; but at that time, amid all the hubbub
of the Hindus streaming in, it was impossible to talk without
interruption. So I agreed to come and see him after dinner, by
which time he hoped the refugees would have settled down for
the night. I got down to the camp about 10.0 p.m. The supply

of more grain was urgent. Nur Mohammad, knowing that I had already gleaned all there was to be had from the mandi, had obtained from leading Hindus a list of temples and other buildings in their wards where sizeable stocks of flour, grain and fuel wood were known or believed to exist. These, if we could lay hands on them before looters seized them, would keep us going for some time. I took the list from him.

Only three or four well-educated Hindus were with him at this hour; the rest had all gone to get what sleep they could. They spoke to me most earnestly about the perils of travelling by rail to India. One and all, they said, wanted to leave the camp and go there, but they had read and heard of terrible train massacres in the Punjab and they did not know how to face the fearful risks of the journey. I told them that they would not have to travel across the Punjab, we would send them out along the branch line running through the State and so could ourselves be responsible for their protection all the way. This seemed to reassure them to some extent, for it was of the Punjab that they were mainly frightened. I also told them that there would be a military escort with every train. They immediately requested that the escorts might be of Gurkha troops. There were a few platoons of Gurkhas in the Bahawalpur Army and we had drawn upon these to provide guards at the jail camp, much to the relief and satisfaction of the Hindus. But I was doubtful whether we could also find Gurkha escorts for the trains. I said that I could not promise this and that in any case a Gurkha escort could not be arranged for the train that was to leave the next morning. I would see what could be done about it in the case of future trains.

I impressed upon them that as we were very short of lorries they must be ready for an early and punctual start the next morning and also see that the lorries were filled expeditiously so that they could make as many trips as possible to the station before the train left. It was agreed to start at 7.00 a.m. Nur Mohammad suggested that tongas should also be utilized for taking the Hindus to the station. I was unnecessarily nervous and did not agree to this. I was afraid that in the explosive atmosphere altercations between the Muslim tonga drivers and their Hindu passengers might lead to outbreaks of violence. In any case I felt that it was too late at that hour of the night to start

calling up tongas for the next morning. However, in the course
of the next day, I was persuaded by Nur Mohammad that it
would be safe to use tongas; and for speeding up the evacuation
there was really no other course. He was quite right. The tonga
drivers were delighted at the opportunity of doing a roaring
trade. The more Hindus they could carry to the station, the
better. They had no wish to cause any fracas which might interrupt this profitable traffic.

I left the camp quite late, probably about 11.30 p.m., and went
with a chaprassi to the city with the list which Nur Mohammad
had given me, in search of the tahsildar. I had been trying to
find him all day, but without success. So far as I recollect he
was reported to be out on tour, but to be due back that afternoon. To reach his house I had to go through various winding
lanes and alleys which were all too plentifully sprinkled with
corpses. I did not like stumbling upon them in the dark. When
we got there we had great difficulty in rousing him, but at last,
after sundry knockings and hallooings, which reverberated in the
silence of the night, an answering shout of 'Kaun hai'[1] came
from the inmost recesses of the house. We proclaimed our
identity, but this did not penetrate to or did not convince the
tahsildar. After a long interval he gingerly opened the door and
emerged in the darkness covering himself with a double-
barrelled gun. He lowered the gun and looked very foolish as
soon as he realized who it was. He was profuse in apologies.
I thought it very ridiculous for the tahsildar, a Muslim, to
show such alarm and take such excessive precautions on being
knocked up in the night, and so I was rather severe with him.
I asked him what on earth he was afraid of? Did he imagine the
city was full of Sikhs? My chaprassi also impertinently interjected some sarcasms and had to be reprimanded. The tahsildar
said he had thought we might be robbers. He could not believe
that the Revenue Minister would be coming to see him at such
a late hour. I told him that he should not carry arms and that it
was absurd for Muslims to behave as though they were in
danger. He promised not to do it again! Actually he was a very
good tahsildar and I liked him. I said I was sorry for disturbing
him in the middle of the night, but there was urgent work for
him to do in the morning. Handing over to him Nur Moham-

[1] 'Who's there?'

mad's list I directed him to collect the supplies from the places indicated therein and have them sent immediately to the new jail. I told him that this must take precedence over all his other duties and that his primary responsibility during the next few days would be to keep the jail camp supplied with food, fuel and other necessities. He could procure them from wherever he could find them in and around the city. If he foresaw any difficulties, he was to let me know.

A fair proportion of the places shown in Nur Mohammad's list yielded supplies more or less intact. Though there was some delay, owing to lack of transport, in getting them to the jail, they tided us over our immediate difficulties and somehow or other we kept going till the evacuation was over. Later, however, we had to bring in considerable supplies of grain from elsewhere to restock the city.

Since the evacuation of the Hindus from the city was not quite complete, I had decided once again to establish myself for the night just outside the city gate. After leaving the tahsildar, I made my way there and sat down on my bed. It was a little after midnight. The city was quite still; there were no rifle shots as during the previous night, but from all directions there came the sound of 'tap, tap, tap; tap, tap, tap' as looters hammered away at safes left behind in the deserted houses of the Hindus. Somehow or other I fell in with the I.N.A. officer with whom I had made friends at Bahawalnagar. He had been helping with the evacuation all day and had either settled himself for the night, like me, just outside the city gate or had strolled over there from the battalion headquarters about two hundred yards away. We sat chatting for some time and then decided, before turning in for the night, to make a round of the city.

We went up the main bazaar and then followed the sound of hammering, first in one direction and then in another; but as soon as we approached, the hammering stopped and the looters eluded us in the darkness. While we were wandering about in this way, a man came running up to us from behind and said that there were some fresh corpses lying in the main bazaar. We were amazed. We had passed up the main bazaar only about fifteen minutes earlier. There had been no corpses there then and since then we had not heard any sound from that direction. We hurried back. There were one or two street lamps in the main bazaar. In the dim light shed by one of these we saw some forms lying in the middle of the roadway. When we got up to them, we found that they were the bodies, still quite warm, of two women and three children. I was stooping down to examine one of the women more closely, when my companion a few yards away exclaimed, 'This one is breathing!' I felt the pulse of the woman near me; it was beating quite strongly. 'This one is also alive,' I said. Just at that moment one of the children, aged about four, sat up and began to talk.

We now guessed that these women must have tried to commit suicide by throwing themselves and their children from the roof of one of the adjoining houses—a fall of twenty-five to thirty feet. For some minutes they continued to feign that they were dead or dying and we could not get them to speak. One of them, the elder of the two, appeared to be quite badly hurt. It was she who at last became a little communicative. We gathered from her that during the day the military had come and taken away their husbands and, being left alone and fearing that the worst would befall them, they had in desperation tried to make away with themselves and their children by jumping from the roof of their house. She also told us that there were some more children, though not hers, inside the house.

This woman was too much injured to rise from the ground. We propped her up and she remained lying there until we could get a lorry to take her to the hospital. The other rather younger woman had only superficial injuries. The smallest of the three children was dead; the second was injured; and the third, who had first sat up and begun to talk, was practically unscathed. We sent a man to fetch a military lorry and another to the hospital to warn them in advance that these patients would be coming. Meanwhile we ourselves went to explore the inside of the house.

We had to go up a narrow passage-way leading from the main street, and then enter the house from the side. In a central room a charming but unexpected sight met our eyes. Laid out on the floor, side by side in rows, each with its own small pillow, were sixteen little children, all fast alseep, sleeping, in truth, the sleep of innocence. Their untroubled slumbers were in strange contrast to the chaos in the city outside and to the agonized despair of the two women. It was an unforgettable scene. We put out the light and tiptoed from the room. My companion kindly undertook to collect these children in the morning and convey them to the hospital or the jail camp, as might seem best.

A lorry arrived quite soon. We lifted into it the women and children who had been lying in the road and my companion went off with them to the hospital. He said that he would make inquiries at the battalion headquarters about their menfolk. It was pretty clear that these women and children—some more women were found in the house later on—were the families of the captured Sikhs about whom the jamadar had spoken to me in the afternoon. My companion had, I think, also heard something about them. The next morning he told me that he had not so far been able to get any trace of them. Fearing the worst, I went and spoke to Gurmani. I explained to him that these Sikhs were said to have been sent over to the battalion headquarters in the school building. I asked him to tell the battalion commander to report where they were. The battalion commander, when questioned, denied all knowledge of them, and the inquiries made by him yielded nothing, or nothing that was ever conveyed to me or to the outside world. These Sikhs, about eight in number, just vanished. My I.N.A. friend quite early on confided to me, with an indignation which, I believe, was genuine, his suspicion that they had all been killed. In a day or two, when no clue to them was forthcoming, this suspicion became a certainty. Where and how they were made away with was never ascertained, but it seems probable that by the time the two women threw themselves from their housetop they were already dead, having been killed and thrown into the river earlier that night. One of them, Amar Singh, was cashier of the local branch of the Imperial Bank of India and had the keys of the strong room containing all the cash not only of the bank but of the State Treasury. The keys vanished with him. For days we could not open the strong room or replenish our stocks of cash, till finally someone came from Lahore with a duplicate set of keys.

No-one was punished, no-one individually was even blamed, for this dark deed. The Bahawalpur Army hid the matter in its own unwritten archives. But I could not rid myself of the sense of my own responsibility for the tragedy. Knowing as I did the feeling against the Sikhs and the army's attitude to them it was idiotic to allow my first apprehensions to be lulled to rest because the jamadar told me that the prisoners had been sent to battalion headquarters. Even there they could not be assumed to be safe. In the light of incidents that had occurred in the Bahawalnagar area, I ought to have abandoned all else and gone in search of them as soon as the jamadar spoke to me about them. I have often thought since that in mentioning them to me at all the jamadar was trying to convey to me that I ought to look to their safety. In the few minutes' conversation I had with him, he struck me as a decent sort of man. He must have known that the Sikhs were in imminent danger and, having seen that I was endeavouring to help the refugees, must have realized that I could be the means of saving them. To give an indirect hint by just referring to them would have been typical of his class. But if he meant to give the hint, I was too dull to take it.

The painful task of breaking the truth to the women devolved on me. For several days, in answer to their repeated inquiries, we said that we were still looking for their husbands. But before they left for India—and, owing to the injuries to one of them, they were among the last to leave—it seemed best to put an end to their suspense and to hopes which we knew to be vain. So I told them that all our searches had been fruitless and we had to presume that their husbands were no more.

My narrative has now run ahead of the course of events and it is necessary to go back a little. After sending off the would-be suicides to the hospital in the middle of the night, I went to bed. Next morning I was up early to supervise the transport of refugees from the camp to the railway station. This did not go at all well. When the first lorries arrived, there were no refugees ready to get into them. Though the jail camp was not an alluring spot, there appeared to be a general reluctance to forsake it for the unknown hazards of a railway journey. I began to doubt whether more than a handful of refugees would be induced to take the plunge and go by the first train. Then presently, after about twenty minutes of seemingly fruitless persuasion, there was a sudden rush and a mad scramble to obtain seats. Nur Mohammad and I tried vainly to impose some kind of order. It was utterly useless and we gave it up. Some of the lorries were not really designed for passengers and were not

easy to get into. Men, women and children crowded round
them, shouting, yelling and weeping, pushing and jostling and
banging one another with their luggage without distinction of
age or sex. In this confusion parents got into lorries without
their children or their luggage, or luggage and children were
thrown in first and the owners were unable to scramble up after
them. It took ages then to sort this out and send a lorry off
without some vital person or package missing. Consequently
the lorries made very few trips and we were able to transport
barely 1,000 people to the station before the train left.

We had reserved the whole train for refugees. The number
that we succeeded in bringing to the station filled but did not
crowd it. Muslims in general and the station staff in particular
considered that the Hindus were being sent off (at the expense
of the Bahawalpur Government) in far too much luxury and
comfort. They wanted them to be packed like sardines, to the
exclusion, if need be, of all luggage. After the first day their wish
on the first point was gratified. With the use of tongas and improved arrangements for loading the lorries we were able to
transport two to three thousand refugees daily to the station in
time for the train. This usually consisted of seven coaches; but
after the first two days we had to agree to the last coach being
kept for ordinary passengers and cram the refugees into the
remainder. This meant that there was no more luxury travel for
them! Many had to cling like locusts to the outside or sit on the
roof in the broiling sun or on the buffers. Since the journey to
Hindumalkot took the whole day, it must have been terribly
uncomfortable and exhausting. But those who travelled in the
first train escaped these hardships.

Among these there was a prominent Hindu named Professor
Mehta. With a view to allaying the general anxiety the Hindu
leaders had arranged with him that he should accompany
those going by the first train and come back and report how
things went. He left with every profession that he would be
seeing us all again the next day. However, having once got
safely through to India, he never returned.

While this train was being sent off, the few Hindus still remaining in the city were being evacuated to the jail camp. I
went back there direct from the station and spoke to the Hindu
leaders about the need to control their people so that in future

there would not be such a mad rush for the lorries in the morning. They said that they were themselves ashamed at what had occurred and were determined that the embarkation should be more orderly in future. They soon effected quite a marked improvement.

Not unnaturally they were at this time very querulous and unhappy, and it was impossible to remove all their complaints or to offer them much consolation in their misery. Several of those in the camp had some close relative in some other part of the State and wanted him or her to join them before they entrained for India. A few of these, in what appeared to be especially deserving cases, were fetched in my car and such other private cars as we could muster, but it was not possible to collect them all, still less to scour the countryside for cousins, aunts and yet more distant relations, as we were repeatedly pressed to do. There were also numerous requests for being escorted back to the city in search of some treasured possession that had been forgotten. Since such requests had ordinarily to be refused, a method was soon devised of obtaining an escort on false pretences. Knowing that we were short of grain, individual Hindus would come forward and say that they had several bags of grain stored in their houses and that they offered these to the camp 'as a free gift'—though they were by now hardly theirs to give. We would then depute escorts to take them to the city so that they could point out their houses and the bags of grain. A few of the early offers were genuine; but a large number were found to be bogus. When the house was reached, there would be no sign of any bags of grain; the donor would say that they must have been looted and immediately begin to search for other of his belongings. We soon had to refuse all such offers.

Apart from these petty matters, there was the question of having Gurkha escorts for the trains. I put the Hindus' request to Gurmani. Like me, he was not very hopeful about it. He discussed it, I think, with Marden who was at this time still lying wounded at Gurmani's house. There were overwhelming objections to it. The use of Gurkha troops at the jail camp had caused some murmuring and their use for the escorts would be regarded by the rest of the Bahawalpur Army as a reflection on themselves and might dangerously excite them. Already there had been some signs of hostility towards the Gurkhas and it was felt that in the changed conditions they would have to be disbanded—some initial steps had, I think, been taken. I was quite convinced, and so was Gurmani, that the wisest course was to lay squarely on the Muslim troops the responsibility for escorting the Hindus safely to Hindumalkot. There seemed reason to think that individual units, when entrusted with a specific task such as escorting a train of refugees, would feel in honour bound to discharge it faithfully. Gurmani took the trouble to speak personally to each of the officers deputed to command the escort of a train and impress on him his responsibility.

The Hindus were very far from being satisfied. I could not disclose to them in full our reasons for not providing Gurkha escorts, but I told them that there were in my judgement good reasons and that it was really safer to give them Muslim troops as escorts. In spite of this they went on incessantly pestering me to provide Gurkha escorts until at last I was driven to take an extreme step. I told them bluntly that the matter had been decided in the manner which we judged to be in their best interests and that if they raised it again, I would wash my hands entirely of their affairs and leave them to get to India as best they could without any further help from me. This had the desired effect. Thereafter they became more amenable to my advice and never mentioned Gurkha escorts again except that one of them, a few days later, had the courtesy to tell me that they now realized our decision had been right and that they had been wrong to press us on the point.

Now that the Hindus had been removed from the city we began the usual process of locking and numbering the abandoned houses and shops and listing their contents, if any. Most of the latter were auctioned. The looters had not left much. I felt it necessary to do something to put a stop to the constant hammering at safes, so in the next few days I had them all collected and stored in the compound of the tahsil. About one hundred were found intact; a much larger number had been broken open. There was one which, according to the tahsildar, was reputed to contain 'much gold' and he did not like to have to assume responsibility for safeguarding it; so this one large and very heavy safe was deposited in my house.

One of the items of loot was livestock. During the day follow-ing the evacuation of the Hindus from the city the grounds of the school, which the military had made their headquarters, gradually became stocked with large numbers of cows, buffaloes and ponies. These caught the eye of Gurmani who was rather incensed at this blatant exhibition of their loot by the military. I was inclined to take a more charitable view of the matter. The animals left behind in the city by the Hindus, I said, had to be fed and watered by someone. As Revenue Minister I was Custodian of Evacuee Property, but I had not yet had time to attend to these animals and was quite glad that the military had provided for them in this way. Gurmani was emphatic that the military intended to appropriate the animals; in any case, he said, the populace, seeing them tethered in the grounds of the battalion headquarters, would conclude that they had done so, and we ought not to permit any such public advertisement of military misconduct. He therefore asked me to take the animals over and see about their disposal; and he ordered the O.C. troops—who rather foolishly disclaimed all knowledge of them—to hand them over to me. But when the tahsildar, on my instructions, went to collect them, only a few inferior ponies were delivered to him. All the valuable milch cattle had dis-appeared—like the Sikhs—no-one could say where.

I had thought that by midday on September 17th all the Hindus still remaining in the city had been removed to the camp with the exception of those we had allowed to stay in the precincts of the Gosain's shrine. Some time in the middle of the afternoon, as I was going up the main bazaar, two or three men stopped me and said that they had heard some shots coming from somewhere off to the right. On my questioning them, they pointed to a narrow doorway and said that some soldiers had gone in that way not long before and they thought that it must be they who had fired the shots. I then realized that this was the entrance to the shrine in which late the previous day some Hindu families, unable to obtain places in the lorries to go to the camp, had taken refuge. I looked about for some V.C.O.[1] as I considered it prudent, so far as possible, to handle the troops through their own officers. I was told that there was a jamadar a little way down the street. Sending my chap-

[1] Viceroy's Commissioned Officer.

rassi off to call him, I hurried through the doorway and up a narrow flight of wooden stairs. These led to a maze of rooms, dark passages and balconies overlooking courtyards down below. I made my way through some of these, then down some more stairs and up another flight, and was beginning to despair of finding anything when I heard voices and sounds of a scuffle a little ahead of me. Coming out on to a flat roof, I saw three soldiers in an open court below and a crowd of Hindus huddled under the roof of a colonnade running along one side of it. The soldiers had their backs towards me, but the Hindus were facing me and saw me up on the roof opposite to them. Many of them raised folded hands towards me and there was a sort of muffled gasp of 'Sahib a gaya'.[1] Some of them pointed to a stairway at one corner by which I could get down into the court. I ran to it and down the stairs, shouting out in Hindustani to an, as yet, imaginary jamadar, 'Come along, this way, jamadar sahib, here they are.'

The soldiers were taken by surprise. I peremptorily ordered them to fall in, and, having got them lined up in a row, tapped one of them on the pocket of his tunic, which was bulging tremendously, and asked him what he had got in there. He pulled out an enormous alarm clock. Meanwhile the other two, with the greatest alacrity, began taking out of their pockets a large assortment of watches, rings, bracelets and fountain-pens. Every one of their pockets was stuffed full. They were very apologetic and repeatedly asked to be forgiven and were so naïve and engaging that my anger began to evaporate. One of them even asked if he might be permitted to retain a particular watch as he liked it very much! I was still collecting the booty from them when my chaprassi and a jamadar appeared on one of the roofs above. I pointed out to them the stairs leading down into the court and, as soon as the jamadar arrived, handed over the soldiers to him and went across to the Hindus. There were thirty or forty of them. Some of the men had begun to pluck up courage and had ventured out into the court to watch the soldiers disgorge their plunder; but several of the women were weeping and I now saw that one grey-haired old woman was lying dead on the floor. She appeared to have been shot through the heart. I called the jamadar and showed him the

[1] 'The Sahib has come.'

dead body, saying, 'Look what your men have done.' He seemed rather appalled and, staring down at the old woman, said two or three times, 'Bara zulm hai, bara zulm hai!'[1] I angrily asked the soldiers why they had shot her. They replied that one of their rifles had gone off by mistake. This produced a violent volley of contradiction from the Hindus. I cut short the beginnings of a fierce altercation and told the jamadar to march his men away. I then handed over to the Hindus their watches and other property and asked them whether they wanted to be sent to the jail camp. They said that they had been waiting for someone to take them there but had been altogether forgotten—which was quite true. So I summoned a lorry and they were all sent off.

I was not called as a witness at the court martial of the soldiers. Marden told me later that it had not been necessary to bother me as the evidence of the jamadar had been sufficient. They were given some kind of punishment; but not, of course, in any way commensurate with the crime of robbery with murder of which they had been guilty. It is possible that they were never charged with murder; in any case their story that the woman had been shot by accident would have had to be accepted as there was no-one, except the Hindus, to prove the contrary and, after their evacuation to India, they were not available to give evidence. I made no particular effort myself to secure the condign punishment of these men. Perhaps secretly I felt some sympathy with them or had become infected with the lax spirit of the times.

So far as I know, this old woman, the murdered Sikhs and the wealthy Nand Kishore were the only casualties in the town of Bahawalpur after the decision was taken to evacuate the Hindus. This decision may be fairly regarded as equivalent in effect to agreements of the type often reached during wars in earlier times, whereby a city was delivered over to be sacked by the soldiery, but the lives of its inhabitants were spared. By and large the Hindus were saved from further slaughter, but their property became legitimate spoil. Certainly the appearance of the Hindu quarters and the bazaars of Bahawalpur after the evacuation conformed to my idea of a city that had been sacked. The casualties before the evacuation totalled two hundred and

[1] Literally: 'It's a great tyranny!'

fifty to three hundred, of which about a third were Hindus from the surrounding villages who had sought refuge in the town. Both absolutely and, still more, relatively to population these casualties were lower than at Bahawalnagar and Hasilpur; but the consternation which they caused among the Hindu population was no less and their ultimate effects far greater; for the enforced evacuation from the capital of many of the oldest Hindu families profoundly shook the confidence of the Hindu community throughout the State.

The reader may have wondered how the disturbances in Bahawalpur city originated and what course they took prior to my arrival late in the afternoon of September 15th. I have so far only recorded the very brief explanations of them which Gurmani gave me that same evening. To this day I have not been able to obtain any full or coherent account of what happened. It is certain, however, that the disturbances were pre-arranged. Some of the Hindus were given warning of the coming trouble by Muslim friends or employees. They repeatedly expressed their uneasiness to Gurmani, Gilani and others in authority, but right up to the last moment they were assured by them that there was no cause for anxiety. On the evening of September 13th at exactly 9.0 p.m. there was a loud explosion in the city just outside the principal mosque. This was the signal for the riot to begin.[1] A Muslim mob, which included some of the relatives of one of the Muslim Ministers, debouched from the mosque into the main bazaar and began looting and setting fire to shops and killing any Hindus they came across. A smaller mob emerged from a second mosque and began doing the same in another quarter of the town. A third mob advanced on the city from outside the walls and did great slaughter among Hindus who had come in from surrounding villages and had been accommodated in a large Hindu school. This mob was said to have been led by a lame man on a white horse alleged to be a member of the Gilani family.

At 10.0 p.m. a curfew was imposed; the streets were gradually cleared, the rioting subsided and the city quietened down for the night. Large numbers of troops were brought in during the

---

[1] During the Mutiny the signal for the sepoys to rise and murder their officers was at many stations given by the firing of a gun or some kind of explosion.

next two days and the city was kept under curfew. The Hindus remained shut up in their houses, too terrified to venture out, while military pickets and Muslim gangs looted such shops and houses as could be easily broken into, killing any stray Hindus that fell into their hands. This was the position when I reached Bahawalpur.

The outbreak of rioting in the city more or less synchronized with a disturbance in the jail. Beginning as a small affair, it developed into an attempt at a mass break-out. The inner wall was breached and it seemed at one time that all the prisoners might escape and join the marauding gangs in the city. Owing to reluctance to fire upon them effectively, it took many hours and a large force of police and military to overpower them and drive them back to their cells.

During the two days of September 14th and 15th when the city was under curfew some endeavour was made to clean up the mess and to clear away the corpses; but the municipal lorry engaged on the latter task broke down before it was completed. By the time I arrived on the scene the dead bodies had been removed from the two main bazaars, but a good many were still lying about in the side-streets and remained there for a number of days. One corpse of a stout Hindu sprawled, completely naked, right across a lane which I went down daily in order to visit the Hindus in the Gosain's shrine. Day by day it became more swollen and bloated. Again and again I and my entourage passed it without comment until one day we came along and found that it was missing from its usual place.

During the period of mass hysteria I found myself in a 'through the looking-glass' world of moral conventions. There was a complete breakdown, or rather reversal, of the ordinary moral values. To kill a Sikh had become almost a duty; to kill a Hindu was hardly a crime. To rob them was an innocent pleasure, carrying no moral stigma; to refrain was a mark not of virtue but of lack of enterprise. On the other hand to try to stop these things was at best folly, at worst a crime. Mild remonstrance, though disliked and despised, could be tolerated, like the babblings in England against betting or blood sports; but effective action was liable to be viewed as a capital offence.

Most of those who in these days robbed and murdered

members of the opposite community might have plausibly put forward a plea of temporary insanity; for they did not know, or had forgotten, the real moral character of their actions. A new scale of values had been introduced and the old one had been almost universally discarded. Certainly my own indignation at their misdeeds, though often very great, was constantly tempered by my awareness of this change in moral values. I was also not blind to the dangers of an excessive zeal for the usual standards.

Well-to-do Muslims expressed more than once to me their fear that the sanctity of life and property having broken down, the mob, after finishing with the Hindus and Sikhs, would turn upon them. These fears were not realized. Between Muslims the normal moral code continued to apply and operated everywhere with all its pristine vigour once the Hindus were out of the way.

The dispatch of the Hindus of Bahawalpur city to India took six days—from September 17th to the 22nd. Such was my anxiety for its safe accomplishment that it seemed more like a fortnight. I used to go to the jail camp every morning and then from there to the railway station to supervise the entraining of the refugees. I had an arrangement with Leghari that I would ring him up on the railway telephone immediately after the train had left and that he would be at the Bahawalnagar railway station at that time to receive the call. I used to tell him the approximate number of refugees we had put on the train that day and he would transmit the information to Hindumalkot and also see that there were adequate supplies of drinking-water and such other refreshment as could be provided for the parched and exhausted refugees when the train passed through Bahawalnagar at about 4.30 p.m. Then again in the evening I would go to the station at a fixed time and Leghari would ring me up and let me know if the train had passed safely through Bahawalnagar and reached Hindumalkot. This arrangement enabled me also to keep in touch with the affairs of the Bahawalnagar area, where another 40,000 Muslim refugees had arrived,[1] and to give directions quickly to Leghari and Fazlur Rahman on any matter that they might wish to refer to me.

The Muslim railway officials at the Baghdad-ul-jadid station

[1] These had marched all the way from Hissar and Rohtak districts. They traversed Bikanir and entered Bahawalpur in the Harunabad area.

were at first rather sulky and did not much like the constant use of their telephone and the trouble that was being taken over the dispatch of the Hindu refugees. But they soon got used to our ways and, after hearing me talking over the phone to Leghari and Fazlur Rahman about measures for the receipt of incoming Muslim refugees, they became quite friendly and obliging and on more than one occasion took much trouble to locate me and call me to the telephone at the station when Leghari wanted me urgently.

Almost up to the last day I remained in constant dread that one of the trains would be attacked, that the escort would fail to repel the assailants with proper vigour and that there would be a massacre of Hindus. At the time of actual entraining I was afraid, not that they would be assaulted, but that they would be robbed or on some pretext relieved of the pitifully small possessions that they were trying to carry away with them. It was mainly to prevent this and other harassment of the refugees that I personally attended the entraining every morning. Muslim feeling in general was against their being allowed to carry away anything at all. There was a sort of idea that all their property belonged really to Pakistan and so should not be taken out of it. Objections were constantly being made that some box or package, which a wretched Hindu had successfully lugged from his house to the camp and then transported to the railway station, was too large or too heavy to go in the train! I overruled all such objections and somehow or other all the luggage brought to the station was squeezed into the train or stacked on the roofs of the carriages. But my rulings were not altogether appreciated. Several times as I stood on the platform watching a train steam slowly from the station, crammed full to overflowing and with men and luggage piled along the roofs of the coaches, Muslim officials would say to me, 'Look how these rich banias are being allowed to leave laden with their belongings, whereas our people are being driven out of India empty-handed.' I had no very adequate answer to this and to some extent I entered into their feelings.[1] So I just used to reply

---

[1] It must be remembered that under the British 'rule of law', Hindu and Sikh moneylenders and shopkeepers in the Punjab, and particularly the Western Punjab, had been allowed to oppress the Muslim peasantry in the most shameful manner.

that Muslims were not as barbarous as the Sikhs or as mean as the Hindus and were expected to behave more chivalrously. 'That is the reason', they would say, 'why we have always come off worst.'

On one occasion, just before the train was about to leave, my attention was drawn to a sick man lying right at the end of the platform. In a weak voice he asked to be put on the train and said he was not being allowed to go. None of his relations were at hand and I concluded that they had deliberately left him on the platform, thinking he was too ill to travel and wanting to be rid of him. I asked where they were, and after a minute some of them jumped out of the train and came running up. I inquired why they were being so heartless as to leave the poor man behind. With tears in their eyes they replied that they wanted him to go with them, but had been prevented from putting him on the train by someone—I think the guard— who said that they must produce a doctor's certificate that he was fit to travel! There was no doctor at hand and they begged me to detain the train till they could go and fetch one. How easily they could be imposed upon by petty officials! The need for a doctor's certificate must have been thought of by someone who hoped to obtain a good tip for graciously waiving its production. I told them that their sick relation could go without doctor or certificate. The train was already packed, but we made some men get out and climb on to the roof and so found room for him.

Yet it would be wrong to convey the impression by these instances of harassment and the desire to rob the outgoing Hindus that their departure was unaccompanied by any signs of friendliness and good feeling. On the contrary, there was daily quite an attendance of Muslims at the station who came to say goodbye to old friends. They helped them to carry their luggage and embraced them affectionately on the platform; and, as each train left, there was from both sides a great waving of farewell. Sentimental affection for the Hindus subsisted along with the desire to benefit from their plight.

There was a particularly large concourse at the station on about the fifth day when the Gosain and all his people were brought from their sanctuary in the city. No doubt he may have been considered by some to be a pious fraud, but he was quite a figure and a well-established institution in the State. He came down to the station wearing a topi and accompanied by a mass of luggage and the I.N.A. Gilani. The latter had assumed charge of his evacuation—an arrangement that was doubtless highly satisfactory to both parties. He was given a privileged seat in the train and a hearty send-off.

There was one incident at the station—probably on the fourth day of evacuation—that gave me some minutes of anxiety. The train was standing at the platform and the refugees were still clambering into it when an officer of the State Forces on duty at the station came up to me and said that in the rear coach, which was reserved for ordinary passengers, there was a Muslim gentleman from the North-West Frontier Province travelling to Harunabad with a bodyguard of eight Pathans, all carrying rifles. He asked whether I thought it would be safe to let these armed men from the Frontier travel on a train crammed with Hindu refugees. He wanted to know what should be done. This was rather a tricky question and inwardly I did not thank him for posing it, though it was quite right of him to do so. The risk that these Pathans, the servants of some wealthy and respectable Muslim gentleman, would get out of hand and use their arms against the Hindus was small, but in these excited times it was not easy to discount it altogether. Moreover there were the feelings of the Hindus to consider. Word would flash down the train that in the rear coach there were Pathans from the Frontier armed with rifles and this would put many of them in an agony of fear throughout the journey. It was indeed likely that before the train left they would importune me to take the arms away. On the other hand the Muslim gentleman might well regard a request to surrender the arms as a quite unnecessary precaution and an insult to himself. I judged that he might prove a difficult customer for to be travelling about with an armed guard was sheer swank and indicated that he must be a pompous fellow with a great sense of his own importance. If he adopted a stiff attitude and declined voluntarily to give up the rifles and we were compelled to take them away by force, then this might lead to a scene and a scuffle and even worse. We might thus wantonly provoke an outbreak of violence which it was our object to avoid.

All these thoughts raced through my mind as I walked down

the platform towards the rear coach. By the time I reached it I had decided that the rifles must be taken away. So I climbed up into the coupé in which the Muslim gentleman was sitting, apologized for the intrusion and requested to speak to him for a minute. He was a stout elderly man and asked me in rather a surly tone what I wanted. I explained to him that we had a lot of frightened Hindus in the train whom we were evacuating to India and requested him, having regard to their feelings and the prevailing tension, to hand over temporarily the rifles which his men were carrying. I said that we would return them later and that if he let me know when he would be coming back, I would have them ready for him at the station. He refused to agree to my request and questioned my right to make it, so I was forced to inquire whether he had a licence to carry all these arms in Bahawalpur State. (I was quite certain that he had not.) He replied grandly that he held an all-India licence. I pointed out that such a licence was valid only in the whole of what had been British India and was not valid in a State, like Bahawalpur, for which a separate licence was required. I had therefore ample right to request him to surrender the arms, since they were in fact unlicensed; and, though in normal times I would never have dreamed of taking him up on such a formality, I must, in the special circumstances already explained to him, repeat my request to him to give them up. This did not please him and he began to bluster. He said that he was a friend of Sir George Cunningham, Sir Rob Lockhart and other famous figures of the Frontier; that he had travelled all over India and never before been questioned about his arms or asked to give them up; that the Nawab of Bahawalpur knew him well and would be very angry when he heard that he had been insulted in this way.

The officers on the platform outside were now telling me that the train was due to leave. Further attempts at persuasion seemed useless, so I said to him, 'Very well then, Khan Bahadar, if you won't tell your men to hand over their arms, I'll have to uncouple your coach and leave you standing here on the line while the rest of the train goes on without you.' I got down from the carriage and gave orders for the rear coach to be uncoupled. This brought him to reason. 'All right, all right,' he growled, coming to the window, 'I'll give them up,' and he leaned out and told his men in the next compartment to hand over their rifles. They immediately complied. I thanked him for so kindly acceding to my request; but he was not to be mollified. 'Why', he asked, 'does Jinnah employ such bad officers?' I had held myself in so far, but I could not now resist the pleasure of exculpating Mr. Jinnah. He was not, I said, in the least to blame as he had got my services quite by accident and was probably not yet even aware of his misfortune. The blame rested on the Nawab of Bahawalpur and Gurmani. I advised him to complain to the latter as the Nawab was away in England!

I was thankful to have got the rifles away from him quietly and without any scuffle. The train went on its way and reached its destination safely.

By the 21st I began to feel confident that the evacuation would be completed without mishap. There were only twelve hundred to fifteen hundred refugees left in the jail camp, and these were all entrained and dispatched safely to Hindumalkot on the 22nd. In all about fifteen thousand were evacuated by train to India from the city of Bahawalpur. In these trains, and in other escorted refugee trains which we sent to Hindumalkot before and after, there was not a single casualty. This is a tribute to the Bahawalpur State Forces. Whatever criticisms may be made of their conduct in these times, their successful escorting of these trains stands conspicuously to their credit. An attempt was made by crowds of villagers to attack one of the trains— probably on the third day—but the escort promptly opened fire and the crowds were scattered. After that no-one again ventured to play any mischief.

So far as Bahawalpur State is concerned, the evacuation of the Hindus from the capital was a decisive event. It was the signal that the State must inevitably lose all its Hindu inhabitants and become a purely Muslim territory. Up till then this had not been a foregone conclusion. Even if West Punjab was emptied of Hindus, it had seemed possible that Bahawalpur, like Sind to the south where no large-scale migration had yet begun, might retain a large proportion of its Hindu population. As recently as September 11th, I had been thinking and talking in terms not merely of retaining Hindus, but of recovering those who had already left. Now all such ideas were seen to be illusions. A few people, it is true, still continued to think in the old terms, but they were persons far removed from the actual scene of events. Those in daily contact with them and able to sense the popular mood knew that to retain any Hindus would be difficult and dangerous and that to recall those who had left and reinstate them in their property was impracticable madness and would provoke a fresh holocaust.

Conscious of the change that had occurred. I had found time while I was at Bahawalpur to run up to Khairpur and Qaimpur and have a talk with the Hindus of those places. Now that all the Hindus from the capital were being sent away to India they were unanimous that they too could no longer remain in the State and requested me to arrange at once for their evacuation. I discussed the matter with Leghari over the phone. He said that all the Hindus still remaining in Chishtian and other places in the eastern part of the State were also now wanting to leave. He suggested that as soon as the evacuation of Bahawalpur city was complete, we should send them all off by train to Hindumalkot. Arrangements were made accordingly and they were also safely evacuated.[1]

Thus by the close of September the Bahawalpur district—rather more than one-half of the State—had been completely denuded of its Hindu and Sikh population. Only a few stray individuals—the Hindu Minister, a Hindu High Court Judge and some Hindu officials attached to the Palace—still remained. The frenzy of slaughter subsided, for in the Bahawalpur district victims were no longer readily available. But in the Rahim Yar Khan district, so far comparatively tranquil, we still had sixty to seventy thousand Hindus; and Muslim refugees were still pouring into the State. Our troubles were diminished, but not over.

[1] This took over a week as Pakistan was now suffering from a coal shortage and a train from Samasatta to Hindumalkot could only be run on alternate days.

XII

Events in Rahim Yar Khan

I N the closing days of September a serious and unexpected calamity befell us. Normally the monsoon slackens in northern India during September and by the beginning of October has come to an end. But this year was an exception. During the last week of September there was unusually heavy rain throughout the Punjab, quenching to some extent the fires of communal fury, but intensifying the miseries of the refugees. We had just completed the evacuation of the Hindus from Bahawalpur city and I was looking forward to a little respite when I was called urgently one evening to the station at Baghdad-ul-jadid to speak to Leghari over the railway telephone. The news he had to give me was most disconcerting. The rain, he said, had caused a heavy flood in the Sutlej; this had arrived with little warning at Suleimanke, broken through the protective embankments, and breached both the two big State canals, the Sadiqia and the Fordwah, taking off from the Suleimanke headworks. The damage to the Sadiqia was reported to be extensive and the irrigation officers thought it would take weeks to repair it.

Coming on the top of all the troubles of the past month, this mishap seemed to me the last straw. The damage to the Fordwah Canal did not so much matter, for this was only a semi-perennial (six-monthly) canal and was in any case due to cease running in about a fortnight's time. But the damage to the Sadiqia, a perennial canal, was disastrous. The sowing time for the rabi crop was at hand; if the Sadiqia could not be re-opened by about the third week of October, there would be no rabi in the vast semi-desert tract which it irrigated. Moreover in this tract the villagers were entirely dependent on the canal for water for themselves and their cattle. Any prolonged interruption of supplies would force them to migrate.

In normal times such a disaster could never have occurred.

H   225

Telegraphic flood warnings would have been sent out from high up the river, where it debouches from the mountains, and the staff at Suleimanke would have had at least twenty-four hours' notice of the flood. They would have immediately started intensive patrolling of the embankments so that any weak points revealed by the rising waters could be promptly strengthened and potential breaches closed before they had been effectually opened. But owing to the division of the Punjab the warning system had broken down and Suleimanke received less than four hours' notice of the flood; and owing to the defects of the Radcliffe line the embankments on the south of the river were not patrolled; for except the first hundred yards these now all fell in Indian territory and the Dogra troops in the area prevented or frightened Muslim canal patrols from venturing along them.

These embankments, which should have held the swollen river in its channel and guided it to the headworks, gave way in several places. The waters poured through the breaches and piled up against the Sadiqia Canal which, running due south at right-angles to the river, lay right athwart their course. The weight of the water caused the bank of the canal to give way; the water then poured into it, filled it to overflowing and, owing to the excessive pressure on the banks, caused breaches in them at intervals over a distance of forty-five to fifty miles. Some of the water also burst through into the Fordwah Canal, which for about one mile south of the headworks runs parallel to and only thirty to fifty yards distant from the Sadiqia.

The breaches in the Sadiqia were biggest and most numerous over the first ten miles of its length. For their speedy repair— two or three of them were seventy to eighty feet wide—a large labour force was required. But in this area no suitable labour . was available. This was the area around Macleodganj Road where the Muslim cultivators had scattered in panic and the numerous Sikh colonists had crossed over into Bikanir. In place of the Sikhs there were now a lot of newly-arrived refugees from the East Punjab. These poor people had barely settled in their new homes after their trek when they had been overwhelmed by the floods and forced to spend days and nights on the roofs of their houses or in the branches of trees. It was futile to expect to get hard labour from these unfortunates. The only course was to bring in labour from elsewhere. Though Roy, the Chief Engineer, was at first sceptical, I had no doubt that the stout-hearted Punjabi colonists at the tail of the canal around Fort Abbas, over a hundred miles away, would readily offer their labour gratis, if the need for it was explained to them—since the reopening of the canal was for them a vital matter. The tahsildar was directed to call for volunteers. There was no lack of them; rather the difficulty was to provide them with suffi-cient baskets or other utensils for carrying the earth required to fill the breaches. The train service between Fort Abbas and Bahawalnagar had been suspended owing to shortage of coal; but we persuaded the railway authorities to put on a special train and transported several hundred sturdy peasants from around Fort Abbas and Harunabad to the Macleodganj area. They brought with them their pots and pans and bedding and we supplied them with flour. The work of repair was admirably organized by the officials of the Irrigation Department—a highly efficient body of men—and within little more than a fort-night the breaches were repaired and the canal was running again.

These floods caused great havoc among the refugees strug-gling in both directions across the Punjab. Many are said to have been swept away and drowned. The actual number who perished in this way may not have been large, but the rain and floods added enormously to the difficulties and discomforts of the refugees and to some extent undermined their stamina.

During most of the month of September the fury of communal frenzy had raged unabated in both halves of the divided Pun-jab. But with October, there began a long period of slow con-valescence. The remnants of the respective minority commu-nities had by now in most places been herded into camps and in consequence killings and disorder became less widespread. Attacks on refugee trains and on columns of refugees moving by road had not yet been fully mastered, but gradually there was an improvement; and as, with the movement of refugees in both directions, the two communities were separated and withdrawn from proximity to one another, the normal moral sanctions reasserted themselves, the bonds of society were renewed and law and order prevailed once more.

But while the disease had burnt itself out at the centre, viz. the Central Punjab, at points on the circumference, where the

communities were still intermingled, there remained a danger
of fresh outbreaks. In Bahawalpur State we still had many thousands of Hindus in the Rahim Yar Khan district, and until
they could be got safely away to India we could never be certain that they might not occasion a fresh outburst of killing.
They remained a constant source of anxiety. Our other problem was how to cope with the continuous stream of incoming
refugees. Throughout October their numbers and, with the
onset of the cold weather, their needs increased; and the sympathy which they had at first excited turned, through no real
fault of theirs, to indifference and even disgust.

Events in the Rahim Yar Khan district and the resettlement
of refugees are, therefore, the main themes of the two concluding chapters of this narrative.

A new factor was introduced into the local situation in Bahawalpur by the return of the Nawab. He arrived back in the State
from his summer residence at Farnham, Surrey, on October
2nd. I was at that time in the Bahawalnagar area, coping with
floods and refugees. Gurmani explained to the Nawab all
that had occurred, whereupon he is said to have expressed the
intention of composing a poem in my honour and reciting it to
me when I came to see him! This was a kind thought, but I am
afraid the recitation never took place. Long before I saw him
there had been a clash between us and his poetic ardour cooled.

The exodus from the State of such a large number of his
'loyal Hindu subjects' affected the Nawab keenly. The
courtiers at the Palace represented that Gurmani and I had
'driven them away' and introduced in their place Punjabi
Muslims with no tradition of loyalty to a Nawab or Maharajah. Gurmani and I had, of course, been at the mercy of
events, but it is certainly true that these had not been favourable to the position of the Nawab as an autocratic ruler. In
Bahawalpur, as in many of the Princely States of India, the
minority community felt a particular allegiance to the Ruler,
for they looked to him, and not in vain, for protection from
oppression by the majority. Thus the Hindus who had left the
State were in a real sense 'loyal' subjects of the Nawab. Their
community had been treated by him and his forefathers with
justice and consideration and they felt some attachment to the
Ruler as such. On the other hand the Punjabi Muslims, who

had flooded in as refugees from East Punjab, cared nothing for the Nawab of Bahawalpur and perhaps had hardly heard of him. The exchange of population which had taken place meant, therefore, for the Nawab the loss of loyal subjects and their replacement by others who would be at best indifferent to him.

Not unnaturally the Nawab was strongly opposed to any more Hindus leaving the State. He also expressed the wish that only refugees from Princely States, e.g. Bikanir, Patiala, Nabha, Bharatpur and Alwar, should be received and settled in Bahawalpur since these, being accustomed to personal rule, would more readily accommodate themselves to our conditions and develop a loyalty to the Ruler. This was a reasonable and desirable proposal, but only to a very limited extent practicable. However much we might prefer refugees from Princely States, we had no means of effectively exercising this preference. We had, as a matter of fact, already received a large number of refugees from the State of Bikanir; but this had been due not to our own volition but to the fact that Bahawalpur, being adjacent, was the natural place for them to come to. To some extent we could pick and choose from among the refugees who actually entered our borders, passing on to the Punjab those whom we did not like or were too numerous for us to absorb. But we could not control or even influence the movement of refugees from India and so determine which of them should enter Bahawalpur territory. Within the narrow limits possible, we did tend to give preference to refugees from Princely States; but not invariably as there might be other overriding considerations. For instance, in November several thousand refugees reached us from a small State in south-east Punjab. They appeared to me to be very poor stuff and likely to be a drag on the economy and so, with Gurmani's approval, they were all pushed over into the Punjab.

The Nawab's views regarding the selection of the incoming refugees did not have much practical effect. But his strong desire not to lose any more of his loyal Hindu subjects affected for some months the fortunes of those still bottled up in Rahim Yar Khan. Here circumstances favoured his views; for, as will be explained later, it was very difficult for us to extricate the Hindus from the Rahim Yar Khan district; nor could they slip away themselves except slowly in small numbers.

The story of the Hindus of the Rahim Yar Khan district
runs on right until the middle of 1948. At no time were there
widespread disturbances, as in the Bahawalpur district, but there
was one bad episode and many small incidents and recurrent
threats of a flare-up. At the beginning of September there was
a good deal of restlessness in the northern portion of the district
and a few stray Hindus were killed. During this period Gurmani
sent out Roy and Duncan (the British Superintending Engineer) in a jeep with a couple of Bahawalpur soldiers to run
about from place to place and try to nip any trouble in the bud.
One incident of their jeep trips requires mention. They were
driving along a canal bank in the northern part of the district
when they saw ahead of them a bullock-cart standing on a
bridge across the canal. There seemed to be some knobbly
things sticking out of it which in the distance looked to Roy like
swedes or turnips; but this puzzled him, as such root crops are
not grown in Bahawalpur. On getting nearer he discerned that
the knobbly things were really the arms, legs and heads of
human beings—the cart was in fact full of corpses which were
being tipped out into the canal. The men with the cart, on
seeing who were in the jeep, jumped over the bridge into the
canal and were quickly carried away by the current. The two
soldiers accompanying Roy and Duncan opened fire on them,
but with the usual lack of aim—no doubt in the water they were
not easy targets—and they all escaped.

The corpses had been brought from a small village or hamlet
not far distant. Roy and Duncan went over to it. At first they
could find no sign of life. The whole population of about two
hundred seemed to have been wiped out and their bodies were
lying about all over the place. The hamlet had been inhabited
by Labana Sikhs whose forefathers had been settled there in the
last century by the then Ruler of Bahawalpur. The penalty had
now been exacted for the crime of being Sikhs! Roy and Duncan
thought at first that not a single living soul was left, but they
did at last find a woman with an infant in her arms still alive
and cowering in the corner of one of the houses. They were the
sole survivors.

Apart from this small group of Labanas the total number of
Sikhs in the Rahim Yar Khan district was only two to three
thousand. Soon after disturbances broke out in the State, they

sensed that they were in danger and by the middle of September
had all congregated for safety at one or two centres; whereas
the Hindus remained for some weeks more scattered throughout
the district and pursuing their normal avocations. Gurmani, who,
it will be recalled, had assumed responsibility for Rahim Yar
Khan, was confronted with the problem of what to do with these
Sikhs. The desideratum was to get them away to India as
quickly as possible; but to put them in one of the main line
trains running through Rahim Yar Khan would have been sheer
murder, and we had not enough lorries to transport them all
the way by road to Samasatta and then send them down the
branch line to Hindumalkot. Gurmani, therefore, proposed
that they should be marched out under escort from the town of
Rahim Yar Khan to the extreme border of the cultivated area
and thence across the desert to the State of Jaisalmir which
adjoins Bahawalpur on the south-east and forms part of India.
There are well-marked tracks across the desert and at the nearest
point the distance from the edge of the cultivated area to the
Jaisalmir border is only a day or two's march. It was thought
that with adequate preparations the journey would not be too
arduous or hazardous. Camels and donkeys could be provided
for the women and children. Gurmani consulted me about this
proposal a day or two after the evacuation of Bahawalpur city
had begun. I felt rather dubious about it, but could suggest
no better alternative. My main misgiving was in regard to the
escort which was to be furnished by the Bahawalpur State forces.
In answer to my doubts Gurmani assured me that the officer
commanding it would be one who could be relied upon to do
his duty. My doubts were not, however, wholly removed. I said
to Gurmani that if the military were to furnish the escort—I
would have myself preferred the police to do so—then at least
a senior civil officer with magisterial powers should accompany
the expedition. I suggested that no less a person than the Deputy
Commissioner of the district should be deputed for this purpose.
A Muslim officer of the State, Maulvi Faiz Ahmad, held this
post and since the outbreak of disturbances had also been given
the powers of District Magistrate. Owing to the loss of one eye
he had, perhaps, a somewhat villainous appearance, but I
knew him to be a man of strong character, well capable of
standing up to the military and not likely to be browbeaten or

bamboozled by them. Gurmani, while agreeing that a civil officer should accompany the column, said that the Deputy Commissioner could not be spared. There was some force in this contention as the whole district was at that time rather bobbery; and so it was settled that the Assistant Commissioner should accompany the Sikh refugees on their march.

My mind was not at rest and I therefore asked Faiz Ahmad to keep me in touch with the progress of this expedition. At the end of September I heard that it had started, and some days later, when I happened to be at Bahawalnagar, I received a copy of a report, signed by the Commanding Officer and countersigned by the Assistant Commissioner, to the effect that the whole column had reached the border in safety and good order and that the refugees had departed with many professions of gratitude for the excellent manner in which they had been looked after and protected from all dangers by the escort of Bahawalpur troops.

The report was written in a vivid colourful style; but somehow or other I didn't believe a word of it. I showed it to Leghari and asked him what he made of it. He said that he thought it was quite false and that reports which had reached him from other sources of his own told quite a different story. He urged me to make further inquiries and satisfy myself as to the real facts. Not long after I had occasion to go to Rahim Yar Khan and while there I questioned the Deputy Commissioner about the report and told him that it did not ring true to me. He was a bit cagey at first and put me off, saying that he would talk to me about it later. After a couple of hours he came back to the rest-house where I was staying and said that, since I had myself cast doubts on the correctness of the report, he had decided to reveal to me the truth. The report, he said, was in fact false; the Assistant Commissioner had now admitted this, and had made a statement, which was corroborated by other witnesses, giving an entirely different account of what had taken place. He had reduced all this evidence to writing and handed it over to me for perusal.

It was a horrible tale of treachery and violence. The column, rather over two thousand strong, had moved off on the afternoon of September 26th from a chak near Rahim Yar Khan where they had all congregated. Before the start there was a slight contretemps. The Sikhs had thought that they would be allowed to carry with them such arms as they possessed, but they were ordered to surrender them. With the usual Sikh lack of docility they were inclined to resist. They said that the Deputy Commissioner had promised them that they would be permitted to take their arms. Fortunately Faiz Ahmad had himself come along with the Commanding Officer to the chak to see them set off on their journey, and through his intervention the matter was amicably settled and they were persuaded peacefully to surrender their arms. They parted from him with expressions of gratitude and goodwill.

On the first evening, when the column had encamped for the night, trouble broke out. The escorting troops began to search the Sikhs and relieve them of their valuables. A certain Karnail Singh resisted. There was a fight; Karnail Singh and several other Sikhs were shot dead and a number were injured. At once there was a great commotion and outcry throughout the camp. This was awkward for the officer commanding the escort. Rahim Yar Khan was still not far distant. Some of the Sikhs might slip away with news of what had happened and bring the Deputy Commissioner on the scene. The Assistant Commissioner, accompanying the column, talked of sending in a report. The Commanding Officer persuaded him that it was best to keep quiet and hush the matter up, while towards the Sikhs he was most conciliatory. He expressed profound regret for what had taken place, said that it was all a mistake and due to some misunderstanding and promised that nothing of the kind would happen again.

Partially reassured the Sikhs continued on their way; but the next evening when they were approaching the edge of the desert and were already far from any hope of succour the Commanding Officer announced that they would be searched and all their belongings taken away. He justified this on the ground that the Muslims who were being driven out of India were not being allowed to bring any of their possessions with them. The Sikhs protested against this betrayal and breach of all the promises made to them; but resistance was useless. During that night and the following day they were all systematically searched and deprived of everything, including the camels and horses on which some of them hoped to cross the desert. The booty was loaded

H*

on to military lorries and driven away to Rahim Yar Khan. The Assistant Commissioner weakly acquiesced in all these proceedings. He perhaps eased his conscience with the thought that the C.O. was acting under some secret instructions not communicated to him.

The Sikhs could now place little faith in the C.O.'s promises. Nevertheless they were assured that there would be no further harassment; and so they journeyed on. They had now reached the farthest limit of the cultivated area and were starting on their march across the open desert in considerable distress for want of sufficient food and water. After two days they had almost reached the border and halted for the night of September 30th only about two miles short of it. Chauki Kishangarh, the nearest inhabited place in Jaisalmir territory, lay some miles farther on. They expected to cross the border and make their way to this place the next morning. But at about 1.0 a.m. the two leaders of the Sikh column, Bakhtawar Singh and Bhag Singh, were roused from their slumbers and told that they must all make ready to start immediately. They protested to the C.O. and expressed their disquiet and suspicion at being suddenly ordered to march at the dead of night. By way of answer they were both bayoneted and fatally injured.

The rest of the column moved off, but after they had gone a short distance firing was heard ahead and they were ordered to halt. They were told that the firing was coming from a gang of armed Hurs,[1] who were waiting to fall upon them, and that special measures must be taken to ensure the safety of the women and children. This was, of course, all a hoax. A portion of the escort had been sent ahead with orders to conceal themselves behind some sand-hills and let off their rifles. However, on the pretext of an imminent attack by Hurs, of which the firing was supposed to provide the evidence, the women were separated from the men under threats of violence. A selection was then made of the younger women who were in due course distributed among the escort and taken back to Rahim Yar Khan.

Having secured their prey the escort were anxious to be rid

---

[1] A fanatical sect of Muslims who had turned outlaws and terrorized parts of Sind during the war. Military operations had to be undertaken to hunt them down. At this time small parties of them still caused an occasional incident.

of the men and of the old women and children. So these were
told that, as there were Hurs prowling around, they had better
make a run for it to the border. At the same time the escort
began firing off their rifles indiscriminately—perhaps to suggest
that they were giving covering fire against the bogus Hurs.
Some of the Sikhs ran wildly forward in the direction of the
border; the rest struggled after them under fire from the escort
behind and from the party concealed behind sand-hills to the
front. In the darkness and confusion an unascertained number
were killed or wounded. From the accounts which the Assistant
Commissioner and others were able to give us it was impossible
at that time to judge how many, if any, of the column had survived and made their way successfully into Indian territory.

Some years later I was able to contact in India members of
this ill-fated expedition. Several hundred of them,[1] I learnt, got
through safely to Chauki Kishangarh and reported what had
befallen them. Camels were sent out from there to the scene
of the firing to bring in the wounded, most of whom were ultimately transported to Jodhpur and admitted to hospital there.

In this affair the Bahawalpur escort certainly showed a well-
judged audacity, but they were wrong in supposing that their
dark deeds far out in the desert would remain unknown. The
bringing in of so much booty and so many female captives to a
small place like Rahim Yar Khan could not pass unnoticed.
The arrival of the lorries laden with spoil, though they came in
under cover of night, set tongues wagging; and later the return
of the escort, accompanied by numbers of Sikh women, quickly
gave rise to open scandal. The women's presence could not in
any case have easily been concealed; and it soon became
notorious; for a number of them escaped from their captors
and hid themselves in the tall standing crops just outside the
town. There followed a regular game of hide-and-seek. In
broad daylight soldiers of the Bahawalpur Army were to be
seen hunting these young women from one millet field to
another round the outskirts of Rahim Yar Khan. Some of
them were recaptured, but three or four got away altogether
and were taken in and given shelter in various houses in the
town. The respectable inhabitants of the place were greatly

[1] I should guess at least 600–700 but the numbers given to me were
considerably less.

shocked. They reported the matter to the Deputy Commissioner and soon the full story of the treachery began to leak out.

When the Assistant Commissioner was confronted by the Deputy Commissioner with the damning evidence afforded by the women, he broke down and made a clean breast of the whole affair, pleading his own helplessness in face of the overbearing attitude of the military. It was with some difficulty that the Deputy Commissioner induced him to present himself before me. I felt sorry for him. He was by no means a bad man, but he did not possess the strength of character equal to the sternness and wickedness of the times.

I returned at once to Bahawalpur and informed Gurmani of all that the Deputy Commissioner and Assistant Commissioner had reported to me. He agreed that the Assistant Commissioner should immediately be suspended from service and the Commanding Officer placed under arrest. Orders were issued accordingly and the Commanding Officer, having been duly arrested by the police, was handed over to the military for custody. The Nawab, who had been consulted by Gurmani about his arrest, was reported to be greatly enraged at his misconduct.

Within a week he had escaped—or been permitted to escape by his military guards—and made his way to Multan. At Multan, which is in the Punjab, he was beyond our jurisdiction. We could not have him rearrested there except with the concurrence of the (West) Punjab Government. Gurmani therefore considered—perhaps with some relief—that the matter was closed. But I was not content. I pointed out that the evidence at our disposal against him disclosed offences of robbery, abduction and murder, or at any rate abetment thereof. These were grave offences and we could ask for his extradition. There was no need for any lengthy investigation at this stage. The statements of the Assistant Commissioner and of the women who had escaped afforded sufficient prima facie evidence to justify a request to the Punjab Government for his immediate extradition.

Gurmani agreed to address them. A few weeks later he told me that they had replied with an absolute refusal. They had not asked for further evidence or explanations on any points but had simply rejected the request for extradition out of hand.

At this stage I gave up the unequal struggle. It was said—with what truth we did not know—that a British military officer of very high rank had intervened with the Punjab Government on the C.O.'s behalf. Whether this was really so I never had time to inquire; but even without any well-meant prompting from a distinguished British military officer, it would have been quite natural and in keeping with current sentiment for the Punjab Government to refuse extradition. Despite noble professions there was no real desire to punish those who robbed, raped and murdered the minority communities; rather there was a disposition to punish those who tried to protect them. This was the main reason why I did not press the matter or attempt to persuade the Punjab Government to reconsider their decision. I had shot my bolt.

There were many incidents in those days both in India and Pakistan far exceeding the story of this ill-starred expedition in horror, atrocity and the extent of the bloodshed; but I know of none that surpass it in calculated perfidy. To me it was more painful and shocking than any other incident that took place in the State of Bahawalpur. Partly this was because there was such an absolute and flagrant breach of trust. On no other occasion did the Bahawalpur Army, when solemnly assigned a specific task, let us down so completely. But partly it was because of my feeling of direct responsibility for the disaster. In authorizing the expedition we had, with our eyes open, taken a fearful risk. We already knew the temper of the troops. One battalion had looted Bahawalnagar, another Bahawalpur. We could not expect that the appetites of the remainder would be any less keen. In entrusting the Sikhs to their protection we were handing them over to ravening wolves. Yet we were, I think, justified in doing so as the consequences of keeping them were almost certain to be worse. Our mistake lay, not in taking the risk, but in failing to take the one measure which could have effectively lessened it, and that was to send the Deputy Commissioner along with the column. I have no doubt that if Faiz Ahmad had gone with it instead of the Assistant Commissioner he would have stood up to the military and all the worst episodes would have been avoided. I also believe that if I had urged this course upon Gurmani with the vehemence which the situation required he would have agreed to it. As it was we contented ourselves with an ineffective half-measure; for the Assistant Commissioner, while he assisted in the end in un-covering the villainy, was not a strong enough man to prevent it.

It is only fair to the Commanding Officer and his troops to point out that the temptation to them to despoil the Sikhs must have been very hard to resist. They had so far had no share of the loot; and everywhere in West Pakistan Sikhs were at that time considered fair game. To spare their lives could be accounted a special favour; to relieve them of their property a normal rou-tine. If the Commanding Officer had ever been brought to trial he might have pleaded in his defence that it was impossible for him to keep his men in check. Certainly the incident on the first evening, when several Sikhs were killed, may well have been due to the unauthorized high-handedness of a section of the troops. The systematic searches on the following evening and the seizure of all that the Sikhs possessed were, according to all evidence, ordered and organized by the C.O. himself; but he might have argued that this was the only way of satisfying the troops and avoiding a repetition of violence and further heavy loss of life. Thus far one may find some excuse. But the general deceitfulness of his proceedings and the final transparent ruse, whereby the women were separated from the men and the latter driven in helpless panic and under a rain of bullets to-wards the border, are very hard to extenuate or defend.

The mistakes of the Bahawalpur Government and the crimes of its employees that have just been narrated may have un-designedly helped to keep the Rahim Yar Khan district com-paratively free from disturbances. If the soldiery had been baulked of their prey and had returned hungry from their escort duties, it is likely that they would have contrived to instigate large-scale assaults on the thousands of Hindus who still re-mained in the district, so as to provide themselves with an opportunity for loot. As it was, they glutted themselves on the Sikh column and were content that the Hindus should remain more or less unmolested. The booty which they had taken from the Sikhs they divided up quietly among themselves; and no questions were asked. Their enjoyment of most of the women was more temporary. In the course of the next year all except twenty-seven were recovered and sent away to India.

During the month of October the Hindus living in the vil-

lages of the Rahim Yar Khan district began gradually to shift
for greater security to the towns. Some planted themselves on
friends and relatives; others took up their abode in serais
or built themselves temporary shelters. This migration was
hastened by a number of small incidents in which Hindus
were robbed or murdered. Most of these were the work of tribesmen from the Dera Ghazi Khan district across the Indus. With
the fall in the river they took it into their heads to make tip-
and-run raids into Bahawalpur territory, directed against
villages where rich Hindus resided. The lead which they gave
was to some extent followed by the local inhabitants.

It was very difficult to stop these raids or to give effective protection to Hindus in the rural areas. Many of them sought safety
by temporarily embracing Islam. Faiz Ahmad and I were
afforded a good first-hand example of this one morning following a big raid in which several villages had been attacked. We
were motoring along the bank of a small canal running through
the affected area and came to a large village where two or three
Hindus had been killed the night before. As we approached it,
a stream of Hindu women was to be seen issuing from the village
and crossing the canal in the direction of a mosque on the other
side around which a number of people were gathered. Faiz
Ahmad, realizing at once what was afoot, jumped out of the
car and began to reason with the women and try to deflect them
from their purpose. It was like trying to deflect a line of ants.
The women were bent on proceeding to the mosque to be received into the Faith and paid not the slightest heed to what the
Deputy Commissioner was saying. They simply backed away
from him, murmuring snatches of the Koran, and then edged
past him over the bridge. He begged them not lightly to
abandon their own religion; he assured them that it was unnecessary and that both he and I had come to protect them. It
was all to no effect. The stream divided and flowed on past him
to the mosque.

As a good Muslim Faiz Ahmad took to heart these enforced
and spurious conversions much more than I did. I was only too
happy that these people should be able to purchase so easily, if
not absolute safety, at any rate a feeling of safety. It seemed to
me to relieve us of a good deal of bother and anxiety. These
crude utilitarian views I conveyed in slightly modified form to

Faiz Ahmad, quoting Gibbon's observation that all the various modes of worship may be considered 'by the philosopher as equally false; and by the magistrate as equally useful'.

By the latter half of November virtually all the Hindus had come away from the villages and were concentrated in the four or five towns of the district. The immediate responsibility for their welfare fell on Faiz Ahmad. It was a great and growing burden. Cut off from their normal places of business and livelihood many of them soon began to find themselves in straits; and so to a constant anxiety for their safety was added the problem of how to support them. Naturally Faiz Ahmad wished to be relieved of the burden; while amongst the Hindus themselves the conviction grew that they had no alternative but to abandon their homes and migrate to India. Some of the more wealthy of them made their way down to Karachi and from there took ship or plane to Bombay. Others by bribery managed to get themselves conveyed in military lorries to some railway station on the Hindumalkot line or even to Hindumalkot itself. In this way several hundred and, as weeks lengthened into months, perhaps some thousands slipped away from the State into India. But a hard core of some sixty thousand Hindus still remained. As in the case of the Sikhs, it was impossible without special trains to move them out along the main Karachi-Lahore line which ran through the district; and we had nothing like sufficient lorries to move them up to some station on the Hindumalkot line and entrain them there. Moreover the Nawab was still wedded to the idea of keeping his 'loyal' Hindu subjects and was even thinking of getting back those who had already left! There was no hope, therefore, of persuading him to ask the Pakistan Government to provide special trains; nor, even if asked, was there much prospect of their being able to comply, for Pakistan was short of everything required for running trains, particularly coal.

Help came from another quarter. A large number of Hindu refugees from Bahawalpur State were by this time gathered at Delhi. They were well posted with all the difficulties of their co-religionists in Rahim Yar Khan and during December they began to agitate vigorously for arrangements to be made for their evacuation. Some threatened to fast before the Governor-General's house; others staged demonstrations at Gandhi's prayer-meetings, appearing with placards on which was written 'Save 70,000 Hindus of Bahawalpur'. Gandhi himself, though sympathetic, was not really in favour of extricating these Hindus from Bahawalpur. His whole aim at this time was to stop and even reverse the movements of migration. But the agitation had some effect on the Government of India and one day in December a British colonel, in the service of the Indian Union, arrived at Bahawalpur with an offer of special trains.

The Nawab and Gurmani were both away at Karachi,[1] so the colonel came to see me. I warmly welcomed the offer but I had no authority to accept it. I explained to him the Nawab's attitude and advised him to go to Karachi and try to see both Gurmani and the Nawab personally. I also wrote to the former strongly urging him to prevail upon the Nawab to accept this opportune offer.

It was all to no effect. The Nawab would not let his people go and the offer was refused.

The unwisdom of this refusal was speedily demonstrated. One afternoon early in January I had met Faiz Ahmad at a place called Khanpur to discuss with him various problems regarding the settlement of incoming refugees. While we were so engaged a message was received that there had been a raid on a small town named Ahmadpur Lamma and that a number of Hindus had been killed. This place lay in the south of the district towards the Sind border some fifty miles from Khanpur. We at once bundled into a car and bumped along as fast as we could over some very bad roads, but did not reach the place till after nightfall. Everything was pitch dark and we found our way with some difficulty to the police station, where a small group of lachrymose Hindus were gathered. As soon as our arrival was known, many more assembled, weeping and wailing and begging to be evacuated forthwith to India. Amid all the hubbub it was hard to obtain any coherent account of what had taken place. It appeared however that about twenty armed men from Dera Ghazi Kkan had suddenly arrived that morning and boldly walked up the bazaar, looting every Hindu shop they came to and shooting anyone who got in their way.

[1] The Nawab had a house a few miles away from Karachi to which he often resorted in the cold weather.

The police, recently reinforced and armed with rifles which would really fire, made not the slightest attempt to interfere —'Dar ke mare',[1] the sub-inspector apologetically explained. Finding that there was no resistance the raiders spent a couple of hours leisurely ransacking the shops and selecting their booty, and left quite unmolested about midday.

We turned from this sorry tale to the exhibits—the corpses which the Hindus were itching to show to us; for the corpses were irrefutable evidence in support of their plea to be sent away to India. It was a mercy, they said, that we had arrived before they were burnt so that we could see them with our own eyes. They were all laid out close to the police station, some on charpoys and some on the ground. A number of police constables were also asleep on charpoys and in the dim light of a hurricane lantern it was hard to distinguish the dead from the living. I kept on confusing a constable for a corpse and a corpse for a constable. These blunders were corrected by my eager guides and with their help I successfully established the existence of ten indubitable corpses. We had come to the end of the row and having, as I thought, finished the inspection I turned to the accompanying Hindus and began to murmur some suitable words of sorrow and sympathy. I spoke too soon; for, just as though they were showing off manure pits or other commendable examples of public spirit, they cried out at once with enthusiasm, 'There're some more, there're some more!'

'Enough, enough!' Faiz Ahmad interjected impatiently, 'we've seen sufficient.'

But the Hindus would not be denied and led me over to the other side of the pathway where another six to eight dead bodies were laid out in a row. I was duly impressed by this ocular evidence of the casualties. I could not, however, give any very straight answer to their urgent request for evacuation to India. The Nawab's views being what they were, Faiz Ahmad and I had to be careful what we said. I dwelt, therefore, on the lack of trains and shortage of coal on account of which, with the best will in the world, we could not immediately get them away. But, not to leave them entirely without hope, I said that possibly the Pakistan Government might be persuaded

[1] Literally: 'Being stricken with fear.'

to furnish trains if His Highness the Nawab himself requested them to do so. I advised them, therefore, to see the Nawab. I happened to know that he was due to return that very night from Karachi to Bahawalpur and that his train would be stopping next morning for ten to fifteen minutes at Sadiqabad—a station about eight miles from Ahmadpur Lamma. I suggested that some of them should go and seek audience of him as he passed through.

They did so, but were rebuffed by the personal staff who said that His Highness was unable to see them. With natural annoyance but little tact they then proceeded to march up and down the platform outside his special coach shouting, 'Dule[1] come out, Dule come out!' But 'Dule' remained firmly in his carriage or in his bed—perhaps quite unaware that some of his 'loyal Hindu subjects' wanted to see him.

The news of the raid on Ahmadpur probably penetrated to Delhi pretty quickly. In any case the Bahawalpuris there were keeping up their agitation. On January 10th it was rumoured that they were going to interrupt the actual reciting of the prayers at Gandhi's prayer-meeting. In the event they refrained from committing this awful sacrilege and were warmly commended by Gandhi for maintaining perfect silence during the prayers and expressing their anguish in a restrained manner. He knew, he said, their sufferings, but he had the word of the Ruler that, though he could not bring the dead back to life, the remaining Hindus could live in Bahawalpur in peace and safety, and no-one would interfere with their religion. The Hindu refugees from Bahawalpur may well have wondered what was the basis for these assurances; but Gandhi himself was only too anxious to accept them at their face value. Like the Nawab, with whom he was at this time in correspondence, he wanted the Hindus to remain where they were so that the tide of migration might be stayed. At the same time, however, he could not ignore the mounting pressure of opinion calling for the evacuation of all Hindus still remaining in West Pakistan. Ultimately, therefore, it was agreed between him and the Nawab that he should send an emissary over to Bahawalpur to discuss with the Hindus their position and try to pacify and reassure them.

[1] An honorific title applied locally to the Ruler, meaning literally: 'generous person'.

Failing this, it was recognized that other measures would have to be taken.

Accordingly about the fourth week of January Dr. Shushila Nair, a lady belonging to Gandhi's intimate circle, arrived in Bahawalpur, accompanied by Mr. Leslie Cross, a member of the Friends Ambulance Association. Both of them were bent on persuading the Hindus not to abandon their homes but to remain and face bravely such dangers as there might be. Both of them seemed to have a sincere belief in the propriety and probable success of their mission.

I was away from headquarters when they arrived, so by the time they came to call on me they had already seen most of the other Ministers, all of whom, echoing the Nawab's sentiments, had expressed warm sympathy with their objectives and given them every assurance regarding the safety of the Hindus. It was left to me to strike a harsh discordant note. With the corpses at Ahmadpur Lamma still fresh in my memory I no doubt expressed myself with more vigour than tact. I told Dr. Shushila Nair that so far as I could judge 90 per cent of the Hindus still remaining in the State wanted to leave it as soon as possible. If she tried to dissuade them, she was assuming a very heavy responsibility. Suppose they agreed to stay on and were then the victims of an assault such as had taken place recently at Ahmadpur, their blood would be on her head. What justification would she then be able to plead for endangering their lives? It was all very well to exhort them to face danger courageously, but with what object was she trying to make heroes out of these timid Hindu shopkeepers? I could not see that any public or private purpose was served by inducing them to stay on in Rahim Yar Khan, especially when in the rest of the State and in the surrounding Punjab districts all Hindus had migrated to India.

She said that the Nawab had personally assured her that he guaranteed their safety. I replied that the Nawab would in April go off to England for the summer. Whether from Farnham, Surrey, he would be able to protect his Hindu subjects in Rahim Yar Khan it was for her to judge. I certainly could not underwrite the guarantee.

I am afraid that both she and Mr. Cross were a little put out by my emphatic and uncompromising hostility to the main objectives of their mission. They did not, however, take it ill and a few days later, after they had toured the Rahim Yar Khan district, they called on me again and good-naturedly admitted that they had quite come round to my way of thinking. Dr. Shushila Nair told me that at each place which she had visited the Hindus had been assembled and she had talked to them alone, putting forward to them all the arguments which she could think of in favour of their remaining in the State. She had then at each place asked those who were willing to remain to hold up their hands. Not a hand was raised. She realized that the desire to migrate to India was overwhelming and unalterable and that for many of them, unable to follow their normal avocations, every day that passed was adding to their distress. In the course of her tour she had also seen and heard enough to realize that the wealthier Hindus were slipping away in military lorries to the Hindumalkot line and were paying through the nose for the privilege.

Everything was now quickly and happily settled. Dr. Shushila Nair went straight from Bahawalpur to Karachi, whither the Nawab had again betaken himself, and told him she must advise both him and Gandhi that the retention of the Hindus in the Rahim Yar Khan district was impossible and that they would have to be evacuated to India. She renewed the offer of special trains and also, at my suggestion, proposed that a liaison officer should be sent from India to help in the evacuation and obviate the possibility of subsequent complaints and misunderstandings. A few days later I received word that everything had been agreed to and that she was on her way back to Delhi. Poor lady! The end of her mission coincided with a tragedy shocking to everyone but particularly painful to her. At Lahore on her return journey from Karachi to Delhi she learnt that Gandhi had been assassinated.

The evacuation was accomplished without any hitch or unpleasantness. Mr. Anand Deva, the liaison officer, came well in advance and was most sensible and helpful. I took the opportunity of his presence to have opened more than a hundred safes which had been recovered intact from the houses of Hindus in Bahawalpur and stored in the tahsil. Nearly all of them were found to be empty and the total amount of cash and valuables which they yielded was quite trifling. One may perhaps conclude that the majority of the Hindus who were evacuated from Bahawalpur city succeeded in taking with them their most valuable possessions and that the numerous safes which looters broke open disappointed their cupidity.

It will be recalled that there was one very large and heavy safe which, according to the tahsildar, was reported to contain 'much gold'. He had on this account been unwilling to assume responsibility for it at the tahsil and so it had been deposited at my house and had remained there for about four months. I was personally present along with Mr. Anand Deva when this massive safe was solemnly prised open. I had visions of it containing gold and ornaments worth about a lac of rupees, but the actual yield was much less spectacular. The 'much gold' of popular imagination turned out to be a few currency notes and some jewellery worth perhaps in all about Rs 1000.

The Hindus of Bahawalpur city had been obliged to leave their homes in haste and confusion at less than twenty-four hours' notice. By contrast the evacuation of the Hindus from the Rahim Yar Khan district was a planned and orderly operation and only undertaken after plenty of time for preparation. For weeks beforehand the Hindus had been selling—no doubt at knock-down prices—such of their movable property as could not easily be transported; but they successfully carried away with them their most treasured possessions, including gold and silver ornaments and cash worth in all about two crores of rupees. The process of evacuation extended over a couple of months. Altogether sixteen special trains were run and the number of persons evacuated was about sixty thousand.

So in the end the Nawab's good intentions towards his 'loyal Hindu subjects' were honourably carried into effect.

XIII

Resettlement

IF the massacres of 1947 showed the Punjabis at their worst, the enforced migrations brought out some of the best of their qualities. The fortitude with which they bore the sudden uprooting from their homes and the vigour with which they set about establishing themselves in new ones were such as few other peoples could have equalled. They showed all the cheerful vitality of birds which, when robbed of their nest, will start immediately to build a fresh one. The conditions were harsh, but not too harsh to suppress or even check the surge of life in these sturdy, virile people. I often wondered whether a more sophisticated society would have survived so easily the violent shock to which the Punjab was subjected in 1947. It seemed to me at the time that if the more highly-strung and highly-organized peoples of the western world had had to undergo such a ruthless transplanting, they would have succumbed in large numbers to sheer exhaustion and *taedium vitae*.

The resettlement of the refugees, or 'displaced persons' as they had to be officially termed, was such a gigantic task and took so much of the time and energies of all the Governments concerned that no account of the upheaval of 1947 would be quite balanced without a few pages devoted to this subject. There are several publications[1] which deal with it in some detail. Here I will only describe briefly how the problem presented itself to us in Bahawalpur.

The first really big wave of refugees struck Bahawalpur in the last few days of August. They came from the Ferozepur district of East Punjab and, as mentioned in an earlier chapter, entered the State near Macleodganj Road. At about the same time most of the Muslim inhabitants of the adjoining State of Bikanir moved across into Bahawalpur by various routes. There was then a slight lull; but about September 20th a second smaller

[1] E.g. *Out of the Ashes* by M. S. Randhawa.

247

wave of forty to fifty thousand refugees poured into the State across the Bikanir border. They had marched all the way from the Rohtak and Hissar districts of south-east Punjab and were in a famished and exhausted condition. Some two thousand of them died within a few days of their arrival in Bahawalpur. Small parties from the same districts and from some of the Princely States south of the Sutlej followed in the next three to four weeks, but by the middle of October the stream had dwindled to a trickle and we concluded that the flow was drying up.

Our plans for coping with this influx were formulated at the end of August immediately after my arrival at Bahawalnagar.[1] At that time we could not tell whether there would be any limit to the number of Muslims forced to leave India. For aught we knew, all of them, or at any rate all those in northern India, might be driven into Pakistan. Certainly many Hindus, in their bitterness at the partition of the country, wanted all Muslims to be expelled and hoped that in this way Pakistan would be smothered at birth. We thought it quite likely that these sentiments would prevail, and during September, as the area of disturbance widened and the Government of India proved incapable of preventing indiscriminate assaults on Muslim lives and property even in Delhi, its own capital, our expectations seemed to be confirmed. It was not till October that the spread of disorder could be seen to be definitely checked. Muslims were still streaming in from East Punjab in accordance with the agreement of September 2nd for exchange of populations between the two halves of the Province; but beyond the confines of East Punjab the Government of India was proving capable of crushing any attempts to harry and drive away the Muslim population. To us in Bahawalpur this successful checking of the assaults on Muslims appeared to be mainly due to Gandhi. We felt that had it not been for his exertions and tremendous moral influence we should have been overwhelmed by a multitude of Muslim immigrants far greater than we could possibly have absorbed. In reality there must have been other forces working in the same direction and certainly Gandhi's efforts were vigorously backed by Nehru—though not equally so by all the leading figures in the Government of India. They were, however, battling

[1] See Chapter IX, p. 158.

against very strong currents of popular opinion, as Gandhi's subsequent assassination all too vividly revealed, and I still believe that his influence with all classes was the decisive factor in halting the disturbances on the Indian side more or less at the borders of the Punjab.

At the end of August we could not foresee that this would be the outcome. We had to be prepared for the worst; and so we thought it advisable to frame our resettlement plans so as to accommodate as many as we could. In the colony areas of Bahawalpur the normal unit of allotment had been the 'square' of twenty-five acres. We decided that we should not allot to any refugee family more than half a square for cultivation and that wherever the canal supplies were reasonably adequate one-quarter of a square or six and a quarter acres should be the unit of allotment. In this way we were able to settle on the land two to three times the number of families that had left it.

Speed was essential if, as we desired, we were to get the refugees on to the land in time to prepare it for the 'rabi' crop. This would have to be in the ground by the middle of November at latest. We made the allotments, therefore, as fast as we could on a temporary six months' basis. The refugees were permitted to gather without payment whatever they could of the standing 'kharif' crops and to hold the land on payment of only the land revenue and water rates until they had reaped the 'rabi' harvest in the following May. Thereafter fresh terms would be settled.

Our principle was to allot land on a uniform basis of one-quarter or one-half of a square per family to all those who owned or cultivated agricultural land in the districts from which they came. We did not at this stage make detailed inquiries about the size of their holdings, but simply tried to satisfy ourselves that those to whom we allotted land were genuine owners or tillers of the soil. We required them to file affidavits to this effect, warning them that we would in due course check the correctness of their statements. This turned out to be a not entirely empty threat, as some time later an agreement was reached between India and Pakistan for an exchange of copies of all the relevant revenue records and so eventually it became possible to verify everybody's claim. Of course a fair number of false affidavits and bogus claims were put in.

Settlement of the refugees in the colony lands evacuated by the Sikhs proceeded at a very rapid pace. The Sikhs had cultivated their holdings themselves and not through tenants and so, with their departure, the land and the villages which they had occupied were left quite vacant and the newcomers could move straight in. Settlement of the old proprietary land owned by the Hindus in the non-colony areas was a slower and more complicated business. This land had mostly been cultivated by Muslim tenants and was often intermingled with other land owned by Muslims. As soon as the Hindus left, the tenants or neighbouring Muslim landowners appropriated it, and it took some time to come to arrangements with the former or to oust the latter. A considerable portion of it had to be left with the tenants.

The settlement of refugees in urban areas followed a similar pattern. In the colony towns, where the buildings were all new and well-constructed and where there were competent municipal staffs, the work proceeded rapidly. The refugees were themselves eager to settle in these towns and in order to accommodate as many as possible we divided up some of the bigger premises. The fixation of rent was comparatively simple as the houses and shops vacated by the Hindus were of a few standard sizes and designs and their valuation for purposes of municipal house tax readily ascertainable.

There was much more difficulty in filling up the old towns with their ramshackle buildings of all shapes and sizes and inefficient or non-existent municipal staff, and several of them remained half-empty throughout the winter.

It was a marvel to me how the incoming Muslims who settled in these urban areas—tradesmen, artisans and ordinary labourers—succeeded from the very start in standing on their own legs with very little help of any kind from the Government. Some of them within a day of arrival dashed off to Multan, laid out their scanty resources on the purchase of wares, and returned to peddle them at the street side pending the allotment of premises. Others began straight away to ply their trades in the roadways, establishing themselves as barbers, cobblers, tailors etc., at whatever seemed a favourable site. It puzzled me how so many more or less destitute people could so quickly find a livelihood by taking in each other's washing. The explanation is that in these colony towns the interchange of goods and services amongst the refugees themselves managed to base itself almost at once on the solid foundation of economic service to the surrounding countryside. These 'mandi' (market) towns fulfilled certain essential functions in the economy of the area, and in the performance of these functions the incoming Muslims were able to step fairly easily into the shoes of the departed Hindus. They were aided by the fact that the harvest was at hand. Large quantities of grain, cotton and oilseeds were about to come into the market and had to be warehoused, bagged, processed or dispatched by rail to other centres. At the same time the cultivators, having received payment for their produce, had money in their hands for buying goods and services in the towns. So the refugees settled into their new quarters at a favourable moment and were soon sustained by the normal flow of economic life which had been only temporarily interrupted.

Most of the grain merchants and other dealers in agricultural produce had been Hindus, but there were a few substantial Muslims in the trade and other local Muslims with a little capital soon set themselves up as grain dealers. We also entered the market wherever necessary, advancing money to agents to buy up stocks on our behalf. There was, therefore, not much difficulty in taking from the cultivators the produce which they had to offer. Only cotton presented a serious problem. This was the principal 'cash' crop in Bahawalpur and the cultivator largely relied on it to provide him with the means of paying his dues to the State Government. Cotton in its natural raw state as plucked from the bush cannot be stocked for any great length of time. The first step is to gin it, that is to separate the cotton from the cotton seeds. Ordinarily most of the crop was bought up at harvest time by the ginning factories, of which there were three or four in Bahawalpur district and about double that number in Rahim Yar Khan. All of them, except perhaps one in Rahim Yar Khan, were owned by Hindus and were worked by them with a predominantly Hindu staff. Those in Bahawalpur district were abandoned during September as a result of the general exodus of Hindus from that district. Some of the factory owners in Rahim Yar Khan also left for India, while those who remained showed no disposition to run their factories. They considered it too dangerous for themselves or their employees to go out into the rural areas to arrange purchases of cotton, nor were they willing to lay out large sums on such purchases when there was no certainty that they would be able to stay on in the State and recover their investment. There was a prospect, therefore, that practically all the ginning factories would remain closed and cotton become unsaleable. How were we to get them working? This was a question which continuously worried us from the beginning of September right on until well into November. It also worried the West Punjab Government. I would say that it was in regard to the working of these ginning factories that the Hindu notion of paralysing Pakistan by withdrawal of essential expertise came nearest to fulfilment.

Somehow or other a solution was found. When it came to a pinch, the Muslims proved to be less lacking in initiative, ingenuity and business capacity than had been imagined and with a little delay enough factories were brought into operation to handle the crop. It became clear quite early on that we should have to provide most of the working capital required. This we did through the State Bank of Bahawalpur at the head of which we were fortunate in having at this time an experienced Muslim banker on loan from the Imperial Bank of India. The difficulty was to find parties, with or without any capital of their own, who had any experience at all of the business and who could be relied on to collect staff capable of starting up one of these ginning factories and keeping it running. There was a danger of being hoodwinked by speculators who, after taking advances for the purchase of cotton and making a show of starting up the factory, would decamp with the money. Even when what seemed to be genuine and reliable parties were forthcoming, the negotiation of terms for the lease of a factory was a tricky business, especially as in some cases they were being simultaneously wooed by the West Punjab authorities and could play us off against each other. The back of our problem was, however, broken when a Muslim who had owned several ginning factories in East Punjab turned up as an applicant for the lease of some of ours. Resisting the blandishments of West Punjab, he did a deal with us and by shifting the Muslim personnel he had brought with him from one factory to another he managed by December to get three or four of the biggest ones into operation. Other lesser fry started up a few more and so we scraped through. We were in such straits that the lessees got the factories on very easy terms and probably some of them made a small fortune out of the one season's working. I was, however, so thankful to see smoke coming out of the factory chimneys and bullock-carts unloading cotton in the factory yards that I did not care if we had dropped a few lacs of rupees in lease money.

The reader may have wondered under what authority we disposed of the land, houses, shops, factories and other premises left by the Hindus and Sikhs. From the very outset we felt the need of some legal basis for our proceedings and in the last few days of August I began to draft an ordinance regarding the custody of evacuee property. To my intense relief I was spared further labour for just about this time the West Punjab Government issued an excellent ordinance on this very subject. It was simple, lucid and comprehensive and with a few modifications could easily be adapted to our needs. We duly promulgated our version of it. It provided *inter alia* for the appointment of the highest revenue authority (in the Punjab the Financial Commissioner and in Bahawalpur the Revenue Minister) as Custodian of Evacuee Property with Deputy and Assistant Custodians under him whose orders were ultimately appealable to him. This gave our proceedings a legal basis and to some extent a judicial character.

By the second half of October we had taken in as many refugees as we could for the moment readily absorb. There were still a number of nooks and crannies into which, with time and careful arrangements, more could be fitted; but for the time being we could not cope with any more. So far we had been fairly lucky, as we had succeeded in passing on to the West Punjab large numbers whom we could not readily accommodate or did not like the look of. We were helped by the fact that for most of the refugees Bahawalpur was only a first haven of refuge and not the ultimate goal. They were really making for the Punjab and most of them were willing of their own accord to proceed there, particularly if no immediate and attractive accommodation was made available to them in Bahawalpur. We refused quite firmly, despite pressure from several quarters, to open any regular refugee camps in the State. At one or two places we made temporary transit arrangements, but we did not undertake to look after, except for a few days, any for whom we could not permanently provide. So we kept the refugees on the move and those who seemed disposed to linger were politely but firmly pushed across the Sutlej into the Punjab.

Everything seemed to be settling down nicely when suddenly at the end of October almost without warning the Government of India began dumping on us at Macleodganj Road thousands of refugees brought there by train from districts around Delhi. Some eighty thousand were deposited in this way during the first half of November. At about the same time the Maharajah of Bikanir wrote to us saying that 150,000 refugees bound for the West Punjab had entered his State from the Hissar and Rohtak districts and that he proposed to pass them into Bahawalpur in the Fort Abbas region, whence they could proceed to the bridge across the Sutlej at the Pallah headworks, instead of conducting them northwards through his own State to the bridge at Suleimanke which was their shortest route. He gave as his reason that there were a number of Sikhs in the north of Bikanir (including many who had recently migrated from Bahawalpur) and he was afraid the column of refugees might be attacked if it passed through that area.

We could not but agree to receive them and give them passage through the State, though we did not like it. To have this column on our hands while simultaneously thousands of unwanted guests were detraining at Macleodganj meant a great strain on our resources; and we feared that many of the column, wearied of their journey and no longer in danger of attack, might halt permanently by the wayside and become our liability. However the column proved to be well-disciplined, and fortunately much of the Bahawalpur territory through which they had to pass was so little removed from sheer desert that they were glad to press on to the Punjab. As they approached Pallah and entered country that was more smiling and attractive, I mobilized all available tongas, donkeys, ponies and camels to assist them over the last laps of their journey. They thanked me profusely for this help, little realizing, I hope, how far from disinterested it was.

The refugees decanted at Macleodganj were more of a

burden. The Government of India insisted on dumping them there because it was easier and safer to do this than to take them by train through the Central Punjab and push them over the frontier between Amritsar and Lahore. The arrangement was most unwelcome to us, and unwelcome also to the Governments of West Punjab and Pakistan, as it meant that at a time when there was an acute shortage of coal in Pakistan, trains had to be provided to move these refugees from Macleodganj into the West Punjab by a long and circuitous route via Samasatta and Multan. An attempt was made to get us to accept responsibility for them. This we declined to do. Our stand throughout was that the Government of Bahawalpur, unlike that of West Punjab or the Federal Government of Pakistan, could not be held responsible for refugees. We had not asked for the creation of Pakistan or even been consulted about it, and therefore anything that we might do to mitigate its consequences by settling refugees within the State was purely *ex gratia*. We had by this time already absorbed nearly two hundred thousand and could not for the present take on any more.

The West Punjab Government had to accept this position and assume responsibility for the refugees at Macleodganj. But they accumulated there much faster than trains could be provided to move them to the Punjab and for two to three weeks we had large numbers on our hands. However, ultimately we got rid of most of them.

We were not alone in passing on refugees to others. The feelings of pity and sympathy which they had initially evoked had become deadened by repeated excitation, and by this time Provincial Governments and district authorities were all alike trying to shift the burden from themselves. The West Punjab Government were particularly overwhelmed and anxious for relief. Owing to weak administration the whole refugee problem had come to appear to them much more intractable than in fact it was. There was no danger now of all the Muslims in northern India being driven out. The flow had been checked and the numbers to be accommodated were, therefore, more or less limited to the Muslims from East Punjab and the adjoining Princely States. Room for all of them could in reality be found fairly easily in the West Punjab, but owing to delays and corruption in the allotment of land and houses this fact was obscured and huge numbers collected in refugee camps or in squatting places of their own choosing where the misery and squalor were appalling. The West Punjab Government, erroneously thinking that most of the available land had already been allotted to bona fide refugees, were at a loss how to empty these camps and were disturbed because in some of them there had been minor demonstrations and cries of 'Pakistan Murdabad'[1] and 'Jinnah Murdabad'. They appealed to the Pakistan Government for assistance and early in December the latter called a conference in Lahore to consider the whole problem.

At this conference a general, if cynical, hope was expressed —though not officially recorded—that with the onset of the really cold weather, due in two to three weeks' time, a good proportion of the refugees would die of pneumonia and so relieve us, partially at least, of our difficulties. But we could not rely on these forces of nature, nor in the event did they give us much aid—the refugees proved remarkably tough. The West Punjab Government had another quite simple solution for the problem and that was, with the backing of the Pakistan Government, to persuade other Governments to take a large number of the refugees off their hands. I was afraid that the Government of Bahawalpur might be one of those expected to come to the rescue and was relieved to find that, with very little persuasion from me, it was generally accepted that we had done our part and could not for the moment be expected to do any more. The two Governments specially earmarked for relieving the Punjab of refugees were those of Sind and the N.W.F.P., particularly the former. Sind had so far escaped the main deluge and had only received some few thousand refugees, arriving by sea and air from Bombay. There was a general belief that they had vast areas of land available for allotment. This was not altogether correct, as a large proportion of the non-Muslim population had not yet left the province. However, Sind were more or less told that they would have to take half a million refugees from the Punjab. They did not clearly accept this liability, but they seemed to acquiesce in the necessity of doing something.

It was proposed to make a start by sending 150,000 refugees on foot to Sind complete with all their bullocks and carts. It would be a long trek and for 125 miles their route would lie

---

[1] 'Down with (death to) Pakistan.'

through Bahawalpur, so our co-operation was desired. We were expected to prepare camping grounds, arrange for water supplies and provide stocks of food, fodder and fuel. Though I was sceptical of both the need and the practicability of the plan, I undertook to do all that was required of us. Suitable halting places were selected, officers deputed to be in charge of them, stocks of fuel etc. laid in and complicated changes made in the rotation of the canals so as to ensure water supplies at the right places and at the right time. After several postponements a date was finally fixed for the commencement of the march. Everything in Bahawalpur was in readiness. But nobody came. The refugees refused to budge from the Punjab and the whole project of sending 150,000 of them on foot to Sind collapsed ignominiously.

The refugees were quite right in their obstinate refusal to move; and slowly it dawned on the West Punjab Government that there was ample land available for accommodating them and for compensating them in full for land abandoned on the other side of the frontier. Ultimately it turned out that, after meeting all just claims, there were several hundred thousand acres surplus.

In Bahawalpur Rao Fazlur Rahman had reported quite early on that owing to the mistakes or corruption of the subordinate revenue staff there had been many cases of over-allotment and double-allotment, and of wrong allotment to persons who were not owners or cultivators of land or were not refugees at all. So in January and February we undertook a thorough scrutiny of all the allotments so far made as a result of which several thousand acres were found to have been improperly allotted and became available for further settlement of refugees. We also took this opportunity to do some reshuffling of the refugees so as to group together those from the same district or belonging to the same tribe, and also so as to ensure that the border areas would be occupied by stout-hearted cultivators with martial traditions who would not run away at the slightest alarm. These reallotments were worked out by the middle of March and scheduled to take effect at the end of May after the 'rabi' harvest had been gathered. It was hoped that after this reshuffling all the allotments would in fact become more or less permanent and that none of the refugees would have to shift

I

again. But it was impossible at this stage, when there had been
no proper verification of claims, to make permanent allotments
and so for the time being they were made on a yearly basis.

In the latter half of February I made an extensive tour
through the eastern parts of the State where the refugees
were most thickly settled. I had rather dreaded it as I feared
that I would everywhere hear nothing but complaints and be
assailed with requests which could not be granted. But not at
all; everywhere the refugees had settled down amazingly
contentedly and were full of thanks for all that had been done
for them. They were particularly grateful to the inhabitants of
adjoining villages who had lent them bullocks or ploughed and
sowed their lands for them and in numerous other ways assisted
them to find their feet in their new quarters. They were looking
forward to a good 'rabi' harvest and seemed already to have
forgotten all their tribulations of a few months earlier.

I have painted on the whole a rosy picture of the refugees.
This is because in Bahawalpur we escaped the worst scenes of
misery. At Vehari and Arifwala and, no doubt, several other
places in the Punjab, hundreds of refugees sat day after day
by the roadside huddled together, half dead or dying, in squalor,
filth, utter wretchedness and dumb despair. In Bahawalpur too,
though the conditions were nowhere so bad, we had a few
black spots. Macleodganj Road was one of them. From the very
outset this place had continuously a large floating population
of refugees. Though certain facilities were available there and
we had a competent staff in charge, at times the numbers out-
ran our resources and the refugees suffered considerable privations. Another bad spot—probably the worst in the State—
was Samasatta. This was a railway junction and nothing more.
There were some railway quarters and a number of railway
sheds and warehouses and a very small bazaar, but no regular
town or municipal services. Large numbers of refugees entering
the State at Macleodganj Road came on by train to Samasatta
and waited there to catch some train going northwards to the
Punjab. For about six weeks, from the end of September till
well into November, a floating population of about two thousand
refugees squatted and defaecated near the station and along
the railway lines. During about half this period there were on
an average six deaths daily—mostly old people and infants.

Very soon the mess and filth in the station precincts became indescribable as there was no-one to clear it up. We then bribed some of the municipal staff of Bahawalpur city with large bonuses to come out periodically in lorries and clean the place up and some improvement was effected. But we were not able to do much for the refugees halting at Samasatta and the condition of many of them was pitiable.

One should also not forget the emotional suffering of the refugees, forced to quit all of a sudden and for ever the familiar scenes of childhood and youth or, maybe, of a lifetime. One scene, riveted in my mind, typifies for me this measureless and meaningless suffering. I had gone over to Macleodganj Road—probably one day in October—in response to an urgent call from Rao Fazlur Rahman. The flour mill at that place had run out of oil and was about to close down, the Muslim owner or his agent having given no warning of any shortage until his stocks of oil were on the point of exhaustion. Fazlur Rahman was faced with the imminent prospect of having no flour to offer to the incoming refugees, and he wanted my authority for requisitioning one of six tank wagons, fully laden with oil, which happened to be standing at the station *en route* from Karachi to India. Together we dragooned the station staff into uncoupling one of these wagons and handing it over to us. Having secured this supply of oil and given orders for the flour mill to be restarted, we turned our attention to the refugees, large numbers of whom had newly arrived by train from India. They were squatting disconsolately along the line for several hundred yards on either side of the station and seemed so stunned by their misfortunes as to be incapable of speech or movement. As we were strolling about among them, trying to reassure them and cheer them up, a long train of open trucks drew into the station from the west, crammed with Hindu refugees from Multan who were being evacuated to India. Thus the two separate sets of refugees, driven in opposite directions by the same impalpable forces, met at Macleodganj station, and for fifteen minutes gazed at each other in lugubrious silence. Not a word was exchanged and the sense of cumulated misery was overpowering. As those standing in the trucks looked down at those sitting by the track and those sitting by the track looked up at those standing in the trucks, an expression of half-dawning comprehension crept into their gloomy, bewildered faces and seemed to say, 'So you're also in just the same plight! God help you!' Then the train started again and steamed slowly out of the station with its load of misery, while the other lot of refugees continued sitting dazed and speechless by the side of the line. All alike had been driven from their homes by the exigencies not of war but of freedom. It did not make sense, but it had to be endured.

XIV

Summing Up

I N this chapter I shall attempt to answer two questions, which may have suggested themselves to the reader, and then conclude with some general remarks regarding the responsibility for these events.

The two questions which I shall try to answer are:

(i) Were the happenings in Bahawalpur typical of the disorders elsewhere?

(ii) Could these massacres and migrations have been prevented?

There is no doubt that the outbreaks of violence in Bahawalpur, even in the eastern part of the State which was most affected, did not compare in scale or savagery with those in the Central and Eastern Punjab. At one stage the Indian press made great play with the Bahawalpur disturbances and produced some ingenious calculations to prove that no less than seventy thousand Hindus and Sikhs had been killed in the State. There were special reasons for this propagandist arithmetic. In some of the Princely States of East Punjab, notably Patiala, Kapurthala and Faridkot, the slaughter of Muslims had been particularly heavy and this had been given great prominence in the Pakistan press. India was tempted to reply with a *tu quoque* and the Bahawalpur disorders, considerably exaggerated, provided convenient material. In actual fact the total casualties in the whole of Bahawalpur State (including the Sikhs from Rahim Yar Khan district killed on the way to Jaisalmir) cannot, on a liberal estimate, have exceeded three thousand, and V. P. Menon's description of it as 'a paradise compared with East Punjab' was not wide of the mark.

In Bahawalpur there were no terrific holocausts such as took place at Sheikupura, where several thousands of Hindus and Sikhs were killed in a few hours, and no large-scale train

261

massacres. On three occasions small parties of Hindus were murdered while travelling in trains within Bahawalpur territory, but there was no successful systematic hold-up of a refugee train, followed by an overpowering or seduction of the armed guard and a wholesale slaughter of all the passengers. Several such sickening outrages were perpetrated elsewhere. There were also in Bahawalpur none of the grosser excesses—no deliberate mutilation of men or women, no sadistic rapes as distinct from seduction, no parading of women naked through the streets such as was widely reported to have occurred in a town in East Punjab.[1]

In general the disturbances in Bahawalpur resembled closely both in scale and character those in the immediately adjoining districts of south-west Punjab. The resemblance was due to a similarity in the composition and temperament of the population, while differences in these same respects gave a somewhat different colour to the disturbances in the Central Punjab. In Bahawalpur and south-west Punjab loot rather than blood was the dominating motive of the majority community. Non-Muslims who resisted the pillagers or got in their way were liable to be bumped off and occasionally, when the Muslims were roused to fury by the sight of injury to any of themselves, blood flowed freely. But there were very few instances of an organized hunt for victims and a delight in killing for its own sake. The Muslim population was less interested in blood than in the quiet enjoyment of Hindu property and Hindu girls.

In the Central Punjab, on the other hand, particularly among the Sikhs, there was a positive lust for blood and consequently casualties were much higher. Individuals boasted—not without exaggeration—of the numbers of the opposite community they had slain. Casualties resulted not merely from chance encounters or sudden gusts of anger but from systematic butchery and hunting down of victims. Many witnesses attest how in East Punjab murderous-looking Sikhs armed with large kirpans prowled about the platforms of railway stations sniffing

[1] It should be noted that a similar story was current during the Mutiny when forty-eight young women were reported to have been paraded naked through the streets of Delhi, ravished in broad daylight and then murdered. This story was classed by Lecky among the 'Fictions connected with the Indian Outbreak of 1857'.

for blood, and when a train halted, searched the carriages for Muslim travellers and, if they discovered any, stabbed them to death. The historian of Lahore records how in the early eighteenth century during the commotions that marked the break-up of the Mogul empire, the Sikhs laid waste the Punjab from Ambala to Lahore. 'They butchered, bayoneted, strangled, shot down, hacked to pieces, and burnt alive every Mohammedan in the place.'[1] History repeated itself in 1947.

The greater ferocity displayed in the Central as compared with the south-western Punjab was in part just a reflection of the differing temperaments of the respective populations. Even in ordinary times the number of murders reported to the police in districts like Lahore, Amritsar and Ferozepur exceeded a hundred per district per annum. There were similar high murder rates in some of the Muslim districts of north-west Punjab. But in the districts of Bahawalpur and south-west Punjab the rate was more like ten than a hundred per annum. The relative docility of the peoples of this area gave a milder character to the disorders.

Apart from this difference of temperament, the more even distribution of the population between the two communities in the central districts was conducive to greater and more widespread violence. Here there was considerable intermingling of Muslims and non-Muslims not merely in the towns but in the rural areas also. In all these central districts Sikh and Muslim villages existed side by side while quite a number had mixed populations. Thus once warfare broke out between the two communities it involved the whole countryside and was very difficult to control. In a number of instances whole villages or sections of villages were practically annihilated.

Moreover the more even the balance between the two communities, the greater the force required for the one in the majority to assert its mastery. The Sikhs were determined to overpower the Muslims on their side of the frontier and to drive them away; and they had armed themselves well for this purpose. But since the Muslims were very numerous in the east-central districts of Amritsar, Ferozepur, Gurdaspur and Jullundur and initially had no thought of leaving their homes, the Sikhs had necessarily to employ force and terror on a consider-

[1] *Lahore, its history*, by Syed Mohammad Latif.

able scale in order to dislodge them; and this in turn set going corresponding Muslim violence in the adjoining districts across the frontier.

The same conditions did not obtain in Bahawalpur or in the western districts of the Punjab generally. Here not only were the Muslims in an overwhelming majority, but, outside the colony areas, the population of the countryside was almost exclusively Muslim. The non-Muslims were concentrated in the towns. In the rural areas there was only a sprinkling of Hindus and Sikhs—shopkeepers, moneylenders and petty officials—and, save for the Sikh colony 'chaks', there existed very few villages with a wholly or largely Hindu or Sikh population. The Sikh 'chaks' in Bahawalpur were nearly all near the eastern border and, as mentioned earlier, their inhabitants at the very outset of the trouble slipped away into Bikanir State with little loss or molestation. The only instance in Bahawalpur of a whole village being wiped out in the style of the Central Punjab was the isolated hamlet of Labana Sikhs whose fate has been re-counted on page 230.

Of the Hindu and Sikh shopkeepers scattered about the villages in small numbers, some were killed, some submitted to forcible conversion, but the majority, sensing their danger in time, made their way to the nearest town where there were larger numbers of their own community and more hope of protection from the authorities. Thus the disorders in the villages, never very considerable, tended to subside rapidly through the elimination of the few non-Muslims, and the towns, large and small, with all that they offered in the way of Hindu property to loot, became the main centres of trouble. In the larger towns disturbances were the work of the local Muslim inhabitants. In the smaller towns the Hindu shops and quarters were liable to be attacked by mobs of Muslim villagers from the surrounding countryside, often with the connivance of the Muslims inside, as happened at Khairpur, Qaimpur, Macleod-ganj Road and Hasilpur and was attempted at Minchinabad.

This was the general pattern of the disorders both in Baha-walpur and throughout most of western Punjab, but towards the north, where the Muslim population was by nature more turbulent, the violence tended to be greater.

The herding of members of the minority community into

keeps or camps where they could be more easily safeguarded
was a common feature throughout the Punjab, and our jail
camp outside the city of Bahawalpur had its counterpart in
places great and small from Delhi to Rawalpindi. We were
lucky in being able to evacuate all the inmates of our camp
within a very few days so they suffered no serious or prolonged
privations. This was not everywhere the case.

Throughout the Punjab—and not merely in Bahawalpur—
the forces of law and order proved unreliable. Their general
apathy and at places active connivance in loot and murder
were a principal cause of the magnitude of the disorders. The
behaviour of the police and military in Bahawalpur in these
respects was not unrepresentative and by no means below the
general level elsewhere—indeed, so far as I can judge, the Bahawalpur troops behaved far better than some of the forces in the
Sikh States of East Punjab. But in Bahawalpur we were at this
disadvantage, that we had nothing to fall back upon. The States
in East Punjab had the Government of India behind them, and
the Government of India, finding many of its forces unreliable,
could and did call in Gurkha and Madrasi troops who were
more or less uncontaminated. We had no option but to do the
best we could with the Bahawalpur Army. Pakistan was hardly
in a position to help us and its own troops were largely infected
with the general contagion.

These troubled times afforded to officials of all ranks unparalleled opportunities for illicit gain and some of them may
have felt, like Clive, astonished at their own moderation.
Money could be made both from the outgoing and from the
incoming refugees. The former, if they had any resources, were
naturally willing to pay for safe evacuation, and they could also
be called upon to pay for the privilege of taking some of their
belongings with them. The theory was put forward—and being
so beneficial to dishonest persons quickly gained wide acceptance—that an evacuee must not take away anything valuable
from the territory he was leaving on the ground that 'it belonged
to Pakistan' or to India as the case might be. On this absurd
pretext evacuees could be searched and their property mis-
appropriated, or they could be compelled to pay a heavy toll.
This system of semi-legalized robbery and extortion, of which
there were many traces in Bahawalpur, flourished extensively in

I*

both halves of the Punjab. An unmolested evacuation such as was arranged in the Rahim Yar Khan district in 1948 would have been hardly possible in 1947.

Much of the movable property left behind by evacuees in shops, factories, business premises and houses fell into the hands of plundering mobs; but articles which they could not easily carry away or dispose of, such as furniture, carpets and cars, were often appropriated by high-ranking officials and their friends either by open seizure or on the plea, true or false, that the owners had consigned them to their care. The inclination to profit from the misfortunes of others was widespread and showed itself in the highest as well as the lowest strata of society. One story illustrative of the general depravity, which particularly shocked Nur Mohammad—a man of rather old-fashioned views—was that of a well-known Muslim prostitute of Delhi. It was said that in return for a large sum of money an influential Muslim family, who were in a position to arrange for their own evacuation by air, permitted her to pose as one of their daughters and take her seat along with them in the plane.

The incoming refugees desired to be allotted and put in possession of vacated land, houses, shops etc., so that they could settle down quickly and begin to earn a livelihood. Those who possessed ready cash or could borrow from relations and friends on the side of the border to which they had migrated, bribed and tipped patwaris and other petty officials according to the custom of the country. This went on in Bahawalpur as elsewhere, but in Bahawalpur the incoming refugees were probably settled more promptly and with less harassment than elsewhere because we had the advantages of an autocratic government, which could take decisions promptly, and of an efficient 'settlement' staff all of whom could be switched at once from their ordinary duties on to 'resettlement' of refugees.

Big money often changed hands when it came to the allotment of factories, mills, and other commercial or industrial undertakings. There were prospects of large profits for anyone with the ability to restart these abandoned establishments, and incoming refugees with business experience and access to banking facilities were prepared to pay handsomely for quick possession. Amid all the golden opportunities for peculation in those days here was the real bonanza for political bosses and high-ranking officials.

Against the general inhumanity and collapse of moral standards must be set numerous individual examples of kindness and compassion, loyalty to friendship, devotion to duty, and courage in shielding and sheltering those whose lives were in danger. In this and in other ways there is a parallel with the Mutiny ninety years earlier. Unfortunately these examples of virtue were not widely appreciated and sometimes received even from the Governments concerned less than lukewarm approbation. While the Governments of India and Pakistan were both genuinely anxious to do the right thing and bank down the fires of hatred, the two new Governments of East and West Punjab were both appreciably influenced by the popular passions to which they were more directly exposed. Consequently officials who were slack in the performance of their duty or even guilty themselves of horrible crimes were allowed to go unpunished, while the few who vigorously and courageously resisted the general frenzy were in several instances frowned upon or victimized.

Most civilized societies have been liable to occasional pogroms. What occurred in the Punjab in 1947 was qualitatively a not uncommon phenomenon; but it was unusual in so far as it affected so many people simultaneously over such a wide area and resulted in such a very heavy death roll. In India the nearest well-authenticated precedent to frenzy on such a scale is afforded by the Mutiny. The parties to the conflict at that time were different, Hindus and Muslims being ranged on one side and Christians of all kinds—European, Eurasian and Indian—on the other; but the passions aroused were much the same and caused the adherents of all three religions alike to sink to the crudest savagery. The mutineers set the standard by shooting their British officers and then murdering their wives and children. This roused in the British such a burning spirit of revenge that British troops, when they got the opportunity, slaughtered 'niggers' indiscriminately without regard to guilt or innocence, age or sex. These ferocious reprisals provoked further outrages by the sepoys, including the hideous massacre of women and children at Cawnpore, and this in turn stimulated the British to more fearful acts of vengeance. Thus one atrocity or the report of it led to another and prompted the irrational massacre of quite innocent persons. A young English Assistant Commissioner, whose sister had undoubtedly been murdered in Delhi by the mutineers, believed that she had first been stripped naked and outraged. The thought of this so worked upon his feelings that on the recovery of Delhi by the British, 'he had put to death', according to his own admission, 'all he had come across, not excepting women and children'. The less sophisticated Punjabi, inflamed by similar provocations, real or rumoured, perpetrated in 1947 many like insensate deeds of violence, though he has probably left no such clear written record of his vengeful exploits.

This review of some of the general features of these massacres and migrations may be rounded off with a few overall statistics. Reliable figures are not available in regard to all matters, but it can be stated compendiously and with certainty that while Muslims lost the most lives, Hindus and Sikhs lost the most property. As regards the number of persons compelled to migrate, reasonably accurate figures are available. Between August 1947 and March 1948 about four and a half million Hindus and Sikhs migrated from West Pakistan to India and about six[1] million Muslims moved in the reverse direction. A great part of this huge migration took place within the short space of three months, that is between the middle of August and the middle of November.

The Hindus and Sikhs who left West Pakistan were as a whole decidedly better-to-do than the Muslims who entered it. The latter were mainly peasants, artisans and labourers with a comparatively small admixture of big landowners and business-men. On the other hand among the Hindu and Sikh refugees there were a considerable number of landlords and capitalists, big or small, and numerous persons holding administrative or clerical posts in industry, trade, banking, and insurance, while the Sikh peasantry, who had to leave the 'colony' areas of West Pakistan, were more prosperous and had larger holdings than the Muslim peasantry of East Punjab. This is reflected in the available statistics. In West Punjab alone the land abandoned by Hindus and Sikhs amounted to 6·7 million acres against 4·7 million acres abandoned by Muslims on the other

[1] Seven million according to Pakistan authorities.

side of the border. Figures regarding the total value of immovable property left on either side are less reliable. In the years immediately after Partition exaggerated claims were made by both sides, but according to more recent and more moderate estimates of the Government of India Rs 500 crores represents the value of property left by Hindus and Sikhs in West Pakistan while the corresponding figure for the property left in India by Muslims who migrated to West Pakistan is put at Rs 100 crores. Even if the disparity was not as much as the five to one indicated by these figures, it was certainly very considerable.

Estimates of casualties are largely a matter of guesswork. During and immediately after the disturbances it was freely stated that millions had lost their lives. Even a later and more sober estimate made by an Indian High Court judge puts the figure at about half a million.[1] An English journalist, Andrew Mellor, thinks[2] that the number killed is unlikely to have been less than two hundred thousand and may well have been far more. The other extreme is represented by an estimate, attributed to Nehru, that twenty to thirty thousand people had been killed in the Punjab. My own guess, based on some rough calculations[3] originally made in December 1947, is not widely different from that of Andrew Mellor. Slightly varying his conclusion I would say that the number killed is unlikely to have been more than two hundred thousand and may well have been appreciably less. This, though lower than most estimates, is an enormous total for civilian casualties in time of peace.

I turn now to the second question, 'Could these massacres and migrations have been prevented?' To answer it one has to be clear about their cause. Succinctly stated their cause was the decision to create Pakistan by dividing the Punjab and thus dividing or threatening to divide the Sikhs. The question, therefore, resolves itself into two parts, viz.:

(i) Could Pakistan have been avoided altogether?
(ii) If not, could the Sikhs have been peacefully accommodated in some agreed way?

These two parts of the question are closely interconnected,

---

[1] *Stern Reckoning*, by G. D. Khosla, p. 299.
[2] *India since Partition*, p. 45.
[3] See note at the end of the chapter.

but for purposes of analysis it will be convenient to consider them separately.

In this narrative the course of events leading to the creation of Pakistan has been traced only from the year 1937; for though Pakistan had its roots much further back in history, as is apparent from the ideas expressed by Sir Syed Ahmad in the nineteenth century, it was only after 1937 that it became a live political issue. I propose, therefore, to examine whether its avoidance was possible only from 1937 onwards and not to dig down deeply into the events of an earlier period. As regards pre-1937, I will dwell only on one significant fact, namely that Gandhi's rise to ascendancy in Congress was more or less coincident with Jinnah's estrangement from it.

In 1917 Jinnah was a member and keen supporter of Congress, noted primarily as an Indian rather than a purely Muslim Nationalist. At that time he was pooh-poohing the threat of Hindu domination. 'Fear not,' he said, 'this is a bogy which is put before you to scare you away from the co-operation and unity which are essential to self-government.' So long as Congress was led by men like G. K. Gokhale, who spoke the familiar language of Western liberalism and constitutionalism, Jinnah felt at home in it. But the growing influence of Gandhi at the end of World War I set it on unconstitutional paths and simultaneously gave it a more pronounced Hindu complexion. To these developments Jinnah could not reconcile himself. He parted from Congress in 1928.

Jinnah's dislike of Gandhi—that 'Hindu revivalist' as he called him—was deep-seated; and he distrusted profoundly his methods of non-co-operation and organized agitation. They 'have already caused split and division', he wrote to him in 1920, 'in almost every institution that you have approached hitherto,' and he predicted that they would 'lead to disaster'— as indeed they did as regards Hindu-Muslim unity, the preservation of which was an objective which at that time both of them shared. The fact is—as Jinnah seems dimly to have perceived—that with Gandhi's decision not to co-operate with the British and to launch a campaign of civil disobedience the seeds of separation were being sown. Civil disobedience involved an appeal to the masses, and an appeal to the masses by an organization headed and symbolized by Gandhi was necessarily

an emotional, semi-religious appeal to the Hindu masses and
not to the Muslims; for Gandhi with all his fads and fastings,
his goat's milk, mud baths, days of silence and fetish of non-
violence was pre-eminently a Hindu. He himself claimed to be
'a Muslim, a Hindu, a Buddhist, a Christian, a Jew, a Parsee'.
But this claim did not cut much ice; indeed who but a Hindu
could entertain such a preposterous hope of being all things to
all men?

Gandhian leadership of Congress was highly successful in
securing for the nationalist movement popular backing from
the Hindus; and popular backing was considered necessary in
order to bring pressure on the British to relax their hold on
India. Whether this view was correct is open to question. It
may well be that the British could have been induced to leave
just as quickly if Congress had stuck to strictly constitutional
methods and had consistently co-operated with the British instead of doing the reverse. However this may be, under Gandhi's
leadership Congress took the opposite course and, instead of
remaining just an organization of the intelligentsia, deliberately
sought to enlist wide popular support. But to appeal to the
masses was to run the risk of rousing the latent Hindu-Muslim
antagonism that existed at mass level. Congress, it is true,
achieved in the N.W.F.P. a limited and deceptive success among
the Muslim masses, and it continued to enjoy the support of a
few distinguished Muslim intellectuals. But in general the more
Gandhi became the idol of the Congress and the more Congress
diffused itself among the masses, the more the Muslims as a
whole stood aloof from it, viewing it coldly as an essentially
Hindu institution.

The danger that his methods would provoke Muslim antipathy was not adequately appreciated by Gandhi who, with
the normal Hindu tendency to prefer dreams to facts, ideals to
reality, could not divest himself of the belief that Congress—
more particularly Congress as personified by himself—could
and did represent everybody, or at any rate everybody that
mattered. This fatal self-deception had already by 1937 done
serious, though not irreparable, damage to the cause of national
unity. What was ultimately to prove worse, Gandhian policies
had also alienated Jinnah who instead of being friendly to
Congress was by now potentially, though not as yet actually,

hostile. No-one, of course, could have foreseen that he would prove such an implacable foe. Unknowingly, however, Gandhi had helped to transform him from a keen nationalist into the chief architect of Pakistan.

At the beginning of 1937 all this was still in the womb of time. Jinnah had no considerable following and his prospective importance was not at all apparent. The question 'Can Pakistan be avoided?' could hardly have been asked, since Pakistan was not yet envisaged as even a remote possibility. Though Hindu-Muslim differences were fairly acute, even Jinnah and the League had not suggested that division of the country was an appropriate or possible solution of them. At this stage Pakistan was still quite easily avoidable. When were the mistakes made which caused it in a few years to become absolutely unavoidable?

When a boat is being carried downstream by the current of a river towards a weir or dangerous rapids, it is difficult to fix the precise moment at which all efforts to save it become vain and nothing can prevent it from being swept to disaster. At a distance from the fall the rowers, if they realize in time the danger ahead of them and exert themselves, will be strong enough to make head against the current. Even if they neglect this opportunity and let the boat drift down to where the current is too much for them, there may still be time to steer it to the safety of the bank. But there comes a point, not exactly identifiable, when the force of the current will take complete charge and draw the boat irresistibly to destruction.

So it was with Pakistan. In 1938 the current making for it was quite discernible, but was not yet too strong to be resisted. By 1942 it had gained tremendously in strength, but there still seemed to be ways of avoiding its worst effects. Even as late as 1946 it appeared at the time that there was a slender chance of steering clear of an absolute division of the country. By the end of that year division was seen to be inevitable.

The crucial years were 1937-42. It was in this period that mistakes were committed and opportunities let slip which made unavailing the later efforts to avoid the division of the country. First came Congress's mistake of declining to form coalition governments with the League in those Provinces in which they had a majority. The mistake was very natural, perhaps unavoidable, and by no means fatal. It could have been retrieved. But Congress did not perceive the importance of retrieving it because they did not appreciate how deep and widespread were the fears which it had aroused among the Muslim intelligentsia. Yet they had sufficient warning. The immediate rallying of all Muslims to the League banner and the doubts which Muslims began to express about submitting to a permanent Hindu majority at the Centre were very plain danger signals. Congress did not read them.

The outbreak of war afforded a splendid opportunity of repairing the damage that had been done. On the plea of a national emergency Congress could have retraced their steps and sought to join with the League in coalitions both in the Provinces and at the Centre. If Congress had entered into such working partnerships with the League while moderate men were still in control of the Muslim masses both in Bengal and the Punjab, the forces of disruption could have been checked. But Congress elected to follow the barren path of non-co-operation —non-co-operation with both the British and the League— and resigned office in all the provinces in which they held it.

From the point of view of preserving Indian unity, this was perhaps the most foolish step Congress ever took. In fairness it must be said that several Congress leaders consented to it with reluctance and misgiving; and Gandhi's own initial instinct was against it. If the British had shown more generosity and imagination the scales might have been tipped the other way. But the chance was missed and Congress, blind to the importance of reaching accommodation with the Muslims while there was yet time and obsessed by their struggle with the British, gave up office and with it the prospect of coalitions with the League. Within six months Jinnah and the League had committed themselves to the demand for Pakistan.

In so far as Jinnah really wanted Pakistan, despite all the calamities which it would necessarily entail, he cannot be held to have been guilty of a mistake in demanding it in 1940. If, however, as seems probable, he did not at this stage really intend to follow the demand through to its logical conclusion, then it was a grave—a criminal—error to raise such a dangerous slogan, and men like Sikander, who clearly foresaw the dangers, were also much to blame for weakly consenting to it. If they were unable to dissuade Jinnah from his course, they should have broken with him at this time instead of giving their tacit blessing to a demand for the absolute division of the country.

Probably the last chance of averting an absolute division came in 1942 with the 'Cripps' offer. If it had been accepted, Congress and the League would at any rate have participated together in the defence of India against the Japanese and the partnership might have prevented an absolute break later. The chance was not taken.

After this all further rescue operations were probably vain. It seemed at the time that the Cabinet Mission of 1946 had an outside chance of saving the unity of India and that this was thrown away through the bad judgement first of Gandhi and then of Nehru. In retrospect this chance appears to have been illusory. The constitution-making machinery proposed by the Cabinet Mission might have been brought into operation, if it had not been for the mistakes of the Congress leaders; but it could hardly have produced an agreed constitution for a single Indian Union. Congress and the League were by this time such poles apart, so much the slaves of their own slogans and animosities, so much imbued with mutual hostility and distrust that the Constituent Assembly as envisaged by the Cabinet Mission, if it had ever started to function, would have broken up in confusion and strife.

To sum up: A general lack of wisdom and statesmanship in the years 1937–42 made Pakistan unavoidable. Thereafter British efforts to preserve the unity of India were sincere and well-conceived—it is difficult to see what more they could have done—but passions had been too deeply aroused for human reason to control the course of events.

I pass to the second part of the question. If Pakistan became unavoidable, could the Sikhs, nevertheless, have been peacefully accommodated in some agreed way? The answer depends on whether one considers that agreement between the Akalis and the Muslim League was inherently possible or inherently impossible. On this opinions may well differ. But one thing is certain. If any possibility of agreement did exist, it was effectively destroyed when the League was excluded from power in the Punjab in the spring of 1946. The formation of the Khizar-Akali-Congress Government so infuriated the Punjabi leaguers

—never very reasonable at the best of times—that thereafter they could never be brought even to attempt to reach agreement with the Sikhs.

Agreement, if at all possible, could only have been reached on the basis of avoiding altogether the partition of the Punjab and reconciling the Sikhs to its inclusion as a whole[1] in Pakistan along with the whole Sikh community. This is what the Muslim leaguers themselves originally wanted, and it might have been made acceptable to the Sikhs, if the League had shown some disposition to safeguard their interests. But the League made no effort at all to conciliate them and there was no-one to act as mediator. Khizar and the moderate Muslims were regarded as traitors and the British were suspect for having connived at the formation of the Khizar Ministry.

It may be thought that agreement might have been reached for a division of the Punjab on the basis of a planned transfer of population. In the circumstances as they actually developed an arrangement of this kind was out of the question. The League claimed the whole of the Punjab for Pakistan and would not think in terms of division till the very last moment. But by that time such violent passions had been aroused and so much blood had been spilt in the Punjab and elsewhere that delicate negotiations for an agreed transfer of population could not possibly have taken place.

There are good reasons for thinking that an agreement on these lines was in any case inherently impracticable. It was no mere coincidence but in the very nature of things that the proposal for the division of the Punjab should find both parties in a very angry mood; for neither party wanted division and each was bound bitterly to blame the other for being the cause of it, the Sikhs holding the Muslims responsible because of their insistence on Pakistan, the Muslims holding the Sikhs responsible because of their refusal to be included in Pakistan.

Apart from this, the great disparity between the assets owned by the Sikhs (and Hindus) in West Punjab and those owned by the Muslims in East Punjab would have been a well-nigh insuperable obstacle to an agreed and planned exchange of populations. The Sikhs would have pressed for the dividing line to be shifted westwards—at the very least, west of Lahore—

[1] Minus, possibly, some predominantly Hindu areas in the south-east.

so that both the transfer of Sikh population and the loss to themselves on the transfer would be diminished. It is, however, difficult to imagine that the Muslims would ever have voluntarily surrendered Lahore or indeed agreed to any dividing line materially different from what they were entitled to on a population basis. Nor would they have consented to pay compensation for any disparity of assets. In reply to such a demand they would have contended that they had no wish to turn out non-Muslims from Pakistan, all of whom were quite welcome to remain and enjoy their property.[1]

For these reasons even in the most favourable circumstances it would hardly have been practicable to negotiate an agreement for the division of the Punjab on the basis of an exchange of population. But suppose it had been, would the populations in those circumstances have moved at all? A negotiated settlement would have implied a calm, peaceful atmosphere. In such conditions millions of people do not abandon for ever their ancestral homes in response merely to official requests and propaganda. Some strong compulsion is required to make them move—the compulsion of fear, famine or the harsh unchallengeable fiat of a Stalin or Nebuchadnezzar. A forcible transfer by government decree in Russian or Babylonian style was hardly conceivable in India at that time. The political leaders and the people at large had been too long accustomed to the mild easygoing ways of the British to employ or submit to such official coercion. The transfer took place in fact—and probably could only have taken place—under the impulse of fear and at the point of the sword.

So the conclusion is that, once Pakistan became inevitable, there was little or no chance of promoting an amicable Sikh-Muslim settlement which would have prevented a holocaust in the Punjab. If any chance existed at all, it vanished when the Sikhs were permitted to combine with Khizar in forming a Government to the exclusion of the League. This fatal step precluded all possibility of a peaceful solution of the Sikh problem.

It will be clear from the previous discussion that by the time

---

[1] The real urge for transfer of population came from the Sikhs—despite the fact that many of them individually would lose so heavily by it—because they did not want their small community to be split between India and Pakistan. This is discussed further on pages 280-1.

Lord Mountbatten arrived in India it was far too late to save the situation. The creation of Pakistan had become unavoidable, and this in turn in the circumstances which had developed was bound to involve a conflagration in the Punjab—indeed the first premonitory outbreaks had occurred shortly before his arrival. No last-minute miracle could prevent this conflagration; on the other hand by lack of decision and dilly-dallying it might easily have been made far worse than it actually was. The vigour and speed with which Lord Mountbatten acted had at least the merit of confining it to the Punjab. Nevertheless there has been criticism, particularly of this very speed of action which was in reality a merit. The critics say that he rushed ahead without realizing the probable consequences and that if he had not been in such a hurry to wind up British rule in India—antedating by some ten months the time limit set by the British Government—the division of the Punjab could have taken place with less carnage and in a more planned and orderly fashion. This criticism may have gained a certain plausibility from the fact that the magnitude and severity of the disturbances in the Punjab in August–September 1947 seemed to take the authorities in India by surprise. That this was in fact the case is confirmed by the frank admission of Mr. V. P. Menon already quoted.[1] Some trouble in the Punjab was expected, but it was optimistically believed that a Boundary Force (quite inadequate both in numbers and composition) would be able to control it. Here undoubtedly there was a miscalculation. But the question arises whether, even if Lord Mountbatten had foreseen more clearly what was going to happen in the Punjab, he could have done any better than he did. While he and the topmost leaders of Congress and the League may all have misjudged the Punjab situation, quite a number of people acquainted with that Province were fully aware, especially after the March disorders, that its proposed division must end in a catastrophe. But none of them were able at the time to offer any practicable suggestions for averting or even minimizing it; nor have those who were wise after the event indicated any alternative course of action which might have promised better results.

All the suggestions that have been put forward really amount

[1] See page 94.

to this, that instead of rushing through the Partition in two and a half months while the Punjab was seething with passion, Lord Mountbatten should have stuck to the time-table originally laid down by the British Government and so enabled the Punjab to be brought under control and tranquillized before the final division took place. If this had been done, the withdrawal of British authority, it is contended, and the setting up of two new governments for the two halves of the Province could have been effected in a more organized manner and in a calmer atmosphere. Tempers would have cooled and there would have been less disposition for Muslims and non-Muslims to set upon one another. There would also have been time to sort out all the Muslim and non-Muslim police, magistracy and other civil officials and settle them in their appropriate stations in West and East Punjab well in advance of the formal Partition, instead of all this reshuffling synchronizing, as it actually did, with the Partition itself, so that at the crucial moment civil officials were still in transit to their posts or had only just reached them and the whole administration in a state of turmoil.

This sounds very plausible; but it all rests on the false premise that the means and the time were available for controlling and tranquillizing the Punjab. In fact they were not, and so the course proposed was a quite impracticable one. After the March disorders, to re-establish law and order firmly in the Punjab required the proclamation of martial law, which would have been politically difficult, and the employment of overwhelming and *reliable* military forces, which simply did not exist; while to assuage the tempers that had been aroused required far more time than the twelve to thirteen months which the British Government's schedule allowed.

As regards military forces it must be remembered that the bulk of the Indian Army was drawn from just those areas and races of northern India in which communal passion was at its height. An attempt to hold down the Punjab with such forces would have been worse than useless. It would have ended at best in a fiasco, like the plan for a Boundary Force, at worst in a civil war in which the armed forces were themselves engaged.

Other comparatively neutral elements of the Indian Army, e.g. Gurkhas, Mahrattas and Madrasis, would have been quite insufficient in numbers for the task, and to have employed them to the exclusion of the rest would have been fraught with political and practical difficulties. In order to muster enough dependable forces, it would have been necessary to bring out to India a large number of additional British troops. In the summer of 1947, with the British scheduled to quit India for good by June 1948 and barely able to scrape together enough troops for occupied Germany, this was plainly not feasible.

But let us suppose that somehow or other enough forces could have been assembled during the summer of 1947 to enable the Punjab situation to be firmly gripped, would this have afforded any solution of the problem? Would tempers have so much cooled and the Province been so much tranquillized by June 1948 that its division and the withdrawal of the controlling forces could have been accomplished comparatively peaceably? At the time there was certainly no reason to think so. On the contrary it seemed clear that any temporary over-awing of the Punjab by a tremendous show of strength—if that were possible —could only put off the evil day at the risk of making it far worse when it ultimately came. I expressed this view in connection with the proposal for a Boundary Force. If it was weak, the Sikhs would simply ignore it—which is what actually happened. If on the other hand it was strong enough to be effective, the Sikhs would bide their time and wait for its withdrawal before launching the attack on the Muslims of East Punjab for which they had long been preparing. The same would have applied to any other short-term measure for holding down the Punjab. There was not the slightest hope of the Sikhs meekly swallowing the insults and outrages which they had suffered and allowing all their revengeful feelings to evaporate in the short space of twelve months.

But apart from these feelings of revenge there was another factor which would have made it impossible to prevent a violent explosion in the Punjab by mere postponement of its division till June 1948. This factor was none other than the determination of the Akali leaders to ensure the survival of the Sikhs as a compact, coherent, undivided community. In the situation which had developed by 1947 this basic objective of Sikh policy could only be realized by the forcible expulsion of Muslims from East Punjab; for only so could accommodation be found on the Indian side of the frontier for the two million Sikhs who would otherwise be left in Pakistan. So in falling upon the Muslims in East Punjab *vi et armis* in August 1947 the Sikhs were not only gratifying their desire for revenge, but also helping to secure a more rational objective—the integral survival of the Sikh community. The migratory movements that were thus set going became, no doubt, largely spontaneous and instinctive, the natural product of fear and danger, but there lay behind them, as the original source of the initial impulse, this rational motivation. To grasp this is to grasp an important clue to the understanding of these events. The determination of the Sikhs to preserve their cohesion was the root cause of the violent exchange of population which took place; and it must have operated with like effect even if the division of the Punjab had been put off for another year.

The Sikhs would, no doubt, vehemently disclaim the part here ascribed to them. They would contend that the root of the trouble was the Muslim desire to expel *all Sikhs* from Pakistan and in support of this would cite the Muslim attacks on Sikhs in March–April 1947. There is, however, little to show that these attacks in the spring of 1947 had any far-reaching strategic motive or were anything more than ill-timed ebullitions of Muslim hooliganism. Jinnah had, it is true, at one stage suggested in general terms an exchange of population, but one cannot infer from this that the Muslims entertained any plan or intention of forcibly expelling all Sikhs or all non-Muslims from Pakistan. I know of no reliable evidence of such a plan or intention, and all that I myself saw and heard in those days was entirely inconsistent with its existence. Moreover such a plan would have been highly dangerous to the Muslims themselves, as it would have been to risk inviting as a reprisal the extrusion into Pakistan of *all* Muslims from India, and Pakistan would not have been large enough to hold them. That this might actually happen was a fear that oppressed us on the Pakistan side of the border during the weeks which followed the beginning of the migratory movements.

For the Sikhs, on the other hand, the preservation of their cohesion was a natural, intelligible objective. It had long been uppermost in the minds of influential Akali leaders. Even as far back as 1942 they had been thinking in terms of concentrating all Sikhs on the Indian side of the border, if the Muslims insisted on Pakistan. When, therefore, Pakistan became inescapable and the Mountbatten Plan for dividing the Punjab —and so the Sikhs—was announced, they accepted it, but, in order to meet it, privily perfected their own plans for Sikh concentration. They were, of course, led to hope that, because of 'other factors', the dividing line would be fixed farther west than it was and consequently that the number of Sikhs from the Pakistan side to be accommodated in East Punjab would be smaller and the Muslim assets available for distribution among them greater than actually proved to be the case. In a measure they were deceived and befooled. But though the Radcliffe line disappointed them, they were committed in advance to accepting it and had no option but to put their plans for Sikh concentration into operation. In order to drive out the Muslims from East Punjab there was need initially for force and terror. The Sikhs, thirsting for revenge and with large stocks of arms at their disposal, were well prepared physically and psychologically for this part of the programme and it did not require many days of their ruthless methods to make all Muslims wish to leave. The other half of the programme, the inflow of Sikhs from the Pakistan side of the border, followed partly as a natural chain reaction without plan or preparation. But not entirely; large numbers of Sikh colonists of the Montgomery and Multan districts, like most of the Sikh colonists in Bahawalpur, left their villages and trekked away to India, unscathed and in good order, before anyone had touched them or the disturbances had spread to their areas. I have no doubt that this was the result of previous Akali propaganda. The only considerable body of Sikhs who did not immediately move were the Sikhs of the colony district of Lyallpur. Protected by their own strength and the efficiency of the Muslim Deputy Commissioner—who did his duty but got into trouble for it—they stood their ground until September when they were evacuated with very little loss.

The policy of concentration ensured the survival of the Sikhs as a single distinct community, but at the cost of much blood and enormous sacrifices by individual Sikhs. If the objective was legitimate—and the Sikhs, being the most homogeneous, integrated and self-conscious community in India, could claim as much right to survival as the Muslims—the policy is defensible. Nay, what else could the Sikhs do? Circumstances which others had created threatened their existence as a distinct community, and their leaders cannot justly be blamed for adopting this policy, despite the bloodshed which it entailed, but only for the brutal savagery with which it was carried out.

Thus—to resume once more the main thread of the argument —Sikh desire for revenge and Akali determination to keep the Sikh community together would have prevented any gains being derived from a temporary postponement of Partition. Holding down the Punjab by overwhelming force till June 1948, if it had been possible, would only have meant deferring till a year later the upheaval of 1947. Even the supposed advantages of having administrations far more ready to assume responsibility in the two halves of the Punjab than was the case in 1947 would have been unappreciable. For the troubles were uncontrollable in 1947 not because Governments and officials were insecurely seated in their saddles, but because the forces of law and order were themselves unreliable. This is well illustrated by our experience in Bahawalpur. The Government and government officials remained practically unchanged. A stable administration, hardly at all affected by transfers or losses of non-Muslim personnel, was available to cope with the troubles. Yet in a situation far less difficult than that in the Central Punjab we failed to prevent disorders because the police and military could not be depended upon. This was also the fundamental weakness in the Punjab and, unless passions had subsided, would have produced the same results in 1948 as in 1947.

Postponement of Partition by ten months could have done no good; and it carried with it dangers of its own. Sparks from suppressed fires in the Punjab were liable to ignite combustible materials in other parts of India. Any delay in separating the armed forces might give occasion, in the excited state of feeling, for clashes between Muslim and non-Muslim units with incalculable consequences. The three parties who had agreed to the Mountbatten Plan might resile from it, if they were given too much time for reflection. Furthermore, from the purely British point of view there was the danger that the drastic measures which would be necessary for keeping the peace in the Punjab would earn them the odium of all three communities and that

they would in the end leave the country amid general exe-
cration.

All things considered, it must really be accounted a mercy
that Lord Mountbatten did not foresee more clearly the magnitude of the calamity that threatened the Punjab. Had he done
so, he might have fumbled and faltered, casting about vainly
for means of avoiding it while the whole country drifted into
civil war. As it was, by driving ahead at top speed with his
plan for Partition he successfully divided the country and the
armed forces before they could be engulfed in universal strife,
and the Punjab alone had to pay in blood the price of freedom.

While Lord Mountbatten may be absolved from blame, the
claim, often put forward, to great merit for the manner of our
departure from India rings somewhat hollow. It is true that the
disturbances of 1947 were more or less confined to the north-
west of the sub-continent and that the tribulations of the Punjab
meant no more to central and southern India than did the
horrors of the Spanish civil war to the rest of Europe. Yet that
the ending of the British Raj, which we had so long foreseen and
so long proclaimed as our goal, should involve a last-minute
division of the country which we had ourselves united, the
sudden rending in twain of two large well-knit provinces, the
precipitate, enforced migration of well over ten million people,
and casualties of the order of 200,000 does seem to argue a
singular want of prevision and failure of statesmanship.

For this the British bear a good share of the responsibility.
The complacency shown by them from 1937 to 1942, when the
demand for Pakistan was first gathering strength, has been
commented upon in earlier chapters. It is possible, though by
no means certain, that if from the outset the British had made
it quite clear that they would never countenance Pakistan, the
division of the country would have been avoided. But it was
very difficult, if not impossible, for them to do this. By the time
the demand for Pakistan was actually put forward by the Muslim
League, World War II had already broken out and the main
Hindu political organization, Congress, was standing aloof in an
attitude of passive hostility. In these circumstances the British
could hardly have been expected to risk antagonizing also the
principal Muslim political party by turning down their demand
out of hand. They were also precluded from doing so by the

repeated assurances given earlier that the wishes and interests of the minorities would not be lightly overridden. The most, therefore, that the British could do at this time was to temporize and to use their best endeavours to bridge the chasm that had opened between Congress and the League. The latter they certainly failed to do in the period 1937 to 1942.

But to understand fully the British responsibility one has to go back further. The root of the trouble lay in the decision to introduce parliamentary democracy into a society which was far from homogeneous and riven with the deep Hindu-Muslim cleavage. The irrevocable step was taken with the Montagu-Chelmsford reforms at the end of World War I. Ten years earlier the liberal Secretary of State, Lord Morley, when introducing his own Morley-Minto reforms, had said that he would have nothing to do with reforms which directly or necessarily led to the establishment of a parliamentary system in India. But by 1919 the tide running in favour of parliamentary democracy was too strong to be resisted. Almost everywhere sceptres and crowns were tumbling down and being replaced by democratic institutions. The Indian intelligentsia, deeply imbued with the ideas of English liberalism, could not think of freedom from foreign rule in any other terms; and even English opinion, lacking for the most part any real insight into Indian conditions, tended to view with equanimity, if not enthusiasm, the export of parliamentary democracy to India. And so there was introduced into a vast country of illiterate peasants, belonging to diverse races and religions and held together only by geography and common subjection to British rule, a system of government which, while it has served the English and some closely kindred peoples well enough, has elsewhere been—and doubtless will continue to be—a constant source of strife, disunity and disruption.

The inherent dangers of this British-sponsored experiment would have been lessened if the British, having once launched it, had hastened to transfer all political power to Indian hands before the constant appeals to the gallery inseparable from democratic processes had time to inflame feelings and accentuate the Hindu-Muslim division. But the British, fighting a stubborn rearguard action, conceded power in the inter-war period only slowly and reluctantly. While it is not true, as is often alleged against them, that in this period they deliberately promoted divisions, they certainly took advantage of the divisions that existed in order to justify the prolongation of their rule, and they failed, until quite near the end, actively to promote unity. Their hesitation to part with power in the inter-war period gave time for the communal situation to deteriorate and the cry of Pakistan to be raised. If in 1929, when the Montagu-Chelmsford reforms came up for review, they had boldly decided to treat Dominion Status as an immediate and not a distant objective and had set about with some determination to frame a constitution on this basis with merely a few transitional safeguards, then by the early thirties a Central Government representative of the major Hindu and Muslim parties would have been installed in power before anyone had occasion to think of Partition. And once the country had virtually reached the goal of independence as a unity, that unity would have been preserved at least for some time; for, apart from the bias of sheer inertia in favour of the *status quo*, the Muslims of the Muslim-majority provinces, with wide control over their provincial affairs, would have had no strong motive for secession. What might ultimately have been the outcome is a matter of speculation, but at least the British would have brought their rule in India to a blameless close.

If therefore the British ever care to ask wherein lay their responsibility for the massacres and migrations of 1947, the answer may be succinctly given. It lay in their belief in the virtues of parliamentary democracy and their reluctance to part with power.

Responsibility did not rest only with the British. Countless Indians and Pakistanis of every walk in life share the guilt for these events. Of those in a position of authority His Highness the Maharajah of Patiala was for many weeks regarded in West Pakistan as one of the blackest villains. Startling tales were in circulation of the atrocities alleged to have been committed by Patiala troops at his orders or instigation, and it was reported that these crimes were so weighing upon his conscience that terrible dreams visited him nightly and prevented him getting any rest. At that time we did not trouble to ask ourselves how any authentic information about the Maharajah of Patiala's dreams could possibly percolate to Bahawalpur. The reports about them, so comfortingly suggestive of divine retribution, were acceptable and were readily accepted. Nevertheless I was very loath to believe that the Maharajah, whom I knew and liked, was really responsible for the crimes attributed to him. Knowing from my own experience how difficult it was in those days to control the armed forces, I preferred to think that he had been powerless or, at worst, insufficiently determined to curb the violence of his Sikh troops. Some time later I inquired the truth of the matter from a friend on the Indian side of the border who knew something of events in Patiala. He substantially confirmed my assessment of the Maharajah's responsibility and went on to point out that he and many others like him were largely the victims of circumstances and that real responsibility rested higher up and ultimately, and in greatest measure, on two persons—Gandhi and Jinnah.

This may be an over-simplification, yet it conveys the essential truth. As the acknowledged leaders of the Hindus and Muslims they undoubtedly share, though perhaps not equally, the main responsibility for the catastrophe in which their leadership resulted. In the ultimate analysis the cause of the disaster was their common worship of the new god—the National State. Utterly dissimilar though they were in temperament and outlook, they resembled each other in this, that both alike were high priests of this modern Moloch—a god which the Akalis in their humbler, cruder way also served—and both, though with different degrees of reluctance, were prepared in the last resort to sacrifice countless victims at the altar. The National States which they had in view were different, but the motivation was basically the same. Western nations should feel no surprise or indignation at this blood-stained worship, seeing that they themselves at the bidding of the same god have accepted the slaughter of two world wars.

Jinnah's responsibility is the more obvious and was certainly the more deliberate. It is a measure of his guilt, but also of his greatness, that without him Pakistan would never have come into being. His career affords a striking illustration of the influence of a single individual—and also of sheer chance—on the broad course of history. Only Jinnah, and none of his lieutenants whether singly or combined, could have mastered all the Muslims of the Punjab and Bengal, dominating or overthrowing their own leaders, and swung them in favour of a policy and objective to which they were originally quite opposed. Yet Jinnah would never have had the opportunity to seize the lead and make Pakistan the goal of all the Muslims had it not been for the accident of fate which removed from the scene in 1936 the great Punjabi Muslim, Sir Fazl-i-Husain, at the comparatively early age of fifty-nine. Sir Fazli was the founder of the Unionist Party, a staunch Muslim, a staunch Punjabi, but also a staunch Nationalist. Like Jinnah he was a man of integrity, and in ability, force of character and renown he was more than his equal. If he had lived to lead the Unionist Party for another ten years instead of dying prematurely and giving place to lesser men, Jinnah would not have been able, and would not even have attempted, to win over the allegiance of the Punjabi Muslims and Pakistan would have remained an 'impracticable students' scheme'. But fate decreed otherwise and by removing Sir Fazli gave Jinnah his chance.

The responsibility for first putting forward 'Pakistan' as the well-nigh unanimous demand of the Muslims rests squarely on Jinnah. It was he who, despite the misgivings of Sir Sikander and many others, transformed it from an esoteric fancy into a powerful political slogan. Even if originally he made the demand only as a tactical move, he stuck to it thereafter so uncompromisingly—only at the time of the Cabinet Mission showing a disposition to accept something less—that a settlement on any other basis became virtually impossible. By his stubborn attitude and refusal to negotiate with anyone except on his own terms he made sure of getting Pakistan, but also of getting it in the worst possible form—a truncated, 'moth-eaten' Pakistan brought into existence by an unnatural division of the Punjab and Bengal with all the miseries that flowed therefrom. At no stage did he show signs of uneasiness at the probable consequences of his policy or seriously attempt to avert them; on the contrary, by consistently rebuffing the Sikhs, he ensured that the partition of the Punjab would take place with the maximum horror. To what extent in all this he acted with his eyes open is not definitely known. Possibly in regard to the facts of the Punjab situation he deliberately preferred to remain ignorant so that knowledge might not inhibit him from the course he wished to pursue. Great achievements in action, whether divine or diabolic, require a certain ruthlessness.

It would be too uncharitable to presume—as some have done —that Jinnah, in pressing the demand for Pakistan, was actuated solely by vainglory and desire for personal power. He must have persuaded himself that some larger interests were at stake. Though not a religious man or deeply steeped in Islamic culture, he may well have genuinely believed that to safeguard the interests of the Muslims as a separate community and to preserve their distinctive character and way of life from insidious Hindu encroachment were objectives of supreme importance. Whether he was right in so believing, a non-Muslim perhaps cannot fairly judge. In any case we move into the sphere of value judgements where there are likely to be differences of opinion. Englishmen had no doubt that to escape Hitler's domination was worth a destructive war. Likewise Jinnah and his Muslim associates might maintain that to save their community from Hindu domination was worth the miseries of Partition.

But was Partition really necessary in order to secure the objectives which he had in view? It is here that the correctness, perhaps even the integrity, of his judgement may be questioned. He was right, no doubt, in distrusting Hindu professions. They might say that Muslims were their brothers, but would in fact treat them as less than stepbrothers. A few leaders might be sincere in their intentions, but the ingrained exclusiveness of most of the high-caste Hindus was bound to assert itself, so that at most only a few hand-picked Muslims would be embraced as brothers and the rest relegated to the position of outcastes. An excellent illustration of what treatment Muslims might expect from the Hindus, if the latter had a free choice, was afforded in the Punjab. In that province most of the commercial, industrial and banking establishments were controlled by Hindus. In none of them was any Muslim employed except in a menial capacity as a coolie or watchman or as an artisan. Well-paid posts and positions of profit were not open to outsiders, but were filled on the basis of family, caste and other similar connections according to the deeply-embedded habits and traditions of Hindu society. That society was not going to change its nature overnight at the pious wish of a Gandhi or a Nehru. Hindu professions were widely different

from Hindu practice, as all Muslims knew. Jinnah's distrust of
them was both genuine and well-founded. But it does not
follow that he was right in thinking that the creation of Pakistan was necessary in order to safeguard Muslim interests. Many
staunch Muslims, who shared his distrust of the Hindus and
had Muslim interests at heart no less than he, were far from
convinced that these could only be secured by the division of
India into two separate National States. Since Muslims were in
a majority in several large provinces, it was felt that, with provincial autonomy and constitutional safeguards at the Centre,
they would become too powerful an element in the Indian
Union for the crafty Hindus to override or circumvent their
interests, however much they might desire to do so. Thus
in the opinion of these Muslims—and in 1940 they were certainly a majority—the creation of Pakistan in the sense of a
separate National State was unnecessary.

On the purely political plane—and in the long run this might
have been all that mattered—they were probably right.
Probably, too, in 1940 Jinnah himself recognized that they
were right and did not intend to press the demand for Pakistan
to the extreme limit. But later the tide of events which he had
himself set going, reinforced by his own and his associates'
personal ambitions, persuaded him that he could accept
nothing less than Pakistan, even though all he could get was the
husk without the kernel and at a cost in human suffering which
he had not initially foreseen.

Whatever judgement may be passed on Jinnah by the moral-
ist, he must ever be venerated by Pakistanis as the man to whom
their State owes its very existence. Nor can outsiders withhold
admiration. To have transformed in little more than seven
years the chimerical idea of Pakistan into a living political
reality was an astonishing achievement. Alike in his tenacity
of purpose and in his calm, cold acceptance of consequences
which would have deeply troubled the conscience of an ordinary man he showed qualities of greatness.

Gandhi's responsibility, though less direct and less deliberate
than Jinnah's, was nevertheless very considerable. He did not,
like Jinnah, wittingly follow a policy calculated to lead to
bloodshed, but unwittingly, as has been pointed out in earlier
chapters, he contributed in many ways to this outcome. More-

K

over, as many of his utterances made clear, in pursuit of the cherished goal of Independence he was prepared, despite his proclaimed dislike of violence, to risk both bloodshed and anarchy, albeit with more reluctance and self-questioning than Jinnah.

The mistakes made by Congress under Gandhi's leadership were due basically to the Gandhian facility for self-deception. Over-conscious of his own good intentions, he clung till too late to the fallacy that Congress could and did represent all Indians including the Muslims. Obsessed by the supposedly evil intentions of the British and unaware that his own methods of appeal were calculated to provoke Muslim antipathy he shut his eyes till too late to the menace of Muslim separatism. It was easy to blame everything on the British and to persuade one-self that with their departure Hindus and Muslims would embrace as brothers. It was easy to decry the League leaders as relics of an outworn feudalism and to believe that owing to the primacy of the economic motive—one of Nehru's pet doctrines which was to be abundantly disproved—the Muslim masses would disown them. With these consoling beliefs Gandhi allowed himself to be deceived. They did not accord with facts, but they obviated the need for facing them, until at last the facts themselves confronted him in all their stark-ness, leaving no room for escape from partition, massacres and migrations.

There was no-one to whom this outcome gave more grief than Gandhi himself. The independence for which he had striven so long seemed hardly worth having when these were its first fruits. The extent of his own responsibility for them he may not have recognized, but at least it can be said of him that he made heroic efforts to atone for his mistakes. The closing months of his life showed his character at its noblest. Unbroken in spirit by the shocks to his own hopes and ideals, he laboured to combat the frenzy that had been aroused with a sincerity and courage which cost him his life but entitle him to be looked upon as a saint and a martyr. Gandhi, indeed, may be classed with those Christian saints of the dark and middle ages who combined astute political manoeuvring (and a certain amount of humbug) with genuine moral earnestness and a courage sustained by more than mundane convictions.

The division of India and its entry into the scale of nations as two sovereign States instead of one, though it accords with twentieth-century trends, seems absolutely contrary to the broad long-term interests of the human race. The dispassionate philosopher, no less than Ghandhi, must deplore that Hindus and Muslims insisted on thinking of themselves as separate peoples. But practical statesmen have to bow to the logic of facts. The original formulation of the demand for Pakistan may have been a mistake and the obstinate adherence to it a blunder as, in their hearts, many of those who are now Pakistanis at one time believed. But by 1946 the creation of Pakistan had become the least of possible evils, and in the following year this was wisely, if regretfully, recognized by all parties concerned. It is indeed fortunate that the final attempts to retain some semblance of political unity failed and were abandoned, for in the state of feeling that had been reached in 1946 a single Union of India would have been a house divided against itself and the end would have been a civil war far more devastating in its effects than the severe but short-lived blood-letting in the Punjab. The whole sub-continent and a whole generation would probably have foundered in Chinese chaos. As it is, ordered life has been successfully maintained both in India and Pakistan and in some directions considerable progress has been achieved.

Will these two countries, within a measurable distance of time, come together again in some form of political union? This is a question which those who knew India before Partition necessarily ask themselves. Few of them, perhaps, would now expect to see such reunion within their own lifetime. The longer India and Pakistan remain separate sovereign States, the more they must tend to grow apart and develop personalities of their own which will be resistant to coalescence. With the passage of years the old bonds between the two populations are gradually being loosened and their old common culture effaced. Within the present century a voluntary reunion under democratic forms seems wholly impossible. Such reunion could come about, if at all, only under an authoritarian system which permits differences only within an iron frame of basic uniformity and rigidly enforced discipline. There is at present only one political system in the world which fulfils these requirements.

Note on Casualties

IN December 1947 I made some calculations regarding the number of persons killed in West Punjab and Bahawalpur. I had a pretty accurate knowledge of the casualties both in Bahawalpur State itself and in the immediately adjacent West Punjab districts. Regarding several other districts I had good information from old subordinates, especially among the magistracy and police, with whom I was in touch. I was thus able to reach fairly precise figures for about half the districts of West Punjab and on the basis of these to make intelligent guesses regarding the remainder. These calculations led me to a certain figure for the total casualties from August onwards in West Punjab and Bahawalpur. I found that Sir Francis Mudie, the Governor of West Punjab, had independently arrived at exactly the same result. The figure was 60,000.

I had no detailed information about casualties elsewhere, but knew that in East Punjab, including the Punjab States, they had been considerably heavier than in West Punjab. I assumed at the time that they might have been about twice as heavy, i.e. 120,000, and that therefore the casualties in the Punjab as a whole, including Bahawalpur and other Punjab States, were about 180,000. Making allowances for outlying areas, where casualties were comparatively lighter, e.g. the States of Bikanir, Alwar and Bharatpur on the one side and the N.W.F.P., Baluchistan and Sind on the other, I concluded that 200,000 would be a fair estimate of the total casualties. Subsequent inquiries have led me to think that the casualties in East Punjab, though undoubtedly higher than in West Punjab, were not, as I had assumed, twice as high and that consequently my final figure of 200,000 was somewhat inflated.

Re-reading *Divide and Quit*

Tapan Raychaudhuri

I

Historical studies, as well as contemporary narratives of historic events, rarely have long lives, so far as readers' interest is concerned. Sir Penderel Moon's *Divide and Quit* is among the more fortunate exceptions. Hardly any study of decolonization in South Asia and the partition of Britain's Indian empire published in the course of the last four decades has failed to use this extraordinarily perceptive book. Sir Penderel's complex explanation of the long and the short-term developments leading to the partition of India and his empathic yet hard-headed narrative of the holocaust as it was experienced in one part of the Punjab, the princely state of Bahawalpur, are still of interest. The lay reader, seeking to understand events which seemed unlikely even a few weeks before they actually took place, continues to find here a combination of objectivity and intelligent analysis rare in the writings of people actually involved in those happenings. It was a wise decision to republish a book which is no longer easily available.

Sir Penderel, like some of his famous predecessors in the Indian Civil Service, was even more successful as a professional scholar and historian than as an administrator: arguably, he lacked the 'flexibility' expected of imperial bureaucrats who aspired to reach the top. His preoccupation with discovering the truth and, worse, telling it to the world could not have helped. Yet he evidently made a worthwhile bargain: lasting fame as a scholar of integrity as against some higher rung in the bureaucratic ladder or cheap popularity as a writer. His judgements are not comforting to either the believers in imperial righteousness or the champions on Indian nationalism. Quite surprisingly, the varied and intensive research over the last thirty five years on many of the themes discussed in his book confirm his judgements far oftener than one might expect.

Yet, *Divide and Quit*, unlike the author's other works (excepting the semi-fictional *Strangers in India*) is not a scholarly tome. It

294

omits all critical apparatus, cites very few sources of information and is not based in archival research. It simply records the considered judgement of an insightful participant-observer who had earned his living as a responsible official in the British Indian administration in the 'thirties' and 'forties'. While doing so, he had also done his best to try and understand the bewildering and tragic reality taking shape under his eyes using both common sense and scholarship. His conclusions offer a curious mixture of imperial stereotypes, profound analysis and some highly idiosyncratic notions.

The list of long-term factors he identified as the ultimate cause of the partition of India began, unpromisingly, with an old familiar. It was first evoked by Sir Syed Ahmad and later used by Muhammed Ali Jinnah and his Muslim League to great purpose in generating a mass movement to achieve Pakistan: 'Two nations—Muslim and Hindu—could not sit on the same throne'. He considers and rejects the other familiar stereotype,— *Divide et Impera*,—as a contributory factor, but perhaps not entirely. The British, in his view, certainly did not generate the communal problem; yet they were happy to make use of the existing divisions in Indian society. As Linlithgow's constitutional adviser put it somewhat blandly, 'That such divisions and conflicts should be used as practical aids to imperial government was only to be expected'.[1] The British were worried when there were signs of Hindu–Muslim disunity and certainly did nothing to resolve the conflict. Communal conflicts, Moon points out, occurred almost exclusively in the British Indian Provinces. The princely states were, for the most part, free from this plague.

In his opinion, the most fundamental cause of the communal rift and its final end products, the partition, massive violence and mass exodus affecting the lives of millions, was not religion, but a more modern preoccupation—nationalism. The struggle was not about faith but about power and the material gains which it might bring. Hindus and Muslims were not interested in converting one to another. If these were the concerns of the ambitious elite, the Pakistan demand accorded with the 'blind impulses' of the Muslim multitude. The British had contributed to these negative developments by introducing the Westminster

[1] H.V. Hodson, *The Great Divide*, quoted in G. Rizvi, *Linlithgow and India: A study in British policy and political impasse in India, 1936-43* (London, 1978), p. 106.

style of electoral process, something totally alien to India's political traditions and entirely unsuitable for her non-literate masses who got caught up in processes of which they had no understanding.

Then there were more proximate causes. The strategies and aspirations of the Indian National Congress and the Muslim League and the leaders of the two organizations led inexorably to a situation where no compromise was possible any longer. Gandhi and the Congress were determined to win freedom for a united India and claimed to speak for all Indians, even after the elections of 1937 and 1945 showed quite conclusively that the vast majority of Muslims were not with them. Mr Jinnah stood forth as the 'sole spokesman' for the Muslims and claimed that the League alone should represent the Muslims even at a time when there were non-League ministries in the Muslim majority provinces. Virtually autonomous regions in the Muslim majority areas, their boundaries and degree of autonomy defined vaguely to begin with, was his stated object. Initially viewed with scepticism, if not horror, by most Muslim leaders, the idea of an autonomous Muslim homeland acquired its own inevitable momentum until the road to a free and united India was firmly blocked. The British, anxiously concerned to preserve the unity they had created, tried to avoid partition far too late in the game.

With apologies to their followers and admirers, Sir Penderel insistently laid the blame at the door of the leaders,—Gandhi, Nehru, Jinnah, Khizr Hyat Khan, Master Tara Singh and Baldev Singh—for the relentless descent into chaos and misery. He blamed the British for doing nothing to stop the journey to disaster when there was still time and for even taking some pleasure in the disarray of the nationalists. He traced how it all happened step by step,—the Congress refusal to form coalitions with the League in 1937 which finally alienated Jinnah, Nehru's Muslim mass contact programme which directly induced Jinnah to try the same game bringing communal politics to the Muslim masses, Linlithgow's uninspiring call for co-operation in the war effort with no inducement offered to the Indian nationalists, the resignation of Congress ministries which was not unwelcome to the British bureaucracy, the failure of the Cripps Mission for which Moon held Gandhi responsible, the 'Quit India' movement which only helped neutralize the Congress for the duration of the war leaving Jinnah free to consolidate his power among the Muslims and the final negotiations for transfer of power in which

Jinnah insisted on the League being the sole representative of the Muslims while Gandhi was adamant that the Congress Muslims should be represented in the interim government. This long litany of unfortunate decisions explains the circumstances leading to partition.

But, in Moon's view, they were less important than the fact that the aspirations of the nationalists and the politicized Muslims had become fundamentally incompatible: the Congress leadership, Gandhi excepted, came to find divided India a more acceptable solution than a loose federation with its two major partners always at loggerheads. Along the road there had been many alternative possibilities which could have led to a different outcome. An effective transfer of power before there was any serious demand for a partition of India, say, around 1929 was one of these. But once Pakistan, however defined, had become the cherished object of Muslim aspirations, partition in fact, if not in name, was an unavoidable result. The wranglings over the precise interpretation of the Cabinet Mission's three-tiered constitutional proposals and the non-cooperation between the Congress and the League ministers in the interim government were symptoms rather than causes of irreconcilable agendas.

If partition had become inevitable after a point in time, the holocaust which accompanied it was the product of contingent rather than long-term factors. Moon's analysis is slightly ambivalent on this issue. He records Sir Sykander Hyat Khan's opinion that 'Pakistan would mean a massacre': the tribesmen and the Baluch, for instance, would be least concerned with the lethal consequences of their orgy of violence for their co-religionists in Hindustan. His not very satisfactory comparison between the communal violence of 1947 and the Indo-British conflict ninety years earlier also suggests a substratum of faith in a colonial stereotype—the historic and undying hatred between Hindus and Muslims. But his emphasis in explaining the tragedy is on the immediate circumstances. The Muslim League which had the overwhelming support of the Punjabi Muslims in 1946 was prevented from forming a ministry by an unacceptable coalition of Khizr Hyat's Unionists with the Akali Sikhs and sundry Hindus. The League's protests were fought with prohibitory orders which could not be imposed leading to the first massacres of Hindus and Sikhs. The seeds of a terrible vendetta were thus sown.

The inclusion of the Punjab in Pakistan would mean the

subjection of the Sikhs, a cohesive community, to Muslim domination. Nothing was done to make the prospect attractive or acceptable to them. And the Sikhs' desire to hold together as a community in one state meant that the partition of the Punjab which divided them did not solve their problem. Revenge for the events of March 1946–7 and the desire to expel all Muslims from Eastern Punjab to find *lebensraum* for Sikhs who would necessarily migrate from the west explain the massive violence which followed. In short, the Punjab tragedy was the end product of events which took place in the last year of British rule. It was a preventable disaster.

But once the cycle of horrors had begun, it had to run its course. The Border Security Force of 50,000 was inadequate to deal with the outbreak. The loyalty of the police, reluctant to fire on their co-religionists, could not be depended upon. Many of the British officials, like the Governor of Bengal who had done little to stop the carnage in August 1946 failed to do even what was possible. One inexperienced official marched his British troops up and down the street of Amritsar without firing a shot. Others advised the Hindus who sought their protection to go to Gandhi, Patel and Nehru who were not exactly in charge in Western Punjab. Even where they were, whether in Eastern Punjab, Delhi, Bihar, or West Bengal, they had a hard struggle bringing things under control. On one point, however, Moon is quite emphatic. The events in the Punjab were in no way triggered off by the bloodshed in eastern India.

II

How far has Moon's analysis of the causes of the Partition, and the horrors which accompanied it, been confirmed by the very extensive research of the last three decades? One has to remember that, his remarkably independent spirit notwithstanding, his perceptions could not entirely shake off the ambience of the colonial discourse which coloured his views on Hindu–Muslim relationships. His own writings are full of examples of varied patterns of understanding between Hindus and Muslims depending on local circumstances. In the two largest Muslim majority provinces, coalition governments including non-Muslims ruled until 1943 and 1945 respectively, while in the North-West frontier with a Muslim population of over ninety per cent a Congress government held sway until 1946. The League secured the loyalty of the majority of the Muslims only in the last few years of British rule. Moon himself projects several alternative scenarios in which Hindus and Muslims could have co-operated in working a federal polity. Yet in his final conclusion he falls back on Sir Syed's simple dictum, that the two could not sit on the same throne. Moon goes further and sees in the policies of the Congress, with its claim to represent all Indians and its demand that the Muslim League in U.P. should virtually merge itself in the Congress as the price for coalition, simply a reflection of the alleged Hindu tendency to absorb all and sundry.

The implication that there are two monolithic communities from time immemorial who inevitably pursued their separate political paths is accepted by only a handful of historians today.[2] The view that Hindus and Muslims as two distinct political constituencies and hence all-India communities with separate and competing political aspirations are the products of constitutional arrangements and executive policies of the colonial state is now widely accepted.[3] This view is not to be equated with the thesis that communal conflicts are derived from a policy of divide and rule. The new thesis implies only that the politicization of communal identities and overarching solidarities covering the entire sub-continent emerged because 'Hindus' and 'Muslims' were the basic categories in the formation of constitutional and executive policies of the British in India. As Ayesha Jalal pointed out in her monograph on Jinnah, the thesis that the 'myriad splits and fissures' in Indian society 'had somehow resolved into a simple line of division between Muslims and Hindus ... is an unacceptable simplification'.[4] Support for the view that communal solidarities, rather than any pan-Indian nationalism were somehow 'natural' foundations for political integration comes from an unlikely quarter: the radical writers who contribute to volumes entitled *Subaltern Studies*.[5] They attribute to the unlettered masses

[2] See, for example, Chaudhri Muhammad Ali, *The Emergence of Pakistan* (New York, London, 1967), R.C. Majumdar's *History of the Freedom Movement* 3 Vols. (New Delhi, 1973) which also basically accepted the two nation thesis.

[3] See Anil Seal's introductory essay in J. Gallagher, *et. al* editors, *Locality, Province and Nation* (Cambridge, 1973).

[4] A. Jalal, *The Sole Spokesman, Jinnah, the Muslim League and the Demand for Pakistan* (Cambridge, 1985), p. 223.

[5] See R. Guha, editor, *Subaltern Studies*, Vols. 1–6 (New Delhi, 1982–93). This thesis is presented quite powerfully in Partha Chatterji, *The Nation and its fragments* (Princeton, 1991) Gyanendra Pandey is currently working on the popular consciousness expressed in the conflicts and violence which attended the partition in the Punjab.

an 'autonomous consciousness' rather than a 'totally blind' feeling manipulated by the elite. Communal loyalty is seen to be a major component of that consciousness.

Moon's view that the introduction of an alien system, constitutional processes based on the Westminster model with its elections and political parties to a society with a totally different political tradition, had a lot to answer for, is indirectly confirmed by recent research, though on terms very different from his. Modern scholars do not share his view that the constitutional structure introduced by the British was a disaster which vitiated the body politic, but acknowledge that it was a major influence on the shape and course of indigenous politics. The constitution of 1919 with its emphasis on autonomy for the provinces and communal electorates opened the road to eventual partition: the fact that Hindus and Muslims would no longer require one another's support in order to get elected virtually meant the creation of two mutually distinct political bodies and the power which the Muslims now enjoyed in the provinces, where they were in the majority, gave them a vested interest in perpetuating provincial autonomy within a loose federal structure. These provinces thus became the future building blocks of Pakistan.[6] This line of argument, however, leaves unexplained the reasons why Pakistan was at first unacceptable to the leadership as well as their mass following in the Muslim majority provinces and their eventual conversion to the ideology of a separate Muslim state. Arguably, the substantial literature on the subject, based on careful analysis of documentary evidence, not accessible to the author of *Divide and Quit*, does not really invalidate the basic line of his argument.

Questions do arise regarding some details of his narrative covering the specific circumstances which led to the transfer of power to two sovereign states. Documents made accessible to scholars in more recent years have disclosed facts which were not known to him. Some of his judgements regarding the unfolding of British policy are also not entirely acceptable.

There is an implied, and at times explicit, assumption in Moon's book that Dominion Status was the accepted goal of British policy in India, at least from the thirties, the hesitation to give up power and profit in the highest circles notwithstanding.

[6] See David Page, *Prelude to Partition* (Oxford, 1982).

The recruiters from Whitehall who went to his school and induced the idealistic teenager to plan a career in the ICS had appealed in terms of the white man's ultimate burden, training Indians for that stated goal. Lord Irwin's famous declaration intended to avert the threatened Civil Disobedience movement did state that Dominion Status in some unstated future was Britain's constitutional plan for India. Yet the expression occurs nowhere in the Simon Commission's report published after the said Declaration nor does it appear in the pages of the 1935 constitution. The federal proposals in the said document, it is now clear, were intended to neutralize the nationalists in the federal legislature with the help of the separately elected Muslim legislators and the large number of representatives nominated by the princes. They were not meant to set the scene for a dress rehearsal preceding the institution of Dominion Status.[7] Contrary to Moon's assumption, it was not obvious to all the decision makers at the beginning of the Second World War that the empire would disappear at its end. Linlithgow, writing to the Secretary of State for India, Amery in 1940, opined that the likely date of British departure from India was still 'very remote' and meanwhile 'it would be a pity to throw too much cold water' on the Pakistan proposal which was welcomed in official circles as a means of checkmating the Congress.[8]

Moon's view that the Cripp's proposal was rejected through Gandhi's influence has also proved to be incorrect. The Congress, it is now known, was willing to accept quasi-cabinet government without change in the constitution for the duration of the war on the basis of an informal understanding given by the Viceroy. But Linlithgow would not stand for the convention of Cabinet Government. In a letter dated 21 January, 1942 he informed Churchill that Burma and India were conquered countries which were in the empire because they were 'kept there by force' and, unknown to Cripps, appealed to the Prime Minister for support on a policy of 'standing firm'. And the reasons why the Mission failed are summed up by Moore as follows:

> Against his long and fiercely held imperialist prejudices, Churchill was forced by the pressure of Cripps, his Labour colleagues,

---

[7] For full discussion of British Policy in India in the late twenties and thirties, see Robin Moore, *The Crisis in Indian Unity* (Oxford, 1974).

[8] See Rizvi, *Linlithgow and India* (London, 1978), p. 119.

and the Americans to acquiesce in the offer of post-war independence and wartime association of the Indian parties with the central government. ... Aided by the like-minded Viceroy, Lord Linlithgow, a reaction among his conservative Cabinet colleagues, ... and a certain American hesitancy, Churchill was able to abort the negotiations.[9]

As an enthusiastic recruit to the ICS, Moon had sought to discuss with some Whitehall mandarins his ideas regarding reform and development in India. He was pointedly told that the British were not in India to teach Indians the art of self-government but to safeguard British investments in the country worth some thousand million pounds.[10] Evidently, every British official and politician was not in a hurry to quit India. The reason power could not be effectively transferred at a time when the conflict between nationalist and Muslim aspirations could still be resolved was that the decision makers in Britain wished to prolong their hold on India as long as possible. It certainly was not in their interest to seek a resolution of that conflict and hence it was no part of their political agenda. Their anxious efforts to prevent partition came much too late in the day.

III

The second part of *Divide and Quit* (Chapters v–xiii), especially the chapters dealing with events in the West Punjab state of Bahawalpur where Moon served as Revenue Minister at the time of Partition, is almost unique in its importance as an eyewitness account of one of the greatest tragedies in human history. Such accounts have a relevance which goes way beyond the limited interest of historical narrative. Our capacity as a species for evil, the mindless infliction of monstrous suffering on fellow creatures is something we are apt to forget. Records which help remind us of this potential, of what man can do to man, are hence essential props for the maintenance of our moral sanity.

Accounts of the holocaust in Germany and the sufferings of the Soviet people under Stalin can be numbered in hundreds. By comparison narratives of the mass killings and migration in

[9] R.J. Moore, *Churchill, Cripps and India, 1939–1945* (Oxford, 1979) pp. 1, 53, 115–25.

[10] See typescript of interview with Sir Penderel Moon deposited at the India Office Library.

the Punjab at the time of the Partition in India are indeed very few. And Moon's objective account of the tragedy based on the day to day experience of a responsible and highly perceptive official is perhaps the only one of its kind. The fact that it is limited to only a small part of the affected territory does not reduce its importance.

Alan Campbell-Johnson has described 'the scale of the killings and the movement of the refugees' in the Punjab as ' even more extensive than those caused by the more formal conflicts of opposing armies' and the two way migration as 'one of the greatest movements of population in recorded history'. On 21 September 1947 he looked down from the Governor General's Dakota on two streams of refugees moving in opposite directions. He estimated one to be over fifty miles in length and the other at least forty-five.[11] Moon estimated the number of casualties at below 180,000 for the Punjab and 200,000 for the subcontinent, excluding eastern India (p. 293). Moore, in a later estimate puts the figure for those killed and maimed at 500,000.[12] To this one has to add the estimated 4,000 killed and 15,000 maimed in Calcutta in 1946.[13] As Hodson pointed out, it was impossible to be sure of the number of casualties because for much of the time in question there was no effective civil authority to report death. Besides, as Major-General Rees in command of the Punjab Border Force reported on one occasion, '... it was impossible to count the victims properly in the confused heap of rubble and corpses'.[14]

The estimates for the scale of the migrations similarly vary. The relevant figures as calculated by Moon are four and a half million Hindus and Sikhs migrating from West Pakistan and six million Muslims moving in the opposite direction (p. 268).

The geographer, O.H.K. Spate, put the total number of refugees at 17 million.[15] According to Campbell-Johnson, in August 1947

[11] See Alan Campbell-Johnson, *Mission with Mountbatten* (London, 1951) pp. 178, 200–1.

[12] R.J. Moore, *Escape from empire: the Attlee government and the Indian problem* (Oxford, 1983), p. 327; R. Jeffrey 'The Punjab Boundary forces and the problem of order; August 1947', *Modern Asian Studies* VII 4 (1974), pp. 491–520.

[13] See A. Jalal, 1985 p. 46.

[14] H.V. Hodson, *The Great Divide* (London, 1969) p. 418.

[15] O.H.K. Spate, 'India and Pakistan: a general and regional geography' (London, 1954) quoted in Jalal (Introduction) 1985.

some ten million people were on the move in an area 'about the size of Wales'.[16] V.P. Menon estimated that the relevant figures were five and a half million each way besides the one and a quarter million each way from East Pakistan. R. Jeffrey, on the basis of detailed calculations arrives at the figure of 12 million, for the Punjab.[17] Yet, as Campbell-Johnson pointed out, these horrors affected the lives of only three per cent of the subcontinent's population and were not comparable in their impact to the Bengal famine of 1943.

Bahawalpur, the region covered in *Divide and Quit* was only the size of Denmark with a population of over one to two million of whom 190,000 were Hindus and 52,000 Sikhs. It was unique in being the only Indian state ruled by a Muslim prince in which the majority of the population were Muslims. It had no record of communal violence and the Nawab took pride in the loyalty of his Hindu subjects. As rumours of communal violence in Eastern Punjab reached the state and refugees with their tales of horror began to arrive, the scene changed. Muslim villagers started pillaging and killing Hindus and Sikhs, especially in the urban areas. Women were abducted as a matter of routine. Killing Sikhs, who were leaving the State in a body and were reported to be up in arms against the Muslims in East Punjab, became a legitimate blood sport. By September, the number of casualties had mounted to a thousand.

The state police, never very effective, were reluctant to fire on co-religionists. Even if they could be disciplined, the army was not to be trusted. Several thousand Sikhs from the district of Rahim Yar Khan were treacherously attacked by the army unit who were to escort them to the border. They had taken the precaution of robbing them first. Their women had also been separated for 'reasons of security' and were later distributed among the soldiers. The commanding officer was arrested, but managed to escape to Pakistan, of which Bahawalpur was not yet an integral part. Extradition was refused, allegedly through the influence of a highly placed British officer. Elsewhere Moon encountered a long column of Hindu women marching to a mosque to seek conversion. No reassurance would stop them.

[16] A Campbell-Johnson (1951), p. 175.
[17] V.P. Menon, *The Transfer of Power in India* (Orient Longmans, 1968 (First published, 1957), p. 439; R. Jeffrey, *Modern Asian Studies* (1974).

Their menfolk had probably been killed already. V.P. Menon, on hearing reports of such happenings in the State, commented that it was 'a paradise compared with East Punjab' (p. 117).

Moon's dead pan description of the said paradise is capped by a comment of great moral significance; ' ... I found myself in a "through the looking glass" world of moral conventions. There was a complete breakdown, or rather reversal, of the ordinary moral values. To kill a Sikh had become almost a duty; to kill a Hindu was hardly a crime. To rob them was an innocent pleasure ... to refrain was not a mark of virtue but of lack of enterprise'. Some years ago, a leading Indian sociologist studied some Punjab villages in the grip of both Khalistani and police terrorism. She found that all the expectations of normal existence and the associated values had disappeared. The only concern was survival and that anyhow.[18] The world of mass hysteria described by Moon has a similar ambience. Yet all human values had not collapsed. The majority of state officials did their duty conscientiously. Rich Muslims offered shelter to Hindus and Sikhs. At the railway station there were moving scenes of Muslims bidding farewell to their Hindu neighbours whom they would never see again. But the twin syndromes of fear and vengeance were the dominant emotions of the day. The present writer was a witness to the Calcutta riot of 1946 and remembers how people whom one had known to be gentle and peaceable, stood forth as great avengers and killed innocent men, women and children on the plea that offence was the best means of defence in the circumstances.

The question as to whether this tragedy could have been averted has been answered in the negative by virtually everyone who has written on the subject. For one thing, no one anticipated violence on such a scale. The civil administration, crippled by the Partition, could not cope with the pervasive defiance of the law. East Punjab had lost 7000 Muslim policemen. Neither soldiers nor the police could be relied upon to restrain their co-religionists. A force at least four times the size of the P.B.F. was required to cope with the crisis. The people had defied their leaders and taken charge.[19] In fact it was surprising that things returned to

---

[18] Paper presented by Veena Das at a seminar on *Subaltern Studies* in Calcutta 1991.

[19] See A. Campbell-Johnson, 1951, pp. 355–7.

'normal' by the end of that fateful year. The circumstances of the Partition rendered the holocaust inevitable. Moon puts the blame mainly on two persons, Gandhi and Jinnah, and their inflexible attitudes regardless of consequences. But his own account shows that the responsibility was far more widely distributed and that Britain's reluctance to quit when there was still time was a prime factor in the tragedy. The holocaust in the final analysis was the end result of human errors, committed in the very last days of colonial rule, rather than of long term trends in the Indian polity. But once these had occurred, the tragedy was not preventable.

IV

Divide and Quit has to be read in the wider context of Moon's perception of British rule in India and of Indian society. That perception was informed by a remarkable degree of objectivity, intellectual honesty and a high-minded view of Britain's duty to India. It also reflects very idiosyncratic opinions which are curious variants of the colonial discourse.[20]

Moon had no doubts regarding the greatness of the British achievement in India—the unification of a vast territory, maintainence of peace, the massive infrastructural developments and an unusually mild rule. He considered it a joint achievement of the British and Indians which future generations would hold in admiration. Admiration for the imperial past was highly and openly popular in England until the end of the Second World War. Academics and intellectuals who still share that enthusiasm would be more hesitant to declare it today, though there are notable exceptions. The blasts of anti-colonial criticism from the Third World and from western liberals have induced a measure of circumspection. It is worth noting, however, that the dominant ideology in the early days of Indian nationalism, in fact as late as 1918, acknowledged the grandeur of the British achievement in India, its many failings notwithstanding. That admiration has no resonances in the intellectual or popular culture of contemporary India. In Britain, expectedly, there is a persistent nostalgia for the imperial past and this is not confined to the politically conservative only. As to how future generations will

---

[20] See his *Strangers in India* (New York, 1945) and typescripts of his interviews given to David Blake deposited in the India Office Library.

assess England's work in India, any prediction is likely to prove premature.

Moon's admiration for the British achievements in India was tempered by serious criticisms of that record. He accused his fellow countrymen of treating Indians 'like scum', of heaping social insults upon them and excluding them from higher ranks of office.[21] He accepted that pre-colonial India had enjoyed relative advantage as compared with the West in economic terms and that she had suffered relative rather than absolute decline. He denied that Britain had a deliberately exploitative policy after the first decades of the post-Plassey era, and affirmed that Indian poverty was the result of population growth which far exceeded the rate of growth in income and resources. But he did not absolve Britain of responsibility for the situation. He considered developmental strategies possible and the grounds on which these had been adopted entirely spurious: in this sphere the Raj made 'difficulties instead of trying to overcome them'.

British policy, in his view, was directly responsible for keeping the Indian peasants in absolute poverty and reducing them to a state of bondage. The introduction of the English legal system, with its emphasis on the inviolability of contract, into a society where the majority were illiterate meant a subjection of the peasant to the moneylender. Introduction of legally guaranteed proprietary rights in land, in an economy where such rights were rudimentary in the past, ensured ruthless exploitation by the landlord. The new legal system which replaced the older practice of consultation with local worthies by a new requirement of evidence from sworn witnesses guaranteed denial of justice and massive corruption. The lower ranks of the colonial bureaucracy were mostly corrupt. The police habitually used torture and were left undisturbed in their practice because it was convenient for the British to do so. And the worst mistake of all was to try and introduce the parliamentary system which was totally alien to the traditions of the country. Of course the Indians were perfec_ly capable of governing themselves but not in terms of an alien system and its unfamiliar standards.[22]

Curiously enough, Moon's critique of the economic consequences of the empire had much in common with the views of the

---

[21] *Strangers in India* pp. 22, 30.
[22] Ibid., chapters 1–3.

nationalists, though he rejected their thesis of absolute impoverish-
ment and deliberate exploitation: he does not even refer to the
thesis of drainage of wealth from India, central to the nationalist
critique. The debate on the implications of the colonial economic
nexus is still far from concluded. There are doughty defences
of the imperial record which suggests that India did well
economically under Pax Britannica. The opposite view now
emphasizes statistical evidence for decline in per capita agricultural
output and executive policies which actually hindered industrial
development and contributed to overall structural stagnation
in the economy.[23]

Not a great deal has been done on the implications of the
judicial and police systems for India's rural society, but it would
be difficult to reject the findings of this astute participant-observer.
The allegations of racism in both social relations and executive
action have been confirmed by later research.[24]

Moon's perception of Indian society and prognostications
for its future were not based only on his observation. It was
informed by colonial stereotypes however much he might disapprove
of his countryman's attitudes. 'Hindus', 'Muslims', 'Sikhs', 'Punjabis'
et al appear in his writings as monolithic and timeless categories
and so do 'Indians'. Parliamentary government was totally
unsuitable for the said Indians. Indians also had a healthy respect
for authority and hence the institution of princely states was a
welcome feature of its polity which would prove useful in the
future. Indian qualities of leadership, especially in matters, military,
were inadequate and hence marriages between the Princes, natural
leaders of the people, and English women might produce the
right kind of human material.[25] In the event, princely states
have disappeared from the Indian scene without anyone shedding

[23] For emphasis on the positive aspects of the imperial record, see *Cambridge
Economic History of India*, Vol. 2 (Cambridge, 1983), D. Fieldhouse's Chapter
in P.J. Marshall, ed., *The Cambridge Illustrated History of the British Empire* (Cambridge,
1996) and Neil Charlesworth, *British rule and the Indian economy, 1800–1914*
(London, 1982). For the opposite view see A.K. Bagchi, *Private investment in
India, 1900–1939*, (Cambridge, 1972); M.D. Morris *et al*, *Indian economy in
the nineteenth century, a symposium* (New Delhi, 1969).

[24] See for example K. Ballhatchet, *Race, sex and class under the Raj: imperial
attitudes and policies and their critics, 1793–1905* (London, 1980).

[25] This idea of Sir Penderel Moon was mentioned by S. Gopal in his
lecture 'All Souls and India' delivered at All Souls College in 1993.

tears for this particular loss. The progeny born of British mothers, have not been prominent in the ranks of India's leaders. Over time, the people of the sub-continent have developed a stake in the parliamentary system of government and, arguably, some understanding of it. Two of the successor states have returned to it after periods of military dictatorship which had the blessings of the western democracies.

Moon believed that Independent India would need British military protection for some time to come, but was sure to fall under the influence of one of the great powers: Britain, Russia or China. Hindu India would have a natural affinity with China or, given the predilection of her intelligentsia, they might fall under Russian influence. The USA , oddly, is not mentioned in his list of great powers. Writing in 1945, he does not anticipate the Cold War and hence neutralism as a possible option. He warmly recommends Soviet style planning for industrialization, especially massive investment in irrigation and hydroelectric projects and was strongly in favour of co-operative farming. In all this his pragmatic preferences came close to Nehru's socialist ones. He accepted the latter's invitation to work as an adviser to the Planning Commission and helped to shape its policies.

His relationship with Indian nationalists had a quality of ambivalence. He evidently shared the British officials' impatient incomprehension of Gandhi, but acknowledged his honesty of purpose and the element of true saintliness in the man. He distrusted the nationalists' preoccupation with parliamentary government. He disapproved even more of high-handed methods in dealing with them, even when they were in open and, in his view, pointless rebellion. Expression of such disapproval cost him his job in 1943.

He was not one to hide his true feelings whatever the situation. During my brief tenure as an official of the National Archives in India, I had to deal with a devastating review he had written of Maulana Azad's introduction to S.N. Sen's *Eighteen Fifty Seven*. The review was meant for a publication of the Education Ministry and the Maulana was the Minister of Education. I went to see Sir Penderel and asked if he would modify the more trenchant comments. He offered to withdraw his review. We were saved further embarrassment when the minister asked us to publish the piece without changing a word. I met Sir Penderel for the last time when he came to give a talk at our weekly South Asian

History Seminar at Oxford. At question time he dropped a sizeable brick, referring to the alleged deficiencies of a certain Indian community. Three members of the said community were sitting in the front row. The speaker was exceptionally quiet later that evening. When we invited him again to speak at our seminar, he declined. He said that he no longer felt very confident as to what he might say. There is no lack of confidence in his written words. Even his idiosyncratic views detract little from their abiding importance.

Bibliography

Ali, C.	*The emergence of Pakistan.* New York/London, 1967.
Bagchi, A.K.	*Private Investment in India, 1900–1939.* London/Cambridge, 1972.
Ballhatchet, K.	*Race, sex and class under the Raj: imperial attitudes and policies and their critics, 1793–1905.* London, 1980.
Campbell-Johnson, A.	*Mission with Mountbatten.* London, 1951.
Charlesworth, N.	*British rule and the Indian Economy, 1800–1914.* London, 1982 (prepared for the Economic History Society).
Chatterji, P.	*The Nation and its fragments.* Princeton, 1991.
Das, V.	Paper presented at *Subaltern Studies* in Calcutta, 1991.
Guha, R. (ed.)	*Subaltern Studies.* 1982–93. New Delhi, Vol 1–6.
Hodson, H.V.	*'The Great Divide' : Britain-India-Pakistan.* First published London, 1969.
Jalal, A.	*The sole Spokesman, Jinnah, the Muslim League and the Demand for Pakistan.* Cambridge, 1985.
Jeffrey, R.	'The Punjab boundary forces and the problem of order: August 1947', in Modern Asian Studies VII 4 (1974), pp. 491–520.
Kumar , D. (ed.)	*Cambridge Economic History of India.* Vol. 2, Cambridge, 1983.
Marshall, P.J. ed.,	*The Cambridge Illustrated History of the British Empire.* Cambridge, 1996.
Majumdar, R.C.	*History of the Freedom movement.* 3 Vols., New Delhi, 1973.

Menon, V.P.	*The Transfer of Power in India.* Bombay, 1968, (first published 1957).
Moon, P.	*Strangers in India.* New York, 1945.
Moon, P.	Unpublished interviews with, housed at India Office Library.
Moore, R.	*The crisis in Indian Unity.* Oxford, 1974.
———	*Churchill, Cripps and India, 1939–1945.* Oxford, 1979.
Moore, R.J.	*Escape from empire: the Attlee government and the Indian Problem.* Oxford, 1983.
Mooris, M.D. *et al.* (eds.)	*Indian economy in the Nineteenth Century, a Symposium,* New Delhi, 1969.
Page, D.J.H.	*Prelude to Partition,* New Delhi, 1976.
Rizvi, G.	*Linlithgow and India—A study in British Policy and Political Impasse in India 1936–43.* London, 1978.
Seal, A.	'Imperialism and Nationalism in India'. *Locality, Province and Nation. Essays on Indian Politics 1870–1940* in J. Gallagher, G. Johnson and A. Seal (eds.) *et al.,* Cambridge, 1973.
Spate, O.H.K	*India and Pakistan: a general and regional geography.* London, 1954. (Revised 1967).

Further suggested reading on the Partition of the Indian Subcontinent

Azad, A.K.	*India wins freedom: The complete version,* Delhi, 1988.
Brown, Judith M.	*Gandhi: Prisoner of Hope.* New Haven and London, 1989.
Das, Surajan	*Communal Riots in Bengal 1905–47,* Delhi, 1991.
Freitag, Sandra	*Collective Action and Community: Public Arenas and the Emergence of Communalism in North India,* Delhi 1980.
Gandhi, Rajmohan,	*Patel; A Life.* Ahmedabad, 1990.
Gilmartin, David.	*Empire and Islam: Punjab and the making of Pakistan.* Delhi, 1989.

Gopal, S.   *Jawaharlal Nehru: A Biography.* Delhi, Vol. 1, 1979.

Gupta, A.K. (ed.)   *Myth and reality: The Struggle for Freedom in India.* Delhi, 1987.

Hardy, Peter   *The Muslims of British India.* Cambridge, 1971.

Hassan,   *India's Partition: Process, strategy and Mobilisation.* Delhi,
Mushirul (ed)   1993.

————   *India Partitioned: The other face of freedom.* New Delhi, Vol. 1 and 2.

Hasan, Mushirul   *Legacy of a Divided Nation: India: Muslims since Independence.* London, 1997.

Jalal, Ayesha   *The sole spokesman: Jinnah, the Muslim league and the demand for Pakistan.* Cambridge, 1985.

Jaffrelot,   *The Hindu Nationalist Movement and Indian Politics*
Christophe   *1925 to the 1990s.* London, 1996.

Jones, Kenneth W.,   *Hindu Consciousness in 19th Century Punjab.* California,
Arya, Daram: 1976.

Joshi, Shashi and   *Struggle for Hegemony in India: Culture Community and*
Josh, Bhagwan,   *Power 1941–47.* Delhi, 1994.

Malik, I.H.   *Sikander Hyat Khan* (1892–1942). Islamabad, 1985.

Moore, R.J.   *The Crisis of Indian Unity, 1917–47.* Oxford, 1974.

Menon, V.P.   *The Transfer of Power in India.* Bombay, 1957.

Nanda, B.R.   *Jawaharlal Nehru: Rebel and Statesman.* Delhi, 1980.

Page, David   *Prelude to partition: The Indian Muslims and the Imperial State System of Control 1920–32.* Delhi, 1982.

Philips, C.H. and   *The Partition of India: Policies and Perspectives 1935–*
Wainwright   *47.* 1970.
M.D. (eds.)

Robinson, Francis   *Separatism Among Indian Muslims 1880–1923.* Cambridge, 1974 (Paperback, 1994).

Shaikh, Farzana   *Community and Consensus in Islam: Muslim Representation in Colonial India, 1860–1974.* Cambridge, 1989.

Singh, Anita Inder   *The Origins of the Partition of India,* 1936–47. Delhi, 1987 (Paperback, 1990).

Talbot, Ian   *Punjab and the Raj: 1849–1947.* Delhi, 1988.

———   *Provinical Politics and the Pakistan Movement: The growth of the Muslim league in North West and North East India, 1937–57.* Karachi, 1988.

——— .   *Khizae Tiwana: The Punjab Unionist Party and the Partition of India.* Surrey, 1996.

———   *Freedom's cry: the popular dimension in the Pakistan Movement and Partition Experience in North West India.* Karachi, 1996.

Wolpert, Stanley   *Jinnah of Pakistan.* New York, 1984.

Index

Abdullah Shah, compound of, 129, 132, 172, 183

Abdul Kalam Azad, Maulana, 3, 23, 41, 55, 58, 309

Afghanistan, 157

Ahmad, Sir Syed, 4–5, 11–12, 63, 270, 295, 299

Ahmadpur Lamma, 241, 243–4

Ajmal Hassan, Mir, Clerk of Court, 153

Akali, Akalis, 4, 31–7, 50; canvass idea of Khalistan, 69 (footnote); 71, 73, 83–4, 86, 92, 122, 274; determination to preserve Sikh cohesion, 279–81, 297

Alexander, Rt. Hon. A.V. (Viscount), 2–3, 43

Alwar State, 110, 229, 293

Amar Singh, Cashier, 208

Ambala, 117, 119, 263

Amery, 301

Amritsar, xiv, 31, 33–6, 38, 74; riots in, 78, 80–2; 88, 94, 96, 109–10, 117, 119–20, 263, 298; district, 90–2, 116, 120

Anand Deva, liaison officer, 245–6

Arifwala, 122, 258

Ashiq Hussain Qureshi, Major, 3, 109–10

Asia, xx

Assam, 14, 17, 19, 40, 45, 48, 52, 57, 61

Atari, 120

Attlee, Rt. Hon. Clement (Earl), xvi, 6, 62–3, 65, 76, 303 (footnote)

Attock district, 78

Aurangzeb, 16, 30

Babar, Lt., 163, 178, 181, 185

Bagh Ali, 180–2

Baghdad-ul-jadid, 203, 218, 225

Bahawal canal, 123–4, 133

Bahawalnagar, 108, 111, 123–4, 132–3, 135, 138, 140, 144, 146–51, 154–5, 159, 161, 165, 168–9, 173–4, 176, 178–9, 182–5, 187–9, 191, 195–6, 209, 216, 218, 227, 232, 237, 248

Bahawalpur, Nawab (Amir) of, xix, 3–4, 83; position in the State, 99–102; 103–6; accedes to Pakistan, 107; 141, 144; assumes title of Amir, 157; 222–3; returns from England, 228; wishes to retain Hindu subjects, 228–9, 240–4; agrees to their evacuation, 245; enraged at misconduct of army officer, 236, 304

Army, State Forces, 104, 108, 123; reported to be unreliable,

135; conduct at Bahawalnagar, 139–40, 144–5, 148; shoot Sikhs, 185; detachments of sent to Suleimanke head-works, 186–7; in Bahawalpur city, 191–4, 198–200; with-drawn from it, 202; 204, 208, 211; escort refugee trains, 223; escort Sikh column to Jaisalmir border, 231–8; 265

Bahawalpur city, 110, 133, 141, 148–9, 158, 182–4; distur-bances in, 189–224; 225, 231, 237, 241, 245–6, 259, 265

district, 103, 141–2, 183; evacuation of Hindus from, 224; 230, 251

State, xv, 3–9, 83, 87–8, 94–6; description of, 97–111; 114, 116, 122; first disturbances in, 124–54 passim; 156–7; mis-conduct of railway personnel in, 165; 166, 174, 176–7, 185; improvement of situation in, 187; 222, 228–31, 237; refugees from, in Delhi, 240–3; 247, 249, 256–8; survey of disorders in, 261–6; 281–2, 293–4, 302, 304

Bakhtawar Singh, 234

Baldev Singh, Sardar, 4, joins Punjab Cabinet, 36; goes to London, 60; accepts Mount-batten Plan, 66; 70; persuades Khizar to form a Coalition Ministry, 71, 73; 84–6, 96; 296

Baluchistan, 19, 45 (footnote), 50–1 (footnote), 293

Bangladesh, xx

Beas river, 35 (footnote), 90

Bengal, xviii, 14, 17, 19, 22, 24, 40, 45, 47–8, 66–70 74, 81, 273, 286–7, 298, 304

East, 58, 68, 79

West, 68, 298

Bengal Government, 58, 68

Bennett, Sir John, 115

Bhag Singh, 234

Bhandari, P.C., 74

Bharatpur State, 110, 229, 293

Bhatinda, 159, 164, 166–7, 170, 203

Bihar, 59, 74, 79, 298

Bikanir State, 97, 99 (footnote), 133, 150–2, 159, 163, 166, 169, 173–5, 187, 218 (foot-note), 226; refugees from cross into Bhawalpur, 173, 229, 247; 248, 254, 264, 293

Maharajah of, 254

Bombay, 4, 13, 57, 240, 256

Bombay Resolution, 57, 59–61

Boundary Commission, 67, 69, 88, 107

Boundary Force, 94–5, 119, 123, 277–9

Burewala, 114

Burma, xv, 2–3, 301

Cabinet Mission, Cabinet Missio Plan, xv–xvi, 1–3, 8, 36, 4: 64 passim, 65, 67, 70, 74, 27 287, 297

Calcutta, 58, 68, 303, 305

Cawnpore, 267

Central India Horse, 32

Chamberlain, Neville, 37

Chenab river, 35, 50, 90

Chhotu Ram, Sir, 40

China, xix, xx, 309

Chishtian, 123, 132, 135, 137–8, 151, 171–2, 182–3, 187, 224

Chuni Lal, Rai Bahadur, 174

Churchill, Winston, xxi, 2, 6, 70, 301–2

Cold War, 309

Congress, Indian National, 1–4, 12–18; fails to conciliate Muslim League, 23–8; 33, 40–4, 46, 49, 52–7, 59–65; accepts Mountbatten Plan, 67; 70; un-responsive to Sikh ambitions, 85; 93; attitude towards Rulers, 105–6; 107, 270; Jinnah's alienation from, 271; mistakes of, 272–4, 290; 277, 283–4, 296–7, 299, 301

Constituent Assembly, 48, 51, 56–62, 66, 274

Craik, Sir Henry, 6, 33

Cripps, Sir Stafford, xv–vi, 2–3, 26, 43, 49, 56, 301

Cripps offer, mission, 1–4, 6, 26–7, 54, 274, 296, 301

Crofton, Sir Richard, 6, 102, 104, 108, 156, 301

Cross, Leslie, 244

Cunningham, Sir George, 222

Curzon, Lord, Viceroy, 101

Darling, Sir Malcolm, 25 (footnote)

Dacca, 58

Daultana, Mumtaz, 120

Delhi, xiii, xviii, 4, 29, 45, 50, 63, 65, 73, 83, 94–6, 106, 110, 117, 240, 243, 245, 248, 262 (footnote), 265–6, 268, 298

Senior Superintendent of Police, 88

Dera Ghazi Khan district, 239, 241

Dera Nawab, 101

Derawar fort, 173

Domimon Status, 300–1

Duncan, Superintending Engineer, 103, 230

Dunga Bunga, 169

Durrani, Lieutenant-Colonel, 104–5

Dyer, Brigadier-General, 80–1

Eustace, J.C.W., 115–16

Faiz Ahmad, Maulvi, Deputy Commissioner, 4, 103, 231–4, 237, 239–42

Faridkot State, 261

Farnham, Surrey, 106, 228, 244

Fateh Chand, Dewan, Hindu Minister, 194, 224

Fazilka, Sub-Divisional Officer of, 180–1

Fazl-i-Husain, Sir, 287

Fazl-ul-Haq, A.K., 22, 40

Fazlur Rahman, Rao, Assistant Settlement Officer, 6, 158, 160, 163; grapples with refugees, 177–9; 181–2; reports on

Suleimanke headworks, 185–6; 218–19; regroups refugees, 257; 259

Ferozepur district, 97, 111, 117, 159, 162, 180–2, 247, 263

headworks, 88, 91, 99, 186 (footnote)

Fordwah Canal, 133, 178, 225–6

Fort Abbas, 150, 161, 169, 173, 227, 254

Gandhi, Indira, xviii, xx

Gandhi, M.K., xv, xxiii, 1, 4, 24; secures rejection of Cripps offer, 27–8; 37, 42, 45; shows sympathy with Sikhs, 50; 51–2; secures rejection of proposals for Interim Government, 54, 56; 59, 61, 63–4, 70 (footnote), 79; allays passions in Bengal, 81; resists evacuation of Hindus, 240–5; assassination of, 245, 249; checks assaults on Muslims, 248; his leadership of Congress alienates Jinnah, 270–1; 273–4, 286, 288; mistakes of, 290; 291, 296–8, 301, 306, 309

Gandhi, Rajiv, xxi

Gilani, ex-army officer, 104–5, 192–3, 201–2, 221

Gilani, High Court Judge, 184, 189, 191, 216

Glancy, Sir Bertrand, xiv, xiv–xvi, 6; 71–2

Gobind Baksh, alias Nur Mohammad, 137, 171–2

Gokhale, G.K., 4, 270

Government of India Act 1935, 2, 12–13, 19, 21, 24, 58, 71, 301

Grand Trunk Road, xiii, 36, 119

Gurdaspur district, 263

Gurkhas, 104, 204, 211–12, 265, 278

Gurmani, Nawab Mushtaq Ahmad, 4, 6, 83–4, 86–8, 90, 94, 102–3, 105–7; reassures minority communities, 108; 109–10, 114, 119, 124–5, 127, 129; indignant at looting, 131; 132, 134–5, 138, 140–2; speaks to military officers, 143–6; 148, 157, 165, 174, 182; opposes evacuation of Hindus, 183–4; 187, 189; deplores inadequacy of military and police, 190–1; 192, 194, 201–2, 208; disinclined to furnish Gurkha escorts, 211–12; 213, 216, 223, 228; evacuation of Sikhs to Jaisalmir, 231–2, 236–7; 241

Harijan (newspaper), 50

Harunabad, 108, 150, 161, 169, 173, 189, 218 (footnote), 221

Hasilpur, 132–7, 171–2, 187, 197, 216, 264

Hastings, Warren, xvi

Himachal Pradesh, xviii

Hindumalkot, 159–60, 164–5; description of, 166; 167, 170, 172, 175–6, 185, 197, 203, 212, 218, 223–4, 231, 240, 245

Hindustan Times, 54

Hissar district, 218 (footnote), 248, 254

Hunter Commission, 188

Hurs, 234–5

Hyderabad State, 107

Imperial Bank of India, 165, 208, 252

Indian Mutiny, 216 (footnote), 262 (footnote), 267

Indian National Army (I.N.A.), 104, 124, 148, 192

Indian (Native, Princely) States, 13, 26, 45–6, 104, 127, 156; refugees from preferred by Nawab of Bahawalpur, 228–9; 248, 255, 261

Indus river, 97, 239

Iqbal, Sir Mohammad, 11 (footnote)

Irwin, Lord, 301

Ismay, General Lord, 86

Jaisalmir State, 97, 231, 234, 261

Jenkins, Sir Evan, xvi, 115

Jinnah, M.A., 1, 5–6, 12–13, 16; describes Pakistan Resolution as a tactical move, 21; 22–30, 37–8; seeks to overthrow Khizar, 39–41; claims to speak for all Muslims, 41–3; 44–6, 48; accepts Cabinet Mission Plan, 49–51; 52–3; charges Viceroy and Mission with breach of faith, 56; 57, 59–60, 63–4, accepts Mountbatten Plan, 66, 68; views on exchange of population, 69; 72; lack of sympathy with Sikhs and ignorance of the Punjab, 37, 82–4, 87; 94; not hostile to Rulers, 105; 118, 223, 256; estrangement from Congress, 270–1; 272–3, 280; responsibility for Pakistan, 286–9, 295–7, 299 (footnote), 306

Jodhpur, 235

Maharajah of, 107

Johnson-Campbell, Alan, 303–4 (footnote)

Jullundur, xiii, 119, 178, 263

Kahrore, 123

Kapurthala State, 261

Karachi, 1, 88, 107, 110, 114, 144, 203, 240–1, 243, 245, 259

Karanpur, 187

Karnail Singh, 233

Kashmir, 4, 19, 107

Kasur, 188

Kerala, xix

Khairpur, 126–8, 132, 136, 151, 155; lawlessness around, 169–71; looted, 172; a third attack forestalled, 173; improvement at, 182–3; evacuation of Hindus from, 224; 264

Khalistan, 69 (footnote), 305

Khalsa National Party, 32 (footnote), 36

Khanpur, 241

Khizar Hyat Tiwana, Malik Sir, becomes Premier of the Punjab, 5–6, 38; expelled from League, 39; 40–1; loses heavily at the elections, 43; heads a Coalition Ministry, 71–4; 75; resigns, 76–7; 180, 274–6, 296–7

Khosla, G.D., 269 (footnote)

Kishangarh, 234–5

Lahore, 29, 32–4, 36, 50, 75; outbreak of rioting in, 77; 81, 86, 88, 90, 92, 94, 96, 107, 109–10; state of on August 15th 1947, 114–17; 120, 203, 208, 240, 245, 255–6, 263, 275–6

district, 95, 114

Lawrence, John, xiv, xvi

Lecky, 262 (footnote)

Leghari, R.K., Superintendent of Police, 5, 138–40, 146–7, 150–2, 154, 159; at Minchinabad, 160–2; 164, 166; endures bitter reproaches, 167–9; 171, 173, 177–8, 182; angry at shooting of Sikhs, 185; 189, 218–19, 224–5, 232

Liaqat Ali Khan, 5, 16, 59

Linlithgow, Marquis of, Viceroy, xv, 2, 5–6, 18, 25–6, 295–6, 301–2

Lockhart, Sir Rob, 222

London, xix, 1, 3, 5, 60, 63

Ludhiana, 117, 119, 170

Lyallpur district, 35, 281

Macleodganj Road, 150, 158–60; looted, 162–3; horrible incident at, 164; 165, 167, 171, 175; refugees pour into, 177–80; 187, 226–7, 247, 254–5; a

black spot, 258; 259, 264

village, 163

Madhopur headworks, 91

Maharatta Light Infantry, 123

Mahrattas, 143, 278

Mailsi, 123

Majithia, Sir Sunder Singh, 36

Mamdot, Nawab of, 90

Manohar Lal, Sir, 118

Marden, Brigadier J.H., 104, 123, 135, 137, 139, 148, 191, 197; is wounded, 201–2; 211, 215

Mason, Philip, xiv, xvi, xxi

Mehta, Professor, 210

Mellor, Andrew, 269

Menon, V.P., 5, 66, 94, 96; visits Bahawalnagar, 174–7; 261, 277, 304–5

Minchinabad, 150; attack on beaten off, 160–2; 177–9, 187, 264

Moghulpura, 116

Mohammad Ali, naib-tahsildar, 91–2

Mohammad Latif, Syed, 263 (footnote)

Montagu-Chelmsford Reforms, xix, 284–5

Montgomery district, 35, 50, 114, 281

town, 121–2

Morley-Minto Reforms, Lord Morley, 284

Mountbatten, Admiral Lord Louis (Earl), Viceroy, 2, 6, 18, 65–7, 81; on transfer of population, 93; persuades Rulers to accede, 106; 277–8, 283, 303 (footnote)

Mountbatten Plan, 65–70 *passim,* 84, 281–2

Mudie, Sir Francis, 293

Multan district, 50, 78–9, 114, 121, 123, 162, 196, 281

city, rioting in, 78; 202, 236, 250, 255, 259

Muslim League, 1–2, 5–6, 13–18; rapid slide towards Pakistan, 21–5; 29, 33, 39–41; success at elections, 43; 44, 46–7, 49, 51–4, 56–7, 59–65, 68, 70; excluded from office in Punjab, 71–4; contest with Punjab Government, 6, 75–7; fails to mollify Sikhs, 82–3; averse to settlement with Sikhs, 84–6; 92–3, 107–8, 143, 180, 272–7, 283–4, 290, 295–9

Mussouri, 52

Nabha State, 229

Nair, Dr. Shushila, 244–5

Nand Kishore, Mehta, 202, 215

Nazimuddin, Khwaja Sir, 40

Nebuchadnezzar, 276

Nehru, Pandit Jawaharlal, xi, xix, 1, 3, 18, 42, 53; demolishes Cabinet Mission Plan, 56–7; 58, 60, 63; accepts Mountbatten Plan, 66; 79, 248, 269, 288, 290, 296, 298, 304, 309

Noakhali district, 59

North West Frontier Province (N.W.F.P.), 14, 19, 40, 42–3, 45 (footnote), 48, 50, 52, 66, 102, 104, 137, 155, 221, 256, 271, 293, 298

Nur Hussain Shah, Commissioner of Police, 104, 124–5, 127–8; joins pursuit of looters, 130–2; disapproves of shoe-beating, 131; takes gloomy view of situation, 140; 148, 183, 189; absents himself from meeting, 192

Nur Mohammad, Khan Bahadur, Settlement Officer, 103–4, 149, 171, 184; takes charge of jail camp, 195–6; 200, 203; advises use of tongas for evacuation, 204–5; supplies list of stocks of grain, 204–6; 209, 266

Okara, 120

Oliver, Deputy Commissioner, 103–4

Pakistan, xx, 1–2, 4–5, 7–8; first idea of, 11–13, 15, 19; Sikander's dislike of, 20–3; 26–7; Sikhs' view of, 29–31, 34–7; 39–40, 45–6; as Sovereign State rejected by Cabinet Mission, 47, 49; 51, 57, 63, 66–9, 72, 79; possibility of inclusion of Sikhs in, 82–7; 91, 94, 96; accession of Bahawalpur to, 105–8; 110, 118, 125; danger of collapse, 154–5; 157, 164, 180; coal shortage in, 224 (footnote), 255; 237, 248–9, 252, 256,

265, 269, 270, 272–7, 280–1, 283, 286–9, 291, 295, 297, 299 (footnote), 300–1, 303, 304

West Pakistan, 9, 11, (footnote), 172, 238, 243, 268–9, 285, 303

Pakistan Government, 93, 110, 144, 157, 255–6

Pakistan Resolution, 21, 25, 38, 40

Pallah (Islam) headworks, 99, 106, 121–3, 179, 254

Panjnad, 97
headworks, 99, 103, 105

Pannikar, Sardar, K.M., 174–6

Patel, Sardar Vallabhai, 53, 79, 174, 176–7, 298

Pathankot, 91

Pathans, in Bahawalpur Army, 1–2, 104, 144; cause massacre at Hasilpur, 136–7; 155, 172, 221

Patiala State, 33, 159, 229, 261, 286
Maharajah of, 285–6

Pethick-Lawrence, Lord, 3, 43, 56

Pindaris, 143

Princes (Rulers), 14, 18–19, 105–6

Punjab, xi, xiii–vi, xviii, 3, 5–6, 7–10, 14, 17, 19–20, 22, 24, 29–41 passim, 42–3, 47–50, 52, 61, 66–96 passim, 97–100, 102–3, 106, 108–111, 114–23

passim, 132–3, 137, 140, 144–6, 154; train massacres in, 169, 204, 262; 187, 225, 227, 249, 253–4, 262–7, 273, 275–83, 286–8, 291, 294, 297–9, 303–5

East Punjab, 9, 35, 68, 79, 84–5, 90 (footnote), 95, 97, 111, 119, 132, 145–7, 155, 175, 298, 304–5; Bahawalpur a paradise compared with, 177, 261; agreement for exchange of populations, 181; 202, 226, 229, 247–8, 252, 255; savagery in, 261–2, 265; 267–8, 275, 278–81, 293

West Punjab, 20, 30, 38, 79, 81–2, 84–5, 88, 90, 298, 302; warning to Hindus in, 93, 111, 117–18, 132, 179, 181, 223, 252–4; refugee problem in 255–8; 267–8, 278, 293, 302

Qaimpur, attacked and looted, 128–31; 132, 136, 151; lawlessness around 169–71; 172, 182; evacuation of Hindus from, 224; 264

'Quit India' demand, rebellion, 1–2, 27–8, 40, 296

Radcliffe award, line, Lord Radcliffe, 91 (footnote), 111; defects of, 186, 226; 281

Rahim Yar Khan district, 4, 103, 106, 176, 224–46 passim, 251, 261. 266. 304

Rai, Mangat, xiii, 304

Rajagopalachari, C., 26–7, 45

Rajputana, 97–8, 106

Randhawa, M.S., 247 (footnote)

Ranjit Singh, Maharajah, 30–1 (footnote), 97, 144

Ravi river, 35 (footnote), 50

Rawalpindi, 78, 265

Red Shirts, 15, 40

Rees, Major-General, 94, 303

Reforms Land, xviii

Revolution Green, xiii, xviii

Rohtak district, 218 (footnote), 248, 254

Roy James, Chief Engineer, 103, 227, 230

Sadiqabad, 243

Sadiqia canal, 152, 154, 173, 178, 185, 225–6

Samasatta, 159, 169, 187, 203, 224 (footnote), 231, 255; a black-spot, 258–9

Sen, Amartya, xx

Shaukat Hyat-Khan, 82

Sheikupura, 261

Short, Major, 31–3; works for Unionist-Akali alliance, 34–6; accompanies Cabinet Mission, 43; 49, 84–6; arrives in Delhi, 96; visit Bahawalnagar, 174–7; visits Bahawalpur, 184

Sikander Hyat-Khan, Sir, 4–6; joins the League, 17; 19; foresees dangers of Pakistan, 20–3; 24; in touch with Congress leaders, 25–6; 29, 32–3; distrusts Akalis, 34; 36; death of, 37; unwilling to stand up to Jinnah, 38; 39, 82, 273, 287, 297

Sikander-Baldev Singh pact, 4, 36–7, 49, 73

Simla, 18, 40, 46–7, 114–17
  Conference, 2–3, 5, 40, 42

Simon Commissio's report, 301

Sind, 13–14, 19, 40, 45 (footnote), 48, 50, 84, 97, 105, 110, 223, 234 (footnote), 241, 256–7, 293

South Asia, xx, 294, 309

South East Asia, xx, 2

Stalin, 276, 302

Suhrawardy, H.S., Chief Minister of Bengal, 58, 68, 70 (footnote)

Suleimanke headworks, 88, 99, 106, 133, 179, 181, 185–6, 225–6

Sutlej river, 35 (footnote), 90, 97, 122, 172, 179, 181, 203, 225, 248, 254

Sutlej Valley Project, 98–100

Tara Singh, Master, 31, 77, 93, 296

Tipperah district, 59

Unionist Party, Unionists, 5–6, 15, 17, 33, agreement with

Akalis, 36; 37; decline of, 39–
40; 41; defeat of, 43, 49, 71;
73, 83, 180, 287, 297

Government, 32–4, 37

United Provinces (U.P.), 5, 15, 17,
164, 299

USA, 309

Vehari, 258

Wagah, 36, 120

Walker, Colonel, 115

Wavell, Field-Marshal (Earl),
Viceroy, xv, 2, 40–2, 57–60
passim; dismissed, 65, 69

Wyatt, Woodrow, 43

Zafrullah Khan, Sir Mohammad,
88, 90, 96, 107

STERN RECKONING

A Survey of the Events Leading Up To and
Following the Partition of India

by

GOPAL DAS KHOSLA

MORTAL Prudence, handmaid of divine Providence,
hath inscrutable reckoning with Fate and Fortune:
We sail a changeful sea through halcyon days and storm,
and when the ship laboureth, our stedfast purpose
trembles like as the compass in a binnacle.
Our stability is but balance, and wisdom lies
in masterful administration of the unforeseen.

ROBERT BRIDGES—Testament of Beauty

CONTENTS

		Page
FOREWORD	.. ..	v
CHAPTER I—THE PARTING OF THE WAYS	.. .. ..	1
CHAPTER II—DIRECT ACTION DAY AND AFTER	.. ..	39
CHAPTER III—THE PUNJAB	. .. .	87
Lahore District	.. ..	120
Sheikhupura ,, ..	.. ..	126
Sialkot ,, ..	.. ..	141
Gujranwala ,, ..	.. ..	149
Gujrat ,, ..	.. ..	153
Montgomery ,, ..	.. ..	160
Lyallpur ,, ..	.. ..	165
Shahpur ,, ..	.. ..	172
Jhang ,, ..	.. ..	177
Multan ,, ..	.. ..	184
Muzaffargarh ,, ..	.. ..	191
Rawalpindi ,, ..	.. ..	196
Jhelum ,, ..	.. ..	199
Attock ,, ..	.. ..	201
Mianwali ,, ..	.. ..	204
Dera Ghazi Khan ,, ..	.. ..	208
Bahawalpur State	.. ..	212
CHAPTER IV—EXODUS ..	.. ..	217
CHAPTER V—SIND	.. ..	235
CHAPTER VI—NORTH-WEST FRONTIER PROVINCE	.. ..	255
CHAPTER VII—RETALIATION ..	.. .. ..	275
CHAPTER VIII—CONCLUSION ..	.. .. ..	293
APPENDIX I—NOTES TO CHAPTERS	.. .. ..	301
APPENDIX II—TABLES AND STATEMENTS	.. ..	319
BIBLIOGRAPHY ..	.. ..	351

FOREWORD

IN the history of communal relations, the years 1946-47 mark a period of unequalled mistrust, acerbity and frenzied warfare in almost all parts of India. Tension between the Muslim and non-Muslim communities increased till the cords that bound them together snapped and flung them apart—it seemed for ever. Came the horrors of Calcutta, Noakhali, Bihar and, after a brief interval, the tragic events enacted in the Punjab, North-West Frontier Province and Sind. Large numbers of Hindus left Calcutta and Noakhali to seek shelter in Bihar and other parts of India. A similar exodus of Muslims from Bihar was witnessed in October 1946. In March 1947 several parts of West Punjab were ablaze and nearly half a million Hindus and Sikhs abandoned their homes and migrated to the eastern districts. They brought harrowing tales of murder, rapine, arson and wholesale destruction of property. Every item of news added to the wrath and horror of the non-Muslims in India and exacerbated still further the bitterness between the two communities. Retaliation followed and during the five months August-December 1947, the provinces of East and West Punjab, the North-West Frontier Province and Sind were convulsed with the pangs of a terrible fratricidal war. And while killing, burning and looting were taking place everywhere, a two-way mass movement of the population added to the confusion. The Muslims were travelling westward to Pakistan and the non-Muslims were leaving Pakistan for India.

Millions of Hindus and Sikhs, forced to leave their homes and migrate eastward, arrived on the soil of the newly born Dominion of India. Every one of them had a grim tale to tell. Some of the stories related by the refugees were, no doubt, exaggerated ; the newspaper reports were not always accurate ; but the total denial of these happenings by the Government of Pakistan was hardly calculated to appease the rising temper of the Indian people. It was necessary that a true and authoritative account of the happenings in West Punjab, the North-West Frontier Province and Sind should be available for the future student of History and, to this end, the Government of India set up a Fact Finding Organization in the beginning of 1948. This Organization examined thousands of refugees and recorded their statements. Every attempt was made to achieve accuracy and check the veracity of the witnesses. Many of them were apt to magnify their sufferings and losses and inflate the figures of casualties. A scaling down of numbers was necessary and much of the evidence had to be rejected for no other reason than that it lacked corroboration. After a careful and detailed study of the evidence so collected the narrative set out in these pages was prepared.

This book is intended to give the reader a survey of the events leading up to the partition of India and an account of the widespread disturbances which took place in the Punjab, North-West Frontier Province and Sind during the year 1947. In the first chapter an attempt has been made to analyse the facts and state the causes which led the Muslim League to make a demand for partition. The second chapter contains an account of the riots in Calcutta, East Bengal and Bihar during the second half of 1946. Chapters Three, Four and Seven deal with the Punjab disturbances and Chapters Five and Six are devoted to the events in Sind and the North-West Frontier Province respectively. Chapters Three to Six are based on the material collected by the Fact Finding Organization. For the material of Chapter Two the writer is indebted to various official and unofficial reports, the accuracy of which is beyond suspicion. In compiling Chapter Seven the writer had to rely mainly on newspaper reports and some official documents which, however, did not give a complete account of what happened. This was inevitable in the nature of things as first-hand evidence of these events was not available. Exaggerated accounts of the atrocities perpetrated in East Punjab have been published in Pakistan ; some of these emanated from official sources. It is not the purpose of this book to answer the charges contained in these reports, nor is it intended that the account given here should be used as propaganda. The sole aim of the writer has been to give a true and objective narrative which would serve as a historical record for the future.

The tables in Appendix II have been compiled from the evidence of witnesses. Only some selected instances from a number of villages in each district have been given. Care has been exercised in selecting the various items and any incident which appeared to be doubtful or exaggerated has been studiously excluded.

The writer is deeply indebted to a number of friends who have read these pages and have made many helpful suggestions.

I

Between man and other animals there are various differences, some intellectual, some emotional. One of the chief emotional differences is that some human desires, unlike those of animals, are essentially boundless and incapable of complete satisfaction.

Imagination is the goad that forces human beings into restless exertion after their primary needs have been satisfied.

To those who have but little of power and glory, it may seem that a little more would satisfy them, but in this they are mistaken: these desires are insatiable and infinite, and only in the infinitude of God could they find repose.

Of the infinite desires of man, the chief are the desires for power and glory.

BERTRAND RUSSELL—*Power*

CHAPTER ONE

THE PARTING OF THE WAYS

THE great upheaval which shook India from one end to the other during a period of about fifteen months commencing with August 16, 1946, was an event of unprecedented magnitude and horror. History has not known a fratricidal war of such dimensions in which human hatred and bestial passions were degraded to the levels witnessed during this dark epoch when religious frenzy, taking the shape of a hideous monster, stalked through cities, towns and countryside, taking a toll of half a million innocent lives. Decrepit old men, defenceless women, helpless young children, infants in arms, by the thousand, were brutally done to death by Muslim, Hindu and Sikh fanatics. Destruction and looting of property, kidnapping and ravishing of women, unspeakable atrocities and indescribable inhumanities were perpetrated in the name of religion and patriotism. To be a Hindu, Sikh or a Muslim became a crime punishable with death. Madness swept over the entire land, in an ever-increasing crescendo, till reason and sanity left the minds of rational men and women, and sorrow, misery, hatred, despair took possession of their souls. A Sikh or a Hindu dared not show his face in the place where he and his forefathers had lived for centuries, and a Muslim was forced to abandon his native soil, his home and his property.

Yet for over a thousand years the various communities had lived together in peace and amity. United India had a population of 389 million (1941) comprising 255 million Hindus (including members of Scheduled Castes), 92 million Muslims, 6.3 million Christians, 5.6 million Sikhs and a number of smaller communities. There were Muslim majority areas (in the North-East and the North-West) and Hindu majority areas, but no part of India was exclusively inhabited by any one community. Everywhere Hindus, Muslims and Sikhs lived together as neighbours. In the urban areas the various communities could not, in the very nature of things, live in separate airtight compartments. There were, no doubt, Hindu *mohallas*, Sikh *mohallas* and Muslim *mohallas*, but these were situated side by side and it could not be said of any town in India that it was owned or inhabited by one community or that any particular area of the town belonged exclusively to the Hindus, Muslims or Sikhs. In the provinces of the Punjab, Sind and Bengal, at least, even the rural population was of a mixed character. There were Hindu villages, Muslim villages and Sikh villages, but all three communities were to be found in greater or smaller numbers in every village. Hindu and Sikh landlords had Muslim tenants and *kamins*.* Muslim landlords had Hindu tenants, and employed Hindus as managers and accountants. Hindu industrialists in towns and factories had Muslim workers. Religion had never interfered with social relations to any great extent. The unifying force of geographical entity, historical and cultural influences, extending over a period of ten centuries, had welded the various elements into a homogeneous whole. This was scarcely surprising for more than 90 per cent of the Muslim and Sikh population consisted of converts from Hinduism and belonged to the same stock, and had the same traditions as the Hindus. The converts in many cases retained even the old religious ceremonies , they differed but little in appearance or dress and behaved as members of the same society. This was particularly true of the rural areas. There had, no doubt, been occasional clashes between the communities but these were sporadic and very short-lived. The direct cause was almost invariably an economic or political disturbance rather than the religious factor. Riots usually occurred among the lower classes and the communal tension among them was spasmodic, though, when it occurred, it took an intense form. The peasant rising around Calcutta in 1831 was hardly a communal riot. The peasants broke into the houses of Muslim and Hindu landlords with perfect impartiality. The Mymensingh disturbance of May 1907 was really nothing more than the rising of the Muslim peasantry against their Hindu landlords and creditors. They would probably have risen with the same ferocity had the landlords and creditors been Muslims. The Mopla Revolt, which is often quoted as one of the worst communal disturbances and which was exploited by the British Government to their great profit, was also a rising of the oppressed and poverty-stricken peasants. The Bombay riots of 1929 were riots between the mill-workers who went on strike and the Pathan strike breakers. Riots in the Punjab were seldom handled with tact or imagination, and the indifference or incompetence of British officials in dealing with communal disturbances was frequently ascribed to the policy of Divide and Rule. Minor differences in

---

* Village menials and labourers in charge of rural crafts, e.g., carpenters, blacksmiths, weavers, shoemakers, potters, tailors, etc.

custom and outlook never stood in the way of the various communities living together in the most amicable and friendly manner. Hindus, Muslims and Sikhs used to meet each other on terms of equality. They dined * at each other's houses and seldom allowed their religious persuasions to interfere with their social and friendly intercourse. In the United Provinces the relations between the Hindus and Muslims were extremely cordial. Muslims went to play *Holi* with their Hindu friends while Hindus always went to their Muslim friends on the occasion of the *Id* festival.

The riots were confined mostly to the urban areas. The rural population, which comprises nearly 90 per cent of the total population of India, has always remained peaceful. Louis Fischer, in his book, " A Week with Gandhi,' refers to this circumstance† which was also observed by the Simon Indian Statutory Commission, who presented a report to the Viceroy in May 1930.‡ This neighbourly feeling rose on occasions to emotional heights, such as during the days of the Khilafat movement when Hindus and Muslims could be seen eating together and drinking from the same bowl. Even in the North-West Frontier Province the turbulent and fanatic Pathan lived on terms of friendship with his Hindu neighbour. Their relations were free from suspicion, bitterness, or any kind of hostility on grounds of religion. Unity in variety has been insisted upon as a peculiar characteristic of India. This was not a piece of wishful thinking but a true statement of the actual state of affairs—a statement reiterated by those who saw that the destructive forces of disruption were beginning to appear in some places.

These disruptive and separatist tendencies had their origin in a movement of national revival which took place during the nineteenth century by way of a moral defence against British domination. The impact of Western thought and civilization in

---

* This is naturally not true of the very orthodox Hindus who never dine outside the narrow limits of their caste and would refuse to eat from the hands of an outsider, Hindu or Muslim.

† " Caroe (the Viceroy's Secretary for Foreign Affairs who worked for many years as a British official in the Punjab) and Jenkins (a high British official in the Department of Supplies) ", I said, " told me that there were no communal differences in the villages, and I heard from others, too, that the relations between the two religious communities are peaceful in the villages. If that is so, that is very important because India is ninety per cent village."

‡ " There is among the Hindu minority in Sind a feeling that the independence of the (British) Commissioner is too great, while on the Mahomedan side there is a well-known cry for separation from Bombay. This demand has gathered strength not so much in the homes of the people or among the Mahomedan cultivators of Sind, as among the leaders of Mahomedan thought all over India to whom the idea of a new Muslim Province, contiguous to the predominantly Muslim areas of Baluchistan, the North-West Frontier Province, and the Punjab, naturally appeals as offering a stronghold against the fear of Hindu domination."

the first half of the nineteenth century led to an awakening of political consciousness and a sense of frustration in the face of British imperialism. In the desire to re-capture self-esteem the Indian mind harked back to the ancient Hindu and Muslim cultures. The Hindu mind sought solace in the memory of the Golden Age of Hindu imperialism and the Vedas. The founding of the Brahmo Samaj by Raja Ram Mohan Roy in 1828, of the Arya Samaj by Swami Daya Nand in 1875, the revival of Shivaji's cult in the Maharashtra and the anti-cow-killing campaign by Bal Gangadhar Tilak marked the various steps in the Hindu revivalist movement. The Hindu mind, in trying to rehabilitate its lost pride, sought an escape in glorifying its ancient achievements towards which the Muslims had made no contribution, and Hindu revivalism, therefore, took a religious and communal form. By a similar psychological process the Muslims took their minds back to the glory of the Prophet, the Khilafat and the Muslim conquest of the countries around the Mediterranean. These trends found expression in the Wahabi movement, the activities of Syed Ahmad of Rae-Bareli and the Mutiny of 1857 in which Hindus and Muslims made common cause against the foreign oppressor. It is to be observed that these revivalist tendencies were faint and hardly noticeable until the latter half of the nineteenth century when the differences between the Hindu and Muslim thought began to get more and more pronounced. Thus it was that, by a most unfortunate process of human psychology, the mental defences raised against foreign domination, and barriers, intended to restore self-esteem and moral rehabilitation, became fissiparous tendencies. As the revivalist movement gathered force, its momentum carried it beyond the limits of safety and sanity. The buffers of reason proved quite inadequate to arrest this emotional rush, and, before the end of the nineteenth century, signs of mutual suspicion and antagonism had begun to appear with disturbing frequency. Hindus and Muslims began to assert themselves as separate entities by withdrawing themselves from each other's festivals, by wearing different dress, observing distinctive manners, and by each demanding a separate language and educational institutions. Hindu culture and Muslim culture were now mentioned as distinct and irreconcilable conceptions.

There arose a desire for power, for communal supremacy and for the assertion of Hindu rule and Muslim rule. The lengths to which the respective protagonists carried their logic was amazing.

A scheme was drafted in all seriousness for organizing a society of workers to achieve a free India which would in effect be a Hindu India:

"Should the Society consist only of Hindus? In my opinion, yes, for—(*a*) A harmonious sentiment, based on common memories, literature and polity can be produced in its full intensity among Hindus.

" (*b*) The peasants will take the Society as their own, if it consists only of Hindus. We should look to the Jats, Rajputs, Sikhs and other Hindu populations and must not be carried away by our advanced notions. Politics is the art of manipulating the passions of large masses of men so as to achieve a desired object.

" (*c*) As no serious man can predict the indissoluble character of the union of Hindus and Mohammedans, it is advisable to lead the Mohammedans by means of Hindus. If you create the idea of political organization and sacrifice among Mohammedans, these are weapons which might be turned against the Hindus in the possible case of an English intrigue. The Mohammedan masses are so susceptible to religious mania that it is probable that if the idea of organization and communal service is accentuated in their midst, it will find its embodiment in a union of Muslims, which would be anti-Hindu in character. It is better to organize the Mohammedans by means of Hindus, for as soon as a Mohammedan worker will appeal to his co-religionists for national unity, his words will rouse only religious passion and the spell of Hindu-Mohammedan unity will be broken. Let us bring the Moham-medans into our camp by means of Hindu workers.

" (*d*) In using the word 'Swarajya' and appealing to the people we arouse Hindu associations. We would ask the Mohammedans to join us, but we must keep their masses under Hindu leadership. If you give them Mohammedan leaders, you tread on dangerous ground.

" (*e*) Many enthusiastic young men, zealous for the freedom of the Fatherland, think that the introduction of Mohammedans will bring in a jarring note. I know more than six or seven young men of the Punjab who will give up all worldly prospects for a Hindu Society, but not for a mixed one. I think Mr. Tilak and Mr. Lajpat Rai will agree in this opinion." *

---

* The scheme was drawn by Lala Hardyal in 1906 when he was in England and sent to Pandit Shyama Krishna Varma for consideration.

The Rashtriya Swayam Sewak Sangh, founded in Maharashtra in 1925, raised the cry of " Hindi, Hindu, Hindustan."

A Muslim writer argued:

" There is not an inch of the soil of India which our fathers did not once purchase with their blood. We cannot be false to the blood of our fathers. India, the whole of it, is therefore our heritage and it must be re-conquered for Islam. Expansion in the spiritual sense is an inherent necessity of our faith and implies no hatred or enmity towards the Hindus. Rather the reverse. Our ultimate ideal should be the unification of India, spiritually as well as politically, under the banner of Islam. The final political salvation of India is not otherwise possible."*

In 1933 Choudhary Rahmat Ali, a Punjabi, residing in Cambridge, evolved a scheme for the partition of India. His original idea was that those portions of India in which the Muslims were in a majority, should be partitioned and made into a sovereign State which would constitute the homeland of the Muslims and Muslim culture. Choudhary Rahmat Ali developed his idea and his imagination expanded the little dark cloud until it covered the entire sky. In the beginning Pakistan was to consist of the Punjab, North-West Frontier Province, Kashmir, Sind and Baluchistan only. Later, encouraged by the reception which was given to it by the Muslim League, in 1940, he initiated the second part of his programme embracing Bangistan, which was to include Bengal and Assam, and Osmanistan, comprising Hyderabad (Deccan). He thus evolved the conception of Dinia and finally of Pakasia, which he called " The Historic Orbit of the Pak Culture." Choudhary Rahmat Ali's naiveté would be amusing, had it not led to so much disaster in the country. He defined 'Dinia' in the following manner:

" Dinia is the new designation and destiny of the old, ante-diluvian 'India,' which is dying its well-deserved death. It is obvious that the word 'Dinia' is composed of the letters of the word 'India' itself and that, in the arrangement of letters, there is only one change. This is the transposition of the letter 'd' in 'India' to the first place. That is all."

Yes, that is all, but what is the implication of 'Dinia'? Choudhary Rahmat Ali says that the old name 'India' was both a misnomer and a menace. " It was a misnomer because it

---

* " The Meaning of Pakistan," by F. K. Khan Durrani.

literally and politically meant that India was the domain of only Caste Hindooism and Caste Hindoos ; . . . It was a menace because it was being systematically exploited by Indians (Caste Hindoos) to 'Indianize' the non-Indians and to make them nationally honourless, rightless and futureless in the lands of their birth." The introduction of democratic institutions involving the counting of heads raised the hopes of the Hindus and shattered the dreams of Muslim domination. A feeling of frustration grew and the Muslim mind began to show signs of a fear complex and an obsession which was used to stir up hatred of everything Hindu. It was said that with a Hindu majority government in power :

" Nothing will be left undone to crush the Islamic spirit and distinctions, destroy the Muslim moral and social fabric, the education and training of future generations and alter the entire phase of Islamic life, e.g., a law may be made that if a Muslim girl marries a non-Muslim the union will be taken as valid. Even forced marriages will obviously be presumed, or, decided to be, voluntary, with non-Muslim Judges to decide such cases. Urdu may be replaced by Hindi as *lingua franca* for India. Conversion to Islam, use of beef for food, or sacrifice, uttering a call for prayer, resentment to noise before mosques at prayer time, teaching or propagating the Holy Quran, building up of mosques and a hundred other Muslim customs and traditions may be stopped by legislation ; and they will have power to execute such laws."*

These effusions, though not authoritative utterances, are fairly representative of the channels in which extremist thought was running.

The differences between the communities were accentuated and magnified by economic factors, commercial competition and professional rivalry. The Muslims did not, as eagerly as the Hindus, take to Western education and Western culture. In the race for employment in Government service and the liberal professions, they started late and the initial handicap persisted. After the Mutiny of 1857 the British Government adopted a policy of repression against the Muslim upper and middle classes on the ground that they were responsible for the Mutiny. Sir Sayed Ahmad saw the dangerous consequences of this line of action and realized that the salvation of Muslims could only be achieved by the spread of Western

---

* S. N. A. Qadri—" A Muslim's Inner Voice."

learning among them and by their unqualified loyalty to the British
rule. He repelled the suggestion that the Muslims were anti-British
or that the Mutiny was an attempt to restore Moghul rule in India.
An essay written by him in 1858 in which he had urged the policy
of " divide and rule " was resuscitated from oblivion and published
in an English translation in 1873. He exhorted the Muslims to
embrace Western culture and study modern science. The
Mahommedan Anglo-Oriental College at Aligarh was founded and
the European Principals of this College played an important part
in leading the Muslim agitation for preferential treatment in
Government posts and the bourgeois professions. During his
later years, Sir Sayed began to evince an obsession of Hindu
domination. The demands for greater Muslim representation
increased with the realization that official position and participation
in the administrative machinery brought power and prestige.

In the business and industrial spheres the non-Muslims had
obtained an initial advantage which increased and multiplied
rapidly. Commercial activity first came to India in parts where
the Muslim influence was least. In Bombay, Madras and Calcutta,
the main centres of the East India Company activities, the non-
Muslims were in a majority and their intellectual and financial
resources enabled them to forge ahead and leave the Muslims
behind. The most important businesses and industries were captured
by them and the Muslims felt that they had irretrievably lost the
position of supremacy once held by them. There was constant
harping on the theme that they had been relegated to the status
of drawers of water and hewers of wood. The Hindus were
accused of exploiting and impoverishing the Muslims. This agitation was conducted solely by the Muslim middle classes, for the
peasantry (which forms the bulk of the Hindu and Muslim population) had no such grievances and it was only among the bourgeois
elements that separatist tendencies were most noticeable. In
the demand for Pakistan the Muslim officials and the Muslim
commercial interests raised the loudest voice. The Muslim writers
and politicians of the nineteenth and early twentieth centuries
were for the most part drawn from the class of Government
servants. Sir Sayed Ahmad Khan was for a time an Additional
Member of the Governor-General's Council and served on a
number of Government Commissions. Chiragh Ali, Professor
Salah-ud-Din Khuda Bakhsh of Calcutta, Abdulla Yusaf Ali whose
writings to a considerable extent shaped the modernist movement

in Islamic thought were all Government servants. When Pakistan became a realizable dream and the partition of India was imminent, Muslim officials and administrators played a very important part in shaping the course of events and precipitating the disastrous results that followed.

These differences were observed by the British Government and exploited in order to further their imperialistic aims in the country. As early as 1843 the Governor-General, Lord Ellenborough, wrote, " I cannot close my eyes to the belief that that race (the Muslims) is fundamentally hostile to us and our true policy is to conciliate the Hindus." Mountstuart Elphinstone advised " *Divide et Impera* was the old Roman motto and it should be ours." It has been already observed that after the Mutiny of 1857 a determined attempt was made to suppress the Muslims. This was soon carried to dangerous limits and a British official, W. W. Hunter, pointed out that the Muslim population was being shut out from official employ and from the recognized professions. He also drew attention to the British spoliation and extermination of the old Muslim educational system. This was a reference to the resumption of rent-free grants of land made by the Muslim rulers in Bengal. The grantees were responsible for financing a large number of Muslim educational institutions. With the establishment and progress of the Indian National Congress the pendulum of British favouritism swung in the opposite direction, and means were sought to provide a counterpoise to Congress aims. Lord Curzon brought about the partition of Bengal in order to " shatter the unity and to disintegrate the feeling of solidarity " in the province. This fostered the growth of Mahommedan power in Eastern Bengal by way of a check to the rapidly growing strength of the Hindu community. The events which culminated in the founding of the Muslim League and the introduction of separate electorates in 1909 make instructive reading. In the winter of 1905-06 the Prince of Wales (afterwards King George V) made a tour of India. On his return to England he told Lord Morley, the Secretary of State for India, that the National Congress was rapidly becoming a great power. On May 11, 1906, Lord Morley wrote to the Viceroy, Lord Minto, and drew his attention to what the Prince of Wales had observed. A week later Lord Minto replied, " I have been thinking a good deal lately of a possible counterpoise to Congress aims." He suggested a Council of Princes of the native Rulers and a few other important persons.

He added, " Subjects for discussion and procedure would have to
be very carefully thought out, but we should get different ideas
from those of the Congress." On June 19, 1906, Lord Morley
again wrote to Lord Minto and warned him that " before long
Muslims will throw in their lot with Congressmen against you."
Mr. Archbold, Principal, Aligarh College, now took a hand and
had a talk with the Private Secretary to the Viceroy. On August
10, 1906, Mr. Archbold wrote to Nawab Mohsin-ul-Mulk a letter
in which he suggested that a deputation of Muslims should wait
upon the Viceroy and ask for certain concessions.* Mr. Archbold
was anxious that his own name should " remain behind the
screen." On October 1, 1906, a Muslim delegation. led by His
Highness the Aga Khan, waited on the Viceroy and presented an
address. Lord Minto in his reply conceded the Muslim demands.
He said, " Your address, as I understand it, is a claim that, in any
system of representation, whether it affects a Municipality, a
District Board, or Legislative Council, in which it is proposed to
introduce or increase an electoral organization, the Mahommedan
community should be represented as a community. . . . I am
entirely in accord with you. . . . I am as firmly convinced as I
believe you to be, that any electoral representation in India would
be doomed to mischievous failure which aimed at granting a
personal enfranchisement, regardless of the beliefs and traditions
of communities composing the population of this continent." The
gratification of Lord Minto and Lady Minto at the successful
conclusion of this episode was recorded in Lady Minto's Diary.†
An official wrote to her commenting on her husband's work of
statesmanship. " It is nothing less," he said, " than the pulling
back of 62 millions of people from joining the ranks of the seditious
opposition." The same year the All-India Muslim Conference
which subsequently became the All-India Muslim League was
founded.

The Minto-Morley Reforms of 1909 introduced separate
electorates and erected a formidable and impregnable barrier
between the two major communities of India. Hindus and
Muslims henceforth began to have distinct and antagonistic
political aspirations. Each community felt little need of canvassing
the support of the other community. The electorate was divided
into watertight compartments and in each compartment communal

---

* For the text of the letter see Appendix I—Note (ii) to Chapter I.
† See Appendix I—Note (iii) to Chapter I.

ferment and communal hostility increased. A Muslim candidate's appeal was formulated only for the Muslim electorate and this had the inevitable result of putting extremist views at a premium. Sectional opinion was thus promoted, at the cost of public opinion, and the interests of the nation were sacrificed to the interests of the community. The poison introduced in 1909 increased and spread throughout the body politic as the franchise was enlarged. In 1909 the electorate numbered only about a million. It was increased in 1919 to more than seven millions and by the Government of India Act of 1935 more than thirty-six million voters were created, every one of whom thought, spoke and acted on communal lines.

Employment in Government service, entry to educational and professional institutions were fixed on communal basis. Communal-minded people, both Hindu and Muslim, were encouraged by being awarded high positions and titles,* while people who worked for inter-communal harmony were in danger of imprisonment. Press censorship was worked on a preferential basis. No restrictions were placed on Muslim papers that advocated murder for apostasy. The British press repeatedly attempted to stir up communal discord in nationalistic movements, e.g., by insinuating that Khudai Khidmatgars were anti-Hindu rather than anti-British. More room was given in London papers to communal questions and very little to nationalist ones. Nationalist Muslims hardly ever found mention in these papers. The split between the communities was gradually widened and, by carefully calculated and judiciously delivered blows, the wedge was driven in deeper on every possible occasion. The Muslim personnel of the Round Table Conference of 1930 and the subsequent Conferences was chosen out of the most communal Muslims. Mian Fazl-i-Husain who was a Member of the Viceroy's Executive Council advised in the choice of the Muslim delegates and the names of nationalist-minded Muslims were removed from the list of nominees. When it was found that Mr. Jinnah did not support all the communal demands at the first Round Table Conference, no invitation was issued to him for the subsequent Conferences. Later, when he changed his views, he was accepted as a leader of all Muslims in spite of the fact that he represented only a small minority of them. The case of forty-five million Momins, the Khudai

---

* A study of the list of title-holders will indicate the extent to which communal-minded individuals, Hindus, Muslims and Sikhs were encouraged and rewarded for their anti-nationalist activities.

Khidmatgars, the Khaksars, the Ahrar Party, the Mansooris and a number of other Muslim bodies who opposed Mr. Jinnah, the Muslim League and Pakistan, was never considered. The Communal Award of 1932 which conceded almost all the demands of the Muslims was a cunning device to perpetuate the Hindu-Muslim differences.

The framers of the British imperialist policy at the top were ably assisted by the local administrators and officials. All possible means were adopted to maintain the strength of the British hold on India. Riots were encouraged and in some cases initiated. The peaceful and non-violent nationalist movement was ruthlessly suppressed. The uprising of the Mopla tenants against their landlords was utilized to spread disaffection among the two communities. The Moplas had committed certain atrocities against Hindus but these were only incidental to the general uprising which, as we have observed earlier, was really the protest of the tenants against their landlords. Photographs of Muslims cutting the *choti* of the Hindus and forcing beef down their throat were exhibited by the Government of the United Provinces in various places and particularly in the vicinity of temples and other sacred Hindu places. They were, for instance, exhibited in Ajudhia. A member of the United Provinces Legislative Assembly* asked a question about these photographs and pamphlets and the Government admitted that this propaganda was done at public expense. Indian officials who showed independence of spirit and integrity of purpose were discouraged, superseded and kept out of key posts, involving the exercise of personal discretion in important matters. Since a dishonest and corrupt official could be relied upon to carry out an anti-national policy, a blind eye was turned on dishonesty and no serious effort was made to stamp out corruption, while sycophants and anti-India officers were rewarded by appreciation and preferment.

The story of a secret deal between Mr. Jinnah and Mr. Churchill was revealed by Michael Foot, M.P., in an article published in the *Daily Herald*, the official organ of the British Labour Party. Louis Fischer commented on the Churchill-Jinnah alliance in an article contributed to the *Hindusthan Standard*.†

During the disturbances of 1947 it was noticed that British and Anglo-Indian officers in Police, Military and Civil employ helped

---

* Mr. Mohan Lal Saksena.
Note (iv) in Appendix I.

the Muslim League organization in a most reprehensible manner. In Orissa it was found that Muslim hooligans were given arms imported from Java by army men and distributed by English and Anglo-Indian officers. Large quantities of arms and ammunition were stolen from and smuggled out of the Ordnance Depot at Jubbulpore and the information of the police was that English Police and Army Officers were concerned in this smuggling. Hawkins, a British Army Officer, was tried and found guilty of possessing unlicensed arms. He was alleged to be a member of a secret organization controlled by the Churchill Group of Conservatives, having agents all over India. These agents had been stirring disaffection among the Muslims and distributing arms to them. The Commander of the Boundary Force in the Punjab, entrusted with the task of maintaining law and order in the areas alongside the boundary between East and West Punjab, was frequently accused of criminal apathy in putting down the disturbances. It was impossible to prove any specific charges, but when the volume of complaints increased, the Government of India removed him from this important post. When it became certain that the British Government had finally decided upon the transfer of power to Indians and a complete relinquishment of authority in India was imminent, the British officials were sullen and angry. They realized that the era of their power and glory was about to come to an end. They predicted the most dire consequences for India and Indians. They had no urge or desire to control the forces of destruction and were quite content to see the break up of *Pax Britannica* which now appeared galling to them in the new political set-up.

Such was the result achieved by a hundred years of "divide and rule" policy.*

While the extreme Hindu and Muslim communal organizations assisted by the British administrators, embittered the once friendly and neighbourly relations of the two communities, the Indian National Congress endeavoured, by every possible means, to bring them together on a common platform, so that they could offer a united front to British imperialism. Founded in 1885, and completely secular in its composition and ideology, it met every year

---

* We make no apology for quoting the following from a letter written by Lord Olivier to the *London Times* on July 10, 1926:

"No one with any close acquaintance of Indian affairs will be prepared to deny that on the whole there is a predominant bias in British officialism in India in favour of the Moslem community, partly on the ground of closer sympathy but more largely as a make-weight against Hindu nationalism."

ana soon mobilized the entire body of political consciousness in the country. Large numbers of Muslims joined the organization and at its Sixth Session held in Calcutta in 1890 there were 156 Muslim delegates out of a total of 702. Several of its sessions were presided over by Muslims.* Many of the foremost leaders of the Muslim community have been members of this nationalist organization. They found that its programme and ideology were not only consistent with Islamic ideals but were calculated to further and promote Islamic culture. According to Professor W. C. Smith,† some Muslims joined the National Congress because they were Muslims and because their religion taught them "freedom, equality of justice and co-operation with and respect for all mankind." Such were Hussain Ahmad Madni, an orthodox Ulema and Principal of the Deoband College, and Obedullah Sindhi, a fire-brand agitator. Then again there were Muslims who joined the Congress because they disapproved of the Muslim League developing into an anti-Hindu organization, e.g., Hakim Ajmal Khan, Dr. Saif-ud-Din Kitchlew, Dr. M. A. Ansari and Maulana Abul Kalam Azad. There were others who joined the Congress because they were nationalist-minded. For them being a Muslim was wholly irrelevant to the question which party they should join. Mr. Badar-ud-Din Tayabji who presided over the Third National Congress and Yusaf Meharally are instances of such nationalist Muslims. Lastly, there were Muslims who had become anti-religious, such as young Muslim intellectuals and communists. The Congress hold on the Muslim mind remained firm until only a few years ago.

The Congress was opposed to sectarian politics and the principle of separate electorates. Unfortunately, the disastrous consequences of the separatist tendencies introduced by the Minto-Morley Reforms of 1909 were not fully realized and, in their anxiety to win over Muslim opinion at any cost whatever, the Congress leaders entered into a pact with the Muslim League in 1916,‡ whereby they accepted separate electorates for Muslims.

---

* E.g., Mr. Badrudin Tayabjee, Maulana Mohammad Ali, Dr. M. A. Ansari, Maulana Abul Kalam Azad.

† " Modern Islam in India " by Wilfred Cantwell Smith.

‡ The Lucknow Pact of 1916 was a draft scheme, in outline, of Constitutional Reforms formulated by the All-India Congress Committee in concert with the Reforms Sub-Committee appointed by the All-India Muslim League, which amongst other constitutional proposals, accepted the principle " One-third of the Indian elected members should be Mohammedans elected by separate Mohammedan electorates in the several Provinces, in the proportion, as may be in which they are represented in the Provincial Legislative Councils by separate Mohammedan electorates."

This course of action may have seemed inevitable at the time but there can be no doubt that it was a most unfortunate sacrifice of nationalist ideals and a major blunder.

The same anxiety to secure the allegiance of the Muslim masses resulted in another sacrifice of secular ideals when, in 1920, the Congress espoused the Khilafat cause and adopted the dangerous course of borrowing religious emotions for gaining political ends. The artificial stimulant applied by the Civil Disobedience movement was followed by an apathetic reaction when the events in Turkey made the achievement of Khilafat a practical impossibility. The neutral attitude adopted by the Congress towards the Communal Award in 1932 was another unfortunate mistake, and alienated the Muslims. It failed to achieve national unity and provided Mr. Jinnah with an opportunity to say some harsh things about the Congress.

We have seen how a hundred years of revivalist tendencies, sixty years of economic rivalry, fostered and promoted by the insidious British policy of "divide and rule," and a generation of separate electorates created and steadily widened the gulf between the Muslims and non-Muslims of India. The efforts of the Congress to bridge this gulf had some measure of success and a final break was avoided for a considerable time. Failure, however, was inevitable and came partly because the British rulers always had the whip-hand and partly because the remedies applied were inadequate and not indicated by a correct diagnosis of the malady. It is in this context that the more recent events of the period 1937-46 must be studied.

The Government of India Act of 1935 was an extremely unsatisfactory measure and scarcely improved the existing position from the Indian standpoint. The powers of the provincial authorities were, no doubt, enlarged and extended, but the terms of the Act intensified the separatist tendencies inherent in the system of separate electorates, fortified the position of the bureaucracy by introducing a number of reservations which increased the scope of its executive functions and the Federal structure was intended to impede any real progress on nationalist lines. The Congress, however, on being assured that the British Governors would behave as gentlemen and not interfere in the day-to-day administration of the provinces, decided to enter the new Councils and work Provincial Autonomy under the Act. The Muslim League also came to a similar decision under the leadership of

Mr. Jinnah and resolved to create a Central Election Board in order to organize the election campaign and undertook "the policy and programme of mass contact."* Mr. Jinnah had scant success in achieving Muslim solidarity on a communal basis. The Muslim majority provinces were not willing to accept Mr. Jinnah's leadership and the results of the elections in 1937 were bitterly disappointing to him. Only 4.4 per cent of the Muslims who went to the polls voted for the Muslim League.† In Bihar, the Central Provinces, the North-West Frontier Province, Orissa and Sind not a single Muslim League candidate was elected. In the Punjab only two candidates (of whom one later resigned from the Muslim League) were returned as against 82 non-League Muslims. The League had partial success in Bengal, Bombay, the United Provinces and Madras, but in these provinces also, the number of non-League candidates returned was greatly in excess of the League candidates.‡ The Congress swept the polls and found itself in a position to form Ministries in eight out of eleven provinces (all except the Punjab, Bengal and Sind). The Muslim League had not expected such a wholesale rout and felt completely left out of the political game. It now began to hope for concessions from the Congress and asked for a share in the administration of the provinces by including Muslim League Ministers in the Cabinets. This request was not so fantastic as the Congress High Command, obsessed with the rules of British Parliamentary etiquette, seemed to think. Indeed in the United Provinces, the Congress had, in some constituencies, supported the League candidate and a tacit understanding appears to have grown up that after the elections a Coalition Ministry would be formed. The Congress did not expect to secure an absolute majority in the

---

* " Some Recent Speeches and Writings of Mr. Jinnah," edited by Jamil-ud-Din Ahmed.
† The total number of Muslim votes cast was 7,319,445 and of these only 321,772 voted for the Muslim League.
‡ The exact position was as follows:

Province							Muslim League	Other Muslims
Madras	..	..	..	..	..	..	11	17
Bombay	..	..	..	..	..	..	20	9
Bengal	..	..	..	..	..	..	40	77
United Provinces	..	..	..	..	..	27	37
Punjab	..	..	..	..	..	..	2	82
Bihar	..	..	..	..	..	..	Nil	39
Central Provinces	..	..	..	..	..	Nil	14
Assam	..	..	..	..	..	..	9	25
North-West Frontier Province	..	..	..	Nil	36
Orissa	..	..	..	..	..	..	Nil	4
Sind	..	..	..	..	..	..	Nil	36
Total	..	..	..	..	..		109	376

Legislature and it was assumed that it would have to rely on League co-operation. The Congress success at the polls was, however, phenomenal and entirely unexpected, and, flush with victory, the nationalist party declined to include a Muslim League member in the Government. The signing of the Congress pledge was made a condition precedent to participation in the Cabinet. There were no doubt good reasons for taking this step. It was argued that "the Congress itself was a kind of coalition or joint front of various groups tied together by the dominating urge for India's independence" and—

"A wider coalition meant a joining up with people whose entire political and social outlook was different, and who were chiefly interested in office and ministerships. Conflict was inherent in the situation, conflict with the representatives of British interest— the Viceroy, the Governor, the superior services; conflict also with vested interests in land and industry over agrarian questions and workers' conditions. The non-Congress elements were usually politically and socially conservative; some of them were pure careerists. If such elements entered Government, they might tone down our whole social programme or at any rate obstruct and delay it. There might even be intrigues with the Governor over the heads of the other Ministers. A joint front against the British authority was essential. Any breach in this would be harmful to our cause. There would have been no binding cement, no common loyalty, no united objective and individual Ministers would have looked and pulled in different directions."*

Mr. Nehru was somewhat impatient of the League and its insistence on separate representation and wanted the whole country to present a united front against the British rulers, but when he declared that "the parties that mattered in India are the Congress and the British, and others should line up with the Congress if they intended to survive," Mr. Jinnah was justifiably angry and retorted, "There is a third party, namely, the Mussalmans. We are not going to be dictated to by anybody. We are willing to co-operate with any group of a progressive and independent

---

* Jawaharlal Nehru, " The Discovery of India."

It might be argued that the results predicted in these words were achieved when the Coalition Interim Government was formed in 1946. There is, however, no analogy between 1937 and 1946. In 1937 there was no question of partition of the country and the League had expressed the intention of working with the Congress.

In 1946 the League was not imbued with the same desire for co-operation as in 1937. In fact, the Muslim leaders openly declared that they had entered the Interim Government in order to achieve Pakistan.

character provided its programme and policy correspond to our own. We are willing to work as equal parties for the welfare of India."

The unwisdom of this parliamentary orthodoxy, however, soon became manifest when its effects on communal relations began to appear. The Muslim League leaders felt frustrated and chagrined. Mr. Jinnah was angry and gave unrestrained expression to his sentiments against Gandhiji and Mr. Nehru.* He called upon the Mussalmans of India to organize, consolidate and establish solidarity and unity. In October 1937, a session of the All-India Muslim League was held at Lucknow. This session was attended by Sir Sikandar Hayat Khan, the Premier of the Punjab, Mr. Fazlul Haq, the Premier of Bengal, and Sir Saadullah Khan, the Premier of Assam, who had hitherto refused to fall into line with Mr. Jinnah. The Muslim League changed its creed from "Full Responsible Government" to "Full Independence," and decided to take immediate steps to "frame and put into effect an economic social and educational programme." This was intended to muster popular support for the League and woo the non-League Muslim groups, e.g., the Coalition Party in the Punjab, the Krishak Proja Party in Bengal. The Sikandar-Jinnah Pact was concluded. An attempt was made to win the sympathies of the Indian Christians and members of the Scheduled Castes. Mr. Jinnah undertook a country-wide tour to establish contact with the masses. The Muslim League began to say that the Congress was a purely Hindu body and was perpetrating atrocities upon the Muslims, in the provinces where it was in power. The allegations regarding atrocities were somewhat vague and undefined but the main grievances may be briefly examined. The *Bande Mataram* was sung on official occasions. It was said that the associations of this song were anti-Muslim. The song occurs in Bankim Chandra Chatterji's novel " Ananda Math " which deals with the struggle of Bhavananda, the hero of the story, against the Muslim power in Bengal. The Congress agreed to retain only the first two stanzas of the song, but this did not satisfy the Muslim agitators. The use of the tricolour Congress flag on official buildings was another atrocity. The contention of the Congress was that the flag represented both the major communities and had been the symbol of the united fight of the Indians

* Mr. Jinnah's statement dated July 26, 1937, in reply to Babu Rajendra Prasad's offer, quoted in " Some Recent Speeches and Writings of Mr. Jinnah."

against British imperialism. The Wardha Scheme of Basic Education was another grievance. It is to be observed that the Committee which drafted this scheme was presided over by Dr. Zakir Hussain who was assisted by Khwaja G. Sayyadain. The scheme was tried with success in Jamia Millia of Delhi, a Muslim institution, and other places. The League also took exception to the Congress attempt to win over the Muslim masses, and it was alleged that this was intended to stifle and destroy Muslim culture. The Hindi-Urdu controversy was another item in the list of atrocities.

The Congress made one or two mistakes which were magnified and exploited by the Muslim League. The United Provinces Cabinet issued a circular letter to the District Officers that they should co-operate and act in consultation with District Congress Committees and its office-bearers. This direction was issued on the ground that the Congress Governments were in the position of national Governments; but there can be no doubt that the direction was ill-advised. At about this time the Shia-Sunni trouble at Lucknow began and even this was utilized by the League leaders for their own purposes. It was alleged that the Congress had brought about this trouble by creating a split in the Muslim ranks. Mr. Jinnah remarked, "One cannot help noting in these unfortunate developments at Lucknow that those who are responsible for leading, rather misleading, sections of both Shias and Sunnis in the fratricidal struggle are prominent Muslim Congressites." The Hindu agitation in Hyderabad was ascribed to Congress instigation.

In April 1938 the Muslim League appointed a Committee to enquire into the Congress oppression of Muslims and the report of this Committee, which came to be known as the Pirpur Report, was submitted on November 15, 1938. In the meantime, Pandit Nehru had been in correspondence with Mr. Jinnah and had tried to evolve a formula on the basis of which the Congress and the Muslim League could work together. Mr. Jinnah, however, was extremely evasive. He had now appointed himself as the sole defender of Muslim rights in India and he set about achieving his ends by developing an ever-increasing proficiency in the art of saying "no".

The fact of the matter is that the League, at this time, was desperate. It had been knocking against a brick wall. Its allegations of ill-treatment against the Congress Ministries could not be substantiated. The Pirpur Report contained, at best, a few minor incidents which could easily be matched by happenings of a much more serious nature in the provinces of the Punjab and Bengal where Muslim Ministries were in power. No one but the League members could be convinced of the truth of the allegations made against the Congress Ministries. The European Governors of the provinces where the Congress was in power declared in unequivocal terms that the administration of the Congress Ministers had been singularly free from communal bias and that they had performed their functions with complete impartiality and justice. Babu Rajendra Prasad, the President of the Congress, offered to have the allegations regarding atrocities enquired into by the Chief Justice of India. Mr. Jinnah, however, declined this offer and said that the matter was now in the hands of the Viceroy. But the League charges were never investigated or adjudicated upon by the Viceroy and the bogey of Hindu oppression was kept alive.

It was at this juncture that the European war came as a godsend to the League. The Viceroy of India immediately announced that India was also at war. This was naturally resented by the Congress as the Viceroy's declaration was made without previous consultation with the Central or Provincial Legislatures or the Congress Ministries representing the vast body of public opinion in the country.

After careful consideration and long deliberation the Congress Working Committee came to the conclusion that the only course open to them, consistent with their honour and dignity, was to call upon all the eight Congress Ministries to resign from office. As soon as this decision was implemented the Provincial Governors suspended the Legislatures and took charge of the administrative machinery under the provisions of section 93 of the Government of India Act of 1935. The Muslim League was jubilant and offered its co-operation in the war effort. It was decided to celebrate the end of the Congress rule by observing a Deliverance Day on December 22, 1939. On that day resolutions were passed at meetings called by the Muslim League in various places. At the same time nationalist Muslims organized counter-demonstrations.

The Congress being now out of power, the League began to strain every nerve to climb into the seat of office. The League leaders realized that the Muslim Ministries in the Punjab and

Bengal had achieved a great deal and if they had failed to achieve more it was because they were not Muslim League Ministries ; and the extremist Muslim leaders now began to think of some concrete way of attaining their aims. They began to talk of the partition of the country. Sir Sikandar Hayat Khan published a Zonal Scheme.* This was not a part of the official Muslim League programme but, in view of the Sikandar-Jinnah Pact of 1937, it showed the direction in which the League politics were beginning to travel. Up to this moment the League had refused to entertain the idea of partition seriously ; but now, partly to mobilize mass emotions and partly to use it as a lever for better bargaining, the Muslim League passed the famous Pakistan Resolution at the Lahore Session of the Muslim League Council on March 26, 1940, the terms of which were:

" 1. While approving and endorsing the action taken by the Council and the Working Committee of the All-India Muslim League as indicated in their resolutions dated the 27th of August, 17th and 18th of September and 22nd of October 1939 and 3rd of February 1940 on the constitutional issue, this Session of the All-India Muslim League emphatically reiterates that the Scheme of Federation embodied in the Government of India Act, 1935, is totally unsuited to, and unworkable in the peculiar conditions of, this country and is altogether unacceptable to Muslim India.

" 2. It further records its emphatic view that while the declaration dated the 18th of October 1939 made by the Viceroy on behalf of His Majesty's Government is reassuring in as far as it declares that the policy and plan on which the Government of India Act, 1935, is based will be reconsidered in consultation with the various parties, interests and communities in India, Muslim India will not be satisfied unless the whole constitutional plan is reconsidered *de novo* and that no revised plan would be acceptable to the Muslims unless it is framed with their approval and consent.

" 3. Resolved that it is the considered view of this Session of the All-India Muslim League that no constitutional plan would be workable in this country or acceptable to the Muslims unless it is designated on the following basic principle, viz., that geographically contiguous units are demarcated into regions which should be so constituted with such territorial readjustments as may be necessary, that the areas in which the Muslims are numerically in a majority as in the North-Western and Eastern Zones of India

---

* The scheme was expounded in the Provincial Assembly on March 11, 1941, but was conceived much earlier.

should be grouped to constitute 'Independent States' in which the Constituent Units shall be autonomous and sovereign.

"That adequate, effective and mandatory safeguards should be specifically provided in the constitution for minorities in these units and in the regions for the protection of their religious, cultural, economic, political, administrative and other rights, and interests in consultation with them ; and in other parts of India where the Mussalmans are in a minority, adequate, effective and mandatory safeguards shall be specifically provided in the constitution for them and other minorities for the protection of their religious, cultural, economic, political, administrative and other rights and interests in consultation with them.

"This Session further authorizes the Working Committee to frame a scheme of Constitution in accordance with these basic principles, providing for the assumption finally by the respective regions of all powers such as defence, external affairs, communication, customs, and such other matters as may be necessary."

The terms of the resolution were vague and amorphous in the extreme. There was no mention of the two-nation theory, though the sole justification for partition rested on Hindus and Muslims being two distinct nations. The word 'Pakistan' was not mentioned and there was a significant reference to territorial adjustments which were left undefined.

The Muslim League's offer of co-operation and Mr. Jinnah's profession of loyalty prompted Lord Linlithgow to make another effort to resolve the political deadlock. Mr. Jinnah immediately made two demands. In the first place, he wanted an assurance that no constitution for the future Government of India would be framed unless the Muslims, who, according to him, meant the Muslim League or himself, agreed. In the second place, he demanded that League representation in the Viceroy's Executive Council should be equal to Congress representation. The Congress could not accept Mr. Jinnah's claim to veto constitutional advance, nor could it agree to Congress-League parity in the Executive Council. The negotiations, therefore, proved fruitless, but Lord Linlithgow on August 8, 1940, made the announcement that His Majesty's Government "could not contemplate the transfer of their present responsibilities to any system of Government whose authority was directly denied by large elements in India's national life" and that they "could not be a party to the coercion of such elements into submission to any such Government." Mr. Jinnah had thus secured a very important point, in that he acquired the right to place a veto on any political advance to which the rest of the country may be agreeable. This episode prompted Edward Thompson to observe that Mr. Jinnah was being treated as a kind of Moslem Mahatma.

The Congress started individual civil disobedience in October 1940 and within a short time between twenty-five and thirty thousand men and women were either in prison or under detention. In June 1941, Germany attacked Russia and then followed a time of great anxiety for the Allied Nations. In December 1941 Japan entered the war and, in the beginning of 1942, India saw the dangers of war rapidly approaching her boundaries. Penang and Singapore fell within a short time and the Japanese moved through Malaya towards Burma and India. The Civil administrative machinery in Burma broke down completely and a large-scale exodus of Indians, Burmese and Europeans began. The Indian National Army under Subhas Bose presented another problem. The Japanese made one or two air attacks on Calcutta and Britain felt the urgency of doing something in order to mobilize Indian resources. Indian opinion was at the time hostile. The Congress was agitating for independence and a Constituent Assembly. The Muslim League had asked for Pakistan even though the demand did not appear to have been made seriously. The fortunes of the war on the Western front were shaping adversely, and American anxiety was increasing. In these circumstances Sir Stafford Cripps, a Socialist member of the British Coalition Cabinet, was sent out to India. He arrived at the Karachi Airport on March 22, 1942, and the next day gave a Press interview at which he stated that he was a friend and admirer of India, that he had come for a fortnight and could not stay longer and within this short time the leaders must make quick decisions, and that the proposals which he brought with him were the result of the unanimous deliberations of the British War Cabinet. This take-it-or-leave-it attitude was neither conciliatory nor flattering to India's self-esteem. He announced his proposals on the radio on March 30. These proposals, contained in a State Paper, dealt with the question of the immediate transfer of power to Indians and a long-term constitutional plan which would be taken up after the end of the war. Gandhiji described the State Paper as a " post-dated cheque, " drawn, according to a member of the Princely Order, on a " crashing bank." The Congress leaders felt depressed on reading these

3

proposals as they contained seeds of disintegration. For the first time "the right of any province of British India that was not prepared to accept the new constitution, to retain its present constitutional position" was recognized. The principle of non-accession, in effect, meant conceding the demand for Pakistan. This, however, was not the ground on which the Cripps Mission failed. The Congress were prepared to accept the proposals in so far as they related to the immediate transfer of power and when Sir Stafford glibly talked of a "Cabinet" consisting of Indians and a "Constitutional Viceroy," the Congress opened negotiations in a trustful and constructive mood. There was difference of opinion about the functions of the Defence Minister, but, when these differences showed signs of resolving, Cripps suddenly made a *volte face* and began to talk of the interests of the minorities. At no time during the discussions had the minority or communal questions been mentioned, and the Congress President was naturally surprised when, in his last letter, Cripps referred to the dangers of having a "permanent and autocratic majority in the Cabinet." Mr. Nehru, who took a prominent part in these negotiations, refers to this sudden change in these terms:

"And, then just when I was most hopeful, all manner of odd things began to happen. Lord Halifax, speaking somewhere in the U.S.A., made a violent attack on the National Congress. Why he should do so just then in far America was not obvious, but he could hardly speak in that manner, when negotiations were actually going on with the Congress, unless he represented the views and policy of the British Government. In Delhi it was well known that the Viceroy, Lord Linlithgow, and the high officials of the Civil Service were strongly opposed to a settlement and to a lessening of their powers. Much happened, which was only vaguely known." *

The fact of the matter was that there was no intention ever to transfer real power to India and Cripps had been sent to India at the urgent request of Mr. Roosevelt who understood the implications of Indian unrest and sympathised with our aspirations. Mr. Churchill was opposed to this move from the beginning and was able to defeat the project with the help of a reactionary Viceroy and Commander-in-Chief. Sir Stafford Cripps went back to England and misrepresented the whole episode by making incorrect statements about what had happened.

---

* Jawaharlal Nehru. "The Discovery of India."

The feeling of frustration in the country was intensified as the conviction was borne in upon all right-thinking men that the salvation of India could not be attained as long as the heel of British imperialism continued to crush free thought and enterprise. The Congress felt desperate and, as the monster of war approached the doors of India, the temper of the people rose. There were some who even welcomed the Japanese advance with a hope born of spite and hatred of the British rule. In this mood of the people, the All-India Congress Committee met at Bombay on August 7 and 8, 1942, and after careful deliberation passed the "Quit India" resolution which was nothing more than a "reasoned argument for the immediate recognition of Indian freedom and the ending of the British rule in India." * Early on the morning of August 9, large numbers of Congress leaders were arrested all over the country.

Months of bitter struggle followed. Thousands of men and women were sent to prison or kept in detention. The Government at first took no action against the Muslims but the news of these happenings agitated the Khudai Khidmatgars in the North-West Frontier Province where they held demonstrations against the Government. They were beaten, fired at, arrested and imprisoned by the thousand. By March 1943, thirty-five thousand Congressmen were in prison and nearly twelve thousand in detention or preventative custody. Mr. Jinnah disapproved of the Congress resolution and tried to show that the Muslims had kept aloof from these anti-British activities. He accused the Congress of "ignoring the Muslims." †

Mr. Jinnah's one aim now was to strengthen his own position by gathering the maximum amount of Muslim support for his idea of Pakistan. With the Congress leaders behind bars he had undisputed command of the political field. "Social cohesion," says Bertrand Russel, "demands a creed, a code of behaviour or a prevailing sentiment." Mr. Jinnah provided his followers with all three. He gave them the creed of Muslim superiority implicit in the idea of Pakistan, a code of anti-Congress and anti-Hindu behaviour and a prevailing sentiment that Islam stood in danger of perishing under Congress rule. To quote Bertrand Russel again:

"In excited times, a politician needs no power of reasoning, no apprehension of impersonal facts, and no shred of wisdom.

---

* Jawaharlal Nehru, "The Discovery of India."
† Mr. Jinnah's address to the Muslim Federation at Bombay on January 24, 1943.

What he must have is the capacity of persuading the multitude that
what they passionately desire is attainable, and that he, through his
ruthless determination, is the man to attain it." *

The times, indeed, were excited and unusual. Danger from
outside combined with internal conditions of food scarcity helped
to spread discontent. The dishonesty and incompetence of officials
and the greed of the business community made matters worse. The
Bengal Famine took a toll of nearly three million lives.† The
activities of the pro-League Muslim officials in the Supply
Departments created a class of *nouveaux riches* Muslims who
identified their interests with the fortunes of the Muslim League.
The bourgeois elements had always dominated the League counsels
and Pakistan contained a fresh appeal to their self-interest. In
Pakistan there would be no risk of competition from the richer
and more experienced Hindus. Promotions of Muslim Government
servants would be more rapid. All the higher appointments and
key posts would be in their hands. Their more efficient Hindu
colleagues had always stood in their path and the only way for
the Muslims to succeed was to oust the Hindu officers and step
into their places. The Muslim industrialists would have the field
clear to themselves and there would be no injurious competition
by the other communities. The Hindus had captured almost the
entire business market and a partition of the country would mean
greater facilities to the Muslim industrialists and possibly State
subsidies to them. This appeal to the pocket of the bourgeoisie
had the desired effect and the League won the support of almost
the entire Muslim middle class, more particularly of the men in
the services who proved to be the staunchest protagonists of the
League. The political leaders would have unchallenged sway in
Pakistan and, as for the masses, Pakistan was a glorious dream, the
realization of which was a matter of secondary importance. It
fired their imagination and they converged all their emotional
energies towards it without realizing its consequences. To this was
added the prospect of acquiring the wealth of the non-Muslims.
The prospect of loot is not an unimportant factor in the success of
a leader's appeal. As an instance of the emotional heat generated
we may quote the undertaking given by Maulvi Mohammad
Bahadur Khan, President of the India States Muslim League, at

---

* Bertrand Russel—*Power.*
† The Famine Commission presided over by Sir John Woodhead estimated the number
of deaths caused by the famine at between fifteen and twenty lakhs but the general opinion
was that nearly thirty lakhs of people died of starvation.

the Muslim League Conference at Karachi in December 1943:
" I solemnly pledge and bear you (Mr. Jinnah) and the
audience as my witness, I bear the air, the shining sun, the stars
and the moon and above all I bear God as my witness that I will
sacrifice my life and everything at your command in the name
of God. I assure you that you will never find me lag behind
even at the most difficult stage of our struggle. Qaid-i-Azam, that
day will be the greatest day of my life when I shall have sacrificed
the last penny in my pocket and the last drop of my blood at the
altar of God. (Voices from the meeting: ' We are with you.')
Today, we do not want those people who want to effloresce into
fragrant sweet flowers on the ' Tree of Millat.' We want the
people who will spill their own blood and give their life for the
life of the nation."

Mr. Jinnah had no desire or intention to come to terms with
the Congress. He maintained an arrogant and unbending attitude
towards all attempts at settlement. He refused even to formulate
concrete demands,* as the giving of a definite shape would have
deprived Pakistan of its emotional appeal, for the human emotion
is seldom stirred by the contemplation of a material substance or
a logical formula. The masterly evasion and intransigence of
Mr. Jinnah prevented the Gandhi-Jinnah talks of September 1944
and the Simla Conference convened by Lord Wavell in 1945 from
bringing about a satisfactory *rapprochement* between the parties.

The war in the West and in the East ended and Churchill's
Government in England was succeeded by a Labour Government,
possessing a clear majority in the House of Commons. Indians
tried to shed their mistrust of British intentions and once more
turned hopeful eyes towards their rulers. Their hopes and
expectations were reinforced by the compelling influences of world
conditions. America had once tried to intervene on behalf of India
during the Cripps' episode,† and was now expected to mould

---

* Mr. Jinnah gave an interview to the representative of the *Daily Worker* of London on
October 5, 1944. He said, " To understand the Pakistan demand in its full significance it
is to be borne in mind that six provinces, namely, the N.W.F.P., Baluchistan, Sind and the
Punjab in the North-West and Bengal and Assam in the North-East, of this sub-continent
have a population of seventy million Muslims and the total population of Muslims would not
be less than 70 per cent." Professor W. C. Smith has pointed out that this statement either
" does not mean what it seems to mean or else Mr. Jinnah either was lying or was grossly
misinformed," for, according to the census of 1941, the Muslim population of these six
provinces is only 55.23 per cent of the total population of these provinces.

† The pressure exercised by Mr. Roosevelt upon the British Government is said to
have been responsible to a great extent for Cripps being sent to India. When the
negotiations were drawing to a conclusion, Louis Johnson, the Personal Representative of
Mr. Roosevelt, tried to intervene but specific instructions received from Mr. Roosevelt
arrived too late and Cripps had already departed.

British attitude towards Indian aspirations. The unrest in the
country showed signs of spreading and it was becoming increasingly
difficult to maintain a firm hold on, what Mr. Churchill called, the
most precious jewel in the British Crown. The trial of the Indian
National Army officers in the Delhi Fort revealed and gave wide
publicity to the story of a Provisional Government of free India,
fighting the British imperialist forces under the leadership of
Subhas Chandra Bose and fired the imagination of the masses.
Riots to protest against the sentences awarded to these officers
broke out in Calcutta in February 1946. A few days later the
mutiny of the Naval ratings in Bombay provoked sympathetic riots
in the cities of Bombay and Calcutta. The Jubbulpore sepoys went
on strike in the end of February, and a week later the Victory
Day Celebrations in Delhi on March 7, were accompanied by hostile
demonstrations and riots, necessitating firing by the Civil and
Military police. The economic position deteriorated every day.
A Parliamentary Delegation representing all political parties in
Britain came to India and, after an extensive tour of observation
and discussion, returned to England. They conveyed their
impressions to the British Government. On February 19, the
British Prime Minister announced that "three Cabinet Ministers
are going to India to discuss with leaders of Indian opinion the
framing of an Indian Constitution."

It had been decided to hold fresh elections for the Central
and Provincial Legislatures and this provided the Muslim League
with an unparalleled opportunity for exacerbating communal
feelings. The winter of 1945-46 stands out as an era of hate and
bitterness. The election campaign of the Muslim League was
one sustained and uncompromising attack on everything and
everyone that did not fall in line with the League ideology. It
was not a political fight but a fight in which the sole attempt of
the Muslim League was to arouse communal passions and work
up the religious frenzy of the ignorant and superstitious masses.
Sajjada Nashins, Pirs and religious leaders of the fanatical school
were impressed into service and sent out to propagate the creed
of hate. The voters were warned against the *kafirs* and they were
told that voting for a nationalist Muslim was a sin that could not
be expiated. Five times a day, after prayers in the mosques,
Fatwas were read out that Unionists (in the Punjab) and nationalist
Muslims were enemies of Islam and working as spies of the Hindu
Congress : and, therefore, anyone casting a vote in their favour

would be excommunicated. It was announced that inasmuch
as voting for a non-Leaguer was tantamount to *kufr* the voter's
marriage would stand automatically dissolved. One or two voters
who died during the elections were actually refused burial in the
Muslim graveyards. The effect of this propaganda on the illiterate
rural masses may well be imagined. District officials, school
teachers, postmen, subordinate Revenue staff, all worked day and
night to influence the minds of the Muslim voters and work up
their emotions by these devices. The Muslim press carried on a
ruthless campaign of hate and anti-Hindu propaganda and its
vitriolic utterances whipped up mass hysteria among the Muslims.

These threats and intimidations were completely successful.
The Muslim League secured all the Muslim seats in the Central
Assembly and .a vast majority of the seats in the Provincial
Assemblies. The analysis of voting, however, shows that nationalist
Muslims secured more than one-fourth of the total Muslim votes
cast. In Sind, they obtained 32 per cent and in the Punjab 30
per cent of the total Muslim votes.* It is instructive to observe
that the Muslim League votes were only 17 per cent of the total
votes (all parties) cast. The demand for Pakistan was, therefore,
supported by less than one-fifth of those who went to the polls.

The League was, however, exultant and victory celebrations
were held throughout India. Mr. Jinnah declared that the League
had secured not less than 90 per cent of the Muslim votes.
Mr. Abdul Hamid Khan of Madras claimed that 99 per cent
Muslims were for Pakistan.† The anti-Hindu campaign increased
in intensity and the speeches at the Convention of the Muslim
League Legislators held in Delhi in the beginning of April
contained wholly unnecessary and unjustifiable attacks on Hindus.
The resolution passed at this Convention described the Hindu
Caste System as " a direct negation of nationalism, equality, democracy and all the noble ideas that Islam stands for." Khan Abdul
Qaiyum Khan threatened that the Muslims would take out the
sword if Pakistan were not conceded. Hindus were referred to
as enemies ; reason and moderation were thrown to the winds and
abusive epithets pushed to the superlative degree were freely
employed.

---

* The Muslim League polled 45,01,156 votes while the non-League Muslims polled
15,86,392 votes. The total number of votes cast was 2,63,55,853. " Mitra's Annual Register
—1946. Vol. I. Jan.-June."

† The Muslim League leaders have never shown any respect for truth. Mr. Jinnah
has given the number of Muslims in India as eighty millions, ninety millions and one
hundred millions on various occasions as it suited him. See also page 29.

On March 15, 1946, Mr. Attlee, in amplification of his announcement of February 19, stated that the Cabinet Delegation was ready to leave for India. He declared that it was the intention of His Majesty's Government to help India "to attain her freedom as speedily and as fully as possible." He added that while "mindful of the rights of minorities" who should be "able to live free from fear," the British people "cannot allow a minority to place a veto on the advance of the majority." This statement indicated a new orientation in British policy and when the Cabinet Delegation arrived at Karachi on March 23, 1946, expectation ran high. After prolonged discussions with the leaders of various parties it was found that no agreement was possible, and on May 16, 1946, the Delegation, with the approval of His Majesty's Government in the United Kingdom, published a Statement by way of an award. This Statement gave reasons for not acceding to the demand for the partition of India and contained a short-term and a long-term Plan. The short-term Plan provided for the formation of an Interim Government consisting of Indians. This meant immediate transfer of power to Indian hands. The long-term Plan provided for the framing of a constitution on certain lines. The provinces of India were divided into three groups. Group A consisted of the Hindu majority provinces of Madras, Bombay, United Provinces, Bihar, Central Provinces and Orissa; Group B consisted of the three Muslim majority provinces in the North-West, namely, the Punjab, North-West Frontier Province and Sind; while Group C comprised the provinces of Bengal and Assam. The provinces were given the right to opt out of their particular Group in accordance with the provisions contained in the Statement. The Groups would have complete autonomy in dealing with all subjects save three, viz., Defence, Communications and Foreign Affairs which would be administered by the Centre. This scheme preserved the unity of India and at the same time presented Mr. Jinnah with a modified Pakistan. The scheme was considered by the Working Committees of the Congress and the Muslim League. The Congress Working Committee, by a resolution passed on May 24, 1946, asked for some further clarification of the scheme envisaged by the Statement. The Working Committee of the Muslim League decided to accept the entire Statement on June 5, and Mr. Jinnah communicated this decision to the Viceroy. The Congress was willing to accept the portion of the Statement relating to the long-term Plan if the question of opting out was clarified but was doubtful about the wisdom of joining the Interim Government on the proposed terms. On June 16, 1946, the Viceroy and the Cabinet Delegation issued another Statement announcing that the Viceroy intended to issue invitations to a number of persons asking them to serve as Members of the Interim Government. Clause 8 of this Statement which became a matter of contention was as follows:

" In the event of two major parties or either of them proving unwilling to join in the setting up of a Coalition Government on the above lines, it is the intention of the Viceroy to proceed with the formation of the Interim Government which will be as representative as possible of those willing to accept the Statement of May 16."

Mr. Jinnah had already communicated to the Viceroy his acceptance of the May 16 Statement. The Muslim League was, therefore eligible to serve on the Interim Government. The Congress was hesitating and Mr. Jinnah hoped that they would refuse. Lord Wavell's original plan was to have an Interim Government of twelve members, five drawn from the Muslim League, five from the Congress, one from the Sikh community and one Indian Christian or Anglo-Indian. If the Congress decided to join the Interim Government Mr. Jinnah had an even chance of securing a majority and having the decisive voice in everything. He had several times courted the favour of the Christians and the Anglo-Indians and had been holding extensive *pourparlers* with the Sikh leaders. If, on the other hand, the Congress refused, Mr. Jinnah hoped, under the terms of clause 8 quoted above, to be in sole charge of the Interim Government.

Lord Wavell revised his original scheme of twelve members of the Interim Government by adding a thirteenth to be drawn from the Scheduled Castes. The Statement of June 16 envisaged an Executive Council of fourteen members. Mr. Jinnah took strong exception to these changes as they decreased his chances of outvoting the Congress members. His hope of Congress refusal, however, sustained him. On June 25, 1946, the Congress Working Committee came to a final decision and this decision was conveyed to the Viceroy the same day. The Congress had accepted the long-term Plan, placing their own interpretation on the clause relating to opting out, but expressed their inability to " accept the proposals for the formation of an Interim Government as contained in the Statement of June 16." Lord Wavell called Mr. Jinnah and apprised him of the exact situation. Mr. Jinnah was told that the formation of the Interim Government would be postponed for the present but that the Government when formed would be a Coalition Government in which the Congress would have a share. Mr. Jinnah's annoyance knew no bounds. He had thought that his adroit moves had brought him to a position from which he could hope to have a decisive say in all matters concerning the Government of India. He argued that because the Congress had not accepted the Statement of May 26, in its entirety, it had disqualified itself from participating in the short-term Plan. The Viceroy should not therefore postpone the formation of the Interim Government but should, according to the provisions of clause 8 of the Statement of June 16, proceed immediately to appoint the personnel of his Executive Council from the Muslim League Party. The Viceroy, however, was not willing to form a Government from which the majority party representing more than 75 per cent of the people of India was excluded. Mr. Jinnah accused the Viceroy of breach of faith, reminded him that "statesmen should not eat their words" and told him that in the altered circumstances, the Muslim League could not offer its co-operation.

*　　　*　　　*　　　*

Reference has been made to the provision regarding the question of opting out by the provinces from the various Groups. At this stage this matter may be examined briefly as it formed the subject-matter of controversy between the Congress and the British Government on the one hand and the Congress and the Muslim League on the other. Clause 15(5) of the Statement of May 16 provided that "Provinces should be free to form Groups with Executive and Legislatures and each Group could determine the Provincial subjects to be taken in common." The procedure for opting out was laid down in clause 19 (v) and (viii): —

" (v) These sections shall proceed to settle the Provincial Constitutions for the Provinces included in each section, and shall also decide whether any Group Constitution shall be set up for those Provinces and, if so, with what provincial subjects the Group should deal. Provinces shall have the power to opt out of the Groups in accordance with the provisions of sub-clause (viii) below:

" (viii) As soon as the new constitutional arrangements have come into operation, it shall be open to any Province to elect to come out of any Group in which it has been placed. Such a decision shall be taken by the new Legislature of the Province after the first general election under the new Constitution."

The question at once arose whether a province like the North-West Frontier Province, placed in Section B, or Assam, which was placed in Section C, would have the right to opt out of the Section assigned to it before the new elections under the new Constitution or after. The Congress Working Committee took the view that under clause 15(5) provinces were free to form Groups and this meant that a province could choose the Group which it wanted to join before the new elections. It was also claimed that the Constituent Assembly would be a sovereign body and would be at liberty to alter any rule of procedure laid down by the Cabinet Mission Plan. The Congress President wrote to Lord Pethick Lawrence on May 20, 1946, drawing attention to these two points. He said, " The Assembly itself, when formed, will in my Committee's opinion be a sovereign body for the purpose of drafting the Constitution unhindered by any external authority.... Further, that it will be open to the Assembly to vary in any way it likes the recommendations and the procedure suggested by the Cabinet Delegation." With regard to the question of opting, he said:

" In your recommendations for the basic form of the Constitution you state that provinces should be free to form Groups with executive and legislatures.... Later on in the Statement, however, on page 5 you state that the provincial representatives to the Constituent Assembly will divide up into three Sections and these Sections shall proceed to settle the Provincial Constitutions for the provinces in each Section and shall also decide whether any Group Constitution shall be set up for these provinces. There appears to us to be a marked discrepancy in these two separate provisions. The basic provision gives full autonomy to a province to do what it likes and subsequently there appears to be a certain compulsion in the matter which clearly infringes that autonomy."

The attitude of the Congress was based on democratic principles and was prompted, to a large extent, by fears regarding the fate of the North-West Frontier Province and of Assam where the Congress Ministries were in power. Section B had a total strength of 35 members in the Constituent Assembly. Of these only three represented the North-West Frontier Province and it

was clear that if the North-West Frontier Province were compelled to go into Section B, before the framing of the Constitution,
the voice of the province would carry no weight whatsoever. The
Constitution of Section B might, therefore, be framed in such a
way that it would become impossible for the North-West Frontier
Province to opt out and join Group A. This could be done by
changing the nature of the electorate or by imposing disabilities
upon candidates for the Assembly. Similarly, in Section C there
were 70 members of the Constituent Assembly and of these only
10 were assigned to Assam and they would be outvoted by the
Bengal members.

The Congress and the Muslim League saw the mischief
pregnant in the procedure laid down for opting out and, while the
Congress took exception to it, the Muslim League was gratified.
Mr. Jinnah saw that the scheme would certainly enable him to get
the Provinces of North-West Frontier and Assam in the two
Sections which would virtually comprise Pakistan. Mr. Jinnah's
attitude in this matter was on a par with his demand that in order
to determine whether a certain province wanted to join Pakistan
or not a plebiscite of the Muslim voters alone should be held
rather than a referendum in which voters of all communities were
free to express their wishes. It was for this reason that the
Congress Working Committee insisted on the contradiction
involved in the basic provisions of the long-term Plan contained
in the Statement of May 16 and sub-clause (viii) When the
matter was debated in the House of Commons on July 18,
Sir Stafford Cripps maintained that " it was an essential feature of
the scheme that the provinces should go into the Sections." In
September, Assam decided not to enter Section C, and it appeared
that there was no way of resolving the deadlock before December
9, on which date the Constituent Assembly was due to meet.
Towards the end of November Indian leaders were invited to
London to discuss the matter with His Majesty's Government.
The discussion, however, failed to bring about a settlement and
the British Government declared that the interpretation accepted
by the League was the correct one. The Congress offer of referring
the matter to the Federal Court of India was rejected, and it was
not till Lord Mountbatten drew up his Plan of June 3, 1947, that
the matter was finally disposed of. This episode shows clearly
that while the Congress took its stand on democratic principles
and insisted that a province should have the right to choose its

destiny, the Muslim League and the British Government introduced an element of compulsion to ensure that the North-West Frontier Province and Assam should join Sections B and C respectively.

*   *   *   *

The Cabinet Delegation left India on June 29. It was announced that they would report to the British Parliament on July 18. Mr. Jinnah now began to search for a weapon with which he could adequately take his revenge and assert his individuality and power. He had declared in March that there was a change of outlook in the Muslim League and that Muslims no longer talked of a mere constitutional fight. The Pakistan demand had been reiterated at the Muslim League Legislators' Convention in the beginning of April, and, as we have seen, the speakers had poured out their anti-Hindu venom in the most violent terms. There had been talk of direct action as early as 1943. In the course of the debate in Parliament on July 18, the Secretary of State for India, in the House of Lords, and Sir Stafford Cripps, in the House of Commons, attributed the failure of negotiations to the intransigence of Mr. Jinnah. This only helped to add fuel to the already raging fire. Mr. Jinnah had called a meeting of the Muslim League Council at Bombay on July 29, 1946, and this Council passed two resolutions, one withdrawing the acceptance of the Cabinet proposals and the other sanctioning direct action. According to the first resolution, " the participation of the Muslims in the proposed constitution-making machinery is fraught with danger and the Council, therefore, hereby withdraws its acceptance of the Cabinet Mission's proposals." The text of the second resolution on Direct Action was as follows:

" Whereas the All-India Muslim League has today resolved to reject the proposals embodied in the Statement of the Cabinet Delegation and the Viceroy dated May 16, 1946, due to the intransigence of the Congress on the one hand and the breach of faith with the Muslims by the British Government on the other ;

" And Whereas Muslim India has exhausted without success all efforts to find a peaceful solution of the Indian problem by compromise and constitutional means ; And Whereas the Congress is bent upon setting up a Caste Hindu Raj in India with the connivance of the British ; And Whereas recent events have shown that power politics and not justice and fair play are deciding factors in Indian affairs ;

" And Whereas it has become abundantly clear that the
Muslims of India would not rest content with anything less than
the immediate establishment of an independent and full sovereign
State of Pakistan and would resist any attempt to impose any
constitution, long-term or short-term, or setting up of any Interim
Government at the Centre without the approval and consent of the
Muslim League, the Council of the All-India Muslim League is
convinced that now the time has come for the Muslim nation to
resort to Direct Action to achieve Pakistan and to get rid of the
present slavery under the British and contemplated future Caste
Hindu domination.

" This Council calls upon the Muslim nation to stand to a
man behind their sole representative organisation,—the All-India
Muslim League and be ready for every sacrifice.

" This Council directs the Working Committee to prepare
forthwith a programme of direct action to carry out the policy
initiated above and to organize the Muslims for the coming
struggle to be launched as and when necessary.

" As a protest against and in token of their deep resentment
of the attitude of the British, this Council calls upon the
Mussalmans to renounce forthwith the titles conferred upon them
by the Alien Government."

II

In an enthusiastic public meeting with whose purpose one is in sympathy, there is a sense of exaltation, combined with warmth and safety: the emotion which is shared grows more and more intense until it crowds out all other feelings except an exultant sense of power produced by the multiplication of the ego. Collective excitement is a delicious intoxication, in which sanity, humanity, and even self-preservation are easily forgotten, and in which atrocious massacres and heroic martyrdom are equally possible.

BERTRAND RUSSELL—*Power*

Now let it work; mischief, thou art afoot.
Take thou what course thou wilt!

SHAKESPEARE—*Julius Cæsar*

CHAPTER TWO
DIRECT ACTION DAY AND AFTER
(i)

THE decision was made and the die was cast. The League leaders announced in no uncertain terms that the two resolutions passed at the Bombay Session of the Council on the July 29, 1946, were intended to be a clarion-call to their followers and a challenge to their enemies. There were " scenes of unparalleled enthusiasm "* inside the Kaisar Bagh where this " most historic act " was performed. Outside, on the road, a small crowd of enthusiastic Muslims waited expectantly, huddled together beneath a canopy of umbrellas, while the rain poured down in a steady fine drizzle, mirroring their mud bespattered shoes in the macadamized surface of the road. The meaning and purport of " Direct Action " were not left in doubt. It meant " good-bye to constitutional methods," the " forging of a pistol " and using it. Mr. Jinnah declared: " What we have done today is the most historic act in our history. Never have we in the whole history of the League done anything except by constitutional methods and by constitutionalism. But now we are obliged and forced into this position. This day we bid good-bye to constitutional methods." The applause which accompanied this declaration encouraged Mr. Jinnah to add that he did not believe in equivocation and meant every word of what he said. He concluded his speech by quoting a couplet of the Persian poet Firdausi in a loud voice resonant with passion:

" *If you seek peace we do not want war*
But if you want war we will accept it unhesitatingly."

" The quotation was drowned in vociferous shouting of League slogans and cheers." †

The Congress might be content to bask in the halo of a self-denying ordinance or struggle on as best it could through the quagmire of constitutionalism and nationalism, the League had chosen to forge ahead with rapid strides towards the seat of power and glory. The means adopted or the cost incurred were matters

---

* The *Dawn*, August 30, 1946.
† *Ibid*

4

of secondary consideration. Not for Mr. Jinnah or his acolytes
the way of peace or true democracy. They had openly abjured
the democratic ideal as a phantom wholly unsuited to Indian
conditions.* What they really meant was that they could not rely
on a democratic vote to give them absolute power and position.
The petulant impatience of Mr. Jinnah could not brook the delays
and uncertainties of a lawful path. He had seen fanatical
audiences vibrate to the sound of his not unmusical voice. He had
silenced refractory criticism with an upraised finger or a stern
look. While yet in his teens, he had successfully conducted an
election campaign in England on behalf of Dadabhoy Naroji, the
Parsi candidate for the British House of Commons. Since his
establishment as the head of the All-India Muslim League in 1937,
he had, within his narrow sphere, wielded all the powers of a
dictator in steadily increasing measure.† With consummate skill
he had manœuvred himself into a seemingly unassailable position
from which all the power and prestige of the Congress could not
dislodge him. In the last chapter we saw how Mr. Jinnah
demanded his right to form an Interim Government without the
Congress, and how this demand was rejected by the Viceroy. To
be thus frustrated when the fruit of his toils was almost within
his grasp was a distressing mortification. His disappointment and
chagrin on this occasion were deeper and more galling than in
1937 when the powers exercised by the Congress Ministries under
the Government of India Act of 1935 were neither so extensive
nor so full-blooded as the declaration of the Cabinet Mission in
1946 seemed to adumbrate. Methods of peaceful negotiations
had failed to bring Mr. Jinnah to the pinnacle of his ambition,
so now he unhesitatingly turned to fanatical violence and decided
to launch a crusade against the so-called oppression of the Bania-
British alliance. He made a call for Direct Action. It was the
commencement of Operation Pakistan in dead earnest.

After the emotional outbursts in Kaisar Bagh, Mr. Jinnah
was asked by a press representative if the resolutions passed by
the League Council ruled out the scope of negotiations. He
retorted : " What are the other nations doing ? Armed to the

---

* Mr. Jinnah discussed this thesis in an article written for " Time and Tide " issued
from New Delhi on February 13, 1940. He expressed the opinion that Western Democracy
was totally unsuited to India, and that its imposition on India was a disease in the body
politic.

† At the open session of the All-India Muslim League held in Delhi, in April, 1943,
Mr. Jinnah was authorized to " take every step or action as he may consider necessary in
furtherance of and relating to the objects of the Muslim League as he deems proper."
See also Note (i) to Chapter II in Appendix I.

teeth with atom bombs, are they not going on talking and discussing? Are they not at the same time going on with preparations to put down any party they like? Why do you want me (the League) alone to sit with folded hands. I am also going to make preparations to meet the situation as and when it arises." Asked if the proposed Direct Action would be violent or non-violent, Mr. Jinnah said, "I am not going to discuss ethics."*

Mr. Liaquat Ali Khan told the Associated Press of America that Direct Action meant " resorting to non-constitutional methods, and that can take any form and whatever form may suit the conditions under which we live." He added, " We cannot eliminate any method. Direct Action means any action against the law." Sardar Abdul Rab Nishtar was reported to have said that Pakistan could only be achieved by shedding blood and, if opportunity arose, the blood of non-Muslims must be shed, for " Muslims are no believers in *ahimsa."* Khwaja Nazimuddin declared that Leaguers were not pledged to non-violence.

This was the interpretation of " Direct Action " given by the leaders themselves. The lower orders of the League hierarchy and the rank and file of Muslim masses heard what their leaders said and knew what was expected of them. Months of insidious propaganda and the emotional excitement of religious fanaticism had filled their minds with jealousy and hatred. The two-nation theory had been dinned into their ears till they came to believe that Congress rule meant Hindu tyranny and the total annihilation of Muslim culture. It was felt that Islam itself was in immediate danger of perishing. The unruly elements who flourish on the fears of the timid during times of lawlessness, and hope to reap a harvest of loot and plunder, were straining at the leash, and the decision of July 29 was the first definite signal for action and a pointer in the direction towards which they had to proceed.

The world at large heard these utterances and felt dismayed. The Western nations had just emerged from the throes of the most murderous war that history has ever known, and still lay panting and exhausted. China was engaged in a fratricidal combat which seemed interminable. Palestine was developing into an incurable cancer. The United Nations had failed to solve satisfactorily a single problem—economic, social or political—arising out of the

---

* *Statesman,* August 1, 1946.

Second World War ; and the killing was yet going on on the continent of Asia. And now the Muslim League had openly and deliberately spurned the way of peaceful negotiation, and decided to have recourse to violent and unlawful means. The decision could not fail to evoke resentment and dismay. The non-Muslims in India were appalled at this scarcely veiled threat ; the British press was all but unanimous in condemning the step taken by Mr. Jinnah. The *Manchester Guardian* ascribed the event to Mr. Jinnah's anger and disappointment because the Viceroy would not let him form the Interim Government without the Congress. According to the *News Chronicle,* " there could be no excuse for the wild language and the abandonment of negotiations which marked " the meeting of the League Council. It asked, " What precisely does Mr. Jinnah think he will achieve by embracing violence and at a moment when so substantial a part of his claim has been conceded ? Does he think that communal strife will benefit India or even the Muslim part of India ? He has only to look at other parts of Asia to see what lies at the end of that journey." The *News Chronicle* concluded on a note of despair, " it is hopeless, of course, if Mr. Jinnah is wedded to complete intransigence, if, as now seems the case, he is really thirsting for a holy war." Other papers expressed similar views.

We have drawn attention to the comments of the British Press in order to show that those who read the terms of the Bombay resolutions and the speeches delivered in their support were under no misconception regarding the aims and intentions of the League. They believed, and rightly so, that Mr. Jinnah was virtually declaring a civil war in India.*

The details of how the Day of Direct Action was to be observed had now to be worked out. Mr. Jinnah and Khwaja Nazimuddin, when questioned on th ~oint immediately after the Bombay session, said that they were not prepared to say anything about the matter. Within a few days, however, Khwaja Nazimuddin was able to say that the Muslim population of Bengal knew very well what " Direct Action " would mean.†

Immediate steps were taken to implement the momentous decision arrived at. A Council of Action was appointed to draw up a programme of Direct Action and devise ways and means of

---

* Mr. Suhrawardy at the Convention of the Muslim League Legislators had said: " We stand for one leader, one voice, one aim. Is Pakistan our last demand ? I will not attempt to give an answer but that is our latest demand. .... If you wage war against us I am not prepared to forecast the future."

† *Amrita Bazaar Patrika,* August 13, 1946.

carrying it through. The meetings of this Council of Action were naturally secret but the results of deliberations conducted behind closed doors, were made manifest a few days later by the events which provided the overture to a long and horrible drama. To these secret conclaves came Khan Iftikhar Hussain Khan of Mamdot, President of the Punjab Muslim League and later the Premier of the West Punjab, and Sardar Shaukat Hayat Khan, the impulsive but ambitious son of Sir Sikandar Hayat Khan. He had been found guilty of corrupt practices and dimissed from the post of a Minister by Sir Khizar Hayat Khan and was anxious to resuscitate his lost reputation. Subsequent events showed that he had not succeeded in curbing his wayward tendencies and there is at present* a proposal to prosecute him for offences committed when he again became a Minister in West Punjab. Begum Shah Nawaz, the daughter of Sir Mohammad Shafi who had broken away from Mr. Jinnah and chosen to co-operate with the British Government at the Round Table Conference, was another Punjabi who attended these meetings. Mr. I. I. Chundrigar President of the Bombay Provincial Muslim League and now a Minister of the Pakistan Government, represented Bombay, while Mr. H. S. Suhrawardy, the Chief Minister of Bengal, spoke on behalf of the more important of the two League Ministries in India at the time.

A great deal of thought and argument went to shape the decision of the League leaders. It was finally decided that Calcutta should be the venue of the opening scene of the dark drama which the whole of India was to witness during the course of the next sixteen months and for this decision there were very good reasons.

There were, at this time, only two League Ministries in India, namely, Bengal and Sind. The position in Sind was not at all satisfactory from the League point of view. Sir Ghulam Hussain Hidayatullah felt extremely insecure in his position as Provincial Premier. He had successfully evaded a censure motion but another had been tabled and it was feared that the opposition might carry it through.† Moreover, the Sind Governor had been interfering in the day-to-day administration of the province; and the Ministry, therefore, did not feel that they could undertake to carry out a programme of Direct Action successfully. Bengal, on the other hand, had a powerful League Ministry with

---

* 1949.   † See page 241 in Chapter V.

Mr. Suhrawardy at its head, and in him the Qaid-i-Azam saw a most efficient instrument for executing his design. Suave of appearance and urbane in his manners, he was a clever politician. He accepted Mr. Jinnah as his leader because, in this course, he saw a splendid opportunity for furthering his own interests. He possessed the necessary skill for provoking a controversy and then turning the situation to his own advantage. He was capable of starting a large-scale and gruesome massacre in Calcutta and then afterwards associating himself with Mahatma Gandhi's peace mission. He was seen to interfere in the working of the police in the Control Room but, when charged with procrastination and criminal neglect, he pleaded that the Commissioner of Police had declined to carry out his orders for restoring peace, and sought shelter behind the wording of section 9 of the Police Act which entrusted "the exclusive direction and control" of the Police Force to the Commissioner of Police. As head of the Government in Bengal he refused to issue petrol coupons to the Muslim League lorries but as a Muslim Leaguer he issued supplementary petrol coupons for hundreds of gallons to the Ministers individually and to himself. This petrol was later used to transport Muslim rioters on Direct Action Day.* He was capable of issuing a statement to the Associated Press of India on the evening of August 16 that conditions were improving when things had been going from bad to worse throughout the city. When questioned on this point later he denied that he had issued such a statement. On August 23, speaking on the radio, he urged the people of Bengal to live in peace and brotherly affection, and within half an hour sent out a special message to the correspondents of the foreign Press which wholly contradicted his radio broadcast. It was probably on his advice that Calcutta was selected for starting a large-scale assault upon the non-Muslims. Khwaja Nazimuddin was an even more conscientious Muslim Leaguer. He was more forthright than Mr. Suhrawardy and was far more hostile to the Hindus. He had more experience of administrative matters and his advice and assistance were of inestimable value in drawing up the programme for the Direct Action Day and in implementing it. He reaped his reward later by succeeding Mr. Jinnah as the Governor-General of Pakistan.

The position of Bengal and, more particularly, of Calcutta was extremely important from the League point of view. Bengal

---

* Dr. Shyamaprasad Mukerjee, speaking in support of a no-confidence motion in the Bengal Legislative Assembly on September 20, 1946, said, "Evidence is available that these coupons were used by lorries moving in Calcutta on those fateful days."

was a Muslim majority province with a Muslim population of 54.3 per cent (1941). The eastern districts had a preponderance of Muslim population while, in the western districts, the Hindus were in a majority. This circumstance had persuaded Lord Curzon to effect a partition of the province in 1905. There was considerable Hindu agitation against this measure, and when, in 1911, the partition was annulled, the Muslims looked upon the decision of the British Government as a wholly unjustifiable surrender to the Hindu desire for domination and a betrayal of the pledges given to the Muslims. The large Muslim majority area of East Bengal-*cum*-Assam where the Muslims might have attained economic domination was broken up and the Muslims of East Bengal were relegated to a subordinate position. They had to contend with the greater ability and experience of the Hindu business men and the better educational qualifications of the Hindu candidates for Government posts. Economic interests were identified with religious persuasion and the Muslims felt that in the re-united Bengal they could not win the prize of power and money with their only slightly superior numerical strength. The solution which presented itself was some form of political readjustment which would reflect correctly the census figures. The Government of India Act of 1935 was scarcely a sovereign remedy, for according to its provisions the Muslims obtained only 117 seats in a Legislature of 250. To give effective protection to British business interests the Europeans and the Anglo-Indians were given a much larger representation than their numbers warranted. In 1946 they had as many as 29 seats in the Assembly whereas they comprised scarcely one per cent of the total population. The Muslims had been allotted only 119 seats. The Muslims could no doubt depend on European and Ango-Indian votes but their uncertain support could not be accepted as a complete panacea for all time and for all the ills with which the Muslims imagined themselves to be afflicted. In this set-up of things Calcutta occupied a position of special importance. It stood on the common line which divided the Muslim and Hindu majority areas and, when the partition of Bengal was being effected for the second time in 1947, the contending parties fought for the prize of this rich city with all the vigour at their command. " In Calcutta Hindus predominate in numbers, commercial and professional wealth and experience, and resources and organization; but the course of events since the re-union of

Bengal has made Calcutta the richest prize in what is now a Muslim majority province.*

Another reason why the choice fell upon Calcutta was that there had been a most unfortunate weakening of the authority responsible for maintaining law and order. Calcutta had in recent years witnessed large-scale breaches of the peace and these, together with the political change in the administrative machinery, had undermined the prestige and power of the authorities. In November 1945 the agitation against the trial, by Court-Martial in Delhi, of certain members of Subhas Bose's Indian National Army had resulted in a clash with the police. The demonstrators were refused permission to lead a procession into the area of Dalhousie Square, and, when they insisted, the police opened fire on them. But they succeeded in breaking through the police cordon and marched in triumph through the prohibited area. This was followed by another demonstration in February 1946, when Abdul Rashid of the Indian National Army was sentenced to a term of imprisonment. On this occasion the military had to be called in to assist the police when the mob became unruly. In July 1946, a large and threatening mob collected in front of the Legislative Assembly and demanded the release of certain political prisoners. Some of the agitators pushed past the policemen on duty and invaded the Assembly building. They were persuaded to leave only when the Chief Minister assured them that he would examine the case of each prisoner and announce his decision within a short time. In the same month (July 1946) the Posts and Telegraph employees went on strike for several weeks and, on Monday, July 29, workers of all types observed a general strike in sympathy with the strikers. "In Calcutta on that day there were no trams, no buses, no taxis, not even rickshaws. Shops were closed and offices, Government and commercial, were heavily picketed. Picketers .... turned away a number of Secretaries and at least one Minister, while the police, under orders not to precipitate a clash which would undoubtedly have involved a general conflagration, looked on. The life of the city was brought to a standstill and thousands of strikers took charge of the city and went where they pleased." †

---

* Note on the Causes of the Calcutta Disturbances, August 1946, published by the Government of Bengal, Home Department, in 1946.

† *Ibid.*

Mr. Suhrawardy was the Minister in charge of the portfolio of Law and Order and this state of affairs was known to him. He expatiated on this theme at considerable length when defending himself in the Bengal Legislative Assembly in the course of a debate on a no-confidence motion. In planning the programme of Direct Action Day he decided to make use of it in shaping the course of events. The fact that in Calcutta the Hindus were in the majority did not deter Mr. Suhrawardy from accepting the responsibility of making a success of the Direct Action Day. Indeed this was an incentive and put him on his mettle. He decided to show to the world what a Muslim minority could do when they were determined to use violence and gangster methods, and the *Dawn* drew the attention of its readers to this circumstance after the events in Calcutta had taken place.* Thus the position of the League Ministry in Bengal, the importance of Calcutta and the weakness of the Administrative Authority made Calcutta eminently suitable for a demonstration of violence on Direct Action Day. Mr. Suhrawardy was just the man for this purpose and he undertook to implement the decision of the League in a befitting manner. It was, therefore, in Calcutta, and Calcutta alone, that so much violence and hooliganism were displayed on Direct Action Day.

Mr. Suhrawardy undertook to shape the course of events in Calcutta in a manner calculated to inspire awe in the minds of the non-Muslims and to demonstrate to the world at large the strength and solidarity of the protagonists of Pakistan. As Minister in charge of the portfolio of Law and Order, he made arrangements for the transfer of Hindu police officers from all key posts. On August 16, twenty-two police stations out of a total of twenty-four were in charge of Muslim officials and the remaining two were controlled by Anglo-Indians. The programme for the fateful day was taken up with feverish activity. On August 4, a conference of the Executive Committees of the Calcutta District and City Muslim Leagues and representatives of Branch Leagues, Mohalia Sardars and labour workers of Calcutta, Howrah, Hoogly, Metiabruz and 24-Parganas was called to consider the matter. A programme was drawn up and this was later elaborated and given the widest publicity in the Muslim Press. Leaflets and pamphlets over the name of Mr. S. M. Usman, Mayor of Calcutta and

---

* The *Dawn*, August 17, 1946, in its editorial " Even Now."

Secretary of the Calcutta Muslim League, were printed and distributed. It was announced in the Press that these could be obtained free of cost from the Muslim League Office at 8, Zakaria Street, Calcutta.

The published programme called for a total *hartal* and complete cessation of business on August 16. To this end Mr. Suhrawardy's Government declared August 16 a public holiday throughout the province. There was naturally considerable opposition to this proposal and it was said that a public holiday would let loose a considerable number of *goondas* and irresponsible characters. An industrial city like Calcutta has a large population of millhands, dockyard workers, casual labour, mischief-makers and professional agitators whose energies are, on ordinary days, expended in the performance of constructive work. To draw them away from their business, send them into the streets and tell them to agitate was tantamount to unleashing the forces of lawlessness and destruction. When the matter came up for discussion in the Legislative Assembly this fact was pointed out to the Ministry. Mr. Suhrawardy's Government, however, ignored the protests of the opposition and, disregarding wiser counsels, determined to carry on with the prearranged programme. Indeed Mr. Suhrawardy suggested that the step contemplated was in the interests of the people, for they would be available to defend themselves and their families instead of being away from home, and leaving their women and children to the mercy of the rioters.

The *hartal* contemplated was to be complete. It was to take the form of a general strike in all spheres of civic, commercial and industrial life. In the published programme it was said that the essential services of water-works, hospitals, physicians' clinics, maternity centres, light, electricity, gas and postal services would continue to function as usual.. This exception was, however, in form only, for when Direct Action began on August 16, the civic life of Calcutta was so completely paralysed that the " essential services " found it impossible to function for several days. Non-Muslims were also exhorted to join the *hartal* and " make common cause with the League in its fight." A mass rally and meeting were to be held at the foot of the Ochterlony Monument from 3 p.m. onwards and Mr. Suhrawardy was to preside over it. The Mayor of Calcutta wanted a million Muslims to congregate in the maidan and give evidence of their united strength. The programme reminded the Muslims of what stuff they were made:

" Muslims must remember that it was in Ramzan that the Quran was revealed. It was in Ramzan that the permission for Jehad was granted by Allah. It was in Ramzan that the battle of Badr, the first open conflict between Islam and Heathenism was fought and won by 313 Muslims ; and again it was in Ramzan that 10,000 under the Holy Prophet conquered Mecca and established the kingdom of Heaven and the commonwealth of Islam in Arabia. The Muslim League is fortunate that it is starting its action in this holy month."

The leaflets issued by Mr. Usman were in the same strain. An Urdu circular bearing the title " Manifesto " contained the following exhortation : —

" Brethren of Islam,
Please explain this circular to the people of your *ilaqa, mohalla,* in mosques, schools, colleges, clubs, tea-stalls and hotels. Ask them to awake, arise and unite under the banner of the Muslim League and make this *hartal* a success. Assemble at the foot of the Ochterlony Monument in processions with the accompaniment of bands at 3 p.m. Lead the procession with such strength and enthusiasm that even the blind, deaf and dumb can appreciate their strength and determination."

Another leaflet containing a special prayer for the crusade is worth quoting in full.

" MUNAJAT FOR THE JEHAD.
(To be said at every mosque after the Jumma prayer.)

It was in this month of Ramzan that the Holy Quran was revealed ! It was in this month of Ramzan that 313 Muslims were victorious through the grace of God over many *Kafers* in the battle of Badr and the *Jehad* of the Muslims commenced ! It was in this month that ten thousand Muslims marched to Mecca and were conquerors and thus there was the establishment of the Kingdom of Islam.

By the grace of God we are ten crores in India but through bad luck we have become slaves of the Hindus and the British. We are starting a *Jehad* in Your Name in this very month of Ramzan. We promise before You that we entirely depend on You. Pray make us strong in body and mind—give Your helping hand in all our actions—make us victorious over the

Kafers—enable us to establish the Kingdom of Islam in India and make proper sacrifices for this *Jehad*—by the grace of God may we build up in India the greatest Islamic kingdom in the world.

The Muslims in China, Manchuria, Mongolia, Malaya, Java and Sumatra are all fighting for their freedom—pray by Your grace they may succeed. May You bring freedom to the Muslims of Turkey, Iran, Iraq, Albania, Arabia, Egypt and the Sudan and also to the Muslims of Tunis, Algiers, Morocco, Africa. May God help us so that Muslims of the world may be able to build up a very strong Islamic kingdom in this world.

(Then followed some Arabic quotations from Quran and Hadis.)

Note.—This form of prayer should be kept with care—must not be touched with the foot or dishonoured in any way."

A Bengali pamphlet ' Mugur ' (Club) concluded with a passionate appeal :

" The Bombay resolution of the All-India Muslim League has been broadcast. The call to revolt comes to us from the Qaid-e-Azam of the Muslim leaders. Braves, this is what we want. This is the policy for the nation of heroes. For so long we have been acting like beggars. We are glad from the core of our hearts to hear this magnificent news. This is what we have been eagerly waiting for. God has granted to the Muslims in the month of Ramzan what they have been clamouring for. The day for an open fight which is the greatest desire of the Muslim nation has arrived. Come, those who want to rise to heaven. Come those who are simple, wanting in peace of mind and who are in distress. *Those who are thieves, goondas, those without the strength of character and those who do not say their prayers—all come.* (Italics ours.) The shining gates of heaven have been opened for you. Let us enter in thousands. Let us all cry out victory to Pakistan, victoy to the Mulim nation and victory to the army which has declared a *Jehad.*"

A leaflet bearing a picture of Mr. Jinnah with a sword in hand, said : —

" The sword of Islam must be shining on the heavens and will subdue all evil designs. . . . We Muslims have had the Crown and have ruled. Do not lose heart. Be ready and take your swords. Think you, Muslims, why we are under the *kafirs* today. The result of loving the *kafirs* is not good. O *kafir* ! Do not be proud and happy. Your doom is not far and the general massacre will come. We shall show our glory with swords in hands and will have a special victory."

Another leaflet asked the Muslims to come into the arena with their swords and change their tactics. "We shall then see who will play with us, for rivers of blood will flow. We shall have the swords in our hands and the noise of *takbir*. Tomorrow will be doom's day."

*   *   *   *

As August 16 approached, the tempo and volume of the preparations increased. Ward Committee meetings were held frequently in various Wards of Calcutta. Transport for League volunteers and Muslim hooligans was arranged. Petrol rationing difficulties were overcome by obtaining supplementary coupons issued to the Ministers personally just before Direct Action Day. A large number of regulation lathis and lethal weapons were imported. In the Basti in Mission Row, Hindu and Muslim cobblers had been living in peace and amity. Suddenly on August 10, the Hindus saw that the Muslims were supplied with *lathis,* spears and daggers. This early discovery made them run away and escape to safety. The *goondas* and bad characters were mobilized. Large numbers of them were imported from outside. A few days before the due date Pathans and suspicious characters were seen prowling about the streets of Calcutta. Mr. Kiron Shankar Roy drew the attention of the police to this circumstance and warned them that the presence of these strange men did not augur well for the peace of Calcutta. Hundreds of bad characters who were in detention during the World War had been released by Government and this force with all its destructive power was available to carry out the behests of the League agitators.

The League leaders made arrangements to treat any persons who might be injured in the riots. Mr. Abdul Wahed Choudhuri, described as the D.G.O.C., Pakistan Ambulance Corps, was called upon to mobilize his men. He took steps to open a First Aid Centre at Curzon Park near the maidan where the mass rally was to be held. He further ordered that five First Aid Units must be held in reserve and an ambulance car bearing flags with a red crescent on a white background should circulate through the city on Direct Action Day. It was also arranged that every major procession should have its own First Aid equipment. Two League representatives were posted at each of the Medical College

Hospitals and also at the Campbell Hospital. Representatives were to hold themselves in readiness to go to other hospitals if necessity arose. It was announced that information about the condition of patients could be obtained at the Calcutta office of the Pakistan Ambulance Corps. These extensive arrangements are indicative not merely of a prudent foresight, but are clear proof of the fact that the local League leaders had foreknowledge of what would happen on Direct Action Day, and had taken steps to provide facilities for the treatment of their injured and wounded.

All kinds of weapons were distributed to the agitators, and the Muslim mobs who formed processions early on the morning of August 16 and paraded the streets were seen to be armed not only with *lathis* but with spears, daggers, hatchets and, in some cases, even firearms. The *goondas* of Howrah were given *lathis* and other weapons through Sharif Khan, M.L.A., who was a trusted henchman of Mr. Suhrawardy. Sharif Khan had been previously convicted of homicide but was later elected as a Member of the Legislative Assembly because he controlled the *goondas* of Howrah. Mr. Usman, the Mayor of Calcutta, visited Howrah with Sharif Khan and incited the people to violent action. On Direct Action Day a huge procession of Muslims armed with *lathis,* spears, daggers, etc., left Howrah for Calcutta to attend the meeting at the Ochterlony Monument. The Control Room at Calcutta was not informed of this circumstance. At 4-30 p.m. this crowd was seen returning to Howrah and was stopped by a European Superintendent of Police at the bridge. They were disarmed and *lathis,* spears, daggers, knives, unburnt torches, empty soda water bottles, tins containing kerosene oil, rags soaked in oil, ready for being used in setting fire to houses, were collected. They filled three trucks and were taken to the Golabari Police Station in Howrah. They were later shown to Mr. Justice Spens, President of the Calcutta Disturbances Enquiry Commission. It is impossible to believe that these men had come out armed in this manner on their own initiative and without any specific instructions having been issued to them in this respect.

Events in the political field had in the meantime proceeded according to a prearranged plan. Negotiations between the Viceroy and Mr. Nehru for the formation of an Interim Government had been started. Mr. Jinnah was invited to participate in these talks. The Viceroy's latest formula offered five seats out of fourteen to the Muslim League and six to the Congress. The remaining three were to be filled up by nomination. Mr. Jinnah had already made up his mind, and spurned this offer of more than 35 per cent League representation in the Central Government. When it was realized, contrary to expectation, that Mr. Jinnah's refusal had failed to bring about the desired deadlock ; and the negotiations proceeded in the absence of the Muslim League, the League leaders gave unrestrained expression to their chagrin. Mr. Suhrawardy immediately raised the standard of rebellion and declared that if the Congress were put in power he would set up an independent and parallel Government in Bengal. No part of the provincial revenues would be paid to the Centre and Bengal would become a separate State having no connection with the rest of India. On the same day Mr. Mohammad Usman, the Mayor of Calcutta, told the representative of the Orient Press that Muslims in Bengal were fully prepared.

On August 13 it was announced that the Viceroy had invited Mr. Nehru to form an Interim Government and on the 15th the breakdown of negotiations between Mr. Jinnah and Mr. Nehru was made known to the public. On the morning of the 16th the *Dawn* brought out a four-page supplement telling its readers that the day for Direct Action had arrived and that "might alone could now secure the right" of Muslims.

*   *   *   *

The progress of these events gave rise to grave apprehensions in the minds of the Bengal Hindus. It was feared that the celebrations of Direct Action Day would inevitably result in extensive clashes between the two major communities. The desire of the Muslim League (as indicated in the published programme) that non-Muslims should also join the *hartal* was resented by the other political parties. The Bengal Provincial Congress Committee characterized the demonstration as communal and anti-national. They took exception to August 16 being declared a public holiday and called upon the nation to protest against the prostitution of governmental authority in order to secure personal and party aims. Surendra Mohan Ghosh, President of the Bengal Provincial Congress Committee, issued a statement on August 15 advising the public to remain peaceful and telling those who did not wish to join in the League demonstration to go about their usual business. A leaflet issued by the Hindu Mahasabha was more categorical.

"The Hindus and non-Muslims of Bengal are strongly opposed to the demand for Pakistan. Under the circumstances, to join or to assist in the *hartal* declared by the Muslim League will amount to supporting the Pakistan demand. The Hindus of Bengal can never act in this way. The League Ministry has had the audacity to declare the day as a public holiday. The object is obvious. By this action they mean to compel the Hindu Government servants to join the *hartal*. The Hindus will have to give a clear answer to this act of effrontery. It is the duty of every Hindu to carry on as usual his normal occupation. The Hindus must make organised efforts to see that no Hindu, non-Muslim or non-League Muslim is forced to join the *hartal*. We, therefore, request the public to continue on that day their normal work. They must not yield to any coercive measures. Remember that to join the *hartal* is to support the demand for Pakistan."

This leaflet marks a certain amount of stiffening in the Hindu attitude towards the League propaganda.

*   *   *   *

The police had received secret information that trouble was afoot. According to the Report of the Commissioner of Police on the Calcutta disturbances, the information received by the Intelligence Department was:

(a) A report that *goonda* elements among the Muslims might create disturbances if non-Muslims did not observe the *hartal* ; and

(b) a report that instructions had been issued to several Muslim hostels to make preparations to set fire to tramcars and military lorries on the 16th.*

There can be no doubt that police information extended much further. Even the military were not wholly ignorant of the extent and nature of the League agitation. When giving evidence before the Spens Enquiry Commission, Brigadier Sixsmith, who was then acting as Area Commander, said that on August 10 General Bucher sent for him and warned him of the possibility of trouble on Muslim League Direct Action Day. General Bucher advised Brigadier Sixsmith to make himself thoroughly conversant with arrangements in the area for internal defence and duties in aid of the civil power. Mr. Suhrawardy later denied that any reports of " preparedness on the part of either the Hindus or the Muslims " were available, but it was in view of these warnings and fears that

---

* Report of the Commissioner of Police on the disturbances and the action taken by the Calcutta Police between the 16th and 20th of August 1946 inclusive, published by the Government of Bengal, Home Department (Political) in 1946.

the Commissioner of Police issued orders to the whole police force on August 15 to "take emergency action." This entailed the establishment of a Control Room at Police Headquarters where information of disturbances from all parts of the city could be received and classified, and correlated mobilization at Headquarters of all Inspectors and Sergeants, of all available constables from the Reserve Force. Further, all Inspectors and Sergeants of Security Control and the Public Vehicles Department, the Traffic Police and all Armed Police, not engaged in essential duties, were to hold themselves in readiness.

*   *   *   *

Such were the hopes and expectations, the fears and forebodings which possessed the citizens of Calcutta when they retired to rest on the evening of August 15. The night brought little rest to many of them and, shortly after dawn, a feverish activity began to spread throughout the vast city. The skies were dark and lowering, but rain held off till the evening, and any slight discouragement that the inclemency of the monsoon weather might have provided was spared the League demonstrators. Unruly crowds, numbering at first not more than fifty or sixty, carrying flags and banners and armed with sticks, daggers, spears and hatchets began roaming about the main streets. They were shouting slogans and inviting their Muslim brethren to join them. As their numbers swelled they became bolder and more provocative. Whenever they saw an open shop they ordered the owner to close it at once. If this peremptory demand was not complied with immediately, the shop-keeper was beaten and his goods were looted or thrown out into the street. The unfortunate victims were almost invariably Hindus for all Muslim shops were observing *hartal*. Anyone seen cycling or motoring was stopped and told to walk. If he showed reluctance or offered resistance he was assaulted and the tyres of his vehicle were deflated. The transport services had suspended business and no trams or buses were running; taxis were off the roads, and apart from a few individuals whose ignorance or hardihood had brought them out, the only vehicles to be seen were Muslim League lorries or jeeps. These, laden with armed hooligans, shouting League slogans, went about the streets freely, encouraging the mobs or issuing directions. The privilege of free movement enjoyed by them indicated a well-laid plan and their numbers evidenced the extent of the League resources.

5

As early as 6 a.m. reports began to pour into the Police
Control Room. The eleven telephones, installed in two separate
rooms, rang so frequently and brought forth so many tales of
distress, so many calls for help and such a stream of appeals for
rescue that it was impossible to keep even a brief record of the
countless messages received. The Police Deputy Commissioner,
Headquarters, himself received over 1,200 such messages. It was
impossible to maintain accurate figures of the crimes committed
during the first four days of this bloody fight or to send assistance
where it was needed most. The resources of the Calcutta Police
were quite unequal to the magnitude of the task involved. The
available police force was both insufficient and inadequate to
cope with the nature and the extent of the disturbances which
held the life of the city in a murderous grip. There can, however, be no doubt that the criminal apathy of the police officials
and the failure of those in authority to deploy the available forces
to the best advantage were mainly responsible for the holocaust
which followed. For two days the police were almost completely
inactive or evasive. Appeals for assistance were answered with,
"We have no orders." Policemen stood watching the burning
and looting of houses with calm indifference. A house opposite
a Traffic Outpost where over a hundred police officers were present was completely ransacked. The Mallick Bazaar was looted
by a mob of hooligans who ran about displaying their booty with
a great show of exultant joy. Police guards joined the looters
in this merry-making. Mr. Fazlul Haq, speaking on the no-
confidence motion in the Legislative Assembly, complained
bitterly of police attitude during the first two days of the riots.
He could not get into touch with the police officers or secure
their assistance.* There were numerous complaints of deliberate
inaction on the part of subordinate police officials of a number
of *thanas*. Timely action in disarming the riotous mobs in the
morning could perhaps have averted serious trouble, but once
the assaults and clashes began, the situation was completely out
of hand and only a determined action by a large military force
could save the city. Unfortunately, the military was not called
until the evening of the 17th, and by that time a great deal of
irreparable damage had been done. For a day and a half the

---

* Mr. Fazlul Haq voted against the no-confidence motion though his speech contained
a violent attack on Mr. Suhrawardy's administration. See Note (ii) to Chapter II in
Appendix I for extracts from the speeches of Messrs. Fazlul Haq and Dhirendra Narayan
Mukherji.

Muslim rioters held their own. The tide of the battle then began to turn and Hindus and Sikhs began to hit back. It was only when this change began to spell disaster for the Muslims, that military assistance was summoned. It was mentioned before the Spens Enquiry Commission that the Civil authorities had been guilty of gross dereliction of duty in failing to call in the military on the afternoon of the 16th when the situation had deteriorated to such an extent that the police were quite unable to deal with it. It was said that, in the February riots of the same year, the military had been called in at once. To add to the embarrassment of the Police Chiefs, Mr. Suhrawardy arrived in the Control Room and established himself there for the space of several hours. He received messages, gave verbal directions, issued written instructions or orders, scribbled on scraps of paper, talked to the Police Heads, overrode the decisions made by them, received visitors, discussed the political events with them and generally interrupted the vital business of those in charge of the Control Room. He ordered that special protection should be given to all mosques and that police pickets should be posted at each one of them ; but nothing was to be done to safeguard the inmates, sanctity or property of any Hindu shrine. He assured the Commissioner of Police that the situation would improve after he had addressed the gathering in the maidan. He would tell the Muslims to go home quietly and they would obey him. When his eloquence failed to soothe the frenzied masses and produce the calm he could not have hoped for, he returned to the Control Room and continued his mischievous activities. Towards evening Inspector Wade, on patrol with a lorry detachment, arrested eight Muslims for looting in Mallick Bazaar Market. Some of the looters were wearing Red Cross bands to give them immunity from police action. The arrested persons and a lorry in which the looted goods were being stocked were taken to the Park Street Police Station. Shortly afterwards Mr. Suhrawardy arrived at the police station and ordered the immediate release of the miscreants on his personal responsibility.* The same evening he reported that firearms had been used against Muslim passers-by by Messrs. Lal Chand and Sons, Ammunition Dealers. The Additional Deputy Commissioner, Security Control, at once went to the spot to

---

* This incident was referred to in the Assembly debate which took place in the month of September. Dr. Shyama Prasad Mookerjee accused the Premier of having set at liberty *goondas* who had been caught red-handed, looting property. Mr. Suhrawardy retorted that Dr. Shyama Prasad Mookerjee himself was a *goonda*. He later admitted having ordered the release of these men.

investigate. He found that this complaint was false and, on his return, reported that a Muslim mob had attacked the shop and attempted to set fire to it. Messrs. Lal Chand and Sons complained that they had sent a message to the police station asking for help but their appeal had been disregarded. The Chief Minister's presence and conduct in the Control Room were a serious impediment to the work of the Police and Army chiefs and a complaint to this effect was made to His Excellency the Governor. A desire was expressed that Mr. Suhrawardy should keep away from the Control Room.

* * * *

It is impossible to give a complete and accurate picture of the Great Calcutta Killing as it came to be called. The reports received by the police were not always true. The noise of a disturbance in the next street, the shouting of slogans from a passing lorry, or the sight of an approaching mob frequently lent substance to an imaginary fear and spread panic through a whole street ; and messages of an actual attack having taken place were sent to the Control Room. On the other hand, hundreds of incidents, some of them the most terrible, went unreported, because the blow fell before anyone could communicate to the authorities or because the injury sustained was past all redress. The local police were in some cases unsympathetic. One police station shut its doors against all appeals for help. When the Commissioner of Police arrived he found the premises closed and the gate barred. Hundreds of messages received could not be recorded and were completely forgotten. Rumours of all kinds, based partly on hearsay but largely on the imagination of the speaker, were accepted as true by a credulous people. Things unprecedented in the whole history of communal warfare were happening all over Calcutta and nothing was beyond belief. The newspaper reporters went round the city under armed protection and tried to give accurate accounts of what they saw, but they could not be everywhere at the same time, and they could not enter the worst affected areas. The Commissioner of Police drew up an official report based on information conveyed to the police and this document is a long and sordid catalogue of crime and human passions at their basest; but it does not pretend to be complete. It reads like the defence plea of a person accused of neglecting his duty. The Spens Enquiry Commission heard a great deal of evidence and brought to light many things, but it

Jawaharlal Nehru and Mohammed Jinnah taking a walk in the garden at the latter's residence.

Mahatma Gandhi and Mohammed Jinnah leaving the latter's residence en route for Delhi for talks with the Viceroy.

Lord and Lady Mountbatten with Mahatma Gandhi.

Sardar Baldev Singh, Minister of Punjab Government in New Delhi.

His Highness The Nawab of Bahawalpur in his regalia.

Sir Richard Crofton, Prime Minister of Bahawalpur with the Nawab (far left).

Mountbatten discloses the Partition of India plan. From left to right, Jawaharlal Nehru, Lord Ismay, Lord Mountbatten, and Mohammed Jinnah.

Bahawalpur station with refugees boarding a train.

Sir Penderel Moon taking tea with Rajendra Prasad, the first President of the Indian Republic, on the verandah of the Viceregal Lodge at Simla.

The second Marquess of Linlithgow, Viceroy Designate of India, leaving his home in London with the Marchioness, en route to India.

*The Cabinet Mission and Jinnah, from left to right, A.V. Alexander,
Mohammed Jinnah, and Lord Pethick-Lawrence.*

A special train used to take Delhi Muslims to Pakistan.

Nehru moves the resolution for an independent Republic in the Constituent Assembly at New Delhi.

was not allowed to conclude its labours and the hearing was brought to an abrupt end by an order of the League Ministry who expressed the opinion that further progress of the Enquiry was likely to exacerbate communal feelings. Some people held the view that the Enquiry had brought forth a great deal of incriminating matter not very palatable to the Chief Minister and his colleagues.

It is not our business here to give full and complete details of the horrible events transacted in Calcutta during these days. Such an undertaking is neither possible nor within the scope of this book. There is nothing that distinguishes the looting and burning of a shop in one street from the looting and burning of another shop in another street. One case of stabbing is very like another. The frenzied mobs behaved in very much the same way in different parts of Calcutta. For individual details the reader is referred to a study of the Police Commissioner's Report and the proceedings of the Spens Enquiry Commission. It will suffice to give in these pages a general outline of the over-all picture and mention a few of the more important incidents.

Reference has already been made to the forcible closing of Hindu shops as the immediate exciting cause of the disturbances. All over Calcutta Muslim crowds demanded the closure of non-Muslim shops. If the slightest resistance was offered the shop was looted and burnt. Very soon the crowds began to break open closed shops and loot them. It is significant that many Muslim shops had been marked in chalk with "Mussalman shop —Pakistan " to save them from the attentions of the mob and this circumstance was mentioned as proving a previous plan to loot all non-Muslim shops. The Muslim League demonstrators soon came into clash with Hindu crowds, and general rioting of a most fierce type broke out in all parts of Calcutta. The houses of prominent Hindus and Congressmen became a special target of the Muslim fury. The house of Dr. B. C. Roy,* Congress leader, was attacked and set on fire. The son-in-law of Mr. Kiron Shankar Roy, leader of the Bengal Congress Parliamentary Party, was stabbed. The office of the Bengal Provincial Congress Committee was heavily stoned. The offices of the News Editor of *Hindusthan Standard* and the *Ananda Bazar Patrika* were attacked and attempts were made to set fire to the buildings.

---

* The present Premier of the Province of West Bengal.

Five garages in Mechubazar Street were broken open and set on fire.   In the Central Avenue a crowd was observed standing round a number of cars.   One of these had already been set on fire when the police arrived.   The fires in Amherst Street section were reported to be very severe.   In the area of Shampukur Police Station several lorries, full of Muslims and loaded with tins of petrol, were seen moving about.   A house in Tara Chand Dutt Street was burnt and it was still on fire on the following day.   The Park Street Police saw a large mob of Muslims carrying sticks with kerosene-soaked rags attached to them.   From a house in Umadas Lane the police recovered a quantity of kerosene-soaked rags, two bottles of nitric acid and a number of soda water bottles and battle axes.   The house belonged to a Muslim and two Muslims were arrested from the premises.   The Regent Cinema was set on fire.   On August 17, Inspector Kinchin found a crowd of Muslims with blazing torches setting fire to the huts near Manicktola Bridge.   The Fire Brigade found it extremely difficult to control these fires because of persistent interference by the Muslim crowds.   The fire engines could only go about with armed escorts but even so they could not always perform their task.   It was found that several hydrants had been opened by the rioters and the consequent decrease in the water pressure created further difficulties.

The house of Mr. D. L. Dutt, Presidency Magistrate, was attacked.   Even Muslims who were known to be supporters of the Congress were not spared.   The residence of Syed Nausher Ali, former Speaker of the Bengal Legislative Assembly, was attacked by a mob on the afternoon of the 16th.   Police help was sent and Syed Nausher Ali informed Inspector Kinchin that he had been flying Congress colours from his house and local Muslims had taken exception to it.   They wanted to take down the Congress flag and fly the Muslim League flag in its place.   There was frequent interference with police lorries.   In at least one instance the police were seen to be taking part in the looting.   On receiving a report of looting in Wellesley Street the Deputy Commissioner, Special Branch, went to the spot in a jeep with two orderlies and a Sergeant-Major armed with tommy guns.   "Arriving at the shop of Sen Law's on the corner of Royd Street and Wellesley Street, the Deputy Commissioner found it was being looted by a mixed mob of Anglo-Indians and Indians.   Outside stood an empty police weapon-carrier and inside, the Deputy Commissioner reports having found three Police Sergeants passively watching the looters and taking no preventive action.* The crowd was driven away but as soon as the Deputy Commissioner, Special Branch, moved away, the looters again entered the shop.

A number of temples were attacked and burnt down. Among these was the Radhakrishna Temple on Cornwallis Road and the Sitla Temple in College Street. The Science College and the Hindu houses in its neighbourhood were persistently attacked for several hours. A mob of Muslim hooligans entered the Carmichael Medical College and began to threaten patients and nurses. An attack was made on the Medical College Hostel in the jurisdiction of Jorasanko Police Station. A number of cars and lorries, marked with the Red Cross or flying Red Cross flags, were going about killing people and looting shops. The looting and killing went on continuously for forty hours in some localities and this sustained energy of the fanatical mobs was an astonishing feature of the riots. The streets were strewn with dead bodies and the corpses lay thus for several days giving out a foul stench. The task of disposing of the corpses seemed at first impossible because there was no one to carry them away and bury or cremate them. The *domes* who usually perform this work had run away and their *bustees* were found to be deserted. Dozens of dead bodies were pushed down manholes and obstructed the sewage of the city. Dead bodies were seen floating in the river. A number of boats had been burnt and sunk and the boatmen were killed or drowned. Bodies lay in houses where they had been done to death. There were stories of children having been hurled down from the roofs of houses. Young children were reported to have been boiled in oil. Others were burnt alive. Women were raped and mutilated and then murdered. A number of hooligans were seen going about the streets, robbing the pockets of dead men. On the other hand, there were many instances of Muslims giving protection to Hindus and Hindus giving protection to Muslims. At Tiretta Bazar the police found three Hindus in the house of Muslims who had given shelter to them. On the evening of August 18 four Sikhs went to the Police Headquarters and stated that they had hidden a number of threatened Muslims in their house and requested that the Muslims be removed so that the Sikhs might not be victimized. The police took a prison van to the house and evacuated fifteen male Muslims from the Sikhs' quarters.

---

* Report of the Commissioner of Police.

For four terrible days this massacre and brutality continued unabated. During this time the life of the city was completely paralysed. Hospitals were full of patients and streams of injured men continued to pour in. The Lake Hospital, recently vacated by the United States Army, was taken over and a number of patients were accommodated there. It was, however, impossible to cope with the number of injured persons and the medical arrangements all but broke down. The problem of feeding the patients and thousands of refugees who had crowded in the hospital compounds was a formidable one. Students and doctors living outside the hospitals, in hostels, sought shelter in hospital buildings and they had to be fed. The total admissions, according to the Report of the Surgeon-General, were well over four thousand. Of these some had been brought in dead while others died in hospital.

The rescue of persons in dangerous localities was another serious problem. Once the disturbances began, Muslims living in Hindu majority areas and Hindus living in Muslim majority areas wanted to be evacuated. They did not dare to venture out without proper escort. Rescue Squads were organized but the transport available was quite inadequate to cope with the demand. It is estimated that over thirty thousand people were moved before the end of the fourth day of the riots. Thousands more left the city of their own accord although this was not easy as the train services had been completely disorganized. The newspaper reporters estimated an exodus of a hundred thousand persons from Calcutta.

Food and sanitation arrangements were completely upset. Many grain ration shops were looted and for four days it was almost impossible to maintain supplies in the city. Although there was no interference with the filtered water-supply, the unfiltered water-supply for sanitary fittings was interrupted in certain sections of the city owing to the low water pressure in the mains because the hydrants were left open by the people. Garbage and rubbish went on piling up in the streets as the Corporation Conservancy Staff did not report for duty. Bleaching powder was sprinkled by military lorries on the rubbish heaps and human and animal corpses, but for days the stench of the city was unbearable.

Until August 18 nothing could be done to remove the dead bodies from the streets. The Government then gave consideration to this matter and, with the assistance of the Anjuman Mofidul Islam and the Hindu Satkar Samiti, began to tackle the problem.

It was decided that all bodies dealt by the Government Organization should be buried. A small force of sixteen *domes* was requisitioned and this proceeded to pick up the dead bodies at 9 p.m. on the 18th. The *domes* worked through the night and lorries, loaded with dead bodies, were taken to the Bagmari Cemetery. The approach to the graves was too narrow for the lorries and the dead bodies had to be transferred to hand-carts and wheeled for nearly a quarter of a mile. The *domes* were now tired out and the dead bodies had to be left unburied. The next day the work was resumed and, with the assistance of Mr. Justice Sharpe and Mr. Justice Hindley of the Calcutta High Court, who volunteered for this extremely unpleasant work, a number of bodies were buried. Some Anglo-Indians later came forward to handle the dead bodies on payment. It was learnt that *domes* would be more willing to work when stimulated by a country liquor known as *paglapani*. This was provided and the work of disposing of the dead bodies proceeded. Corpses were recovered from streets, houses, temples, mosques, manholes, the river and the canals and buried in large trenches. The Hindu Satkar Samiti cremated over a thousand bodies. By the 27th almost all the dead bodies had been disposed of. High Government officials including two High Court Judges already named, Mr. Mitra of the Indian Civil Service, Mr. Auden of the Geological Survey, Mr. Hodge of the B.A. Railway, worked for hours at a stretch, in an overpowering stench, to accomplish this task. But for *paglapani* and liberal payment to the *domes,* beer and high wages to the Anglo-Indians who handled the corpses, this work could not have been performed. The following table gives the number of dead bodies collected and disposed of :

By Government Organization	...	...	...	1,182
By Anjuman Mofidul Islam	...	...	...	761
By Hindu Satkar Samiti	...	...	...	1,230
			Total ...	3,173

This figure does not represent the total number of deaths caused in the riots. Many dead bodies were burnt in houses, many others floated down the river to the sea. The loss of property by arson and looting was estimated at several crores. Accurate figures are not available but an examination of the individual reports submitted by Fire officers who supervised action at the various fires shows that the ownership of the various properties which suffered from arson is in the following ratio:

(a) Hindu ownership   ...   . 65 per cent
(b) Muslim ownership   ...   . 20 per cent
(c) Ownership either joint Hindu/Muslim
    not known, European or Government. 15 per cent*

Comparative figures of persons wounded or killed in the course of the riots are not available. The report of the Surgeon-General based on the admissions to the various hospitals is to the following effect:

A. *Classified*

	Admissions	Brought in dead	Deaths
Hindus	2,322	11	151
Muslims	1,832	12	138
Others	222	11	62

B. *Unclassified*

Brought in dead   174
Deaths   11

These figures give a total of 570 dead only. It is estimated that more than five thousand persons were killed and more than fifteen thousand injured, and if the hospital figures are accepted as a basis for determining the ratio of the Muslim and Hindu casualties it will be clear that the Muslims fared almost as badly the Hindus. When this circumstance came to light the Muslim League leaders and the Muslim League Press asserted vehemently that the rioting was started by the supporters of the Congress and some of them even went so far as to say that the Hindus had prepared a deeply laid plan to commit wholesale murder of Muslims on Direct Action Day in order to discredit the Muslim League. On the other hand, it was said that the Muslims had an efficient transport and ambulance corps and all their dead and injured were taken to hospital, while Hindu dead bodies were for the most part burnt or destroyed and, therefore, did not figure in the official statistics.

*   *   *   *

It is convenient here to anticipate the chronology of events and say a few words about what happened in Calcutta during the following twelve months. Complete peace did not return to the

---

* Report of the Commissioner of Police.

city even after the fury of these four days was over. There were days on which no incidents took place. Then followed days and weeks during which stray and sporadic assaults were reported from different quarters of the city. On some days there were as many as ten murders. Muslims and non-Muslims both took part in these criminal acts. In the beginning of August 1947, when the partition of the province was imminent and the Government of the future East Bengal was ready to leave Calcutta, attacks on Muslims increased. Calcutta appeared to be on the verge of another catastrophe similar to the one in which it had been plunged a year previously. Mahatma Gandhi then came to the rescue and decided to live in Calcutta until peace was restored. Accompanied by Mr. Suhrawardy, he took up his residence in the house of a Muslim and, braving the anger of the Hindus, began to preach his gospel of non-violence. On one occasion a Hindu mob attacked the house in which he was living and a *lathi* was actually thrown at him. He stood his ground undaunted and his courage worked a veritable miracle in Calcutta. Sanity returned to the people and on August 15, when the independence of India was celebrated in the city, Hindus and Muslims joined hands as brothers and went through the streets shouting " Hindu-Muslim *ek ho.*"

(ii)

The results of the Calcutta episode did not, in the ultimate analysis, prove very gratifying to the Muslim League leaders. The Hindus suffered grievously both in life and in property. Large numbers of them left their habitation and migrated to the neighbouring districts of West Bengal and Bihar. The exhibition of Muslim strength and solidarity had, however, failed to intimidate the non-Muslims. A large number of Muslims was killed or wounded and the damage to Muslim property was not inconsiderable. This was not what Mr. Suhrawardy or Mr. Usman had hoped for or anticipated. It was small consolation to lay the entire responsibility of the tragic events on the shoulders of the Congress. It was clear that Direct Action Day plans had miscarried and some vindication of this disastrous failure was necessary. The passions aroused in Calcutta found a more satisfying release in the district of Noakhali where Maulvi Ghulam Sarwar, an ex-M.L.A. and a religious Pir, succeeded in working up the Muslim passions by spreading grossly exaggerated stories of what had happened in Calcutta. In that city stray assaults had continued after August 20. On September 2, the day on which the Congress Interim Government assumed office, rioting broke out in the Muslim quarters in the city of Bombay and continued for several days, taking a toll of over two hundred killed and nearly a thousand injured. On September 5, the papers reported recrudescence of trouble at Calcutta and, during the weeks that followed, the tension showed no signs of easing. Then in the beginning of October Noakhali and Tippera were in flames.

* * * *

The district of Noakhali is a narrow strip of land 55 miles long and 22 miles broad, lying along the Bay of Bengal. It also includes a number of small islands situated in the Bay. Tippera lies to the north of Noakhali. The two districts are flanked by rivers and numerous streams flow through them. Towards the end of the monsoon, communications present serious difficulties and, in some parts, means of transport are restricted to small country boats which proceed along the hyacinth-covered waterways at the rate of one mile per hour. Travelling on foot in these areas is more speedy and often more convenient. A few roads also serve the two districts but when disturbances broke out the roads were breached in several places and some bridges were destroyed. The passage of cars and lorries was thus almost completey stopped. It is, therefore, not surprising that for some days no news of the great upheaval reached the outside world and it was not till October 14 that Calcutta heard of anything wrong or unusual occurring in Noakhali. By that date a great deal had happened. Hundreds of murders had been committed, thousands of women had been dishonoured and carried away or compelled to marry Muslims. Whole villages had been burnt down and razed to the ground. Almost the entire Hindu population of the district had been robbed of all they possessed and then forcibly converted to Islam.

Anti-Hindu propaganda was started in Noakhali towards the end of August. Meetings were held throughout the district on August 29 which was the occasion of the *Id* festival. Rumours were spread through the district that bands of armed Sikhs had been imported from outside with the object of assaulting and murdering Muslims. The Maulvis in their *waaz* (sermon) preached hatred against the non-Muslims and warned the Muslims to be on their guard. Soon afterwards looting of Hindu shops and houses in various parts of the district began.

Temples were desecrated and idols were broken. There were a few cases of forcible conversion. In the beginning of September Pir Ghulam Sarwar took a hand. This gentleman was originally opposed to the Muslim League and had openly disapproved of the *hartal* of August 16. He, however, joined the Muslim League in the first week of September and at once began to use all the influence at his command in disseminating unrest among his followers. He addressed large audiences and exhorted them to avenge the massacre of Muslims in Calcutta. He threatened police officers and told them to doctor the reports of his utterances. When the *Puja* festival drew near, Hindus travelling by boat were held up and deprived of their ornaments and valuables. Some dacoities were committed in Hindu houses in a number of villages in the district. There were reports of buffaloes being butchered in public near mosques and other places. Mr. Haran Chandra Ghosh Chowdhury, speaking on an adjournment motion in the Bengal Legislative Assembly on February 6, mentioned a number of incidents which took place between August 29 and October 10.

" Debi Prasanna Guha of Babupur was murdered on the *Id* day and the Congress office in front of his house was burnt to ashes ; one of his brothers and a servant were also assaulted.

" While fishing in the Feny River, a group of fishermen were attacked with deadly weapons resulting in the death of one and serious injuries to two others.

" Chandra Kumar Karmakar of Monpura was murdered near Jamalpur on the *Id* day.

" Jamini Dey, a servant of the hotel, while proceeding to Ghoshbag on the *Id* day, was murdered on the way. A dead body in a decomposed condition with his clothes was found later.

" Nine fishermen of Charuriah, less than a mile from the town, were seriously assaulted with deadly weapons. Seven of them were admitted into hospital. They were prevented from coming out and lodging any complaint with the police.

" Shops of Kamini Kumar Paul and Jadav Chandra Saha were looted at Chandraganj and Jadav Chandra Saha was beaten.

" Hindu shops of Koresh Munshi Hat in Feni Sub-division were looted.

" Three boats full of clothes were looted at Bholakot.

" Temple of the family diety of Harendra Ghose of Rajpur was desecrated by butchering a calf and throwing it inside the temple.

" Shiva Temple of Dr. Jadunath Majumdar of Chandipur was similarly desecrated.

" Family deities of Nagendra Majumdar and Rajkumar Choudhury of Dadpur were desecrated and stolen.

" Many Hindu shops and two pharmacies of Kankirhat were looted.

" All the properties of six or seven families of Kanur Char were looted.

" A gang armed with deadly weapons entered the house of Jadav Mojumdar of Karpara, assaulted Nakul Mojumdar and looted properties worth Rs. 1,500.

" Hindu shopkeepers of Tajmohammad Hat were victimised and driven away.

" Some Hindu shops of Shahapur Bazar were looted.

" Ashu Sen of Debsingpur was severely beaten near Tajumiarhat at Char Parbati.

" House of Sj. Prasanna Mohan Chakravorty, B.L., at Tatarkhil, was looted and Durga image was broken. A buffalo was butchered.

" Rajkumar Choudhury of Banspara was brutally assaulted on his way home.

" Durga images of Sj. Iswar Chandra Pathak, Kethuri, Sj. Kedareswar Chakravorty of Merkachar and Sj. Ananta Kumar De of Angrapara were also broken.

"Houses of Nabin Chandra Nath of Miralipur and of Radhacharan Nath of Latipur were raided. Nobin Chandra and Radha Charan and five members of his family were injured.

" Shop of Subal Chandra Banik of Nandanpur was looted at Sonapur Bazar."

The total population of the district is twenty-two lakhs of which 80 per cent are Muslims. The Hindu minority found itself completely helpless. Many of them did not dare to lodge any complaint with the police for fear of further oppression and harassment. Some complainants were actually harassed and assaulted because they had had the temerity to report against the Muslims. The disturbances spread and increased in intensity at a rapid rate and, in the beginning of October, Muslim mobs began attacking Hindu houses on the pretext of searching for Sikh and Hindu *goondas* who were alleged to have been brought to Noakhali for the purpose of attacking Muslims. Another method adopted was to make demands for large sums of money in order to relieve the sufferings of the Calcutta Muslims. In some cases, as much as a thousand rupees were demanded from an individual. The demand was almost invariably followed by looting and burning. A school master of Khilpara stated that his house was attacked in this manner by seven different gangs each numbering about three hundred or four hundred. All images and sacred pictures were desecrated and smashed and he and his family were then forcibly converted to Islam. This is typical of what was happening all over the district of Noakhali. A crowd of Muslims drawn from a number of contiguous villages would proceed to a chosen village, loot and burn all the Hindu houses and then convert the non-Muslim population to Islam *en masse,* on pain of death. They would carry away the womenfolk and give them in marriage to Muslims. It was estimated that at least 95 per cent of the non-Muslim population of Noakhali District was, in this manner, converted to Islam and their women dishonoured. The converted persons were made to read *kalma,* slaughter cows and eat their flesh. The conch-shell bangles of the women were broken and the *sandhoor* mark was removed before they were made to marry into Muslim families. The converted persons were given Muslim dress to wear including caps printed with League flags, a map of Pakistan and the slogan " Pakistan *Zindabad.*" Thousands of these caps had been imported into the district and distributed in the various villages. It is astonishing how the enormous quantity of cloth used in the manufacture of these caps was obtained in those days of strict cloth control.

On October 10, the Lakshmi *Puja* Day, a meeting was held at the Sahapur English High School and this meeting was attended by about fifteen thousand Muslims. Pir Ghulam Sarwar exhorted the Muslims to attack the *kutchery bari* of Babu Surendra Nath Bose, Zemindar of Narayanpur, and the house of Rai Sahib Rajendra Lal Roy Chowdhury of Karapra. Immediately after this the Hindu shops in Sahapur Bazar were burnt down by the mob in the presence of the Sub-Inspector of Police. The mob then attacked Narayanpur Kutchery and set fire to it. When the house was in flames Surendra Babu jumped down from the first floor and fell in front of the Muslim mass who immediately set upon him and hacked him to pieces. They then threw the pieces into the flames and presented the head to the Pir Sahib who was standing at a short distance. The house of Rajendra Babu was then attacked and set fire to. The inmates climbed up to the roof and some of the hooligans fired shots at them. The unfortunate victims took shelter behind the garret. A portion of the roof collapsed and some of them fell into the flames and lost their lives. A number of hooligans cut down a tall coconut tree and, using it as a ladder, climbed on to the roof. " One by one the male inmates were brought down and mercilessly butchered on the spot. The female inmates were brought down and cordoned off and taken to the Pir Sahib who was waiting in a boat at a distance. He ordered them to be taken to some other house. The heads of Rajendra Babu and some others were reported to have been presented to the Pir Sahib. Thirty-four persons, including about half a dozen unknown figures, were killed on the spot." *

The trouble in Noakhali spread to the neighbouring district of Tippera where too the same methods of looting, burning and converting the non-Muslims were adopted. The number of murders was not very large. Estimates vary between 250 and 5,000. There is no satisfactory evidence on this point and an I.C.S. officer of the Bengal Government who went to investigate local conditions reported that about 250 persons only had been killed. This figure is certainly an understatement, but the indications are that the loss of life in Noakhali and Tippera was not considerable. The aim of the Noakhali Muslims was to terrorize the Hindus, dishonour their women, plunder their property, desecrate their gods and convert them to Islam.

Footpaths and roads leading to villages were watched by Muslim hooligans and the egress and ingress of everyone was stopped. A party of Government officials proceeding to Haemchar Bazar by boat found their progress arrested by a barricade across the stream, built of banana trees and water hyacinth. They had to cut a channel through this barrier. It was observed that a number of small Muslim boys were watching the scene and when they saw the boat approach they gave warning to someone who could not be seen. The police were either indifferent or helpless. Conditions in the *thana* of Raypur in the district of Noakhali were

---

* Proceedings of the Bengal Legislative Assembly. February 6, 1947.

appalling. When the disturbances began all Hindus of Raypur left their homes and took refuge in the *thana*. A mob of Muslims arrived and demanded that all male Hindus should be handed over for conversion. The police officer in charge of the *thana* immediately complied with this demand although he had a number of muskets with him. The result was that all these males were dragged away by the mob and converted to Islam. A prominent Brahmin merchant was murdered in the *thana* compound. A few days later when a Government official specially sent by the Bengal Government arrived at Raypur he found that the non-Muslim public had lost all confidence, and even in the *thana* compound Hindus were afraid to wear their own clothes and were obliged to walk about in Muslim dress. Hundreds of written complaints were made to the police but on very few of them was any action taken. In the police station of Ramgunje 777 complaints had been lodged upto November 3 and, although each complaint named between two and ten accused persons, the police had arrested only fifty-four individuals. Within two miles of the police station resided two Muslim ringleaders who had been named in several complaints. Both of them were gun licence-holders. The police did not arrest them or apply for the cancellation of their licences. The state of affairs in the other police stations was no better. Hundreds of Muslims accused of very serious offences were not arrested or, when arrested, were released on bail in small amounts. It was said that the whereabouts of Maulvi Ghulam Sarwar were not known although he went about the district freely, disseminating his poison among receptive fanatics. On the other hand, a number of counter-cases against Hindus were registered and the police showed extraordinary zeal in prosecuting them. There were some cases even against police officials and military men who had tried to quell the riots, and complaints were made that these cases hampered the work of the police and the army. The raiders were frequently helped by ex-servicemen who had experience of blowing up bridges and roads. In some cases of arson stirrup-pumps were used to spray the houses with petrol or kerosene. The damage done to Hindu houses was so complete that in affected villages hardly a single Hindu house stood. The disturbances began on a mass scale on October 10 and spread through Noakhali and Tippera during the following days. On the 13th and 14th the rioting reached its peak and then began to decrease gradually. Normal conditions were not, however, restored for a considerable time as non-Muslims found it impossible to go back to their homes and live peacefully.

During the disturbances the districts were visited by Acharya Kripalani, President of the Congress. He flew over some of the affected area on October 19 and remained touring in the district until the 26th. On his way to Comilla, on the morning of the 19th, he flew very low over the area north of Begumganj and Chitansi and saw houses burning in ten or fifteen villages. On the 20th he again flew over Noakhali and saw fresh fires burning in Faridganj, Raypur, Chandpur and Ramgunje areas. In Charhain village he found that every non-Muslim house was completely devastated. Hindu houses had been burnt down and looted of all movables including ornaments, utensils, clothes and foodgrains. The cattle had been driven away. In Khalpara and Hipara all Hindu shops had been looted and League flags were flying on them. Soon after the President's visit the Bengal Government sent one I.C.S. officer to tour the district of Noakhali and another to Tippera to investigate conditions at the spot. These officers saw a part of the havoc perpetrated by the Muslim fanatics. In Noakhali it was found that almost every Hindu house in the affected villages had been thoroughly looted. The looting was thorough and complete. " Floors were dug up, courtyards were dug up, even adjacent pools of water into which many of the victims had thrown their utensils, etc., in a last minute effort to hide them, were dragged and the booty fished out." The victims were left with only the clothes they stood in. The houses were then burnt and all that could be seen was a heap of blackened and twisted corrugated iron lying on the plinth of the house. It was estimated that 99 per cent of the non-Muslim houses had been looted and between 70 and 90 per cent of the houses had been burnt down. In Tippera the conditions were equally distressing. Here, too, the looting and arson had been on a very wide scale. The Special Officer said in his report, " I was appalled by what I saw in such villages as Paikpara and Haemchar. It is, however, not enough to speak of merely two villages by name. In all the affected villages, the scenes of wreckage cannot be adequately described. Large homesteads have ceased to exist and loss of property has been very considerable. No description of the condition of Haemchar Bazar can be sufficiently vivid ; it must be visited to be appreciated," and again, " In the affected villages, there is chaos, destruction of homesteads, an absence of any sign of movable property, despondency and apprehension ; the few who have remained are anxious to leave. The destruction is so complete that, except for sheets of corrugated iron, the looting of which is in progress each night even at present, nothing remains but pathetic wreckage. . . . Large numbers of small personal temple-huts have been burnt out, images have been pulled down and smashed and at least one large and brick-built temple has been looted and desecrated." This was written on November 5, 1946.

The condition of refugees was deplorable. Foodstuffs were unavailable and the price of rice when it could be obtained was Rs. 2 per seer. A large number of refugees had congregated at different places and their state was pitiable. At Faridganj on November 2 there were about six thousand refugees huddled on boats and sheltering in huts ashore. Many of them were suffering from dysentery and other diseases. Rescue parties sent from Calcutta were refused police protection and had to go back.

Gandhiji heard of these tragic events and, on October 22, he resolved to go to East Bengal. He said he wanted to wipe away the tears of the outraged womanhood of Noakhali. Soon after this decision was made, serious rioting broke out in Bihar; and large numbers of Muslims suffered at the hands of the Hindus. Gandhiji went on a partial fast and, before leaving Calcutta for Noakhali, he sent a message to the Bihar Hindus that unless they stopped their mad orgy, he would fast unto death. Bihar returned to peace and sanity within a very short time. In the meantime Gandhiji arrived in Noakhali on November 6 and began to preach his gospel of brotherly love and *ahimsa*. He stayed for almost exactly four months and went from village to village telling the Hindus to shed their fear and have faith in God. He asked the Muslims to love their Hindu brethren.

The first village he stayed at was Choumhoni. The place presented a sorry spectacle. The Hindu habitations had been reduced to a mass of rubble and shapeless mud. All around lay the charred remains of human flesh and bone. The stains of blood on what were once door-steps were still visible and the smell of corpses hung in the air. Clusters of arecanut and coconut palms dotting the landscape intensified the tragedy of human suffering. The few women who were present came and sobbed out their sorrow at Gandhiji's feet. The same story was repeated in every village he went to. He listened in silence and tried to give comfort to the crucified souls. "My heart weeps before God," he would say, "although my eyes have no tears." He spoke to the Muslims and invited them to his prayer meetings. After a few days he decided to disperse his party and send individual members to different villages. He asked them to stay there and act as hostages for the safety and security of the Hindu residents. He himself made Srirampur his headquarters and stayed there for forty-one days. He visited all the neighbouring villages and held prayer meetings in which he brought Hindus and Muslims together and spoke to them of brotherly love. He accepted invitations to distant villages and returned home at the dead of night, in boats tugged through dense hyacinth-logged canals. On January 2, he began his great lonely march. Staff in hand and walking barefoot through slush and mud, through palm groves and bamboo thickets, this dark frail man of 77, trudged on and on, day after day, from village to village, carrying the torch of truth and *ahimsa*. Thorns pricked his feet and made the soles bleed, but he declined the offer of shoes, saying he was on a pilgrimage and a pilgrim must walk barefoot. His programme was one night one village, and he visited twenty-nine villages. In the course of this march he made the acquaintance of Muslim men and women and won their affection and co-operation. He brought the light of reason and sanity to mad Noakhali. Large numbers of Muslims came forward and pledged to protect the Hindu minorities. Confidence once again returned, the Hindus cast away their fears and began to go back to their homes.

On February 4 Gandhiji left East Bengal.

There can be very little doubt that the Noakhali and Tippera disturbances were the result of a planned attempt to intimidate the Hindus and make war upon their religion. The manner in which the rioting began in a large number of villages and the procedure adopted by the mobs are clear proof of this. The help rendered by the ex-servicemen, the use of stirrup-pumps, the mode of conversion employed and the distribution of thousands of Muslim League caps is wholly inconsistent with the hypothesis of a sudden and spontaneous uprising on the part of a few hooligans who attacked the rich Hindus with the object of looting them and then as suddenly brought their activities to an end. There was, no doubt, a determined attempt to loot and destroy Hindu property but the assault on their religion and their womenfolk was made with even greater intensity. The riots were preceded by virulent propaganda carried out all over the district by fanatical Muslim Leaguers, and there can be no doubt that in East Bengal they were able to achieve results far more satisfactory than in Calcutta on the official Direct Action Day.

The presence of Gandhiji brought peace and confidence to the Hindu minority but only temporarily. With the establishment of Pakistan on August 15, 1947, the atmosphere was once again polluted and a large-scale exodus of the non-Muslim population started. This still continues.*

(iii)

The events in Calcutta and Noakhali could not fail to have repercussions in the neighbouring Province of Bihar. Calcutta was the workshop and business premises of thousands of Biharis drawn from all parts of Bihar and particularly from the Gangetic districts of Saran, Patna, Muzaffarpur, Darbhanga, Monghyr and Bhagalpur. The ghastly drama enacted on August 16, 1946, and the following days at Calcutta gave them a feeling of insecurity and, leaving their adopted homes, their business and employment, they returned to their native towns and villages. The harrowing tales of massacre, rape, arson and plunder which they related stirred the emotions of the Bihar Hindus. Newspapers published accounts and pictures of the atrocities perpetrated by the Muslims. Even the sober and aloof indifference of the European-owned *Statesman* was moved to a passionate condemnation of the mob rule prevailing in the city of Calcutta. It may be presumed that the refugees smarting under the injury (personal and financial) did not understate the situation, and the imagination of the listeners was fired by sympathy for the sufferers and a desire to take revenge. The attitude of the Bihar Muslims had contributed very little towards a peaceful solution of the problems which presented themselves to the minds of the Bihar Hindus or towards appeasing the sullen tempers which grew more sullen with every item of gruesome news arriving from Calcutta. Peace had prevailed throughout the province on Direct Action Day and one or two stray cases of conflict in Gaya, Jamalpur and Bhagalpur were too insignificant to give the authorities cause for alarm or even anxiety. The League spokesmen had exercised no restraint in their utterances on August 16. At a meeting held in the Anjuman Islamia Hall, some of the speakers referred to the strength of the sword, by which alone the Muslims had achieved whatever they had achieved in the past. They held out promises

---

* For the later activities of Pir Ghulam Sarwar see Note (iii) to Chapter II, Appendix I.

of like success if like means were adopted. One speaker, Syed Muhammad Abdul Jalil, categorically said that the Qaid-e-Azam and Messrs. Nazimuddin and Suhrawardy had unequivocally said that non-violence was not a creed of the Muslims and that the Muslims were free to use any weapons that might be of assistance to them:

" *Unka hamla aur unka tarz-i-amal* non-violence *hota hai lekin main saf kah dena chahta hun keh hamare numaindagan* Qaid-e-Azam, Nazimuddin *aur* Suhrawardy *nen is cheez ko saf kar diya hai ki hamare samne* non-violence *hargiz koi cheez nahin hai. Ham jab jang karna chahenge to jo cheez hamare pas hogi usko ham hathiyar banayenge aur ham usko istemal karenge.*"

(Their attack and their conduct is based on non-violence but I want to make it clear to you that our representatives, Qaid-e-Azam, Nazimuddin and Suhrawardy have made it clear that to us non-violence means nothing. When we want to fight we shall make use of whatever weapons we have.)

Shaheedul Haq of the Muslim Students' Federation was particularly provocative and declared that for a Muslim the way to heaven lay both by killing and by being killed by a Hindu.

These fulminations and indiscreet outbursts of the Muslim leaders caused a great deal of resentment, and the gloomy foreboding to which they gave rise caused unrest and brought about a feeling of insecurity. The tension increased every day as news of greater and more extensive disasters from Calcutta was received. On August 18, the *Statesman* of Calcutta announced that over 170 persons had been killed and 1,000 injured. On August 19, the news was that 270 had been killed and 1,600 injured. On the 20th the *Statesman* announced that the death roll was between 2,000 and 3,000. Thousands of refugees began to leave Howrah ; and the Bihar Government, fearing an outbreak in the province, issued instructions to the magistracy and the police asking them to exercise special vigilance in maintaining law and order. They were enjoined to enforce not only the ordinary law but also the Emergency War Legislation which had not yet expired and was to remain in force until the end of September. The Provincial Armed Police Reserve were moved to strategic centres, e.g. , Patna, Muzaffarpur, Monghyr and Gaya. On August 28, the *Statesman* annnounced that 3,468 bodies had so far been accounted for in Calcutta. The

Interim Central Government was expected to take over charge at Delhi on September 2, 1946, and this further complicated matters because the Muslim League had not joined the Government and their attitude was fraught with danger to the public peace. On August 27, the Provincial Government issued telegrams to all District Magistrates calling upon them to warn all important communal-minded persons. At the same time the officiating President of the Provincial Congress Committee sent instructions to all Congressmen to abstain from doing anything which might cause offence to any party or group in the country. The situation at the moment was so tense that at Ranchi the news of a buffalo fight caused a panic. Shops were shut down and frightened women ran home. The Provincial Government distributed a large number of leaflets issued over the signatures of the Premier and leaders of both communities. These leaflets asked the people to keep calm, check rumours and show a spirit of tolerance, and, at all cost, avoid a repetition of the unfortunate happenings at Calcutta. As the result of these efforts the occasion of the *Idul-Fitr* (August 29, 1946) passed off without any incidents. Even on September 2, no untoward incident happened and the Muslims who were not in sympathy with the Interim Central Government happily flew black flags on their houses. An undercurrent of tension, however, continued during the following weeks although there were no incidents of any type.

The first serious riot occurred on September 27, at Benibad district Muzaffarpur. News had gone round that a local Muslim had brought a Bengali Hindu girl from Calcutta and was keeping her against her wishes. Investigation proved that the girl had in fact been brought from Calcutta but she had voluntarily embraced Islam and had married her Muslim lover. The truth, however, was not known till later, and in the meantime a riot broke out. A police truck bringing magistrates and armed force to the village in order to quell the disturbance had a breakdown on the way and was delayed. This unfortunate incident precipitated events and resulted in a serious deterioration of the communal situation throughout North Bihar. Fuel was added to the fire by a singularly stupid and provocative act of the President of the Muslim League at Biharsharif. This gentleman was the Secretary of the Cloth Distribution Committee and in this capacity handled cloth ration cards. He stamped every ration card with the words " *Allah-ho-Akbar, Leyke rahenge* Pakistan." Nothing more unfortunate in the circumstances can be imagined. The trouble was, however, still local and confined to a small area. It was overcome and the following days showed an improvement in the communal situation. *Dussehra*, which fell on October 2 to 5, was peaceful, there being just one incident in Monghyr District where the police had to open fire because the Sub-Divisional Officer and an armed police party were stoned by the mob.

In this state of tension the news of the Noakhali lawlessness began to arrive. The first announcement was contained in the *Statesman* of October 16, 1946, and the issues of the subsequent days brought tales of horror, murder, loot and arson. The Muslim League had joined the Interim Government on October 17, but the utterances of the Muslim League leaders showed that their decision did not contemplate co-operation with the Congress. In fact, Ghaznafar Ali Khan, speaking at Lahore, said:

"We are going into the Interim Government to get a foothold to fight for our cherished goal of Pakistan. . . . The Interim Government is one of the fronts of the Direct Action Campaign and we shall most scrupulously carry out the order of Mr. Jinnah on any front that we are called upon to serve."

The happenings at Calcutta and Noakhali were associated with the Direct Action plan of the League. The Hindus could not help thinking that the campaign of murder and loot in Calcutta and East Bengal was part of a well-laid and pre-conceived design to intimidate and terrify the Hindus and the Congress so that they should be forced to concede Pakistan. Leaflets containing direct incitement to violence were recovered from Muslims in various parts of Bihar. In some leaflets, printed in Delhi, over the name of one Muhammad Bari, Hindus were described as the enemies of Islam and the writer referred to himself in the words of Saadi as "one whose head is to be found besmeared with the blood and dust of the battle-field." These leaflets were traced to the Secretary of the local Muslim League in South Bihar. In the second week of October two Maulvis from Hyderabad (Deccan) were found in possession of three leaflets. These purported to have been issued by Allama Amiruddin Sahib of Najore, North-Western Frontier Province. One of them was addressed to Mr. Jinnah and contained the following message:

"So far we have given sufficient time to Indian infidels. It is time to remove the darkness of infidelity and illuminate the whole universe by resplendent Islam. To accomplish this sublime cause we must slaughter the˚ infidels as was done in the early days."

Another leaflet, found in circulation, was signed by one Habibur Rahman of Calcutta. This leaflet purported to contain the verbal directions of Mr. Jinnah and set forth elaborate instructions for the destruction of Hindu religion and culture, conversion and murder of Hindus, murder of nationalist Muslims, Congress leaders, and bestial attacks on Hindu women. No wonder the Hindu public of Bihar thought that the happenings at Calcutta and Noakhali were merely an implementation of the directions and plans contained in these leaflets.

On October 25, a number of meetings all over Bihar were organized to protest against the atrocities committed on the Hindus in East Bengal. The authorities took stock of the situation and after giving the matter their most careful consideration came to the conclusion that it would be unwise to prohibit these meetings as a prohibition in the circumstances would merely result in an unhealthy bottling up of emotions. Directions were given to the speakers to exercise restraint and moderation in their utterances. At least, in one place, namely, Bhagalpur, these directions were scrupulously respected. The Government had issued a circular from which the following passage may be quoted:

"I need hardly emphasise the importance which the Provincial Government attach to the maintenance of communal peace which, except for a few isolated outbreaks, has been maintained in this Province. The Emergency War Legislation . . . is of course no longer in force, but you should not hesitate to use the provisions of the ordinary law where you consider it necessary and you should have no hesitation in dealing with *agents provocateurs,* and persons whose acts or utterances may lead to trouble, whatever their status, party or creed. Officers who have done their duty to the best of their ability and judgment should rest assured that they will have full support of the Provincial Government in taking whatever action they consider necessary to prevent a dangerous outbreak."

These precautions, directions and exhortations were, however, of no avail and October 25 saw a serious outbreak of trouble which spread and increased during the follow ng days, reached its peak on November 3 and 4, and then rapidly died down. During these twelve dark days the Hindus of Bihar let their passions loose upon their Muslim brethren and drank deep of the cup of revenge. Trouble began at Chapra, the headquarters of Saran District. A meeting had been arranged in order to condemn the Noakhali outrages; but, before the meeting could be held, rioting started in the town beginning with a fatal attack on a Muslim League protagonist who had been marked down by the hooligans for his communal activities. In the course of the afternoon and evening there were eight or nine different riots in the town and altogether fifty incidents were reported. The police opened fire on three separate occasions at three different places and the military was sent for. Trouble also started at Jamalpur in Monghyr District where the celebration of the Kali *Puja* by the Hindus was interfered with by some Muslims who threw brickbats. The disturbance was temporarily controlled. At Bhagalpur there was a similar incident and the Kali image was stoned during the night. On the 26th, the rioting gathered intensity and began to spread to fresh localities. The rural areas in the vicinity of Chapra were aflame and a Hindu mob advancing towards Chapra was stopped only when the police opened fire on them. In Monghyr town rioting had begun and twenty-two persons were injured. In village Chichraun a Kali procession was attacked by a Muslim mob and the image was damaged by them. The Hindus were compelled to leave the image in the fields and this gave rise to a great deal of resentment against the Muslims. A riot broke out in Bhagalpur and in the Tarapur area in Monghyr District.

On November 2, Pandit Jawaharlal Nehru arrived in Patna and began an extensive whirlwind tour of the disturbed areas by car, train and plane. He visited Biharsharif, Jetli, Mouzipur, Fatwa, Khusrupur, Bakhtiarpur, Patna City, Hilsa, Jehanabad, Gaya, and numerous other places. He rebuked the Hindus and told them that retaliation would only bring fresh trouble and ruin upon both communities. He comforted the Muslims and told them to show courage and remain peaceful. The Hindus were openly hostile to Pandit Nehru and he had to face an angry audience at Patna after a Hindu mob had been ordered to be fired upon at Nagarnausa. On November 3 and 4 trouble in all the districts of Patna, Saran, Bhagalpur, Gaya and Monghyr was at its height. There were cases of cold-blooded murders of Muslims, dead bodies were thrown in wells and property was looted and burnt. There were some instances of Muslims attacking Hindus and these only exacerbated feelings further. From two villages in Hilsa area it was reported that Muslims armed with guns had attacked Hindu houses and killed several people without provocation. This resulted in a terrible exhibition of mob frenzy and the punishment exacted by the Hindus was severe. The killing in Tilhar, Telonar, Masathu and Nagarnausa was on a large scale. The military and the police had to open fire several times. News now came that Gandhiji had started a partial fast to do penance for the Bihar atrocities. He had declared his resolve to fast unto death unless conditions in Bihar showed immediate improvement. Leaflets announcing Gandhiji's resolve and asking the people to put an end to this mad orgy were dropped from the air over the troubled areas. The Government mobilized all its machinery and resources to attain the desired end. The Provincial Congress Organization turned its whole attention to this purpose, and at once an improvement was noticeable. When the seriousness of Gandhiji's resolve was realized, the mad frenzy which had suddenly seized the people of Bihar towards the end of October and had raged unabated for little more than a whole week, died down almost completely on November 7. When Pandit Jawaharlal Nehru left Bihar on November 9 after a week's stay the situation had returned to what might be described as normal, and on November 14 he made a statement in the Legislative Assembly in the course of which he said:

" The Bihar situation was brought completely under control after a week and is quiet now. . . . This mass uprising lasted almost exactly a week. Just as it started suddenly it ended also equally suddenly. This rapid ending of a widespread movement which was on the verge of spreading to other districts was remarkable. The military, of course, came in at some later stage and helped in restoring order. But a much more powerful factor in this restoration of order was the fact that a large number of persons, chiefly Biharis, spread out all over the villages and faced the masses. News of the Mahatma's proposed fast also had a powerful effect."

The happenings in the five above-mentioned districts of Bihar are not a chapter of which the Biharis or the Provincial Government are proud. There has been no attempt to understate either the terrible nature of the catastrophe or the losses, but it must be made clear that exaggerated and garbled accounts of what actually occurred were spread by frightened or interested individuals. The number of murders was increased out of all proportion to reality.

It was alleged that a large number of Muslim women had been kidnapped and converted to Hinduism. Some Muslims carried the skulls of victims to the North-Western Frontier Province and exhibited them in the town of Hazara, inciting the spectators to exact vengeance from the *kafirs*. While it is not possible to prepare an accurate statement of the number of persons killed and wounded, a very careful and detailed enquiry made by the Provincial Government has brought to light the figures contained in the following table:

STATEMENT A

Districts	Muslims killed	Hindus killed	Total killed	Muslims injured	Hindus injured	Total injured
Saran	114	8	122	101	24	125
Patna ..	3,388	143	3,531	407	172	579
Gaya ..	547	19	566	113	7	120
Monghyr	1,021	48	1,069	436	1	437
Bhagalpur	158	6	164	94	89	183
Saharsa	8	—	8	2	2	4
Santal Parganas	47	—	47	209	—	209
E.I. Railway ..	44	—	44	85	8	93
O.T. Railway..	7	—	7	4	—	4
Grand total	5,334	224*	5,558	1,451	303*	1,754

Some women must undoubtedly have been abducted but almost all of them were recovered. There were hardly any conversions and when, after the return of peace, an announcement was made inviting the Muslims to give names of abducted women, no names were mentioned. In the second week of November 1946 an assurance was given to Mian Iftikhar Hussain Khan of Mamdot that immediate action would be taken if the Relief Committee of the Muslim League or any other organization gave information regarding abducted women. The Khan, however, did not report a single case. The Relief Committee of the Muslim League reported one or two cases upon which prompt action was taken. The President of the Muslim League promised to give a list of abducted women to the Additional District Magistrate of Patna but no list was furnished. A Muslim lady M.L.A. was asked to give such a list but she, too, did not communicate any information to the Additional District Magistrate. Even Gandhiji at a meeting on March 30, 1947, observed:

" Since my arrival in Bihar I have been telling those Muslims who told me about the kidnapped girls to give me the names

---

* The majority of the Hindu casualties resulted from police and military firing on the riotous mobs.

and the family connection of such girls in order to help them finding out if they were still alive ; but up till now not one name has been submitted to me. I again ask you to submit names of these unfortunate girls."

Gandhiji, however, received no names. Some stray reports of kidnapping were received by the District Officers and prompt action was taken on every one of these. It may be mentioned that in some cases the information given was of a vague and nebulous type and searches carried out on the basis of such information proved fruitless. On January 15, 1948, eighteen women remained untraced and a reward of Rs. 1,000 for the recovery of each one of them was offered by the Government.

Mention has been made of the numerous occasions on which the police and military were ordered to open fire on the Hindu mobs in order to stop the rioting. The following tables give complete information on this point:

STATEMENT B
By Police

Serial No.	Districts	Occasions	Rounds	Killed	Injured
1	Saran	11	58	3	8
2	Saharsa	1	30	—	1
3	Muzaffarpur	1	4	—	—
4	O.T. Railway	—	nil	—	—
5	Patna	30	351	Over 57	15
6	Gaya	10	35	5	6
7	Monghyr	6	74	4	1
8	Bhagalpur	2	2 plus a few	—	—
9	Santal Parganas ..	1	2	—	—
10	E.I. Railway	—	—	—	—
	Total ..	62	556 plus a few	Over 69	About 31

STATEMENT B-1
By Military

Serial No.	Districts	Occasions	Rounds	Killed	Injured
1	Saran	—	—	—	—
2	Saharsa	—	—	—	—
3	Muzaffarpur	—	—	—	—
4	O.T. Railway	—	—	—	—
5	Patna	23	1,516	319	68
6	Gaya	3	54	4	—
7	Monghyr	1	60	1	—
8	Bhagalpur	—	—	—	—
9	Santal Parganas ..	—	—	—	—
10	E.I. Railway	—	—	—	—
	Total ..	27	1,630	324	68

The ordinary law was enforced with the utmost rigour and the following table shows the number of criminal cases brought against the persons concerned in these riots:

STATEMENT C

Serial No.	Districts	No. of persons sent up in criminal cases	No. of houses searched	No. of cases instituted
1	Saran	1,982	444	243
2	Patna	9,668	4,690	1,304
3	Gaya	1,003	1,783	159
4	Monghyr	2,980	876	449
5	Bhagalpur	1,524	649	492
6	Santal Parganas	239	86	14
7	Saharsa	79	177	7
8	E.I. Railway	49	72	17

It is to be noted that the disturbances were confined to only a small area of the province. The number of Muslims killed has been estimated at 5,334 and Muslims injured at 1,451. As against this, 224 Hindus lost their lives and 303 were injured. Most of the Hindu casualties resulted from police and military firing on the riotous mobs. Out of a total of fifty-four sub-divisions only fifteen were affected and no sub-division was affected in its entirety. Out of a total of 18,869 villages in Bihar, riots broke out in 750 villages only. The total number of houses in Bihar according to the census of 1941 is 6.96 millions and a fairly comprehensive enquiry shows that only 9,869 were damaged or destroyed. Thousands of Muslim families who had left the province during the troubles have returned. Compensation on an average of Rs. 200 per family has been given for purposes of rehabilitation. Building advances were also made by the Provincial Government. Gandhiji paid three visits to Bihar in the early part of 1947 and toured the rural areas which had been affected during the riots. It was his threatened fast which brought the orgy to a rapid conclusion and his subsequent visits helped to establish complete confidence in the minds of the Muslim population.

III

Tuez !

Que fait hors des maisons ce peuple? Qu'il s'en aille!
Soldats, mitraillez-moi toute cette canaille !
Feu ! feu ! Tu voteras ensuite, ô peuple-roi !
Sabrez l'honneur, sabrez le droit, sabrez la loi !
Que sur les boulevards le sang coule en rivières !
Du vin plein les bidons ! des morts plein les civières !
Qui veut de l'eau-de-vie? En ce temps pluvieux
Il faut boire. Soldats, fusillez-moi ce vieux,
Tuez-moi cet enfant. Qu'est-ce que cette femme ?
C'est la mère? tuez. Que tout ce peuple infâme
Tremble, et que les pavés rougissent ses talons !

*   *   *   *

C'est fait, réposez-vous ; et l'on entend sonner
Dans les fourreaux le sabre et l'argent dans les poches.
De la banque aux bivouacs on vide les sacoches.
Ceux qui tuaient le mieux at qui n'ont pas bronché
Auront la croix d'honneur par-dessus le marché.
Les vainqueurs en hurlant dansent sur les décombres.
Des tas de corps saignants gisent dans les coins sombres.
Le soldat, gai, féroce, ivre, complice obscur,
Chancelle, et, de la main dont il s'appuie au mur,
Achève d'écraser quelque cervelle humaine.
On boit, on rit, on chante, on ripaille, on amène
Des vaincus qu'on fusille, hommes, femmes, enfants.
Les généraux dorés galopent triomphants,
Regardés par les morts tombés à la renverse.

V. Hugo—*Les Chatiments*

CHAPTER THREE

THE PUNJAB

THESE convulsions left the tranquillity of the Punjab undisturbed. News of the events in Calcutta, Noakhali and Bihar horrified the people and gave rise to a feeling of insecurity but produced no repercussions. Riots took place in Allahabad on August 23, 1946, and at Garh Mukteshwar in the Meerut District on November 6, 7 and 8 of the same year, and it seemed as if the murderous monster were approaching. On August 16, 1946, life in the Punjab had followed a normal and uneventful course. The Muslim League held meetings throughout the province and passed reso utions reaffirming their demand for Pakistan, but these demonstrations were entirely peaceful. It was not till March 4, 1947, that the storm of lawlessness broke over the province, but, when it came, it continued unabated (except for a few lulls) for several months and attained a degree of horror and destruction unequalled anywhere else.

There were several factors which contributed to bring about this phenomenon. The Punjab has always occupied a peculiar position in the history, economy and politics of India. A continuous procession of invading hordes from the west made it difficult for the province to have a settled and stable Government for any length of time. The Punjabi did not develop a peculiar indigenous culture. Political instability and frequent infusion of fresh ideas made him singularly prone to imitate and accept foreign notions about life and social behaviour. The birth and rise of the Sikh religion helped to promote the virile and unorthodox spirit, native to the soil of this dry and vigorous land. The Punjab has for long been the land of peasant proprietors, and a comparatively even distribution of wealth resulting from this circumstance has made for contentment and lack of interest in political affairs. This indifference towards national aspirations often made politicians lose their patience and accuse the Punjabis of impeding the progress of the country and being a drag on the rest of India. The British rulers kept a firm hold on this strategic province and prevented the growth of political discontent. They came to the Punjab as conquerors, established themselves in the seat of power in a remarkably short time and, at one stroke, annexed the whole province. They preserved the existing system of land tenure which prevented the accumulation of wealth in the hands of a few idle landlords, and the growth of an industrialist class. The Government of the province was conducted on the lines of a beneficent despotism. The ablest officers of the Indian Civil Service were encouraged to choose the Punjab and they were allowed a great deal of latitude in administrative matters. The District Officer in the Punjab had far more power and prestige than his prototype in, for instance, the United Provinces, where his attitude was not so aloof or godlike. Small wonder that the Punjab was called the Ulster of India and Congressmen despaired of finding a satisfactory response to nationalist cries in the robust heart of the Punjabi.

The population of the united Punjab, as recorded at the census of 1941, was 28.4 millions, comprising 16.2 millions Muslims, 7.5 millions Hindus and 3.7 millions Sikhs (the rest of the population was made up of Christians, etc.). The western districts were predominantly Muslim while the eastern districts were predominantly Hindu, or perhaps more correctly non-Muslim.* In the central districts the communities were evenly divided. The Sikhs were concentrated for the most part in the central districts of Ludhiana, Jullundur, Ferozepore, Amritsar, Lahore, Montgomery, Sheikhupura, Lyallpur and Gujranwala. The population in the towns did not show a pronounced bias in favour of any particular community though non-Muslim interests in property, commerce and industry predominated in all the urban areas.

When the arid lands in Sheikhupura, Lyallpur and Montgomery Districts were made culturable by the incidence of canal irrigation, the peasants from the central areas were persuaded to go and colonize these lands. Large numbers of enterprising Sikhs set up homes in the new colonies and their skill and industry brought prosperity to these hitherto unproductive districts. The Sikh soldiery, disbanded after the annexation of the Punjab, found employment in the areas irrigated by the Upper Bari Doab canal. Lyallpur has been described † as the daughter of Central Punjab.

---

* In the Ambala Division the percentage of Muslims was only 28.07. In the Jullundur Division it was 34.53 per cent, whereas in the western districts this figure rose as high as 90.42 per cent in Attock, 89.42 per cent in Jhelum and 86.42 per cent in Muzaffargarh. Muslims in Rawalpindi Division were 85.52 per cent and in the Multan Division 75.43 per cent.

† By Sir Malcolm Darling.

More than a hundred thousand Sikhs from Amritsar District alone went to Lyallpur and helped to colonize it. In Montgomery there were a hundred and ten thousand Sikh military grantees. Population in the eastern districts was always more congested than in the western districts, and the establishment of these colonies provided a measure of relief in the east and helped to increase production in the west.* These Sikh colonists had their roots in the eastern districts and the setting up of new homes in the west did not involve a break with their original homes and villages. It meant, in the majority of cases, nothing more than a division of the family, some members of which remained in charge of the old ancestral lands while others went over to the colony. This preserved the family ties and kept alive the old association with home and village. This circumstance assumed great importance when the question of partitioning the province was bruited, and was responsible for much bloodshed in West as well as in East Punjab.

Another factor which contributed towards the malevolence and acrimony of the communal relations during and after the riots was the peculiarity of the Punjab land tenure system. Reference has already been made to this circumstance, but it is necessary to devote a little more attention to it. Ninety-four per cent of the landowners in the province paid less than Rs. 50 each as land revenue ; yet they contributed nearly 60 per cent of the total land revenue of the province. Of these a very large number (17.59 lakhs) paid Rs. 5 or less per annum. There were no more than thirty-six persons paying a land revenue of more than five thousand rupees per annum. This meant that a very large proportion of the population had a stake in the land and was attached to the soil. Among the non-Muslims especially, the floating population engaged in labour or menial tasks was almost negligible, whereas a large number of Muslims, residing more particularly in the eastern districts, had no proprietary interest in land. The Census Returns of 1931 showed that the Muslim population of the Punjab was 14.9 millions and of these no less than 4.7 millions or more than one-third, were weavers, cobblers, herdsmen, potters, mussalis (sweepers), carpenters, oilmen, beggars, bards, barbers, blacksmiths, butchers, washermen and mirasis. Again, the western

---

* The population density in the twelve eastern districts which now comprise East Punjab was 327 persons per sq. mile as compared to 264 persons per sq. mile in the western districts. The production of the eastern districts was, however, only 29 per cent as compared to the remaining 71 per cent of the western districts.

districts were far more productive than the eastern districts, the ratio of productivity being 71 per cent (west) to 29 per cent (east). Cotton was grown almost exclusively in the west where there was also a greater abundance of wheat and rice.*

The Sikhs thus had a very important landed interest in the districts of Gujranwala, Sheikhupura, Lyallpur and Montgomery, which now form part of Pakistan. Some of their shrines possessing deep emotional and cultural associations were also situated in this area. Nankana Sahib, for instance, where there are several Gurdwaras commemorating the birth of Guru Nanak, the founder of the Sikh religion, is in Sheikhupura District. Another famous shrine, known as the Gurdwara of Sacha Sauda, is situated in the same district. The Sikhs were, therefore, attached to some of the western districts by secular as well as spiritual ties. Such being the state of affairs, it is not surprising that their presence was a source of annoyance to the Muslims and a hindrance to the achievement of economic supremacy by them. Nor need we wonder at the extent of resentment and the desire for revenge displayed by the Sikhs when they were uprooted from the land they had developed and enriched, and were driven out of their homes.

*   *   *   *

Constitutional Reforms and Local Self-Government came to the Punjab slowly and late. Until 1920 the Lieutenant-Governor ruled the province without the advice or assistance of Executive Councillors or of any non-official individual. He thus maintained a firm hold on the administrative machinery. With the exception of Sir Fazl-i-Hussain and Chaudhry Chhotu Ram, the Ministers appointed under the Chelmsford Reforms, were effete and ineffective. After the Government of India Act of 1935 Sir Fazl-i-Hussain attempted to form a non-communal party representing the interests of the Punjab zemindars. He realized that the alignment of parties on a purely religious or communal basis would lead to a stalemate, as no party would be in a position to command a clear majority or form a stable Ministry. The Unionist Party organized by him had Hindu, Muslim and Sikh members. Sir Fazl-i-Hussain died on July 9, 1936, before the elections were held, and the leadership of the Party devolved upon the shoulders

---

* The wheat produced in the eastern districts was only 15.7 *per capita* of the population as compared to 26.3 lbs. in the west. Only 14.4 per cent of the total rice produced in the province came from the eastern districts.

of Sir Sikandar Hayat Khan, a somewhat lukewarm and timid politician whose anxiety to keep himself in office frequently led him into difficult and thorny paths, extrication from which was only possible by a sacrifice of truth and integrity. He was thus driven into situations where prevarication and suppression of truth became necessary. His compromises with Mr. Jinnah and Sardar Baldev Singh succeeded only in discrediting him both with the Muslim League and the Sikhs.

The elections of 1937 resulted in a majority for the Unionist Party. The Muslim League succeeded in winning two seats only and one of the members resigned as soon as the Assembly met and joined the Unionist Party. The Punjab had thus given a decisive verdict against the Muslim League. Mr. Jinnah was anxious to secure the support of a Muslim majority province and invited Sir Sikandar Hayat Khan to the Lucknow Session of the All-India Muslim League in October 1937. The Sikandar-Jinnah Pact * thus came into existence and Sir Sikandar Hayat Khan divided his loyalties between the Muslim League and the non-Muslim members of his Unionist Party. On the sudden death of Sir Sikandar at the peak of his glory in December 1942, Sir Khizar Hayat Khan Tiwana succeeded him as the Provincial Premier. His attitude towards the Muslim League was a little more robust than that of his predecessor and entailed a definite breach with Mr. Jinnah. The dismissal of Sardar Shaukat Hayat Khan from the Ministry on charges of corruption and nepotism created a bitter and vociferous opponent of Sir Khizar Hayat Khan and the Unionist Party.

The provincial elections, held in the beginning of 1946, were marked by a display of unprecedented acerbity and vituperation. The Unionist candidates were dubbed as heretics and slaves of the *kafir* Hindus. Muslim students from Aligarh were imported to spread disaffection against the non-Muslims. Khizar Hayat Khan found that, in this election campaign, Muslim officials were ranged against him. The story is told of a District Inspector of Schools telling the voters that unless they voted for the Muslim League candidate their sons would fail in their school examinations. He issued instructions to all school masters subordinate to him to implement his wishes in this respect. He then went to see the Deputy Commissioner and, believing him to be a Muslim, spoke of his activities with a glow of pride. Unfortunately for him, the Deputy Commissioner was a Christian with a Muslim name and

---

* See notes to Chapter III in Appendix I.

the matter was reported to the higher authorities. Brailsford, the well-known journalist who was an eye-witness of this election, wrote as follows:

"Three great powers confront the Muslim peasants—the feudal landlord, the Government and the League. Of these three only the League can reach his emotions, and it has been in action everywhere on behalf of the Muslim League. It has created a fear that Islam is in danger. The clergy tells the peasants that their hope of salvation depends on their voting for the League and sometimes they enforce this appeal by parading the roads with a copy of the Quran. I have heard the loudspeaker on their cars shouting the slogan ' A curse on the infidel Hindus.' The result is that a wave of communal feeling has gripped the Muslims of this province, who form a slight majority of its population, and, with rare exceptions, they have rallied to the demand for Pakistan. Few have thought it out in detail, but in Lahore, the average man who can read a newspaper, the clerk or the shopkeeper, does at least know dimly what it means. He will tell you that he wants a State in which the Muslims will rule. I got no further in questioning the well-educated upper stratum. When I asked whether Pakistan would build a tariff wall against Hindustan, even the candidates answered: ' That is for the leaders to decide.' The well-bred upper class is not fanatical. . . . Fanaticism is the expedient they use to win the masses." *

The result of the elections was an overwhelming success for the Muslim League. The position of the parties stood as follows: Muslim League 75, Congress 51 (including one Muslim), Akalis 22, Unionists 20 (including 13 Muslims) and Independents 7. The Muslim League was thus the largest party in the Legislature but it did not possess a clear majority. Anxious and prolonged negotiations between the various parties foll ved and finally Sir Khizar Hayat Khan was able to secure the support of the Congress and Akali members, and announce the personnel of his Cabinet. The Muslim League leaders were indignant and started a bitter campaign against the Ministry.

Soon after the passing of the Direct Action resolution at Bombay, a Provincial Committee of Action was appointed.† An

---

* *The Tribune*, February 26, 1946.
† The Committee consisted of Khan Iftikhar Hussain Khan of Mamdot, President, Raja Ghazanfar Ali Khan Convenor, Sardar Shaukat Hayat Khan, Malik Feroze Khan Noon, Sheikh Karamat Ali, Mian Iftikhar-ud-Din and Mian Abdul Aziz, members. Mian Mumtaz Daultana was its ex officio member as he was on the Central Committee of Action.

appeal was made to Muslim lawyers to go forth as "shock troops" and mobilize the masses in anticipation of the coming struggle. Students were enjoined to be ready for all emergencies and Muslim women were called upon to learn First Aid. Sardar Shaukat Hayat Khan was assigned the task of enrolling National Guard volunteers. Maulana Shabir Ahmad Usmani, President, All-India Jamiat-ul-Ulema-i-Islam, declared: "To maintain discipline in the ranks when the war is on, to train our soldiers in the technique of that war, to provide for its means and material, to ensure its uninterrupted prosecution, to keep co-operation throughout the country and to arrange for meeting the requirements of the families of those who lose their lives are matters which call for immediate planning on an extensive scale." * A programme of Direct Action containing twenty-three points was received from Calcutta and communicated to the League workers. The programme contained detailed instructions for stabbing non-Muslims, setting fire to their houses and terrorizing them.†

The National Guards were provided with army helmets purchased from the Military Disposal Department and many of them were given firearms. They wore uniforms and were taught army drill. Group physical training was also undertaken by members of the Rashtriya Swayam Sewak Sangh on an increasing scale though there is no evidence of the members of this organization possessing any arms at this stage. During December 1946 and January 1947 processions of National Guards in military formation began to parade the streets of Lahore, shouting provocative slogans. This display of what can only be called a hostile private army compelled the Punjab Government to declare the National Guards and the Rashtriya Swayam Sewak Sangh unlawful bodies on January 24, 1947. The Rashtriya Swayam Sewak Sangh submitted to the order and allowed its premises to be searched and locked up, but the Muslim National Guards took up a refractory attitude and, when the police arrived at their Lahore headquarters, they offered resistance. The members of the Muslim League Working Committee, Mian Iftikhar-ud-Din, Sir Feroze Khan Noon, Mian Mumtaz Daultana, Sardar Shaukat Hayat Khan and Khan Iftikhar Hussain Khan of Mamdot, hurried to the spot and refused to allow the search. They were immediately placed under arrest and the premises were broken open. Over a thousand steel helmets, uni-

---

* *Dawn* September 21, 1946.
† See note (ii) in Appendix I, page 313.

forms and a mass of inflammatory literature were recovered by the police. It was said at the time that firearms and daggers lay concealed in the residential houses of the League leaders and the name of Mian Amir-ud-Din, Mayor of Lahore, was particularly mentioned in this connection. Subsequent events showed that the suspicions were not unfounded, for during the riots firearms were seen to be used from the house of Mian Amir-ud-Din on several occasions.

The next day Mr. Liaquat Ali Khan declared that the National Guards were an integral part of the Muslim League and that, therefore, an attack on them was an attack on the Muslim League. This statement, coupled with the arrest of the Punjab League leaders, was the signal for starting a ruthless agitation by the Muslim League. The cases against League leaders were withdrawn on January 26 and the ban placed on the Muslim League National Guards and the Rashtriya Swayam Sewak Sangh was revoked on the 28th, but " the League reaction to this was open defiance " * and the war of nerves continued. The agitation was ostensibly against the Khizar Ministry but, as this Ministry was supported by the Congress and Akali Parties, it assumed a communal shape. Every day meetings were held outside the Mochi Gate and violent speeches were delivered. Processions of students and women were organized and sent to march through the streets of Lahore in a most aggressive manner. Provocative slogans were shouted, e.g., " *Leyke rahengey Pakistan—Jaise liya tha Hindustan*" (" We will take Pakistan just as we once took Hindustan "), " *Khizar kanjar hai hai*" (" Khizar, the procurer is dead ; O sorrow "), *Pakistan zindabad* (" Long live Pakistan "), " Unionist Ministry *murdabad*" (" Death to the Unionist Ministry "), etc.

The processions usually terminated near the Assembly Hall where the police made temporary arrests. A number of persons who claimed to be leading the procession were taken into custody and driven out of Lahore for a distance of ten or fifteen miles and then left on the road. This was an extremely stupid way of dealing with the situation, for the Muslim League workers took a number of cars and followed the police vans. As soon as the arrested persons were put out on the road they were brought back to Lahore in the League cars within a few minutes. The public naturally took the view that the Khizar Ministry was not firm

* Punjab Government Press *communique—Civil and Military Gazette*, January 29 1947.

enough in suppressing this agitation because Khizar himself was to some extent in sympathy with them. This may or may not have been true, nevertheless, the fact remains that this agitation and the farce of putting it down continued for a period of thirty-four days. The processionists were not always peaceful. They stopped cars on the Mall and interfered with the traffic. On one occasion a huge procession entered the premises of the Lahore High Court, wandered about the corridors, entered and damaged Judges' chambers, broke windows and articles of furniture. Some of the agitators climbed on to the roof and replaced the Union Jack by a Muslim League flag. The Union Jack was then burnt. The damage caused to the premises of the High Court was estimated at several thousand rupees. On another occasion a procession of these hooligans went to the District Courts and smashed window-panes, doors and chairs. The police tried to disperse these processionists by firing tear-gas bombs at them, but the agitators soon learnt that a wet handkerchief placed against the nose is impervious to tear gas. One day a number of respectable Muslim women led by Lady Shafi went to the house of the Premier on the excuse of interviewing him. They entered his drawing room and began to do *siyapa* as if the owner of the house were dead. The Premier's womenfolk were deeply affected by this incident but no steps were taken to put a stop to these unpleasant, and at times dangerous, activities.

On February 20, 1947, the British Prime Minister announced that it was the considered intention of His Majesty's Government to transfer political power to Indian hands by June 1948 at the latest and that this decision would not be affected by the happenings n this country. This added to Mr. Jinnah's anxiety and placed Sir Khizar on the horns of a dilemma. Mr. Jinnah had now a little more than a year to consolidate his position in Western Pakistan, and efforts to reach a settlement in the Punjab and North-West Frontier Province were started. On February 25, the Punjab Government agreed to place before the Assembly certain Ordinances containing provisions prohibiting processions and militant organizations. This was hardly satisfactory from the League point of view as Khizar's Government had a majority in the House and these Ordinances would almost certainly be ratified. On the other hand, Khizar's position was unenviable. He felt that he had lost the support of the Muslim masses and the agitation against him was gathering force and venom. The official report of Mr. Akhtar Hussain, Chief Secretary to the Punjab Government, for the month of February describes the state of affairs in the province:

"The agitation which the Muslim League commenced on the 24th of January has continued until the time of drafting this report. It has affected all districts in the province in ' a varying degree and in places there have been situations of some seriousness. The campaign is one of deliberate disobedience and defiance of law conducted with a definite undemocratic political motive. So far there has been no sign that the Muslim League leaders at large or in jail have been persuaded to a sense of responsibility or to reasonableness. In the circumstances, the early restoration of the province to its normal life cannot confidently be expected. . . . The law and order field may be further and adversely affected if the Muslim League puts certain of its threats into action. These include interference with communications and a campaign of non-payment of taxes. . . . In three places—Amritsar, Jullundur and Ambala—the police were forced to resort to firing to control unruly violent crowds and there were casualties on both sides, some of them of a serious kind. . . .

"Among Hindus and Sikhs resentment to the agitation is growing and part cularly in the case of the latter in an ominous degree. On the 12th of February . . . Master Tara Singh declared that it was communal in its essentials and had as its purpose the domination of the Punjab by Muslims. He called on the Sikhs to prepare themselves to face the Muslim League onslaught and towards this end, to organize the Akal Fauj."

In the circumstances Khizar could not look forward to the continued support of his Hindu and Sikh colleagues as the course of events in the Punjab was widening the gulf between the Muslims and the non-Muslims. The ties that bound the various elements in the Unionist Party were extremely tenuous. Moreover, the Punjab was part of Group B which had a preponderance of Muslim population and the future of a Punjab politician rested on Muslim support. Khizar had deemed it impolitic to deal with the League agitation with a firm hand and his indecision had earned him the odium of Muslims and non-Muslims alike. The former thought that his continuance in office was keeping the Muslim League out of power while the latter interpreted his mildness as sympathy for the League. The compelling force of

Mr. Attlee's statement demanded an immediate decision but a decision in the circumstances was no easy matter. Conditions in the province were fast approaching a state of anarchy while his own political future was dark and uncertain. Finally, realizing that whether he were in office or out he could exercise no influence on the future affairs of the Punjab, he decided to quit and on March 2, 1947, tendered his resignation. He justified his action by saying that the declaration of His Majesty's Government of February 20 had completely changed the position and that he must resign in order to let the Muslim League seek the co-operation of other parties and form a Government.

Events now moved with a rapidity that made "masterful administration" of their course impossible. The Muslim League was triumphant and celebrated the occasion by illuminating their houses and business premises in the evening. Crowds began to roam about the streets shouting League slogans and congratulating Khizar on having displayed so much wisdom and good sense. Khizar, the toady, the procurer and butcher was transformed overnight into a dear brother. Young boys stopped passers-by on the road and asked them, "Have you heard the latest? Khizar is our brother!" On March 3, the Governor summoned Khan Iftikhar Hussain Khan of Mamdot, the leader of the Muslim League Party in the Legislature, and asked him to form a Government. Khan Iftikhar Hussain Khan agreed and promised to give the names of his Ministers on the following day.

A wave of resentment spread through the Congress and Panthic Parties. All the fears engendered by the events of Calcutta and Noakhali seemed about to be realized. The Muslim League could not form a Ministry without their co-operation and they determined to withhold it. They held a joint meeting in the Assembly Chamber and discussed the situation. A large crowd of Muslims who had collected outside kept up a continuous barrage of provocative Muslim League slogans. They said that they would take Pakistan by force, if necessary. As soon as the meeting was over Master Tara Singh and a number of Sikh and Congress leaders came out of the Assembly Chamber. Master Tara Singh stood on the stairs facing the hostile Muslim crowd and taking out his *kirpan* flourished it in front of him. He shouted, "*Kat ke deynge apni jan maggar nahin deynge Pakistan*" ("We shall kill ourselves and give you our lives but will never concede Pakistan"). This somewhat childish prank was about to develop into a most ugly incident when the police intervened and dispersed the crowd. The same evening non-Muslims held a mammoth meeting in the grounds of Kapurthala House and the leaders gave vent to their pent-up anger against the Muslim League attitude. For six weeks they had remained silent spectators of the Muslim League campaign but Khizar's resignation and the prospect of a Muslim League Government put too great a strain on their patience. Master Tara Singh had, on February 28, given a Press interview to a representative of the *New York Times* and had remarked, " I do not see how we can avoid civil war. There can be no settlement if the Muslims want to rule the Punjab. We cannot trust the Muslims under any circumstances. The Sikhs had the ability to keep the Muslims out of Eastern Punjab but why should we stop there. We shall drive them out of the Punjab entirely. The Sikhs have started to reorganize their own private volunteer army in response to the Muslim League month-old agitation against the Coalition Ministry of the Punjab in which the Sikhs are represented." In his speech on March 3, in the grounds of Kapurthala House, he was even more categorical.

" O Hindus and Sikhs ! Be ready for self-destruction like the Japanese and the Nazis. Our motherland is calling for blood and we shall satiate the thirst of our mother with blood. By crushing Moghulistan we shall trample Pakistan. I have been feeling for many a day now that mischief has been brewing in the province and for that reason I started reorganizing the Akali Party. If we can snatch the Government from the Britishers no one can stop us from snatching the Government from the Muslims. We have in our hold the legs and the limbs of the Muslim League and we shall break them. Disperse from here on the solemn affirmation that we shall not allow the League to exist. The world has always been ruled by minorities. The Muslims snatched the kingdom from the Hindus, and the Sikhs grabbed it from the hands of the Muslims, and the Sikhs ruled over the Muslims with their might and the Sikhs shall even now rule over them. We shall rule over them and will get the Government, fighting. I have sounded the bugle. Finish the Muslim League."

Giani Kartar Singh reminded his audience that the yellow flag of the Sikhs used to fly on the Fort at Lahore and hoped that the same flag would fly again. The Congress speakers were not violent but the audience could not overlook the fact that they spoke from the same platform.

These pompous and boastful utterances were mere empty threats. The Akal Fauj of Master Tara Singh existed only in his imagination and the preparedness of the Sikhs was nothing more than a piece of wishful thinking. The folly of these provocative speeches was abundantly demonstrated by the manner in which the non-Muslims and more particularly the Sikhs suffered in the March riots. They found themselves without any means of self-defence and perished in thousands.

On the following morning the non-Muslim students of Lahore were to hold a meeting in the Gol Bagh.* The meeting was banned and did not take place. Some of the students, however, collected in the square in front of the Government College and tried to organize a *hartal*. The Principal, Mr. Bukhari, called the police and the peaceful crowd was subjected to indiscriminate firing by the police. A number of persons were killed. Another procession of non-Muslim students later in the afternoon was attacked by the Muslim National Guards. This was the prelude to the stabbing of non-Muslims in various parts of the city. Rioting now started in right earnest and a number of Hindu shops in Sua Bazaar and Chowk Rang Mahal were set on fire. By the evening thirty-seven cases of non-Muslim casualties were reported in the Mayo Hospital.

The Governor abandoned the negotiations with the Muslim League leader and took over the administration of the province under section 93 of the Government of India Act. This did not improve the situation and in no way helped to check the terror which had been let loose by the Muslims upon the city of Lahore. Rioting at the same time broke out in the cities of Amritsar, Rawalpindi and Multan and the rural areas of Rawalpindi, Multan, Jhelum and Attock Districts. The similarity of the pattern followed by the Muslim rioters in all these places indicated a preconceived and well-developed plan.

On March 5, rioting had spread to almost all parts of the city of Lahore. Hindus and Sikhs were stabbed in Gumti Bazaar, Kinari Bazaar, Kasera Bazaar and Rang Mahal. The police pickets suddenly disappeared from these localities. Shops were looted and burnt. A Muslim mob assisted by National Guards arrived in Rang Mahal and began to loot the shops. The non-Muslim residents offered resistance. Thereupon a Muslim Sub-Inspector with a police party arrived on the scene and opened fire

---

* The Gol Bagh is situated near the District Courts and opposite the Government College.

upon the non-Muslim defenders. A Hindu young man had the temerity to make a protest to the Sub-Inspector and, on this, the Sub-Inspector overpowered him and shot him dead. Instances of this type were reported from several localities of Lahore. A number of houses and shops in different parts of the city, all owned or occupied by non-Muslims, were destroyed by fire. There was hardly any traffic on the Mall. Schools were closed down and it became unsafe for children to venture out even in the middle of the day. Tension and anxiety increased on all sides, though the first fury of the rioting died down after three or four days, and, on March 11, there was quiet in the city although the streets were completely deserted and all shops were shut. On March 14, Mr. Nehru and Sardar Baldev Singh paid a visit to Lahore and were horrified to see the damage done by the hooligans.

Riots began in Amritsar almost simultaneously. On March 6 the train from Batala was stopped by a Muslim mob at Sharifpura, a suburb of Amritsar. Several Hindu and Sikh passengers were killed and when the train reached Amritsar, pools of blood were seen in many compartments. The women's compartment contained a number of dead bodies. A Hindu Magistrate posted at Amritsar had gone to Lahore for a day's holiday. He hurried back to duty, and, outside the railway station, he saw a crowd of frightened and excited men rushing from the direction of the city. They were shouting that firing had begun. Picking his way with difficulty through this mob he reached home and rang up the District Magistrate for instructions. To his astonishment, the District Magistrate ordered him to go to the hospital and record the statements of injured persons. At the hospital he saw heads almost severed from bodies, bellies ripped open with intestines protruding from the wounds, arms and legs chopped off and all kinds of horrible injuries. Many of the patients could hardly speak and anything they said could not stay the holocaust proceeding in the city. On March 7, Amritsar was reported to be a veritable inferno. Fires were raging in different parts of the city. Non-Muslim shops in Hall Bazaar, Katra Jaimal Singh and the surrounding areas were destroyed or greatly damaged. By the next day 140 deaths had been recorded at the mortuary; the number of casualties treated in the two main hospitals was 275. The actual number of dead and wounded far exceeded these figures. Many dead bodies were consumed by the fire, others were buried under the debris of fallen buildings.

It appeared at first that the British Deputy Commissioner and the Police officers had lost their heads and did not possess the ability or the courage to deal with the situation. The District Magistrate displayed an amazing degree of indifference towards all calls for help, and the Muslim Deputy Superintendent of Police declined to risk the lives of his policemen and proceed to the city from where huge columns of fire and smoke could be seen rising, while the shrieks of the frenzied mob and their victims added to the confusion and horror of the scene. It was, however, soon clear that this indifference and lack of courage were due to a callous disregard of non-Muslim life and property, for it was observed that very few Muslims suffered during this preliminary phase of the disturbances. All factories, save one, owned by non-Muslims within the jurisdiction of 'D' Division Police Station, were burnt down. The Jawala Flour Mill alone stood intact and supplied food to the city. If this mill were destroyed the whole of Amritsar would starve. The Deputy Inspector-General of Police was persuaded to depute a guard of Hindu policemen for its protection. A day later the Hindu policemen were replaced by Muslims, apparently under the directions of the Muslim Deputy Superintendent of Police. When a Hindu Magistrate rang up the District Magistrate and asked him to call in the military and declare Martial Law, the latter merely swore and banged the telephone receiver down. The non-Muslim officers were placed in positions from which they could make no contribution towards efforts to restore peace. They were entrusted with routine duties of patrolling the Civil Lines and the suburbs. They were frequently sent out on a wild-goose chase to stop imaginary Sikh *jathas* said to be converging towards the town. Muslim Magistrates assisted by Muslim Police officials were in charge of the city and lent their support and connivance to the miscreants. The Muslim hooligans were well-organized mobs carrying their own ambulance arrangements. Doctors in white overalls and stretcher-bearers accompanied them on their raids. The Muslim League agitation of January and February had prepared them for this event and they had acquired a sense of cohesion and solidarity. On the other hand, weeks of quasi-peaceful processions, when no open conflict between the communities took place, had lulled the non-Muslims into a false sense of security, and when the Muslim assault began they were taken completely unawares. They suffered grievously both in life and in property.

The devastation caused by fire and the difficulties of leading a normal life during long curfew hours were aggravated by the breakdown of essential services. The scavenging staff disappeared, the water-pipes in many places were broken or cut, electric supply became uncertain. Heaps of night soil and dirt covered the streets from end to end. Broken wires, electric poles and mounds of rubble lying everywhere added to the gloom and desolation of the city. Only the rationing service continued to function throughout. The Rationing Controller* worked day and night and saw that every depot was well supplied with flour. Inside the city he distributed bags of flour to trusted residents, Muslim and non-Muslim alike, and gave them directions that they were to supply the needs of the entire street or block of houses.

The rioting continued for a whole week before it was brought under control.

In Multan, too, clashes began on March 5. The Hindu and Sikh students of the local schools and colleges took out a procession to protest against the shooting of peaceful students in Lahore. A mob of Muslims armed with *lathis,* daggers and spears and shouting " *Leyke rahenge Pakistan, Pakistan zindabad* " † attacked the procession near Bohar Gate and inflicted injuries on several students. Within a short time trouble spread to other parts of the city and Muslim hooligans ran about the streets murdering Sikhs and Hindus, looting their shops and houses and setting fire to them. This state of affairs continued for the space of three days. Of the first eight persons killed, seven were Sikhs. Thirty-eight injured persons were admitted into hospital on March 5. The victims had been attacked with swords, daggers or hatchets. Several houses and shops were on fire and Muslim crowds were reported to be obstructing the operations of the Fire Brigade.

A fanatical Muslim mob invaded the Shri Krishan Bhagwan Tuberculosis Hospital outside Delhi Gate and began to butcher the miserable patients in their beds. The Hindu compounder who tried to argue with the hooligans was immediately killed. Every sick man, woman or child in the hospital was done to death and then the hospital building was set on fire. Blocks of houses near the railway bridge, known as Serai Wan Wattan, were sprayed with petrol and set ablaze. About twenty-five houses owned by Hindus

---

* Mr. R. D. Mathur.
† ' We shall not rest till we get Pakistan. Long live Pakistan.''

on Circular Road were burnt down. All houses and shops on the road leading from the Town Hall to Kotla Tola Khan, the houses in Khuni Burj, the shops in Sabzi Mandi were looted and destroyed by fire. The palatial house of Seth Kalyan Das was attacked and burnt down. The owner came out to reason with the mob but he was cut to pieces in front of his door. Dr. Saif-ud-Din Kitchlew, the well-known Congress leader, was at the time staying with Seth Kalyan Das. He was recognized and was immediately surrounded by a mob. A number of Muslim Leaguers took him to a house and offered to release him if he signed the Muslim League pledge. Dr. Kitchlew refused and tried to make his way to the railway station. He was attacked and beaten but was able to escape alive.

The temples and Gurdwaras in the city were looted and desecrated. Many of them were burnt down. The old Dharamsala of Bawa Sant Das, the Shivala in Serai Wan Wattan, the Jain temple outside Delhi Gate, the shrine of Baba Safra, Kultarianwali Dharamsala, the local Gaushala, were all reduced to ashes. The temple of Jog Maya and the Ram Tirath Temple were desecrated, the idols were smashed and thrown out. The devotees living on the premises were slaughtered. The Devpura Temple and Devta Khu were similarly attacked and the inmates done to death.

A number of young girls were kidnapped. An Army officer patrolling the town saw four non-Muslim girls being driven in a tonga. They cried to him for help and he was able to rescue them.

The police took no steps to quell these disturbances which were wholly one sided. At least one Sub-Inspector of Police was seen shooting at unoffending Hindus and Sikhs. An Army officer arrested him but he was released on the orders of the Deputy Commissioner and the Superintendent of Police. The military finally brought the situation under control in the city of Multan on March 7, but, in the meantime, the rural areas were ablaze and looting and burning of villages started on a large scale. An Army officer while on patrol duty saw fires in the villages of Aliwala, Thulwala, Chak, Bhikwala, Kotwala, Kuruwala, Sukhanwala, Bhandewala, Godhawala, Isawala, Turger, Chandhar and Khujan. This continued for several days and it was not till a large Army force was sent out with instructions not to brook hooliganism at any cost that comparative peace was restored.

A number of other districts were involved. In the words of Mr. Akhtar Hussain, Chief Secretary to Government, Punjab,

8

" With the news of grave events radiating from Lahore, there has
been bloodshed and burning in many districts and rural areas
have paid the price levied by insensate fury as well as towns." The
district of Rawalpindi was the worst affected area and the non-
Muslims who were in a small minority in the rural areas perished
in large numbers.

On the morning of March 6, a crowd of Muslims collected in
Raja Bazaar, Rawalpindi, and began to raise the usual provocative
slogans. Soon another crowd of non-Muslims faced them, shouting
counter-slogans. A clash was averted but that night the Muslim
residents of Ratta Amral, a Muslim majority area on the outskirts
of Rawalpindi, attacked the Sikh and Hindu houses. The houses
were set on fire and some of the inmates were mercilessly butchered.
Many Sikhs were forcibly converted to Islam and their hair and
beards were removed. There were clashes in the city also but there
the communities were evenly balanced and the Muslims suffered as
much as the non-Muslims. By the next morning large numbers of
Muslims from the neighbouring villages had invaded the city and
the Hindus and Sikhs were outnumbered. The British Deputy
Commissioner was apathetic. Perhaps he did not possess the ability
to cope with the extraordinary situation. The Muslim Additional
District Magistrate openly connived at the misdeeds of the Muslim
mobs and, when a senior Sikh Advocate asked him for police assistance, the Additional District Magistrate accused him of spreading
false rumours and added that he was only endangering his own life.
The next day a Muslim police constable tried to shoot this Sikh
Advocate. Military pickets were posted in various parts of the city
but they did nothing beyond standing and looking on as interested
spectators of the looting and killing taking place within a few yards
of them. They said they had no orders to leave their posts. For
three days rioting went on in the city. Shots were continuously
fired from the Jumma Mosque at Hindus and Sikhs residing in the
locality. On March 7 or 8,* the President of the Cantonment
Muslim League invited eleven Hindus and Sikhs to form a Peace
Committee for re-establishing communal amity. The meeting was
held in the house of the President which stands at a little distance
from the main *abadi*. No sooner had the members of the Peace
Committee collected there than Muslims began to arrive as if by

---

* The witnesses who related this incident were making their statements after several
months and could not remember the exact date.

previous arrangement with the host. Seven of the eleven non-Muslim members were murdered at the spot. Another two who succeeded in escaping remained under medical treatment for a considerable time. The police refused to register the case. The son of one of the murdered persons was the stenographer of Mr. Scott, Deputy Inspector-General of Police. Mr. Scott ordered that the case should be registered but his order was not carried out for several days. It is scarcely necessary to add that the murderers were never brought to book.

Conditions in the rural areas of Rawalpindi beggar description. On March 6, 1947, meetings were held in the village mosques and the Muslims were told that the Jumma Mosque at Rawalpindi had been razed to the ground by Hindus and Sikhs and that the city streets were littered with Muslim corpses. The audience were exhorted to avenge these wrongs. The village population of the district of Rawalpindi has a large proportion of Muslim military pensioners possessing firearms and other weapons. These men, incited in this manner, rose up against the non-Muslim residents and attacked one village after another. The *modus operandi* was almost invariably the same. A mob of Muslims armed with all kinds of weapons, shouting slogans and beating drums, approached a selected village and surrounded it from all sides. A few non-Muslim residents were immediately killed to strike terror throughout the village. The rest were asked to embrace Islam. If they refused or showed reluctance a ruthless assault was launched upon non-Muslim life and property. Some members of the mob started looting and burning their houses and shops. Others searched out young and good-looking girls and carried them away. Not infrequently young women were molested and raped in the open, while all around them frenzied hooligans rushed about shouting, looting and setting fire to houses. Most of the non-Muslims would leave their houses and run to the local Gurdwara or a house affording some measure of protection or defence and there men, women and children, huddled together, would hear the noise of carnage, see the smoke rising from their burning homes and wait for the end. The horror of what they saw or heard made them insensible to pain or suffering. Some women would commit suicide or suffer death at the hands of their relations with stoic indifference, others would jump into a well or be burnt alive uttering hysterical cries. The men would come out and meet death in a desperate sally against the marauders.

Some villages were completely wiped out. Houses and shops were looted and then burnt down and demolished. Conversion saved the lives of many but not their property. Refusal to accept Islam brought complete annihilation. The men were shot or put to the sword. In some cases small children were thrown in cauldrons of boiling oil. In one village men and women who refused to embrace Islam were collected together and after a ring of brambles and firewood had been placed around them they were burnt alive. A woman threw her four-month old baby to save it from burning. The infant was impaled upon a spear and thrown back into the fire. In Murree nearly a hundred houses belonging to non-Muslims were systematically marked and burnt down.

In as many as 110 villages, attacks of this nature were made by Muslim mobs. A conservative estimate, based on the evidence of over two hundred witnesses, places the number of persons killed at two thousand and five hundred, the number of persons forcibly converted at more than three thousand and the number of girls kidnapped at two hundred.*

It is impossible to give a detailed account of these happenings. We content ourselves by giving a few representative instances.†

The Muslim League leaders of Kahuta sent out messages to the Muslims of the neighbouring villages inviting them to collect at Kahuta on March 7, and take part in a flag-hoisting ceremony. A huge gathering was held in the local mosque but what transpired at this meeting remained secret. Early on the following morning many thousands of armed Muslims arrived in Kahuta. The non-Muslims approached the Tehsildar and also invoked the help of the Sub-Inspector of Police. Telegrams were sent by the Lambardar but it transpired later that the Muslim Sub-Postmaster did not transmit them. By chance a detachment of a British Army unit, on patrol duty, arrived at Kahuta but they were sent back by the Tehsildar who assured them that there was no danger of any disturbance occuring. Within a short time of the detachment leaving the town, a determined attack was launched by the Muslims. The towers of the mosque and the hillocks surrounding the town were occupied by gunmen and a volley of shots was fired to frighten away the non-Muslims. Crowds then ran into the town, sprinkled

---

* These figures relate to the rural areas only and do not include the casulties of a number of smaller villages where disturbances are reported to have occurred but from where no witnesses were examined. See also page 112 for the official figures.

† See also the table given in Appendix II.

petrol on houses and set them on fire. Large quantities of movables were removed and carried away on camels, donkeys, mules and motor lorries. The annual examinations were being held in the Government Girls' School. The Assistant District Inspectress asked the Sub-Inspector of Police to depute two policemen to guard the school. This request was refused and a little later the school was attacked by a mob of Muslims. The Tehsildar himself was seen shooting at non-Muslims with his gun while his orderly carried his box of cartridges. The Hindus and Sikhs of the village sought refuge in the Gurdwara and remained in a state of siege for twenty-seven hours without food, water or sanitary arrangements. Shots fired at the Gurdwara caused the death of a few non-Muslims. On the afternoon of March 9, the military arrived and evacuated the non-Muslims to the Civil Rest House from where they were escorted to safety. They were, however, compelled to leave all their movable and immovable property behind.

Bewal was a village of mixed population, the Sikhs numbering about four hundred. On the morning of March 10, some of the Sikh residents tried to travel to Gujar Khan but the Muslim lorry driver refused to carry them on the ground that the Sub-Inspector of Police had forbidden the issue of lorry tickets to Sikhs. The same afternoon a large crowd of Muslims shouting "*Ya Ali, Ya Ali,*" to the beating of drums, was seen approaching. The non-Muslim villagers entrenched themselves in two improvised shelters. At 11 p.m. the raiders set fire to a number of non-Muslim houses on the outskirts of the village. The siege of the village continued throughout the night, and, on the morning of March 11, fresh gangs of raiders arrived. The assault on the non-Muslim sanctuaries was now opened. Houses around the Gurdwara, where many of the Sikh residents had taken shelter, were set on fire. The fire spread to the Gurdwara and those inside were almost all burnt alive. The house of a retired Extra Assistant Commissioner, in which the rest of the non-Muslims had collected, was also attacked in a similar manner. Very few of the four hundred Sikh residents escaped alive. Many women and girls saved their honour by self-immolation. They collected their beddings and cots in a heap and when the heap caught fire they jumped on to it, raising cries of "*Sat Sri Akal.*" The raiders behaved in a most cruel manner and subjected the few men whom they captured to torture. The eyes of Mukand Singh, one of the residents, were removed from their sockets and he was dragged by the legs till he died.

Doberan had a population of seventeen hundred of whom a very large majority were Sikhs. On the morning of March 10, swarms of armed raiders from the neighbouring villages began to collect in front of Doberan. The non-Muslim residents sought shelter in the local Gurdwara. The raiders began to loot the houses thus deserted and set fire to them. The Sikhs had a few firearms and fought the raiders from the Gurdwara. They, however, suffered heavily and soon ran out of ammunition. The raiders asked them to surrender their arms and promised not to molest them. About three hundred of them came out and they were placed in the house of one Barkat Singh. During the night the roof was ripped open, kerosene oil was poured in, and those inside were burnt alive. In the morning the doors of the Gurdwara were broken open. The remaining Sikhs dashed out sword in hand and died fighting the raiders. Very few escaped from this hideous massacre. The total loss of life in this village is estimated at 506.

In Qazian, a village five miles from Gujar Khan, the atmosphere on the morning of March 7 was tense. Qazi Ghulam Hussain, a retired Government official, assured the Sikh residents that there was no cause for alarm and that they were perfectly safe in his village. On the morning of March 9, a large crowd of Muslims began to assemble near the village *abadi* on the pretence of holding a *kabaddi* match. A few hours later this crowd encircled the village. The Muslims advanced with the beat of drums and began setting fire to the Sikh houses and Gurdwara. Shots were fired at the raiders and they retreated. On the following morning they came back, reinforced, in larger numbers. Qazi Ghulam Hussain asked the Sikhs to come to his house for the night with their valuables. A number of Sikhs accepted this invitation and went there with their women and children. At 4 p.m. the raiders appeared in front of Qazi Ghulam Hussain's house and the Qazi then asked his guests to surrender their arms and leave his house. When the unarmed Sikhs emerged from the house they were set upon by the raiders and murdered. Three young girls were raped in public. Sant Singh, a Sikh resident, had on the previous day killed one of the Muslim raiders and had then hidden himself. He was sent for by Qazi Ghulam Hussain and, while he was talking to him, a rope was flung round his neck and he was dragged to a firewood stall where he and his son were hacked to bits and then burnt. The survivors were evacuated to Gujar Khan by military lorries on the night of the 11th.

Nara village is situated in a hilly tract. It had a majority of
Sikhs but the neighbouring villages were all predominantly Muslim. At about 4 p.m. on March 9, Muslim mobs were seen
approaching the village and, late at night, the village was attacked
and the outlying houses were set on fire. One of the residents,
Makhan Singh and his wife and daughter were burnt alive in their
house. The looting and burning continued on the following day.
Some of the raiders had firearms and they appeared to be ex-
military men. On March 11 the number of raiders swelled to several
thousands and the village was encircled. As the ring narrowed
the Sikh residents offered a stubborn resistance. The raiders
seized a number of women and children and threw them into the
blaze of a burning house. A few women committed suicide by
jumping into a well. Over a hundred men were killed ; about fifty
were forcibly converted to Islam. The survivors were evacuated
to Gujar Khan.

Moghal was a Muslim majority village with a population of
about two hundred Sikhs. On the midnight of March 9, the village
was attacked by a large mob of Muslims. A number of Sikh
houses were set on fire. The Sikhs collected themselves in the
Gurdwara and, with the two rifles which they possessed, returned
the fire of the raiders. The fight continued till the evening of
March 10 and there was loss of life on both sides. Then a Muslim
ringleader, Qazim Khan of Dadochha, swore by the Quran that
the Muslims had no wish to do injury to men of such courage,
and undertook not to molest the Sikhs if they came out unarmed.
Sikhs had exhausted their ammunition and had no choice left but
to accept Qazim Khan's terms. When they came out of the
Gurdwara the rioters fell upon them and hacked them to pieces.

At Dhamali, a village in Tehsil Kahuta, a mob of over
a thousand raiders arrived on the evening of March 9. There
was exchange of fire and the raiders retreated. The next
day, a bigger crowd appeared but this also retreated after
an exchange of fire. On March 12 a crowd of several thousands
arrived and began to set fire to the village. A Hindu resident of
the village offered terms of peace and the raiders demanded fourteen
thousand rupees for the safety of the village. The money was paid
and the raiders left. The next day (March 13) the raiders again
appeared in the afternoon. The non-Muslim residents, now desperate, ran out with whatever weapons they had and attacked the
raiders. Very few of them, however, escaped and it is estimated

that not less than five hundred non-Muslims of the village were killed. When Dhamali lay in ruins and almost the entire non-Muslim population had been decimated, military lorries arrived to render assistance to the Hindus and Sikhs. It was then too late.

Almost every village in the Rawalpindi District where non-Muslims lived was attacked and plundered in this manner and Hindus and Sikhs were murdered and subjected to indescribable barbarities. In Thoha Khalsa some Sikh women were thrown into a well, others jumped in of their own free will to save themselves from being raped. A mob of several thousand Muslims raided Harilal, the birth-place of the Akali leader Master Tara Singh. Master Tara Singh's house was razed to the ground and his uncle, Gokal Singh, was killed. Kuri Dalal and Dehra Khalsa were looted and burnt. In Kallar the residents resisted the raiders for a time stubbornly, but the village was eventually looted and burnt, and large numbers of residents murdered.

This wholesale massacre and plunder in Rawalpindi District ceased in the middle of March and there was comparative peace for several months. The Muslms had achieved a decisive victory in the opening battle of the war for Pakistan. Mr. Williams, Home Secretary to Government, Punjab, in a note written on July 26, 1947, gave the comparative figures of casualties as follows:

Number of persons killed

Non-Muslims	...	...	...	...	2,263
Muslims	...	...	...	...	38

Number of persons injured

Non-Muslims	...	...	...	...	234
Muslims	...	...	...	...	126

These figures, however, nowhere approach accuracy as " owing to the widespread nature of disturbances and breakdown of normal administrative machinery " more accurate statistics could not be prepared. The information given was collected from the number of cases registered with the police. " They do not include losses inflicted where whole families were wiped out and no claims were made." The non-Muslim population of West Punjab feared that these incidents were merely a foretaste of what awaited them in the future State of Pakistan. The Chief Secretary of the Punjab recorded, " It is safe to say that feelings between them were never so strained or chances of their coming together ever so remote.

Invisibly but definitely all non-Muslims have been drawn together and there has been a manifest stiffening in their resolve neither to collaborate with the Muslims nor suffer their domination. . . . The prospect is not improved by the brutality of some of the acts committed by the majority community (Muslims) in the areas most affected." On April 2, Hindu and Sikh leaders made a demand for the partition of the Punjab and asked Mr. Nehru to exercise his influence in this direction.

Lord Wavell's pro-League attitude and his clumsy handling of the political situation forced the British Government to recall him and send out Lord Mountbatten in his place. The demand for the partition of the Punjab was placed before the new Viceroy. On April 15, he was able to persuade Mr. Jinnah to join Gandhiji in issuing a joint appeal for peace. This appeal was received well in the foreign Press and the London *Times* observed that it marked " an important change in the outlook of the Muslim League." It did not, however, improve the situation in India one whit. Many thought that Mr. Jinnah had been persuaded into issuing this appeal against his wishes and that he was, at heart, glad at the course of events in the Punjab. Muslim preparations for a large-scale offensive continued. The Chief Secretary reported in April 1947 that an additional 5,630 National Guards had been recruited. " In the Eastern Punjab active training has been confined mainly to Simla, Ambala Cantonment and Panipat where Guards have bee exercising secretly in *lathi* fighting." He estimated that the number of Muslim League National Guards was about thirty-nine thousand.

Three days before this appeal was issued (on April 12) there was a recrudescence of trouble in Amritsar, after a respite of nearly five weeks. Fifteen men were killed and thirty-two injured. Fourteen places, including two factories in Qila Bhangian, three shops in Kucha Chhappar Wala and eight houses in Kucha Saroop Singh were entirely gutted. The fire brigade recovered some pieces of cloth soaked in kerosene oil and a broken bottle of kerosene oil from in front of several houses. From now onwards there was no peace in Amritsar or Lahore. Arson and stabbing cases became a normal state of affairs and ceased to arouse surprise. The residents began to pursue their usual avocations regularly. But there was no peace of mind, no feeling of security ; a lurking fear haunted the men whether they were at home or outside. A man walking along the Mall would suddenly turn round to make sure that he was not about to be stabbed in the back. People stopped going out to lonely places or paying friendly calls after dark. The non-Muslims took special precautions for safeguarding their personal property. In the narrow lanes of the city of Lahore, barred iron gates were put up and these were closed at sundown. Women did not go out to shop unless accompanied by male members of their family. Underneath the apparently normal life a continuous fear and tension gnawed at the hearts of men, and the universal opinion was that worse things were yet to happen.

On May 9, serious trouble again broke out in Amritsar. On the following day a party of twelve Sikhs was returning to the city after cremating the body of a child. They were waylaid by a gang of armed Muslims who beat them and then, after sprinkling petrol upon them, set fire to the bodies. Seven of the party died at the spot while the remaining five sustained severe wounds and burns. Other incidents followed and the Chief Secretary in his official report said, " Some of the acts committed (by the Muslims) were shocking in their stark brutality, and an attack on a funeral party of a child in which six Sikhs and one Hindu were killed has added to an already over-long list of Muslim atrocities." * When the Muslim *badmashes* of Amritsar noticed that trouble had not simultaneously broken out at Lahore they sent some glass bangles to that city. The present was intended to bring home to the Lahore Muslims their cowardice and effeminacy in not vindicating the honour of Islam. Trouble at once broke out in Lahore and, on May 14, there were several stabbing cases in different parts of the city. Nine persons were killed and twenty injured. A Muslim mob, armed with hatchets, swords and lathis, invaded the Shahalmi Gate area and set fire to a shop. Early the following morning reports of gunshots could be heard from the direction of Mochi Gate.

During the night an exchange of brickbats and bottles containing explosive material had taken place and a number of fires were started. " Delirious noisy slogans and war cries rent the sky." † Bitter fighting continued throughout the night. People stood on the roofs of their houses shouting and hurling down brickbats, crude country-made incendiary bombs and fire-balls. On May 16, the intensity and bitterness of the conflict achieved a new record. The whole of the city seemed to be ablaze with a

---

* The Chief Secretary, it must be remembered, was a Muslim officer of the Indian Civil Service (Mr. Akhtar Hussain).
* *Civil and Military Gazette*, May 16, 1947.

dozen mighty fires raging in different localities. The stabbing went on unabated. This state of affairs continued for several days. Entire streets and rows of houses were consumed by fire and reduced to a heap of rubble and ashes. The bazaar inside Shahalmi Gate, once the main centre of the provisions trade, was reduced to a complete wreck. Mounds of hot smouldering building material made the road impassable. The demolition of burnt or half-burnt houses to prevent the spread of fire added to the desolation. The bazaar inside Akbari Gate was a hot glowing oven. Every shop and house had been destroyed in the non-Muslim blocks and bare blackened walls lined the street. Hindus and Sikhs began to leave the city and, each day, during the hours when curfew was suspended, long lines of these unfortunate people, smitten by the scourge of religious frenzy, could be seen moving from all gates of the inner city and converging towards the railway station. They carried beddings on their heads, small bundles in their hands; the women carried young children and bundles of clothes hurriedly tied up in a duster or old *dopatta*. They had left the major portion of their belongings to perish or to be looted. They had abandoned their houses and shops to the future State of Pakistan. Their faces grim with the memory of what they had seen, their eyes full of a vague fear of the future, their minds darkened by the shadow that hung over their heads, their one conscious thought was ' flight,' though the end of the journey was not in sight. And so these pitiable processions of mute humanity continued to move day after day in an ever-increasing volume. From Multan, Gujranwala, Jhelum and Rawalpindi people were moving eastward in batches of dozens and scores. Soon this exodus became the rout of a helpless and defeated people.

The Muslim police and some of the Muslim Magistrates made a very important contribution to these destructive operations. The Hindu and Sikh police personnel were kept on routine duty in the Police Lines while the Muslim constables and officers were entrusted with the duty of maintaining peace and enforcing the curfew orders. The curfew was seen to work solely for the benefit of the Muslims. During curfew hours Muslims were seen to move about freely. A party of them would enter a Hindu shop or house and set fire to it with the help of petrol or fire-balls.*

---

* The fire-ball or fire-*gola*, as it came to be known, was a new invention manufactured during the riots. It consisted of a large roll of string and a cloth soaked in coal-tar and petrol. It could remain alight for a considerable time and proved to be a very efficient weapon for spreading fire.

When the owners rushed out to extinguish the fire they were arrested or shot for violating the curfew orders. If there were danger of the fire spreading to a Muslim building, a Muslim group would arrive and, with the help of the police and the fire brigade, control the fire. This procedure was adopted on a large scale in the Mozang area. Here the houses in the front line belonging to the non-Muslims were burnt down while scarcely a single Muslim house was damaged. The activities of a Muslim Magistrate became notorious in Lahore. He was personally responsible for the death of Mr. Sethi, a Sub-Divisional Officer of the Electricity Department, who came out at night to attend to his official duties. Mr. Sethi had a curfew pass but the Muslim Magistrate ordered him to be arrested and within a few minutes he was shot. When a privately owned fire brigade came to attend to a fire in a block of Hindu houses, the water-hose was cut under the orders of the same Muslim Magistrate. He remarked that the Municipal Fire Brigade was the only one entitled to attend to these fires.

It was about this time (May 1947) that the non-Muslims in Lahore and Amritsar began to hit back. Rumours went round that the Rashtriya Swayam Sewak Sangh had taken upon themselves the duty of defending Hindu life and property. There were cases of Muslims being stabbed both in Lahore and in Amritsar. The results achieved by the Rashtriya Swayam Sewak Sangh were, however, grossly exaggerated. The Hindus frequently boasted that they had not lacked courage in striking back. The Sikhs also bragged about what they had accomplished. There can be very little doubt, however, that in Lahore the Hindu and Sikh casualties far exceeded those of the Muslims, while the Muslim loss in property was almost negligible. In Amritsar it was reported that the score was about even * though, there also, the Hindu loss in property was several times the Muslim loss.

In the meantime discussions and negotiations between the various political leaders and the Viceroy were proceeding. The Congress was anxious to avoid a partition of the country and was prepared to make many concessions in order to retain the integral unity of India. Mr. Jinnah, on the other hand, was insistent on his demand for Pakistan. The non-Muslims of the Punjab wanted a partition of the province if a separate Muslim State were set up.

---

* In the month of May a Hindu lawyer paid a visit to a Muslim Judge of the High Court and during the course of this visit a telephone message was received from Amritsar. The Muslim Judge said laughingly that the score in Amritsar was even and that the Muslims had not done so badly.

They said it would be impossible for them to live in Pakistan and pointed out that the events in the Muslim majority areas of West Punjab had amply demonstrated the utter futility of expecting the Muslims to safeguard their life and property or treat them with justice. The eastern districts had a predominantly non-Muslim population and there was no justification for including them in the Muslim State of Pakistan. Mr. Jinnah twisted this argument in his own favour and urged the immediate necessity of dividing the country into Muslim majority and Hindu majority areas, each independent of the other. This, he maintained, was the only solution and the only way of putting an end to the fratricidal war. The inexorable logic of separatism and the two-nation theory forced Mr. Jinnah to accept the partition of the Punjab and Bengal. " The moth-eaten and truncated Pakistan " which he had spurned a few years previously was now the only choice before him. But he was adamant and unequivocally declared that he must have a separate independent Muslim State and a Muslim homeland. Once, during the discussions, when the unwisdom of cutting up the country and setting up two widely separated and attenuated States of Pakistan was pointed out to him he picked up a box of matches and, striking a dramatic pose, exclaimed with considerable heat: " Even if I get *so* much territory for a separate State of Pakistan I shall insist on partition." Further argument was useless. Months of anxiety and tension had weakened the resisting power of the Congress leaders. They had been struggling with the Muslim League both inside the Government and outside. The policy of the Muslim League members of the Interim Government had been one of avowed obstruction. They maintained that they had entered office merely to fight for Pakistan. They were able to defeat almost every progressive measure which the Congress members were desirous of adopting. The Interim Government had no unity or cohesion and the different departments of administration frequently pulled in different directions. All over the country unrest and lawlessness were spreading and, in the Punjab, conditions bordering on utter anarchy prevailed. Mr. Nehru and his colleagues felt tired and helpless. Frustration and chaos stared them in the face. Years of suffering and hard labour had brought them to a blind alley and the only alternatives were ignominious retreat or a way out by the acceptance of partition. They agreed to partition. They withdrew their opposition to the establishment of a separate independent State carved out of a united India. They, however, insisted that the demand of the Sikhs for the partition of the Punjab and of the West Bengal Hindus for the partition of Bengal must be conceded by Mr. Jinnah. Lord Mountbatten saw the justness of this demand and, in this matter, gave his full support to the Congress and Sikh leaders. The Punjab and Bengal were to be divided ; the district of Sylhet was to be separated from Assam and joined to East Bengal. The boundaries would be demarcated by two Boundary Commissions specially set up for this purpose.

The Mountbatten Plan of June 3, 1947, was thus drawn up and agreed to by the various party leaders. This was the first occasion on which the different warring elements in the country had attained some measure of unanimity, and it was hoped that with the implementation of this scheme, sanity would return to the land and constructive action take the place of disorder and despair. It is not necessary to discuss the Mountbatten Plan and its implications or the difficulties and dangers inherent in the mode of partition proposed. The Boundary Commissions and their terms of reference were subjected to bitter criticism in many quarters. It was said that the whole thing was a complete farce and only silly people could expect a fair and just decision from a tribunal whose Chairman did not attend a single hearing, though it was he and he alone in whose hands rested the ultimate decision.* There was, however, no other way in which this matter could be disposed of as expeditiously or with greater satisfaction to all concerned. Time was a vital consideration. Conditions in the Punjab showed little improvement, the attitude of the Muslim League was hardening and the British Government had agreed to hand over power on August 15, 1947. Everything had to be rushed through at break-neck speed, for it was hoped that, with the transference of power and the establishment of Pakistan, the feeling of frustration among the Muslim masses would disappear and their anger would be appeased. The Congress leaders did not envisage the complete collapse of the administrative machinery and the stampede that followed the attainment of independence. Attacks by Muslims in West Punjab were followed by counter-attacks by Sikhs and Hindus in East Punjab. Reprisal followed retaliation till the whole province was one seething cauldron of hate and bestial passions. The poison infected the unlettered and ignorant masses as well as the educated

---

* Sir Cyril Radcliffe was the Chairman of both the Boundary Commissions. He did not attend the hearings personally but verbatim reports of the proceedings were sent him every day by air. After the hearings were concluded he held discussions with the members of the Commissions and then communicated his decision or Award to the Viceroy.

middle classes; it spread to the officials upon whom rested the duty of maintaining law and order, it corrupted the police and the army who were entrusted with the safety and security of the citizens; it antagonized friends and neighbours till they turned upon each other with murderous frenzy. Muslims and non-Muslims vied with each other in degrading themselves to the lowest level of barbarity. What had been happening in West Punjab since March began to happen in East Punjab in August and the grim sport of murder and rapine was played on both sides with equal ferocity. But while the Government of India and the East Punjab Government mobilized all their resources to quell the disturbances, the West Punjab Government gave encouragement to the rowdy elements by many official and unofficiall acts. The first of these was the release of all Muslims who had been detained under the Punjab Public Safety Act or who had been convicted of crimes committed during communal riots. Even persons who had been sentenced to long terms of imprisonment on charges of murder and other acts of violence were released. The restriction on the carrying of swords was removed the day after Pakistan was established. Muslims were encouraged to carry swords and District Magistrates were instructed to grant arms licences freely to Muslims. *

The following pages contain a brief account of the main incidents in the various districts of West Punjab during August and the following months. Considerations of space and time make it impossible to give full and complete details of the atrocities committed by the Muslims or the suffering to which the non-Muslims were subjected. An attempt has, however, been made to give a true overall picture of these happenings. The reader will notice many important omissions but it is hoped that he will not find false or exaggerated stories. Every effort has been made to verify and check the correctness of the narrative, and drab understatement has been preferred to picturesque probability. Allowance had frequently to be made for the angry mood of the refugees, their tendency to exaggerate their suffering and invite sympathy by magnifying the extent of their losses. It is, however, believed that the account given in these pages is as near the truth as is possible in any historical narrative.

---

* Many months later when Muslims had been completely evacuated the East Punjab Government also issued similar instructions. These instructions were intended to check the border disturbances which were assuming serious proportions.

Lahore District

Lord Louis Mountbatten paid a visit to Lahore on July 22, 1947, and as a measure of caution or anticipation directed the shadow Government of East Punjab to move their headquarters to Simla. He, at the same time, gave assurance to the residents of Lahore that there was no finality about this move; Simla was, in any case, the summer capital of the Punjab and if Lahore eventually fell to the share of India the Government could move back without great inconvenience. In the meantime, a Boundary Force would be constituted and this would furnish adequate protection to the life and property of all communities. The Viceroy's declaration heartened the Muslims and they interpreted it as an indication that Lahore would be assigned to Pakistan. To the non-Muslims, it came as a hideous shock, as they had entertained high hopes of the Boundary Commission. According to the terms of reference, the boundary between the two countries was to be drawn on the basis of contiguous majority areas,* but other factors would also be taken into consideration The non-Muslims naturally assumed that " other factors " meant financial, economic, strategic and social interests. Lahore had been built with non-Muslim capital and enterprise; 80 per cent of the property in Lahore was owned by non-Muslims and the social life of the city centred round the Hindus and Sikhs. The Ravi (if not the Chenab) was the only feasible boundary from the geographical and strategic point of view and the non-Muslims had been happy in the thought that the claim of Pakistan based merely on census figures was effete and untenable. The Viceroy's order directing a move to Simla shattered these hopes and many non-Muslims felt that they would have to migrate to India in the immediate or distant future. There were others who believed that once Pakistan, as an independent State, were established and recognized, peaceful conditions would return and members of all communities would be able to live and pursue their avocations undisturbed and unmolested. To them the proposal to constitute a Boundary Force came as a great relief, for they felt that the Army, at any rate, would not take sides and would enforce law and order with complete impartiality. These hopes, alas, did not find realization.

---

* This was a somewhat vague term as it did not specify what the unit of the area was to be: whether it was to be a district, a tehsil, a zail or a village. Broadly speaking, it was intended that Muslim majority areas (excluding islands) should be assigned to Pakistan and the Hindu majority areas to India.

On August 8, some members of the Boundary Commission came back to Lahore after having held discussion with Sir Cyril Radcliffe in Simla. The next day, all over Lahore, posters purporting to have been issued by some Muslim Associations were put up. They proclaimed that if Lahore were awarded to India the Muslims of Lahore would not accept the Award of the Boundary Commission and would retain the town by force. On the nights of August 10 and 11, meetings were held in various mosques in the city and Muslims were called upon to make a ruthless attack on non-Muslims. On the 11th morning, it was generally known in Lahore that very soon it would become impossible for non-Muslims to live there. Some Muslims issued warnings to their non-Muslim friends and advised them to leave the town at once. Trouble began inside the city early on the morning of the 11th and on the following days spread to the whole town and to the Cantonment area.

Mohalla Kharasian was attacked by a mob of five hundred armed Muslims, led by National Guards and a Sub-Inspector of Police. Mohalla Sarin was attacked in the afternoon. Fires were started in various parts of the city and by the evening the residents of the Civil Lines saw a huge wall of flames and smoke standing against the sky. Throughout the day groups of Muslims armed with guns, pistols, spears, hatchets and *lathis* wandered about the streets, attacking non-Muslims and setting fire to shops and houses. Non-Muslims remained imprisoned in their houses. Some of them were dragged out by the hooligans and slaughtered. The official *communiqué* stated that there were twenty-five fires blazing in Lahore on that day, of which eight were of a serious nature. The Mayo Hospital received fifty-six dead bodies and one hundred and twenty injured persons. Thirty injured persons were received at Sir Ganga Ram Hospital. It is needless to say that only those persons who required medical treatment were carried to the hospital and the deaths of many others who were killed at the spot were not even reported. On the 12th, the Mayo Hospital received eighty-seven dead bodies and two hundred injured. Bharat Nagar and Mohan Lal Road were subjected to a bitter attack during the course of which many non-Muslims perished. Several houses in Bharat Nagar were looted and set fire to. Kalibari Mandir was looted and defiled. Non-Muslims were being killed all over the city, in the presence of police constables, and their property was being looted. At the railway station one hundred and twenty non-

9

Muslims were waiting to catch a train for Amritsar. On the platform were twenty-five Sindi Muslim constables guarding treasury chests. Some Muslims threw stones at the police constables and, according to a prearranged plan, the constables at once began to fire at the Hindus waiting for their train. Fifteen persons were killed and twelve wounded.

The Lahore Railway Station became a veritable death-trap between August 12 and August 18. The riots in the city compelled the non-Muslims to leave, and their only avenue of escape was the railway station, because journey by road was far more perilous. On the evening of August 11, the railway station was packed with passengers. The coolies dictated their own terms for carrying luggage and were able to get fantastic sums of money. There was a general state of tension and anxiety and when news came that the Sind Express, on its way to Lahore, had been attacked by Muslims, panic spread among the passengers. The Sind Express arrived soon afterwards, and the non-Muslim volunteers rushed forward to bring out the dead bodies from the various compartments. They found that men, women and children had been brutally murdered and were lying in pools of blood. The dead bodies were carried across several platforms and a hush fell upon the intending non-Muslim passengers who stood rooted to the ground and watched their luggage with vague and grim forebodings while all that was visible of the city of Lahore was a huge tower of smoke. Fortunately a Muslim refugee train arrived from Amritsar at this time and the Muslim volunteers became engaged in bringing out the Muslim passengers and their luggage. The passengers who left by the Frontier Mail were attacked near Wahga. The Bhatinda Express, however, reached its destination safely. The next day, it became impossible for non-Muslims even to reach the railway station. They were caught and massacred on the way. The Baluch Regiment took a very prominent part in this slaughter. On August 14 and 15, the railway station became a scene of wholesale carnage. According to one witness there was a continuous rain of bullets at the railway station. The military shot and plundered non-Muslims freely. The passengers from a refugee train from Sacha Sauda came out to get drinking water, and thirteen of them were shot dead. A Hindu passenger was pushed into the compartment of a moving train and found himself surrounded by Baluchis. He was robbed of everything he had, his clothes were taken off till he was stark naked and then the Baluchis began to kick him and strangle him ; they continued this game of slow torture till the man fell senseless. His unconscious body was then thrown out as dead, but he succeeded in struggling back to life and lived to tell his horrible tale.

The Liaison Officer of the East Punjab Government wrote: " In Lahore you will not find a single Hindu or Sikh anywhere in the city or the Civil Station walking about. In some places, however, people in hundreds are living together in a small room to avoid slaughter." A number of important officials were picked out and murdered in a shameless manner. The District Engineer, Mr. S. P. R. Sawhney, had gone to Dalhousie on leave during August. He returned to Lahore on September 11 and was advised by his Muslim friends and colleagues to leave immediately. He went to his office on September 12 to hand over charge, and in his office he was attacked by some Muslims who dragged him out, tied him to a post and then sawed his body into several pieces in a diabolical manner that baffles comprehension.

Mr. Vir Bhan, the Deputy Director of Industries, had opted for India and made arrangements to leave Lahore on August 9. He had, however, to postpone his departure as he was entrusted with certain work connected with the partition of his Department. When the disturbances began on August 11, a police force of about ten constables was posted at his house for his protection. On August 14, the situation in Lahore took a turn for the worse. Mr. Vir Bhan decided to send his family away to Simla. He accordingly asked his wife to pack her things and himself went to his office to arrange for a truck which had been placed at his disposal. Before leaving the house he asked his orderly to get some coolies for loading the truck. It appears that the Muslim orderly brought four coolies and concealed them somewhere in the house. Mr. Vir Bhan returned with the military truck and told his orderly to have the luggage placed on it. He was standing in the drawing room, reading a letter, when he was suddenly attacked by four men who began to stab him with daggers. On hearing his cries, his wife ran up and she, too, was stabbed. Mr. Vir Bhan staggered out of the room and collapsed in the verandah. His daughter was dressing in her room and when she came out she saw her parents lying in pools of blood while the Muslim orderly and the four murderers were carrying away luggage from the house. The police guard pointed their guns at her and accused her of murdering her father. These policemen searched the persons of Mr. and Mrs. Vir Bhan and removed a wrist watch and currency notes while the pool girl stood watching the grim drama, completely helpless. It was with considerable difficulty that Mrs. Vir Bhan was allowed to be taken to the hospital to receive medical treatment.

Mr. Madan Gopal Singh, the Registrar of the Punjab University, was asked to go to Lahore towards the end of August and an assurance was given to him that he would be protected and provided with an armed escort and trucks for evacuating the non-Muslim staff of the University. He accordingly went to Lahore by air on August 24. No escort was, however, provided and, when Mr. Singh saw the Governor of West Punjab, he was told that trucks would be made available on September 2. On the morning of September 1, a peon of the University went to Mr. Singh's house and told him that the new Registrar, Mr. Bashir, wished to see him in his office. Mr. Singh went to the office at 9 a.m. but did not find Mr. Bashir there. He was told that Mr. Bashir had gone up to see the Vice-Chancellor whose office was on the first floor of the building. Mr. Singh came out of the room to go upstairs and in the verandah he was attacked by three men who inflicted nine wounds on his person and then ran away. Some members of the University staff were working in the rooms near the verandah but no one came out to answer Mr. Singh's cries. Mr. Singh was still alive and he was placed in a car and driven to the hospital. The car, however, was driven at an extremely slow pace and the distance of two miles is said to have been covered in forty-five minutes. When the car arrived at the hospital Mr. Singh's life was extinct.

The massacre of the non-Muslims who had taken shelter in Gurdwara Hargobind on Temple Road was another incident of extreme barbarity. About three hundred and fifty non-Muslims were confined in this Gurdwara which was being guarded by a unit of Hindu military. On August 14, the Hindu guard was replaced by a Muslim guard. The same evening a number of fire balls were thrown inside the Gurdwara and when the non-Muslims, driven by these flames, came out they were shot dead by the Muslim guard or stabbed by members of the Muslim National Guards. Every one of the three hundred and fifty was killed in this manner. The attack had been carefully planned and a member of the National Guards had spoken of it to a Hindu friend a day before. This Hindu friend had been temporarily converted to Islam and later related the story of the attack. Most of the dead bodies were carried away in military trucks and only a few were left lying in front of the Gurdwara.

Model Town was attacked on August 14, and the National Guards shot several non-Muslims who had taken shelter in a camp. The fortunate arrival of Dogra soldiers prevented what might have been a wholesale slaughter of the camp dwellers. On August 28, a paint and varnish factory was attacked and the National Guards carried away the machinery, raw material, furniture and other goods from the premises in bullock-carts. It took them a week to do this, and the bullock-carts had to make four hundred trips for the purpose but no policeman or military man interfered. Single lorries carrying non-Muslims through the town were frequently attacked. On one occasion the police fired shots at the tyres of a lorry to stop it. The driver and the passengers were ordered to get down and stand in a row. The police constables then began to shoot them one by one.

In the Cantonments looting and arson began on August 16. The Fire Brigade was summoned but the Muslims did not allow it to function. The disturbance spread to all parts of the Cantonments and, between August 21 and September 1, the whole of the Cantonment area was plundered and the non-Muslim houses occupied by Muslims.

Thousands of non-Muslims left the city and found shelter in a camp set up in the D.A.V. College. Of the three lakhs non-Muslims living in Lahore before the trouble began only ten thousand were left on August 19, and, by the end of August, there were not more than a few Hindus and Sikhs in houses and these, too, were waiting for an opportunity to go away.

Conditions in the rural areas were equally bad. It was, however, easy for the villagers to escape from a border district and run away to India. There were numerous mob attacks resulting in considerable loss of life and property. Pattoki was attacked on August 20 and nearly two hundred and fifty non-Muslims were killed. The non-Muslim shops were looted and set fire to. The Baluch military participated in this attack. Many non-Muslim houses in Kasur were burnt down and destroyed. Rioting broke out in this town on August 18, and about ninety non-Muslims were

killed and many more injured. Non-Muslims waiting at the Kasur
Railway Station were attacked and several of them were killed.*

Sheikhupura District

The British Government had declared that the interests of the
Sikh community would receive special consideration in determining the mode of partition and demarcating the boundary line
between India and Pakistan. The district of·Sheikhupura was a
Muslim majority area† but the Sikhs formed a substantial minority
comprising 18.85 per cent of the total population. They were
almost mainly responsible for the agricultural development of the
district and had important religious and cultural associations in
Nankana Sahib, the birth-place of Guru Nanak, the founder of the
Sikh religion, and in Sacha Sauda, an important shrine glorifying 'the piety of his childhood days.‡ The fears of the non-
Muslims in the district were therefore somewhat allayed by the hope
that the Boundary Commission would allot the district to India
and they would be permitted to keep their homes and lands. For
this reason no large-scale exodus from Sheikhupura took place
before August 17, on which date the Radcliffe Award was announced
and a stampede for safety began. The minorities were taken at
a disadvantage, arrangements for evacuation could not be made
immediately, every possible obstacle was placed in their way by
the Civil Administration and the military, and for several days no
escape was possible; and, while men, women and children,
uprooted from their homes, ran hither and thither like hunted
animals and crowded into refugee camps, a most ruthless campaign of murder, rape, arson and loot was launched upon them.
Wherever they went horror and despair faced them; bloodthirsty
gangs of marauders confronted them on the country roads, in
towns, in refugee camps, even in trains. Sheikhupura became
a by-word during the months that followed. In West Punjab
Muslim hooligans used it to intimidate the minorities into handing
over their property, accepting Islam or quitting their homes. " If
you do not do as you are told," they said, " we shall enact another
Sheikhupura here." The horror and wrath which it continued to

---

* See also table in Appendix II for incidents in rural areas.

† Muslims numbered 63.62 per cent of the total population

Tradition has it that Nanak's father once gave him some money and sent him to buy
provisions for setting up a shop. The young Nanak used the money to feed some sadhus
and returned home empty-handed. He told his father that he had invested the money
in the commerce of Truth.

evoke in the hearts of the non-Muslims for months afterwards cannot be gauged by a future student of History. Nothing of this nature or on this scale had ever taken place in India, and understanding is staggered at the depth and extent of the murderous fury displayed alike by the unruly Muslim hooligans and the disciplined Police and Army personnel stationed at Sheikhupura. To give a picture of the events which took place at Sheikhupura we cannot do better than quote from the eye-witness accounts of a few persons who were fortunate enough to survive the massacre which continued for three whole days. These statements 'have been chosen on grounds of sincerity and for their lack of exaggeration. The first of these was given by the Civil Surgeon of Sheikhupura.

" Mr. C. H. Disney, the Deputy Commissioner, was mostly away from Sheikhupura during the month of August 1947. He was camping at Nankana Sahib. The Additional District Magistrate, Pir Karam Shah, P.C.S., used to be in charge of the administration at District Headquarters during the absence of Mr. Disney. Pir Karam Shah is a case of high blood pressure and I had to visit him daily, morning and evening, since the trend of events always worried him and brought about symptoms of high blood pressure. These visits afforded me many opportunities to come in contact with people who were to control and order the butchering of Hindus and Sikhs.

" During one of these visits, on August 11 or so, a Canal telegram was received by the Additional District Magistrate that Sikhs had actually attacked Joyanwala Canal Colony and the Muslims living there. Mr. Mohammad Anwar, a local lawyer and the President of the Muslim League, was there. A hasty consultation was held between the Additional District Magistrate and Mr. Mohammad Anwar. The military and police were despatched to Joyanwala and, later on, returned to the Additional District Magistrate's house to report that no such attack had taken place. The Sub-Divisional Officer (Canals), thinking that the Canal Colony was predominantly Muslim, had sent that telegram in panic. Mr. Mohammad Anwar told the Additional District Magistrate that four Sikhs, fully armed, had been spied by the Muslim League volunteers going to Kot Pindi Das, a village with purely Hindu and Sikh population. Mr. Mohammad Anwar was of the opinion that unless strong action were taken Muslim lives in the whole district were in danger. At this Mr. Ahmad Shaffi,

Section 30 Magistrate, who was also present, suddenly flared up and said that in the very near future strong action with a capital S would be taken in the district. I was naturally alarmed at t'-is remark. As about ten Hindu and Sikh' gazetted officers were stranded at Sheikhupura without any means of going to India, a joint representation was made to the Deputy Commissioner to afford us facilities to leave Sheikhupura. This representation was treated with the utmost discourtesy. In fact, we were told that there were many Muslim gazetted officers who were stranded in India and were being murdered daily. We made desperate efforts to leave Pakistan but in vain, as the rings put round us were very tight. All vehicular traffic, motor cars, tongas, cycles, going out of Sheikhupura were stopped except with the written permission of the Additional District Magistrate, on August 20 or so. People were flocking into Sheikhupura town from Gujranwala District and its rural areas as Sheikhupura was considered the safest place in Pakistan. This caused great congestion in the town.

" Another factor to be noted is that Muslim refugees began to arrive in Sheikhupura from August 21 onwards. They related hysterical tales about their sufferings. The Muslm League volunteers and Mr. Ahmad Shaffi, P.C.S., used to promise early revenge even in my presence.

" Mr. Mohammad Anwar, the Muslim League President, was always consulted by the Additional District Magistrate or the Magistrates whenever any conference about the disturbed conditions in the district took place. In fact, he used to dictate the action to be taken against non-Muslims.

" Mr. C. H. Disney, the Deputy Commissioner, came back from Nankana Sahib on August 24, and amidst all sorts of rumours about the disturbed conditions in the Sheikhupura District a curfew was clamped on the town from 6 p.m. to 6 a.m. This was the first time that a curfew had been promulgated in the town even though there had been Muslim League and Sikh agitation before. The people received the news as a very bad omen. The Hindus and Sikhs had been stabbed in trains running between Lahore and Lyallpur from August 21 onwards. The stabbers were particularly active at Sheikhupura Railway Station. Unknown bodies of about twelve Hindus and Sikhs had been sent in for *post mortem* examination with stab or gunshot wounds.

Naturally people took this curfew order to mean their extinction and it proved to be so.

"At about 2 a.m. on August 25, the town was ablaze. Some Hindu and Sikh shops in the main bazaar had been set on fire. The military and police reached the spot and anybody coming out of their houses to extinguish the fire was shot at. The Deputy Commissioner reached the spot later on. He decided to lift the curfew then and there, and so it was announced by him and by the police. The people rushed to extinguish the fire. The Baluch soldiers of the Punjab Boundary Force stationed there for protective purposes began to shoot these people. One died on the spot and another, Hakim Lachhman Singh, was hit by a bullet at about 2-30 a.m. in the main street near the place where the fire was raging. He was not allowed to be moved to the hospital till 7 a.m. next morning. He died of the gunshot wound in his chest a few hours later, as nothing could be done to save his life after so much time. About four Sikhs and two Hindus were also stabbed in running trains. One of the Sikhs was a police constable. A medico-legal certificate about his injuries was issued to him by me. His statement was not recorded by the police even on repeated requests in my presence as some people of the Sheikhupura town were involved in that stabbing. Another feature, most alarming to the people, was the disarming of the Sikh and Hindu police at Sheikhupura from Sub-Inspector down to constables. All of them were asked to deposit their kit and their arms in the Civil Lines Police Station and to quit the Police Lines. God only knows their fate. August 25 dawned with all bad omens. The town began to be evacuated. The people began to go to the villages. They were ordered to stay in the town by the local authorities and anybody leaving the town was liable to be shot. The people then began to flock to the Civil Lines. Each bungalow in the Civil Lines became a refugee centre for the people from the city.

"At about 10 a.m. people began to talk of the curfew being again imposed from 2-30 p.m. on August 25 to 6 a.m. on August 26. This curfew order was never promulgated. A Baluch Officer came and asked the Superintendent of the Deputy Commissioner's office who was my neighbour to get the curfew order promulgated in the town. There were no peons, no conveyances and no men available to do this. The Military officer was informed accordingly. He left the place, saying that he had orders to contact the Superintendent only. If the Superintendent had no arrangements he should see the Deputy Commissioner himself. The Deputy Commissioner was not on the 'phone ; the stabbers were out in the town and no one was safe on the roads. The publicity van was not used for this purpose even on repeated requests. And so the curfew order was never promulgated. It will not be out of place to mention here that all the Punjab Boundary Force stationed at Sheikhupura consisted of Baluch Muslims with the exception of six Hindus who were kept in the office for paper work.

"The real trouble started· at about 2-30 p.m. The Armed Police was stationed on all the level crossings and all the outlets of the town. One of the policemen told me that the Sikhs were attacking the town and the Baluch soldiers had gone in action against them from Ramgarh side. Smoke was issuing from Ramgarh, a suburb of Sheikhupura, and from the bazaar. Later on it was found that the Sikh and Hindu shops were on fire. The reports of firing increased in intensity and reached a real firing line type. Jeeps carrying Baluch soldiers were seen hurrying to the town. There was no mistaking from the cries of the town people as to who were the victims. The fire came nearer and nearer the hospital. At about 6-30 p.m. a mob of Muslims, headed by Dr. Salimi and his son and some policemen in uniform, crying *"Ya Ali, Ya Ali,'* attacked the house of Mr. Des Raj, Advocate, about a hundred yards from my bungalow. They shot Des Raj's son and one daughter. They kidnapped two of his daughters and the wife of Mr. Barlow, a Sub-Judge, who was staying there as a guest. Then the house was set on fire and completely burnt down. Three helmeted policemen in uniform and one man from the mob entered the hospital compound and came towards my quarters: These people bolted all the doors of my house from outside and went away. We were naturally alarmed at this.

"At night the fury, both of the burning fires and of shooting, increased to an alarming degree. The Hindus and Sikhs, in the name of their gods, were crying for mercy, but apparently in vain, as an incident narrated below showed.

"At about midnight Lt. Shephard of the Baluch Regiment brought to the hospital a Sikh child who, in the words of the Lieutenant, had been ' *halal karoed.'* He told me that the whole family of seven men and women had been murdered and that people were being horribly massacred in the town. He also said that the two English Lieutenants were on duty in the camp and not in the town.

"Throughout the night the burning of the town and the killing of the people, as evidenced by their cries of mercy, continued. Twice the mob entered the hospital crying '*Ya Ali, Ya Ali,*' and passed through it and then attacked the houses on the other side of the hospital.

"In the midst of burning fires and the shooting of guns August 26 dawned. During the night the old city, Ramgarh, the main bazaar and adjoining portions were completely burnt out. On the morning of the 26th it was proclaimed by the police that the rice mills had been chosen as refugee camps and people in difficult circumstances should go there for safety as military and police would protect them there.

"The firing on the 26th was most concentrated in Guru Nanak Pura, a locality adjacent to the hospital. Here we saw the most ghastly sights and the most organized butchering of Hindus and Sikhs. The technique was as follows. First the Baluch soldiers and police came and shot at everybody on the road or on the houses. Following them were persons carrying tins of kerosene oil, etc. These people soaked rags in petrol or kerosene oil and set fire to the houses. When the houses were ablaze the inmates either came out on the road, where the military got them, or they crossed over to the adjacent houses and thus caused congestion in particular localities. This especially occurred in the Government quarters of the Clerical Establishment. The stabbers were then let loose on these houses. These fiends broke open the doors with axes and hammers and butchered the inmates, men and women, and abducted the girls within their sight. Whosoever tried to run away fell a victim to the shots of the Baluchis and the policemen. Having thus cleared away all the living population the looters began to ransack the houses under the very nose of the policemen. At about 10 o'clock, trench-mortar fire was heard in Guru Nanak Pura locality. In all we heard about ten mortar shots. Since the firing came nearer and nearer to the hospital and the people had been killed under our very noses, we hid ourselves in the dark room attached to the X-ray Department of the hospital. It proved to be the safest place. While hiding there in the dark room we heard woeful cries of Hindu and Sikh children as they were done to death by the Muslim mob. The cry of one child was particularly heart-rending. At about 2 p.m.

we heard the cry, ' Do not cut my throat. Do not cut my throat. You have already killed my parents. Take me with you.' He was killed in the hospital verandah about twenty paces from us.

" A hospital cook, Gopal by name, being the toughest and the most trustworthy servant, volunteered to stay out of the dark room and tell us at guarded moments what was happening outside. In case he had to communicate with us, the pass word was ' Sheikh Sahib,' shouted thrice with intervals. Until he did this no one of us in the dark room was to reply. At about 3 p.m. Gopal gave us a warning that the military men were in the hospital and that some children had been killed in the hospital compound. He returned after a while to report that my house had been surrounded by about fifty soldiers. Here Gopal got a brain wave. He told the military men that I and the dispenser with a few servants had left the hospital to go to some village and that the mob had found us and murdered us. Gopal said that our dead bodies were lying in the fields. He was intimidated but stuck to his story. A short while afterwards the firing in the hospital increased in fury and hand-grenades were heard bursting. Gopal told us afterwards that the military had attacked my house and, finding it empty, they had their revenge on the hospital patients. There were eight patients in the hospital, all Hindus and Sikhs, Muslims having left *en bloc* a day previously. None of these patients was alive on August 27. Gopal told me afterwards that Qazi Ahmad Shaffi, P.C.S., and K. S. Bakar Hussain, Super- intendent of Police, were present for two hours in the hospital compound directing the fire, especially at my house. The firing in the hospital died down at about 6 p.m. The groans of the injured, nearing their end, were heard from all round the hospital. We remained in the dark room till the 27th morning.

" All the injured who were brought to the hospital by the military told us that they had been shot by the Baluch soldiers or stabbed in their presence by Muslim mobs on the 25th or 26th. The injured also told me that the Baluch soldiers had collected the Hindus and Sikhs in the rice mills on the false pretext of protecting them. Having got these men in these places the military first asked them to hand over their valuables and then mercilessly killed them.

" The Hindu and Sikh Military Force arrived on the 27th evening and we heaved a sigh of relief.

" The number of the injured swelled to four hundred indoor patients and about two hundred walking patients. Besides these there were women and young girls in all forms of nakedness. Even the ladies of most respectable families had the misfortune of having undergone this most terrible experience. The wife of an Advocate had practically nothing on when she came to the hospital. The casualties among the males and females were about equal. About a hundred wounded children were amongst the casualties.

" The Officer Commanding the Baluch Para Troops, 1st Battalion, came to the hospital at about noon. I had a talk with him. His words were ' All this has happened because the senior officers had gone on leave.' The Commanding Officer placed the services of his Unit Medical Officer, Captain Zia-ul-Hussan, I.A.M.C., at my disposal. This officer, though always at the hospital, never dressed a single case nor administered any medicine to any Hindu or Sikh wounded. He was always an obstacle in the way of getting amenities and treatment for the patients. . . .

" In the end I feel honour-bound to record that the lives of my children and those of about six hundred educated Hindus and Sikhs, male and female, of the Civil Lines, were saved by the efforts of some God-fearing Muslims who gave them shelter in their houses, even at the risk of their lives."

What happened at the rice mills is related by an eye-witness in the following terms:

" On August 26, at about 7 a.m., I reached the mill of Sardar Atma Singh. There were about seven or eight thousand non-Muslim refugees from all parts of the town collected there. At about 8 a.m. the Muslim Baluch military surrounded the mill and then a shot was fired which resulted in the death of a woman inside the mill. After that, Swami Anand Singh, President of the Congress Committee, went to the military men with a green flag in his hand and asked them what they wanted. He said that the entire non-Muslim property in the town had been burnt and looted. The military men demanded twenty-six hundred rupees which were paid. After this another shot was fired and a man was killed, and, on being again requested by Swami Anand Singh, they demanded another twelve hundred rupees which were also paid. But after this they told us that they wanted to search all the refugees and that we should come out and whosoever remained in would be shot dead. All the seven thousand or eight thousand refugees went out and then they were told that they should give up all cash and valuables which they had. Swami Anand Singh advised the unfortunate refugees to comply with this demand. In a short while a pile of seven or eight maunds of gold was collected at the spot and about thirty or forty lakhs of rupees. All this wealth was taken away by the military men. Then they began to pick and choose young girls from the refugees, but when this was being done Swami Anand Singh objected, upon which he was shot dead. Thereafter one of the Muslim Baluch military men took hold of a young girl and began to molest her in the presence of all the non-Muslim refugees. This became intolerable and a young Hindu attacked the Baluch soldier. Thereupon all the Baluch soldiers began to fire upon the refugees, and while the front rows of the refugees stood up the non-Muslims began to kill their young girls to save their honour. In the meantime the firing upon the refugees continued and people began to fall and die on the spot. I lay down on the ground behind a tree. After some time, seeing that it would be impossible to survive if I remained there, in a hysterical state of mind, I stood up and, under the shower of bullets, I scaled the adjoining wall and jumped down on the other side. During this interval there was a rain of bullets over my head and under my feet and I cannot imagine how I remained alive. On the other side, a Baluch soldier who was standing on guard aimed his gun at me when I was very close to him, but I jumped and rushed at him and was able to snatch away his gun. I struck him with the butt-end and he became unconscious. All the time there were showers of bullets around me but I ran with the greatest speed that I could gather and went away into the fields and ultimately found shelter in an adjoining mill under the jute bags lying there. I heard reports of guns being fired inside the mill and, after two or three hours, fearing that I might be discovered, I went up to the mill inside a room, where two young unfortunate Hindu girls had also taken refuge. From that place of vantage I could see what was happening to the non-Muslim refugees in the mill which I had left. Those who could escape alive from the bullets of the Baluch soldiers were being attacked by an armed Muslim mob outside and were being killed on the spot in a most savage fashion. In one instance they snatched a young child from the arms of his mother, cut it into two and stabbed the mother with a spear.

" After some time, seeing that it was impossible to escape alive from there, I could think of no means of escape, but seeing a Mohammedan constable who was an old friend of mine I came down with the two refugee Hindu girls pretending that they were my sisters. The Mohammedan constable was near by when we were about to be attacked by other raiders. I beckoned to him and begged him to save mine and my sisters' lives. Fortunately he agreed and took us away stealthily to a village Malian Kalan."

The experience of a rich Reis is also worth recording.

" . . . The Muslim military came looting the houses and shops of Hindus and Sikhs on our side. We saw the house of Sardar Bahadur Buta Singh which was opposite mine being looted. The goods were removed in a truck by twenty men. This made us certain that we would be the next victims. My wife immediately ran into the inner room of the house and took some poison, while we were watching through the window and awaiting the arrival of the looters. My old mother did the same. A military tank entered from one gate and passing in front of my house left by the other gate. It had come either to warn us or to scare us away.

" We waited for the night to come. At 8 on the night of the 26th, we left the house, leaving the bodies of my wife and mother uncremated and covered with a sheet. Servants carried my five children and we passed through the Mission Ahata and across the railway line safely. After we had run about a hundred yards we met sixty men, armed with spears and swords. To our great good fortune they took pity on me and my children and allowed us to pass. We decided to go towards Gujranwala and cross the Ravi river and reach India. We continued walking the whole night and the next day at about 3-30, we reached Tallianwala. Unfortunately we were not allowed to enter the village as the villagers were afraid that we might cause a disturbance. We selected a spot where there was a small forest. To my surprise I came to know in the evening that there were about fifteen thousand Hindus and Sikhs assembled in the neighbourhood. Some of them were from Sheikhupura while the majority of them were from different villages which had been attacked by the military." This witness and his children finally reached the refugee camp at Chuharkana.

All the three camps set up in Sheikhupura on the morning of August 26, were attacked in this manner. Some non-Muslims collected in the Namdhari Dharamshàla. Among them was a teacher of the Government High School, Sheikhupura, whose story is as follows:

" At about 3-30 p.m. from our roofs we saw that the rioters had come into the courtyard round which our houses were situated. The military was patrolling around this area and once they even came into the courtyard. They pointed guns at us but did not fire, nor did they interfere with the rioters. Soon after this, the rioters who were Muslims set fire to some of the houses. The military were purely Baluch. The rioters looted the houses and drove away the cattle which were tied in the courtyard. The looted houses were then set fire to. Some women were also taken away by the rioters. When the residents of the houses went up to the roofs the military shot them. I saw this with my own eyes. The houses on three sides of the courtyard were in this manner looted and burnt by about 4 a.m. the following night. A large crowd of non-Muslims had collected in my house where they had sought refuge. A large number of rioters came to our house but we raised cries of ' Sat Siri Akal ' and they went away. Almost immediately afterwards they returned and began to fire at us. Our impression was that it was the Baluch military who were firing. Two of our men were killed and two were injured. Wherever we could see there were fires raging all round us. We thought we would go out in the open and leave the rioters to loot our houses but the general opinion was against this step and so we stayed on inside the houses till the morning. The fire on one side died down and then we came out. We met the military who told us that it was safe for us to go away.

" We left and soon afterwards we heard reports of firing. I took shelter in the Namdhari Dharamsala where there were about a thousand non-Muslims collected. At 9 a.m. about sixty rioters, accompanied by about twenty soldiers, arrived and began to fire at us. The rioters were carrying iron tube-like contraptions about 18 inches long and 3 inches in diameter. I was told that this implement was used for throwing bombs or grenades. The rioters were carrying swords but not guns. There were so many of us in the small room of the Gurdwara that we could scarcely breathe. Many men cut off the heads of their wives and daughters and threw them down the well. We could not get water from this well as the bucket would not go down. The well became full of blood. After a little while we were told to come out and were

made to sit in the courtyard of the Dharamsala. It was the military
who gave this order. They asked us to give whatever valuables
we had and every one of us handed out whatever he had, and
then we were sent one by one to the cremation ground which was
near the Dharamsala. There we saw hundreds of dead bodies
lying. We were made to sit in rows and in small groups at different points of the cremation ground. Then the rioters came there
with swords and other weapons ready to kill us. We asked these
people to convert us to Islam but they refused. There were no
soldiers there. They had gone away after taking part of our valuables in the Gurdwara courtyard. Many Sikhs bared their heads
and asked the rioters to cut off their hair and convert them to
Islam but they said that they were thirsty for the blood of the
non-Muslims. At this time an aeroplane passed over our heads
and we made signals of distress by waving turbans, clothes or
women's veils. The rioters did not make a wholesale attack on
us. They took a few of us at a time behind a house near the
cremation ground to kill. This was about 2 p.m. I cannot say
how many of us were killed. We heard cries and shrieks from
behind the house. After a time the rioters went away and we
returned to the Dharamsala. There also we found hundreds of
dead bodies lying. I cannot say if these were the bodies of people
who were originally in the Dharamsala or if they had been brought
there afterwards to kill. There were no rioters or military in sight.

"We had heard rumours that the rioters wanted to loot and
set fire to Chuharkana. Thinking that this was a good opportunity
to escape, about forty of us left to run away to a neighbouring
village. A second party of about a hundred persons left a little
later when it was getting dark. I was in this party. We did not
go by the main roads but through the rice fields. We reached a
Sikh village, Ranjit Kot, three and a half miles away, at about
10 p.m. that night. We met a party of about forty Muslims just
outside the village. They were armed with daggers and swords
and they told us that all the Sikhs and Hindus had already left.
They saw that many of us were wounded. These Muslims did not
attack us. They told us that they could not give us any food as
it was too late and advised us to go away if we valued our lives.
As I have already said, we were about a hundred in number
but we had no arms of any kind. There were women and children
also among us. We approached another village but from there
we heard sounds of firing. We spent the night in a wet ploughed

10

field. In the morning we went to a village near Mirza. Around this village I noticed that a ditch had been dug, apparently for purposes of protection. This ditch was full of water. I noticed similar ditches around several other villages which I visited during the course of the next few days. I was going round the villages in order to make enquiries about my wife and daughter. I did not come across any police or military during this time. There was a general movement, on a large scale, of non-Muslims. People were moving in and out of villages. I did not come across any rioting during these few days. I saw a crowd of about forty Muslims outside the village near Mirza, but the number of non-Muslims in this village was large. The Sikhs were saying that the Muslims were telling them to go away if they did not want to be killed. There was a party of about sixty persons, Hindus and Sikhs, led by a dacoit, Bahadur Singh, who offered to protect us. Some of these persons had firearms. There were about a thousand of us and Bahadur Singh told us to sit together and said that he would protect us as long as he lived.

" We used to visit different villages and the Sikh residents gave us food and served us. Then we heard that refugee camps were being opened near Sheikhupura and Sacha Sauda. I went to the camp at Sacha Sauda. On the way I met crowds of people walking like ants. They had left their houses and were making for the refugee camps. At Sacha Sauda there were about one and a quarter lakh refugees. The only food which was available for them was wheat and gram which was being distributed by the officer in charge. People were bringing sugarcanes from the neighbouring fields. I thought that I would die of cholera in these conditions and decided to go to Sheikhupura. Seeing two Baluch lorries coming along the road I asked the Baluch soldiers to take me to Sheikhupura. They took me there and I went to the Sikh Girls' School which had been converted into a refugee camp. There in the hospital, some patients told me that my wife and daughter had been taken away safely. At Sacha Sauda no lorries came and I was told that some days ago ten lorries had come to take refugees away and after that no transport had arrived although telephonic messages had been sent. Three or four days later I found accommodation in a truck and went to the D.A.V. College Camp at Lahore. Two or three days later some trucks for Government servants came and I travelled by one of these to Amritsar where I found my wife and daughter.

" The story given by my wife and daughter was this:

" ' When we left our house and went on to the main road the
military collected about 150 of us and took us on one side. They
made us sit down and gave us water to drink and some fruits and
biscuits which had been looted from a shop. They told us to eat
these as our end was near. Then they made us sit in a row and
began to kill us one by one. (I cannot say if these were the rioters
or the military but the military was present.) The military carried
away some girls in lorries. They wanted to take my daughter away
also but she said that she should rather be shot. A military soldier
pointed his gun at her but it appears that these men were busy looting and carrying away the booty and so my daughter escaped.
The killing started from one end of the row and, getting an opportunity, about twenty-five of us from the other side ran and escaped
into a narrow lane near the temple.'

"My wife and daughter were separated. My wife took shelter
in one house and my daughter in another. My daughter tried to
put an end to her life by persuading a lawyer's son to strangle her.
Three attempts were made to do this but my daughter survived
though she remained unconscious for some time. There were one
or two other girls in this house also and they prepared a pyre with
some quilts and *charpoys*. They spent about two days in this house
and during this time my wife joined my daughter. Then the military came and rescued them and took them to Amritsar. My
daughter was an Assistant Mistress in the Government High School
at Sargodha and was staying with me during the holidays at
that time."

A Hindu lawyer who found shelter in the house of a friendly
Muslim relates that he heard Mr. Disney, Malik Mohammad Anwar
and Mr. Ghulam Hussain Chhatta * holding the following conversation:

" *Mr. Disney*: ' In the last twenty-four hours practically the
whole town is decimated. What more do you want? '

" *Malik Mohammad Anwar*: ' We have to continue this work
till we receive further instructions from higher authorities at
Lahore.'

" *Mr. Disney*: ' I am a little upset about this carnage.'

" *Malik Mohammad Anwar*: ' But orders are to be obeyed
and we have to carry on till we get further instructions. We
apprehend danger from Sikhs of neighbouring villages.'

---

* Afterwards a Parliamentary Secretary in the West Punjab Government.

"*Mr. Disney*: 'But no Sikh can come in the presence of Muslim military and the police.'

"*Mr. Chhatta*: 'But orders are orders. We will phone up Lahore just now for further instructions.'"

It would be superfluous to make any comment on this amazing conversation.

The total death roll at Sheikhupura has been variously estimated between eight thousand and twenty-five thousand. A conservative estimate based on the evidence of the most reliable witnesses would put the figure at about ten thousand.

The Sacha Sauda refugee camp was situated near the railway line and was a good target for anyone firing from a railway train passing by. Baluch soldiers, travelling in trains, fired at refugees in the camp on three different occasions and each time heavy loss of life was occasioned. These attacks were admitted by the West Punjab Government and the explanation given by them was that the refugees had taken up a threatening attitude towards the armed Muslim military in the trains who had fired shots in self-defence. It is difficult to imagine a more unconvincing and evasive explanation of these savage attacks on innocent and unarmed refugees who had been driven out from their homes and were subsisting on extremely meagre rations before means for evacuating them could be made available.

At Sangla Hill, the local Sub-Inspector of Police demanded a heavy bribe for protecting the non-Muslims. The money was paid but the non-Muslims were attacked on August 28, and large numbers of them were murdered. Looting and burning of Hindu shops and houses followed. On September 7, the non-Muslims were told that they must leave within an hour. They were then driven out from their houses at the point of the bayonet. Anyone who tried to take his valuables away was robbed. The non-Muslims were kept in a camp in one of the factories for several days. Some of them were forcibly converted. One of the factory owners was compelled to write a letter admitting that he had leased his factory to a Muslim for five years. About three hundred men in the refugee camp died from an epidemic of cholera which broke out owing to the insanitary conditions prevailing there.

Some shops in Chuharkana were burnt on August 20, but a major tragedy was averted by the arrival of some non-Muslim military officers. In Chak No. 10 four hundred men were killed in the course of an assault by a Muslim mob accompanied by Pakistan military. Over a hundred young girls were kidnapped. Bhalair and Jandiala Sher Khan were attacked in a similar manner. Several foot convoys of non-Muslims were attacked in different parts of the district. A railway train was attacked near Moman and fifty non-Muslims were killed. Their dead bodies were thrown in the canal. Some of them were recovered the next day by the residents of Sangla. All twenty passengers in a truck, escorted by Baluch soldiers, were done to death on their way to Lahore. Their dead bodies were found lying in the canal by a foot caravan. A large party of non-Muslims from Sheikhwan was attacked on September 3 and, in the course of the attack, forty persons lost their lives, a hundred more were injured and fourteen girls were kidnapped.

Sialkot District

Sialkot has many historical, religious and romantic associations with the past. According to popular legends the city was founded by Raja Sala, the uncle of the Pandavas and re-founded, in the time of Vikramaditya, by Raja Salivahan who built the fort and the city on their present sites. Puran Bhagat, the saint and hero of popular romances, who refused the incestuous advances of his step-mother and was made to undergo horrible tortures, was the son of this Salivahan. The well in which he was thrown by the order of the wicked Rani lies a few miles from Sialkot and, until its desecration and partial demolition by the Muslims in August 1947, used to be a place of pilgrimage. There is a Sikh shrine dedicated to Guru Nanak and near it Darbar Baoli Sahib, a covered well, built by a Rajput disciple of Baba Nanak. Both places are held in great veneration by the Sikh community.

During the Moghul times, Sialkot became the headquarters of a fiscal district and has remained so to the present day. The Emperor Jahangir passed through the district on his way to Kashmir and recorded in his diary that he found the surroundings delightful.* In more recent years the district acquired a certain amount of notoriety during the Ahrar agitation of 1932-33 when bands of Ahrars, bound for Kashmir, invaded the district. The city of Sialkot is associated with the firm of Uberoi, the well-known manufacturers of sports goods ; and numerous other firms, big and

---

* The name of the town Pasrur is said to be a corruption of the word " *pursaroor* " used by Jehangir, meaning full of delight.

small, dealing in sports goods, surgical and scientific instruments ; and a number of rubber factories recently set up gave it considerable importance in the commercial world. It was a flourishing trade centre and an important depot for agricultural produce. A large cantonment situated near the city added to its importance.

The total population of the district at the census of 1941 was 11.9 lakhs including 7.39 lakhs, or 62 per cent Muslims. It became one of the border districts during the days of notional division. As the result of the Radcliffe Award it was augmented by the addition of Shakargarh Tehsil which originally formed part of the district of Gurdaspur. The river Ravi then became its eastern boundary along its entire length. This circumstance added to the difficulties and sufferings of the non-Muslim refugees running eastward to escape from the bands of Muslim marauders who roamed the countryside committing murder, loot and arson during the months of August and September 1947.

Hindu-Muslim relations in the district had always been cordial and were seldom marred by communal riots. The agitation against the Coalition Ministry during January and February 1947, however, helped to awaken communal consciousness and, in the beginning of March, an incident occurred in the city of Sialkot which led to the stabbing of a dozen non-Muslims. The situation was controlled immediately and no further trouble was witnessed until July 11, when someone threw a bomb in one of the main bazaars. There was a sudden though short-lived flare up and three non-Muslims were stabbed. Exactly a month later three Sikhs were fatally stabbed. The next day, August 12, six more non-Muslims were attacked and killed. Panic spread through the city, Hindus and Sikhs closed their shops and locked themselves up in their houses. Muslim League National Guards and Muslim hooligans began to move about the city in a threatening manner. On August 13, a mob of several thousand Muslims armed with all kinds of weapons, firearms, hatchets, swords, daggers and sticks was seen collecting. At this time the Deputy Commissioner and the Superintendent of Police were both Muslims. They were informed of what was happening but they left for Narowal without making any arrangements to safeguard the life and property of the citizens. The first victim of mob fury was a Sikh Advocate whose house was looted and burnt. Before the morning was well advanced, almost all the Hindu Mohallas and bazaars were in flames. The sports goods factories and the rubber mills were plundered and set fire to.

A huge mob attacked the rice factory of **Munshi Ram-Gian Chand** and began to loot it. A number of hooligans caught the proprietor and cut off his fingers. They stood around him, jeered at him and asked him: " Where are your Nihang protectors we heard so much about? Call them now." They then threw petrol all over his clothes and burnt him alive. His brothers, who were watching this gruesome scene from a distance, jumped into a well with their wives and children. The mob ran up and threw brickbats down the well till all of them were killed. The rest of the family and the staff working in the mill were done to death. The Gurdwara Baoli Sahib was surrounded and burnt. Thirty-two non-Muslims including a Sikh police constable, lost their lives in this fire. Groups of hooligans accompanied by National Guards and Muslim police-men rushed about the streets of the city in a mad frenzy, shouting " *Allah-O-Akbar*," " *Ya Ali, Ya Ali* " and burnt and looted non-Muslim houses. Only the Muslim houses and shops displaying pieces of green cloth or Muslim League flags were spared. Any Sikh or Hindu who was rash or foolish enough to venture out was shot or stabbed. An Inspector of Police and a head constable were seen leading one of the mobs. Curfew was imposed late on the evening of the 14th, but even then it could not be enforced against the Muslims. A refugee camp was set up in the Canton-ments and some non-Muslims succeeded in finding their way to it. They were searched and deprived of all they possessed. Non-Muslim officers posted at Sialkot sought refuge in the Police Lines and remained confined there for four days. On August 18, these wretched officers were taken out of the Police Lines, forcibly dis-armed and thrown out on the road to fend for themselves. They sought shelter in the refugee camp. The non-Muslim police officials found themselves in serious peril of their lives. A Sub-Inspector of Police was told by his own subordinates to give up his revolver. A Sikh Prosecuting Sub-Inspector, while walking in the Police Lines, was shot at by a Muslim constable but was able to save himself by lying flat on the ground. The non-Muslim police officials took refuge in a private bungalow where they remained for two nights before moving to the refugee camp.

A train from Wazirabad which arrived at Sialkot on August 14, was found to contain fifty dead bodies of non-Muslim men, women and children. Young infants had been butchered and two of them were found clinging to their mothers with gashing wounds and completely covered with blood. This train had been stopped at Naizam Abad by the Muslim driver who saw a mob waiting near the railway line. The train was attacked and the non-Muslim passengers were brutally slaughtered. The dead bodies were removed from the compartments under the supervision of a Magistrate and the train was loaded with non-Muslims of Sialkot wishing to leave for Jammu. The train was derailed three miles from Sialkot near Dalowali and a mob of four or five thousand Muslims was seen approaching. The military escort fired at the mob and kept them at bay for a time. Fortunately a body of Sikh soldiers, living in the military barracks near by, ran up and averted what might have proved a most gruesome massacre.

Two or three days later another train carrying non-Muslim passengers was derailed at the same place. The Muslim mob was again driven away, as on the previous occasion, and the train was taken back to Sialkot. Owing to the curfew orders, the passengers could not leave the station and go home. They had to stay on the platform, surrounded by an angry Muslim mob for several hours, while a leading Advocate was making efforts to obtain the permission of the District Magistrate to their going home. They were finally taken to a private camp at Puran Nagar.

From August 16 to August 20 a marked improvement in the situation was observed. A Minister of the West Punjab Government then paid a visit to Sialkot and held a secret conference with the Muslim League leaders behind closed doors, while the District Magistrate and the Superintendent of Police waited outside. After the Minister left Sialkot, disturbances re-commenced with even greater fury. The general impression was that the District Magistrate was sincerely anxious to put an end to this carnage but the police openly flouted his authority and he felt completely helpless. He called the Secretary and the President of the local Muslim League to a meeting at the City Police Station and told them that their leadership had failed because they had been unable to influence their followers and stop the rioting in the city. The office-bearers resented this remark and left the meeting in anger. Three days later the District Magistrate was transferred to Lahore.

A refugee train was scheduled to leave Sialkot for Jammu at 9 a.m. on August 20. The train was packed with non-Muslim passengers and provided with a non-Muslim escort. The engine driver refused to start unless the personnel of the escort were changed and until Muslim police and military were sent with the train. A report was made to the District Magistrate who ordered the engine driver to be arrested. The man was adamant and he was supported by the Muslim National Guards who openly declared that they would murder him if he left with the non-Muslim escort. This train did not leave and the passengers had to go back to the refugee camp.

The proprietor of the firm of Uberoi saw many of his non-Muslim employees murdered; others ran away. He himself escaped and reached Jammu. When he returned a few days later, he found that the local authorities, with the assistance of the Police and National Guards, had taken possession of his factory. Large quantities of his stocks lying in the factory and his personal goods including carpets, furniture and jewellery from his house were removed in trucks. A dummy directorate was set up and an attempt was made to operate upon the firm's bank account.

A Hindu Advocate left his house in a tonga with a few belongings and proceeded on the road to Jammu. He was stopped by the National Guards and deprived of all his goods. He returned to Sialkot after peace was restored but was unable to remove either his library or any other part of his personal effects. Thousands of non-Muslims perished in the course of this rioting and lost all their property. Many girls were kidnapped and dishonoured.

Rioting in the rural areas started almost simultaneously. Every village in the district was attacked by mobs of Muslim hooligans. In many instances the mobs were led by members of the Muslim League National Guards or police officials. The pattern of the assault was the same everywhere with a few variations prompted by individual genius or the peculiarity of local conditions. In some cases the local Muslims promised safety and protection to the non-Muslim residents and swore upon the Quran that no harm would come to them; but, when the village was attacked by men from the neighbouring villages, these promises were forgotten and the local Muslims joined the marauders in looting and murdering their co-villagers. In other villages heavy bribes were demanded and paid, but this only increased the greed of the bribe-takers, and the non-Muslim residents were soon afterwards robbed of everything they had. Conversion to Islam was frequently offered as the price of safety, and if the victims exhibited any reluctance or religious scruples they were subjected to duress and torture. The hair of Sikhs was cut off, their beards were trimmed and beef was cooked and forced down their throats. Some of them were circumcised. Young women and girls were molested and carried away. Reason and decency were completely banished by fanatical zeal ; and young innocent girls were raped in public. In one village the relations of a girl were made to stand around in a ring while she was raped by several men in succession. Parties of non-Muslims running away from such horrible scenes were set upon and murdered. Even when armed escorts accompanied these parties there was no respite from these ordeals, in fact, the guards were not unwilling to share in the loot. When the refugees reached the banks of the Ravi and safety appeared to be within sight, the problem of crossing the river presented serious difficulties. Heavy rains had made the river unfordable, boats were rarely available and the Muslim boatmen demanded exorbitant fares. Delays occurred and, while the refugees waited, they were attacked by Muslim hooligans. In some cases a whole week had to be spent, out in the open, without food or shelter. Young children and old men could not survive exposure and starvation during the monsoon months and large numbers of them died. Trains were stopped and attacked on the way. Their passage was delayed and food and drink were deliberately withheld from the unfortunate passengers. Appeals for a drop of water were met with the argument that the water of Pakistan would disagree with the stomachs of those who were running away to India.

During the months of August and September two hundred and thirty-eight villages were attacked and looted. There were thirty-three distinct attacks on refugees proceeding to India by road and six on those travelling by train. A few village incidents chosen at random are given below. A few others will be found in a table in Appendix II.

A mob of armed Muslims raided Rajiana Rattan on August 22, 1947, at 9 a.m. An Assistant Sub-Inspector of Police and twelve police constables accompanied the mob. The non-Muslims of the village were asked to embrace Islam if they wanted to live peacefully. They had to make their decision within two hours and inform the Assistant Sub-Inspector. They met in a *haveli* to discuss the matter and decided against conversion. Torrential rain coming at this juncture drove the Muslims to seek shelter in houses. The non-Muslims ran out and hid themselves in the fields near the village. As soon as the rain stopped, the Muslims came out and plundered the empty houses. They then went out to the fields in order to round up the non-Muslims. Ten of them were killed but the rest were able to escape to Jammu State.

On August 23, the non-Muslims of village Gol decided to leave their homes on hearing persistent rumours of attacks on the neighbouring villages. A large party of them left at noon but they had gone only a short distance when they were confronted by a mob of armed Muslims accompanied by some policemen and military soldiers. They ran back to the village and took shelter in the house of Chaudhry Raghbir Singh Zaildar. The Zaildar took his gun and climbed up to the roof. The house was surrounded by the Muslims and the Zaildar was shot dead. Some of the hooligans went up to the roof, made a hole in the ceiling and dropped a number of bombs inside. Many people were killed and injured. Some, opening the door, ran out. These, too, were attacked. Others hid themselves in the fields till it was dark, and then they walked to the river Ravi and succeeded in being taken across.

On August 17, five thousand non-Muslims drawn from thirty-two villages went to the Daska Camp and after staying there for a fortnight started for Dera Baba Nanak, escorted by the Pakistan military. The convoy arrived at Alipur Saidan Railway Station, and stopped there for the night. A mob of two hundred Muslims, armed with fire arms, spears and swords, had come to Alipur Saidan the previous day and they were entertained by the local Muslims. They planned to attack the non-Muslims camping at the station. When the convoy left in the morning the Muslim mob attacked it. The military escort joined the mob and the attack continued for two hours and a half. Eight hundred non-Muslims were killed and seventy were injured. A number of girls were kidnapped. Property valued at several thousand rupees was looted. The providential arrival of a train from Sialkot enabled two thousand of the survivors to leave Alipur Saidan. The rest had to be left behind for lack of accommodation in the train. These were saved by some Hindu soldiers who arrived on the following day and escorted them to Dera Baba Nanak.

Baidana remained peaceful until September 18, although there was considerable panic and tension as several villages in the neighbourhood were being attacked by Muslim mobs. On September 18, Jajjar, a village one mile from Badiana, was attacked. The Zaildar of the Ilaqa took a Muslim chaukidar with him and tried to persuade the Muslim mob to spare Badiana. The Zaildar was attacked and beaten. The next day the non-Muslims from the adjoining villages collected and marched out to meet the Muslims.

In the clash that ensued both sides suffered casualties. On September 24, a huge mob of Muslims attacked village Fatehpur which is close to Badiana. This mob was led by a Sub-Inspector of Police and four constables armed with rifles. The Sikh residents of Fatehpur resisted and the mob went back. The non-Muslims of Badiana then left their village and made their way to Pasrur. At the Pasrur Camp the refugees were attacked and fifteen of them were killed by Muslim troops. The refugees left Pasrur for Dera Baba Nanak and, on the way, there were again attacked near Narowal. Fortunately, a band of Hindu soldiers arrived and dispersed the attackers. At Jassar the non-Muslims were again attacked. Finally they reached Ramdas on Indian territory, their numbers considerably attenuated by successive attacks.

Dhavad, a village six miles from Narowal, was attacked by a Muslim mob on September 2, at 9 a.m. The Muslims were armed with firearms, swords, daggers and spears and were accompanied by a Sub-Inspector of Police. The non-Muslims of the village were rounded up and told that they would be killed. They were forced to hand over their cash and ornaments. They were then brought to the bank of the river Ravi, a distance of two miles, and left there. Shortly afterwards the same mob again attacked them and looted all their property. About eighteen girls were kidnapped and the women were stripped and searched. The survivors arranged with two Muslim boatmen to take them across the river. When they were in midstream the boatmen threatened to overturn the boats unless they were paid five hundred rupees and a gold ring. The money was paid and the boats were taken across.

On September 4, some Muslim National Guards entered the house of one Nand Lal in Rupo Chak and shot him dead. The house was then ransacked and plundered. The matter was reported to the Muslim Zaildar, and he promised to exert his influence in preventing the recurrence of such incidents if he were paid a sum of three thousand rupees. The money was paid but on September 15, Chhanga Mal, a moneylender, and the members of his family were murdered at night by the Muslims. Their dead bodies were thrown on a heap of garbage. The Zaildar again demanded a large sum of money for guaranteeing the security of the non-Muslims and the money was paid. On November 5, some police constables arrived and asked the non-Muslims to get ready to go to Zafarwal. They were told to take only two beddings per family and nothing else. The non-Muslims loaded their belongings on three bullock-carts and left for Zafarwal. The police constables were paid three thousand rupees for escorting them safely. At Zafarwal the non-Muslims were housed in a temple, but the bullock-carts with their belongings were taken to the police station and then removed to the headquarters of the Muslim National Guards. The policemen told the refugees that the bullock-carts contained Pakistan property which could not be taken to India. At midnight a number of Muslims armed with Bren guns and rifles invaded the temple. They seized any cash and jewellery the refugees had hidden on their persons. In the morning the refugees were removed to the Arya Samaj Camp where they were kept until November 13. They were then removed to Sialkot and, on November 16, boarded a goods train bound for India.

Gujranwala District

The March disturbances had no serious repercussions in the Gujranwala District though, in the month of April, the burning of a sweet-seller's shop at Wazirabad caused a great deal of panic in that town. Many residents of Wazirabad left but they came back on receiving assurances of peace and security from the local Muslims. In the second week of August, stabbings of non-Muslims began in the town of Gujranwala. On August 14, a number of houses, shops and factories owned by non-Muslims were set on fire. Then followed a brief lull but the town was, once again, shaken by serious disturbances which spread through all quarters. Muslim hooligans were seen wandering about the streets and looting non-Muslim shops. Trouble increased day by day and, on August 27, a Muslim mob assisted by two constables looted the shops in Bazaar Hari Singh Nalwa. Dr. Tej Bhan, a leading Medical Practitioner, was foully murdered by a Sub-Inspector of Police who first searched his house and then shot him and all members of his family who were at home. Wazirabad fared much worse. Almost the whole of this town was set on fire and the flames were seen for many miles. The town was attacked on August 13, by a large Muslim mob which came from the direction of Nizamabad. Non-Muslim shops and houses were freely looted and then burnt. Wazirabad was the scene of a most ruthless and barbarous attack on a train of refugees proceeding to Jammu. The train was stopped about a mile outside Wazirabad where the track was found to be blocked. A large mob of armed Muslims then attacked the train and a veritable orgy of loot and murder began. Several hundred non-Muslims were killed in the course of this attack and many women were kidnapped. Almost the entire belongings of the passengers were carried away. It may be mentioned here that Nizamabad, situated a mile from Wazirabad, was a centre of the cutlery cottage industry and large quantities of knives and daggers were sent from this place to various parts of India. Several cases of this deadly merchandise addressed to Muslim League agitators were captured by the police.

Eminabad and Kamoke are important trade and factory centres where non-Muslims owned considerable property. At Eminbad, on August 11, a Hindu, proceeding in a tonga, was foully murdered. His assailants were arrested and sent up to stand their trial. Two days after the partition of the province they were discharged and allowed to return to their village. On their arrival they openly proclaimed that they would not allow any non-Muslim to live in Eminabad. On August 19, a large mob of Muslims with whom were some members of the National Guard began to loot and burn the non-Muslim shops. The grain market was almost completely destroyed. The disturbance gathered volume and, on August 20, there was more looting and burning. The Gurdwara Rohri Sahib was desecrated and set on fire. Some Sikhs in the Gurdwara were murdered. Almost all the factories in Kamoke were set on fire on August 22 and 23. Most of the non-Muslims left the village and in their absence their houses and shops were plundered. Many of those who were left behind were murdered and then burnt by pouring kerosene oil over the corpses. The worst massacre in the district, perhaps, took place at Akalgarh, an important trade centre on the railway line between Wazirabad and Lyallpur. The business and Zemindara interests were all in the hands of non-Muslims who comprised a moiety of the total population. The surrounding villages were chiefly inhabited by Muslims and when the disturbances began the non-Muslims from these villages began to move into Akalgarh in the hope of finding greater security. The number of these refugees soon swelled into thousands and five different refugee camps were set up in Akalgarh. Till September 2, Hindu military was stationed at Akalgarh and conditions remained peaceful. A Baluch regiment then replaced the Hindu military and, within a few days, conditions changed. On September 7, it was announced that all Hindus and Sikhs must surrender their weapons immediately. Extensive searches were carried out through the town and the refugee camps, and even ordinary knives were taken away. Two retired Sikh Subedars of the Army protested against this order. They were attacked by the Baluch soldiers and murdered. Their dead bodies were thrown into the canal. The search for weapons provided the police and the army with an excuse for taking away all the cash and jewellery in possession of the refugees. Boxes and trunks were rifled. Women were stripped naked and molested. The weapons collected were placed in a large heap in front of the police station and were then distributed to the Muslims who came in from the neighbouring villages. That evening a large mob of Muslims, assisted by Baluch soldiers, attacked the refugee camp in the Government High School. The men were separated from the women and then about forty girls were selected and told to march out. Some of the girls resisted and were shot. The mob attacked the men and killed several of them. The refugee camp in Sanatan Dharam Mandir was attacked next. Some parents, knowing the designs of the Muslims, tried to conceal their young girls by wrapping them up inside their beddings. The girls were discovered, taken out and led up to a room on the top storey where they were raped by Baluch soldiers. Some girls jumped into a well to save themselves from such foul treatment. The Muslim mob looted the refugees and killed several hundreds of them. The dead bodies were carried in trucks to the canal bank and thrown in the water. A young girl was found dying on the roadside four days later. She had been raped by several Muslims and then left for dead. The Sub-Inspector of Police, Akalgarh, issued directions that no Muslim should grind wheat for the refugees or sell any provisions to them. The looted property from the refugee camps and houses was carried away in military trucks. The Muslim residents of the neighbouring villages took away a share of the loot in bullock-carts. The arrival of the Dogra military, on September 8, saved the town and the refugees from total annihilation. The refugees were finally evacuated at the end of October. It is estimated that over two thousand people were killed in Akalgarh on September 7 and 8, and about two hundred girls were abducted.

Towards the end of September, Kamoke witnessed a most gruesome attack on a refugee train carrying non-Muslims from West Punjab. The train contained over three thousand refugees, most of whom had been placed in open cattle wagons. At Kamoke the train was made to stop for a whole night as it was said that the track had been damaged. During the night parties of Muslims were seen moving about near the train, and by the morning, a large mob had collected. At 12 noon, the train was attacked and almost the entire body of passengers was killed. About six hundred young girls were carried away. One of them, who was afterwards recovered, was taken to village Pandorian by a Kashmiri who kept her in his house for five days. The girl's story is that the Kashmiri tried to kill her. "I had 16 *tolas* of gold sewn into my under-garments. I requested him not to kill me and offered him the gold which he took and made over to his brother. In the house, the Kashmiri raped me and then suggested that I should marry his nephew Din Mohammad. Owing to the shock and the atrocities my brain became ·unbalanced. A month later Gurkha military came to the village. I was concealed in a Muslim refugee's house. For some hours the Gurkha military searched for me in vain and went away. Three months later the military again came to the village. Neither the Kashmiri nor Din Mohammad were in the house. I had been concealed in a corn bin. The soldiers were going to leave when a Muslim woman told them of my whereabouts. The soldiers returned to the house in which I was concealed and hearing their foot-steps I came out and fell down senseless." The abducted girls who had the good fortune to be recovered and restored to their relations have related many horrible stories of the atrocities to which they were subjected.

The town of Hafizabad was attacked on August 24, and looting and arson on a very large scale took place.

In the rural areas disturbances on a large and extensive scale took place throughout the district. Whole villages were ransacked and the non-Muslim residents compelled to embrace Islam. Rumours of an imminent attack made the non-Muslim residents of Talwandi leave their village. Those who were left behind were forcibly converted to Islam. In Wanike-Tarar the Sub-Inspector announced that all Sikhs had been declared disloyal by the Pakistan Government. He said he had instructions to drive out all the Sikhs from the village. The village was raided soon after this and all the Sikhs were mercilessly butchered. Their dead bodies were carried to the river Chenab, in a truck, and thrown in the stream. The Sikh houses and shops were plundered. The Muslims undertook to spare the Hindus but the next day they were told that they must be converted to Islam. All the Hindus, numbering about two hundred, were taken to the local mosque and converted. Thatta Parothian was attacked and burnt on August 26. Many of the residents lost their lives in the fire. Looting continued throughout the night and hundreds of cattle, belonging to the non-Muslims, were driven away. The Hindus of Kale Ki Mandi were told, on August 26, that they would be murdered unless they embraced Islam. They agreed to this but refused to hand over their girls to the Muslims. On this the Muslims attacked them, killing ten and injuring about fifty. On August 27, two lorries carrying Muslim police and military arrived in the village. They joined the Muslim mob in a brutal attack on the Hindus, entered Hindu houses and dishonoured Hindu women. Some women committed suicide by taking poison. In village Jokhian, a house in which a number of Hindus were locked up was set on fire. The Hindus escaped through one of the doors but they were pursued and put to death. At Joara, while a peace committee of Hindus and Muslims was deliberating and devising means of preserving peace, a Muslim mob attacked the village. A Sub-Inspector of Police, police constables and Baluch soldiers accompanied the mob. Some Sikhs were killed and many houses were looted. A second attack was made on the village a fortnight later. On this occasion, thirty-five non-Muslims were killed and the rest of the houses were looted. The remaining non-Muslims were converted to Islam. Baddoki Gosain was attacked and looted on August 24. Non-Muslim refugees of Madiala Panach and Mandi Sukhoke were attacked on the way by Muslim mobs. A number of people lost their lives and many young women were abducted. The attack on Chak Ghazi by a Muslim mob was averted by the efforts of Fateh Mohammad Lambardar and Mian Rehmat Khan. These two men escorted the non-Muslims of their village safely to Akalgarh. In Chak Bhatti there was a difference of opinion among the local Muslims. Some of them wanted to exterminate the " *kafirs* " while others were of the opinion that they should be converted and then allowed to stay unmolested. The timely arrival of a Hindu Army officer with a number of trucks saved the situation and the non-Muslim residents were evacuated from the village.

Gujrat District

The district of Gujrat touches Kashmir State along its northern boundary. The Grand Trunk Road passes through the headquarter town of Gujrat. The district is a predominantly Muslim one and its population at the census of 1941 was recorded

11

as 85.58 per cent Muslim. Gujrat, Lalamusa, Malakwal, Mandi Baha-ud-Din, Dinga and Kunjah are among the important places in the district.

There were no disturbances in the district during the month of March. In June, after the Mountbatten Plan had been announced, the attitude of the Muslims towards the Hindus and Sikhs began to change and, with the advance of time, the minorities became apprehensive of their safety. Many began to leave the urban and the rural areas and, before the 15th of August, a large number of Hindus and Sikhs had left the town of Gujrat and some of the villages. On August 12, three Hindus were stabbed in Gujrat, in broad daylight. This spread panic through the town. A day or two later, some non-Muslims who were travelling by train were murdered and their dead bodies were thrown out. It was said that Muslim butchers had been specially engaged for the purpose. More incidents of this type occurred and travelling became unsafe. The railway authorities cancelled a number of trains as adequate arrangements for the safety of the passengers could not be made. At about this time, Muslim refugees from East Punjab began to arrive and, on August 18, after *Id* prayers, a rumour was spread through the town that a large mob of Sikhs from the neighbouring villages of Tahli Sahib and Shadiwal was preparing to attack the Muslims. The rumour was wholly baseless but it provided the Muslims with an excuse to collect in large numbers and make an attack on the non-Muslim localities. All the shops in the Railway Station Bazaar belonging to the non-Muslims were looted and burnt. The disturbance spread to other parts of the town and Bazaar Sarafan was also plundered and burnt. On August 19, a group of Muslims entered the Lakshmi Narain Temple, threw out the images and pictures and set fire to the building. Khanna Gurdwara, situated near the railway station, was similarly desecrated. The Punjab National Bank, the Grain Market and the Imperial Bank were burnt. About one hundred and fifty non-Muslims were killed in these two days, and a number of girls were kidnapped. A refugee camp for non-Muslims was set up, while looting in the town continued. Travelling by train became more and more unsafe and every train, arriving from the north-west, was found to contain dead bodies of Hindus and Sikhs. Trains were stopped on the way and attacked by mobs of Muslim hooligans. The neighbouring village of Tahli Sahib was a predominantly Sikh village and the residents offered a certain amount of resistance to the Muslim attack on August 18. Many of them lost their lives in the conflict that followed. The attack was, however, repulsed and two men who were clean-shaven offered to go to Amritsar and get military assistance. When they reached the Wazirabad Railway Station they found that all non-circumcised passengers were being put to death. They, therefore, came back to their village. They made another attempt and reached Wazirabad by road. They were able to see a Hindu Army officer who promised to arrange for their evacuation. A few days later, a foot convoy under military escort was arranged. Some members of this convoy lost their lives in a stream which was then in spate. When the convoy arrived at Wazirabad all men and women were searched by members of the National Guard and deprived of all their valuables. After their departure the Gurdwara Tahli Sahib was looted and burnt.*

At Lalamusa also a rumour about Sikhs preparing themselves for an attack was spread through the town and, immediately afterwards, a Muslim mob, assisted by members of the National Guard, began setting fire to the shops and houses of non-Muslims. Gurdwara Singh Sabha was desecrated and burnt. The Granthi and the members of his family were murdered. The Gurdwara in Santpur was also burnt and its Granthi killed. This happened on August 18. On the following day a Madras military contingent arrived and prevented further mischief. The Madrasis remained in Lalamusa until October 2, and, during their stay, no untoward incident occurred. They were then replaced by a Baluch regiment. There were many complaints of harassment by the Baluch military and some women from the refugee camp were molested by them. The houses vacated by non-Muslims were looted and occupied. Evacuation from the camp began on October 11. Before evacuation non-Muslims were searched and deprived of their valuables.

The events in Malakwal followed a similar course. Here, too, a rumour of a contemplated attack by the Sikhs of village Shumari was heard and the Sub-Inspector left Malakwal to enquire into its truth. In his absence, the local Muslims began to loot non-Muslim houses and shops. Forty shops in Rail Bazaar were destroyed in this manner on August 19. On August 28, a mob of several thousand Muslims attacked Malakwal and burnt a major

---

* This incident was deposed to by one hundred and thirty-nine witnesses.

portion of the town. Several hundred non-Muslims were killed. The survivors were escorted to Mandi Baha-ud-Din where a large camp had been set up.

Mandi Baha-ud-Din was an important trade centre. It was a railway station, the headquarters of a *thana* and the seat of a Subordinate Judge and an Honorary Magistrate. Three Boys High Schools and a Girls' High School were located in the town. On August 15, Hindus took part in a public function arranged to celebrate the establishment of Pakistan and offered their co-operation to the new Government. On August 18, the local Muslims spread a rumour that a large mob of Sikhs was preparing to attack them. That evening a number of villages, including Kunjah and Jalalpur Jattan, were attacked by Muslim mobs. There was Hindu military in Mandi Baha-ud-Din and nothing untoward occurred in the town until August 27 on which date Hindu military was replaced by Muslim military, in charge of one Major Aslam. According to all the available evidence this officer did everything in his power to safeguard the lives of the non-Muslims, and the local Hindus offered to present him with a gold shield if they remained unmolested. In the early hours of September 1, the noise of drums was heard and soon afterwards a mob of Muslims opened an attack on the Hindu and Sikh houses in Mohalla Rampura. With the mob were a number of Pathan labourers who had come from the Rasul Head Works. The military resisted this attack and one Pathan was shot dead. Major Aslam then sent a wireless message to Jhelum and a contingent of Hindu military with six tanks arrived in Mandi Baha-ud-Din and saved further loss of non-Muslim lives. Conditions were, however, far from satisfactory in the refugee camp where several thousand non-Muslims were living. The food and drink supplied to the non-Muslims in the camp were poisoned on several occasions and this caused considerable loss of life. Reports regarding the number of casualties vary but it would be safe to say that nearly a thousand persons lost their lives from food poisoning.

On September 5, a huge Muslim mob attacked the town of Dinga. Over a thousand non-Muslims are alleged to have been massacred and about three hundred girls were kidnapped.* A A witness saw dead bodies lying naked in the streets, some of

---

* Some of these were later recovered.

them had been horribly mutilated. The town was looted and a large portion of it was burnt down. A lorry containing Gurkha soldiers arrived on the night of September 7 and the survivors were evacuated to a camp. On September 9, some Muslim Army men went to the camp and carried away a considerable quantity of cash and ornaments. On September 19, the refugees were taken to the camp at Mandi Baha-ud-Din. According to the available evidence members of the National Guards and the police took part in the massacre and looting.

Village Kunjah was similarly attacked on August 18. The shops of the non-Muslims were broken open and looted and then the entire bazaar was burnt down. The town was completely sacked. About three hundred and fifty non-Muslims were murdered and about one hundred and fifty Sikhs were forcibly converted to Islam. About twenty girls were kidnapped. Village Bhairowal was attacked on August 31. The shops and houses were looted and about one hundred and eighty persons were murdered. The survivors agreed to accept Islam but when they were being escorted to Haveli Manu Basal, a neighbouring *abadi*, they were set upon by a Muslim mob and thrown into the river Chenab. Nearly a hundred girls were carried away. The same Muslim mob then went to the neighbouring village of Makhdoom and killed a number of non-Muslims. They carried away thirty-five women. Karianwala, Daulat Nagar, Gakhar Kalan, Gobindpura, Kalu and Jalalpur Jattan were also subjected to very severe attacks and the loss of life in these villages was considerable. The residents of Barsala, Ram Garhwal, Gotriala, Sudewal, Dhal, Lahri, Ara, Samithal, Dhamthal and Alamgarh, near the border of Jammu State, were frequently attacked while proceeding to seek refuge in the State territory. Their villages were looted and burnt.* The happenings in Chak No. 26, a Sikh village, are best described in the words of its Lambardar Sant Singh, an extract from whose statement is given below:

"Chak No. 26 was a Sikh Chak colonised by Sikh Rajputs of the Rathor clan, popularly known as Labana Sikhs. It was populated by two thousand Sikhs and a few Muslim *kamins* or tenants. The adjoining villages of Chak No. 23, Chak No. 25, Chak No. 35, Jara, Sat Basal, Chak No. 11, Mona, Chak Makoh, etc., were all predominantly Muslim. Prior to the formation of

---

* In the table in Appendix II, which is by no means exhaustive, are mentioned a number of other villages in which the attacks were most severe.

Pakistan, the relations between the Sikhs and the Muslims were cordial and friendly. Between June 3 and August 15, the Muslim attitude towards the Sikhs steadily changed. They felt that the Sikhs were aggrieved and would not put up with Pakistan. The agitation by the Sikhs that they would not be content with partition unless the boundary were demarcated along the river Chenab greatly annoyed the Muslims and they began looking upon the Sikhs as the stumbling block in their way. We, the Sikhs, were undoubtedly aggrieved as the result of the partition but we trusted the professions of friendship by the Muslims and their pretentions to protect the minorities.

" In order to ward off an attack in the event of any disturbance, the villagers had taken the following precautions. They had built a surrounding wall 7 feet high round the village *abadi* which extended over two squares of land and a ditch, 4 feet deep beyond the wall. There were four openings in the wall with *pucca* doors. A Shahidi Jatha had been organized with Jethedars and duties were assigned to them. We had sent out spies into the Muslim villages to find out their plans.

" On August 15, a meeting was convened by Jahan Khan, an M.L.A. and a prominent Muslim League worker of Basal village. The Sub-Inspector of Miana. Gondal was also in the meeting. On August 16, one Mohammad Shafi, a compounder of the Civil Hospital, who held me in great respect, informed me that it was not possible for the Sikhs to remain in the district any longer. We sent Sant Singh, Dewan Singh, Gurmukh Singh, Budh Singh, Lambardars and Giani Takhat Singh, Thakar Singh and Bhag Singh to Mona, the Army Remount Depot, to inform the Officer Commanding about the schemes of the Muslims and ask for assistance in the event of an attack. The officer promised his help.

" On August 17, friendly messages came from the neighbouring villages that our chak was in danger. On that day, Prem Singh Nihang, who had lands in Chak No. 21, was returning home with his two sons, aged 12 and 13, when he was attacked by a number of Muslims. The two boys ran into the *rakh* close by but Prem Singh was set upon and shot dead. When the boys came to our village and told us of the attack I went with the Sub-Inspector of Police who had come to our village by chance, to Chak No. 21, and found Prem Singh's dead body lying on the road. The Sub-Inspector then went away. On the night between August 17 and 18, we heard the beating of drums, which was the signal for the attack. Large crowds of Muslims were seen collecting in the neighbouring villages.

"We organized our defence in the following way. Two hundred men of the Akal Regiment were posted in batches of fifty each on the four gates in the wall. All the women were armed with *kirpans*. They wore male dress, i.e., turbans on their heads and *salwars* round their waists. *Thalis* (metal dishes) were tied on the chest by way of shields. One hundred women were detailed to supply water to the defenders. The men were divided in two parts. Half were placed in front of the women and half behind them. The building of the village Gurdwara is a tall one, and a Sikh was posted on top with a telescope. The Muslim mob was seen to possess ladders, camels and spades besides all kinds of firearms and leathal weapons.

"According to our plan we had to remain on the defensive, but when we saw that the Muslim mob was very large and strong we changed our tactics. We also began to beat the *dhol maru* (battle drum) and came out of our fortress. This made the Muslims think, and Jahan Khan sent us a message through Mohammad Din Lohar that we should send four of our men to talk to four of their men and come to terms. The two parties met half-way and Jahan Khan said, 'It is Muslim Raj now. Pakistan has been established. We are the rulers and the Hindus *ryot*. The Sikhs will have to fly the Pakistan flag and obey the orders and injunctions of the Muslim Government and pay them land revenue and other dues.' We replied that we would obey all just and honourable orders but nothing beyond that. In reply to our question Jahan Khan said that he had heard of Sikh attacks on several villages but that the news was found to be false. He then agreed to go back and the mob retreated.

"Mr. Lich, who was the Commanding Officer posted at the Mona Remount Depot, now arrived on the scene with a contingent of sepoys, but returned on seeing that the Muslim mob was retreating.

"We again sent four men (including myself) on horseback to Mona Depot to ask for an escort to evacuate us from the village. We were met by a number of Muslims on the way and told to return home. We said that we were going to see the Police officers in Chak No. 28. A little further we met another group of seven Muslims who tried to attack us. We opened fire on them and they ran away. We finally reached Mona and saw the officer in charge. He gave us four trucks and these, doing two trips daily, began to transport the men of our village. We were not allowed to take any luggage as there was no room in the trucks. We could only take a few clothes, rations and ornaments.

"On August 24, the Sub-Inspector of Police ordered that further evacuation should stop as the Sikhs and the Sikh military sepoys had burnt alive some Muslims and set their houses on fire. At this stage three hundred men were left in Chak No. 26. They were expected to bring some of the valuable property with them. The Sub-Inspector came to the village with a posse of armed police and stopped the evacuation. The sound of drums was again heard from Muslim villages and the Sikhs formed a *morcha* for their defence. A mob of fifteen hundred Muslims armed with .303 rifles attacked the village in the evening at about 8 p.m. The firing started and went on for a long time. The Sikhs had to take shelter in the Gurdwara. The mob entered the village. Bullets pierced through the walls of the Gurdwara. The Sikhs became desperate and came out to fight. One hundred of them were killed and fifty were injured. The remaining one hundred and fifty escaped and reached Mona. Our houses and the Gurdwara were looted and burnt."

This statement was corroborated by eleven other witnesses.

Montgomery District

The Sikhs had an important stake in the district of Montgomery as their enterprise was mainly responsible for developing the colony area and adding to the agricultural prosperity of the district. The Hindus had an important share in the industrial economy of the district* and these considerations, among many others, were urged before the Boundary Commission in support of the non-Muslim claim to a part of this district, although the Muslims comprised 69 per cent of the total population. The Muslim response to this claim was one of open and bitter hostility, directed towards both Hindus and Sikhs but, more particularly, towards the Sikhs. This increased after the announcement of the Radcliffe Award and a most determined and sustained attempt was made to eliminate the Sikh element from the district. The Sikh villages were subjected to ruthless attacks ; men, women and children were brutally slaughtered and their houses were reduced to ashes ; those who fled from their burning homes were pursued

---

* All the thirty-one joint stock companies in the district were controlled by non-Muslims.

or waylaid by the murderous hoards who infested the whole countryside. Day after day foot caravans of refugees, on the way to the Dominion of India, were attacked ; men and women were butchered, young girls were carried away and property was looted. The progress of trains carrying non-Muslim refugees was delayed, there were frequent and quite inexplicable halts on the way, food and drink were denied to the passengers and mobs of armed hooligans attacked them at different stages of the journey. The Muslim military escorts adopted an apathetic, if not acutally hostile, attitude while the non-Muslim escorts found themselves powerless against greater numbers, though in some instances they were successful in driving away the assailants. There was very heavy loss of life in the district and numerous cases of mass conversion.

Upto August 10, Mr. Said Zaman held the office of Deputy Commissioner and till then the district remained peaceful. According to general opinion, his impartiality and firmness kept the unruly elements in check. He was succeeded by Raja Hassan Akhtar, an avowed Muslim Leaguer, whose arrival appeared to encourage the Muslim gangsters. A few days after he took charge, an alarm was raised in the town of Montgomery that some Muslim girls had been molested by Sikh boys. The basis of this outcry was that a Muslim . girl who had purchased some sweets from a Sikh boy had refused to pay for them. Muslim *goondas* began to collect and rioting spread through the city. Three Sikhs and two Hindus were stabbed to death. Curfew was imposed but, the moment it was lifted, twenty-four non-Muslims going to the railway station were set upon and killed. On this, curfew was re-imposed. On the night of August 19, two Muslims, walking in the street during curfew hours, were fatally shot by Sikh soldiers on patrol duty. The next morning a huge funeral procession was taken out through the main streets, and it was openly said that the deaths of these two Muslims would be adequately avenged. The Saw Mill of Dewan Chand and a number of shops in the bazaar were set fire to. Hooligans then looted Okara Mill and the Delhi Cloth Mills retail shop. A Hindu Magistrate, posted at Montgomery, at the time, attended a meeting in the Deputy Commissioner's room on August 24. The Deputy Commissioner openly said that all Sikhs must be shot or killed at sight and that the Hindus could, for the time being, be spared. Some Muslim refugees from East Punjab had, by now, arrived in Montgomery, and they were located in a camp near the railway

station. Their presence made it impossible for any non-Muslim
to reach the railway station with any degree of safety. The non-
Muslims, waiting for trains at the railway station, were frequently
attacked and, on August 25, they were fired upon. Muslim
policemen were seen taking part in the attack. Conditions in the
non-Muslim camp were extremely distressing. Provisions were
scarce and frequently unobtainable. In one case, fruit sold to
refugees was found to be poisoned. The Muslim guard did not
permit water to be carried to the camp, nor were the refugees
allowed to bring it from the canal which ran at a distance of a
few hundred feet. They were frequently forced to get drinking
water from a small water-course in which carcasses of dead dogs
had been thrown by the Muslims.

The non-Muslim policemen were all disarmed under the
orders of the Superintendent of Police on August 14, and they
were kept in a *serai* near the railway station as virtual prisoners.
The Deputy Commissioner and the Superintendent of Police
announced that they could not give any protection to the non-
Muslim minorities. Condition in the town made it impossible for
the non-Muslims to live there. A well in Sabzi Mandi was full
of dead bodies and the stench emanating from it proclaimed the
fate in store for the non-Muslims. It was not till August 25,
when Mr. Belcher, Commissioner, Multan Division, paid a visit to
Montgomery that arrangements for the evacuation of some of the
non-Muslims by train were made.

Hujra Shah Mukim was attacked on August 23, by a Muslim
mob assisted by a Sub-Inspector of Police and Muslim
military. A wholesale slaughter and burning of the houses of non-
Muslim residents ensued. The frenzy of the mob prompted many
women to commit suicide by jumping into burning houses. The
depth of suffering and the anguish resulting from this brutal attack
can be assessed by the fact that many men took the extreme step
of putting their own women and children to death, to save them
from a worse fate at the hands of the hooligans. One man was
seen throwing his infant son, four days old, into the flames. Out
of a total population of nearly a thousand non-Muslims, only one
hundred and sixty survived. At village Kasowal a she-buffalo
was slaughtered by the Muslims in full view of the Hindu residents. A protest merely made the Muslims more aggressive in
their attitude. The Sub-Inspector of Police tried to pacify the
two communities and, for the time being, a clash was averted.
A few days later, a Muslim mob accompanied by members of the

Pakistan Army and a police constable arrived in the village. These men came in military trucks, on horseback and on foot. They laid a siege around the village and then attacked it from all sides. For a time the non-Muslims defended themselves but many of them were shot down by the Muslim soldiers. The mob then ran wild and began an indiscriminate slaughter of non-Muslims. Some, in their frenzy, impaled young children and infants on spears and flourished them in front of their mothers. Nearly four hundred Hindus and Sikhs perished in the course of this assault. Many young girls were carried away by the raiders. While this holocaust was still in progress, a contingent of Hindu and Sikh soldiers, on patrol duty, arrived and, on seeing them, the mob dispersed and ran away.

Pakpattan was attacked and looted on August 23 and 24. The next day a large convoy of non-Muslims left the town. The convoy was stopped by the police at a distance of two furlongs and detained for several hours, during which time the non-Muslims were searched and looted of a large part of their valuables. Proceeding further, they found dead bodies of non-Muslims strewn all along the route. Near Chak No. 22, they saw a lorry lying on its side with the dead body of its Hindu driver near by. A little further, they saw dead bodies of twenty-five non-Muslims by the roadside. In Chak Daula Bala the Zaildar announced that he had received orders from the Deputy Commissioner and the Superintendent of Police to exterminate the Sikhs in his zail. He said that this was merely the price which the Sikhs had to pay for what their co-religionists had done to the Muslims in East Punjab. He offered safety to the Hindus if they agreed to embrace Islam. News of an attack on a neighbouring village where thirty non-Muslims were murdered was received in Chak Daula Bala and this argument persuaded the non-Muslims to accept conversion. The non-Muslims were finally evacuated by Hindu military on September 29. The non-Muslim residents of Chak No. 123/E.B. loaded their belongings on bullock-carts and left the village. They were stopped on the way by the police and told to go back. The following morning the village was surrounded by a huge mob of Muslims. The villagers ran to the police station in the hope of finding shelter there. They were pursued and many who had lagged behind were murdered. The village was then looted and burnt down. The Sub-Inspector advised the non-Muslims to go to Arifwala. On the way the convoy was again attacked and some young girls were carried away. The timely arrival of some Dogra soldiers on patrol duty saved the remaining non-Muslims and they were escorted to Arifwala and thence to Ferozepore. Chak No. 44 was attacked by a Muslim mob on August 22, and the non-Muslims escaped to Chak No. 47. On August 28, Chak No. 47 was attacked by a large mob, assisted by some Police officials and Muslim soldiers. The mob made a large breach in the canal embankment and the whole village was flooded. The non-Muslims resisted the attack for a time but nearly a thousand of them perished. Many young women were kidnapped.

The non-Muslim convoy from village Kandianwala was attacked just outside the village on August 19, and ten persons were killed. On August 22, a similar convoy from Mandi Hira Singh Wala was attacked. Nine non-Muslims were killed and almost the entire property of the convoy looted. On August 23, non-Muslims, living in village Bhila Gulab Singh, were attacked. Over a hundred persons were killed. On August 24, a large caravan which left Chak No. 4/14L with bullock-carts and cattle was attacked by a Muslim mob accompanied by Muslim military. The attack resulted in many deaths and the looting of considerable property. There were attacks on convoys on August 25 at Rattake, and on August 26 at Arifwala where there was an exchange of shots between the non-Muslim escort and some Muslim soldiers. The Canal Head Works at Sulemanke, which became a bottleneck for the refugees crossing over into the Indian Dominion, was the scene of numerous attacks by Muslim mobs. In some parts of the district, the road runs parallel and close to the railway line and, on at least one occasion, Baluch military travelling by train fired upon a foot convoy killing many non-Muslims.

There were three very serious attacks on trains in the district. On August 15, a number of non-Muslims left Okara by the Sind Express. This train was attacked at Harappa and of about three hundred non-Muslims who were in two bogies only twelve survived. The train from Pakpattan was attacked near Basirpur Railway Station and many persons were murdered. On September 26, an east-bound train arrived at Pakpattan. The Mahratta escort was replaced by a Baluch escort. After several hours' delay at Pakpattan, the train left at 11 p.m. It was stopped a mile beyond the station and a Muslim mob, shouting "*Ya Ali, Ya Ali*," attacked it. About four hundred non-Muslims were killed in the course of this assault and over a hundred girls were carried away. Almost the entire property of the passengers was looted. The train did not start till 6 a.m. next morning. In the middle of October, a train arrived at Montgomery at 9 p.m. and was then driven back a distance of two miles and stopped. In the darkness of the night, a mob of Muslims came out of the cotton fields on either side of the railway track and attacked the passengers who were travelling in open goods wagons. There was considerable loss of life. Almost every east-bound train passing through Montgomery or Pakpattan was attacked at some stage of its journey. Some of these attacks took place in the area of Lahore District and some of the worst massacres were witnessed at Raiwind Railway Station.

Lyallpur District

The district of Lyallpur was the most prosperous and productive of the colony areas and one of the richest in the whole province. The cotton crop made a substantial contribution to the wealth of Lyallpur, and apart from adding to the prosperity of the agriculturists it was responsible for the establishment of several industrial concerns. There were many important grain markets in the district, e.g., Lyallpur, Jaranwalla, Gojra, Tandlianwala, all of which were controlled and run by non-Muslims. Large amounts of Hindu capital had been sunk in setting up cotton ginning and weaving factories and flour and sugar mills. On the agricultural side a very large share of the holdings in the colony area was in the hands of the Sikhs who contributed the major portion of the land revenue. So extensive were the financial and proprietary interests of the non-Muslims* in this district that even after the enforcement of the Radcliffe Award, when Lyallpur became part of Pakistan, and when the life and property of the minorities were seen to be in jeopardy, the non-Muslims did not migrate as readily as from some of the other districts of the Punjab. They lingered on, hoping that the state of madness would soon pass away and the return of normal conditions would enable them to live peaceful lives. They received assurances of protection from the Deputy Commissioner, Mr. Hamid, whose impartial

---

* The Sikhs owned 75 per cent of the total holdings and, in the colony areas, they paid 80 per cent of the land revenue. The non-Muslims controlled sixty joint stock companies as against two such companies controlled by Muslims ; of the seventy-two factories in the district fifty-seven were owned by non-Muslims. The figures of the taxes paid by the Muslims and non-Muslims were

	Non-Muslims Rs. (lakhs)	Muslims Rs. (lakhs)
Property tax	1.4	0.2
Sales tax	3.0	0.1
Income-tax	59.5	5.0

and helpful attitude kept the lawless elements in check for a considerable time. Unqualified tributes are paid to his indefatigable energies in this direction and large numbers of refugees have expressed the opinion that, but for his exertions, the loss of non-Muslim life would have been much greater. The emotional wave of communal frenzy, however, proved too strong in the end, and the arrival of large numbers of Muslim refugees from East Punjab who had suffered the retaliatory wrath of the Sikhs made it impossible to preserve the safety of the non-Muslims. The Sikhs, in particular, were singled out and made to pay heavily for the crimes of their co-religionists in Amritsar, Ferozepore, Ludhiana and Jullundur. Lyallpur witnessed three horrific holocausts and, at Jaranwala and Gojra, gruesome tragedies of murder and rapine were enacted. In the rural areas, village after village was attacked by Muslim mobs, assisted, in many cases, by Muslim military and police personnel. Foot and lorry convoys were held up and the travellers subjected to ruthless and inhuman barbarities. An analysis of the evidence recorded shows that, in all, seventy-three different villages and towns were attacked and there were ninety distinct major incidents. In addition, on thirty-nine different occasions, foot convoys on lorries were attacked. The total loss of life was considerable and the value of property, looted or destroyed, ran into several crores of rupees.

The first major incident in the district was a mass attack on Tandlianwala, an important grain market and a police station. There was a large concentration of non-Muslims in Tandlianwala, drawn from the local residents and from the neighbouring villages. On August 26, a huge Muslim mob attacked the Sikh Gurdwara lying on the outskirts of the town. The Gurdwara was burnt and razed to the ground. In it perished many Sikhs who had taken shelter there. Two days later, a larger mob attacked the town, in the afternoon. A large house in Ward No. 6 was burnt down. A gate erected in front of Ward No. 4 was stoned and demolished It is estimated that over two thousand persons were killed during the course of this attack and many young girls were kidnapped. A small batch of Hindu troops under the command of a Sikh officer arrived at midnight and tried to drive away the raiders. The troops were attacked and the Sikh officer lost his life. The next morning the surviving non-Muslims were escorted to Lyallpur.

Jaranwala was attacked on September 8, by a large Muslim mob accompanied by Muslim police and military who fired on the non-Muslims during the course of the assault. The attack continued through the night and large numbers of non-Muslims were done to death. Their property was looted and many of their girls were carried away in trucks. A witness saw pools of blood and dead bodies lying in the streets. The next morning, the Muslims announced that Sikhs would not be allowed to live in Jaranwala. On hearing this, many Sikhs had their beards cut as they believed that a Hindu appearance would ensure their safety. Large numbers of them took shelter in the Gurdwara, and the building was stoned several times. On September 12, the non-Muslims formed a caravan and left the town. They were searched and looted of their valuables. The caravan was attacked and many persons lost their lives. In this attack the Baluch military escort is alleged to have taken a prominent part. A refugee camp had been set up at Jaranwala and conditions in this camp were extremely distressing. The water taps were closed and the refuse of the town was thrown near it. Provisions were scarce and unobtainable and an epidemic of cholera which broke out in the camp took a toll of several lives.

The Hindu military, stationed at Kamalia to protect the non-Muslims, was replaced, on September 1, by Muslim troops. Nawab Saadat Ali Khan and a number of other Muslim Zemindars of the *ilaqa* made very gallant efforts to protect the Hindu and Sikh residents and offered their assistance. The town was attacked on September 6 by a huge Muslim mob. It is said that ammunition was given to this mob by some Muslim soldiers who arrived in Kamalia by a refugee train. The mob invaded the whole town, attacked the Khalsa High School, the Gurdwara Prem Sati, Arya Putri Pathshala and the house of Bahadur Chand Zemindar where non-Muslims had collected. In the course of a determined attack, made by the Muslims, large numbers of Hindus and Sikhs perished. Many young women were kidnapped. On September 7, a Hindu Army officer arrived with two military trucks to evacuate members of his family. He had an armed escort with him and the non-Muslims of Kamalia begged him to stay and lead them to a place of safety. The officer had a small military escort which was quite inadequate to protect a convoy of several thousands. He, therefore, left. Deprived of this avenue of escape the non-Muslims despaired of surviving the bitter attack. The next day, however, Nawab Saadat Ali Khan appealed to the good sense of the Muslims. It is said that he went to them with folded hands and his turban round his neck and asked them to spare the non-Muslims. The fury of the mob had abated and they desisted from continuing their brutal attack. The non-Muslims were, a few days later, evacuated in military trucks and refugee trains.

Gojra was attacked on September 9 by a Muslim mob assisted by Muslim soldiers. About a hundred Sikhs who had taken shelter in the local Gurdwara were murdered. The non-Muslim shops, houses and factories were pillaged. The non-Muslims of Toba Tek Singh were disarmed on September 4, and the next day a Muslim mob attacked the town. The gates of the Gurdwara, where a number of Sikhs had taken shelter, were broken down. Some Sikh residents escaped by wearing women's clothes and removing their beards. The town was subjected to wholesale looting. The inmates of the local refugee camp had to pay large sums of money to the Muslim military in charge. Despite this, neither their life nor the honour of their womenfolk could be assured. On September 6, a foot caravan which started from the town was attacked by a Muslim mob and the Baluch military escort. A non-Muslim refugee train which arrived at Toba Tek Singh was attacked and over a thousand passengers were murdered. Many young women were kidnapped. The Sikh Assistant Station Master of Bhalike and his father-in-law were murdered at the railway station. A young woman of his family was carried away.

Arauti witnessed a most horrible holocaust in which a large number of non-Muslims lost their lives. Syed Nasir Ali Shah, an ex-Unionist member of the Punjab Legislative Assembly who had joined the Muslim League in June, took a prominent part in this incident. A large number of non-Muslims from the neighbouring villages, within a radius of six or seven miles, had congregated at Arauti and Syed Nasir Ali Shah, at first, assured them that they would not be molested. He advised them not to go to the refugee camp and, when conditions in the neighbourhood began to deteriorate, he told them to accept Islam if they valued their lives. On September 12, a large number of Muslims from the adjoining villages gathered in Arauti and made an attack on the non-Muslims in the afternoon. Large numbers of them were killed and the killing continued through the night. The next morning several fires were lit and the dead bodies were burnt. Even the wounded who were alive were not spared and many of them were burnt alive. Some non-Muslims had sought shelter in the houses of local Muslims. These were combed out and put to death. Many young girls attempted suicide by jumping into wells. Some of them were rescued and carried away. The entire non-Muslim property was then pooled and divided among the rioters. It is said that Syed Nasir Ali Shah received a large share of this loot. In a neighbouring village, Sandilianwali, about six hundred non-Muslims had sought shelter. Syedani Anwar Bibi and her son who wielded a great deal of influence in the village refused to permit an attack on these refugees and, be it said to their credit, they called their followers and escorted the non-Muslims to the refugee camp at Mian Channu safely. Samundri and Khihala Kalan were subjected to severe attacks and large numbers of non-Muslims lost their lives in these villages. In Samundri the dead bodies were carried away in trucks to destroy the evidence of the horrible crime.

At Lyallpur conditions remained comparatively peaceful until the end of September. The Deputy Commissioner strained every nerve to avert an attack on the non-Muslims, of whom a large number had collected in the town. On September 3, while he was holding a meeting of the Magistrates, the dead body of a Sikh was brought in. This spread panic in the town and there were a few stabbing cases. A cotton ginning factory was looted by the Muslim employees. The West Punjab Government were anxious to drive out all non-Muslims and more particularly the Sikhs. On September 5 the Governor, Sir Francis Mudie, had written to Mr. Jinnah: " I am telling everyone that I do not care how the Sikhs get across the border: the great thing is to get rid of them as soon as possible. There is still little sign of the three lakh Sikhs in Lyallpur moving, but in the end they too will have to go."* On September 6, Sir Francis Mudie came to Lyallpur and told the Deputy Commissioner that all Sikhs should be moved to the refugee camp as a preliminary step to their being evacuated to India. This direction appears to have given a lead to the local Muslims and tension in the town increased. The first major incident occurred on the morning of October 1. A large non-Muslim foot convoy from Sargodha was passing through Lyallpur and, when a part of it had crossed the railway level crossing, near Tarkabad, the gates of the crossing were closed. A mob of armed Muslims then fell upon the portion of the convoy left

---

* See Notes to Chapter III in Appendix I.

12

behind and began a ruthless massacre. Pandemonium broke out. Screaming women and children began to run hither and thither and the Baluch military escort opened fire upon them. The property loaded in bullock-carts was looted and, as the assault continued through the day the ground was strewn with dead bodies. The Deputy Commissioner recalled the Baluch military in charge of the convoy and deputed a police guard in its place. Soon afterwards a contingent of Gurkha military arrived and led the convoy to safety. The same night an attack was made on the refugee camp in Khalsa College where many of the non-Muslims who had survived the assault on the foot convoy had taken shelter. The Muslim military in charge of the camp took part in the killing and looting. A large number of non-Muslims lost their lives and many young girls were carried away. Men and women were searched for valuables on their persons. The next night the Arya School Refugee Camp was attacked in a similar manner. The Baluch soldiers in charge of this camp had been molesting the inmates for many days. They had frequently searched them for cash and valuables. They used to carry away women at night and rape them. The attack on the night of October 2, however, resulted in a veritable holocaust. The camp was attacked from several sides simultaneously and the Muslim military opened fire on the inmates. All the property in the camp was looted. It is impossible to make an exact estimate of the loss of life occasioned as it is said that large numbers of dead bodies were carried away in military trucks during the night and thrown in the river Chenab. When the Deputy Commissioner arrived in the morning he found a hundred and fifty dead bodies still lying in the camp. The general opinion, however, is that more than two thousand persons in the camp were killed. The Deputy Commissioner replaced the Baluch military by a police guard. This attack was carefully planned and the Agent of the Imperial Bank heard his police guard talking boastfully, in the morning, that the school camp would be attacked in the evening. He did not, however, attach any importance to this talk, otherwise the tragedy might possibly have been averted.

A canal bridge at Saloonijhal in Tehsil Samundri was the scene of persistent attacks on non-Muslim convoys passing over it. Scarcely a single foot convoy was allowed to pass without serious mishap. On September 11, a convoy from Samundri was attacked and sixty persons were killed. The next day a convoy from Kamalia was similarly set upon and nine persons were killed.

Foot caravans from Toba Tek Singh, Chak No. 44, Chak No. 46, Chak No. 531, Chak No. 91, a caravan from Jodha Nagari, another one from Chak No. 293/J.B., a convoy of lorries from Chak No. 203/G.B. and another convoy from Chak No. 360 were attacked at different times. In every case the refugees were looted and their girls were carried away.

The residents of village Tiba Dhak Salha were told on August 23, that their safety lay in departure. The local Zaildar offered to help them in going away to a place of safety. The non-Muslims accordingly collected their more precious belongings and left the village, in a procession, on August 24. They passed Tandlianwala and crossed the river Ravi by boat, intending to go to Okara. Across the river some Muslims met them and told them to return to their village as it was unsafe to go further. The refugees spent the night on the bank of the river. The next morning the Sub-Inspector and the Zaildar, however, assured them that it was inadvisable to return and the more prudent course lay in proceeding on their journey. They gave them an escort of Muslim villagers. Near village Burj Jiwa Khan some Muslim soldiers opened fire on the convoy. The non-Muslims ran back towards the river. The soldiers were joined by a large Muslim mob, armed with deadly weapons, and an attack was launched on the refugees. The stragglers were cut down or shot. Those who reached the riverside safely spent the night in anxious dread, as no boats were available. The next morning the sound of drums was heard and, soon after, the Muslims opened a fresh assault. Many jumped into the river and were drowned. One woman strapped her three children to her waist and entered the river; the two younger children were drowned. Almost the entire convoy was decimated within a few hours. The Muslims carried away many young girls and the property of the caravan. One young girl was taken by the ruffians to village Burj Jiwa Khan. On the way she saw dead bodies lying everywhere in the fields, on the roads and in the canal minors. She was kept at Burj Jiwa Khan for four days in the house of a Muslim. At night she succeeded in escaping but was overtaken and beaten. She jumped into a canal minor and her pursuers, believing her to be drowned, went away. She says, "I swam for a mile or so and then, getting out, went to a village near the canal bank. An old Muslim took pity on me and bandaged my bleeding wounds. The next day he asked me to leave the village. Eleven days later I found myself in my own village, Tiba Dhak Salha. I cannot explain how God helped me to reach my village." A few other survivors also reached their native village in this manner and were finally evacuated to India.*

A convoy of three trucks carrying passengers from Lyallpur on August 25 was stopped near Sharakpur and attacked. The passengers were made to pay a heavy ransom for their safety, and were then allowed to proceed on their way. Another truck which left Lyallpur on September 27, with twenty-five passengers, was also stopped near Sharakpur. The Muslim driver picked up two Pathan passengers and then drove on. A little further, he left the road which had been breached by recent floods and drove the truck through some fields. A mob of armed Muslims attacked the truck and killed some of the passengers. All the property in the truck was looted and some of the girls were taken away to Sharakpur. They were kept in a house where a number of kidnapped women were already present. Some of the women were later rescued and escorted to India. A convoy of four lorries proceeding to Lahore on October 24, was attacked and looted in a similar manner. The truck containing women was subjected to a thorough search and some of the women were stripped naked to see if they had any valuables on their persons. Some young girls were raped by the roadside. The passengers were then asked to get down and the trucks were driven back to Lyallpur. The next morning a military truck containing some Gurkhas arrived and escorted them to Lahore.

Shahpur District

Shahpur is another colony district though the colonists are drawn not from Central Punjab but from the north-western districts and are, for the most part, Muslim. The non-Muslim population of the district was not more than 15 per cent. There was a sprinkling of Sikh villages but the majority of the non-Muslims were concentrated in the towns and the depots for agricultural produce. Sargodha, Bhera, Khushab, Loon Miani and Bhaironwal were places in which many well-to-do and even wealthy non-Muslims resided. The March riots affected only a few villages in the Shahpur District and were soon suppressed. In Sargodha, the headquarters of the district, there was peace almost throughout. There was however, considerable tension owing to the happenings in the neighbourhood. A peculiar feature

---

* Foot convoys were attacked near Roshanwala, Khu Burj, Chak No. 27, Tandlianwala, Row Korn Bungalow, Rodo Koro and other places.

of the district was that forcible conversions took place on a very large scale in the rural areas. The Hindus found themselves greatly outnumbered and, when given the offer of conversion to Islam as the price of safety, had no other choice but to submit. In some villages they were able to live in peace after their decision but, when they were evacuated to India under military escort, they had to leave behind all their belongings. Another feature of the district was that in Sargodha a number of false cases were brought against rich and prominent non-Muslims alleging that they owed money to Muslims. Warrants were issued for their arrest and, in some cases, the victims were taken into custody. They could only leave Sargodha on payment of heavy ransoms. Ornaments pawned with non-Muslim *sahukars* were returned without the debts being discharged. In many villages the non-Muslims were not attacked and were told to quit and make room for the Muslims. They were not allowed to take any property with them. In some of the western villages Pathans looted non-Muslim property. Camps were set up near Sargodha and Phulerwan and the conditions in these camps were far from satisfactory. Foodstuffs were not available and at Phulerwan the general complaint was that owing to curfew orders non-Muslims could not even go out to ease themselves although Muslims moved about freely. Except in a few places the killing of non-Muslims was not on a large scale, and the loss of life was not so heavy as in some other districts. The loss of property, however, was considerable.

In Bhaironwal, a Muslim mob attacked the village towards the end of August. The non-Muslims abandoned their houses and shops and took shelter in a Gurdwara. The shops and houses were looted and a mass massacre of the non-Muslims in the Gurdwara followed. The survivors were forcibly converted to Islam and were made to eat beef. The dead bodies were thrown in the river Chenab near by. Mitha Tiwana was attacked on August 19, and the attack continued for four days. The Batra family, who owned several thousand acres of land and possessed eight licensed guns, defended their *mohalla* by mounting guard on the roof of their house. They were, however, deprived of their guns, taken into custody and charged with the offence of attempted murder. This was due to the fact that shots fired by them in self-defence had injured two men. In Khushab there was some trouble in the month of March and the Mahant of the Bairagi shrine was murdered. In August the non-Muslim shops were looted and many of them were ejected from their houses. Eight non-Muslims left Bhalwal on August 17, with the intention of going to Sargodha. They were attacked and murdered at the railway station by Muslim League National Guards. The residents of Khwaja Ahmad were converted to Islam - and robbed of their belongings. They were taken to the Jumma Mosque in Sargodha from where they were rescued by the Gurkha military. In Mandi Warchhan a number of non-Muslims refused conversion. They were promptly murdered. Their dead bodies were then taken to a Hindu temple and burnt. About sixty residents of Raipur left their village with their valuables but they were stopped on the way by the police who searched them and deprived them of their valuables. They proceeded further and were persuaded to return home by two local Muslim Zemindars who gave them assurances of safety. On the way back they were attacked by a Muslim mob who killed several of them and abducted a number of young girls. The residents of Chak Ramdas were saved by the timely arrival of a European military officer when a Muslim mob was preparing to attack them. The massacre of Loon Miani and the events of Bhera can best be described in the words of two witnesses, extracts from whose statements are given below. These statements were chosen because the deponents are simple unsophisticated persons who have given a fair and unadorned account of what occurred and have not hesitated to mention facts in favour of the Muslim officials.

Statement of Lakhmi Das, a labourer, of Loon Miani:

"Malakwal, a town near my town, was reported to have been attacked in the beginning of September and we were feeling nervous. The Sub-Inspector of Police, who was a Mohammedan and had come recently from Khushab or Nowshera, assured us that as long as he was there we would suffer no danger or loss. He had taken the place of a Sikh Sub-Inspector of Police. We, the non-Muslims of Miani, felt satisfied by the assurances given by the Muslim Sub-Inspector. There were three attempts on Miani by Muslim *goondas* of adjoining villages in the first week of September 1947, but the Sub-Inspector beat off these attacks and arrested some of the *goondas* of the assaulting party. The arrested persons were made to sit the whole day at the police station and then released in the evening. The non-Muslims of Miani thought that the Sub-Inspector was a strong man and would really safeguard their interests and protect them. On September however, drums continued beating the whole night. We felt afraid but the Sub-Inspector told us that there was nothing to fear; the military had arrived and he had police arrangements also and so no harm would come to us. He had also told previously that he was arranging for our evacuation.

" On one side we were hearing drums being beaten and were feeling nervous. On the other hand, there was an assurance by the Sub-Inspector and by the local Muslims who had behaved well so far. Nothing happened that night but on September 10, at about 12 noon, there was a sudden attack on Miani. First, we heard shots being fired and we thought that the military were firing at the mob. But, after a little time, we were astonished to find that the mob of Muslim *goondas* and dacoits, armed with all sorts of weapons, aided by the police constables, a head constable and an Assistant Sub-Inspector of Police who had a cut on his upper lip, and Baluch military, had attacked and were shooting the Hindus indiscriminately. The head constable and the Assistant Sub-Inspector were proclaiming that even a suckling baby would not be spared. The firing continued till 4 p.m. and the non-Muslims were threatened with death if they did not give up their cash and valuables, but, when they handed over their valuables, they were mercilessly beaten, assaulted and murdered. Some babies were even cut into pieces. People were thrown from the house-tops like balls. Young girls were abducted. Their number was about sixty. My daughter-in-law was killed. A granddaughter of mine was also killed. I and my son Krishan Lal were seriously injured and left as dead. In my vicinity about two hundred persons lay dead or injured. In all about nine hundred persons died and four hundred were wounded. Some of the mob were killing and inflicting injuries, some were looting and some were engaged in breaking open locks and doors. When I saw that the dacoits had left, I got up and cried for water. Someone replied that he was coming and shortly afterwards the head constable, Qureshi, and a constable, accompanied by some military men, came and told us that the survivors should come out and that we would be taken to the camp in the house of Jawala Sahai Chadda. We went there and water was supplied to us by one of the constables. Later Qureshi head constable told us that curfew had been relaxed and that we could go home and bring our belongings and luggage. I brought a bedding first and left it in the camp. Then I went again and brought a small trunk and a small bedding containing some children's clothes and a quilt. This latter load was snatched away by the said Qureshi on the way.

"The Sub-Inspector was not seen the whole day. The Assistant Sub-Inspector asked the able-bodied among us to remove the corpses and we accordingly collected about four hundred by the evening and burnt them.   Meanwhile Hindu military accompanied by some Muslim soldiers reached the camp and gave first aid to the injured.   The remaining five hundred bodies were collected the next morning and burnt with wood and kerosene oil. We were then transferred to Phulerwan Hospital and from there I, my son and about a hundred others were transferred to the Sargodha Hospital.   From Sargodha we have come to the Amritsar Refugee Camp."

The second statement was given by Shrimati Ram Piari, a resident of Bhera :

"On August 20, 1947, a Muslim mob armed with *chhavis, kulharis,* etc., numbering about four or five hundred, entered our street.   With the mob were members of the National Guards and the local police.   They openly and loudly said that we should vacate the houses and run away; otherwise we would be killed, and that everything lying in our houses belonged to Pakistan. Eight persons in Bhandawali Galli were killed and four or five others were wounded.   The Muslims tried to break open our doors and when they could not do so they abused us.   They said that they would kidnap our young girls and marry them to Muslims.   The sweepers were forbidden to clean our streets and remove the night-soil from our houses. On August 22, we left our houses and reached the railway station.   We had to leave all our luggage at home.   There was no train that day and on August 24, we again went to the railway station.   The lorry-driver, who was a Muslim, charged us five rupees per passenger upto the railway station.   The National Guards and the police charged us four rupees each railway fare for Mandi Baha-ud-Din, although the real fare is only ten annas.   Only some of us could go on the 24th and the rest, including myself, went on the 25th. During the night the Sikh officer and his non-Muslim subordinates, who formed our escort, undertook to protect us.   They remained awake the whole night.   On the way the train was stopped as the trunk of a huge tree lay across the line.   A Muslim mob attacked us with guns, hatchets etc., shouting " *Allah-o-Akbar.*"   The non-Muslim escort defended us and killed many

Muslims. The train reached Mandi Baha-ud-Din at 1-30 p.m. It was very hot and we asked for water. There was none available as the water taps at the station had been closed. Even our babies were not given water and the Muslims said that they were ready to supply us with their urine. A child in our compart ment died of thirst. We were taken to a camp one and a half miles from the railway station and here, too, we found that the water taps had been removed. We arranged to get water from the wells by letting down vessels tied to bed-sheets strung together. In the camp the rations were not free and we could only buy three *chhattaks* every other day. The non-Muslims in Mandi Baha-ud-Din sometimes sold us *atta* at four seers per rupee but the police removed these non-Muslims and brought them to the camp Their stocks were left behind and taken possession of by the Muslims. Cholera spread and, as the result of it, many non-Muslims died. As the Muslim National Guards, the local police and the Muslim military had taken possession of all the fuel wood in the Mandi, the non-Muslims in the camp used to light fire for cremating the dead bodies by chopping up their boxes. This, 'however, was not enough and, frequently, dead bodies remained uncremated. On September 27 and 28, thirty-two trucks sent by the Indian Union arrived but the Muslim military permitted only those persons to go in the trucks who paid heavy bribes. I was allowed to sit in a truck at the request of a Subedar.

" On September 10, sixty non-Muslims died after taking milk. It was said that the milk was poisoned."

Jhang District

Mass massacres of Hindus and Sikhs and wholesale plunder of non-Muslim property in the towns of Jhang-Magiana, Masan, Shorkot and Chiniot were the salient features of the events in Jhang District. Similar tragedies on a smaller scale, though not less gruesome in their intensity or in the suffering occasioned to the individual victims, took place in almost all the villages in the rural areas. A study of all the availabe evidence, consisting of the statements of hundreds of refugees from the district, leaves no doubt whatever that these results were achieved by the vitriolic utterances of Pir Mubarak Ali Shah, the local Muslim League member of the Provincial Legislative Assembly, and the assistance given to him and to his *goonda* followers by Mr. Zaffar-ul-Haq Khan, District Magistrate, Mr. Mohammad Akbar,

Additional District Magistrate and Mr. Hasnat Ahmad, City Magistrate.

In the month of March the post of the Deputy Commissioner was held by a Sikh officer and the peace of the district remained undisturbed. The Superintendent of Police was a British officer and his attitude towards the minorities was sympathetic and protective. In August Mr. Zaffar-ul-Haq Khan assumed charge as District Magistrate and Mr. Hasnat Ahmad was appointed City Magistrate. Signs of unrest were observed soon after August 15, and Muslims took out processions through the streets of Jhang in defiance of prohibitory orders under section 144, Criminal Procedure Code. The processionists openly asked the Hindus to leave the town. When an appeal was made to Mr. Hasnat Ahmad he merely retorted that his own house in Amritsar had been burnt by the Sikhs, and he made no secret of his resentment against the non-Muslims. His attitude could not but encourage the gangster element in the town. Pir Mubarak Ali Shah went to Karachi in the middle of August to attend a conference of the Muslim League. He returned to Jhang on the 21st, and soon afterwards Muslim hostility became more open and more intense. On August 24, Mr. Ryan, the Superintendent of Police, went to Lahore to consult the Deputy Inspector-General of Police. It was said that his departure from the district was due to a cunning move on the part of the District Magistrate and Pir Mubarak Ali Shah who wanted to have him out of the way in order to carry out their plans successfully. The events which followed support this hypothesis. On the morning of August 25, trouble began in the city of Jhang-Maghiana. Two persons were stabbed near the Canal Office and one in front of the Sessions House. The news of these assaults spread through the town like wild-fire and, while the non-Muslims took shelter in their houses, the Muslim hooligans became openly rowdy and ran about, assaulting unwary non-Muslims and setting fire to their houses and shops. By the afternoon the whole of the town was affected and large fires were seen blazing in different quarters. The wife of the Hindu Station Master came to the city with her clothes soaked in blood and crying that her husband and son had been brutally stabbed at the railway station. The following night was comparatively quiet but, on the morning of August 26, utter lawlessness broke out, and the Muslim mobs began to attack Hindus and Sikhs with redoubled fury. The military and the police patrolled the city in a leisurely fashion as if nothing serious were happening and looked on calmly while murder and arson were committed under their very eyes. In some cases they even gave open support to the hooligans by shooting at the Hindus and looting their property. Some soldiers handed over their guns to the Muslim marauders. Pir Mubarak Ali Shah was seen firing from a .303 rifle and leading the mobs. Houses and shops in Sultanwala, Budhewala, Hasnana, Dhupsari and Railway Bazaar were looted. Dozens of houses were burnt and destroyed. This state of affairs continued throughout the day on the 26th and the following night. It is estimated that nearly two thousand non-Muslims perished in this brutal attack ; about four hundred girls were carried away and some who were later recovered were found to have been raped in a most horrible and inhuman manner. On the morning of August 27, when the fury of the marauders had abated somewhat, the non-Muslims came out of their houses and, taking their cash and valuables, formed a procession with the intention of going to the bungalow of the District Magistrate and appealing to him for help. On the way they were stopped by a military and police picket who ordered them to leave their property behind. Complaints made to the Additional District Magistrate and the City Magistrate were of no avail. The processionists were forced to comply with the orders of the police and continued their journey without their belongings. The District Magistrate told them to go to a refugee camp which had been set up in the school premises.

The District Magistrate had, on August 25, passed two orders. One of these prohibited the departure of any lorry without the specific permission of the District Magistrate and the other placed a ban on the removal of all property. A copy of this latter order was sent to the President, Town Committee, Lalian, and this copy was brought out by one of the refugees. Its text is given below : —

"ORDER

I, Zaffar-ul-Haq Khan, District Magistrate, Jhang, do hereby order that none leaving the Jhang District, shall export any goods of any description whatsoever, except the necessary wearing apparel, and the bedding enjoined by weather.

Any contravention of this order is a penal offence under the Public Safety Act.

T. O. Jhang will please contact the Police and make necessary arrangements that the contents of this order are faithfully carried out.

25th August, 1947.

(Sd.) ZAFFAR-UL-HAQ KHAN.
District Magistrate, Jhang.

District Magistrate's Office, Jhang.
No. 6012 *dated* 25-8-1947.

Copy forwarded to the President, Town Committee, Lalian, for wide publicity by beat of drum.

(Sd.)
For District Magistrate, Jhang.
25-8-1947."

This order was strictly enforced throughout the district and its terms were invoked to deprive the residents of Maghiana of all their valuable before they left the district. Some of their property was taken away even before they arrived in the refugee camp.

Conditions in the refugee camp can best be described by quoting the words of a local medical practitioner who lived in the camp.

" In the refugee camp I was placed in charge of the sick and the injured by the leaders of refugees. I had no medicines or instruments with me to perform operations and to dress the wounds of the injured. We wrote to the authorities to let us have medicines and surgical instruments from our own clinics but the Government took no action. Therefore, without the help of any instruments, we had to perform major operations with second-hand shaving blades which also were available with considerable difficulty. We were lucky to get some boric acid and a very small quantity of potassium permanganate from some shops in the Mandi and we were compelled to use ordinary oil which was unsterilized and unmedicated for dressing wounds.

"In place of gauze we used rags from tailors' shops. There were no bandages and we had to leave the wounds uncovered. Cotton, too, was not available. Most of the injured had bullet wounds and we had to cut their flesh with blades and extract the bullets with our fingers. Some of the bullets were very big in size and were fired from .303 rifles. I took out bullets from the bodies of over a hundred persons. A large number of the injured had grievous wounds inflicted by spears and other sharp-edged weapons, and almost all injured persons had multiple injuries on their bodies. I came across the case of a goldsmith's wife belonging to village Sagla, at that time residing in Mohalla Sultanwala, who said that her infant daughter of about six months was rent into pieces by her thighs being pulled apart, and her son was stabbed to death by Wali Mohammad, Municipal Commissioner of Jhang.

"Apart from the injured from Jhang-Maghiana town, over five hundred persons, seriously wounded, were brought to the refugee camp from adjoining villages. One of the cases that I treated was of a woman from village Chund Bharwana who was the wife of a railway porter. One of her hands was chopped off above the wrist and then she was thrown into the fire as the result of which her lower portion got burnt. But she escaped from there and was then thrown into a well with her two daughters and one son. She was taken out of the well later on and brought to the refugee camp. Her children died in the well but one of her daughters survived and she had a deep cut from the temple to the cheek cutting the bone also. Her eldest daughter aged 18 had been abducted earlier. . . .

"The chief types of injuries inflicted on the wounded were (1) amputation of limbs, hands and forearms, (2) skull and temple injuries, (3) stab wounds penetrating the abdomen and chest, (4) bullet and gunshot wounds, (5) amputation of breasts of women (six such cases of chopped off breasts were brought to the refugee camp and all of them proved fatal), (6) circumcision wounds performed on the male organs of many young men and old men, (7) cut throat cases and (8) burns. . . .

"In the refugee camp at Jhang, due to insanitary conditions, and, due to total lack of any facilities for sanitation on behalf of the authorities and lack of proper diet, many diseases sprang up amongst the refugees and it became a gigantic problem for us doctors. Besides this, one of our big problems was the handling of maternity cases. On an average six to seven births were daily taking place in our camp. Quite a large number of deliveries was premature, due to the panic and excitement and the discomforts to which the mothers were not accustomed. There was no place to confine these unfortunate women and deliveries had to take place in the open and in the presence of men and women. We did not even have the elementary things for use on such occasions and our requests to the authorities to supply them were turned down. They had no clothes to change and no soap to wash and clean the clothes they were wearing, at the time of delivery. A very poignant case was that of a women who was forced to walk three miles from Jhang city to the Mandi along with other refugees. She had hardly covered one mile when she gave birth to a child by the roadside. Many maternity cases became septic."

Food and water in the refugee camps were scarce. Fortunately the residents of Lyallpur came to the rescue of the refugees in the Jhang Camp and began to send them a lorry-load of *chappattis* and other foodstuffs every day. There were no latrines in the refugee camp. The inmates had to defecate in buckets and then carry the buckets out themselves.

Dhupsari and Hasnana are two suburbs of Jhang-Maghiana and there, too, disturbances broke out on August 25. The residents of Dhupsari saw the city of Maghiana ablaze on the evening of August 25, and collected in the house of one Panju Ram. A Muslim mob attacked the suburb and many houses were set on fire. Sixty persons are said to have lost their lives in the course of this assault and thirty young girls were kidnapped. In Hasnana the entire inmates of one house were butchered and the City Magistrate was shown a heap of thirty corpses lying in the house. Some residents took shelter in the house of Amir Lambardar who had promised to protect the non-Muslims. This house was attacked by a Muslim mob and the owner was compelled to ask his neighbours to leave the house. Almost all of them were murdered by the Muslims.

Jhang City, which is situated at a distance of a mile and a half from Jhang-Maghiana, did not suffer to the same extent. The total loss of life in the city is said to have been not more than thirty or forty. The entire property of the non-Muslims was, however, looted after they had left for the refugee camp. The property of the residents of Mohalla Gulabwala was carried away on trucks, camels and donkeys.

At Shorkot the sound of drums was heard on the evening of August 19, and a rumour was spread through the town that a mob of Sikhs was preparing to attack the Muslims. This rumour was wholly baseless and it transpired that the drum-beating was merely intended to collect the Muslims by way of a rehearsal of the major attack which took place on August 26. On the morning of that day it was found that all the Muslim houses were displaying Muslim League flags to distinguish them from the non-Muslim houses. In the course of the assault which took place during the day one hundred and fifty non-Muslims lost their lives and two hundred more were injured. Muslim military on arriving joined the mob and shot, at the non-Muslims. The town was then pillaged by the Muslim police, military and Muslim National Guards together with the Muslim mob. Masan, a village eight miles from Jhang, was attacked on August 26. The village was surrounded on all sides by a Muslim mob and the Hindus took shelter in a Gurdwara near the police station. The Zaildar of the *ilaqa* was a Hindu and he was done to death. Two of his daughters were abducted. Scarcely a handful of the non-Muslim population of the village escaped this brutal massacre. On August 22, a large mob of Muslims assisted by members of the National Guards, the police force and some Baluch soldiers, surrounded Chiniot. A sadhu, sitting in his hut, was murdered and his dead body was thrown into a well. Two young boys were stabbed and thrown on a mound near by. The next day Muslim National Guards were seen spraying kerosene oil with stirrup-pumps on Hindu houses and shops. The houses were then set on fire. The disturbances continued on the following day. The Deputy Superintendent of Police, who was in Chiniot, when appealed to, demanded a sum of three thousand rupees for stopping the massacre. The money was paid but the police remained inactive. In the course of three days four hundred persons lost their lives in Chiniot. The survivors took shelter in the premises of the local school. They loaded their goods on some trucks but the trucks were driven away to the police station and the property was shared among the police and the Muslim mob. Some of the residents had concealed their valuables and they were asked to give details of their whereabouts. The valuables were most probably removed by the police as the owners were never able to recover them. In the refugee camp no fuel for cremating the dead was available and the doors, windows and benches of the school were used to make up funeral pyres. A Muslim mob attacked village Chela on August 28. Some of the non-Muslims found shelter in the house of a sympathetic Muslim resident. His house was surrounded and he was threatened with death unless he ejected all those who had come under his protection. When the non-Muslims came out they were attacked and forty of them were killed. Some young girls were kidnapped. About one hundred and fifty non-Muslims were forcibly converted to Islam. These were subsequently evacuated by Hindu military on September 4. An armed mob assisted by

Muslim police and Muslim National Guards attacked Lalian on the night between August 27 and August 28. The houses of non-Muslims were looted for two days. A contingent of Hindu soldiers arrived on the third day and remained stationed at Lalian till September 25 when they were replaced by a Muslim military guard. On October 13, the non-Muslims were again attacked when they were in a refugee camp and seven persons were killed. Ten girls were kidnapped. The villages of Rajana, Ubhana and Chak No. 232 were similarly attacked resulting in the loss of several non-Muslim lives. In Chak No. 232, the non-Muslims were converted to Islam and made to eat beef. They were then set upon and several of them were done to death.

Multan District

The March riots had resulted in a decisive victory for the Muslim League gangsters and, as August 15 approached, the non-Muslim residents of the towns and villages in the district began to get apprehensive of what lay in store for them in the future State of Pakistan. Some of them began to leave their native towns and habitations but difficulties of transport, risks of train and road journeys and the desire to cling to one's property to the last prevented a large-scale exodus. The non-Muslims were in a small minority in the district, and, in the rural areas particularly, they found themselves isolated and at the mercy of their Muslim neighbours. The advent of Pakistan took them at a disadvantage if not unawares.

Looting and burning of villages commenced towards the end of August and continued throughout the month of September. In some of the out ying villages the non-Muslims were compelled to accept Islam as they realized that, unless they adopted this course, they would be immediately done to death. In these villages loss of life was negligible and the converted persons were in due course escorted to safety by the Military Evacuation Organization.* There was, however, wholesale looting and the non-Muslims lost all their property. During September, groups of non-Muslims travelling by road were attacked in almost all parts of the district. There were altogether no less than twenty-eight distinct attacks resulting in considerable loss of life. There were five attacks on trains. The recorded evidence shows a hundred and five different attacks on

---

* Wholesale conversion took place in the following villages :—Bandra, Baqraon, Bhalli, Bati Qoiser, Chak No. 42, Chak No. 119, Mughal-Da-Bait, Chah Pipilwala, Chah Kalu Mohtamwala, Chah Gaban Wala, Dera Mulla Fazal, Gehlawala, Ghafoor, Haveli Lang, Mauzabet Kaich, Khaki Panjani, Khakhan Jalalpur, Khaki Paunta, Khanpur, Basti Miani, Nawabpur, Basti Rajputan, Ranewan and Basti Shel Khan.

villages. In a large number of these there was considerable loss of life and in every case looting and burning of non-Muslim property were witnessed. The massacre of Rampur and Jalalpur Pirwala in Tehsil Shujabad was perhaps one of the worst incidents in the district.

In Multan a large crowd of about four thousand non-Muslims went to the Cantonment Railway Station, intending to take an eastbound train. The authorities in charge of evacuation, however, allowed only a few Government officials to enter the platform. The rest of the crowd waited outside hopefully. in the meantime a large mob of Muslims began to collect and, soon after the train had left, the non-Muslims were attacked. Members of the Muslim League National Guards took part in the attack. Fifteen non-Muslims were killed and twenty-five injured. Ten young girls were kidnapped. Fortunately a contingent of Mahratta military arrived and saved the situation. Conditions in the city deteriorated and utter lawlessness prevailed. Non-Muslims, venturing out of their houses to visit a bank, or on their way to the railway station or the aerodrome, were attacked and looted. Many persons lost their lives in this manner. Groups of Muslim hooligans would bring hand-carts or bullock-carts to the doors of Hindu and Sikh houses and calmly remove all the property, whether the residents were at home or not. The police did not choose to interfere. Some non-Muslims tried to sell their furniture and other movables for a pittance and, for some days, radio sets, bicycles and gramophones were sold for a few rupees each. Then information was sent to the city that the Hindus would be leaving their property behind in any case and it was unwise and unnecessary for the Muslims to pay money for it. Hindu and Sikh officials were refused their salary for the month of August as the Accountant-General of West Punjab had sent out instructions that no salary should be paid to officials who were not expected to remain in Pakistan. The Police officers were all disarmed and even the licenced weapons privately owned by them were taken away. They were then turned out of their barracks and their rations were stopped. It was with the greatest difficulty that the Deputy Superintendent of Police allowed them to stay in the Gurdwara and the Police Lines. One of the constables who was dark complexioned and, in appearance, somewhat like a Muslim, grew a short beard and wore a Jinnah cap; and, thus disguised, he went out to get rations for his colleagues, confined in the Gurdwara and the Police Lines. On

13

September 17, a number of Muslim Police officials from East Punjab arrived in Multan and launched an attack on the Hindu and Sikh Police officials. Many of them were injured and deprived of their belongings. The timely arrival of the Deputy Superintendent of Police prevented loss of life on this occasion, but a little later two Sikhs were murdered and a Hindu Prosecuting Sub-Inspector who rushed to their help was given a severe beating.

An Army officer posted at Shujabad in the beginning of August made a tour of the neighbouring villages. He described what he saw as follows:

" On September 3, 1947, I was proceeding to Chadhar and Khojan and the surrounding villages on patrol duty with four Sikh and one Dogra sepoys. We had one Bren gun, one tommy-gun, one pistol and three .303 rifles, one box of hand-grenades and one thousand .303 bullets. When we reached Chadhar, we saw a big blaze of fire in the direction of Rampur. I ordered the driver to take our jeep to that side. When we reached near Rampur we saw a very big Muslim mob of about six or seven thousand persons armed with rifles and sharp-edged weapons with an Assistant Sub-Inspector of Police and many police constables all armed. The village was burning. We took our stand at a distance of about five hundred yards from the village and began firing on the Muslim mob. The hooligans ran. Some men in the mob tried to surround us but persistent firing kept them at a distance. Many men in the mob were killed. We saw heaps of dead bodies in the village, some burnt, some half burnt, some killed by shots and some stabbed to death. There was a smell of flesh and blood burning and we felt choked. In my estimate the number of dead bodies might have been nearly two thousand. The non-Muslims of the neighbouring villages had come to Rampur, believing it to be more safe, as the Hindu landlords of that place had licensed arms with them. I saw the Assistant Sub-Inspector of Police in possession of the guns of the Hindus. I could find only eleven persons alive in the village. They had concealed themselves in strange places. Of them I found two women concealed between the wall and the iron safe of their house."

The Assistant Sub-Inspector of Karor Pucca visited village Khaji Wala on the morning of August 25, and witnessed a horrible spectacle. Over a hundred non-Muslim men, women and children had been tied together and placed on a heap of burning straw. As the flames killed them slowly they writhed and groaned in a most dreadful manner. In the neighbouring villages much murder and looting had taken place. Every time non-Muslims went to the Shujabad Railway Station to board a train, they were searched and deprived of all their belongings. The first train left on August 25, and the search was carried out thoroughly and ruthlessly. The passengers were not allowed to take anything with them. The second train left on September 14. On this occasion the passengers were allowed to take away a few clothes and one light bedding each. The third train left on September 25, and on this occasion the search was somewhat relaxed. This train was attacked at Pakpattan and thoroughly looted. On October 11, the non-Muslims were ordered to leave their houses in Shujabad within two hours and go to the refugee camp which consisted of a plot of open ground flooded with water. After some time the refugees were removed to a number of houses on the outskirts of the town. They were continuously harassed by the Baluch military and there were many reports of women having been taken away and raped by the soldiers.

The Naib Tehsildar of Shujabad was a witness of the happenings in Khan Bela. His story is given in his own words:

"On September 3, news was received in Shujabad that Ghazipur, a village about seven miles from Jalalpur Pirwala, was burnt down and pillaged by the Muslims on the previous night and over a hundred persons had been murdered in cold blood. Many of the residents were terrified into accepting Islam. Quite a number of young women were abducted. On the afternoon of September 3, some people of Jalalpur Pirwala informed me that that village stood in great danger of being burnt and looted. I thought it was no use going to the Tehsildar who was a Muslim and was well known for his communal tendencies. I, therefore, went to the Officer Commanding of the Military Unit stationed in Shujabad. He needed a good deal of persuading to send some of his men to Jalalpur Pirwala but finally agreed to do so. I accompanied the Officer Commanding.

"We left Shujabad at about 9 p.m. in a jeep. On the way we met another jeep coming from Ghazipur and the Officer Commanding directed this jeep also to follow us. We reached Jalalpur Pirwala shortly after 10. The people were awake and shaking with terror. We made a round of the town and told the people to be on their guard. At the police station the Sub-Inspector informed me that he had received a report about a huge mob having gathered at Khan Bela in the evening. Khan Bela is seven miles to the west of Jalalpur Pirwala and had a population of about 2,500 persons. I asked the Sub-Inspector if he would accompany us there but he refused to do so. I was of the opinion that we should go to Khan Bela. About two miles from Jalalpur Pirwala the road was under water and our jeeps could not go across. We left the jeeps with two soldiers to keep a watch on them and went forward on foot. We could see the holocaust from quite a long distance and hear the report of gunfire. As we drew near we could see that the whole village was ablaze and we could hear the groans of the injured persons. We passed a lane which was full of smoke. Brickbats began to be thrown at us from house-tops and suddenly someone began to fire at us. We withdrew and went to another part of the village where we saw people coming out after committing loot, murder and arson. Most of them were carrying looted property and some of them were dragging non-Muslim women. We opened fire at them and most of them ran away. Some fell down dead as the result of our firing. In an hour's time the village was almost clear of them. I saw that over one hundred Hindus were lying dead in the village and enquiries showed that about fifty young women had been kidnapped."

The Officer Commanding went back to Jalalpur Pirwala and saw that, in his absence, the village had been subjected to a brutal and determined attack by a huge Muslim mob. Over a thousand persons had been butchered. Many residents committed suicide. The whole village was then ransacked. The Officer Commanding, on seeing this wreckage, sent a wireless message to Multan, asking for more troops, but the reply received by him was that he should not expose his men to unnecessary risk. The Zaildar of the *ilaqa* led out a number of non-Muslims, on the following day, promising to escort them to Shujabad. On the way the caravan was attacked and most of the men were killed and the young women abducted. Some men from Jalalpur Pirwala left in two trucks after having bribed the Sub-Inspector of Police heavily. The trucks were attacked on the way, and almost all the male passengers were killed. All the young girls were kidnapped.

Village Budhe was attacked towards the end of August and almost the entire population was wiped out. In Chak No. 16/10R the non-Muslims tried to defend themselves and two of them, who had licensed arms, returned the fire of Muslim raiders but the villagers were heavily outnumbered and it is said that nearly a thousand of them were killed and many of their young girls were carried away. Mian Chànnu was attacked on August 20. A foot caravan of non-Muslims from the neighbouring villages coming to Mian Channu was stopped and accused of planning to attack the Muslims. The non-Muslims were deprived of their weapons and their goods. A mob of Muslims then attacked these poor refugees and killed many of them. A convoy of seventeen trucks left Mian Channu on September 15. One of the trucks had engine trouble on the way and had to stop. A Muslim mob suddenly appeared from nowhere and attacked the passengers. Six girls were carried away and the remaining non-Muslims were all murdered. The Sikhs of village Belewala sought shelter in the house of a local Muslim Pir. While they were on their way some of their young girls were kidnapped. After they had entered the house, the doors were sprayed with kerosene oil and set ablaze. When the Sikhs ran out they were set upon by their Muslim neighbours and mercilessly butchered. Village Makhdumpur Pahoran, the camp at Talamba and the Hindu residents in Hamand Cantal Rest House were attacked by Muslim mobs in the end of August.

As an instance of the conditions of train travel in these days we may quote from the statement of an Advocate of Multan who left Mailsi on October 7.

"Our train (consisting of open roofless trucks) with about three thousand and five hundred refugees started at noon from Mailsi under a Mahratta military escort headed by Subedar——, a very sympathetic and dutiful young military officer, on October 7. After Kutubpur Station a mob consisting of more than fifteen hundred armed Muslims came out from behind some sand-hills. The railway line was blocked with stones and logs of wood. Our train, therefore, stopped. The mob fired at the train. The Subedar and the members of the escort got down from the train and returned the fire. Three or four persons from among the mob were killed, while as many more were injured. The Subedar brought back a rifle and a helmet which belonged to the leader of the mob. The raiders then fled away and the train started once again. The train stopped at Khanewal Junction at sunset. There was no engine to continue the journey and we spent the night at Khanewal. We were told at night that a Magistrate had come and recorded the statements of the Subedar and the engine driver. We left in the morning and reached Harappa at 9 a.m. but we were not allowed to proceed further as orders to detain us had been issued by the District Magistrate of Multan or Montgomery. At 5 p.m. the Commissioner, Multan, the Deputy Commissioner, Montgomery, two big military officers, three or four police officials and some sixty or seventy Muslim soldiers arrived. The Commissioner and others interrogated the Subedar at length and he had to repeat his story several times. We learnt that the leader of the mob who had been killed by our military escort was a Sub-Divisional Officer of Canals posted there and that he was a very near relation of the Prime Minister of Pakistan. For this reason all the big local officers were afraid of his participation in the assault becoming known in India. After the interrogation was over, our train was taken back to Mian Channu and stopped at a distance of half a mile from the railway station. Next day, at noon, an armed mob of Muslims appeared. There was an exchange of shots between the mob and our military escort. The Muslim soldiers from Mian Channu now appeared on the scene and persuaded the mob to go back. After some time our Mahratta Subedar was called aside by a Muslim military officer who came from Mian Channu. After this interview the Subedar came to us and told us with tears in his eyes that the position had become serious and there was no other alternative for us but to leave the train within fifteen minutes and take with us only so much luggage as we could carry on our heads. The confusion that followed after hearing this sudden announcement can better be imagined than described. We had to leave most of our luggage in the train. The armed mob of Muslims again approached near us. We were placed in a garden covering two *qillas* of land at a distance of one and a half miles from the train. It was within this small space that we had to cremate some twenty refugees who had died of starvation.

" As soon as we left the train the Muslim mob dispersed and the train was taken possession of by the Muslim military. Not a single article was removed by any member of the mob. We came to know later that all our luggage from the train was taken to the *malkhana* and converted into Pakistan Government property. We were kept almost locked up in that garden for five days. No Pakistan official ever enquired whether we had anything to eat and how we managed to subsist. They gave us no provisions. Some of the local refugees shared their scanty provisions with us.

"On the sixth day we were taken back to the same goods train which was now in charge of a Gurkha military escort. We finally reached Attari on October 15."

This is a case in which the refugees travelled in comparative comfort and safety. There was only one attack and this was repulsed successfully. The hardship that the passengers, however, suffered entailed the loss of several lives on the way. There was no food and many died of starvation. They had to remain for many days in the open, by day and by night, and exposure took a toll of nearly twenty-five persons. It was learnt later that the Mahratta Subedar was accused of killing the Sub-Divisional Officer by shooting at him from the running train while the Sub-Divisional Officer was performing his duties on the canal bank.

Muzaffargarh District

Muzaffargarh District is bounded on the north by the district of Mianwali and on the west by the river Indus. The river Chenab runs along the greater part of its eastern boundary. Muslims comprised 86.42 per cent of its total population before partition. Not many Sikhs lived in the district; their number was probably not much more than six thousand in all,* and they lived mostly in the rural areas concentrated in a handful of *bastis* surrounded by predominantly Muslim villages. When disturbances began in the month of September they found it difficult either to defend themselves or to escape to places of comparative safety. As they formed a special target of the fanatical attack on the minorities many of them perished; the rest were forcibly converted to Islam. These last were eventually evacuated under police or military escort. Mass conversion of Hindus and Sikhs was a special feature of the Muzaffargarh District and there were many villages in which the entire non-Muslim population was compelled to embrace Islam, under threat of annihilation. In these villages the loss of life was inconsiderable,† though conversion did not prevent their entire property from being looted and their young women from being kidnapped and subjected to the barbarous lust of the marauders. Here, as elsewhere, there were numerous cases of neighbourly kindness and protection offered by local Muslims and the Muslim

---

* At the census of 1941 the figure was 5,882.

† Wholesale conversion took place in the villages of Serwala, Warra Sera, Sohal, Ratta Ram, Dogar Kalasra, Subani Wasti, Pakki Labhana, Makhan Bela, Tarpur, Sahhani, Basti Qazi (seven non-Muslims who were unwilling were murdered), Tibbi Nizam, Usman Kuria and Mariwala.

police officers. Only rarely, however, did these efforts succeed in evading or counteracting the hideous forces of murder and rapine. In a few instances the kidnapped girls were restored to their relations after they had agreed to accept Islam. The evacuation of these converted persons presented serious difficulties to our Liaison Agency and the Military Organization in charge of evacuation, as they were stranded in small and all but inaccessible pockets. Sometimes their very existence was not known as they had moved from their last habitation. The available evidence regarding their whereabouts was meagre and a diligent search had to be made in very difficult conditions.

At the time of partition Raja Sultan Lal Hussain was the Deputy Commissioner and during his tenure of office the district remained peaceful. He left on August 20, and soon afterwards disturbances began and spread to all parts of the district. The first recorded incident is an attack on a Sikh passenger on August 20, at the Sanawan Railway Station. The victim escaped and sought refuge in a Hindu temple. He was pursued by a mob of Muslims who demanded that he should be handed over to them. They threatened to destroy the whole city if the man were not given up. They succeeded in capturing the Sikh and murdering him. A fortnight later the railway station was attacked again and two Hindu railway officials were murdered. There were simultaneous attacks on a number of other railway stations on the solitary line which runs through this district. At Dorata a Sikh Station Master and seven members of his family were murdered. At Jaman Shah a Hindu Station Master was murdered and his two daughters were kidnapped. At Karor twenty-one non-Muslim railway employees including the Assistant Station Master were murdered. Two girls were abducted. At Dera Dinpanah a Hindu porter was murdered. The daughter of the Station Master of Gurmani was kidnapped. These attacks struck terror in the hearts of the non-Muslim railway employees. The murders at the railway stations were followed by attacks on the villages. A large mob of two thousand Muslims surrounded village Sanawan and murdered a large number of non-Muslims. The women of the village had been placed in a separate house which was attacked by a mob of Muslims. About ten old women were murdered and then all the ornaments and valuables were plundered. Fifteen young girls were carried away. The Sub-Inspector of Police took the non-Muslims to the railway station and helped in evacuating

them to Muzaffargarh. A member of the West Punjab Legislative
Assembly and a Muslim Recruiting Officer were observed encouraging and helping the Muslim mob.

At Karor a most horrible massacre of non-Muslims was
enacted. Karor is a small town situated in the extreme north
of the district. There were a police station, a High School, Civil
and Veterinary Hospitals in the town and a large number of
non-Muslims resided there. With the outbreak of disturbances
the non-Muslims of the neighbouring villages arrived in Karor
and, in the beginning of September, nearly ten thousand Hindus
and Sikhs had congregated in the town. On September 3, a Hindu
while crossing a stream was murdered. The same night the railway station was attacked. During the days that followed, the
town was subjected to several attacks. A Hindu, writing on September 5, said that dogs and vultures were eating the corpses of
non-Muslims lying in the streets of Karor. The neighbouring villages suffered heavy losses in life and property. Almost all the
villages in the neighbourhood of Karor and Leiah were attacked
on September 4 and 5. The simultaneity of the attack indicated
a pre-conceived plan. On September 7 a large Muslim mob
attacked Dedhe Lal, a small village near Rohillanwali, in the
southern part of the district. The non-Muslims abandoned their
houses and took shelter in the house of Chaudhry Lila Kishen.
The Muslims began to loot the houses and shops and the pillage
continued through the night. The next morning the village Lambardar took the non-Muslims to his house and sent a messenger
to Muzaffargarh for military aid. In the afternoon ten Baluch
soldiers arrived in the village and asked the Lambardar to turn
the non-Muslims out. The soldiers wanted the women to be
placed in a separate house but, on being paid a bribe of two
hundred rupees, agreed to let them stay with the men. During the
night some young women were raped by the Baluch soldiers. On
September 9, the non-Muslims were asked to embrace Islam. While
these negotiations were proceeding, a local Pleader brought a truck
to the village and, in this truck, twenty non-Muslims were carried
to Muzaffargarh. The remaining non-Muslims took shelter in a
room but the local Muslims assisted by the Baluch soldiers made
a hole in the roof of the *kotha* and, pouring kerosene oil inside,
set fire to it. Sixty-five persons are said to have been burnt in this
kotha. The Sub-Inspector of Kinjar told the local non-Muslims,
on September 5, that he could not guarantee their safety. He,
however, asked the Muslim Zemindars to try and protect their

co-villagers. The village was attacked early on the morning of
September 7. The Sufaidposh and the Zaildar who had given
assurances of safety to the non-Muslims were seen to be taking
part in the assault. The mob entered the village shouting "*Pakistan Zindabad*" and "*Jinnah Zindabad.*" They broke open the
locks of houses and shops and began to loot them. About two
hundred shops and houses were set fire to and any non-Muslims
found in the streets were set upon and murdered. The Sub-
Inspector of Police sat in the rural dispensary gossiping with the
doctor. He was either completey indifferent to what was going
on in the village or, what is more probable, quite powerless to
stop it. Later, when the fury of the mob had somewhat abated,
the Sub-Inspector took the non-Muslims to the police station and
kept them there for a week. Rations were extremely meagre and
attempts to carry provisions to the police station were foiled by
the Zaildar and the local Muslims. On September 15, a number
of lorries were hired and the non-Muslims were evacuated. The
village, however, was reduced to a ruin. Chaudhri Lal Chand, a
resident of Kamal Kurai, a village five miles from .Kinjar, was
robbed of his cash and ornaments while he was proceeding to
Kinjar on September 5. He reported the matter to the Sub-
Inspector at Kinjar who paid a visit to his village but was unable
to trace the culprits. When Lal Chand went to Kinjar on September 7 with a list of the stolen property he found the village in
flames. He went back to Kamal Kurai and found it surrounded
by a Muslim mob. The Hindu residents collected at the house of
Chaudhri Asu Ram and handed over the keys of their houses and
shops to the Muslims who immediately began to loot them. All
the cattle owned by the non-Muslims were driven out and some
of the houses were burnt down. The next morning the attack
was renewed and the non-Muslims were asked to embrace Islam.
Some of them agreed and publicly took off their sacred threads.
Those who hesitated or did not agree were set upon and murdered. The converted persons were taken to a Muslim house in a
neighbouring village, and some of the girls who had been kidnapped were restored to them. These unfortunate persons were
rescued about three weeks later by the military.

The Sikh Bastis Kothiwala, Shihnwala, Kartarpur and
Basantpura were attacked on September 6 and 7. The majority
of the residents perished and the rest were forcibly converted to
Islam. Those who tried to escape were waylaid and done to
death. Many girls were carried away by the marauders. The

total loss of life in these four Bastis was several hundred. The
Muslims of village Chandian were divided in their attitude towards
the non-Muslims. Some of them were of the opinion that if the
non-Muslims were willing to accept Islam they should not be
molested while others thought that immediate death was the only
suitable end for all non-Muslims. Sardar' Khan Chandian, who
was the leader of the first party, took the non-Muslims to a
mosque and converted them to Islam. They were all made to
remove their sacred threads and *chotis* and recite the *Kalma.*
They spent a night in the mosque and, in the morning, ate beef
which was given to them. The second party of Muslims was,
however, not satisfied and launched an attack on the mosque.
Over a hundred persons were done to death and a number of
young girls were kidnapped. Their houses were then looted.
Sardar Khan took the survivors to his Chak and finally helped in
evacuating them to Muzaffargarh. The residents of Basti Miran-
pur were saved through the good offices of the local Muslims who
converted them to Islam and finally helped to send them to Kinjar
from where they were evacuated. In villages Serin Dewan Wali
and Gujrat a wholesale murder of non-Muslims took place. In
village Gangian the non-Muslims accepted the offer of conversion
but many of them were nevertheless done to death. The Sikh
residents of village Mangal Singh were attacked on September 9
and many of them were burnt alive in a house where they had
taken shelter. Others who tried to rush out were slaughtered and
a large heap of dead bodies was seen lying in the village.

A large number of non-Muslims ran to Muzaffargarh from
the neighbouring villages and sought shelter in the refugee camp
near the railway station. Muzaffargarh itself did not witness
disturbances on a large scale but there were many cases of murder
and loot. Exit from Muzaffargarh was made difficult because the
bridge over the Chenab, connecting the districts of Muzaffargarh
and Multan, was continuously watched by Muslim mobs who
attacked and murdered anyone trying to cross it. This bridge was
seen to be strewn with dead bodies. All the roads leading from
Muzaffargarh were infested by murderous gangs of Muslims and
it was not till the end of September, when a large-scale evacuation with the help of the Military Evacuation Organization began,
that the non-Muslims in the district were able to escape to safety.
The refugees from Dera Ghazi Khan had to pass through
Muzaffargarh and this added to the numbers in the refugee camps
and to the problems of providing food for them. On September 12,

the Deputy Inspector-General of Police, Multan Range, came to the district and was instrumental in checking the disturbances. Non-Muslims from different villages were brought to the nearest Tehsil headquarters and placed in nineteen different camps. The number of camps was gradually reduced and evacuation by railway began on October 23. Indian military arrived on October 25, and this further helped to restore confidence.

Rawalpindi District

Rawalpindi was a predominantly Muslim district. The census returns of 1941 recorded a population of 7.85 lakhs of whom 6.28 lakhs, representing 80 per cent of the total, were Muslims. Sikhs in appreciable numbers resided both in the town of Rawalpindi and in the rural areas. They occupied a not unimportant position in the civic life of the district, as some of them were very wealthy and owned large properties in the urban areas of Rawalpindi and Murree and also in the villages. The people of the district are robust in physique and warlike in spirit; and provide good material for Army recruitment. Every village counted among its residents a few Army pensioners who owned firearms and knew how to use them effectively. There are few roads and some of the outlying villages are difficult of access. The extent and intensity of the March riots had driven out almost the entire non-Muslim population from the rural areas. The August riots were, therefore, confined for the most part to Rawalpindi proper and Chaklala, a military base four miles away.

The headquarters of the Northern Command were situated in Rawalpindi and a large Army force was stationed in the Cantonment. The presence of so many troops should have ensured the safety of the town but, after the March happenings, the non-Muslims lost all confidence in the ability or, at any rate, the impartiality of the Army personnel in affording protection to them.

The August trouble at Rawalpindi began with the arrival of some Muslim refugees from East Punjab. The Deputy Commissioner, Mr. Anwar-ul-Haq, made a gallant attempt to control the situation but he received no assistance from his subordinates or the police. Indeed, their attitude and conduct were calculated to revive and exacerbate the hostilities between the communities. Added to this was the factor that many of the culprits responsible for committing offences, during the March riots, were released on bail. This circumstance was utilized by the Muslim League agitators to their benefit, for they were able to say that, with the establishment of Pakistan, they had been able to redeem the pledges given to these criminals and any future acts of a similar nature committed by them would be condoned by the authorities. These hooligans, therefore, thought that they were free to murder and loot the minorities in the district.

On the morning of August 15, a number of non-Muslims were stabbed. On the following day Kartarpura Mohalla was attacked by armed Muslims and completely plundered. Many of the non-Muslim residents were killed. On August 17, the Khalsa High School and the Khalsa College suffered the same fate. The *Id* festival was celebrated on August 18, and, after the morning prayers, Muslims ran about the city, in a fit of exultant frenzy, looting and burning non-Muslim property. Hindus and Sikhs were freely attacked and beaten. The Hindu Civil Surgeon, Mr. Sondhi, was severely wounded and his car was damaged as he was on his way to the hospital to give medical aid to the riot casualities. A Hindu physician was shot dead in the street. Murderous gangs lurked behind every street corner and inside every mosque. If a Hindu or a Sikh were seen approaching he was pounced upon and killed. Mosques were used as arsenals and vantage points for attack. The authorities raided a mosque in the city and found a large dump of firearms, hand-grenades and other lethal weapons. Hindu and Sikh shrines were desecrated. Rioting continued upto the end of September except for a few temporary lulls. Mai Veero-ki-Banni, Pul Shah Nazar, Nimak Mandi, Momanpura and Mohalla Talwaran were all looted. On September 11, about two hundred non-Muslim subjects of Poonch State left Rawalpindi in eleven trucks under military escort. They were first subjected to a thorough search at the railway station, under the supervision of an Anglo-Indian Magistrate, Mr. Ross. They were then stopped at the octroi post and another search which lasted several hours was carried out. The trucks finally left but, when they had travelled for about six miles, they were set upon by a mob of armed Muslims. The military escort sat by the roadside and took no steps to defend the non-Muslims. The last two trucks were able to turn round and return to Rawalpindi but the remaining nine trucks were thoroughly looted and almost all the passengers were killed. Many girls were kidnapped.

If a non-Muslim temporarily left his house he found, on his return, that it had been occupied by Muslim refugees with the help of National Guards. In some cases non-Muslims were forcibly ejected from their houses. A prominent Advocate had to go to Delhi on business and, before he left, the Deputy Commissioner assured him that his house would be safe. At Delhi, however, news was received by this Advocate that the Tehsildar and the Naib Tehsildar had gone to his house and taken possession of it. His motor car was also taken away. Some luggage which he had packed up in crates was lost.

Non-Muslims experienced great difficulty in travelling to India. Mr. Ross was in charge of evacuation and he exerted all his influence in harassing and victimizing the non-Muslims. Not a single train left Rawalpindi for India between September 1 and October 18, except Military Specials in which civil refugees could not ordinarily travel. Mr. Ross refused to arrange for transport on the ground that there was no reciprocal movement of rolling stock from India. This was not true because at least two trains carrying Muslim Refugees from East Punjab arrived in Rawalpindi during this period.* A train was announced to leave Chaklala Railway Station on September 18. Rolling stock and engines were available. Tickets for the journey to India were issued to non-Muslims but, when the intending travellers arrived at Chaklala, they learnt that the train had been cancelled. No reasons for this decision were assigned. Arrangements were finally made for a train to leave on October 18. Large numbers of passengers with their luggage arrived at Chaklala. They had to pay fifty rupees per package to the coolies, but their luggage was finally brought to the station platform. A Muslim Magistrate, accompanied by a number of police constables, now arrived and ordered all the non-Muslim to leave the station premises. Some of them had to be driven out at the point of the bayonet. After they had left, almost the entire luggage was looted by members of the National Guards. When the train arrived at 5 p.m., the passengers had to get in without their luggage.†

Gujar Khan was attacked by a Muslim mob towards the end of August. A number of non-Muslims were stabbed and several more injured. The non-Muslims were forcibly ejected from their houses and they were told that the goods in their shops were Pakistan property. The non-Muslims then left the town.

---

* Bakshi Mehtab Singh, a senior Advocate, says that he himself saw these trains arrive and visited the Muslim Refugee Camp.

† Many Government officials took part in the loot and received a share of the property thus stolen. Action was taken against them by the Pakistan Government, many recoveries were made and some of the official were actually suspended.

Hindu houses were ransacked and some of the shops were burnt down. The remaining non-Muslim population was compelled to embrace Islam and every one of them was circumcised. The non-Muslim residents of Choti Zarin left their village on August 30, leaving behind seventeen young men to look after the property. On August 31, a Muslim mob attacked the village and killed eight of these young men. They then burnt their bodies after sprinkling kerosene oil on them. The Hindu shops and houses were completely looted. The residents of the villages surrounding Vahowa abandoned their homes and collected at Vahowa. They remained there for some time and were finally escorted to Dera Ghazi Khan from where they were evacuated to Muzaffargarh and India. At Dajal forty non-Muslims lost their lives in the course of a mob attack on September 13. A Sub-Inspector of Police drove away the raiders and escorted the survivors to Dera Ghazi Khan in trucks. A mob attack was made on Ghajaniyan on September 3. Twenty-seven persons were killed and seven injured. The arrival of Dogra soldiers prevented the loss of further life, and the survivors were taken to Dera Ghazi Khan. Mamori was attacked by a Muslim mob on August 30. A number of persons were killed and four girls were kidnapped. The remaining non-Muslims were forcibly converted to Islam. Eight days later they were rescued by the military and escorted to Dera Ghazi Khan. The non-Muslim residents of Chah Patoli Wala ran away to the fields on seeing a Muslim mob approaching the village on the evening of August 31. The Hindu houses and shops were looted while the owners passed the night hiding in the fields. The next morning they escaped to Samina from where the police escorted them to Dera Ghazi Khan. The villages of Suleman Kasha Dhingana, Gadaie, Paro and Harnand were similarly looted. In each village a few persons lost their lives and looting, on an extensive scale, took place. In Mangrotha Sharqi there were about a hundred houses and a dozen shops, owned by Hindu traders. Towards the end of August, the neighbouring villages of Sokar and Buglani were attacked by the Muslims. All the residents of Mangrotha Sharqi took fright and left the village after locking up their shops and houses on September 3. They took shelter in the police station Taunsa. As soon as they had left, their houses were broken open and looted. A goldsmith who had remained behind was murdered. The next day, a Daffedar of the Border Constabulary arrived and reported the matter to

Party and for some time held the office of Minister. He exerted himself in preserving peace in the district and his influence was a strong steadying factor. The Deputy Commissioner and the Superintendent of Police also took timely action in checking the forces of law essness and sent for Gurkha military, to guard the towns and refugee camps, and patrol the countryside. It is also gratifying to record that the Muslim police and the Border Constabulary displayed, on the whole, a commendable sense of duty, though in a few instances their conduct was marred by an apathetic indifference towards the safety of the non-Muslims in their charge. In one or two cases they even gave support and assistance to the hooligans and shared the loot.

There were no large-scale mass murders of non-Muslims in the district. The total number of Hindus and Sikhs was less than seventy thousand, comprising only 13 per cent of the population, and they resided, for the most part, in the towns of Dera Ghazi Khan, Jampur, Rajanpur and Taunsa. In the villages a few scattered families handled the rural commerce and trade. When news of disturbances across the Indus reached Dera Ghazi Khan and signs of unrest began to show, these isolated pockets were vacated and the non-Muslims moved to places of comparative safety. As soon as they left, the Muslims looted the entire property left behind. In some outlying villages, the non-Muslim residents were attacked and forcibly converted to Islam. Those who resisted were put to death. In a few cases, refugees travelling to Dera Ghazi Khan or Rajanpur were attacked, on the way, and looted There were a few instances of arson in villages but these stopped when someone gave currency to a supposedly official announcement that the property of the non-Muslims belonged to Pakistan and should not be destroyed. The total loss of life in the district was not considerable though the non-Muslims were deprived of almost all their property. A number of girls were kidnapped and subsequently recovered. The converted persons were, in due course, evacuated to India under escort.

Almost the first outbreak of lawlessness occurred, curiously enough, in Choti, the headquarters of the Laghari chief. It is said that Mohammad Khan, the son of the chief, was responsible for this disturbance. A number of non-Muslims were massacred and the survivors were converted to Islam. Kotla Muglan was attacked by a Muslim mob, in the beginning of September, and five Hindus lost their lives. Many more were injured and the

In the town of Jhelum disturbances broke out during September. The attack on the residents of Machine Mohalla was a particularly brutal one. On September 25, a mob of armed Muslims carrying machine-guns, revolvers and other weapons attacked the non-Muslim houses. The victims had been warned of this attack and they entrenched themselves in five or six houses in Mohalla Gobindpura, the doors of which were barricaded. The attack lasted for several hours and some of the houses in the Mohalla were set fire to. A contingent of Muslim military arrived and asked the non-Muslims to send their women and girls in trucks to a place of safety. This direction was complied with. The women and girls were never heard of again. Immediately afterwards the non-Muslim males were set upon and a general massacre followed. Hundreds of men were killed and their dead bodies were thrown in the Jhelum River. It is said that only about three hundred persons out of a total of two thousand non-Muslims living in this Mohalla survived. The houses were then looted and even the dead bodies were searched and robbed. The bungalow of Sardarni Lachhmi of Wahali was attacked and she and her brother's wife were brutally murdered by a Muslim mob. Their entire property was then looted.

Murid, a village six miles from Chakwal, was attacked, on September 10, by a mob of several thousand Muslims. The houses and shops of the non-Muslims were ransacked, the Gurdwara was desecrated and the religious books were burnt. To add to the sacrilege, cows were butchered inside the Gurdwara. Bhaun, a village eight miles from Chakwal, was attacked on August 11. The raiders brought camels, donkeys and bullock-carts with them and carried away large quantities of loot. The non-Muslims were then told to leave their village if they valued their lives. Haranpur was attacked on August 13, and it is said that the Sub-Divisional Magistrate of Pind Dadan Khan and a Sub-Inspector of Police came with the raiders and shared the loot. The residents of Haranpur were later evacuated to the Pind Dadan Khan refugee camp under military escort. On September 19, five thousand refugees from this camp boarded a train bound for Amritsar. This train was attacked several times on the way, and the majority of the passengers were killed. Many girls and young women were abducted. Some residents of Balkassar tried to run away by stealing out of the village at night. They were attacked on the way and three of them were murdered. Some reached Chakwal and

The evidence relating to disturbances in the rural areas during the months of August and September is somewhat meagre, partly because most of the non-Muslims had already left after the March disturbances and partly because the few who were left did not survive to tell their story. Chak Shahbad, a village about six miles from Rawalpindi, was attacked on the afternoon of August 28. All the non-Muslim houses were plundered, and about ten non-Muslims were killed. The rest escaped to Rawalpindi and were evacuated to India. The villages of Chak Shadadpur, Hanaysar, Nara and Daultala were similarly attacked.

Jhelum District

Jhelum was another predominantly Muslim District. The total number of Hindu and Sikh residents was only about sixty-five thousand or a little more than 10 per cent of the total population. The inhabitants of the rural areas possessed a strong physique and the district shared with Rawalpindi the honour of providing an endless supply of Army recruits. Large sums of money were poured into the district annually by way of military pensions, and the tiresome vocation of tilling the land was not the only means of livelihood open to the people. Their moral fibre, however, was weak and they were prone to be swayed by base and selfish considerations. It was not religious emotion or aggressive chauvinism which prompted them to attack the Hindu and Sikh minorities living in their midst, but the prospect of personal gain. This was truer of the people of Jhelum than of, perhaps, any other district in the Punjab.

The March riots affected some of the rural areas and in Gah, a village in Tehsil Chakwal, a general massacre of non-Muslims took place in that month. Eighty houses were burnt and thirty persons lost their lives in this fire. Village Warwal was also attacked in a similar manner. Nine persons were killed and many more injured. At Hasal a large Muslim mob arrived and forced the non-Muslims to embrace Islam. Those who refused were murdered. The village was then looted. A military picket was posted in the village and there was no further trouble until August. Narang, Mangwal, Rasala, Sarkal, and Minwal were similarly attacked and the non-Muslims were forced to accept Islam. Chakwal was subjected to several attacks but the local Muslims advised the raiders to go back. On March 12, military was posted in the town and normal conditions returned.

returned home but some whose confidence was completely shaken stayed on in the camp. When attacks by Muslim mobs began, in August, the Hindus once again hurried to find safety in the Basal Camp. They were subsequently removed to the larger camp at Wah.

Campbellpur, Talagang, and Fatehjang where the Hindus lived in appreciable numbers were all attacked. It must be recorded that the Gurdwara of Panja Sahib was not attacked as it remained well guarded throughout. There were few Hindus left in the rural areas and the evidence discloses only thirty-one cases of attacks on villages. The number of road incidents recorded is eight while two trains were attacked.

Talagang was attacked on the morning of September 18, by a mob of five thousand Muslims. A number of women and girls who had gone out into the fields to answer the call of nature were kidnapped. The raiders surrounded the village and exchanged shots with the non-Muslim residents. The siege lasted two days and when the ammunition of the defenders was exhausted the 'Muslims attacked the town and began to slaughter the non-Muslims and loot their houses and shops. It is estimated that about three hundred and fifty Hindus were done to death and many more injured. Some were forcibly converted to Islam. Several young girls were kidnapped. Two days later, the Baluch military arrived and the survivors were taken to a camp set up in the local school. A fortnight later, they were escorted to the Wah Camp by lorry and train ; but, before leaving, they were deprived of their money and valuables. The train was attacked on the way, near Golra Railway Station, by a mob of Muslims who had concealed themselves in *bajra* fields. Eleven of the Hindu passengers were wounded but the train was safely brought to Wah.

Some non-Muslim residents of Lava left the village on September 3. The remaining two hundred or two hundred and fifty could not make any transport arrangements and had to stay behind. On September 5, a Muslim mob attacked the village killing a number of persons and forcibly converting others. The entire village was then looted.

On August 30, a convoy of non-Muslims, passing through Fatehjang, was attacked. Twenty Hindus were killed and fifteen wounded. Koti Gul was attacked on September 5. Two Hindus were killed and seven injured ; the rest of the non-Muslims were forcibly converted to Islam. The Hindu shops were looted. About one thousand non-Muslims lived in Tamman. On August 15, a crowd of Muslims attacked some Hindu houses on the western side of the village and looted them. Twelve Hindus were killed. The Zaildar then proclaimed that Hindus had no right to live in Pakistan and should prepare themselves to leave the village. A crowd of Pathans from Mianwali arrived and demanded a share of the loot from the local Muslims. A clash ensued and the Hindus, seeing a chance of escape, ran from the village. They were pursued by the police who had taken a prominent part in planning the attack and were deprived of whatever valuables they had. They eventually reached Talagang from where they were taken to Wah. A band of Baluch soldiers in plain clothes raided the barracks occupied by Hindu employees of the M.E.S. on September 29. Eleven Hindus, sleeping in the verandah, were dragged to an adjoining field and assaulted. The hands of a Gurkha were first chopped off and then he was killed. Only one out of these eleven escaped; the dead bodies of the remaining ten were seen lying in the fields the next day. All the non-Muslims of the town were then collected and taken to a Gurdwara where a camp had been set up. No provisions were supplied to the refugees and the only food they had was some bags of parched gram lying in the Gurdwara. After a fortnight, the refugees were asked to get ready to go to the railway station where a train, bound for India, was waiting for them. No conveyance for luggage was provided and the refugees were not allowed to carry anything except small packages. A convoy of lorries carrying non-Muslims of Campbellpur to Wah, on September 29, was attacked by a Muslim mob two miles from Campbellpur. The military escort took no steps to ward off this attack. It is said that some shots were fired by the European Officer in charge of the escort but the Muslim soldiers remained passive spectators of the assault. More than two hundred non-Muslims are said to have lost their lives in this incident.

Attacks were also made on road convoys proceeding from Khaur, Pindi Gheb, Fatehjang and Pind Sultani.

Mianwali District

The Mianwali District is a boot-shaped area with a long and narrow strip of land lying along the Indus River. It was a predominantly Muslim district and the Muslims numbered 86.16 per cent of the total population. On March 11, a crowd of several thousand Muslims from the neighbouring villages arrived at Mianwali with the intention of plundering the town. The Deputy Commissioner, however, succeeded in persuading this mob to go away. On the way back, they killed a few non-Muslims but there was no serious trouble in the district until September. In the month of August, a number of trains were stopped and searched and there were a few stray stabbing cases. A more serious incident was the murder of Captain Grewal, a Sikh officer, at the Paikhel Railway Station on August 26. The happenings in the neighbouring districts had spread panic in Mianwali and, on August 30, the Deputy Commissioner announced his plan of evacuating the non-Muslims from the district. He appointed differ-,ent dates for different villages. This announcement appeared to encourage the Muslims to lawlessness as they thought that the departing Hindus and Sikhs were entirely at their mercy. There is some indication of a pre-conceived plan to launch an attack throughout the district. On September 2, nearly twenty villages were attacked by Muslim mobs and, on September 3, the trouble spread to many more. A mounted messenger brought the news of an attack on Wan Bachran, and, when military aid was sent, the Muslim hooligans ran into the neighbouring village of Shadia and killed a number of Hindus. They were pursued to Shadia and trouble broke out afresh at Wan Bachran.

On September 3, two houses in village Alluhwali were attacked. The residents were asked to pay a large sum of money and, when they refused, were shot down. Their houses were then looted. On September 6, the Hindus left their houses and collected at the house of one Jamna Das in the hope of being able to defend themselves better from one place. The Muslims looted the houses thus vacated. The next morning the Mianwali train brought a number of Muslim hooligans who joined the local Muslims and attacked some Hindus who had taken shelter in a *serai* near the railway station, killing twenty-five of them and plundering all their goods. The survivors agreed to accept Islam and were escorted to the mosque of Ramzan Arain. A barber was summoned and he began to shave the non-Muslim heads in order to make them conform to Muslim appearance. The Assistant Sub-Inspector of Police, however, did not trust the new converts, and, at his instigation, several of them were killed as they came out of the mosque. A train carrying refugees arrived at this juncture and the military escort rescued the few Hindu survivors.

On September 3, Behl was attacked. The main bazaar was looted and burnt down and then a general massacre of the non-Muslims began. This continued throughout the night and the Muslim soldiers posted in the village took part in the looting and killing. Over a hundred girls were kidnapped. In the morning the dead bodies, some half burnt and others mutilated, were thrown into a well and the survivors were asked to embrace Islam. Many of the converts were later killed. One of the kidnapped girls, relating her experience, said that she had been raped in a most inhuman manner and passed on from man to man till she completely lost all sense of feeling.

Kundian was attacked, on September 4, by a huge mob of Muslims, led by the Zaildar and the local Lambardars. The Headmaster of the school and members of the National Guards were seen helping and encouraging the hooligans. A number of houses were set on fire and over a hundred non-Muslims were killed. At Piplan the non-Muslims were escorted to the railway station for the ostensible purpose of being taken to Mianwali. They hopefully crowded into three bogies sanding at the platform, but the engine steamed away, leaving the bogies behind and the intending travellers were set upon by a Muslim mob and slaughtered like sheep. A train carrying non-Muslim refugees from Mari Indus and the neighbouring villages was attacked at Daud Khel on September 12, and looted. The military escort merely fired a few shots in the air.

September 6 was the appointed date for the evacuation of village Harnoli. That day a Muslim mob collected and launched an attack on the non-Muslims at 2-30 p.m. The Hindus defended themselves from previously prepared *morchas* and shot some of the raiders. News of this was carried to Mianwali and the Deputy Commissioner was informed that the Hindus had perpetrated horrible atrocities on the Muslims and had burnt the mosque. A contingent of Baluch military and a number of tanks were sent to restore peace in Harnoli. The Hindu residents of Mianwali saw these tanks pass and shuddered at the fate which awaited their co-religionists. The military threw a ring round the village and attacked the Hindu strongholds. The *morchas* were blown up and the town was sacked. The streets were littered with dead bodies and some of the Baluch soldiers indulged in the most inhuman barbarities. Men were hung upon trees and shot.

arranged to send military trucks to the village and this enabled the remaining non-Muslims to escape to safety. Wahali was attacked on September 2, and the big *haveli* of Sardar Hari Singh was burnt down. Forty non-Muslims are said to have been murdered. In village Lehr Sultanpur, there was only one non-Muslim family. When they were leaving the village they were attacked and looted. In the beginning of October the Police Sub-Inspector of Dina ordered the non-Muslims to leave their village. They were not allowed to take anything with them. When the non-Muslims arrived in Mirpur they were attacked by a Muslim mob and many of them were killed. The survivors escaped to Jammu and finally found their way to Amritsar. In contrast to this, it is agreeable to record that in village Pahdri no incident took place and that the Muslims helped to evacuate the non-Muslims and carried their luggage on their own heads up to the place where lorries were available. At Jhelum, however, the luggage was looted.

Attock District

Attock, a small village on the banks of the Indus, is the last Punjab outpost on the Grand Trunk Road. When the head-quarters of the district were set up at Campbellpur, Attock lost its civic importance and the village was almost completely deserted. A garrison, posted in the fort, remained to watch the frontier of the province and guard the bridge which strides across the Indus as its torrent rushes through a narrow gorge flanked by rocky precipices. The Grand Trunk Road winds down to the bridge and crosses over into the territory of the North-West Frontier Province. Long stretches of undulating sandy fields, dotted with small stone-built villages, alternate with wooded hilly tracts. A number of streams which suddenly swell up during the monsoon rains to unfordable dimensions run through the district. There are remains of several Moghul buildings including a Rest House situated amid the picturesque surroundings of the Wah springs and a *Baradari* at Attock. The Sikh shrine of Panja Sahib at Hassan Abdal was visited by Sikh pilgrims from all parts of India.

The population of the district according to the census of 1941, was 6.75 lakhs the vast majority of whom (6.11 lakhs comprising 90.42 per cent) were Muslims. In March 1947 several villages in the eastern part of the district were affected by the disturbances in the rural areas of Rawalpindi District.

On March 9 a Muslim mob, shouting slogans and beating drums, entered village Jhari. The non-Muslims ran to take shelter

14

in the Gurdwara but, when they found that they would be over-powered, they escaped from the back door and ran out into the jungle. The next morning they came back, on learning that the mob had left. That afternoon the Zaildar asked all non-Muslims to embrace Islam. The barbers were called and the hair of the Sikhs was removed. The next morning the newly converted people were asked to eat beef and give their daughters in marriage to the Muslims. The Gurdwara Granthi argued that the Quran did not make these things compulsory for Muslims. On this the converts were attacked and more than a hundred of them were done to death. Logs of wood were thrown into the pit of a well under construction and a huge fire was lit. A number of women were thrown into this pit and burnt alive ; several young girls were kidnapped ; children were impaled on spears and displayed in the village. In village Parial the Sub-Inspector of Police asked the Sikhs to become Muslims if they wanted to live in safety. Master Thakar Singh, President of the Gurdwara Panchayat, refused. The next day a Muslim mob attacked the village. Master Thakar Singh was captured and murdered. His dead body was taken to the Gurdwara on spears, and the Sikhs in the Gurdwara were told that unless they embraced Islam they would meet the same fate. The Sikhs appeared to show some reluctance and the Gurdwara was set on fire. Over a hundred persons were burnt alive or murdered by the Muslim mob. In village Mithial, a number of persons were murdered and ten children were burnt alive. In Rajar a mass massacre of Sikhs, involving the death of one hundred and fifty persons, took place. In Dheri thirteen persons were murdered and two burnt alive because they refused to embrace Islam. The remaining non-Muslims were then converted. Mass conversions took place in Chak Belikhan, Ghela Kalan, Mial, Dhalwali, Mohra, Sihal, Sanghral, Saroha, etc.

A Muslim mob attacked village Basal on March 11, killing four Hindus and injuring fifteen. A number of Hindu houses and shops were looted. The neighbouring village of Kisran was similarly attacked and several persons were murdered. Basal was attacked a second time, on March 13, and in the course of this attack twenty-seven Hindus lost their lives. Altogether seventy-two villages in the district were attacked during the March riots. A camp was set up near the Basal Railway Station and the non-Muslims of the neighbouring villages sought shelter there. When the Rawalpindi trouble subsided most of the refugees

Little infants were dashed to the ground or had their limbs torn. Young girls were raped in a horrible manner and then slaughtered.

Bhakkar was attacked three times. On September 3, a Muslim mob surrounded the town and set fire to a number of houses. About ten non-Muslims were killed. The Sub-Divisional Officer had recently come from Gurdaspur and, when an appeal for help was made to him, he merely replied that he had seen horrible things done to his Muslim brethren in East Punjab. The Inspector of Police said that he had lost everything in East Punjab and that he was not sorry to see the Hindus of Bhakkar suffering. The arrival of the military, however, prevented further mischief. A second attack was made on September 10. On this occasion also a few houses were burnt and a few non-Muslims were killed. Gurkha soldiers were at the time posted in the town and they immediately restored peace. A few days later, Muslim military replaced the Gurkhas and conditions in the town changed. There were reports of young women and girls being raped by the Muslim soldiers. On October 8, the Muslim military were to leave and, on that day, a determined and large-scale attack was made on the people of Bhakkar. The Muslim military were seen helping the hooligans, and looting continued the whole day. There was considerable loss of life and property. Many houses were set on fire and over three hundred persons were killed.

At Darya Khan, a Muslim mob attacked the town on October 2. The non-Muslims were placed in a house, on the upper storey of which Muslim soldiers mounted guard. During the night the house was attacked by a Muslim mob and several hundred persons were killed. The military guard merely fired shots in the air. Some of them even shot at the people under their protection. There was large-scale killing and looting at Hassan Shah.

In Mianwali there was peace until the end of September. The Deputy Commissioner had, however, passed an order, on September 15, that all non-Muslims must surrender their arms. The matter was represented to the Governor when he visited the town, a few days later, but the non-Muslims continued to remain without any means of defending themselves against a possible attack. Many non-Muslims moved into a camp set up near the Deputy Commissioner's house. This camp was attacked on the evening of September 28. The town was attacked the same night and the attack continued for three or four days. The shops in the bazaar were broken open and set on fire. Within a short time the whole town seemed to be ablaze. An eye-witness said: " I, along with

my family members and with about two hundred other non-
Muslims, was taking shelter in a deserted house. The Muslim
mob surrounded us and gave us an ultimatum that either we should
embrace Islam or we would be put to death and our womenfolk
would be carried away to the villages. All of us agreed to embrace
Islam. In spite of our declaration we were all dragged out and
our womenfolk were molested and disgraced in our presence.
They were searched and stripped of their last jewellery
and many of them were beaten. On coming out we saw that a
big Muslim mob along with military was standing there and
women and virgin girls were being loaded forcibly in military
trucks. The whole town wore a ghastly appearance and the
streets were full of heaps of dead. We had to walk on dead
bodies as we went to the mosque. In our presence many young
children were dashed against walls. Suckling babies were
snatched from the arms of their mothers and torn into bits.
Goondas and Muslim mobs with the military were busy in a
general massacre and looting. Groups of men were pouring in,
carrying rifles, daggers, hatchets and other deadly weapons. We
were taken to the house of Haji Abdur Rehman Khan, a Muslim
League leader. On all sides the town presented a dreadful scene
which we could not bear. The attackers had sacked the whole
town. Not a single shop or house, belonging to a non-Muslim, was
left which had not been swept clean. The pillaged houses had a
desolate look with the doors wide open as if no one had ever
lived in them."

Dera Ghazi Khan District

The importance of the Muslim League and its programme of
establishing an exclusively Muslim theocratic State of Pakistan
were almost unknown in the far-flung district of Dera Ghazi Khan.
The river Indus acted as a barrier against extraneous influences.
There is no railway in the district and the only means of transport
available to the people are motor lorries, bullock-carts or camels.
A number of ferries ply at various points on the river and a boat
bridge, during the winter months, furnishes access to Muzaffargarh. During the summer months, when the volume of water in
the Indus increases, the boat bridge is dismantled and the crossing is made by steamer. The local politics were inspired and
controlled by the tribal chiefs, of whom the most important was
the head of the Laghari Tribe. He was a member of the Unionist

the Superintendent of Police. All the residents of Mangrotha Sharqi were safely escorted to Dera Ghazi Khan. A Hindu resident of Basti Jhok Hafiz Nur Hassan was murdered on August 31, and his property was looted. The next day, four of the culprits were caught and produced before the Zaildar who reported the matter to the police. Some of the stolen property was recovered from the culprits. The arrival of the Mounted Constabulary, at village Chorhatta, saved the non-Muslims from the assault of a Muslim mob. Village Mehrawala was subjected to a most brutal attack on the evening of September 3. A number of men were massacred and some women were raped. Four girls were carried away. There was extensive looting and burning of shops. The survivors were compelled to accept Islam and all the males were circumcised. Gurkha military arrived the next day and rescued the survivors.

On the evening of September 9 a large mob was seen approaching Rajanpur. Gurkha military drove them away and one of them who was wounded by a shot fired by Gurkha soldiers, was caught and prosecuted. Near Rajanpur occurred probably the worst tragedy in this district. On October 25, a convoy of thirteen trucks, carrying more than four hundred non-Muslims, left Rojhan for Rajanpur. The convoy was accompanied by a Muslim military escort. The refugees were all searched by the Sub-Inspector of Police before they left and deprived of their cash and valuables. Twelve miles from Rojhan, the convoy was attacked by a mob of Muslims. Two Advocates of Rajanpur who had gone to Rojhan to bring out the refugees were with the convoy, and one of them lost his life while trying to defend himself. In all forty-six persons from this convoy were killed and sixty injured. Seven girls were carried away. The military escort is alleged to have helped the Muslim mob in attacking this convoy. A number of non-Muslims, travelling on camelback to Vahowa, were attacked on September 8. Nine of them were killed and their property was looted. A lorry, containing twelve Hindus from Taunsa, was attacked near Pir Adal and looted, in the end of October. Some of the passengers were killed. On October 6, a lorry from Vahowa on way to Dera Ghazi Khan was attacked by a Muslim mob and seven persons were killed. A lorry, travelling from Paiga to Dera Ghazi Khan, was attacked and looted.

In a number of outlying villages, there was little or no loss of life but the residents were forcibly converted and their property was looted.*

Bahawalpur State

Bahawalpur was a predominantly Muslim State and in the months of April and May 1947, the news of the happenings in Lahore, Rawalpindi and Multan and the persistent demand for the partition of the country gave rise to a feeling of insecurity among the non-Muslims. Large numbers of them left the State. They, however, returned home, as the State remained peaceful and their Muslim neighbours gave them assurances of safety. The Ruler acceded to Pakistan and, within a few days of August 15, attacks on non-Muslim life and property began. The Nawab was away in England and did not return till October 1 by which date, out of a total of two and a half lakhs non-Muslims, only about seventy thousand were left alive in the State. Between seventy and eighty thousand had migrated to India and the rest (one lakh) could not be accounted for. They had either perished in the mass massacres which took place throughout Bahawalpur or had been forcibly converted to Islam. The Muslims proclaimed in triumph that the loss of Muslim life in Patiala, Kapurthala and Faridkot had been amply compensated by what happened in Bahawalpur and felt satisfied that the measure of retribution was exemplary rather than adequate.

Almost the first important event in the State was the murder of a number of Sikh passengers at Bahawal Nagar Railway Station on August 19. When the noon train from Bhatinda arrived, the Sikh passengers were dragged out and done to death in a most brutal manner. Soon afterwards rioting broke out in the town and, during the next few days, many stray assaults on non-Muslims were reported. On August 22, several shops in Dhaban Bazaar were looted. On August 26, Muslim hooligans, assisted by the military, launched a determined and large-scale

---

* In villages Batal Goleewara, Haidar Vahan, Hajipur, Kotla Sher Mohammad, Jakra Imam Shah, Chah Jamal Wala, Basti Malkhaniwala, Basti Nasir, Naushera Sharqi, Basti Nur Wahi, Basti Rekh, Samina, Sarangwala, Shampur and Udhanewala looting and mass conversions took place.

In Ahmadani Basti, Batah Imam, Chah Bhathari Wala, Bindi, Bohar, Buglani, Basti Chhabri Zarin, Chuni, Fazalipur, Basti Ghali, Basti Ghuman, Hero Garbi, Haut, Kalol Kalan, Kohar, Kotani, Kotla Dad, Kot Mithan, Basti Lund Shawan, Luteri Shamali, Basti Mad Kasuran, Basti Mari Magrabi, Mirkhar, Phaphari, Pir Adal, Pir Bakhsh Khas, Basti Rai Khana, Basti Ranjehwala, Basti Raman, Ratera, Shniwala Shah Sadar Din and Vadwar looting a one took place. The residents of these villages left, out of fear, and, as soon as they had gone, the Muslims looted their houses and shops.

attack on non-Muslim life and property. Curfew was imposed on the town but this did not stop the carnage as Muslims defied the order and roamed about the streets with impunity, killing, looting and burning. It is estimated that over four hundred persons were killed and many girls were kidnapped. About fifty houses were reduced to ashes.

Travelling by train became a perilous undertaking for the Sikhs and Hindus and attacks on trains from all parts of the State were reported. The news of these attacks, and, more particularly, the murder of the Sikhs at the Bahawal Nagar Railway Station, spread panic in the neighbouring town of Minchinabad and several hundred non-Muslims rushed to the railway station with their luggage, intending to leave for India. A mob of Muslims, accompanied by two Tehsil peons and the Octroi clerk, came up and told them to go back as the Tehsildar had forbidden their departure. The members of the mob began to carry away the luggage and valuables of the non-Muslims who were forced to return home, dejected and deprived of their property. Later, in the evening, the Muslim residents of Minchinabad, assisted by the local police, started looting Hindu shops. Looting continued on the following day, locks on houses and shops were broken open, cattle were driven away and a state of complete lawlessness prevailed. The Sub-Inspector of Police arrived in the evening and tried to restore a semblance of order by firing a number of rounds in the air. He also arrested some of the ruffians. For the next few days there was comparative calm and the non-Muslims began to leave the town on foot, in parties of one hundred or two hundred each. The people had to pay heavy bribes to the police and the military escorting them. The last batch of about three hundred left on September 24. They carried their belongings in fifty-nine bullock-carts. The convoy was stopped near the boundary of Bikaner State and subjected to a malevolent and harassing search in the course of which many valuables and ornaments were taken away, the womenfolk were molested and one young girl was kidnapped. A complaint was made to the Bikaner authorities who immediately retaliated by refusing to let a Muslim convoy go further unless the girl was restored. Fortunately wiser counsels prevailed, the kidnapped girl was restored and both convoys were able to proceed on their way.

Left alone to themselves, the Muslims of Minchinabad plundered whatever was left of the non-Muslim property and desecrated the temples and Gurdwaras.

On August 18, a mob of several thousand armed Muslims attacked the town of Allahabad. The raiders began to loot non-Muslim shops and murder any Hindus and Sikhs they met in the streets. A message was sent to the Hindu Tehsildar that if the non-Muslims agreed to embrace Islam their lives would be spared. Hurried consultations were held and it was decided to accept the terms offered by the Muslims. Several hundred Hindus were marched off to a selected spot and converted to Islam. The next day a Muslim State official arrived and enquired if the Hindus had agreed to be converted of their own free will. His attitude appeared to be sympathetic and the Hindus replied that they had been forced to do so. On this the Muslims prepared to attack the converts, but the State official arrested the leader of the hooligans and ordered his troops to open fire on the Muslims if they attempted to create a disturbance. The non-Muslims were taken to a camp and finally evacuated.

Mitti Roya was attacked, on August 20, by a Muslim mob, assisted by the State forces. About twenty non-Muslims were killed and ten wounded. Their houses were plundered. Further mischief was stopped by the arrival of some British military officers.

A mob of a thousand armed Muslims invaded village Goth Mehro and called upon the non-Muslims to hand over all their cash and valuables. When this demand was complied with, the Muslims fell upon the unfortunate victims of this robbery and began to butcher them. Some women jumped into a well and committed suicide. A number of villagers ran away and concealed themselves in the fields outside. Looting and killing continued till midnight and was resumed in the morning. Over two hundred non-Muslims perished in the course of this holocaust. The few remaining survivors were ceremoniously converted to Islam. The young boys were circumcised, beef was cooked and served to everyone.

In Khankah Mubarak about six hundred non-Muslims were killed. Their shrines were desecrated, and nearly a hundred girls were carried away. The mother of a young boy ran up to save him and offered all her ornaments to a murderous ruffian. The man took the ornaments and, with a bestial laugh, hacked the boy to pieces with his hatchet before the eyes of his mother.

A Muslim Sub-Inspector of Police from Ferozepore came to Mandi Sadiq Ganj, on August 20, and spread the news that he had been driven out of his home, and the Sikhs had desecrated the mosques by tying their horses inside them. This story, coming a day after the massacre of Sikh passengers at Bahawal Nagar, was the signal for a mass attack on non-Muslim life and property which continued for four days. The Muslim military took part in this assault and shot many unoffending Hindus and Sikhs who tried to run away from the town. The Gurdwaras and temples were desecrated. All non-Muslim houses, shops and factories were ruthlessly pillaged.

In Bahawalpur itself, signs of unrest were witnessed towards the end of August. A Muslim mob collected in front of the house of the Education Minister and, from there, proceeded to the temple of Sanwal Shah. The mob was led by a butcher, Bakhsha, who rode on horseback. When the mob arrived in front of the temple, Bakhsha got down and murdered the temple Pujari. The mob then went back to the city and broke the images in the Kalladhari Temple. News of disturbances in other parts of the State began to arrive and it was rumoured that a mass attack on the non-Muslims of Bahawalpur had been planned for September 13. A Peace Committee consisting of members of all communities had tried to maintain calm in the town but, on September 12, the Muslim members did not attend the meeting of this Committee. The next day it was reported that Muslim tailors had removed their sewing machines from Hindu shops where they were usually kept. At 9 p.m. shouting was heard from the mosque in Chowk Bazaar. Soon afterwards fires were seen rising from a number of non-Muslim houses. The owners who ran out of the burning houses were shot by the military. The disturbances became more widespread and increased in intensity on the following two days, and for the space of three days murder, loot and arson went on in the town of Bahawalpur. It is estimated that nearly one thousand non-Muslims lost their lives and two thousand more were injured. About forty shops and houses were destroyed by fire. The surviving non-Muslims were then taken to a camp and finally evacuated to India.

The worst incident in Bahawalpur State was the massacre of a convoy of Sikhs which left Bhattian Camp on September 26. There were over two thousand men, women and children living in the camp and, when it was found impossible to evacuate them by train, a foot convoy, in charge of a Magistrate and a military escort, commanded by a Muslim Colonel, was arranged. The convoy left for Jesalmer State. At the first halt, the military escort conducted a wholly unauthorized search for valuables and cash. The refugees resisted and the military opened fire upon them. About forty persons were killed. The convoy then proceeded on its way and, when they arrived at the boundary of Jesalmer State, they were stopped and all the women and girls were separated. The refugees were then completely looted and the men were left to continue their journey to Jesalmer. They were told to be on their guard and warned against a possible attack by the Hurs who might be lying in wait for them. The goat-skins containing the drinking water of the refugees were bayoneted by the soldiers so that they found themselves without any water for their long journey through the desert. A few hours earlier, the Colonel in charge of the escort had sent forward a number of soldiers who concealed themselves round the route of the convoy. When the refugees entered Jesalmer, the soldiers, lying in ambush, opened fire upon them and the refugees were told that they were being attacked by the Hurs. The remaining escort, on the pretext of shooting at the Hurs, began to shoot the refugees and almost the entire caravan was decimated in this manner. The women and girls were taken away and the Officer Commanding received a considerable portion of the loot and the best-looking kidnapped girls. The Magistrate was later suspended and the Commanding Officer taken into custody. He was soon afterwards released and no further action was taken against him.

Hasilpur was another place where the loss of non-Muslim life was very great. The village was attacked, on August 26, by a huge Muslim mob who killed more than four hundred non-Muslims and set fire to almost the entire non-Muslim property. Many young girls were kidnapped. Of these some were later returned. The survivors were forcibly converted to Islam. They were eventually rescued by a British officer. There were many villages in which there was little or no loss of life as the non-Muslims were completely overpowered and, at once, agreed to be converted to Islam.*

---

* Chak No. 122 is alleged to have been completely looted after the non-Muslims had left.

In the following villages there was no loss of life and the non-Muslims were converted to Islam :

Ablani, Asbani, Asrani, Behli, Bhinda Samad Khan, Bhinda Shahra Lakhvera, Bunga Balochan, Chak No. 10, Chak No. 11, Chak No. 36/3R, Chak No. 147, Chak No. 169, Chhina, Deda, Ghulam Ali, Ghulan Arain, Goth Ali, Goth Lal, Inayati, Jhandani, Jhangi Wali, Jhok Gola, Kaura Bhutna, Kilanjwala, Kirpal, Kukara, Maharan Sharif Marhi Jethi, Mochi Wali, Mohammad Pur, Mubarakpur, Naharwali, Nurpur, Nurpur Nauranga, Pallah, Rathar, Shahr Farid, Sheikhwahen, Sultanarain. Tibbi Sehajan and Zohrkot.

Why didst thou promise such a beauteous day,
And make me travel forth without my cloak,
To let base clouds o'ertake me in my way,
Hiding thy bravery in their rotten smoke?
'Tis not enough that through the cloud thou break,
To dry the rain on my storm-beaten face,
For no man well of such a salve can speak,
That heals the wound and cures not the disgrace:

IV

Nor can thy shame give physic to my grief;
Though thou repent, yet I have still the loss:
The offender's sorrow lends but weak relief
To him that bears the strong offence's cross.
Ah! but those tears are pearl which thy love sheds,
And they are rich and ransom all ill deeds.

WILLIAM SHAKESPEARE—Sonnets

Why didst thou promise such a beauteous day,
And make me travel forth without my cloak,
To let base clouds o'ertake me in my way,
Hiding thy bravery in their rotten smoke?
'Tis not enough that through the cloud thou break,
To dry the rain on my storm-beaten face,
For no man well of such a salve can speak
That heals the wound and cures not the disgrace:
Nor can thy shame give physic to my grief;
Though thou repent, yet I have still the loss:
The offender's sorrow lends but weak relief
To him that bears the strong offence's cross.
Ah, but those tears are pearl which thy love sheds,
And they are rich and ransom all ill deeds.

WILLIAM SHAKESPEARE—*Sonnets*

CHAPTER FOUR

EXODUS

THE Muslim League demand for Pakistan was based on the hypothesis that Hindus and Muslims constitute two separate nations, each entitled to a separate and exclusive homeland where they would be free to develop their culture, tradition, religion and polity. On any other ground, the partition of the country and the setting up of a separate independent State for the Muslims would have been indefensible. But the two-nation theory brought the problem of minorities into greater prominence than ever before, and partition, instead of offering a solution, made it even more difficult and more complicated. No matter where the line of demarcation were drawn, there would be Hindus, Muslims and Sikhs on either side of it, in a majority or in a substantial minority ; and, whatever the geographical boundaries of Pakistan, large numbers of Hindus and Sikhs would, overnight, become aliens and foreigners in their own homes. Mr. Jinnah made desperate efforts to evade the issue by promising protection and rights of citizenship to the minorities, but the nature of his demand was wholly inconsistent with these promises. How could millions of foreigners acquire rights of citizenship and equal status with the nationals of Pakistan ; and if they could, why divide India, why not let Muslims continue as nationals of India? Mr. Jinnah could find no answer to these questions and he was finally compelled to suggest an exchange of population. This was such a fantastic idea that he referred to it, first, in a vague and hesitating manner, as if he were doing no more than throwing out a feeler to watch the reactions it brought forth. All he said was: "It is possible that there will have to be exchange of population if it can be done on a purely voluntary basis."* No one took Mr. Jinnah seriously and, for a year, very little was said about the possibility contemplated by him. To the Muslim League, however, it was a matter of great urgency as it offered a complete answer to the opponents of Pakistan. Exchange on a voluntary basis was an impossibility. The non-Muslims of the Punjab, North-West Frontier Province, Sind and Bengal could never consent to leave their lands, the industry and commerce they had built up with

---

* Mr. Jinnah's interview to the Special Correspondent of the Associated Press of India on December 10, 1945, published in *Dawn* of December 12, 1945.

their money and labour, and become beggars and nomads to satisfy a whim of Mr. Jinnah's ; nor would the Muslims of the United Provinces, Bombay, Madras, Bihar and Central Provinces be willing to abandon their native soil, give up everything they owned and made life worth living, and migrate to distant lands. Human beings take moral and cultural roots in the soil where they live and prosper for generations, and the ties that bind them to the native village and town are not easily severed. The dream of exchanging populations on a voluntary basis was impossible of realization and the Muslim League had to find another way of resolving the difficulty.

The Calcutta experiment did not produce very satisfactory results but it achieved a certain measure of success in that large numbers of non-Muslims were intimidated into leaving their homes even though for a temporary period. The experience gained, proved useful in Noakhali and Tippera. A change of tactics, better organization and more favourable conditions enabled the Muslim League to strike terror into the hearts of the non-Muslims, destroy their property, their self-respect and the honour of their women, and convert them wholesale to Islam. This was a more effective way of dealing with the minorities and obviated the difficulties involved in an exchange of population. The events in Bihar compelled many Muslims to leave the province and seek shelter in Sind, and the question of exchange arose once again. It was now taken up by the League leaders and put forward in all seriousness and with all the vehemence at their command. They became more and more uncompromising on this issue and answered all criticism by uttering scarcely veiled threats, and predicted a horrible doom for those who disagreed with them. On November 25, 1946, Mr. Jinnah, addressing a Press Conference at Karachi expressed the opinion that "the authorities, both Central and Provincial, should take up immediately the question of exchange of population."* This brought forth a storm of protest from non-Muslims all over India. Sir Chimanlal Setalvad, the Liberal leader, described the idea as "hopelessly impracticable." Sardar Swaran Singh said, "the Sikhs in the Punjab would not tolerate any move to this end." Sardar Patel, addressing the Nagpur University Convocation, characterized Mr. Jinnah's proposal as "absurd" and one which "can never materialize." The Muslim League leaders, on the other hand,

---

* *Dawn.* November 26. 1946.

expressed their wholehearted approval of the scheme. Khan Iftikhar Hussain Khan of Mamdot declared, with great enthusiasm, that "the exchange of population offered a most practical solution of the multifarious problems " of the Muslims. " We are not going to ask Sardar Patel or Dr. Khare for it, but we will get it by our own inherent strength. The exchange of population will wipe out the most important argument against Pakistan which has been persistently fired from the Congress armoury."* The frank avowal and the unabashed threat, implicit in this utterance, were hardly calculated to inspire confidence in the minorities. Pir Ilahi Bux, the Sind leader, said he " welcomed an exchange of population for the safety of minorities" as such an exchange would put an end to all communal disturbances.† Sir Evan Jenkins, the Governor of the Punjab, observed that by advocating an exchange of population the Muslim League was thinking of forcibly driving away the Hindus from the Punjab. This brought forth a protest from Raja Ghaznafar Ali Khan. " This is certainly not so," he said, "the Muslim League will do everything possible to protect the minorities living in the Muslim majority areas and will even be prepared to give what help is possible for any plans of strengthening the sense of security among Hindus where they happen to be living as a scattered minority." But, lest his professions of sympathy were misconstrued, he added darkly : "After what has happened, the present position cannot be accepted with equanimity and minorities which are too scattered and helpless owing to the smallness of their numbers must not be left as a tempting prey to those who can arrange organized lawlessness."‡

Sir Feroze Khan Noon had already threatened to re-enact the murderous orgies of Changez Khan and Halaqu Khan if the non-Muslims took up a refractory attitude.§ Everything was now ready and, in the month of January 1947, the agitation against the Punjab Coalition Ministry was started. We have seen in the previous chapter how it promoted lawlessness and utter disregard of authority, and provided an opportunity for the Muslim League to organize their forces and rehearse the great *putsch* which would solve the problem of minorities once and for all. The agitation culminated in the resignation of the Khizar Ministry and when the prospect of a League Government provoked the Sikh

---

* *Dawn*, December 3, 1946.   † *Dawn*, December 4, 1946.
‡ *Dawn*, December 19, 1946.
§ Speech at the Convention of the Muslim League legislators on April 9, 1946.

leaders into giving vent to their anger and fears in somewhat stupid and boastful words, their utterances were made the excuse for launching a bloody assault on non-Muslim life and property.   The Sikhs had opposed the partition of India with even greater vigour than the Hindus, because they felt that as a community they could only expect disaster in Pakistan ; it was, therefore, against the Sikhs that the spear-point of the Muslim League attack was first aimed.   In the March riots, the Sikhs of Rawalpindi faced annihilation and large numbers of them left the district.   Within a few weeks almost the entire Sikh population (save those who were killed or converted) had migrated from the district.   On a somewhat smaller scale a movement of the Hindus from Multan, Jhelum, Attock and Bahawalpur also took place. Some of these non-Muslims went back when peaceful conditions were restored during the months of April, May, June and July.

In Lahore and Amritsar the cauldron of hate and communal passion continued to simmer and boil.   In May riots broke out once again with redoubled fury.   The Sikhs had asked for the partition of the Punjab and the Congress leaders had taken the matter up with the Viceroy and Mr. Jinnah.   There was a danger that Pakistan might lose Lahore, as the Sikhs were agitating for the Chenab as the boundary line between the two countries.   The battle for Lahore thus began in May and continued unabated till the city was clear of non-Muslims.   Persons residing inside the walled city were stabbed and intimidated, their habitations were destroyed by fire.   Homeless and deprived of the means of livelihood, many of them began to leave the city and the volume of exodus increased day by day, till it became a pitiable and ignominious stampede in the month of August.

Towards the end of July, signs of unrest began to manifest themselves in Amritsar and the neighbouring villages. Refugees from West Punjab had been for months relating their sufferings and losses.   Tales of misery, anguish and horror received wide currency.   Indignation and resentment went on mounting till they passed the limits of human endurance.   Every day brought fresh cause for revenge and retaliation.   The storm of rage bottled up for so long burst forth in the beginning of August and the Sikhs began to attack the Muslims in the rural areas.   In the city of Amritsar, the loss of Muslim life was almost equal to the loss of non-Muslim life during May and June, though non-Muslims sustained considerably heavier losses in property.   In Lahore, too, the non-Muslims had begun to hit back and the Rashtriya Swayam Sewak Sangh volunteers boasted that they had saved many lives by taking the offensive in some cases. There, however, the non-Muslims were fighting a losing battle as the Muslim magistracy and police were openly supporting the Muslim League hooligans and giving active assistance to them in every possible way. On August 11, another determined and, what proved to be the conclusive, attack was launched on the non-Muslims of Lahore. The exchange of population had begun in grim earnest and was going to be achieved by the "inherent strength" of the Muslims. A two-way traffic of men, women and children, hounded out of their homes and running to seek shelter in unknown lands, started and continued for several months. None but those who have travelled in a refugee train or seen a foot caravan on its slow and interminable march can gauge the magnitude of the problems which the Government of India and the Government of East Punjab had to cope with, or the difficulties of transporting, feeding, housing, looking after and providing medical aid to four million people.

The exodus gathered volume and momentum so rapidly that it took some time to organize the machinery for protecting and transporting the refugees and putting it in effective working order. All over West Punjab non-Muslims felt the urgency of leaving Pakistan where, within a day or two, conditions of life became impossible and destruction was the only alternative left. From hamlets and villages the people ran like hunted animals to seek shelter in towns where they hoped to find safety, in large numbers. They were not permitted to take their cattle, their household effects or their cherished belongings. On the way they were harassed, searched and looted ; their young women were molested and carried away. Those who had the misfortune of living in outlying places and isolated pockets found escape impossible. In the towns and cities large concentrations of refugees grew up, and hundreds of thousands of them watched and waited, huddled together in camps like herds of cattle. Food and drink were denied them and they were subjected to frequent attacks. From large villages started foot caravans on the long and perilous journey to the Dominion of India. Some of these caravans were more than a mile long, and progressed slowly, in their long march, from Sagodha, Lyallpur, Montgomery, Balloki on to Ferozepore. From other places evacuation was undertaken by train and motor lorry. The supply of rolling stock was inadequate and accommodation was extremely limited. Every train was packed inside and outside ; people climbed on to the roof and sat balanced precariously on the curved surface. They stood on the footboards, clinging to door-handles, exposed to the hazards of a shower of stones or a volley of bullets. For hours the trains were stopped, for no ostensible reason, while the passengers suffered the agonies of exposure to the sweltering heat of the sun. No food was provided, water was unobtainable, and if anyone left the train, for any purpose, he ran the risk of not being able to return alive. Small children and infants died of thirst and starvation. When babies in arms cried for a drop of water till no sound came from their parched throats, fathers and mothers in despair gave them their own urine to drink. Train after train was attacked by bands of hooligans and armed National Guards, assisted by Baluch soldiers who had been sent as protectors. Evacuation by motor lorries and trucks was neither safer nor more comfortable. The trucks were for the most part roofless transport vans, and the passengers had to stand so that more of them could be accommodated. They travelled thus for hours, along roads infested by murderous gangs. The trucks were frequently attacked and looted. In the foot caravans, decrepit old men and women, unable to withstand the rigours of a long and painful march, lay down by the roadside and expired without uttering a groan till the whole route was littered with bloated and putrefying corpses, animal and human skeletons. There was no time to pause and grieve over the dead ones. The caravan had to march on—a caravan of a defeated people in flight.

It was of this exodus that Mr. Jinnah spoke in his tirade against the non-Muslims. " We have been the victims of a deeply-laid and well-planned conspiracy, executed with utter disregard of the elementary principles of honesty, chivalry and honour." To his own people he said : " Do not for a moment imagine that your enemies can ever succeed in their designs, but at the same time do not make light of the situation facing you. . . . You have only to develop the spirit of the *mujahids*."

There was no co-operation from the officials of the West Punjab Government. Complaints were made that the rolling stock of the trains carrying Muslim refugees from East Punjab was not returned in full. West-bound trains normally consisted of twenty-five bogies drawn by two engines. The trains, sent back, contained only twelve bogies drawn by one engine. Unauthorized searches continued at all places in spite of Inter-Dominion agreements to the contrary. In Sind, the Premier openly repudiated the authority of the Central Government to prohibit searches. The personnel of the escort was too frequently Muslim* in whom the refugees had no confidence. Their fears were often justified. Insufficient food was supplied to camps and to the refugees on the march. The Government of India did all they could to alleviate the sufferings of their people. Aeroplanes carried foodstuffs to feed the starving refugees. On September 9, six Dakotas loaded with provisions were sent. On October 2, 32,000 lbs. of food were dropped, on October 17 and 18, 12,138 lbs. and on October 21 and 22, 24,924 lbs. of food were dropped.

As an instance of the difficulties encountered by the Liaison Agency in evacuating outlying pockets of non-Muslims and the lack of co-operation from Pakistan officials, the story of how the non-Muslims of Isakhel were evacuated may be narrated.† Isakhel lies beyond the Indus at a distance of about fifty miles from Kala Bagh. It is near the border and not far from tribal territory. When disturbances began in the various districts of West Punjab some Hindus of Isakhel decided to send their families to India, while they themselves remained behind to look after their lands and business. As the situation deteriorated and transport difficulties increased, the relatives in India became anxious for the safety of those who had been left in Isakhel and sent persistent appeals to the Government of India asking them to bring out these unfortunate persons. The Chief Liaison Officer accompanied by Brigadier Keenen paid a visit to Mianwali and contacted the Deputy Commissioner. The Chief Liaison Officer told him that he wanted to see the local conditions for himself and make arrangements for the evacuation of the Hindus of Isakhel. The Deputy Commissioner disapproved of the Liaison Officer's proposal and said that all the Hindus of Isakhel had been voluntarily converted to Islam and that none of them wished to go to India. He offered to show the Liaison Officer statements of converted Hindus, recorded by a First Class Magistrate. The Deputy Commissioner added that any attempt to rescue these men was fraught with the greatest danger and that he would not be responsible if anything untoward happened. The tribesmen, returning from Mirpur (Jammu State), were present in the area

---

* See an instance of this on page 144.
† The account has been prepared from the records of the Chief Liaison Officer

and they would resist any attempt to take the converts away. According to Islam, the tribesmen believed, a converted person was liable to suffer death if he became apostate and anyone attempting to reclaim such a converted man was subject to the same penalty. The Liaison Officer, however, insisted on going to the spot himself and the Deputy Commissioner had to agree. When Brigadier Keenen approached the Pakistan Commander at Mianwali for help in procuring transport, similar objections were raised and the Pakistan Commander insisted that the Hindus in Isakhel had no right to be evacuated even if they expressed a wish to go to India. Finally, however, the Commander was prevailed upon to place a few trucks at the disposal of the Liaison Officer.

Leaving Mianwali early in the morning, the party arrived at Isakhel at about noon. Anticipating the difficulty of establishing contact with the Hindu converts in Isakhel, a dozen intelligent men from Mianwali had been taken with the party. On arrival at Isakhel, these men were sent out into the city to warn the Hindu converts that Indian troops under Hindu officers had arrived to rescue them, and that now was the opportunity for them to escape. The information received by the Liaison Agency was that the converts had been frightened and intimidated to such an extent that, whenever any enquiry was made from them regarding their desire to go to India, they always replied in the negative. They feared that if they set out on a journey they would be robbed and butchered on the way. The information conveyed by the men from Mianwali, however, reassured them and the converts prepared to leave Isakhel. Objections were raised by the local Commander and the Nawabs of Isakhel who said that the converts did not wish to be evacuated. The Commander came forward with a proposal that the representatives of the Hindu converts were present and wished to speak to the Liaison Officer and Brigadier Keenen. The Liaison Officer, however, replied that the officers of the Indian Dominion had no intention of holding a discussion with the converts or interviewing them. Their orders were simply to have it notified in the city, by beat of drum, that those who were willing to be evacuated should come out and no persuasion of any kind was to be allowed. The Liaison Officer learnt that the Deputy Commissioner had warned the Commander of his visit and that arrangements had been made to tutor some of the converts. The Deputy Commissioner had agreed to promulgate section 144 of the Criminal Procedure Code in the city, and all residents were required to remain indoors for the whole day. Before the Liaison Officer entered the city, the local Commander of Pakistan troops tried to impose a condition that Indian troops should not enter the city and only Pakistan troops should bring the Hindu converts from the city area. The Liaison Officer did not agree as the whole object of his visit to Isakhel would have been defeated by the acceptance of this condition. Finally, it was agreed that the Pakistan and Indian troops would act jointly and enter the city together. A man chosen from the Indian Army and one from the Pakistan Army were accordingly sent in pairs. The Liaison Officer, accompanied by Brigadier Keenen, himself made a round of the city and saw that, on the roof of every second house, an armed tribesman and a member of the Muslim League National Guard with a rifle were present. Their object was to terrify the Hindu converts and not allow them to exercise their free will. The information given by the men from Mianwali and the presence of Indian troops, however, reassured the converts and in about two hours almost every man, woman and child, with as much luggage as they could carry, came out of the city and were placed in trucks waiting near the city wall. The local officers did not provide transport of any kind so that these unfortunate people could only take with them what they could themselves carry. In this manner six hundred and thirty-four persons were rescued.

The convoy, escorted by Indian and Pakistan troops, left Isakhel at about 5 p.m. When the convoy was near village Qamar Mushani, between Kala Bagh and Isakhel, it was waylaid and fired at by a crowd of Muslims. The Gurkha troops returned the fire, killing half a dozen men. Fortunately the convoy reached Mianwali without further mishap.

The District Liaison Officer of Montgomery had a most distressing experience when he went to evacuate some non-Muslims from village Harditpur on July 19, 1948. The Liaison Officer was escorted by two Muslim foot constables while a Hindu driver was in charge of the car in which he travelled. At the village a large number of people assembled, among whom were some sepoys of the Pakistan Boundary Police The District Liaison Officer was stopped by these sepoys and told not to talk with the non-Muslims whom he had come to evacuate. The sepoys then conducted him and his party to the Jemadar, and reported that Hindus had entered the boundary of Pakistan without permits. The Liaison Officer informed the Jemadar who he was, but the Jemadar was not satisfied and proceeded to arrest him, his escort and the driver of his car. The Jemadar then searched the party and removed cash and other articles which he found. The Muslim constables of the escort were disarmed and their ammunition was taken away. The Liaison Officer was conducted to village Makhana and produced before an officer who finally allowed him to go away. The non-Muslims could not be evacuated.

There were several attacks on refugee trains. Some of these have been referred to in Chapter Three. A train which left Pind Dadan Khan on September 19, was attacked at three different points of its journey and the loss of life and property suffered was considerable. Near Chalisa the train was stopped by a Muslim mob which carried away nearly two hundred women and killed a large number of men and women. It was attacked a second time near Mughalpur and a third time at Harbanspura. The attack at Mughalpura took place at about noon. Hundreds of people were seen marching along the canal bank to waylay the train and attack the passengers. The authorities did not stop or discourage them and took no preventative action.

On September 24, a refugee train from Wah was attacked near Wazirabad. The train was diverted towards Sialkot as its journey to Lahore was considered unsafe. A mile from Wazirabad it was derailed and a Muslim mob came out of the surrounding fields and attacked the passengers. The Hindu escort drove the mob away and the train was brought back to Wazirabad. At Wazirabad the train was subjected to incessant firing during the night and many refugees were killed.

On October 23, a large batch of non-Muslim refugees left Sialkot by train. The track beyond Jassar was out of order and the District Liaison Officer, Sialkot, informed the Deputy Commissioner that it was inadvisable to send refugees by this train as they would have to leave the train and continue the journey on foot through territory infested by Muslim hooligans. The Deputy Commissioner, however, insisted on sending the train and, at Jassar, all the refugees had to get down and start walking. The convoy had proceeded for half a mile when it was attacked by a large mob of armed Muslims who had been hiding in the sugarcane fields. The attack continued for two hours and the refugees ran in all directions to save themselves. The military escort instead of defending the refugees began to shoot at them. One of the Sikh guards was shot dead. A number of women were raped at the spot and many young girls were kidnapped. The entire property of the refugees was looted and many of them reached the Indian border, deprived even of the clothes they had been wearing. A conservative estimate places the number of persons killed at five hundred and the number of girls kidnapped at two hundred and fifty. About five hundred persons were injured. A military officer who flew over the place where the attack took place saw the whole area littered with rags and dead bodies.

The attack on a train of refugees from Bannu, at the Gujrat Railway Station in January 1948, resulted in another horrible massacre of non-Muslims. Two trains carrying about two thousand and four hundred non-Muslims left Bannu on January 10. When the trains arrived at Mari Indus the passengers were transferred to one train which left on the morning of the 11th. At Khushab the train was stopped for four hours, and the reason given was that the route via Sargodha and Lyallpur was unsafe, and arrangements were, therefore, being made for the train to run via Lalamusa and Gujrat. The train ultimately left Khushab at 7 p.m. It arrived at Gujrat at 11-30 p.m. It was escorted by a contingent of the Bihar Regiment consisting of a Sikh Captain and sixty soldiers. The driver of the train was a Muslim. At the Gujrat Railway Station the engine was disconnected and driven off. In the dead of night, two sepoys of the escort who went to get water from a tap were attacked by Pathans. One of them was killed and the other was injured ; the guns of both were taken away. Soon afterwards the train was fired at. The military escort replied and firing continued till the morning when the escort found that their ammunition was exhausted. A mob of between two thousand and three thousand armed Pathans now attacked the train. Windows and doors were broken open. The passengers were dragged out and done to death. The train was ransacked and thoroughly looted. The number of persons killed was not less than five hundred. The passengers were well-to-do Hindus from Bannu and they had brought a large quantity of valuables with them. It was said that this attack had been carefully planned and that the train was deliberately brought to Gujrat where armed Pathans in large numbers were present. In was also said that the Pir of Manki Sharif was at that time in Gujrat and was seen supervising and directing the attack.

One of the worst attacks on a lorry convoy took place near Lahore on August 26, 1947. A convoy of thirty-five military trucks, packed with non-Muslim refugees, left Sialkot in the morning. The convoy was in charge of a British officer and Muslim military. The lorries arrived at the Chhota Ravi bridge at 2 p.m. and were stopped. The British officer went back to Sialkot saying that he had to report there for duty. The Muslim lorry drivers went away on the pretext of taking tea. At about 4 p.m. a large mob of Muslims armed with spears and hatchets attacked the trucks. The Muslim sepoys took no steps to beat off this attack and no one from Lahore came to the assistance of the non-Muslims. There was heavy loss of life and when the trucks finally reached Amritsar they were found to contain large numbers of dead bodies and injured persons. Lorries and trucks travelling alone or in twos or threes were frequently attacked. As late as July 1948 travelling by lorry on roads in West Punjab was wholly unsafe.

A foot convoy of more than five thousand persons left Lyallpur on September 11, 1947. It was escorted by Muslim military. It arrived at Balloki Head on September 15, and was attacked by a Muslim mob. The escort joined the mob and began to shoot the refugees indiscriminately. It is estimated that nearly a thousand persons lost their lives. A huge convoy, nearly six miles in length, was attacked at various points of its journey. The refugees in this convoy were without food for days together and, but for the provisions supplied by the Government of India, most of them might have perished on the way.

The kidnapping of young women and the treatment to which they were subjected constitute a sordid chapter in the histoy of human relations. Poor innocent girls, young married women, sometimes with infants in their arms, were forcibly taken away to distant places. They were molested and raped, passed on from man to man, bartered and sold like cheap chattel. Sometimes it was impossible to trace their whereabouts. When representatives of the Indian Dominion went to recover them they were concealed and denied access to their relations. Large numbers of them, when recovered, were brought to a refugee camp at Kunjah. Conditions in this camp beggar description. A young woman of 21, describing her experiences, said: " I stayed in the camp for two months. Camp life was very miserable. We were given *chappatis* full of lime and were constantly molested by the soldiers. Maulvis used to come and preach to us against the Indian Dominion. They told us that we would go to heaven if we lived with them. They said that it was foolish on our part to go to India as flour was selling there at Rs. 5 per seer, salt at Rs. 10 per seer and the difficulties of obtaining cloth were insurmountable. According to them the Sikhs were not allowing Hindu girls to go beyond Amritsar and were raping them and cutting up their hearts." A party of young women who were brought to the camp said: "We reached the camp on the fifteenth day. It was nothing less than hell. The flour was mixed with lime and drinking water smelt so foul that it made us ill to drink it. When the Muslims gave us food they taunted us by saying that they were feeding witches. Sick children were given wrong medicines and some of them became blind and died as the result of the poisons given to them. The military guards brought their friends at night and molested the young girls in the camp. They pinched our breasts and made indecent jokes ; those who were pregnant were shot down. One day a man caught me by my breast and dragged me. When I moaned and wailed he kicked me and then left me to weep. A young girl of 14 or 15 sleeping by my side was dragged away and raped. When she resisted they kicked her. Her face in the morning looked as if it had been scratched by a knife." A young woman who was forcibly married to a Muslim named Sultan said: "Whenever Sultan came to know of the arrival of the Indian military he would take me out and hide me in pits which were covered from above, leaving very little space for breathing air. Thus he deceived the military several times. One day, the military reached the station unawares. Sultan locked me up in the house and went out. The soldiers called out loudly that if there was any Hindu woman about she should come out. I peeped out of a window and, seeing the soldiers, became frightened, but their assurances convinced me. I was taken out of the house through that window and brought to Lahore."

In some rare instances the girls had the good fortune of receiving kind treatment. There is, at least, one recorded case of a Muslim willingly escorting his Hindu wife to the military camp and making her over to her relatives. A young woman of 22 who was travelling with a foot convoy from Lyallpur said: "When I grew up I found myself an orphan. The people with whom I was living sold me to an old man named Tara Singh. He married me for the purpose of having children and paid Rs. 500

for me. He treated me kindly. When the convoy left Lyallpur we all joined it. The military had robbed us of everything before we left our house. First they took away our arms, then our valuables. On the way, I was separated from my people. I saw men being murdered and women being raped on the wayside. If someone protested he was killed. One woman was raped by many men. I was also raped by three men in succession. A man, at last, took me to his house and kept me there for eight days. He treated me in a beastly manner. He subjected me to physical torture, forced cow bones into my mouth so that I should be converted to Islam, and, when I objected, he thrashed me and made me lie under his bed. He put my hands under the *charpoy* legs and sat down on it to say his prayers. He asked me to repeat the prayers while I suffered agonies of pain. When I could not pronounce the words he uttered, he threatened to shoot me with his gun. After eight days of this torture, the military recovered me. I was taken to Amritsar and then brought to the Gandhi Vanita Ashram." The Lady Fact Finding Officer who took the statement of this unfortunate woman noticed that the extent of her suffering had unbalanced her mind.

A young girl of 12 gave the following story: " The news of the communal troubles in the cities used to frighten us, but the villagers always said, ' Let us wait till the 15th of August and then we will go away.' Trouble came to the neighbouring villages and then my relations collected a group of people and we came out of the village. We had gone only a little way when a mob of Muslims attacked us. I was stabbed in five places. ·Many people were killed and many ran away. I was separated from my parents. When I recovered my senses I saw two boys of my age lying near me and eight or nine dead bodies. The boys and I were bleeding. We got up and started to go towards the village. A Muslim, Wazir by name, caught me, took me to his village and left me with his sister. I did what his sister told me while Wazir used to go out to attack other villages. Wazir then sent me to his relatives in another village. I became ill and the women in that house were kind to me. When I recovered, the master of the house wanted to marry me. His first wife told me privately not to obey the priest even if I were beaten or threatened. I did what she said and when the priest went away the man gave me a good beating. The old man came to my bed, scratched my face and removed my clothes. I cried out for help to the mistress of the house, but the man did not listen to her. She then brought her son, and, hearing his voice, the old man left me. After a few days the old man's son sent me to Sir Ganga Ram Hospital at Lahore with a Muslim, but that Muslim took me to the Lahore Jail where many Hindu girls were living at that time. In the evening the wife of Anwar, a Muslim, took me to her house. She had two more girls staying with her already. All three of us used to sleep in one room. Anwar's wife told me that she would marry me to her son when he finished his studies. He was then reading in the ninth class. I stayed in this house for two months. My father was looking for me in Lahore. The military one day came and surrounded the house and rescued me."

Slowly and step by step, the situation was brought under control as the Civil Administration and the Military Evacuation Organization mobilized their resources. There were fatal and agonising delays in procuring transport and escorts, in sending help to the isolated pockets in outlying areas, in searching out the kidnapped women. The Government had to labour against heavy odds. Unprecedented floods broke down the lines of communication. Portions of the railway track in East Punjab were washed away, roads were damaged beyond repair, telephone and telegraph systems were frequently out of order. All the while, refugees in distress continued to make loud and frantic appeals for help to all departments of Government. Some had faith only in the highest and sent personal letters to Mr. Nehru and Sardar Patel.

The correspondence bag of the Prime Minister for the months of August, September and October 1947 contained a curious assortment of letters from all kinds of people. There were letters begging him to exercise his personal intervention to save a son or a wife, a father or a more distant relative. The Prime Minister was asked sometimes to rescue a factory, some piece of machinery, a cash box or an article of furniture. There were letters complaining of the indecision of the Government of India, letters accusing the Prime Minister of lack of sympathy for the non-Muslims, letters charging him with enjoying the fruits of victory at the expense of the Hindus of West Punjab, letters giving details of property left in Pakistan, descriptions of relatives whose whereabouts had not been heard of, apologetic letters, complaining letters, letters informing him of things he knew only too well, letters which began by saying that the writer was taking the opportunity of addressing the greatest man in the world, letters

16

from persons who claimed to have met the Prime Minister on some occasion, years previously, letters from avowedly total strangers, letters from officials, business men, shopkeepers, rich men, poor men, men in agony, deprived of their property, men asking for a job. One letter began: " Dear Sir, I am a poor and dirty man in the world. I have written one letter for you till now there is no reply. You are enjoying now for the independence. I am sorrowing now for the cause of money." Another correspondent said: " My Lord! I, with heavy heart, state you my whole miserable autobiography." The writer who described himself as a poor student then went on to give a narrative of his scholastic career. A retired headmaster unable to trace his son-in-law wrote as follows: " Worthy of reverence Panditji. It is after the greatest hesitation that I write this to you, knowing that your time is very precious. What has compelled me to write this to you is the fact that in casting about my eyes I fail to find anyone in the world except you who can help me in my calamity."

Day after day, week after week, non-Muslims from West Punjab continued to pour across the border in trains, lorries, aeroplanes, bullock-carts and on foot, till, by the end of December 1947, four millions of them had come to India. All of them had left behind their property and valuables, the majority of them had suffered bereavement ; their bodies sick and wounded, their souls bruised with the shock of horror, they came to a new home. There was discomfort in the refugee camps and the future held out uncertain hopes but, at last, their lives were free from danger and the honour of their womenfolk was safe. As they crossed the boundary line and entered the Dominion of India a cry of joy arose from their tired and almost voiceless throats with the spontaneity of a reflex action. Many of them wept with sheer relief as they uttered the salutation, " Jai Hind."

V

Let there be in Pakistan, the separate centre of Islam,
We shall not in Pakistan have to look at faces of non-
    Muslims.
The abode of the Muslim Nation will brighten up only,
When in Pakistan there remain no idolatrous thorns.
They (Hindus) whose function is to be slaves have no right
    to participate in Government,
Nowhere have they succeeded in governing.

—Song recited at the Muslim League
Conference at Sultankot (Sind)

"Let the Hindus of Sind leave Sind and go elsewhere.
Let them go while the going is good and possible, else I
warn them that a time is fast coming when in their flight
from Sind, they may not be able to get a horse or an ass
or a gari or any other means of transport."

—MR. KHURRO

CHAPTER FIVE

SIND

EVENTS in the newly created* Province of Sind followed a peculiar course of their own. This portion of India was one of the first to be conquered by the Muslims and has always remained a Muslim stronghold. During the British regime it formed part of the Bombay Presidency for administrative purposes until March 31, 1937. The province was not economically rich and, before the Karachi Port attained its present proportions, it was considered to be a drag on the finances of Bombay. The Hindu leaders of the Bombay Presidency were anxious to throw off this burden and often pressed for the separation of Sind from Bombay. At first, however, this proposal was not entertained as the British Government considered it impracticable. The pendulum gradually swung in the opposite direction, when income from the port of Karachi increased, and the Muslims of Sind began to agitate for its separation from Bombay. They demanded that the income from customs should be paid towards the Provincial Revenues in order to make it a self-supporting province. While the British Government were making up their mind about the matter, His Highness the Aga Khan offered to purchase the province in lieu of his loyal services to the British Crown extending over a number of years, and to these he agreed to add a substantial amount drawn from his much accumulated cash and gold. The prospect of his becoming the Nawab of Sind was not unpleasing to a number of persons and the Aga Khan found a great deal of support for his proposition, particularly in the die-hard element of the British peerage. Indian opinion was strongly opposed to this retrograde step as it would have meant the creation of a quite unnecessary autocracy, and, when the Secretary of State for India announced that the Aga Khan's petition had been rejected, the news was received with great relief. Shortly afterwards the Government of India Act, 1935, was passed and Sind became a separate province.

According to the census of 1941 the total population of the province was 45.35 lakhs, of whom no less than 70.7 per cent were Muslims. The economy of the province depends mainly

---

* Sind was separated from the Bombay Province by the Government of India Act, 1935.

upon agriculture and there are few industries of any importance. It is to be observed that only a little over one-half of the total area is culturable as there are large sandy tracts where nothing grows. Actually, a little less than one-fifth of the total area is under cultivation. The province has spent large sums of money on schemes of irrigation and, in spite of the fact that the annual irrigation expenses amount to Rs. 170.67 lakhs, the total income from land revenue and water cess is only Rs. 125.56 lakhs. Before the partition of the country Sind used to receive a subvention of Rs. 105 lakhs from the Central Revenues and without this contribution it was impossible to balance the provincial budget. These facts give some idea of the poverty of this small province.* The Hindus were mostly petty shopkeepers, poor labourers or tenants of Muslim Zemindars. Although there was a substantial number of Hindus, living in urban areas, who were engaged in business or industries, they represented only a small proportion of the total Hindu population. There were also a few Hindu Zemindars but their number was not considerable. The Hindus of Sind were not aggressive or bellicose like the non-Muslims of the Punjab. They were not given to indulging in political agitation or clamouring for their rights. The impression one gains is that the Hindus had resigned themselves to the theory that the Muslims of Sind belonged to a superior class and were entitled to treat the Hindus as their underlings. The labourers and the poor cultivators were particularly timid and were, at no time, prepared to offer resistance to the Muslim hooligans or to insist upon retaining whatever rights they had in property. Their first impulse, when the disturbances began, was to run away rather than stay and offer fight.

The result of the first elections held under the Government of India Act of 1935 showed that it would not be an easy matter to form a stable Ministry in Sind. The constitution of the parties was such that no single party commanded an absolute majority in the Legislature. The Muslim League secured only eight out of sixty seats. The largest number of seats was won by independent persons belonging to no political party. After a certain amount of unsavoury bargaining with self-seeking legislators, Sir Ghulam Hussain Hidayatullah succeeded in forming a Ministry. He did

---

* No mention is made in these figures of the income derived from Central subjects which forms the contribution towards the Central Revenues. Nor is any mention made of the expenses incurred by the Centre on account of Defence and other matters from which the province benefits. The net result, therefore, is what has been pointed out above.

not, however, stay in office long and was defeated by a combination of the Congress and the Allah Bux Group. Mr. Allah Bux now became the Premier and began to seek the assistance of the Congress for the support of his cause. Mr. Allah Bux himself had shown strong national leanings and was not disposed to endorse the Muslim League programme. He even offered to join the Congress and take all his supporters with him, if the Congress would help him to form a stable Ministry. Maulana Abul Kalam Azad who was deputed to deal with this matter, however, advised that it would be better in the interests of the province to form a united Muslim Party which should devote its energy and attention to economic and social progress. Had Mr. Allah Bux succeeded in doing this, the Muslim League would have ceased to count as a force in Sind. Mr. Jinnah, however, successfully prevented the formation of such a united Muslim Party and the Muslim League members declined to give their support to Mr. Allah Bux. Even the Hindu Party joined hands with the Muslim League opposition. The position of Mr. Allah Bux thus became precarious. He suffered a defeat on February 13, 1940, and, six days later, tendered his resignation to the Governor. He was, however, asked to continue in office until a stable Ministry could be formed. On February 26, a no-confidence motion against the Ministry was brought forward in the Assembly and Mr. Allah Bux resisted this attempt to dislodge him from office, though he had not withdrawn his resignation, and still professed his readiness to quit. He survived the censure, implicit in a no-confidence motion, by the casting vote of the Speaker. This narrow majority showed that Mr. Allah Bux's position was extremely insecure and on March 18, 1940, his resignation was accepted. Mr. Bundeh Ali Khan, on being called by the Governor, formed the new Ministry. He proved quite unequal to the task of administration, and the peace and economy of the province deteriorated a great deal by his incompetence and self-interest. Maulana Abul Kalam Azad was once again asked to resolve the tangled skein of Sind politics ; and he drew up what was popularly called the Azad Pact, the terms of which were that Mr. Bundeh Ali Khan was to resign his office as Premier and allow Mr. Allah Bux or Sir Ghulam Hussain Hidayatullah to take his place as head of the Government. The new Government would not be a League Government though it would include League Ministers and would also have the support of the Congress Party. Mr. Bundeh Ali Khan agreed to implement this Pact but, subsequently, on the advice of Mr. Jinnah, retracted his promise. The Ministry was overthrown on March 8, 1941, and Mr. Allah Bux once again returned to office. His nationalist leanings had now become more pronounced and he openly took instructions from the Congress High Command in administrative matters. The events which followed the " Quit India " resolution of the Congress in August 1942 agitated him a great deal and he renounced his title of Khan Bahadur. He communicated his decision to the Viceroy in a strongly-worded letter * and the result was that, within two days, the Governor of Sind summoned him to Government House and summarily dismissed him from the post of Provincial Premier. A few months after this Mr. Allah Bux was murdered.† Among the persons tried for this crime was Mr. Khurho who had occupied the post of a Minister in the Cabinets of Sir Ghulam Hussain Hidayatullah and Mr. Bundeh Ali Khan. At the time of Mr. Allah Bux's murder also he was a Minister and was removed from office to stand his trial. Subsequently he became the Premier of Sind.‡

On October 10, 1942, Sir Ghulam Hussain Hidayatullah was again invited to form a Ministry. He thus returned to power and continued to share it with the Provincial Governor in a varying degree, until the establishment of Pakistan, when he was himself raised to the post of the Governor. He was far from easy in his position as Premier. There was a great deal of opposition even among the Muslim League members, and on February 14, 1945, the Ministry was defeated with the help of some Muslim League votes. Hidayatullah behaved like a chastised child and declared " Sind is not fit for reforms. We in this House are teaching how to be treacherous," and then went away to sulk. As the result of this defeat, however, he reconstituted his Ministry by taking Khan Bahadur Haji Moula Bux into his Cabinet and continued in office. Moula Bux, a brother of Mr. Allah Bux, was not a member of the Muslim League and he was naturally asked to sign the League pledge. Moula Bux refused and Hidayatulla was ordered by the League High Command to reconstitute his Cabinet once again. On March 12, 1945, Hidayatullah resigned and proceeded to reform his Ministry. In the meantime, Moula Bux went to the Governor and told him that *he* was in a position to form a stable

---

* For text of the letter see Appendix I.
† May 14, 1943.
‡ He was once again removed from his post, tried on charges of corruption and theft and convicted.

Ministry if he were given twelve hours' time. The Governor, how-ever, saw no reason why Moula Bux's bargaining should stabilize matters more effectively than the negotiations in which Hidayat-ullah was engaged. He, therefore, declined to entertain this proposal.

Hidayatullah's new Ministry ran a somewhat dubious and erratic course but succeeded in surviving, mainly, because the members of the Congress Assembly Party were not allowed to attend the session. Attempts were now made to overthrow Hidayatullah and G. M. Syed, President of the Sind Provincial Muslim League, led the opposition. G. M. Syed was promptly expelled from the League. On February 8, 1946 Hidayatullah again reconstituted his Cabinet. The members of the new Ministry were all Muslim Leaguers. The other groups now formed a coalition opposition under the leadership of G. M. Syed. On March 19, 1946, a no-confidence motion was moved against one of the Ministers. This was defeated by one vote, thirty voting against the motion and twenty-nine for it. The Assembly was then prorogued before any further injury could be inflicted on this drooping and sapless Ministry. The Assembly met again on July 11, 1946, to elect members for the All-India Constituent Assembly. A no-confidence motion was once again tabled but, on the first day, its discussion was avoided by taking up a technical objection and, the next day, the Assembly was prorogued by the Governor. G. M. Syed now appealed to the Governor and asked him to compel the League Ministry to resign. The Governor did not agree. A motion of no-confidence was tabled against the Min-istry and it was due to come up for discussion on September 10, 1946. The Ministry hoped to have the support of twenty-nine votes while the opposition consisted of thirty votes. The sixtieth mem-ber occupied the position of the Speaker who belonged to the Muslim League, but naturally could not vote. It was expected, therefore, that the no-confidence motion would be passed by one vote. To meet this unfortunate event, the Speaker resigned from his post of enforced and helpless impartiality so that he could vote against the no-confidence motion. The parties now numbered thirty each. The Deputy Speaker, Miss Jethi T. Sipahimalani, would have to sit in the chair, on the day the motion came up for discussion, and this would mean the reduction of the opposition party by one. The resignation of the Speaker had, therefore, re-versed the situation and the no-confidence motion must be lost by one vote. To meet this eventuality Miss Sipahimalani resigned from the post of Deputy Speaker. The result was that there was no one left to sit in the Speaker's chair. Mr. Fraser, a European member, had on previous occasions occupied the chair when both the Speaker and the Deputy Speaker were not available. It is said that he expressed his willingness to take the chair, but as he was the supporter of the Government this would have meant reducing the support of the Ministry by one vote. A stalemate had been reached and expectation ran high as to how this seeming impasse would be resolved. The Governor came to the rescue by exercising his special powers of dissolving the Assembly and ordering a general election.

During the interim period the Hidayatullah Ministry continued in office and exercised every kind of pressure and influence in shaping the course of the elections. The voters were intimidated, threatened and directed to support the Muslim League candidates. Sayad Murad Ali Shah, a supporter of Mr. G. M. Syed, was shot dead in his village by a Muslim League worker. Sayad Jandial Shah, another supporter of the Coalition Party, was arrested and refused bail. Haji Moula Bux stood against a Muslim League candidate and was declared elected. League hooligans avenged their defeat by assaulting him outside the office of the Revenue Commissioner and Returning Officer. He was abused and beaten in the presence of the Returning Officer and the police, but no one chose to interfere. Haji Moula Bux's son, Mansoor, was also belaboured by Muslim League hooligans. Independent Hindu Mukhtarkars were transferred just before the elections. Muslim Presiding Officers, known for their integrity, were made to resign. An official took leave and openly worked for a League candidate. A rich Zemindar undergoing a sentence of twenty years' imprisonment was prematurely released. Land was given to another on condition he helped Sir Ghulam Hussain's son, Anwar. Five hundred persons were brought from Hyderabad (Sind) to impersonate voters in Karachi District. Mr. G. M. Syed complained of last minute changes in his polling stations and Presiding and Polling Officers, indicating a plan of impersonation on a large scale. The election results showed that these efforts had succeeded in attaining the desired object. The Muslim League secured thirty-five seats out of a total of sixty and thus obtained an absolute majority in the new House.

On the creation of Pakistan, Hidayatullah became Governor of Sind. His previous supporter and rival, Mr. Khurho, became the Premier but he was very soon dismissed by Hidayatullah under Mr. Jinnah's instructions and was placed before a Special Tribunal to stand an enquiry into charges of corruption and malpractices. Pir Illahi Bux succeeded Mr. Khurho as Premier. Five daily newspapers of Karachi, soon afterwards, started a campaign against him and demanded his instant removal. As the result of an election petition against him, his election was declared invalid on the ground of corrupt practices and he was forced to resign.

This brief narrative of the political events in Sind shows that Provincial Government was reduced to a travesty of the administrative machinery. Party alignment was based on considerations of personal gain rather than on moral conviction or a desire to do public good. The voting in the General Election of 1945-46, which was fought on the issue of Pakistan, showed that only 46.3 per cent of the Muslim votes were cast for the League candidates ; and only 20.8 per cent of the total electorate voted for the Muslim League. Thus, although the population was predominantly Muslim, the support for the Muslim League was extremely meagre. In the circumstances, it is not surprising that the Ministers were weak and liable to be swayed from their resolve by petty intrigues. Sir Hugh Dow took over the Governorship of the province in April 1941, and, soon afterwards, began to interfere in the day-to-day administration of Government. Mr. Allah Bux, who was the Premier at that time, felt greatly agitated by this circumstance and brought the matter up in the Assembly. He, however, felt helpless and said that he had referred the question to the Viceroy, and added that it was no use his " resigning in a huff." He, no doubt, realized that if he went out of office the Governor would at once be able to find someone more accommodating and less protesting. When personal advancement is the main moving force in politics and where the various parties are unstable and subject to constant change, the Government cannot retain a firm hold on administration and maintain law and order. The various Ministries which held office in Sind never made a serious attempt to deal with this important problem. Disorders were at various times allowed to spread over large areas and undermine the administration. The Pir of Pagaro and the activities of his nefarious band of marauders contributed, in no small measure, to this unfortunate state of affairs, and, in 1942, the Pir's disciples, whose numbers extend into several thousands, terrorized whole districts by indulging in wholesale murder, sabotage and dacoity. It was only after Martial Law was proclaimed in Sind on June 1942, that these fanatical followers of the Pir could be brought under control. Their suppression was no easy matter, for the Hurs, as these disciples are called, were skilled gangsters, having behind them a history of seventy years of crime. Their chief arm was the axe, although they also possessed large quantities of firearms and ammunition. They had succeeded in overawing the population by using the weapon of reprisal against all unfriendly acts. Their main hide-out was in a thick forest where they could easily evade arrest. The Hurs were essentially a criminal tribe and their activities were not of a communal nature ; but, after their suppression, the spirit of lawlessness which they had disseminated in the province gave rise to a strong anti-Hindu feeling and this was utilized by the Muslim League protagonists in arousing the Muslim masses. A prominent Hur was tried and convicted of the murder of Mr. Allah Bux who had refused to line up with the Muslim League.

The Muslim leaders had, for some time before the establishment of Pakistan, carried on a ruthless anti-Hindu propaganda and their utterances were not calculated to promote peace. Mr. Khurho during his election campaign for the Sind Legislative Assembly in 1945-46 is reported to have said, " I am looking forward to the day when the Hindus in Sind will be so impoverished or economically weakened that their women, even like poor Muslim women now, will be constrained to carry on their heads the midday food to their husbands, brothers and sons toiling in the fields and market places." * Later on, when he became Minister for Public Works, he declared, " Let the Hindus of Sind leave Sind and go elsewhere. Let them go while the going is good and possible, else I warn them that a time is fast coming when in their flight from Sind, they may not be able to get a horse or an ass or a *gari* or any other means of transport."† Agha Badaruddin Ahmad, M.L.A., Deputy Speaker of the Sind Legislative Assembly, in a letter, addressed to the Sukkur District Muslim League Conference, said : " These Muslims are anxiously and restlessly straining their ears to hear the sound of the hooves of galloping horses, the rattling of the swords and the sky-rending slogans of ' *Allah-o-Akbar* ' of Muslim crusaders."‡ Pir Ilahi Bux, Minister for

---

* Quoted by Parsram V. Tahilramani in " Why the Exodus from Sind."
† " Why the Exodus from Sind," by Parasram V. Tahilramani.
‡ *Alwahid*, Karachi, dated April 9, 1947.

Education and Local Self-Government,* in the course of a speech which he delivered at Jacobabad in April 1947, said that the Muslims would give the Hindus a fourth battle of Panipat where the Hindus would meet their Waterloo. The Muslim Press in Sind was equally violent. *Dawn,* which is the official organ of the Muslim League, in its issue of September 13, 1947, called upon the Muslim League National Guards to help in searching the baggage and persons of Hindu passengers, both male and female, who were leaving for India. The *Hilal-e-Pakistan,* a Sindhi daily of Hyderabad, published a fanatical article on October 6, 1947, and called upon the Muslim criminals and hooligans to devote their energies in victimising Hindus.

" You should neither kill nor rob Muslims. On the contrary, your full strength, valour and weapons should be used to wreak vengeance on those people with whom even today thousands of Muslim women are prisoners. . . . Every Muslim who casts his eye on this article and happens to know any dacoit, thief, aggressor or a *Patharidar* should carry our request to him and should instruct him to convey the exact sense of our appeal to members of his Jamiat. . . . You should inform us about your Association or meet us so that we may give you requisite instructions and directions."

This was published after the partition of the country and shows the extent to which the emotions of the Muslim masses were being worked up.

The lead given by the Muslim leaders was quickly followed by religious preceptors and the local Zemindars who saw in this anti-Hindu propaganda an opportunity for the satisfaction of personal greed. The Pir of Barchundi of Ubavero Taluqa in Sukkur District had a large following of *murids* (disciples). He had always supported the League candidates in the Assembly elections and, therefore, enjoyed the confidence of the League Ministers. He began to exhort his disciples to terrorize the Hindus and deprive them of their crops and lands. Qazi Fazal Ullah of District Larkhana is reported to have said, " Take your sword in one hand and your Quran in the other and win for Islam a superior position." The smaller Zemindars urged their tenants to harass Hindus, deprive them of their crops and plunder their houses. The seeds

---

* Now the Premier of Sind.

of unrest and communal hatred sown in this manner soon bore fruit.

The attitude of the Sind Muslims towards the Hindus became increasingly arrogant and overbearing. The element of financial gain was, of course, predominant in shaping their conduct. The authorities responsible for keeping law and order were indifferent to this state of affairs and they had no real desire to maintain peace among the two communities. Some time before the partition of the country, a few sporadic attacks on Hindu person and property began in the southern districts of Sind. There were, however, no extensive disorders until the Muslim refugees from East Punjab began to arrive and spread stories of atrocities to which they had been subjected by the non-Muslims. They had been uprooted from their homes. They had seen massacre and looting on a large scale and were not slow to wreak vengeance upon the Sind Hindus and Sikhs. The initiative taken by them was followed up by the Sind Muslims. In some few cases the local Muslims tried to intervene. They promised protection to the Hindus and made half-hearted and feeble attempts to ward off the attacks made by the Muslim fanatics but very soon they, too, joined the band of marauders, in the hope of enriching themselves at the cost of the Hindus. There is mention of one Khan Bahadur Sardar Jogan Khan of village Jogan in Sukkur District who assured the Hindu villagers that he would safeguard their life and property. After the partition, however, he took a prominent part in looting them. Faqir Ghulam Ali, the headman of village Kandri, is mentioned as having saved the lives of the Hindu villagers but not their property, in which he took his due share.

There were two distinct lines of attack upon Sind Hindus. Of these the most important was economic pressure brought to bear from all sides, and, in this, the Muslim officials took a very prominent part. Mention has been made of the attitude of the Muslim Zemindars towards the Hindu and Sikh population. This manifested itself in the deprivation of the crops of the Hindu tenants by the Muslim landlords. The Zemindars refused to give a share of the crop to the Hindu *haris*. The Muslim *haris* refused to hand over the crops of the Hindu Zemindars. The Revenue Authorities demanded payment of land revenue before the due date ; and the Muslim *haris* were instructed not to hand over any portion of the crops until the receipts for land revenue were shown to them. They openly carted away the harvested grain while the

Hindu owners looked on helplessly. In one case a Muslim land-lord carried away the entire crop reaped by a Hindu tenant. The tenant sued the landlord but, one day, when he was returning to his village, he was waylaid and murdered. Hindus were not allowed to sell movable or immovable property. Even where they succeeded in securing a purchaser, they had to part with their goods for a mere pittance. One shopkeeper in village Bambro in Tharparkar District had to part with his entire stock-in-trade worth several thousand rupees for the paltry sum of Rs. 15. A medical dispensary at Phulji Railway Station was sold for Rs. 100. The District Magistrate of Larkana issued a proclamation that any Hindu selling property would be committing an offence punishable with six months' imprisonment. Three Hindus were actually detained for a number of days upon this charge. Thefts of Hindu property in the rural areas assumed alarming proportions. Cattle were driven away from the grazing fields. Houses and shops were broken into and the goods therein carried away in broad daylight. A curious feature of these thefts was that even doors and windows of houses were removed and carried away. There were cases of dacoities in which the culprits were armed with firearms and battle-axes. One Sub-Inspector of Police removed the tiles from a religious institution in Dadu District. He used the tiles for his own house. The Mukhtarkar in village Ladhedero, District Dadu, asked the Muslim *haris* if they had celebrated Pakistan, which meant if they had looted the Hindu Zemindar of his produce.

Hindu occupiers of houses were driven out and Muslim refugees put in their place. In some cases Muslim refugees were billeted in Hindu quarters and their presence compelled the Hindus to leave. In one case a Hindu factory owner was served with notice that his factory would be taken over unless he purchased a certain quantity of rice for his factory within four days. The owner protested that his factory was working and that he had the requisite raw materials in stock. He was, thereupon, directed to hand the factory over to a Muslim. Millowners were told to take Muslims as their partners on pain of their mills being confiscated. In one case a Hindu was ordered to hand over his mill to a Muslim without any reasons being assigned. In village Daon-Vallo, District Sukkur, the Hindus were asked to leave the village and go to a place of safety under police escort. As soon as they had left, their houses were occupied by Muslim refugees who appropriated all the movable property left behind.

An order was issued by the local authorities calling upon Hindu business men and moneylenders to deposit all ornaments and valuables which the Muslims had pawned with them. These were then returned to the Muslim owners without discharging the debts due from them. Bhoja Mal, a moneylender of Dadu, had the temerity to ask for the payment of his dues. He was attacked and made to read the *Kalma*. He was then forced to drink curd from the same bowl as a Muslim and, after this indignity, he was told to go away. Hindus everywhere were asked to contribute towards Mr. Jinnah's Fund for the relief of refugees. In district Nawabshah, where Hindu oppression was at its worst, the District Magistrate declared that the Hindus must collect a sum of one lakh of rupees, otherwise they.would not be allowed to leave the district.

When a large-scale exodus from the province began, the Government introduced a permit system. On February 15, 1948, the Sind Government announced that no non-Muslim would be allowed to leave unless he was in possession of a permit issued by the proper authority. This led to gross abuse of powers and corruption on a very large scale. Only a limited number of permits was issued each day and the applicants had to pay heavily for them. Before a permit could be issued, the intending emigrant had to produce as many as eight certificates proving that he had discharged all his liabilities in Sind. This requirement prompted the Muslims to lay false claims against the Hindus, which meant delay and the expenditure of more money, for the Hindu had no other choice but to pay the blackmailer and obtain a certificate of discharge. Even after securing a permit, the troubles of the Hindu emigrant were not ended. He had to bribe the booking clerk heavily to buy a railway ticket. He was subjected to extensive searches and gross indignities. His womenfolk were undressed and searched under the gaze of men. The searchers took away valuables and ornaments without giving any receipt for them. In some cases even the food intended for consumption on the journey was taken away. An inter-Dominion agreement had been arrived at that no searches would be made and Mr. Liaquat Ali Khan, the Prime Minister of Pakistan, assured the Indian High Commissioner in Pakistan that evacuees would not be searched. The searches, however, continued and when the matter was brought to the notice of Mr. Khurho, the Sind Premier, he said: " I do not agree with the Pakistan Government that no searches should be made of the outgoing passengers. Their order seems to be unworkable as it would only mean putting a premium on dishonesty." * This was the manner in which the inter-Dominion agreement was respected by the Provincial Government. In Nawabshah the District Magistrate announced that no Hindu could carry away more than ten rupees with him. The luggage placed in the brake van was removed and, at the end of the journey, the owner found himself without any redress. Muslims entered crowded compartments and drove the Hindu passengers out in order to make room for themselves and, in the process, deprived them of a part of their belongings. Non-Muslim travellers were searched at several stages of their journey, and each time some part of their property was taken away. Sometimes when they arrived at their destination, they found themselves dispossessed of everything they had except the clothes they wore. Non-Muslims about to leave Refugee Camps in Karachi by boat were subjected to further searches. A juggler was deprived of his entire apparatus although it was of no use to the searchers.

Large numbers of temples and places of worship were desecrated by Muslim hooligans. In some cases the object was to loot, but more often the purpose was to give offence to the religious susceptibilities of the non-Muslims. Images were broken and thrown out of temples. The holy books were torn up, thrown in the mud and trampled upon. In many cases they were set fire to and burnt. If resistance was offered by the priest he was attacked and beaten and, in a few cases, murdered. The Sikhs from whose hands the Muslim refugees appeared to have suffered most in East Punjab were made the special target of attack and there were few Gurdwaras which escaped the attention of the looters.

This state of affairs made life impossible for the non-Muslims in Sind. Even where their life was safe their property and means of livelihood were taken away from them. When they wanted to leave, innumerable difficulties were placed in their way and *en route* they were subjected to all types of harassing indignities. In this way the bulk of the non-Muslim population emigrated from Sind. The figure given by the Pakistan Government in a *communique* published in the *Hindustan Times* in its issue of January 19, 1949, is 8,21,000, but it is estimated that out of 12 lakh non-Muslims, nearly 10 lakhs have already left and the exodus has not yet ended.

---

* Mr. Khurho was subsequently found guilty of having in his possession property stolen from non-Muslims.

The loss of life in Sind was not on the same scale as in West Punjab and the North-West Frontier Province but the number of murders, conversions and abductions was by no means inconsiderable. It is not possible to obtain exact figures though the murders must run into thousands and the number of persons forcibly converted to Islam cannot be less. The number of women abducted is probably not very large and the evidence of Hindu refugees shows that it was the poor labourers and *Odds* who suffered most in this respect. In the urban areas there were numerous cases of dacoities, in the course of which murders were committed. Soon after the arrival of Muslim refugees from East Punjab, crimes of violence increased rapidly. Mention is made, in the evidence of refugees, of marriage parties being attacked and looted. These attacks were invariably accompanied by loss of life. Lorries of refugees leaving villages were waylaid and attacked. In the town of Dadu, five Hindu families were forcibly converted to Islam and paraded through the streets, in a procession. There were a few attacks on trains involving loss of life. In village Madeji, district Sukkur, a Muslim mob attacked a Hindu lorry, murdering a number of persons. The culprits were identified and later apprehended by the police but then released, without further action being taken against them. The District Magistrate of Nawabshah openly declared that he wanted to do something for the Muslim refugees, and this emboldened them to such an extent that they made indiscriminate attacks on the lives of Hindus.

Particular mention must be made of the disturbances which took place in Quetta, Hyderabad and Karachi. Quetta is in Baluchistan but it is convenient to deal with that town in this chapter.

There was a general feeling of unrest in the minds of the Quetta Hindus but they decided to join hands with the Muslims in celebrating the establishment of Pakistan. On August 19, 1947, a number of Muslim refugees arrived in the town, and the stories of what they had been through greatly agitated the local Muslims. An extensive plan to attack Hindu houses was prepared and at about 9 p.m. on the 20th, a crowd of several thousand Muslims, drawn from among these refugees and the neighbouring villages, surrounded the entire town. Rumours had been whispered through the town that such an attack was contemplated and some prominent Hindus brought the matter to the notice of the police. No steps, were, however, taken to prevent the massacre that followed. Hindu houses all over the town were attacked, looted and burnt. The rioting went on throughout the night and the Hindus suffered very heavy casualties. There was a brief lull for about three hours on the morning of the 21st, and then at 9 a.m. the attack was resumed. Large numbers of Hindus and Sikhs lost their lives. Property worth over a crore of rupees was destroyed and it is estimated that more than a thousand persons were murdered. On the afternoon of the 21st, the Dogra troops entered the town and controlled the situation.

When news of the massacre in Quetta reached Sind a panic spread among the Hindus. Their fears were enhanced by a number of robberies and assaults which appeared to have been inspired by the happenings in Quetta. There was, however, no large-scale killing until December 17, 1947, when extensive rioting broke out in the town of Hyderabad. On December 16, 1947, a meeting was held in Hyderabad at which speakers gave false and exaggerated accounts of the burning of Ajmer Sharif and the murder of hundreds of Muslims. It was said that a train carrying large numbers of Muslim corpses was due to arrive at Hyderabad on the 17th. A huge mob of Muslims gathered at the railway station before the arrival of the train. When the train came it did not contain any corpses, but several Muslims who had come from Ajmer Sharif related their tales of suffering. These stories worked up the frenzy of the Muslim mob who at once left the railway station and invaded the entire town and started killing and looting. Hindu property and schools were attacked and burnt. It is estimated that over two hundred and fifty Hindus were killed in the course of this furious assault, while a thousand houses were looted. It is stated that Qazi Mohammad Akbar, Parliamentary Secretary, also took part in the looting. Hyderabad was a large and prosperous town with a majority of Hindu population. The business was almost entirely owned by Hindus who, therefore, suffered a great deal in this rioting. Trains of Hindu refugees from the rural areas were attacked and looted. The disturbance continued for several hours before it could be controlled.

These disorders in the southern districts of Sind compelled the non-Muslims to leave their homes, and large numbers of them arrived in Karachi on their way to the Indian Dominion. Some had to go by train, others by boat. Some of them were living with friends and relations in different parts of the city, while others had been housed in temporary refugee camps. Towards the end of 1947, the city of Karachi was overcrowded with these evacuees. On the morning of January 6, 1948, a party of Sikhs, numbering between two and three hundred, including women and children, arrived in Karachi. This party had travelled under police escort but no information of their arrival was given to India's Deputy High Commissioner in Pakistan who was stationed at Karachi. A mob of Punjabi Muslims saw the Sikhs arrive on the railway station and immediately showed signs of great agitation. The authorities responsible for keeping law and order displayed a reprehensive degree of indifference in regard to the safety of these Sikhs, and, instead of conveying the Sikhs under strong police or military escort, they sent them in open carriages to the Gurdwara of Ratan Talao which, at this stage, was surrounded by houses occupied by Muslim refugees.

News of the arrival of these Sikhs spread throughout the city and, within a very short time, a large crowd of Sindhi and Punjabi Muslims armed with hatchets, swords, knives, crowbars and *lathis* arrived in front of the Gurdwara and began to stone it. The Sikhs had locked themselves inside the Gurdwara but some of the crowd scaled the walls and entered the Gurdwara compound. They, however, found further progress barred. The Muslim neighbours on seeing this began to throw bags of live coal into the Gurdwara and soon the entire buiding was on fire. Many of the Sikhs were burnt alive. Those who tried to escape by coming out were set upon by the mob and done to death. At about 1-30 p.m., while this wholly one-sided battle was in progress, the police arrived with two trucks in order to remove the Sikhs from the Gurdwara. When the trucks were full the mob prevented the departure of the trucks, and all the passengers were butchered on the roadside. An eye-witness stated: " The crowd tried to break open the doors (of the Gurdwara) but they could not do so. There was one building in between the Gurdwara and the Ram Mandir and that building was occupied by Muslims. The inmates of that house threw coal bags from the top of the building in the Gurdwara compound for setting fire to it. At this stage a party of twenty armed constables arrived on the scene and asked the mob to disperse but the crowd refused to do so. The police kept silent." Another eye-witness stated: " At about 1-30 p.m., when this bloodshed was going on inside the Gurdwara, the police officials tried to remove the Sikhs in two trucks but the *goondas* did not allow the trucks to go and broke open the doors and

windows and started killing them in the trucks under the very
nose of the police."

The rioting continued in front of the Gurdwara till after
2 p.m. and the hooligans carried away a number of girls from the
spot. The mob was not pacified by this massacre ; in fact, their
frenzy increased and they rushed into other quarters of the city
shouting : " Kill the *kafirs*. Kill the Hindus. Loot the *kafirs*."
The hooligans indulged in an orgy of indiscriminate stabbing and
killing and many innocent women and children lost their lives in
the course of the afternoon. A mob went to the railway station
and attacked Hindu passengers. Some men entered the house of
a Gujerati Hindu and carried away three young girls. Their
mother was so overcome with grief that she picked up her two
infant children who had been left behind and jumped from the
balcony of her house. All three were killed instantaneously. The
father was thrown down from the same balcony by the hooligans
and he met the same fate. Some *goondas* were seen attacking a
young boy of seven. They stabbed him and then tearing his legs
apart threw the pieces of bleeding flesh on the ground. Dharma-
salas and refugee camps containing large numbers of Hindus
were attacked. The inmates were murdered and looted and a
number of young girls were abducted, women were raped and
subjected to horrible tortures.

At the railway station, the Hindu passengers, waiting on the
platforms and arriving by trains, passed through a terrible ordeal.
As soon as a train arrived, murderous-looking individuals surrounded it and started stabbing and looting Hindu passengers.
The Hindus rushed into the waiting rooms but there, too, they
were not safe. A big Zemindar of Sind who was formerly a
member of the Legislative Assembly arrived in Karachi that
morning and, when he saw the train being attacked by Muslim
goondas, he took out his gun to defend himself. A Sub-Inspector
of Police arrived and took away the gun from him, saying that
he had left his own behind. The Sub-Inspector then disappeared
with the gun and the Muslim crowd attacked the Zemindar's carriage and carried away his entire luggage. The Hindus, marooned
in the waiting rooms, could not get food or drink and policemen
posted to protect them charged as much as a rupee for a glass of
water.

The temples and Gurdwaras in the city were attacked and
desecrated. Guru Ramdas Durbar, the Jagannath Temple, the
Chidan Kashi Mandir, the temple of Bhai Vassyaram, the temple

of Guru Nanak, the Gurdwara near Rambaugh Garri Khata, the temples of Hanumanji in Ranchore Lines, the Sitla Mandir on Lawrence Road, the Jethmal Gurdwara in Garri Khata, the Swami Narain Temple, the Bhagnari Temple, and the Sharda Mandir were all attacked and wherever the mob could find any holy books they tore them or set fire to them.

In these disturbances the *goonda* element predominated but there is unimpeachable evidence showing the participation of large numbers of persons belonging to the middle classes. Even Government officials took part in the plunder. Well-dressed men were seen going about looting Hindu shops and houses and carrying away whatever could be of use to them. Members of the Pakistan Secretariat staff were subsequently found in possession of large quantities of looted property. There was considerable agitation against the action of Government in searching the houses of these officials and a deputation on their behalf represented to the Pakistan Authorities the unwisdom of this seemingly pro-Hindu conduct.

The rioting in Karachi continued for two days before the fury of the mob was spent. No accurate estimate of the casualties is possible. Several lorry-loads of dead bodies were taken to the cremation ground, piled up in heaps, sprayed with petrol and burnt. The number of those killed cannot have been less than three hundred and the number of injured about twice this number.

The events in Sind show that apart from the massacres of Hyderabad and Karachi there was no large-scale or organized attempt on the part of the Sind Muslims to exterminate the Hindus. The insidious propaganda which the League leaders had been carrying on throughout India for a number of years had made the Muslims arrogant and hostile towards the Hindus. This propaganda, coming at a time when the spirit of lawlessness had spread throughout Sind, gave rise to a feeling of insecurity and this further emboldened the Muslims. The prospect of loot and financial gain made them callous and regardless of the Hindu sufferings. The arrival of the Muslim refugees from East Punjab acted as a spark on this mass of inflammable material and set the whole province ablaze. In the southern districts, murders, dacoities and robberies with violence were on a much larger scale than in the northern districts where the hooligans mostly confined themselves to looting the property of the Hindus and driving them away from their homes.

V]

Last came Anarchy: he rode
On a white horse, splashed with blood;
He was pale even to the lips,
Like Death in the Apocalypse.

And he wore a kingly crown;
And in his grasp a sceptre shone;
On his brow this mark I saw—
'I AM GOD, AND KING, AND LAW!'

And a mighty troop around,
With their trampling shook the ground,
Waving each a bloody sword;
For the service of their Lord.

And each dweller, panic-stricken,
Felt his heart with terror sicken
Hearing the tempestuous cry
Of the triumph of Anarchy.

Then all cried with one accord,
'Thou art King, and God, and Lord;
Anarchy, to thee we bow,
Be thy name made holy now!'

And Anarchy, the Skeleton,
Bowed and grinned to every one.

PERCY BYSSHE SHELLEY—*The Mask of Anarchy*

CHAPTER SIX

NORTH-WEST FRONTIER PROVINCE

THE North-West Frontier Pathan is a curious mixture of brutality and kindness, greed and generous hospitality, unstinted loyalty and venomous treachery. He combines a fanatical jealousy for the honour of his womenfolk with a notorious perversity in his sexual relations. He will kidnap a woman or a man with wealthy and influential connections for the sake of a rich ransom, and risk his life and liberty to steal food for his hostage. He will expose himself to any danger in order to protect a worthless neighbour, and kill his greatest friend if he suspects him of having an impure thought about his wife or daughter. Quick-tempered and easily excitable, he is ready to use his gun or dagger at the slightest provocation. It has been said that he loves his gun more than his brother. But more than either of these, he loves his personal freedom which he exalts to the level of licence. He makes a fetish of his honour and never forgives what he considers an insult or slight to his self-esteem. Seven hundred years of Indian influence have not obliterated his distinct racial character, and though he has imbibed the culture of his adopted home, and intermarriage has diluted his race purity, he is easily recognizable by the peculiar cast of his features ; he speaks a different language ; and observes different customs. His songs and dances are redolent of his far-flung origin and have more in common with the folk art of Central Asia than the forms in which the Hindus and Muslims of India express their emotional complexes.

At the census of 1941 the total population of the North-West Frontier Province was 30.38 lakhs of which 91.79 per cent were Muslims. The districts of Dera Ismail Khan and Bannu had the largest proportion of non-Muslims who comprised 14.2 and 13 per cent respectively. In Mardan there were only 2.1 per cent Hindus and in Hazara only 3.8 per cent. In the rural areas the Hindus formed a very small and helpless minority of the population. The members of their community were mostly petty shopkeepers and traders. In some villages there were not more than two or three Hindu families and their safety depended entirely on the goodwill and friendly relations of their Muslim neighbours. The position of the Hindus in the cities was stronger. Their business was more lucrative and they wielded greater financial power. They paid 80 per cent of the total income-tax of the province.

Life in the Pathan country is hard and economically precarious. Food is scarce and industrial occupation is negligible. Scarcely one-fourth of the total province is under cultivation. To earn a living by productive effort is not always easy. Agriculture, fruit farming, trade and ordnance factories, both licit and illicit, do not provide employment for all, and a considerable proportion of the population lives on blackmail, hush money, kidnapping fees, moneylending and looting. Primitive, illiterate and ungovernable, the Pathan is singularly susceptible to catch-phrases and slogans.

This malleable and inflammable material was subjected during recent years to two distinct and opposing forces. The two Khan brothers, Dr. Khan Sahib and Khan Abdul Ghaffar Khan, strove to shape the Pathan ideology in the mould of Gandhian ethics and achieved a remarkable degree of success. Dr. Khan Sahib as the head of three Congress Ministries piloted the province through some difficult times, while his younger brother, Khan Abdul Ghaffar Khan, a rich landlord, who give up a life of luxury and ease, organized the Red Shirt movement. The " Red Shirts " was the popular name of the army of Khudai Khidmatgars who wore a distinctive red-coloured shirt and pledged themselves to peace, non-violence and public service. They were followers of Gandhiji whom they referred to as " Malang Baba." * Their numbers ran into thousands and their leader, Khan Abdul Ghaffar Khan or Badshah Khan, as he was sometimes called, soon came to be known as the Frontier Gandhi. The manner in which thousands of unruly and turbulent Pathans accepted the creed of *ahimsa* and practised it, evoked the wonder and admiration of all, and it was said that Khan Abdul Ghaffar Khan had worked a veritable miracle in the Frontier. The Red Shirts remained non-violent under the gravest provocation and on, at least, one occasion brought peace to the city of Peshawar at a most critical moment.

The other force at work was the sinister influence of the Muslim League exercised through Sardar Aurangzeb Khan and Abdul Rab Nishtar assisted by the local British and Muslim officials. During the election campaign of 1937 these officials opposed the Congress Party and the Khudai Khidmatgars in every

---

* Literally an ascetic *faqir*.

conceivable manner. Khan Abdul Ghaffar Khan, Pandit Nehru, Sardar Vallabhbhai Patel and Bhulabhai Desai were not allowed to enter the province. The nomination papers of Khudai Khidmatgar candidates were rejected by Returning Officers on scarcely tenable technical grounds. " A Deputy Commissioner forcibly prevented the voters from going to cast their votes with the result that about six hundred people could not record their verdict. Another officer, in charge of conducting the elections throughout the province, openly conspired with the rivals of the Congress and helped them to choose places and dates of polling, and gave a free hand to the Polling Officers to act in their interests." *

It is to be remembered that the Governor and the officials of the North-West Frontier Province exercised dual functions. In respect of the non-tribal areas the officials were under the Ministry, and the Governor acted through his Ministers. In respect of the tribal area, however, the Governor acted as the agent of the Governor-General and was not answerable to the Ministry in power. The officials also acted independently of the Ministry. Thus a Secretary was answerable to the Ministry for acts and orders relating to the non-tribal area, but he was answerable only to the Governor (as agent to the Governor-General) for all acts and orders relating to the tribal area. This somewhat anomalous position placed the majority of the officials beyond the strict control of the Ministry and enabled them to take an active part in supporting the League agitation.

So strong, however, was the hold of the Congress over the Pathan mind that no Muslim Leaguer was returned to the first elected Legislature. Mr. Jinnah paid a visit to the province, but his cries of appeal fell on deaf ears. In his own words he " was, to put in one word, dismissed from the Province."† Thus, until 1938, there was no Muslim League Party in the Provincial Legislative Assembly. In January of that year several Muslim agitators, including Maulana Zafar Ali Khan and Maulana Shaukat Ali Khan, were sent to the North-West Frontier Province and their efforts succeeded in winning a measure of support for the Muslim League. Eight members of the Assembly elected on the Independent ticket formed themselves into a nucleus of the Muslim League Party in the Legislature and, by the end of 1945, their number had swelled to eighteen. This figure fell to seventeen

---

* " Frontier Speaks," Mohammed Yunus, 1942.
† *Pakistan Times*, April 20, 1948.

after the General Elections of 1945-46. At about this time, Sardar Aurangzeb Khan lost the active support of the League High Command, owing to his incompetence and inability to deal with corruption and maladministration; and Khan Abdul Qaiyum Khan, originally a staunch nationalist and Deputy Leader of the Congress Party in the Central Legislature, came into prominence as a leader of the Muslim League Party. He is the present* Premier of the North-West Frontier Province.

We shall presently see what results were brought about by these two opposing forces and in what manner; but for the correct appreciation of these matters it is necessary to review briefly the recent political events in the Frontier.

The Government of India Act of 1935 provided for a Provincial Legislature of fifty members. The first elections under the Act were held in 1937, and the party position was as follows: Congress 19 (including 15 Muslims), Hindu and Sikh Nationalist Party 7 and Independents 24 (including 21 Muslims). The Congress Party did not come forward to form a Ministry at once as negotiations between the Congress High Command and the British Government regarding the exact position of the Provincial Governors in administrative matters were proceeding, and Sir George Cunningham, the Governor of the North-West Frontier Province, invited Nawabzada Sir Abdul Qayyum to form a Ministry. This invitation was accepted. Sir Abdul Qayyum was able to secure the support of some independent members and the Hindu and Sikh members of the Nationalist Party. The Ministry, however, did not command a majority in the Assembly and Sir Abdul Qayyum's tenure of office was very brief. For some months the Assembly was not convened but, as soon as it met, a no-confidence motion, tabled by Dr. Khan Sahib on September 3, 1937, was carried by twenty-seven votes to twenty-two. Four days later Dr. Khan Sahib formed a new Ministry and this remained in office till October 1939. Its achievements, during this brief period of a little over two years, included the abolition of the institution of Honorary Magistrates and the removal of Zaildars and Muafidars. These individuals had constituted a body of corrupt, sycophantic supporters of the British officials and their dismissal deprived the bureaucracy of a permanent and reliable instrument of their designs. Their own discontent made them walk into the League camp.†

---

* 1949.
† See note in Appendix I, page 317.

After the declaration of war, the Congress High Command issued instructions to all the Congress Ministries to resign. Dr. Khan Sahib's Ministry complied with this order and the Governor took over the administration of the province under the provisions of section 93, Government of India Act of 1935. This state of affairs continued till May 25, 1943. The proclamation under section 93 was then revoked and the Governor invited Sardar Aurangzeb Khan to form a Ministry. During the movement of 1942, ten members of the Congress Party in the Provincial Legislature had been arrested and imprisoned. Six of these were later released. The Ministry formed by Sardar Aurangzeb Khan did not command a majority but the Congress Party, attenuated by the incarceration of four members and the indisposition of one more who was in hospital, did not take any part in the Assembly proceedings and remained absent from the autumn session of 1943. The position of the minority Ministry was somewhat precarious and it felt compelled to offer the bribe of money and office to its supporters. Its first Legislative Act was to pass a Bill increasing the salaries of the Ministers to almost three times the previous amount. The number of Ministers was increased from three to five, and seven of its supporters were given various other posts as Speaker, Deputy Speaker and Parliamentary Secretaries.

These artificial props, however, did not succeed in keeping the Ministry long in power and on March 12, 1945, Dr. Khan Sahib again tabled a no-confidence motion against the Ministry and this motion was carried by twenty-four votes to eighteen. He had received instructions from the Congress High Command to accept office and form a Ministry after the defeat of the Aurangzeb Khan Cabinet. The strength of the ministerial party at this time was twenty-seven. The Muslim League Party, as stated above, numbered eighteen. General elections were again held in 1945-46 and these elections witnessed the activities of the alliance formed between the Muslim League and the officials. Mr. Jinnah again visited the province. A number of students from Aligarh were sent to preach communal hatred. The Congress voters were threatened and intimidated by Police and Civil officials. Khan Abdul Ghaffar Khan said : " I know for certain that women voters in the constituency of Qazi Attaullah Khan, Education Minister, were waylaid by certain armed *goondas* and, even when they managed to reach the polling booth, they were not permitted to poll. Because of this about three hundred ladies could not vote. Similarly, another of our candidates was deprived of about four hundred votes in Razzar Constituency. In one constituency the ballot-box of the Congress candidate had been broken."* In spite of these efforts the Congress was victorious at the polls. The party strength was: Congress 30, Muslim League 17, Jamiat-ul-Ulema-i-Hind (Nationalist Muslims supporting the Congress programme) 2 and Akali 1. The voting showed that only 25 per cent of the total electorate voted for the Muslim League. The Congress defeated the Muslim League candidate in as many as nineteen contests while the Congress suffered a defeat in eight cases only.

The Congress, with a clear majority in the new Legislature, now formed a Ministry under the leadership of Dr. Khan Sahib and remained in office until August 22, 1947. Mr. Jinnah wanted Lord Mountbatten to make the Ministry resign. Sir Olaf Caroe, who was then the Provincial Governor, did his best to make Dr. Khan Sahib give up office. He called Dr. Khan Sahib on March 18, 1947, and referred to the presence of a large number of Red Shirts in Peshawar in most deprecating terms. A few days later he summoned the Cabinet and said, " The Englishman who did not allow the reforms to be introduced into the North-West Frontier Province in 1920 was a fool. He sent the Pathans into the Congress arms. I shall see that this mistake is rectified." He added that, since the last elections, the Muslim League had gained strength in the province and, therefore, the Assembly and the Ministry no longer represented the people. He asked Dr. Khan Sahib to form a Coalition Government with the Muslim League and ended by making a categorical demand: " Coalition Cabinet or general elections." The Ministry refused to choose either alternative, and this was the beginning of an open war between Sir Olaf Caroe and Dr. Khan Sahib's Ministry.

To resolve this impasse and carry out the plan of making the Frontier Province accede to Pakistan the device of holding a referendum was adopted. Ordinarily, the Provincial Assembly should have been asked to decide this issue. Mr. Jinnah and the British Government, however, took the view that the Assembly did not represent the people of the Frontier Province and, therefore, a referendum was necessary. The Pathan leaders wanted the issue of Pathanistan to go before the electorate so that the Pathans could decide whether (*a*) to accede to Hindustan, (*b*) to accede to Pakistan or (*c*) to remain independent of either Dominion. The Viceroy, however, refused to offer the alternative of Pathanistan and in the

---

* " The Pathan votes against Pakistan." Congress Central Election Board Pamphlet No. 11.

referendum the only issues were India or Pakistan. The Red Shirts and the Congress Party boycotted the referendum and the result was overwhelmingly in favour of Pakistan. It is to be observed, however, that the number of voters who went to the polls was less than fifty-one per cent of the total electorate.* The usual Muslim League methods were adopted during this referendum. The Pir of Manki Sharif or Manki Mullah, as he was called, assisted by a number of fanatical Maulvis, conducted a most virulent propaganda among the electors. Accession to India was interpreted as being synonymous with subordination to Hindu Raj, unislamic conduct and heresy. It is to be remembered that this referendum was held in an atmosphere of heat and poison brought about by months of communal bitterness and rioting. The susceptibilities of the ignorant and emotional Pathan were played upon and he was told that he had to choose between the Quran and the Gita. Men in *burqa*, posing as women, went to the polling booths over and over again and helped to swell the number of actual votes cast. The result was thus a foregone conclusion.

With the creation of Pakistan, Mr. Jinnah had obtained from Lord Mountbatten special powers as Governor-General of Pakistan to dismiss Provincial Ministries.† Within a week of assuming office he had recourse to these powers and Dr. Khan Sahib's Ministry was dismissed on August 22, 1947. Khan Abdul Qaiyum Khan then formed a purely Muslim League Ministry although he was still in a minority.‡

*   *   *   *

The rioting, killing and other anti-Hindu activities in the North-West Frontier passed through three successive phases ; (1) from the beginning of 1946 till about the third week of February

---

* The total electorate of the North-West Frontier Province consisted of 572,798 and of these only 289,244 voted for Pakistan.

† The Pakistan (Provincial Constitution) Order, 1947, (Notification No. G.G.O. 22, published in the *Gazette of India Extraordinary* dated the 14th August, 1947) amended sub-section (5) of section 51 of the Government of India Act, 1935, to read " (5) In the exercise of his functions under this section with respect to choosing and summoning and the dismissal of ministers, the Governor shall be under the general control of, and comply with such particular directions, if any, as may from time to time be given to him by the Governor-General."

‡ Dr. Khan Sahib gave the following account of this unsavoury episode:

" Before August 15, 1947, Mr. Jinnah tried to persuade Lord Mountbatten to make the Frontier Ministry resign, and several times the then Governor of the North-West Frontier Province, Sir Olaf Caroe, personally asked me to either tender resignation or take one Muslim League member in the Cabinet which I, of course, refused, as I was constitutionally installed as the Premier of the majority party in the Legislature. This attempt having failed, Mr. Jinnah tried again to prevail on Lord Mountbatten to dismiss the Ministry. This time the matter was referred to the then Secretary of State for India who refused to take such steps on the ground that it would be unconstitutional to interfere with the majority Ministry. After August 15, the newly appointed Governor, Sir George Cunningham, at once called upon me to resign which I flatly refused as on past occasions. As a sequel to this finally the unconstitutional step was taken by the Governor-General of Pakistan and my Ministry was straightaway dismissed." *Hindustan Times,* June 24, 1948.

1947 ; (2) from February 20, 1947, till August 22, 1947 ; and (3) from August 22, 1947, till the beginning of 1948.

The defeat of the Muslim League in the general elections of February 1946 had given rise to a feeling of frustration, and the chagrin of the League leaders was intensified when the Congress formed an Interim Government at the Centre on September 2, 1946. The Muslim Leaguers started a vigorous propaganda against the Sikhs, the Khudai Khidmatgars and the Congress. They proclaimed that "Hindu Nehru" was responsible for the bombing of the Waziri Tribes and that the Khudai Khidmatgars owed their victory to the support of the infidel Hindu. When Pandit Nehru announced his intention of visiting the Frontier, the League Party conducted an intensive campaign throughout the province. Sir Olaf Caroe had advised Pandit Nehru not to visit the Frontier but his advice was not accepted. Subsequent events showed that Sir Olaf did not disapprove of the League activities against him. Pandit Nehru was described as the murderer of the Muslims in Calcutta ; and, when he arrived at the Peshawar aerodrome, he was confronted by a violent and hostile demonstration led by no less a person than Khan Abdul Qaiyum Khan, the erstwhile Deputy Leader of the Congress Party at the Centre.* On the eve of his visit to the Khyber Agency, the Pir of Manki Sharif made a speech at Jamrud in which he incited the Afridis not to let the murderer of Muslims return alive. Pandit Nehru was met with hostile demonstrations organized by the Muslim League wherever he went and it was the influence of the Khan brothers and their vigilance that prevented the mischievous elements from doing any harm to his person. The tribal areas were, as has been pointed out above, under the direct control of the Provincial Governor and he was responsible for controlling or inspiring these disturbances.

Soon after Pandit Nehru's visit, the news of the unfortunate happenings in Bihar arrived, and this gave further opportunity to the Muslim Leaguers to intensify their campaign against the Khudai Khidmatgars and the non-Muslims. Batches of Muslim Leaguers from all over the province and the tribal area were sent to Bihar to see things for themselves. What had happened in Bihar was gruesome enough, but these Muslim Leaguers, on their return, gave accounts which were grossly exaggerated and distorted. They took out processions shouting " *Bihar ka badla Sarhad men leynge* " (" We will avenge Bihar in the Frontier ") and " *Khoon*

---

* The present Premier of the North-West Frontier Province.

ka badla khoon" ("Blood will be avenged by blood"). Some processionists marched through Hazara, exhibiting a number of skulls which they said were the remains of Muslims murdered in Bihar. They showed photographs of atrocities committed in Bihar, blood-stained clothes of children and torn and mutilated leaves of the Quran. It has been said that the skulls exhibited by the processionists were dug out of local graveyards. The exhibition, however, had the desired effect of arousing the bitterest type of communal feelings. A *khooni mushaira* (blood recital) was held in a hall, the entrance of which was decorated with human skulls and bones. A portrait of Khan Abdul Ghaffar Khan at one of Gandhiji's meetings was exhibited and it was pointed out that a Muslim was worshipping a Hindu Bania. It was said that he had committed a sin against God in allowing his son, Ghani, to marry a Parsi woman who was a fire-worshipper. Dr. Khan Sahib was maligned in a similar manner and the people were reminded that his daughter, Mariam, had married an Indian Christian. Bricks, said to belong to a mosque in Bihar which had been desecrated and demolished by Hindu rioters, were carried about and shown around. These demonstrations could not but result in arousing the wrath of the excitable Pathans beyond control.

Rioting began in a number of villages of the Hazara District in the beginning of December 1946. Oghi, Shamdhara, Batal, Balakot, Patan Kalan, Rangaryal, Manakrai, Bairkund and some other villages were attacked by the Muslim mobs. The Hindu population of these villages was small and quite unable to defend itself. The Hindu and Sikh shops were looted and set fire to. In some villages a few non-Muslims were murdered. There were instances of desecration of Gurdwaras and temples, but the energies of the Muslim mobs were concentrated chiefly on looting and burning. The disturbances spread to the hilly tracts of the district round about Nathia Galli and continued through the month of January 1947. Rajoia, a village ten miles from Abottabad, was attacked on January 1, and about eighty shops and houses, belonging to non-Muslims, were looted and burnt. Havelian was attacked on January 2, and the temples and Gurdwaras were plundered. Mori, Manshera, Nambal, Patan Khurd and Mulia were also attacked, in a similar manner, during the month of January 1947. A Sikh woman whose husband was murdered by the rioters was abducted in the end of December, and forcibly married to a Muslim. The matter was reported to the authorities and a Muslim
18

Magistrate was appointed to examine the woman. As the result of the statement made by her, Dr. Khan Sahib directed that the woman should be returned to her relations. This naturally caused resentment among the kidnappers and agitation was started against Dr. Khan Sahib. At about this time a number of by-elections in Hazara District had resulted in the victory of the Muslim League candidates, and, to celebrate this victory, a procession was taken out in the town of Mardan. The processionists went to the residence of the Deputy Commissioner and demanded the return of the Sikh girl who had been restored to her relations. The Deputy Commissioner promulgated an order prohibiting processions and public speeches under section 144, Criminal Procedure Code. Khan Abdul Qaiyum Khan defied this order and addressed the Muslim League procession. He was arrested on February 20, 1947, and this circumstance was utilized by the Leaguers in inciting further opposition to Dr. Khan Sahib's Ministry. A large mob attacked the residence of Dr. Khan Sahib in Peshawar and threw stones at it. Dr. Khan Sahib himself escaped but his son-in-law was injured.

The districts of Hazara and Dera Ismail Khan constitute the non-Pushto-speaking areas, and, in these two districts, the Punjabi influence predominates, whereas, in the remaining districts of the province which constitute the Pushto-speaking area the Congress had a strong hold over the Pathans. The Muslim League was, therefore, strongest in the districts of Hazara and Dera Ismail Khan, and the rioting in these two districts was much more violent than in the other districts. Hitherto trouble had been confined mainly to the district of Hazara although there had been stray incidents in Kohat, in which district the village Toghbala was attacked by a Muslim mob in the month of January. The civil disobedience movement, started by the Muslim League towards the end of February 1947, began to poison the atmosphere in the entire province and disturbances were witnessed in almost all the districts. A number of stabbing and shooting incidents took place in the city and cantonments of Peshawar, in the beginning of March. In the neighbouring villages, the Muslim Leaguers had begun to convert Hindus to Islam, and many of them had to be evacuated under military escort. The news of these happenings brought about a state of panic among the non-Muslim residents of Peshawar. For ten days they remained confined to their houses and did not dare to venture out in the streets. The Provincial Assembly was at the time holding its

Budget Session. The Ministry felt that if they took any drastic action the Governor might take the extreme step of dissolving the Assembly. They, therefore, kept their counsel until the budget was passed. Then they held a secret meeting and decided to call in the assistance of the Red Shirts. Whips were sent out in the evening and by the next morning ten thousand Red Shirts had arrived in Peshawar. They were posted throughout the city and their presence brought confidence to the people and normal conditions were restored.

In April 1947, Dera Ismail Khan was in flames. On the 14th and 15th attacks were made on the villages surrounding the town of Dera Ismail Khan and, on the 15th, a large mob invaded the city and began to loot and set fire to the non-Muslim shops and houses. The entire non-Muslim population withdrew and entrenched themselves in a distant quarter of the city from where they watched the destruction of their property in helpless despair. The assault continued for three whole days and it is estimated that about twelve hundred shops owned by non-Muslims were destroyed. This devastating attack reduced the city to a smouldering ruin at the end of three days. Attacks on other villages in the district followed and in some cases the entire non-Muslim population was killed or forcibly converted. Kulachi, a Tehsil headquarter town where about two thousand non-Muslims resided, was attacked by a mob of several thousands on April 22. The Frontier Constabulary present in the town did nothing to help or protect the non-Muslims and allowed the mob to loot and burn their houses. On May 2, Kulachi was again attacked by a Muslim mob led by a member of the Frontier Legislative Assembly and a Sub-Inspector of Police. During this month a number of villages in Kohat District was attacked by Muslim mobs. The casualties in these villages were not large because the number of non-Muslims was extremely small. These unfortunate people found themselves entirely at the mercy of the attackers and, when asked to embrace Islam, saw no other alternative but to submit. The non-Muslim residents of Kalagoth, on hearing of the trouble at Dera Ismail Khan, left their village in a body on April 16, 1947. They were, however, waylaid and attacked. They ran back to their village, pursued by the Muslims who burnt their houses and plundered the village Gurdwara. Village Paroa was attacked on April 15 and the attack continued through the night. The non-Muslim residents of the village tried to defend themselves as best they could. The attack was repeated the next night when the

Muslim mobs succeeded in breaking open a number of houses. On April 22, the police brought lorries in order to evacuate the non-Muslims. The lorries were attacked by a mob of Pathans who killed twelve Hindus and injured fifteen. In village Malana about sixty non-Muslim families lived. The village was attacked on April 15. Sixty houses and shops were looted and burnt and fifty-two persons were killed by a Muslim mob. It will be tiresome to repeat instances but there is overwhelming evidence to prove that almost every village in the district, containing non-Muslims, was attacked and looted in this way.

For some weeks there was comparative peace although stray attacks in towns and villages continued. For instance, village Lachi in district Kohat was attacked in the month of May. Village Teli in Waziristan was attacked in June, and in the same month a number of Hindus who left village Thal by train were attacked by a Muslim mob. Forty persons were killed and five women were abducted. Village Ambar Kalan in district Hazara was attacked in the end of July. But the efforts of Dr. Khan Sahib's Ministry were, to some extent, responsible for stemming the tide of lawlessness.

On August 15, 1947, Pakistan was established, and Mr. Jinnah found himself possessed with powers to dismiss a recalcitrant Congress Ministry. As soon as Khan Abdul Qaiyum Khan was installed in office, he began a virulent propaganda against the non-Muslims. Exaggerated accounts of the events in East Punjab and the atrocities to which the Muslims had been subjected, were spread throughout the province in order to arouse the passions of the Pathans. A deputation of the Muslim Leaguers was sent to East Punjab and the accounts which they gave on their return aggravated the situation. In the last week of August rioting on a very large scale broke out in the town of Haripur. Almost the entire Hindu property in the town was destroyed. The Hindu population, numbering several thousands, was taken to a refugee camp but the camp was attacked by Muslims and three hundred refugees were killed. The temples and Gurdwaras in Haripur were sacked and burnt. On August 27, village Lalogali in district Hazara was attacked and the Hindus were forcibly converted to Islam. Trouble spread to other districts and to Waziristan. The influence of the Khudai Khidmatgars in Bannu and in Mardan and Charsadda Tehsils was strong and there the disturbances did not assume large proportions. In the beginning of September arson, looting and killing started in Peshawar City. The attack this time was more determined and the Red Shirts could not come to the rescue. The assault began with the usual stories, spread by the Muslim Leaguers, that a mob of Sikhs had collected to attack the Muslims. In order to ward off this attack the Muslims were asked to arm and collect themselves in large numbers. The mob then proceeded against the imaginay Sikh assailants and attacked the suburbs of Peshawar. They invaded the city and went about looting, burning and killing. Some of the rioters were seen going about in jeeps and cars. Khan Abdul Qaiyum Khan, the Premier, had to go to Rawalpindi to meet the West Punjab Premier and rioting began soon after he left Peshawar on September 7. The following is an account given by an official of the Government of India posted at Peshawar at the time:

" Khan Abdul Qaiyum Khan could hardly have left Peshawar when Leaguers went about in a car in Peshawar City proclaiming that a Sikh regiment was going to attack Muslims. Similar emissaries went about in different parts of Peshawar Cantonment and adjoining villages on cycles, asking people to come out with guns and pistols to repel the Sikh attack. It was a Sunday and the shops were closed. Panic-stricken Hindus and Sikhs ran to their houses and shut themselves up in their *mohallas* and blocks. The myth of a Sikh attack has invariably been the signal for the butchery of minorities in the Frontier. On many occasions this false alarm has been successfully used, and the minorities in Peshawar at once sensed that the fateful hour had arrived.

" In the Cantonment, police guards at Salwan Refugee Camp and some other prominent shops and houses at once fled to the police station at this false alarm signal. To appeals from Hindus and Sikhs for posting of police and military and enforcement of curfew, the only answer given by the authorities was that Sikh and Muslim troops were fighting among themselves and all the force available was occupied there. This was again a myth which has been exploded by the military spokesman in New Delhi.

" Khan Abdul Qaiyum Khan has been loud in proclaiming to the outside world that enemies of Pakistan, i.e., Khudai Khidmatgars and Zalm-i-Pukhtoon, were responsible for the circulation of this false rumour. But his own clerk who answered the telephone call on the 7th, in his absence, repeated the story of Sikh and Muslim troops having clashed. The Deputy Commissioner and the Inspector-General of Police could not be contacted on the telephone. They were all out. But their clerks and orderlies who answered the telephone further harped on the same theme.

"Asked whether Khan Abdul Qaiyum Khan had been informed about the situation that was developing, his Personal Assistant replied that it was for the C.I.D. to do so.

"Thus the field was left open for the *goondas* to start murder and arson. Curfew was not even formally imposed till 5-30 p.m. The forces of law and order were either away from the scene or acted as full-fledged partisans. Little boys, servants and *malis* of Government officers, sweepers and riff-raff in the cantonments, absolutely unarmed, were seen breaking open the locks of shops and helping themselves to the goods while constables stood gossiping here and there. Occasionally they claimed their share of the loot when they saw something attractive.

"As the news of this universal loot spread to the adjoining villages, League Khans got into their cars with armed servants and carried back cart-loads of looted property. Within a couple of hours, threatening armed gangs from the neighbouring villages entered the City and Cantonments. They were guided by police or some local Leaguers to Hindu and Sikh shops. They broke open the locks by firing shots and escaped with lorry-loads of goods.

"More gruesome tragedies happened in the Civil Quarters and Railway Quarters where Hindu and Sikh Government servants along with their women and children were done to death. . . .

"For nearly twelve hours the non-Muslims fought the ruffians heroically while flames enveloped them and bullets were being showered on them. Some brave women committed suicide. The Civil Quarters are a stone's-throw from the Lines of the Frontier Constabulary. We cannot believe that the authorities were unaware of these happenings. Curfew was imposed at 5-30 p.m. The Deputy Commissioner himself told one of us on the telephone at about 6 p.m. that unfortunately there had been considerable loss of life in the Cantonments. The mob at the Civil Quarters was not very big. It is difficult to understand why no effort was made by him to rescue the non-Muslims till one of them managed to escape and knocked for help at his bungalow at about 10 p.m.

"In spite of the curfew, till Khan Abdul Qaiyum Khan arrived at 5 p.m. on Monday the 8th, loot, arson and murder went on unchecked. Fire consumed a part of the city. Shots rang on all sides. League-minded Muslim shopkeepers dumped the looted property in their shops and houses to be cleared at night by lorries, trucks, tongas and carts.

" While the Delhi Cloth Mills shop in Peshawar Cantonments was being looted at 1 p.m. on Monday the 8th, during curfew hours, both the West Police Station and the Deputy Commissioner were informed on the telephone of this happening. Military arrived on the spot and saw that bales were being removed. But after some ' chitchat ' with the ringleaders they went away. So did the police.

" The Private Secretary to the Governor was informed of the situation on the telephone on the 7th, i.e., Sunday evening. His reply was ' What can H.E. do? Ask the police.' The Chief Secretary gave the same reply on the 10th morning.

" It is difficult to assess the total number of deaths and the loss of property. Dead bodies were being removed from isolated houses in Cantonments for many days after these happenings. Conditions for several weeks did not permit free movement on the part of any member of the minorities. Two Hindus were shot dead in the city when they went from the refugee camp to their shops to collect their goods, a few days after the loot."

With the arrival of the Premier in Peshawar on the 8th evening, the situation was to some extent controlled, but this only diverted the attack from Peshawar to Nowshera where trouble broke out the same day. Nowshera Cantonment was attacked by a large riotous mob. In Nowshera the non-Muslims are in a majority but they found themselves helpless when assaulted suddenly by a furious armed mob. A number of bungalows and houses were set on fire. When the residents tried to escape they were shot dead. In one house a number of persons were burnt alive. The attack continued throughout the Cantonment until the afternoon of the 9th when the Jat military arrived and controlled the situation. It is estimated that about two thousand persons lost their lives and about four hundred women were abducted. Of these nearly half were restored subsequently.

The town of Abbottabad was subjected to a fierce attack on the night between the 6th and 7th December 1947. Mahasha Shiv Ram, a member of the Provincial Legislative Assembly who was in the military camp, was murdered.

We shall conclude this chapter by giving a brief account of the gruesome tragedy enacted at Parachinar towards the end of January 1948. Parachinar is a Kurram Agency Headquarters situated amongst the hills at a height of nearly six thousand feet. The Grand Trunk Road connects it with Thal and Kohat and there was a regular lorry service between Kohat and Parachinar. The railway station for Parachinar is Thal. The population of Parachinar was about eleven thousand persons of whom nearly two thousand were non-Muslims. Business and trade were almost entirely in the hands of Hindus and Sikhs who also owned a large area of agricultural land in the Kurram Agency. For some months, before the fighting in Kashmir began, arms were freely distributed among the Muslims who were asked to volunteer and join the raiders. On October 20, 1947, a Muslim dead body was brought from Kashmir to a village, five miles from Parachinar, and given a public burial. This infuriated the Muslims and they attacked the Hindus and Sikhs living in the village. The incident was regarded as a danger-signal by the non-Muslim residents of the neighbouring villages and they began to leave. The Assistant Political Agent; however, asked them to stay on, and gave them assurances of safety. On October 26, 1947, a Muslim mob, supported by the militia, made an attack on the Hindu quarter of Parachinar. They burnt some houses and desecrated the Gurdwara. Conditions deteriorated, and on November 4, 1947, the non-Muslims were asked to proceed to a camp near the Fort of Parachinar. They were allowed to take only twenty-two *seers* of personal luggage and some food. The camp was set up outside the walls of Parachinar Fort at a distance of about three miles from the town. The arms and ammunition of the non-Muslims who went to the camp were seized and taken away.

There were about fifteen hundred non-Muslims in this camp but the arrangements for their food and drink were far from satisfactory. They had to purchase their rations privately at exorbitant prices. The militia who were posted for their safety had to be bribed, and the officials demanded heavy bribes for escorting them to a place of safety. They agreed to evacuate them on promise of being paid Rs. 65,000. By the middle of November some more non-Muslims had arrived in the camp from the neighbouring villages and the total number rose to about two thousand. On December 5, 1947, Sir George Cunningham, the Provincial Governor, paid a visit to the camp. The refugees laid their difficulties before him and asked for immediate evacuation from the camp. The Governor, however, told them that he could make no arrangements for their transport, and returned to Peshawar. On

December 8, 1947, the Assistant Political Agent asked the refugees to go back to their houses and even had some of the tents pulled down in order to force them to leave the camp. It was bitterly cold at the time and some women and children died of exposure. The refugees, however, did not leave the camp as life in the villages was fraught with the gravest danger. A few days later the refugees were told that they would be forcibly ejected. This state of affairs continued until January 20, 1948, when the refugees heard that a Muslim mob was getting ready to attack the camp. On the following day, telegrams were sent to the Political Agent and other persons for help. On January 22, at about 11 a.m., some officers arrived and asked the refugees to get ready for removal to Arawali Camp. The refugees packed up their things and waited till 4 p.m. At that hour three lorries arrived to transport two thousand refugees. No one was prepared to leave the camp in these circumstances, but the militia beat the refugees and arrested four of them on the ground that they were spreading disaffection and dissuading the others from leaving the camp. That evening the camp was attacked by a large Muslim mob armed with guns, spears, hatchets, etc. The attack continued till 8-30 p.m. and the militia, numbering about five or six hundred, joined the attackers. One hundred and thirty-eight Hindus and Sikhs were killed, one hundred and fifty more were injured and two hundred and twenty-three women were carried away. The mob looted the entire property of the non-Muslims and some of them were seen searching the dead bodies.

When the news of this horrible massacre arrived in Delhi it was feared that communal rioting might once again disturb the peace of the metropolis, but extensive police precautions and the counsel of the saner elements were successful in preserving an atmosphere of calm and tranquillity.

VII

*Tous les hommes se ressemblent si fort qu'il n'y a point
de peuple dont les sottises ne nous doivent faire trembler.*

FONTENELLE

*Cet animal est très méchant
Quand on l'attaque il se défend.*

THEODORE

CHAPTER SEVEN

RETALIATION

THE events described in the preceding chapters could not but fail to arouse horror and indignation all over India, and more particularly in the eastern districts of the Punjab, where the arrival of large numbers of non-Muslims from West Punjab furnished concrete proof of the manner in which the plans and designs of the Muslim League were being executed. The burning and killing which took place in the towns of Lahore, Multan and Rawalpindi and in the rural areas of the districts of Rawalpindi, Multan and Jhelum, in the beginning of March, compelled thousands of Hindu and Sikh residents to leave their homes and seek temporary or permanent shelter in the comparative security of the Muslim minority districts. They related the tales of their sufferings and, as their anger mounted, they spoke of revenge and retaliation. During the months that followed, the pressure was kept up by the recrudescence of trouble in Lahore and by the constant influx of refugees from all parts of West Punjab. Hopes of a peaceful settlement and a satisfactory *rapprochement* receded with every fresh outbreak of communal frenzy. Resentment grew with the arrival of every batch of bereaved and impoverished persons. These people, bruised in their minds and bodies, deprived of their property and their means of livelihood, did not hesitate to exaggerate the severity of the blows inflicted upon them or the extent of their suffering. They had been unable to hit back at their assailants who heavily outnumbered them ; but the desire for revenge remained and, towards the end of July, began to assume the proportions of a categorical imperative. Stories began to be heard of small groups of Sikhs roaming the countryside in Amritsar District, and attacking a lonely Muslim or setting fire to a Muslim house. Serious trouble broke out in the town of Amritsar, in the beginning of August, and there was considerable loss of Muslim life and property. Lahore was once again ablaze, and the news of the happenings in that town had serious repercussions in several towns of East Punjab. The intensity of the rioting in Amritsar achieved a new record and began to spread to other districts. The division of the Punjab was given effect to on the midnight between the 14th and 15th of August 1947, although the Award of the

Boundary Commission was not announced till two days later. The terms of the Award caused a great deal of disappointment and frustration. The Sikhs made no secret of the resentment they felt at losing their historic shrinès and almost the entire rich colony area. They felt that the division of their community into two halves would result in the lowering of their political status in both parts of the Punjab. The Muslims had also lost some areas in which they had had a majority of population. The loss of Lahore and the consequent deprivation of a large number of cultural and educational institutions, of their property and wealth was keenly felt by the Hindus. At the same time, partition brought a certain measure of relief, for the non-Muslims in East Punjab felt that they had gained independence, though at a terrible cost. The feeling grew that Hindus and Sikhs could now retaliate with impunity and avenge some, at least, of the wrongs suffered at the hands of the Muslims in West Punjab.

The new regime in East Punjab started functioning in circumstances which were extremely abnormal. Not only did the new Government inherit a legacy of serious lawlessness and disorder from their predecessors ; but, for want of a suitable place to locate their headquarters, they had to split up their administrative machinery into several parts in order to find accommodation for the various offices and staff. The machinery for law and order, which had worked under a great strain for several months, was thrown completely out of gear by large-scale desertions of Muslim policemen, who predominated in the Force.* The lack of experienced and well-disciplined officers and hurried transfers and postings, even of senior officers, deprived them of the benefit of local knowledge and, to that extent, impaired their ability to deal with the difficult problems that faced them. Certain sections of people, who had been kept down by ruthless force by the previous administration, took advantage of this situation and started trouble both in towns and villages. The cumulative effect of it all was that the administration virtually broke down for about a week and there was considerable chaos and lawlessness in a large part of the province.

---

* 74.1 per cent of the regular Police Force in the united Punjab was Muslim and 78.2 per cent of the Additional Police was Muslim. In the Ambala Range, out of a total of 3,695 constables 1,861 were Muslims. In the Jullundur Range, out of a total of 3,368 police constables 2,119 were Muslims. In the Lahore Range, there were 5,403 Muslim constables out of a total of 7,205. The Government of East Punjab thus found themselves depleted of more than half of the available Police Force.

The Government and the leaders of all communities earned a great deal of criticism and odium at the hands of the public, during the first fortnight of the new regime. This was especially so among the Sikhs because their leaders had encouraged fond hopes of getting them their Gurdwaras and a part of the colony lands. An impression gained ground that Sikh leadership had proved unequal to the occasion, and the leaders had committed blunders which had resulted in the community being nearly ruined. The Congress leaders were accused of having brought this calamity on the non-Muslims of the Punjab by following a policy of appeasement towards Muslims and it was freely said that the intransigence of Mr. Jinnah had not been dealt with firmly. The Government were charged with inefficiency and tardiness in dealing with the border incidents, the evacuation and rehabilitation of refugees. East Punjab had no Press or other means of publicity to counteract this propaganda and this un-informed criticism held the field for a considerable time.

Following upon the disturbances in Amritsar, rioting, arson and murder broke out in the districts of Gurdaspur, Jullundur, Hoshiarpur, Ludhiana and Ferozepore. The trouble soon spread to the rural areas and there were reports of attacks and counter-attacks, on a large scale, in almost all districts of the Jullundur Division. It is impossible to make a correct estimate of the total number of persons killed but, it is feared, that several thousand persons lost their lives. Muslim losses in these riots were naturally much heavier than non-Muslim losses, but the loss of Hindu property was considerable. The news from West Punjab, where massacre and looting of non-Muslims on a large scale were taking place, continued to agitate the public mind. The atrocity stories led to flare-ups in several places and the authorities had the greatest difficulty in bringing the situation under control. As the refugees progressed eastward, communal trouble followed in their wake. By the end of August the atmosphere throughout East Punjab had become very tense, and it was realized that more trouble was in store.

The scale and extent of these riots had not been correctly foreseen and the arrangements made to deal with them proved inadequate. The Punjab Boundary Force, which had been specially set up to deal with disputes in connection with the de-marcation of the boundary, did useful work to start with, but the troops did not take long to become infected with communalism, and complaints of wanton and unprovoked excesses began coming in from several quarters. In answer to an insistent demand by the public, a decision to disband the Boundary Force was taken towards the end of August. Economic factors added to the troubles of Government and to the discontent in East Punjab. The food arrangements in rationed towns were thrown out of gear by the arrival of a very large number of refugees and, at some places, the position was precarious, indeed even dangerous. Complaints of shortages began to pour in from a number of districts and, with the complete dislocation of transport, food stocks could not be moved easily from the surplus to the deficit areas. This state of affairs led in various places to the looting of Muslim property.

During the month of September, communal incidents continued to occur in all parts of the province of East Punjab and rendered resumption of normal life difficult, except perhaps in some towns where the exist of the Muslim population and its replacement by Hindu and Sikh refugees gave some semblance of restoration of normal conditions. Border incidents were continuously reported in Ferozepore and Amritsar Districts. There were several instances of Muslim League National Guards and the West Punjab Police trespassing into East Punjab territory and taking away cattle and other property. Military vehicles were also alleged to have entered some districts with stocks of illicit arms for distribution among Muslims. The main theatres of trouble during the first fortnight of September were the three districts of the Hariana Tract—Karnal, Rohtak and Hissar. Trouble on a lesser scale also occurred in some districts of the Jullundur Division. Even Simla and Kangra Districts were affected and there were reports of sporadic cases of murder, arson and looting. The vernacular Press added fuel to the fire of frenzy by giving highly coloured and unilateral accounts of the unfortunate happenings on both sides of the border. We must also confess that there was a regrettable lack of honesty of purpose on the part of the police and certain other agencies in charge of the maintenance of law and order. This was found especially marked in the Railway Police in Ambala and a number of their men had to be arrested. A large number of arrests of policemen had to be made on charges of looting and murder in other districts also. This apathy of the police, combined with their inadequacy, made matters very difficult indeed. People who had suffered at the hands of the

Muslims in West Punjab, and they included non-Muslim police-men, found it difficult to resist or prevent the temptation of loot or to connive at damage to Muslim life and property.

Towards the end of August, a camp for about six thousand Muslims was set up in Hansi, district Hissar. A sweeping attack on this camp was made by Jats, Rajputs, Sikhs and Banias. The attack lasted for several days and resulted in very heayy loss of Muslim life.

Relations between the Muslims and the non-Muslims in the Ambala District had been strained for many years, particularly over the vexed question of cow-slaughter during *Id*. In previous years firing had been resorted to, in order to control the situation. Feeling in the Rupar Sub-Division had been particularly bitter owing to the grant of a new licence for cow-slaughter, three years before the partition took place, in a Muslim village, surrounded on all sides by Sikh villages, of which many were in the territory of the Patiala State. Every year military aid was called in to maintain peace in this village. Ambala occupied a central position for the evacuation of Muslim and non-Muslim refugees by rail, road and air. Non-Muslim refugees arrived in hundreds of thousands by trains and in thousands by planes for dispersal to the different districts of East Punjab. The proximity of five States (Patiala, Bilaspur, Nalagarh, Sirmur and Kalsia) was another handicap for the Ambala authorities in maintaining order. These States provided convenient spring-boards for marauders who launched their offensive and then quickly retreated before they could be appre-hended or dealt with. A camp for about sixty thousand Muslims was set up at Kurali (Rupar Sub-Division). Severe rioting broke out in several parts of Ambala District and the loss of Muslim life was heavy, particularly in the Rupar Sub-Division where it is estimated that between ten and twelve thousand Muslims lost their lives. Some other parts of the district were also affected and the Muslim evacuee camp at Kalka was attacked by an armed mob who opened fire and threw some hand-grenades, killing ten and injuring fifty. The assailants were driven off by the military guard. But Ambala City and Cantonments remained almost free from trouble. There was a large camp of nearly 180,000 Muslims near Ambala City and between thirty and forty thousand Muslims were living in their homes in the city of Ambala. The total loss of Muslim life in Ambala City and Cantonments was less than one hundred, though there was a certain amount of looting of Muslim property even after the Muslims had been evacuated.

19

Belongings of Muslims had been collected in dumps at convenient centres for safe custody, and much of this property was stolen and looted. It must be recorded that the Muslim refugees spoke very highly of the police arrangements made for their safety at the District Headquarters.

Trouble started in Simla on September 9. Owing to bitter communal tension in the police ranks, the Muslim police constables had to be disarmed. No military assistance was available and arson and looting on a considerable scale broke out. There were also several cases of stabbing. The exploding of two hand-grenades, in the Muslim refugee camp, resulted in the death of thirteen Muslims and the wounding of fifteen others. It was reported that bands of Sikh marauders from Patiala were mainly responsible for the trouble in Simla. The Bishop of Lahore who was at the time staying in Simla, wrote: "Two days ago I buried an old friend of mine who died of cancer. We had the greatest difficulty in getting her body to the cemetery as our bier-bearers were all Muslims. We got police escort in the end. On the way we came across one Muslim hacked to death: on the way back two or three more—coolies carrying loads who had no chance of defending themselves."

There were several attacks on trains between Jullundur and Ludhiana and between Ludhiana and Rajpura. Sikh *jathas* from Patiala were said to be responsible for these attacks. The authorities, at this time, were dismayed to see that there was "very little evidence of willingness on the part of the Sikhs to cry a halt." It will be remembered that, by this time, the Sikhs had become special targets of Muslim fury in West Punjab. A Sikh was not safe anywhere and was killed at sight.

Serious trouble broke out at Hoshiarpur towards the end of August. The situation at Ludhiana showed no sign of improving.

Delhi had been used as a base by the Muslim League and the police had received reports of underground activities on the part of the League National Guards. An abortive attempt to create disorder, in November 1946, failed but Muslim preparations continued, and there is abundant evidence to show that arms were being secretly collected by the Muslims. Riots broke out in Delhi in the beginning of September, and for a fortnight, beginning September 6, large-scale looting of property and stabbing in almost all localities of the capital took place. In these riots Muslims were found to be heavily armed. They used automatic weapons, country-made cannons, rifles, bombs, mortars and other missiles. It was reported that Muslim ammunition dealers had restricted the sale of ammunition to members of their own community and this sale was on a fairly liberal scale. One Haji Obedullah played a prominent part in the riots in the area of Subzimandi and he was responsible for importing large quantities of weapons into Delhi. The shops of Muslim blacksmiths and motor mechanics were converted into small arsenals where spears, mortars and crude muzzle-loading guns were manufactured. After the riots, it was discovered that many Muslim localities had been provided with a wireless transmitter and receiving set ; and these instruments were used for exchanging messages between the various areas. As many as thirteen wireless transmitters were recovered by the police. A burnt Signal Corps Radio Transmitter was recovered from the remains of the *Dawn* Press which had been set on fire. In Subzimandi area a tunnel was discovered in which a large quantity of arms and ammunition had been stored. Loss of Muslim life in the Delhi riots was considerable and, although the exact numbers cannot be determined, the police received reports of five hundred and seven Muslims killed and two hundred and ninety-seven injured. It is almost certain that an equal number of killed and wounded was not reported to the police and the total casualties may, therefore, be placed at more than one thousand killed and an equal number injured. As against this seventy-six Hindus were reported to have been killed and ninety-seven injured. These figures, however, do not correctly indicate the provocation given by the Muslims. The first incident occurred on August 21, 1947, when an explosion took place in Shahadara, in a house belonging to a Muslim student. It was believed that the student was trying to prepare a bomb which exploded accidentally. On August 25, four Muslim workers of the Birla Mills were killed during a scuffle between the Hindu and Muslim workers. On the night of September 3, a bomb exploded in a Hindu locality in Qarol Bagh. A rumour spread through the locality that the bomb had been thrown by a Muslim. Whether this rumour was correct or false, it led to a sudden flare-up of communal frenzy and rioting began in the Qarol Bagh area. A mob of rowdy Muslims was seen parading the streets and Dr. Joshi, a resident of Qarol Bagh, went out to reason with them. He was shot dead by Dr. Qureshi who was in the mob. This incident had serious repercussions in other parts of Delhi.* Rioting spread soon afterwards to Subzimandi, Turkman Gate, Paharganj, Phatak Habash Khan and other parts of the city.

The Delhi Police Force was sixty per cent Muslim and the Civil Authorities found it difficult to control the situation. There was constant firing by the Muslims in Paharganj, Subzimandi and Turkman Gate. The Khaksars confined in the District Jail attacked and killed a Hindu warder, and the police had to open fire upon them. In the Subzimandi area a veritable battle between the Muslims and the police lasted for a whole day. The official account says: " On September 8, at 7 a.m., a police patrol, headed by a Sub-Inspector on duty in Subzimandi area, heard sounds of firing. They proceeded to the scene of occurrence and saw the Muslims firing on Hindus of the locality. The police party returned the fire but many of them were wounded, including an Assistant Sub-Inspector who had to be sent to hospital. As the police force available was inadequate, military help was sought and a posse of military arrived at the spot with a Magistrate. The Muslims opened fire on the military also and wounded several men. Another Assistant Sub-Inspector of Police was fatally shot by the Muslims. The Subzimandi Police Station was also fired at, and the battle continued till 6 p.m. when the Muslims surrendered and asked to be evacuated to a safe place."

Reports of these occurrences exacerbated the non-Muslim feeling in the capital and large-scale looting and burning of Muslim property was reported from several quarters of the city. There were also attacks on Muslim life and in the course of four days several hundred Muslims were murdered. There was a great deal of disturbance in the rural areas surrounding the capital. Muslim villages were attacked and set on fire and the residents were murdered. In many instances, the Muslims were found to be armed with firearms, but they were heavily outnumbered and quickly overpowered. In some villages trouble was started by the Meo residents. Hindu villages were attacked and burnt down. The Meos were ultimately driven out and many of them were wiped out in the neighbouring State of Alwar.

---

* Dr. Qureshi was tried on a charge of murder and convicted, and his conviction was upheld on appeal by the East Punjab High Court. He was subsequently transferred to Pakistan in pursuance of the inter-Dominion agreement for the exchange of prisoners. As soon as he arrived at Lahore he was released unconditionally and feted as a patriot and a hero

The police found several heaps of dead bodies, burning on both sides of the railway track near Badli Railway Station. It transpired that two passenger trains had been attacked by an armed mob and Muslim passengers had been dragged out and murdered. Village Barwala was attacked by a mob of armed non-Muslims. It was reported that about fifty houses were burnt down and three hundred and eighty-nine Muslims were murdered. Police help was sent but the mob defied the police firing and continued the massacre and depredation till a heavy contingent of armed police and military reserve reached the spot. On September 4, a number of Hindu labourers of the Delhi Cloth Mills, on their way home, killed every Muslim they met. On September 7 and 8, the Muslim shops in Connaught Circus were looted and burnt down. The police and military were ordered to shoot at sight, and the Prime Minister of India himself visited the spot at the risk of his life. On September 9, a number of wagons containing goods booked for Pakistan were standing in the station yard of the Delhi Main Railway Station. Four of these were set on fire and four more were looted. Almost the entire Muslim population was forced to leave and seek refuge in a number of refugee camps set up by the Administration. Nearly all of them have now returned to their original homes and are leading a peaceful life. Stray cases of assault continued until the end of September, when the situation was finally brought under control. Besides a number of unlicensed guns, daggers and knives, one hundred and fifty-four bombs, forty-five mortars, one thousand nine hundred and fifty rounds of rifle ammunition, thirteen wireless transmitters, a number of hand-grenades, Sten gun cartridges and a quantity of chemicals were recovered by the police from Muslim houses.

Heavy rains in the province during the second half of September caused widespread distress and loss of life and property. The Sutlej, Beas and Ravi overflowed their banks and wiped out several villages. The Hydro-electric Power Station at Jogindernagar was thrown out of order; and, besides stoppages in industrial and business undertakings, several towns were plunged into darkness for a period of nine days. The floods interfered seriously with the means of communication. The main rail and road bridges on the Grand Trunk Road, seven miles south of Jullundur, were completely washed away. Traffic between Hamira and Beas was held up for ten days as road and rail communications were breached. The communications between Ferozepore and Qasubegu were interrupted.

A road breach, one and a half miles long, was caused between Fazilka and Sulemanki. The Chakki Bridge on the Gurdaspur-Kangra Road was washed away. The road between Jullundur and Hoshiarpur was seriously breached five miles south of Hoshiarpur and the railway line was destroyed. The Indian Army Sappers were rushed to the various affected parts and restored communications within a few days, but in the meantime a great deal of damage both to life and property was caused. The heavy rains on the 24th and 25th added to the immense sufferings of the unfortunate refugees. Several hundred thousands of them had to stay on the roadside during these days without any cover. The road between Beas and Kartarpur was completely inundated and a large number of refugees was·washed away. The countryside was strewn with dead bodies which floated down the river in spate. Because of the suddenness and extent of the calamity, many villages and towns were isolated and very little could be achieved in the way of rescue operations.

Two great tragedies were enacted during the last week of September. One was an attack on a Muslim refugee train at Amritsar on the evening of September 22. Mention has been made of the non-Muslim refugee train from Pind Dadan Khan which was attacked at three different places.* When this train arrived at Amritsar, the news of the attack and the heavy loss of non-Muslim life spread through Amritsar and caused bitter resentment. On the evening of September 22, a Muslim refugee train on its way to Lahore was held up and attacked. It is feared that the loss of Muslim life was very heavy. Earlier the same day there had been an attack on a Muslim road convoy, though the number of people killed was less than fifty. The second great tragedy was an attack on a Muslim foot convoy in Ferozepore a few days later. The official report of this incident reads as follows:

" A large column, strength not known but estimated approximately at ten thousand, entered Ferozepore District from Kapurthala State, over the railway bridge near Makhu. The column included approximately three hundred persons who had previously migrated from Ferozepore District to Kapurthala State.

" A Muslim, named Mehdi, persuaded the column to proceed to Lahore via Makhu and the Sutlej Bridge. He promised, in return for some remuneration, to arrange military escort for

---

* See page 228, *ante*.

the column from Makhu. The movement of the column was kept secret.

" Mehdi had apparently arranged with some agents of his to leave the column and to ferry his own family across the Sutlej soon after entering Ferozepore District; and this he did. The column traversed through Ferozepore District without any escort and, on the way, was set upon by recently settled Sikh refugees from Pakistan. The number of casualties suffered by the column is estimated at between five hundred and one thousand, killed or wounded. In addition, a number of girls were abducted.

" No information regarding the entry of the column into Ferozepore District was received from the State authorities or from any other quarter. The first time that the local Army authorities came to know about the presence of the column was when the head of the column appeared at the Sutlej Bridge near Ferozepore City. The police of Makhu and Malanwala Police Stations, through whose jurisdiction the column passed, failed to report the passage of the column through their areas to the authorities of the headquarters of the district. If a report had been made, the headquarter authorities would have been able to arrange a suitable escort, and in all probability the attack would not have taken place or at least the number of casualties would have been much smaller.

" On receipt of information, the Deputy Commissioner and the Superintendent of Police made immediate arrangements for the collection and safe passage of the travellers and also for the recovery of abducted women. As a result of their efforts two hundred and fifty refugee stragglers were collected and transported safely to Kasur and over two hundred Muslim girls were recovered and sent to Pakistan.

" Severe action has been taken against the police for failure to report the arrival of the column in Ferozepore District. The Station House Officers of Makhu and Malawala Police Stations have been withdrawn and placed under arrest."

The Muslim villages round the town of Rewari were subjected to heavy attacks and Muslim houses were burnt and looted. Loss of life was not heavy as the inhabitants were evacuated to refugee camps. In one village, however, nearly one thousand Muslims were reported to have been killed. Large numbers of Meos left the district but later returned when conditions became normal.

A number of raiders assisted by the local Sangh people burnt down evacuated Muslim huts in Rewari. The damage, however, was not very great and the raiders were dispersed by the military and six of them were arrested.

In Tehsil Sonepat there were casualties at two places, Ghanaur and Akbarpur Barota. The loss of life was not considerable. The Muslims at Sonepat were attacked by a large mob who were driven off by the military.

In the end of September, Master Tara Singh and Udham Singh Nagoke issued a statement calling upon the Sikhs to stop the murder of Muslims. The appeal, however, was not happily worded and came in for a great deal of criticism from the Pakistan Authorities. While pointing out that the Sikhs and Hindus had been "guilty of most shameful attacks upon women and children in the communal warfare" and asking them to "stop all retaliation" the Sikh leaders said, " We do not desire friendship of the Muslims and we may never befriend them. We may have to fight again but we shall fight a clean fight—man killing man. This killing of women and children and those who seek asylum must cease at once. . . . There should be no attacks on refugee trains, convoys and caravans. We ask you to do so chiefly in the interests of your own communities, reputations, character and tradition than to save the Muslims." An exhortation of this type was scarcely calculated to check the non-Muslim frenzy in East Punjab.

A Hindu Advocate who visited a number of places in the Jullundur Division and the Patiala State, relating his observations, said:

" While the happenings in West Punjab have been indescribably tragic and unimaginably barbarous, the tragic happenings in East Punjab and Patiala State have not been less gruesome or less barbarous. Almost all Muslim men, women and children, whether urban or rural, have been either killed or turned out of their homes. There has been large-scale looting and destruction of property left by them, including standing crops. A large number of Muslim girls has been forcibly married, mostly to Sikhs. In certain villages Muslim population has been either wholly or mainly wiped out. Nature and epidemics are doing what man has failed to do.

" From Ambala to Jullundur roadsides and other areas are stinking with foul and poisonous smell. There is filth and dirt everywhere.

" What has happened in Patiala State is even worse. The Muslim population of the State was about one-third which has been virtually either wiped out or expelled. It is in very few cases that the Muslims started trouble and in good many places they adopted a submissive attitude. I can say, on the strength of my personal testimony, that my own ancestral village, mostly inhabited by Muslim Rajputs, received the worst treatment, though there was no loss of life owing to the peaceful and voluntary withdrawal of more than two thousand Muslims. All the valuable buildings of the Muslim Rajputs were wantonly destroyed and all the building material, including girders, was removed. This destruction and loot of all valuables, including a large quantity of foodgrains, by the neighbouring villages continued for days. All this was done mostly by the Sikh gangs aided by a few Hindus. I went to Rajpura to contact the police and military officers and found two of them, of whom one was a Muslim, under the influence of liquor."

An observer who watched the progress of a column of Muslim refugees from the Kapurthala State, said, " I saw a long column of Muslim men, women and children proceeding from Kapurthala to Jullundur. The column was guarded by a few military sepoys. It was ten or twelve deep, the women and children walking in the centre, flanked on either side by men. Groups of armed Sikhs stood about in the fields on either side of the road. Every now and again one of these groups would make a sudden sally at the column of Muslims, drag out two or three women and run away with them. In the process they would kill or injure the Muslims who tried to resist them. The military sepoys did not make a serious attempt to beat off these attacks. By the time the column arrived at Jullunder almost all the women and young girls had been kidnapped in this manner."

Reports of happenings in Patiala were grossly exaggerated by the Pakistan officials, but there can be no doubt that there was heavy loss of Muslim life among the Patiala Muslims.

Exposure and starvation took a heavy toll of the Muslims proceeding to Pakistan by foot convoys. It was reported that from a convoy of eighty thousand proceeding on its slow march to Amritsar and Lahore fifteen hundred Muslims died of exposure and starvation.

The disturbances in East Punjab resulted in the evacuation of almost the entire Muslim population to Pakistan. The loss of

Muslim life was not less than the loss of non-Muslim life in West Punjab. Indeed, there are many who boast that the total number of Muslims killed was more than the number of Hindus and Sikhs who perished in West Punjab, though the latter suffered greater losses in property. It is impossible to estimate even approximately the number of persons killed. What happened in West Punjab was re-enacted in East Punjab on an equally large scale and with equal ferocity. The same barbarities, inhuman murders, savage outrages, atrocities against women and children were witnessed. It must, however, be remembered that the attacks on the Muslims were by way of retaliation and began only after several months of a determined and sustained effort to drive the non-Muslims out of West Punjab. It was the tales brought by the sufferers from the West which set the East Punjab ablaze and no major incident happened in the eastern districts till the end of July. The mass killing and looting really began after the partition of the country and continued for about six weeks till the end of September. Those who took part in this holocaust were merely repeating the terrible lesson they had learnt from their Muslim preceptors in West Punjab. A great deal has been said by the Pakistan Press about a Sikh plan to drive out the Muslims and take possession of their lands and houses. A careful examination of the evidence, however, shows that no such plan was formulated up to the 15th of August 1947. The Hindu and Sikh leaders continued to appeal to the minorities in West Punjab to stay in their homes. The uncompromising Master Tara Singh told the Associated Press of India on June 26, 1947, that " he was of the considered opinion that non-Muslims of Western Punjab should continue to stay on in their homes."* Lala Avtar Narain of Jhelum, member, Constituent Assembly, Pakistan, issued a Press statement to the same effect and asked the minorities to become good citizens of Pakistan.† At a Minority Convention held at Rawalpindi on July 7, 1947, Dewan Pindi Das Sabharwal and Sardar Sant Singh exhorted the minorities not to leave their homes. Mr. Bhimsen Sachar, Lala Avtar Narain, Dr. Lehna Singh and Parbodh Chander, M.L.A., participated in this Convention. Goswami Ganesh Dutt also sent a message to this Convention. Mr. Mehr Chand Khanna, Finance Minister, North-West Frontier Province, exhorted the Hindus and Sikhs who had

---

* *Tribune*, June 29, 1947. † *Vir Bharat*, July 8, 1947.

migrated from the Frontier Province to return to their homes.* As late as August 10, 1947, Sardar Swaran Singh, in the course of an appeal to the people of Lahore, said, "In spite of the division of the country, all of us—Muslims, Hindus and Sikhs—have to live together. Let us, therefore, live in peace so that the poor and downtrodden may, in the new freedom that we have achieved, get enough to eat and to cover their naked bodies, leading to a happier and fuller life."† With the influx of large numbers of refugees from West Punjab the conviction was borne in upon the non-Muslims that it was impossible for them to live in Pakistan. They then launched large-scale attacks on Muslims by way of retaliation. It was only then that they realized that to drive out the Muslims would furnish an easy solution of their economic problems. They felt that they could not trust the Muslims and their presence in East Punjab was greatly resented. The exodus of Muslims provided them with the opportunity of securing land for the refugees from West Punjab and the drive became widespread and relentless till almost the entire Muslim population was evacuated.

---

* *Vir Bharat,* July 13, 1947.
† *Civil and Military Gazette,* August 12, 1947.

VIII

I do not endeavour either by triumphs of confutation, or pleadings of antiquity, or assumption of authority, or even by the veil of obscurity, to invest these inventions of mine with any majesty... I have not sought nor do I seek either to force or ensnare men's judgments, but I lead them to things themselves and the concordances of things, that they may see for themselves what they have, what they can dispute, what they can add and contribute to the common stock.

FRANCIS BACON—*Preface to the Great Instauration*

CHAPTER EIGHT

CONCLUSION

THE task of a writer of contemporary history is not an easy one. He finds it difficult to achieve objectivity because he has himself played a role, however unimportant, in the unfolding of events. There is a tendency, nay a temptation, to seek an interpretation consistent only with his own personal prepossessions. If he or anyone upon whom his affections are centred has suffered in person or in property, the loss assumes undue proportions and the desire to castigate those responsible for it is correspondingly greater. Then again, he has been too near a spectator and his field of vision too large to enable him to view everything in its true perspective. What happens in his neighbourhood or his own sphere of life, an incident (not perhaps of any great moment) which he sees with his own eyes, or hears narrated with the poignancy of freshness, may obscure a more significant occurrence in another part of the country. It is only with the passage of time that the mind can, as it were, draw itself away from the panorama of history and assume a position from which the various happenings of a critical period, their causes and their ultimate influences can be seen, in their true perspective. Finally, the wealth of material available is a serious handicap, for it makes the business of selection difficult. In the writing of history " selection is not merely expedient, it is the essence " of the historian's work ; he must pick out what is relevant from a vast quantity of evidence, before he can give an intelligible explanation of the events presented to the reader. The process of selection is rendered more difficult by a realization of the fact that he does not know how his story will end. He must nevertheless study all the available material and make up his mind before he begins to write. A haphazard and colourless narrative intended to provide a purely objective account of what happened will not achieve the dignity of history, for it will fail to accomplish the real business of the historian which is "to establish causal relations between events."

The writer of these pages has endeavoured to present a true and coherent account of the partition of India and what it cost the people of this great country in terms of life, property and mental suffering. The questions he asked himself were many and

puzzling ; what were the real causes that led to the partition :
who was responsible for breaking up the integral unity of India :
was it necessary to concede the demand for Pakistan : was it not
possible to avoid so much bloodshed and wholesale destruction
of property; can such things happen again and how can we guard
against them? To some of these questions the reader will find
a satisfactory answer while others will provoke a controversy, for
everyone will answer them in his own way and so long, at least,
as the wounds inflicted by partition are fresh, opinion on many
issues will differ. There will be some who will accuse the Congress leaders of pursuing a wholly unnecessary policy of appeasement towards Mr. Jinnah and the Muslim League ; while others
will hold the view that the majority of Congressmen were indifferent to the economic welfare and the political aspirations of the
Muslims and made no attempt to remove their genuine grievances.

That there are, and have always been, differences between
the beliefs, habits and outlook of the Muslims and the non-Muslims
cannot be denied; but it is equally true that these differences were
no more than an expression of individual personality such as may
be observed in members of one family where the peculiar traits and
features of one branch may be marked enough to distinguish it
from another branch, but do not give rise to temperamental in-
compatibility or open hostility. For over a thousand years Muslims and non-Muslims had lived as neighbours and friends, despite these differences, and it was not till the impact of British
imperialism forced them to raise mental and moral defences
around themselves that consciousness of their distinctive character
was forced upon them. This consciousness was accentuated and
exploited by the British rulers. Economic factors brought a sense
of frustration to the Muslims, for the Hindus, preferred and favoured by the British, rapidly achieved prosperity. The pendulum
of British attention than swung in the opposite direction, and
Muslims were urged to make demands for a subsidized existence,
in economic and political spheres. These demands were no
sooner made than conceded, on an ever-increasing scale, till the
population was divided into two hostile and warring camps. The
Congress refusal to form coalition ministries in 1937 was a serious
blunder and during the war years 1939-46 when the Congress
had voluntarily gone into the wilderness, the Muslim League
gained power and cohesion. The demand for the partition of
India was a logical corollary to the loyal and inspired address

presented to Lord Minto in 1906. Power no doubt corrupts, but it is equally true that corruption seeks power and it was this desire for power that led Mr. Jinnah to assume an uncompromising attitude and say 'no' to every proposal which did not concede the first place to him. Forty years of separate electorates and British favouritism had brought about a state of affairs from which it was impossible to escape except by dismembering the country and disrupting its integral unity.

The professed creed of the Muslim League, its avowedly communal composition, its frankly sectarian objectives and its espousal of unconstitutional methods led inevitably to a widespread conflict of arms. We have seen how the tempo and volume of the venomous propaganda carried on by the League swelled into an ever-increasing crescendo, till leaders like Sir Feroze Khan Noon threatened to repeat the orgies perpetrated by Halaku Khan and Changez Khan. Violence as a means of securing political power began to be preached freely from the Muslim League platform and the Muslim Press made hysterical appeals for a mass rising against the Hindus. A massive drive for the recruitment of Muslim League National Guards was launched; manufacture and collection of arms began on a large scale and the National Guards soon assumed the proportions of a private army, ready, at a moment's notice, to open an assault on non-Muslim life and property. These National Guards proved, after partition, to be the most ruthless enemies of the non-Muslims in Pakistan. They defied the Civil Administration and carried on a relentless campaign of murder, loot and arson against unoffending non-Muslims even when the police and civil officers were anxious to restore normal conditions.

That League ideology and the line of conduct pursued by it were mainly and directly responsible for the horrible drama, narrated in these pages, is clearly demonstrated by the inexorable logic of chronology. The speeches delivered at the Convention of the Muslim League legislators in April 1946, were an open incitement to violence. On July 29, the Direct Action resolution frankly abjured peaceful and constitutional methods and, on August 16, the campaign of violence was opened at Calcutta under the command and guidance of Mr. Suhrawardy. In October came the tragedy of Noakhali and Tippera. Almost immediately afterwards retaliation followed in Bihar. Then for some months there was

20

a lull while a major operation in the North-west was being planned. With the riots of March 1947 began the genocide of the non-Muslims. These disturbances were confined to the Muslim majority areas only and the victims were almost invariably Hindus and Sikhs. In May and June there was another flare-up in Lahore. It was not till the end of July that reprisals began in the eastern districts and the mass killing of Muslims took place between August 15 and September 30, 1947, when the arrival of large numbers of refugees from West Punjab and the tales told by them provoked the non-Muslims to retaliate. They were joined by the newly arrived refugees and the grim story of West Punjab was repeated in East Punjab and Delhi.

It is not possible to make an accurate estimate of the total loss of life or the extent of damage to property caused by these riots. Figures computed on the population basis must, of necessity, prove extremely misleading. The census returns of 1941 were not accurate even at the time they were compiled. They became hopelessly wrong, at the end of six years, when a general increase in population and local movements made it impossible to determine, with any degree of accuracy, how many non-Muslims were living in West Punjab, the North-West Frontier Province and Sind. Nor is it possible to know the total number of Hindu and Sikh refugees who later arrived in India. Rough estimates of the total number of refugees, prepared for purposes of rehabilitation and allotment to the various provinces, do not give a true picture ; and the total number of non-Muslims killed or converted cannot be calculated by substracting the number of refugees in India from the number of non-Muslims residing in the area which now comprises Pakistan, for the simple reason that both numbers will be grossly inaccurate. Figures based on the statements of refugee eye-witnesses are a surer guide though even these can, at best, be only approximate. The Fact Finding Organization examined nearly fifteen thousand witnesses and they bear testimony to the murder of fifty thousand non-Muslims. The incidents deposed to by these witnesses, however, represent only a fraction of the total devastation caused. Thousands of villages where riots are known to have taken place do not figure in the material collected by the Organization,* and no account has been taken of incidents not

---

* Out of a total of 19,914 villages in West Punjab only 2,094 are covered by the evidence collected by the Fact Finding Organization. The figures for the North-West Frontier Province are 2,826 and 362 respectively, and for Bhawalpur 2,376 and 216 respectively.

deposed to by eye-witnesses. Taking these factors into consideration the loss of non-Muslim life has been estimated at a figure between 200,000 and 250,000. It is believed that an equal number of Muslims perished in the course of the riots in India. The loss of non-Muslim property is estimated at about twenty thousand million rupees.

This was a heavy price and the memory of this painful and costly transaction will linger for years and continue to embitter and enrage the refugees. Perhaps there are some who will take warning from this sad chapter in our history and endeavour to guard against a repetition of these events. So long as sectarianism and narrow provincialism are allowed to poison the minds of the people, so long as there are ambitious men with corruption inside them, seeking power and position, so long will the people continue to be deluded and misled, as the Muslim masses were deluded and misled by the League leaders and so long will discord and disruption continue to threaten our peace and integrity.

APPENDIX I

APPENDIX I

NOTES TO CHAPTERS

Notes to Chapter One

(i)

THE "Seven Commandments of Destiny" enunciated by Choudhary Rehmat Ali in "The Millat and the Mission" (1942) are as follows:—

(1) Avoid Minorityism, which means that we must not leave our minorities in Hindu lands, even if the British and the Hindus offer them the so-called constitutional safeguards. For no safeguards can be a substitute for nationhood which is their birthright. Nor must we keep Hindu or Sikh minorities in our own lands, even if they themselves were willing to remain with or without any special safeguards. For they will never be of us. Indeed, while in ordinary times they will retard our national reconstruction, in times of crisis they will betray us and bring about our re-destruction.

(2) Avow Nationalism. We must assert and demand the recognition of the distinct national status of our minorities in the Hindu majority regions of Dinia and its dependencies, and reciprocally offer to give similar status to the Hindu and Sikh minorities in Pakistan, Bangistan and Osmanistan.

(3) Acquire proportional territory to create Siddiqistan, Faruqistan, Haideristan, Muinistan, Moplistan, Sufistan and Nasaristan. Now in the orbit of Pakasia we form about one-fourth of the total population, and, according to the laws of nature and nations, are entitled to about one-fourth of its area. We must, therefore, press our claims to the proportional areas in all such regions of the Continent and do so without delay.

(4) Consolidate the individual nations. It is dangerous to leave dispersed our minorities in the Hindu-majority regions of Dinia and in Ceylon, we must unify and consolidate them as nations in the countries that will comprise the proportional areas acquired under the previous commandment.

(5) Co-ordinate the nations under the Pak Commonwealth of Nations. To us the Pakistanians, union is not only a source of strength but also a sacred duty.

(6) Convert the sub-continent of India into the continent of Dinia. We must write *finis* to the most deceptive fiction in the world that India is the sphere of Indianism.

(7) Organize the continent of Dinia and its dependencies into the orbit of Pakasia. This is the last commandment and is meant to consolidate the results of the previous commandments. Pakasia connotes that part of Asia wherein our Pak culture is actually or potentially, predominant, and geographically it includes the Continent of Dinia.

(ii)

The text of Mr. Archbold's letter to Nawab Mohsin-ul-Mulk:

"Colonel Dunlop Smith (Private Secretary to the Viceroy) now writes to me that the Viceroy is prepared to receive the deputation of Mussalmans and intimates me that a formal petition be submitted for it. In this connection, the following matters require consideration.

"The first question is that of sending the petition. To my mind it would be enough that some leaders of Mussalmans, even though they may not have been elected, should put their signatures to it. The second is the question as to who the members of the deputation should be. They should be representatives of all the provinces. The third question is of the contents of the address. In this connection my opinion is that in the address loyalty should be expressed, that thanks should be offered that, in accordance with the settled policy, steps are going to be taken in the direction of self-government according to which the door will be opened for Indians to offices. But apprehension should be expressed that by introducing election injury will be done to Mussalman minority and hope should be expressed that in introducing the system of nomination or granting representation on religious basis the opinion of Mussalmans will be given due weight. The opinion should also be given that in a country like India it is necessary that weight should be attached to the views of zemindars.

" My personal opinion is that the wisest thing for Mussalmans to do would be that they support the system of nomination because the time for introducing election has not yet come. Besides, it will be very difficult for them if the system of election is introduced to secure their proper share.

" But in all these matters I want to remain behind the screen and this move should come from you. You are aware how anxious I am for the good of the Mussalmans and I would, therefore, render all help with the greatest pleasure. I can prepare and draft the address for you. If it be prepared in Bombay then I can revise it because I know the art of drawing up petitions in good language. But Nawabsaheb, please remember that if, within a short time, any great and effective action has to be taken then you should act quickly."

(iii)

Lady Minto recorded in her diary:

" This has been a very eventful day: as someone said to me, ' an epoch in Indian history.' We are aware of the feeling of unrest that exists throughout India, and the dissatisfaction that prevails amongst people of all classes and creeds. The Mohamedan population which numbers 62 millions, who have always been intensely loyal, resent not having proper representation and consider themselves slighted in many ways, preference having been given to the Hindus. The agitators have been most anxious to foster this feeling and have naturally done their utmost to secure the co-operation of this vast community. The younger generation were wavering, inclined to throw in their lot with advanced agitators of the Congress, and a howl went up that the loyal Mohamedans were not to be supported, and that the agitators were to obtain their demands through agitation. The Mohamedans decided, before taking action, that they would bring an address before the Viceroy, mentioning their grievances. The meeting was fixed for today and about 70 delegates from all parts of India have arrived. The ceremony took place this morning in the Ball-room. The girls and I went in by a side door to hear the proceedings while Minto advanced up the room with his staff and took his seat on the dais. The Aga Khan is the spiritual head of the Khoja Moslem community. He claims to be descended from Ali and is their Ruler by divine right, but without territory. The Prince was selected to read the very long but excellent Address stating all their grievances and aspirations. Minto then read his answer which he had thought out most carefully—' You need not ask my pardon for telling me that representative institutions of the European type are entirely new to the people of India or that their introduction here requires the most earnest thought and care I should be very far from welcoming all the political machinery of the western world among the hereditary traditions and instincts of Eastern races . . . . Your address, as I understand it, is a claim that, in any system of representation, whether it affects a Municipality, a District Board, or Legislative Council, in which it is proposed to introduce or increase an electoral organization, the Mohamedan community should be represented as a community You point out that in many cases electoral bodies, as now constituted, cannot be expected to return a Mohamedan candidate, and that if by chance they did so, it could only be at the sacrifice of such candidate's views to those of a majority opposed to his own community, whom he would in no way represent, and you justly claim that your position should be estimated not merely on your numerical strength but in respect to the political importance of your community and the service it has rendered to the Empire. I am entirely in accord with you. . . . I am as firmly convinced as I believe you to be, that any electoral representation in India would be doomed to mischievous failure which aimed at granting a personal enfranchisement, regardless of the beliefs and traditions of the communities composing the population of this continent."

(iv)

Louis Fischer wrote in the *Hindustan Standard:*

" Winston Churchill remains the implacable enemy of India's independence. He has never disguised his views. Many members of his party differ with him on the question of Indian Freedom, but Churchill's imperialistic policy dominates.

" Mohamed Ali Jinnah has not in recent years given any proof of a devotion to the cause of India's liberation from foreign rule. Nor has the Muslim League over which he presides. Landlords, who bulk large in the counsels of the League, stand to lose by the establishment of a new India, which would certainly alter the present land tenure to the disadvantage of landlords, Muslims as well as Hindus, and to the advantage of all peasants.

" What could be more natural, therefore, than that Churchill and Jinnah should have been in correspondence, in recent months, over the fate of India ? They have quietly exchanged letters and messages. It was shortly after the receipt of one such secret communication from Churchill that the Muslim League reconsidered its acceptance of the British Cabinet Mission's long-term proposals and decided instead to boycott the coming Assembly which is to draw up a constitution for a new free India.

" The Cabinet Mission laboured hard and on the whole successfully to prepare the way for the transfer of political power from British to Indian hands. Churchill and Jinnah are now attempting to undermine the effort."

Notes to Chapter Two

(i)

Mr. Jinnah's love of pageantry grew as he came to be accepted as the sole leader of Muslims in India. At the 30th session of the All-India Muslim League held in April 1943 at Delhi, the President, Mr. Jinnah, was taken out in a huge procession led by a number of decorated elephants who were followed by camels and a squad of Muslim National Guards, on bicycles, displaying Muslim League flags. Muslim National Guards on foot, playing bands and in military formation, followed next. The processionists were raising slogans of " *Allah-o-Akbar*," " *Qaid-i-Azam Zindabad*," " *Pakistan Zindabad*" and " Rulers of Islamic countries *Zindabad*."

At the next session held, in December, at Karachi, Mr. Jinnah was taken out with even greater pomp and show. The procession was led by a rider on horseback carrying a huge League flag. National Guards in uniform marched behind him like an army battallion. They numbered nearly two thousand and were drawn from all the provinces of India. Then followed representatives of the Muslim students and various other Anjumans. There were more than fifty Sindhi horsemen. Then came a formation of camels with men in Sindhi dress riding them. Then a number of camels with riders in Arab dress. Physical culturists, students and boy scouts followed. Then came 50 camels and 50 caparisoned horses, all mounted by Hajis in Arab costumes. Shouts of " *Allah-o-Akbar,*" " *Pakistan Zindabad,*" " *Shahinshah-i-Pakistan Zindabad,*" " *Faateh-i-Congress Zindabad* " and " *Qaīd-i-Azam Zindabad* " were raised on all sides as Mr. Jinnah's decorated carriage came into view.

(ii)

Mr. Fazalul Haq, speaking on a no-confidence motion against the Ministry, moved by Mr. Dhirendra Nath Datta in the Bengal Legislative Assembly on September 19, 1946, said :—

" Sir, during the dark days or nights of the Great Killing, I watched events from the point of view of a member of the Opposition. The news that came to me trickling down from various sources was unfavourable to the Ministers in power. I was very deeply impressed with the fact that during the whole of these disturbances the machinery of Government had completely broken down in this city. Sir, I pondered deeply over the situation, and if I have risen to say a few words on these motions I wish to tell my comrades in this Assembly what I feel very strongly and which I think ought to be raised before the people of Bengal, if Bengal is to be saved at all from utter extermination. There have been Hindu-Muslim quarrels in the past all over India. In many of these quarrels, when cases had been started, I had the privilege of defending the Muslim accused almost all over the country. But, Sir, I have never in the whole course of my life seen anything like the purely fiendish fury with which both Hindus and Muslims have murdered not merely men or women but even small children. I do not know to satisfy what impulse—human or dévilish—which seems to have possessed the Bengalees for those fateful days and nights that my countrymen indulged.

" Sir, so far as the Ministers are concerned, I am going to obey the Party mandate and I will cast my votes against the motions before the House. But that is only because I feel constitutionally that we cannot, when a motion like this is tabled, leave the Ministers of our choice to the tender mercies of the Opposition. But if that is so as regards the Ministers, the guardians of law and order who control the police force in Calcutta can claim no protection from us.

" Sir, I will not take much time of the House, but I will refer to a few instances which have been an eye-opener to me. I have felt that the greatest disturbances did not rise in a moment out of the moon but seem to be the result of a well-planned action—may be on one side or may be on both sides. I do not know—God alone knows. The future alone will disclose what is the truth.

" Sir, on Friday morning I received telephone messages from various parts of the city from both Hindus and Muslims that troubles had broken out. I thought it was one of those unfortunate affairs which have shown to the world that although the Bengalees or Indians generally are amongst the most intellectual races of the world, they do not know the virtue of toleration. But, then the situation worsened gradually. I advised those who were telephoning to me, to seek police protection. It was then I came to know that the police were being appealed to and in some cases the police said that they had received no orders. Wonder of wonders ! What are the police here for, what are they being paid for, if they do not know that whenever there is a disturbance of the public peace and tranquillity, their first duty is to jump into the situation, if necessary, and to defend public peace and tranquillity with their lives ?

" Then, Sir, in the afternoon of that day the Mallick Bazar was looted. It is within about half a mile of my house. I was then standing on the verandah and I found people in great glee and merriment rushing all sides with booty in their hands and police *paharawalas* accompanying them. Everyone was very happy as if they were members of a marriage procession !

" Then, Sir, that night the Park Circus market was looted. I sent one of my nephews and Mr. Khairul Anam, Editor of the *Mohammadi*, to the

Park Circus outpost. Will the House be surprised to hear that the Officer-in-charge was there and he said that he had no time to go and see what was happening. Certainly some change had come over the Calcutta Police !

" Then, Sir, the next day, I believe it was the 17th, the Mahisadal Raj House was looted. That building is about 40 yards from my house and in front of that building on the other side of the road there was a Traffic Police Outpost where there are at least 100 police officers. The House will be surprised to hear—and I am an eye-witness—that the whole of that house was ransacked. It took two hours to clear that house of all its belongings and the police were looking on. I sent one of my clerks to interfere and stop because the Raja was not in the house; he had left previously. The reply my clerk got was ' those people are taking to whom the property belongs ' and, Sir, people came out with all their booty and I received a report that a member of a certain Provincial Service went home with a silver tea tray as a part of the loot.

" I am not here concerned with the details of this nauseating event. I do not wish to discuss how these disturbances began, who was responsible, but I certainly want the House to consider why is it that the trouble was allowed to grow to gigantic proportions, and, within 24 hours, the entire situation was out of control. Now, Sir, I have not been an eye-witness of everything that occurred but one who has suffered most. I am not a young man with a stout heart but, Sir, I am supposed to have something like that sort of grit which can face unpleasant situation, but this time my nerves completely broke down. We could not sleep, batch after batch of ruffians knocked at our doors and every moment seemed to be our last. It seemed, Sir, that not only had British rule ended but that some modern Nadir Shah had come upon Calcutta and had given up the city to rapine, plunder and pillage. Sir, each time I tried to get into touch with police officers I was told that I was to contact the Control Room. I do not know, Sir, who was controlling the Control Room, but whenever I wanted some kind of help the reply came that my complaint has been noted and will be attended to in proper time. Then, Sir, I sometimes tried to get into touch with high officials of Government House. I was told that none but Government servants were allowed to use the telephone to get into touch with the household of His Excellency the Governor. Police officers would not listen, the Control Office would not control, the Government House would not listen, Sir, in these circumstances the Great Killing went on and it is undisputed that this thing would never have happened if the police and the military had taken strong measures on Friday, the 16th, when the trouble began. It would have been nipped in the bud that very day, and, therefore, the conclusion is inevitable that although the police may not be responsible for the origin of disturbances, they are directly responsible for the great loss of human life, and if an impartial enquiry is held and these police officers can be spotted, my opinion is that they deserve to be hanged, drawn and quartered publicly, on charges of murder and abetment of murder. . . .

" Quite within a stone's throw of Lalbazar, the Scotland Yard of Calcutta, Limton Watch Company, at the junction of Bowbazar and Dalhousie Square, was looted. The whole ceremony of looting took about 2 or 2½ hours. Police officers came but only to take part in the loot. One of my friends who somehow managed to see what was going on told me that half an hour after the loot people were seen rushing out with wrist watches and other articles of value and most of them were policemen."

Mr. Dhirendra Narayan Mukherji who had accompanied· Mr. Suhrawardy on a tour of the affected areas, describing his experiences, said :

" We turned towards the Bowbazar Street but could not proceed far, as the other crowd blocked the way. I got down and tried to persuade them to disperse. There was an Assistant Commissioner of Police with a lorry-load of policemen, some of them armed with rifles, but they merely looked on. As the crowd was in no mood to listen to him the Chief Minister decided to leave, and while the car was turning back, brickbats were thrown at it. The picture given by the Chief Minister in the Upper House about the violent mood of the crowd, has been too much overcoloured and had he stayed on, I am sure his courage and sincerity would have been eventually appreciated even by a Hindu mob. I stayed on, tried to pacify the crowd, and was successful.

" While there, I learnt that some *bustee* at the corner of Bowbazar Street and Amherst Street had been set on fire. I rushed there, and arranged to bring out the Fire Brigade by using a phone from Bandhab Bastralaya. The police were patrolling the streets but not helping to disperse the crowd or stop the fire. At the corner I was persuading a large crowd to disperse; while doing so a police lorry came, and a European officer pointed a gun at me and fired a shot. Immediately the whole crowd melted away. It was tear gas, and I asked the officer why he fired without warning. He said he wanted to disperse the crowd and I pointed out to him that as the crowd was already on the point of dispersing at my persuasion, the tear gas would only irritate them and might have resulted in a shower of brickbats, and retaliatory shots fired by sergeants. I complained that patrol police merely looked on, making no attempt to stop the fire. The officer, Mr. Barnes, a Deputy Commissioner of Police, then left. The altercation with him gave me an advantage—the police must have thought me a person of importance. I managed to restore peace in the locality and at 1 o'clock I was told there that rioting had broken out at Sealdah corner. I hastened to the spot and found fighting going on between Hindus and Muslims inside Baithakhana Bazar. I was successful in putting a stop to it. Just as I came out on the Bowbazar Street, I found a wine shop in the Circular Road-Bowbazar corner ablaze, and both Muslims and policemen in uniform busy taking away the bottles. Some of the bottles I found stored in the police lorry. I caught hold of a policeman carrying away two bottles from the shop, and dragged him before the Police Sergeant, but no action was taken and the man ran away.

" I saw that a very big Muslim procession had come to the Sealdah corner from the Upper Circular Road side. They were carrying swords, *lathis*, etc., and wanted aggressively to pass through Bowbazar Street. I moved towards them and suggested, they might go to the maidan, by continuing through the Circular Road and Dharamtalla Street instead of forcing their way through Bowbazar. All of a sudden, some of them began to break open the shops on Circular Road and loot them. Some rushed and surrounded me and began to beat me. One young Muslim, apparently a student, gave me a blow, declaring he would break my teeth. Another brandished his long knife shouting that he was thirsty for my blood. Further mischief was prevented by some who must have appreciated my motives. Just then, one of the Sergeants who had been with Mr. Barnes rushed with two armed policemen into the crowd and brought me back to comparative safety. Anyway, the processionists changed their mind and passed on through Circular Road, as I had suggested, instead of trying to force their way through Bowbazar. Meanwhile, another armed and a more violent crowd came up from Beliaghata side and wanted to force their way through Bowbazar. Policemen, both ordinary and armed, about 50 in number, were there in two lorries under the direction of Sergeants. I suggested to the Sergeants that the two lorries might be placed blocking the entrance to Bowbazar Street, and the police should fire to prevent the clash between the two crowds. The Sergeants paid no heed. The Beliaghata crowd looted the aerated waters shop at the corner and began to hurl the bottles and rushed in to Bowbazar Street, and proceeded two to three hundred yards. I could not prevent them forcing in, nor could I persuade them to get back. Instead, I got *lathi* blows on my arms. This crowd was prevented from passing through Bowbazar Street by a shower of brickbats.

" I learnt that processionists passing through Circular Road were rushing inside the lanes leading to west, and assaulting the local residents. I went round and saw at Dixon Lane one gentleman lying dead in the street with his throat gashed, blood still spouting up.   He was a Hindu, who was coming through Circular Road, and had been chased by the *goondas*.   This was about a hundred yards from Circular Road."

(iii)

Alec Reid, who paid a visit to Noakhali in February 1949, wrote as follows:

"I have given, in a previous article, some idea of the great work being carried on in Noakhali by those who have devoted the past two years of their lives to the Gandhi Camps—men and women who have fearlessly succoured those who suffered as a result of the communal passions let loose in the district towards the end of 1946.

"But there is another side to the picture and to appreciate it properly, let me first introduce you to Sah Sayed Gulam Sarwar Hussaini, Pir of Daira-Shariff, Dhampur, Noakhali   That is what he calls himself, but for the sake of brevity let me simply refer to him as Gulam Sarwar by which name he has been most widely known in Bengal these past two years.

"It was just after the great Calcutta Massacre that he first came into real prominence.   Noakhali was aflame with communal hate and stories trickled through to Calcutta connecting this man with the affair.   Then the military moved in and Mr. Sarwar disappeared from the public eye; he was reported to have been locked up   Came partition and, according to officials in Dacca, he was pardoned owing to ' insufficient evidence ' and also the fact that ' no prosecution witnesses had come forward.'   How could they?—many must have been dead, others must have fled westwards or perhaps those that remained found it healthier not to proceed with their charges.

"At any rate, Mr. Sarwar is now as large as life in Noakhali District—and he is a man with a mission.   He does not like those people who run the Gandhi Camps and he thinks they should be closed.   He told me that himself when I met him in his home village one Sunday afternoon three weeks ago. It all came about like this.

"I had heard in Dacca that it had been reported that Sarwar was making inflammatory speeches.   According to a leading official, he had sent to Noakhali for a report (afterwards I asked the authorities there whether they had received that report; they said they had not).   So I determined to see Sarwar and ask him what he felt about things in general.

"Our meeting was arranged after some trouble in the school of his village. I was told that the local *thana* had been suggested as a rendezvous, but apparently Mr. Sarwar had raised some objection.   At any rate, I arrived at the appointed hour—11-30 a.m.—and was received by one of the schoolmasters. That something unusual was afoot had spread through the village, for a large crowd had gathered and the windows of the room where our meeting was to take place were lined with interested spectators who had taken up their positions early to avoid the rush.

"We settled down to a cup of tea and the master informed me that a message had been sent to Sarwar's house to inform him that I had arrived. Shortly after noon it was announced that he was having a bath and he would be along in a few minutes.   We waited.   I grew impatient, for I had far to go that afternoon.   Another emissary was sent and back came the reply that he was more or less on his way.   The audience had increased.   Our room was now invaded with interested spectators.   It was not every day that the big man received a Press representative.

"At the stroke of one there was a hush—within and without.   He was approaching.   Then through the windows came a chorus of *salaams*.   The door shot open and, in the flowing robes of a spiritual leader, stood Sarwar.   With an arrogant stare he surveyed the room; his thick sensuous lips pouted as his followers rose with one accord to greet him. He looked me up and down and with a flourish sat at the head of the table.

" Then there followed much formality. He demanded paper and ink, declaring that everything must be duly noted down. The schoolmaster was appointed scribe, interpreter, master of ceremonies. Our interview lasted three hours, for not only did I interview Sarwar but he insisted on interviewing me. While the hunt for paper and ink went on, he sat back in his chair and surveyed me while I surveyed him. I felt it would be, appropriate if at a given signal somebody shouted, ' Seconds out of the ring.'

" An aged lieutenant sat on his left hand and on his right a gentleman in the garb of a Hindu. Where did he fit into the picture, I pondered. I got the answer two and a half hours later; he was the Trump Card. The lieutenant seemed to be enjoying the situation. He sucked noisily through his teeth—I suspected they were false—and leered wickedly at some of his companions as much as to say, ' We're in for a good afternoon's entertainment.'

" All was ready at last. There was silence as I put my first question: what was the feeling locally about refugees coming back to the district? The reply was prompt. ' The feeling is very hopeful and brotherly and akin to peace. The Muslims will receive the Hindu ladies as their mothers and their sisters and their menfolk as their brothers.'

" On went my questions and back came the replies with Sarwar careful not to commit himself in any way. The scribe—at times almost overcome with his efforts—took copious notes while his pen screeched in protest. Tea and fruit were ordered, for it was thirsty work, and as the afternoon wore on we consumed many cups.

" The interest, so far as the audience were concerned, never flagged; there was for them never a dull moment. But there was an awkward one all the same. Sarwar had proudly informed me that he had over 20,000 followers and when I remarked on the frightful condition of the roads and suggested that he might use his influence and manpower to good account by having them repaired, for (with an eye to the audience) I pointed out that the villagers and farm workers would in the end suffer untold hardships if their already slender lines of communication broke down altogether. Mr. Sarwar was annoyed. Some of his younger followers glanced at each other. His chief lieutenant sucked noisily through his teeth. The Trump Card winced. The scribe scratched furiously at his minutes. The feuhrer's face clouded. He gave me a nasty look, then snapped back that he was much too busy with other things to organize such a scheme.

" After an hour I had finished my questioning. It was now his turn. We talked of many things. I was asked my views on the future of the two Dominions, the international situation ; on Linlithgow, Wavell and Mountbatten, on others who had played a part in the Indian scene. Sarwar seemed quite a glutton for knowledge. At any rate the audience were interested and the schoolmaster wrote much more than he had for many a long day. There was a pause. I sensed that something out of the ordinary was coming; the gathering had leaned forward with fresh interest. Sarwar had sat back. He glanced round the room, pushed his arms outwards to their full length and stretched his fingers as if he were about to strangle some imaginary foe. This was obviously the *pièce de resistance*. Then he broke the silence with the words— ' And now let me tell you about the Gandhi Camps.'

" There followed a recitation of ' facts.' Sarwar makes continual use of them in the meetings he addresses up and down the countryside. The leaders of the Camps did not follow the ideals laid down by their founder. The Camps were filled with fifth columnists, members of the R.S.S. and Communists and their main object was to create disturbances to interfere in the brotherly relations of Hindus and Muslims. They must be closed. The Gandhi Camp workers wanted to control the Muslims of East Pakistan in every possible way by adopting a ' Nazi and Fascist policy.'

" When he had finished Sarwar turned to the gentleman. on his right. It was then that I learned that he was the Trump Card. He was a Hindu, a man well known locally, and he would corroborate all that had been said. And this unfortunate individual did so with great zest. I learned afterwards that he acted as Sarwar's chairman at his various meetings throughout the countryside: it was alleged that he had had a hand in ' planting ' evidence used in some of the prosecutions that had been started against several Gandhi Camp workers. It was the old, old technique. The Nazis developed it to a fine art. Repeat the same lies and abuse against your opponents over and over again and produce someone belonging to your adversaries' community and make him say that you are speaking the truth. There was once a man called Quisling who lived in Norway.

" I stopped at a village the next day. Two local Muslims said they wanted to have a word with me. This is what they had to say: ' We have had a lot of trouble in this district. We have had enough of it; we want to live in peace with the Hindus. We have no quarrel with them; we never really had. But there are several in this district who go about making speeches which do no good. Gulam Sarwar says he intends coming here. We have sent a special request to the District Magistrate at Noakhali to stop him. We don't want him.'

" My next interview was in Noakhali with the District Magistrate. I told him of my visit to the Gandhi Camps and of the excellent work that was being done there. A mild-mannered man, he listened with courteous attention. I told him of Sarwar's allegations and when I asked him his views, he very guardedly and with much hesitation, admitted that the Camps were there for the common good.

" We were joined by the Superintendent of Police, but what he had to say was without the slightest hesitation whatsoever. I wanted to know what he thought about the Gandhi Camps. Well, I would have it. With hands that shook with emotion as he lit a cigarette, he went even further than Gulam Sarwar. According to him, in the first place the coming of Gandhiji to Noakhali was just a ' hoax ' designed to draw attention to the communal disturbances there, which had been in seriousness ' exaggerated beyond all proportion.' Gandhiji had been hesitant to leave even when the Bihar riots started as he wanted to ' divert attention ' to East Bengal.

" Then the police official got into his full stride on the question of the Camps themselves. They were filled with Communists, members of the R.S.S., various types of fifth columnists who were ' agents of the Government of Hindustan.' Why were they supplied with so much money; he demanded. Their chief job was to cause disaffection in the surrounding countryside. I looked at the District Magistrate as this tirade continued. He appeared to have forgotten his earlier conversation with me and now seemed in complete agreement with the representative of the police. The latter thundered on.

" As for the Gandhi Camp workers, he dealt with several of them individually and ' scoundrel ' was the least of the various epithets he applied to them while enumerating their various ' crimes.' But, according to him, they were an uncommonly wily crew. Attempts had been made to intercept their mail to India, but they sent it by special couriers and they ' disguised ' themselves as Muslims ' while carrying communications between the various Camps, which were nothing less than ' nests of intrigue.' They said they were loyal to the East Bengal Government—why then did they not fly the Pakistan flag ? He would see they did on next Independence Day. But in the meantime the Camps must be closed. The authorities could not tolerate the present state of affairs any longer. As to when exactly they would be closed, he spoke of possible immediate ' repercussions ' in view of the various inter-Dominion talks, but whatever happened they were determined that they would be closed sooner or later. And so he went on for over an hour.

"What are the various 'crimes' that several of the Gandhi Camp workers are charged with? Chief among the accused is Col. Jiwan Singh, formerly of the I.N.A. He was arrested some months ago on a fantastic charge of abducting a Hindu woman for immoral purposes. He was interned in Noakhali while I was there and had to report twice a day to the *thana*. When Gandhiji was in Bengal Col. Jiwan Singh became one of his most devout followers. Gandhiji personally put him in charge of several of the Camps. He faced with bravery the dangers of carrying on the work. He is a man of the highest integrity. To say that the charge against him is 'fantastic' is putting it mildly. After several farcical hearings it was found that there was not sufficient evidence against him and so the authorities were willing to stop the proceedings (but at the same time not clear his name) if the Colonel left East Bengal. He refused.

"Two other Camp workers have been implicated in a charge of murder. One, a trusted follower of Gandhiji, was marched many miles by road handcuffed. Other charges are pending against several more men of the same calibre.

"Thus the campaign of repression goes on. The authorities seem determined to 'frame' as many of the Camp workers as they can. Beyond doubt their aim is gradually to freeze the Camps out of existence by such diabolical methods. What price justice in Noakhali District?

"What is the purpose of this campaign against the Gandhi Camps? Dacca has been kept fully informed of their work and the authorities there know of the repressive measures being used against them. Why is it that they do not silence Gulam Sarwar? There was once a Superintendent of Police in Noakhali who was sympathetic towards the Camps—why was he transferred? These questions require an answer.

"Is it that the authorities in East Bengal do not want a meeting ground for both communities? Is it that they do not wish a Hindu minority once more to arise and take its place in the working of the State? Is this the prelude to the founding of a true Islamic State?

"Already certain members of the East Bengal Government have visited the Camps and expressed themselves satisfied as to their *bona fides*. But they have done nothing on their return to Dacca. Perhaps the time is now ripe, in the interests of inter-Dominion peace, for a commission of inquiry to be sent from Karachi. If properly conducted it will find that the Camps are not 'nests of intrigue' but starting points for communal peace."

—"The Mission of Gulam Sarwar: What price justice in East Bengal?" *The Hindustan Times*, March 22, 1949. (By courtesy of *The Hindustan Times*.)

Notes to Chapter Three

(i)

The Sikandar-Jinnah Pact drawn up at Lucknow, October 15, 1937:

(1) That on his return to the Punjab Sir Sikandar Hayat will convene a special meeting of his Party and advise all Muslim members of his party who are not members of the Muslim League already to sign its creed and join it. As such they will be subject to the rules and regulations of the Central and Provincial Boards of the All-India Muslim League. This will not affect the continuance of the present coalition and of the Unionist Party;

(2) That in future elections and by-elections for the Legislature after the adoption of this arrangement, the Groups constituting the present Unionist Party will jointly support the candidates put up by their respective Groups;

(3) That the Muslim members of the Legislature who are elected on or accept the League ticket will constitute the Muslim League Party within the Legislature. It shall be open to the Muslim League Party so formed to maintain or enter into coalition or alliance with any other party consistently with the fundamental principles, policy and programme of the League. Such alliances may be evolved upon after the elections. The existing combinations shall maintain its present name " The Unionist Party."

(ii)

Printed and cyclostyled copies of the following circular were secretly distributed among the Muslims of India:

(1) All Muslims of India should die for Pakistan.

(2) With Pakistan established whole of India should be conquered.

(3) All people of India should be converted to Islam.

(4) All Muslim kingdoms should join hands with the Anglo-American exploitation of the whole world.

(5) One Muslim should get the right of five Hindus, i.e., each Muslim is equal to five Hindus.

(6) Until Pakistan and Indian Empire is established, the following steps should be taken:—

(a) All factories and shops owned by Hindus should be burnt, destroyed, looted and loot should be given to League Office.

(b) All Muslim Leaguers should carry weapons in defiance of order.

(c) All nationalist Muslims if they do not join League must be killed by secret Gestapo.

(d) Hindus should be murdered gradually and their population should be reduced.

(e) All temples should be destroyed.

(f) Muslim League spies in every village and district of India.

(g) Congress Leaders should be murdered, one in one month by secret method.

(h) Congress upper offices should be destroyed by secret Muslim Gestapo, single person doing the job.

(i) Karachi, Bombay, Calcutta, Madras, Goa, Vizagapatam should be paralysed by December 1946 by Muslim League volunteers.

(j) Muslim should never be allowed to work under Hindus in Army, Navy, Government services or private firms.

(k) Muslim should sabotage whole of India and Congress Government for the final invasion of India by Muslims.

(l) Financial resources are given by Muslim League. Invasion of India by Nizam communist, few Europeans, Khoja by Bhopal, few Anglo-Indians, few Parsis, few Christians, Punjab, Sind and Bengal will be places of manufacture of all arms, weapons for Muslim Leaguers invasion and establishing of Muslim Empire of India.

(m) All arms, weapons should be distributed to Bombay, Calcutta, Delhi, Madras, Bangalore, Lahore, Karachi, branches of Muslim League.

(n) All sections of Muslim League should carry minimum equipment of weapons, at least pocket knife at all times to destroy Hindus and drive all Hindus out of India.

(o) All transport should be used for battle against Hindus.

(p) Hindu women and girls should be raped, kidnapped and converted into Muslims from October 18, 1946.

(q) Hindu culture should be destroyed.

(r) All Leaguers should try to be cruel at all times to Hindus and boycott them socially, economically and in many other ways.

(s) No Muslim should buy from Hindu dealers. All Hindu produced films should be boycotted. All Muslim Leaguers should obey these instructions and bring into action by September 15, 1946.

(iii)

No. 2.

GOVERNMENT HOUSE, LAHORE,

5th September, 1947.

DEAR MR. JINNAH,

Many thanks for your letter of 26th August, which arrived just after you left on Monday. I will certainly write to you more often than once a fortnight to keep you in touch with the situation here. I will also, as you asked me to, write quite frankly.

The law and order position here has improved very definitely, but there are still great dangers. I got a telephone message from the Commissioner Multan last night that Muzaffargarh was giving trouble, and Dera Ghazi Khan is still disturbed. I think that the raiders took a pretty severe knock. There was serious trouble in Jhang, due, partly at least I think, to the incapacity and low morale of the Deputy Commissioner, but it seems to be quiet now. I am apprehensive about Lyallpur. In the next two days I am visiting Multan, Lyallpur and Jhang. I had hoped to go to Dera Ghazi Khan, but cannot get a light aeroplane, which is the only way of getting there quickly. So I have asked the Deputy Commissioner to meet me in Multan and bring the Nawab Leghari with him, if he can. I expect trouble in all the Western districts. The refugee problem is assuming gigantic proportions. The only limit that I can see to it is that set by the Census reports. According to reports, the movement across the border runs into a *lakh* or so a day. At Chuharkana in the Sheikhupura District I saw between a *lakh* and a *lakh* and a half of Sikhs collected in the town and round it, in the houses, on the roofs and everywhere. It was exactly like the Magh Mela in Allahabad. It will take 45 trains to move them, even at 4,000 people per train; or, if they are to stay there, they will have to be given 50 tons of *ata* a day. At Govindgarh in the same district there was a collection of 30,000 or 40,000 Mazhbi Sikhs with arms. They refused even to talk to the Deputy Commissioner, an Anglo-Indian, who advanced with a flag of truce. They shot at him and missed. Finally arrangements were made to evacuate the lot. I am telling every one that I don't care how the Sikhs get across the border; the great thing is to get rid of them as soon as possible. There is still little sign of 3 *lakh* Sikhs in Lyallpur moving, but in the end they too will have to go.

The most serious recent development is the very rapid deterioration in the reliability of the Army. Yesterday Pathans in a Frontier Force Rifle battalion in Gujranwala seized their arms and established a road block on the main road, and their officers could do nothing with them. Brigadier McDonald, who belongs to the regiment and can talk Pushto, was sent out this morning and the situation is now under control. I do not know quite what the mutiny was about. I imagine that the real trouble was that the Commanding Officer is a *bania* and the Second in Command a Sikh! All the Hindus and Sikhs of the Battalion are being sent today across the border. The Muslims will, as soon as possible, be sent to Jhelum. Anyhow, this and other incidents—

I understand that things are worse in this respect in N.W.F. Province—have convinced the Military that their own non-Muslim troops are number one priority for evacuees. And yet a proposal was seriously put forward that the Military should take over our police.

I am getting very doubtful—and so is the General—whether the plan of protecting evacuee camps by troops of their own nationality will work in practice. But we will have to try it and keep the two armies absolutely apart. I think that we could secure the safety of non-Muslim camps on our side, but I doubt very much whether any Muslim camps in the East would be safe with a Sikh guard. Se we will have to do our best to work the scheme on our side in order to keep it going on the other.

From various sources I hear that the political situation is deteriorating. Yesterday there was a minor refugee demonstration with shouts of " Pakistan Murdabad "—I am told that Shaukat is afraid to show his face in the Muslim Refugee Camp here. I warned my Ministry about a week ago that this sort of thing was inevitable, that when things go wrong on a large scale it is always the Government that gets the blame. At first they were inclined to attribute any unpopularity they may have sensed to the machinations of Firoz, Khaksars, etc. This was mere self-delusion and very dangerous. This feeling of resentment against things in general and against the Government in particular is bound to grow. The ways in which, as far as I can see, it can be countered are (a) propaganda reiterating what Government is doing for the refugees and (b) an efficient administration.

Efficiency with my present staff is out of the question. We have one Financial Commissioner, instead of a normal two or three, and our present one, Akhtar Hussain, though loyal and a good technical revenue officer, is certainly not capable of doing two men's work. Out of three Commissioners of Divisions we have only one, and he is from all accounts, hardly up to the job. Out of five D.I.Gs. Police we have only three and two are recently joined outsiders, one from U.P. and one from C.P. Finally to crown all, we have no Chief Secretary—the Finance Secretary, a mediocre officer, is supposed to be doing both jobs. In all these matters the Ministry had to adopt the attitude of the ostrich.

They have got a " new scheme " by which no Chief Secretary is required: a senior departmental Secretary to Government apparently is called Chief Secretary and draws the pay. The shortage of Commissioners is to be met partially by abolishing the post of Commissioner of Lahore.

I have not yet troubled them on the subject of the Chief Secretaryship but on the general question of staff and, incidentally, that of the Commissionership of the Lahore Division. I called in Liaquat and Mohammad Ali and had a joint meeting with them and my Ministers. Largely by Liaquat's help I got the Ministers to agree to our trying to get back a number of ex-Punjab and ex-U.P. British I.C.S. officers and to the retention of the Lahore Division. Shaukat was a bit difficult, I don't quite know why.

We had, from our point of view, a successful meeting with Nehru, Patel and company on Wednesday. Your Ministers and we had the day before drawn up a paper on refugee policy, which went through after about four hours rather desultory talk with only drafting amendments. The main fight was over certain proposals of East Punjab by which their troops or officers would be allowed to enter West Punjab on various pretexts. Finally, I had it conveyed to Nehru that the conference would break down unless they gave way, which they did. I enclose a copy of the final paper for your Excellency's information.

Patel kept silence for the first three hours and then said that we were all wasting our time, and delivered a lecture on how things should have been done months ago. According to Liaquat the mistakes which he claimed had been made were largely due to his own attitude in the Partition Council. He was really getting at Nehru, who sat with closed eyes, half asleep. After the meeting when my A.D.C. was waiting to show Trivedi and Patel into their car he heard the following conversation:

" *Trivedi :* Panditji looks quite done up.

Patel: So he deserves to be, flying all over the country and making fools of us all."

I hope that we have now seen an end of the visits to this province of Nehru and his fellow politicians. By his hectoring manner he did considerable damage to the morale of the District Administration of Sheikhupura. Besides, he brings newspaper-men like Durga Das with him. I hope that it will be possible to prevent further visits to Lahore.

This all sounds very gloomy, but we are all in quite good heart. Moss and Amin-ud-Din are pillars of strength. If we can get some of our old officers back, the whole situation will change.

I do not know whether I have addressed you in this letter as you wish to be addressed. If not, will you please let me know?

Yours sincerely,

(Sd.) Francis Mudie.

His Excellency Qaid-i-Azam Mohammad Ali Jinnah,
      Governor General of Pakistan,
          Karachi.

Note to Chapter Five

The letter of Khan Bahadur Allah Bux to the Viceroy renouncing his titles:

" I have decided to renounce both the honours (K.B. and O.B.E.) I hold from the British Government, as I feel I cannot, consistently with my views and convictions, retrain them any longer. India has been struggling for her national freedom for a long time past. Upon the outbreak of the present war, it was hoped that, under the very principles and ideology in defence of which the Allies were waging a titanic conflict, India would be made free to participate in the world struggle as a free country. Convinced as I am that India has every right to be free and that the people of India should have conditions in which they could live in peace and harmony, the declaration and action of the British Government have made it clear that, instead of giving co-operation to various Indian parties and communities in settling their differences and parting with power to the people of the land and allowing them to live happily in freedom and mould the destinies of their country according to their birth-right, the policy of the British Government has been to continue their imperialistic hold on India and persist in keeping her under subjection, use political and communal differences for propaganda purposes and crush the national forces to serve their own imperialistic aims and intentions. The latest speech delivered by Mr. Winston Churchill in the House of Commons has caused the greatest disappointment to all men of goodwill who wish to see justice rendered to India—which is long due to her. As that hapless pronouncement withholds such justice from India and adds to the volume of evidence that Britain has no desire to give up her imperialistic hold on India, I feel I cannot retain the honours I hold from the British Government which, in the circumstances that have arisen, I cannot but regard as tokens of British imperialism."

Note to Chapter Six

That is what Khan Abdul Qaiyum Khan says in "Gold and Guns on the Pathan Frontier": "The first to go were the Honorary Magistrates. Their powers were henceforth to be exercised by the regular Courts. These old-fashioned gentlemen were mostly corrupt, some were illiterate, almost all were ignorant of the first principles of Criminal Law. Powers had been conferred on such people because they acted as the intermediaries through whom the British hoped to control the masses. . . . The Zaildars who were placed over the headmen of a number of villages were mostly corrupt. They were often employed by the police for cooking up false cases and also sometimes as intermediaries for collecting bribes for dishonest officials. They too shared the fate of the Honorary Magistrates. Then there were the Muafidars (Muafi is the cash remission of land revenue granted to a person) who were no better than parasites. The Muafidars were mainly Government informers, unpatriotic men always anxious to create trouble for those who believed in freedom. . . . The Zaildars, the Honorary Magistrates and the Muafidars soon became the champions of Islam and with the cry of 'Islam in danger' were the Frontier's first recruits to the Muslim League, of which, in this province, they still formed the backbone. This class saw an admirable opportunity in the Muslim League, where, while posing as champions of Islam, they could protect their own vested interests and settle old scores against the progressive forces."

APPENDIX II

APPENDIX II
TABLES AND STATEMENTS

DISTRICT LAHORE

Sl. No.	Name of village	Date	Number of witnesses	Nature of incident	Number of casualties		Number of converted	Number of kidnapped or abducted
					Killed	Injured		
1	Pattoki	Mid. Aug.	5	Murder and desecration	195	300	—	—
2	Thakipur	16-8-47	3	Murder and loot	15	—	—	—
3	Manhala Kalan	17-8-47	8	Murder, loot, abduction, conversion and desecration.	15	Several	—	Several
4	Halloki	19-8-47	2	Murder and kidnapping..	32	—	—	—
5	Deo Sid	Do.	6	Murder, loot, arson & abduction.	400	Many	—	8
6	Bhikhiwind	Do.	2	Murder, loot and abduction	17	Many	—	11
7	Raja Jang	20-8-47	12	Murder, loot and conversion	50	—	Many	—
8	Shahpur Kanjra	24-8-47	3	Murder, loot and conversion	15	Many	Many	—
9	Padhana	20-8-47	5	Murder, loot, arson & abduction	8	25	400	4
10	Bugri	Do	3	Murder and loot	125	—	—	—
11	Bhasin	Do.	5	Murder and loot	38	—	—	—
12	Wagha	Do.	5	Murder, loot and arson	26	—	—	—
13	Kacha Pucca	20-8-47	3	Murder and conversion ..	15	—	Whole village	—
14	Luliani	23-8-47	18	Murder, loot and desecration	24	200	—	—
15	Gagon	22-8-47	3	Murder and loot	125	5	—	—
16	Ganjay Sadhu	23-8-47	6	Murder, loot, arson and abduction	27	5	—	10
		Do.			22			
17	Kahna Kachha	Do.	6	Murder, loot and abduction	3•	—	—	2
18	Mokal	Do.	2	Murder and loot	27	—	—	—
19	Jia Bagga	24-8-47	4	Murder, loot and abduction	80	—	—	—
20	Niaz Beg	28-8-47	5	Murder, conversion & abduction	30	—	24	4

DISTRICT SHEIKHUPURA

No.	Village	Date		Nature of crime				Abducted / Raped
1	Hardey	17-8-47	8	Murder, abduction, rape and loot.	150	200	—	70 abducted, 20 raped
2	Sharakpur	18-8-47	1	Murder, abduction, conversion and loot.	150	—	15	10
3	Jatri Vikran	21-8-47	12	Murder, loot and desecration	400	130	—	—
4	Bhuller	21-8-47 / 22-8-47	1	Murder, abduction and loot. (aided by Muslim League National Guards and military).	650	—	—	—
5	Gangapur	22-8-47	2	Murder, abduction and loot	500	—	—	450
6	Bhaini	23-8-47	1	Loot and desecration	—	—	—	—
7	Dhaban Singh	24-8-47	35	Murder and loot	89	—	—	—
8	Awan	24-8-47	1	Murder, abduction, loot and conversion.	100	—	160	125
9	Malakpur	25-8-47	1	Murder, arson, loot & abduction	11	E.F.N.A.	—	29
10	Kile, near Shahdra	27-8-47	1	Murder and loot.	6	—	—	—
		7-9-47	1	Murder (by military).	100	48	—	—
11	Faridabad	28-8-47	6	Murder, conversion and loot	30	—	—	—
12	Gaji Andriooni	29-8-47	1	Murder and abduction (aided by military).	54	E.F.N.A.	E.F.N.A.	10
13	Gopalpura	Aug. 47	2	Murder, abduction and loot (aided by military and police).	67	—	—	4
14	Gazi Mudwala	Aug. 47	10	Murder, burning alive, loot, arson, abduction and rape (aided by military).	67	—	—	4
15	Gobindgarh	2-9-47	1	Murder	E.F.N.A.	—	—	—
		22-9-47	1	Murder and loot (by police and military).	30	60	—	—
16	Chak No. 11 G.B.	3-9-47	1	Murder and loot	60	100	—	—
17	Machhike	17-9-47	1	Murder and loot (by military)	150	3	—	—
18	Bucheki	—	10	Murder, loot, arson and death by starvation.	11	—	—	—
19	Chak No. 5	—	7	Murder, arson, loot and abduction (by military).	500	70	30	—
	Ambekalia	—	7	Murder, abduction and loot	80	20	—	20

E.F.N.A.—Exact figures not available.

Sl. No.	Name of village	Date	Number of witnesses	Nature of incident	Number of casualties		Number of converted	Number of kidnapped or abducted
					Killed	Injured		
20	Feroz Wattuan	—	3	Murder, loot, abduction and conversion.	3	—	E.F.N.A.	6
21	Bahalwala	—	3	Murder, loot, abduction and arson.	1,000	500	Do.	100
22	Chak No. 58	—	2	Murder and loot (by military)	100	70	—	—
23	Kalike	—	5	Murder, abduction and loot	15	12	50	50
	Do.	—	5	Attack on running train (by military).	150	—	—	—
24	Bandeki	—	2	Murder, abduction and loot	16	—	—	4
25	Warburton	—	32	Murder and loot (by military)	120	—	—	—
	DISTRICT SIALKOT							
1	Kalian	28-8-47	2	Arson, abduction and loot	—	—	—	2
2	Umho Chak	14-8-47	1	Murder and loot	18	—	—	40
3	Ranghar	16-8-47	2	Murder, abduction, loot and conversion.	300	—	15	—
4	Rangpur	15-8-47	1	Murder, loot and arson	5	16	—	—
5	Gondal	15-8-47	2	General loot	—	—	—	—
6	Kullowal	15-8-47	2	Murder, loot, abduction and conversion.	200	53	15	250
7	Sukhial	16-8-47	1	Murder, loot and arson	7	—	—	—
8	Othian	16-8-47	43	Murder, loot and conversion	62	140	—	30
9	Udho Khir	16-8-47	2	Loot, murder and arson	2	E.F.N.A.	—	—
10	Halowal	16-8-47	1	Murder, abduction, loot and arson.	100	—	—	500
11	Killa	17-8-47	1	Murder, conversion, abduction, loot and arson.	1	—	30	3

No.	Place	Date		Nature of crime				
12	Kartarpur Bostan	17-8-47	5	Conversion, loot and arson	—	—	1,000	—
13	Dharewal	17-8-47	1	Murder and loot	10	4	—	—
14	Rangpura	18-8-47	2	Murder, loot and arson	12	—	—	—
15	Ramal	18-8-47	1	Murder, loot and arson	25	—	—	—
16	Nadala	18-8-47		Murder, loot and arson	8	—	—	—
17	Taranwala	18-8-47	2	Murder, general loot and arson.	2	—	—	—
18	Kuluwal	18-8-47	13	Murder, abduction, loot and arson (aided by M.L.N.G.).	600	200	—	15
19	Nainia	18-8-47	1	Murder, loot and arson	6	—	—	—
20	Beli	18-8-47	1	Murder and loot	40	—	—	—
21	Darman	18-8-47	1	Murder, abduction, loot and arson.	15	—	—	7
22	Kanjrur Dattan	18-8-47	14	Murder, mass conversion, loot and arson (aided by M.L.N.G. and Muslim military).	500	300	80	300
23	Adamkeychima	18-8-47	2	Murder, general loot and arson.	14	—	—	—
24	Jadhowali	18-8-47	5	Murder and loot	150	—	—	—
25	Jadhola	18-8-47	9	General loot and arson.	1	—	—	—
26	Gill	18-8-47	2	Murder, abduction, loot and arson.	50	—	—	7
27	Gharowal	18-8-47	1	Murder and loot	30	20	—	6
28	Bhatta	19-8-47	1	General loot and abduction	7	—	—	1
29	Shalla	19-8-47		Loot and murder.	2	—	—	—
30	Gangwal	19-8-47	2	Murder, abduction and loot	125	—	—	—
31	Jassar	19-8-47	10	Murder, loot and arson	40	E.F.N.A.	—	E.F.N.A.
32	Ahtulal	19-8-47	1	Murder, loot and arson (aided by military and Muslim police).	18	—	8	—
33	Janglora	20-8-47	2	Murder, loot and arson	5	—	—	—
34	Ikhlaspur	20-8-47	2	Murder, loot and arson	3	—	—	—
35	Seer	20-8-47	2	Murder, loot and arson	10	—	—	—
36	Theli	21-8-47	3	Murder, abduction, general loot and arson (aided by M.L.N.G.)	80	20	—	20
37	Shahzaida	20-8-47	8	Murder, abduction, loot and arson.	900	50	—	125
38	Pindi Dunian	20-8-47	1	Arson, abduction, murder and loot.	2	—	—	2
39	Manga Bran	20-8-47	4	Murder, loot and arson	6	—	—	—

E.F.N.A.—Exact figures not available.   M.L.N.G.—Muslim League National Guards.

Sl. No.	Name of village	Date	Number of witnesses	Nature of incident	Number of casualties — Killed	Number of casualties — Injured	Number of converted	Number of kidnapped or abducted
40	Gari Bhura	20-8-47	3	Murder, loot and arson	4	—	—	1
41	Chak Kotla	20-8-47	1	Murder and loot	22	—	—	—
42	Doaba	21-8-47	1	Murder, abduction, loot and arson	18	—	—	2
43	Ban Bajwa	21-8-47	1	Murder, conversion, abduction, loot and arson	E.F.N.A.	E.F.N.A.	150	1
44	Gulbahar	21-8-47	1	Murder, abduction and loot	13	40	—	E.F.N.A.
45	Amirshah	21-8-47	1	Murder, loot and arson	16	—	—	—
46	Kushal Garh	21-8-47	1	Murder and loot	6	—	—	—
47	Bhyochak	21-8-47	1	Murder, loot and arson (aided by police and Muslim military)	11	—	—	7
48	Peerkot	22-8-47	2	Murder and loot	100	E.F.N.A.	—	—
49	Mattanwala	22-8-47	1	Murder, abduction, loot and arson	150			18
50	Bhatan Wala	22-8-47	2	Murder and loot	3	—	—	—
51	Nirgal	22-8-47	1	Murder, abduction and loot	2	—	—	1
52	Dhabliwala	22-8-47	1	Murder, abduction, loot and arson	Many	—	—	60
53	Chak Bika	22-8-47	1	Murder, loot and arson	E.F.N.A.	—	—	—
54	Gangran	23-8-47	3	General loot, arson and murder	12	—	—	9
55	Randhawa	23-8-47	2	Murder, abduction and loot	10	12	—	—
56	Dhattal	23-8-47	1	Conversion, loot and arson	—		E.F.N.A.	2
57	Sankhatra	24-8-47	6	Murder, conversion, abduction, loot and arson	30	E.F.N.A.	60	2
58	Dudwan	24-8-47	1	Murder, abduction and loot	3	—	—	2
59	Dhapai	24-8-47	3	Murder, abduction, conversion, general loot and arson	300	Many	45	60
60	Bari	24-8-47	1	Murder, abduction, loot and arson	6	—	—	3

No.	Village	Date	No.	Nature of outrage				
61	Kandansian ..	25-8-47	1	General loot, arson and conversion.	—	—	E.F.N.A.	—
62	Garmola ..	25-8-47	2	Murder, abduction, loot and arson.	150	—	—	6
63	Beli	25-8-47	10	Murder, loot of property worth several lakhs.	40	—	50	—
64	Mundeke Berian ..	25-8-47	1	Murder, conversion and loot	5	—	—	—
65	Jangike ..	25-8-47	2	Murder and general loot	5	—	—	30
66	Dera Brahwan ..	25-8-47	1	Murder, abduction and loot	20	200	—	—
67	Jarwal ..	25-8-47	5	Murder and loot	E.F.N.A.	—	—	—
68	Qaimpur ..	25-8-47	2	Murder, abduction, loot and arson.	20	—	—	3
69	Poong ..	25-8-47	1	Murder, abduction and loot	22	7	—	2
70	Mallah ..	25-8-47	5	Mass murder, abduction, conversion, loot and arson.	400	60	39	34
71	Gojra ..	26-8-47	4	Murder, conversion, abduction and loot.	22	Many	40	10
72	Charwah ..	26-8-47	1	Murder, abduction, loot and arson.	55	1	—	2
73	Lala Aulakh ..	27-8-47	3	Murder, abduction, loot and arson.	90/100	18/20	—	25
74	Bhureki ..	27-8-47	3	Murder, abduction, loot and arson.	100	—	—	40
75	Wadala Sidhwan ..	28-8-47	1	Murder, conversion, abduction, loot and arson.	100	100	E.F.N.A.	20
76	Dhungi ..	28-8-47	1	Murder, abduction, loot and arson.	22	—	—	7
77	Pura Nekka ..	28-8-47	3	Conversion and loot	—	—	150	—
78	Olkan ..	28-8-47	3	Murder, abduction and loot	80	20	—	—
79	Bharike ..	28-8-47	1	Murder, abduction and conversion.	200	—	E.F.N.A.	50
80	Habipur ..	28-8-47	8	Murder, abduction, conversion and loot.	350	E.F.N.A.	45	60
81	Lallia ..	28-8-47	1	Murder, abduction, loot and arson (aided by M.L.N.G.).	225	—	—	55
82	Throgh ..	28-8-47	1	Murder, loot and arson	25	100	—	—

E.F.N.A.—Exact figures not available.   M.L.N.G.—Muslim League National Guards.

Sl. No.	Name of village	Date	Number of witnesses	Nature of incident	Killed	Injured	Number of converted	Number of kidnapped or abducted
83	Hubipur	28-8-47	2	Murder, conversion, abduction, loot and arson.	350	50	30	160
84	Phorpian	28-8-47	2	Murder, abduction, loot and arson.	600	300	—	400
85	Dakki	28-8-47	9	Murder, abduction, arson and general loot.	160	70	—	100
86	Baddomali	29-8-47	1	Murder, conversion, abduction, loot and arson.	1,000	—	1,600	200
87	Ghug	30-8-47	2	Loot and arson	2	—	E.F.N.A.	—
88	Jandran	31-8-47	1	Murder, conversion, abduction and loot.	20	—		21
89	Lalewali	31-8-47	4	Murder and loot	15	—	—	—
90	Sadanwala	31-8-47	2	Murder, conversion, abduction and loot.	8	—	80	15
91	Shesian	1-9-47	3	General loot and wholesale arson.	·	—	—	—
92	Mihal	2-9-47	2	Murder, loot and arson	20	—	—	—
93	Sagar	2-9-47	2	Murder and loot	70	—	—	—
94	Mashrala	2-9-47	1	Murder, conversion, abduction and loot.	150	—	100	10
95	Dawood	2-9-47	1	Murder, abduction and loot	7	—	—	14
96	Chakarwala	3-9-47	1	Murder and loot (aided by Baluch military and Muslim police).	25	—	—	—
97	Hailbeywan	6-9-47	2	Murder and loot	14	—	—	—
98	Parthanwala	15-9-47	1	Murder, abduction, loot and arson.	50	—	—	2
99	Kansharpur	18-9-47	6	Murder and loot	3	15	—	—
100	Kusharpur	18-9-47	5	Murder, conversion and loot	1	15	1 family	—

No.	Village	Date		Nature of outrage				
101	Naina Kot	19-9-47	1	Murder and loot	11	50	—	—
102	Sarangian	22-9-47	2	Murder and general loot	30	—	—	5
103	Mastpur Jattan	21-9-47	1	Murder, loot and arson	21	—	25	10
104	Thakarpur and Ganga Nahanga.	29-9-47	2	General loot and forcible conversion.	—	—	—	—
105	Machrala	29-9-47	8	Murder, abduction, loot and arson (bribery of Rs. 3,000).	158	80	—	—
106	Chagri	Sept. 1947	2	Murder, conversion and loot	8	—	E.F.N.A.	—
107	Balloke	—	1	Murder, loot and arson	5	—	—	—
108	Karola	22-11-47	3	Murder and loot	9	—	—	—
109	Pindi Panjara	Nov. 1947	1	Murder, abduction, loot and arson.	123	—	—	6
110	Bhola Musa	Do.	5	Murder, conversion and loot	1	—	E.F.N.A.	—
111	Bhunga Nehanga	Do.	2	Murder and loot	13	—	—	—
112	Dalaki	Do.	1	Murder and loot. Loss of Rs. 20,00,000. Killed in Gurdwara (women and children).	75	—	—	—
113	Karola	Dec. 1947	1	Murder and loot	500	1	—	—
114	Khrota	Do.	10	Murder, abduction and loot	9	—	E.F.N.A.	2
115	Khokarwali	Do.	1	Murder, conversion and loot	9	—	E.F.N.A.	—
116	Ladhar	Do.	2	Murder, abduction and loot	100	—	—	—
117	Mian Hospal	Dec. 1947	1	Murder and loot (desecration of Gurdwaras).	33	—	—	16
118	Palar	Do.	1	Murder and loot	100	—	—	—
119	Ranwa	Do.	1	Murder, loot and arson	10	—	—	—
120	Sansian	Do.	1	Murder, conversion, general loot and arson.	100	—	40	—
121	Sangla Chak	Do.	1	Murder and loot (aided by police)	6	—	—	—
122	Sambrial	Do.	2	Murder, general loot and arson.	5	—	—	—
123	Solehpur	Do.	1	Murder and loot (aided by Muslim police).	15	—	—	—
124	Thorta	Do.	1	Murder and general loot	9	8	—	—

E.F.N.A.—Exact figures not available.

DISTRICT GUJRANWALA

Sl. No.	Name of village	Date	Number of witnesses	Nature of incident	Number of casualties		Number of converted	Number of kidnapped or abducted
					Killed	Injured		
1	Wayanwali (Gujranwala Camp).	16-8-47	5	Murder, loot, arson and food poisoning.	150	—	—	—
	Deodian (Gujranwala Camp).	10-9-47	5	Murder, loot, arson and food poisoning.	E.F.N.A.	—	—	—
2	Attal	16-8-47	3	Loot, arson, murder and desecration.	50	12	—	—
3	Ram Nagar	17-8-47	10	Murder, arson, conversion and desecration.	1	—	E.F.N.A.	—
4	Thata-Jat Mianwala.	Do.	2	Loot and evacuation (aided by police).	—	—	—	—
5	Karula	Do.	1	Murder, arson, conversion and desecration (aided by M.L.N.G., police and military).	150	—	100	—
6	Garmula	18-8-47	3	Murder, conversion and loot	120	5	40	—
7	Ghorian	Do.	2	Murder, abduction, conversion and loot.	10	—	17	5
8	Gilt Gitta	19-8-47	1	Murder, conversion and loot	35	18	9	5
9	Ajan Chak	19-8-47	1	Conversion and loot	—	—	150	20
		10-9-47		Murder, abduction and rape	20	—	—	1
10	Durgapur	20-8-47	2	Murder, conversion, loot, arson and abduction.	8	—	5	—
11	Mansoorwali	21-8-47	1	Murder, mass conversion and loot.	200	—	E.F.N.A.	—
12	Udhowali	Do.	1	Murder, conversion, arson, desecration and loot.	30	—	10	—
13	Buddo Ratta	Do.	2	Murder and loot (aided by military and police).	79	43	—	—

							E.F.N.A.	
14	Patala Sham Singh	21-8-47	2	Murder, conversion and loot ..	5	—	145	—
15	Jalal	Do.	2	Murder, abduction, mass conversion and loot.	17	—	83	7
16	Wazir-ke-Chatta	Do.	1	Mass conversion, murder and loot.	22	—		—
17	Baladpur	22-8-47	1	Murder, arson, rape and loot	20	2	—	5
18	Hardo Deori	23-8-47	1	Murder, arson and loot ..	25	2	—	—
19	Chicharwali Kalan	Do.	3	Murder and loot	19	—	—	—
20	Kuryala	Do.	11	Murder, burning alive, arson, conversion and loot.	50	—	150	200
21	Kehar Wali	Do.	1	Murder, abduction, conversion, desecration and loot.	250	—	770	—
22	Dandian Saloke	Do.	1	Murder, abduction, conversion, desecration and loot.	9	—	13	2
23	Chakrali	24-8-47	2	Murder and abduction ..	70	20	—	20
24	Babbar	Do.	11	Murder, burning alive, arson, conversion and loot.	24	3	249	7
25	Killa Didarsingh	Do.	2	Murder, arson, conversion and loot.	200	—	200	3
26	Deodhi	Do.	1	Murder, arson, conversion and loot (aided by police).	22	—	180	—
27	Dhinse	25-8-47	1	Murder, arson, conversion and loot (aided by police).	22	—	70	—
28	Kakekaula	26-8-47	1	Murder, conversion, arson and loot (aided by police).	30	—	12	—
29	Thata Chima	26-8-47	1	Murder, conversion and loot (aided by police).	200	—	135	—
30	Landewala Chima	27-8-47	2	Murder, abduction and loot ..	110	13	—	2
31	Chak Khalil	Do.	5	Murder and loot ..	23	—	—	—
32	Wazirabad (train incident).	28-8-47	1	Murder and loot	150	—	—	—
33	Mandal Chattak	Do.	1	Murder, conversion and loot (aided by M.L.N.G.)	43	—	43	—
34	Bhango	Do.	1	Murder and loot ..	7	2	—	—
	Bhango (near Alipur Saidan).	Sept. 1947		Murder (aided by military)	1,000	—	—	—

E.F.N.A.—Exact figures not available.　　　　　M.L.N.G.—Muslim League National Guards.

Sl. No.	Name of village	Date	Number of witnesses	Nature of incident	Number of casualties		Number of converted	Number of kidnapped or abducted
					Killed	Injured		
35	Dharowal	28-8-47	1	Conversion and loot	—	—	125	—
36	Majhu Chak	29-8-47	1	Murder, loot, abduction and desecration.	150	—	—	22
37	Jaura Sian	30-8-47	1	Murder, abduction, conversion, arson, loot and desecration.	76	—	25	20
38	Gojargola	31-8-47	1	Mass conversion, murder and loot.	3	1	E.F.N.A.	—
39	Wazirke	Do.	9	Murder, conversion, loot and abduction.	26	—	200	4
40	Kot Nakka	Aug. 1947	1	Murder and loot	30	—	—	—
41	Chowdry Chak	Do.	5	Murder, desecration, rape and conversion.	27	30	11	1
42	Butla Jhanda	Do.	1	Forcible conversion	—	—	20	—
43	Hamidpur	Do.	3	Murder, conversion, loot and abduction.	26	1	7	1
44	Chak Purian	Aug. 1947	2	Murder and mass conversion	3	—	70	—
45	Chinne	Do.	1	Mass conversion (aided by military).	—	—	150	—
46	Sodhra	Do.	1	Murder, arson, conversion and desecration (aided by police).	150	—	100	—
47	Doresh	Do.	6	Murder, mass conversion, abduction and loot.	32	—	200	—
48	Bhudopur	Do.	3	Murder, mass conversion, loot and abduction.	12	—	40	1
49	Akbar Vikran	Do.	9	Murder, conversion, loot and desecration (aided by police).	96	—	100	1
50	Adulakh Bhai	Do.	2	Murder, conversion and loot	2	—	10	—

No.	Name of village	Date		Nature of outrage				
				murder, arson, abduction and loot (aided by police).	50	—	—	11
52	Kalewale	10-9-47	4	Murder, mass conversion, arson and loot (aided by police).	5	—	300	3
53	Walikay Tador	Do.	2	Murder, mass conversion, abduction, rape and loot.	180	—	700	6
54	Kot Fatehwal	14-9-47	5	Murder, arson, conversion, and loot (aided by military and police).	25	—	12	—
55	Dhirowali	Sept. 1947	2	Murder, loot, arson, conversion, abduction and rape.	4	—	55	2
56	Hardeo	Do.	2	Murder and drowning	3	—	—	—
	Sansa Trada	Do.		Murder	80	50	—	—
	Mallah Vikran	Do.		Murder and loot (aided by military).	3	—	—	—

DISTRICT GUJRAT

No.	Name of village	Date		Nature of outrage				
1	Mangot	18-8-47	4	Murder, loot, desecration (aided by police).	32	E.F.N.A.	—	—
2	Panerewala	Do.	1	Murder, food poisoning, and loot (aided by military).	45	—	—	—
3	Dhoka Wada Lak	Do.	1	Mass conversion and loot	—	—	E.F.N.A.	100
4	Thakar Kalan	Do.	3	Murder, abduction, arson and loot.	E.F.N.A.	—	—	—
5	Nowshera Miana	Do.	1	Murder and loot (aided by military).	Large number	—	—	—
6	Nizamabad	Do.	1	Murder, and train attack	700	200	200	—
	Jalalpur Jattan	Do.	1	Murder, burning alive, desecration and loot (aided by military and police).	Large number	—	—	—
7	Jora	Do.	1	Conversion and loot	1	—	—	—
8	Ajjowal	Do.	1	Murder, conversion, and loot (aided by military).	7	—	E.F.N.A.	193
9	Fatehpur	Do.	1	Conversion and loot	5	—	45	—
10	Higgarwala	19-8-47	3	Loot	—	6	—	—
11	Sohbitian	Do.	1	Murder, loot and arson	3	—	—	—

E.F.N.A.—Exact figures not available.

Sl. No.	Name of village	Date	Number of witnesses	Nature of incident	Number of casualties		Number of converted	Number of kidnapped or abducted
					Killed	Injured		
12	Seera	20-8-47	7	Murder, food poisoning, conversion, desecration and loot.	5	—	E.F.N.A.	—
13	Ratto	22-8-47	1	Conversion and loot	—	—	18	—
14	Heggarkurd	Do.	1	Murder, food poisoning, arson and loot.	Large number	—	—	—
15	Bhagowal	23-8-47	1	Murder, conversion, loot and desecration.	1	1	170	—
16	Tanda	25-8-47	3	Murder, abduction, arson and loot.	E.F.N.A.	—	—	100
17	Chak No. 21	26-8-47	2	Conversion and loot	—	—	105	—
18	Shadiwal	27-8-47	1	Murder, abduction and loot	53	—	—	12
19	Wasu	Do.	3	Loot	—	—	E.F.N.A.	—
20	Bhairowal	29-8-47	4	Murder, abduction and mass conversion.	1,400	—	—	100
21	Lassuri Kalan	Do.	2	Loot	—	—	—	—
22	Mian Gondal	30-8-47	1	Mass conversion	—	—	1,000	—
23	Musa Khurd	Do.	7	Murder, loot and desecration	70	—	—	—
24	Jajur	Do.	3	Murder and mass conversion	1	—	299	—
25	Rerka	Do.	3	Conversion	—	—	1,000	—
26	Tahali Sahib	Aug. 1947	2	Murder, loot and arson	6	—	E.F.N.A.	—
27	Thatta Par	Do.	1	Mass conversion and loot	—	—	—	—
28	Malakpur	Do.	10	Murder, abduction and loot	60	—	98	4
29	Ran	Do.	3	Murder, conversion, loot and abduction.	1	—	—	1
30	Gorhi	Do.	5	Conversion and loot	—	—	170	—
31	Bahaudin	1-9-47	4	Murder, loot, arson and desecration (aided by police).	500	—	60	—
32	Jassowal	2-9-47	1	Conversion and loot	—	—	300	—

No.	Place	Date		Nature of crime				
33	Qadarbad ..	Do.	2	Murder, abduction, rape and loot.	27	200	—	17
34	Saidulla ..	4-9-47	2	Murder ...	15	—	—	400
35	Dinga ..	5-9-47	4*	Murder, food poisoning and abduction.	Large number	—	—	—
36	Malikpur ..	Do.	3	Murder and loot (aided by police)	25	5	500	—
37	Hassanwali ..	Do.	2	Mass conversion and loot	—	—	100	—
38	Bagrianwala ..	Do.	1	Conversion, murder, arson and loot.	75	—	—	2
39	Chak No. 2 ..	6-9-47	3	Murder, conversion, abduction and loot.	40	—	750	—
40	Chachian ..	7-9-47	3	Murder, desecration and conversion.	1	—	48	—
41	Chak Sada ..	8-9-47	2	Murder and conversion	2	—	E.F.N.A.	—
42	Shahdra ..	14-9-47	3	Murder (aided by military)	5	6	—	—
43	Nadhir ..	18-9-47	5	Murder, conversion and loot	4	—	125	—
44	Chak Raib ..	Oct./Nov. 1947	3	Murder, desecration, conversion and loot.	1	—	E.F.N.A.	—
	DISTRICT MONTGOMERY							
1	Diptianwala ..	15-8-47	1	Murder and loot (aided by M.L.N.G., police and military).	18	—	—	—
2	Qila Sonda Singh ..	16-8-47	5	Murder, arson and loot	61	—	—	—
3	Huzrashah Mukim	17-8-47	1	Murder and loot ..	Many	—	—	—
4	Chak No. 33/1 A.L.	18-8-47	2	Murder and loot ...	15	—	2,500	2
5	Jandarkar ..	Do.	1	Murder, arson, mass conversion, desecration, loot and abduction.	1	—	—	—
6	Noor Shah ..	19-8-47	5	Murder and loot ..	125	—	—	—
7	Dipalpur City ..	Do.	1	Murder and loot (aided by police and Tehsildar).	15	—	—	—
8	Renala Khurd ..	20-8-47	8	Murder and loot (aided by Baluch military).	60	—	—	—
9	Basidpur ..	21-8-47	1	Murder, abduction and loot (aided by police and military).	Large number	—	—	10

E.F.N.A.—Exact figures not available.

M.L.N.G.—Muslim League National Guards.

Sl. No.	Name of village	Date	Number of witnesses	Nature of incident	Number of casualties		Number of converted	Number of kidnapped or abducted
					Killed	Injured		
10	Wazirpur	21-8-47	10	Murder, loot and abduction (aided by police and military).	300	—	—	50
11	Chak No. 37/9 L.	22-8-47	1	Murder and loot	7	—	—	—
12	Beli Gunj	Do.	1	Murder and loot	10	20	—	—
13	Chak No. 53-SB.	Do.	1	Murder and loot (aided by M.L.N.G. and police).	2	—	—	—
14	Mauza Mirdad Maufi.	Do.	1	Murder and loot	32	—	—	20
15	Malka Hans	Do.	1	Murder, arson, conversion and abduction.	15	—	40 families	2
16	Chichawatni	22-8-47	1	Murder, abduction and loot (aided by police).	200	—	—	2
17	Chak No. 116/9-L.	23-8-47	7	Murder and loot	30	—	—	—
18	Chak No. 11	Do.	2	Murder and loot	5	1	—	—
19	Kumbhariwala	24-8-47	5	Murder, mass conversion, loot abduction and desecration.	50	—	E.F.N.A.	15
20	Kanda	25-8-47	2	Murder, mass conversion, loot and abduction.	9	E.F.N.A.	Do.	2
21	Ambli Moti	26-8-47	6	Murder, loot and mass conversion.	28	—	Do.	—
22	Chak No. 105	Do.	2	Murder and loot (aided by police and military).	Large number	—	—	—
23	Chak No. 39/14L	26-8-47	1	Loot, murder and arson	52	15	—	—
24	Chak No. 70/5L	28-8-47	5	Loot	—	—	—	70
25	Chak No. 47/5-L	Do.	1	Murder, abduction, conversion and loot (aided by military).	Large number	—	60	—
26	Boladuba	30-8-47	4	Murder and abduction	33	—	—	70
27	Chak No. 60/12-L.	Aug. 1947	3	Murder and loot	6	—	—	5

DISTRICT LYALLPUR

	Place	Date		Nature of outrage				
1	Chak No. 224 ..	17-8-47	2	Murder, and arrest of leaders (aided by police).	48	100	—	—
2	Parel ..	20-8-47	1	Murder, abduction and loot	5	—	—	4
3	Chak No. 189	Do.	5	Murder	5	—	—	—
	Tohan ..	Do.	5	Murder	100	—	200	—
4	Dhaulri ..	21-8-47	10	Murder, abduction, loot and mass conversion.	83	—	—	E.F.N.A.
5	Chak No. 127	22-8-47	12	Murder, abduction and loot	200	50	—	15
6	Gangapur ..	23-8-47	3	Murder and loot	400	—	—	—
7	Chak No. 58	Do.	3	Murder, loot and abduction	2,000	E.F.N.A.	—	800
	Khila Kalan	28-8-47	6	Murder, loot and arrest of leaders (aided by Muslim League National Guards and military).	106	43	—	—
8	Bhuller ..	29-8-47	3	Murder, arson, loot and rape ..	300	250	—	Abduction 15 rape 20
9	Gujersinghwala ..	Aug. 1947	3	Murder (aided by military)	12	5	—	7
10	Chak No. 362	31-8-47	7	Murder, loot and abduction	60	10	—	—
	Chak No. 53 J.B. ..	Aug. 1947	4	Murder and loot	1	—	—	—
11	Louki	Do.	4	Murder ..	80	—	—	—
	Chak No. 518	2-9-47	3	Murder and loot	10	—	—	—
12	Chak No. 50	3-9-47	2	Murder and loot	6	2	—	—
13	Attarwali ..	4-9-47	2	Murder and loot	14	—	—	—
14	Mamakanjar	5-9-47	2	Murder, abduction, rape, desecration and arson.	175	125	—	Abduction 20 Rape 20
15	Chak No. 447	8-9-47	6	Murder and loot	20	—	—	—
16	Chak No. 29	12-9-47	4	Murder and loot	60	7	—	—
17	Chak No. 58	2-10-47	5	Murder, abduction and loot	500	300	—	300
18	Gangapur ..	—	4	Murder, loot, arson, rape and abduction.	50	150	—	14
19	Chak No. 294	—	4	Murder, loot and abduction	10	—	—	E.F.N.A.
20	Chak No. 297 J.B.	—	2	Murder and loot	9	—	—	—

E.F.N.A.—Exact figures not available.   M.L.N.G.—Muslim League National Guards.

DISTRICT SHAHPORE

Sl. No.	Name of village	Date	Number of witnesses	Nature of incident	Number of casualties		Number of converted	Number of kidnapped or abducted
					Killed	Injured		
1	Dera Murad	15-8-47	1	Forcible conversion	—	—	E.F.N.A.	E.F.N.A.
2	Lak	16-8-47	2	Rape, conversion and loot	—	—	Do.	E.F.N.A.
3	Chak Misra	19-8-47	1	Murder and loot	4	—	—	—
4	Ranjha	20-8-47	2	Roasting of children	3	—	—	—
5	Mian Kot	23-8-47	2	Conversion (by military)	—	—	40	—
6	Chawa	24-8-47	2	Conversion and loot	—	—	45	—
7	Nali	25-8-47	3	Conversion and loot	—	—	30	—
8	Chaus Mohd. Wala	26-8-47	4	Conversion and evacuation	—	—	9 families	—
9	Nur Pur	Do.	12	Abduction and murder (aided by police).	—	—	9	—
10	Gurna Patana	28-8-47	2	Loot	—	—	—	—
11	Lila Hani	29-8-47	9	Conversion, murder and loot (police involved).	—	9	120	—
12	Doda	Do.	8	Conversion and loot (aided by police).	—	—	E.F.N.A.	—
13	Chak No. 120 S.B.	31-8-47	1	Murder and loot	E.F.N.A.	—	—	—
14	Takhat Hazara	Do.	15	Murder, conversion and desecration.	4	—	22	—
15	Mian Hazara	Do.	15	Conversion	—	—	E.F.N.A.	—
16	Homoka	Aug. 1947	1	Loot and conversion	—	—	4	—
17	Chak Gandewala	Do.	4	Conversion and loot	—	—	E.F.N.A.	—
	Chak No. 87	Do.	5	Murder and conversion (aided by police).	1	—	Do.	—
18	Kot Moman	Do.	2	Murder and conversion (aided by police).	8	—	60	—

No.	Place	Date	No.	Nature of crime				
19	Chak No. 23	Do.	3	Murder, conversion and loot	1	—	E.F.N.A.	—
20	Kai Kalyan	1-9-47	1	Conversion and loot	—	—	Do.	—
21	Kupri	Do.	2	Desecration and loot	—	—	35	—
22	Jallap	Do.	1	Murder, conversion and loot	E.F.N.A.	—	E.F.N.A.	—
23	Mid Ranja	3-9-47	5	Conversion and loot (aided by police and military).	—	—	—	—
24	Chikrala	5-9-47	1	Loot (aided by police).	—	—	—	11
25	Adhikot	6-9-47	8	Murder, abduction and loot	16	—	E.F.N.A.	—
26	Bab Rani	Do.	2	Murder and conversion	3	—	Do.	—
27	Khizarabad	Do.	3	Murder, conversion and loot	36	—	30	—
28	Jabi	Do.	1	Murder and arson	1	—	—	—
29	Chak No. 51	7-9-47	1	Murder and conversion	2	—	E.F.N.A.	—
30	Langarwala	Do.	3	Conversion	—	—	Do.	—
31	Khanpur Wadhre	8-9-47	1	Rape and conversion	—	21	Do.	—
32	Girot	10-9-47	6	Murder and loot	5	—	—	E.F.N.A.
	Malakwal (train attack).	Do.	6	Murder and loot	2	—	—	5
33	Fatehbad	Do.	3	Loot and conversion	10	—	E.F.N.A.	—
34	Jalwal	Do.	4	Murder, kidnapping and conversion.	10	—	Do.	—
35	Tantiwala	16-9-47	1	Murder and loot	10	—	E.F.N.A.	—
36	Choha	18-9-47	3	Conversion and loot	—	—	160	—
37	Golewala	24-9-47	3	Conversion and loot	—	—	E.F.N.A.	—
38	Kotla Sachdan Wala	25-9-47	2	Conversion and loot	8	—	—	—
39	Faruka	—	5	Murder and loot	90	—	E.F.N.A.	—
40	Haveli Mothiram	—	1	Murder and conversion	—	—	Do.	—
41	Chak No. 8-A	—	3	Loot and conversion	—	—	—	—
42	Rangpur	—	5	Desecration and loot	1	—	E.F.N.A.	—
43	Salaam	—	2	Murder, conversion and loot	—	—	Do.	—
44	Warcha Mandi	—	2	Desecration, conversion and loot.	—	—	Do.	—
45	Wirkanwali	—	5	Conversion and loot (aided by police).	—	—	—	—
46	Chak No. 49	—	2	Murder, conversion and loot	E.F.N.A.	—	Do.	—

E.F.N.A.—Exact figures not available.

DISTRICT JHANG

Sl. No.	Name of village	Date	Number of witnesses	Nature of incident	Number of casualties		Number of converted	Number of kidnapped or abducted
					Killed	Injured		
1	Rampur	22-8-47	3	Murder, loot and abduction	300	—	—	20
2	Chhatta Baksha	24-8-47	4	Murder, loot, abduction and mass conversion.	30	25	180	7
3	Girmala	25-8-47	1	Murder, abduction and loot	100	—	—	6
4	Waryam	26-8-47	3	Murder, abduction, mass conversion and loot.	1	—	72	4
5	Nikka Daulatana	Do.	4	Murder, abduction and loot (aided by police).	125	—	E.F.N.A.	25
6	Kot Shakir	Do.	10	Murder and burning	21	—	Do.	—
7	Khekwa	Do.	4	Mass conversion and loot	—	—	Do.	—
8	Kot Khera	Do.	3	Murder, abduction and loot	114	—	—	36
9	Satiana	Do.	1	Murder, mass conversion and abduction.	3	—	Do.	48
10	Basti Makkaram	27-8-47	2	Murder, loot, conversion and abduction.	3	—	Do.	3
11	Pir Abdul Rehman	Do.	1	Mass conversion	—	—	Do.	—
12	Mauza Kabli	Do.	1	Mass conversion	—	—	500	—
13	Kot Khan	Do.	2	Mass conversion and loot	—	—	150	—
14	Basti Makkaranwali	Do.	2	Murder, loot and abduction	3	—	—	4
15	Dharopa	Do.	8	Murder, loot, arson and mass conversion.	E.F.N.A.	—	1,200	40
16	Hassowali	27/28-8-47	3	Murder, abduction, loot and mass conversion.	148	—	E.F.N.A.	30
17	Ghuman	27-8-47	4	Murder, loot, arson and abduction.	25	—	—	5
18	Nithoke	Do.	4	Murder, loot and abduction (aided by police).	15	—	—	6

No.	Place	Date		Nature of incident				
19	Sewa	28-8-47	1	Murder, loot, conversion and desecration.	40	35	15	—
20	Ahmedpur Sial	Do.	2	Murder, loot and mass conversion.	50	—	E.F.N.A.	—
21	Chah Pahwanwala	Do.	2	Murder, loot and arson ..	45	—	—	—
22	Kakki Nau	Do.	1	Mass conversion and loot ..	—	—	15,000	—
23	Kallur	29-8-47	1	Murder, loot and mass conversion.	2	—	70	—
24	Mangan	Do.	3	Murder, conversion, loot and arson.	23	—	100	—
25	Mari Shah Sakhira.	Aug. 1947	3	Murder, loot and arson	12	—	—	—
26	Harsu Sheikh	—	4	Murder, loot, arson and conversion.	16	—	90	—

DISTRICT MULTAN

No.	Place	Date		Nature of incident				
1	Jahan Pur	15-8-47	1	Murder, conversion, loot and arson.	40	—	E.F.N.A.	—
2	Chak No. 117	17/18-8-47	3	Murder and loot	20	—	—	—
3	Daivran	18-8-47	5	Murder, loot, conversion and arson.	3	18	E.F.N.A.	—
4	Chak No. 509	25-8-47	3	Murder, loot and arson aided by police.	500	—	—	E.F.N.A
5	Aulaksandu	25-8-47	2	Murder and arson	6	—	—	—
	Arjaniwala	26-8-47	}	Murder, loot and conversion	E.F.N.A.	—	E.F.N.A.	—
6	Amirpur Siddat	27-8-47	7	Murder, loot, arson and conversion.	125	50	E.F.N.A.	—
7	Mira Mallah	27/28-8-47	3	Murder, loot and arson	45	—	E.F.N.A.	—
8	Bhawal Garh	27-8-47	17	Murder, loot and conversion	300	—	E.F.N.A.	—
9	Bharnot	28-8-47	4	Murder, loot and arson	9	—	E.F.N.A.	—
10	Fateh Pur	30-8-47	2	Murder, abduction, loot and arson.	15	—	—	5
11	Jhalar Lakhar Singh.	30-8-47	4	Murder, loot and conversion	10	E.F.N.A.	Do.	75
12	Khan Bhela	31-8-47	19	Murder, abduction and loot	150	—	—	40
13	Ladha	31-8-47	2	Murder, abduction, loot and arson.	E.F.N.A.	—	—	—
14	Lodhran	31-8-47	1	Loot and abduction	—	—	—	1

E.F.N.A.—Exact figures not available.

Sl. No.	Name of village	Date	Number of witnesses	Nature of incident	Number of casualties		Number of converted	Number of kidnapped or abducted
					Killed	Injured		
15	Mohal Siai	31-8-47	1	Murder, abduction, loot and arson.	Large number	—	—	22
16	Berwala	Aug. 1947	1	Murder, conversion and loot	35	—	70	—
17	Kajiwala	Do.	2	Burnt alive and abduction	105	—	—	15
18	Telok Pur	Do.	7	Murder, conversion, abduction and loot (aided by Baluch military).	105	—	E.F.N.A.	E.F.N.A.
19	Ghazipur	1-9-47	1	Murder, abduction, loot and arson.	160	—	—	—
20	Shahpur	2-9-47	3	Murder and loot	5	—	—	—
21	Kabir Wala (train attack)	3-9-47	1	Murder, abduction and loot	34	—	—	6
22	Qitta Jhumarmal-wala.	3-9-47	2	Murder and loot	9	—	—	—
23	Faquirwala	3-9-47	4	Murder, loot and arson	7	11	—	—
24	Kassi Kundan Mal	4-9-47	2	Murder and loot	E.F.N.A.	—	—	—
25	Chak No. 67	10-9-47	1	Murder, abduction, loot and arson (aided by M.L.N.G.).	35	—	—	—
26	Chak No. Karmali. 7/8	25-9-47	3	Murder, loot and arson	7	E.F.N.A.	—	—
27	Chak No. 104	26-9-47	2	Murder, loot and arson (aided by Muslim military).	45	E.F.N.A.	—	—
28	Talamba	27-9-47	4	Murder, loot (aided by Muslim military and police).	12	—	—	—

DISTRICT MUZAFFARGARH

No.	Village	Date		Nature of offence	87	27	53	13
1	Chand-di-Wasti	15-8-47	1	Murder, burning alive, arson loot and conversion.	20	E.F.N.A.	—	E.F.N.A.
2	Koti	Do.	1	Murder and loot	200	Do.	—	Do.
3	Gobindpura	17-8-47	1	Murder, burning alive and arson.	—	50	20	Do.
4	Sirke	22-8-47	1	Conversion and loot	—	E.F.N.A.	—	Do.
5	Bakiana	24-8-47	1	Murder, burning alive, arson and loot.	100	—	—	Do.
6	Nachank and Dhade Dal.	Do.	1	Murder and mass conversion (aided by military).	62	—	148	Do.
7	Jalal Kurai	25-8-47	1	Murder, kidnapping and loot	Many	25	—	100
8	Buchiwala	27-8-47	1	Murder and loot.	E.F.N.A.	—	—	—
9	Wasti Sujan Singh.	29-8-47	1	Mass murder, arson and loot (aided by military).	100	—	—	—
10	Bet Duami	1-9-47	2	Conversion and loot	6	—	50	—
11	Patti Jhanda	2-9-47	2	Murder and loot (aided by police)	7	—	43	—
12	Chah Mathianwala	3-9-47	5	Murder, mass conversion and loot.	—	—	—	—
13	Chah Kuara	Do.	5	Murder and conversion (aided by police).	7	—	43	—
14	Nasheb Karor	4-9-47	4	Murder	130	—	—	—
15	Tibbi Khurd	Do.	4	Murder and loot	30	3	E.F.N.A.	—
16	Jharkal	Do.	4	Murder, conversion and loot	10	2	E.F.N.A.	—
17	Shinwala	5-9-47	4	Murder, conversion and loot	Many	—	50	—
18	Wadhewali	Do.	4	Mass conversion and loot	—	—	E.F.N.A.	—
19	Khotan	5-9-47 10-9-47	1	Loot and mass conversion / Murder and loot	15 / 120	—	4	2
20	Langewala	5-9-47	2	Murder, kidnapping, conversion and loot.	70	—	—	—
21	Mauza Shinwala	Do.	4	Murder, mass conversion and loot.	—	25	70	—
22	Mahra	6-9-47	5	Murder, mass conversion and loot.	6	—	770	—
23	Gangian	6-9-47 8-9-47	3	Mass conversion	15	—	100	E.F.N.A.
24	Sabri Dewan	6-9-47	1	Murder, abduction and loot, con- version and loot.	125	1	20	30

E.F.N.A.—Exact figures not available.   M.L.N.G.—Muslim League National Guards.

Sl. No.	Name of village	Date	Number of witnesses	Nature of incident	Number of casualties		Number of converted	Number of kidnapped or abducted
					Killed	Injured		
25	Mochi Wala	6-9-47	4	Murder, kidnapping, arson and loot.	85	—	50	—
26	Shah Mara	Do.	3	Murder, mass conversion and loot.	5	—	E.F.N.A.	—
27	Nanduwala	Do.	3	Murder, loot, arson and abduction (aided by police).	107	8	—	25
28	Chak Maulvi	7-9-47	4	Murder, burning alive, loot, arson, conversion and rape.	20	—	110	20
29	Kharak	Do.	4	Murder, mass conversion and loot.	12	—	74	—
30	Shariff Chajra	Do.	2	Murder, abduction, loot and arson.	1	—	45	—
31	Umarpur	Do.	1	Murder, conversion, arson and loot.	2	—	148	—
32	Serin Dewanwali	8-9-47	1	Murder, conversion, loot and abduction.	45	—	80	25
33	Khan Garh	Do.	5	Murder, conversion and loot	18	4	5	—
34	Nach ke Basti	9-9-47	1	Murder, mass conversion and loot.	60	—	140	—
35	Isanwali	Do.	1	Murder, conversion and loot	70	—	130	—
36	Sabuwala	13-9-47	11	Murder, rape and loot	3	—	12	—
37	Ghazi Ghat	14-9-47	6	Murder, abduction, arson, desecration and loot.	400	—	—	70
38	Nurewala	Sept. 1947	4	Murder and loot	10	—	—	—
39	Khokarewala	Do.	1	Murder, abduction and loot	150	—	—	17
40	Bukharian	Do.	3	Murder, abduction, rape, arson and loot.	480	—	—	4

41	Budh ..	Do.	2	Murder, burning alive and mass conversion.	5	—	395	—
42	Basti Sewa Singh ..	9-10-47	9	Murder, arson, desecration and loot.	6	4	—	17
43	Basti Chah Yerwala.	Do.	9	Murder, abduction, conversion, loot and desecration.	22	—	24	—
44	Paharpur ..	13-10-47	8	Murder, conversion and loot ..	3	10	20	—
			2	Murder, abduction and conversion, aided by military.	Large number			
45	Sikhan-di-Basti and Sanwan.	—	2	Murder, abduction and loot ..	216	—	—	20

DISTRICT RAWALPINDI

1	Dhok Ratta ..	6-3-47 / 7-3-47	8	Murder and loot assisted by police.	20	—	—	—
2	Tanch Batta ..	6-3-47	4	Murder, rape, arson, with police help.	18	—	—	—
3	Keeka Khurd ..	7-3-47	1	Burning, looting and murder ..	A few	—	—	—
4	Dhamial ..	7-3-47 / 8-3-47	2	Murder, loot and arson ..	E.F.N.A.	—	—	—
5	Rawel ..	7-3-47	2	Murder, loot and arson ..	1	—	—	—
6	Wani ..	7-3-47	2	Murder and loot ..	3	—	—	—
7	Bunda ..	7-3-47 / 8-3-47	4	Murder, loot and conversion ..	13	—	2	—
8	Taxilla ..	7-3-47	3	Arson, loot and rape ..	—	—	—	One rape case. 16
9	Mogul ..	7-3-47	4	Murder, loot and abduction ..	140	—	20	—
10	Basali ..	8-3-47	4	Murder, loot, arson and conversion.	52	—	100	—
11	Sagri ..	8-3-47	4	Loot and murder ..	E.F.N.A.	—	—	—
12	Kuri ..	8-3-47	6	Murder, loot, abduction and conversion.	50	—	Many	2
13	Addiyala ..	9-3-47	2	Murder, arson and loot ..	12	—	—	—
14	Harnaul ..	9-3-47	3	Murder and conversion ..	13	—	1	1
15	Bhagpur ..	10-3-47	2	Murder, conversion and abduction.	34	—	1	—
16	Machhia ..	10-3-47 / 11-3-47	4	Murder, conversion and abduction.	6	—	70	8

E.F.N.A.—Exact figures not available.

Sl. No.	Name of village	Date	Number of witnesses	Nature of incident	Number of casualties		Number of converted	Number of kidnapped or abducted
					Killed	Injured		
17	Kauntrila	11-3-47	5	Murder, conversion and abduction.	3	—	20	13
18	Sayed Kasran	11-3-47	13	Murder, conversion and abduction.	16	—	14	2
19	Choha Khalsa	12-3-47	6	Murder, loot and conversion	175	—	85	1
20	Baner Kaswal	14-3-47	1	Murder and conversion	10	—	7	—
21	Looni	Mid March 1947	3	Murder, loot and conversion	10	—	3	—

In the villages of Baghar, Belhar, Hathla, Panjar, Panjora, Khandol, etc., mass conversions took place.

DISTRICT JHELUM

Sl. No.	Name of village	Date	Number of witnesses	Nature of incident	Number of casualties		Number of converted	Number of kidnapped or abducted
					Killed	Injured		
1	Bhagwal	Aug. 1947	3	Loot	—	—	—	—
2	Kandwal	Do.	3	Conversion and loot	—	—	E.F.N.A.	—
3	Khurd	Do.	1	Loot	—	—	—	—
4	Katas Raj	18-8-47	1	Murder, desecration-and loot	6	—	—	—
5	Pran	19-8-47	1	Murder, kidnapping and loot	2	—	—	—
6	Sanghoi	22-8-47	3	Murder, arson and loot	32	E.F.N.A.	—	2
7	Kala Gujran	25-8-47	1	Murder and loot	2	—	—	—
8	Dalmola	28-8-47	1	Murder and loot	10	—	—	—
9	Pind	1-9-47	4	Loot	—	—	—	—
10	Rohtas	3-9-47	4	Murder, kidnapping and loot	100	—	—	—
11	Dalwal	4-9-47	6	Murder, kidnapping and loot	17	150	—	E.F.N.A. 5
12	Sadhwal	5-9-47	1	Murder and loot	3	—	—	—
13	Drab	10-9-47	1	Murder, loot and kidnapping	1	—	—	—
14	Wagh	11-9-47	1	Murder, arson and loot	E.F.N.A.	—	—	1

DISTRICT MIANWALI

No.	Place	Date		Nature of crime				
1	Gokul	3-8-47	4	Murder, loot, abduction and arson.	10	—	—	2
2	Chah Lachman and Singh Wala.	21-8-47	5	Mass conversion, loot and desecration.	—	—	75	—
3	Bhari	29-8-47	1	Mass conversion	20	—	40	—
4	Shah Khel	2-9-47	3	Murder, conversion and loot (by military and police).			35	—
5	Isakhel	Do.	2	Mass conversion, arson and loot (aided by police and military).	19	—		E.F.N.A.
6	Dhor Nakka	Do.	5	Murder, loot and arson	5		—	—
7	Kalur	2-9-47	3	Mass conversion and loot	—		75	—
8	Saitan Khel and Mela Khel.	Do.	3	Mass conversion and loot	—		15	E.F.N.A.
9	Kellur Kot	4-9-47	1	Murder and abduction (aided by police).	80	—	E.F.N.A.	
10	Piplan R.S.	Do.	1	Murder and abduction	500	200		Do.
11	Abwali R.S.	Do.	1	Murder and abduction	200	—		Do.
12	Chikrala	Do.	1	Murder, loot, abduction and conversion.	25	—	1	4
13	Deli Namdar	5-9-47	2	Murder, burning alive and loot.	E.F.N.A.	20	E.F.N.A.	16
14	Kanjar	Do.	5	Murder, loot, conversion and abduction.	16			Many
15	Darya Khan Camp.	5-10-47	5	Murder, conversion, abduction, and loot.	Large number		500	
16	Nava Jhandanwala	5-9-47	3	Murder, loot, mass conversion and desecration.	32	25	2,500	
17	Panj Girian	Do.	11	Murder, mass conversion, loot and abduction (aided by military).	200		1,500	25
18	Jandawala	6-9-47	3	Murder, arson, loot and conversion.	23	—	E.F.N.A.	—
19	Ghulama	Do.	1	Mass conversion and loot	—	—	Do.	—
20	Gohar Wala	7-9-47	11	Murder, burning alive, arson, loot and abduction.	62	—	—	13
21	Bhakkar	8-9-47	4	Murder, abduction and loot	250	—	—	10

E.F.N.A.—Exact figures not available.

R.S.—Railway station.

Sl. No.	Name of village	Date	Number of witnesses	Nature of incident	Number of casualties		Number of converted	Number of kidnapped or abducted
					Killed	Injured		
22	Kala Bagh	19-9-47	2	Murder and conversion (aided by military).	10	20	10	—
23	Kot Keri	3-9-47 25-9-47	3	Murder and loot Murder (aided by police and Baluch military).	6 200	5 50	— —	40
	DISTRICT DERA GHAZI KHAN							
1	Choti	15-8-47	2	Murder, loot and mass conversion.	15	—	985	—
2	Khanpur	25-8-47	2	Murder, arson, mass conversion and loot.	5	—	100	—
3	Qayamwala	29-8-47	5	Murder, mass conversion and loot.	E.F.N.A.	—	E.F.N.A.	—
4	Chote Bala	Do.	2	Murder, loot, burning alive, arson, rape and mass conversion.	32	11	Do.	—
5	That Gabolan	30-8-47	5	Murder, loot and conversion	2	—	48	1
6	Basti Mariwala	Do.	3	Murder, loot and abduction	9	50	—	
7	Choti Ziran	Do.	8	Murder, loot and abduction	3	5	—	5
8	Sikhaniwala	Do.	2	Arson, abduction and loot	—	30	—	15
9	Alliwala	31-8-47	5	Murder, conversion, arson and loot.	8	—	3	
10	Lasheta	Do.	2	Murder, arson, abduction, loot and mass conversion.	18	10	293	24
11	Dastiwala	Do.	2	Murder, abduction, conversion and loot.	1	3	15	1
	Basti Mallana	Do.	7	Murder, loot and arson	6	2	—	—

13	Sheru Basti	Do.	3	Murder, arson, abduction, mass conversion and loot.	18	4	260	28
14	Basti Sakhi Sarwar	Do.	1	Murder, abduction, rape and loot.	40	21	—	E.F.N.A.
15	Rakar	1-9-47	5	Murder, mass conversion and loot.	2	—	198	—
16	Shakhani	1-9-47 3-9-47	5	Murder, arson and loot (aided by police).	2	6	—	—
17	Basti Kalewali	1-9-47	5	Murder, arson, loot and conversion.	13	E.F.N.A.	13	—
18	Basti Ahmedani	Do.	4	Murder, arson, desecration, mass conversion and loot.	8	7	1,900	1
19	Malkani Kalan	Do.	5	Murder, loot and mass conversion.	3	E.F.N.A.	95	—
20	Basti Jhoke Utra	Do.	6	Murder, arson, mass conversion abduction and loot.	7	17	500	7
21	Lutkani	Do.	3	Murder, loot and conversion ..	8	7	1	—
22	Shankarpura	Do.	9	Murder, loot, abduction, rape, mass conversion and arson.	5	20	2,000	8
23	Chah Bhanuwala	2-9-47	2	Murder, loot and mass conversion.	6	—	E.F.N.A.	—
24	Mahrewala	Do.	5	Murder, abduction, loot and mass conversion.	E.F.N.A.	16	Do.	5
25	Notak Mahamin	3-9-47	4	Murder, loot and mass conversion.	7	—	43	—
26	Saukar	3-9-47 13-9-47	1	Murder, loot, arson and conversion (aided by Sub-Inspector of police).	5	—	E.F.N.A.	—
27	Numberdar Shamali	9-9-47 12-9-47	9	Murder, loot and arson	2	—	E.F.N.A.	E.F.N.A.
28	Kotla Mughlan		2	Forcible mass conversion, rape and loot.	—	—	E.F.N.A.	E.F.N.A.
	Jhog Utra	12-9-47	2	Murder, loot and mass conversion.	200	—	800	—
29	Kot Garh	Sept. 1947	4	Murder, arson, conversion and loot (aided by police).	10	—	8	—
30	Mahtam	1-12-47	6	Murder, abduction, loot and mass conversion.	11	20	E.F.N.A.	1

E.F.N.A.—Exact figures not available.

BAHAWALPUR STATE

Sl. No.	Name of village	Date	Number of witnesses	Nature of incident	Number of casualties		Number of converted	Number of kidnapped or abducted
					Killed	Injured		
1	Tawakal	Mid Aug.	3	Loot and conversion	—	—	90	—
2	Hazariwala	Do.	2	Murder, loot and conversion	3	—	70	—
3	Gudpura	Do.	4	Murder, loot and conversion	5	—	150	All the girls of the village abducted
4	Chak No. 88	Do.	3	Murder and abduction	44	—	—	
5	Chak Bhura Mal	Do.	5	Murder, loot, conversion and abduction.	40	—	40	10
6	Chak Nihala Mal	Do.	5	Do.	6	8	—	2
7	Boonga	Do.	6	Murder, loot and abduction	34		—	
8	Lal Suhara	19-8-47	4	Murder and loot	8	1	1	11 male children and 21 young women.
9	Tajeka	20-8-47	2	Murder, loot and abduction	20	1	50	
10	Kharal							
11	Lal Dera	Do.	5	Murder, arson and desecration	15	—	—	4
12	Chak Sarkari	21-8-47	1	Murder and abduction	57	—	—	100
13	Khanpur Kotora-wala.	Do.	4	Murder and abduction	150	100	—	
14	Khairpur Tamewali	Do.	3	Murder, loot, conversion and abduction.	150	—	750	5 married girls.
15	Nasirpur	22-8-47	4	Attack and loot	—	1	—	

No.	Village	Date		Nature of crime				
16	Chak Salamat	23-8-47	2	Loot and conversion	—	—	60	17
17	Jamalpur	23-8-47	5	Loot, abduction, conversion and arson.	—	—	270	—
18	Tahli Talbani	24-8-47	4	Loot and conversion	—	—	50	—
19	Lala Amar Singh	Do.	6	Murder, loot and desecration	3	10	—	—
20	Bindara	Do.	3	Murder, loot and conversion	7	—	193	—
21	Qasamke	25-8-47	3	Murder and loot	50	—	—	—
22	Behramka	Do.	3	Loot, conversion and desecration.	—	—	114	—
23	Abbas Nagar	Do.	5	Murder, loot and conversion	5	—	200	—
24	Dhurpur	Do.	4	Murder, loot, conversion and arson.	1	—	17	—
25	Chishtian	Do.	2	Murder and loot	4,000	—	—	—
26	Risalpur	Do.	2	Murder and loot	1,500	—	—	—
27	Qaimpur	Do.	2	Murder and loot	800	—	—	—
28	Shekhwahan	Do.	2	Murder and loot	1,000	—	—	—
29	Dera Bakhan	Do.	2	Murder and loot	700	—	—	—
30	Lalsuhara	26-8-47	2	Murder, loot and arson	32	22	450	—
31	Mari Qasam Shah	27-8-47	3	Murder, loot and conversion	15	—	—	—
32	Chak Chopa	28-8-47	5	Murder and loot	2	—	—	—
33	Chak Nihala	Do.	5		—	—	—	—
34	Chak Bhura	Do.	5	Murder, abduction, conversion and desecration	40	—	E.F.N.A.	—
35	Kanani	Do.	5	Murder, loot and abduction	440	150	200	113
36	Karani	30-8-47	3	Murder, loot and conversion	19	3	—	—
37	McLeodganj	Mid Sept.	6	Murder and loot	1	—	50 families	—
38	Bharian	Do.	1	Murder and conversion	4	—	144	—
39	Bahadurke	Do.	3	Murder, loot and conversion	6	3	—	—
40	Swanak	15-9-47	13	Loot and conversion	—	—	180	—
41	Purana Samasata	16-9-47	2	Murder, loot and abduction	50	—	—	5 young women.
42	Khuh Manga Ram	26-9-47	1	Murder, loot and conversion	2	1	20 families	—

E.F.N.A.—Exact figures not available.

BIBLIOGRAPHY

Ambedkar, B. R.		*Thoughts on Pakistan*
Beni Prasad		*India's Hindu Muslim Questions*
Durrani, F. K. Khan		*The Meaning of Pakistan*
Gandhi, M. K.		*Story of my Experiments with Truth*
,, ,,		*To the Protagonists of Pakistan* (Gandhi Series)
Gauba, K. L.		*Inside Pakistan*
Haq, Ch. Afzal		*Pakistan and Untouchability*
Hussain, Azim		*Fazl-i-Husain*
Jinnah, M. A.		*Some Recent Speeches and Writings of Mr. Jinnah*—Edited by Jamil-ud-Din Ahmad.
Kabir, Hamayun		*Muslim Politics (1906-1942)*
Kailash Chandra		*The Tragedy of Jinnah*
Mukherji, S.		*Communalism in Muslim Politics and Troubles over India*
M. R. T.		*Muslim India* (Home Studies Circle)
Naik, V. N.		*Mr. Jinnah (A Political Study)*
Nanda, J.		*Punjab Uprooted*
Nehru, J. L.		*Autobiography*
,, ,,		*The Discovery of India*
Noman, Mohammad		*Muslim India*
Prasad, Rajendra		*India Divided*
Smith, W. C.		*Modern Islam in India*
,, ,,		*Muslim League*
Tahilramani, Parsram V		*Why the Exodus from Sind*
Vairanapillai, Dr. Samuel		*Are We Two Nations*
Ziaul Islam		*Side Lights on Muslim Politics*